Benchmark Series

Microsoft® Office 2010

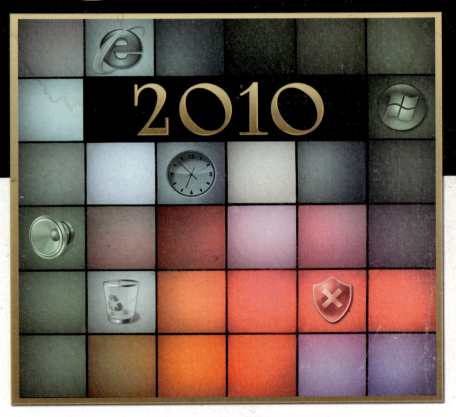

Nita Rutkosky
Pierce College at Puyallup
Puyallup, Washington

Audrey Rutkosky Roggenkamp
Pierce College at Puyallup
Puyallup, Washington

St. Paul • Indianapolis

Managing Editor	Sonja Brown
Senior Developmental Editor	Christine Hurney
Production Editor	Donna Mears
Copy Editor	Susan Capecchi
Cover and Text Designer	Leslie Anderson
Desktop Production	Ryan Hamner, Julie Johnston, Jack Ross
Proofreader	Laura Nelson
Indexer	Sandi Schroeder

Acknowledgements: The authors, editors, and publisher thank the following instructors for their helpful suggestions during the planning and development of the books in the Benchmark Office 2010 Series: Somasheker Akkaladevi, Virginia State University, Petersburg, VA; Ed Baker, Community College of Philadelphia, Philadelphia, PA; Lynn Baldwin, Madison Area Technical College, Madison, WI; Letty Barnes, Lake Washington Technical College, Kirkland, WA; Richard Bell, Coastal Carolina Community College, Jacksonville, NC; Perry Callas, Clatsop Community College, Astoria, OR; Carol DesJardins, St. Clair County Community College, Port Huron, MI; Stacy Gee Hollins, St. Louis Community College--Florissant Valley, St. Louis, MO Sally Haywood, Prairie State College, Chicago Heights, IL; Dr. Penny Johnson, Madison Technical College, Madison, WI; Jan Kehm, Spartanburg Community College, Spartanburg, SC; Jacqueline Larsen, Asheville Buncombe Tech, Asheville, NC; Sherry Lenhart, Terra Community College, Fremont, OH; Andrea Robinson Hinsey, Ivy Tech Community College NE, Fort Wayne, IN; Bari Siddique, University of Texas at Brownsville, Brownsville, TX; Joan Splawski, Northeast Wisconsin Technical College, Green Bay, WI; Diane Stark, Phoenix College, Phoenix, AZ; Mary Van Haute, Northeast Wisconsin Technical College, Green Bay, WI; Rosalie Westerberg, Clover Park Technical College, Lakewood, WA.

The publishing team also thanks the following individuals for their contributions to this project: checking the accuracy of the instruction and exercises—Robertt (Rob) W. Neilly, Traci Post, and Lindsay Ryan; developing lesson plans, supplemental assessments, and supplemental case studies—Jan Davidson, Lambton College, Sarnia, Ontario; writing rubrics to support end-of-chapter and end-of-unit activities—Robertt (Rob) W. Neilly, Seneca College, Toronto, Ontario; writing test item banks—Jeff Johnson; writing online quiz item banks—Trudy Muller; and developing PowerPoint presentations—Janet Blum, Fanshawe College, London, Ontario.

Trademarks: Access, Excel, Internet Explorer, Microsoft, PowerPoint, and Windows are trademarks or registered trademarks of Microsoft Corporation in the United States and/or other countries. Some of the product names and company names included in this book have been used for identification purposes only and may be trademarks or registered trade names of their respective manufacturers and sellers. The authors, editors, and publisher disclaim any affiliation, association, or connection with, or sponsorship or endorsement by, such owners.

We have made every effort to trace the ownership of all copyrighted material and to secure permission from copyright holders. In the event of any question arising as to the use of any material, we will be pleased to make the necessary corrections in future printings. Thanks are due to the aforementioned authors, publishers, and agents for permission to use the materials indicated.

Paradigm Publishing is independent from Microsoft Corporation, and not affiliated with Microsoft in any manner. While this publication may be used in assisting individuals to prepare for a Microsoft Business Certification exam, Microsoft, its designated program administrator, and Paradigm Publishing do not warrant that use of this publication will ensure passing a Microsoft Business Certification exam.

ISBN 978-0-76383-809-6 (Text)
ISBN 978-0-76383-811-9 (Text + CD)

© 2011 by Paradigm Publishing, Inc.
875 Montreal Way
St. Paul, MN 55102
Email: educate@emcp.com
Website: www.emcp.com

All rights reserved. No part of this publication may be adapted, reproduced, stored in a retrieval system, or transmitted in any form or by any means, electronic, mechanical, photocopying, recording, or otherwise, without prior written permission from the publisher.

Printed in the United States of America

19 18 17 16 15 14 13 12 11   2 3 4 5 6 7 8 9 10

Preface	ix
Getting Started in Office 2010	Introduction 1
Using Windows 7	Introduction 13
Browsing the Internet Using Internet Explorer 8.0	Introduction 41

Microsoft Word Level 1

Unit 1 Editing and Formatting Documents — 1

Chapter 1 Preparing Documents — 3
Model Answers	4
Opening Microsoft Word	5
Creating, Saving, Printing, and Closing a Document	5
Using the New Line Command	7
Saving a Document	8
Naming a Document	9
Printing a Document	9
Closing a Document	10
Creating a New Document	11
Opening a Document	12
Pinning a Document	13
Saving a Document with Save As	14
Exiting Word	14
Editing a Document	15
Moving the Insertion Point to a Specific Page	16
Browsing in a Document	16
Moving the Insertion Point with the Keyboard	16
Inserting and Deleting Text	18
Selecting Text	18
Selecting Text with the Mouse	19
Selecting Text with the Keyboard	20
Using the Undo and Redo Buttons	21
Checking the Spelling and Grammar in a Document	22
Using Help	25
Getting Help in a Dialog Box or Backstage View	27
Chapter Summary, Commands Review, Concepts Check, Skills Check, Visual Benchmark, Case Study	28

Chapter 2 Formatting Characters and Paragraphs — 35
Model Answers	36
Changing Fonts	37
Choosing a Typestyle	40
Choosing a Font Effect	41
Using Keyboard Shortcuts	42
Formatting with the Mini Toolbar	42
Changing Fonts at the Font Dialog Box	45
Applying Styles from a Quick Styles Set	47
Changing the Quick Styles Set	47
Applying a Theme	49
Changing Themes	49
Changing Paragraph Alignment	50
Changing Alignment at the Paragraph Dialog Box	52
Indenting Text in Paragraphs	54
Spacing Before and After Paragraphs	57
Repeating the Last Action	57
Formatting with Format Painter	59
Changing Line Spacing	60
Changing Paragraph Spacing with the Change Styles Button	61
Revealing Formatting	62
Comparing Formatting	63

Chapter 3 Customizing Paragraphs — 73
Model Answers	74
Applying Numbering and Bullets	75
Numbering Paragraphs	75
Bulleting Paragraphs	78
Inserting Paragraph Borders and Shading	79
Inserting Paragraph Borders	79
Adding Paragraph Shading	80
Customizing Borders and Shading	82
Sorting Text in Paragraphs	84
Manipulating Tabs	85
Manipulating Tabs on the Ruler	85
Manipulating Tabs at the Tabs Dialog Box	88
Cutting, Copying, and Pasting Text	91
Deleting Selected Text	91
Cutting and Pasting Text	91
Moving Text by Dragging with the Mouse	92
Using the Paste Options Button	93
Copying and Pasting Text	94
Using the Clipboard	95

Chapter 4 Formatting Pages — 105
Model Answers	106
Changing the View	109
Displaying a Document in Draft View	109
Displaying a Document in Full Screen Reading View	109
Navigating Using the Navigation Pane	110
Hiding/Showing White Space in Print Layout View	112
Changing Page Setup	113
Changing Margins	113
Changing Page Orientation	113
Changing Page Size	114
Changing Margins at the Page Setup Dialog Box	115
Changing Paper Size at the Page Setup Dialog Box	115
Inserting a Page Break	117
Inserting a Blank Page	118
Inserting a Cover Page	118
Inserting Predesigned Page Numbering	120
Inserting Predesigned Headers and Footers	122
Removing a Header or Footer	123
Editing a Predesigned Header or Footer	124
Formatting the Page Background	125
Inserting a Watermark	125
Changing Page Color	126
Inserting a Page Border	127
Changing Page Border Options	127
Finding and Replacing Text and Formatting	130
Finding and Replacing Text	132
Choosing Check Box Options	133
Finding and Replacing Formatting	135

Unit 1 Performance Assessment — 145

Unit 2 Enhancing and Customizing Documents — 151

Chapter 5 Applying Formatting and Inserting Objects — 153
Model Answers	154
Inserting a Section Break	156
Creating Columns	157
Creating Columns with the Columns Dialog Box	158
Removing Column Formatting	159
Inserting a Column Break	159
Balancing Columns on a Page	160
Hyphenating Words	161
Automatically Hyphenating Words	161
Manually Hyphenating Words	161
Creating a Drop Cap	162
Inserting Symbols and Special Characters	163
Inserting the Date and Time	165

These activities appear at the end of every chapter.

Using the Click and Type Feature	166
Vertically Aligning Text	167
Inserting an Image	169
Customizing and Formatting an Image	169
Sizing an Image	169
Moving an Image	169
Inserting a Picture	170
Inserting a Clip Art Image	173
Inserting and Customizing a Pull Quote	176
Drawing Shapes	178
Copying Shapes	178
Drawing and Formatting a Text Box	180
Creating and Modifying WordArt Text	181
Creating and Inserting a Screenshot	183
Chapter 6 Maintaining Documents	**197**
Model Answers	198
Maintaining Documents	200
Using Print Screen	200
Creating a Folder	201
Renaming a Folder	202
Selecting Documents	202
Deleting Documents	203
Copying and Moving Documents	204
Renaming Documents	205
Deleting a Folder	205
Opening Multiple Documents	205
Sharing Documents	206
Sending a Document Using Email	207
Saving to SkyDrive	208
Saving to SharePoint	208
Saving a Document as a Blog Post	208
Saving a Document in a Different Format	210
Saving in PDF/XPS Format	213
Working with Windows	214
Opening and Arranging Windows	215
Maximizing, Restoring, and Minimizing Documents	215
Splitting a Window	216
Viewing Documents Side by Side	217
Inserting a File	218
Printing and Previewing a Document	219
Previewing Pages in a Document	219
Printing Pages in a Document	220
Creating and Printing Envelopes	223
Creating and Printing Labels	226
Changing Label Options	226
Creating a Document Using a Template	229
Chapter 7 Creating Tables and SmartArt	**241**
Model Answers	242
Creating a Table	243
Entering Text in Cells	244
Moving the Insertion Point within a Table	244
Using the Insert Table Dialog Box	246
Changing the Table Design	247
Selecting Cells	249
Selecting in a Table with the Mouse	249
Selecting in a Table with the Keyboard	250
Changing Table Layout	251
Selecting with the Select Button	252
Viewing Gridlines	252
Inserting and Deleting Rows and Columns	252
Merging and Splitting Cells and Tables	254
Customizing Cell Size	256
Changing Cell Alignment	258
Repeating a Header Row	258
Inserting a Quick Table	259
Changing Cell Margin Measurements	260
Changing Cell Direction	262
Changing Table Alignment	263
Changing Table Size with the Resize Handle	264
Moving a Table	264
Converting Text to a Table	266
Converting a Table to Text	266
Drawing a Table	267
Sorting Text in a Table	268
Performing Calculations in a Table	268
Creating SmartArt	271
Inserting and Formatting a SmartArt Diagram	271
Arranging and Moving a SmartArt Diagram	273
Creating an Organizational Chart with SmartArt	275
Chapter 8 Merging Documents	**289**
Model Answers	290
Completing a Merge	293
Creating a Data Source File	293
Creating a Main Document	295
Previewing a Merge	298
Checking for Errors	298
Merging Documents	298
Merging Envelopes	300
Merging Labels	302
Merging a Directory	304
Editing a Data Source File	306
Selecting Specific Records	306
Editing Records	308
Inputting Text during a Merge	311
Merging Using the Mail Merge Wizard	313
Unit 2 Performance Assessment	**325**
Word Level 1 Index	**337**

Microsoft Excel 2010 Level 1

Unit 1 Editing and Formatting Documents	**1**
Chapter 1 Preparing an Excel Workbook	**3**
Model Answers	4
Creating a Worksheet	5
Saving a Workbook	8
Editing Data in a Cell	10
Printing a Workbook	11
Closing a Workbook	12
Exiting Excel	13
Using Automatic Entering Features	13
Using AutoComplete and AutoCorrect	13
Using AutoFill	15
Opening a Workbook	16
Inserting Formulas	17
Using the AutoSum Button to Add Numbers	17
Using the AutoSum Button to Average Numbers	18
Using the Fill Handle to Copy a Formula	18
Selecting Cells	19
Selecting Cells Using the Mouse	19
Selecting Cells Using the Keyboard	20
Selecting Data within Cells	20
Applying Basic Formatting	21
Changing Column Width	21
Merging and Centering Cells	21
Formatting Numbers	22
Using Help	24
Getting Help at the Help Tab Backstage View	25
Getting Help on a Button	25
Getting Help in a Dialog Box or Backstage View	26
Customizing Help	27

Chapter 2 Inserting Formulas in a Worksheet — 37
Model Answers — 38
Writing Formulas with Mathematical Operators — 40
    Copying a Formula with Relative Cell References — 41
    Copying Formulas with the Fill Handle — 42
    Writing a Formula by Pointing — 43
    Using the Trace Error Button — 43
Inserting Formulas with Functions — 45
    Writing Formulas with Statistical Functions — 47
    Displaying Formulas — 51
    Writing Formulas with Financial Functions — 51
    Writing Formulas with Date and Time Functions — 53
    Writing a Formula with the IF Logical Function — 54
    Writing IF Formulas Containing Text — 56
Using Absolute and Mixed Cell References in Formulas — 57
    Using an Absolute Cell Reference in a Formula — 57
    Using a Mixed Cell Reference in a Formula — 59

Chapter 3 Formatting an Excel Worksheet — 69
Model Answers — 70
Changing Column Width — 71
    Changing Column Width Using Column Boundaries — 71
    Changing Column Width at the Column Width Dialog Box — 72
Changing Row Height — 73
Inserting and Deleting Cells, Rows, and Columns — 74
    Inserting Rows — 74
    Inserting Columns — 75
    Deleting Cells, Rows, or Columns — 76
    Clearing Data in Cells — 77
Applying Formatting — 77
    Applying Font Formatting — 78
    Formatting with the Mini Toolbar — 78
    Applying Alignment Formatting — 78
Applying a Theme — 81
Formatting Numbers — 82
    Formatting Numbers Using Number Group Buttons — 82
    Formatting Numbers Using the Format Cells Dialog Box — 84
Formatting Cells Using the Format Cells Dialog Box — 86
    Aligning and Indenting Data — 86
    Changing the Font at the Format Cells Dialog Box — 88
    Adding Borders to Cells — 90
    Adding Fill and Shading to Cells — 92
    Repeating the Last Action — 92
Formatting with Format Painter — 94
Hiding and Unhiding Columns and/or Rows — 94

Chapter 4 Enhancing a Worksheet — 107
Model Answers — 108
Formatting a Worksheet Page — 109
    Changing Margins — 109
    Centering a Worksheet Horizontally and/or Vertically — 110
    Changing Page Orientation — 112
    Changing the Page Size — 112
    Inserting and Removing Page Breaks — 112
    Printing Column and Row Titles on Multiple Pages — 115
    Scaling Data — 116
    Inserting a Background Picture — 117
    Printing Gridlines and Row and Column Headings — 118
    Printing a Specific Area of a Worksheet — 118
Inserting Headers and Footers — 120
Customizing Print Jobs — 125
Completing a Spelling Check — 126
Using Undo and Redo — 126
Finding and Replacing Data and Cell Formatting in a Worksheet — 128

Sorting Data — 133
    Completing a Custom Sort — 133
    Sorting More Than One Column — 134
Filtering Data — 135

Unit 1 Performance Assessment — 149

Unit 2 Enhancing the Display of Workbooks — 155

Chapter 5 Moving Data within and between Workbooks — 157
Model Answers — 158
Creating a Workbook with Multiple Worksheets — 161
Cutting, Copying, and Pasting Selected Cells — 161
    Moving Selected Cells — 162
    Copying Selected Cells — 163
    Using the Paste Options Button — 163
    Using the Office Clipboard — 165
    Pasting Values Only — 166
    Inserting a Worksheet — 167
Managing Worksheets — 169
    Hiding a Worksheet in a Workbook — 171
    Formatting Multiple Worksheets — 171
    Printing a Workbook Containing Multiple Worksheets — 173
    Splitting a Worksheet into Windows and Freezing and Unfreezing Panes — 174
Working with Ranges — 177
Working with Windows — 178
    Opening Multiple Workbooks — 179
    Arranging Workbooks — 179
    Hiding/Unhiding Workbooks — 181
    Sizing and Moving Workbooks — 182
Moving, Copying, and Pasting Data — 182
Moving Data — 183
    Linking Data — 184
    Copying and Pasting Data between Programs — 185

Chapter 6 Maintaining Workbooks — 197
Model Answers — 198
Maintaining Workbooks — 200
    Creating a Folder — 201
    Renaming a Folder — 202
    Selecting Workbooks — 202
    Deleting Workbooks and Folders — 203
    Deleting to the Recycle Bin — 203
    Copying Workbooks — 204
    Sending Workbooks to a Different Drive or Folder — 205
    Cutting and Pasting a Workbook — 205
    Renaming Workbooks — 206
    Deleting a Folder and Its Contents — 207
Managing the Recent List — 207
    Displaying a Quick List — 208
    Pinning a Workbook — 208
    Recovering an Unsaved Workbook — 209
    Clearing the Recent Workbooks List — 209
Managing Worksheets — 210
    Copying a Worksheet to Another Workbook — 210
    Moving a Worksheet to Another Workbook — 211
Formatting with Cell Styles — 214
    Applying a Style — 214
    Defining a Cell Style — 215
    Modifying a Style — 219
    Copying Styles to Another Workbook — 220
    Removing a Style — 220
    Deleting a Style — 221
Inserting Hyperlinks — 222
    Linking to an Existing Web Page or File — 222
    Navigating Using Hyperlinks — 223
    Linking to a Place in the Workbook — 224

Linking to a New Workbook	224
Linking Using a Graphic	225
Linking to an Email Address	225
Modifying, Editing, and Removing a Hyperlink	226
Using Excel Templates	227

Chapter 7 Creating a Chart in Excel — 239
Model Answers	240
Creating a Chart	241
Sizing, Moving, and Deleting a Chart	242
Editing Data	243
Printing a Chart	245
Changing the Chart Design	245
Choosing a Custom Chart Style	246
Changing the Data Series	246
Changing Chart Layout and Style	247
Changing Chart Location	248
Deleting a Chart	248
Changing the Chart Layout	251
Inserting, Moving, and Deleting Chart Labels	251
Inserting Shapes	255
Moving, Sizing, and Deleting Shapes	255
Inserting Images	257
Changing the Chart Formatting	258

Chapter 8 Adding Visual Interest to Workbooks — 271
Model Answers	272
Inserting Symbols and Special Characters	273
Inserting an Image	275
Customizing and Formatting an Image	276
Sizing and Moving an Image	276
Inserting a Clip Art Image	278
Creating Screenshots	279
Inserting and Copying Shapes	281
Inserting a Picture	284
Drawing and Formatting a Text Box	285
Inserting a Picture as a Watermark	287
Inserting a SmartArt Diagram	288
Entering Data in a Diagram	289
Sizing, Moving, and Deleting a Diagram	289
Changing the Diagram Design	290
Changing the Diagram Formatting	291
Creating WordArt	293
Sizing and Moving WordArt	293

Unit 2 Performance Assessment — 305
Excel Level 1 Index — 313

Microsoft Access 2010 Level 1

Unit 1 Creating Tables and Queries — 1

Chapter 1 Managing and Creating Tables — 3
Model Answers	4
Exploring a Database	5
Opening and Closing a Database	6
Opening and Closing Objects	8
Managing Tables	10
Inserting and Deleting Records	10
Inserting, Moving, and Deleting Fields	13
Changing Column Width	15
Printing a Table	16
Previewing a Table	17
Changing Page Size and Margins	17
Changing Page Layout	18
Designing a Table	21
Creating a Table	22
Renaming a Field Heading	26
Inserting a Name, Caption, and Description	26
Inserting Quick Start Fields	28
Assigning a Default Value	28
Assigning a Field Size	28
Changing the AutoNumber Field	28

Chapter 2 Creating Relationships between Tables — 43
Model Answers	44
Creating Related Tables	45
Determining Relationships	46
Defining the Primary Key	46
Relating Tables in a One-to-Many Relationship	50
Specifying Referential Integrity	51
Printing a Relationship	52
Showing Tables	56
Editing a Relationship	56
Deleting a Relationship	56
Inserting and Deleting Records in Related Tables	59
Creating a One-to-One Relationship	61
Displaying Related Records in a Subdatasheet	64

Chapter 3 Performing Queries — 79
Model Answers	80
Performing Queries	84
Designing a Query	84
Establishing Query Criteria	86
Sorting Fields in a Query	94
Modifying a Query	96
Designing Queries with *Or* and *And* Criteria	97
Performing a Query with the Simple Query Wizard	101
Creating a Calculated Field	108
Designing Queries with Aggregate Functions	109
Creating a Crosstab Query	113
Creating a Find Duplicates Query	116
Creating a Find Unmatched Query	119

Chapter 4 Creating and Modifying Tables in Design View — 131
Model Answers	132
Creating a Table in Design View	134
Assigning a Default Value	138
Using the Input Mask	139
Validating Field Entries	143
Using the Lookup Wizard	143
Inserting, Moving, and Deleting Fields in Design View	144
Inserting a Total Row	145
Sorting Records	149
Printing Specific Records	149
Formatting Table Data	150
Completing a Spelling Check	154
Finding and Replacing Data	156
Using Help	159
Getting Help at the Help Tab Backstage View	159
Getting Help on a Button	161
Getting Help in a Dialog Box or Backstage View	161

Unit 1 Performance Assessment — 173

Unit 2 Creating Forms and Reports — 183

Chapter 5 Creating Forms — 185
Model Answers	186
Creating a Form	188
Creating a Form with the Form Button	188
Changing Views	188
Printing a Form	188
Navigating in a Form	189
Adding and Deleting Records	191
Sorting Records	191
Creating a Form with a Related Table	192
Customizing a Form	194
Applying Themes	195
Inserting Data in the Form Header	195

Modifying a Control Object	195
Inserting a Control	196
Arranging Objects	199
Formatting a Form	203
Applying Conditional Formatting	205
Adding Existing Fields	208
Creating a Split Form	211
Creating a Multiple Items Form	214
Creating a Form Using the Form Wizard	215

Chapter 6 Creating Reports and Mailing Labels — 229

Model Answers	230
Creating a Report	234
Creating a Report with the Report Button	234
Modifying Control Objects	235
Sorting Records	236
Displaying a Report in Print Preview	236
Creating a Report with a Query	238
Customizing a Report	240
Grouping and Sorting Records	243
Creating a Report Using the Report Wizard	247
Preparing Mailing Labels	251

Chapter 7 Modifying, Filtering, and Viewing Data — 263

Model Answers	264
Filtering Data	265
Filtering Using the Filter Button	265
Removing a Filter	266
Filtering on Specific Values	268
Filtering by Selection	270
Filtering by Shortcut Menu	271
Using *Filter by Form*	272
Viewing Object Dependencies	274
Using Options at the Info Tab Backstage View	276
Compacting and Repairing a Database	276
Encrypting a Database with a Password	277
Viewing and Customizing Database Properties	278
Customizing the Recent Tab Backstage View	281
Displaying a Quick List	282
Pinning a Database	282
Clearing the *Recent Databases* List	282
Saving a Database and Database Object	283

Chapter 8 Importing and Exporting Data — 295

Model Answers	296
Exporting Data	299
Exporting Data to Excel	299
Exporting Data to Word	302
Merging Access Data with a Word Document	304
Merging Query Data with a Word Document	305
Exporting an Access Object to a PDF or XPS File	308
Importing and Linking Data to a New Table	309
Importing Data to a New Table	309
Linking Data to an Excel Worksheet	311
Using the Office Clipboard	312

Unit 2 Performance Assessment — 323

Access Level 1 Index — 331

Microsoft PowerPoint 2010

Unit 1 Creating and Formatting PowerPoint Presentations — 1

Chapter 1 Preparing a PowerPoint Presentation — 3

Model Answers	4
Creating a PowerPoint Presentation	5
Opening a Presentation	7
Starting a Presentation	8
Closing a Presentation	8
Planning a Presentation	9
Creating a Presentation Using a Theme Template	10
Inserting Text in Slides	10
Choosing a Slide Layout	11
Inserting a New Slide	11
Saving a Presentation	11
Changing Views	14
Navigating in a Presentation	14
Printing and Previewing a Presentation	16
Running a Slide Show	20
Creating a Presentation from an Existing Presentation	22
Applying a Design Theme	25
Deleting a Presentation	26
Preparing a Presentation from a Blank Presentation	27
Preparing a Presentation in the Slides/Outline Pane	27
Adding Transition and Sound Effects	29
Adding Transitions	30
Adding Sounds	30
Removing Transitions and Sounds	30
Advancing Slides Automatically	32

Chapter 2 Modifying a Presentation and Using Help — 41

Model Answers	42
Checking Spelling	43
Managing Text in Slides	45
Inserting and Deleting Text in Slides	46
Finding and Replacing Text in Slides	47
Cutting, Copying, and Pasting Text in Slides	49
Rearranging Text in the Slides/Outline Pane	51
Sizing and Rearranging Placeholders in a Slide	52
Managing Slides	54
Inserting and Deleting Slides	54
Moving Slides	54
Copying a Slide	55
Copying a Slide between Presentations	56
Duplicating Slides	57
Reusing Slides	59
Creating Sections within a Presentation	60
Using Help	62
Getting Help at the Help Tab Backstage View	63
Getting Help on a Button	63
Getting Help in a Dialog Box or Backstage View	65

Chapter 3 Formatting Slides — 75

Model Answers	76
Formatting a Presentation	77
Applying Font Formatting	77
Formatting with Format Painter	81
Formatting Paragraphs	83
Customizing Bullets	90
Customizing Numbering	92
Customizing Placeholders	94
Changing Internal Margins	94
Modifying Theme Colors and Fonts	98
Changing Slide Background	98
Changing Page Setup	101
Creating Custom Themes	103
Creating Custom Theme Colors	103
Creating Custom Theme Fonts	105
Saving a Custom Theme	106
Editing Custom Themes	107
Deleting Custom Themes	107

Chapter 4 Inserting Elements in Slides — 119

Model Answers	120
Inserting and Formatting Text Boxes	120
Formatting a Text Box	121
Selecting Multiple Objects	121
Aligning Text Boxes	121
Setting Tabs in a Text Box	125
Inserting, Formatting, and Copying Shapes	127

Displaying Rulers, Gridlines, and Guides	129
Grouping/Ungrouping Objects	134
Inserting an Image	135
Customizing and Formatting an Image	135
Sizing, Cropping, and Moving an Image	136
Arranging Objects	136
Inserting a Picture	137
Inserting a Picture as a Slide Background	140
Inserting a Clip Art Image	141
Sizing, Rotating, and Positioning Objects	143
Copying Objects within and between Presentations	145
Creating Screenshots	146
Creating WordArt Text	148
Formatting WordArt Text	148
Inserting Symbols	150
Inserting Headers and Footers	151
Unit 1 Performance Assessment	**171**

Unit 2 Customizing and Enhancing PowerPoint Presentations — 179

Chapter 5 Creating Tables, Charts, and SmartArt Graphics — 181

Model Answers	182
Creating a Table	183
Entering Text in Cells	183
Selecting Cells	183
Changing Table Design	185
Changing Table Layout	187
Creating SmartArt	189
Modifying SmartArt Design	190
Formatting SmartArt	192
Creating a SmartArt Graphic with Bulleted Text	194
Inserting Text in the Text Pane	196
Creating a Chart	197
Changing Chart Design	200
Formatting Chart Layout	202
Changing Chart Formatting	203
Creating a Photo Album	207
Editing and Formatting a Photo Album	208
Formatting Pictures	211

Chapter 6 Using Slide Masters and Action Buttons — 223

Model Answers	224
Customizing Slide Masters	225
Applying Themes to Slide Masters	226
Applying and Formatting Backgrounds	228
Deleting Placeholders	228
Deleting Slide Master Layouts	228
Inserting Slides in a Customized Presentation	229
Inserting Elements in a Slide Master	231
Creating and Renaming a Custom Slide Layout	232
Inserting Placeholders	232
Creating Custom Prompts	233
Inserting a New Slide Master	234
Preserving Slide Masters	235
Changing Page Setup	235
Saving a Presentation as a Template	238
Customizing the Handout Master	240
Customizing the Notes Master	242
Using View Tab Options	244
Inserting Action Buttons	246
Applying an Action to an Object	248
Inserting Hyperlinks	250

Chapter 7 Applying Custom Animation and Setting Up Shows — 263

Model Answers	264
Applying and Removing Animation Effects	266
Applying Animation Effects	269
Applying Animations with Animation Painter	269
Modifying Animation Effects	270
Reordering Items	271
Customizing Animation Effects at the Animation Pane	273
Applying a Build	276
Animating Shapes and Images	277
Animating a SmartArt Graphic	278
Animating a Chart	279
Creating a Motion Path	281
Applying a Trigger	282
Setting Up a Slide Show	284
Running a Presentation without Animation	284
Setting Up a Presentation to Loop Continuously	285
Setting Automatic Times for Slides	287
Recording Narration	288
Hiding Slides	290
Setting Up Monitors	290
Creating a Custom Show	291
Running a Custom Show	292
Editing a Custom Show	292
Printing a Custom Show	293
Inserting Audio and Video Files	294
Inserting an Audio File	294
Inserting a Video File	295
Trimming a Video File	297
Playing an Audio File throughout a Presentation	297

Chapter 8 Integrating, Sharing, and Protecting Presentations — 309

Model Answers	310
Importing a Word Outline	311
Copying and Pasting Data	312
Sharing Presentations	315
Saving and Sending a Presentation	316
Saving a Presentation in a Different Format	317
Embedding and Linking Objects	325
Embedding Objects	325
Linking Objects	327
Editing Linked Objects	328
Downloading Designs	328
Using Comments	330
Managing Presentation Information	333
Managing Presentation Properties	333
Protecting a Presentation	336
Encrypting a Presentation	336
Adding a Digital Signature	337
Inspecting a Presentation	339
Checking the Accessibility of a Presentation	340
Checking the Compatibility of a Presentation	342
Managing Versions	342
Unit 2 Performance Assessment	**355**
PowerPoint Index	**365**

Office 2010 Integrating Project — IP1

Preface

Benchmark Microsoft Office 2010 is designed for students who want to learn how to use the new version of Microsoft's popular suite to enhance their productivity for educational, workplace, and home use. Throughout this text, students are expected to develop and execute strategies for solving information processing and management problems using Word 2010; for solving numeric and mathematical problems using Excel 2010; for organizing, querying, and retrieving data using Access 2010; and for writing, creating, and producing presentations using PowerPoint 2010. After successfully completing a course using this textbook, students will be able to

- Analyze, synthesize, and evaluate school, work, or home information-processing needs and use application software to meet those needs efficiently and effectively
- Access the Internet and use the browse, search, and hyperlink capabilities of web browsers
- Create, design, and produce professional documents using word processing software
- Process, manipulate, and represent numeric data using spreadsheet software
- Plan, structure, and create databases for efficient data access and retrieval using database software
- Use presentation software to design and create informational and motivational slide shows that contain hyperlinks, tables, images, and animation
- Learn strategies for merging and integrating source data from different applications

In addition to mastering essentials Word, Excel, Access, and PowerPoint skills, students will learn the basic features and functions of computer hardware, the Windows 7 operating system, and Internet Explorer 8.0. Upon completing the text, they can expect to be proficient in using the major applications of the Office 2010 suite to organize, analyze, and present information.

Achieving Proficiency in Office 2010

Since its inception several Office versions ago, the Benchmark Series has served as a standard of excellence in software instruction. Elements of the book function individually and collectively to create an inviting, comprehensive learning environment that produces successful computer users. The following visual tour highlights the structure and features that comprise the highly popular Benchmark model.

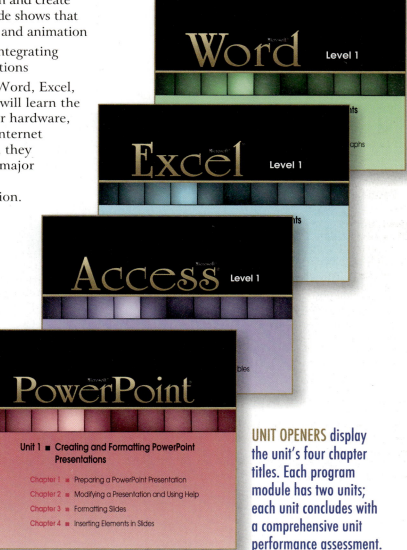

UNIT OPENERS display the unit's four chapter titles. Each program module has two units; each unit concludes with a comprehensive unit performance assessment.

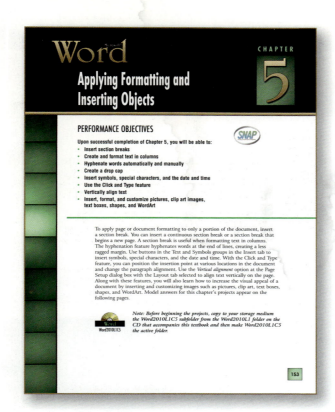

CHAPTER OPENERS present the performance objectives and an overview of the skills taught.

SNAP interactive tutorials are available to support chapter-specific skills at www.snap2010.emcp.com.

DATA FILES are provided for each chapter. A prominent note reminds students to copy the appropriate chapter data folder and make it active.

PROJECT APPROACH: Builds Skill Mastery within Realistic Context

MODEL ANSWERS provide a preview of the finished chapter projects and allow students to confirm they have created the materials accurately.

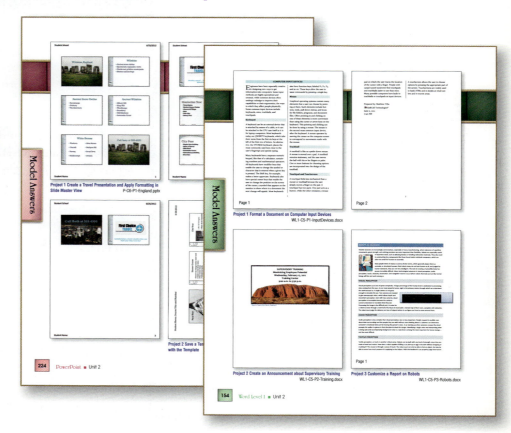

MULTIPART PROJECTS provide a framework for the instruction and practice on software features. A project overview identifies tasks to accomplish and key features to use in completing the work.

QUICK STEPS provide feature summaries for reference and review.

HINTS provide useful tips on how to use features efficiently and effectively.

Between project parts, the text presents instruction on the features and skills necessary to accomplish the next section of the project.

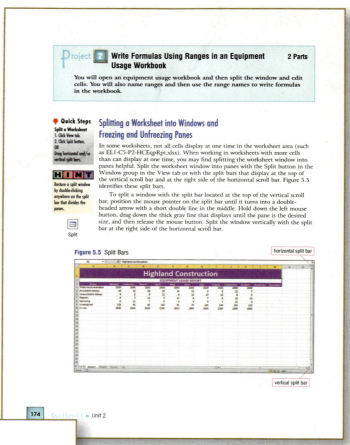

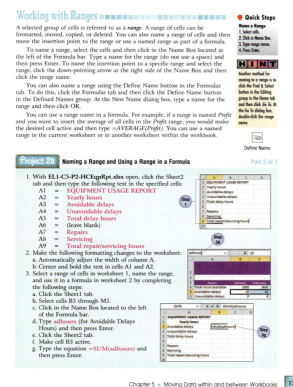

STEP-BY-STEP INSTRUCTIONS guide students to the desired outcome for each project part. Screen captures illustrate what the student's screen should look like at key points.

MAGENTA TEXT identifies material to type.

Typically, a file remains open throughout all parts of the project. Students save their work incrementally. At the end of the project, students save, print, and then close the file.

CHAPTER REVIEW ACTIVITIES: A Hierarchy of Learning Assessments

CHAPTER SUMMARY captures the purpose and execution of key features.

COMMANDS REVIEW summarizes visually the major features and alternative methods of access.

CONCEPTS CHECK questions assess knowledge recall.

Office 2010 ■ Preface

SKILLS CHECK exercises ask students to develop both standard and customized types of word processing, spreadsheet, database, or presentation documents without how-to directions.

VISUAL BENCHMARK assessments test students' problem-solving skills and mastery of program features.

CASE STUDY requires analyzing a workplace scenario and then planning and executing multipart projects.

Students search the Web and/or use the program's Help feature to locate additional information required to complete the Case Study.

Preface xiii

UNIT PERFORMANCE ASSESSMENT: Cross-Disciplinary, Comprehensive Evaluation

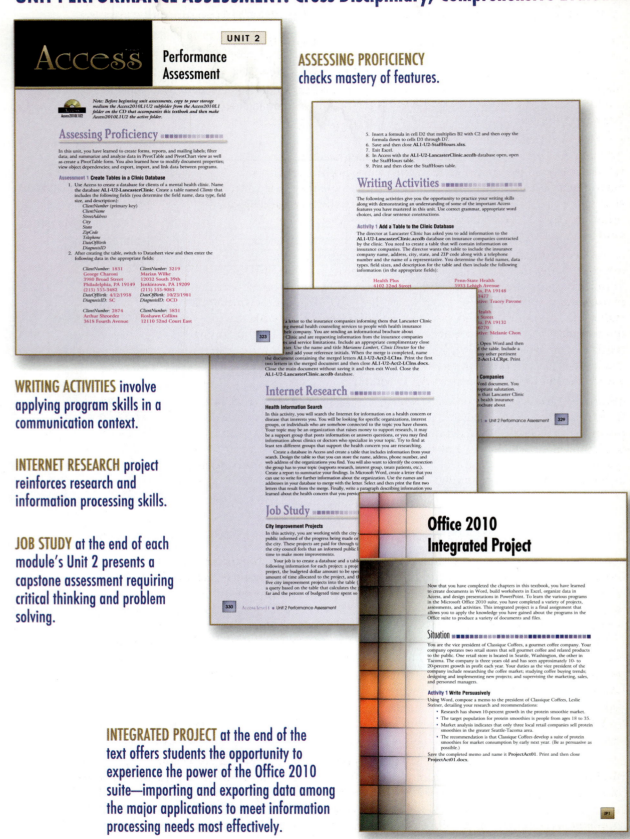

ASSESSING PROFICIENCY checks mastery of features.

WRITING ACTIVITIES involve applying program skills in a communication context.

INTERNET RESEARCH project reinforces research and information processing skills.

JOB STUDY at the end of each module's Unit 2 presents a capstone assessment requiring critical thinking and problem solving.

INTEGRATED PROJECT at the end of the text offers students the opportunity to experience the power of the Office 2010 suite—importing and exporting data among the major applications to meet information processing needs most effectively.

Student Courseware

Student Resources CD Each Benchmark Series textbook is packaged with a Student Resources CD containing the data files required for completing the projects and assessments. A CD icon and folder name displayed on the opening page of chapters reminds students to copy a folder of files from the CD to the desired storage medium before beginning the project exercises. Directions for copying folders are printed on the inside back cover.

Internet Resource Center Additional learning tools and reference materials are available at the book-specific website at www.emcp.net/Benchmark10. Students can access the same files that are on the Student Resources CD along with study aids, web links, and tips for using computers effectively in academic and workplace settings.

SNAP Training and Assessment SNAP is a web-based program offering an interactive venue for learning Microsoft Office 2010, Windows 7, and Internet Explorer 8.0. Along with a web-based learning management system, SNAP provides multimedia tutorials, performance skill items, document-based assessments, a concepts test bank, an online grade book, and a set of course planning tools. A CD of tutorials teaching the basics of Office, Windows, and Internet Explorer is also available if instructors wish to assign additional SNAP tutorial work without using the web-based SNAP program.

eBook For students who prefer studying with an eBook, the texts in the Benchmark Series are available in an electronic form. The web-based, password-protected eBooks feature dynamic navigation tools, including bookmarking, a linked table of contents, and the ability to jump to a specific page. The eBook format also supports helpful study tools, such as highlighting and note taking.

Instructor Resources

Instructor's Guide and Disc Instructor support for the Benchmark Series includes an *Instructor's Guide and Instructor Resources Disc* package. This resource includes planning information, such as Lesson Blueprints, teaching hints, and sample course syllabi; presentation resources, such as PowerPoint slide shows with lecture notes and audio support; and assessment resources, including an overview of available assessment venues, live model answers for chapter activities, and live and PDF model answers for end-of-chapter exercises. Contents of the *Instructor's Guide and Instructor Resources Disc* package are also available on the password-protected section of the Internet Resource Center for this title at www.emcp.net/Benchmark10.

Computerized Test Generator Instructors can use the EXAMVIEW® Assessment Suite and test banks of multiple-choice items to create customized web-based or print tests.

Blackboard Cartridge This set of files allows instructors to create a personalized Blackboard website for their course and provides course content, tests, and the mechanisms for establishing communication via e-discussions and online group conferences. Available content includes a syllabus, test banks, PowerPoint presentations with audio support, and supplementary course materials. Upon request, the files can be available within 24–48 hours. Hosting the site is the responsibility of the educational institution.

System Requirements

This text is designed for the student to complete projects and assessments on a computer running a standard installation of Microsoft Office 2010, Professional Edition, and the Microsoft Windows 7 operating system. To effectively run this suite and operating system, your computer should be outfitted with the following:

- 1 gigahertz (GHz) processor or higher; 1 gigabyte (GB) of RAM
- DVD drive
- 15 GB of available hard-disk space
- Computer mouse or compatible pointing device

Office 2010 will also operate on computers running the Windows XP Service Pack 3 or the Windows Vista operating system.

Screen captures in this book were created using a screen resolution display setting of 1280 × 800. Refer to the *Customizing Settings* section of *Getting Started in Office 2010* following this preface for instructions on changing your monitor's resolution. Figure G.10 on page 10 shows the Microsoft Office Word ribbon at three resolutions for comparison purposes. Choose the resolution that best matches your computer; however, be aware that using a resolution other than 1280 × 800 means that your screens may not match the illustrations in this book.

About the Authors

Nita Rutkosky began teaching business education courses at Pierce College in Puyallup, Washington, in 1978. Since then she has taught a variety of software applications to students in postsecondary Information Technology certificate and degree programs. In addition to *Benchmark Office 2010,* she has co-authored *Marquee Series: Microsoft Office 2010, 2007,* and *2003; Signature Series: Microsoft Word 2010, 2007,* and *2003;* and *Using Computers in the Medical Office: Microsoft Word, Excel, and PowerPoint 2007* and *2003.* She has also authored textbooks on keyboarding, WordPerfect, desktop publishing, and voice recognition for Paradigm Publishing, Inc.

Audrey Rutkosky Roggenkamp has been teaching courses in the Business Information Technology department at Pierce College in Puyallup since 2005. Her courses have included keyboarding, skill building, and Microsoft Office programs. In addition to this title, she has co-authored *Marquee Series: Microsoft Office 2010 and 2007; Signature Series: Microsoft Word 2010 and 2007;* and *Using Computers in the Medical Office 2007* and *2003* for Paradigm Publishing, Inc.

Getting Started in Office 2010

In this textbook, you will learn to operate several computer application programs that combine to make an application "suite." This suite of programs is called Microsoft Office 2010. The programs you will learn to operate are the software, which includes instructions telling the computer what to do. Some of the application programs in the suite include a word processing program named Word, a spreadsheet program named Excel, a database program named Access, and a presentation program named PowerPoint.

Identifying Computer Hardware

The computer equipment you will use to operate the suite of programs is referred to as hardware. You will need access to a microcomputer system that should consist of the CPU, monitor, keyboard, printer, drives, and mouse. If you are not sure what equipment you will be operating, check with your instructor. The computer system shown in Figure G.1 consists of six components. Each component is discussed separately in the material that follows.

Figure G.1 Microcomputer System

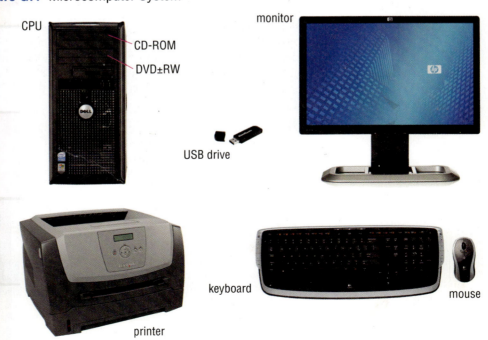

CPU

CPU stands for Central Processing Unit and it is the intelligence of the computer. All the processing occurs in the CPU. Silicon chips, which contain miniaturized circuitry, are placed on boards that are plugged into slots within the CPU. Whenever an instruction is given to the computer, that instruction is processed through circuitry in the CPU.

Monitor

The monitor is a piece of equipment that looks like a television screen. It displays the information of a program and the text being input at the keyboard. The quality of display for monitors varies depending on the type of monitor and the level of resolution. Monitors can also vary in size—generally from 15-inch size up to 26-inch size or larger.

Keyboard

The keyboard is used to input information into the computer. Keyboards for microcomputers vary in the number and location of the keys. Microcomputers have the alphabetic and numeric keys in the same location as the keys on a typewriter. The symbol keys, however, may be placed in a variety of locations, depending on the manufacturer. In addition to letters, numbers, and symbols, most microcomputer keyboards contain function keys, arrow keys, and a numeric keypad. Figure G.2 shows an enhanced keyboard.

Figure G.2 Keyboard

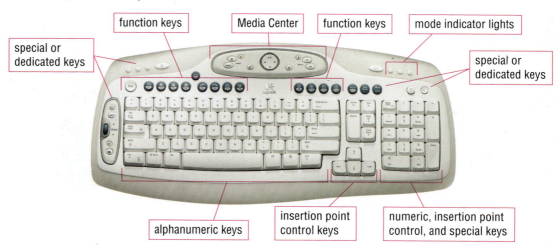

The 12 keys at the top of the keyboard, labeled with the letter F followed by a number, are called *function keys*. Use these keys to perform functions within each of the suite programs. To the right of the regular keys is a group of *special* or *dedicated keys*. These keys are labeled with specific functions that will be performed when you press the key. Below the special keys are arrow keys. Use these keys to move the insertion point in the document screen.

A keyboard generally includes three mode indicator lights. When you select certain modes, a light appears on the keyboard. For example, if you press the Caps Lock key, which disables the lowercase alphabet, a light appears next to Caps Lock. Similarly, pressing the Num Lock key will disable the special functions on the numeric keypad, which is located at the right side of the keyboard.

Disk Drives

Depending on the computer system you are using, Microsoft Office 2010 is installed on a hard drive or as part of a network system. Whether you are using Office on a hard drive or network system, you will need to have available a DVD or CD drive and a USB drive or other storage medium. You will insert the CD (compact disc) that accompanies this textbook in the DVD or CD drive and then copy folders from the CD to your storage medium. You will also save documents you complete at the computer to folders on your storage medium.

Printer

A document you create in Word is considered soft copy. If you want a hard copy of a document, you need to print it. To print documents you will need to access a printer, which will probably be either a laser printer or an ink-jet printer. A laser printer uses a laser beam combined with heat and pressure to print documents, while an ink-jet printer prints a document by spraying a fine mist of ink on the page.

Mouse

Many functions in the suite of programs are designed to operate more efficiently with a mouse. A mouse is an input device that sits on a flat surface next to the computer. You can operate a mouse with the left or the right hand. Moving the mouse on the flat surface causes a corresponding mouse pointer to move on the screen. Figure G.1 shows an illustration of a mouse.

Using the Mouse

The programs in the Microsoft Office suite can be operated with the keyboard and a mouse. The mouse may have two or three buttons on top, which are tapped to execute specific functions and commands. To use the mouse, rest it on a flat surface or a mouse pad. Put your hand over it with your palm resting on top of the mouse and your wrist resting on the table surface. As you move the mouse on the flat surface, a corresponding pointer moves on the screen.

When using the mouse, you should understand four terms — point, click, double-click, and drag. When operating the mouse, you may need to point to a specific command, button, or icon. Point means to position the mouse pointer on the desired item. With the mouse pointer positioned on the desired item, you may need to click a button on the mouse. Click means quickly tapping a button on the mouse once. To complete two steps at one time, such as choosing and then executing a function, double-click a mouse button. Double-click means to tap the left mouse button twice in quick succession. The term drag means to press and hold the left mouse button, move the mouse pointer to a specific location, and then release the button.

Using the Mouse Pointer

The mouse pointer will change appearance depending on the function being performed or where the pointer is positioned. The mouse pointer may appear as one of the following images:

- The mouse pointer appears as an I-beam (called the I-beam pointer) in the document screen and can be used to move the insertion point or select text.

- The mouse pointer appears as an arrow pointing up and to the left (called the arrow pointer) when it is moved to the Title bar, Quick Access toolbar, ribbon, or an option in a dialog box.

- The mouse pointer becomes a double-headed arrow (either pointing left and right, pointing up and down, or pointing diagonally) when performing certain functions such as changing the size of an object.

- In certain situations, such as moving an object or image, the mouse pointer displays with a four-headed arrow attached. The four-headed arrow means that you can move the object left, right, up, or down.

- When a request is being processed or when a program is being loaded, the mouse pointer may appear with a circle beside it. The moving circle means "please wait." When the process is completed, the circle is removed.

- The mouse pointer displays as a hand with a pointing index finger in certain functions such as Help and indicates that more information is available about the item. The mouse pointer also displays as a hand when you hover the mouse over a hyperlink.

Choosing Commands

Once a program is open, you can use several methods in the program to choose commands. A command is an instruction that tells the program to do something. You can choose a command using the mouse or the keyboard. When a program such as Word or PowerPoint is open, the ribbon contains buttons for completing tasks and contains tabs you click to display additional buttons. To choose a button on the Quick Access toolbar or in the ribbon, position the tip of the mouse arrow pointer on a button and then click the left mouse button.

The Office suite provides access keys you can press to use a command in a program. Press the Alt key on the keyboard to display KeyTips that identify the access key you need to press to execute a command. For example, press the Alt key in a Word document with the Home tab active and KeyTips display as shown in Figure G.3. Continue pressing access keys until you execute the desired command. For example, if you want to begin spell checking a document, you would press the Alt key, press the R key on the keyboard to display the Review tab, and then press the letter S on the keyboard.

Choosing Commands from Drop-Down Lists

To choose a command from a drop-down list with the mouse, position the mouse pointer on the desired option and then click the left mouse button. To make a selection from a drop-down list with the keyboard, type the underlined letter in the desired option.

Figure G.3 Word Home Tab KeyTips

Some options at a drop-down list may be gray-shaded (dimmed), indicating that the option is currently unavailable. If an option at a drop-down list displays preceded by a check mark, that indicates that the option is currently active. If an option at a drop-down list displays followed by an ellipsis (...), a dialog box will display when that option is chosen.

Choosing Options from a Dialog Box

A dialog box contains options for applying formatting to a file or data within a file. Some dialog boxes display with tabs along the top providing additional options. For example, the Font dialog box shown in Figure G.4 contains two tabs — the Font tab and the Advanced tab. The tab that displays in the front is the active tab. To make a tab active using the mouse, position the arrow pointer on the desired tab and then click the left mouse button. If you are using the keyboard, press Ctrl + Tab or press Alt + the underlined letter on the desired tab.

Figure G.4 Word Font Dialog Box

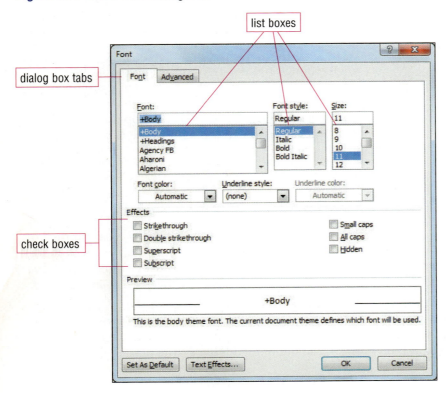

Getting Started in Office 2010

To choose options from a dialog box with the mouse, position the arrow pointer on the desired option and then click the left mouse button. If you are using the keyboard, press the Tab key to move the insertion point forward from option to option. Press Shift + Tab to move the insertion point backward from option to option. You can also hold down the Alt key and then press the underlined letter of the desired option. When an option is selected, it displays with a blue background or surrounded by a dashed box called a marquee. A dialog box contains one or more of the following elements: text boxes, list boxes, check boxes, option buttons, measurement boxes, and command buttons.

List Boxes

Some dialog boxes such as the Word Font dialog box shown in Figure G.4 may contain a list box. The list of fonts below the *Font* option is contained in a list box. To make a selection from a list box with the mouse, move the arrow pointer to the desired option and then click the left mouse button.

Some list boxes may contain a scroll bar. This scroll bar will display at the right side of the list box (a vertical scroll bar) or at the bottom of the list box (a horizontal scroll bar). You can use a vertical scroll bar or a horizontal scroll bar to move through the list if the list is longer than the box. To move down through a list on a vertical scroll bar, position the arrow pointer on the down-pointing arrow and hold down the left mouse button. To scroll up through the list in a vertical scroll bar, position the arrow pointer on the up-pointing arrow and hold down the left mouse button. You can also move the arrow pointer above the scroll box and click the left mouse button to scroll up the list or move the arrow pointer below the scroll box and click the left mouse button to move down the list. To move through a list with a horizontal scroll bar, click the left-pointing arrow to scroll to the left of the list or click the right-pointing arrow to scroll to the right of the list.

To make a selection from a list using the keyboard, move the insertion point into the box by holding down the Alt key and pressing the underlined letter of the desired option. Press the Up and/or Down Arrow keys on the keyboard to move through the list.

In some dialog boxes where enough room is not available for a list box, lists of options are inserted in a drop-down list box. Options that contain a drop-down list box display with a down-pointing arrow. For example, the *Underline style* option at the Word Font dialog box shown in Figure G.4 contains a drop-down list. To display the list, click the down-pointing arrow to the right of the *Underline style* option box. If you are using the keyboard, press Alt + U.

Check Boxes

Some dialog boxes contain options preceded by a box. A check mark may or may not appear in the box. The Word Font dialog box shown in Figure G.4 displays a variety of check boxes within the *Effects* section. If a check mark appears in the box, the option is active (turned on). If the check box does not contain a check mark, the option is inactive (turned off). Any number of check boxes can be active. For example, in the Word Font dialog box, you can insert a check mark in any or all of the boxes in the *Effects* section and these options will be active.

To make a check box active or inactive with the mouse, position the tip of the arrow pointer in the check box and then click the left mouse button. If you are using the keyboard, press Alt + the underlined letter of the desired option.

Text Boxes

Some options in a dialog box require you to enter text. For example, the boxes below the *Find what* and *Replace with* options at the Excel Find and Replace dialog box shown in Figure G.5 are text boxes. In a text box, you type text or edit existing text. Edit text in a text box in the same manner as normal text. Use the Left and Right Arrow keys on the keyboard to move the insertion point without deleting text and use the Delete key or Backspace key to delete text.

Option Buttons

The Word Insert Table dialog box shown in Figure G.6 contains options in the *AutoFit behavior* section preceded by option buttons. Only one option button can be selected at any time. When an option button is selected, a blue circle displays in the button. To select an option button with the mouse, position the tip of the arrow pointer inside the option button and then click the left mouse button. To make a selection with the keyboard, hold down the Alt key and then press the underlined letter of the desired option.

Measurement Boxes

Some options in a dialog box contain measurements or numbers you can increase or decrease. These options are generally located in a measurement box. For example, the Word Paragraph dialog box shown in Figure G.7 contains the *Left*, *Right*, *Before*, and *After* measurement boxes. To increase a number in a measurement box, position the tip of the arrow pointer on the up-pointing arrow to the right of the desired option and then click the left mouse button. To decrease the number, click the down-pointing arrow. If you are using the keyboard, press Alt + the underlined letter of the desired option and then press the Up Arrow key to increase the number or the Down Arrow key to decrease the number.

Command Buttons

In the Excel Find and Replace dialog box shown in Figure G.5, the boxes along the bottom of the dialog box are called command buttons. Use a command button to execute or cancel a command. Some command buttons display with an ellipsis (...). A command button that displays with an ellipsis will open another dialog box. To choose a command button with the mouse, position the arrow pointer on the desired button and then click the left mouse button. To choose a command button with the keyboard, press the Tab key until the desired command button contains the marquee and then press the Enter key.

Figure G.5 Excel Find and Replace Dialog Box

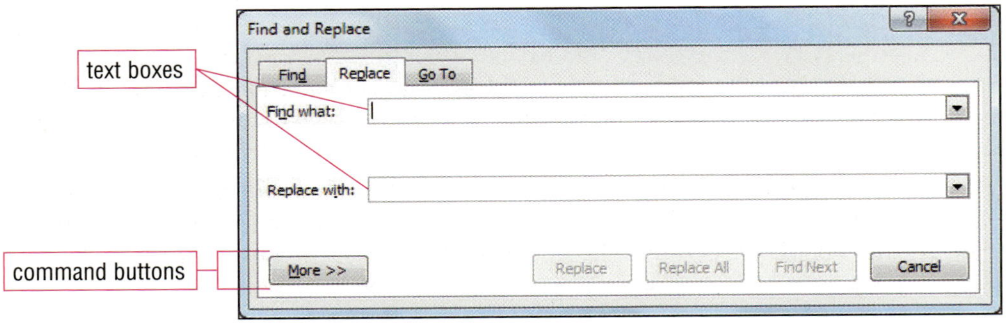

Figure G.6 Word Insert Table Dialog Box

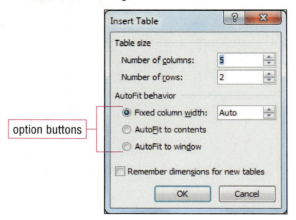

Figure G.7 Word Paragraph Dialog Box

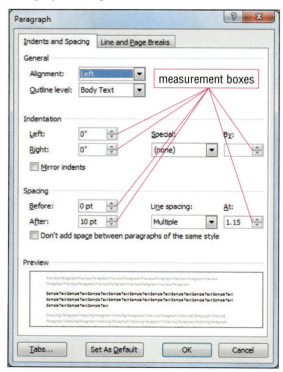

Choosing Commands with Keyboard Shortcuts

Applications in the Office suite offer a variety of keyboard shortcuts you can use to execute specific commands. Keyboard shortcuts generally require two or more keys. For example, the keyboard shortcut to display the Open dialog box in an application is Ctrl + O. To use this keyboard shortcut, hold down the Ctrl key, type the letter O on the keyboard, and then release the Ctrl key. For a list of keyboard shortcuts, refer to the Help files.

Choosing Commands with Shortcut Menus

The software programs in the suite include menus that contain commands related to the item with which you are working. A shortcut menu appears in the file in the location where you are working. To display a shortcut menu, click the right mouse button or press Shift + F10. For example, if the insertion point is positioned in a paragraph of text in a Word document, clicking the right mouse button or pressing Shift + F10 will cause the shortcut menu shown in Figure G.8 to display in the document screen (along with the Mini toolbar).

To select an option from a shortcut menu with the mouse, click the desired option. If you are using the keyboard, press the Up or Down Arrow key until the desired option is selected and then press the Enter key. To close a shortcut menu without choosing an option, click anywhere outside the shortcut menu or press the Esc key.

Working with Multiple Programs

As you learn the various programs in the Microsoft Office suite, you will notice how executing commands in each is very similar. For example, the steps to save, close, and print are virtually the same whether you are working in Word, Excel, or PowerPoint. This consistency between programs greatly enhances a user's ability to transfer knowledge learned in one program to another within the suite. Another appeal of Microsoft Office is the ability to have more than one program open at the same time. For example, you can open Word, create a document, and then open Excel, create a spreadsheet, and copy the spreadsheet into Word.

Figure G.8 Word Shortcut Menu

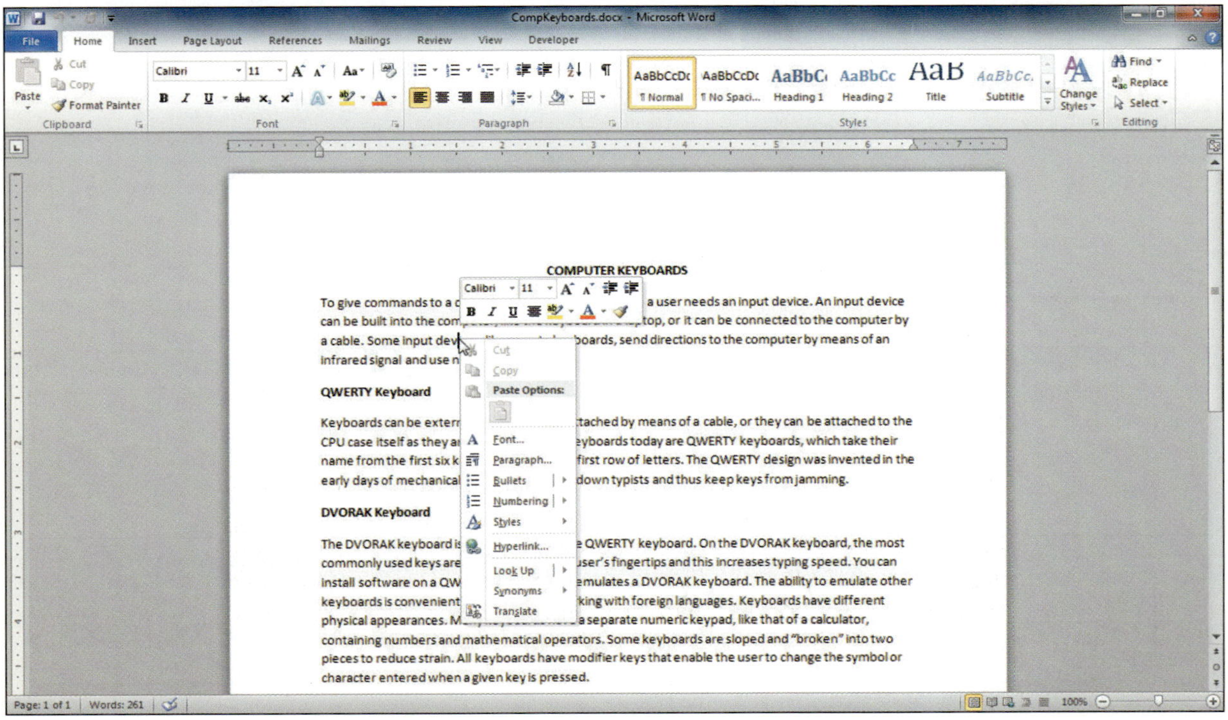

Figure G.9 Taskbar with Word, Excel, and PowerPoint Open

When you open a program, a button displays on the Taskbar containing an icon representing the program. If you open another program, a button containing an icon representing the program displays to the right of the first program button. Figure G.9 shows the Taskbar with Word, Excel, and PowerPoint open. To move from one program to another, click the button on the Taskbar representing the desired program file.

Customizing Settings

Before beginning computer projects in this textbook, you may need to customize the monitor settings and turn on the display of file extensions. Projects in the chapters in this textbook assume that the monitor display is set at 1280 by 800 pixels and that the display of file extensions is turned on.

Changing Monitor Resolutions

Before you begin learning the applications in the Microsoft Office 2010 suite, take a moment to check the display settings on the computer you are using. The ribbon in the Microsoft Office suite adjusts to the screen resolution setting of your computer monitor. Computer monitors set at a high resolution will have the ability to show more buttons in the ribbon than will a monitor set to a low resolution. The illustrations in this textbook were created with a screen resolution display set at 1280 × 800 pixels. In Figure G.10 the Word ribbon is shown three ways: at a lower screen resolution (1024 × 768 pixels), at the screen resolution featured

Figure G.10 Monitor Resolution

1024 × 768 screen resolution

1280 × 800 screen resolution

1440 × 900 screen resolution

throughout this textbook, and at a higher screen resolution (1440 × 900 pixels). Note the variances in the ribbon in all three examples. If possible, set your display to 1280 × 800 pixels to match the illustrations you will see in this textbook.

Project 1 Setting Monitor Display to 1280 by 800

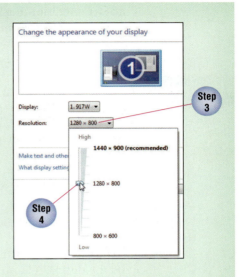

1. At the Windows 7 desktop, click the Start button and then click *Control Panel*.
2. At the Control Panel dialog box, click the *Adjust screen resolution* option in the Appearance and Personalization category.
3. At the Control Panel Screen Resolution window, click the Resolution option button. (This displays a drop-down slider bar. Your drop-down slider bar may display differently than what you see in the image at the right.)
4. Drag the slider bar button on the slider bar until *1280 × 800* displays to the right of the slider button.
5. Click in the Control Panel Screen Resolution window to remove the slider bar.
6. Click the Apply button.
7. Click the Keep Changes button.
8. Click the OK button.
9. Close the Control Panel window.

Project 2 Displaying File Extensions

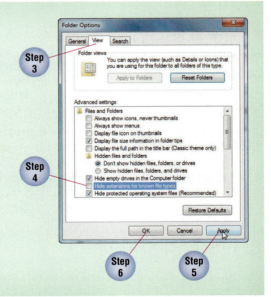

1. At the Windows 7 desktop, click the Start button and then click *Computer*.
2. At the Computer window, click the Organize button on the toolbar and then click *Folder and search options* at the drop-down list.
3. At the Folder Options dialog box, click the View tab.
4. Click the *Hide extensions for known file types* check box to remove the check mark.
5. Click the Apply button.
6. Click the OK button.
7. Close the Computer window.

Getting Started in Office 2010   11

Completing Computer Projects ▪▪▪▪▪▪▪▪▪▪▪▪▪▪▪▪

Some computer projects in this textbook require that you open an existing file. Project files are saved on the Student Resources CD that accompanies this textbook. The files you need for each chapter are saved in individual folders. Before beginning a chapter, copy the necessary folder from the CD to your storage medium (such as a USB flash drive) using the Computer window. If storage capacity is an issue with your storage medium, delete any previous chapter folders before copying a chapter folder onto your storage medium.

Project 3 Copying a Folder from the Student Resources CD

1. Insert the CD that accompanies this textbook in the CD drive. At the AutoPlay window that displays, click the Close button located in the upper right corner of the window.
2. Insert your USB flash drive in an available USB port. If an AutoPlay window displays, click the Close button.
3. At the Windows desktop, open the Computer window by clicking the Start button and then clicking *Computer* at the Start menu.
4. Double-click the CD drive in the Content pane (displays with the name *BM10StudentResources* preceded by the drive letter).
5. Double-click the desired program folder name in the Content pane.
6. Click once on the desired chapter subfolder name to select it.
7. Click the Organize button on the toolbar and then click *Copy* at the drop-down list.
8. In the Computer window Content pane, click the drive containing your storage medium.
9. Click the Organize button on the toolbar and then click *Paste* at the drop-down list.
10. Close the Computer window by clicking the Close button located in the upper right corner of the window.

Project 4 Deleting a Folder

Note: Check with your instructor before deleting a folder.

1. Insert your storage medium (such as a USB flash drive) in the USB port.
2. At the Windows desktop, open the Computer window by clicking the Start button and then clicking *Computer* at the Start menu.
3. Double-click the drive letter for your storage medium (drive containing your USB flash drive such as *Removable Disk (F:)*).
4. Click the chapter folder in the Content pane.
5. Click the Organize button on the toolbar and then click *Delete* at the drop-down list.
6. At the message asking if you want to delete the folder, click the Yes button.
7. Close the Computer window by clicking the Close button located in the upper right corner of the window.

Using Windows 7

A computer requires an operating system to provide necessary instructions on a multitude of processes including loading programs, managing data, directing the flow of information to peripheral equipment, and displaying information. Windows 7 is an operating system that provides functions of this type (along with much more) in a graphical environment. Windows is referred to as a ***graphical user interface*** (GUI—pronounced *gooey*) that provides a visual display of information with features such as icons (pictures) and buttons. In this introduction, you will learn these basic features of Windows 7:

- Use desktop icons and the Taskbar to launch programs and open files or folders
- Add and remove gadgets
- Organize and manage data, including copying, moving, creating, and deleting files and folders; and create a shortcut
- Explore the Control Panel and personalize the desktop
- Use the Windows Help and Support features
- Use search tools
- Customize monitor settings

Before using one of the software programs in the Microsoft Office suite, you will need to start the Windows 7 operating system. To do this, turn on the computer. Depending on your computer equipment configuration, you may also need to turn on the monitor and printer. If you are using a computer that is part of a network system or if your computer is set up for multiple users, a screen will display showing the user accounts defined for your computer system. At this screen, click your user account name and, if necessary, type your password and then press the Enter key. The Windows 7 operating system will start and, after a few moments, the desktop will display as shown in Figure W.1. (Your desktop may vary from what you see in Figure W.1.)

Exploring the Desktop

When Windows is loaded, the main portion of the screen is called the ***desktop***. Think of the desktop in Windows as the top of a desk in an office. A business person places necessary tools—such as pencils, pens, paper, files, calculator—on the desktop to perform functions. Like the tools that are located on a desk, the desktop contains tools for operating the computer. These tools are logically grouped and placed in dialog boxes or panels that you can display using icons on the desktop. The desktop contains a variety of features for using your computer and software programs installed on the computer. The features available on the desktop are represented by icons and buttons.

Figure W.1 Windows 7 Desktop

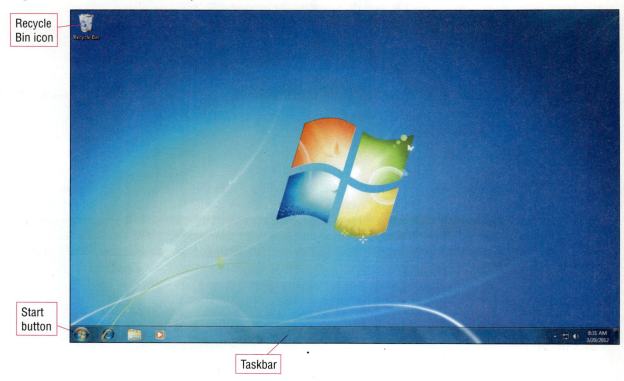

Using Icons

Icons are visual symbols that represent programs, files, or folders. Figure W.1 identifies the Recycle Bin icon located on the Windows desktop. The Windows desktop on your computer may contain additional icons. Programs that have been installed on your computer may be represented by an icon on the desktop. Also, icons may display on your desktop representing files or folders. Double-click an icon and the program, file, or folder it represents opens on the desktop.

Using the Taskbar

The bar that displays at the bottom of the desktop (see Figure W.1) is called the Taskbar. The Taskbar, shown in Figure W.2, contains the Start button, pinned items, a section that displays task buttons representing active tasks, the notification area, and the Show Desktop button.

Figure W.2 Windows 7 Taskbar

Click the Start button, located at the left side of the Taskbar, and the Start menu displays as shown in Figure W.3 (your Start menu may vary). You can also display the Start menu by pressing the Windows key on your keyboard or by pressing Ctrl + Esc. The left side of the Start menu contains links to the most recently and frequently used programs. The name of the currently logged on user displays at the top of the darker right portion of the menu followed by the user's libraries. The two sections below the personal libraries provide links to other Windows features, such as games, the Control Panel, and Windows Help and Support. Use the Shut down button to put the system in a power-conserving state or into a locked, shut down, or sleep mode.

To choose an option from the Start menu, drag the arrow pointer to the desired option (referred to as *pointing*) and then click the left mouse button. Pointing to options at the Start menu that are followed by a right-pointing arrow will cause a side menu to display with additional options. When a program is open, a task button representing the program appears on the Taskbar. If multiple programs are open, each program will appear as a task button on the Taskbar (a few specialized tools may not).

Manipulating Windows

When you open a program, a defined work area displays on the screen, which is referred to as a *window*. A Title bar displays at the top of a window and contains buttons at the right side for closing the window and minimizing, maximizing, and restoring the size of the window. You can open more than one window at a time and the open windows can be cascaded or stacked. Windows 7 contains a Snap feature that causes a window to "stick" to the edge of the screen when the window

Figure W.3 Start Menu

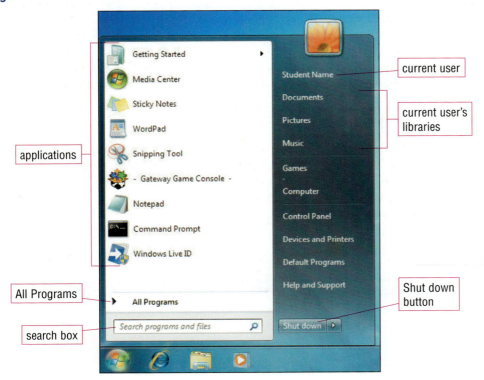

is moved to the left or right side of the screen. Move a window to the top of the screen and the window is automatically maximized. If you drag down a maximized window, the window is automatically restored down.

In addition to moving and sizing a window, you can change the display of all open windows. To do this, position the mouse pointer on the Taskbar and then click the right mouse button and a pop-up list displays with options for displaying multiple open windows. You can cascade the windows, stack the windows, and display the windows side by side.

Project 1 Opening Programs, Switching between Programs, and Manipulating Windows

1. Open Windows 7. (To do this, turn on the computer and, if necessary, turn on the monitor and/or printer. If you are using a computer that is part of a network system or if your computer is set up for multiple users, you may need to click your user account name and, if necessary, type your password and then press the Enter key. Check with your instructor to determine if you need to complete any additional steps.)
2. When the Windows 7 desktop displays, open Microsoft Word by completing the following steps:
   a. Position the arrow pointer on the Start button on the Taskbar and then click the left mouse button.
   b. At the Start menu, click *All Programs* and then click *Microsoft Office* (this displays programs in the Office suite below Microsoft Office).
   c. Drag the arrow pointer down to *Microsoft Word 2010* and then click the left mouse button.
   d. When the Microsoft Word program is open, notice that a task button representing Word displays on the Taskbar.

   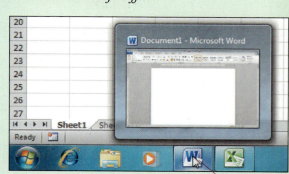
   Step 2d

3. Open Microsoft Excel by completing the following steps:
   a. Position the arrow pointer on the Start button on the Taskbar and then click the left mouse button.
   b. At the Start menu, click *All Programs* and then click *Microsoft Office*.
   c. Drag the arrow pointer down to *Microsoft Excel 2010* and then click the left mouse button.
   d. When the Microsoft Excel program is open, notice that a task button representing Excel displays on the Taskbar to the right of the task button representing Word.
4. Switch to the Word program by clicking the task button on the Taskbar representing Word.
5. Switch to the Excel program by clicking the task button on the Taskbar representing Excel.

Step 4

Using Windows 7

6. Restore down the Excel window by clicking the Restore Down button that displays immediately left of the Close button in the upper right corner of the screen. (This reduces the Excel window so it displays along the bottom half of the screen.)
7. Restore down the Word window by clicking the Restore Down button located immediately left of the Close button in the upper right corner of the screen.

8. Position the mouse pointer on the Word window Title bar, hold down the left mouse button, drag to the left side of the screen until an outline of the window displays in the left half of the screen, and then release the mouse button. (This "sticks" the window to the left side of the screen.)
9. Position the mouse pointer on the Excel window Title bar, hold down the left mouse button, drag to the right until an outline of the window displays in the right half of the screen, and then release the mouse button.

10. Minimize the Excel window by clicking the Minimize button that displays in the upper right corner of the Excel window Title bar.
11. Hover your mouse over the Excel button on the Taskbar and notice the Excel window thumbnail that displays above the button and then click the thumbnail. (This displays the Excel window at the right side of the screen.)
12. Cascade the Word and Excel windows by positioning the arrow pointer on an empty area on the Taskbar, clicking the right mouse button, and then clicking *Cascade windows* at the pop-up list.

13. After viewing the windows cascaded, display them stacked by right-clicking an empty area on the Taskbar and then clicking *Show windows stacked* at the pop-up list.
14. Display the desktop by right-clicking an empty area on the Taskbar and then clicking *Show the desktop* at the pop-up list.
15. Display the windows stacked by right-clicking an empty area on the Taskbar and then clicking *Show open windows* at the pop-up list.

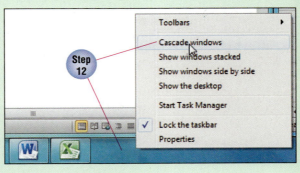

16. Position the mouse pointer on the Word window Title bar, hold down the left mouse button, drag the window to the top of the screen, and then release the mouse button. This maximizes the Word window so it fills the screen.
17. Close the Word window by clicking the Close button located in the upper right corner of the window.
18. At the Excel window, click the Maximize button located immediately left of the Close button in the upper right corner of the Excel window.
19. Close the Excel window by clicking the Close button located in the upper right corner of the window.

Using the Pinned Area

The icons that display immediately right of the Start button are pinned programs. Clicking an icon opens the program associated with the icon. Click the first icon to open the Internet Explorer web browser, click the second icon to open a window containing Libraries, and click the third icon to open the Windows media player window.

Exploring the Notification Area

The notification area is located at the right side of the Taskbar and contains icons that show the status of certain system functions such as a network connection or battery power. It also contains icons you can use to manage certain programs and Windows 7 features. The notification area also contains the system clock and date. Click the time or date in the notification area and a window displays with a clock and a calendar of the current month. Click the Change date and time settings hyperlink that displays at the bottom of the window and the Date and Time dialog box displays. To change the date and/or time, click the Change date and time button and the Date and Time Settings dialog box displays similar to the dialog box shown in Figure W.4. (If a dialog box displays telling you that Windows needs your permission to continue, click the Continue button.)

Change the month and year by clicking the left-pointing or right-pointing arrow at the top of the calendar in the *Date* section. Click the left-pointing arrow to display the previous month(s) and click the right-pointing arrow to display the next month(s).

To change the day, click the desired day in the monthly calendar that displays in the dialog box. To change the time, double-click either the hour, minute, or seconds and then type the appropriate time or use the up- and down-pointing arrows in the spin boxes to adjust the time.

Some programs, when installed, will add an icon to the notification area of the Taskbar. Display the name of the icon by positioning the mouse pointer on the icon and, after approximately one second, the icon label displays. If more icons have been inserted in the notification area than can be viewed at one time, an up-pointing arrow button displays at the left side of the notification area. Click this up-pointing arrow button and the remaining icons display.

Setting Taskbar Properties

You can customize the Taskbar with options from the Taskbar shortcut menu. Display this menu by right-clicking on an empty portion of the Taskbar. The Taskbar shortcut menu contains options for turning on or off the display of specific toolbars, specifying the display of multiple windows, displaying the Start Task Manager dialog box, locking or unlocking the Taskbar, and displaying the Taskbar and Start Menu Properties dialog box.

With options in the Taskbar and Start Menu Properties dialog box shown in Figure W.5, you can change settings for the Taskbar as well as the Start menu. Display this dialog box by right-clicking on an empty area on the Taskbar and then clicking *Properties* at the shortcut menu.

Each property is controlled by a check box. Property options containing a check mark are active. Click the option to remove the check mark and make the option inactive. If an option is inactive, clicking the option will insert a check mark in the check box and turn on the option (make it active).

Figure W.4 Date and Time Settings Dialog Box

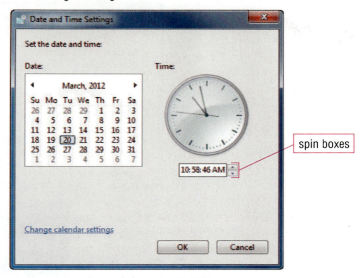

Figure W.5 Taskbar and Start Menu Properties Dialog Box

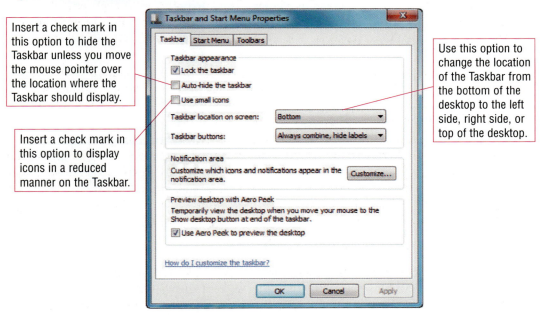

Project 2 — Changing Taskbar Properties

1. Make sure the Windows 7 desktop displays.
2. Change Taskbar properties by completing the following steps:
   a. Position the arrow pointer on any empty area on the Taskbar and then click the right mouse button.
   b. At the shortcut menu that displays, click *Properties*.

c. At the Taskbar and Start Menu Properties dialog box, click the *Auto-hide the taskbar* check box to insert a check mark.
d. Click the *Use small icons* check box to insert a check mark.
e. Click the button (displays with the word *Bottom*) that displays at the right side of the *Taskbar location on screen* option and then click *Right* at the drop-down list.
f. Click OK to close the dialog box.

3. Since the *Auto-hide the taskbar* check box contains a check mark, the Taskbar does not display. Display the Taskbar by moving the mouse pointer to the right side of the screen. Notice that the icons on the Taskbar are smaller.

4. Return to the default settings for the Taskbar by completing the following steps:
a. Move the mouse pointer to the right side of the screen to display the Taskbar.
b. Right-click any empty area on the Taskbar and then click *Properties* at the shortcut menu.
c. Click the *Auto-hide the taskbar* check box to remove the check mark.
d. Click the *Use small icons* check box to remove the check mark.
e. Click the button (displays with the word *Right*) that displays at the right side of the *Taskbar location on screen* option and then click *Bottom* at the drop-down list.
f. Click OK to close the dialog box.

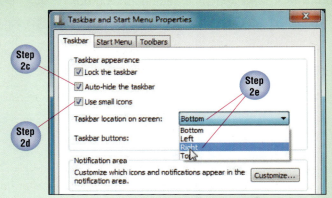

Powering Down the Computer

If you want to shut down Windows, close any open programs, click the Start button on the Taskbar, and then click the Shut down button as shown in Figure W.6. Click the button containing a right-pointing triangle that displays at the right side of the Shut down button and a drop-down list displays with options for powering down the computer.

In a multi-user environment, click the *Switch user* option to change users or click the *Log off* option to log off your computer, which shuts down your applications and files and makes system resources available to other users logged on to the system. If you need to walk away from your computer and you want to protect your work, consider locking the computer by clicking the *Lock* option. When you lock the computer, the desktop is hidden but the system is not shut down and the power is not conserved. To unlock the computer, click the icon on the desktop representing your account, type your password, and then press Enter. Click the *Restart* option to shut down and then restart the computer and click

Figure W.6 Shut Down Button and Power Options Button

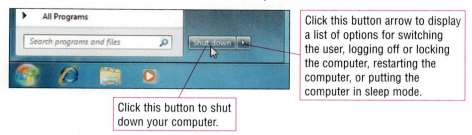

the *Sleep* option to save power without having to close all files and applications. In sleep mode, Windows saves files and information about programs and then powers down the computer to a low-power state. To "wake" the computer back up, quickly press the computer's power button.

Using Gadgets

You can add gadgets to your desktop. A gadget is a mini program providing information at a glance and easy access to frequently used tools. For example, you can add a Clock gadget to your desktop that shows the current time, a Weather gadget that displays the current temperature where you live, or a Calendar gadget that displays the current date. Gadgets are added to the Sidebar, which is a location at the right side of the Windows 7 desktop.

To view available gadgets, right-click in a blank area on the desktop and then click *Gadgets* at the shortcut menu. This displays the gadget gallery similar to what you see in Figure W.7. To add a gadget to the Sidebar, double-click the desired gadget. To remove a gadget from the Sidebar, hover the mouse pointer over the gadget and then click the Close button that displays at the upper right side of the gadget. ***Note: The Gadget option on the shortcut menu may be missing if the computer you are using is located in a school setting where customization options have been disabled. If you do not see* Gadget *on the shortcut menu, please skip Project 3.***

Figure W.7 Gadget Gallery

Using Windows 7

Project 3 **Adding and Removing Gadgets**

1. At the Windows 7 desktop, right-click in a blank area on the desktop and then click *Gadgets* at the shortcut menu.
2. At the Gadgets Gallery, double-click the *Clock* gadget.
3. Double-click the *Weather* gadget.
4. Double-click the *Calendar* gadget.
5. Close the Gadget Gallery by clicking the Close button located in the upper right corner of the gallery.
6. Hover your mouse over the Calendar gadget until buttons display at the right side of the gadget and then click the Larger size button. (This expands the calendar to display the days of the month.)
7. Hover your mouse over the Weather gadget and then click the Options button.
8. At the Weather dialog box that displays, type in the *Select current location* text box the name of your city followed by your state (or province) and then press Enter.
9. If a drop-down list displays with city names, scroll down the list to display your city and then click your city and state (or province).
10. Click OK to close the Weather dialog box.
11. After viewing the gadgets, remove the Clock gadget by hovering the mouse over the clock and then clicking the Close button that displays at the upper right side of the clock.
12. Close the Weather gadget by hovering the mouse over the gadget and then clicking the Close button that displays.
13. Close the Calendar gadget by hovering the mouse over the gadget and then clicking the Close button that displays.

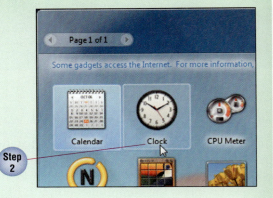

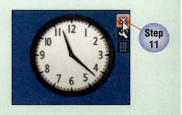

Managing Files and Folders

As you begin working with programs in Windows 7, you will create files in which data (information) is saved. A file might contain a Word document, an Excel workbook, or a PowerPoint presentation. As you begin creating files, consider creating folders into which those files will be stored. You can complete file management tasks such as creating a folder and copying and moving files and folders at the Computer window. To display the Computer window shown in Figure W.8, click the Start button on the Taskbar and then click *Computer*. The various components of the Computer window are identified in Figure W.8.

Figure W.8 Computer Window

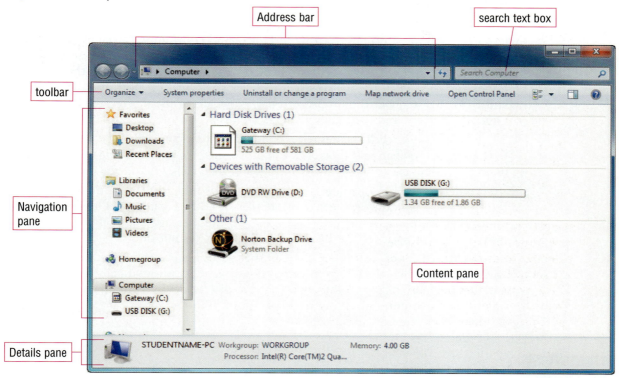

In the Content pane of the Computer window, icons display representing each hard disk drive and removable storage medium such as a CD, DVD, or USB device connected to your computer. Next to each storage device icon, Windows provides the amount of storage space available as well as a bar with the amount of used space shaded with color. This visual cue allows you to see at a glance the proportion of space available relative to the capacity of the device. Double-click a device icon in the Content pane to change the display to show the contents stored on the device. You can display contents from another device or folder using the Navigation pane or the Address bar on the Computer window.

Copying, Moving, and Deleting Files and Folders

File and folder management activities might include copying and moving files or folders from one folder or drive to another, or deleting files or folders. The Computer window offers a variety of methods for copying, moving, and deleting files and folders. This section will provide you with steps for copying, moving, and deleting files and folders using options from the Organize button on the toolbar and the shortcut menu.

To copy a file to another folder or drive, first display the file in the Content pane by identifying the location of the file. If the file is located in the Documents folder, click the *Documents* folder in the *Libraries* section in the Navigation pane and then click the file name in the Content pane that you want to copy. Click the Organize button on the toolbar and then click *Copy* at the drop-down list. In the Navigation pane, click the location where you want to copy the file. Click the Organize button and then click *Paste* at the drop-down list. You would complete similar steps to copy and paste a folder to another location.

If the desired file is located on a storage medium such as a CD, DVD, or USB device, double-click the device in the section of the Content pane labeled *Devices with Removable Storage*. (Each removable device is assigned an alphabetic drive letter by Windows, usually starting at F or G and continuing through the alphabet depending on the number of removable devices that are currently in use.) After double-clicking the storage medium in the Content pane, navigate to the desired folder and then click the file to select it. Click the Organize button on the toolbar and then click *Copy* at the drop-down list. Navigate to the desired folder, click the Organize button, and then click *Paste* at the drop-down list.

To move a file, click the desired file in the Content pane, click the Organize button on the toolbar, and then click *Cut* at the drop-down list. Navigate to the desired location, click the Organize button, and then click *Paste* at the drop-down list.

To delete a file(s) or folder(s), click the file or folder in the Content pane in the Computer window or select multiple files or folders. Click the Organize button and then click *Delete* at the drop-down list. At the message asking if you want to move the file or folder to the Recycle Bin, click the Yes button.

In Project 4, you will insert the CD that accompanies this book into the DVD or CD drive. When the CD is inserted, the drive may automatically activate and a dialog box may display telling you that the disc or device contains more than one type of content and asking what you want Windows to do. If this dialog box displays, click the Cancel button.

Project 4 — Copying a File and Folder and Deleting a File

1. Insert the CD that accompanies this textbook into the appropriate drive. If a dialog box displays telling you that the disc or device contains more than one type of content and asking what you want Windows to do, click the Cancel button.
2. Insert your storage medium (such as a USB flash drive) in the USB port (or other drive). If an AutoPlay window displays, click the Close button.
3. At the Windows 7 desktop, click the Start button and then click *Computer* located at the right side of the Start menu.
4. Copy a file from the CD that accompanies this textbook to the drive containing your storage medium by completing the following steps:
   a. Double-click the CD drive in the Content pane containing the CD from the book.
   b. Double-click the *StudentDataFiles* folder in the Content pane.
   c. Double-click the *Windows7* folder in the Content pane.
   d. Click **WordDocument01.docx** in the Content pane.
   e. Click the Organize button on the toolbar and then click *Copy* at the drop-down list.

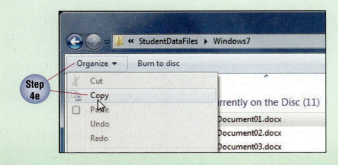

 f. In the Computer section in the Navigation pane, click the drive containing your storage medium. (You may need to scroll down the Navigation pane.)
 g. Click the Organize button and then click *Paste* at the drop-down list.
5. Delete **WordDocument01.docx** from your storage medium by completing the following steps:
 a. Make sure the contents of your storage medium display in the Content pane in the Computer window.
 b. Click **WordDocument01.docx** in the Content pane to select it.
 c. Click the Organize button and then click *Delete* at the drop-down list.
 d. At the message asking if you want to permanently delete the file, click the Yes button.
6. Copy the Windows7 folder from the CD to your storage medium by completing the following steps:
 a. With the Computer window open, click the drive in the *Computer* section in the Navigation pane that contains the CD that accompanies this book.
 b. Double-click *StudentDataFiles* in the Content pane.
 c. Click the *Windows7* folder in the Content pane.
 d. Click the Organize button and then click *Copy* at the drop-down list.
 e. In the *Computer* section in the Navigation pane, click the drive containing your storage medium.
 f. Click the Organize button and then click *Paste* at the drop-down list.
7. Close the Computer window by clicking the Close button located in the upper right corner of the window.

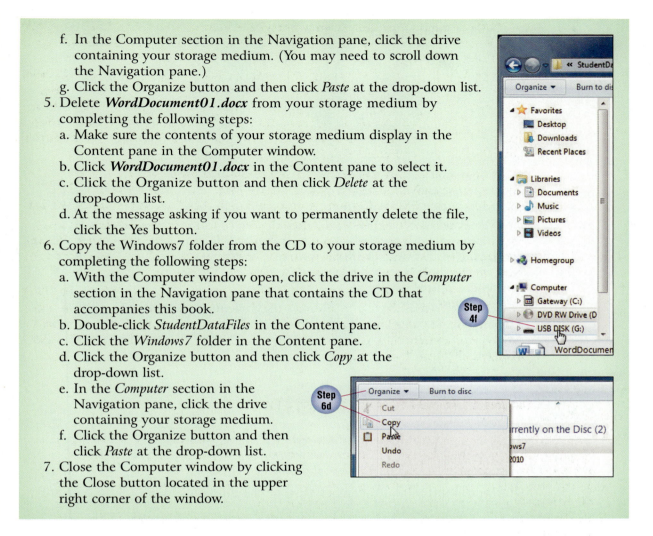

 In addition to options in the Organize button drop-down list, you can use options in a shortcut menu to copy, move, and delete files or folders. To use a shortcut menu, select the desired file(s) or folder(s), position the mouse pointer on the selected item, and then click the right mouse button. At the shortcut menu that displays, click the desired option such as Copy, Cut, or Delete.

Selecting Files and Folders

You can move, copy, or delete more than one file or folder at the same time. Before moving, copying, or deleting files or folders, select the desired files or folders. To make selecting easier, consider changing the display in the Content pane to List or Details. To change the display, click the Views button arrow on the toolbar in the Computer window and then click *List* or *Details* at the drop-down list. You can also cycle through the various views by clicking the Views button. Hover your mouse over the Views button and the ScreenTip *Change your view* displays.

 To select adjacent files or folders, click the first file or folder, hold down the Shift key, and then click the last file or folder. To select nonadjacent files or folders, click the first file or folder, hold down the Ctrl key, and then click any other files or folders.

Project 5 — Copying and Deleting Files

1. At the Windows 7 desktop, click the Start button and then click *Computer*.
2. Copy files from the CD that accompanies this textbook to the drive containing your storage medium by completing the following steps:
    a. Make sure the CD that accompanies this textbook and your storage medium are inserted in the appropriate drives.
    b. Double-click the CD drive in the Content pane in the Computer window.
    c. Double-click the *StudentDataFiles* folder in the Content pane.
    d. Double-click the *Windows7* folder in the Content pane.
    e. Change the display to List by clicking the Views button arrow on the toolbar and then clicking *List* at the drop-down list.
    f. Click **WordDocument01.docx** in the Content pane.
    g. Hold down the Shift key, click **WordDocument05.docx**, and then release the Shift key. (This selects five documents.)
    h. Click the Organize button and then click *Copy* at the drop-down list.
    i. In the *Computer* section in the Navigation pane, click the drive containing your storage medium.
    j. Click the Organize button and then click *Paste* at the drop-down list.

Step 2e

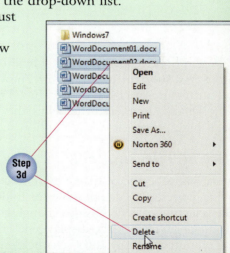

Steps 2f-2g

3. Delete the files from your storage medium that you just copied by completing the following steps:
    a. Change the view by clicking the Views button arrow bar and then clicking *List* at the drop-down list.
    b. Click **WordDocument01.docx** in the Content pane.
    c. Hold down the Shift key, click **WordDocument05.docx**, and then release the Shift key.
    d. Position the mouse pointer on any selected file, click the right mouse button, and then click *Delete* at the shortcut menu.
    e. At the message asking if you are sure you want to permanently delete the files, click Yes.
4. Close the Computer window by clicking the Close button located in the upper right corner of the window.

Step 3d

Manipulating and Creating Folders

As you begin working with and creating a number of files, consider creating folders in which you can logically group the files. To create a folder, display the Computer window and then display in the Content pane the drive or folder where you want to create the folder. Position the mouse pointer in a blank area in the Content pane, click the right mouse button, point to *New* in the shortcut menu, and then click *Folder* at the side menu. This inserts a folder icon in the Content pane and names the folder *New folder*. Type the desired name for the new folder and then press Enter.

Project 6 Creating a New Folder

1. At the Windows 7 desktop, open the Computer window.
2. Create a new folder by completing the following steps:
    a. Double-click in the Content pane the drive that contains your storage medium.
    b. Double-click the *Windows7* folder in the Content pane. (This opens the folder.)
    c. Click the Views button arrow and then click *List* at the drop-down list.
    d. Position the mouse pointer in a blank area in the Content pane and then click the right mouse button.
    e. Point to *New* in the shortcut menu and then click *Folder* at the side menu.

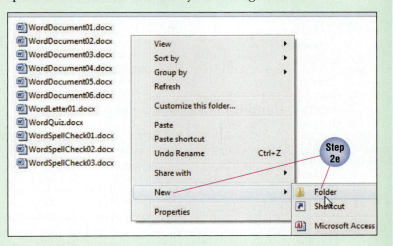

    f. Type **SpellCheckFiles** and then press Enter. (This changes the name from *New folder* to *SpellCheckFiles*.)
3. Copy **WordSpellCheck01.docx**, **WordSpellCheck02.docx**, and **WordSpellCheck03.docx** into the SpellCheckFiles folder you just created by completing the following steps:
    a. Click the Views button arrow and then click *List* at the drop-down list. (Skip this step if *List* is already selected.)
    b. Click once on the file named **WordSpellCheck01.docx** located in the Content pane.
    c. Hold down the Shift key, click once on the file named **WordSpellCheck03.docx**, and then release the Shift key. (This selects three documents.)

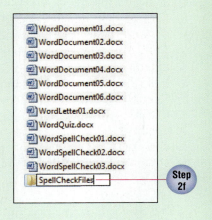

    d. Click the Organize button and then click *Copy* at the drop-down list.
    e. Double-click the *SpellCheckFiles* folder in the Content pane.
    f. Click the Organize button and then click *Paste* at the drop-down list.

Using Windows 7 27

4. Delete the SpellCheckFiles folder and its contents by completing the following steps:
   a. Click the Back button (contains a left-pointing arrow) located at the left side of the Address bar.
   b. With the SpellCheckFiles folder selected in the Content pane, click the Organize button and then click *Delete* at the drop-down list.
   c. At the message asking you to confirm the deletion, click Yes.
5. Close the window by clicking the Close button located in the upper right corner of the window.

Using the Recycle Bin

Deleting the wrong file can be a disaster but Windows 7 helps protect your work with the Recycle Bin. The Recycle Bin acts just like an office wastepaper basket; you can "throw away" (delete) unwanted files, but you can "reach in" to the Recycle Bin and take out (restore) a file if you threw it away by accident.

Deleting Files to the Recycle Bin

A file or folder or selected files or folders you delete from the hard drive are sent automatically to the Recycle Bin. If you want to permanently delete files or folders from the hard drive without first sending them to the Recycle Bin, select the desired file(s) or folder(s), right click on one of the selected files or folders, hold down the Shift key, and then click *Delete* at the shortcut menu.

Files and folders deleted from a USB flash drive or disc are deleted permanently. (Recovery programs are available, however, that will help you recover deleted files or folders. If you accidentally delete a file or folder from a USB flash drive or disc, do not do anything more with the USB flash drive or disc until you can run a recovery program.)

You can delete files in the manner described earlier in this section and you can also delete a file by dragging the file icon to the Recycle Bin. To do this, click the desired file in the Content pane in the Computer window, drag the file icon on top of the Recycle Bin icon on the desktop until the text *Move to Recycle Bin* displays, and then release the mouse button.

Restoring Files from the Recycle Bin

To restore a file from the Recycle Bin, double-click the Recycle Bin icon on the desktop. This opens the Recycle Bin window shown in Figure W.9. (The contents of the Recycle Bin will vary.) To restore a file, click the file you want restored and then click the Restore this item button on the toolbar. This removes the file from the Recycle Bin and returns it to its original location. You can also restore a file by positioning the mouse pointer on the file, clicking the right mouse button, and then clicking *Restore* at the shortcut menu.

Figure W.9 Recycle Bin Window

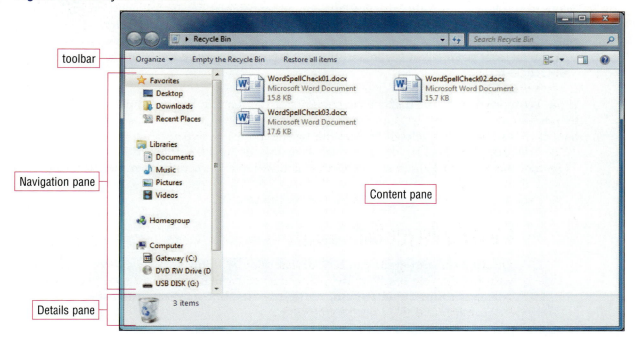

Project 7 Deleting Files to and Restoring Files from the Recycle Bin

Before beginning this project, check with your instructor to determine if you can copy files to the hard drive.

1. At the Windows 7 desktop, open the Computer window.
2. Copy files from your storage medium to the Documents folder on your hard drive by completing the following steps:
   a. Double-click in the Content pane the drive containing your storage medium.
   b. Double-click the *Windows7* folder in the Content pane.
   c. Click the Views button arrow and then click *List* at the drop-down list. (Skip this step if *List* is already selected.)
   d. Click **WordSpellCheck01.docx** in the Content pane.
   e. Hold down the Shift key, click **WordSpellCheck03.docx**, and then release the Shift key.
   f. Click the Organize button and then click *Copy* at the drop-down list.
   g. Click the *Documents* folder in the *Libraries* section in the Navigation pane.
   h. Click the Organize button and then click *Paste* at the drop-down list.

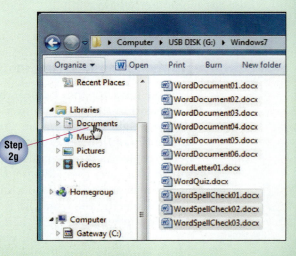

Using Windows 7   29

3. Delete to the Recycle Bin the files you just copied by completing the following steps:
   a. With **WordSpellCheck01.docx** through **WordSpellCheck03.docx** selected in the Content pane, click the Organize button and then click *Delete* at the drop-down list.
   b. At the message asking you if you are sure you want to move the items to the Recycle Bin, click Yes.
4. Close the Computer window.
5. At the Windows 7 desktop, display the contents of the Recycle Bin by double-clicking the Recycle Bin icon.
6. Restore the files you just deleted by completing the following steps:
   a. Select **WordSpellCheck01.docx** through **WordSpellCheck03.docx** in the Recycle Bin Content pane. (If these files are not visible, you will need to scroll down the list of files in the Content pane.)
   b. Click the Restore the selected items button on the toolbar.

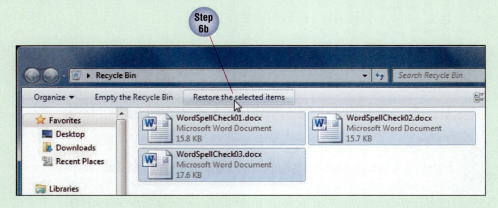

7. Close the Recycle Bin by clicking the Close button located in the upper right corner of the window.
8. Display the Computer window.
9. Click the *Documents* folder in the *Libraries* section in the Navigation pane.
10. Delete the files you restored.
11. Close the Computer window.

Emptying the Recycle Bin

Just like a wastepaper basket, the Recycle Bin can get full. To empty the Recycle Bin, position the arrow pointer on the Recycle Bin icon on the desktop and then click the right mouse button. At the shortcut menu that displays, click the *Empty Recycle Bin* option. At the message asking if you want to permanently delete the items, click Yes. You can also empty the Recycle Bin by displaying the Recycle Bin window and then clicking the Empty the Recycle Bin button on the toolbar. At the message asking if you want to permanently delete the items, click Yes. To delete a specific file from the Recycle Bin window, click the desired file in the Recycle Bin window, click the Organize button, and then *Delete* at the drop-down list. At the message asking if you want to permanently delete the file, click Yes. When you empty the Recycle Bin, the files cannot be recovered by the Recycle Bin or by Windows 7. If you have to recover a file, you will need to use a file recovery program.

Project 8 Emptying the Recycle Bin

Before beginning this project, check with your instructor to determine if you can delete files/folders from the Recycle Bin.

1. At the Windows 7 desktop, double-click the Recycle Bin icon.
2. At the Recycle Bin window, empty the contents by clicking the Empty the Recycle Bin button on the toolbar.
3. At the message asking you if you want to permanently delete the items, click Yes.
4. Close the Recycle Bin by clicking the Close button located in the upper right corner of the window.

Step 2

Creating a Shortcut

If you use a file or program on a consistent basis, consider creating a shortcut to the file or program. A shortcut is a specialized icon that represents very small files that point the operating system to the actual item, whether it is a file, a folder, or an application. If you create a shortcut to a Word document, the shortcut icon is not the actual document but a path to the document. Double-click the shortcut icon and Windows 7 opens the document in Word.

One method for creating a shortcut is to display the Computer window and then make active the drive or folder where the file is located. Right-click the desired file, point to *Send To*, and then click *Desktop (create shortcut)*. You can easily delete a shortcut icon from the desktop by dragging the shortcut icon to the Recycle Bin icon. This deletes the shortcut icon but does not delete the file to which the shortcut pointed.

Project 9 Creating a Shortcut

1. At the Windows 7 desktop, display the Computer window.
2. Double-click the drive containing your storage medium.
3. Double-click the *Windows7* folder in the Content pane.
4. Change the display of files to a list by clicking the Views button arrow and then clicking *List* at the drop-down list. (Skip this step if *List* is already selected.)
5. Create a shortcut to the file named **WordLetter01.docx** by right-clicking **WordLetter01.docx**, pointing to *Send to*, and then clicking *Desktop (create shortcut)*.

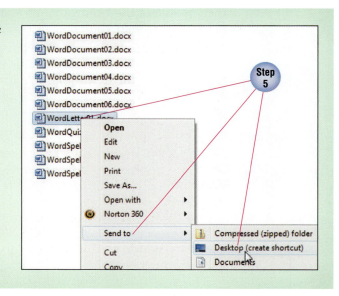

Step 5

Using Windows 7   **31**

6. Close the Computer window.
7. Open Word and the file named **WordLetter01.docx** by double-clicking the *WordLetter01.docx* shortcut icon on the desktop.
8. After viewing the file in Word, exit Word by clicking the Close button that displays in the upper right corner of the window.
9. Delete the *WordLetter01.docx* shortcut icon by completing the following steps:
    a. At the desktop, position the mouse pointer on the *WordLetter01.docx* shortcut icon.
    b. Hold down the left mouse button, drag the icon on top of the Recycle Bin icon, and then release the mouse button.

Step 7

Exploring the Control Panel

The Control Panel, shown in Figure W.10, contains a variety of icons you can use to customize the appearance and functionality of your computer as well as access and change system settings. Display the Control Panel by clicking the Start button on the Taskbar and then clicking *Control Panel* at the Start menu. The Control Panel organizes settings into categories to make them easier to find. Click a category icon and the Control Panel displays lower-level categories and tasks within each of them.

Hover your mouse over a category icon in the Control Panel and a ScreenTip displays with an explanation of what options are available. For example, if you hover the mouse over the Appearance and Personalization icon, a ScreenTip displays with information about the tasks available in the category such as changing the appearance of desktop items, applying a theme or screen saver to your computer, or customizing the Start menu and Taskbar.

If you click a category icon in the Control Panel, the Control Panel displays all of the available subcategories and tasks in the category. Also, the categories display in text form at the left side of the Control Panel. For example, if you click the Appearance and Personalization category icon, the Control Panel displays as shown in Figure W.11. Notice how the Control Panel categories display at the left side of the Control Panel and options for changing the appearance and personalizing your computer display in the middle of the Control Panel.

By default, the Control Panel displays categories of tasks in what is called Category view. You can change this view to *Large icons* or *Small icons*. To change the view, click the down-pointing arrow that displays at the right side of the text *View by* that displays in the upper right corner of the Control Panel, and then click the desired view at the drop-down list (see Figure W.10).

Figure W.10 The Control Panel

Figure W.11 Appearance and Personalization Window

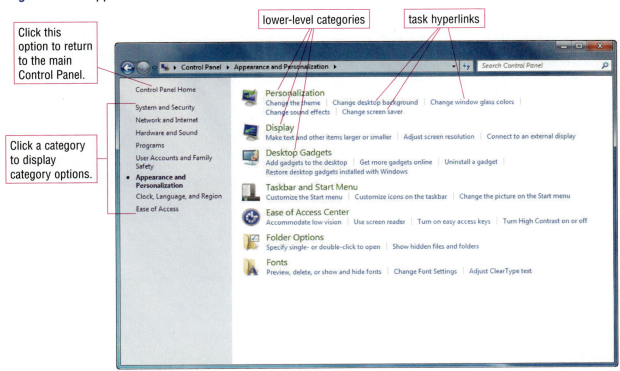

Project 10 — Changing the Desktop Theme

1. At the Windows 7 desktop, click the Start button and then click *Control Panel* at the Start menu.
2. At the Control Panel, click the Appearance and Personalization category icon.

3. Click the Change the theme hyperlink that displays below the Personalization category in the panel at the right in the Control Panel.
4. At the window that displays with options for changing visuals and sounds on your computer, click the *Landscapes* theme.

5. Click the Desktop Background hyperlink that displays in the lower left corner of the panel at the right.
6. Click the button that displays below the text *Change picture every* and then click *10 Seconds* at the drop-down list. (This tells Windows to change the picture on your desktop every 10 seconds.)
7. Click the Save changes button that displays in the lower right corner of the Control Panel.
8. Click the Close button located in the upper right corner to close the Control Panel.
9. Look at the picture that displays as the background at the desktop. Wait for 10 seconds and then look at the second picture that displays.
10. Click the Start button and then click *Control Panel* at the Start menu.
11. At the Control Panel, click the Appearance and Personalization category icon.
12. Click the Change the theme hyperlink that displays below the Personalization category in the panel at the right.

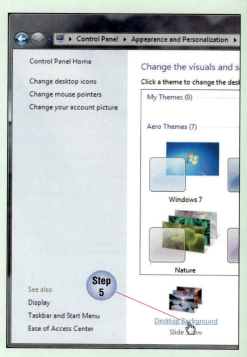

13. At the window that displays with options for changing visuals and sounds on your computer, click the *Windows 7* theme in the *Aero Themes* section. (This is the default theme.)
14. Click the Close button located in the upper right corner of the Control Panel.

Searching in the Control Panel

The Control Panel contains a large number of options for customizing the appearance and functionality of your computer. If you want to customize a feature and are not sure where the options for the feature are located, search for the feature. To do this, display the Control Panel and then type the name of the desired feature. By default, the insertion point is positioned in the *Search Control Panel* text box. When you type the feature name in the Search Control Panel, options related to the feature display in the Control Panel.

Project 11 Customizing the Mouse

1. Click the Start button and then click *Control Panel*.
2. At the Control Panel, type **mouse**. (The insertion point is automatically located in the *Search Control Panel* text box when you open the Control Panel. When you type *mouse*, features for customizing the mouse display in the Control Panel.)
3. Click the Mouse icon that displays in the Control Panel.
4. At the Mouse Properties dialog box, notice the options that display. (The *Switch primary and secondary buttons* option might be useful, for example, if you are left-handed and want to switch the buttons on the mouse.)
5. Click the Cancel button to remove the dialog box.
6. At the Control Panel, click the <u>Change the mouse pointer display or speed</u> hyperlink.

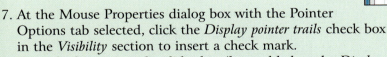

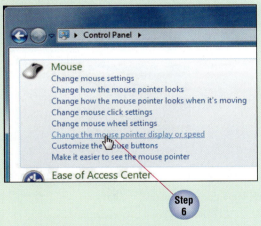

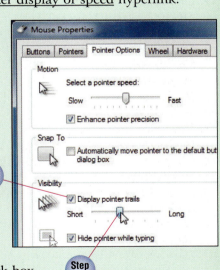

7. At the Mouse Properties dialog box with the Pointer Options tab selected, click the *Display pointer trails* check box in the *Visibility* section to insert a check mark.
8. Drag the button on the slider bar (located below the *Display pointer trails* check box) approximately to the middle of the bar.
9. Click OK to close the dialog box.
10. Close the Control Panel.
11. Move the mouse pointer around the screen to see the pointer trails as well as the speed at which the mouse moves.

Displaying Personalize Options with a Shortcut Command

In addition to the Control Panel, you can display customization options with a command from a shortcut menu. Display a shortcut menu by positioning the mouse pointer in the desired position and then clicking the right mouse button. For example, display a shortcut menu with options for customizing the desktop by positioning the mouse pointer in an empty area on the desktop and then clicking the right mouse button. At the shortcut menu that displays, click the desired shortcut command.

Project 12 Customizing with a Shortcut Command

1. At the Windows 7 desktop, position the mouse pointer in an empty area on the desktop, click the right mouse button, and then click *Personalize* at the shortcut menu.
2. At the Control Panel Appearance and Personalization window that displays, click the Change mouse pointers hyperlink that displays at the left side of the window.
3. At the Mouse Properties dialog box, click the Pointer Options tab.
4. Click in the *Display pointer trails* check box to remove the check mark.
5. Click OK to close the dialog box.
6. At the Control Panel Appearance and Personalization window, click the Screen Saver hyperlink that displays in the lower right corner of the window.
7. At the Screen Saver Settings dialog box, click the option button below the *Screen saver* option and then click *Ribbons* at the drop-down list.
8. Check the number in the *Wait* text box. If a number other than *1* displays, click the down-pointing arrow in the spin box at the right side of the text box until *1* displays. (This tells Windows to display the screen saver after one minute of inactivity.)
9. Click OK to close the dialog box.
10. Close the Control Panel by clicking the Close button located in the upper right corner of the window.

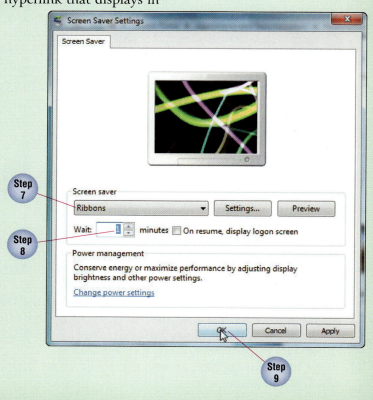

36 Using Windows 7

11. Do not touch the mouse or keyboard and wait over one minute for the screen saver to display. After watching the screen saver, move the mouse. (This redisplays the desktop.)
12. Right-click in an empty area on the desktop and then click *Personalize* at the shortcut menu.
13. At the Control Panel Appearance and Personalization window, click the <u>Screen Saver</u> hyperlink.
14. At the Screen Saver Settings dialog box, click the option button below the *Screen saver* option and then click *(None)* at the drop-down list.
15. Click OK to close the dialog box.
16. Close the Control Panel Appearance and Personalization window.

Exploring Windows Help and Support

Windows 7 includes an on-screen reference guide providing information, explanations, and interactive help on learning Windows features. Get help at the Windows Help and Support window shown in Figure W.12. Display this window by clicking the Start button and then clicking *Help and Support* at the Start menu. Use buttons in the window toolbar to display the opening Windows Help and Support window, print the current information, display a list of contents, get customer support or other types of services, and display a list of Help options.

Figure W.12 Windows Help and Support Window

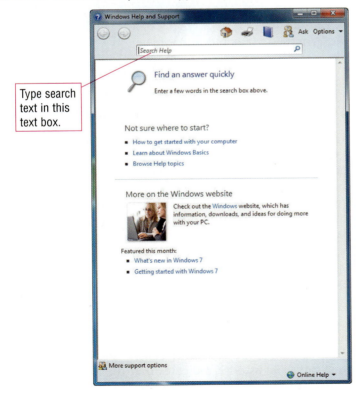

Using Windows 7   37

Project 13 — Getting Help

1. At the Windows 7 desktop, click the Start button and then click *Help and Support* at the Start menu.
2. At the Windows Help and Support window, click the Learn about Windows Basics hyperlink.
3. Click a hyperlink that interests you, read the information, and then click the Back button on the Windows Help and Support window toolbar. (The Back button is located in the upper left corner of the window.)
4. Click another hyperlink that interests you and then read the information.
5. Click the Help and Support home button that displays on the window toolbar. (This returns you to the opening Windows Help and Support window.)
6. Click in the *Search Help* text box, type **delete files**, and then press Enter.
7. Click the Delete a file or folder hyperlink that displays in the window.
8. Read the information that displays about deleting files or folders and then click the Print button on the window toolbar.
9. At the Print dialog box, click the Print button.
10. Click the Close button to close the Windows Help and Support window.

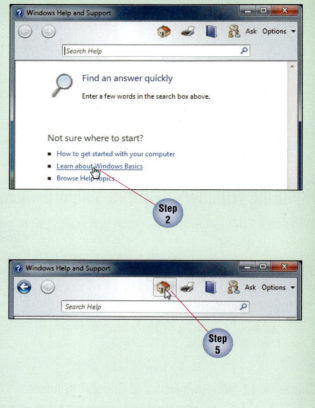

Using Search Tools

The Start menu contains a search tool you can use to quickly find a program or file on your computer. To use the search tool, click the Start button and then type the first few characters of the program or file for which you are searching in the *Search programs and files* text box. As you type characters in the text box, a pop-up list displays with program names or file names that begin with the characters. As you continue typing characters, the search tool refines the list.

You can also search for programs or files with the search text box in the Computer window. The search text box displays in the upper right corner of the Computer window at the right side of the Address bar. If you want to search a specific folder, make that folder active in the Content pane and then type the search text in the text box.

When conducting a search, you can use the asterisk (*) as a wildcard character in place of any letters, numbers, or symbols within a file name. For example, in the following project you will search for file names containing *check* by typing ***check** in the search text box. The asterisk indicates that the file name can start with any letter but it must contain the letters *check* somewhere in the file name.

Project 14 — Searching for Programs and Files

1. At the Windows 7 desktop, click the Start button.
2. With the insertion point positioned in the *Search programs and files* text box, type **paint**. (Notice as you type the letters that Windows displays programs and/or files that begin with the same letters you are typing or that are associated with the same letters in a keyword. Notice that the Paint program displays below the heading *Programs* at the top of the list. Depending on the contents stored in the computer you are using, additional items may display below Paint.)

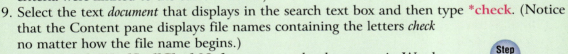

3. Click *Paint* that displays below the *Programs* heading.
4. Close the Paint window.
5. Click the Start button and then click *Computer*.
6. At the Computer window, double-click the icon representing your storage medium.
7. Double-click the *Windows7* folder.
8. Click in the search text box located at the right of the Address bar and then type **document**. (As you begin typing the letters, Windows filters the list of files in the Content pane to those that contain the letters you type. Notice that the Address bar displays *Search Results in Windows7* to indicate that the files that display matching your criteria were limited to the current folder.)
9. Select the text *document* that displays in the search text box and then type ***check**. (Notice that the Content pane displays file names containing the letters *check* no matter how the file name begins.)
10. Double-click **WordSpellCheck02.docx** to open the document in Word.
11. Close the document and exit Word by clicking the Close button located in the upper right corner of the window.
12. Close the Computer window.

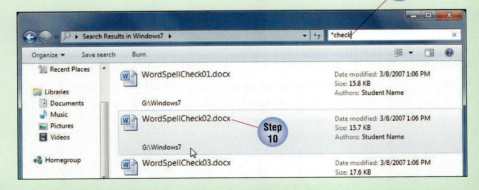

Using Windows 7 39

Browsing the Internet Using Internet Explorer 8.0

Microsoft Internet Explorer 8.0 is a web browser program with options and features for displaying sites as well as navigating and searching for information on the Internet. The ***Internet*** is a network of computers connected around the world. Users access the Internet for several purposes: to communicate using instant messaging and/or email, to subscribe to newsgroups, to transfer files, to socialize with other users around the globe in chat rooms, and also to access virtually any kind of information imaginable.

Using the Internet, people can find a phenomenal amount of information for private or public use. To use the Internet, three things are generally required: an Internet Service Provider (ISP), a program to browse the Web (called a ***web browser***), and a ***search engine***. In this section, you will learn how to:

- Navigate the Internet using URLs and hyperlinks
- Use search engines to locate information
- Download web pages and images

You will use the Microsoft Internet Explorer web browser to locate information on the Internet. Uniform Resource Locators, referred to as URLs, are the method used to identify locations on the Internet. The steps for browsing the Internet vary but generally include: opening Internet Explorer, typing the URL for the desired site, navigating the various pages of the site, navigating to other sites using links, and then closing Internet Explorer.

To launch Internet Explorer 8.0, click the Internet Explorer icon on the Taskbar at the Windows desktop. Figure IE.1 identifies the elements of the Internet Explorer, version 8.0, window. The web page that displays in your Internet Explorer window may vary from what you see in Figure IE.1.

If you know the URL for the desired website, click in the Address bar, type the URL, and then press Enter. The website's home page displays in a tab within the Internet Explorer window. URLs (Uniform Resource Locators) are the method used to identify locations on the Internet. The format of a URL is *http://server-name.path*. The first part of the URL, *http*, stands for HyperText Transfer Protocol, which is the protocol or language used to transfer data within the World Wide Web. The colon and slashes separate the protocol from the server name. The server name is the second component of the URL. For example, in the URL http://www.microsoft.com, the server name is *microsoft*. The last part of the URL specifies the domain to which the server belongs. For example, *.com* refers to "commercial" and establishes that the URL is a commercial company. Examples of other domains include *.edu* for "educational," *.gov* for "government," and *.mil* for "military."

Figure IE.1 Internet Explorer Window

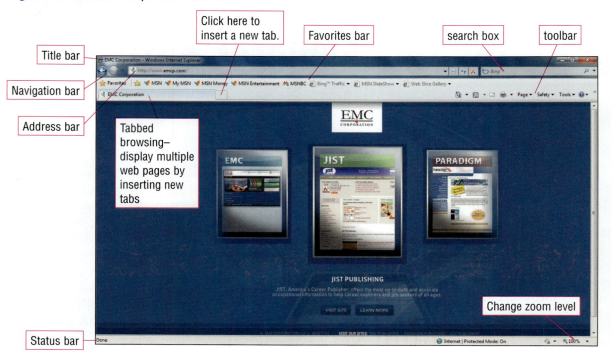

Project 1 — Browsing the Internet Using URLs

1. Make sure you are connected to the Internet through an Internet Service Provider and that the Windows desktop displays. (Check with your instructor to determine if you need to complete steps for accessing the Internet such as typing a user name and password to log on.)
2. Launch Microsoft Internet Explorer by clicking the Internet Explorer icon located on the Taskbar located at the bottom of the Windows desktop.
3. At the Internet Explorer window, explore the website for Yosemite National Park by completing the following steps:
   a. Click in the Address bar, type **www.nps.gov/yose**, and then press Enter.
   b. Scroll down the home page for Yosemite National Park by clicking the down-pointing arrow on the vertical scroll bar located at the right side of the Internet Explorer window.
   c. Print the home page by clicking the Print button located on the Internet Explorer toolbar. (Some websites have a printer friendly button you can click to print the page.)

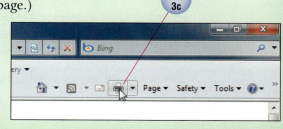

Browsing the Internet Using Internet Explorer 8.0

4. Explore the website for Glacier National Park by completing the following steps:
   a. Click in the Address bar, type **www.nps.gov/glac**, and then press Enter.
   b. Print the home page by clicking the Print button located on the Internet Explorer toolbar.
5. Close Internet Explorer by clicking the Close button (contains an X) located in the upper right corner of the Internet Explorer window.

Step 4a

Navigating Using Hyperlinks

Most web pages contain "hyperlinks" that you click to connect to another page within the website or to another site on the Internet. Hyperlinks may display in a web page as underlined text in a specific color or as images or icons. To use a hyperlink, position the mouse pointer on the desired hyperlink until the mouse pointer turns into a hand, and then click the left mouse button. Use hyperlinks to navigate within and between sites on the Internet. The navigation bar in the Internet Explorer window contains a Back button that, when clicked, takes you to the previous web page viewed. If you click the Back button and then want to return to the previous page, click the Forward button. You can continue clicking the Back button to back your way out of several linked pages in reverse order since Internet Explorer maintains a history of the websites you visit.

Project 2 Navigating Using Hyperlinks

1. Make sure you are connected to the Internet and then click the Internet Explorer icon on the Taskbar.
2. At the Internet Explorer window, display the White House web page and navigate in the page by completing the following steps:
   a. Click in the Address bar, type **whitehouse.gov**, and then press Enter.
   b. At the White House home page, position the mouse pointer on a hyperlink that interests you until the pointer turns into a hand, and then click the left mouse button.
   c. At the linked web page, click the Back button. (This returns you to the White House home page.)
   d. At the White House home page, click the Forward button to return to the previous web page viewed.
   e. Print the web page by clicking the Print button on the Internet Explorer toolbar.
3. Display the website for Amazon.com and navigate in the site by completing the following steps:
   a. Click in the Address bar, type **www.amazon.com**, and then press Enter.

Step 2c

Step 3a

Browsing the Internet Using Internet Explorer 8.0   43

b. At the Amazon.com home page, click a hyperlink related to books.
c. When a book web page displays, click the Print button on the Internet Explorer toolbar.
4. Close Internet Explorer by clicking the Close button (contains an X) located in the upper right corner of the Internet Explorer window.

Searching for Specific Sites

If you do not know the URL for a specific site or you want to find information on the Internet but do not know what site to visit, complete a search with a search engine. A search engine is a software program created to search quickly and easily for desired information. A variety of search engines are available on the Internet, each offering the opportunity to search for specific information. One method for searching for information is to click in the search box located to the right of the Address bar, type a keyword or phrase related to your search, and then click the Search button or press Enter. Another method for completing a search is to visit the website for a search engine and use options at the site.

Bing is Microsoft's online search portal and is the default search engine used by Internet Explorer. Bing organizes search results by topic category and provides related search suggestions.

Project 3 Searching for Information by Topic

1. Start Internet Explorer.
2. At the Internet Explorer window, search for sites on bluegrass music by completing the following steps:
   a. Click in the search box (may display *Bing*) located at the right side of the Address bar.
   b. Type **bluegrass music** and then press Enter.
   c. When a list of sites displays in the Bing results window, click a site that interests you.
   d. When the page displays, click the Print button.
3. Use the Yahoo! search engine to find sites on bluegrass music by completing the following steps:
   a. Click in the Address bar, type **www.yahoo.com**, and then press Enter.
   b. At the Yahoo! website, with the insertion point positioned in the search text box, type **bluegrass music** and then press Enter. (Notice that the sites displayed vary from sites displayed in the earlier search.)
   c. Click hyperlinks until a website displays that interests you.
   d. Print the page.

4. Use the Google search engine to find sites on jazz music by completing the following steps:
   a. Click in the Address bar, type **www.google.com**, and then press Enter.
   b. At the Google website, with the insertion point positioned in the search text box, type **jazz music** and then press Enter.
   c. Click a site that interests you.
   d. Print the page.
5. Close Internet Explorer.

Using a Metasearch Engine

Bing, Yahoo!, and Google are search engines that search the Web for content and display search results. In addition to individual search engines, you can use a metasearch engine, such as Dogpile, that sends your search text to other search engines and then compiles the results in one list. With a metasearch engine, you type the search text once and then access results from a wider group of search engines. The Dogpile metasearch engine provides search results from Google, Yahoo!, Bing, and Ask.

Project 4   Searching with a Metasearch Search Engine

1. At the Windows desktop, click the Internet Explorer icon on the Taskbar.
2. Click in the Address bar.
3. Type **www.dogpile.com** and then press Enter.
4. At the Dogpile website, type **jazz music** in the search text box and then press Enter.
5. Click a hyperlink that interests you.
6. Close the Internet Explorer window.

Browsing the Internet Using Internet Explorer 8.0

Completing Advanced Searches for Specific Sites

Web Search

The Internet contains an enormous amount of information. Depending on what you are searching for on the Internet and the search engine you use, some searches can result in several thousand "hits" (sites). Wading through a large number of sites can be very time-consuming and counterproductive. Narrowing a search to very specific criteria can greatly reduce the number of hits for a search. To narrow a search, use the advanced search options offered by the search engine.

Project 5 Narrowing a Search

1. Start Internet Explorer.
2. Search for sites on skydiving in Oregon by completing the following steps:
    a. Click in the Address bar, type **www.yahoo.com**, and then press Enter.
    b. At the Yahoo! home page, click the Web Search button next to the search text box.
    c. Click the more hyperlink located above the search text box and then click Advanced Search at the drop-down list.
    d. At the Advanced Web Search page, click in the search text box next to *all of these words*.
    e. Type **skydiving Oregon tandem static line**. (This limits the search to web pages containing all of the words typed in the search text box.)
    f. Click the Yahoo! Search button.
    g. When the list of websites displays, click a hyperlink that interests you.
    h. Click the Back button until the Yahoo! Advanced Web Search page displays.
    i. Click in the *the exact phrase* text box and then type **skydiving in Oregon**.
    j. Click the *Only .com domains* in the *Site/Domain* section.
    k. Click the Yahoo! Search button.
    l. When the list of websites displays, click a hyperlink that interests you.
    m. Print the page.
3. Close Internet Explorer.

46 Browsing the Internet Using Internet Explorer 8.0

Downloading Images, Text, and Web Pages from the Internet

The image(s) and/or text that display when you open a web page as well as the web page itself can be saved as a separate file. This separate file can be viewed, printed, or inserted in another file. The information you want to save in a separate file is downloaded from the Internet by Internet Explorer and saved in a folder of your choosing with the name you specify. Copyright laws protect much of the information on the Internet. Before using information downloaded from the Internet, check the site for restrictions. If you do use information, make sure you properly cite the source.

Project 6 — Downloading Images and Web Pages

1. Start Internet Explorer.
2. Download a web page and image from Banff National Park by completing the following steps:
   a. Search for sites on the Internet for Banff National Park.
   b. From the list of sites that displays, choose a site that contains information about Banff National Park and at least one image of the park.
   c. Save the web page as a separate file by clicking the Page button on the Internet Explorer toolbar and then clicking *Save As* at the drop-down list.
   d. At the Save Webpage dialog box, type **BanffWebPage**.
   e. Navigate to the drive containing your storage medium and then click the Save button.

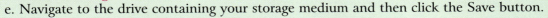
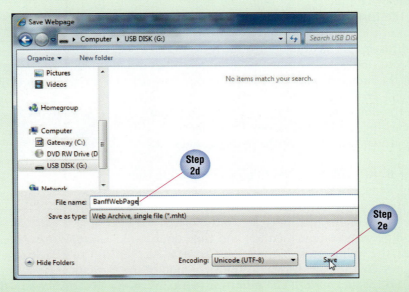

Browsing the Internet Using Internet Explorer 8.0   47

3. Save an image file by completing the following steps:
   a. Right-click an image that displays at the website. (The image that displays may vary from what you see below.)
   b. At the shortcut menu that displays, click *Save Picture As*.
   c. At the Save Picture dialog box, type **BanffImage** in the *File name* text box.

Step 3b

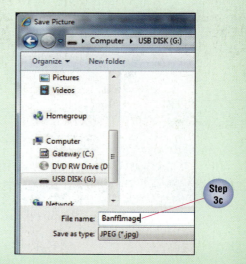

Step 3c

   d. Navigate to the drive containing your storage medium and then click the Save button.
4. Close Internet Explorer.

Project 7 — Opening the Saved Web Page and Image in a Word Document

1. Open Microsoft Word by clicking the Start button on the Taskbar, clicking *All Programs*, clicking *Microsoft Office*, and then clicking *Microsoft Word 2010*.
2. With Microsoft Word open, insert the image in a document by completing the following steps:
   a. Click the Insert tab and then click the Picture button in the Illustrations group.
   b. At the Insert Picture dialog box, navigate to the drive containing your storage medium and then double-click *BanffImage.jpg*.
   c. When the image displays in the Word document, print the document by pressing Ctrl + P and then clicking the Print button.
   d. Close the document by clicking the File tab and then clicking the Close button. At the message asking if you want to save the changes, click *Don't Save*.
3. Open the **BanffWebPage.mht** file by completing the following steps:
   a. Click the File tab and then click the Open button.
   b. At the Open dialog box, navigate to the drive containing your storage medium and then double-click *BanffWebPage.mht*.
   c. Preview the web page(s) by pressing Ctrl + P. At the Print tab Backstage view, preview the page shown at the right side of the Backstage view.
4. Close Word by clicking the Close button (contains an X) that displays in the upper right corner of the screen.

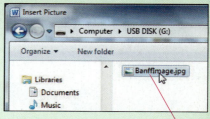

Step 2b

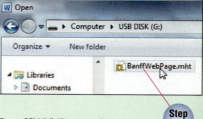

Step 3b

Microsoft® Word Level 1

Unit 1 ■ Editing and Formatting Documents

Chapter 1 ■ Preparing Documents

Chapter 2 ■ Formatting Characters and Paragraphs

Chapter 3 ■ Customizing Paragraphs

Chapter 4 ■ Formatting Pages

Microsoft Word

CHAPTER 1

Preparing Documents

PERFORMANCE OBJECTIVES

Upon successful completion of Chapter 1, you will be able to:
- Open Microsoft Word
- Create, save, name, print, open, and close a Word document
- Exit Word
- Edit a document
- Move the insertion point within a document
- Scroll within a document
- Select text in a document
- Use the Undo and Redo buttons
- Check spelling and grammar in a document
- Use the Help feature

In this chapter, you will learn to create, save, name, print, open, close, and edit a Word document as well as complete a spelling and grammar check. You will also learn about the Help feature, which is an on-screen reference manual providing information on features and commands for each program in the Office suite. Before continuing, make sure you read the *Getting Started* section presented at the beginning of this book. This section contains information about computer hardware and software, using the mouse, executing commands, and exploring Help files. Model answers for this chapter's projects appear on the following page.

Note: Before beginning the projects, copy to your storage medium the Word2010L1C1 subfolder from the Word2010L1 folder on the CD that accompanies this textbook. Steps on how to copy a folder are presented on the inside of the back cover of this textbook. Do this every time you start a chapter's projects.

Project 1 Prepare a Word Document

The traditional chronological resume lists your work experience in reverse-chronological order (starting with your current or most recent position). The functional style deemphasizes the "where" and "when" of your career and instead groups similar experience, talents, and qualifications regardless of when they occurred.

Like the chronological resume, the hybrid resume includes specifics about where you worked, when you worked there, and what your job titles were. Like a functional resume, a hybrid resume emphasizes your most relevant qualifications in an expanded summary section, in several "career highlights" bullet points at the top of your resume, or in project summaries.

Created:
Thursday, December 6, 2012
Note: The two paragraphs will become the 2nd and 3rd paragraphs in the 5th section.

WL1-C1-P1-Computers.docx

Project 2 Save and Edit a Word Document

The majority of new jobs being created in the United States today involve daily work with computers. Computer-related careers include technical support jobs, sales and training, programming and applications development, network and database administration, and computer engineering.

A technician is an entry-level worker who installs and maintains hardware and/or software. Technical sales and technical training jobs emphasize interpersonal skills as much as they do technical skills. Programming is one of the most difficult and highly skilled jobs in the industry. Programmers create new software, such as Microsoft Windows or computer games, and often have college degrees. Software engineers are programmers trained to create software in teams with other programmers. Application developers are similar to programmers, but they use existing software such as a database to create applications for business solutions. Application development jobs include database administration, network administration, and systems analysis. Database and network administration involve overseeing and maintaining databases and networks, respectively. Systems analysts design information systems or evaluate and improve existing ones.

WL1-C1-P2-CompCareers.docx

Project 4 Insert and Delete Text

COMPUTER KEYBOARDS

To enter commands into a computer or to enter data into it, a user needs an input device. An input device can be built into the computer, like the keyboard in a laptop, or it can be connected to the computer by a cable. Some input devices, like remote keyboards, send directions to the computer by means of an infrared signal.

Keyboards can be external devices that are attached by a cable, or they can be attached to the CPU case itself as they are in laptops. Most keyboards today are QWERTY keyboards, which take their name from the first six keys at the left of the first row of letters. The QWERTY design was invented in the early days of mechanical typewriters to slow down typists and thus keep keys from jamming.

The DVORAK keyboard is an alternative to the QWERTY keyboard. On the DVORAK keyboard, the most commonly used keys are placed close to the user's fingertips and this increases typing speed. You can install software on a QWERTY keyboard that emulates a DVORAK keyboard. The ability to emulate other keyboards is convenient especially when working with foreign languages.

WL1-C1-P4-CompKeyboards.docx

Project 5 Complete a Spelling and Grammar Check

ON THE HORIZON

The march of computer technology continues to change the nature of our jobs and workplaces. Considering the global economic and technology scene, some major changes in occupations involve changes in communications media, work locations, and communications tools.

Communications Media

One key to being successful in our modern, technological world is spotting a trend early and adjusting one's career direction accordingly. For example, 80 percent of daily newspaper readers are over 50 years old. Young readers are not as interested in the printed word, and each year the industry suffers from a shrinking number of subscriptions. The young are still reading, but they are reading online media sites rather than the printed page. Websites make excellent dynamic newspapers, as they can be changed at will, they require no printing or distribution costs, and they do not require the newspaper delivery person to go door to door asking for payment. This gradual switch to the new media is causing many jobs to change. The number of printing and lithography jobs is shrinking, but web developers and graphic artists are in demand.

Industry-morphing trends are sweeping away many traditional approaches to the marketing and distribution of products. Increasingly, music and movies are being downloaded versus being bought on a disc. Fewer movies are being rented, while more people are watching them on-demand through their cable systems. Once a successful approach is discovered, every type of media that can be digitized rather than produced and distributed in physical form will come under increasing pressure to modernize in order to match the competition. Individuals managing career paths need to be aware of these trends and avoid becoming part of a downsizing effort.

Telecommuting

Telecommuting, sometimes called telework, involves working via computer from home or while traveling rather than going to the office on a daily basis. Approximately 25 million Americans telecommute at least one day per week. Telework plans have been especially successful for commissioned salespeople, who are often more productive when away from the office environment.

WL1-C1-P5-TechOccTrends.docx

> **Project 1 Prepare a Word Document**   **2 Parts**
>
> You will create a short document containing information on computers and then save, print, and close the document.

Opening Microsoft Word

Microsoft Office 2010 contains a word processing program named Word that you can use to create, save, edit, and print documents. The steps to open Word may vary depending on your system setup. Generally, to open Word, you would click the Start button on the Taskbar at the Windows desktop, point to *All Programs*, click *Microsoft Office*, and then click *Microsoft Word 2010*.

Start

▼ **Quick Steps**

Open Word
1. Click Start button.
2. Point to *All Programs*.
3. Click *Microsoft Office*.
4. Click *Microsoft Word 2010*.

Creating, Saving, Printing, and Closing a Document

When Microsoft Word is open, a blank document displays as shown in Figure 1.1. The features of the document screen are described in Table 1.1.

At a blank document, type information to create a document. A document is any information you choose — for instance, a letter, report, term paper, table, and so on. Some things to consider when typing text are:

- **Word Wrap:** As you type text to create a document, you do not need to press the Enter key at the end of each line because Word wraps text to the next line. A word is wrapped to the next line if it begins before the right margin and continues past the right margin. The only times you need to press Enter are to end a paragraph, create a blank line, or end a short line.

- **AutoCorrect:** Word contains a feature that automatically corrects certain words as you type them. For example, if you type the word *adn* instead of *and*, Word automatically corrects it when you press the spacebar after the word. AutoCorrect will also superscript the letters that follow an ordinal number (a number indicating a position in a series). For example, if you type *2nd* and then press the spacebar or Enter key, Word will convert this ordinal number to 2nd.

- **Automatic Spell Checker:** By default, Word will automatically insert a red wavy line below words that are not contained in the Spelling dictionary or automatically corrected by AutoCorrect. This may include misspelled words, proper names, some terminology, and some foreign words. If you type a word not recognized by the Spelling dictionary, leave it as written if the word is correct. However, if the word is incorrect, you have two choices — you can delete the word and then type it correctly, or you can position the I-beam pointer on the word, click the right mouse button, and then click the correct spelling in the pop-up list.

- **Automatic Grammar Checker:** Word includes an automatic grammar checker. If the grammar checker detects a sentence containing a grammatical error, a green wavy line is inserted below the sentence. You can leave the sentence as written or position the mouse I-beam pointer on the sentence, click the *right* mouse button, and a pop-up list will display with possible corrections.

- **Spacing Punctuation:** Typically, Word uses Calibri as the default typeface, which is a proportional typeface. (You will learn more about typefaces in Chapter 2.) When typing text in a proportional typeface, space once (rather than twice) after

HINT
To avoid opening the same program twice, use the Taskbar to see which programs are open.

HINT
A book icon displays in the Status bar. A check mark on the book indicates no spelling errors detected in the document by the spell checker, while an X in the book indicates errors. Double-click the book icon to move to the next error. If the book icon is not visible, right-click the Status bar and then click the *Spelling and Grammar Check* option at the pop-up list.

Figure 1.1 Blank Document

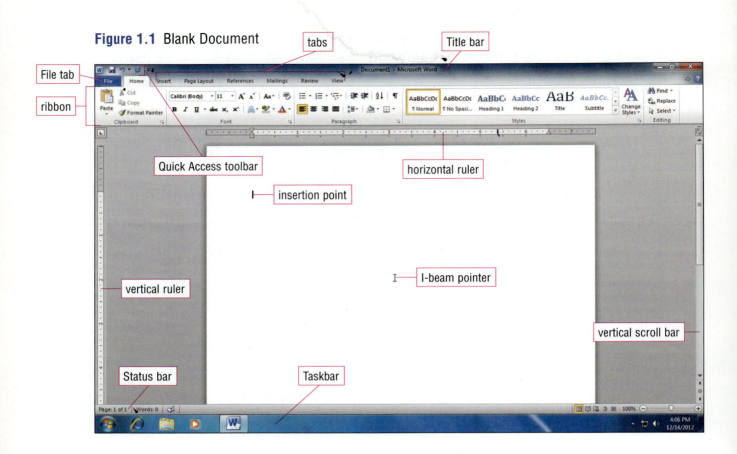

Table 1.1 Microsoft Word Screen Features

Feature	Description
File tab	Click the File tab and the Backstage view displays containing buttons and tabs for working with and managing documents
Horizontal ruler	Used to set margins, indents, and tabs
I-beam pointer	Used to move the insertion point or to select text
Insertion point	Indicates location of next character entered at the keyboard
Quick Access toolbar	Contains buttons for commonly used commands
Ribbon	Area containing the tabs and commands divided into groups
Status bar	Displays number of pages and words, View buttons, and the Zoom slider bar
Title bar	Displays document name followed by program name
Tabs	Contains commands and features organized into groups
Taskbar	Divided into three sections—the Start button, the task buttons area, and the notification area
Vertical ruler	Used to set top and bottom margins
Vertical scroll bar	Used to view various parts of the document

end-of-sentence punctuation such as a period, question mark, or exclamation point, and after a colon. Proportional typeface is set closer together, and extra white space at the end of a sentence or after a colon is not needed.

- **Option Buttons:** As you insert and edit text in a document, you may notice an option button popping up in your text. The name and appearance of this option button varies depending on the action. If a word you type is corrected by AutoCorrect, if you create an automatic list, or if autoformatting is applied to text, the AutoCorrect Options button appears. Click this button to undo the specific automatic action. If you paste text in a document, the Paste Options button appears near the text. Click this button to display the Paste Options gallery with buttons for controlling how the pasted text is formatted.
- **AutoComplete:** Microsoft Word and other Office applications include an AutoComplete feature that inserts an entire item when you type a few identifying characters. For example, type the letters *Mond* and *Monday* displays in a ScreenTip above the letters. Press the Enter key or press F3 and Word inserts *Monday* in the document.

Using the New Line Command

A Word document is based on a template that applies default formatting. Some basic formatting includes 1.15 line spacing and 10 points of spacing after a paragraph. Each time you press the Enter key, a new paragraph begins and 10 points of spacing is inserted after the paragraph. If you want to move the insertion point down to the next line without including the additional 10 points of spacing, use the New Line command, Shift + Enter.

Project 1a Creating a Document   Part 1 of 2

1. Follow the instructions in this chapter to open Microsoft Word or check with your instructor for specific instructions.
2. At a blank document, type the information shown in Figure 1.2 with the following specifications:
    a. Correct any errors highlighted by the spell checker as they occur.
    b. Space once after end-of-sentence punctuation.
    c. After typing *Created:* press Shift + Enter to move the insertion point to the next line without adding 10 points of additional spacing.
    d. To insert the word *Thursday* located towards the end of the document, type **Thur** and then press F3. (This is an example of the AutoComplete feature.)
    e. To insert the word *December*, type **Dece** and then press the Enter key. (This is another example of the AutoComplete feature.)
    f. Press Shift + Enter after typing *December 6, 2012*.
    g. When typing the last line (the line containing the ordinal numbers), type the ordinal number text and AutoCorrect will automatically convert the letters in the ordinal numbers to superscript.
3. When you are finished typing the text, press the Enter key once.

Figure 1.2 Project 1a

The traditional chronological resume lists your work experience in reverse-chronological order (starting with your current or most recent position). The functional style deemphasizes the "where" and "when" of your career and instead groups similar experience, talents, and qualifications regardless of when they occurred.

Like the chronological resume, the hybrid resume includes specifics about where you worked, when you worked there, and what your job titles were. Like a functional resume, a hybrid resume emphasizes your most relevant qualifications in an expanded summary section, in several "career highlights" bullet points at the top of your resume, or in project summaries.

Created:
Thursday, December 6, 2012
Note: The two paragraphs will become the 2nd and 3rd paragraphs in the 5th section.

Saving a Document

▼ **Quick Steps**

Save a Document
1. Click Save button.
2. Type document name.
3. Click Save button in dialog box.

Save a document if you want to use it in the future. You can use a variety of methods to save a document such as clicking the Save button on the Quick Access toolbar, clicking the File tab and then clicking the Save As button, or using the keyboard shortcut Ctrl + S. To save a document, click the Save button on the Quick Access toolbar. At the Save As dialog box shown in Figure 1.3, type the name of the document and then press Enter or click the Save button located in the lower right corner of the dialog box.

Save

Save a document approximately every 15 minutes or when interrupted.

Figure 1.3 Save As Dialog Box

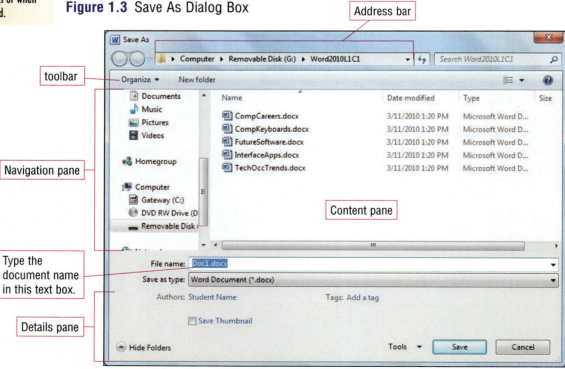

Naming a Document

Document names created in Word and other applications in the Office suite can be up to 255 characters in length, including drive letter and any folder names, and may include spaces. File names cannot include any of the following characters:

HINT
You cannot give a document the same name first in uppercase and then lowercase letters.

- forward slash (/)
- backslash (\)
- greater than sign (>)
- less than sign (<)
- asterisk (*)
- question mark (?)
- quotation mark (")
- colon (:)
- semicolon (;)
- pipe symbol (|)

Printing a Document

Click the File tab and the Backstage view displays as shown in Figure 1.4. Use buttons and tabs at this view to work with and manage documents such as opening, closing, saving, and printing a document. If you want to remove the Backstage view without completing an action, click the File tab, click any other tab in the ribbon, or press the Esc key on your keyboard.

Many of the computer exercises you will be creating will need to be printed. A printing of a document on paper is referred to as *hard copy* and a document displayed in the screen is referred to as *soft copy*. Print a document with options at the Print tab Backstage view shown in Figure 1.5. To display this view, click the File tab and then click the Print tab. You can also display the Print tab Backstage view by pressing the keyboard shortcut, Ctrl + P.

The left side of the Print tab Backstage view displays three categories—Print, Printer, and Settings. Click the Print button in the Print category to send the

▼ **Quick Steps**

Print a Document
Click Quick Print button.
OR
1. Click File tab.
2. Click Print tab.
3. Click Print button.

Close a Document
1. Click File tab.
2. Click Close button.
OR
Press Ctrl + F4.

Figure 1.4 Backstage View

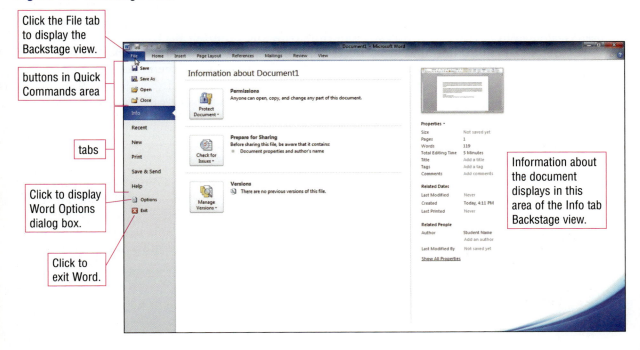

Figure 1.5 Print Tab Backstage View

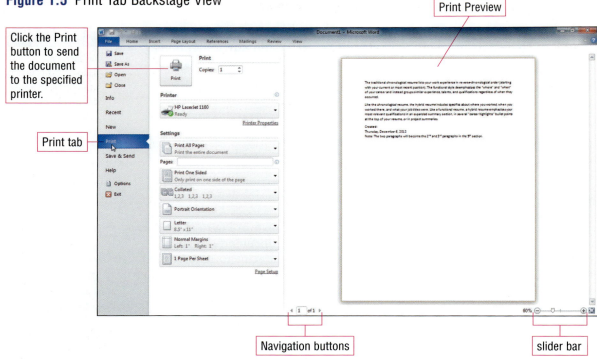

document to the printer and specify the number of copies you want printed with the *Copies* option. Use the gallery in the Printer category to specify the desired printer. The Settings category contains a number of galleries, each with options for specifying how you want your document printed such as whether or not you want the pages collated when printed; the orientation, page size, and margins of your document; and how many pages of your document you want to print on a page.

Quick Print

Another method for printing a document is to insert the Quick Print button on the Quick Access toolbar and then click the button. This sends the document directly to the printer without displaying the Print tab Backstage view. To insert the button on the Quick Access toolbar, click the Customize Quick Access Toolbar button that displays at the right side of the toolbar and then click *Quick Print* at the drop-down list. To remove the Quick Print button from the Quick Access toolbar, right-click on the button and then click the *Remove from Quick Access Toolbar* option that displays in the drop-down list.

Closing a Document

When you save a document, it is saved on your storage medium and remains in the document screen. To remove the document from the screen, click the File tab and then click the Close button or use the keyboard shortcut, Ctrl + F4. When you close a document, the document is removed and a blank screen displays. At this screen, you can open a previously saved document, create a new document, or exit the Word program.

Project 1b Saving, Printing, and Closing a Document   Part 2 of 2

1. Save the document you created for Project 1a and name it **WL1-C1-P1-Computers** (for Word Level 1, Chapter 1, Project 1 and the document refers to computers) by completing the following steps:
   a. Click the Save button on the Quick Access toolbar.
   b. At the Save As dialog box, navigate to the Word2010L1Cl folder on your storage medium. (To do this, click the drive representing your storage medium in the Navigation pane and then double-click the Word2010L1C1 folder.
   c. Click in the *File name* text box (this selects any text in the box), type **WL1-C1-P1-Computers**, and then press Enter.
2. Print the document by clicking the File tab, clicking the Print tab, and then at the Backstage view, clicking the Print button.

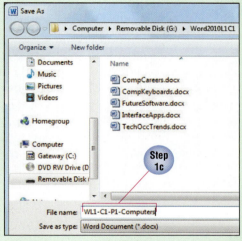
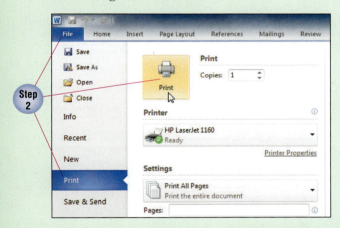

3. Close the document by clicking the File tab and then clicking the Close button.

Project 2 Save and Edit a Word Document   2 Parts

You will open a document located in the Word2010L1C1 folder on your storage medium, add text to the document, and then save the document with a new name.

Creating a New Document

When you close a document, a blank screen displays. If you want to create a new document, display a blank document. To do this, click the File tab, click the New tab, and then click the Create button that displays below the image of the blank document at the right side of the New tab Backstage view. You can also open a new document using the keyboard shortcut, Ctrl + N, or by inserting a New

▼ Quick Steps

Create a New Document
1. Click File tab.
2. Click New tab.
3. Click Create button.

button on the Quick Access toolbar. To insert the button, click the Customize Quick Access Toolbar button that displays at the right side of the toolbar and then click *New* at the drop-down list.

Opening a Document

▼ **Quick Steps**

Open a Document
1. Click File tab.
2. Click Open button.
3. Double-click document name.

After you save and close a document, you can open it at the Open dialog box shown in Figure 1.6. To display this dialog box, click the File tab and then click the Open button. You can also display the Open dialog box using the keyboard shortcut, Ctrl + O, or by inserting an Open button on the Quick Access toolbar. To insert the button, click the Customize Quick Access Toolbar button that displays at the right side of the toolbar and then click *Open* at the drop-down list. At the Open dialog box, open a document by double-clicking the document name.

If you want to see a list of the most recently opened documents, click the File tab and then click the Recent tab. This displays the Recent tab Backstage view containing a list of the most recently opened documents. To open a document from the list, scroll down the list and then click the desired document.

The Recent tab Backstage view contains the *Quickly access this number of Recent Documents* option that displays at the bottom of the screen. Click the option to insert a check mark in the check box and the four most recently opened document names display below the four options (*Save*, *Save As*, *Open*, and *Close*) in the Quick Commands area. By default, four document names display. You can change this number with the option box that displays at the right side of the *Quickly access this number of Recent Documents* option.

Figure 1.6 Open Dialog Box

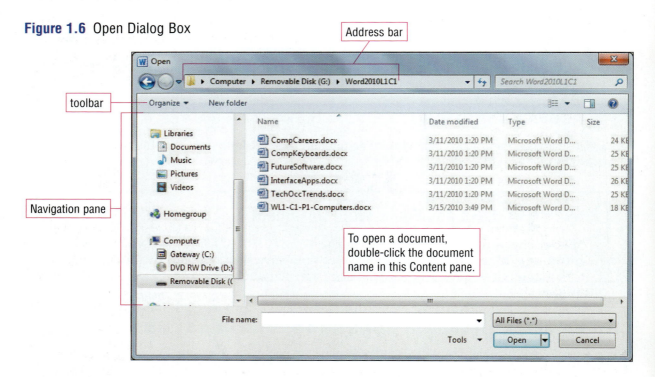

Pinning a Document

When you click the File tab and then click the Recent tab, the Recent Documents list displays with the most recently opened documents. If you want a document to remain in the list, "pin" the document to the list by clicking the pin button that displays at the right side of the document name. This changes the dimmed gray stick pin to a blue stick pin. The next time you display the Recent Documents list, the document you "pinned" displays at the top of the list. To "unpin" the document, click the pin button to change it from a blue pin to a dimmed gray pin. You can pin more than one document to the list.

Project 2a   Opening and Pinning/Unpinning a Document   Part 1 of 2

1. Open the **CompCareers.docx** document by completing the following steps:
   a. Click the File tab and then click the Open button in the Quick Commands area.
   b. At the Open dialog box, make sure the Word2010L1C1 folder on your storage medium is the active folder.
   c. Double-click *CompCareers.docx* in the Content pane.
2. Close **CompCareers.docx**.
3. Open **FutureSoftware.docx** by completing steps similar to those in Step 1.
4. Close **FutureSoftware.docx**.
5. Pin the **CompCareers.docx** document to the Recent Documents list by completing the following steps:
   a. Click the File tab. (If the Recent tab Backstage view does not display, click the Recent tab.)
   b. Click the dimmed gray stick pin that displays at the right side of the document **CompCareers.docx**. (This moves the document to the top of the list and changes the dimmed gray stick pin to a blue stick pin.)

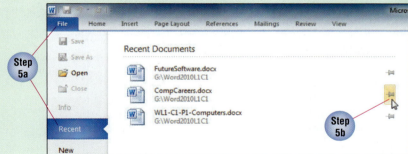

6. Click *CompCareers.docx* at the top of the Recent Documents list to open the document.
7. With the insertion point positioned at the beginning of the document, type the text shown in Figure 1.7.
8. Unpin the **CompCareers.docx** from the Recent Documents list by completing the following steps:
   a. Click the File tab and then click the Recent tab.
   b. At the Recent Documents list, click the blue stick pin that displays at the right of the **CompCareers.docx** document name. (This changes the pin from a blue stick pin to a dimmed gray stick pin.)
   c. Click the File tab to return to the document.

Chapter 1 ■ Preparing Documents   13

Figure 1.7 Project 2a

The majority of new jobs being created in the United States today involve daily work with computers. Computer-related careers include technical support jobs, sales and training, programming and applications development, network and database administration, and computer engineering.

▼ Quick Steps

Save a Document with Save As
1. Click File tab.
2. Click Save As button.
3. Navigate to desired folder.
4. Type document name.
5. Press Enter.

Exit Word
1. Click File tab.
2. Click Exit button.
OR
Click Close button.

Save any open documents before exiting Word.

Saving a Document with Save As

If you open a previously saved document and want to give it a new name, use the Save As button at the Backstage view rather than the Save button. Click the File tab and then click the Save As button and the Save As dialog box displays. At this dialog box, type the new name for the document and then press Enter.

Exiting Word

When you are finished working with Word and have saved all necessary information, exit Word by clicking the File tab and then clicking the Exit button located below the Help tab. You can also exit the Word program by clicking the Close button located in the upper right corner of the screen.

Project 2b Saving a Document with Save As   Part 2 of 2

1. With **CompCareers.docx** open, save the document with a new name by completing the following steps:
   a. Click the File tab and then click the Save As button.
   b. At the Save As dialog box, press the Home key on your keyboard to move the insertion point to the beginning of the file name and then type **WL1-C1-P2-**. (Pressing the Home key saves you from having to type the entire document name.)
   c. Press the Enter key.
2. Print the document by clicking the File tab, clicking the Print tab, and then clicking the Print button at the Print tab Backstage view. (If your Quick Access toolbar contains the Quick Print button, you can click the button to send the document directly to the printer.)
3. Close the document by pressing Ctrl + F4.

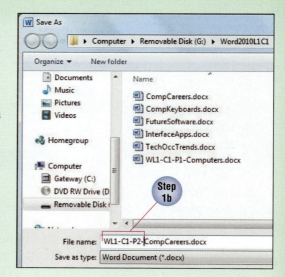

Step 1b

Project 3 | **Scroll and Browse in a Document** | **2 Parts**

You will open a previously created document, save it with a new name, and then use scrolling and browsing techniques to move the insertion point to specific locations in the document.

Editing a Document

When editing a document, you may decide to insert or delete text. To edit a document, use the mouse, the keyboard, or the mouse combined with the keyboard to move the insertion point to specific locations in the document. To move the insertion point using the mouse, position the I-beam pointer where you want the insertion point located and then click the left mouse button.

You can also scroll in a document, which changes the text display but does not move the insertion point. Use the mouse with the *vertical scroll bar*, located at the right side of the screen, to scroll through text in a document. Click the up scroll arrow at the top of the vertical scroll bar to scroll up through the document and click the down scroll arrow to scroll down through the document. The scroll bar contains a scroll box that indicates the location of the text in the document screen in relation to the remainder of the document. To scroll up one screen at a time, position the arrow pointer above the scroll box (but below the up scroll arrow) and then click the left mouse button. Position the arrow pointer below the scroll box and click the left button to scroll down a screen. If you hold down the left mouse button, the action becomes continuous. You can also position the arrow pointer on the scroll box, hold down the left mouse button, and then drag the scroll box along the scroll bar to reposition text in the document screen. As you drag the scroll box along the vertical scroll bar in a longer document, page numbers display in a box at the right side of the document screen.

Project 3a | **Scrolling in a Document** | **Part 1 of 2**

1. Open **InterfaceApps.docx** (from the Word2010L1C1 folder you copied to your storage medium.)
2. Save the document with Save As and name it **WL1-C1-P3-InterfaceApps**.
3. Position the I-beam pointer at the beginning of the first paragraph and then click the left mouse button.
4. Click the down scroll arrow on the vertical scroll bar several times. (This scrolls down lines of text in the document.) With the mouse pointer on the down scroll arrow, hold down the left mouse button and keep it down until the end of the document displays.
5. Position the mouse pointer on the up scroll arrow and hold down the left mouse button until the beginning of the document displays.
6. Position the mouse pointer below the scroll box and then click the left mouse button. Continue clicking the mouse button (with the mouse pointer positioned below the scroll box) until the end of the document displays.
7. Position the mouse pointer on the scroll box in the vertical scroll bar. Hold down the left mouse button, drag the scroll box to the top of the vertical scroll bar, and then release the mouse button. (Notice that the document page numbers display in a box at the right side of the document screen.)
8. Click in the title at the beginning of the document. (This moves the insertion point to the location of the mouse pointer.)

Moving the Insertion Point to a Specific Page

Previous Page

Select Browse Object

Next Page

Along with scrolling options, Word also contains navigation buttons for moving the insertion point to specific locations. Navigation buttons display toward the bottom of the vertical scroll bar and include the Previous Page button, the Select Browse Object button, and the Next Page button. The full names of and the tasks completed by the Previous and Next buttons vary depending on the last navigation completed. Click the Select Browse Object button and a palette of browsing choices displays. You will learn more about the Select Browse Object button in the next section.

Word includes a Go To option you can use to move the insertion point to a specific page within a document. To move the insertion point to a specific page, click the Find button arrow located in the Editing group in the Home tab and then click *Go To* at the drop-down list. At the Find and Replace dialog box with the Go To tab selected, type the page number in the *Enter page number* text box and then press Enter. Click the Close button to close the dialog box.

Browsing in a Document

The Select Browse Object button located toward the bottom of the vertical scroll bar contains options for browsing through a document. Click this button and a palette of browsing choices displays. Use the options on the palette to move the insertion point to various features in a Word document. Position the arrow pointer on an option in the palette and the option name displays above the options (the option name may display below the options). The options on the palette and the location of the options vary depending on the last function performed.

Moving the Insertion Point with the Keyboard

To move the insertion point with the keyboard, use the arrow keys located to the right of the regular keyboard. You can also use the arrow keys on the numeric keypad. If you use these keys, make sure Num Lock is off. Use the arrow keys together with other keys to move the insertion point to various locations in the document as shown in Table 1.2.

When moving the insertion point, Word considers a word to be any series of characters between spaces. A paragraph is any text that is followed by a stroke of the Enter key. A page is text that is separated by a soft or hard page break. If you open a previously saved document, you can move the insertion point to where the insertion point was last located when the document was closed by pressing Shift + F5.

Table 1.2 Insertion Point Movement Commands

To move insertion point	Press
One character left	Left Arrow
One character right	Right Arrow
One line up	Up Arrow
One line down	Down Arrow

continues

Table 1.2 Insertion Point Movement Commands, continued

To move insertion point	Press
One word to the left	Ctrl + Left Arrow
One word to the right	Ctrl + Right Arrow
To end of a line	End
To beginning of a line	Home
To beginning of current paragraph	Ctrl + Up Arrow
To beginning of next paragraph	Ctrl + Down Arrow
Up one screen	Page Up
Down one screen	Page Down
To top of previous page	Ctrl + Page Up
To top of next page	Ctrl + Page Down
To beginning of document	Ctrl + Home
To end of document	Ctrl + End

Project 3b Moving the Insertion Point and Browsing in a Document   Part 2 of 2

1. With **WL1-C1-P3-InterfaceApps.docx** open, move the insertion point to page 3 by completing the following steps:
   a. Click the Find button arrow located in the Editing group in the Home tab and then click *Go To* at the drop-down list.
   b. At the Find and Replace dialog box with the Go To tab selected, type **3** in the *Enter page number* text box and then press Enter.
   c. Click the Close button to close the Find and Replace dialog box.
2. Click the Previous Page button located immediately above the Select Browse Object button on the vertical scroll bar. (This moves the insertion point to page 2.)

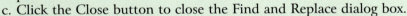

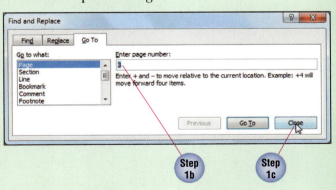

3. Click the Previous Page button again. (This moves the insertion point to page 1.)
4. Click the Next Page button located immediately below the Select Browse Object button on the vertical scroll bar. (This moves the insertion point to the beginning of page 2.)

Chapter 1 ■ Preparing Documents   17

5. Move to the beginning of page 3 by completing the following steps:
   a. Click the Select Browse Object button.
   b. At the palette of browsing choices, click the last choice in the bottom row (*Browse by Page*). (This moves the insertion point to page 3.)
6. Press Ctrl + Home to move the insertion point to the beginning of the document.
7. Practice using the keyboard commands shown in Table 1.2 to move the insertion point within the document.
8. Close **WL1-C1-P3-InterfaceApps.docx**.

Project 4 Insert and Delete Text   2 Parts

You will open a previously created document, save it with a new name, and then make editing changes to the document. The editing changes include selecting, inserting, and deleting text.

Inserting and Deleting Text

Editing a document may include inserting and/or deleting text. To insert text in a document, position the insertion point in the desired location and then type the text. Existing characters move to the right as you type the text. A number of options are available for deleting text. Some deletion commands are shown in Table 1.3.

Selecting Text

You can use the mouse and/or keyboard to select a specific amount of text. Once selected, you can delete the text or perform other Word functions involving the selected text. When text is selected, it displays with a blue background as shown in Figure 1.8 and the Mini toolbar displays in a dimmed fashion and contains options for common tasks. Move the mouse pointer over the Mini toolbar and it becomes active. (You will learn more about the Mini toolbar in Chapter 2.)

Table 1.3 Deletion Commands

To delete	Press
Character right of insertion point	Delete key
Character left of insertion point	Backspace key
Text from insertion point to beginning of word	Ctrl + Backspace
Text from insertion point to end of word	Ctrl + Delete

Figure 1.8 Selected Text and Mini Toolbar

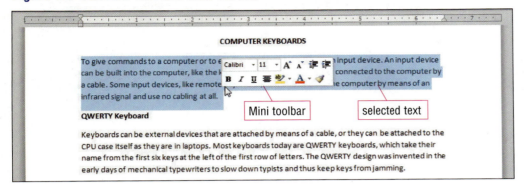

Selecting Text with the Mouse

Use the mouse to select a word, line, sentence, paragraph, or the entire document. Table 1.4 indicates the steps to follow to select various amounts of text. To select a specific amount of text such as a line or a paragraph, the instructions in the table tell you to click in the selection bar. The selection bar is the space located toward the left side of the document screen between the left edge of the page and the text. When the mouse pointer is positioned in the selection bar, the pointer turns into an arrow pointing up and to the right (instead of to the left).

To select an amount of text other than a word, sentence, or paragraph, position the I-beam pointer on the first character of the text to be selected, hold down the left mouse button, drag the I-beam pointer to the last character of the text to be selected, and then release the mouse button. You can also select all text between the current insertion point and the I-beam pointer. To do this, position the insertion point where you want the selection to begin, hold down the Shift key, click the I-beam pointer at the end of the selection, and then release the Shift key. To cancel a selection using the mouse, click anywhere in the document screen outside the selected text.

HINT To select text vertically, hold down the Alt key while dragging with the mouse.

Table 1.4 Selecting with the Mouse

To select	Complete these steps using the mouse
A word	Double-click the word.
A line of text	Click in the selection bar to the left of the line.
Multiple lines of text	Drag in the selection bar to the left of the lines.
A sentence	Hold down the Ctrl key, then click anywhere in the sentence.
A paragraph	Double-click in the selection bar next to the paragraph or triple-click anywhere in the paragraph.
Multiple paragraphs	Drag in the selection bar.
An entire document	Triple-click in the selection bar.

Selecting Text with the Keyboard

If text is selected, any character you type replaces the selected text.

To select a specific amount of text using the keyboard, turn on the Selection Mode by pressing the F8 function key. With the Selection Mode activated, use the arrow keys to select the desired text. If you want to cancel the selection, press the Esc key and then press any arrow key. You can customize the Status bar to display text indicating that the Selection Mode is activated. To do this, right-click any blank location on the Status bar and then click *Selection Mode* at the pop-up list. When you press F8 to turn on the Selection Mode, the words *Extend Selection* display on the Status bar. You can also select text with the commands shown in Table 1.5.

Project 4a — Editing a Document — Part 1 of 2

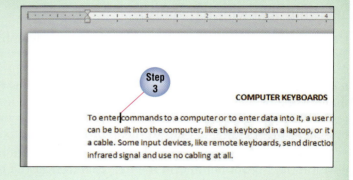

1. Open **CompKeyboards.docx**. (This document is located in the Word2010L1C1 folder you copied to your storage medium.)
2. Save the document with Save As and name it **WL1-C1-P4-CompKeyboards**.
3. Change the word *give* in the first sentence of the first paragraph to *enter*.
4. Change the second *to* in the first sentence to *into*.
5. Delete the words *means of* in the first sentence in the *QWERTY Keyboard* section.
6. Select the words *and use no cabling at all* and the period that follows located at the end of the last sentence in the first paragraph, and then press the Delete key.
7. Insert a period immediately following the word *signal*.
8. Delete the heading line containing the text *QWERTY Keyboard* using the Selection Mode by completing the following steps:
    a. Position the insertion point immediately before the *Q* in *QWERTY*.
    b. Press F8 to turn on the Selection Mode.
    c. Press the Down Arrow key.
    d. Press the Delete key.
9. Complete steps similar to those in Step 8 to delete the heading line containing the text *DVORAK Keyboard*.
10. Begin a new paragraph with the sentence that reads *Keyboards have different physical appearances.* by completing the following steps:
    a. Position the insertion point immediately left of the *K* in *Keyboards* (the first word of the fifth sentence in the last paragraph).
    b. Press the Enter key.
11. Save **WL1-C1-P4-CompKeyboards.docx**.

Table 1.5 Selecting with the Keyboard

To select	Press
One character to right	Shift + Right Arrow
One character to left	Shift + Left Arrow
To end of word	Ctrl + Shift + Right Arrow
To beginning of word	Ctrl + Shift + Left Arrow
To end of line	Shift + End
To beginning of line	Shift + Home
One line up	Shift + Up Arrow
One line down	Shift + Down Arrow
To beginning of paragraph	Ctrl + Shift + Up Arrow
To end of paragraph	Ctrl + Shift + Down Arrow
One screen up	Shift + Page Up
One screen down	Shift + Page Down
To end of document	Ctrl + Shift + End
To beginning of document	Ctrl + Shift + Home
Entire document	Ctrl + A or click Select button in Editing group and then Select All

Using the Undo and Redo Buttons

If you make a mistake and delete text that you did not intend to, or if you change your mind after deleting text and want to retrieve it, you can use the Undo or Redo buttons on the Quick Access toolbar. For example, if you type text and then click the Undo button, the text will be removed. You can undo text or commands. For example, if you add formatting such as bolding to text and then click the Undo button, the bolding is removed.

HINT You cannot undo a save.

If you use the Undo button and then decide you do not want to reverse the original action, click the Redo button. For example, if you select and underline text and then decide to remove underlining, click the Undo button. If you then decide you want the underlining back on, click the Redo button. Many Word actions can be undone or redone. Some actions, however, such as printing and saving, cannot be undone or redone.

Undo

Word maintains actions in temporary memory. If you want to undo an action performed earlier, click the Undo button arrow. This causes a drop-down list to display. To make a selection from this drop-down list, click the desired action and the action, along with any actions listed above it in the drop-down list, is undone.

Redo

Project 4b Undoing and Redoing Deletions   Part 2 of 2

1. With **WL1-C1-P4-CompKeyboards.docx** open, delete the last sentence in the last paragraph using the mouse by completing the following steps:
   a. Position the I-beam pointer anywhere in the sentence that begins *All keyboards have modifier keys . . . .*
   b. Hold down the Ctrl key and then click the left mouse button.

   > install software on a QWERTY keyboard that emulates a DVORAK keyboard. The ability to emulate other keyboards is convenient especially when working with foreign languages.
   >
   > Keyboards have different physical appearances. Many keyboards have a separate numeric keypad, like that of a calculator, containing numbers and mathematical operators. Some keyboards are sloped and "broken" into two pieces to reduce strain. All keyboards have modifier keys that enable the user to change the symbol or character entered when a given key is pressed.

   Steps 1a-1b

   c. Press the Delete key.
2. Delete the last paragraph by completing the following steps:
   a. Position the I-beam pointer anywhere in the last paragraph (the paragraph that begins *Keyboards have different physical appearances*).
   b. Triple-click the left mouse button.
   c. Press the Delete key.
3. Undo the deletion by clicking the Undo button on the Quick Access toolbar.
4. Redo the deletion by clicking the Redo button on the Quick Access toolbar.
5. Select the first sentence in the second paragraph and then delete it.
6. Select the first paragraph in the document and then delete it.
7. Undo the two deletions by completing the following steps:
   a. Click the Undo button arrow.
   b. Click the *second* Clear listed in the drop-down list. (This will redisplay the first sentence in the second paragraph as well as displaying the first paragraph. The sentence will be selected.)
8. Click outside the sentence to deselect it.
9. Save, print, and then close **WL1-C1-P4-CompKeyboards.docx**.

Step 3

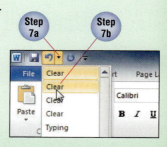

Step 7a Step 7b

Project 5 Complete a Spelling and Grammar Check   1 Part

You will open a previously created document, save it with a new name, and then check the spelling and grammar in the document.

Checking the Spelling and Grammar in a Document ■■■

Two tools for creating thoughtful and well-written documents include a spelling checker and a grammar checker. The spelling checker finds misspelled words and offers replacement words. It also finds duplicate words and irregular capitalizations. When you spell check a document, the spelling checker compares the words in your document with the words in its dictionary. If the spelling checker finds a match, it passes over the word. If a match is not found for the word, the spelling checker will stop, select the word, and offer replacements.

The grammar checker will search a document for errors in grammar, punctuation, and word usage. The spelling checker and the grammar check can help you create a well-written document, but do not replace the need for proofreading. To complete a spelling and grammar check, click the Review tab and then click the Spelling & Grammar button in the Proofing group. You can also begin spelling and grammar checking by pressing the keyboard shortcut, F7. As the spelling and grammar checker selects text, make a choice from some of the options in the Spelling and Grammar dialog box as shown in Table 1.6.

By default, a spelling and grammar check are both completed on a document. If you want to check only the spelling in a document and not the grammar, remove the check mark from the *Check grammar* check box located in the lower left corner of the Spelling and Grammar dialog box. When spell checking a document, you can temporarily leave the Spelling and Grammar dialog box, make corrections in the document, and then resume spell checking by clicking the Resume button.

▼ **Quick Steps**

Check Spelling and Grammar
1. Click Review tab.
2. Click Spelling & Grammar button.
3. Change or ignore errors.
4. Click OK.

HINT

Complete a spelling and grammar check on a portion of a document by selecting the text first and then clicking the Spelling & Grammar button.

Spelling & Grammar

Table 1.6 Spelling and Grammar Dialog Box Buttons

Button	Function
Ignore Once	During spell checking, skips that occurrence of the word; in grammar checking, leaves currently selected text as written
Ignore All	During spell checking, skips that occurrence of the word and all other occurrences of the word in the document
Ignore Rule	During grammar checking, leaves currently selected text as written and ignores the current rule for remainder of the grammar check
Add to Dictionary	Adds selected word to the spelling check dictionary
Delete	Deletes the currently selected word(s)
Change	Replaces selected word in sentence with selected word in *Suggestions* list box
Change All	Replaces selected word in sentence with selected word in *Suggestions* list box and all other occurrences of the word
AutoCorrect	Inserts selected word and correct spelling of word in AutoCorrect dialog box
Explain	During grammar checking, displays grammar rule information about the selected text
Undo	Reverses most recent spelling and grammar action
Next Sentence	Accepts manual changes made to sentence and then continues grammar checking
Options	Displays a dialog box with options for customizing a spelling and grammar check

Chapter 1 ■ Preparing Documents

Project 5   **Checking the Spelling and Grammar in a Document**   Part 1 of 1

1. Open **TechOccTrends.docx**.
2. Save the document with Save As and name it **WL1-C1-P5-TechOccTrends**.
3. Click the Review tab.
4. Click the Spelling & Grammar button in the Proofing group.
5. The spelling checker selects the word *tecnology*. The proper spelling is selected in the *Suggestions* list box, so click the Change button (or Change All button).
6. The spelling checker selects the word *occupatoins*. The proper spelling of the word is selected in the *Suggestions* list box, so click the Change button (or Change All button).
7. The grammar checker selects the sentence that begins *One key to being successful . . .* and displays *trends* and *a trend* in the *Suggestions* list box. Click *a trend* in the *Suggestions* list box and then click the Change button.

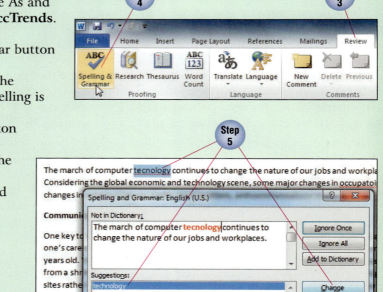

8. The grammar checker selects the sentence that begins *Young reader are not as interested . . .* and displays *reader is* and *readers are* in the *Suggestions* text box. Click the Explain button, read the information about subject-verb agreement that displays in the Word Help window,

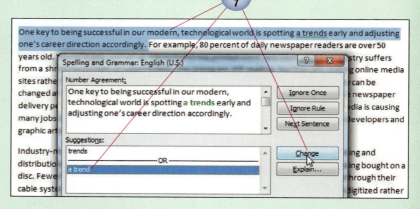

and then click the Close button located in the upper right corner of the Word Help window.
9. Click *readers are* in the *Suggestions* text box and then click the Change button.
10. The spelling checker selects *excelent*. The proper spelling is selected in the *Suggestions* list box, so click the Change button.
11. The grammar checker selects the sentence that begins *The number of printing and lithography job's is shrinking . . . .* Click the Explain button, read the information about plural or possessive that displays in the Word Help window, and then click the Close button located in the upper right corner of the Word Help window.
12. With *jobs* selected in the *Suggestions* list box, click the Change button.
13. The spelling checker selects the word *successful* and offers *successful* in the *Suggestions* text box. Since this word is misspelled in another location in the document, click the Change All button.

14. The spelling checker selects the word *are* that is used twice in a row. Click the Delete button to delete the word.
15. When the message displays telling you that the spelling and grammar check is complete, click the OK button.
16. Save, print, and then close **WL1-C1-P5-TechOccTrends .docx**.

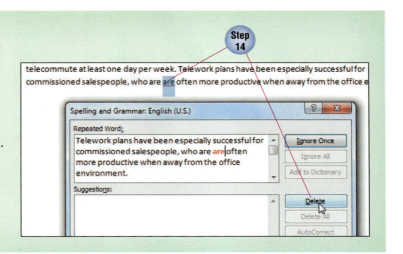

Project 6 Use the Help Feature   2 Parts

You need to learn more about selecting text and saving a document so you decide to use Help to research these features.

Using Help

Word's Help feature is an on-screen reference manual containing information about all Word features and commands. Word's Help feature is similar to Windows Help and the Help features in Excel, PowerPoint, and Access. Get help by clicking the Microsoft Word Help button located in the upper right corner of the screen (a question mark in a circle) or by pressing the keyboard shortcut, F1. This displays the Word Help window. In this window, type a topic, feature, or question in the Search text box and then press Enter. Topics related to the search text display in the Word Help window. Click a topic that interests you. If the topic window contains a Show All hyperlink in the upper right corner, click this hyperlink and the information expands to show all help information related to the topic. When you click the Show All hyperlink, it becomes the Hide All hyperlink.

▼ **Quick Steps**

Use Help Feature
1. Click Microsoft Word Help button.
2. Type topic, feature, or question.
3. Press Enter.
4. Click desired topic.

The Help tab Backstage view, shown in Figure 1.9, contains an option for displaying the Word Help window as well as other options. To display the Help tab Backstage view, click the File tab and then click the Help tab. At the Help tab Backstage view, click the Microsoft Office Help button in the *Support* section to display the Word Help window and click the Getting Started button to access the Microsoft website that displays information about getting started with Word 2010. Click the Contact Us button in the *Support* section and the Microsoft Support website displays. Click the Options button in the *Tools for Working With Office* section and the Word Options dialog box displays. You will learn about this dialog box in a later chapter. Click the Check for Updates button and the Microsoft Update website displays with information on available updates. The right side of the Help tab Backstage view displays information about Office and Word.

Figure 1.9 Help Tab Backstage View

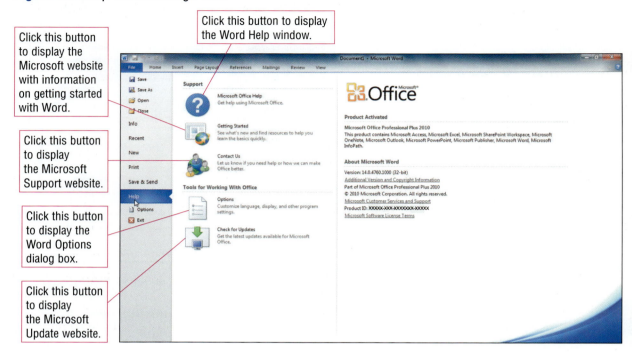

Click this button to display the Microsoft website with information on getting started with Word.

Click this button to display the Word Help window.

Click this button to display the Microsoft Support website.

Click this button to display the Word Options dialog box.

Click this button to display the Microsoft Update website.

Project 6a Using the Help Feature   Part 1 of 2

1. At a blank document, click the Microsoft Word Help button located in the upper right corner of the screen.
2. At the Word Help window, type **save a document** in the Search text box.
3. Press the Enter key.
4. When the list of topics displays, click the Save a document in Word hyperlink. (If your Word Help window does not display the online options, check the lower right corner of the window. If the word *Offline* displays, click *Offline* and then click the *Show content from Office.com* option at the drop-down list.)
5. Click the Show All hyperlink that displays in the upper right corner of the window.

6. Read the information about saving a document.
7. Print the information by clicking the Print button located toward the top of the Word Help window.
8. At the Print dialog box, click the Print button.
9. Click the Close button to close the Word Help window.
10. Click the File tab and then click the Help tab.
11. Click the Getting Started button in the *Support* section. (You must be connected to the Internet to display the web page.)

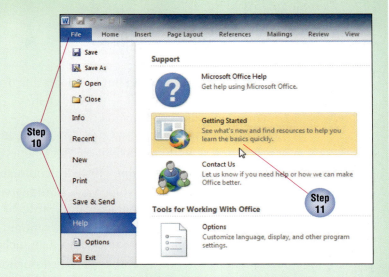

12. Look at the information that displays at the website and then click the Close button located in the upper right corner of the web page.
13. Click the File tab and then click the Help tab.
14. Click the Contact Us button, look at the information that displays at the website, and then close the web page.

Getting Help in a Dialog Box or Backstage View

Some dialog boxes, as well as the Backstage view, contain a Help button you can click to display a help window with specific information about the dialog box or Backstage view. After reading and/or printing the information, close a dialog box by clicking the Close button located in the upper right corner of the dialog box or close the Backstage view by clicking the File tab or clicking any other tab in the ribbon.

Project 6b Getting Help in a Dialog Box and Backstage View   Part 2 of 2

1. At a blank document, click the File tab and then click the Save As button.
2. At the Save As dialog box, click the Help button located in the upper right corner of the dialog box.
3. Read the information about saving files and then click the Close button located in the upper right corner of the dialog box.
4. Close the Save As dialog box.
5. Click the File tab.
6. At the Backstage view, click the Help button located in the upper right corner of the window.
7. Click the Introducing Backstage hyperlink.
8. Read the information about the Backstage view.
9. Close the Word Help window and then click the File tab to return to the document.

Chapter 1 ■ Preparing Documents   27

Chapter Summary

- Refer to Figure 1.1 and Table 1.1 for a listing of key word screen features.
- The Quick Access toolbar is located above the File tab and contains buttons for commonly used commands.
- Click the File tab and the Backstage view displays containing tabs and buttons for working with and managing documents
- The ribbon area contains tabs with commands and options divided into groups.
- The insertion point displays as a blinking vertical line and indicates the position of the next character to be entered in the document.
- Document names can contain a maximum of 255 characters, including the drive letter and folder names, and may include spaces.
- The insertion point can be moved throughout the document without interfering with text by using the mouse, the keyboard, or the mouse combined with the keyboard.
- The scroll box on the vertical scroll bar indicates the location of the text in the document in relation to the remainder of the document.
- Click the Select Browse Object button located at the bottom of the vertical scroll bar to display options for browsing through a document.
- You can move the insertion point by character, word, screen, or page, and from the first to the last character in a document. Refer to Table 1.2 for keyboard insertion point movement commands.
- You can delete text by character, word, line, several lines, or partial page using specific keys or by selecting text using the mouse or the keyboard.
- You can select a specific amount of text using the mouse or the keyboard. Refer to Table 1.4 for information on selecting with the mouse and refer to Table 1.5 for information on selecting with the keyboard.
- Use the Undo button on the Quick Access toolbar if you change your mind after typing, deleting, or formatting text and want to undo the action. Use the Redo button to redo something that had been undone with the Undo button.
- The spelling checker matches the words in your document with the words in its dictionary. If a match is not found, the word is selected and possible corrections are suggested. The grammar checker searches a document for errors in grammar, style, punctuation, and word usage. When a grammar error is detected, display information about the error by clicking the Explain button at the Spelling & Grammar dialog box.
- Word's Help feature is an on-screen reference manual containing information about all Word features and commands. Click the Microsoft Word Help button or press F1 to display the Word Help window.
- Click the File tab and then click the Help tab to display the Help tab Backstage view.
- Some dialog boxes, as well as the Backstage view, contain a Help button you can click to display information specific to the dialog box or Backstage view.

Commands Review

FEATURE	RIBBON TAB, GROUP	BUTTON, OPTION	FILE TAB	KEYBOARD SHORTCUT
Close document			Close	Ctrl + F4
Exit Word		X	Exit	
Find and Replace dialog box with Go To tab selected	Home, Editing	, Go To		Ctrl + G
Help tab Backstage view			Help	
New blank document			New, Create	Ctrl + N
Open dialog box			Open	Ctrl + O
Print tab Backstage view			Print	Ctrl + P
Save document		💾	Save	Ctrl + S
Select document	Home, Editing	, Select All		Ctrl + A
Spelling and Grammar dialog box	Review, Proofing	ABC		F7
Word Help window		?		F1

Concepts Check   Test Your Knowledge

Completion: In the space provided at the right, indicate the correct term, symbol, or command.

1. This toolbar contains the Save button. _____

2. Click this tab to display the Backstage view. _____

3. This is the area located toward the top of the screen that contains tabs with commands and options divided into groups. _____

4. This bar, located toward the bottom of the screen, displays number of pages and words, View buttons, and the Zoom slider bar. _____

5. This tab is selected by default. _____

6. This feature automatically corrects certain words as you type them. _____

7. This feature inserts an entire item when you type a few identifying characters and then press Enter or F3. _____

8. This is the keyboard shortcut to display the Print tab Backstage view. _____

9. This is the keyboard shortcut to close a document. _____

10. This is the keyboard shortcut to display a new blank document. _____

11. Use this keyboard shortcut to move the insertion point to the beginning of the previous page. _____

12. Use this keyboard shortcut to move the insertion point to the end of the document. _____

13. Press this key on the keyboard to delete the character left of the insertion point. _____

14. Using the mouse, do this to select one word. _____

15. To select various amounts of text using the mouse, you can click in this bar. _____

16. Click this tab to display the Spelling & Grammar button in the Proofing group. _____

17. This is the keyboard shortcut to display the Word Help window. _____

Skills Check Assess Your Performance

Assessment

1 TYPE AND EDIT A DOCUMENT ON FUZZY LOGIC

1. Open Word and then type the text in Figure 1.10. Correct any errors highlighted by the spell checker and space once after end-of-sentence punctuation.
2. Make the following changes to the document:
   a. Delete *AI* in the first sentence of the first paragraph and then insert *artificial intelligence*.
   b. Insert the words *for approximations and* between the words *allowing* and *incomplete* located in the first sentence of the first paragraph.
   c. Insert the words *or numerical* between the words *yes/no* and *information* in the second sentence of the first paragraph.
   d. Delete the words *hard to come by* in the last sentence of the first paragraph and replace with the word *rare*.
   e. Insert the letters *SQL* between the words *logic* and *database* in the last sentence of the second paragraph.

f. Move the insertion point immediately left of the period at the end of the last sentence of the last paragraph, type a comma, and then insert the words *and trade shares on the Tokyo Stock Exchange*. Delete the word *and* before the words *automobile transmissions* in the last sentence.
   g. Join the first and second paragraphs.
   h. Delete the name *Marie Solberg* and then type your first and last names.
3. Save the document and name it **WL1-C1-A1-FuzzyLogic**.
4. Print and then close **WL1-C1-A1-FuzzyLogic.docx**.

Figure 1.10 Assessment 1

Fuzzy Logic

The fuzzy logic branch of AI attempts to model human reasoning by allowing incomplete input data. Instead of demanding precise yes/no information, fuzzy logic systems allow users to input "fuzzy" data. The terminology used by the system is deliberately vague and includes terms such as very probable, somewhat decreased, reasonable, or very slight. This is an attempt to simulate real-world conditions, where precise answers are hard to come by.

A fuzzy logic system attempts to work more naturally with the user by piecing together an answer in a manner similar to that used by a traditional expert system. Fuzzy logic database queries seem significantly more human than traditional queries.

Fuzzy logic systems are much more common in Japan than they are in the United States, where traditional expert systems and neural networks tend to be favored. In Japan, microprocessors specially designed by Toshiba and Hitachi to use fuzzy logic operate subways, consumer electronics, and automobile transmissions.

Created by Marie Solberg
Monday, October 1, 2012
Note: Please insert this information between 4th and 5th sections.

Assessment 2

CHECK THE SPELLING AND GRAMMAR OF A COMPUTER SOFTWARE DOCUMENT

1. Open **FutureSoftware.docx**.
2. Save the document with Save As and name it **WL1-C1-A2-FutureSoftware**.
3. Complete a spelling and grammar check on the document. You determine what to change and what to leave as written.
4. Insert the sentence *Wizards are small programs designed to assist users by automating tasks.* between the third and fourth sentences in the *User-Friendly System Software* section.
5. Move the insertion point to the end of the document, type your first and last names, press Shift + Enter, and then type the current date.
6. Save, print, and then close **WL1-C1-A2-FutureSoftware.docx**.

Assessment

3 CREATE A DOCUMENT DESCRIBING KEYBOARD SHORTCUTS

1. Click the Microsoft Word Help button, type **keyboard shortcuts**, and then press Enter.
2. At the Word Help window, click the Keyboard shortcuts for Microsoft Word hyperlink.
3. At the keyboard shortcut window, click the Show All hyperlink.
4. Read through the information in the Word Help window.
5. Create a document describing four keyboard shortcuts.
6. Save the document and name it **WL1-C1-A3-KeyboardShortcuts**.
7. Print and then close **WL1-C1-A3-KeyboardShortcuts.docx**.

Visual Benchmark Demonstrate Your Proficiency

CREATE A COVER PAGE

1. At a blank document, press the Enter key three times and then type the personal business letter shown in Figure 1.11 on the next page by following the directions in red.
2. Save the completed letter and name it **WL1-C1-VB-CoverLtr**.
3. Print and then close the document.

Figure 1.11 Visual Benchmark

4520 South Park Street *(press Shift + Enter)*
Newark, NJ 07122 *(press Shift + Enter)*
(Current date) *(press Enter two times)*

Mrs. Sylvia Hammond *(press Shift + Enter)*
Sales Director, Eastern Division *(press Shift + Enter)*
Grand Style Products *(press Shift + Enter)*
1205 Sixth Street *(press Shift + Enter)*
Newark, NJ 07102 *(press Enter)*

Dear Mrs. Hammond: *(press Enter)*

Thank you for agreeing to meet with me next Wednesday. Based on our initial conversation, it seems that my ability to sell solutions rather than products is a good fit for your needs as you seek to expand your visibility in the region. *(press Enter)*

As noted in the enclosed resume, I have led an under-performing product division to generating 33 percent of total revenue (up from 5 percent) at our location, and delivering, from a single location, 25 percent of total sales for our 20-site company. Having completed this turnaround over the last 5 years, I'm eager for new challenges where my proven skills in sales, marketing, and program/event planning can contribute to a company's bottom line. *(press Enter)*

I have been thinking about the challenges you described in building your presence at the retail level, and I have some good ideas to share at our meeting. I am excited about the future of Grand Style Products and eager to contribute to your growth. *(press Enter)*

Sincerely, *(press Enter two times)*

(Student Name) *(press Enter)*

Enclosure

Case Study   Apply Your Skills

Part 1

You are the assistant to Paul Brewster, the training coordinator at a medium-sized service-oriented business. You have been asked by Mr. Brewster to prepare a document for Microsoft Word users within the company explaining how to use the Save As command when saving a document rather than the Save command. Save the document and name it **WL1-C1-CS-P1-SaveAs**. Print and then close the document.

Part 2

Mr. Brewster would like a document containing a brief summary of some basic Word commands for use in Microsoft Word training classes. He has asked you to prepare a document containing the following information:

- A brief explanation on how to move the insertion point to a specific page
- Keyboard shortcuts to move the insertion point to the beginning and end of a text line and beginning and end of a document
- Commands to delete text from the insertion point to the beginning of the word and from the insertion point to the end of the word
- Steps to select a word, a sentence, a paragraph, and an entire document using the mouse.
- Keyboard shortcut to select the entire document

Save the document and name it **WL1-C1-CS-P2-WordCommands**. Print and then close the document.

Part 3

According to Mr. Brewster, the company is considering updating the Resources Department computers to Microsoft Office 2010. He has asked you to use the Internet to go to the Microsoft home page at www.microsoft.com and then use the search feature to find information on the system requirements for Office Professional Plus 2010. When you find the information, type a document that contains the Office Professional Plus 2010 system requirements for the computer and processor, memory, hard disk space, and operating system. Save the document and name it **WL1-C1-CS-P3-SystemReq**. Print and then close the document.

Microsoft Word

Formatting Characters and Paragraphs

CHAPTER 2

PERFORMANCE OBJECTIVES

Upon successful completion of Chapter 2, you will be able to:
- Change the font and font effects
- Format selected text with buttons on the Mini toolbar
- Apply styles from Quick Styles sets
- Apply themes
- Change the alignment of text in paragraphs
- Indent text in paragraphs
- Increase and decrease spacing before and after paragraphs
- Repeat the last action
- Automate formatting with Format Painter
- Change line spacing in a document
- Reveal and compare formatting

A Word document is based on a template that applies default formatting. Some of the default formats include 11-point Calibri, line spacing of 1.15, 10 points of spacing after each paragraph, and left-aligned text. The appearance of a document in the document screen and how it looks when printed is called the *format*. In this chapter, you will learn about character formatting that can include such elements as changing the typeface, type size, and typestyle as well as applying font effects such as bolding and italicizing. The Paragraph group in the Home tab includes buttons for applying formatting to paragraphs of text. In Word, a paragraph is any amount of text followed by the press of the Enter key. In this chapter, you will learn to apply paragraph formatting to text such as changing text alignment, indenting text, applying formatting with Format Painter, and changing line spacing. Model answers for this chapter's projects appear on the following pages.

Word2010L1C2

Note: Before beginning the projects, copy to your storage medium the Word2010L1C2 subfolder from the Word2010L1 folder on the CD that accompanies this textbook and then make Word2010L1C2 the active folder.

Model Answers

Project 1 Apply Character Formatting
WL1-C2-P1-CompTerms.docx

GLOSSARY OF TERMS

A

Access time: The time a storage device spends locating a particular file.
Aggregation software: E-commerce software application that combines online activities to provide *one-stop shopping* for consumers.
Analog signals: Signals composed of continuous waves transmitted at a certain frequency range over a medium, such as a telephone line.

B

Backup: A second copy kept of valuable data.
Bandwidth: The number of *bits* that can be transferred per second over a given medium or network.
Beta-testing: One of the last steps in software development that involves allowing outside people to use the software to see if it works as designed.

C

Chinese abacus: Pebbles strung on a rod inside a frame. Pebbles in the upper part of an abacus correspond to 5 x 10⁰, or 5, for the first column; 5 x 10¹, or 50, for the second column; 5 x 10², or 500, for the third column; and so on.
Chip: A thin wafer of *silicon* containing electronic circuitry that performs various functions, such as mathematical calculations, storage, or controlling computer devices.
Cluster: A group of two or more sectors on a disk, which is the smallest unit of storage space used to store data.
Coding: A term used by programmers to refer to the act of writing source code.
Crackers: A term coined by computer hackers for those who intentionally enter (or hack) computer systems to damage them.

CREATED BY SUSAN ASHBY
WEDNESDAY, FEBRUARY 22, 2012

Project 2 Apply Styles and Themes
WL1-C2-P2-SoftwareCycle.docx

COMMERCIAL LIFE CYCLE
The software life cycle is the term used to describe the phases involved in the process of creating, testing, and releasing new commercial software products. This cycle is similar to the process used in developing information systems, except that in this case the cycle focuses on the creation and release of a software program, not the development of a customized information system. The commercial software life cycle is repeated every time a new version of a program is needed. The phases in the software life cycle include the following: proposal and planning, design, implementation, testing, and public release.

PROPOSAL AND PLANNING
In the proposal and planning phase of a new software product, software developers will describe the proposed software program and what it is supposed to accomplish. In the case of existing software, the proposal and planning stage can be used to describe any new features and improvements. Older software programs are often revised to take advantage of new hardware or software developments and to add new functions or features.

DESIGN
Developers are ready to begin the design process once the decision has been made to create or upgrade a software program. This step produces specifications documenting the details of the software to be written by programmers. Developers use problem-solving steps to determine the appropriate specifications.

IMPLEMENTATION
The implementation phase of the software life cycle is usually the most difficult. Development teams often spend late nights and weekends writing code and making it work. If the planning and design efforts have been successful, this phase should go well, but unanticipated problems inevitably crop up and have to be solved. The end result of the implementation phase is the production of a prototype called an alpha product, which is used by the development team for testing purposes. The alpha product can be revised to incorporate any improvements suggested by team members.

TESTING
A quality assurance (QA) team usually develops a testing harness, which is a scripted set of tests that a program must undergo before being considered ready for public release. These tests might cover events such as very large input loads, maximum number of users, running on several different platforms, and simulated power outages. Once testing is finished, a beta version of the software program is created for testing outside of the development group, often by a select group of knowledgeable consumers. Any suggestions they make can be used to improve the product before it is released to the general public. Once the beta version is finalized, the user manual can be written or updated. At this point, the software developers would send the master CDs to duplicators for mass production.

PUBLIC RELEASE AND SUPPORT
When the product is deemed ready for widespread use, it is declared "gold" and released to the public. The software life cycle now goes back to the beginning phases as software developers think of new ways to improve the product.

Project 3 Apply Paragraph Formatting and Use Format Painter
WL1-C2-P3-IntelProp.docx

PROPERTY PROTECTION ISSUES

The ability to link computers through the Internet offers many advantages. With linked computers, we can quickly and easily communicate with other users around the world, sharing files and other data with a few simple keystrokes. The convenience provided by linking computers through the Internet also has some drawbacks. Computer viruses can travel around the world in seconds, damaging programs and files. Hackers can enter into systems without authorization and steal or alter data. In addition, the wealth of information on the Web and the increased ease with which it can be copied have made plagiarizing easy. Plagiarism is using others' ideas and creations (their intellectual property) without permission.

All of these ethical issues revolve around property rights, the right of someone to protect and control the things he or she owns. A solid legal framework ensuring the protection of personal property exists, but computers have created many new issues that challenge conventional interpretations of these laws.

Intellectual Property

Intellectual property includes just about anything that can be created by the agency of the human mind. To encourage innovation and improvement and thus benefit society as a whole, our legal system grants patents to those who invent new and better ways of doing things. A patent awards ownership of an idea or invention to its creator for a fixed number of years. This allows the inventor the right to charge others for the use of the invention. To encourage and protect artistic and literary endeavors, authors and artists are awarded copyrights to the material they create, allowing them the right to control the use of their works and charge others for their use. Patent and copyright violation is punishable by law, and prosecutions and convictions are frequent. The legal framework protecting intellectual property has come under constant challenge as technology has moved forward.

With the Internet, accessing and copying written works that may be protected is easy. Today, authors are increasingly dismayed to find copies of their works appearing on the Internet without their permission. The same problem occurs with graphic and artistic images on the Internet, such as photographs and artwork. Once placed on the Web, they can be copied and reused numerous times. Unauthorized copying of items appearing on websites is difficult and sometimes even technically impossible to prevent.

Page 1

Fair Use

Situations exist in which using work written by others is permissible. Using another person's material without permission is allowed as long as the use is acknowledged, is used for noncommercial purposes, and involves only the use of limited excerpts of protected material, such as no more than 300 words of prose and one line of poetry. Such a right is called fair use and is dealt with under the U.S. Copyright Act, Section 107. Here, in part, is what the Fair Use law states:

> [A] copyrighted work, including such use by reproduction in copies of phonorecords or by any other means specified by that section, for purposes such as criticism, comment, news reporting, teaching (including multiple copies for classroom use), scholarship, or research, is not an infringement of copyright.

Even under the Fair Use provision, describing the source of the material is important. Plagiarism may be punished by law, and in many educational institutions it can result in suspension or even expulsion.

Intellectual Property Protection

The problem faced by intellectual property owners in the digital age is twofold. First, new technology has presented new difficulties in interpreting previous understandings dealing with the protection of intellectual property, such as difficulties applying the Fair Use provision to Internet material. Second, the new technical capabilities brought about by digital technologies have greatly increased the ease with which intellectual property can be appropriated and used without authorization, making policing and protecting intellectual property very difficult. Intellectual property owners have formed new organizations to ensure the protection of their property.

REFERENCES

Fuller, Floyd and Brian Larson. (2010) *Computers: Understanding Technology* (pp. 659-661). St. Paul, MN: Paradigm Publishing.

Myerson, Jean A. (2008) *Intellectual Properties* (pp. 123-126). New Orleans, LA: Robicheaux Publishing House.

Patterson, Margaret and Montgomery Littleton. (2011) *Issues of Plagiarism*. Chicago, IL: Lansing and Edelman Publishers.

Page 2

Talbot, Lenora J. and Marcella S. Angleton. (2010) *Internet Considerations*. Portland, OR: Pacific Blue Publishing Group.

Prepared by Clarissa Markham
Edited by Joshua Streeter

Page 3

Solving Problems

In groups or individually, brainstorm possible solutions to the issues presented.

- Computers currently offer both *visual* and *audio* communications. Under development are devices and technologies that will allow users to smell various types of products while looking at them in the computer screen. What are some new applications of this technology for the food industry? Can you think of other industries that could use this capability?
- Picture yourself working in the Information Technology department of a mid-sized company. Your responsibilities include evaluating employees' computer system needs and recommending equipment purchases. Recently, the company president hired a new employee and you must evaluate her computer system needs. Considering that you have a budget of $5,500 for equipping the new employee with the computer system (or systems), research possible configurations and prepare a report outlining your recommendations, including costs. Assume that for her office she needs a complete system, including a system unit, monitor, printer, speakers, keyboard, and mouse.

Project 4 Format Computer Issues Document

WL1-C2-P4-CompIssues.docx

Project  Apply Character Formatting   4 Parts

You will open a document containing a glossary of terms, add additional text, and then format the document by applying character formatting.

Changing Fonts

The Font group shown in Figure 2.1 contains a number of buttons you can use to apply character formatting to text in a document. The top row contains buttons for changing the font and font size as well as buttons for increasing and decreasing the size of the font changing the text case, and clearing formatting. You can remove character formatting (as well as paragraph formatting) applied to text by clicking the Clear Formatting button in the Font group. Remove only character formatting from selected text by pressing the keyboard shortcut, Ctrl + spacebar. The bottom row contains buttons for applying typestyles such as bold, italic, and underline and for applying text effects, highlighting, and color.

A Word document is based on a template that formats text in 11-point Calibri. You may want to change this default to some other font for such reasons as changing the mood of the document, enhancing the visual appeal, and increasing the readability of the text. A font consists of three elements—typeface, type size, and typestyle.

A typeface is a set of characters with a common design and shape and can be decorative or plain and either monospaced or proportional. Word refers to typeface as ***font***. A monospaced typeface allots the same amount of horizontal space for each

Change the default font by selecting the desired font at the Font dialog box and then clicking the Set As Default button.

Use a serif typeface for text-intensive documents.

Figure 2.1 Font Group Buttons

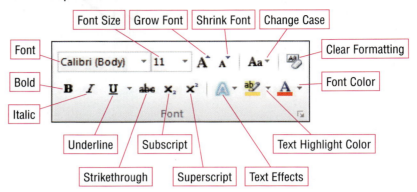

character while a proportional typeface allots a varying amount of space for each character. Proportional typefaces are divided into two main categories: *serif* and *sans serif*. A serif is a small line at the end of a character stroke. Consider using a serif typeface for text-intensive documents because the serifs help move the reader's eyes across the page. Use a sans serif typeface for headings, headlines, and advertisements.

Microsoft added six new fonts in Office 2007 that are available in Office 2010 including the default, Calibri, as well as Cambria, Candara, Consolas, Constantia, and Corbel. Calibri, Candara, and Corbel are sans serif typefaces; Cambria and Constantia are serif typefaces; and Consolas is monospaced. These six typefaces as well as some other popular typefaces are shown in Table 2.1.

Type size is generally set in proportional size. The size of proportional type is measured vertically in units called *points*. A point is approximately $1/72$ of an inch — the higher the point size, the larger the characters. Within a typeface, characters may have a varying style. Type styles are divided into four main categories: regular, bold, italic, and bold italic.

Use the Font button in the Font group to change the font and the Font Size button to change the size. When you select text and then click the Font button arrow, a drop-down gallery displays of font options. Hover your mouse pointer over a font option and the selected text in the document displays with the font applied. You can continue hovering your mouse pointer over different font options to see how the selected text displays in the specified font. The Font button drop-down gallery is an example of the *live preview* feature, which allows you to see how the font formatting affects your text without having to return to the document. The live preview feature is also available when you click the Font Size button arrow.

Table 2.1 Serif and Sans Serif Typefaces

Serif Typefaces	Sans Serif Typefaces	Monospaced Typefaces
Cambria	Calibri	Consolas
Constantia	Candara	Courier New
Times New Roman	Corbel	Lucida Console
Bookman Old Style	Arial	MS Gothic

Project 1a Changing the Font Part 1 of 4

1. Open **CompTerms.docx**.
2. Save the document with Save As and name it **WL1-C2-P1-CompTerms**.
3. Change the typeface to Cambria by completing the following steps:
   a. Select the entire document by pressing Ctrl + A. (You can also select all text in the document by clicking the Select button in the Editing group and then clicking *Select All* at the drop-down list.)
   b. Click the Font button arrow, scroll down the Font drop-down gallery until *Cambria* displays, and then hover the mouse pointer over *Cambria*. This displays a live preview of the text set in Cambria.
   c. Click the mouse button on *Cambria*.

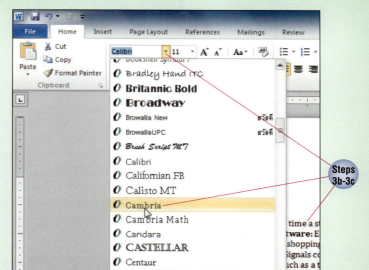

4. Change the type size to 14 by completing the following steps:
   a. With the text in the document still selected, click the Font Size button arrow.
   b. At the drop-down gallery that displays, hover the mouse pointer on *14* and look at the live preview of the text with 14 points applied.
   c. Click the left mouse button on *14*.
5. At the document screen, deselect the text by clicking anywhere in the document.
6. Change the type size and typeface by completing the following steps:
   a. Press Ctrl + A to select the entire document.
   b. Click three times on the Shrink Font button in the Font group. (This decreases the size to 10 points.)
   c. Click twice on the Grow Font button. (This increases the size of the font to 12 points.)

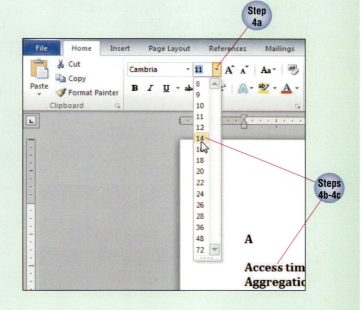

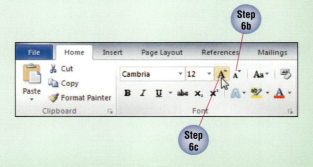

Chapter 2 ■ Formatting Characters and Paragraphs

    d. Click the Font button arrow, scroll down the drop-down gallery, and then click *Constantia*. (The most recently used fonts display at the beginning of the document, followed by a listing of all fonts.)
7. Save **WL1-C2-P1-CompTerms.docx**.

Choosing a Typestyle

Apply a particular typestyle to text with the Bold, Italic, or Underline buttons in the bottom row in the Font group. You can apply more than one style to text. For example, you can bold and italicize the same text or apply all three styles to the same text. Click the Underline button arrow and a drop-down gallery displays with underlining options such as a double line, dashed line, and thicker underline. Click the *Underline Color* option at the Underline button drop-down gallery and a side menu displays with color options.

Project 1b Applying Character Formatting to Text as You Type   Part 2 of 4

1. With **WL1-C2-P1-CompTerms.docx** open, press Ctrl + Home to move the insertion point to the beginning of the document.
2. Type a heading for the document by completing the following steps:
    a. Click the Bold button in the Font group. (This turns on bold.)
    b. Click the Underline button in the Font group. (This turns on underline.)
    c. Type **Glossary of Terms**.
3. Press Ctrl + End to move the insertion point to the end of the document.

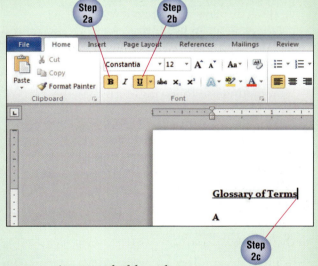

4. Type the text shown in Figure 2.2 with the following specifications:
    a. While typing the document, make the appropriate text bold as shown in the figure by completing the following steps:
        1) Click the Bold button in the Font group. (This turns on bold.)
        2) Type the text.
        3) Click the Bold button in the Font group. (This turns off bold.)
    b. While typing the document, italicize the appropriate text as shown in the figure by completing the following steps:
        1) Click the Italic button in the Font group.
        2) Type the text.
        3) Click the Italic button in the Font group.
5. After typing the text, press the Enter key twice and then press Ctrl + Home to move the insertion point to the beginning of the document.

6. Change the underlining below the title by completing the following steps:
   a. Select the title Glossary of Terms.
   b. Click the Underline button arrow and then click the third underline option from the top of the drop-down gallery.
   c. Click the Underline button arrow, point to the *Underline Color* option, and then click the Red color (second color option from the left) in the *Standard Colors* section.

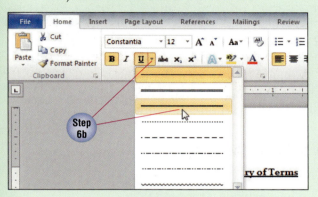
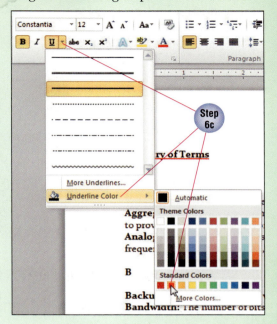

7. With the title still selected, change the font size to 14 points.
8. Save **WL1-C2-P1-CompTerms.docx**.

Figure 2.2 Project 1b

C

Chip: A thin wafer of *silicon* containing electronic circuitry that performs various functions, such as mathematical calculations, storage, or controlling computer devices.

Cluster: A group of two or more *sectors* on a disk, which is the smallest unit of storage space used to store data.

Coding: A term used by programmers to refer to the act of writing source code.

Crackers: A term coined by computer hackers for those who intentionally enter (or hack) computer systems to damage them.

Choosing a Font Effect

Apply font effects with some of the buttons in the top and bottom rows in the Font group or clear all formatting from selected text with the Clear Formatting button. Change the case of text with the Change Case button drop-down list. Click the Change Case button in the top row in the Font group and a drop-down list displays with the options *Sentence case*, *lowercase*, *UPPERCASE*, *Capitalize Each Word*, and *tOGGLE cASE*. You can also change the case of selected text with the keyboard shortcut, Shift + F3. Each time you press Shift + F3, selected text cycles through the case options.

Change Case

Clear Formatting

Strikethrough

Subscript

Superscript

Text Effects

Text Highlight Color

Font Color

The bottom row in the Font group contains buttons for applying font effects. Use the Strikethrough button to draw a line through selected text. This has a practical application in some legal documents in which deleted text must be retained in the document. Use the Subscript button to create text that is lowered slightly below the line such as the chemical formula H_2O. Use the Superscript button to create text that is raised slightly above the text line such as the mathematical equation four to the third power (written as 4^3). Click the Text Effects button in the bottom row and a drop-down gallery displays with effect options. Use the Text Highlight Color button to highlight specific text in a document and use the Font Color button to change the color of text.

Using Keyboard Shortcuts

Several of the buttons in the Font group have keyboard shortcuts. For example, you can press Ctrl + B to turn on bold or press Ctrl + I to turn on italics. Position the mouse pointer on a button and an enhanced ScreenTip displays with the name of the button; the keyboard shortcut, if any; a description of the action performed by the button; and sometimes access to the Word Help window. Table 2.2 identifies the keyboard shortcuts available for buttons in the Font group.

Formatting with the Mini Toolbar

When you select text, the Mini toolbar displays in a dimmed fashion above the selected text. Hover the mouse pointer over the Mini toolbar and it becomes active. Click a button on the Mini toolbar to apply formatting to selected text.

HINT Press Ctrl +] to increase font size by one point and press Ctrl + [to decrease font size by one point.

Table 2.2 Font Button Keyboard Shortcuts

Font Group Button	Keyboard Shortcut
Font	Ctrl + Shift + F
Font Size	Ctrl + Shift + P
Grow Font	Ctrl + Shift + >
Shrink Font	Ctrl + Shift + <
Bold	Ctrl + B
Italic	Ctrl + I
Underline	Ctrl + U
Subscript	Ctrl + =
Superscript	Ctrl + Shift + +
Change Case	Shift + F3

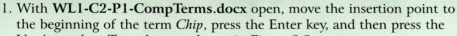

Project 1c Applying Font Effects   Part 3 of 4

1. With **WL1-C2-P1-CompTerms.docx** open, move the insertion point to the beginning of the term *Chip*, press the Enter key, and then press the Up Arrow key. Type the text shown in Figure 2.3. Create the superscript numbers by clicking the Superscript button, typing the number, and then clicking the Superscript button.

2. Change the case of text and remove underlining from the title by completing the following steps:
   a. Select the title *Glossary of Terms*.
   b. Click the Change Case button in the Font group and then click UPPERCASE at the drop-down list.
   c. Click the Underline button to remove underlining.
   d. Click the Text Effects button in the font group and then click the *Gradient Fill - Blue, Accent 1* option (fourth option from the left in the third row) at the drop-down gallery.

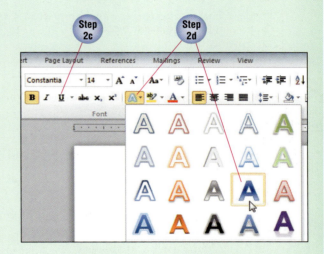

3. Strike through text by completing the following steps:
   a. Select the words and parentheses *(or hack)* in the *Crackers* definition.
   b. Click the Strikethrough button in the Font group.

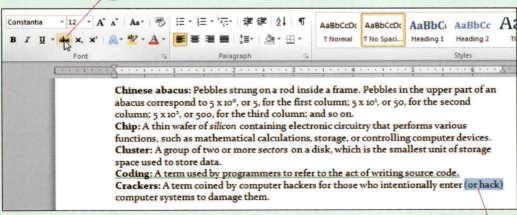

4. Change the font color by completing the following steps:
   a. Press Ctrl + A to select the entire document.

Chapter 2 ■ Formatting Characters and Paragraphs   43

b. Click the Font Color button arrow.
c. Click the Dark Red color (first color option in the *Standard Colors* section) at the drop-down gallery.
d. Click in the document to deselect text.
5. Highlight text in the document by completing the following steps:
   a. Click the Text Highlight Color button arrow in the Font group and then click the yellow color at the drop-down palette. (This causes the mouse pointer to display as an I-beam pointer with a highlighter pen attached.)
   b. Select the term *Beta-testing* and the definition that follows.
   c. Click the Text Highlight Color button arrow and then click the turquoise color (third color from the left in the top row).
   d. Select the term *Cluster* and the definition that follows.
   e. Click the Text Highlight Color button arrow and then click the yellow color at the drop-down gallery.
   f. Click the Text Highlight Color button to turn off highlighting.
6. Apply italic formatting using the Mini toolbar by completing the following steps:
   a. Select the text *one-stop shopping* located in the definition for the term *Aggregation software*. (When you select the text, the Mini toolbar displays.)
   b. Click the Italic button on the Mini toolbar.
   c. Select the word *bits* located in the definition for the term *Bandwidth* and then click the Italic button on the Mini toolbar.
7. Save **WL1-C2-P1-CompTerms.docx**.

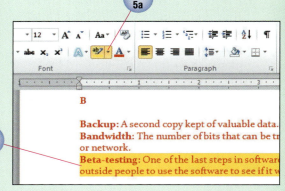
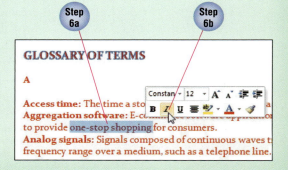

Figure 2.3 Project 1c

Chinese abacus: Pebbles strung on a rod inside a frame. Pebbles in the upper part of an abacus correspond to 5×10^0, or 5, for the first column; 5×10^1, or 50, for the second column; 5×10^2, or 500, for the third column; and so on.

Figure 2.4 Font Dialog Box

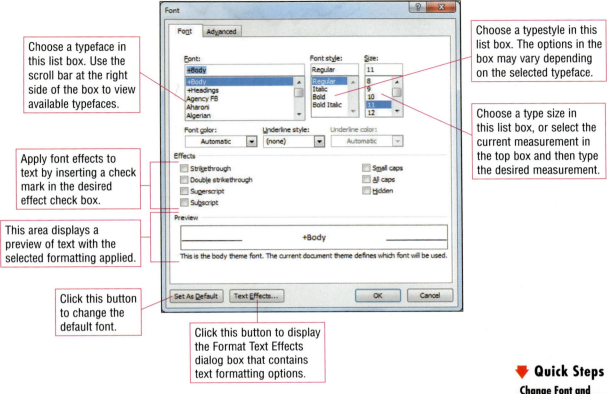

Changing Fonts at the Font Dialog Box

In addition to buttons in the Font group, you can use options at the Font dialog box shown in Figure 2.4 to change the typeface, type size, and typestyle of text as well as apply font effects. Display the Font dialog box by clicking the Font group dialog box launcher. The dialog box launcher is a small square containing a diagonal-pointing arrow that displays in the lower right corner of the Font group.

▼ **Quick Steps**

Change Font and Apply Effects
1. Select text if necessary.
2. Click Font group dialog box launcher.
3. Choose desired options at dialog box.
4. Click OK.

Project 1d Changing the Font at the Font Dialog Box   Part 4 of 4

1. With **WL1-C2-P1-CompTerms.docx** open, press Ctrl + End to move the insertion point to the end of the document. (Make sure the insertion point is positioned a double space below the last line of text.)
2. Type **Created by Susan Ashby** and then press the Enter key.
3. Type **Wednesday, February 22, 2012**.
4. Change the font to 13-point Candara and the color to dark blue by completing the following steps:
   a. Press Ctrl + A to select the entire document.
   b. Click the Font group dialog box launcher.

Chapter 2 ■ Formatting Characters and Paragraphs   45

c. At the Font dialog box, click the up-pointing arrow at the right side of the *Font* list box to scroll up the list box and then click *Candara*.
d. Click in the *Size* text box and then type **13**.
e. Click the down-pointing arrow at the right side of the *Font color* list box and then click a dark blue color of your choosing at the drop-down color palette.
f. Click OK to close the dialog box.
5. Double underline text by completing the following steps:
   a. Select *Wednesday, February 22, 2012*.
   b. Click the Font group dialog box launcher.
   c. At the Font dialog box, click the down-pointing arrow at the right side of the *Underline style* option box and then click the double-line option at the drop-down list.

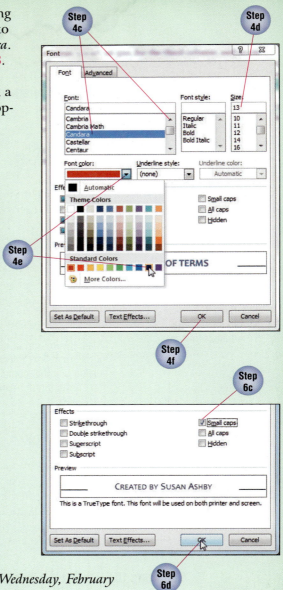

   d. Click OK to close the dialog box.
6. Change text to small caps by completing the following steps:
   a. Select the text *Created by Susan Ashby* and *Wednesday, February 22, 2012*.
   b. Display the Font dialog box.
   c. Click the *Small caps* option in the *Effects* section. (This inserts a check mark in the check box.)
   d. Click OK to close the dialog box.
7. Save, print, and then close **WL1-C2-P1-CompTerms.docx**.

Project 2 Apply Styles and Themes   3 Parts

You will open a document containing information on the life cycle of software, apply styles to text, and then change the Quick Styles set. You will also apply a theme and then change the theme colors and fonts.

Applying Styles from a Quick Styles Set

A Word document contains a number of predesigned formats grouped into style sets called Quick Styles. Several thumbnails of the styles in the default Quick Styles set display in the Styles group in the Home tab. Display additional styles by clicking the More button that displays at the right side of the style thumbnails. This displays a drop-down gallery of style choices. To apply a style, position the insertion point in the text or paragraph of text to which you want the style applied, click the More button at the right side of the style thumbnails in the Styles group, and then click the desired style at the drop-down gallery.

A Word document contains some default formatting including 10 points of spacing after paragraphs and a line spacing of 1.15. (You will learn more about these formatting options later in this chapter.) You can remove this default formatting as well as any character formatting applied to text in your document by applying the No Spacing style to your text. This style is located in the Styles group.

Changing the Quick Styles Set

Word contains a number of Quick Styles sets containing styles you can use to apply formatting to a document. To change to a different Quick Styles set, click the Change Styles button in the Styles group in the Home tab and then point to Style Set. This displays a side menu with Quick Styles sets. Click the desired set and the style formatting changes for the styles in the set.

▼ **Quick Steps**

Apply a Style
1. Position insertion point in desired text or paragraph of text.
2. Click More button in Styles group.
3. Click desired style.

Change Quick Styles Set
1. Click Change Styles button.
2. Point to *Style Set*.
3. Click desired set.

More

Change Styles

Project 2a — Applying Quick Styles — Part 1 of 3

1. Open **SoftwareCycle.docx**.
2. Save the document with Save As and name it **WL1-C2-P2-SoftwareCycle**.
3. Remove the 10 points of spacing after paragraphs and change the line spacing to 1 by completing the following steps:
    a. Press Ctrl + A to select the entire document.
    b. Click the No Spacing style in the Styles group in the Home tab.

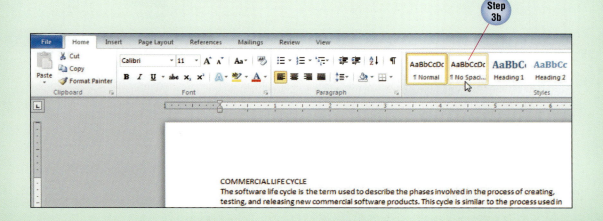

4. Position the insertion point on any character in the title COMMERCIAL LIFE CYCLE and then click the Heading 1 style that displays in the Styles group.
5. Position the insertion point on any character in the heading *Proposal and Planning* and then click the Heading 2 style that displays in the Styles group.
6. Position the insertion point on any character in the heading *Design* and then click the Heading 2 style in the Styles group.
7. Apply the Heading 2 style to the remaining headings (*Implementation*, *Testing*, and *Public Release and Support*).
8. Click the Change Styles button in the Styles group, point to *Style Set*, and then click *Modern*. (Notice how the Heading 1 and Heading 2 formatting changes.)

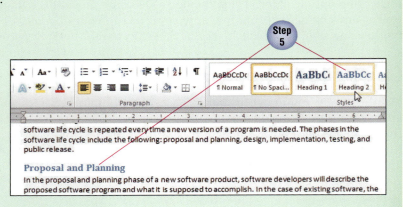

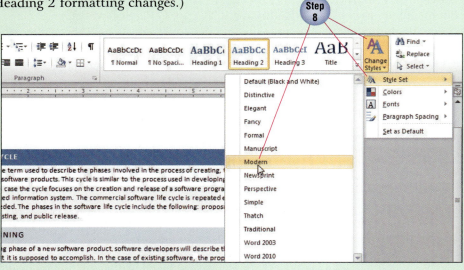

9. Save and then print **WL1-C2-P2-SoftwareCycle.docx**.

Applying a Theme

Word provides a number of themes you can use to format text in your document. A theme is a set of formatting choices that include a color theme (a set of colors), a font theme (a set of heading and body text fonts), and an effects theme (a set of lines and fill effects). To apply a theme, click the Page Layout tab and then click the Themes button in the Themes group. At the drop-down gallery that displays, click the desired theme. You can hover the mouse pointer over a theme and the live preview feature will display your document with the theme formatting applied. With the live preview feature you can see how the theme formatting affects your document before you make your final choice. Applying a theme is an easy way to give your document a professional look.

▼ **Quick Steps**
Apply a Theme
1. Click Page Layout tab.
2. Click Themes button.
3. Click desired theme.

Themes

Project 2b — Applying a Theme to Text in a Document — Part 2 of 3

1. With **WL1-C2-P2-SoftwareCycle.docx** open, click the Page Layout tab and then click the Themes button in the Themes group.
2. At the drop-down gallery, hover your mouse pointer over several different themes and notice how the text formatting changes in your document.
3. Scroll down the drop-down gallery and then click the *Module* theme.
4. Save and then print **WL1-C2-P2-SoftwareCycle.docx**.

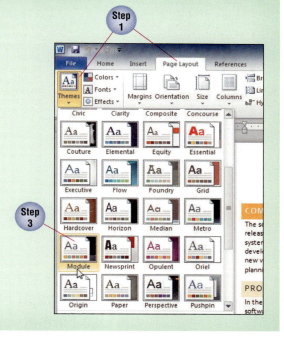

Changing Themes

You can change a theme with the three buttons that display at the right side of the Themes button. A theme contains specific color formatting, which you can change with options from the Theme Colors button in the Themes group. Click this button and a drop-down gallery displays with named color schemes. The names of the color schemes correspond to the names of the themes. Each theme applies specific fonts, which you can change with options from the Theme Fonts button in the Themes group. Click this button and a drop-down gallery displays with font choices. Each font group in the drop-down gallery contains two choices. The first choice in the group is the font that is applied to headings and the second choice is the font that is applied to body text in the document. If you are formatting a document containing graphics with lines and fills, you can apply a specific theme effect with options at the Theme Effects drop-down gallery.

▼ **Quick Steps**
Change Theme Color
1. Click Page Layout tab.
2. Click Theme Colors button.
3. Click desired theme color.

Change Theme Fonts
1. Click Page Layout tab.
2. Click Theme Fonts button.
3. Click desired theme fonts.

Theme Colors

Theme Fonts

Theme Effects

Chapter 2 ■ Formatting Characters and Paragraphs

The buttons in the Themes group display a visual representation of the current theme. If you change the theme colors, the small color squares in the Themes button and the Theme Colors button reflect the change. Changing the theme fonts and the *As* on the Themes button as well as the uppercase *A* on the Theme Fonts button reflect the change. If you change the theme effects, the circle in the Theme Effects button reflects the change.

Project 2c   Changing a Theme   Part 3 of 3

1. With **WL1-C2-P2-SoftwareCycle.docx** open, click the Theme Colors button in the Themes group and then click *Foundry* at the drop-down gallery. (Notice how the colors in the title and headings change.)
2. Click the Theme Fonts button and then click the *Apex* option. (Notice how the document text font changes.)
3. Save, print, and then close **WL1-C2-P2-SoftwareCycle.docx**.

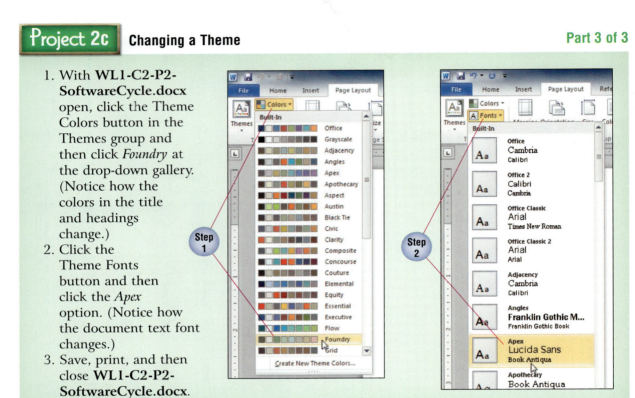

Project 3   Apply Paragraph Formatting and Use Format Painter   6 Parts

You will open a report on intellectual property and fair use issues and then format the report by changing the alignment of text in paragraphs, applying spacing before and after paragraphs of text, and repeating the last formatting action.

Changing Paragraph Alignment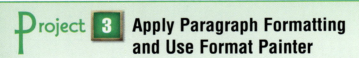

By default, paragraphs in a Word document are aligned at the left margin and ragged at the right margin. Change this default alignment with buttons in the Paragraph group in the Home tab or with keyboard shortcuts as shown in Table 2.3.

You can change the alignment of text in paragraphs before you type the text or you can change the alignment of existing text. If you change the alignment before typing text, the alignment formatting is inserted in the paragraph mark.

Table 2.3 Paragraph Alignment Buttons and Keyboard Shortcuts

To align text	Paragraph Group Button	Keyboard Shortcut
At the left margin		Ctrl + L
Between margins		Ctrl + E
At the right margin		Ctrl + R
At the left and right margins		Ctrl + J

As you type text and press Enter, the paragraph formatting is continued. For example, if you click the Center button in the Paragraph group, type text for the first paragraph, and then press the Enter key, the center alignment formatting is still active and the insertion point displays centered between the left and right margins. To display the paragraph symbols in a document, click the Show/Hide ¶ button in the Paragraph group. With the Show/Hide ¶ button active (displays with an orange background), nonprinting formatting symbols display such as the paragraph symbol ¶ indicating a press of the Enter key or a dot indicating a press of the spacebar.

To return paragraph alignment to the default (left-aligned), click the Align Text Left button in the Paragraph group. You can also return all paragraph formatting to the default with the keyboard shortcut, Ctrl + Q. This keyboard shortcut removes paragraph formatting from selected text. If you want to remove all formatting from selected text including character and paragraph formatting, click the Clear Formatting button in the Font group.

To change the alignment of existing text in a paragraph, position the insertion point anywhere within the paragraph. You do not need to select the entire paragraph. To change the alignment of several adjacent paragraphs in a document, select a portion of the first paragraph through a portion of the last paragraph. You do not need to select all of the text in the paragraphs.

HINT Align text in a document so the message of the document can be followed and the page is attractive.

Project 3a Changing Paragraph Alignment — Part 1 of 6

1. Open **IntelProp.docx**. (Some of the default formatting in this document has been changed.)
2. Save the document with Save As and name it **WL1-C2-P3-IntelProp**.
3. Click the Show/Hide ¶ button in the Paragraph group in the Home tab to turn on the display of nonprinting characters.

Step 3

4. Press Ctrl + A to select the entire document and then change the alignment to Justify by clicking the Justify button in the Paragraph group in the Home tab.
5. Press Ctrl + End to move the insertion point to the end of the document.
6. Press the Enter key once.
7. Press Ctrl + E to move the insertion point to the middle of the page.
8. Type **Prepared by Clarissa Markham**.
9. Press Shift + Enter and then type **Edited by Joshua Streeter**.

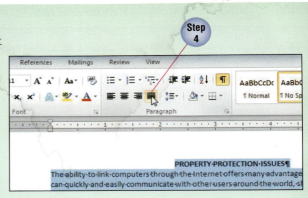

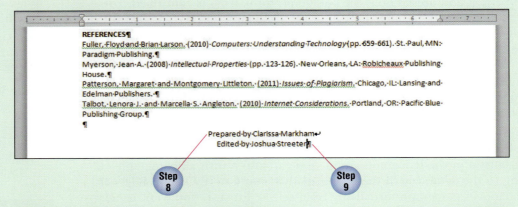

10. Click the Show/Hide ¶ button in the Paragraph group in the Home tab to turn off the display of nonprinting characters.
11. Save **WL1-C2-P3-IntelProp.docx**.

Changing Alignment at the Paragraph Dialog Box

▼ **Quick Steps**

Change Paragraph Alignment
Click desired alignment button in Paragraph group in Home tab.
OR
1. Click Paragraph group dialog box launcher.
2. Click *Alignment* option down-pointing arrow.
3. Click desired alignment.
4. Click OK.

Along with buttons in the Paragraph group and keyboard shortcuts, you can also change paragraph alignment with the Alignment option at the Paragraph dialog box shown in Figure 2.5. Display this dialog box by clicking the Paragraph group dialog box launcher. At the Paragraph dialog box, click the down-pointing arrow at the right side of the *Alignment* option box. At the drop-down list that displays, click the desired alignment option and then click OK to close the dialog box.

Figure 2.5 Paragraph Dialog Box with Alignment Options

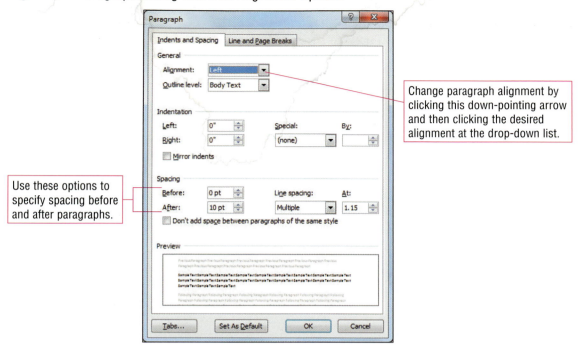

Project 3b — Changing Paragraph Alignment at the Paragraph Dialog Box — Part 2 of 6

1. With **WL1-C2-P3-IntelProp.docx** open, change paragraph alignment by completing the following steps:
   a. Select the entire document.
   b. Click the Paragraph group dialog box launcher.
   c. At the Paragraph dialog box with the Indents and Spacing tab selected, click the down-pointing arrow at the right of the *Alignment* list box and then click *Left*.
   d. Click OK to close the dialog box.
   e. Deselect the text.
2. Change paragraph alignment by completing the following steps:
   a. Press Ctrl + End to move the insertion point to the end of the document.
   b. Position the insertion point on any character in the text *Prepared by Clarissa Markham*.
   c. Click the Paragraph group dialog box launcher.
   d. At the Paragraph dialog box with the Indents and Spacing tab selected, click the down-pointing arrow at the right of the *Alignment* list box and then click *Right*.

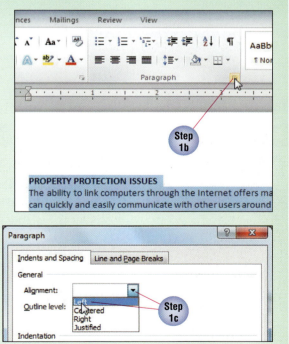

Chapter 2 ■ Formatting Characters and Paragraphs

e. Click OK. (The line of text containing the name *Clarissa Markham* and the line of text containing the name *Joshua Streeter* are both aligned at the right since you used the New Line command, Shift + Enter, to separate the lines of text without creating a new paragraph.)

3. Save and then print **WL1-C2-P3-IntelProp.docx**.

Indenting Text in Paragraphs

▼ **Quick Steps**

Indent Text in Paragraph
Drag indent marker(s) on Ruler.
OR
Press keyboard shortcut keys.
OR
1. Click Paragraph group dialog box launcher.
2. Insert measurement in *Left, Right,* and/or *By* text box.
3. Click OK.

By now you are familiar with the word wrap feature of Word, which ends lines and wraps the insertion point to the next line. To indent text from the left margin, the right margin, or both, use the indent buttons in the Paragraph group, in the Page Layout tab, keyboard shortcuts, options from the Paragraph dialog box, markers on the Ruler, or use the Alignment button on the Ruler. Figure 2.6 identifies indent markers and the Alignment button on the Ruler. Refer to Table 2.4 for methods for indenting text in a document. If the Ruler is not visible, display the Ruler by clicking the View Ruler button located at the top of the vertical scroll bar.

Figure 2.6 Ruler and Indent Markers

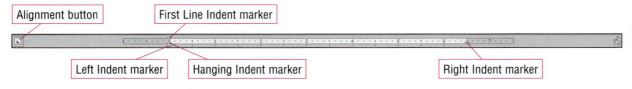

Table 2.4 Methods for Indenting Text

Indent	Methods for Indenting
First line of paragraph	• Press the Tab key.
	• Display Paragraph dialog box, click the down-pointing arrow to the right of the *Special* list box, click *First line*, and then click OK.
	• Drag the First Line Indent marker on the Ruler.
	• Click the Alignment button located at the left side of the Ruler until the First Line Indent button displays and then click on the Ruler at the desired location.

continues

Table 2.4 Methods for Indenting Text, continued

Indent	Methods for Indenting
Text from left margin	• Click the Increase Indent button in the Paragraph group in the Home tab to increase the indent or click the Decrease Indent button to decrease the indent. • Insert a measurement in the *Indent Left* measurement button in the Paragraph group in the Page Layout tab. • Press Ctrl + M to increase the indent or press Ctrl + Shift + M to decrease the indent. • Display the Paragraph dialog box, type the desired indent measurement in the *Left* measurement box, and then click OK. • Drag the left indent marker on the Ruler.
Text from right margin	• Insert a measurement in the *Indent Right* measurement button in the Paragraph group in the Page Layout tab. • Display the Paragraph dialog box, type the desired indent measurement in the *Right* measurement box, and then click OK. • Drag the right indent marker on the Ruler.
All lines of text except the first (called a hanging indent)	• Press Ctrl + T. (Press Ctrl + Shift + T to remove hanging indent.) • Display the Paragraph dialog box, click the down-pointing arrow to the right of the *Special* list box, click *Hanging*, and then click OK. • Click the Alignment button located at the left side of the Ruler until the Hanging Indent button displays and then click on the Ruler at the desired location.
Text from both left and right margins	• Display the Paragraph dialog box, type the desired indent measurement in the *Left* measurement box, type the desired measurement in the *Right* measurement box, and then click OK. • Insert a measurement in the *Indent Right* and *Indent Left* measurement buttons in the Paragraph group in the Page Layout tab. • Drag the left indent marker on the Ruler; then drag the right indent marker on the Ruler.

Project 3c Indenting Paragraphs   Part 3 of 6

1. With **WL1-C2-P3-IntelProp.docx** open, indent the first line of text in paragraphs by completing the following steps:
    a. Select the first two paragraphs of text in the document (the text after the title *PROPERTY PROTECTION ISSUES* and before the heading *Intellectual Property*.
    b. Position the mouse pointer on the First Line Indent marker on the Ruler, hold down the left mouse button, drag the marker to the 0.5-inch mark, and then release the mouse button.

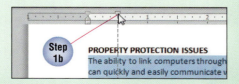

Step 1b

c. Select the paragraphs of text in the *Intellectual Property* section and then drag the First Line Indent marker on the Ruler to the 0.5-inch mark.
d. Select the paragraphs of text in the *Fair Use* section, click the Alignment button located at the left side of the Ruler until the First Line Indent button displays, and then click on the Ruler at the 0.5-inch mark.

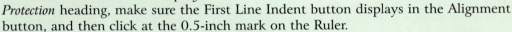

e. Position the insertion point on any character in the paragraph of text below the *Intellectual Property Protection* heading, make sure the First Line Indent button displays in the Alignment button, and then click at the 0.5-inch mark on the Ruler.

2. Since the text in the second paragraph in the *Fair Use* section is a quote, you need to indent the text from the left and right margins by completing the following steps:
    a. Position the insertion point anywhere within the second paragraph in the *Fair Use* section (the paragraph that begins *[A] copyrighted work, including such . . .*).
    b. Click the Paragraph group dialog box launcher.
    c. At the Paragraph dialog box, with the Indents and Spacing tab selected, select the current measurement in the *Left* measurement box and then type **0.5**.
    d. Select the current measurement in the *Right* measurement box and then type **0.5**.
    e. Click the down-pointing arrow at the right side of the *Special* list box and then click *(none)* at the drop-down list.
    f. Click OK or press Enter.

3. Create a hanging indent for the first paragraph in the *REFERENCES* section by positioning the insertion point anywhere in the first paragraph below *REFERENCES* and then pressing Ctrl + T.

4. Create a hanging indent for the second paragraph in the *REFERENCES* section by completing the following steps:
    a. Position the insertion point anywhere in the second paragraph in the *REFERENCES* section.
    b. Make sure the Ruler is displayed. (If it is not, click the View Ruler button located at the top of the vertical scroll bar.)
    c. Click the Alignment button located at the left side of the Ruler until the Hanging Indent button displays.
    d. Click on the 0.5-inch mark on the Ruler.

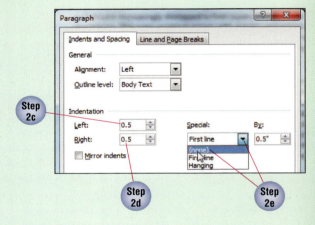

5. Create a hanging indent for the third and fourth paragraphs by completing the following steps:
   a. Select a portion of the third and fourth paragraphs.
   b. Click the Paragraph group dialog box launcher.
   c. At the Paragraph dialog box with the Indents and Spacing tab selected, click the down-pointing arrow at the right side of the *Special* list box and then click *Hanging* at the drop-down list.
   d. Click OK or press Enter.
6. Save **WL1-C2-P3-IntelProp.docx**.

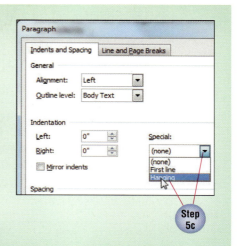

Step 5c

Spacing Before and After Paragraphs

By default, Word applies 10 points of additional spacing after a paragraph. You can remove this spacing, increase or decrease the spacing, and insert spacing above the paragraph. To change spacing before or after a paragraph, use the *Spacing Before* and *Spacing After* measurement boxes located in the Paragraph group in the Page Layout tab, or the *Before* and/or *After* options at the Paragraph dialog box with the Indents and Spacing tab selected. You can also add spacing before and after paragraphs at the Line and Paragraph Spacing button drop-down list.

Spacing before or after a paragraph is part of the paragraph and will be moved, copied, or deleted with the paragraph. If a paragraph, such as a heading, contains spacing before it, and the paragraph falls at the top of a page, Word ignores the spacing.

Spacing before or after paragraphs is added in points and a vertical inch contains approximately 72 points. To add spacing before or after a paragraph you would click the Page Layout tab, select the current measurement in the *Spacing Before* or the *Spacing After* measurement box, and then type the desired number of points. You can also click the up- or down-pointing arrows at the right side of the *Spacing Before* and *Spacing After* measurement boxes to increase or decrease the amount of spacing.

HINT Line spacing determines the amount of vertical space between lines while paragraph spacing determines the amount of space above or below paragraphs of text.

Repeating the Last Action

If you apply formatting to text and then want to apply the same formatting to other text in the document, consider using the Repeat command. To use this command, apply the desired formatting, move the insertion point to the next location where you want the formatting applied, and then press the F4 function key or press Ctrl + Y.

 Quick Steps
Repeat Last Action
Press F4.
OR
Press Ctrl + Y.

Project 3d Spacing Before and After Paragraphs and Repeating Last Action Part 4 of 6

1. With **WL1-C2-P3-IntelProp.docx** open, add 6 points of spacing before and after each paragraph in the document by completing the following steps:
    a. Select the entire document.
    b. Click the Page Layout tab.
    c. Click once on the up-pointing arrow at the right side of the *Spacing Before* measurement box in the Paragraph group (this inserts *6 pt* in the box).
    d. Click once on the up-pointing arrow at the right side of the *Spacing After* measurement box in the Paragraph group (this inserts *6 pt* in the text box).

2. Add an additional 6 points of spacing above the headings by completing the following steps:
    a. Position the insertion point on any character in the heading *Intellectual Property* and then click once on the up-pointing arrow at the right side of the *Spacing Before* measurement box (this changes the measurement to *12 pt*).

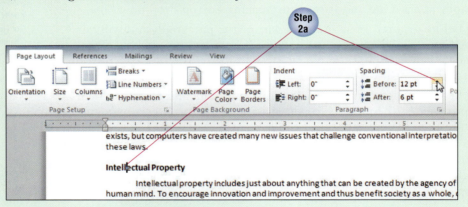

   b. Position the insertion point on any character in the heading *Fair Use* and then press F4. (F4 is the Repeat command.)
   c. Position the insertion point on any character in the heading *Intellectual Property Protection* and then press F4.
   d. Position the insertion point on any character in the heading *REFERENCES* and then press Ctrl + Y. (Ctrl + Y is also the Repeat command.)
3. Save **WL1-C2-P3-IntelProp.docx**.

Formatting with Format Painter

The Clipboard group in the Home tab contains a button for copying formatting and displays in the Clipboard group as a paintbrush. To use the Format Painter button, position the insertion point on a character containing the desired formatting, click the Format Painter button, and then select text to which you want the formatting applied. When you click the Format Painter button, the mouse I-beam pointer displays with a paintbrush attached. If you want to apply formatting a single time, click the Format Painter button once. If you want to apply the formatting in more than one location in the document, double-click the Format Painter button and then select text to which you want formatting applied. When you are finished, click the Format Painter button to turn it off. You can also turn off Format Painter by pressing the Esc key.

▼ Quick Steps

Format with Format Painter
1. Format text.
2. Double-click Format Painter button.
3. Select text.
4. Click Format Painter button.

Format Painter

Project 3e — Formatting Headings with the Format Painter — Part 5 of 6

1. With **WL1-C2-P3-IntelProp.docx** open, click the Home tab.
2. Select the entire document and then change the font to 12-point Cambria.
3. Select the title *PROPERTY PROTECTION ISSUES*, click the Center button in the Paragraph group, and then change the font to 16-point Candara bold.
4. Apply 16-point Candara bold formatting to the *REFERENCES* heading by completing the following steps:
   a. Click on any character in the title *PROPERTY PROTECTION ISSUES*.
   b. Click once on the Format Painter button in the Clipboard group.
   c. Press Ctrl + End to move the insertion point to the end of the document and then click on any character in the heading *REFERENCES*. (This applies the 16-point Candara bold formatting and centers the text.)

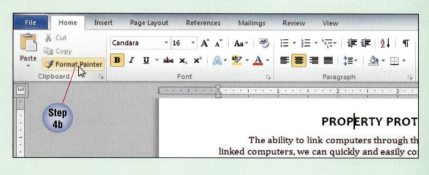

5. With the insertion point positioned on any character in the heading *REFERENCES*, add an additional 6 points of spacing before the heading (for a total of 12 points before the heading).
6. Select the heading *Intellectual Property* and then change the font to 14-point Candara bold.
7. Use the Format Painter button and apply 14-point Candara bold formatting to the other headings by completing the following steps:
   a. Position the insertion point on any character in the heading *Intellectual Property*.
   b. Double-click the Format Painter button in the Clipboard group.
   c. Using the mouse, select the heading *Fair Use*.
   d. Using the mouse, select the heading *Intellectual Property Protection*.
   e. Click once on the Format Painter button in the Clipboard group. (This turns off the feature.)
   f. Deselect the heading.
8. Save **WL1-C2-P3-IntelProp.docx**.

Changing Line Spacing

The default line spacing for a document is 1.15. (The line spacing for the **IntelProp.docx** document, which you opened at the beginning of Project 3, had been changed to single.) In certain situations, Word automatically adjusts the line spacing. For example, if you insert a large character or object such as a graphic, Word increases the line spacing of that specific line. But you also may sometimes encounter a writing situation in which you decide to change the line spacing for a section or for the entire document.

Change line spacing using the Line and Paragraph Spacing button in the Paragraph group in the Home tab, with keyboard shortcuts, or with options from the Paragraph dialog box. Table 2.5 displays the keyboard shortcuts to change line spacing.

You can also change line spacing at the Paragraph dialog box with the *Line spacing* option or the *At* option. If you click the down-pointing arrow at the right side of the *Line spacing* option, a drop-down list displays with a variety of spacing options. For example, to change the line spacing to double you would click *Double* at the drop-down list. You can type a specific line spacing measurement in the *At* text box. For example, to change the line spacing to 1.75, type 1.75 in the *At* text box.

Quick Steps

Change Line Spacing
1. Click Line and Paragraph Spacing button in Paragraph group.
2. Click desired option at drop-down list.

OR

Press shortcut command keys.

OR

1. Click Paragraph group dialog box launcher.
2. Click *Line Spacing* option down-pointing arrow.
3. Click desired line spacing option.
4. Click OK.

OR

1. Click Paragraph group dialog box launcher.
2. Type line measurement in *At* text box.
3. Click OK.

Line and Paragraph Spacing

Table 2.5 Line Spacing Keyboard Shortcuts

Press	To change line spacing to
Ctrl + 1	single spacing
Ctrl + 2	double spacing
Ctrl + 5	1.5 line spacing

Project 3f Changing Line Spacing Part 6 of 6

1. With **WL1-C2-P3-IntelProp.docx** open, change the line spacing for all paragraphs to double spacing by completing the following steps:
   a. Select the entire document.
   b. Click the Line and Paragraph Spacing button located in the Paragraph group in the Home tab.
   c. Click *2.0* at the drop-down list.
2. With the entire document still selected, press Ctrl + 5. (This changes the line spacing to 1.5 line spacing.)

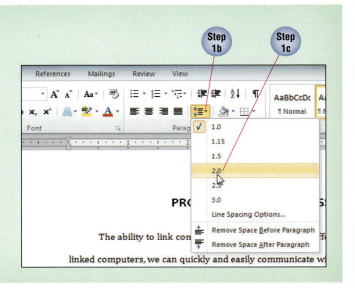

3. Change the line spacing to 1.3 using the Paragraph dialog box by completing the following steps:
    a. With the entire document still selected, click the Paragraph group dialog box launcher.
    b. At the Paragraph dialog box, make sure the Indents and Spacing tab is selected, click inside the *At* text box, and then type **1.3**. (This text box is located to the right of the *Line spacing* list box.)
    c. Click OK or press Enter.
    d. Deselect the text.
4. Save, print, and then close **WL1-C2-P3-IntelProp.docx**.

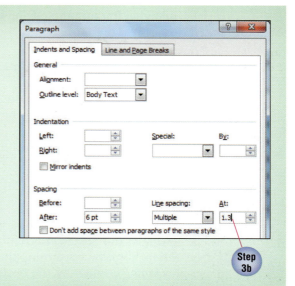

Step 3b

 Project 4 **Format Computer Issues Document** **3 Parts**

You will open a document containing two computer-related problems to solve, apply predesigned paragraph spacing, reveal the formatting, compare the formatting, and make formatting changes.

Changing Paragraph Spacing with the Change Styles Button

The Change Styles button in the Styles group in the Home tab contains a Paragraph Spacing option you can use to apply predesigned paragraph spacing to text in a document. Click the Change Styles button and then point to *Paragraph Spacing* and a side menu displays. Hover your mouse over an option at the side menu and, after a moment, a ScreenTip displays with information about the formatting applied by the option. For example, if you hover the mouse over the *Compact* option at the side menu, a ScreenTip displays telling you that the Compact option will change the spacing before paragraphs to zero points, the spacing after paragraphs to four points, and the line spacing to one. Use options at the *Paragraph Spacing* side menu to quickly apply paragraph spacing to text in your document.

Project 4a — Applying Paragraph Spacing with the Change Styles Button — Part 1 of 3

1. Open **CompIssues.docx**.
2. Save the document with Save As and name it **WL1-C2-P4-CompIssues**.
3. Change the paragraph spacing using the Change Styles button by completing the following steps:
    a. Click the Change Styles button in the Styles group in the Home tab.
    b. Point to *Paragraph Spacing* at the drop-down list.
    c. Hover the mouse over each of the paragraph spacing options beginning with *Compact* and read the ScreenTip that displays for each option explaining the paragraph spacing applied by the option.
    d. Click the *Double* option at the side menu.
4. Scroll through the document and notice the paragraph spacing.
5. Change the paragraph spacing by clicking the Change Styles button, pointing to *Paragraph Spacing*, and then clicking *Relaxed* at the side menu.
6. Save **WL1-C2-P4-CompIssues.docx**.

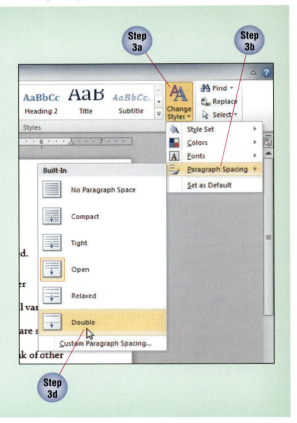

Revealing Formatting

Display formatting applied to specific text in a document at the Reveal Formatting task pane as shown in Figure 2.7. The Reveal Formatting task pane displays font, paragraph, and section formatting applied to text where the insertion point is positioned or to selected text. Display the Reveal Formatting task pane with the keyboard shortcut Shift + F1. Generally, a minus symbol precedes *Font* and *Paragraph* and a plus symbol precedes *Section* in the *Formatting of selected text* section of the Reveal Formatting task pane. Click the minus symbol to hide any items below a heading and click the plus symbol to reveal items. Some of the items below headings in the *Formatting of selected text* section are hyperlinks. Click a hyperlink and a dialog box displays with the specific option.

Project 4b — Revealing Formatting — Part 2 of 3

1. With **WL1-C2-P4-CompIssues.docx** open, press Shift + F1 to display the Reveal Formatting task pane.
2. Click anywhere in the heading *Solving Problems* and then notice the formatting information that displays in the Reveal Formatting task pane.
3. Click in the bulleted paragraph and notice the formatting information that displays in the Reveal Formatting task pane.

Figure 2.7 Reveal Formatting Task Pane

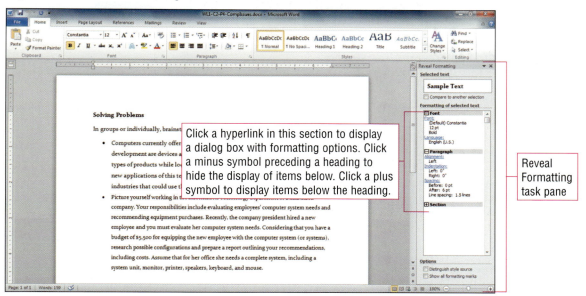

Comparing Formatting

Along with displaying formatting applied to text, you can use the Reveal Formatting task pane to compare formatting of two text selections to determine what formatting is different. To compare formatting, select the first instance of formatting to be compared, click the *Compare to another selection* check box, and then select the second instance of formatting to compare. Any differences between the two selections display in the *Formatting differences* list box.

▼ Quick Steps

Compare Formatting
1. Press Shift + F1 to display Reveal Formatting task pane.
2. Click or select text.
3. Click *Compare to another selection* check box.
4. Click or select text.

Project 4c Comparing Formatting   Part 3 of 3

1. With **WL1-C2-P4-CompIssues.docx** open, make sure the Reveal Formatting task pane displays. If it does not, turn it on by pressing Shift + F1.
2. Select the first bulleted paragraph (the paragraph that begins *Computers currently offer both . . .*).
3. Click the *Compare to another selection* check box to insert a check mark.
4. Select the second bulleted paragraph (the paragraph that begins *Picture yourself working in the . . .*).
5. Determine the formatting differences by reading the information in the *Formatting differences* list box. (The list box displays *12 pt -> 11 pt* below the Font: hyperlink, indicating that the difference is point size.)
6. Format the second bulleted paragraph so it is set in 12-point size.
7. Click the *Compare to another selection* check box to remove the check mark.
8. Select the word *visual* that displays in the first sentence in the first bulleted paragraph.

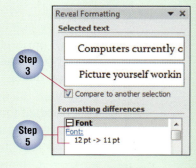

Chapter 2 ■ Formatting Characters and Paragraphs   63

9. Click the *Compare to another selection* check box to insert a check mark.
10. Select the word *audio* that displays in the first sentence of the first bulleted paragraph.
11. Determine the formatting differences by reading the information in the *Formatting differences* list box.
12. Format the word *audio* so it matches the formatting of the word *visual*.
13. Click the *Compare to another selection* check box to remove the check mark.
14. Close the Reveal Formatting task pane by clicking the Close button (contains an X) that displays in the upper right corner of the task pane.
15. Save, print, and then close **WL1-C2-P4-CompIssues.docx**.

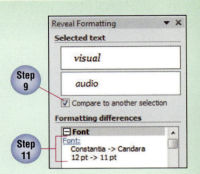

Chapter Summary

- A font consists of three parts: typeface, type size, and typestyle.
- A typeface (font) is a set of characters with a common design and shape. Typefaces are either monospaced, allotting the same amount of horizontal space to each character, or proportional, allotting a varying amount of space for each character. Proportional typefaces are divided into two main categories: serif and sans serif.
- Type size is measured in point size; the higher the point size, the larger the characters.
- A typestyle is a variation of style within a certain typeface. You can apply typestyle formatting with some of the buttons in the Font group.
- With some of the buttons in the Font group, you can apply font effects such as superscript, subscript, and strikethrough.
- The Mini toolbar automatically displays above selected text. Use buttons on this toolbar to apply formatting to selected text.
- With options at the Font dialog box, you can change the font, font size, and font style and apply specific effects. Display this dialog box by clicking the Font group dialog box launcher.
- A Word document contains a number of predesigned formats grouped into style sets called Quick Styles. Change to a different Quick Styles set by clicking the Change Styles button in the Styles group in the Home tab, pointing to Style Set, and then clicking the desired set.
- Apply a theme and change theme colors, fonts, and effects with buttons in the Themes group in the Page Layout tab.
- By default, paragraphs in a Word document are aligned at the left margin and ragged at the right margin. Change this default alignment with buttons in the Paragraph group, at the Paragraph dialog box, or with keyboard shortcuts.

- To turn on or off the display of nonprinting characters such as paragraph marks, click the Show/Hide ¶ button in the Paragraph group.
- Indent text in paragraphs with indent buttons in the Paragraph group in the Home tab, buttons in the Paragraph group in the Page Layout tab, keyboard shortcuts, options from the Paragraph dialog box, markers on the Ruler, or use the Alignment button on the Ruler.
- Increase and/or decrease spacing before and after paragraphs using the *Spacing Before* and *Spacing After* measurement boxes in the Paragraph group in the Page Layout tab, or using the *Before* and/or *After* options at the Paragraph dialog box.
- Use the Format Painter button in the Clipboard group in the Home tab to copy formatting already applied to text to different locations in the document.
- Change line spacing with the Line and Paragraph Spacing button in the Paragraph group in the Home tab, keyboard shortcuts, or options from the Paragraph dialog box.
- Display the Reveal Formatting task pane to display formatting applied to text. Use the *Compare to another selection* option in the task pane to compare formatting of two text selections to determine what formatting is different.

Commands Review

FEATURE	RIBBON TAB, GROUP	BUTTON	KEYBOARD SHORTCUT
Bold text	Home, Font	B	Ctrl + B
Center-align text	Home, Paragraph		Ctrl + E
Change case of text	Home, Font	Aa	Shift + F3
Change Quick Styles set	Home, Styles		
Clear all formatting	Home, Font		
Clear character formatting			Ctrl + spacebar
Clear paragraph formatting			Ctrl + Q
Decrease font size	Home, Font	A	Ctrl + <
Display nonprinting characters	Home, Paragraph	¶	Ctrl + Shift + *
Font	Home, Font	Calibri (Body)	
Font color	Home, Font	A	
Font dialog box	Home, Font		Ctrl + Shift + F

FEATURE	RIBBON TAB, GROUP	BUTTON	KEYBOARD SHORTCUT
Format Painter	Home, Clipboard		Ctrl + Shift + C
Highlight text	Home, Font		
Increase font size	Home, Font		Ctrl + >
Italicize text	Home, Font		Ctrl + I
Justify-align text	Home, Paragraph		Ctrl + J
Left-align text	Home, Paragraph		Ctrl + L
Line spacing	Home, Paragraph		Ctrl + 1 (single) Ctrl + 2 (double) Ctrl + 5 (1.5)
Paragraph dialog box	Home, Paragraph		
Repeat last action			F4 or Ctrl + Y
Reveal Formatting task pane			Shift + F1
Right-align text	Home, Paragraph		Ctrl + R
Spacing after paragraph	Page Layout, Paragraph	After: 0 pt	
Spacing before paragraph	Page Layout, Paragraph	Before: 0 pt	
Strikethrough text	Home, Font		
Subscript text	Home, Font		Ctrl + =
Superscript text	Home, Font		Ctrl + Shift + +
Text Effects	Home, Font		
Theme Colors	Page Layout, Themes		
Theme Effects	Page Layout, Themes		
Theme Fonts	Page Layout, Themes		
Themes	Page Layout, Themes		
Underline text	Home, Font		Ctrl + U

Concepts Check   Test Your Knowledge

Completion: In the space provided at the right, indicate the correct term, symbol, or command.

1. The Bold button is located in this group in the Home tab. _____

2. Click this button in the Font group to remove all formatting from selected text. _____

3. Proportional typefaces are divided into two main categories, serif and this. _____

4. This is the keyboard shortcut to italicize selected text. _____

5. This term refers to text that is raised slightly above the regular text line. _____

6. This automatically displays above selected text. _____

7. Click this to display the Font dialog box. _____

8. A Word document contains a number of predesigned formats grouped into style sets called this. _____

9. Apply a theme and change theme colors, fonts, and effects with buttons in the Themes group in this tab. _____

10. This is the default paragraph alignment. _____

11. Click this button in the Paragraph group to turn on the display of nonprinting characters. _____

12. Return all paragraph formatting to normal with this keyboard shortcut. _____

13. Click this button in the Paragraph group in the Home tab to align text at the right margin. _____

14. In this type of paragraph, the first line of text remains at the left margin and the remaining lines of text are indented to the first tab. _____

15. Repeat the last action by pressing F4 or with this keyboard shortcut. _____

16. Use this button in the Clipboard group in the Home tab to copy formatting already applied to text to different locations in the document. _____

17. Change line spacing to 1.5 with this keyboard shortcut. _____

18. Press these keys to display the Reveal Formatting task pane. _____

Chapter 2 ■ Formatting Characters and Paragraphs

Skills Check Assess Your Performance

Assessment

1 APPLY CHARACTER FORMATTING TO A LEASE AGREEMENT DOCUMENT

1. Open **LeaseAgrmnt.docx**.
2. Save the document with Save As and name it **WL1-C2-A1-LeaseAgrmnt**.
3. Press Ctrl + End to move the insertion point to the end of the document and then type the text shown in Figure 2.8. Bold, italicize, and underline text as shown.
4. Select the entire document and then change the font to 12-point Candara.
5. Select and then bold *THIS LEASE AGREEMENT* located in the first paragraph.
6. Select and then bold *DOLLARS* located in the *Rent* section.
7. Select and then bold *DOLLARS* located in the *Damage Deposit* section.
8. Select and then italicize 12 o'clock midnight in the *Term* section.
9. Select the title *LEASE AGREEMENT* and then change the font to 18-point Corbel and the font color to dark blue. (Make sure the title retains the bold formatting.)
10. Select the heading *Term*, change the font to 14-point Corbel, and apply small caps formatting. (Make sure the heading retains the bold formatting.)
11. Use Format Painter to change the formatting to small caps in 14-point Corbel for the remaining headings (*Rent*, *Damage Deposit*, *Use of Premises*, *Condition of Premises*, *Alterations and Improvements*, *Damage to Premises*, *Inspection of Premises*, *Default*, and *Late Charge*).
12. Save, print, and then close **WL1-C2-A1-LeaseAgrmnt.docx**.

Figure 2.8 Assessment 1

Inspection of Premises

Lessor shall have the right at all reasonable times during the term of this Agreement to exhibit the Premises and to display the usual *for sale, for rent,* or *vacancy* signs on the Premises at any time within <u>forty-five</u> days before the expiration of this Lease.

Default

If Lessee fails to pay rent when due and the default continues for <u>seven</u> days thereafter, Lessor may declare the entire balance immediately due and payable and may exercise any and all rights and remedies available to Lessor.

Late Charge

In the event that any payment required to be paid by Lessee is not made by the 10th day of the month, Lessee shall pay to Lessor a *late fee* in the amount of **$50**.

Assessment 2

APPLY STYLES, A QUICK STYLES SET, AND A THEME TO A HARDWARE TECHNOLOGY DOCUMENT

1. Open **FutureHardware.docx**.
2. Save the document with Save As and name it **WL1-C2-A2-FutureHardware**.
3. Apply the Heading 1 style to the title *ON THE HORIZON*.
4. Apply the Heading 2 style to the headings in the document (*Increased Optical Disc Storage Capacity*, *Improved Monitors*, *Holographic Storage*, and *Electronic Paper*).
5. Change the Quick Styles set to *Fancy*.
6. Apply the *Foundry* theme.
7. Change the theme colors to *Aspect*.
8. Change the theme fonts to *Flow*.
9. Change the paragraph spacing to Relaxed. *Hint: Use the* **Paragraph Spacing** *option at the Change Styles button drop-down list.*
10. Highlight the second sentence in the *Increased Optical Disc Storage Capacity* section.
11. Highlight the second sentence in the *Holographic Storage* section.
12. Save, print, and then close **WL1-C2-A2-FutureHardware.docx**.

Assessment 3

APPLY CHARACTER AND PARAGRAPH FORMATTING TO AN EMPLOYEE PRIVACY DOCUMENT

1. Open **WorkplacePrivacy.docx**.
2. Save the document with Save As and name it **WL1-C2-A3-WorkplacePrivacy**.
3. Move the insertion point to the beginning of the document and then type WORKPLACE PRIVACY centered.
4. Select text from the beginning of the first paragraph to the end of the document (make sure you select the blank line at the end of the document) and then make the following changes:
   a. Change the line spacing to 1.5.
   b. Change the spacing after to 0 points.
   c. Indent the first line of each paragraph 0.5 inch.
   d. Change the alignment to Justify.
5. Move the insertion point to the end of the document and, if necessary, drag the First Line Indent marker on the Ruler back to 0″. Type the text shown in Figure 2.9. (Hang indent text as shown in Figure 2.9.)
6. Select the entire document and then change the font to Constantia.
7. Select the title *WORKPLACE PRIVACY* and then change the font to 14-point Calibri bold and apply the *Gradient Fill - Orange, Accent 6, Inner Shadow* text effect (second option from the left in the fourth row in the Text Effects button drop-down gallery).
8. Apply the same formatting to the title *BIBLIOGRAPHY* that you applied to the title *WORKPLACE PRIVACY*.
9. Save, print, and then close **WL1-C2-A3-WorkplacePrivacy.docx**.

Figure 2.9 Assessment 3

BIBLIOGRAPHY

Amaral, H. G. (2011). *Privacy in the workplace,* 2nd edition (pp. 103-112). Denver, CO: Goodwin Publishing Group.

Cuevas, R. A. (2010). *Employer and employee rights* (pp. 18-35). Los Angeles, CA: North Ridge Publishing Company.

Forsyth, S. M. (2011). *Protecting your privacy* (pp. 23-31). San Francisco, CA: Roosevelt & Carson Publishing.

Visual Benchmark   Demonstrate Your Proficiency

CREATE AN ACTIVE LISTENING REPORT

1. At a blank document, press the Enter key twice, and then type the document shown in Figure 2.10. Set the body text in 12-point Cambria, the title in 16-point Candara bold, the headings in 14-point Candara bold, change the paragraph spacing after the headings to 6 points, and then apply additional formatting so the document appears as shown in the figure.
2. Save the document and name it **WL1-C2-VB-ActiveListen**.
3. Print and then close the document.

Figure 2.10 Visual Benchmark

ACTIVE LISTENING SKILLS

Speaking and listening is a two-way activity. When the audience pays attention, the speaker gains confidence, knowing that his or her message is being received and appreciated. At the same time, alert listeners obtain information, hear an amusing or interesting story, and otherwise benefit from the speaker's presentation.

Become an Active Listener

Active listeners pay attention to the speaker and to what is being said. They are respectful of the speaker and eager to be informed or entertained. In contrast, *passive listeners* "tune out" the presentation and may even display rudeness by not paying attention to the speaker. Here are ways in which you can become an active listener:

Listen with a purpose: Stay focused on what the speaker is saying and you will gain useful information or hear a suspenseful story narrated well. Try to avoid letting your attention wander.

Be courteous: Consider that the speaker spent time preparing for the presentation and thus deserves your respect.

Take brief notes: If the speaker is providing information, take brief notes on the main ideas. Doing so will help you understand and remember what is being said. If you have questions or would like to hear more about a particular point, ask the speaker for clarification after the presentation.

Practice Active Listening Skills in Conversation

Most people have had the experience of being in a one-way conversation in which one person does all the talking and the others just listen. In fact, this is not a conversation, which is by definition an exchange of information and ideas. In a true conversation, everyone has the chance to be heard. Do not monopolize the conversation. Give the other person or persons an opportunity to talk. Pay attention when others are speaking and show your interest in what is being said by making eye contact and asking questions. Avoid interrupting since this shows your disinterest and also suggests that what you have to say is more important.

Case Study Apply Your Skills

Part 1

You work for your local chamber of commerce and are responsible for assisting the Office Manager, Teresa Alexander. Ms. Alexander would like to maintain consistency in articles submitted for publication in the monthly chamber newsletter. She wants you to explore various decorative and plain fonts. She would like you to choose two handwriting fonts, two decorative fonts, and two plain fonts and then prepare a document containing an illustration of each of these fonts. Save the document and name it **WL1-C2-CS-P1-Fonts**. Print and then close the document.

Part 2

Ms. Alexander has asked you to write a short article for the upcoming chamber newsletter. In the article, she would like you to describe an upcoming event at your school, a local college or university, or your local community. Effectively use at least two of the fonts you wrote about in the document you prepared for Case Study Part 1. Save the document and name it **WL1-C2-CS-P2-Article**. Print and then close the document.

Part 3

When preparing the monthly newsletter, additional fonts may be necessary. Ms. Alexander has asked you to research the steps needed to install new fonts on your computer. Use the Help feature to research the steps and then prepare a document listing the steps. Format the document with appropriate headings and fonts. Save the document and name it **WL1-C2-CS-P3-DownloadFonts**. Print and then close the document.

Microsoft Word

Customizing Paragraphs

CHAPTER 3

PERFORMANCE OBJECTIVES

Upon successful completion of Chapter 3, you will be able to:
- Apply numbering and bulleting formatting to text
- Insert paragraph borders and shading
- Apply custom borders and shading
- Sort paragraph text
- Set, clear, and move tabs on the Ruler and at the Tabs dialog box
- Cut, copy, and paste text in a document
- Copy and paste text between documents

As you learned in Chapter 2, Word contains a variety of options for formatting text in paragraphs. In this chapter you will learn how to insert numbers and bullets in a document, how to apply borders and shading to paragraphs of text in a document, how to sort paragraphs of text, and how to manipulate tabs on the Ruler and at the Tabs dialog box. Editing some documents might include selecting and then deleting, moving, or copying text. You can perform this type of editing with buttons in the Clipboard group in the Home tab or with keyboard shortcuts. Model answers for this chapter's projects appear on the following pages.

Note: Before beginning the projects, copy to your storage medium the Word2010L1C3 subfolder from the Word2010L1 folder on the CD that accompanies this textbook and then make Word2010L1C3 the active folder.

Model Answers

Project 1 Format a Document on Computer Technology
WL1-C3-P1-TechInfo.docx

Technology Information Questions
1. Is programming just for professionals?
2. Could a bit of training as a programmer help your career?
3. Which elements in the procedure of creating a macro are similar to the steps in developing a program?
4. What kinds of networks are used in your local area?
5. How can networks improve efficiency?

Technology Timeline: Computers in the Workplace
- 1900 to 1930: Most Americans grow up on farms and live in rural communities.
- 1930 to 1940: Number of factory workers increases and cities swell in population; soon they outnumber rural communities.
- 1950s: Computers invade the business environment and the number of office "white-collar" workers increases.
- 1980: Personal computers enter the workplace and office workers become knowledge workers. Office workers outnumber factory workers in the job market.
- 1993: The Internet becomes publicly available and millions go online. Farmers number less than three percent of the population.
- 2002 to 2010: Seven of the ten fastest-growing occupations, according to the U.S. Department of Labor, are computer-specific jobs. The other three are desktop publishers, personal and home-care aides, and medical assistants.

Technology Career Questions
1. What is your ideal technical job?
2. Which job suits your personality?
3. Which is your first-choice certificate?
4. How does the technical job market look in your state right now? Is the job market wide open or are the information technology career positions limited?

Project 2 Customize a Document on Online Shopping
WL1-C3-P2-OnlineShop.docx

Online Shopping

Online shopping, also called electronic shopping or e-shopping, is defined as using a computer, modem, browser, and the Internet to locate, examine, purchase, and pay for products.

Many businesses encourage consumers to shop online because it saves employee time, thus reducing staff needs and saving money for the company. For example, some major airlines offer special discounts to travelers who purchase their tickets over the Internet, and most are eliminating paper tickets altogether.

Advantages of Online Shopping

For the consumer, online shopping offers several distinct advantages over traditional shopping methods. Some of these conveniences include:
- Convenience. With e-shopping, you can browse merchandise and make purchases whenever you want from the privacy and comfort of your home or office.
- Ease of comparison shopping. E-shopping allows you to quickly find comparable items at similar stores and locate those venues with the best quality and lowest prices.
- Greater selection. Because they are not restricted by available shelf space, online stores can offer you an almost unlimited number of products.
- More product information. At many online stores, you can find detailed information about a wide variety of products, an advantage often unavailable in traditional stores.

Online Shopping Venues

Just as consumers can visit a variety of bricks-and-mortar retail outlets, such as stores and shopping malls, Internet shoppers can browse several types of online shopping venues, including online stores, superstores, and shopping malls.

Online Shopping Safety Tips

The number one concern about shopping online is security. The truth is, shopping online is safe and secure if you know what to look for. Following these guidelines can help you avoid trouble.
1. Only buy at secure sites.
2. Never provide your social security number.
3. Look for sites that follow privacy rules from a privacy watchdog such as TRUSTe.
4. Find out the privacy policy of shopping sites before you buy.
5. Keep current on the latest Internet scams.
6. Answer only the minimum questions when filling out forms.

REFERENCES

Claussen, Morgan. "Online Shopping Tips," *Technology Bytes*, October 2, 2012.
Fairmont, Gerald. "Securing Your Privacy," emcpnews.com, August 5, 2012.
Weyman, Jennifer. "Safe Online Shopping," *Computing Standards*, September 10, 2012.

Project 3 Prepare a Document on Workshops and Training Dates
WL1-C3-P3-Tabs.docx

WORKSHOPS

Title	Price	Date
Quality Management	$240	Friday, February 3
Staff Development	229	Friday, February 17
Streamlining Production	175	Monday, March 5
Managing Records	150	Tuesday, March 27
Customer Service Training	150	Thursday, March 29
Sales Techniques	125	Tuesday, April 10

TRAINING DATES

January 3	February 7
January 12	February 15
January 24	February 21
January 26	February 23

TABLE OF CONTENTS

Computers and Creativity	1
Graphics Software	8
Page Layout Software	14
Multimedia Software	21
Educational and Reference Software	34
Programming Software	43

Project 4 Move and Copy Text in a Document on Online Shopping Tips
WL1-C3-P4-ShoppingTips.docx

Online Shopping Safety Tips

The number one concern about shopping online is security. The truth is, shopping online is safe and secure if you know what to look for. Following these guidelines should help you avoid trouble.

Find out the privacy policy of shopping sites before you buy. Ask what information they gather, how that information will be used, and whether they share that information.

Only buy at secure sites. Secure sites use encryption to scramble your credit card information so that no one except the site can read it. When you enter a secure site, you'll get a pop-up notice in your browser, and then an icon of a closed lock will appear at the bottom of the browser.

Keep current with the latest Internet scams. The U.S. Consumer Gateway reports on Internet scams and tells you what actions the Federal Trade Commission has taken against Internet scammers. The Internet Fraud Watch, run by the National Consumers League, is a great source as well.

Never provide your social security number. A legitimate site will not ask you for your social security number.

Look for sites that follow privacy rules from a privacy watchdog such as TRUSTe. TRUSTe (www.truste.org) is a nonprofit group that serves as a watchdog for Internet privacy. It allows sites to post an online seal if the site adheres to TRUSTe's Internet privacy policies.

Answer only the minimum questions when filling out forms. Many sites put an asterisk next to the questions that must be answered, so only answer those.

Project 5 Copy Text in a Staff Meeting Announcement
WL1-C3-P5-StaffMtg.docx

Project 6 Create a Contract Negotiations Document
WL1-C3-P6-NegotiateItems.docx

Project 1 Format a Document on Computer Technology 5 Parts

You will open a document containing information on computer technology, type numbered text in the document, and apply numbering and bullet formatting to paragraphs in the document.

Applying Numbering and Bullets

Automatically number paragraphs or insert bullets before paragraphs using buttons in the Paragraph group. Use the Bullets button to insert bullets before specific paragraphs and use the Numbering button to insert numbers.

Numbering

Bullets

Numbering Paragraphs

If you type 1., press the spacebar, type a paragraph of text, and then press the Enter key, Word indents the number approximately 0.25 inch from the left margin and then hang indents the text in the paragraph approximately 0.5 inch from the left margin. Additionally, 2. is inserted 0.25 inch from the left margin at the beginning of the next paragraph. Continue typing items and Word inserts the next number in the list. To turn off numbering, press the Enter key twice or click the Numbering button in the Paragraph group. (You can also remove paragraph formatting from a paragraph, including automatic numbering, with the keyboard shortcut, Ctrl + Q. Remove all formatting including character and paragraph formatting from selected text by clicking the Clear Formatting button in the Font group.)

 Quick Steps

Type Numbered Paragraphs
1. Type 1.
2. Press spacebar.
3. Type text.
4. Press Enter.

Chapter 3 ■ Customizing Paragraphs

Define new numbering by clicking the Numbering button arrow and then clicking Define New Number Format.

If you press the Enter key twice between numbered paragraphs, the automatic number is removed. To turn it back on, type the next number in the list (and the period) followed by a space. Word will automatically indent the number and hang indent the text.

When the AutoFormat feature inserts numbering and indents text, the AutoCorrect Options button displays. Click this button and a drop-down list displays with options for undoing and/or stopping the automatic numbering. An AutoCorrect Options button also displays when AutoFormat inserts automatic bulleting in a document. If you want to insert a line break without inserting a bullet or number, you do not need to turn off the automatic numbering/bulleting and then turn it back on again. Instead, simply press Shift + Enter to insert the line break.

Project 1a Typing Numbered Paragraphs   Part 1 of 5

1. Open **TechInfo.docx**.
2. Save the document with Save As and name it **WL1-C3-P1-TechInfo**.
3. Press Ctrl + End to move the insertion point to the end of the document and then type the text shown in Figure 3.1. Bold and center the title *Technology Career Questions*. When typing the numbered paragraphs, complete the following steps:
    a. Type 1. and then press the spacebar.
    b. Type the paragraph of text and then press the Enter key. (This moves the insertion point down to the next line, inserts 2. indented 0.25 inch from the left margin, and also indents the first paragraph of text approximately 0.5 inch from the left margin. Also, the AutoCorrect Options button displays. Use this button if you want to undo or stop automatic numbering.)
    c. Continue typing the remaining text. (Remember, you do not need to type the paragraph number and period — these are automatically inserted.)
    d. After typing the last question, press the Enter key twice. (This turns off paragraph numbering.)
4. Save **WL1-C3-P1-TechInfo.docx**.

Figure 3.1 Project 1a

Technology Career Questions

1. What is your ideal technical job?
2. Which job suits your personality?
3. Which is your first-choice certificate?
4. How does the technical job market look in your state right now? Is the job market wide open or are the information technology career positions limited?

If you do not want automatic numbering in a document, turn off the feature at the AutoCorrect dialog box with the AutoFormat As You Type tab selected as shown in Figure 3.2. To display this dialog box, click the File tab and then click the Options button located below the Help tab. At the Word Options dialog box, click the *Proofing* option located in the left panel and then click the AutoCorrect Options button that displays in the *AutoCorrect options* section of the dialog box. At the

Figure 3.2 AutoCorrect Dialog Box with AutoFormat As You Type Tab Selected

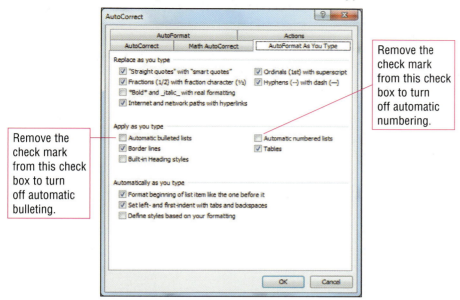

AutoCorrect dialog box, click the AutoFormat As You Type tab and then click the *Automatic numbered lists* check box to remove the check mark. Click OK to close the AutoCorrect dialog box and then click OK to close the Word Options dialog box.

You can also automate the creation of numbered paragraphs with the Numbering button in the Paragraph group. To use this button, type the text (do not type the number) for each paragraph to be numbered, select the paragraphs to be numbered, and then click the Numbering button in the Paragraph group. You can insert or delete numbered paragraphs in a document.

▼ **Quick Steps**

Create Numbered Paragraph
1. Select text.
2. Click Numbering button.

Project 1b Inserting Paragraph Numbering Part 2 of 5

1. With **WL1-C3-P1-TechInfo.docx** open, apply numbers to paragraphs by completing the following steps:
   a. Select the five paragraphs of text in the *Technology Information Questions* section.
   b. Click the Numbering button in the Paragraph group.

Chapter 3 ■ Customizing Paragraphs

2. Add text between paragraphs 4 and 5 in the *Technology Information Questions* section by completing the following steps:
   a. Position the insertion point immediately to the right of the question mark at the end of the fourth paragraph.
   b. Press Enter.
   c. Type **What kinds of networks are used in your local area?**
3. Delete the second question (paragraph) in the *Technology Information Questions* section by completing the following steps:
   a. Select the text of the second paragraph. (You will not be able to select the number.)
   b. Press the Delete key.
4. Save **WL1-C3-P1-TechInfo.docx**.

Bulleting Paragraphs

Quick Steps

Type Bulleted Paragraphs
1. Type *, >, or - symbol.
2. Press spacebar.
3. Type text.
4. Press Enter.

Create Bulleted Paragraphs
1. Select text.
2. Click Bullets button.

In addition to automatically numbering paragraphs, Word's AutoFormat feature will create bulleted paragraphs. You can also create bulleted paragraphs with the Bullets button in the Paragraph group. Bulleted lists with hanging indents are automatically created when a paragraph begins with the symbol *, >, or -. Type one of the symbols, press the spacebar, type text, and then press Enter. The AutoFormat feature inserts a bullet approximately 0.25 inch from the left margin and indents the text following the bullet another 0.25 inch. The type of bullet inserted depends on the type of character entered. For example, if you use the asterisk (*) symbol, a round bullet is inserted and an arrow bullet is inserted if you type the greater than symbol (>). Like the numbering feature, you can turn off the automatic bulleting feature at the AutoCorrect dialog box with the AutoFormat As You Type tab selected.

You can also create bulleted paragraphs with the Bullets button in the Paragraph group. To create bulleted paragraphs using the Bullets button, type the text (do not type the bullet) of the paragraphs, select the paragraphs, and then click the Bullets button in the Paragraph group.

Project 1c Typing and Inserting Bulleted Text   Part 3 of 5

1. With **WL1-C3-P1-TechInfo.docx** open, press Ctrl + End to move the insertion point to the end of the document and then press the Enter key once.
2. Type the text shown in Figure 3.3. Bold and center the title *Technology Timeline: Computer Design*. Create the bulleted paragraphs by completing the following steps:
   a. With the insertion point positioned at the left margin of the first paragraph to contain a bullet, type the greater than symbol (>).
   b. Press the spacebar once.
   c. Type the text of the first bulleted paragraph.
   d. Press the Enter key once and then continue typing the text after the bullets.

3. After typing the last bulleted paragraph, press the Enter key twice (this turns off bullets).
4. Format the paragraphs of text in the *Technology Timeline: Computers in the Workplace* section as a bulleted list by completing the following steps:
   a. Select the paragraphs of text in the *Technology Timeline: Computers in the Workplace* section.
   b. Click the Bullets button in the Paragraph group. (Word will insert the same arrow bullets that you inserted in Step 2. Word keeps the same bullet formatting until you choose a different bullet style.)
5. Save and then print **WL1-C3-P1-TechInfo.docx**. (This document will print on two pages.)

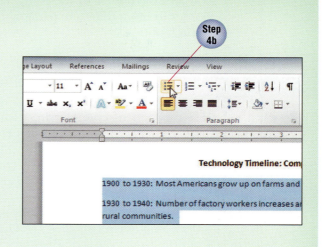

Figure 3.3 Project 1c

Technology Timeline: Computer Design

➢ 1937: Dr. John Atanasoff and Clifford Berry design and build the first electronic digital computer.
➢ 1958: Jack Kilby, an engineer at Texas Instruments, invents the integrated circuit, thereby laying the foundation for fast computers and large-capacity memory.
➢ 1981: IBM enters the personal computer field by introducing the IBM-PC.
➢ 2004: Wireless computer devices, including keyboards, mice, and wireless home networks, become widely accepted among users.

Inserting Paragraph Borders and Shading

Every paragraph you create in Word contains an invisible frame. You can apply a border to the frame around the paragraph. You can apply a border to specific sides of the paragraph or to all sides, you can customize the type of border lines, and you can add shading and fill to the border. Add borders and shading to paragraphs in a document using the Borders and Shading buttons in the Paragraph group or options from the Borders and Shading dialog box.

Inserting Paragraph Borders

When a border is added to a paragraph of text, the border expands and contracts as text is inserted or deleted from the paragraph. You can create a border around a single paragraph or a border around selected paragraphs. One method for creating a border is to use options from the Borders button in the Paragraph group. Click the Borders button arrow and a drop-down list displays. At the drop-down list, click the option that will insert the desired border. For example, to insert a border at the bottom of the paragraph, click the *Bottom Border* option. Clicking an option

▼ **Quick Steps**
Apply Border
1. Select text.
2. Click Borders button.

Borders

will add the border to the paragraph where the insertion point is located. To add a border to more than one paragraph, select the paragraphs first and then click the desired option.

 Adding Borders to Paragraphs of Text — Part 4 of 5

1. With **WL1-C3-P1-TechInfo.docx** open, select text from the beginning of the title *Technology Timeline: Computer Design* through the four bulleted paragraphs of text below and then press the Delete key.
2. Insert an outside border to specific text by completing the following steps:
   a. Select text from the title *Technology Information Questions* through the five numbered paragraphs of text.
   b. In the Paragraph group, click the Borders button arrow.
   c. At the Borders drop-down list, click the *Outside Borders* option.
3. Select text from the title *Technology Timeline: Computers in the Workplace* through the six bulleted paragraphs of text and then click the Borders button in the Paragraph group. (The button will apply the border option that was previously selected.)
4. Select text from the title *Technology Career Questions* through the four numbered paragraphs of text below and then click the Borders button in the Paragraph group.
5. Save and then print **WL1-C3-P1-TechInfo.docx**.

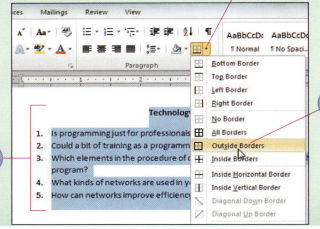

Adding Paragraph Shading

Quick Steps
Apply Shading
1. Select text.
2. Click Shading button.

Shading

With the Shading button in the Paragraph group you can add shading to text in a document. Select text you want to shade and then click the Shading button. This applies a background color behind the text. Click the Shading button arrow and a Shading drop-down gallery displays.

Paragraph shading colors display in themes in the drop-down gallery. Use one of the theme colors or click one of the standard colors that displays at the bottom of the gallery. Click the *More Colors* option and the Colors dialog box displays. At the Colors dialog box with the Standard tab selected, click the desired color or click the Custom tab and then specify a custom color.

Project 1e Applying Shading to Paragraphs   Part 5 of 5

1. With **WL1-C3-P1-TechInfo.docx** open, apply paragraph shading and change border lines by completing the following steps:
   a. Position the insertion point on any character in the title *Technology Information Questions*.
   b. Click the Borders button arrow and then click *No Border* at the drop-down list.
   c. Click the Borders button arrow and then click *Bottom Border* at the drop-down list.
   d. Click the Shading button arrow and then click the *Purple, Accent 4, Lighter 60%* option.

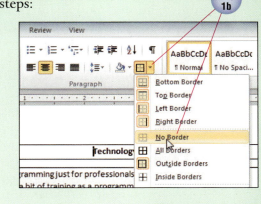

2. Apply the same formatting to the other titles by completing the following steps:
   a. With the insertion point positioned on any character in the title *Technology Information Questions*, double-click the Format Painter button in the Clipboard group.
   b. Select the title *Technology Timeline: Computers in the Workplace*.
   c. Select the title *Technology Career Questions*.
   d. Click the Format Painter button in the Clipboard group.

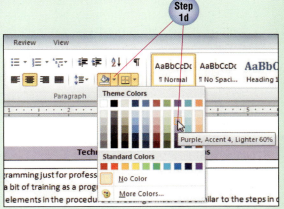

3. Remove the paragraph border and apply shading to paragraphs by completing the following steps:
   a. Select the numbered paragraphs of text below the *Technology Information Questions* title.
   b. Click the Borders button arrow and then click *No Border* at the drop-down list.
   c. Click the Shading button arrow and then click the *Purple, Accent 4, Lighter 80%* option.

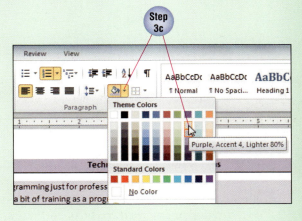

4. Select the bulleted paragraphs of text below the *Technology Timeline: Computers in the Workplace* title, click the Borders button, and then click the Shading button. (Clicking the Borders button will apply the previous border option, which was *No Border*. Clicking the Shading button will apply the previous shading option, which was *Purple, Accent 4, Lighter 80%*.)
5. Select the numbered paragraphs of text below the *Technology Career Questions* title, click the Borders button, and then click the Shading button.
6. Save, print, and then close **WL1-C3-P1-TechInfo.docx**.

Project 2 Customize a Document on Online Shopping   2 Parts

You will open a document containing information on online shopping, apply and customize borders and shading, and then sort text in the document.

Customizing Borders and Shading

If you want to further customize paragraph borders and shading, use options at the Borders and Shading dialog box. Display this dialog box by clicking the Borders button arrow and then clicking *Borders and Shading* at the drop-down list. Click the Borders tab and options display for customizing the border; click the Shading tab and shading options display. As you learned in a previous section, you can add borders to a paragraph with the Borders button in the Paragraph group. If you want to further customize borders, use options at the Borders and Shading dialog box with the Borders tab selected as shown in Figure 3.4. At the Borders and Shading dialog box, specify the desired border, style, color, and width. Click the Shading tab and the dialog box displays with shading options.

Figure 3.4 Borders and Shading Dialog Box with the Borders Tab Selected

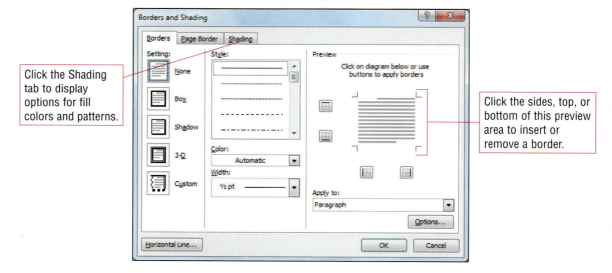

Project 2a Adding a Customized Border and Shading to a Document   Part 1 of 2

1. Open **OnlineShop.docx**.
2. Save the document with Save As and name it **WL1-C3-P2-OnlineShop**.
3. Make the following changes to the document:
    a. Insert 12 points of space before and 6 points of space after the headings *Online Shopping, Advantages of Online Shopping, Online Shopping Venues, Online Shopping Safety Tips,* and *REFERENCES*. (Do this with the *Spacing Before* and *Spacing After* measurement boxes in the Page Layout tab.)
    b. Center the *REFERENCES* title.

4. Insert a custom border and add shading to a heading by completing the following steps:
    a. Move the insertion point to any character in the heading *Online Shopping*.
    b. Click the Borders button arrow and then click *Borders and Shading* at the drop-down list.
    c. At the Borders and Shading dialog box with the Borders tab selected, click the down-pointing arrow at the right side of the *Color* option box and then click the *Dark Blue* color in the *Standard Colors* section.
    d. Click the down-pointing arrow at the right of the *Width* option box and then click *1 pt* at the drop-down list.

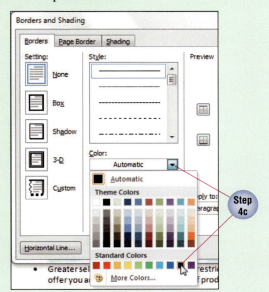
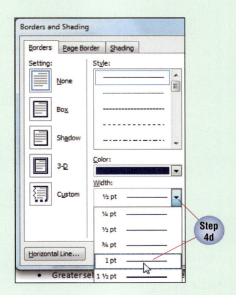

    e. Click the top border of the box in the *Preview* section of the dialog box.
    f. Click the down scroll arrow in the *Style* list box and then click the first thick/thin line.
    g. Click the down-pointing arrow at the right side of the *Color* option box and then click the *Dark Blue* color in the *Standard Colors* section.
    h. Click the bottom border of the box in the *Preview* section of the dialog box.

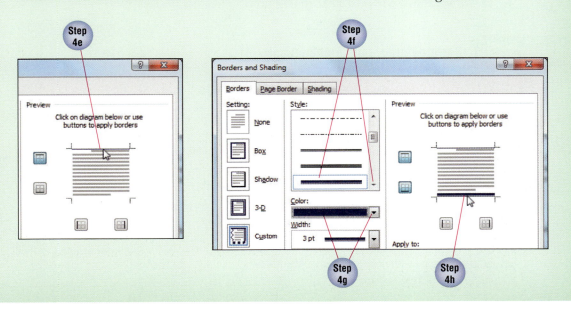

Chapter 3 ■ Customizing Paragraphs   83

i. Click the Shading tab.
   j. Click the down-pointing arrow at the right side of the *Fill* option box and then click *Olive Green, Accent 3, Lighter 60%*.
   k. Click OK to close the dialog box.
5. Use Format Painter to apply the same border and shading formatting to the remaining headings by completing the following steps:
   a. Position the insertion point on any character in the heading *Online Shopping*.
   b. Double-click the Format Painter button in the Clipboard group in the Home tab.
   c. Select the heading *Advantages of Online Shopping*.
   d. Select the heading *Online Shopping Venues*.
   e. Select the heading *Online Shopping Safety Tips*.
   f. Click the Format Painter button once.
6. Move the insertion point to any character in the heading *Online Shopping* and then remove the 12 points of spacing above.
7. Save **WL1-C3-P2-OnlineShop.docx**.

Sorting Text in Paragraphs

Sort

Quick Steps

Sort Paragraphs of Text
1. Click Sort button.
2. Make any needed changes at Sort Text dialog box.
3. Click OK.

You can sort text arranged in paragraphs alphabetically by the first character. The first character can be a number, symbol (such as $ or #), or letter. Type paragraphs you want to sort at the left margin or indented to a tab stop. Unless you select specific paragraphs for sorting, Word sorts the entire document.

To sort text in paragraphs, open the document. If the document contains text you do not want sorted, select the specific paragraph you do want sorted. Click the Sort button in the Paragraph group and the Sort Text dialog box displays. At this dialog box, click OK. If you select text and then display the dialog box the *Sort by* option is set at *Paragraphs*. If the text you select is numbers, then *Numbers* displays in the Sort Text dialog box.

Project 2b Sorting Paragraphs Alphabetically   Part 2 of 2

1. With **WL1-C3-P2-OnlineShop.docx** open, sort the bulleted text alphabetically by completing the following steps:
   a. Select the bulleted paragraphs in the *Advantages of Online Shopping* section.
   b. Click the Sort button in the Paragraph group.
   c. At the Sort Text dialog box, make sure *Paragraphs* displays in the *Sort by* option box and the *Ascending* option is selected.
   d. Click OK.
2. Sort the numbered paragraphs by completing the following steps:
   a. Select the numbered paragraphs in the *Online Shopping Safety Tips* section.

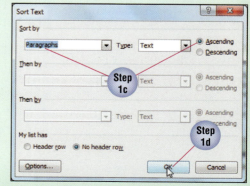

b. Click the Sort button in the Paragraph group.
c. Click OK at the Sort Text dialog box.
3. Sort alphabetically the three paragraphs of text below the *REFERENCES* title by completing the following steps:
   a. Select the paragraphs of text below the *REFERENCES* title.
   b. Click the Sort button in the Paragraph group.
   c. Click the down-pointing arrow at the right side of the *Type* list box and then click *Text* at the drop-down list.
   d. Click OK.
4. Save, print, and then close **WL1-C3-P2-OnlineShop.docx**.

Step 3c

Project 3 Prepare a Document on Workshops and Training Dates   **4 Parts**

You will set and move tabs on the Ruler and at the Tabs dialog box and type tabbed text about workshops, training dates, and a table of contents.

Manipulating Tabs

When you work with a document, Word offers a variety of default settings such as margins and line spacing. One of these defaults is a left tab set every 0.5 inch. In some situations, these default tabs are appropriate; in others, you may want to create your own. Two methods exist for setting tabs. Tabs can be set on the Ruler or at the Tabs dialog box.

Manipulating Tabs on the Ruler

Use the Ruler to set, move, and delete tabs. If the Ruler is not visible, click the View Ruler button located at the top of the vertical scroll bar. The Ruler displays left tabs set every 0.5 inch. These default tabs are indicated by tiny vertical lines along the bottom of the Ruler. With a left tab, text aligns at the left edge of the tab. The other types of tabs that can be set on the Ruler are center, right, decimal, and bar. Use the Alignment button that displays at the left side of the Ruler to specify tabs. Each time you click the Alignment button, a different tab or paragraph alignment symbol displays. Table 3.1 shows the tab alignment buttons and what type of tab each will set.

Table 3.1 Tab Alignment Buttons

Tab Alignment Button	Type of Tab	Tab Alignment Button	Type of Tab
L	Left tab	⊥	Decimal tab
⊥	Center tab	I	Bar tab
⌐	Right tab		

Chapter 3 ■ Customizing Paragraphs

Setting Tabs

▼ **Quick Steps**

Set Tabs on Ruler
1. Click Alignment button on Ruler.
2. Click desired location on Ruler.

To set a left tab on the Ruler, make sure the left alignment symbol (see Table 3.1) displays in the Alignment button. Position the arrow pointer just below the tick mark (the marks on the Ruler) where you want the tab symbol to appear and then click the left mouse button. When you set a tab on the Ruler, any default tabs to the left are automatically deleted by Word. Set a center, right, decimal, or bar tab on the Ruler in a similar manner.

Before setting a tab on the Ruler, click the Alignment button at the left side of the Ruler until the appropriate tab symbol displays and then set the tab. If you change the tab symbol in the Alignment button, the symbol remains until you change it again or you exit Word. If you exit and then reenter Word, the tab symbol returns to the default of left tab.

When setting tabs on the Ruler, a dotted guideline displays to help align tabs.

If you want to set a tab at a specific measurement on the Ruler, hold down the Alt key, position the arrow pointer at the desired position, and then hold down the left mouse button. This displays two measurements in the white portion in the Ruler. The first measurement displays the location of the arrow pointer on the Ruler in relation to the left margin. The second measurement is the distance from the location of the arrow pointer on the Ruler to the right margin. With the left mouse button held down, position the tab symbol at the desired location and then release the mouse button and the Alt key.

Position the insertion point in any paragraph of text, and tabs for the paragraph appear on the Ruler.

If you change tab settings and then create columns of text using the New Line command, Shift + Enter, the tab formatting is stored in the paragraph mark at the end of the columns. If you want to make changes to the tab settings for text in the columns, position the insertion point anywhere within the columns (all of the text in the columns does not have to be selected) and then make the changes.

Project 3a   **Setting Left, Center, and Right Tabs on the Ruler**   Part 1 of 4

1. At a new blank document, type **WORKSHOPS** centered and bolded as shown in Figure 3.5.
2. Press the Enter key and then return the paragraph alignment back to left and turn off bold for the new paragraph.
3. Set a left tab at the 0.5-inch mark, a center tab at the 3.25-inch mark, and a right tab at the 6-inch mark by completing the following steps:
   a. Click the Show/Hide ¶ button in the Paragraph group in the Home tab to turn on the display of nonprinting characters.
   b. Make sure the Ruler is displayed. (If not, click the View Ruler button located at the top of the vertical scroll bar.)
   c. Make sure the left tab symbol displays in the Alignment button at the left side of the Ruler.
   d. Position the arrow pointer on the 0.5-inch mark on the Ruler and then click the left mouse button.

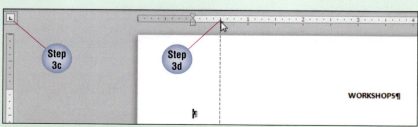

e. Position the arrow pointer on the Alignment button at the left side of the Ruler and then click the left mouse button until the center tab symbol displays (see Table 3.1).
f. Position the arrow pointer below the 3.25-inch mark on the Ruler. Hold down the Alt key and then the left mouse button. Make sure the first measurement on the Ruler displays as *3.25"* and then release the mouse button and the Alt key.

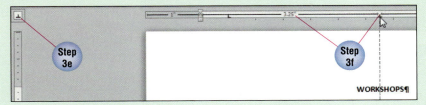

g. Position the arrow pointer on the Alignment button at the left side of the Ruler and then click the left mouse button until the right tab symbol displays (see Table 3.1).
h. Position the arrow pointer below the 6-inch mark on the Ruler. Hold down the Alt key and then the left mouse button. Make sure the first measurement on the Ruler displays as *6"* and then release the mouse button and the Alt key.

4. Type the text in columns as shown in Figure 3.5. Press the Tab key before typing each column entry and press Shift + Enter after typing the text in the third column.
5. After typing the last column entry, press the Enter key twice.
6. Press Ctrl + Q to remove paragraph formatting (tab settings).
7. Click the Show/Hide ¶ button to turn off the display of nonprinting characters.
8. Save the document and name it **WL1-C3-P3-Tabs**.

Figure 3.5 Project 3a

Title	Price	Date
	WORKSHOPS	
Quality Management	$240	Friday, February 3
Staff Development	229	Friday, February 17
Streamlining Production	175	Monday, March 5
Managing Records	150	Tuesday, March 27
Customer Service Training	150	Thursday, March 29
Sales Techniques	125	Tuesday, April 10

Moving Tabs and Deleting Tabs

After a tab has been set on the Ruler, it can be moved to a new location. To move a tab, position the arrow pointer on the tab symbol on the Ruler, hold down the left mouse button, drag the symbol to the new location on the Ruler, and then release the mouse button. To delete a tab from the Ruler, position the arrow pointer on the tab symbol you want deleted, hold down the left mouse button, drag the symbol down into the document, and then release the mouse button.

Project 3b Moving Tabs Part 2 of 4

1. With **WL1-C3-P3-Tabs.docx** open, position the insertion point on any character in the first entry in the tabbed text.
2. Position the arrow pointer on the left tab symbol at the 0.5-inch mark, hold down the left mouse button, drag the left tab symbol to the 1-inch mark on the Ruler, and then release the mouse button. *Hint: Use the Alt key to help you precisely position the tab symbol.*

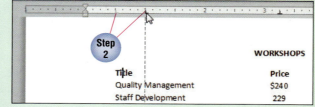

3. Position the arrow pointer on the right tab symbol at the 6-inch mark, hold down the left mouse button, drag the right tab symbol to the 5.5-inch mark on the Ruler, and then release the mouse button. *Hint: Use the Alt key to help you precisely position the tab symbol.*
4. Save **WL1-C3-P3-Tabs.docx**.

Manipulating Tabs at the Tabs Dialog Box

▼ **Quick Steps**

Set Tabs at Tabs Dialog Box
1. Click Paragraph group dialog box launcher.
2. Click Tabs button.
3. Specify tab positions, alignments, and leader options.
4. Click OK.

Use the Tabs dialog box shown in Figure 3.6 to set tabs at a specific measurement. You can also use the Tabs dialog box to set tabs with preceding leaders and clear one tab or all tabs. To display the Tabs dialog box, click the Paragraph group dialog box launcher. At the Paragraph dialog box, click the Tabs button located in the bottom left corner of the dialog box.

Figure 3.6 Tabs Dialog Box

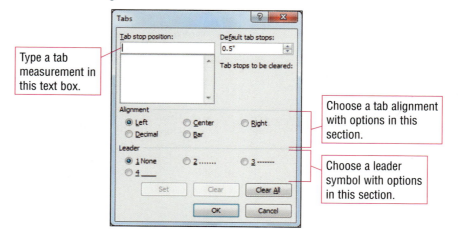

Clearing Tabs and Setting Tabs

At the Tabs dialog box, you can clear an individual tab or all tabs. To clear all tabs, click the Clear All button. To clear an individual tab, specify the tab position, and then click the Clear button.

At the Tabs dialog box, you can set a left, right, center, or decimal tab as well as a bar. (For an example of a bar tab, refer to Figure 3.7.) You can also set a left, right, center, or decimal tab with preceding leaders. To change the type of tab at the Tabs dialog box, display the dialog box and then click the desired tab in the Alignment section. Type the desired measurement for the tab in the *Tab stop position* text box.

Project 3c — Setting Left Tabs and a Bar Tab at the Tabs Dialog Box — Part 3 of 4

1. With **WL1-C3-P3-Tabs.docx** open, press Ctrl + End to move the insertion point to the end of the document.
2. Type the title **TRAINING DATES** bolded and centered as shown in Figure 3.7, press the Enter key, return the paragraph alignment back to left, and then turn off bold.
3. Display the Tabs dialog box and then set left tabs and a bar tab by completing the following steps:
   a. Click the Paragraph group dialog box launcher.
   b. At the Paragraph dialog box, click the Tabs button located in the lower left corner of the dialog box.
   c. Make sure *Left* is selected in the *Alignment* section of the dialog box.
   d. Type **1.75** in the *Tab stop position* text box.
   e. Click the Set button.
   f. Type **4** in the *Tab stop position* text box and then click the Set button.
   g. Type **3.25** in the *Tab stop position* text box, click *Bar* in the *Alignment* section, and then click the Set button.
   h. Click OK to close the Tabs dialog box.

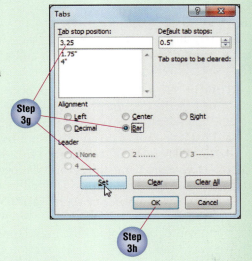

4. Type the text in columns as shown in Figure 3.7. Press the Tab key before typing each column entry and press Shift + Enter to end each line.
5. After typing *February 23*, complete the following steps:
   a. Press the Enter key.
   b. Clear tabs by displaying the Tabs dialog box, clicking the Clear All button, and then clicking OK.
   c. Press the Enter key.
6. Remove the 10 points of spacing after the last entry in the text by completing the following steps:
   a. Position the insertion point on any character in the *January 26* entry.
   b. Click the Page Layout tab.
   c. Click twice on the down-pointing arrow at the right side of the *Spacing After* measurement box. (This changes the measurement to *0 pt*.)
7. Save **WL1-C3-P3-Tabs.docx**.

Figure 3.7 Project 3c

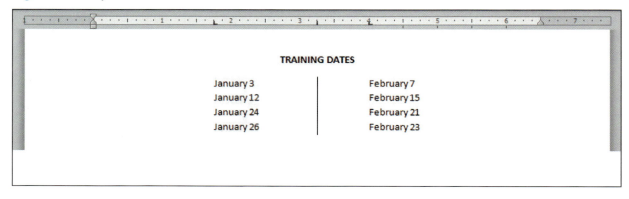

Setting Leader Tabs

The four types of tabs can also be set with leaders. Leaders are useful in a table of contents or other material where you want to direct the reader's eyes across the page. Figure 3.8 shows an example of leaders. Leaders can be periods (.), hyphens (-), or underlines (_). To add leaders to a tab, click the type of leader desired in the *Leader* section of the Tabs dialog box.

Project 3d — Setting a Left Tab and a Right Tab with Dot Leaders — Part 4 of 4

1. With **WL1-C3-P3-Tabs.docx** open, press Ctrl + End to move the insertion point to the end of the document.
2. Type the title **TABLE OF CONTENTS** bolded and centered as shown in Figure 3.8.
3. Press the Enter key and then return the paragraph alignment back to left and turn off bold.
4. Set a left tab and a right tab with dot leaders by completing the following steps:
   a. Click the Paragraph group dialog box launcher.
   b. Click the Tabs button located in the lower left corner of the Paragraph dialog box.
   c. At the Tabs dialog box, make sure *Left* is selected in the *Alignment* section of the dialog box.
   d. With the insertion point positioned in the *Tab stop position* text box, type **1** and then click the Set button.
   e. Type **5.5** in the *Tab stop position* text box.
   f. Click *Right* in the *Alignment* section of the dialog box.
   g. Click *2 ......* in the *Leader* section of the dialog box and then click the Set button.
   h. Click OK to close the dialog box.
5. Type the text in columns as shown in Figure 3.8. Press the Tab key before typing each column entry and press Shift + Enter to end each line.
6. Save, print, and then close **WL1-C3-P3-Tabs.docx**.

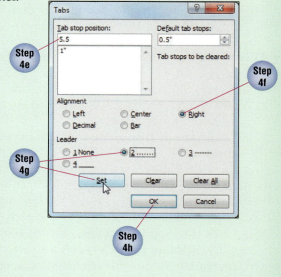

Figure 3.8 Project 3d

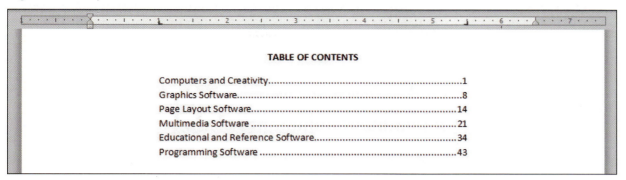

 **Move and Copy Text in a Document on Online Shopping Tips** **2 Parts**

You will open a document containing information on online shopping safety tips and then cut, copy, and paste text in the document.

Cutting, Copying, and Pasting Text

When editing a document, you may need to delete specific text, move text to a different location in the document, and/or copy text to various locations in the document. You can complete these activities using buttons in the Clipboard group in the Home tab.

Cut

Paste

Deleting Selected Text

Word offers different methods for deleting text from a document. To delete a single character, you can use either the Delete key or the Backspace key. To delete more than a single character, select the text, and then press the Delete key on the keyboard or click the Cut button in the Clipboard group. If you press the Delete key, the text is deleted permanently. (You can restore deleted text with the Undo button on the Quick Access toolbar.) The Cut button in the Clipboard group will remove the selected text from the document and insert it in the *Clipboard*. Word's Clipboard is a temporary area of memory. The Clipboard holds text while it is being moved or copied to a new location in the document or to a different document.

HINT The Clipboard contents are deleted when the computer is turned off. Text you want to save permanently should be saved as a separate document.

Cutting and Pasting Text

To move text to a different location in the document, select the text, click the Cut button in the Clipboard group, position the insertion point at the location where you want the text inserted, and then click the Paste button in the Clipboard group.

You can also move selected text with a shortcut menu. To do this, select the text and then position the insertion point inside the selected text until it turns into an arrow pointer. Click the right mouse button and then click *Cut* at the shortcut menu. Position the insertion point where you want the text inserted, click the right mouse button, and then click *Paste* at the shortcut menu. Keyboard shortcuts are also available for cutting and pasting text. Use Ctrl + X to cut text and Ctrl + V to insert text.

Quick Steps
Move Selected Text
1. Select text.
2. Click Cut button.
3. Move to desired location.
4. Click Paste button.

Chapter 3 ■ Customizing Paragraphs   91

▼ **Quick Steps**

Move Text with Mouse
1. Select text.
2. Position mouse pointer in selected text.
3. Hold down left mouse button and drag to desired location.

When selected text is cut from a document and inserted in the Clipboard, it stays in the Clipboard until other text is inserted in the Clipboard. For this reason, you can paste text from the Clipboard more than just once. For example, if you cut text to the Clipboard, you can paste this text in different locations within the document or other documents as many times as desired.

Moving Text by Dragging with the Mouse

You can also use the mouse to move text. To do this, select text to be moved and then position the I-beam pointer inside the selected text until it turns into an arrow pointer. Hold down the left mouse button, drag the arrow pointer (displays with a gray box attached) to the location where you want the selected text inserted, and then release the button. If you drag and then drop selected text in the wrong location, immediately click the Undo button.

Project 4a — Moving and Dragging Selected Text — Part 1 of 2

1. Open **ShoppingTips.docx**.
2. Save the document with Save As and name it **WL1-C3-P4-ShoppingTips**.
3. Move a paragraph by completing the following steps:
   a. Select the paragraph that begins with *Only buy at secure sites.* including the blank line below the paragraph.
   b. Click the Cut button in the Clipboard group in the Home tab.
   c. Position the insertion point at the beginning of the paragraph that begins with *Look for sites that follow . . . .*
   d. Click the Paste button in the Clipboard group. (If the first and second paragraphs are not separated by a blank line, press the Enter key once.)

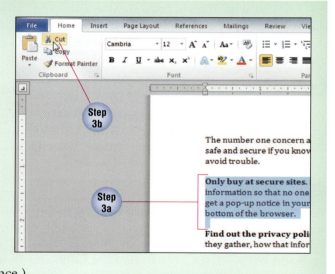

4. Following steps similar to those in Step 3, move the paragraph that begins with *Never provide your social . . .* so it is positioned before the paragraph that begins *Look for sites that follow privacy . . .* and after the paragraph that begins *Only buy at secure . . . .*
5. Use the mouse to select the paragraph that begins with *Keep current with the latest Internet . . .* including one blank line below the paragraph.
6. Move the I-beam pointer inside the selected text until it becomes an arrow pointer.
7. Hold down the left mouse button, drag the arrow pointer (displays with a small gray box attached) so that the insertion point, which displays as a grayed vertical bar, is positioned at the beginning of the paragraph that begins with *Never provide your social . . .* , and then release the mouse button.
8. Deselect the text.
9. Save **WL1-C3-P4-ShoppingTips.docx**.

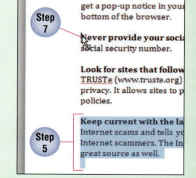

Using the Paste Options Button

Paste Options

When selected text is pasted, the Paste Options button displays in the lower right corner of the text. Click this button (or press the Ctrl key on the keyboard) and the *Paste Options* gallery displays as shown in Figure 3.9. Use options from this gallery to specify how you want information pasted in the document. Hover the mouse over a button in the gallery and the live preview displays the text in the document as it will appear when pasted. By default, pasted text retains the formatting of the selected text. You can choose to match the formatting of the pasted text with the formatting where the text is pasted or paste only the text without retaining formatting. To determine the function of a button in the *Paste Options* gallery, hover the mouse over a button and a ScreenTip displays with an explanation of the button function as well as the keyboard shortcut. For example, hover the mouse pointer over the first button from the left in the *Paste Options* gallery and the ScreenTip displays with the information *Keep Source Formatting (K)*. Click this button or press the letter *K* on the keyboard and the pasted text keeps its original formatting.

Figure 3.9 Paste Options Button Drop-down List

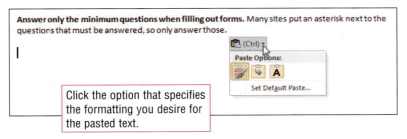

Click the option that specifies the formatting you desire for the pasted text.

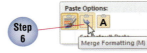 **Using the Paste Options Button** Part 2 of 2

1. With **L1-C3-P4-ShoppingTips.docx** open, open **Tip.docx**.
2. Select the paragraph of text in the document including the blank line below the paragraph and then click the Copy button in the Clipboard group.
3. Close **Tip.docx**.
4. Move the insertion point to the end of the document.
5. Click the Paste button in the Clipboard group.
6. Click the Paste Options button that displays at the end of the paragraph and then click the middle button in the Paste Options gallery (Merge Formatting (M) button). (This changes the font so it matches the formatting of the other paragraphs in the document.)
7. Save, print, and then close **WL1-C3-P4-ShoppingTips.docx**.

Project 5 Copy Text in a Staff Meeting Announcement   1 Part

You will copy and paste text in a document announcing a staff meeting for the Technical Support Team.

Copying and Pasting Text

Quick Steps

Copy Selected Text
1. Select text.
2. Click Copy button.
3. Move to desired location.
4. Click Paste button.

Copy

Copying selected text can be useful in documents that contain repetitive portions of text. You can use this function to insert duplicate portions of text in a document instead of retyping the text. After you have selected text, copy the text to a different location with the Copy and Paste buttons in the Clipboard group in the Home tab or using the mouse. You can also use the keyboard shortcut, Ctrl + C, to copy text.

To use the mouse to copy text, select the text and then position the I-beam pointer inside the selected text until it becomes an arrow pointer. Hold down the left mouse button and hold down the Ctrl key. Drag the arrow pointer (displays with a small gray box and a box containing a plus symbol) to the location where you want the copied text inserted (make sure the insertion point, which displays as a grayed vertical bar, is positioned in the desired location) and then release the mouse button and then the Ctrl key.

Project 5 Copying Text   Part 1 of 1

1. Open **StaffMtg.docx**.
2. Save the document with Save As and name it **WL1-C3-P5-StaffMtg**.
3. Copy the text in the document to the end of the document by completing the following steps:
   a. Select all of the text in the document and include one blank line below the text. *Hint: Click the Show/Hide ¶ button to turn on the display of nonprinting characters. When you select the text, select one of the paragraph markers below the text.*
   b. Click the Copy button in the Clipboard group.
   c. Move the insertion point to the end of the document.
   d. Click the Paste button in the Clipboard group.
4. Copy the text again at the end of the document. To do this, position the insertion point at the end of the document and then click the Paste button in the Clipboard group. (This inserts a copy of the text from the Clipboard.)
5. Select all of the text in the document using the mouse and include one blank line below the text. (Consider turning on the display of nonprinting characters.)
6. Move the I-beam pointer inside the selected text until it becomes an arrow pointer.
7. Hold down the Ctrl key and then the left mouse button. Drag the arrow pointer (displays with a box with a plus symbol inside) to the end of the document, release the mouse button, and then release the Ctrl key.
8. Deselect the text.

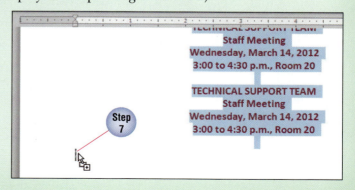
Step 7

94 Word Level 1 ■ Unit 1

9. Make sure all text fits on one page. If not, consider deleting any extra blank lines.
10. Save, print, and then close **WL1-C3-P5-StaffMtg.docx**.

Project 6 — **Create a Contract Negotiations Document** — **1 Part**

You will use the Clipboard to copy and paste paragraphs to and from paragraphs in separate documents to create a contract negotiations document.

Using the Clipboard

Use the Clipboard to collect and paste multiple items. You can collect up to 24 different items and then paste them in various locations. To display the Clipboard task pane, click the Clipboard group dialog box launcher located in the lower right corner of the Clipboard group. The Clipboard task pane displays at the left side of the screen in a manner similar to what you see in Figure 3.10.

Select text or an object you want to copy and then click the Copy button in the Clipboard group. Continue selecting text or items and clicking the Copy button. To insert an item, position the insertion point in the desired location and then click the option in the Clipboard task pane representing the item. Click the Paste All button to paste all of the items in the Clipboard into the document. If the copied item is text, the first 50 characters display beside the button on the Clipboard task pane. When all desired items are inserted, click the Clear All button to remove any remaining items.

▼ **Quick Steps**

Use Clipboard
1. Click Clipboard group dialog box launcher.
2. Select and copy desired text.
3. Move to desired location.
4. Click desired option in Clipboard task pane.

You can copy items to the Clipboard from various Office applications and then paste them into any Office file.

Clear All

Figure 3.10 Clipboard Task Pane

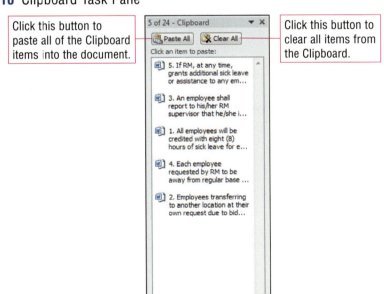

Click this button to paste all of the Clipboard items into the document.

Click this button to clear all items from the Clipboard.

Chapter 3 ■ Customizing Paragraphs   95

Project 6 Collecting and Pasting Paragraphs of Text   Part 1 of 1

1. Open **ContractItems.docx**.
2. Turn on the display of the Clipboard task pane by clicking the Clipboard group dialog box launcher. (If the Clipboard task pane list box contains any text, click the Clear All button located toward the top of the task pane.)
3. Select paragraph 1 in the document (the 1. is not selected) and then click the Copy button in the Clipboard group.
4. Select paragraph 3 in the document (the 3. is not selected) and then click the Copy button in the Clipboard group.
5. Close **ContractItems.docx**.
6. Paste the paragraphs by completing the following steps:
    a. Press Ctrl + N to display a new blank document. (If the Clipboard task pane does not display, click the Clipboard group dialog box launcher.)
    b. Type **CONTRACT NEGOTIATION ITEMS** centered and bolded.
    c. Press the Enter key, turn off bold, and return the paragraph alignment back to left.
    d. Click the Paste All button in the Clipboard task pane to paste both paragraphs in the document.
    e. Click the Clear All button in the Clipboard task pane.
7. Open **UnionContract.docx**.
8. Select and then copy each of the following paragraphs:
    a. Paragraph 2 in the *Transfers and Moving Expenses* section.
    b. Paragraph 4 in the *Transfers and Moving Expenses* section.
    c. Paragraph 1 in the *Sick Leave* section.
    d. Paragraph 3 in the *Sick Leave* section.
    e. Paragraph 5 in the *Sick Leave* section.
9. Close **UnionContract.docx**.
10. Make sure the insertion point is positioned at the end of the document and then paste the paragraphs by completing the following steps:
    a. Click the button in the Clipboard task pane representing paragraph 2. (When the paragraph is inserted in the document, the paragraph number changes to 3.)
    b. Click the button in the Clipboard task pane representing paragraph 4.
    c. Click the button in the Clipboard task pane representing paragraph 3.
    d. Click the button in the Clipboard task pane representing paragraph 5.
11. Click the Clear All button located toward the top of the Clipboard task pane.
12. Close the Clipboard task pane.
13. Save the document and name it **WL1-C3-P6-NegotiateItems**.
14. Print and then close **WL1-C3-P6-NegotiateItems.docx**.

Step 2

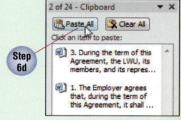

Step 6d

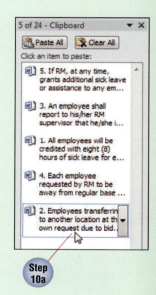

Step 10a

Step 11

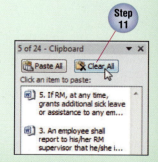

Chapter Summary

- Number paragraphs with the Numbering button in the Paragraph group in the Home tab and insert bullets before paragraphs with the Bullets button.
- Remove all paragraph formatting from a paragraph by pressing the keyboard shortcut, Ctrl + Q, and remove all character and paragraph formatting by clicking the Clear Formatting button in the Font group.
- The AutoCorrect Options button displays when the AutoFormat feature inserts numbers. Click this button to display options for undoing and/or stopping automatic numbering.
- Bulleted lists with hanging indents are automatically created when a paragraph begins with *, >, or -. The type of bullet inserted depends on the type of character entered.
- You can turn off automatic numbering and bullets at the AutoCorrect dialog box with the AutoFormat As You Type tab selected.
- A paragraph created in Word contains an invisible frame and you can insert a border around this frame. Click the Borders button arrow to display a drop-down list of border choices.
- Apply shading to text by clicking the Shading button arrow and then clicking the desired color at the drop-down gallery.
- Use options at the Borders and Shading dialog box with the Borders tab selected to add a customized border to a paragraph or selected paragraphs and use options with Shading tab selected to add shading or a pattern to a paragraph or selected paragraphs.
- With the Sort button in the Paragraph group in the Home tab, you can sort text arranged in paragraphs alphabetically by the first character, which includes numbers, symbols, or letters.
- By default, tabs are set every 0.5 inch. These settings can be changed on the Ruler or at the Tabs dialog box.
- Use the Alignment button at the left side of the Ruler to select a left, right, center, or decimal tab. When you set a tab on the Ruler, any default tabs to the left are automatically deleted.
- After a tab has been set on the Ruler, it can be moved or deleted using the mouse pointer.
- At the Tabs dialog box, you can set any of the four types of tabs as well as a bar tab at a specific measurement. You can also set tabs with preceding leaders and clear one tab or all tabs. Preceding leaders can be periods, hyphens, or underlines.
- Cut, copy, and paste text using buttons in the Clipboard group or with keyboard shortcuts.
- When selected text is pasted, the Paste Options button displays in the lower right corner of the text. Click the button and the *Paste Options* gallery displays with buttons for specifying how you want information pasted in the document.
- With the Office Clipboard, you can collect up to 24 items and then paste them in various locations in a document.

Commands Review

FEATURE	RIBBON TAB, GROUP	BUTTON, OPTION	KEYBOARD SHORTCUT
Borders	Home, Paragraph		
Borders and Shading dialog box	Home, Paragraph	, Borders and Shading	
Bullets	Home, Paragraph		
Clear character and paragraph formatting	Home, Font		
Clear paragraph formatting			Ctrl + Q
Clipboard task pane	Home, Clipboard		
Copy text	Home, Clipboard		Ctrl + C
Cut text	Home, Clipboard		Ctrl + X
New Line command			Shift + Enter
Numbering	Home, Paragraph		
Paragraph dialog box	Home, Paragraph		
Paste text	Home, Clipboard		Ctrl + V
Shading	Home, Paragraph		
Sort Text dialog box	Home, Paragraph		
Tabs dialog box	Home, Paragraph	, Tabs	

Concepts Check Test Your Knowledge

Completion: In the space provided at the right, indicate the correct term, symbol, or command.

1. The Numbering button is located in this group in the Home tab. _____

2. Automate the creation of bulleted paragraphs with this button in the Home tab. _____

3. This button displays when the AutoFormat feature inserts numbers. _____

4. You can turn off automatic numbering and bullets at the AutoCorrect dialog box with this tab selected. _____

5. Bulleted lists with hanging indents are automatically created when you begin a paragraph with the asterisk symbol (*), the hyphen (-), or this symbol. _____

6. The Borders button is located in this group in the Home tab. _____

7. Use options at this dialog box to add a customized border to a paragraph or selected paragraphs. _____

8. Sort text arranged in paragraphs alphabetically by the first character, which includes numbers, symbols, or this. _____

9. By default, each tab is set apart from the other by this measurement. _____

10. This is the default tab type. _____

11. When setting tabs on the Ruler, choose the tab type with this button. _____

12. Tabs can be set on the Ruler or here. _____

13. This group in the Home tab contains the Cut, Copy, and Paste buttons. _____

14. To copy selected text with the mouse, hold down this key while dragging selected text. _____

15. With this task pane, you can collect up to 24 items and then paste the items in various locations in the document. _____

Skills Check Assess Your Performance

Assessment

1 APPLY PARAGRAPH FORMATTING TO A COMPUTER ETHICS DOCUMENT

1. Open **CompEthics.docx**.
2. Save the document with Save As and name it **WL1-C3-A1-CompEthics**.
3. Move the insertion point to the end of the document and then type the text shown in Figure 3.11. Apply bullet formatting as shown in the figure.
4. Change the Quick Styles set to *Formal*.
5. Apply the Heading 1 style to the three headings in the document.
6. Apply the Paper theme.
7. Select the paragraphs of text in the *COMPUTER ETHICS* section and then apply numbering formatting.
8. Select the paragraphs of text in the *TECHNOLOGY TIMELINE* section and then apply bullet formatting.
9. Insert the following paragraph of text between paragraphs 2 and 3 in the *Computer Ethics* section: **Find sources relating to the latest federal and/or state legislation on privacy protection.**

10. Apply Blue-Gray, Accent 6, Lighter 60% paragraph shading to the three headings in the document.
11. Apply Gold, Accent 3, Lighter 80% paragraph shading to the numbered paragraphs in the COMPUTER ETHICS section and the bulleted paragraphs in the TECHNOLOGY TIMELINE and ACLU FAIR ELECTRONIC MONITORING POLICY sections.
12. Save, print, and then close **WL1-C3-A1-CompEthics.docx**.

Figure 3.11 Assessment 1

ACLU Fair Electronic Monitoring Policy

➢ Notice to employees of the company's electronic monitoring practices
➢ Use of a signal to let an employee know he or she is being monitored
➢ Employee access to all personal data collected through monitoring
➢ No monitoring of areas designed for the health or comfort of employees
➢ The right to dispute and delete inaccurate data
➢ A ban on the collection of data unrelated to work performance
➢ Restrictions on the disclosure of personal data to others without the employee's consent

---

Assessment 2

TYPE TABBED TEXT AND APPLY FORMATTING TO A COMPUTER SOFTWARE DOCUMENT

1. Open **ProdSoftware.docx**.
2. Save the document with Save As and name it **WL1-C3-A2-ProdSoftware**.
3. Move the insertion point to the end of the document and then type the tabbed text as shown in Figure 3.12. Before typing the text in columns, set left tabs at the 0.75-inch, 2.75-inch, and 4.5-inch marks on the Ruler.
4. Apply the Heading 1 style to the three headings in the document (*Productivity Software*, *Personal-Use Software*, and *Software Training Schedule*).
5. Change the Quick Styles set to *Distinctive*.
6. Apply the Elemental theme.
7. Select the productivity software categories in the PRODUCTIVITY SOFTWARE section (from *Word processing* through *Computer-aided design*) and then sort the text alphabetically.
8. With the text still selected, apply bullet formatting.
9. Select the personal-use software categories in the PERSONAL-USE SOFTWARE section (from *Personal finance software* through *Games and entertainment software*) and then sort the text alphabetically.
10. With the text still selected, apply bullet formatting.
11. Apply a single-line border to the top and a double-line border to the bottom of the three headings in the document and then apply paragraph shading of your choosing to each heading.
12. Position the insertion point on the first line of tabbed text below the SOFTWARE TRAINING SCHEDULE heading and then insert 12 points of spacing before the paragraph.
13. Select the text in columns and then move the tab symbols on the Ruler as follows:
    a. Move the tab at the 0.75-inch mark to the 1-inch mark.
    b. Move the tab at the 4.5-inch mark to the 4-inch mark.
14. Save, print, and then close **WL1-C3-A2-ProdSoftware.docx**.

Figure 3.12 Assessment 2

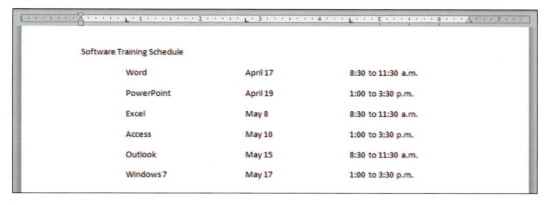

Assessment 3 — TYPE AND FORMAT A TABLE OF CONTENTS DOCUMENT

1. At a new blank document, type the document shown in Figure 3.13 with the following specifications:
   a. Change the font to 11-point Cambria.
   b. Bold and center the title as shown.
   c. Before typing the text in columns, display the Tabs dialog box and then set left tabs at the 1-inch mark and the 1.5-inch mark, and a right tab with dot leaders at the 5.5-inch mark.
2. Save the document and name it **WL1-C3-A3-TofC**.
3. Print **WL1-C3-A3-TofC.docx**.
4. Select the text in columns and then move the tab symbols on the Ruler as follows:
   a. Delete the left tab symbol that displays at the 1.5-inch mark.
   b. Set a new left tab at the 0.5-inch mark.
   c. Move the right tab at the 5.5-inch mark to the 6-inch mark.

Figure 3.13 Assessment 3

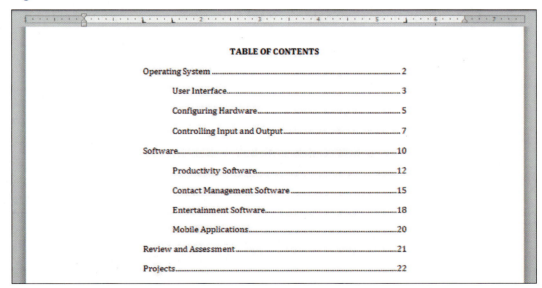

5. Apply paragraph borders and shading of your choosing to enhance the visual appeal of the document.
6. Save, print, and then close **WL1-C3-A3-TofC.docx**.

Assessment

4 FORMAT A BUILDING CONSTRUCTION AGREEMENT DOCUMENT

1. Open **ConstructAgrmnt.docx**.
2. Save the document with Save As and name it **WL1-C3-A4-ConstructAgrmnt**.
3. Select and then delete the paragraph that begins *Supervision of Work*.
4. Select and then delete the paragraph that begins *Exclusions*.
5. Move the paragraph that begins *Financing Arrangements* above the paragraph that begins *Start of Construction*.
6. Open **AgrmntItems.docx**.
7. Turn on the display of the Clipboard and then clear all the contents, if necessary.
8. Select and then copy the first paragraph.
9. Select and then copy the second paragraph.
10. Select and then copy the third paragraph.
11. Close **AgrmntItems.docx**.
12. With **WL1-C3-A4-ConstructAgrmnt.docx** open, turn on the display of the Clipboard and then paste the *Supervision* paragraph *above* the *Changes and Alterations* paragraph and merge the formatting. (Make sure you position the insertion point *above* the paragraph before you paste the text.)
13. Paste the *Pay Review* paragraph *above* the *Possession of Residence* paragraph and merge the formatting.
14. Clear all items from the Clipboard and then close the Clipboard.
15. Check the spacing between paragraphs. Insert or delete blank lines to maintain consistent spacing.
16. Save, print, and then close **L1-C3-A4-ConstructAgrmnt.docx**.

Assessment

5 HYPHENATE WORDS IN A REPORT

1. In some Word documents, especially documents with left and right margins wider than 1 inch, the right margin may appear quite ragged. If the paragraph alignment is changed to justified, the right margin will appear even, but there will be extra space added throughout the line. In these situations, hyphenating long words that fall at the end of the text line provides the document with a more balanced look. Use Word's Help feature to learn how to automatically hyphenate words in a document.
2. Open **InterfaceApps.docx**.
3. Save the document with Save As and name it **WL1-C3-A5-InterfaceApps**.
4. Automatically hyphenate words in the document, limiting the consecutive hyphens to 2. *Hint: Specify the number of consecutive hyphens at the Hyphenation dialog box.*
5. Save, print, and then close **WL1-C3-A5-InterfaceApps.docx**.

Visual Benchmark — Demonstrate Your Proficiency

CREATE A RESUME

1. At a blank document, click the No Spacing style and then type the resume document shown in Figure 3.14. Apply character and paragraph formatting as shown in the figure. Insert six points of spacing after the heading *PROFESSIONAL EXPERIENCE* and after the heading *EDUCATION*. Change the font size of the name, DEVON CHAMBERS, to 16 points.
2. Save the document and name it **WL1-C3-VB-Resume**.
3. Print and then close the document.

Case Study — Apply Your Skills

Part 1

You are the assistant to Gina Coletti, manager of La Dolce Vita, an Italian restaurant. She has been working on updating and formatting the lunch menu. She has asked you to complete the menu by opening the **Menu.docx** document (located in the Word2010L1C3 folder), determining how the appetizer section is formatted, and then applying the same formatting to the *Soups and Salads*; *Sandwiches, Calzones and Burgers*; and *Individual Pizzas* sections. Save the document and name it **WL1-C3-CS-P1-Menu**. Print and then close the document.

Part 2

Ms. Coletti has reviewed the completed menu and is pleased with the menu but wants to add a page border around the entire page to increase visual interest. Open **WL1-C3-CS-P1-Menu.docx** and then save the document and name it **WL1-C3-CS-P2-MenuPgBorder**. Display the Borders and Shading dialog box with the Page Border tab selected and then experiment with the options available. Apply an appropriate page border to the menu (consider applying an art page border). Save, print, and then close **WL1-C3-CS-P2-MenuPgBorder.docx**.

Part 3

Each week, the restaurant offers daily specials. Ms. Coletti has asked you to open and format the text in the **MenuSpecials.docx** document. She has asked you to format the specials menu in a similar manner as the main menu but to make some changes to make it unique from the main menu. Apply the same page border to the specials menu document that you applied to the main menu document. Save the document and name it **WL1-C3-CS-P3-MenuSpecials**. Print and then close the document.

Part 4

You have been asked by the head chef to research a new recipe for an Italian dish. Using the Internet, find a recipe that interests you and then prepare a Word document containing the recipe and ingredients. Use bullets before each ingredient and use numbering for each step in the recipe preparation. Save the document and name it **WL1-C3-CS-P4-Recipe**. Print and then close the document.

Figure 3.14 Visual Benchmark

DEVON CHAMBERS

344 North Anderson Road – Oklahoma City, OK 73177 – (404) 555-3228

PROFILE
Business manager with successful track record at entrepreneurial start-up and strong project management skills. Keen ability to motivate and supervise employees, strong hands-on experience with customer service, marketing, and operations. Highly organized and motivated professional looking to leverage strengths in leadership and organizational skills in a project coordinator role.

PROFESSIONAL EXPERIENCE

Midwest Deli, Oklahoma City, OK ....02/10 to present
Assistant Manager
- Coordinated the opening of a new business, which included budgeting start-up costs, establishing relationships with vendors, ordering supplies, purchasing and installing equipment, and marketing the business to the community
- Manage business personnel, which includes recruitment, interviewing, hiring, training, motivating staff, and conflict resolution
- Manage daily business operations through customer satisfaction, quality control, employee scheduling, process improvement, and maintaining product inventory

Marin Associates, Shawnee, OK..06/08 to 06/09
Projects Coordinator
- Developed and maintained a secure office network and installed and repaired computers
- Provided support for hardware and software issues
- Directed agency projects such as equipment purchases, office reorganization, and building maintenance and repair

Moore Insurance Agency, Shawnee, OK..04/06 to 04/08
Administrative Assistant
- Prepared documents and forms for staff and clients
- Organized and maintained paper and electronic files and scheduled meetings and appointments
- Disseminated information using the telephone, mail services, websites, and email

EDUCATION

Associate of Arts, Business 2010
Oklahoma City Community College

TECHNOLOGY SKILLS
- Proficient in Microsoft Word, Excel, and PowerPoint
- Knowledgeable in current and previous versions of the Windows operating system
- Experience with networking, firewalls, and security systems

REFERENCES
Professional and personal references available upon request.

CHAPTER 4

Formatting Pages

PERFORMANCE OBJECTIVES

Upon successful completion of Chapter 4, you will be able to:
- Change document views
- Navigate in a document with the Navigation pane
- Change margins, page orientation, and paper size in a document
- Format pages at the Page Setup dialog box
- Insert a page break, blank page, and cover page
- Insert page numbering
- Insert and edit predesigned headers and footers
- Insert a watermark, page color, and page border
- Find and replace text and formatting

A document generally displays in Print Layout view. You can change this default view with buttons in the View area on the Status bar or with options in the View tab. Use the Navigation pane to navigate in a document. A Word document, by default, contains 1-inch top, bottom, left, and right margins. You can change these default margins with the Margins button in the Page Setup group in the Page Layout tab or with options at the Page Setup dialog box. You can insert a variety of features in a Word document including a page break, blank page, and cover page as well as page numbers, headers, footers, a watermark, page color, and page border. Use options at the Find and Replace dialog box to search for specific text or formatting and replace with other text or formatting. Model answers for this chapter's projects appear on the following pages.

Note: Before beginning the projects, copy to your storage medium the Word2010L1C4 subfolder from the Word2010L1 folder on the CD that accompanies this textbook and then make Word2010L1C4 the active folder.

Model Answers

Project 2 Format a Document on Online Etiquette Guidelines
WL1-C4-P2-Netiquette.docx

Project 3 Customize a Report on Computer Input and Output Devices
WL1-C4-P3-CompDevices.docx

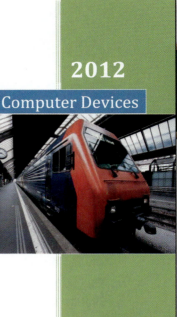

Page 3

COMPUTER OUTPUT DEVICES

To get information into a computer, a person uses an input device. To get information out, a person uses an output device. Some common output devices include monitors, printers, and speakers.

MONITOR

A monitor, or screen, is the most common output device used with a personal computer. A monitor creates a visual display and is either built into the CPU case or attached as an external device by means of a cable. Sometimes the cable is connected to a circuit board called a video card placed into an expansion slot in the CPU.

The most common monitors use either a thin film transistor (TFT) active matrix liquid crystal display (LCD) or a plasma display. Plasma displays have a very true level of color reproduction compared with LCDs. Emerging display technologies include surface-conduction electron-emitter displays (SED) and organic light emitting diodes (OLED).

PRINTER

After monitors, printers are the most important output devices. The print quality produced by these devices is measured in dpi, or dots per inch. As with screen resolution, the greater the number of dots per inch, the better the quality. The earliest printers for personal computers were dot matrix printers that used perforated computer paper. These impact printers worked something like typewriters, transferring the image of a character by using pins to strike a ribbon.

A laser printer uses a laser beam to create points of electrical charge on a cylindrical drum. Toner, composed of particles of ink with a negative electrical charge, sticks to the charged points on the

Page 1

FUTURE OF THE INTERNET

The Internet is having trouble keeping up with the rapid increase in users and the increased workload created by the popularity of bandwidth-intensive applications such as music and video files. The broadband connections needed to enjoy these new applications are not evenly distributed. Several ongoing projects promise to provide solutions for these problems in the future. Once these connectivity problems are dealt with, people around the world will be able to enjoy the new web services that are only a few short years away.

SATELLITE INTERNET CONNECTIONS

Many people living in remote or sparsely populated areas are not served by broadband Internet connections. Cable or optical fiber networks are very expensive to install and maintain, and ISPs are not interested in providing service to areas or individuals unless they think it will be profitable. One hope for people without broadband connections is provided by satellite TV networks. Remote ISPs connect to the satellite network using antennae attached to their servers. Data is relayed to and from ISP servers to satellites, which are in turn connected to an Internet backbone access point. While the connection speeds might not be as fast as those offered by regular land-based broadband access, they are faster than the service twisted-pair cable can offer and much better than no access at all.

SECOND INTERNET

A remedy for the traffic clogging the information highway is **Internet2**, a revolutionary new type of Internet currently under development. When fully operational, Internet2 will enable large research universities in the United States to

May 4, 2012

Project 4 Add Elements to a Report on the Future of the Internet
WL1-C4-P4-InternetFuture.docx

Page 2

collaborate and share huge amounts of complex scientific information at amazing speeds. Led by over 170 universities working in partnership with industry and government, the Internet2 consortium is developing and deploying advanced network technologies and applications.

Internet2 is a testing ground for universities to work together and develop advanced Internet technologies such as telemedicine, digital libraries, and virtual laboratories. Internet2 universities will be connected to an ultrahigh-speed network called the Abilene backbone. Each university will use state-of-the-art equipment to take advantage of transfer speeds provided by the network.

INTERNET SERVICES FOR A FEE

Industry observers predict that large portals such as AOL, MSN, and Yahoo! will soon determine effective structures and marketing strategies to get consumers to pay for Internet services. This new market, called bring-your-own-access (BYOA), will combine essential *content*, for example, news and weather, with *services*, such as search, directory, email, IM, and online shopping, into a new product with monthly access charges. But to entice current and potential customers into the BYOA market, ISP and telecom companies must offer improvements in the area of security, privacy, and ease of use. Additionally, they are expected to develop new ways to personalize content and add value to the current range of Internet services.

May 4, 2012

Page 3

INTERNET IN 2030

Ray Kurzweil, a computer futurist, has looked ahead to the year 2030 and visualized a Web that offers no clear distinctions between real and simulated environments and people. Among the applications he sees as very possible are computerized displays in eyeglasses that could offer simultaneous translations of foreign language conversations, nanobots (microscopic robots) that would work with our brains to extend our mental capabilities, and sophisticated avatars (simulated on-screen persons) that people will interact with online. Technologies that allow people to project their feelings as well as their images and voices may usher in a period when people could "be" with another person even though they are physically hundreds or even thousands of miles apart.

May 4, 2012

Model Answers

Project 5 Format a Report on Robots

Page 1

ROBOTS AS ANDROIDS

Robotic factories are increasingly commonplace, especially in heavy manufacturing, where tolerance of repetitive movements, great strength, and untiring precision are more important than flexibility. Robots are especially useful in hazardous work, such as defusing bombs or handling radioactive materials. They also excel in constructing tiny components like those found inside notebook computers, which are often too small for humans to assemble.

Most people think of robots in science fiction terms, which generally depict them as androids, or simulated humans. Real robots today do not look human at all and, judged by human standards, they are not very intelligent. The task of creating a humanlike body has proven incredibly difficult. Many technological advances in visual perception, audio perception, touch, dexterity, locomotion, and navigation need to occur before robots that look and act like human beings will live and work among us.

VISUAL PERCEPTION

Visual perception is an area of great complexity. A large percentage of the human brain is dedicated to processing data coming from the eyes. As our most powerful sense, sight is the primary means through which we understand the world around us. A single camera is not good enough to simulate the eye. Two cameras are needed to give stereoscopic vision, which allows depth and movement perception. Even with two cameras, visual perception is incomplete because the cameras cannot understand or translate what they see. Processing the image is the difficult part. In order for a robot to move through a room full of furniture it must build a mental map of that room, complete with obstacles. The robot must judge the distance and size of objects before it can figure out how to move around them.

AUDIO PERCEPTION

Audio perception is less complex than visual perception, but no less important. People respond to audible cues about their surroundings and the people they are with without even thinking about it. Listeners can determine someone's emotional state just by hearing the person's voice. A car starting up when someone crosses the street prompts the walker to glance in that direction to check for danger. Identifying a single voice and interpreting what is being said amid accompanying background noise is a task that is among the most important for human beings—and the most difficult.

Page 2

TACTILE PERCEPTION

Tactile perception, or touch, is another critical sense. Robots can be built with any level of strength, since they are made of steel and motors. How does a robot capable of lifting a car pick up an egg in the dark without dropping or crushing it? The answer is through a sense of touch. The robot must not only be able to feel an object, but also be able to sense how much pressure it is applying to that object. With this feedback it can properly judge how hard it should squeeze. This is a very difficult area, and it may prove that simulating the human hand is even more difficult than simulating the human mind.

Related to touch is the skill of dexterity, or hand-eye coordination. The challenge is to create a robot that can perform small actions, such as soldering tiny joints or placing a chip at a precise spot in a circuit board within half a millimeter.

LOCOMOTION

Locomotion includes broad movements such as walking. Getting a robot to move around is not easy. This area of robotics is challenging, as it requires balance within an endlessly changing set of variables. How does the program adjust for walking up a hill, or down a set of stairs? What if the wind is blowing hard or a foot slips? Currently most mobile robots work with wheels or treads, which limits their mobility in some circumstances but makes them much easier to control.

NAVIGATION

Related to perception, navigation deals with the science of moving a mobile robot through an environment. Navigation is not an isolated area of artificial intelligence, as it must work closely with a visual system or some other kind of perception system. Sonar, radar, mechanical "feelers," and other systems have been subjects of experimentation. A robot can plot a course to a location using an internal "map" built up by a navigational perception system. If the course is blocked or too difficult, the robot must be smart enough to backtrack so it can try another plan.

WL1-C4-P5-Robots.docx

Project 6 Format a Lease Agreement Document

Page 1

RENT AGREEMENT

THIS RENT AGREEMENT (hereinafter referred to as the "Agreement") is made and entered into this ___ day of _____, 2012, by and between Tracy Hartford and Michael Iwami.

Term

Tracy Hartford rents to Michael Iwami and Michael Iwami rents from Tracy Hartford the described premises together with any and all appurtenances thereto, for a term of _____ year(s), such term beginning on _____, and ending at 12 o'clock midnight on _____.

Rent

The total rent for the term hereof is the sum of _____ DOLLARS ($_____) payable on the _____ day of each month of the term. All such payments shall be made to Tracy Hartford at Tracy Hartford's address on or before the due date and without demand.

Damage Deposit

Upon the due execution of this Agreement, Michael Iwami shall deposit with Tracy Hartford the sum of _____ DOLLARS ($_____), receipt of which is hereby acknowledged by Tracy Hartford, as security for any damage caused to the Premises during the renting term hereof. Such deposit shall be returned to Michael Iwami, without interest, and minus any set off for damages to the Premises upon the termination of this renting Agreement.

Use of Premises

The Premises shall be used and occupied by Michael Iwami and Michael Iwami's immediately family, exclusively, as a private single family dwelling, and no part of the Premises shall be used at any time during the term of this Agreement by Michael Iwami for the purpose of carrying on any business, profession, or trade of any kind, or for any purpose other than as a private single family dwelling. Michael Iwami shall not allow any other person, other than Michael Iwami's immediate family or transient relatives and friends who are guests of Michael Iwami, to use or occupy the Premises without first obtaining Tracy Hartford's written consent to such use.

Condition of Premises

Michael Iwami stipulates, represents, and warrants that Michael Iwami has examined the Premises, and that they are at the time of this Agreement in good order, repair, and in a safe, clean, and tenantable condition.

Alterations and Improvements

Michael Iwami shall make no alterations to the buildings or improvements on the Premises without the prior written consent of Tracy Hartford. Any and all alterations, changes, and/or improvements

Page 2

built, constructed, or placed on the Premises by Michael Iwami shall, unminus otherwise provided by written agreement between Tracy Hartford and Michael Iwami, be and become the property of Tracy Hartford and remain on the Premises at the expiration or earlier termination of this Agreement.

Damage to Premises

In the event Premises are destroyed or rendered wholly unlivable, by fire, storm, earthquake, or other casualty not caused by the negligence of Michael Iwami, this Agreement shall terminate from such time except for the purpose of enforcing rights that may have then accrued hereunder.

WL1-C4-P6-LeaseAgrmnt.docx

 **Project 1 Navigate in a Report on Computer Input and Output Devices** **2 Parts**

You will open a document containing information on computer input and output devices, change document views, navigate in the document using the Navigation pane, and show and hide white space at the top and bottom of pages.

Changing the View

By default a Word document displays in Print Layout view. This view displays the document on the screen as it will appear when printed. Other views are available such as Draft and Full Screen Reading. Change views with buttons in the View area on the Status bar or with options in the View tab. The buttons in the View area on the Status bar are identified in Figure 4.1. Along with the View buttons, the Status bar also contains a Zoom slider bar as shown in Figure 4.1. Drag the button on the Zoom slider bar to increase or decrease the size of display, or click the Zoom Out button to decrease size and click the Zoom In to increase size.

HINT Click the 100% that displays at the left side of the Zoom slider bar to display the Zoom dialog box.

Displaying a Document in Draft View

Change to Draft view and the document displays in a format for efficient editing and formatting. At this view, margins and other features such as headers and footers do not display on the screen. Change to Draft view by clicking the Draft button in the View section on the Status bar or click the View tab and then click the Draft button in the Document Views group.

Zoom Out

Zoom In

Displaying a Document in Full Screen Reading View

The Full Screen Reading view displays a document in a format for easy viewing and reading. Change to Full Screen Reading view by clicking the Full Screen Reading button in the View section on the Status bar or by clicking the View tab and then clicking the Full Screen Reading button in the Document Views group.

Draft

Navigate in Full Screen Reading view using the keys on the keyboard as shown in Table 4.1. You can also navigate in Full Screen Reading view with options from the View Options button that displays toward the top right side of the screen or with the Next Screen and Previous Screen buttons located at the top of the window and also located at the bottom of each page.

You can customize the Full Screen Reading view with some of the options from the View Options drop-down list. Display this list by clicking the View Options button located in the upper right corner of the Full Screen Reading window.

Full Screen Reading

Figure 4.1 View Buttons and Zoom Slider Bar

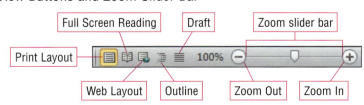

Chapter 4 ■ Formatting Pages   **109**

Table 4.1 Keyboard Commands in Full Screen Reading View

Press this key	To complete this action
Page Down key or spacebar	Move to the next page or section
Page Up key or Backspace key	Move to the previous page or section
Right Arrow key	Move to next page
Left Arrow key	Move to previous page
Home	Move to first page in document
End	Move to last page in document
Esc	Return to Print Layout

Navigating Using the Navigation Pane

▼ **Quick Steps**

Display Navigation Pane
1. Click View tab.
2. Click *Navigation Pane* check box.

Word includes a number of features you can use to navigate in a document. Along with the navigation features you have already learned, you can also navigate using the Navigation pane shown in Figure 4.2. When you click the *Navigation Pane* check box in the Show group in the View tab, the Navigation pane displays at the left side of the screen and includes a Search text box and a pane with three tabs. Click the first tab to display titles and headings with styles applied in the Navigation pane. Click a title or heading in the pane to move the insertion point to that title or heading. Click the second tab to display thumbnails of each page in the pane. Click a thumbnail to move the insertion point to the specific page. Click the third tab to browse the current search results in the document. Close the Navigation pane by clicking the *Navigation Pane* check box in the Show group in the View tab or by clicking the Close button located in the upper right corner of the pane.

Figure 4.2 Navigation Pane

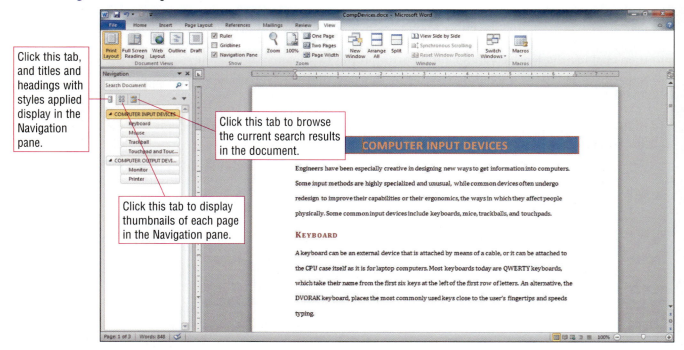

Project 1a Changing Views and Navigating in a Document   Part 1 of 2

1. Open **CompDevices.docx**.
2. Click the Draft button located in the View section on the Status bar.
3. Using the mouse, drag the Zoom slider bar button to the left to decrease the size of the document display to approximately 60%. (The percentage displays at the left side of the Zoom Out button.)
4. Drag the Zoom slider bar button back to the middle until *100%* displays at the left side of the Zoom Out button.
5. Click the Print Layout button in the View section on the Status bar.
6. Click the Full Screen Reading button located in the View section on the Status bar.
7. Click the View Options button located toward the top of the viewing window and then click *Show Two Pages* at the drop-down list.
8. Click the Next Screen button to display the next two pages in the viewing window.
9. Click the Previous Screen button to display the previous two pages.
10. Click the View Options button located toward the top of the viewing window and then click *Show One Page* at the drop-down list.
11. Practice navigating using the actions shown in Table 4.1. (Try all of the actions in Table 4.1 except pressing the Esc key since that action will close Full Screen Reading view.)
12. Increase the size of the text by clicking the View Options button and then clicking the *Increase Text Size* option.
13. Press the Home key to display the first viewing page.
14. Decrease the size of the text by clicking the View Options button and then clicking the *Decrease Text Size* option.
15. Click the Close button located in the upper right corner of the screen.

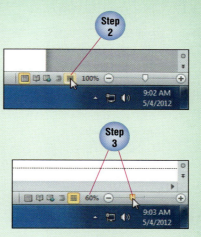
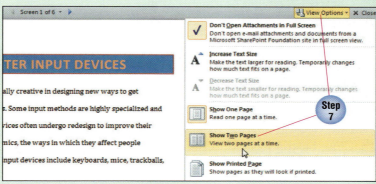
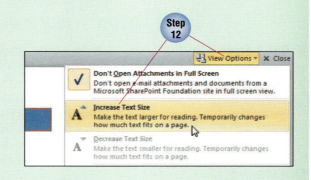

Chapter 4 ■ Formatting Pages

16. Click the View tab and then click the *Navigation Pane* check box.
17. Click the *COMPUTER OUTPUT DEVICES* title that displays in the Navigation pane.

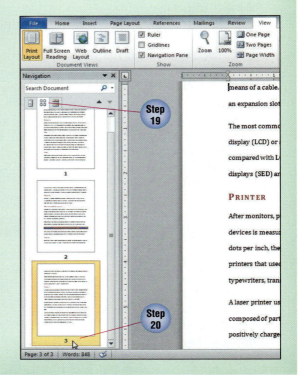

18. Click the *Keyboard* heading that displays in the Navigation pane.
19. Click the middle tab in the Navigation pane. (This displays page thumbnails in the pane.).
20. Click the number 3 thumbnail in the Navigation pane.
21. Click the number 1 thumbnail in the Navigation pane.
22. Close the Navigation pane by clicking the Close button located in the upper right corner of the Navigation pane.

Hiding/Showing White Space in Print Layout View

▼ **Quick Steps**

Hide White Space
1. Position mouse pointer at top of page until pointer displays as *Hide White Space* icon.
2. Double-click left mouse button.

Show White Space
1. Position mouse pointer on thin line separating pages until pointer displays as *Show White Space* icon.
2. Double-click left mouse button.

In Print Layout view, a page displays as it will appear when printed including the white space at the top and bottom of the page representing the default margins. To save space on the screen in Print Layout view, you can remove the white space by positioning the mouse pointer at the top edge or bottom edge of a page or between pages until the pointer displays as the *Hide White Space* icon and then double-clicking the left mouse button. To redisplay the white space, position the mouse pointer on the thin, black line separating pages until the pointer turns into the *Show White Space* icon and then double-click the left mouse button.

Hide White Space

Show White Space

Project 1b Hiding/Showing White Space   Part 2 of 2

1. With **CompDevices.docx** open, make sure the document displays in Print Layout view.
2. Press Ctrl + Home to move the insertion point to the beginning of the document.
3. Hide the white spaces at the top and bottom of pages by positioning the mouse pointer at the top edge of the page until the pointer turns into the *Hide White Space* icon and then double-clicking the left mouse button.
4. Scroll through the document and notice the display of pages.
5. Redisplay the white spaces at the top and bottom of pages by positioning the mouse pointer on any thin, black, horizontal line separating pages until the pointer turns into the *Show White Space* icon and then double-clicking the left mouse button.
6. Close **CompDevices.docx**.

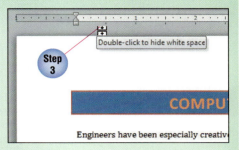

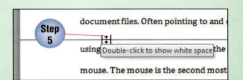

Project 2 Format a Document on Online Etiquette Guidelines 2 Parts

You will open a document containing information on guidelines for online etiquette and then change the margins, page orientation, and page size.

Changing Page Setup

The Page Setup group in the Page Layout tab contains a number of options for affecting pages in a document. With options in the group you can perform such actions as changing margins, orientation, and page size and inserting page breaks. The Pages group in the Insert tab contains three buttons for inserting a page break, blank page, and cover page.

Changing Margins

Change page margins with options at the Margins drop-down list as shown in Figure 4.3. To display this list, click the Page Layout tab and then click the Margins button in the Page Setup group. To change the margins, click one of the preset margins that display in the drop-down list. Be aware that most printers contain a required margin (between one-quarter and three-eighths inch) because printers cannot print to the edge of the page.

Changing Page Orientation

Click the Orientation button in the Page Setup group in the Page Layout tab and two options display—*Portrait* and *Landscape*. At the portrait orientation, which is the default, the page is 11 inches tall and 8.5 inches wide. At the landscape orientation, the page is 8.5 inches tall and 11 inches wide. Change the page orientation and the page margins automatically change.

Margins

▼ **Quick Steps**
Change Margins
1. Click Page Layout tab.
2. Click Margins button.
3. Click desired margin option.

Change Page Orientation
1. Click Page Layout tab.
2. Click Orientation button.
3. Click desired orientation.

Chapter 4 ■ Formatting Pages   113

Figure 4.3 Margins Drop-down List

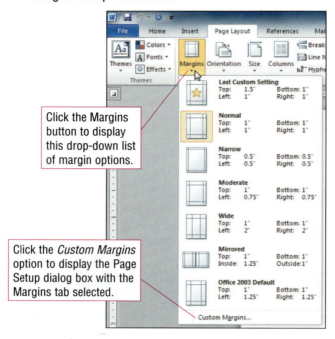

Click the Margins button to display this drop-down list of margin options.

Click the *Custom Margins* option to display the Page Setup dialog box with the Margins tab selected.

▼ **Quick Steps**

Change Page Size
1. Click Page Layout tab.
2. Click Size button.
3. Click desired size option.

Size

Changing Page Size

By default, Word uses a page size of 8.5 inches wide and 11 inches tall. You can change this default setting with options at the Size drop-down list. Display this drop-down list by clicking the Size button in the Page Setup group in the Page Layout tab.

Project 2a — Changing Margins, Page Orientation, and Size — Part 1 of 2

1. Open **Netiquette.docx**.
2. Save the document with Save As and name it **WL1-C4-P2-Netiquette**.
3. Click the Page Layout tab.
4. Click the Margins button in the Page Setup group and then click the *Office 2003 Default* option.
5. Click the Orientation button in the Page Setup group.
6. Click *Landscape* at the drop-down list.

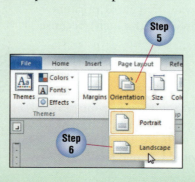

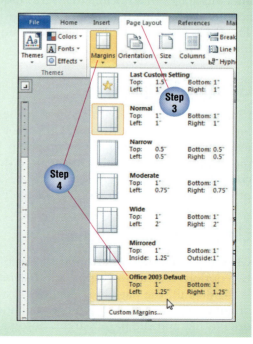

Word Level 1 ■ Unit 1

7. Scroll through the document and notice how the text displays on the page in landscape orientation.
8. Click the Orientation button in the Page Setup group and then click *Portrait* at the drop-down list. (This changes the orientation back to the default.)
9. Click the Size button in the Page Setup group.
10. Click the A5 option (displays with *5.83" × 8.27"* below *A5*). If this option is not available, choose an option with a similar size.
11. Scroll through the document and notice how the text displays on the page.
12. Click the Size button and then click *Legal* (displays with *8.5" × 14"* below *Legal*).
13. Scroll through the document and notice how the text displays on the page.
14. Click the Size button and then click *Letter* (displays with *8.5" × 11"* below *Letter*). (This returns the size back to the default.)
15. Save **WL1-C4-P2-Netiquette.docx**.

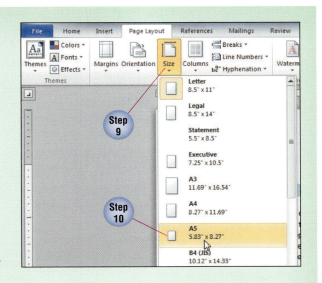

Changing Margins at the Page Setup Dialog Box

The Margins button in the Page Setup group provides you with a number of preset margins. If these margins do not fit your needs, you can set specific margins at the Page Setup dialog box with the Margins tab selected as shown in Figure 4.4. Display this dialog box by clicking the Page Setup group dialog box launcher or by clicking the Margins button and then clicking *Custom Margins* at the bottom of the drop-down list.

To change margins, select the current measurement in the *Top*, *Bottom*, *Left*, or *Right* text box, and then type the new measurement. You can also increase a measurement by clicking the up-pointing arrow at the right side of the text box. Decrease a measurement by clicking the down-pointing arrow. As you make changes to the margin measurements at the Page Setup dialog box, the sample page in the *Preview* section illustrates the effects of the margin changes.

Changing Paper Size at the Page Setup Dialog Box

The Size button drop-down list contains a number of preset page sizes. If these sizes do not fit your needs, you can specify page size at the Page Setup dialog box with the Paper tab selected. Display this dialog box by clicking the Size button in the Page Setup group and then clicking *More Paper Sizes* that displays at the bottom of the drop-down list.

▼ **Quick Steps**

Change Margins at Page Setup Dialog Box
1. Click Page Layout tab.
2. Click Page Setup group dialog box launcher.
3. Specify desired margins.
4. Click OK.

Change Page Size at Page Setup Dialog Box
1. Click Page Layout tab.
2. Click Size button.
3. Click *More Paper Sizes* at drop-down list.
4. Specify desired size.
5. Click OK.

Figure 4.4 Page Setup Dialog Box with Margins Tab Selected

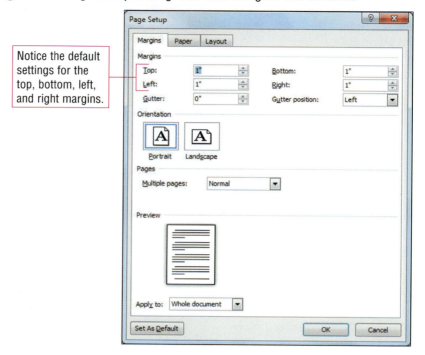

Notice the default settings for the top, bottom, left, and right margins.

Project 2b — Changing Margins at the Page Setup Dialog Box

Part 2 of 2

1. With **WL1-C4-P2-Netiquette.docx** open, make sure the Page Layout tab is selected.
2. Click the Page Setup group dialog box launcher.
3. At the Page Setup dialog box with the Margins tab selected, click the down-pointing arrow at the right side of the *Top* text box until *0.5"* displays.
4. Click the down-pointing arrow at the right side of the *Bottom* text box until *0.5"* displays.
5. Select the current measurement in the *Left* text box and then type **0.75**.
6. Select the current measurement in the *Right* text box and then type **0.75**.
7. Click OK to close the dialog box.
8. Click the Size button in the Page Setup group and then click *More Paper Sizes* at the drop-down list.
9. At the Page Setup dialog box with the Paper tab selected, click the down-pointing arrow at the right side of the *Paper size* option, scroll down the list box, and then click *A4* at the drop-down list.
10. Click OK to close the dialog box.

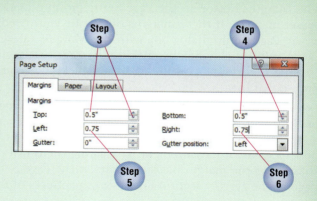

116 Word Level 1 ■ Unit 1

11. Scroll through the document and notice how the text displays on the page.
12. Click the Size button in the Page Setup group and then click *Letter* at the drop-down list.
13. Save, print, and then close **WL1-C4-P2-Netiquette.docx**.

Project 3 Customize a Report on Computer Input and Output Devices — 3 Parts

You will open a document containing information on computer input and output devices and then insert page breaks, a blank page, a cover page, and page numbering.

Inserting a Page Break

With the default top and bottom margins of one inch, approximately nine inches of text print on the page. At approximately the ten-inch mark, Word automatically inserts a page break. You can insert your own page break in a document with the keyboard shortcut, Ctrl + Enter, or with the Page Break button in the Pages group in the Insert tab.

A page break inserted by Word is considered a *soft* page break and a page break inserted by you is considered a *hard* page break. Soft page breaks automatically adjust if you add or delete text from a document. A hard page break does not adjust and is therefore less flexible than a soft page break. If you add or delete text from a document with a hard page break, check the break to determine whether it is still in a desirable location. In Draft view, a hard page break displays as a row of dots with the words *Page Break* in the center. To delete a page break, position the insertion point immediately below the page break and then press the Backspace key or change to Draft view, position the insertion point on the page break, and then press the Delete key.

▼ Quick Steps

Insert Page Break
1. Click Insert tab.
2. Click Page Break button.
OR
Press Ctrl + Enter.

Page Break

Project 3a Inserting Page Breaks — Parts 1 of 3

1. Open **CompDevices.docx**.
2. Save the document with Save As and name it **WL1-C4-P3-CompDevices**.
3. Change the top margin by completing the following steps:
   a. Click the Page Layout tab.
   b. Click the Page Setup group dialog box launcher.
   c. At the Page Setup dialog box, click the Margins tab and then type **1.5** in the *Top* text box.
   d. Click OK to close the dialog box.
4. Insert a page break at the beginning of the heading *Mouse* by completing the following steps:
   a. Position the insertion point at the beginning of the heading *Mouse* (located toward the bottom of page 1).

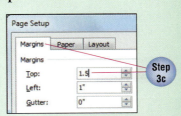
Step 3c

b. Click the Insert tab and then click the Page Break button in the Pages group.
5. Move the insertion point to the beginning of the title *COMPUTER OUTPUT DEVICES* (located at the bottom of page 2) and then insert a page break by pressing Ctrl + Enter.
6. Move the insertion point to the beginning of the heading *Printer* and then press Ctrl + Enter to insert a page break.
7. Delete the page break by completing the following steps:
   a. Click the Draft button in the view area on the Status bar.
   b. With the insertion point positioned at the beginning of the heading *Printer*, press the Backspace key. (This displays the page break in the document.)
   c. Press the Backspace key again to delete the page break.
   d. Click the Print Layout button in the view area of the Status bar.
8. Pressing the Backspace key removed the formatting from the Printer heading. Apply formatting by completing the following steps;
   a. Move the insertion point to any character in the heading *Monitor*.
   b. Click the Home tab and then click once on the Format Painter button.
   c. Select the heading *Printer*.
9. Save **WL1-C4-P3-CompDevices.docx**.

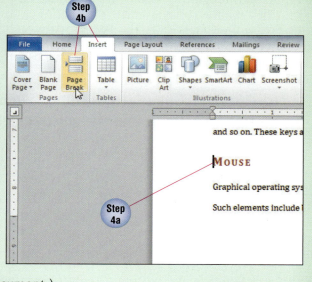

Blank Page

Cover Page

▼ **Quick Steps**

Insert Blank Page
1. Click Insert tab.
2. Click Blank Page button.

Insert Cover Page
1. Click Insert tab.
2. Click Cover Page button.
3. Click desired cover page at drop-down list.

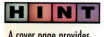

A cover page provides a polished and professional look to a document.

Inserting a Blank Page

Click the Blank Page button in the Pages group in the Insert tab to insert a blank page at the position of the insertion point. This might be useful in a document where you want to insert a blank page for an illustration, graphic, or figure.

Inserting a Cover Page

If you are preparing a document for distribution to others or you want to simply improve the visual appeal of your document, consider inserting a cover page. With the Cover Page button in the Pages group in the Insert tab, you can insert a predesigned and formatted cover page and then type personalized text in specific locations on the page. Click the Cover Page button and a drop-down list displays. The drop-down list provides a visual representation of the cover page. Scroll through the list and then click the desired cover page.

A predesigned cover page contains location placeholders where you can enter specific information. For example, a cover page might contain the placeholder *[Type the document title]*. Click anywhere in the placeholder text and the placeholder text is selected. With the placeholder text selected, type the desired text. You can delete a placeholder by clicking anywhere in the placeholder text, clicking the placeholder tab, and then pressing the Delete key.

Project 3b — Inserting a Blank Page and a Cover Page — Part 2 of 3

1. With **WL1-C4-P3-CompDevices.docx** open, create a blank page by completing the following steps:
    a. Move the insertion point to the beginning of the heading *Touchpad and Touchscreen* located on the second page.
    b. Click the Insert tab.
    c. Click the Blank Page button in the Pages group.
2. Insert a cover page by completing the following steps:
    a. Press Ctrl + Home to move the insertion point to the beginning of the document.
    b. Click the Cover Page button in the Pages group.
    c. At the drop-down list, scroll down and then click the *Motion* cover page.
    d. Click anywhere in the placeholder text *[Type the document title]* and then type **Computer Devices**.

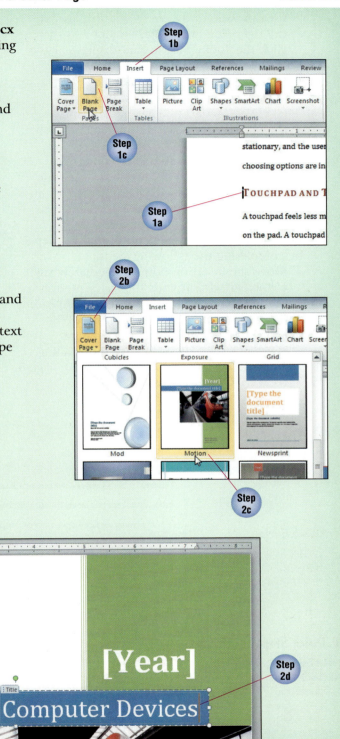

Chapter 4 ■ Formatting Pages   119

e. Click the placeholder text *[Year]*. Click the down-pointing arrow that displays at the right side of the placeholder and then click the Today button that displays at the bottom of the drop-down calendar.
f. Click anywhere in the placeholder text *[Type the company name]* and then type **Drake Computing**. (If a name displays in the placeholder, select the name and then type **Drake Computing**.)
g. Click anywhere in the placeholder text *[Type the author name]* and then type your first and last names. (If a name displays in the placeholder, select the name and then type your first and last names.)

3. Remove the blank page you inserted in Step 1 by completing the following steps:
   a. Move the insertion point immediately right of the period that ends the last sentence in the paragraph of text in the *Trackball* heading (located toward the bottom of page 3).
   b. Press the Delete key on the keyboard approximately six times until the heading *Touch Pad and Touch Screen* displays on page 3.
4. Save **WL1-C4-P3-CompDevices.docx**.

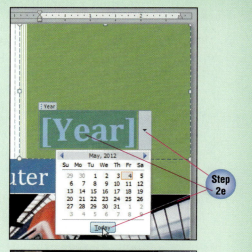
Step 2e

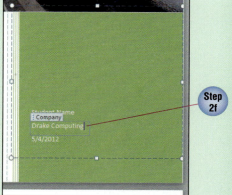
Step 2f

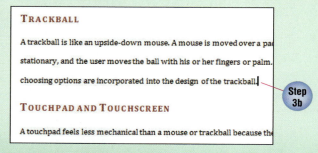
Step 3b

Inserting Predesigned Page Numbering

Quick Steps

Insert Page Numbering
1. Click Insert tab.
2. Click Page Number button.
3. Click desired option at drop-down list.

Page Number

Word, by default, does not print page numbers on a page. If you want to insert page numbering in a document, use the Page Number button in the Header & Footer group in the Insert tab. When you click the Page Number button, a drop-down list displays with options for specifying the page number location. Point to an option at this list and a drop-down list displays of predesigned page number formats. Scroll through the options in the drop-down list and then click the desired option. If you want to change the format of page numbering in a document, double-click the page number, select the page number text, and then apply the desired formatting. You can remove page numbering from a document by clicking the Page Number button and then clicking *Remove Page Numbers* at the drop-down list.

Project 3c Inserting Predesigned Page Numbering

Part 3 of 3

1. With **WL1-C4-P3-CompDevices.docx** open, insert page numbering by completing the following steps:
   a. Move the insertion point so it is positioned on any character in the title *COMPUTER INPUT DEVICES*.
   b. Click the Insert tab.
   c. Click the Page Number button in the Header & Footer group and then point to *Top of Page*.
   d. Scroll through the drop-down list and then click the *Brackets 2* option.

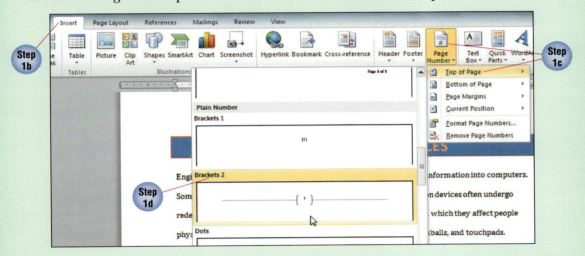

2. Double-click the document to make it active and then scroll through the document and notice the page numbering that displays at the top of each page except the cover page. (The cover page and text are divided by a section break, which you will learn more about in Chapter 5. Word considers the cover page as page 1 but does not include the numbering on the page.)
3. Remove the page numbering by clicking the Insert tab, clicking the Page Number button, and then clicking *Remove Page Numbers* at the drop-down list.
4. Click the Page Number button, point to *Bottom of Page*, scroll down the drop-down list and then click the *Accent Bar 2* option.
5. Double-click in the document to make it active.
6. Save, print, and then close **WL1-C4-P3-CompDevices.docx**.

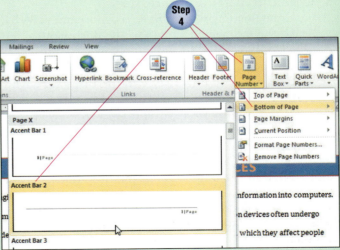

Chapter 4 ■ Formatting Pages   121

Project 4 Add Elements to a Report on the Future of the Internet   3 Parts

You will open a document containing information on the future of the Internet, insert a predesigned header and footer in the document, remove a header, and format and delete header and footer elements.

Inserting Predesigned Headers and Footers

▼ **Quick Steps**

Insert Predesigned Header
1. Click Insert tab.
2. Click Header button.
3. Click desired option at drop-down list.
4. Type text in specific placeholders in header.

Header

Text that appears at the top of every page is called a *header* and text that appears at the bottom of every page is referred to as a *footer*. Headers and footers are common in manuscripts, textbooks, reports, and other publications. Insert a predesigned header in a document by clicking the Insert tab and then clicking the Header button in the Header & Footer group. This displays the Header drop-down list. At this list, click the desired predesigned header option and the header is inserted in the document. Headers and footers are visible in Print Layout view but not Draft view.

A predesigned header or footer may contain location placeholders where you can enter specific information. For example, a header might contain the placeholder *[Type the document title]*. Click anywhere in the placeholder text and all of the placeholder text is selected. With the placeholder text selected, type the desired text. You can delete a placeholder by clicking anywhere in the placeholder text, clicking the placeholder tab, and then pressing the Delete key.

Project 4a Inserting a Predesigned Header in a Document   Part 1 of 3

1. Open **InternetFuture.docx**.
2. Save the document with Save As and name it **WL1-C4-P4-InternetFuture**.
3. Make the following changes to the document:
   a. Select the entire document, change the line spacing to *2*, and then deselect the document.
   b. Apply the Heading 1 style to the title *FUTURE OF THE INTERNET*.
   c. Apply the Heading 2 style to the headings *Satellite Internet Connections*, *Second Internet*, *Internet Services for a Fee*, and *Internet in 2030*.
   d. Change the Quick Styles set to *Formal*. **Hint: Use the Change Styles button in the Styles group in the Home tab**.
   e. Apply the Origin theme by clicking the Page Layout tab, clicking the Themes button, and then clicking *Origin* at the drop-down gallery.
   f. Move the insertion point to the beginning of the heading *INTERNET IN 2030* (located toward the bottom of page 2) and then insert a page break by clicking the Insert tab and then clicking the Page Break button in the Pages group.

4. Press Ctrl + Home to move the insertion point to the beginning of the document and then insert a header by completing the following steps:
   a. If necessary, click the Insert tab.
   b. Click the Header button in the Header & Footer group.
   c. Scroll to the bottom of the drop-down list that displays and then click *Tiles*.
   d. Click anywhere in the placeholder text *[Type the document title]* and then type **Future of the Internet**.
   e. Click anywhere in the placeholder text *[Year]* and then type the current year.
   f. Double-click in the document text. (This makes the document text active and dims the header.)
5. Scroll through the document to see how the header will print.
6. Save and then print **WL1-C4-P4-InternetFuture.docx**.

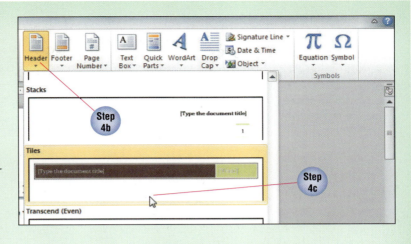

Insert a predesigned footer in the same manner as inserting a header. Click the Footer button in the Header & Footer group in the Insert tab and a drop-down list displays similar to the Header drop-down list. Click the desired footer and the predesigned footer formatting is applied to the document.

Removing a Header or Footer

Remove a header from a document by clicking the Insert tab and then clicking the Header button in the Header & Footer group. At the drop-down list that displays, click the *Remove Header* option. Complete similar steps to remove a footer.

▼ Quick Steps

Insert Predesigned Footer
1. Click Insert tab.
2. Click Footer button.
3. Click desired option at drop-down list.
4. Type text in specific placeholders in footer.

Footer

Project 4b — Removing a Header and Inserting a Predesigned Footer — Part 2 of 3

1. With **WL1-C4-P4-InternetFuture.docx** open, press Ctrl + Home to move the insertion point to the beginning of the document.

Chapter 4 ■ Formatting Pages   123

2. Remove the header by clicking the Insert tab, clicking the Header button in the Header & Footer group, and then clicking the *Remove Header* option at the drop-down menu.
3. Insert a footer in the document by completing the following steps:
   a. Click the Footer button in the Header & Footer group.
   b. Click *Alphabet* at the drop-down list.

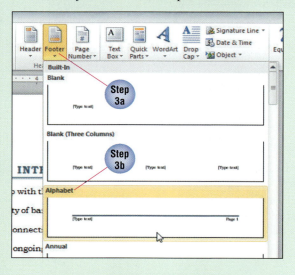

   c. Click anywhere in the placeholder text *[Type text]* and then type **Future of the Internet**.
   d. Double-click in the document text. (This makes the document text active and dims the footer.)
4. Scroll through the document to see how the footer will print.
5. Save and then print **WL1-C4-P4-InternetFuture.docx**.

You can double-click a header or footer in Print Layout view to display the header or footer pane for editing.

Editing a Predesigned Header or Footer

Predesigned headers and footers contain elements such as page numbers and a title. You can change the formatting of the element by clicking the desired element and then applying the desired formatting. You can also select and then delete an item.

Project 4c — Formatting and Deleting Header and Footer Elements — Part 3 of 3

1. With **WL1-C4-P4-InternetFuture.docx** open, remove the footer by clicking the Insert tab, clicking the Footer button, and then clicking *Remove Footer* at the drop-down list.

2. Insert and then format a header by completing the following steps:
   a. Click the Header button in the Header & Footer group in the Insert tab, scroll in the drop-down list, and then click *Motion (Odd Page)*. (This header inserts the document title as well as the page number.)
   b. Delete the document title from the header by clicking anywhere in the text FUTURE OF THE INTERNET, selecting the text, and then pressing the Delete key.
   c. Double-click in the document text.
3. Insert and then format a footer by completing the following steps:
   a. Click the Insert tab.
   b. Click the Footer button, scroll down the drop-down list, and then click *Motion (Odd Page)*.
   c. Click on any character in the date that displays in the footer, select the date, and then type the current date.
   d. Select the date, turn on bold, and then change the font size to 12.
   e. Double-click in the document text.
4. Scroll through the document to see how the header and footer will print.
5. Save, print, and then close **WL1-C4-P4-InternetFuture.docx**.

Project 5 Format a Report on Robots   2 Parts

You will open a document containing information on the difficulties of creating a humanlike robot and then insert a watermark, change page background color, and insert a page border.

Formatting the Page Background

The Page Background group in the Page Layout tab contains three buttons for customizing a page background. Click the Watermark button and choose a predesigned watermark from a drop-down list. If a document is going to be viewed on-screen or on the Web, consider adding a page color. In Chapter 3, you learned how to apply borders and shading to text at the Borders and Shading dialog box. This dialog box also contains options for inserting a page border.

Inserting a Watermark

A *watermark* is a lightened image that displays behind text in a document. Using watermarks is an excellent way to add visual appeal to a document. Word provides a number of predesigned watermarks you can insert in a document. Display these watermarks by clicking the Watermark button in the Page Background group in the Page Layout tab. Scroll through the list of watermarks and then click the desired option.

Quick Steps

Insert Watermark
1. Click Page Layout tab.
2. Click Watermark button.
3. Click desired option at drop-down list.

Change Page Color
1. Click Page Layout tab.
2. Click Page Color button.
3. Click desired option at color palette.

Watermark

Changing Page Color

Page Color

Use the Page Color button in the Page Background group to apply background color to a document. This background color is intended for viewing a document on-screen or on the Web. The color is visible on the screen but does not print. Insert a page color by clicking the Page Color button and then clicking the desired color at the color palette.

Project 5a — Inserting a Watermark and Page Color — Part 1 of 2

1. Open **Robots.docx** and then save the document with Save As and name it **WL1-C4-P5-Robots**.
2. Apply the Heading 1 style to the title *ROBOTS AS ANDROIDS* and the Heading 3 style to the five headings in the document. (You may need to click the Heading 2 style to display the Heading 3 style.)
3. Change the Quick Styles set to *Thatch* and then center the document title *ROBOTS AS ANDROIDS*.
4. Change the top margin to 1.5 inches.
5. Apply the Aspect theme.
6. Insert a page break at the beginning of the heading *Tactile Perception*.
7. Insert a watermark by completing the following steps:
    a. Move the insertion point to the beginning of the document.
    b. Click the Page Layout tab.
    c. Click the Watermark button in the Page Background group.
    d. At the drop-down list, click the *CONFIDENTIAL 1* option.

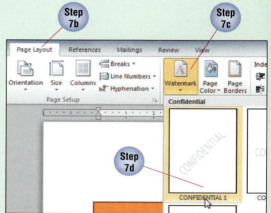

8. Scroll through the document and notice how the watermark displays behind the text.
9. Remove the watermark and insert a different one by completing the following steps:
    a. Click the Watermark button in the Page Background group and then click *Remove Watermark* at the drop-down list.
    b. Click the Watermark button and then click *DO NOT COPY 1* at the drop-down list.

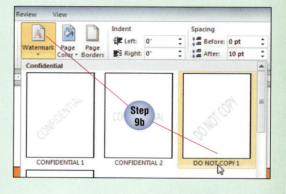

10. Scroll through the document and notice how the watermark displays.
11. Move the insertion point to the beginning of the document.
12. Click the Page Color button in the Page Background group and then click *Dark Green, Accent 4, Lighter 80%* at the color palette.
13. Save **WL1-C4-P5-Robots.docx**.

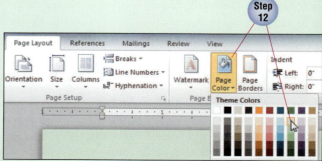

Inserting a Page Border

To improve the visual appeal of a document, consider inserting a page border. When you insert a page border in a multiple-page document, the border prints on each page. To insert a page border, click the Page Borders button in the Page Background group in the Page Layout tab. This displays the Borders and Shading dialog box with the Page Border tab selected as shown in Figure 4.5. At this dialog box, you can specify the border style, color, and width.

The dialog box contains an option for inserting a page border containing an image. To display the images available, click the down-pointing arrow at the right side of the *Art* list box. Scroll down the drop-down list and then click the desired image. (This feature may need to be installed the first time you use it.)

Changing Page Border Options

By default, a page border displays and prints 24 points from the top, left, right, and bottom edges of the page. Some printers, particularly inkjet printers, have a nonprinting area around the outside edges of the page that can interfere with the printing of a border. Before printing a document with a page border, click the File tab and then click the Print tab. Look at the preview of the page at the right side of the Print tab Backstage view and determine whether the entire border is visible. If a portion of the border is not visible in the preview page (generally at the bottom and right side of the page), consider changing measurements at the Border and Shading Options dialog box shown in Figure 4.6. You can also change measurements at the Border and Shading Options dialog box to control the location of the page border on the page.

Display the Border and Shading Options dialog box by clicking the Page Layout tab and then clicking the Page Borders button. At the Borders and Shading dialog box with the Page Border tab selected, click the Options button that displays in the lower right corner of the dialog box. The options at the Border and Shading Options dialog box change depending on whether you click the Options button at the Borders and Shading dialog box with the Borders tab selected or the Page Border tab selected.

▼ **Quick Steps**

Insert Page Border
1. Click Page Layout tab.
2. Click Page Borders button.
3. Specify desired options at dialog box.

Page Borders

Figure 4.5 Borders and Shading Dialog Box with Page Border Tab Selected

Figure 4.6 Border and Shading Options Dialog Box

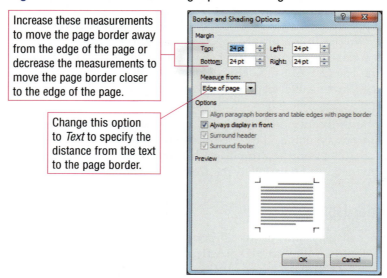

Increase these measurements to move the page border away from the edge of the page or decrease the measurements to move the page border closer to the edge of the page.

Change this option to *Text* to specify the distance from the text to the page border.

If your printer contains a nonprinting area and the entire page border will not print, consider increasing the spacing from the page border to the edge of the page. Do this with the *Top*, *Left*, *Bottom*, and/or *Right* measurement boxes. The *Measure from* option box has a default setting of *Edge of page*. You can change this option to *Text*, which changes the top and bottom measurements to *1 pt* and the left and right measurements to *4 pt* and moves the page border into the page. Use the measurement boxes to specify the distance you want the page border displayed and printed from the text in the document.

Project 5b Inserting a Page Border   Part 2 of 2

1. With **WL1-C4-P5-Robots.docx** open, remove the page color by clicking the Page Color button in the Page Background group in the Page Layout tab and then clicking *No Color* at the color palette.
2. Insert a page border by completing the following steps:
   a. Click the Page Borders button in the Page Background group in the Page Layout tab.
   b. Click the *Box* option in the *Setting* section.
   c. Scroll down the list of line styles in the *Style* list box until the end of the list displays and then click the third line from the end.
   d. Click the down-pointing arrow at the right of the *Color* list box and then click *Red, Accent 2, Darker 25%* at the color palette.
   e. Click OK to close the dialog box.

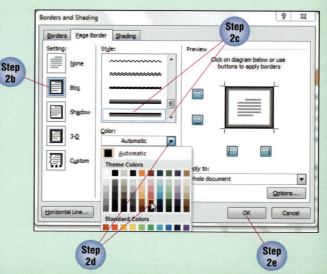

3. Increase the spacing from the page border to the edges of the page by completing the following steps:
   a. Click the Page Borders button in the Page Background group in the Page Layout tab.
   b. At the Borders and Shading dialog box with the Page Border tab selected, click the Options button located in the lower right corner.
   c. At the Border and Shading Options dialog box, click the up-pointing arrow at the right side of the *Top* measurement box until *31 pt* displays. (This is the maximum measurement allowed.)
   d. Increase the measurement for the *Left, Bottom,* and *Right* measurement boxes to *31 pt*.
   e. Click OK to close the Border and Shading Options dialog box.
   f. Click OK to close the Borders and Shading dialog box.
4. Save **WL1-C4-P5-Robots.docx** and then print only page 1.
5. Insert an image page border and change the page border spacing options by completing the following steps:
   a. Click the Page Borders button in the Page Background group in the Page Layout tab.
   b. Click the down-pointing arrow at the right side of the *Art* list box and then click the border image shown below (located approximately one-third of the way down the drop-down list).
   c. Click the Options button located in the lower right corner of the Borders and Shading dialog box.
   d. At the Border and Shading Options dialog box, click the down-pointing arrow at the right of the *Measure from* option box and then click *Text* at the drop-down list.
   e. Click the up-pointing arrow at the right of the *Top* measurement box until *10 pt* displays.
   f. Increase the measurement for the *Bottom* measurement to *10 pt* and the measurement in the *Left* and *Right* measurement boxes to *14 pt*.
   g. Click the *Surround header* check box to remove the check mark.
   h. Click the *Surround footer* check box to remove the check mark.
   i. Click OK to close the Border and Shading Options dialog box.
   j. Click OK to close the Borders and Shading dialog box.
6. Save, print, and then close **WL1-C4-P5-Robots.docx**.

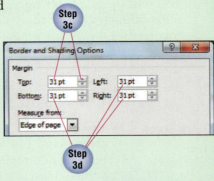
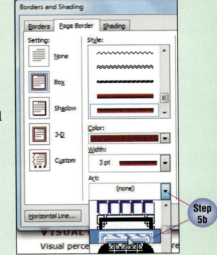
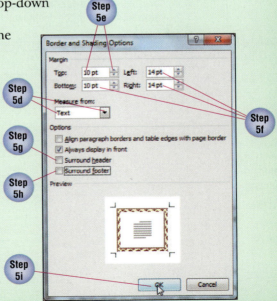

Chapter 4 ■ Formatting Pages

Project 6 Format a Lease Agreement Document   4 Parts

You will open a lease agreement document, search for specific text and replace it with other text, and then search for specific formatting and replace it with other formatting.

Finding and Replacing Text and Formatting

Quick Steps

Find Text
1. Click Find button in Home tab.
2. Type search text.
3. Click Next Search Result button.

Find

Replace

With Word's Find feature you can search for specific characters or formatting. With the Find and Replace feature, you can search for specific characters or formatting and replace them with other characters or formatting. The Find button and the Replace button are located in the Editing group in the Home tab.

Click the Find button in the Editing group in the Home tab (or press the keyboard shortcut, Ctrl + F) and the Navigation pane displays at the left side of the screen with the third tab selected. Hover the mouse over the third tab and a ScreenTip displays with the information *Browse the results from your current search*. With this tab selected, type search text in the Search text box and any occurrence of the text in the document is highlighted and a fragment of the text surrounding the search text displays in a thumbnail in the Navigation pane. For example, search for *Lessee* in the WL1-C4-P6-LeaseAgrmnt.docx document and the screen displays as shown in Figure 4.7. Notice that any occurrence of *Lessee* displays highlighted in yellow in the document and the Navigation pane displays thumbnails of text surrounding the occurrences of *Lessee*.

Figure 4.7 Navigation Pane Showing Search Results

130 Word Level 1 ■ Unit 1

Click a text thumbnail in the Navigation pane and the occurrence of the search text is selected in the document. If you hover your mouse over a text thumbnail in the Navigation pane, the page number location displays in a small box near the mouse pointer. You can also move to the next occurrence of the search text by clicking the Next Search Result button located towards the upper right side of the Navigation pane. Click the Previous Search Result button to move to the previous occurrence of the search text.

Click the down-pointing arrow at the right side of the Search text box and a drop-down list displays with options for displaying dialog boxes such as the Find Options dialog box or the Find and Replace dialog box and also options for specifying what you want to find in the document such as figures, tables, and equations.

You can also highlight search text in a document with options at the Find and Replace dialog box with the Find tab selected. Display this dialog box by clicking the Find button arrow in the Editing group in the Home tab and then clicking *Advanced Find* at the drop-down list. You can also display the Find and Replace dialog box by clicking the down-pointing arrow at the right side of the Search text box in the Navigation pane with the Find tab selected and then clicking the *Advanced Find* option at the drop-down list. To highlight find text, type the search text in the *Find what* text box, click the Reading Highlight button, and then click *Highlight All* at the drop-down list. All occurrences of the text in the document are highlighted. To remove highlighting, click the Reading Highlight button and then click *Clear Highlighting* at the drop-down list.

Project 6a Finding and Highlighting Text   Part 1 of 4

1. Open **LeaseAgrmnt.docx** and then save the document with Save As and name it **WL1-C4-P6-LeaseAgrmnt**.
2. Find all occurrences of *lease* by completing the following steps:
   a. Click the Find button in the Editing group in the Home tab.
   b. Type **lease** in the search text box in the Navigation pane.
   c. After a moment, all occurrences of *lease* in the document are highlighted and text thumbnails display in the Navigation pane. Click a couple of the text thumbnails in the Navigation pane to select the text in the document.
   d. Click the Previous Search Result button to select the previous occurrence of *lease* in the document.
3. Use the Find and Replace dialog box with the Find tab selected to highlight all occurrences of *Premises* in the document by completing the following steps:
   a. Click in the document and press Ctrl + Home to move the insertion point to the beginning of the document.
   b. Click the down-pointing arrow at the right side of the search text box in the Navigation pane and then click *Advanced Find* at the drop-down list.

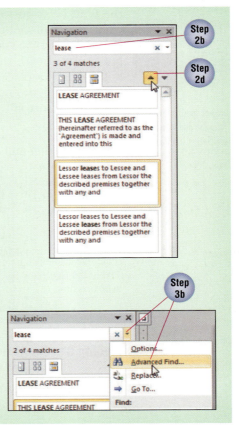

c. At the Find and Replace dialog box with the Find tab selected (and *lease* selected in the *Find what* text box), type **Premises**.
d. Click the Reading Highlight button and then click *Highlight All* at the drop-down list.
e. Click in the document to make it active and then scroll through the document and notice the occurrences of highlighted text.
f. Click in the dialog box to make it active.
g. Click the Reading Highlight button and then click *Clear Highlighting* at the drop-down list.
h. Click the Close button to close the Find and Replace dialog box.
4. Close the Navigation pane by clicking the Close button that displays in the upper right corner of the pane.

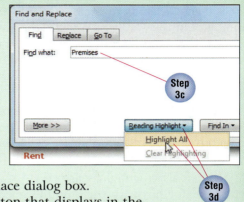

Finding and Replacing Text

Find and Replace Text
1. Click Replace button in Home tab.
2. Type search text.
3. Press Tab key.
4. Type replace text.
5. Click Replace or Replace All button.

HINT If the Find and Replace dialog box is in the way of specific text, drag the dialog box to a different location.

To find and replace text, click the Replace button in the Editing group in the Home tab or use the keyboard shortcut, Ctrl + H. This displays the Find and Replace dialog box with the Replace tab selected as shown in Figure 4.8. Type the text you want to find in the *Find what* text box, press the Tab key, and then type the replacement text.

The Find and Replace dialog box contains several command buttons. Click the Find Next button to tell Word to find the next occurrence of the characters. Click the Replace button to replace the characters and find the next occurrence. If you know that you want all occurrences of the characters in the *Find what* text box replaced with the characters in the *Replace with* text box, click the Replace All button. This replaces every occurrence from the location of the insertion point to the beginning or end of the document (depending on the search direction). Click the Cancel button to close the Find and Replace dialog box.

Figure 4.8 Find and Replace Dialog Box with the Replace Tab Selected

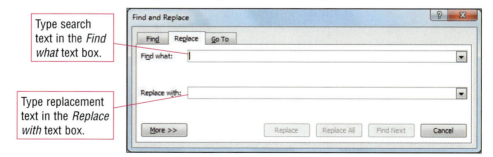

Project 6b — Finding and Replacing Text — Part 2 of 4

1. With **WL1-C4-P6-LeaseAgrmnt.docx** open, make sure the insertion point is positioned at the beginning of the document.

2. Find all occurrences of *Lessor* and replace with *Tracy Hartford* by completing the following steps:
   a. Click the Replace button in the Editing group in the Home tab.
   b. At the Find and Replace dialog box with the Replace tab selected, type **Lessor** in the *Find what* text box.
   c. Press the Tab key to move the insertion point to the *Replace with* text box.
   d. Type **Tracy Hartford**.
   e. Click the Replace All button.
   f. At the message *Word has completed its search of the document and has made 11 replacements*, click OK. (Do not close the Find and Replace dialog box.)
3. With the Find and Replace dialog box still open, complete steps similar to those in Step 2 to find all occurrences of *Lessee* and replace with *Michael Iwami*.
4. Close the Find and Replace dialog box.
5. Save **WL1-C4-P6-LeaseAgrmnt.docx**.

Choosing Check Box Options

The Find and Replace dialog box contains a variety of check boxes with options you can choose for completing a search. To display these options, click the More button located at the bottom of the dialog box. This causes the Find and Replace dialog box to expand as shown in Figure 4.9. Each option and what will occur if

Figure 4.9 Expanded Find and Replace Dialog Box

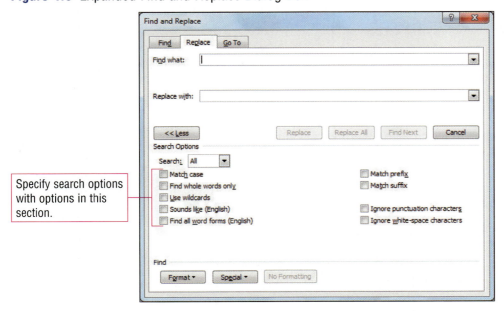

Specify search options with options in this section.

Chapter 4 ■ Formatting Pages   133

it is selected is described in Table 4.2. To remove the display of options, click the Less button. (The Less button was previously the More button.) Note that if you make a mistake when replacing text, you can close the Find and Replace dialog box and then click the Undo button on the Quick Access toolbar.

Table 4.2 Options at the Expanded Find and Replace Dialog Box

Choose this option	To
Match case	Exactly match the case of the search text. For example, if you search for *Book* and select the *Match case* option, Word will stop at *Book* but not *book* or *BOOK*.
Find whole words only	Find a whole word, not a part of a word. For example, if you search for *her* and did not select *Find whole words only*, Word would stop at t*her*e, *her*e, *her*s, etc.
Use wildcards	Search for wildcards, special characters, or special search operators.
Sounds like	Match words that sound alike but are spelled differently such as *know* and *no*.
Find all word forms	Find all forms of the word entered in the *Find what* text box. For example, if you enter *hold*, Word will stop at *held* and *holding*.
Match prefix	Find only those words that begin with the letters in the *Find what* text box. For example, if you enter *per*, Word will stop at words such as *perform* and *perfect* but skip words such as *super* and *hyperlink*.
Match suffix	Find only those words that end with the letters in the *Find what* text box. For example, if you enter *ly*, Word will stop at words such as *accurately* and *quietly* but skip over words such as *catalyst* and *lyre*.
Ignore punctuation characters	Ignore punctuation within characters. For example, if you enter *US* in the *Find what* text box, Word will stop at *U.S.*
Ignore white space characters	Ignore spaces between letters. For example, if you enter *F B I* in the *Find what* text box, Word will stop at *FBI*.

Project 6c — Finding and Replacing Word Forms and Suffixes — Part 3 of 4

1. With **WL1-C4-P6-LeaseAgrmnt.docx** open, make sure the insertion point is positioned at the beginning of the document.
2. Find all word forms of the word *lease* and replace with *rent* by completing the following steps:
    a. Click the Replace button in the Editing group in the Home tab.
    b. At the Find and Replace dialog box with the Replace tab selected, type **lease** in the *Find what* text box.

c. Press the Tab key and then type **rent** in the *Replace with* text box.
d. Click the More button.
e. Click the *Find all word forms (English)* option. (This inserts a check mark in the check box.)
f. Click the Replace All button.
g. At the message telling you that Replace All is not recommended with Find All Word Forms, click OK.
h. At the message *Word has completed its search of the document and has made 6 replacements*, click OK.
i. Click the *Find all word forms* option to remove the check mark.
3. Find the word *less* and replace with the word *minus* and specify that you want Word to find only those words that end in *less* by completing the following steps:
a. At the expanded Find and Replace dialog box, select the text in the *Find what* text box and then type **less**.
b. Select the text in the *Replace with* text box and then type **minus**.
c. Click the *Match suffix* check box to insert a check mark and tell Word to find only words that end in *less*.
d. Click the Replace All button.
e. At the message telling you that 2 replacements were made, click OK.
f. Click the *Match suffix* check box to remove the check mark.
g. Click the Less button.
h. Close the Find and Replace dialog box.
4. Save **WL1-C4-P6-LeaseAgrmnt.docx**.

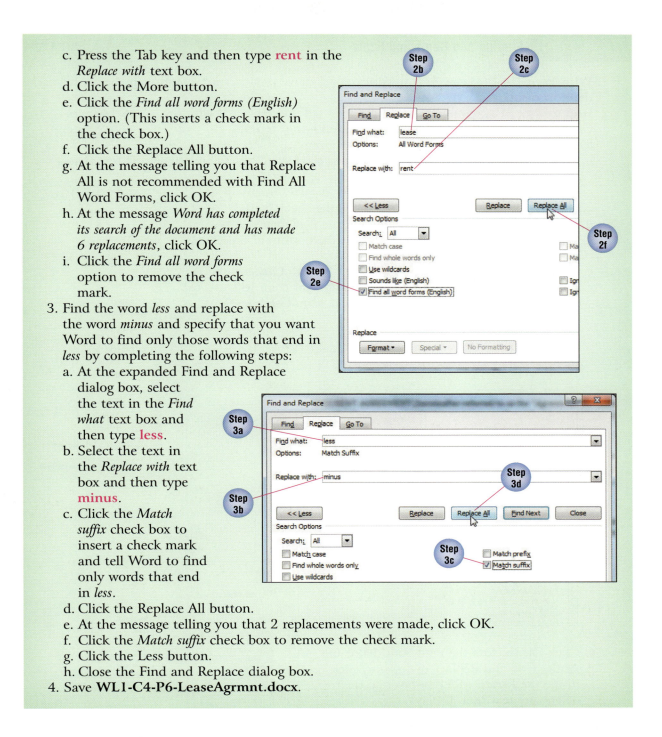

Finding and Replacing Formatting

With options at the Find and Replace dialog box with the Replace tab selected, you can search for characters containing specific formatting and replace them with other characters or formatting. To specify formatting in the Find and Replace dialog box, click the More button and then click the Format button that displays toward the bottom of the dialog box. At the pop-up list that displays, identify the type of formatting you want to find.

Project 6d Finding and Replacing Fonts   Part 4 of 4

1. With **WL1-C4-P6-LeaseAgrmnt.docx** open, move the insertion point to the beginning of the document.
2. Find text set in 12-point Candara bold dark red and replace it with text set in 14-point Calibri bold dark blue by completing the following steps:
    a. Click the Replace button in the Editing group.
    b. At the Find and Replace dialog box, press the Delete key. (This deletes any text that displays in the *Find what* text box.)
    c. Click the More button. (If a check mark displays in any of the check boxes, click the option to remove the check mark.)
    d. With the insertion point positioned in the *Find what* text box, click the Format button located toward the bottom of the dialog box and then click *Font* at the pop-up list.
    e. At the Find Font dialog box, change the Font to *Candara*, the Font style to *Bold*, the Size to *12*, and the Font color to *Dark Red* (first color option from the left in the *Standard Colors* section).

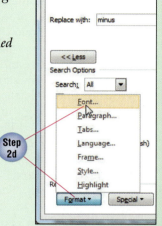

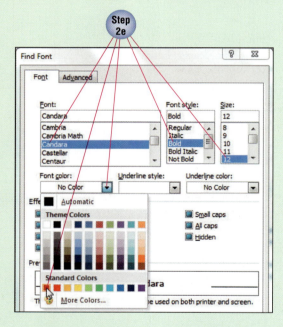

    f. Click OK to close the Find Font dialog box.
    g. At the Find and Replace dialog box, click inside the *Replace with* text box and then delete any text that displays.
    h. Click the Format button located toward the bottom of the dialog box and then click *Font* at the pop-up list.
    i. At the Replace Font dialog box, change the Font to *Calibri*, the Font style to *Bold*, the Size to *14*, and the Font color to *Dark Blue* (second color option from the right in the *Standard Colors* section).
    j. Click OK to close the Replace Font dialog box.

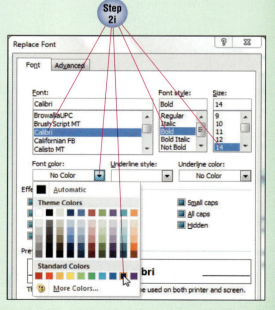

k. At the Find and Replace dialog box, click the Replace All button.
l. At the message telling you that the search of the document is complete and eight replacements were made, click OK.
m. Click in the Find what text box and then click the No Formatting button.
n. Click in the Replace with text box and then click the No Formatting button.
o. Click the Less button.
p. Close the Find and Replace dialog box.
3. Save, print, and then close **WL1-C4-P6-LeaseAgrmnt.docx**.

Chapter Summary

- You can change the document view with buttons in the View section on the Status bar or with options in the View tab.
- Print Layout is the default view, which can be changed to other views such as Draft view or Full Screen Reading view.
- The Draft view displays the document in a format for efficient editing and formatting.
- Use the Zoom slider bar to change the percentage of the display.
- Full Screen Reading view displays a document in a format for easy viewing and reading.
- Navigate in a document using the Navigation pane. Display the pane by clicking the *Navigation Pane* check box in the Show group in the View tab.
- By default, a Word document contains 1-inch top, bottom, left, and right margins. Change margins with preset margin settings at the Margins button drop-down list or with options at the Page Setup dialog box with the Margins tab selected.
- The default page orientation is portrait, which can be changed to landscape with the Orientation button in the Page Setup group in the Page Layout tab.
- The default page size is 8.5 by 11 inches, which can be changed with options at the Size drop-down list or options at the Page Setup dialog box with the Paper tab selected.
- The page break that Word inserts automatically is a soft page break. A page break that you insert is a hard page break. Insert a page break with the Page Break button in the Pages group in the Insert tab or by pressing Ctrl + Enter.
- Insert a predesigned and formatted cover page by clicking the Cover Page button in the Pages group in the Insert tab and then clicking the desired option at the drop-down list.
- Insert predesigned and formatted page numbering by clicking the Page Number button in the Header & Footer group in the Insert tab, specifying the desired location of page numbers, and then clicking the desired page numbering option.
- You can insert predesigned headers and footers in a document with the Header button and the Footer button in the Header & Footer group in the Insert tab.
- A watermark is a lightened image that displays behind text in a document. Use the Watermark button in the Page Background group in the Page Layout tab to insert a watermark.

- Insert page color in a document with the Page Color button in the Page Background group. Page color is designed for viewing a document on-screen and does not print.
- Click the Page Borders button in the Page Background group and the Borders and Shading dialog box with the Page Border tab selected displays. Use options at this dialog box to insert a page border or an image page border in a document.
- Use the Find feature to search for specific characters or formatting. Use the Find and Replace feature to search for specific characters or formatting and replace with other characters or formatting.
- At the Find and Replace dialog box, click the Find Next button to find the next occurrence of the characters and/or formatting. Click the Replace button to replace the characters or formatting and find the next occurrence, or click the Replace All button to replace all occurrences of the characters or formatting.
- Click the More button at the Find and Replace dialog box to display additional options for completing a search.

Commands Review

FEATURE	RIBBON TAB, GROUP	BUTTON, OPTION	KEYBOARD SHORTCUT
Blank page	Insert, Pages		
Borders and Shading dialog box with Page Border tab selected	Page Layout, Page Background		
Border and Shading Options dialog box	Page Layout, Page Background	, Options	
Cover page	Insert, Pages		
Draft view	View, Document Views		
Find and Replace dialog box with Find tab selected	Home, Editing	, Advanced Find	
Find and Replace dialog box with Replace tab selected	Home, Editing		Ctrl + H
Footer	Insert, Header & Footer		
Full Screen Reading view	View, Document Views		
Header	Insert, Header & Footer		
Margins	Page Layout, Page Setup		
Navigation Pane	View, Show		Ctrl + F
Orientation	Page Layout, Page Setup		
Page break	Insert, Pages		Ctrl + Enter

FEATURE	RIBBON TAB, GROUP	BUTTON, OPTION	KEYBOARD SHORTCUT
Page color	Page Layout, Page Background		
Page numbering	Insert, Header & Footer		
Page Setup dialog box with Margins tab selected	Page Layout, Page Setup	, Custom Margins OR	
Page Setup dialog box with Paper tab selected	Page Layout, Page Setup	, More Paper Sizes	
Page size	Page Layout, Page Setup		
Print Layout view	View, Document Views		
Watermark	Page Layout, Page Background		

Concepts Check Test Your Knowledge

Completion: In the space provided at the right, indicate the correct term, symbol, or command.

1. This is the default measurement for the top, bottom, left, and right margins.

2. This view displays a document in a format for efficient editing and formatting.

3. This view displays a document in a format for easy viewing and reading.

4. The Navigation pane check box is located in this group in the View tab.

5. To remove white space, double-click this icon.

6. This is the default page orientation.

7. Set specific margins at this dialog box with the Margins tab selected.

8. Press these keys on the keyboard to insert a page break.

9. The Cover Page button is located in the Pages group in this tab.

10. Text that appears at the top of every page is called this.

11. A footer displays in Print Layout view, but not this view.

12. A lightened image that displays behind text in a document is called this. _____

13. Change the position of the page border from the edge of the page with options at this dialog box. _____

14. The Page Borders button displays in this group in the Page Layout tab. _____

15. If you want to replace every occurrence of what you are searching for in a document, click this button at the Find and Replace dialog box. _____

16. Click this option at the Find and Replace dialog box if you are searching for a word and all of its forms. _____

Skills Check Assess Your Performance

Assessment

1 FORMAT A SOFTWARE LIFE CYCLE DOCUMENT AND CREATE A COVER PAGE

1. Open **SoftwareCycle.docx** and then save the document with Save As and name it **WL1-C4-A1-SoftwareCycle**.
2. Select the entire document, change the line spacing to *2*, and then deselect the document.
3. Apply the Heading 1 style to the title of the document and apply the Heading 2 style to the headings in the document.
4. Change the Quick Styles set to *Fancy*.
5. Select the entire document and then remove italic formatting.
6. Change the theme colors to *Elemental*. (Make sure you change the theme colors and not the theme.)
7. Insert a page break at the beginning of the heading *Testing*.
8. Move the insertion point to the beginning of the document and then insert the *Austere* cover page.
9. Insert the following text in the specified fields:
    a. Insert the current year in the *[Year]* placeholder.
    b. Insert your school's name in the *[Type the company name]* placeholder. (If a company displays, select the name and then type your school's name.)
    c. If a name displays below your school's name, select the name and then type your first and last names.
    d. Insert **software life cycle** in the *[TYPE THE DOCUMENT TITLE]* placeholder (the placeholder will convert the text you type to all uppercase letters).
    e. Click the text below the document title, click the Abstract tab, and then press the Delete key.
10. Move the insertion point to any character in the title *COMMERCIAL LIFE CYCLE* and then insert the *Thin Line* page numbering at the bottom of the pages (the page numbering will not appear on the cover page).
11. Save, print, and then close **WL1-C4-A1-SoftwareCycle.docx**.

Assessment 2 FORMAT AN INTELLECTUAL PROPERTY REPORT AND INSERT HEADERS AND FOOTERS

1. Open **IntelProp.docx** and then save the document with Save As and name it **WL1-C4-A2-IntelProp**.
2. Select text from the beginning of the first paragraph of text to just above the *REFERENCES* title located toward the end of the document and then indent the first line to 0.25 inch.
3. Apply the Heading 1 style to the titles *PROPERTY PROTECTION ISSUES* and *REFERENCES* (located toward the end of the document).
4. Apply the Heading 2 style to the headings in the document.
5. Change the Quick Styles set to *Distinctive* and change the paragraph spacing to *Relaxed*. (Use the Change Styles button to make these changes.)
6. Center the *PROPERTY PROTECTION ISSUES* and *REFERENCES* titles.
7. Select and then hang indent the paragraphs below the *REFERENCES* title.
8. Insert a page break at the beginning of the *REFERENCES* title.
9. Move the insertion point to the beginning of the document and then insert the *Exposure* header. Type **Property Protection Issues** in the *[Type the document title]* placeholder and, if necessary, insert the current date in the *[Pick the date]* placeholder.
10. Insert the *Pinstripes* footer and type your first and last names in the *[Type text]* placeholder.
11. Save and then print **WL1-C4-A2-IntelProp.docx**.
12. Remove the header and footer.
13. Insert the *Austere (Odd Page)* footer and then make the following changes:
    a. Delete the *[Type the company name]* placeholder.
    b. Select the text and page number in the footer and then change the font size to 12 and turn on bold.
14. Insert the *DRAFT 1* watermark in the document.
15. Insert a page border of your choosing to the document.
16. Display the Border and Shading Options dialog box and then change the top, left, bottom, and right measurements to *31 pt*. **Hint: Display the Border and Shading Options dialog box by clicking the Options button at the Borders and Shading dialog box with the Page Border tab selected.**
17. Save, print, and then close **WL1-C4-A2-IntelProp.docx**.

Assessment 3 FORMAT A REAL ESTATE AGREEMENT

1. Open **REAgrmnt.docx** and then save the document with Save As and name it **WL1-C4-A3-REAgrmnt**.
2. Find all occurrences of *BUYER* (matching the case) and replace with *James Berman*.
3. Find all occurrences of *SELLER* (matching the case) and replace with *Mona Trammell*.
4. Find all word forms of the word *buy* and replace with *purchase*.
5. Search for 14-point Tahoma bold formatting in dark red and replace with 12-point Constantia bold formatting in black.
6. Insert page numbers at the bottom center of each page.
7. Save, print, and then close **WL1-C4-A3-REAgrmnt.docx**.

Visual Benchmark — Demonstrate Your Proficiency

FORMAT A RESUME STYLES REPORT

1. Open **ResumeStyles.docx** and then save it with Save As and name it **WL1-C4-VB-ResumeStyles**.
2. Format the document so it appears as shown in Figure 4.10 with the following specifications:
   - Change the top margin to 1.5 inches.
   - Apply the Heading 1 style to the title and the Heading 2 style to the headings.
   - Change the Quick Styles set to *Formal*.
   - Apply the Aspect theme and then change the theme colors to *Origin*.
   - Insert the *Tiles* header and the *Tiles* footer. Insert the appropriate text in placeholders and/or delete placeholders so your headers and footers display similar to what you see in Figure 4.10.
   - Apply other formatting so your document appears the same as the document shown in the figure.
   - Insert the *Tiles* cover page and insert the text in the placeholders and/or delete placeholders so your coverage page displays similar to what you see in Figure 4.10.
3. Save, print, and then close **WL1-C4-VB-ResumeStyles.docx**.

Case Study — Apply Your Skills

Part 1

You work for Citizens for Consumer Safety, a nonprofit organization providing information on household safety. Your supervisor, Melinda Johansson, has asked you to attractively format a document on smoke detectors. She will be using the document as an informational handout during a presentation on smoke detectors. Open the document named **SmokeDetectors.docx** and then save the document with Save As and name it **WL1-C4-CS-P1-SmokeDetectors**. Apply a theme to the document and apply appropriate styles to the title and headings. Ms. Johansson has asked you to change the page orientation and then change the left and right margins to 1.5 inches. She wants the extra space at the left and right margins so audience members can write notes in the margins. Use the Help feature or experiment with the options in the Header & Footer Tools Design tab and figure out how to number pages on every page but the first page. Insert page numbering in the document that prints at the top right side of every page except the first page. Save, print, and then close **WL1-C4-CS-P1-SmokeDetectors.docx**.

Figure 4.10 Visual Benchmark

Part 2

After reviewing the formatted document on smoke detectors, Ms. Johansson has decided that she wants the document to print in the default orientation and she is not happy with the theme and style choices. She also noticed that the term "smoke alarm" should be replaced with "smoke detector." She has asked you to open and then format the original document. Open **SmokeDetectors.docx** and then save the document with Save As and name it **WL1-C4-CS-P2-SmokeDetectors**. Apply a theme to the document (other than the one you chose for Part 1) and apply styles to the title and headings. Search for all occurrences of *smoke alarm* and replace with *smoke detector*. Insert a cover page of your choosing and insert the appropriate information in the page. Use the Help feature or experiment with the options in the Header & Footer Tools Design tab and figure out how to insert an odd-page and even-page footer in a document. Insert an odd-page footer that prints the page number at the right margin and insert an even-page footer that prints the page number at the left margin. You do not want the footer to print on the cover page so make sure you position the insertion point below the cover page before inserting the footers. After inserting the footers in the document, you decide that they need to be moved down the page to create more space between the last line of text on a page and the footer. Use the Help feature or experiment with the options in the Header & Footer Tools Design tab to figure out how to move the footers down and then edit each footer so they display 0.3" from the bottom of the page. Save, print, and then close **WL1-C4-CS-P2-SmokeDetectors.docx**.

Part 3

Ms. Johansson has asked you to prepare a document on infant car seats and car seat safety. She wants this informational car seat safety document available for distribution at a local community center. Use the Internet to find websites that provide information on child and infant car seats and car seat safety. Write a report on the information you find that includes at least the following information:

- Description of the types of car seats (such as rear-facing, convertible, forward-facing, built-in, and booster)
- Safety rules and guidelines
- Installation information
- Specific child and infant seat models
- Sites on the Internet that sell car seats
- Price ranges
- Internet sites providing safety information

Format the report using a theme and styles and include a cover page and headers and/or footers. Save the completed document and name it **WL1-C4-CS-P3-CarSeats**. Print and then close the document.

UNIT 1

Performance Assessment

Note: Before beginning unit assessments, copy to your storage medium the Word2010L1U1 subfolder from the Word2010L1 folder on the CD that accompanies this textbook and then make Word2010L1U1 the active folder.

Assessing Proficiency

In this unit, you have learned to create, edit, save, and print Word documents. You also learned to format characters, paragraphs, and pages.

Assessment 1 Format *Designing an Effective Website* Document

1. Open **Website.docx** and then save the document with Save As and name it **WL1-U1-A1-Website**.
2. Complete a spelling and grammar check.
3. Select from the paragraph that begins *Make your home page work for you.* through the end of the document and then apply bullet formatting.
4. Select and then bold the first sentence of each bulleted paragraph.
5. Apply paragraph border and shading to the document title.
6. Save and then print **WL1-U1-A1-Website.docx**.
7. Change the top, left, and right margins to 1.5 inches.
8. Select the bulleted paragraphs, change the paragraph alignment to justified, and then insert numbering.
9. Select the entire document and then change the font to 12-point Cambria.
10. Insert the text shown in Figure U1.1 after paragraph number 2. (The number 3. should be inserted preceding the text you type.)
11. Save, print, and then close **WL1-U1-A1-Website.docx**.

Figure U1.1 Assessment 1

> **Avoid a cluttered look.** In design, less is more. Strive for a clean look to your pages, using ample margins and white space.

Assessment 2 Format *Accumulated Returns* Document

1. Open **ReturnChart.docx** and then save the document with Save As and name it **WL1-U1-A2-ReturnChart**.
2. Select the entire document and then make the following changes:
   a. Click the No Spacing style.
   b. Change the line spacing to 1.5.

c. Change the font to 12-point Cambria.
d. Apply 6 points of spacing after paragraphs.
3. Select the title *TOTAL RETURN CHARTS*, change the font to 14-point Corbel bold, change the alignment to center, and apply paragraph shading of your choosing.
4. Bold the following text that appears at the beginning of the second through the fifth paragraphs:
   Average annual total return: *Annual total return:*
   Accumulation units: *Accumulative rates:*
5. Select the paragraphs of text in the body of the document (all paragraphs except the title) and then change the paragraph alignment to justified.
6. Select the paragraphs that begin with the bolded words, sort the paragraphs in ascending order, and then indent the text 0.5 inch from the left margin.
7. Insert a watermark that prints *DRAFT* diagonally across the page.
8. Save, print, and then close **WL1-U1-A2-ReturnChart.docx**.

Assessment 3 Format Computer Ethics Report

1. Open **FutureEthics.docx** and then save the document with Save As and name it **WL1-U1-A3-FutureEthics.docx**.
2. Apply the Heading 1 style to the titles *FUTURE OF COMPUTER ETHICS* and *REFERENCES*.
3. Apply the Heading 2 style to the headings in the document.
4. Change the paragraph spacing to *Relaxed*. **Hint: Do this with the Change Styles button**.
5. Change the Quick Styles set to *Thatch*.
6. Apply the Hardcover theme and then change the theme colors to *Concourse*.
7. Center the two titles (*FUTURE OF COMPUTER ETHICS* and *REFERENCES*).
8. Hang indent the paragraphs of text below the *REFERENCES* title.
9. Insert page numbering that prints at the bottom center of each page.
10. Save, print, and then close **WL1-U1-A3-FutureEthics.docx**.

Assessment 4 Set Tabs and Type Division Income Text in Columns

1. At a new blank document, type the text shown in Figure U1.2 with the following specifications:
   a. Bold and center the title as shown.
   b. You determine the tab settings for the text in columns.
   c. Select the entire document and then change the font to 12-point Arial.
2. Save the document and name it **WL1-U1-A4-Income**.
3. Print and then close **WL1-U1-A4-Income.docx**.

Figure U1.2 Assessment 4

INCOME BY DIVISION			
	2009	2010	2011
Public Relations	$14,375	$16,340	$16,200
Database Services	9,205	15,055	13,725
Graphic Design	18,400	21,790	19,600
Technical Support	5,780	7,325	9,600

Assessment 5 Set Tabs and Type Table of Contents Text

1. At a blank document, type the text shown in Figure U1.3 with the following specifications:
   a. Bold and center the title as shown.
   b. You determine the tab settings for the text in columns.
   c. Select the entire document, change the font to 12-point Bookman Old Style (or a similar serif typeface), and then change the line spacing to 1.5.
2. Save the document and name it **WL1-U1-A5-TofC**.
3. Print and then close **WL1-U1-A5-TofC.docx**.

Figure U1.3 Assessment 5

TABLE OF CONTENTS	
Online Shopping	2
Online Services	4
Peer-to-Peer Online Transactions	5
Transaction Payment Methods	8
Transaction Security and Encryption	11
Establishing a Website	14

Assessment 6 Format Union Agreement Contract

1. Open **LaborContract.docx** and then save the document with Save As and name it **WL1-U1-A6-LaborContract**.
2. Find all occurrences of *REINBERG MANUFACTURING* and replace with *MILLWOOD ENTERPRISES*.
3. Find all occurrences of *RM* and replace with *ME*.
4. Find all occurrences of *LABOR WORKERS' UNION* and replace with *SERVICE EMPLOYEES' UNION*.
5. Find all occurrences of *LWU* and replace with *SEU*.
6. Select the entire document and then change the font to 12-point Cambria and the line spacing to double.
7. Select the numbered paragraphs in the *Transfers and Moving Expenses* section and change to bullets.
8. Select the numbered paragraphs in the *Sick Leave* section and change to bullets.
9. Change the page orientation to landscape and the top margin to 1.5".
10. Save and then print **WL1-U1-A6-LaborContract.docx**.
11. Change the page orientation to portrait and the left margin (previously the top margin) back to 1".
12. Insert the *Alphabet* footer and type **Union Agreement** in the *[Type text]* placeholder.
13. Insert the *Alphabet* cover page and insert *UNION AGREEMENT* as the document title and *Millwood Enterprises* as the document subtitle. Include any additional information required by the cover page.
14. Save, print, and then close **WL1-U1-A6-LaborContract.docx**.

Assessment 7 Copy and Paste Text in Health Plan Document

1. Open **KeyLifePlan.docx** and then save the document with Save As and name it **WL1-U1-A7-KeyLifePlan**.
2. Open **PlanOptions.docx** and then turn on the display of the Clipboard task pane. Make sure the Clipboard is empty.
3. Select the heading *Plan Highlights* and the six paragraphs of text below the heading and then copy the selected text to the clipboard.
4. Select the heading *Plan Options* and the two paragraphs of text below the heading and then copy the selected text to the clipboard.
5. Select the heading *Quality Assessment* and the six paragraphs of text below the heading and then copy the selected text to the clipboard.
6. Close **PlanOptions.docx**.
7. With **WL1-U1-A7-KeyLifePlan.docx** open, display the Clipboard task pane.
8. Move the insertion point to the beginning of the *Provider Network* heading, paste the *Plan Options* item from the Clipboard, and merge the formatting.
9. With the insertion point positioned at the beginning of the *Provider Network* heading, paste the *Plan Highlights* item from the Clipboard, and merge the formatting.
10. Move the insertion point to the beginning of the *Plan Options* heading, paste the *Quality Assessment* item from the Clipboard, and merge the formatting.
11. Clear the Clipboard and then close it.
12. Apply the Heading 1 style to the title, *KEY LIFE HEALTH PLAN*.
13. Apply the Heading 2 style to the headings in the document.
14. Change the top margin to 1.5 inches.
15. Change to the *Modern* Quick Styles set.
16. Apply the Grid theme.
17. Insert a double line, dark red page border.
18. Insert the *Sideline* header and type **Health Plans** in the *[Type the document title]* placeholder. Insert the *Sideline* footer.
19. Add the *Sideline* cover page. Delete the company name and document subtitle placeholders. Insert your first and last names in the Author placeholder and the current date in the Date placeholder.
20. Save, print, and then close **WL1-U1-A7-KeyLifePlan.docx**.

Writing Activities

The following activities give you the opportunity to practice your writing skills along with demonstrating an understanding of some of the important Word features you have mastered in this unit. Use correct grammar, appropriate word choices, and clear sentence constructions. Follow the steps explained on the next page to improve your writing skills.

The Writing Process

Plan Gather ideas, select which information to include, and choose the order in which to present the information.
- *Checkpoints*
  - What is the purpose?
  - What information does the reader need in order to reach your intended conclusion?

Write Following the information plan and keeping the reader in mind, draft the document using clear, direct sentences that say what you mean.
- *Checkpoints*
  - What are the subpoints for each main thought?
  - How can you connect paragraphs so the reader moves smoothly from one idea to the next?

Revise Improve what is written by changing, deleting, rearranging, or adding words, sentences, and paragraphs.
- *Checkpoints*
  - Is the meaning clear?
  - Do the ideas follow a logical order?
  - Have you included any unnecessary information?
  - Have you built your sentences around strong nouns and verbs?

Edit Check spelling, sentence construction, word use, punctuation, and capitalization.
- *Checkpoints*
  - Can you spot any redundancies or clichés?
  - Can you reduce any phrases to an effective word (for example, change *the fact that* to *because*)?
  - Have you used commas only where there is a strong reason for doing so?
  - Did you proofread the document for errors that your spell checker cannot identify?

Publish Prepare a final copy that could be reproduced and shared with others.
- *Checkpoints*
  - Which design elements, such as boldface or different fonts, would help highlight important ideas or sections?
  - Would charts or other graphics help clarify meaning?

Activity 1 Write Hyphenation Steps and Hyphenate Text in Document

Use Word's Help feature to learn about hyphenating text in a document. Learn how to hyphenate text automatically as well as manually. Create a document following these instructions:

1. Include an appropriate title that is bolded and centered.
2. Write the steps required to automatically hyphenate text in a document.
3. Write the steps required to manually hyphenate text in a document.

Save the document and name it **WL1-U1-Act1-Hyphen**. Print and then close **WL1-U1-Act1-Hyphen.docx**. Open **WL1-U1-A3-FutureEthics.docx** and then save the document with Save As and name it **WL1-U1-Act1-FutureEthics**. Manually hyphenate text in the document. Save, print, and then close **WL1-U1-Act1-FutureEthics.docx**.

Activity 2 Write Information on Customizing Spelling and Grammar

Use Word's Help feature to learn about grammar and style options. Learn about grammar options and what they detect and style options and what they detect. Also, learn how to set rules for grammar and style. Once you have determined this information, create a document describing at least two grammar options and at least two style options. Also include in this document the steps required to change the writing style from grammar only to grammar and style. Save the completed document and name it **WL1-U1-Act2-CustomSpell**. Print and then close **WL1-U1-Act2-CustomSpell.docx**.

Internet Research

Research Business Desktop Computer Systems

You hold a part-time job at a local newspaper, *The Daily Chronicle*, where you conduct Internet research for the staff writers. Mr. Woods, the editor, has decided to purchase new desktop computers for the staff. He has asked you to identify at least three PCs that can be purchased directly over the Internet, and he requests that you put your research and recommendations in writing. Mr. Woods is looking for solid, reliable, economical, and powerful desktop computers with good warranties and service plans. He has given you a budget of $1,300 per unit.

Search the Internet for three desktop PC computer systems from three different manufacturers. Consider price, specifications (processor speed, amount of RAM, hard drive space, and monitor type and size), performance, warranties, and service plans when making your choice of systems. Print your research findings and include them with your report. (For helpful information on shopping for a computer, read the articles "Buying and Installing a PC" and "Purchasing a Computer," posted in the Course Resources section of this book's Internet Resource Center, either at www.emcp.net/BenchmarkOffice10 or www.emcp.net/BenchmarkWord10.)

Using Word, write a brief report in which you summarize the capabilities and qualities of each of the three computer systems you recommend. Include a final paragraph detailing which system you suggest for purchase and why. If possible, incorporate user opinions and/or reviews about this system to support your decision. At the end of your report, include a table comparing the computer system. Format your report using the concepts and techniques you learned in Unit 1. Save the report and name it **WL1-U1-InternetResearch**. Print and then close the file.

Microsoft Word Level 1

Unit 2 ■ Enhancing and Customizing Documents

Chapter 5 ■ Applying Formatting and Inserting Objects

Chapter 6 ■ Maintaining Documents

Chapter 7 ■ Creating Tables and SmartArt

Chapter 8 ■ Merging Documents

Microsoft Word

Applying Formatting and Inserting Objects

CHAPTER 5

PERFORMANCE OBJECTIVES

Upon successful completion of Chapter 5, you will be able to:
- **Insert section breaks**
- **Create and format text in columns**
- **Hyphenate words automatically and manually**
- **Create a drop cap**
- **Insert symbols, special characters, and the date and time**
- **Use the Click and Type feature**
- **Vertically align text**
- **Insert, format, and customize pictures, clip art images, text boxes, shapes, and WordArt**

To apply page or document formatting to only a portion of the document, insert a section break. You can insert a continuous section break or a section break that begins a new page. A section break is useful when formatting text in columns. The hyphenation feature hyphenates words at the end of lines, creating a less ragged margin. Use buttons in the Text and Symbols groups in the Insert tab to insert symbols, special characters, and the date and time. With the Click and Type feature, you can position the insertion point at various locations in the document and change the paragraph alignment. Use the *Vertical alignment* option at the Page Setup dialog box with the Layout tab selected to align text vertically on the page. Along with these features, you will also learn how to increase the visual appeal of a document by inserting and customizing images such as pictures, clip art, text boxes, shapes, and WordArt. Model answers for this chapter's projects appear on the following pages.

Note: Before beginning the projects, copy to your storage medium the Word2010L1C5 subfolder from the Word2010L1 folder on the CD that accompanies this textbook and then make Word2010L1C5 the active folder.

153

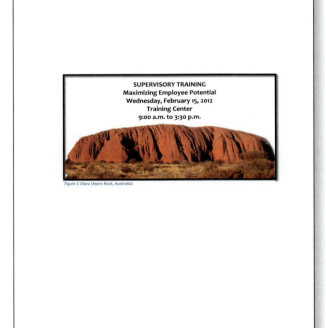

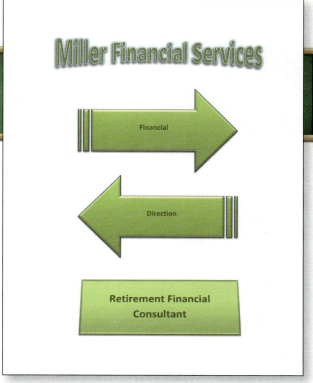

Project 4 Prepare a Company Flyer

WL1-C5-P4-FinConsult.docx

Project 5 Create and Format Screenshots

WL1-C5-P5-BackstageViews.docx

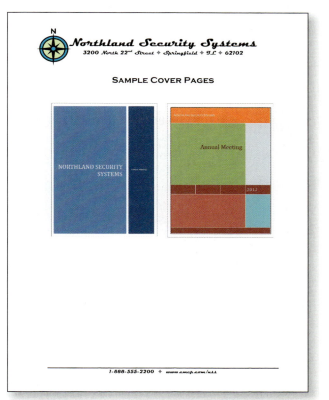

WL1-C5-P5-NSSCoverPages.docx

Project 1 Format a Document on Computer Input Devices   8 Parts

You will format into columns text in a document on computer input devices, improve the readability of the document by hyphenating long words, and improve the visual appeal by inserting a drop cap.

Inserting a Section Break

▼ Quick Steps

Insert a Section Break
1. Click Page Layout tab.
2. Click Breaks button.
3. Click section break type in drop-down list.

HINT
If you delete a section break, the text that follows the section break takes on the formatting of the text preceding the break.

Breaks

You can change the layout and formatting of specific portions of a document by inserting section breaks. For example, you can insert section breaks and then change margins for the text between the section breaks. If you want to format specific text in a document into columns, insert a section break.

Insert a section break in a document by clicking the Page Layout tab, clicking the Breaks button in the Page Setup group, and then clicking the desired option in the *Section Breaks* section of the drop-down list. You can insert a section break that begins a new page or a continuous section break that does not begin a new page. A continuous section break separates the document into sections but does not insert a page break. Click one of the other three options in the *Section Breaks* section of the Breaks drop-down list if you want to insert a section break that begins a new page.

A section break inserted in a document is not visible in Print Layout view. Click the Draft button and a section break displays in the document as a double row of dots with the words *Section Break* in the middle. Depending on the type of section break you insert, text follows *Section Break*. For example, if you insert a continuous section break, the words *Section Break (Continuous)* display in the middle of the row of dots. To delete a section break, change to Draft view, position the insertion point on the section break, and then press the Delete key.

Project 1a Inserting a Continuous Section Break   Part 1 of 8

1. Open **InputDevices.docx** and then save it with Save As and name it **WL1-C5-P1-InputDevices**.
2. Insert a continuous section break by completing the following steps:
   a. Move the insertion point to the beginning of the *Keyboard* heading.
   b. Click the Page Layout tab.
   c. Click the Breaks button in the Page Setup group and then click *Continuous* in the *Section Breaks* section of the drop-down list.
3. Click the Draft button in the view area on the Status bar and then notice the section break that displays across the screen.
4. Click the Print Layout button in the view area on the Status bar.

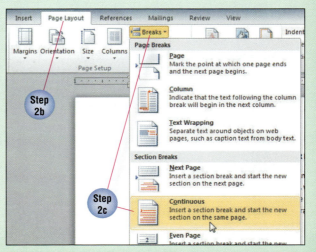

5. With the insertion point positioned at the beginning of the *Keyboard* heading, change the left and right margins to 1.5 inches. (The margin changes affect only the text after the continuous section break.)
6. Save and then print **WL1-C5-P1-InputDevices.docx**.

Creating Columns

When preparing a document containing text, an important point to consider is the readability of the document. Readability refers to the ease with which a person can read and understand groups of words. The line length of text in a document can enhance or detract from the readability of text. If the line length is too long, the reader may lose his or her place on the line and have a difficult time moving to the next line below. To improve the readability of some documents such as newsletters or reports, you may want to set the text in columns. One common type of column is newspaper, which is typically used for text in newspapers, newsletters, and magazines. Newspaper columns contain text that flows up and down in the document.

Create newspaper columns with the Columns button in the Page Setup group in the Page Layout tab or with options from the Columns dialog box. The Columns button creates columns of equal width. Use the Columns dialog box to create columns with varying widths. A document can include as many columns as room available on the page. Word determines how many columns can be included on the page based on the page width, the margin widths, and the size and spacing of the columns. Columns must be at least one-half inch in width. Changes in columns affect the entire document or the section of the document in which the insertion point is positioned.

▼ **Quick Steps**
Create Columns
1. Click Page Layout tab.
2. Click Columns button.
3. Click on desired number of columns.

Columns

Project 1b Formatting Text into Columns   Part 2 of 8

1. With **WL1-C5-P1-InputDevices.docx** open, make sure the insertion point is positioned below the section break and then return the left and right margins to 1 inch.
2. Delete the section break by completing the following steps:
   a. Click the Draft button in the view area on the Status bar.
   b. Position the insertion point on the section break.

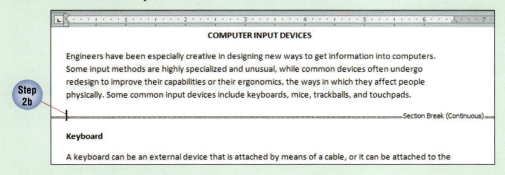

   c. Press the Delete key.
   d. Click the Print Layout button in the view area on the Status bar.

3. Move the insertion point to the beginning of the first paragraph of text in the document and then insert a continuous section break.
4. Format the text into columns by completing the following steps:
   a. Make sure the insertion point is positioned below the section break.
   b. Click the Page Layout tab.
   c. Click the Columns button in the Page Setup group.
   d. Click *Two* at the drop-down list.
5. Save **WL1-C5-P1-InputDevices.docx**.

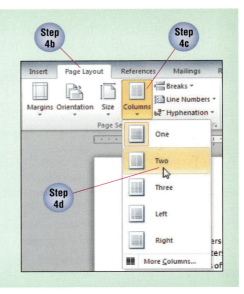

Creating Columns with the Columns Dialog Box

Quick Steps

Create Columns with Columns Dialog Box
1. Click Page Layout tab.
2. Click Columns button.
3. Click *More Columns* at the drop-down list.
4. Specify column options.
5. Click OK.

You can use the Columns dialog box to create newspaper columns that are equal or unequal in width. To display the Columns dialog box shown in Figure 5.1, click the Columns button in the Page Setup group of the Page Layout tab and then click *More Columns* at the drop-down list.

With options at the Columns dialog box you can specify the style and number of columns, enter your own column measurements, and create unequal columns. You can also insert a line between columns. By default, column formatting is applied to the whole document. With the *Apply to* option at the bottom of the Columns dialog box, you can change this from *Whole document* to *This point forward*. At the *This point forward* option, a section break is inserted and the column formatting is applied to text from the location of the insertion point to the end of the document or until other column formatting is encountered. The *Preview* section of the dialog box displays an example of how the columns will appear in your document.

Figure 5.1 Columns Dialog Box

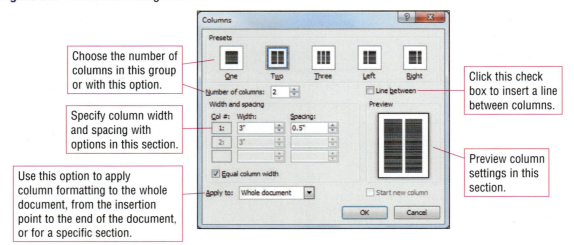

Removing Column Formatting

To remove column formatting using the Columns button, position the insertion point in the section containing columns, click the Page Layout tab, click the Columns button, and then click *One* at the drop-down list. You can also remove column formatting at the Columns dialog box by selecting the *One* option in the *Presets* section.

Inserting a Column Break

When formatting text into columns, Word automatically breaks the columns to fit the page. At times, column breaks may appear in an undesirable location. You can insert a column break by positioning the insertion point where you want the column to end, clicking the Page Layout tab, clicking the Breaks button, and then clicking *Column* at the drop-down list.

HINT You can also insert a column break with the keyboard shortcut, Ctrl + Shift + Enter.

Project 1c — Formatting Columns at the Columns Dialog Box — Part 3 of 8

1. With **WL1-C5-P1-InputDevices.docx** open, delete the section break by completing the following steps:
    a. Click the Draft button in the view area on the Status bar.
    b. Position the insertion point on the section break and then press the Delete key.
    c. Click the Print Layout button in the view area on the Status bar.
2. Remove column formatting by clicking the Columns button in the Page Setup group in the Page Layout tab and then clicking *One* at the drop-down list.
3. Format text in columns by completing the following steps:
    a. Position the insertion point at the beginning of the first paragraph of text in the document.
    b. Click the Columns button in the Page Setup group and then click *More Columns* at the drop-down list.
    c. At the Columns dialog box, click *Two* in the *Presets* section.
    d. Click the down-pointing arrow at the right of the *Spacing* option box until *0.3"* displays.
    e. Click the *Line between* check box to insert a check mark.
    f. Click the down-pointing arrow at the right side of the *Apply to* option box and then click *This point forward* at the drop-down list.
    g. Click OK to close the dialog box.

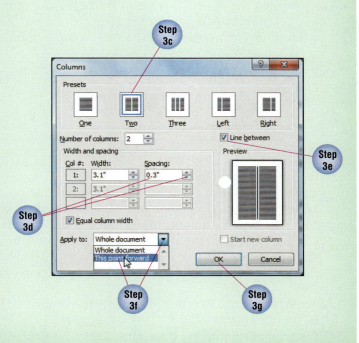

Chapter 5 ■ Applying Formatting and Inserting Objects   159

4. Insert a column break by completing the following steps:
   a. Position the insertion point at the beginning of the *Mouse* heading.
   b. Click the Breaks button in the Page Setup group and then click *Column* at the drop-down list.
5. Save and then print **WL1-C5-P1-InputDevices.docx**.

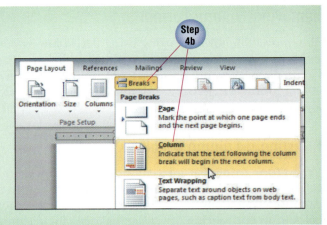

Balancing Columns on a Page

In a document containing text formatted into columns, Word automatically lines up (balances) the last line of text at the bottom of each column, except the last page. Text in the first column of the last page may flow to the end of the page, while the text in the second column may end far short of the end of the page. You can balance columns by inserting a continuous section break at the end of the text.

Project 1d Formatting and Balancing Columns of Text   Part 4 of 8

1. With **WL1-C5-P1-InputDevices.docx** open, delete the column break by completing the following steps:
   a. Position the insertion point at the beginning of the *Mouse* heading.
   b. Click the Draft button in the view area on the Status bar.
   c. Position the insertion point on the column break.

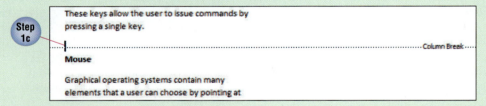

   d. Press the Delete key.
   e. Click the Print Layout button in the view area on the Status bar.
2. Select the entire document and then change the font to 12-point Constantia.
3. Move the insertion point to the end of the document and then balance the columns by clicking the Page Layout tab, clicking the Breaks button, and then clicking *Continuous* at the drop-down list.
4. Apply the Aqua, Accent 5, Lighter 60% paragraph shading to the title *COMPUTER INPUT DEVICES*.
5. Apply the Aqua, Accent 5, Lighter 80% paragraph shading to each of the headings in the document.
6. Insert page numbering that prints at the bottom of each page.
7. Save **WL1-C5-P1-InputDevices.docx**.

Hyphenating Words

In some Word documents, especially documents with left and right margins wider than 1 inch, or text set in columns, the right margin may appear quite ragged. To improve the display of text lines by making line lengths more uniform, consider hyphenating long words that fall at the end of a text line. When using the hyphenation feature, you can tell Word to hyphenate words automatically in a document or you can manually insert hyphens.

Automatically Hyphenating Words

To automatically hyphenate words in a document, click the Page Layout tab, click the Hyphenation button in the Page Setup group, and then click *Automatic* at the drop-down list. Scroll through the document and check to see if hyphens display in appropriate locations within the words. If, after hyphenating words in a document, you want to remove all hyphens, immediately click the Undo button on the Quick Access toolbar. This must be done immediately after hyphenating since the Undo feature undoes only the last function.

▼ **Quick Steps**

Automatic Hyphenation
1. Click Page Layout tab.
2. Click Hyphenation button.
3. Click *Automatic* at drop-down list.

Manual Hyphenation
1. Click Page Layout tab.
2. Click Hyphenation button.
3. Click *Manual* at drop-down list.
4. Click Yes or No to hyphenate indicated words.
5. When complete, click OK.

Manually Hyphenating Words

If you want to control where a hyphen appears in a word during hyphenation, choose manual hyphenation. To do this, click the Page Layout tab, click the Hyphenation button in the Page Setup group, and then click *Manual* at the drop-down list. This displays the Manual Hyphenation dialog box as shown in Figure 5.2. (The word in the *Hyphenate at* text box will vary.) At this dialog box, click Yes to hyphenate the word as indicated in the *Hyphenate at* text box, click No if you do not want the word hyphenated, or click Cancel to cancel hyphenation. You can also reposition the hyphen in the *Hyphenate at* text box. Word displays the word with syllable breaks indicated by a hyphen. The position where the word will be hyphenated displays as a blinking black bar. If you want to hyphenate at a different location in the word, position the blinking black bar where you want the hyphen and then click Yes. Continue clicking Yes or No at the Manual Hyphenation dialog box. Be careful with words ending in *-ed*. Several two-syllable words can be divided before that final syllable, for example, *noted*. However, one-syllable words ending in *-ed* should not be divided. An example is *served*. Watch for this type of occurrence and click No to cancel the hyphenation. At the hyphenation complete message, click OK.

Avoid dividing words at the ends of more than two consecutive lines.

Hyphenation

Figure 5.2 Manual Hyphenation Dialog Box

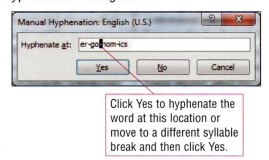

Click Yes to hyphenate the word at this location or move to a different syllable break and then click Yes.

If you want to remove all hyphens in a document, immediately click the Undo button on the Quick Access toolbar. To delete a few, but not all, of the optional hyphens inserted during hyphenation, use the Find and Replace dialog box. To do this, you would display the Find and Replace dialog box with the Replace tab selected, insert an optional hyphen symbol in the *Find what* text box (to do this, click the More button, click the Special button and then click *Optional Hyphen* at the pop-up list), and make sure the *Replace with* text box is empty. Complete the find and replace, clicking the Replace button to replace the hyphen with nothing or clicking the Find Next button to leave the hyphen in the document.

Project 1e Automatically and Manually Hyphenating Words   Part 5 of 8

1. With **WL1-C5-P1-InputDevices.docx** open, hyphenate words automatically by completing the following steps:
    a. Press Ctrl + Home and then click the Page Layout tab.
    b. Click the Hyphenation button in the Page Setup group and then click *Automatic* at the drop-down list.

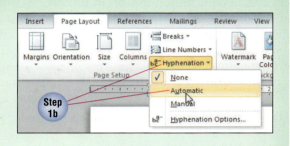

2. Scroll through the document and notice the automatic hyphenations.
3. Click the Undo button to remove the hyphens.
4. Manually hyphenate words by completing the following steps:
    a. Click the Hyphenation button in the Page Setup group and then click *Manual* at the drop-down list.
    b. At the Manual Hyphenation dialog box, make one of the following choices:
        • Click Yes to hyphenate the word as indicated in the *Hyphenate at* text box.
        • Move the hyphen in the word to a more desirable location, and then click Yes.
        • Click No if you do not want the word hyphenated.
    c. Continue clicking Yes or No at the Manual Hyphenation dialog box.
    d. At the hyphenation complete message, click OK.
5. Save **WL1-C5-P1-InputDevices.docx**.

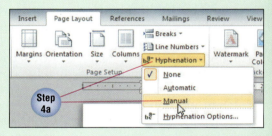

Creating a Drop Cap

▼ **Quick Steps**

Create Drop Cap
1. Click Insert tab.
2. Click Drop Cap button.
3. Click desired type in drop-down list.

Drop Cap

Use a drop cap to enhance the appearance of text. A ***drop cap*** is the first letter of the first word of a paragraph that is set into a paragraph. Drop caps identify the beginning of major sections or parts of a document. Create a drop cap with the Drop Cap button in the Text group in the Insert tab. You can choose to set the drop cap in the paragraph or in the margin. At the Drop Cap dialog box, you can specify a font, the numbers of lines you want the letter to drop, and the distance you want the letter positioned from the text of the paragraph. You can drop cap the first word by selecting the word first and then clicking the Drop Cap button.

Project 1f Inserting Drop Caps   Part 6 of 8

1. With **WL1-C5-P1-InputDevices.docx** open, create a drop cap by completing the following steps:
   a. Position the insertion point on the first word of the first paragraph of text (*Engineers*).
   b. Click the Insert tab.
   c. Click the Drop Cap button in the Text group.
   d. Click *In margin* at the drop-down gallery.
2. Looking at the drop cap, you decide that you do not like it in the margin and want it to be a little smaller. To change the drop cap, complete the following steps:
   a. With the E in the word *Engineers* selected, click the Drop Cap button in the Text group and then click *None* at the drop-down gallery.
   b. Click the Drop Cap button and then click *Drop Cap Options* at the drop-down gallery.
   c. At the Drop Cap dialog box, click *Dropped* in the *Position* section.
   d. Change the font to *Times New Roman*.
   e. Change the *Lines to drop* option to *2*.
   f. Click OK to close the dialog box.
   g. Click outside the drop cap to deselect it.
3. Save **WL1-C5-P1-InputDevices.docx**.

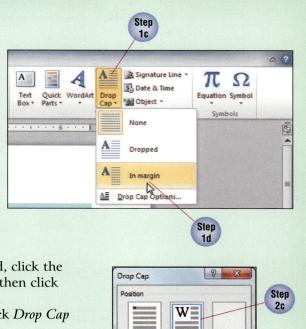

Inseting Symbols and Special Characters

You can use the Symbol button in the Insert tab to insert special symbols in a document. Click the Symbol button in the Symbols group in the Insert tab and a drop-down list displays with the most recently inserted symbols along with a *More Symbols* option. Click one of the symbols that displays in the list to insert it in the document or click the *More Symbols* option to display the Symbol dialog box as shown in Figure 5.3. At the Symbol dialog box, double-click the desired symbol, and then click Close; or click the desired symbol, click the Insert button, and then click Close.

At the Symbol dialog box with the Symbols tab selected, you can change the font with the *Font* option. When you change the font, different symbols display in the dialog box. Click the Special Characters tab at the Symbol dialog box and a list of special characters displays along with keyboard shortcuts to create the special character.

▼ **Quick Steps**

Insert a Symbol
1. Click Insert tab.
2. Click Symbol button.
3. Click desired symbol in drop-down list.
OR
1. Click Insert tab.
2. Click Symbol button.
3. Click *More Symbols*.
4. Double-click desired symbol.
5. Click Close.

Symbol

Figure 5.3 Symbol Dialog Box with Symbols Tab Selected

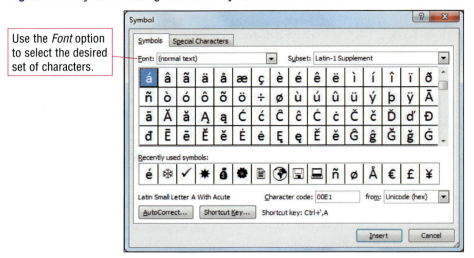

Use the *Font* option to select the desired set of characters.

Project 1g Inserting Symbols and Special Characters — Part 7 of 8

1. With **WL1-C5-P1-InputDevices.docx** open, press Ctrl + End to move the insertion point to the end of the document.
2. Press the Enter key once, type **Prepared by:**, and then press the spacebar once.
3. Type the first name **Matthew**.
4. Insert the last name *Viña* by completing the following steps:
    a. Type **Vi**.
    b. Click the Symbol button in the Symbols group in the Insert tab.
    c. Click *More Symbols* at the drop-down list.
    d. At the Symbol dialog box, make sure the *Font* option displays as *(normal text)* and then double-click the ñ symbol (located in approximately the twelfth row).
    e. Click the Close button.
    f. Type **a**.
5. Press Shift + Enter.
6. Insert the keyboard symbol (⌨) by completing the following steps:
    a. Click the Symbol button and then click *More Symbols*.
    b. At the Symbol dialog box, click the down-pointing arrow at the right side of the *Font* option and then click *Wingdings* at the drop-down list. (You will need to scroll down the list to display this option.)
    c. Double-click ⌨ (located approximately in the second row).
    d. Click the Close button.
7. Type **SoftCell Technologies**.

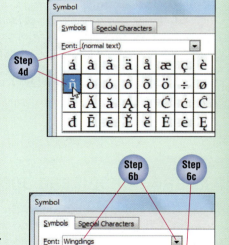

8. Insert the registered trademark symbol (®) by completing the following steps:
   a. Click the Symbol button and then click *More Symbols*.
   b. At the Symbol dialog box, click the Special Characters tab.
   c. Double-click the ® symbol (tenth option from the top).
   d. Click the Close button.
   e. Press Shift + Enter.
9. Select the keyboard symbol () and then change the font size to 18.
10. Save **WL1-C5-P1-InputDevices.docx**.

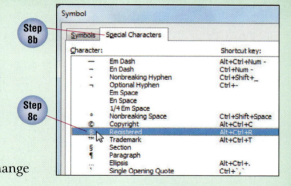

Inserting the Date and Time

Use the Date & Time button in the Text group in the Insert tab to insert the current date and time in a document. Click this button and the Date and Time dialog box displays as shown in Figure 5.4. (Your date will vary from what you see in the figure.) At the Date and Time dialog box, click the desired date and/or time format in the *Available formats* list box.

If the *Update automatically* check box does not contain a check mark, the date and/or time are inserted in the document as normal text that you can edit in the normal manner. You can also insert the date and/or time as a field. The advantage to inserting the date or time as a field is that the field can be updated with the Update Field keyboard shortcut, F9. Insert a check mark in the *Update automatically* check box to insert the data and/or time as a field. You can also insert the date as a field using the keyboard shortcut Alt + Shift + D, and insert the time as a field with the keyboard shortcut Alt + Shift + T.

▼ **Quick Steps**

Insert Date and Time
1. Click Insert tab.
2. Click Date and Time button.
3. Click option in list box.
4. Click OK.

Date & Time

Figure 5.4 Date and Time Dialog Box

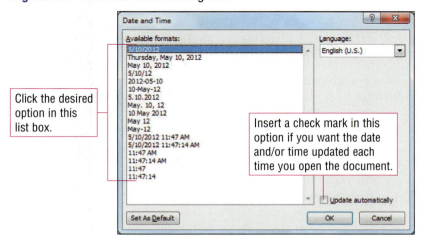

Chapter 5 ■ Applying Formatting and Inserting Objects

Project 1h — Inserting the Date and Time — Part 8 of 8

1. With **WL1-C5-P1-InputDevices.docx** open, press Ctrl + End and make sure the insertion point is positioned below the company name.
2. Insert the current date by completing the following steps:
    a. Click the Date & Time button in the Text group in the Insert tab.
    b. At the Date and Time dialog box, click the third option from the top in the *Available formats* group.
    c. Click in the *Update automatically* check box to insert a check mark.
    d. Click OK to close the dialog box.
3. Press Shift + Enter.
4. Insert the current time by pressing Alt + Shift + T.
5. Save **WL1-C5-P1-InputDevices.docx**.
6. Update the time by clicking the time and then pressing F9.
7. Save, print, and then close **WL1-C5-P1-InputDevices.docx**.

Project 2 — Create an Announcement about Supervisory Training — 3 Parts

You will create an announcement about upcoming supervisory training and use the click and type feature to center and right align text. You will vertically center the text on the page and insert and format a picture to add visual appeal to the announcement.

Using the Click and Type Feature

Word contains a click and type feature you can use to position the insertion point at a specific location and alignment in the document. This feature allows you to position one or more lines of text as you type, rather than typing the text and then selecting and reformatting the text, which requires multiple steps.

To use click and type, make sure the document displays in Print Layout view and then hover the mouse pointer at the location where you want the insertion point positioned. As you move the mouse pointer, you will notice that the pointer displays with varying horizontal lines representing the alignment. Double-click the mouse button and the insertion point is positioned at the location of the mouse pointer.

If the horizontal lines do not display next to the mouse pointer when you double-click the mouse button, a left tab is set at the position of the insertion point. If you want to change the alignment and not set a tab, make sure the horizontal lines display near the mouse pointer before double-clicking the mouse.

▼ **Quick Steps**

Use Click and Type
1. Hover mouse at left margin, between left and right margins, or at right margin.
2. Double-click left mouse button.

Project 2a **Using Click and Type** Part 1 of 3

1. At a blank document, create the centered text shown in Figure 5.5 by completing the following steps:
   a. Position the I-beam pointer between the left and right margins at about the 3.25-inch mark on the horizontal ruler and the top of the vertical ruler.
   b. When the center alignment lines display below the I-beam pointer, double-click the left mouse button.

   c. Type the centered text shown in Figure 5.5. Press Shift + Enter to end each text line.
2. Change to right alignment by completing the following steps:
   a. Position the I-beam pointer near the right margin at approximately the 1.5-inch mark on the vertical ruler until the right alignment lines display at the left side of the I-beam pointer.
   b. Double-click the left mouse button.
   c. Type the right-aligned text shown in Figure 5.5. Press Shift + Enter to end the text line.
3. Select the centered text and then change the font to 14-point Candara bold and the line spacing to double.
4. Select the right-aligned text, change the font to 10-point Candara bold, and then deselect the text.
5. Save the document and name it **WL1-C5-P2-Training**.

Figure 5.5 Project 2a

SUPERVISORY TRAINING
Maximizing Employee Potential
Wednesday, February 15, 2012
Training Center
9:00 a.m. to 3:30 p.m.

Sponsored by
Cell Systems

Vertically Aligning Text

Text in a Word document is aligned at the top of the page by default. You can change this alignment with the *Vertical alignment* option at the Page Setup dialog box with the Layout tab selected as shown in Figure 5.6. Display this dialog box by clicking the Page Layout tab, clicking the Page Setup group dialog box launcher, and then clicking the Layout tab at the Page Setup dialog box.

Figure 5.6 Page Setup Dialog Box with Layout Tab Selected

[Page Setup dialog box screenshot with Layout tab selected. Callout: "Click this down-pointing arrow to display a list of vertical alignment options."]

Quick Steps

Vertically Align Text
1. Click Page Layout tab.
2. Click Page Setup dialog box launcher.
3. Click Layout tab.
4. Click desired alignment.
5. Click OK.

The *Vertical alignment* option from the Page Setup dialog box contains four choices — *Top*, *Center*, *Justified*, and *Bottom*. The default setting is *Top*, which aligns text at the top of the page. Choose *Center* if you want text centered vertically on the page. The *Justified* option will align text between the top and the bottom margins. The *Center* option positions text in the middle of the page vertically, while the *Justified* option adds space between paragraphs of text (not within) to fill the page from the top to bottom margins. If you center or justify text, the text does not display centered or justified on the screen in the Draft view, but it does display centered or justified in the Print Layout view. Choose the *Bottom* option to align text in the document vertically along the bottom of the page.

Project 2b Vertically Centering Text   Part 2 of 3

1. With **WL1-C5-P2-Training.docx** open, click the Page Layout tab and then click the Page Setup group dialog box launcher.
2. At the Page Setup dialog box, click the Layout tab.
3. Click the down-pointing arrow at the right side of the *Vertical alignment* option box and then click *Center* at the drop-down list.
4. Click OK to close the dialog box.
5. Save and then print **WL1-C5-P2-Training.docx**.

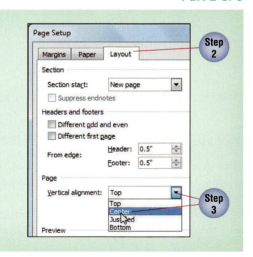

168 Word Level 1 ■ Unit 2

Inserting an Image

You can insert an image such as a picture or clip art in a Word document with buttons in the Illustrations group in the Insert tab. Click the Picture button to display the Insert Picture dialog box where you can specify the desired picture file or click the Clip Art button and then choose from a variety of images available at the Clip Art task pane. When you insert a picture or a clip art image in a document, the Picture Tools Format tab displays. Use options on the Picture Tools Format tab to customize and format the image.

Customizing and Formatting an Image

With options in the Adjust group in the Picture Tools Format tab you can remove unwanted portions of the image, correct the brightness and contrast, change the image color, apply artistic effects, compress the size of the image file, change to a different image, and reset the image back to the original formatting. Use buttons in the Picture Styles group to apply a predesigned style to the image, change the image border, or apply other effects to the image. With options in the Arrange group, you can position the image on the page, specify how text will wrap around it, align the image with other elements in the document, and rotate the image. Use the Crop button in the Size group to remove any unnecessary parts of the image and specify the image size with the *Shape Height* and *Shape Width* measurement boxes.

Crop

In addition to the Picture Tools Format tab, you can customize and format an image with options at the shortcut menu. Display this menu by right-clicking the image. With options at the shortcut menu, you can change the picture, insert a caption, choose text wrapping, size and position the image, and display the Format Picture dialog box.

Sizing an Image

You can change the size of an image with the *Shape Height* and *Shape Width* measurement boxes in the Size group in the Picture Tools Format tab or with the sizing handles that display around the selected image. To change size with a sizing handle, position the mouse pointer on a sizing handle until the pointer turns into a double-headed arrow and then hold down the left mouse button. Drag the sizing handle in or out to decrease or increase the size of the image and then release the mouse button. Use the middle sizing handles at the left or right side of the image to make the image wider or thinner. Use the middle sizing handles at the top or bottom of the image to make the image taller or shorter. Use the sizing handles at the corners of the image to change both the width and height at the same time.

Resize a selected object horizontally, vertically, or diagonally from the center outward by holding down the Ctrl key and then dragging a sizing handle.

Moving an Image

Move an image to a specific location on the page with options from the Position button drop-down gallery. The Position button is located in the Arrange group in the Picture Tools Format tab. When you choose an option at the Position button drop-down gallery, the image is moved to the specified location on the page and square text wrapping is applied to the image.

Position

You can also move the image by dragging it to the desired location. Before dragging an image, you must first choose a text wrapping style by clicking the Wrap Text button in the Arrange group and then clicking the desired wrapping style at the drop-down list. After choosing a wrapping style, move the image by positioning the mouse pointer on the image border until the arrow pointer turns into a four-headed arrow. Hold down the left mouse button, drag the image to the desired position, and then release the mouse button. To help precisely position an image, consider turning on gridlines. Do this by clicking the Align button in the Arrange group in the Picture Tools Format tab and then clicking *View Gridlines*.

Rotate the image by positioning the mouse pointer on the green, round rotation handle until the pointer displays as a circular arrow. Hold down the left mouse button, drag in the desired direction, and then release the mouse button.

▼ **Quick Steps**

Insert Picture
1. Click Insert tab.
2. Click Picture button.
3. Double-click desired picture in Insert Picture dialog box.

Picture

Inserting a Picture

To insert a picture in a document, click the Insert tab and then click the Picture button in the Illustrations group. At the Insert Picture dialog box, navigate to the folder containing the desired picture and then double-click the picture. Use buttons in the Picture Tools Format tab to format and customize the picture. You can insert a picture from a Web page by opening the Web page, opening a Word document, and then dragging the picture from the Web page to the document. If the picture is linked, the link (rather than the image) will display in your document.

Project 2c **Inserting and Customizing a Picture** Part 3 of 3

1. With **WL1-C5-P2-Training.docx** open, return the vertical alignment back to *Top* by completing the following steps:
   a. Click the Page Layout tab.
   b. Click the Page Setup group dialog box launcher.
   c. At the Page Setup dialog box, click the Layout tab.
   d. Click the down-pointing arrow at the right side of the *Vertical alignment* option box and then click *Top* at the drop-down list.
   e. Click OK to close the dialog box.
2. Select and then delete the text *Sponsored by* and the text *Cell Systems*.
3. Select the remaining text and change the line spacing to single.
4. Move the insertion point to the beginning of the document and then press the Enter key until the first line of text displays at approximately the 3-inch mark on the vertical ruler.
5. Insert a picture by completing the following steps:
   a. Click the Insert tab.
   b. Click the Picture button in the Illustrations group.
   c. At the Insert Picture dialog box, navigate to your Word2010L1C5 folder.
   d. Double-click *Uluru.jpg* in the list box.
6. Crop the picture by completing the following steps:
   a. Click the Crop button in the Size group.
   b. Position the mouse pointer on the bottom, middle crop handle (displays as a short black line) until the pointer turns into the crop tool (displays as a small, black T).

c. Hold down the left mouse button, drag up to just below the mountain as shown at the right, and then release the mouse button.
d. Click the Crop button in the Size group to turn off the feature.
7. Change the size of the picture by clicking in the *Shape Height* measurement box in the Size group, typing 3, and then pressing Enter.
8. Move the picture behind the text by clicking the Wrap Text button in the Arrange group and then clicking *Behind Text* at the drop-down list.
9. Rotate the image by clicking the Rotate button in the Arrange group and then clicking *Flip Horizontal* at the drop-down list.

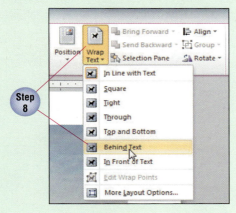

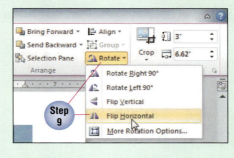

10. Change the picture color by clicking the Color button in the Adjust group and then clicking the second option from the right in the *Color Saturation* section (*Saturation: 300%*).
11. After looking at the coloring, you decide to return to the original color by clicking the Undo button on the Quick Access toolbar.
12. Sharpen the picture by clicking the Corrections button in the Adjust group and then clicking the second option from the right in the *Sharpen and Soften* section (*Sharpen: 25%*).

Chapter 5 ■ Applying Formatting and Inserting Objects   171

13. Change the contrast of the picture by clicking the Corrections button in the Adjust group and then clicking the third option from the left in the bottom row of the *Brightness and Contrast* section [*Brightness: 0% (Normal) Contrast: +40%*].
14. Apply a picture style by clicking the More button at the right side of the thumbnails in the Picture Styles section and then clicking the first option from the left in the second row (*Simple Frame, Black*).

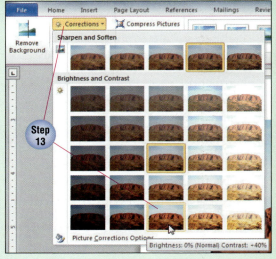

Step 13

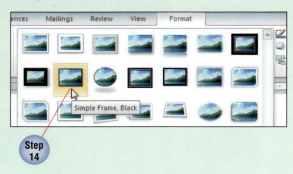

Step 14

Step 15a

15. Compress the picture by completing the following steps:
    a. Click the Compress Pictures button in the Adjust group.
    b. At the Compress Pictures dialog box, make sure a check mark displays in both options in the *Compression options* section and then click OK.
16. Position the mouse pointer on the border of the selected picture until the pointer displays with a four-headed arrow attached and then drag the picture so the text is positioned in the sky above Ayres Rock.
17. If the text does not fit in the sky above the rock, increase the height of the picture. To do this, position the mouse pointer on the top border middle sizing handle until the pointer displays as a two-headed arrow pointing up and down. Hold down the left mouse button, drag up until the text displays approximately one-half inch below the top border of the picture, and then release the mouse button.
18. Save and then print **WL1-C5-P2-Training.docx**.
19. With the picture selected, remove the background by completing the following steps:
    a. Click the Remove Background button in the Adjust group in the Picture Tools Format tab.
    b. Using the left middle sizing handle, drag the left border to the left side of the image.

Step 16

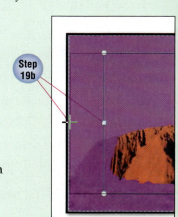

Step 19b

c. Drag the right middle sizing handle to the right side of the image.
   d. Drag the bottom middle sizing handle to the bottom border of the image.
   e. Click the Keep Changes button in the Close group in the Background Removal tab. (The picture should now display with the sky removed.)
20. Insert a caption by completing the following steps:
   a. Right-click the picture. (This displays the shortcut menu.)
   b. Click the *Insert Caption* option at the shortcut menu.
   c. At the Caption dialog box with the insertion point positioned in the *Caption* text box, press the spacebar and then type **Uluru (Ayers Rock, Australia)**.
   d. Click OK. (The caption displays below and at the left side of the picture.)
21. Save, print, and then close **WL1-C5-P2-Training.docx**.

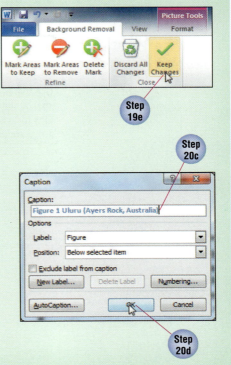

Project 3 Customize a Report on Robots   2 Parts

You will open a report on robots and then add visual appeal to the report by inserting and formatting a clip art image and a built-in text box.

Inserting a Clip Art Image

Microsoft Office includes a gallery of media images you can insert in a document such as clip art, photographs, and movie images, as well as sound clips. To insert an image in a Word document, click the Insert tab and then click the Clip Art button in the Illustrations group. This displays the Clip Art task pane at the right side of the screen as shown in Figure 5.7.

To view all picture, sound, and motion files, make sure the *Search for* text box in the Clip Art task pane does not contain any text and then click the Go button. When the desired image is visible, click the image to insert it in the document. Use buttons in the Picture Tools Format tab to format and customize the clip art image.

Unless the Clip Art task pane default settings have been customized, the task pane displays all illustrations, photographs, videos, and audio files. The *Results should be* option has a default setting of *Selected media file types*. Click the down-pointing arrow at the right side of this option to display media types. To search for a specific media type, remove the check mark before all options at the drop-down list except for the desired type. For example, if you are searching only for photograph images, remove the check mark before *Illustrations*, *Videos*, and *Audio*.

▼ **Quick Steps**

Insert Clip Art Image
1. Click Insert tab.
2. Click Clip Art button.
3. Type search word or topic.
4. Press Enter.
5. Click desired image.

You can drag a clip art image from the Clip Art task pane to your document.

Clip Art

Figure 5.7 Clip Art Task Pane

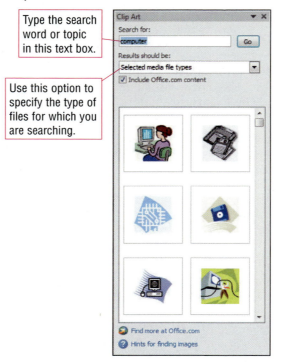

Type the search word or topic in this text box.

Use this option to specify the type of files for which you are searching.

If you are searching for specific images, click in the *Search for* text box, type the desired topic, and then click the Go button. For example, if you want to find images related to business, click in the *Search for* text box, type **business**, and then click the Go button. Clip art images related to *business* display in the viewing area of the task pane. If you are connected to the Internet, Word will search for images at the Office Online website matching the topic.

Project 3a — Inserting an Image — Part 1 of 2

1. Open **Robots.docx** and then save the document with Save As and name it **WL1-C5-P3-Robots**.
2. Apply the Heading 1 style to the title *ROBOTS AS ANDROIDS* and apply the Heading 2 style to the headings in the document.
3. Change the Quick Styles set to *Modern*. **Hint: Do this with the Change Styles button in the Styles group in the Home tab.**
4. Insert a clip art image by completing the following steps:
   a. Move the insertion point so it is positioned at the beginning of the first paragraph of text (the sentence that begins *Robotic factories are increasingly . . .*).
   b. Click the Insert tab.
   c. Click the Clip Art button in the Illustrations group.
   d. At the Clip Art task pane, select any text that displays in the *Search for* text box, type **computer**, and then press Enter.
   e. Click the computer image in the list box as shown at the right.

f. Close the Clip Art task pane by clicking the Close button (contains an X) located in the upper right corner of the task pane.
5. Format the clip art image by completing the following steps:
a. Click the More button at the right side of the thumbnails in the Picture Styles group and then click the *Drop Shadow Rectangle* option (fourth option from the left in the top row).
b. Click the Color button in the Adjust group and then click the *Blue, Accent color 1 Dark* option (second option from the left in the second row).
c. Click in the *Shape Height* measurement box in the Size group, type 3, and then press Enter.
6. Reset the image and the image size by clicking the Reset Picture button arrow in the Adjust group and then clicking the *Reset Picture & Size* option at the drop-down list.
7. Crop the clip art image by completing the following steps:
a. Click the Crop button in the Size group.
b. Position the mouse pointer on the top middle crop handle (displays as a short black line) until the pointer turns into the crop tool.
c. Hold down the left mouse button, drag down to just above the top of the computer as shown at the right, and then release the mouse button.
d. Click the Crop button in the Size group to turn off the feature.
8. Decrease the size of the picture by clicking in the *Shape Height* measurement box in the Size group, typing 1.3, and then pressing Enter.
9. Change the text wrapping by clicking the Wrap Text button in the Arrange group and then clicking *Square* at the drop-down list.
10. Rotate the image by clicking the Rotate button in the Arrange group and then clicking *Flip Horizontal* at the drop-down list.
11. Click the Corrections button in the Adjust group and then click the third option from the left in the bottom row [*Brightness: 0% (Normal) Contrast: +40%*].
12. Click the Picture Effects button in the Picture Styles group, point to *Shadow*, and then click the last option in the top row of the *Outer* section (*Offset Diagonal Bottom Left*).

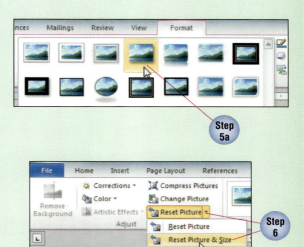

Step 5a

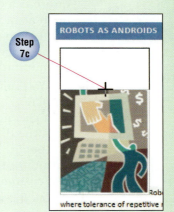

Step 6

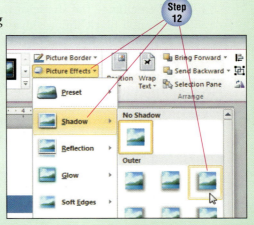

Step 7c

Step 12

Chapter 5 ■ Applying Formatting and Inserting Objects 175

13. Position the mouse pointer on the border of the selected picture until the pointer turns into a four-headed arrow and then drag the picture so it is positioned as shown at the right.
14. Click outside the clip art image to deselect it.
15. Save **WL1-C5-P3-Robots.docx**.

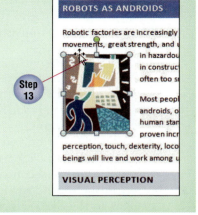

Step 13

Inserting and Customizing a Pull Quote

Quick Steps

Inserting Pull Quote
1. Click Insert tab.
2. Click Text Box button.
3. Click desired pull quote.

Text Box

Use a pull quote in a document such as an article to attract attention. A **pull quote** is a quote from an article that is "pulled out" and enlarged and positioned in an attractive location on the page. Some advantages of pull quotes are that they reinforce important concepts, summarize your message, and break up text blocks to make them easier to read. If you use multiple pull quotes in a document, keep them in order to ensure clear comprehension for readers.

You can insert a pull quote in a document with a predesigned built-in text box. Display the available pull quote built-in text boxes by clicking the Insert tab and then clicking the Text Box button in the Text group. Click the desired pull quote from the drop-down list that displays and the built-in text box is inserted in the document. Type the quote inside the text box and then format the text and/or customize the text box. Use buttons in the Drawing Tools Format tab to format and customize the built-in text box.

At the Drawing Tools Format tab, use options in the Insert Shapes group to insert a shape in the document. Click the Edit Shape button in the Insert Shapes group and a drop-down list displays. Click the *Change Shape* option if you want to change the shape of the selected text box. Click the *Edit Points* option and small black squares display at points around the text box. Use the mouse on these points to increase or decrease a point of the text box. Apply predesigned styles to a text box with options in the Shape Styles group. You can also change the shape fill, outline, and effects. Change the formatting of the text in the text box with options in the WordArt Styles group. Click the More button that displays at the right side of the WordArt style thumbnails and then click the desired style at the drop-down gallery. You can further customize text with the Text Fill, Text Outline, and Text Effects buttons in the Text group. Use options in the Arrange group to position the text box on the page, specify text wrapping in relation to the text box, align the text box with other objects in the document, and rotate the text box. Specify the text box size with the *Shape Height* and *Shape Width* measurement boxes in the Size group.

Project 3b Inserting a Built-in Text Box   Part 2 of 2

1. With **WL1-C5-P3-Robots.docx** open, click the Insert tab.
2. Click the Text Box button in the Text group.
3. Scroll down the drop-down list and then click the *Contrast Quote* option.
4. Type the following text in the text box: "The task of creating a humanlike body has proven incredibly difficult."
5. Make sure the Drawing Tools Format tab is active.
6. Click the More button at the right side of the style thumbnails in the Shape Styles group and then click the *Subtle Effect - Blue, Accent 1* option (second option from the left in the fourth row).

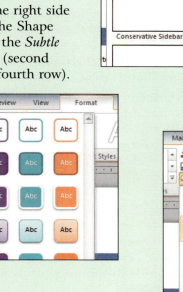

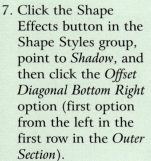

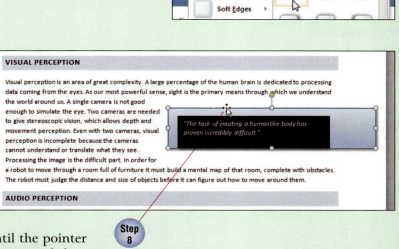

7. Click the Shape Effects button in the Shape Styles group, point to *Shadow*, and then click the *Offset Diagonal Bottom Right* option (first option from the left in the first row in the *Outer Section*).
8. Position the mouse pointer on the border of the selected text box until the pointer turns into a four-headed arrow and then drag the text box so it is positioned as shown above.
9. Save, print, and then close **WL1-C5-P3-Robots.docx**.

Chapter 5 ■ Applying Formatting and Inserting Objects

Project 4 Prepare a Company Flyer   3 Parts

You will prepare a company flyer by inserting and customizing shapes, text boxes, and WordArt.

▼ **Quick Steps**

Draw a Shape
1. Click Insert tab.
2. Click Shapes button.
3. Click desired shape at drop-down list.
4. Drag in document screen to create shape.

HINT

To draw a square, choose the Rectangle shape and then hold down the Shift key while drawing the shape. To draw a circle, choose the Oval shape and then hold down the Shift key while drawing the shape.

Shapes

Drawing Shapes

Use the Shapes button in the Insert tab to draw shapes in a document including lines, basic shapes, block arrows, flow chart shapes, stars and banners, and callouts. Click a shape and the mouse pointer displays as crosshairs (plus sign). Position the crosshairs where you want the shape to begin, hold down the left mouse button, drag to create the shape, and then release the mouse button. This inserts the shape in the document and also displays the Drawing Tools Format tab. Use buttons in this tab to change the shape, apply a style to the shape, arrange the shape, and change the size of the shape. This tab contains many of the same options and buttons as the Picture Tools Format tab and the Text Box Tools Format tab.

If you choose a shape in the *Lines* section of the drop-down list, the shape you draw is considered a ***line drawing***. If you choose an option in the other sections of the drop-down list, the shape you draw is considered an ***enclosed object***. When drawing an enclosed object, you can maintain the proportions of the shape by holding down the Shift key while dragging with the mouse to create the shape.

Copying Shapes

To copy a shape, select the shape and then click the Copy button in the Clipboard group in the Home tab. Position the insertion point at the location where you want the copied image and then click the Paste button. You can also copy a selected shape by holding down the Ctrl key while dragging the shape to the desired location.

Project 4a Drawing Arrow Shapes   Part 1 of 3

1. At a blank document, press the Enter key twice and then draw an arrow shape by completing the following steps:
   a. Click the Insert tab.
   b. Click the Shapes button in the Illustrations group and then click the *Striped Right Arrow* shape in the *Block Arrows* section.
   c. Position the mouse pointer (displays as crosshairs) in the document at approximately the 1-inch mark on the horizontal ruler and the 0.5-inch mark on the vertical ruler.
   d. Hold down the Shift key and the left mouse button, drag to the right until the tip of the arrow is positioned at approximately the 5.5-inch mark on the horizontal ruler, and then release the mouse button and the Shift key.

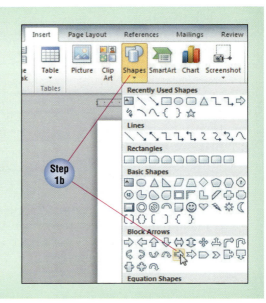
Step 1b

2. Format the arrow by completing the following steps:
    a. Click in the *Shape Height* measurement box in the Size group, type 2.4, and then press Enter.
    b. Click in the *Shape Width* measurement box in the Size group, type 4.5, and then press Enter.
    c. Click the More button at the right side of the thumbnails in the Shape Styles group and then click the *Intense Effect – Olive Green, Accent 3* option (fourth option from the left in the sixth row).

Step 2c

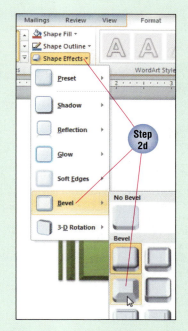

Step 2d

    d. Click the Shape Effects button in the Shape Styles group, point to *Bevel*, and then click the *Angle* option (first option from the left in the second row in the *Bevel* section).
    e. Click the Shape Outline button arrow in the Shape Styles group and then click the Dark Blue color (second color from the right in the *Standard Colors* section).
3. Copy the arrow by completing the following steps:
    a. With the mouse pointer positioned in the arrow (mouse pointer displays with a four-headed arrow attached), hold down the Ctrl key and the left mouse button.
    b. Drag down until the outline of the copied arrow displays just below the top arrow, release the mouse button, and then release the Ctrl key.
    c. Copy the arrow again by holding down the Ctrl key and the left mouse button and then dragging the outline of the copied arrow just below the second arrow.
4. Flip the middle arrow by completing the following steps:
    a. Click the middle arrow to select it.
    b. Click the Rotate button in the Arrange group in the Drawing Tools Format tab and then click *Flip Horizontal* at the drop-down gallery.
5. Insert the text *Financial* in the top arrow by completing the following steps:
    a. Click the top arrow to select it.
    b. Type **Financial**. (The text will appear in the middle of the arrow.)
    c. Select *Financial*.
    d. Click the Home tab.
    e. Change the font size to 16, turn on bold, and then change the font color to *Olive Green, Accent 3, Darker 50%*.
6. Complete steps similar to those in Step 5 to insert the word *Direction* in the middle arrow.
7. Complete steps similar to those in Step 5 to insert the word *Retirement* in the bottom arrow.
8. Save the document and name it **WL1-C5-P4-FinConsult**.
9. Print the document.

Drawing and Formatting a Text Box

▼ **Quick Steps**

Draw a Text Box
1. Click Insert tab.
2. Click Text Box button in Text group.
3. Click *Draw Text Box*.
4. Drag in document screen to create box.

You can use the built-in text boxes provided by Word or you can draw your own text box. To draw a text box, click the Insert tab, click the Text Box button in the Text group, and then click *Draw Text Box* at the drop-down list. The mouse pointer displays as crosshairs. Position the crosshairs in the document and then drag to create the text box. You can also just click in the document. When a text box is selected, the Text Box Tools Format tab displays. Use buttons in this tab to format text boxes in the same manner as formatting built-in text boxes.

Project 4b Inserting and Formatting a Text Box   Part 2 of 3

1. With **WL1-C5-P4-FinConsult.docx** open, delete the bottom arrow by completing the following steps:
   a. Click the bottom arrow. (This displays a border around the arrow.)
   b. Position the mouse pointer on the border (displays with four-headed arrow attached) and then click the left mouse button. (This changes the dashed border to a solid border.)
   c. Press the Delete key.
2. Insert, size, and format a text box by completing the following steps:
   a. Click the Insert tab.
   b. Click the Text Box button in the Text group and then click *Draw Text Box* at the drop-down list.
   c. Click in the document at about the one-inch mark on the horizontal ruler and about one inch below the bottom arrow. (This inserts a text box in the document.)
   d. Click in the *Shape Height* measurement box in the Size group and then type **1.7**.
   e. Click in the *Shape Width* measurement box, type **4.5**, and then press Enter.
   f. Click the More button at the right side of the thumbnails in the Shape Styles group and then click the *Intense Effect – Olive Green, Accent 3* option at the drop-down gallery (fourth option from the left in the sixth row).
   g. Click the Shape Effects button in the Shape Styles group, point to *Bevel*, and then click the *Soft Round* option at the side menu (second option from the left in the second row in the *Bevel* section).

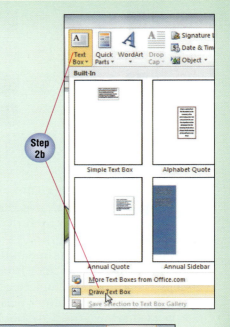

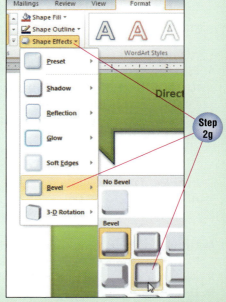

h. Click the Shape Effects button in the Shape Styles group, point to *3-D Rotation*, and then click the *Perspective Above* option (first option from the left in the second row in the *Perspective* section).

3. Insert and format text in the text box by completing the following steps:
   a. Press the Enter key twice. (The insertion point should be positioned in the text box.)
   b. Click the Home tab.
   c. Change the font size to 24 points, turn on bold, and change the font color to Olive Green, Accent 3, Darker 50%.
   d. Click the Center button in the Paragraph group.
   e. Type **Retirement Financial Consulting**. (Your text box should appear as shown below.)

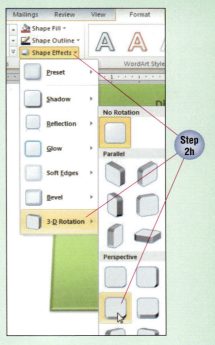

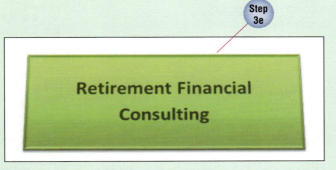

4. Save **WL1-C5-P4-FinConsult.docx**.

Creating and Modifying WordArt Text

With the WordArt feature, you can distort or modify text to conform to a variety of shapes. This is useful for creating company logos, letterheads, flyer titles, or headings. To insert WordArt in a document, click the Insert tab and then click the WordArt button in the Text group. At the drop-down list that displays, click the desired option and a WordArt text box is inserted in the document containing the words *Your text here* and the Drawing Tools Format tab is active. Type the desired WordArt text and then format the WordArt with options in the Drawing Tools Format tab.

▼ Quick Steps
Create WordArt Text
1. Click Insert tab.
2. Click WordArt button.
3. Click desired WordArt option at drop-down list.
4. Type WordArt text.

WordArt

Project 4c Inserting and Modifying WordArt   Part 3 of 3

1. With **WL1-C5-P4-FinConsult.docx** open, press Ctrl + Home to move the insertion point to the beginning of the document.
2. Insert WordArt text by completing the following steps:
   a. Click the Insert tab.

b. Click the WordArt button in the Text group and then click the *Fill – Olive Green, Accent 3, Outline – Text 2* option.
c. Type **Miller Financial Services**.

3. Format the WordArt text by completing the following steps:
   a. Click the outside border of the WordArt text so the border displays as a solid line instead of a dashed line.
   b. Click the Text Fill button arrow in the WordArt Styles group in the Drawing Tools Format tab and then click the *Olive Green, Accent 3, Darker 25%* option.
   c. Click the Text Effects button in the WordArt Styles group, point to *Glow*, and then click the *Aqua, 5 pt glow, Accent color 5* option in the *Glow Variations* section.

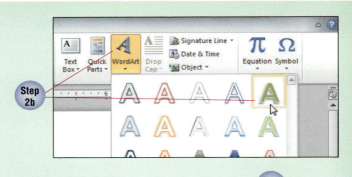
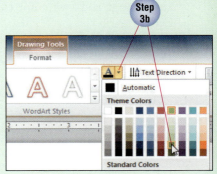
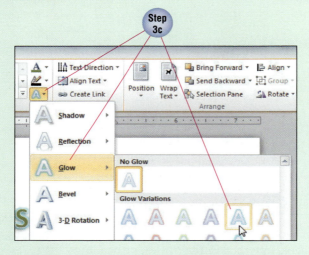
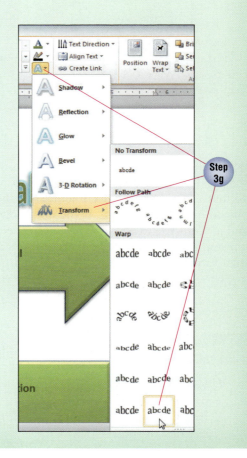

   d. Click the Text Effects button in the WordArt Styles group, point to *3-D Rotation*, and then click the *Perspective Above* option in the *Perspective* section.
   e. Click in the *Shape Height* measurement box in the Size group and then type **1**.
   f. Click in the *Shape Width* measurement box in the Size group, type **6**, and then press Enter.
   g. Click the Text Effects button in the WordArt Styles group, point to *Transform*, and then click the *Deflate* option in the *Warp* section (second option from the left in the sixth row).

h. Click the Position button in the Arrange group and then click the second option from the left in the first row in the *With Text Wrapping* section (*Position in Top Center with Square Text Wrapping*).

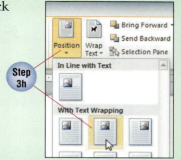
Step 3h

4. Check to make sure that the WordArt, the two arrows, and the text box all fit on one page. If they do not, consider moving and/or sizing the arrows or text box to ensure that they fit on one page.
5. Save, print, and then close **WL1-C5-P4-FinConsult.docx**.

Project 5   Create and Format Screenshots   2 Parts

You will create screenshots of the Print tab and Save & Send tab Backstage views and then create screen clippings of cover pages and create a sample cover pages document.

Creating and Inserting a Screenshot

The Illustrations group in the Insert tab contains a Screenshot button, which you can use to capture the contents of a screen as an image or capture a portion of a screen. If you want to capture the entire screen, open a new document, click the Insert tab, click the Screenshot button in the Illustrations group, and then click the desired screen thumbnail at the drop-down list. The currently active document does not display as a thumbnail at the drop-down list, only any other documents or files that you have open. When you click the desired thumbnail, the screenshot is inserted as an image in the open document, the image is selected, and the Picture Tools Format tab is active. Use buttons in this tab to customize the screenshot image.

Screenshot

Project 5a   Inserting and Formatting Screenshots   Part 1 of 2

1. Open a blank document.
2. Open a second blank document, type **Print Tab Backstage View** at the left margin, and then press the Enter key.
3. Save the document and name it **WL1-C5-P5-BackstageViews**.
4. Click the Word button on the Taskbar, click the thumbnail representing the blank document, and then display the Print tab Backstage view by clicking the File tab and then clicking the Print tab.

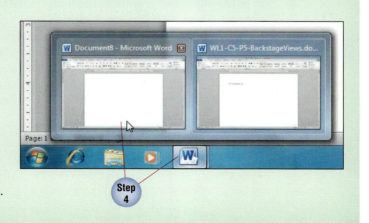
Step 4

Chapter 5 ■ Applying Formatting and Inserting Objects   183

5. Click the Word button on the Taskbar and then click the thumbnail representing **WL1-C5-P5-BackstageViews.docx**.
6. Insert and format a screenshot of the Print tab Backstage view by completing the following steps:
   a. Click the Insert tab.
   b. Click the Screenshot button in the Illustrations group and then click the thumbnail that displays in the drop-down list. (This inserts a screenshot of the Print tab Backstage view in the document.)
   c. With the screenshot image selected, click the More button that displays at the right side of the thumbnails in the Picture Styles group and then click the *Drop Shadow Rectangle* option.
   d. Select the measurement in the *Shape Width* measurement box in the Size group, type 5.5, and then press Enter.
7. Press Ctrl + End and then press the Enter key twice. (This moves the insertion point below the screenshot image.)
8. Type **Save & Send Tab Backstage View** at the left margin and then press the Enter key.
9. Click the Word button on the Taskbar and then click the thumbnail representing the blank document.
10. At the Backstage view, click the Save & Send tab. (This displays the Save & Send tab Backstage view.)
11. Click the Word button on the Taskbar and then click the thumbnail representing **WL1-C5-P5-BackstageViews.docx**.
12. Insert and format a screenshot of the Save & Send tab Backstage view by completing Step 6.
13. Press Ctrl + Home to move the insertion point to the beginning of the document.
14. Save, print, and then close **WL1-C5-P5-BackstageViews.docx**.
15. At the Save & Send tab Backstage view, click the Close button to close the document without saving it.

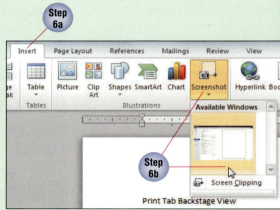

In addition to making a screenshot of an entire screen, you can make a screenshot of a specific portion of the screen by clicking the *Screen Clipping* option at the Screenshot button drop-down list. When you click this option, the other open document, file, or Windows desktop displays in a dimmed manner and the mouse pointer displays as a crosshair. Using the mouse, draw a border around the specific area of the screen you want to capture. The specific area you identified is inserted in the other document as an image, the image is selected, and the Picture Tools Format tab is active. If you have only one document or file open when you click the Screenshot tab, clicking the *Screen Clipping* option will cause the Windows desktop to display.

Project 5b — **Creating and Formatting a Screen Clipping** — Part 2 of 2

1. Open **NSSLtrhd.docx** and save it with Save As and name it **WL1-C5-P5-NSSCoverPages**.
2. Type the text **Sample Cover Pages** and then press the Enter key twice.
3. Select the text you just typed, change the font to 18-point Copperplate Gothic Bold, and then center the text.
4. Press Ctrl + End to move the insertion point below the text.
5. Open the document named **NSSCoverPg01.docx**.
6. Click the Word button on the Taskbar and then click the thumbnail representing **WL1-C5-P5-NSSCoverPages.docx**.
7. Create and format a screenshot screen clipping by completing the following steps:
    a. Click the Insert tab.
    b. Click the Screenshot button in the Illustrations group and then click *Screen Clipping*.
    c. When the **NSSCoverPg01.docx** displays in a dimmed manner, position the mouse crosshairs in the upper left corner of the cover page, hold down the left mouse button, drag down to the lower right corner of the cover page, and then release the mouse button. (See image at the right.)
    d. With the cover page screenshot image inserted in **WL1-C5-P5-NSSCoverPages.docx**, make sure the image is selected (sizing handles display around the cover page image).
    e. Click the Wrap Text button in the Arrange group in the Picture Tools Format tab and then click *Square* at the drop-down gallery.
    f. Select the current measurement in the *Shape Width* measurement box in the Size group, type 3, and then press Enter.
8. Click the Word button on the Taskbar and then click the thumbnail representing **NSSCoverPg01.docx** and then close the document.
9. Open **NSSCoverPg02.docx**.
10. Click the Word button on the Taskbar and then click the thumbnail representing **WL1-C5-P5-NSSCoverPages.docx**.
11. Create and format a screenshot by completing steps similar to those in Step 7.
12. Position the two cover page screenshot images so they are side by side in the document.
13. Save, print, and then close **WL1-C5-P5-NSSCoverPages.docx**.
14. Close **NSSCoverPg02.docx**.

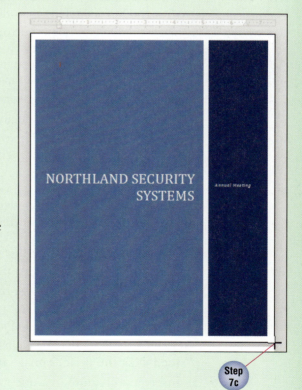

Chapter 5 ■ Applying Formatting and Inserting Objects

Chapter Summary

- Insert a section break in a document to apply formatting to a portion of a document. You can insert a continuous section break or a section break that begins a new page. View a section break in Draft view since section breaks are not visible in Print Layout view.
- Set text in columns to improve readability of documents such as newsletters or reports. Format text in columns using the Columns button in the Page Setup group in the Page Layout tab or with options at the Columns dialog box.
- Remove column formatting with the Columns button in the Page Layout tab or at the Columns dialog box. Balance column text on the last page of a document by inserting a continuous section break at the end of the text.
- Improve the display of text lines by hyphenating long words that fall at the end of the line. You can automatically or manually hyphenate words in a document.
- To enhance the appearance of text, use drop caps to identify the beginning of major sections or parts of a paragraph. Create drop caps with the Drop Cap button in the Text group in the Insert tab.
- Insert symbols with options at the Symbol dialog box with the Symbols tab selected and insert special characters with options at the Symbol dialog box with the Special Characters tab selected.
- Click the Date & Time button in the Text group in the Insert tab to display the Date and Time dialog box. Insert the date or time with options at this dialog box or with keyboard shortcuts. If the date or time is inserted as a field, update the field with the Update Field key, F9.
- Use the click and type feature to center, right-align, and left-align text.
- Vertically align text in a document with the *Vertical alignment* option at the Page Setup dialog box with the Layout tab selected.
- Insert an image such as a picture or clip art with buttons in the Illustrations group in the Insert tab.
- Customize and format an image with options and buttons in the Picture Tools Format tab. Size an image with the *Shape Height* and *Shape Width* measurement boxes in the Size group in the Picture Tools Format tab or with the sizing handles that display around the selected image.
- Move an image with options from the Position button drop-down gallery located in the Picture Tools Format tab or by choosing a text wrapping style and then moving the image by dragging it with the mouse.
- To insert a picture, click the Insert tab, click the Picture button, navigate to the desired folder at the Insert Picture dialog box, and then double-click the picture.
- To insert a clip art image, click the Insert tab, click the Clip Art button, and then click the desired image in the Clip Art task pane.
- Insert a pull quote in a document with a built-in text box by clicking the Insert tab, clicking the Text Box button, and then clicking the desired built-in text box at the drop-down list.
- Draw shapes in a document by clicking the Shapes button in the Illustrations group in the Insert tab, clicking the desired shape at the drop-down list, and

then dragging in the document to draw the shape. Customize a shape with options at the Drawing Tools Format tab. Copy a shape by holding down the Ctrl key while dragging the selected shape.
- Draw a text box by clicking the Text Box button in the Text group in the Insert tab, clicking *Draw Text Box* at the drop-down list, and then clicking in the document or dragging in the document. Customize a text box with buttons at the Drawing Tools Format tab.
- Use WordArt to distort or modify text to conform to a variety of shapes. Customize WordArt with options at the Drawing Tools Format tab.
- Use the Screenshot button in the Illustrations group in the Home tab to capture the contents of a screen or capture a portion of a screen.
- Use buttons in the Picture Tools Format tab to customize a screenshot image.

Commands Review

FEATURE	RIBBON TAB, GROUP	BUTTON, OPTION	KEYBOARD SHORTCUT
Continuous section break	Page Layout, Page Setup	, Continuous	
Columns dialog box	Page Layout, Page Setup	, More Columns	
Columns	Page Layout, Page Setup		
Hyphenate words automatically	Page Layout, Page Setup	, Automatic	
Manual Hyphenation dialog box	Page Layout, Page Setup	, Manual	
Drop cap	Insert, Text		
Symbol dialog box	Insert, Symbols		
Date and Time dialog box	Insert, Text		
Insert date			Alt + Shift + D
Insert time			Alt + Shift + T
Update field			F9
Page Setup dialog box	Page Layout, Page Setup		
Insert Picture dialog box	Insert, Illustrations		
Clip Art task pane	Insert, Illustrations		
Pull quote (Built-in text box)	Insert, Text		

FEATURE	RIBBON TAB, GROUP	BUTTON, OPTION	KEYBOARD SHORTCUT
Shapes	Insert, Illustrations		
Text box	Insert, Text		
WordArt	Insert, Text		
Screenshot	Insert, Illustrations		

Concepts Check Test Your Knowledge

Completion: In the space provided at the right, indicate the correct term, symbol, or command.

1. View a section break in this view.

2. Format text into columns with the Columns button located in this group in the Page Layout tab.

3. Balance column text on the last page of a document by inserting this type of break at the end of the text.

4. The first letter of the first word of a paragraph that is set into a paragraph is called this.

5. The Symbol button is located in this tab.

6. This is the keyboard shortcut to insert the current date.

7. Use this feature to position the insertion point at a specific location and alignment in a document.

8. Vertically align text with the *Vertical alignment* option at the Page Setup dialog box with this tab selected.

9. Insert an image in a document with buttons in this group in the Insert tab.

10. Customize and format an image with options and buttons in this tab.

11. Size an image with the sizing handles that display around the selected image or with these measurement boxes in the Picture Tools Format tab.

12. Click the Picture button in the Insert tab and this dialog box displays.

13. Click the Clip Art button in the Insert tab and this displays at the right side of the screen. _____

14. This is the term for a quote that is enlarged and positioned in an attractive location on the page. _____

15. Apply predesigned styles to a text box with options in this group. _____

16. The Shapes button is located in this tab. _____

17. To copy a selected shape, hold down this key while dragging the shape. _____

18. Use this feature to distort or modify text to conform to a variety of shapes. _____

19. To capture a portion of a screen, click the Screenshot button in the Illustrations group in the Insert tab and then click this option at the drop-down list. _____

Skills Check Assess Your Performance

Assessment

1 ADD VISUAL APPEAL TO A REPORT ON THE FUTURE OF THE INTERNET

1. Open **Internet2.docx** and then save the document with Save As and name it **WL1-C5-A1-Internet2**.
2. Apply the Heading 1 style to the title of the report and apply the Heading 3 style to the headings in the report. ***Hint: You may need to click the Heading 2 style to display the Heading 3 style.***
3. Change the Quick Styles set to *Thatch* and then center the title.
4. Apply the Elemental theme and then change the theme colors to *Solstice*.
5. Format the text from the first paragraph to the end of the document into two columns with 0.4 inches between columns.
6. Balance the text on the second page.
7. Insert a clip art image related to *satellite*. (Choose the clip art image that is available with Word and does not require downloading. This clip art image is blue and black and contains a satellite and a person holding a telephone and a briefcase.)
8. Make the following customizations to the clip art image:
   a. Change the height to 1.2".
   b. Apply tight text wrapping.
   c. Change the color of the clip art image to *Aqua, Accent color 1 Light*.
   d. Correct the contrast to Brightness: 0% (Normal) Contrast: −20%.
   e. Drag the image so it is positioned at the left margin in the *Satellite Internet Connections* section.

9. Insert the *Alphabet Quote* built-in text box and then make the following customizations:
   a. Type the following text in the text box: "A remedy for the traffic clogging the information highway is Internet2."
   b. Select the text and then change the font size to 12 and change the line spacing to 1.15.
   c. Apply the Subtle Effect - Aqua, Accent 1 style to the text box (second option from the left in the fourth row).
   d. Apply the Offset Bottom shadow effect to the text box.
   e. Drag the box so it is positioned above the SATELLITE INTERNET CONNECTIONS heading in the first column, below the SECOND INTERNET heading in the second column, and centered between the left and right margins.
10. Press Ctrl + End to move the insertion point to the end of the document. (The insertion point will be positioned below the continuous section break you inserted on the second page to balance the columns of text.)
11. Change back to one column.
12. Press the Enter key twice and then draw a shape using the *Plaque* shape (located in the second row in the *Basic Shapes* section) and make the following customizations:
    a. Recolor the shape to match the color formatting in the document or the built-in text box.
    b. Position the shape centered between the left and right margins.
    c. Make any other changes to enhance the visual appeal of the shape.
    d. Type the following text inside the shape: ☙ Felicité Compagnie ❧. Insert the ☙ and ❧ symbols at the Symbol dialog box with the Wingdings font selected. Insert the é symbol at the Symbol dialog box with the *(normal text)* font selected.
    e. Insert the current date below ☙ Felicité Compagnie ❧ and insert the current time below the date.
13. Manually hyphenate the document (do not hyphenate headings or proper names).
14. Create a drop cap with the first letter of the word *The* that begins the first paragraph of text.
15. Save, print, and then close **WL1-C5-A1-Internet2.docx**.

Assessment

2 CREATE A SALES MEETING ANNOUNCEMENT

1. Create an announcement about an upcoming sales meeting with the following specifications:
   a. Insert the company name *Inlet Corporation* as WordArt text.
   b. Insert the following text in the document:
      National Sales Meeting
      Northwest Division
      Ocean View Resort
      August 20 through August 22, 2012
   c. Insert the picture named **Ocean.jpg** and size and position the picture behind the text.
   d. Make any formatting changes to the WordArt, text, and picture to enhance the visual appeal of the document.
2. Save the announcement document and name it **WL1-C5-A2-SalesMtg**.
3. Print and then close **WL1-C5-A2-SalesMtg.docx**.

Assessment

3 CREATE AN ANNOUNCEMENT

1. At a blank document, create the announcement shown in Figure 5.8. Insert the caduceus clip art image as shown in the figure with the following specifications:
   a. Use the word *medicine* to locate the clip art image.
   b. Change the text wrapping to *Tight*.
   c. Change the clip art image color to *Blue, Accent color 1 Dark*.
   d. Correct the brightness and contrast to *Brightness: +20% Contrast: −20%*.
   e. Size and move the clip art image as shown in the figure.
2. Apply character (set the heading in 28-point Candara and the remaining text in 14-point Candara), paragraph, and page formatting so your document appears the same as the document in Figure 5.8.
3. Save the completed announcement and name it **WL1-C5-A3-FirstAidCourse**.
4. Print and then close **WL1-C5-A3-FirstAidCourse.docx**. (If some of the page border does not print, consider increasing the measurements at the Border and Shading Options dialog box.)

Figure 5.8 Assessment 3

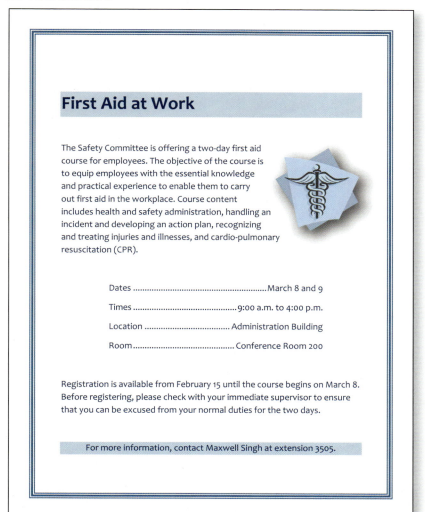

Assessment

4 INSERT SCREENSHOTS IN A MEMO

1. Open **FirstAidMemo.docx** and then save it with Save As and name it **WL1-C5-A4-FirstAidMemo**.
2. Insert screenshots so your document appears as shown in Figure 5.9. (Insert your initials in place of the XX located toward the end of the document.) Use the **FirstAidAnnounce.docx** document located in your Word2010L1C5 folder to create the first screenshot and use the document **WL1-C5-A3-FirstAidCourse.docx** you created in Assessment 3 for the second screenshot. *Hint: Decrease the size of the document so the entire document is visible on the screen*.
3. Save, print, and close **WL1-C5-A4-FirstAidMemo.docx**.

Figure 5.9 Assessment 4

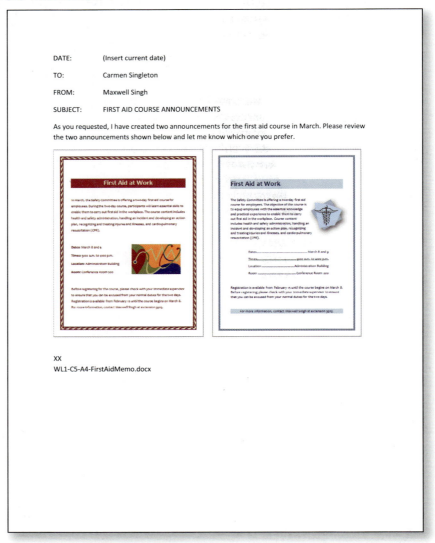

Visual Benchmark Demonstrate Your Proficiency

CREATE A SHAPE

1. At a blank document create the document shown in Figure 5.10 with the following specifications:
   a. Draw the shape using the *Quad Arrow Callout* located in the *Block Arrows* section.
   b. Apply the *Subtle Effect – Olive Green, Accent 3* shape style to the shape.
   c. Change the shape effect to *Soft Round* bevel.
   d. Change the height and width of the shape to 5 inches.
   e. Type the text in the shape as shown and set the text in 16-point Copperplate Gothic Bold and change the text color to dark green.
   f. Insert the truck clip art image and size and position it as shown in Figure 5.10. (If this truck clip art image is not available, choose another truck clip art image. Change the text wrap to *In Front of Text*.)
2. Center the shape on the page.
3. Save the document and name it **WL1-C5-VB1-FourCorners**.
4. Print and then close the document.

Figure 5.10 Visual Benchmark

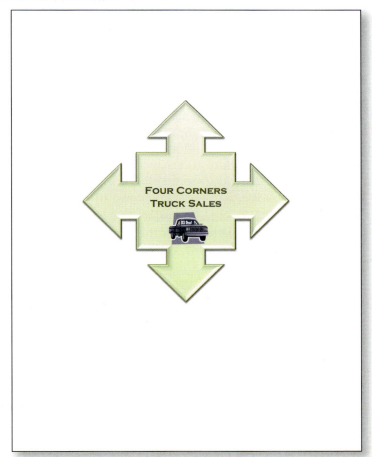

FORMAT A REPORT

1. Open **Resume.docx** and then save it with Save As and name it **WL1-C5-VB2-Resume**.
2. Format the report so it appears as shown in Figure 5.11 with the following specifications:
   a. Insert the WordArt text *Résumé Writing* with the following specifications:
      - Use the *Gradient Fill – Blue, Accent 1* option (fourth option from the left in the third row).
      - Type the text **Résumé Writing** and insert the é symbol using the Insert Symbol dialog box.
      - Change the position to *Position in Top Center with Square Text Wrapping* (middle option in the top row of the *With Text Wrapping* section).
      - Change the width of the WordArt to 5.5 inches and the height to 0.9 inch.
      - Apply the *Can Up* transform text effect. **Hint: Use the Transform** *option from the Text Effects button drop-down list*.
   b. Apply the Heading 3 style to the two headings in the report.
   c. Change the Quick Styles set to *Modern*.
   d. Change the theme to *Aspect* and change the theme colors to *Flow*.
   e. Format the report into two columns beginning with the first paragraph of text and balance the columns on the second page.
   f. Insert the pull quote with the following specifications:
      - Use the *Austere Quote*.
      - Type the text shown in the pull quote in Figure 5.11. (Use the Insert Symbol dialog box to insert the two é symbols in the word résumé.)
      - Change the pull quote text color to dark blue.
      - Select the text box (make sure the border displays as a solid line), make the Drawing Tools Format tab active, and then change the shape outline color to blue.
   g. Insert the cake clip art image with the following specifications:
      - Insert the clip art image shown in the figure. If this image is not available, choose a similar image of a cake.
      - Change the image color to *Blue, Accent color 1 Light*.
      - Change the width to 1.2 inches.
      - Change the text wrapping to *Tight*.
      - Position the cake image as shown in Figure 5.11.
   h. Insert the *Conservative* footer.
   i. Manually hyphenate text in the document.
3. Save, print, and then close **WL1-C5-VB2-Resume.docx**.

Figure 5.11 Visual Benchmark

Résumé Writing

To produce the best "fitting" résumé, you need to know about yourself and you need to know about the job you are applying for. Before you do anything else, ask yourself why you are preparing a résumé. The answer to this question is going to vary from one person to the next, and here are our top ten reasons for writing a résumé:

1. You have seen a job advertised in the paper that appeals to you.
2. You want to market yourself to win a contract or a proposal, or be elected to a committee or organization.
3. You have seen a job on an Internet job site that appeals to you.
4. Your friends or family told you of a job opening at a local company.
5. You want to work for the local company and thought that sending a résumé to them might get their attention.
6. You have seen a job advertised internally at work.
7. You are going for a promotion.
8. You are feeling fed up and writing down all your achievements will cheer you up and might motivate you to look for a better job.
9. You are thinking "Oh, so that's a résumé! I suppose I ought to try to remember what I've been doing with my life."
10. You are about to be downsized and want to update your résumé to be ready for any good opportunities.

"Updating your résumé from time to time is a good idea so you do not forget important details..."

All of these certainly are good reasons to write a résumé, but the résumé serves many different purposes. One way of seeing the differences is to ask yourself who is going to read the résumé in each case.

Résumés 1 through 5 will be read by potential employers who probably do not know you. Résumés 6 and 7 are likely to be read by your boss or other people who know you. Résumés 8 through 10 are really for your own benefit and should not be considered as suitable for sending out to employers.

THE RIGHT MIX

Think about the list of reasons again. How else can you divide up these reasons? An important difference is that, in some cases, you will have a good idea of what the employer is looking for because you have a job advertisement in front of you and can tailor your résumé accordingly. For others, you have no idea what the reader might want to see. Updating your résumé from time to time is a good idea so you do not forget important details, but remember that the result of such a process will not be a

Page 1

---

winning résumé. It will be a useful list of tasks and achievements.

Writing a résumé is like baking a cake. You need all the right ingredients: flour, butter, eggs, and so on. It is what you do with the ingredients that makes the difference between a great résumé (or cake) and failure. Keeping your résumé up-to-date is like keeping a stock of ingredients in the pantry—it's potentially very useful, but do not imagine that is the end of it!

INFORMATION ABOUT THE JOB

You should tailor the information in your résumé to the main points in the job advertisement. Get as much information about the job and the company as you can. The main sources of information about a job are normally the following:

- A job advertisement
- A job description
- A friend in the company
- The media
- Gossip and rumor
- Someone already doing the job or something similar

There is no substitute for experience. Talking to someone who does a job similar to the one you wish to apply for in the same company may well provide you with a good picture of what the job is really like. Bear in mind, of course, that this source of information is not always reliable. You may react differently than the way that person does, and therefore their experience with a company may be very different from yours. However, someone with reliable information can provide a golden opportunity. Make sure you do not waste the chance to get some information.

Page 2

Case Study — Apply Your Skills

Part 1

You work for Honoré Financial Services and have been asked by the office manager, Jason Monroe, to prepare an information newsletter. Mr. Monroe has asked you to open the document named **Budget.docx** and then format it into columns. You determine the number of columns and any additional enhancements to the columns. He also wants you to proofread the document and correct any spelling and grammatical errors. Save the completed newsletter and name it **WL1-C5-CS-P1-Budget** and then print the newsletter. When Mr. Monroe reviews the newsletter, he decides that it needs additional visual appeal. He wants you to insert visual elements in the newsletter such as WordArt, clip art, a built-in text box, and/or a drop cap. Save **WL1-C5-CS-P1-Budget.docx** and then print and close the document.

Part 2

Honoré Financial Services will be offering a free workshop on Planning for Financial Success. Mr. Monroe has asked you to prepare an announcement containing information on the workshop. You determine what to include in the announcement such as the date, time, location, and so forth. Enhance the announcement by inserting a picture or clip art and by applying formatting such as font, paragraph alignment, and borders. Save the completed document and name it **WL1-C5-CS-P2-Announce**. Print and then close the document.

Part 3

Honoré Financial Services has adopted a new slogan and Mr. Monroe has asked you to create a shape with the new slogan inside. Experiment with the shadow and 3-D shape effects available at the Drawing Tools Format tab and then create a shape and enhance the shape with shadow and/or 3-D effects. Insert the new Honoré Financial Services slogan "Retirement Planning Made Easy" in the shape. Include any additional enhancements to improve the visual appeal of the shape and slogan. Save the completed document and name it **WL1-C5-CS-P3-Slogan**. Print and then close the document.

Part 4

Mr. Monroe has asked you to prepare a document containing information on teaching children how to budget. Use the Internet to find websites and articles that provide information on how to teach children to budget their money. Write a synopsis of the information you find and include at least four suggestions on how to teach children to manage their money. Format the text in the document into newspaper columns. Add additional enhancements to improve the appearance of the document. Save the completed document and name it **WL1-C5-CS-P4-ChildBudget**. Print and then close the document.

Microsoft Word

Maintaining Documents

CHAPTER 6

PERFORMANCE OBJECTIVES

Upon successful completion of Chapter 6, you will be able to:
- Create and rename a folder
- Select, delete, copy, move, rename, and print documents
- Save documents in different file formats
- Open, close, arrange, split, maximize, minimize, and restore documents
- Insert a file into an open document
- Print specific pages and sections in a document
- Print multiple copies of a document
- Print envelopes and labels
- Create a document using a Word template

Almost every company that conducts business maintains a filing system. The system may consist of documents, folders, and cabinets; or it may be a computerized filing system where information is stored on the computer's hard drive or other storage medium. Whatever type of filing system a business uses, daily maintenance of files is important to a company's operation. In this chapter, you will learn to maintain files (documents) in Word, including such activities as creating additional folders and copying, moving, and renaming documents. You will also learn how to create and print documents, envelopes, and labels and create a document using a Word template. Model answers for this chapter's projects appear on the following pages.

Word2010L1C6

Note: Before beginning the projects, copy to your storage medium the Word2010L1C6 subfolder from the Word2010L1 folder on the CD that accompanies this textbook and then make Word2010L1C6 the active folder.

Project 1 Manage Documents

WL1-C6-P1-CompKeyboards.docx

WL1-C6-P1-AptLease-PlainTxt.txt

WL1-C6-P1-AptLease-RichText.rtf

Project 2 Manage Multiple Documents

WL1-C6-P2-CommIndustry.docx

SECTION 2: COMPUTERS IN COMMUNICATION

Computers have become central to the communications industry. They play a vital role in telecommunications, publishing, and news services.

TELECOMMUNICATIONS

The industry that provides for communication across distances is called telecommunications. The telephone industry uses computers to switch and route calls automatically over telephone lines. Today, many kinds of information move over such lines, including the spoken word, faxes, and computer data. Data can be sent over telephone lines from computer to computer using a device known as a modem. One kind of data sent by modem is electronic mail, or email, which can be sent from person to person via the Internet or an online service. A recent innovation in telecommunications is teleconferencing, which allows people in various locations to see and hear one another and thus hold virtual meetings.

PUBLISHING

Just twenty years ago, a book manuscript had to be typeset mechanically or on a typesetting machine and then reproduced on a printing press. Now anyone who has access to a computer and either a modem or a printer can undertake what has come to be known as electronic publishing. Writers and editors use word processing applications to produce text. Illustrations and photographs are digitized, or turned into computer-readable files, by means of inexpensive scanners. Artists and designers use drawing and painting applications to create original graphics. Typesetters use personal computers to combine text, illustrations, and photographs. Publishers typically send computer-generated files to printers for production of the film and plates from which books and magazines are printed.

NEWS SERVICES

News providers rely on reporters located worldwide. Reporters use email to send, or upload, their stories to wire services. Increasingly, individuals get daily news reports from online services. News can also be accessed from specific providers, such as the *New York Times* or *U.S.A. Today*, via the Internet. One of the most popular Internet sites provides continuously updated weather reports.

Page 2

SECTION 3: COMPUTERS IN EDUCATION

The widespread use of home computers has brought about an increase in the availability of educational and reference software, making the computer a popular learning and reference tool. Examples of educational and reference software include encyclopedias, dictionaries, and learning tutorials.

ENCYCLOPEDIAS AND DICTIONARIES

Almost everyone has used an encyclopedia or dictionary at one time or another. An encyclopedia is a comprehensive reference work containing detailed articles on a broad range of subjects. Before computers, encyclopedias were only available in book form. They are now available electronically and many new PCs include a CD-based encyclopedia.

A standard dictionary is a reference work containing an alphabetical listing of words, with definitions that provide the word's meaning, pronunciation, and usage. Examples include *Webster's Dictionary* and *Webster's New World Dictionary of Computer Terms*. Other specialized dictionaries, such as multi-language dictionaries, contain words along with their equivalent in another language for use in translation. Many dictionaries are available on CD.

LEARNING TUTORIALS

Many people learn skills by using CD- or Internet-based tutorials. A tutorial is a form of instruction in which students are guided step-by-step through the learning process. Tutorials are available for almost any subject, including learning how to assemble a bicycle, use a word processor, or write a letter. Once an electronic tutorial is accessed, students need only follow the instructions displayed on the screen. Many tutorials include graphics to help guide students during the learning process.

Page 3

Project 3 Create and Print Envelopes

WENDY STEINBERG
4532 S 52 ST
BOSTON MA 21002-2334

GREGORY LINCOLN
4455 SIXTH AVE
BOSTON MA 21100-4409

WL1-C6-P3-Env.docx

Project 4 Create Mailing Labels

DAVID LOWRY	MARCELLA SANTOS	KEVIN DORSEY
12033 S 152 ST	394 APPLE BLOSSOM	26302 PRAIRIE DR
HOUSTON TX 77340	FRIENDSWOOD TX 77533	HOUSTON TX 77316

AL AND DONNA SASAKI	JACKIE RHYNER	MARK AND TINA ELLIS
1392 PIONEER DR	29039 107 AVE E	607 FORD AVE
BAYTOWN TX 77903	HOUSTON TX 77302	HOUSTON TX 77307

WL1-C6-P4-Labels.docx

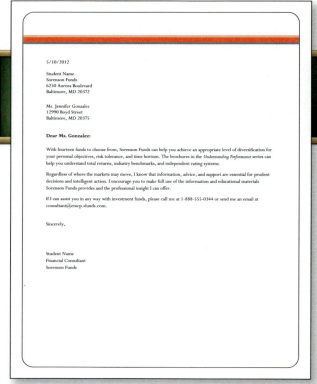

WL1-C6-P4-LAProg.docx

Project 5 Use a Template to Create a Business Letter

WL1-C6-P5-SFunds.docx

Project 1 Manage Documents   8 Parts

You will perform a variety of file management tasks including creating and renaming a folder; selecting and then deleting, copying, cutting, pasting, and renaming documents; deleting a folder; and opening, printing, and closing a document.

Maintaining Documents

Many file (document) management tasks can be completed at the Open dialog box (and some at the Save As dialog box). These tasks can include copying, moving, printing, and renaming documents; opening multiple documents; and creating a new folder and renaming a folder.

Using Print Screen

Keyboards contain a Print Screen key that you can use to capture the contents of the screen into a file. That file can then be inserted in a Word document. The Print Screen feature is useful for file management in that you can print folder contents to help you keep track of documents and folders. To use the Print Screen key, display the desired information on the screen and then press the Print Screen key on your keyboard (generally located in the top row). When you press the Print Screen key, nothing seems to happen but, in fact, the screen image is captured in a file that is inserted in the Clipboard. To insert this file in a document, display a blank document and then click the Paste button in the Clipboard group in the Home tab. You can also paste the file by right-clicking in a blank location in a document screen and then clicking the *Paste* option at the shortcut menu.

Creating a Folder

Word documents, like paper documents, should be grouped logically and placed in *folders*. The main folder on a storage medium is called the ***root folder*** and you can create additional folders within the root folder. At the Open or Save As dialog box, documents display in the Content pane preceded by a document icon and folders are preceded by a folder icon. Create a new folder by clicking the New folder button located on the dialog box toolbar. This inserts a folder in the Content pane that contains the text *New folder*. Type a name for the folder (the name you type replaces *New folder*) and then press Enter. A folder name can contain a maximum of 255 characters. Numbers, spaces, and symbols can be used in the folder name, except those symbols explained in Chapter 1 in the "Naming a Document" section.

▼ **Quick Steps**
Create a Folder
1. Display Open dialog box.
2. Click New folder button.
3. Type folder name.
4. Press Enter.

New Folder

To make the new folder active, double-click the folder name in the Open dialog box Content pane. The current folder path displays in the Address bar in the Open dialog box. The path includes the current folder as well as any previous folders. If the folder is located in an external storage device, the drive letter and name may display in the path. For example, if you create a folder named *Correspondence* in the Word2010L1C6 folder on your storage medium, the Address bar will display *Word2010L1C6* followed by a right-pointing triangle and then *Correspondence*. Two left-pointing arrows display before *Word2010L1C6*. These arrows indicate that *Word2010L1C6* is a subfolder within a folder. Click the two left-pointing arrows and a drop-down list displays with the folder name or drive letter that is up one level from *Word2010L1C6*. The drop-down list also includes other common folders and locations.

Back

Project 1a Creating a Folder   Part 1 of 8

1. Display the Open dialog box.
2. In the *Computer* list box in the Navigation pane, click the drive containing your storage medium. (You may need to scroll down the list to display the drive.)
3. Double-click the *Word2010L1C6* folder in the Content pane.
4. Click the New folder button on the dialog box toolbar.
5. Type **Correspondence** and then press Enter.
6. Print the screen contents and insert the file in a document by completing the following steps:
    a. With the Open dialog box displayed, press the Print Screen key on your keyboard (generally located in the top row of your keyboard).

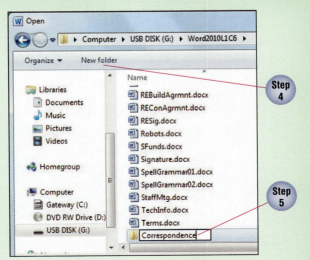

Chapter 6 ■ Maintaining Documents   201

b. Close the Open dialog box.
c. At the blank document, click the Paste button in the Clipboard group in the Home tab. (If a blank document does not display on your screen, press Ctrl + N to open a blank document.)
d. With the print screen file inserted in the document, print the document by clicking the File tab, clicking the Print tab, and then clicking the Print button at the Print tab Backstage view.
7. Close the document without saving it.
8. Display the Open dialog box and make Word2010L1C6 the active folder.

▼ **Quick Steps**

Rename a Folder
1. Display Open dialog box.
2. Right-click folder.
3. Click *Rename*.
4. Type new name.
5. Press Enter.

Organize

Renaming a Folder

As you organize your files and folders, you may decide to rename a folder. Rename a folder using the Organize button on the toolbar in the Open or Save As dialog box or using a shortcut menu. To rename a folder using the Organize button, display the Open or Save As dialog box, click the folder you want to rename, click the Organize button located on the toolbar in the dialog box, and then click *Rename* at the drop-down list. This selects the folder name and inserts a border around the name. Type the new name for the folder and then press Enter. To rename a folder using a shortcut menu, display the Open dialog box, right-click the folder name in the Content pane, and then click *Rename* at the shortcut menu. Type a new name for the folder and then press Enter.

Project 1b — Renaming a Folder — Part 2 of 8

1. With the Open dialog box open, right-click the *Correspondence* folder name in the Content pane.
2. Click *Rename* at the shortcut menu.
3. Type **Documents** and then press Enter.

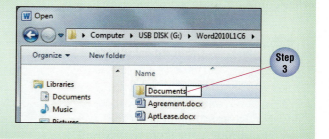

Selecting Documents

You can complete document management tasks on one document or selected documents. To select one document, display the Open dialog box, and then click the desired document. To select several adjacent documents (documents that display next to each other), click the first document, hold down the Shift key, and then click the last document. To select documents that are not adjacent, click the first document, hold down the Ctrl key, click any other desired documents, and then release the Ctrl key.

Deleting Documents

At some point, you may want to delete certain documents from your storage medium or any other drive or folder in which you may be working. To delete a document, display the Open or Save As dialog box, select the document, click the Organize button on the toolbar, and then click *Delete* at the drop-down list. At the dialog box asking you to confirm the deletion, click Yes. To delete a document using a shortcut menu, right-click the document name in the Content pane, click *Delete* at the shortcut menu, and then click Yes at the confirmation dialog box.

Documents deleted from the hard drive are automatically sent to the Recycle Bin. If you accidentally send a document to the Recycle Bin, it can be easily restored. To free space on the drive, empty the Recycle Bin on a periodic basis. Restoring a document from or emptying the contents of the Recycle Bin is completed at the Windows desktop (not in Word). To display the Recycle Bin, minimize the Word window, and then double-click the *Recycle Bin* icon located on the Windows desktop. At the Recycle Bin, you can restore file(s) and empty the Recycle Bin.

▼ **Quick Steps**

Delete Folder/ Document
1. Display Open dialog box.
2. Click folder or document name.
3. Click Organize button.
4. Click *Delete* at drop-down list.
5. Click Yes.

HINT
Remember to empty the Recycle Bin on a regular basis.

Project 1c   **Selecting and Deleting Documents**   Part 3 of 8

1. Open **FutureHardware.docx** and then save the document with Save As and name it **WL1-C6-P1-FutureHardware**.
2. Close **WL1-C6-P1-FutureHardware.docx**.
3. Delete **WL1-C6-P1-FutureHardware.docx** by completing the following steps:
   a. Display the Open dialog box.
   b. Click *WL1-C6-P1-FutureHardware.docx* to select it.
   c. Click the Organize button on the toolbar and then click *Delete* at the drop-down list.
   d. At the question asking if you want to delete **WL1-C6-P1-FutureHardware.docx**, click Yes.
4. Delete selected documents by completing the following steps:
   a. At the Open dialog box, click **CompCareers.docx**.
   b. Hold down the Shift key and then click **CompEthics.docx**.
   c. Position the mouse pointer on a selected document and then click the right mouse button.
   d. At the shortcut menu that displays, click *Delete*.
   e. At the question asking if you want to delete the items, click Yes.
5. Open **CompKeyboards.docx** and then save the document with Save As and name it **WL1-C6-P1-CompKeyboards**.
6. Save a copy of the **WL1-C6-P1-CompKeyboards.docx** document in the Documents folder by completing the following steps. (If your system does not contain this folder, check with your instructor to determine if another folder is available for you to use.)
   a. With **WL1-C6-P1-CompKeyboards.docx** open, click the File tab and then click the Save As button.

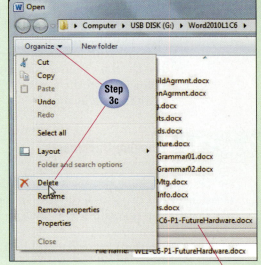

b. At the Save As dialog box, double-click the *Documents* folder located at the beginning of the Content. (Folders are listed before documents.)
  c. Click the Save button located in the lower right corner of the dialog box.
7. Close **WL1-C6-P1-CompKeyboards.docx**.
8. Display the Open dialog box and then click *Word2010L1C6* in the Address bar.

Step 8

Copying and Moving Documents

Quick Steps

Copy Documents
1. Display Open dialog box.
2. Right-click document name.
3. Click *Copy*.
4. Navigate to desired folder.
5. Right-click blank area in Content pane.
6. Click *Paste*.

You can copy a document to another folder without opening the document first. To do this, use the *Copy* and *Paste* options from the Organize button drop-down list or the shortcut menu at the Open or Save As dialog box. You can copy a document or selected documents into the same folder. When you do this, Word inserts a hyphen followed by the word *Copy* to the document name. You can copy one document or selected documents into the same folder.

Remove a document from one folder and insert it in another folder using the *Cut* and *Paste* options from the Organize button drop-down list or the shortcut menu at the Open dialog box. To do this with the Organize button, display the Open dialog box, select the desired document, click the Organize button, and then click *Cut* at the drop-down list. Navigate to the desired folder, click the Organize button, and then click *Paste* at the drop-down list. To do this with the shortcut menu, display the Open dialog box, position the arrow pointer on the document to be removed (cut), click the right mouse button, and then click *Cut* at the shortcut menu. Navigate to the desired folder, position the arrow pointer in a blank area in the Content pane, click the right mouse button, and then click *Paste* at the shortcut menu.

Project 1d Copying Documents   Part 4 of 8

1. At the Open dialog box with Word2010L1C6 the active folder, copy a document to another folder by completing the following steps:
   a. Click **CompTerms.docx** in the Content pane, click the Organize button, and then click *Copy* at the drop-down list.
   b. Navigate to the Documents folder by double-clicking *Documents* at the beginning of the Content pane.
   c. Click the Organize button and then click *Paste* at the drop-down list.
2. Change back to the Word2010L1C6 folder by clicking *Word2010L1C6* in the Address bar.
3. Copy several documents to the Documents folder by completing the following steps:
   a. Click once on ***IntelProp.docx***. (This selects the document.)
   b. Hold down the Ctrl key, click ***Robots.docx***, click ***TechInfo.docx***, and then release the Ctrl key. (You may need to scroll down the Content pane to display the three documents and then select the documents.)
   c. Position the arrow pointer on one of the selected documents, click the right mouse button, and then click *Copy* at the shortcut menu.
   d. Double-click the *Documents* folder.

e. Position the arrow pointer in any blank area in the Content pane, click the right mouse button, and then click *Paste* at the shortcut menu.
4. Click *Word2010L1C6* in the Address bar.
5. Move **CompIssues.docx** to the Documents folder by completing the following steps:
   a. Position the arrow pointer on **CompIssues.docx**, click the right mouse button, and then click *Cut* at the shortcut menu.
   b. Double-click *Documents* to make it the active folder.
   c. Position the arrow pointer in any blank area in the Content pane, click the right mouse button, and then click *Paste* at the shortcut menu.
6. Print the screen contents and insert the file in a document by completing the following steps:
   a. With the Open dialog box displayed, press the Print Screen key on your keyboard.
   b. Close the Open dialog box.
   c. At the blank document, click the Paste button in the Clipboard group in the Home tab. (If a blank document does not display on your screen, press Ctrl + N to open a blank document.)
   d. With the print screen file inserted in the document, print the document by clicking the File tab, clicking the Print tab, and then clicking the Print button at the Print tab Backstage view.
7. Close the document without saving it.
8. Display the Open dialog box and make Word2010L1C6 the active folder.

Renaming Documents

At the Open dialog box, use the *Rename* option from the Organize button drop-down list to give a document a different name. The *Rename* option changes the name of the document and keeps it in the same folder. To use Rename, display the Open dialog box, click once on the document to be renamed, click the Organize button, and then click *Rename* at the drop-down list. This causes a black border to surround the document name and the name to be selected. Type the desired name and then press Enter. You can also rename a document by right-clicking the document name at the Open dialog box and then clicking *Rename* at the shortcut menu. Type the desired name for the document and then press the Enter key.

▼ **Quick Steps**
Rename a Document
1. Display Open dialog box.
2. Click document name.
3. Click Organize button, *Rename*.
4. Type new name.
5. Press Enter.

Deleting a Folder

As you learned earlier in this chapter, you can delete a document or selected documents. Delete a folder and all its contents in the same manner as deleting a document.

Opening Multiple Documents

To open more than one document, select the documents in the Open dialog box, and then click the Open button. You can also open multiple documents by positioning the arrow pointer on one of the selected documents, clicking the right mouse button, and then clicking *Open* at the shortcut menu.

HINT
Open a recently opened document by clicking the File tab and then clicking the document in the *Recent Documents* list box.

Chapter 6 ■ Maintaining Documents   205

Project 1e Renaming and Opening Documents and Deleting a Folder   Part 5 of 8

1. Rename a document located in the Documents folder by completing the following steps:
   a. At the Open dialog box with the Word2010L1C6 folder open, double-click the *Documents* folder to make it active.
   b. Click once on **Robots.docx** to select it.
   c. Click the Organize button.
   d. Click *Rename* at the drop-down list.
   e. Type **Androids** and then press the Enter key.

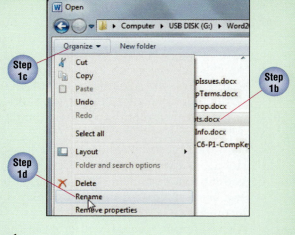

2. Print the screen contents and insert the file in a document by completing the following steps:
   a. Press the Print Screen key on your keyboard.
   b. Close the Open dialog box.
   c. At the blank document, click the Paste button in the Clipboard group in the Home tab. (If a blank document does not display on your screen, press Ctrl + N to open a blank document.)
   d. With the print screen file inserted in the document, print the document.
3. Close the document without saving it.
4. Display the Open dialog box and make Word2010L1C6 the active folder.
5. At the Open dialog box, click the *Documents* folder to select it.
6. Click the Organize button and then click *Delete* at the drop-down list.
7. At the question asking if you want to remove the folder and its contents, click Yes.
8. Select **CompIndustry.docx**, **CompKeyboards.docx**, and **CompTerms.docx**.
9. Click the Open button located toward the lower right corner of the dialog box.
10. Close the open documents.

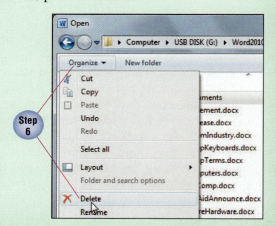

Sharing Documents

Click the File tab and then click the Save & Send tab and the Save & Send tab Backstage view displays as shown in Figure 6.1. With options at this view, you can share a document by sending it as an email attachment or a fax, save your document as a different file type, and post your document to a special location such as a blog.

Figure 6.1 Save & Send Tab Backstage View

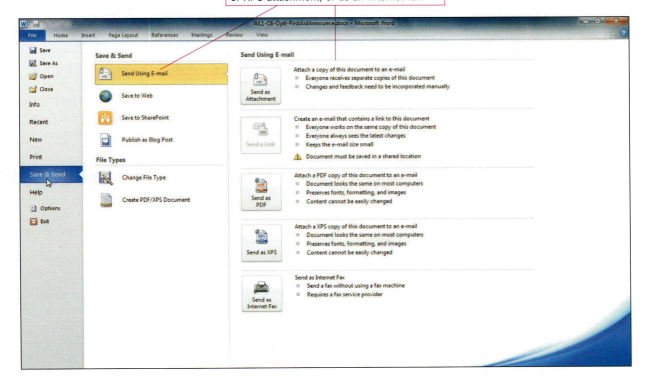

Sending a Document Using Email

When you click the *Send Using E-mail* option in the Save & Send category, options for sending a document display, such as sending a copy of the document as an attachment to an email, creating an email that contains a link to the document, attaching a PDF or XPS copy of the open document to an email, and sending an email as an Internet fax. To send the document as an attachment, you need to set up an Outlook email account. If you want to create an email that contains a link to the document, you need to save the document to a web server. Use the last button, Send as Internet Fax, to fax the current document without using a fax machine. To use this button, you must be signed up with a fax service provider. If you have not previously signed up for a service, you will be prompted to do so.

With the remaining two buttons in the Send Using E-mail category of the Save & Send tab Backstage view, you can send the document in PDF or XPS format. The letters *PDF* stand for *portable document format*, which is a document format developed by Adobe Systems® that captures all of the elements of a document as an electronic image. An XPS document is a Microsoft document format for publishing content in an easily viewable format. The letters *XPS* stand for *XML paper specification* and the letters *XML* stand for *Extensible Markup Language*, which is a set of rules for encoding documents electronically. The options below *Attach a PDF copy of this document to an e-mail* and below *Attach a XPS copy of this document to an e-mail* describe the format and the advantages of sending a document in the PDF or XPS format.

A file's format is indicated by a three- or four-letter extension after the file name.

Saving to SkyDrive

If you want to share documents with others, consider saving documents to SkyDrive, which is a file storage and sharing service that allows you to upload files that can be accessed from a web browser. To save a document to SkyDrive, you need a Windows Live ID account. If you have a Hotmail, Messenger, or Xbox LIVE account, you have a Windows Live ID account. To save a document to SkyDrive, open the document, click the File tab, click the Save & Send tab, and then click the *Save to Web* option in the Save & Send category. In the Save to Windows Live category, click the Sign In button. At the connecting dialog box, type your email address, press the Tab key, type your password, and then press Enter. Once you are connected to your Windows Live ID account, specify whether you want the file saved to your personal folder or saved to your shared folder, and then click the Save As button. At the Save As dialog box, click the Save button or type a new name in the *File name* text box and then click the Save button. One method for accessing your file from SkyDrive is to log into your Windows Live ID account and then look for the SkyDrive hyperlink. Click this hyperlink and your personal and shared folder contents display.

Saving to SharePoint

Microsoft SharePoint is a collection of products and software that includes a number of components. If your company or organization uses SharePoint, you can save a document in a library on your organization's SharePoint site so you and your colleagues have a central location for accessing documents. To save a document to a SharePoint library, open the document, click the File tab, click the Save & Send tab, and then click the *Save to SharePoint* option.

Saving a Document as a Blog Post

You can save a Word document as a blog post with the *Publish as Blog Post* option in the Save & Send tab Backstage view. To save a blog post, you must have a blog site established. Click the *Publish as Blog Post* option and information about supported blog sites displays at the right side of the Save & Send tab Backstage view. To publish a document as a blog post, open the document, click the File tab, click the Save & Send tab, click the *Publish as Blog Post* option in the Save & Send category, and then click the *Publish as Blog Post* option in the Publish as Blog Post category. If you have a blog site established, the document will open in a new window. Type a title for the blog post and then click the Publish button that displays in the Blog group in the Blog Post tab.

Optional Project — Sending a Document as an Email Attachment, Saving to SkyDrive, and Publishing as a Blog Post

Before completing this optional exercise, check with your instructor to determine if you have Outlook set up as your email provider, if you have a Windows Live ID account, and if you have a blog site established for use in the course.

1. Open **FirstAidAnnounce.docx** and then save the document with Save As and name it **WL1-C6-Optl-FirstAidAnnounce**.
2. Send the document as an email attachment by completing the following steps:

a. Click the File tab, click the Save & Send tab, and then make sure the *Send Using E-mail* option is selected.
b. Click the Send as Attachment button in the Send Using E-mail category.
c. At the Outlook window, type your instructor's email address in the *To* text box.
d. Click the Send button.

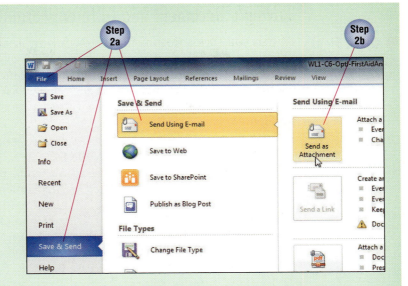

3. With **WL1-C6-Optl-FirstAidAnnounce.docx** open, save the document to SkyDrive by completing the following steps:
   a. Click the File tab, click the Save & Send tab, and then click the *Save to Web* option in the Save & Send category.
   b. In the Save to Windows Live category, click the Sign In button.
   c. At the connecting dialog box, type your email address, press the Tab key, type your password, and then press Enter.
   d. Once you are connected to your Windows Live ID account, specify whether you want the file saved to your personal folder or saved to your shared folder, and then click the Save As button.
   e. At the Save As dialog box, click the Save button.
   f. Close **WL1-C6-Optl-FirstAidAnnounce.docx**.

4. If you have a blog site established, save the first aid announcement as a blog post by completing the following steps:
   a. Open the **WL1-C6-Optl-FirstAidAnnounce.docx** document.
   b. Click the File tab, click the Save & Send tab, and then click the *Publish as Blog Post* option in the Save & Send category.
   c. Click the Publish as Blog Post button in the Publish as Blog Post category.
   d. If you have a blog site established, the document will open in a new window. Type a title for the blog post and then click the Publish button that displays in the Blog group in the Blog Post tab.
   e. Close the blog post document.
5. Close **WL1-C6-Optl-FirstAidAnnounce.docx**.

Saving a Document in a Different Format

▼ **Quick Steps**

Save Document in Different Format
1. Click File tab.
2. Click Save & Send tab.
3. Click *Change File Type* option in File Types category.
4. Click desired format in Change File Type category.
5. Click Save As button.

When you save a document, the document is saved automatically as a Word document. If you need to share a document with someone who is using a different word processing program or a different version of Word, you may want to save the document in another format. At the Save & Send tab Backstage view, click the *Change File Type* option in the File Types category and the view displays as shown in Figure 6.2.

With options in the *Document File Types* section, you can choose to save a Word document with the default file format, save the document in a previous version of Word, save the document in the OpenDocument Text format, or save the document as a template. The OpenDocument Text format is an XML-based file format for displaying, storing, and editing files such as word processing, spreadsheet, or presentation files. OpenDocument Text format is free from any licensing, royalty payments, or other restrictions and, since technology changes at a rapid pace, saving a document in the OpenDocument Text format ensures that the information in the file can be accessed, retrieved, and used now and in the future.

Additional file types are available in the *Other File Types* section. If you need to send your document to another user who does not have access to Microsoft Word, consider saving the document in plain text or rich text file format. Use the *Plain Text (*.txt)* option to save the document with all formatting stripped, which is good for universal file exchange. Use the *Rich Text Format (*.rtf)* option to save the

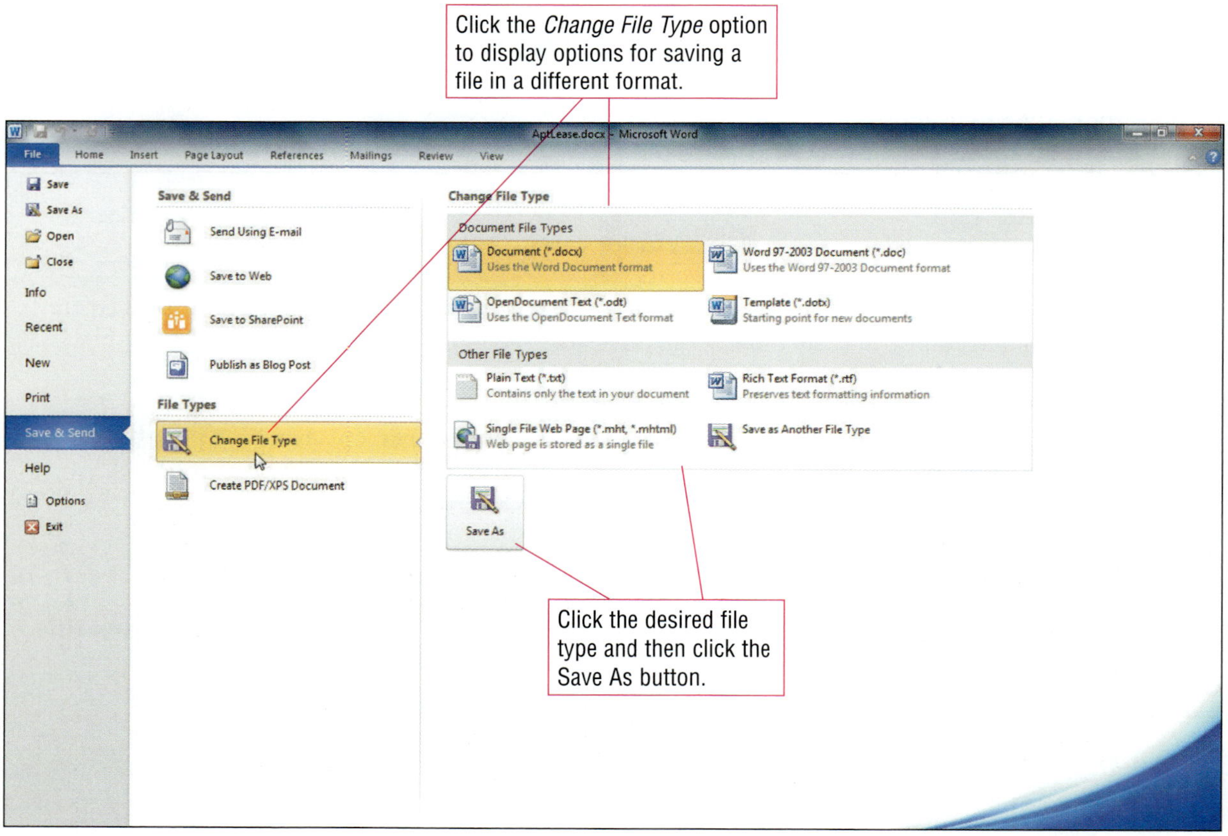

Figure 6.2 Save & Send Tab Backstage View with *Change File Type* Option Selected

document with most of the character formatting applied to text in the document such as bold, italic, underline, bullets, and fonts as well as some paragraph formatting such as justification. Before the widespread use of Adobe's portable document format (PDF), rich text format was the most portable file format used to exchange files. With the *Single File Web Page (*.mht, *.mhtml)* option, you can save your document as a single page web document. Click the *Save as Another File Type* option and the Save As dialog box displays. Click the *Save as type* option box and a drop-down list displays with a variety of available file type options.

Project 1f   Saving a Document in Different File Formats   Part 6 of 8

1. Open **AptLease.docx** and then save the document in Word 07-2003 format by completing the following steps:
   a. Click the File tab and then click the Save & Send tab.
   b. At the Save & Send tab Backstage view, click the *Change File Type* option in the File Types category.
   c. Click the *Word 97-2003 Document (*.doc)* option in the *Document File Types* section and then click the Save As button.

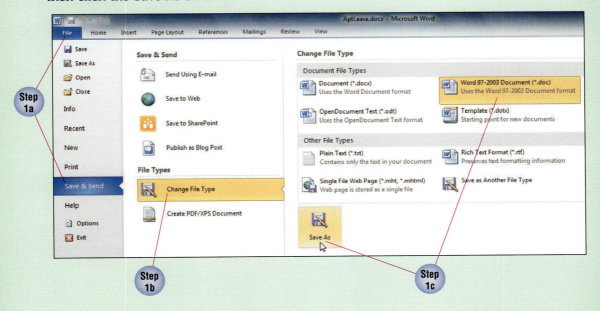

   d. At the Save As dialog box with the *Save as type* option changed to *Word 97-2003 Document (*.doc)*, type **WL1-C6-P1-AptLease-Word97-2003** and then press Enter.
2. At the document, notice the title bar displays the words *[Compatibility Mode]* after the document name.
3. Click the Page Layout tab and notice the buttons in the Themes group are dimmed. (This is because the themes features were not available in Word 97 through 2003.)
4. Close **WL1-C6-P1-AptLease-Word97-2003.doc**.
5. Open **AptLease.docx**.
6. Save the document in plain text format by completing the following steps:
   a. Click the File tab and then click the Save & Send tab.
   b. At the Save & Send tab Backstage view, click the *Change File Type* option in the File Types category.

c. Click the *Plain Text (*.txt)* option in the *Other File Types* section and then click the Save As button.
   d. At the Save As dialog box, type **WL1-C6-P1-AptLease-PlainTxt** and then press Enter.
   e. At the File Conversion dialog box, click OK.
7. Close **WL1-C6-P1-AptLease-PlainTxt.txt**.
8. Display the Open dialog box and, if necessary, display all files. To do this, click the file type button at the right side of the *File name* text box and then click *All Files (*.*)* at the drop-down list.
9. Double-click **WL1-C6-P1-AptLease-PlainTxt.txt**. (If a File Conversion dialog box displays, click OK. Notice that the character and paragraph formatting has been removed from the document.)
10. Close **WL1-C6-P1-AptLease-PlainTxt.txt**.

▼ **Quick Steps**

Save Document in Different Format at Save As Dialog Box
1. Open document.
2. Click File tab, click Save As button.
3. Type document name.
4. Click *Save as type* option box.
5. Click desired format at drop-down list.
6. Click Save button.

In addition to options in the Save & Send tab Backstage view with the *Change File Type* option selected, you can save a document in a different format using the *Save as type* option box at the Save As dialog box. Click the *Save as type* option box and a drop-down list displays containing all available file formats for saving a document.

Project 1g   Saving a Document in a Different Format Using the *Save as type* Option Box   Part 7 of 8

1. Open **AptLease.docx**.
2. Save the document in rich text format by completing the following steps:
   a. Click the File tab and then click the Save As button.
   b. At the Save As dialog box, type **WL1-C6-P1-AptLease-RichTxt** in the *File name* text box.
   c. Click in the *Save as type* option box.
   d. Click *Rich Text Format (*.rtf)*.
   e. Click the Save button.
3. Close the document.
4. Display the Open dialog box and, if necessary, display all files.
5. Double-click **WL1-C6-P1-AptLease-RichText.rtf**. (Notice that the formatting was retained in the document.)
6. Close the document.

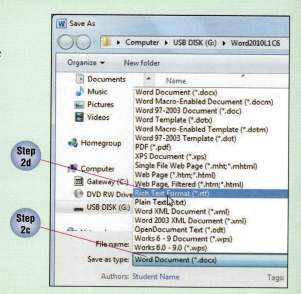

Saving in PDF/XPS Format

As you learned earlier, the portable document format (PDF) captures all of the elements of a document as an electronic image, and the XPS document format is a format for publishing content in an easily viewable format. To save a document in PDF or XPS format, click the File tab, click the Save & Send tab, click the *Create PDF/XPS Document* option in the File Types category, and then click the Create a PDF/XPS button in the *Create a PDF/XPS Document* section of the Backstage view. This displays the Publish as PDF or XPS dialog box with the *PDF (*.pdf)* option selected in the *Save as type* option box. If you want to save the document in XPS format, click in the *Save as type* option box and then click *XPS Document (*.xps)* at the drop-down list. At the Save As dialog box, type a name in the *File name* text box and then click the Publish button. If you save the document in PDF format, the document opens in Adobe Reader, and if you save the document in XPS format, the document opens in your browser window.

You can open a PDF file in Adobe Reader or in your web browser, and you can open an XPS file in your web browser. To open a PDF file or XPS file in your web browser, click File in the browser Menu bar and then click *Open* at the drop-down list. At the Open dialog box, click the Browse button. At the browser window Open dialog box, change the *Files of type* to *All Files (*.*)*, navigate to the desired folder, and then double-click the document.

▼ Quick Steps

Save Document in PDF/XPS Format
1. Open document.
2. Click File tab.
3. Click Save & Send tab.
4. Click *Create PDF/XPS Document* option.
5. Click Create PDF/XPS button.
6. At Publish as PDF or XPS dialog box, specify if you want to save in PDF or XPS format.
7. Click Publish button.

Project 1h Saving a Document in PDF Format   Part 8 of 8

1. Open **NSS.docx**
2. Save the document in PDF file format by completing the following steps:
   a. Click the File tab and then click the Save & Send tab.
   b. At the Save & Send tab Backstage view, click the *Create PDF/XPS Document* option in the File Types category.
   c. Click the Create PDF/XPS button.

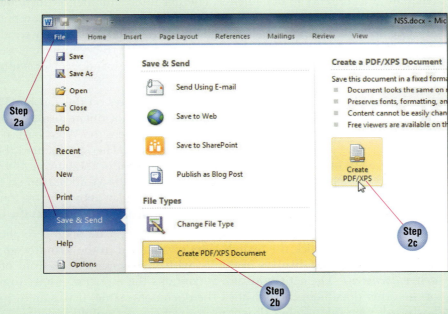

Chapter 6 ■ Maintaining Documents   213

d. At the Publish as PDF or XPS dialog box, make sure *PDF (*.pdf)* is selected in the *Save as type* option box and then click the Publish button.
3. Scroll through the document in Adobe Reader.
4. Click the Close button located in the upper right corner of the window to close Adobe Reader.
5. Close **NSS.docx**.
6. Print the screen contents of the Word2010L1C6 folder by completing the following steps:
  a. Display the Open dialog box with the Word2010L1C6 folder active.
  b. Make sure the Files of type displays as *All Files (*.*)*. (If necessary, scroll down the content pane to display your completed project documents.)
  c. Press the Print Screen key.
  d. Close the Open dialog box.
  e. At a blank document, click the Paste button.
  f. Print the document and then close the document without saving it.

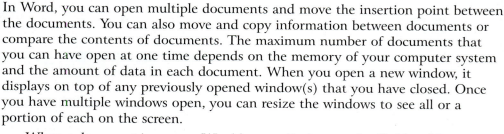

Working with Windows

Press Ctrl + F6 to switch between open documents.

In Word, you can open multiple documents and move the insertion point between the documents. You can also move and copy information between documents or compare the contents of documents. The maximum number of documents that you can have open at one time depends on the memory of your computer system and the amount of data in each document. When you open a new window, it displays on top of any previously opened window(s) that you have closed. Once you have multiple windows open, you can resize the windows to see all or a portion of each on the screen.

Press Ctrl + W or Ctrl + F4 to close the active document window.

When a document is open, a Word button displays on the Taskbar. Hover the mouse over this button and a thumbnail of the document displays above the button. If you have more than one document open, the Word button on the Taskbar displays another layer in a cascaded manner. The layer behind the Word button displays only a portion of the edge at the right of the button. If you have multiple documents open, hovering the mouse over the Word button on the Taskbar will cause thumbnails of all of the documents to display above the button. To change to the desired document, click the thumbnail that represents the document.

Another method for determining what documents are open is to click the View tab and then click the Switch Windows button in the Window group. The document name that displays in the list with the check mark in front of it is the ***active document***. The active document contains the insertion point. To make one of the other documents active, click the document name. If you are using the keyboard, type the number shown in front of the desired document.

Opening and Arranging Windows

If you open a document, click the View tab, and then click the New Window button in the Window group, Word opens a new window containing the same document. The document name in the Title bar displays followed by *:2*. Changes you make to one document are reflected in the other document.

If you have more than one document open, you can arrange them so a portion of each document displays. The portions that display are the titles (if present) and opening paragraphs of each document. To arrange a group of open documents, click the View tab and then click the Arrange All button in the Window group.

Maximizing, Restoring, and Minimizing Documents

Use the Maximize and Minimize buttons in the active document window to change the size of the window. The Maximize button is the button in the upper right corner of the active document immediately to the left of the Close button. (The Close button is the button containing the *X*.) The Minimize button is located immediately to the left of the Maximize button.

If you arrange all open documents and then click the Maximize button in the active document, the active document expands to fill the document screen. In addition, the Maximize button changes to the Restore button. To return the active document back to its size before it was maximized, click the Restore button. If you click the Minimize button in the active document, the document is reduced and a button displays on the Taskbar representing the document. To maximize a document that has been minimized, click the button on the Taskbar representing the document.

▼ **Quick Steps**

Open New Window
1. Open document.
2. Click View tab.
3. Click New Window button.

Arrange Windows
1. Open documents.
2. Click View tab.
3. Click Arrange All button.

Arrange All   Maximize

Minimize   Restore

Project 2a   Arranging, Maximizing, Restoring, and Minimizing Windows   Part 1 of 6

Note: If you are using Word on a network system that contains a virus checker, you may not be able to open multiple documents at once. Continue by opening each document individually.

1. Open the following documents: **AptLease.docx**, **IntelProp.docx**, **NSS.docx**, and **CommIndustry.docx**.
2. Arrange the windows by clicking the View tab and then clicking the Arrange All button in the Window group.
3. Make **IntelProp.docx** the active document by positioning the arrow pointer on the title bar for **IntelProp.docx** and then clicking the left mouse button.
4. Close **IntelProp.docx**.
5. Make **NSS.docx** active and then close it.
6. Make **CommIndustry.docx** active and minimize it by clicking the Minimize button in the upper right corner of the active window.
7. Maximize **AptLease.docx** by clicking the Maximize button at the right side of the Title bar. (The Maximize button is the button at the right side of the Title bar, immediately left of the Close button.)
8. Close **AptLease.docx**.
9. Restore **CommIndustry.docx** by clicking the button on the Taskbar representing the document.
10. Maximize **CommIndustry.docx**.

Step 6

Step 9

Splitting a Window

You can divide a window into two *panes*, which is helpful if you want to view different parts of the same document at one time. You may want to display an outline for a report in one pane, for example, and the portion of the report that you are editing in the other. The original window is split into two panes that extend horizontally across the screen.

Quick Steps

Split Window
1. Open document.
2. Click View tab.
3. Click Split button.
4. Click in document at desired split point.
OR
Drag split bar.

Split

Split a window by clicking the View tab and then clicking the Split button in the Window group. This causes a wide gray line to display in the middle of the screen and the mouse pointer to display as a double-headed arrow pointing up and down with a small double line between. Move this double-headed arrow pointer up or down, if desired, by dragging the mouse or by pressing the up- and/or down-pointing arrow keys on the keyboard. When the double-headed arrow is positioned at the desired location in the document, click the left mouse button or press the Enter key.

You can also split the window with the split bar. The split bar is the small black horizontal bar above the View Ruler button and up scroll arrow on the vertical scroll bar. To split the window with the split bar, position the arrow pointer on the split bar until it turns into a short double line with an up- and down-pointing arrow. Hold down the left mouse button, drag the double-headed arrow into the document screen to the location where you want the window split, and then release the mouse button. With the window split, you may decide you want to move certain objects or sections of text. Do this by selecting the desired object or text and then dragging and dropping it across the split bar.

When a window is split, the insertion point is positioned in the bottom pane. To move the insertion point to the other pane with the mouse, position the I-beam pointer in the other pane, and then click the left mouse button. To remove the split line from the document, click the View tab and then click the Remove Split button in the Window group. You can also double-click the split bar or drag the split bar to the top or bottom of the screen.

Project 2b   Moving Selected Text between Split Windows   Part 2 of 6

1. With **CommIndustry.docx** open, save the document with Save As and name it **WL1-C6-P2-CommIndustry**.
2. Click the View tab and then click the Split button in the Window group.
3. With the split line displayed in the middle of the document screen, click the left mouse button.
4. Move the first section below the second section by completing the following steps:
    a. Click the Home tab.
    b. Select the *SECTION 1: COMPUTERS IN COMMUNICATION* section from the title to right above *SECTION 2: COMPUTERS IN ENTERTAINMENT*.
    c. Click the Cut button in the Clipboard group in the Home tab.
    d. Position the arrow pointer at the end of the document in the bottom window pane and then click the left mouse button.
    e. Click the Paste button in the Clipboard group in the Home tab.

Word Level 1 ■ Unit 2

f. Change the number in the two titles to *SECTION 1: COMPUTERS IN ENTERTAINMENT* and *SECTION 2: COMPUTERS IN COMMUNICATION*.
5. Remove the split from the window by clicking the View tab and then clicking the Remove Split button in the Window group.
6. If the Section 2 title displays at the bottom of the first page, move the insertion point to the beginning of the title and then press Ctrl + Enter to insert a page break.
7. Save **WL1-C6-P2-CommIndustry.docx**.
8. Open a new window with the **WL1-C6-P2-CommIndustry.docx** document by clicking the New Window button in the Window group in the View tab. (Notice the document name in the Title bar displays followed by *:2*.)
9. Close the second version of the document by hovering the mouse pointer over the Word button on the Taskbar and then clicking the Close button in the upper right corner of the *WL1-C6-P2-CommIndustry.docx:2* thumbnail (the thumbnail that displays above the Word button on the Taskbar).

Viewing Documents Side by Side

If you want to compare the contents of two documents, open both documents, click the View tab, and then click the View Side by Side button in the Window group. Both documents are arranged in the screen side by side as shown in Figure 6.3. By default synchronous scrolling is active. With this feature active, scrolling in one document causes the same scrolling to occur in the other document. This feature is useful in situations where you want to compare text, formatting, or other features between documents. If you want to scroll in one document and not the other, click the Synchronous Scrolling button in the Window group in the View tab to turn it off.

▼ **Quick Steps**
View Side by Side
1. Open two documents.
2. Click View tab.
3. Click View Side by Side.

View Side by Side

Figure 6.3 Viewing Documents Side by Side

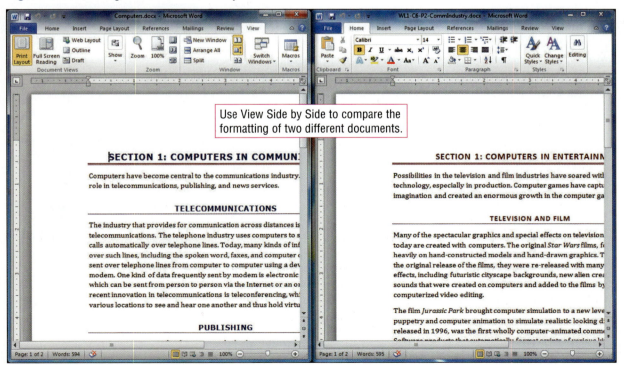

Chapter 6 ■ Maintaining Documents   217

Project 2c — Viewing Documents Side by Side — Part 3 of 6

1. With **WL1-C6-P2-CommIndustry.docx** open, open **Computers.docx**.
2. Click the View tab and then click the View Side by Side button in the Window group.
3. Scroll through both documents simultaneously. Notice the difference between the two documents. (The title and headings are set in a different font and color.) Select and then format the title and headings in **WL1-C6-P2-CommIndustry.docx** so they match the formatting in **Computers.docx**.
4. Save **WL1-C6-P2-CommIndustry.docx**.
5. Make **Computers.docx** the active document and then close it.

Step 2

Inserting a File

Quick Steps

Insert a File
1. Click Insert tab.
2. Click Object button arrow.
3. Click *Text from File*.
4. Navigate to desired folder.
5. Double-click document.

If you want to insert the contents of one document into another, use the Object button in the Text group in the Insert tab. Click the Object button arrow and then click *Text from File* and the Insert File dialog box displays. This dialog box contains similar features as the Open dialog box. Navigate to the desired folder and then double-click the document you want to insert in the open document.

Object

Project 2d — Inserting a File — Part 4 of 6

1. With **WL1-C6-P2-CommIndustry.docx** open, move the insertion point to the end of the document.
2. Insert a file into the open document by completing the following steps:
    a. Click the Insert tab.
    b. Click the Object button arrow in the Text group.
    c. Click *Text from File* at the drop-down list.
    d. At the Insert File dialog box, navigate to the Word2010L1C6 folder and then double-click **EduComp.docx**.
3. Check the formatting of the inserted text and format it to match the formatting of the original text.
4. Save **WL1-C6-P2-CommIndustry.docx**.

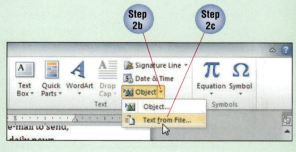

Step 2b, Step 2c

Printing and Previewing a Document

With options at the Print tab Backstage view shown in Figure 6.4, you can specify what you want to print and also preview the pages before printing. To display the Print tab Backstage view, click the File tab and then click the Print tab.

Previewing Pages in a Document

When you display the Print tab Backstage view, a preview of the page where the insertion point is positioned displays at the right side (see Figure 6.4). Click the Next Page button (right-pointing arrow), located below and to the left of the page, to view the next page in the document and click the Previous Page button (left-pointing arrow) to display the previous page in the document. Use the Zoom slider bar to increase/decrease the size of the page, and click the Zoom to Page button to fit the page in the viewing area in the Print tab Backstage view.

Zoom to Page

Figure 6.4 Print Tab Backstage View

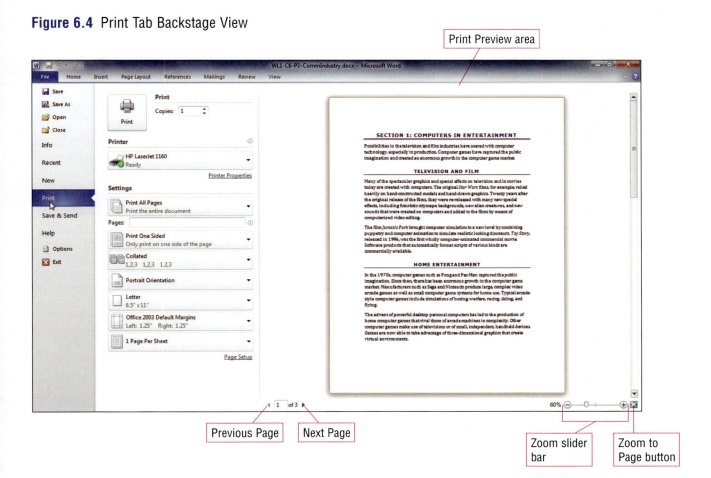

Project 2e Previewing the Document   Part 5 of 6

1. With **WL1-C6-P2-CommIndustry.docx** open, press Ctrl + Home to move the insertion point to the beginning of the document.
2. Preview the document by clicking the File tab and then clicking the Print tab.
3. At the Print tab Backstage view, click the Next Page button located below and to the left of the preview page. (This displays page 2 in the preview area.)
4. Click twice on the plus symbol that displays at the right side of the Zoom slider bar. (This increases the size of the preview page.)
5. Click four times on the minus symbol that displays at the left side of the Zoom slider bar. (This displays the two pages of the document in the preview area.)
6. Change the zoom at the Zoom dialog box by completing the following steps:
   a. Click the percentage number that displays at the left side of the Zoom slider bar.
   b. At the Zoom dialog box, click the *Many pages* option in the *Zoom to* section.
   c. Click OK to close the dialog box. (Notice that all pages in the document display as thumbnails in the preview area.)
7. Click the Zoom to Page button that displays at the right side of the Zoom slider bar. (This returns the page to the default size.)
8. Click the File tab to return to the document.

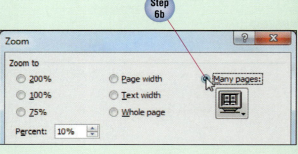
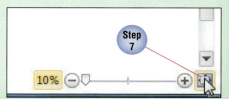

Printing Pages in a Document

HINT Save a document before printing it.

If you want control over what prints in a document, use options at the Print tab Backstage view. Click the first gallery in the Settings category and a drop-down list displays with options for printing all pages in the document, selected text, the current page, or a custom range of pages in the document. If you want to select and then print a portion of the document, choose the *Print Selection* option.

With this option, only the text that you have selected in the current document prints. (This option is dimmed unless text is selected in the document.) Click the *Print Current Page* option to print only the page on which the insertion point is located. With the *Print Custom Range* option, you can identify a specific page, multiple pages, or a range of pages to print. If you want specific pages printed, use a comma (,) to indicate *and* and use a hyphen (-) to indicate *through*. For example, to print pages 2 and 5, you would type 2,5 in the *Pages* text box. To print pages 6 through 10, you would type 6-10.

With the other galleries available in the Settings category of the Print tab Backstage view, you can specify on what sides of the pages you want to print, change the page orientation (portrait or landscape), specify how you want the pages collated, choose a page size, specify margins, and specify how many pages you want to print on a page.

If you want to print more than one copy of a document, use the *Copies* text box located to the right of the Print button. If you print several copies of a document that has multiple pages, Word collates the pages as they print. For example, if you print two copies of a three-page document, pages 1, 2, and 3 print, and then the pages print a second time. Printing collated pages is helpful for assembly but takes more printing time. To reduce printing time, you can tell Word *not* to print collated pages. To do this, click the Collated gallery in the Settings category and then click *Uncollated*.

If you want to send a document directly to the printer without displaying the Print tab Backstage view, consider adding the Quick Print button to the Quick Access toolbar. To do this click the Customize Quick Access Toolbar button located at the right side of the toolbar and then click *Quick Print* at the drop-down gallery. Click the Quick Print button and all pages of the active document print.

Project 2f Printing Specific Text and Pages   Part 6 of 6

1. With **WL1-C6-P2-CommIndustry.docx** open, print selected text by completing the following steps:
   a. Select the heading *Television and Film* and the two paragraphs of text that follow it.
   b. Click the File tab and then click the Print tab.
   c. At the Print tab Backstage view, click the first gallery in the Settings category and then click *Print Selection* at the drop-down list.
   d. Click the Print button.
2. Change the margins and page orientation and then print only the first page by completing the following steps:
   a. Press Ctrl + Home to move the insertion point to the beginning of the document.

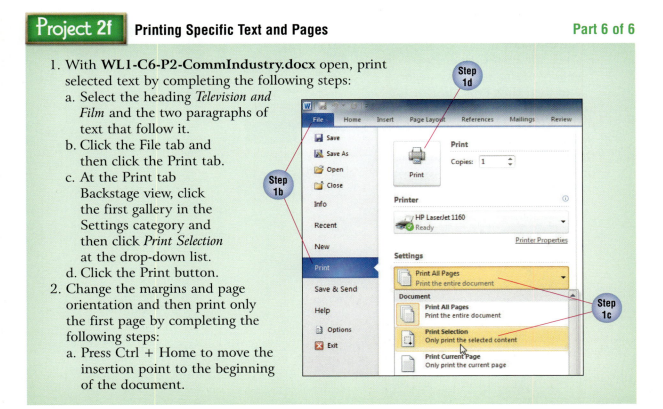

b. Click the File tab and then click the Print tab.
c. At the Print tab Backstage view, click the *Portrait Orientation* gallery in the Settings category and then click *Landscape Orientation* at the drop-down list.
d. Click the *Custom Margins* gallery in the Settings category and then click *Narrow* at the drop-down list.
e. Click the *Print All Pages* gallery in the Settings category and then click *Print Current Page* at the drop-down list.
f. Click the Print button. (The first page of the document prints in landscape orientation with 0.5-inch margins.)

3. Print all of the pages as thumbnails on one page by completing the following steps:
   a. Click the File tab and then click the Print tab.
   b. At the Print tab Backstage view, click the *1 Page Per Sheet* gallery in the Settings category and then click *4 Pages Per Sheet* at the drop-down list.
   c. Click the *Print Current Page* gallery in the Settings category and then click *Print All Pages* at the drop-down list.
   d. Click the Print button.

4. Select the entire document, change the line spacing to *1.5*, and then deselect the text.

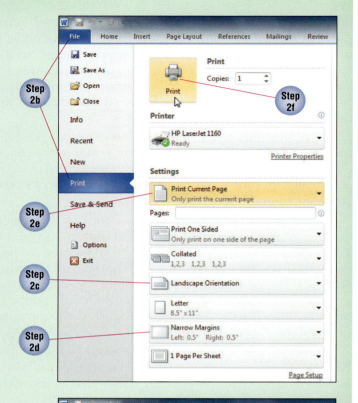

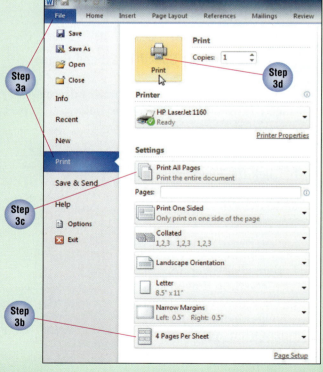

5. Print two copies of specific pages by completing the following steps:
   a. Click the File tab and then click the Print tab.
   b. Click the *Landscape Orientation* gallery in the Settings category and then click *Portrait Orientation* in the drop-down list.
   c. Click in the *Pages* text box located below the *Print Custom Range* gallery in the Settings category and then type *1,3*.
   d. Click the up-pointing arrow at the right side of the *Copies* text box (located to the right of the Print button) to display *2*.
   e. Click the *Collated* gallery in the Settings category and then click *Uncollated* at the drop-down list.
   f. Click the *4 Pages Per Sheet* gallery in the Settings category and then click *1 Page Per Sheet* at the drop-down list.
   g. Click the Print button. (The first page of the document will print twice and then the third page will print twice.)
6. Save and then close **WL1-C6-P2-CommIndustry.docx**.

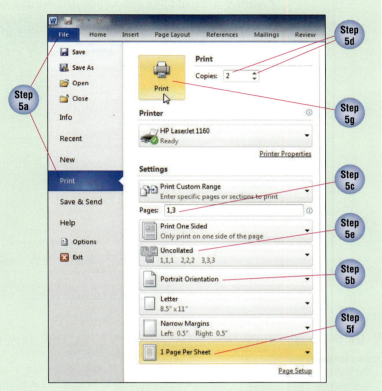

Project 3 Create and Print Envelopes   2 Parts

You will create an envelope document and type the return address and delivery address using envelope addressing guidelines issued by the United States Postal Service. You will also open a letter document and then create an envelope using the inside address.

Creating and Printing Envelopes

Word automates the creation of envelopes with options at the Envelopes and Labels dialog box with the Envelopes tab selected as shown in Figure 6.5. Display this dialog box by clicking the Mailings tab and then clicking the Envelopes button in the Create group. At the dialog box, type the delivery address in the *Delivery address* text box and the return address in the *Return address* text box. You can send the envelope directly to the printer by clicking the Print button or insert the envelope in the current document by clicking the Add to Document button.

Envelopes

Figure 6.5 Envelopes and Labels Dialog Box with Envelopes Tab Selected

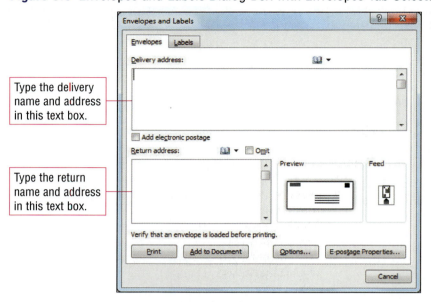

If you enter a return address before printing the envelope, Word will display the question *Do you want to save the new return address as the default return address?* At this question, click Yes if you want the current return address available for future envelopes. Click No if you do not want the current return address used as the default. If a default return address displays in the *Return address* section of the dialog box, you can tell Word to omit the return address when printing the envelope. To do this, click the *Omit* check box to insert a check mark.

The Envelopes and Labels dialog box contains a *Preview* sample box and a *Feed* sample box. The *Preview* sample box shows how the envelope will appear when printed and the *Feed* sample box shows how the envelope should be inserted into the printer.

When addressing envelopes, consider following general guidelines issued by the United States Postal Service (USPS). The USPS guidelines suggest using all capital letters with no commas or periods for return and delivery addresses. Figure 6.6 shows envelope addresses following the USPS guidelines. Use abbreviations for street suffixes (such as *ST* for *Street* and *AVE* for *Avenue*). For a complete list of address abbreviations, visit the www.emcp.net/usps site and then search for *Official USPS Abbreviations*.

▼ Quick Steps

Create Envelope
1. Click Mailings tab.
2. Click Envelopes button.
3. Type delivery address.
4. Click in *Return address* text box.
5. Type return address.
6. Click Add to Document button or Print button.

Project 3a Printing an Envelope   Part 1 of 2

1. At a blank document, create an envelope that prints the delivery address and return address shown in Figure 6.6. Begin by clicking the Mailings tab.
2. Click the Envelopes button in the Create group.
3. At the Envelopes and Labels dialog box with the Envelopes tab selected, type the delivery address shown in Figure 6.6 (the one containing the name *GREGORY LINCOLN*). (Press the Enter key to end each line in the name and address.)
4. Click in the *Return address* text box. (If any text displays in the *Return address* text box, select and then delete it.)

5. Type the return address shown in Figure 6.6 (the one containing the name *WENDY STEINBERG*). (Press the Enter key to end each line in the name and address.)
6. Click the Add to Document button.
7. At the message *Do you want to save the new return address as the default return address?*, click No.
8. Save the document and name it **WL1-C6-P3-Env**.
9. Print and then close **WL1-C6-P3-Env.docx**. *Note: Manual feed of the envelope may be required. Please check with your instructor.*

Figure 6.6 Project 3a

```
WENDY STEINBERG
4532 S 52 ST
BOSTON MA 21002-2334


                    GREGORY LINCOLN
                    4455 SIXTH AVE
                    BOSTON MA 21100-4409
```

If you open the Envelopes and Labels dialog box in a document containing a name and address (the name and address lines must end with a press of the Enter key and not Shift + Enter), the name and address are automatically inserted in the *Delivery address* section of the dialog box. To do this, open a document containing a name and address and then display the Envelopes and Labels dialog box. The name and address are inserted in the *Delivery address* section as they appear in the letter and may not conform to the USPS guidelines. The USPS guidelines for addressing envelopes are only suggestions, not requirements.

Chapter 6 ■ Maintaining Documents

Project 3b Creating an Envelope in an Existing Document Part 2 of 2

1. Open **LAProg.docx**.
2. Click the Mailings tab.
3. Click the Envelopes button in the Create group.
4. At the Envelopes and Labels dialog box (with the Envelopes tab selected), make sure the delivery address displays properly in the *Delivery address* section.
5. If any text displays in the *Return address* section, insert a check mark in the *Omit* check box (located to the right of the *Return address* option). (This tells Word not to print the return address on the envelope.)
6. Click the Print button.
7. Close **LAProg.docx** without saving changes.

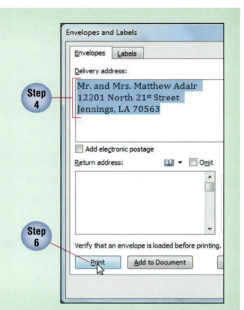

Project 4 Create Mailing Labels 2 Parts

You will create mailing labels containing names and addresses and then create mailing labels containing the inside address of a letter.

Creating and Printing Labels

Quick Steps

Create Labels
1. Click Mailings tab.
2. Click Labels button.
3. Type desired address(es).
4. Click New Document button or Print button.

Use Word's labels feature to print text on mailing labels, file labels, disc labels, or other types of labels. Word includes a variety of predefined formats for labels that can be purchased at an office supply store. To create a sheet of mailing labels with the same name and address using the default options, click the Labels button in the Create group in the Mailings tab. At the Envelopes and Labels dialog box with the Labels tab selected as shown in Figure 6.7, type the desired address in the *Address* text box. Click the New Document button to insert the mailing label in a new document or click the Print button to send the mailing label directly to the printer.

Labels

Changing Label Options

Click the Options button at the Envelopes and Labels dialog box with the Labels tab selected and the Label Options dialog box displays as shown in Figure 6.8. At the Label Options dialog box, choose the type of printer, the desired label product, and the product number. This dialog box also displays information about the selected label such as type, height, width, and paper size. When you select a label, Word automatically determines label margins. If, however, you want to customize these default settings, click the Details button at the Label Options dialog box.

Figure 6.7 Envelopes and Labels Dialog Box with Labels Tab Selected

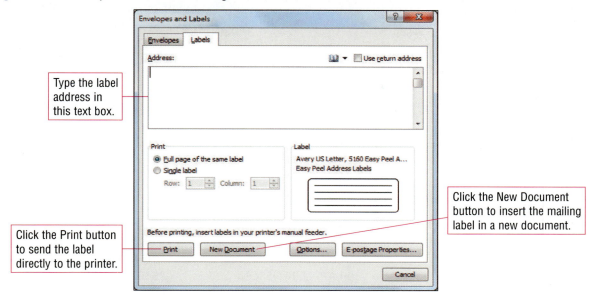

Figure 6.8 Label Options Dialog Box

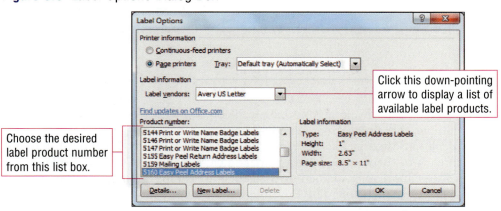

Project 4a — Creating Customized Mailing Labels   Part 1 of 2

1. At a blank document, click the Mailings tab.
2. Click the Labels button in the Create group.
3. At the Envelopes and Labels dialog box with the Labels tab selected, click the Options button.
4. At the Label Options dialog box, click the down-pointing arrow at the right side of the *Label vendors* option and then click *Avery US Letter* at the drop-down list.
5. Scroll down the *Product number* list box and then click *5160 Easy Peel Address Labels*.
6. Click OK or press Enter.

Chapter 6 ■ Maintaining Documents

7. At the Envelopes and Labels dialog box, click the New Document button.
8. At the document screen, type the first name and address shown in Figure 6.9 in the first label.
9. Press the Tab key twice to move the insertion point to the next label and then type the second name and address shown in Figure 6.9.
10. Continue in this manner until all names and addresses in Figure 6.9 have been typed.
11. Save the document and name it **WL1-C6-P4-Labels**.
12. Print and then close **WL1-C6-P4-Labels.docx**.
13. At the blank document, close the document without saving changes.

Figure 6.9 Project 4a

```
DAVID LOWRY            MARCELLA SANTOS         KEVIN DORSEY
12033 S 152 ST         394 APPLE BLOSSOM       26302 PRAIRIE DR
HOUSTON TX 77340       FRIENDSWOOD TX 77533    HOUSTON TX 77316

AL AND DONNA SASAKI    JACKIE RHYNER           MARK AND TINA ELLIS
1392 PIONEER DR        29039 107 AVE E         607 FORD AVE
BAYTOWN TX 77903       HOUSTON TX 77302        HOUSTON TX 77307
```

If you open the Envelopes and Labels dialog box with the Labels tab selected in a document containing a name and address, the name and address are automatically inserted in the *Address* section of the dialog box. To enter different names in each of the mailing labels, start at a clear document screen, display the Envelopes and Labels dialog box with the Labels tab selected, and then click the New Document button. The Envelopes and Labels dialog box is removed from the screen and the document displays with label forms. The insertion point is positioned in the first label form. Type the name and address in this label and then press the Tab key once or twice (depending on the label) to move the insertion point to the next label. Pressing Shift + Tab will move the insertion point to the preceding label.

Project 4b   Creating Mailing Labels   Part 2 of 2

1. Open **LAProg.docx** and create mailing labels with the delivery address. Begin by clicking the Mailings tab.
2. Click the Labels button in the Create group.

3. At the Envelopes and Labels dialog box with the Labels tab selected, make sure the delivery address displays properly in the *Address* section.
4. Click the New Document button.
5. Save the mailing label document and name it **WL1-C6-P4-LAProg.docx**.
6. Print and then close **WL1-C6-P4-LAProg.docx**.
7. Close **LAProg.docx**.

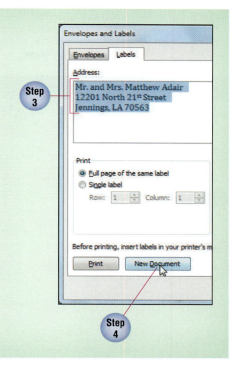

 **Use a Template to Create a Business Letter** 1 Part

You will use a letter template provided by Word to create a business letter.

Creating a Document Using a Template

Word includes a number of template documents formatted for specific uses. Each Word document is based on a template document with the *Normal* template the default. With Word templates, you can easily create a variety of documents, such as letters, faxes, and awards, with specialized formatting. Display templates by clicking the File tab and then clicking the New tab. This displays the New tab Backstage view as shown in Figure 6.10.

Click the Sample templates button in the Available Templates category and installed templates display. Click the desired template in the *Sample templates* list box and a preview of the template displays at the right side of the screen. With options below the template preview, you can choose to open the template as a document or as a template. Click the Create button and the template opens and displays on the screen. Locations for personalized text display in placeholders in the template document. Select the placeholder text and then type the personalized text.

If you are connected to the Internet, you can download a number of predesigned templates that Microsoft offers. Templates are grouped into categories and the category names display in the *Office.com Templates* section of the New tab Backstage view. Click the desired template category and available templates display. Click the desired template and then click the Download button.

▼ **Quick Steps**

Create Document Using a Template
1. Click File tab.
2. Click New tab.
3. Click Sample templates button.
4. Double-click desired template.

Chapter 6 ■ Maintaining Documents   **229**

Figure 6.10 New Tab Backstage View

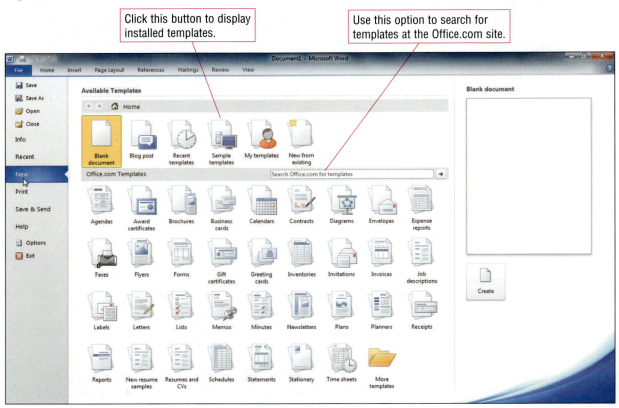

Project 5 — Creating a Letter Using a Template — Part 1 of 1

1. Click the File tab and then click the New tab.
2. At the New tab Backstage view, click the Sample templates button in the Available Templates category.

3. Double-click the *Equity Letter* template.

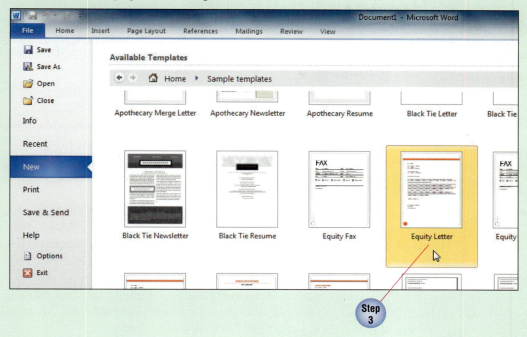

Step 3

4. At the letter document, click the placeholder text *[Pick the date]*, click the down-pointing arrow at the right side of the placeholder, and then click the Today button located at the bottom of the calendar.
5. Click in the name that displays below the date, select the name, and then type your first and last names.
6. Click the placeholder text *[Type the sender company name]* and then type **Sorenson Funds**.
7. Click the placeholder text *[Type the sender company address]*, type **6250 Aurora Boulevard**, press the Enter key, and then type **Baltimore, MD 20372**.
8. Click the placeholder text *[Type the recipient name]* and then type **Ms. Jennifer Gonzalez**.
9. Click the placeholder text *[Type the recipient address]*, type **12990 Boyd Street**, press the Enter key, and then type **Baltimore, MD 20375**.
10. Click the placeholder text *[Type the salutation]* and then type **Dear Ms. Gonzalez:**.
11. Insert a file in the document by completing the following steps:
    a. Click anywhere in the three paragraphs of text in the body of the letter and then click the Delete key.
    b. Click the Insert tab.
    c. Click the Object button arrow in the Text group and then click *Text from File* at the drop-down list.
    d. At the Insert File dialog box, navigate to the Word2010L1C6 folder on your storage medium and then double-click **SFunds.docx**.
12. Click the placeholder text *[Type the closing]* and then type **Sincerely,**.
13. Delete one blank line above Sincerely.
14. Click the placeholder text *[Type the sender title]* and then type **Financial Consultant**.
15. Save the document and name it **WL1-C6-P5-SFunds**.
16. Print and then close **WL1-C6-P5-SFunds.docx**.

Chapter Summary

- Group Word documents logically into folders. Create a new folder at the Open or Save As dialog box.
- You can select one or several documents at the Open dialog box. Copy, move, rename, delete, or open a document or selected documents.
- Use the *Cut*, *Copy*, and *Paste* options from the Organize button drop-down list or the Open dialog box shortcut menu to move or copy a document from one folder to another.
- Delete documents and/or folders with the *Delete* option from the Organize button drop-down list or shortcut menu.
- With options at the Save & Send tab Backstage view, you can send a document as an email attachment, save your document to SkyDrive and SharePoint, save your document in a different file format, and post your document to a special location such as a blog.
- Click the Change File Type button in the File Types category at the Save & Send tab Backstage view, and options display for saving the document in a different file format. You can also save documents in a different file format with the *Save as type* option box at the Save As dialog box.
- Move among the open documents by clicking the button on the Taskbar representing the desired document, or by clicking the View tab, clicking the Switch Windows button in the Window group, and then clicking the desired document name.
- View a portion of all open documents by clicking the View tab and then clicking the Arrange All button in the Window group.
- Use the Minimize, Restore, and Maximize buttons located in the upper right corner of the window to reduce or increase the size of the active window.
- Divide a window into two panes by clicking the View tab and then clicking the Split button in the Window group. This enables you to view different parts of the same document at one time.
- View the contents of two open documents side by side by clicking the View tab, and then clicking the View Side by Side button in the Window group.
- Insert a document into the open document by clicking the Insert tab, clicking the Object button arrow, and then clicking *Text from File* at the drop-down list. At the Insert File dialog box, double-click the desired document.
- Preview a document at the Print tab Backstage view. Scroll through the pages in the document with the Next Page and the Previous Page buttons that display below the preview page. Use the Zoom slider bar to increase/decrease the display size of the preview page.
- At the Print tab Backstage view you can customize the print job by changing the page orientation, size, and margins; specify how many pages you want to print on one page; the number of copies and whether or not to collate the pages; and specify the printer.
- With Word's envelope feature you can create and print an envelope at the Envelopes and Labels dialog box with the Envelopes tab selected.

- If you open the Envelopes and Labels dialog box in a document containing a name and address (with each line ending with a press of the Enter key), that information is automatically inserted in the *Delivery address* text box in the dialog box.
- Use Word's labels feature to print text on mailing labels, file labels, disc labels, or other types of labels.
- Word includes a number of template documents you can use to create a variety of documents. Display the list of template documents by clicking the File tab, clicking the New tab, and then clicking the Sample templates button.

Commands Review

FEATURE	RIBBON TAB, GROUP	BUTTON, OPTION	KEYBOARD SHORTCUT
Open dialog box	File	Open	Ctrl + O
Save As dialog box	File	Save As	
Print tab Backstage view	File	Print	Ctrl + P
Arrange all documents	View, Window		
Minimize document			
Maximize document			Ctrl + F10
Restore			
Split window	View, Window		Alt + Ctrl + S
View documents side by side	View, Window		
Insert file	Insert, Text	Text from File	
Envelopes and Labels dialog box with Envelopes tab selected	Mailings, Create		
Envelopes and Labels dialog box with Labels tab selected	Mailings, Create		
New tab Backstage view	File	New	

Concepts Check Test Your Knowledge

Completion: In the space provided at the right, indicate the correct term, command, or number.

1. Create a new folder with this button at the Open or Save As dialog box. _____

2. At the Open dialog box, the current folder path displays in this. _____

3. Using the mouse, select nonadjacent documents at the Open dialog box by holding down this key while clicking the desired documents. _____

4. Documents deleted from the hard drive are automatically sent here. _____

5. Copy a document to another folder without opening the document at the Open or Save As dialog box with the Organize button drop-down list or this menu _____

6. The letters PDF stand for this. _____

7. Saving a document in this format strips out all formatting. _____

8. Click this button in the Window group in the View tab to arrange all open documents so a portion of each document displays. _____

9. Click this button and the active document fills the editing window. _____

10. Click this button to reduce the active document to a button on the Taskbar. _____

11. To display documents side by side, click this button in the Window group in the View tab. _____

12. Display the Insert File dialog box by clicking the Object button arrow in the Insert tab and then clicking this option. _____

13. Type this in the *Pages* text box at the Print tab Backstage view to print pages 3 through 6 of the open document. _____

14. Type this in the *Pages* text box at the Print tab Backstage view to print pages 4 and 9 of the open document. _____

15. The Envelopes button is located in the Create group in this tab. _____

16. Click the Sample templates button at this Backstage view to display a list of templates. _____

Skills Check Assess Your Performance

Assessment

1 MANAGE DOCUMENTS

1. Display the Open dialog box with Word2010L1C6 the active folder and then create a new folder named *CheckingTools*.
2. Copy (be sure to copy and not cut) all documents that begin with *SpellGrammar* into the CheckingTools folder.
3. With the CheckingTools folder as the active folder, rename **SpellGrammar01.docx** to **Technology.docx**.
4. Rename **SpellGrammar02.docx** to **Software.docx**.
5. Print the screen contents by completing the following steps:
   a. With the Open dialog box displayed, press the Print Screen key on your keyboard.
   b. Close the Open dialog box.
   c. At a blank document, click the Paste button.
   d. Print the document.
   e. Close the document without saving it.
6. Display the Open dialog box and make Word2010L1C6 the active folder.
7. Delete the CheckingTools folder and all documents contained within it.
8. Open **StaffMtg.docx**, **Agreement.docx**, and **Robots.docx**.
9. Make **Agreement.docx** the active document.
10. Make **StaffMtg.docx** the active document.
11. Arrange all of the windows.
12. Make **Robots.docx** the active document and then minimize it.
13. Minimize the remaining documents.
14. Restore **StaffMtg.docx**.
15. Restore **Agreement.docx**.
16. Restore **Robots.docx**.
17. Maximize and then close **StaffMtg.docx** and then maximize and close **Robots.docx**.
18. Maximize **Agreement.docx** and then save the document and name it **WL1-C6-A1-Agreement**.
19. Open **AptLease.docx**.
20. View the **WL1-C6-A1-Agreement.docx** document and **AptLease.docx** document side by side.
21. Scroll through both documents simultaneously and notice the formatting differences between the title and headings in the two documents. Change the font and apply shading to the title and headings in **WL1-C6-A1-Agreement.docx** to match the font and shading of the title and headings in **AptLease.docx**.
22. Make **AptLease.docx** active and then close it.
23. Save **WL1-C6-A1-Agreement.docx**.
24. Move the insertion point to the end of the document and then insert the document named **Terms.docx**.
25. Apply formatting to the inserted text so it matches the formatting of the original text.

26. If the heading, *Damage to Premises*, displays at the bottom of page 1, insert a page break at the beginning of the heading.
27. Move the insertion point to the end of the document and then insert the document named **Signature.docx**.
28. Save, print, and then close **WL1-C6-A1-Agreement.docx**.

Assessment 2

CREATE AN ENVELOPE

1. At a blank document, create an envelope with the text shown in Figure 6.11.
2. Save the envelope document and name it **WL1-C6-A2-Env**.
3. Print and then close **WL1-C6-A2-Env.docx**.

Figure 6.11 Assessment 2

```
DR ROSEANNE HOLT
21330 CEDAR DR
LOGAN UT 84598


                            GENE MIETZNER
                            4559 CORRIN AVE
                            SMITHFIELD UT 84521
```

Assessment 3

CREATE MAILING LABELS

1. Create mailing labels with the names and addresses shown in Figure 6.12. Use a label option of your choosing. (You may need to check with your instructor before choosing an option.)
2. Save the document and name it **WL1-C6-A3-Labels**.
3. Print and then close **WL1-C6-A3-Labels.docx**.
4. At the clear document screen, close the document screen without saving changes.

Figure 6.12 Assessment 3

SUSAN LUTOVSKY	JIM AND PAT KEIL	IRENE HAGEN
1402 MELLINGER DR	413 JACKSON ST	12930 147TH AVE E
FAIRHOPE OH 43209	AVONDALE OH 43887	CANTON OH 43296
VINCE KILEY	LEONARD KRUEGER	HELGA GUNDSTROM
14005 288TH S	13290 N 120TH	PO BOX 3112
CANTON OH 43287	CANTON OH 43291	AVONDALE OH 43887

Assessment 4 PREPARE A FAX

1. Open the Equity fax template at the New tab Backstage view with sample templates selected and then insert the following information in the specified fields.
   To: Frank Gallagher
   From: (your first and last names)
   Fax: (206) 555-9010
   Pages: 3
   Phone: (206) 555-9005
   Date: (insert current date)
   Re: Consultation Agreement
   CC: Jolene Yin
   Insert an X in the *For Review* check box.
   Comments: Please review the Consultation Agreement and advise me of any legal issues.
2. Save the fax document and name it **WL1-C6-A4-Fax**.
3. Print and then close the document.

Assessment 5 SAVE A DOCUMENT AS A WEB PAGE

1. Experiment with the Save as type button at the Save As dialog box and figure out how to save a document as a single file web page.
2. Open **NSS.docx**, display the Save As dialog box, and then change Save as Type to a single file web page. Click the Change Title button that displays in the Save As dialog box. At the Enter Text dialog box, type **Northland Security Systems** in the *Page title* text box and then close the dialog box by clicking the OK button. Click the Save button in the Save As dialog box.
3. Close the **NSS.mht** file.
4. Open your web browser and then open the **NSS.mht** file.
5. Close your web browser.

Assessment 6 CREATE PERSONAL MAILING LABELS

1. At a blank document, type your name and address and then apply formatting to enhance the appeal of the text (you determine the font, font size, and font color).
2. Create labels with your name and address (you determine the label vendor and product number).
3. Save the label document and name it **WL1-C6-A6-PersonalLabels**.
4. Print and then close the document.

Assessment

7 DOWNLOAD AND COMPLETE A STUDENT AWARD CERTIFICATE

1. Display the New tab Backstage view and then search for and download a student of the month award certificate template in the *Office.com Templates* section of the Available Templates category. (To find a student of the month award, click the *Award certificates* option in the *Office.com Templates* section, click the *Academic* folder, and then look for the *Basic certificate for student of the month* template.)
2. Insert the appropriate information in the award template placeholder identifying yourself as the recipient of the student of the month award.
3. Save the completed award and name the document **WL1-C6-A7-Award**.
4. Print and then close the document.

Visual Benchmark Demonstrate Your Proficiency

CREATE CUSTOM LABELS

1. You can create a sheet of labels with the same information in each label by typing the information in the Address text box at the Envelopes and Labels dialog box or you can type the desired information, select it, and then create the label. Using this technique, create the sheet of labels shown in Figure 6.13 with the following specifications:
   - Open **NSSLabels.docx**.
   - Set the text in 12-point Magneto.
   - Select the entire document and then create the labels by displaying the Envelopes and Labels dialog box with the Labels tab selected. Change to the Avery US Letter label, product number 5161, and then click the New Document button.
2. Save the label document and name it **WL1-C6-VB-NSSLabels**.
3. Print and then close the document.
4. Close **NSSLabels.docx** without saving it.

Figure 6.13 Visual Benchmark

 Northland Security Systems
3200 North 22nd Street
Springfield, IL 62102

 Northland Security Systems
3200 North 22nd Street
Springfield, IL 62102

 Northland Security Systems
3200 North 22nd Street
Springfield, IL 62102

 Northland Security Systems
3200 North 22nd Street
Springfield, IL 62102

 Northland Security Systems
3200 North 22nd Street
Springfield, IL 62102

 Northland Security Systems
3200 North 22nd Street
Springfield, IL 62102

 Northland Security Systems
3200 North 22nd Street
Springfield, IL 62102

 Northland Security Systems
3200 North 22nd Street
Springfield, IL 62102

 Northland Security Systems
3200 North 22nd Street
Springfield, IL 62102

 Northland Security Systems
3200 North 22nd Street
Springfield, IL 62102

 Northland Security Systems
3200 North 22nd Street
Springfield, IL 62102

 Northland Security Systems
3200 North 22nd Street
Springfield, IL 62102

 Northland Security Systems
3200 North 22nd Street
Springfield, IL 62102

 Northland Security Systems
3200 North 22nd Street
Springfield, IL 62102

 Northland Security Systems
3200 North 22nd Street
Springfield, IL 62102

 Northland Security Systems
3200 North 22nd Street
Springfield, IL 62102

 Northland Security Systems
3200 North 22nd Street
Springfield, IL 62102

 Northland Security Systems
3200 North 22nd Street
Springfield, IL 62102

 Northland Security Systems
3200 North 22nd Street
Springfield, IL 62102

 Northland Security Systems
3200 North 22nd Street
Springfield, IL 62102

Case Study   Apply Your Skills

Part 1

You are the office manager for the real estate company, Macadam Realty, and have been asked by the senior sales associate, Lucy Hendricks, to organize contract forms into a specific folder. Create a new folder named *RealEstate* and then copy into the folder documents that begin with the letters "RE." Ms. Hendricks has also asked you to prepare mailing labels for Macadam Realty. Include the name, Macadam Realty, and the address 100 Third Street, Suite 210, Denver, CO 80803, on the labels. Use a decorative font for the label and make the *M* in *Macadam* and the *R* in *Realty* larger and more pronounced than surrounding text. **Hint: Format text in the label by selecting text, right-clicking in the selected text, and then choosing the desired option at the shortcut menu.** Save the completed document and name it **WL1-C6-CS-P1-RELabels**. Print and then close the document.

Part 2

One of your responsibilities is to format contract forms. Open the document named **REConAgrmnt.docx** and then save it and name it **WL1-C6-CS-P2-REConAgrmnt**. The sales associate has asked you to insert signature information at the end of the document and so you decide to insert at the end of the document the file named **RESig.docx**. With **WL1-C6-CS-P2-REConAgrmnt.docx** still open, open **REBuildAgrmnt.docx**. Format the **WL1-C6-CS-P2-REConAgrmnt.docx** document so it is formatted in a manner similar to the **REBuildAgrmnt.docx** document. Consider the following when specifying formatting: margins, fonts, and paragraph shading. Save, print, and then close **WL1-C6-CS-P2-REConAgrmnt.docx**. Close **REBuildAgrmnt.docx**.

Part 3

As part of the organization of contracts, Ms. Hendricks has asked you to insert document properties for the **REBuildAgrmnt.docx** and **WL1-C6-CS-P2-REConAgrmnt.docx** documents. Use the Help feature to learn how to insert document properties. With the information you learn from the Help feature, open each of the two documents separately, display the Info tab Backstage view, click the Show All Properties hyperlink, and then insert document properties in the following fields (you determine the information to type): *Title*, *Subject*, *Categories*, and *Company*. Print the document properties for each document (change the first gallery in the Settings category in the Print tab Backstage view to *Document Properties*). Save each document with the original name and close the documents.

Part 4

A client of the real estate company, Anna Hurley, is considering purchasing several rental properties and has asked for information on how to locate real estate rental forms. Using the Internet, locate at least three websites that offer real estate rental forms. Write a letter to Anna Hurley at 2300 South 22nd Street, Denver, CO 80205. In the letter, list the websites you found and include information on which site you thought offered the most resources. Also include in the letter that Macadam Realty is very interested in helping her locate and purchase rental properties. Save the document and name it **WL1-C6-CS-P4-RELtr**. Create an envelope for the letter and add it to the letter document. Save, print, and then close **WL1-C6-CS-P4-RELtr.docx**. (You may need to manually feed the envelope in the printer.)

Microsoft Word

CHAPTER 7

Creating Tables and SmartArt

PERFORMANCE OBJECTIVES

Upon successful completion of Chapter 7, you will be able to:
- **Create, edit, and format a table**
- **Change the table design and layout**
- **Sort text in a table**
- **Perform calculations on data in a table**
- **Create and format a SmartArt diagram**
- **Create and format a SmartArt organizational chart**

Some Word data can be organized in a table, which is a combination of columns and rows. With the Tables feature, you can insert data in columns and rows. This data can consist of text, values, and formulas. In this chapter you will learn how to create and format a table and insert and format data in the table. Word includes a SmartArt feature that provides a number of predesigned diagrams and organizational charts. Use this feature to create and then customize a diagram or organizational chart. Model answers for this chapter's projects appear on the following pages.

Note: Before beginning the projects, copy to your storage medium the Word2010L1C7 subfolder from the Word2010L1 folder on the CD that accompanies this textbook and then make Word2010L1C7 the active folder.

Model Answers

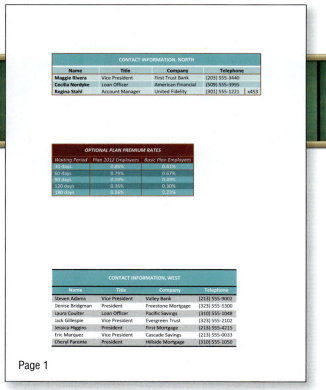

Page 1

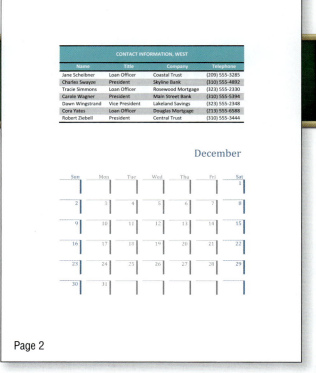

Page 2

Project 1 Create and Format Tables with Company Information
WL1-C7-P1-Tables.docx

Project 2 Create and Format Tables with Employee Information
WL1-C7-P2-TSPTables.docx

Project 3 Sort and Calculate Sales Data
WL1-C7-P3-TSPSalesTables.docx

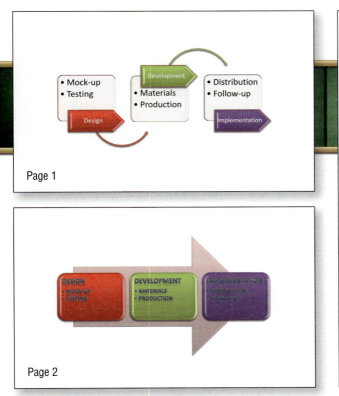

Page 1

Page 2

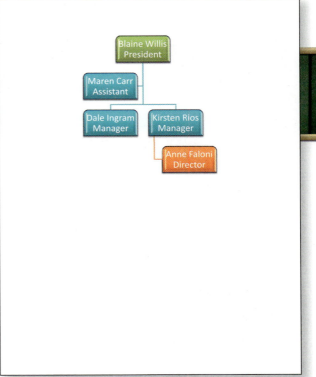

Project 4 Prepare and Format a Diagram
WL1-C7-P4-Diagrams.docx

Project 5 Prepare and Format a Company Organizational Chart
WL1-C7-P5-OrgChart.docx

Project 1 Create and Format Tables with Company Information — 9 Parts

You will create a table containing contact information and another containing information on plans offered by the company. You will then change the design and layout of both tables.

Creating a Table

Use the Tables feature to create boxes of information called *cells*. A cell is the intersection between a row and a column. A cell can contain text, characters, numbers, data, graphics, or formulas. Create a table by clicking the Insert tab, clicking the Table button, dragging down and to the right until the correct number of rows and columns displays, and then clicking the mouse button. You can also create a table with options at the Insert Table dialog box. Display this dialog box by clicking the Table button in the Tables group in the Insert tab and then clicking *Insert Table* at the drop-down list.

Figure 7.1 shows an example of a table with three columns and four rows. Various parts of the table are identified in Figure 7.1 such as the gridlines, move table column marker, end-of-cell marker, end-of-row marker, and the resize handle. In a table, nonprinting characters identify the end of a cell and the end of a row. To view these characters, click the Show/Hide ¶ button in the Paragraph group in the Home

▼ Quick Steps

Create a Table
1. Click Insert tab.
2. Click Table button.
3. Drag to create desired number of columns and rows.
4. Click mouse button.
OR
1. Click Insert tab.
2. Click Table button.
3. Click *Insert Table*.
4. Specify number of columns and rows.
5. Click OK.

 Table

Chapter 7 ■ Creating Tables and SmartArt   **243**

Figure 7.1 Table

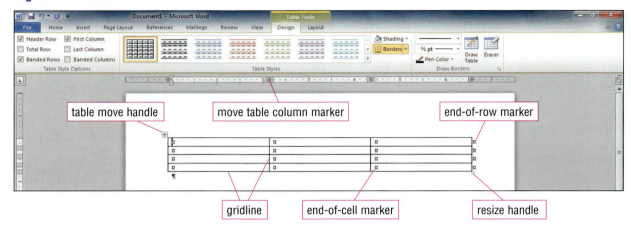

You can create a table within a table, creating a *nested* table.

Pressing the Tab key in a table moves the insertion point to the next cell. Pressing Ctrl + Tab moves the insertion point to the next tab within a cell.

tab. The end-of-cell marker displays inside each cell and the end-of-row marker displays at the end of a row of cells. These markers are identified in Figure 7.1.

When you create a table, the insertion point is located in the cell in the upper left corner of the table. Cells in a table contain a cell designation. Columns in a table are lettered from left to right, beginning with *A*. Rows in a table are numbered from top to bottom beginning with *1*. The cell in the upper left corner of the table is cell A1. The cell to the right of A1 is B1, the cell to the right of B1 is C1, and so on.

When the insertion point is positioned in a cell in the table, move table column markers display on the horizontal ruler. These markers represent the end of a column and are useful in changing the width of columns. Figure 7.1 identifies a move table column marker.

Entering Text in Cells

With the insertion point positioned in a cell, type or edit text. Move the insertion point to other cells with the mouse by clicking in the desired cell. If you are using the keyboard, press the Tab key to move the insertion point to the next cell or press Shift + Tab to move the insertion point to the previous cell.

If the text you type does not fit on one line, it wraps to the next line within the same cell. Or, if you press Enter within a cell, the insertion point is moved to the next line within the same cell. The cell vertically lengthens to accommodate the text, and all cells in that row also lengthen. Pressing the Tab key in a table causes the insertion point to move to the next cell in the table. If you want to move the insertion point to a tab stop within a cell, press Ctrl + Tab. If the insertion point is located in the last cell of the table and you press the Tab key, Word adds another row to the table. Insert a page break within a table by pressing Ctrl + Enter. The page break is inserted between rows, not within.

Moving the Insertion Point within a Table

To move the insertion point to a different cell within the table using the mouse, click in the desired cell. To move the insertion point to different cells within the table using the keyboard, refer to the information shown in Table 7.1.

Table 7.1 Insertion Point Movement within a Table Using the Keyboard

To move the insertion point	Press these keys
To next cell	Tab
To preceding cell	Shift + Tab
Forward one character	Right Arrow key
Backward one character	Left Arrow key
To previous row	Up Arrow key
To next row	Down Arrow key
To first cell in the row	Alt + Home
To last cell in the row	Alt + End
To top cell in the column	Alt + Page Up
To bottom cell in the column	Alt + Page Down

Project 1a   Creating a Table   Part 1 of 9

1. At a blank document, turn on bold, and then type the title **CONTACT INFORMATION** shown in Figure 7.2.
2. Turn off bold and then press the Enter key.
3. Create the table shown in Figure 7.2. To do this, click the Insert tab, click the Table button in the Tables group, drag down and to the right until the number above the grid displays as *3x5*, and then click the mouse button.
4. Type the text in the cells as indicated in Figure 7.2. Press the Tab key to move to the next cell or press Shift + Tab to move to the preceding cell. (If you accidentally press the Enter key within a cell, immediately press the Backspace key. Do not press Tab after typing the text in the last cell. If you do, another row is inserted in the table. If this happens, immediately click the Undo button on the Quick Access toolbar.)
5. Save the table and name it **WL1-C7-P1-Tables**.

Figure 7.2 Project 1a

CONTACT INFORMATION		
Maggie Rivera	First Trust Bank	(203) 555-3440
Les Cromwell	Madison Trust	(602) 555-4900
Cecilia Nordyke	American Financial	(509) 555-3995
Regina Stahl	United Fidelity	(301) 555-1221
Justin White	Key One Savings	(360) 555-8966

Chapter 7 ■ Creating Tables and SmartArt

Using the Insert Table Dialog Box

You can also create a table with options at the Insert Table dialog box shown in Figure 7.3. To display this dialog box, click the Insert tab, click the Table button in the Tables group, and then click *Insert Table*. At the Insert Table dialog box, enter the desired number of columns and rows and then click OK.

Figure 7.3 Insert Table Dialog Box

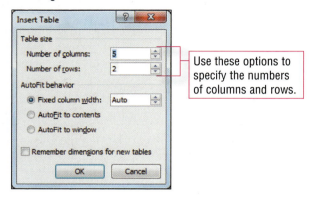

Project 1b Creating a Table with the Insert Table Dialog Box   Part 2 of 9

1. With **WL1-C7-P1-Tables.docx** open, press Ctrl + End to move the insertion point below the table.
2. Press the Enter key twice.
3. Turn on bold and then type the title **OPTIONAL PLAN PREMIUM RATES** shown in Figure 7.4.
4. Turn off bold and then press the Enter key.
5. Click the Insert tab, click the Table button in the Tables group, and then click *Insert Table* at the drop-down list.
6. At the Insert Table dialog box, type 3 in the *Number of columns* text box. (The insertion point is automatically positioned in this text box.)
7. Press the Tab key (this moves the insertion point to the *Number of rows* text box) and then type 5.
8. Click OK.
9. Type the text in the cells as indicated in Figure 7.4.
   Press the Tab key to move to the next cell or press Shift + Tab to move to the preceding cell. To indent the text in cells B2 through B5 and cells C2 through C5, press Ctrl + Tab to move the insertion to a tab within cells and then type the text.
10. Save **WL1-C7-P1-Tables.docx**.

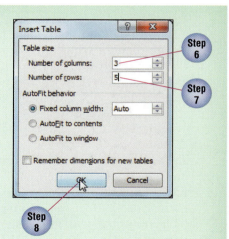

Figure 7.4 Project 1b

OPTIONAL PLAN PREMIUM RATES		
Waiting Period	Basic Plan Employees	Plan 2012 Employees
60 days	0.67%	0.79%
90 days	0.49%	0.59%
120 days	0.30%	0.35%
180 days	0.23%	0.26%

Changing the Table Design

When you create a table, the Table Tools Design tab is selected and the tab contains a number of options for enhancing the appearance of the table as shown in Figure 7.5. With options in the Table Styles group, apply a predesigned style that applies color and border lines to a table. Maintain further control over the predesigned style formatting applied to columns and rows with options in the Table Style Options group. For example, if your table contains a total column, you would insert a check mark in the *Total Row* option. Apply additional design formatting to cells in a table with the Shading and Borders buttons in the Table Styles group. Draw a table or draw additional rows and/or columns in a table by clicking the Draw Table button in the Draw Borders group. Click this button and the mouse pointer turns into a pencil. Drag in the table to create the desired columns and rows. Click the Eraser button and the mouse pointer turns into an eraser. Drag through the column and/or row lines you want to erase in the table.

Draw a freeform table by clicking the Insert tab, clicking the Table button, and then clicking the *Draw Table* option. Drag in the document to create the table.

Shading

Draw Table

Figure 7.5 Table Tools Design Tab

Project 1c Applying Table Styles   Part 3 of 9

1. With **WL1-C7-P1-Tables.docx** open, click in any cell in the top table.
2. Apply a table style by completing the following steps:
   a. Make sure the Table Tools Design tab is active.
   b. Click the More button at the right side of the table style thumbnails in the Table Styles group.
   c. Click the *Medium Grid 3 - Accent 5* style (second table style from the right in the tenth row in the *Built-in* section).

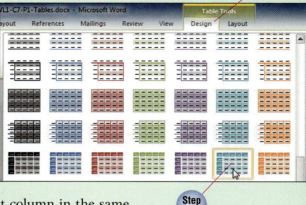

3. After looking at the table, you realize that the first row is not a header row and the first column should not be formatted differently than the other columns. To format the first row and first column in the same manner as the other rows and columns, click the *Header Row* check box and the *First Column* check box in the Table Style Options group to remove the check marks.
4. Click in any cell in the bottom table, apply the Dark List - Accent 5 table style (second option from the right in the eleventh row in the Built-in section), and then remove the check mark from the *First Column* check box.

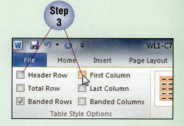

5. Add color borders to the top table by completing the following steps:
   a. Click in any cell in the top table.
   b. Click the Pen Color button arrow in the Draw Borders group and then click the *Orange, Accent 6, Darker 50%* color.
   c. Click the Line Weight button arrow in the Draw Borders group and then click *1 ½ pt* at the drop-down list. (When you choose a line weight, the Draw Table button is automatically activated.)

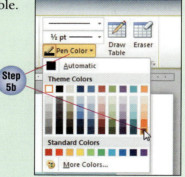
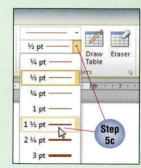

   d. Using the mouse (mouse pointer displays as a pen), drag along each side of the table. (As you drag with the mouse, a thick, brown border line is inserted. If you make a mistake or the line does not display as you intended, click the Undo button and then continue drawing along each side of the table.)
6. Drag along each side of the bottom table.
7. Click the Line Weight button in the Draw Borders group and then click *1 pt* at the drop-down list.
8. Drag along the row boundary separating the first row from the second row in the bottom table.
9. Click the Draw Table button to turn off the feature.
10. Save **WL1-C7-P1-Tables.docx**.

Selecting Cells

You can format data within a table in several ways. For example, you can change the alignment of text within cells or rows, select and then move or copy rows or columns, or you can add character formatting such as bold, italic, or underlining. To format specific cells, rows, or columns, you must first select them.

Selecting in a Table with the Mouse

Use the mouse pointer to select a cell, row, column, or an entire table. Table 7.2 describes methods for selecting a table with the mouse. The left edge of each cell, between the left column border and the end-of-cell marker or first character in the cell, is called the ***cell selection bar***. When you position the mouse pointer in the cell selection bar, it turns into a small, black arrow pointing up and to the right. Each row in a table contains a ***row selection bar***, which is the space just to the left of the left edge of the table. When you position the mouse pointer in the row selection bar, the mouse pointer turns into a white arrow pointing up and to the right.

Table 7.2 Selecting in a Table with the Mouse

To select this	Do this
A cell	Position the mouse pointer in the cell selection bar at the left edge of the cell until it turns into a small, black arrow pointing up and to the right and then click the left mouse button.
A row	Position the mouse pointer in the row selection bar at the left edge of the table until it turns into an arrow pointing up and to the right and then click the left mouse button.
A column	Position the mouse pointer on the uppermost horizontal gridline of the table in the appropriate column until it turns into a short, black down-pointing arrow and then click the left mouse button.
Adjacent cells	Position the mouse pointer in the first cell to be selected, hold down the left mouse button, drag the mouse pointer to the last cell to be selected, and then release the mouse button.
All cells in a table	Click the table move handle or position the mouse pointer in the row selection bar for the first row at the left edge of the table until it turns into an arrow pointing up and to the right, hold down the left mouse button, drag down to select all rows in the table, and then release the left mouse button.
Text within a cell	Position the mouse pointer at the beginning of the text and then hold down the left mouse button as you drag the mouse across the text. (When a cell is selected, the cell background color changes to blue. When text within cells is selected, only those lines containing text are selected.)

Selecting in a Table with the Keyboard

In addition to the mouse, you can also use the keyboard to select specific cells within a table. Table 7.3 displays the commands for selecting specific amounts of a table.

If you want to select only text within cells, rather than the entire cell, press F8 to turn on the Extend mode and then move the insertion point with an arrow key. When a cell is selected, the cell background color changes to blue. When text within a cell is selected, only those lines containing text are selected.

Table 7.3 Selecting in a Table with the Keyboard

To select	Press
The next cell's contents	Tab
The preceding cell's contents	Shift + Tab
The entire table	Alt + 5 (on numeric keypad with Num Lock off)
Adjacent cells	Hold down Shift key and then press an arrow key repeatedly.
A column	Position insertion point in top cell of column, hold down Shift key, and then press down-pointing arrow key until column is selected.

Project 1d Selecting, Moving and Formatting Cells in a Table   Part 4 of 9

1. With **WL1-C7-P1-Tables.docx** open, move two rows in the top table by completing the following steps:
   a. Position the mouse pointer in the row selection bar at the left side of the row containing the name *Cecilia Nordyke*, hold down the left mouse button, drag down to select two rows (the *Cecilia Nordyke* row and the *Regina Stahl* row).
   b. Click the Home tab and then click the Cut button in the Clipboard group.
   c. Move the insertion point so it is positioned at the beginning of the name *Les Cromwell* and then click the Paste button in the Clipboard group.

2. Move the third column in the bottom table by completing the following steps:
   a. Position the mouse pointer on the top border of the third column in the bottom table until the pointer turns into a short, black, down-pointing arrow and then click the left mouse button. (This selects the entire column.)
   b. Click the Cut button in the Clipboard group in the Home tab.
   c. With the insertion point positioned at the beginning of the text *Basic Plan Employees*, click the Paste button in the Clipboard group in the Home tab. (Moving the column removed the right border.)
   d. Insert the right border by clicking the Table Tools Design tab, clicking the Line Weight button arrow, and then clicking *1 ½ pt* at the drop-down list.

e. Hold down the left mouse button and then drag along the right border of the bottom table.
   f. Click the Line Weight button arrow and then click *1 pt* at the drop-down list.
   g. Click the Draw Table button to turn off the feature.
3. Apply shading to a row by completing the following steps:

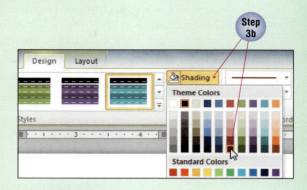

   a. Position the mouse pointer in the row selection bar at the left edge of the first row in the bottom table until the pointer turns into an arrow pointing up and to the right and then click the left mouse button. (This selects the entire first row of the bottom table.)
   b. Click the Shading button arrow in the Table Styles group and then click the *Red, Accent 2, Darker 50%* color.
4. Apply a border line to a column by completing the following steps:
   a. Position the mouse pointer on the top border of the first column in the bottom table until the pointer turns into a short, black, down-pointing arrow and then click the left mouse button.
   b. Click the Borders button arrow in the Table Styles group and then click *Right Border* at the drop-down list. (This inserts a 1 point dark orange border line at the right side of the column.)

5. Complete steps similar to those in Step 2 to insert a border line at the right side of the second column.
6. Apply italic formatting to a column by completing the following steps:
   a. Position the insertion point in the first cell of the first row in the top table.
   b. Hold down the Shift key and then press the Down Arrow key four times. (This should select all cells in the first column.)
   c. Press Ctrl + I.
7. Save **WL1-C7-P1-Tables.docx**.

Changing Table Layout

To further customize a table, consider changing the table layout by inserting or deleting columns and rows and specifying cell alignments. Change table layout with options at the Table Tools Layout tab shown in Figure 7.6. Use options and buttons in the tab to select specific cells, delete and insert rows and columns, merge and split cells, specify cell height and width, sort data in cells, and insert a formula.

HINT Some table layout options are available at a shortcut menu that can be viewed by right-clicking a table.

Figure 7.6 Table Tools Layout Tab

Chapter 7 ■ Creating Tables and SmartArt   **251**

Select

View Gridlines

Insert Above

Insert Below

Insert Left

Insert Right

Delete

Selecting with the Select Button

Along with selecting cells with the keyboard and mouse, you can also select specific cells with the Select button in the Table group in the Table Tools Layout tab. To select with this button, position the insertion point in the desired cell, column, or row and then click the Select button. At the drop-down list that displays, specify what you want to select — the entire table or a column, row, or cell.

Viewing Gridlines

When you create a table, cell borders are identified by horizontal and vertical thin, black gridlines. You can remove a cell border gridline but maintain the cell border. If you remove cell border gridlines or apply a table style that removes gridlines, nonprinting gridlines display as dashed lines. This helps you visually determine cell borders. You can turn on or off the display of these nonprinting, dashed gridlines with the View Gridlines button in the Table group in the Table Tools Layout tab.

Inserting and Deleting Rows and Columns

With buttons in the Rows & Columns group in the Table Tools Layout tab, you can insert a row or column and delete a row or column. Click the button in the group that inserts the row or column in the desired location such as above, below, to the left, or to the right. Add a row to the bottom of a table by positioning the insertion point in the last cell and then pressing the Tab key. To delete a table, row, or column, click the Delete button and then click the option identifying what you want to delete. If you make a mistake while formatting a table, immediately click the Undo button on the Quick Access toolbar.

Project 1e Selecting, Inserting, and Deleting Columns and Rows   Part 5 of 9

1. Make sure **WL1-C7-P1-Tables.docx** is open.
2. The table style applied to the bottom table removed row border gridlines. If you do not see dashed gridlines in the bottom table, turn on the display of these nonprinting gridlines by positioning your insertion point in the table, clicking the Table Tools Layout tab, and then clicking the View Gridlines button in the Table group. (The button should display with an orange background indicating it is active.)
3. Select a column and apply formatting by completing the following steps:
    a. Click in any cell in the first column in the top table.
    b. Click the Select button in the Table group and then click *Select Column* at the drop-down list.
    c. With the first column selected, press Ctrl + I to remove italics and then press Ctrl + B to apply bold formatting.
4. Select a row and apply formatting by completing the following steps:
    a. Click in any cell in the first row in the bottom table.
    b. Click the Select button in the Table group and then click *Select Row* at the drop-down list.
    c. With the first row selected in the bottom table, press Ctrl + I to apply italic formatting.

5. Insert a new row in the bottom table and type text in the new cells by completing the following steps:
   a. Click in the cell containing the text *60 days*.
   b. Click the Insert Above button in the Rows & Columns group.
   c. Type **30 days** in the first cell of the new row, type **0.85%** in the middle cell of the new row (make sure you press Ctrl + Tab before typing the text), and type **0.81%** in the third cell of the new row. (Make sure you press Ctrl + Tab before typing the text.)

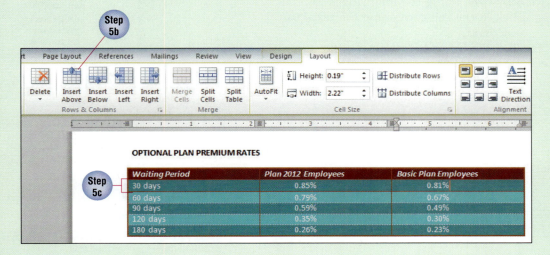

6. Insert three new rows in the top table and type text in the new cells by completing the following steps:
   a. Select the three rows of cells that begin with the names *Cecilia Nordyke*, *Regina Stahl*, and *Les Cromwell*.
   b. Click the Insert Below button in the Rows & Columns group.
   c. Type the following text in the new cells:

Teresa Getty	**Meridian Bank**	**(503) 555-9800**
Michael Vazquez	**New Horizon Bank**	**(702) 555-2435**
Samantha Roth	**Cascade Mutual**	**(206) 555-6788**

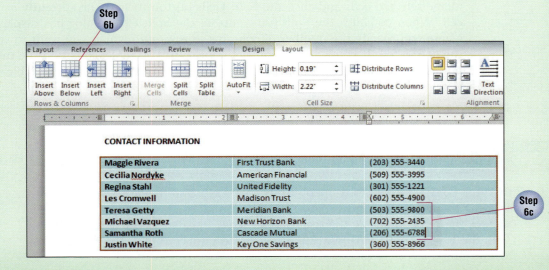

Chapter 7 ■ Creating Tables and SmartArt 253

7. Delete a row by completing the following steps:
   a. Click in the cell containing the name *Les Cromwell*.
   b. Click the Delete button in the Rows & Columns group and then click *Delete Rows* at the drop-down list.
8. Insert a new column and type text in the new cells by completing the following steps:
   a. Click in the cell containing the text *First Trust Bank*.
   b. Click the Insert Left button in the Rows & Columns group.
   c. Type the following text in the new cells:
      B1 = Vice President
      B2 = Loan Officer
      B3 = Account Manager
      B4 = Branch Manager
      B5 = President
      B6 = Vice President
      B7 = Regional Manager
9. Save **WL1-C7-P1-Tables.docx**.

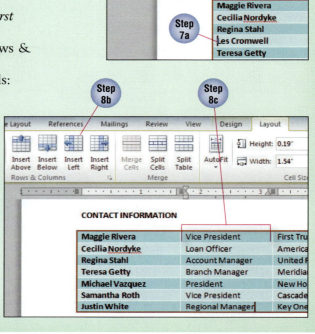

Merging and Splitting Cells and Tables

Merge Cells

Split Cells

Split Table

Click the Merge Cells button in the Merge group in the Table Tools Layout tab to merge selected cells and click the Split Cells button to split the currently active cell. When you click the Split Cells button, the Split Cells dialog box displays where you specify the number of columns or rows into which you want to split the active cell. If you want to split one table into two tables, position the insertion point in a cell in the row that you want to be the first row in the new table and then click the Split Table button.

Project 1f   Merging and Splitting Cells and Splitting a Table   Part 6 of 9

1. With **WL1-C7-P1-Tables.docx** open, insert a new row and merge cells in the row by completing the following steps:
   a. Click in the cell containing the text *Waiting Period* (located in the bottom table).
   b. Click the Insert Above button in the Rows & Columns group in the Table Tools Layout tab.

254   Word Level 1 ■ Unit 2

c. With all of the cells in the new row selected, click the Merge Cells button in the Merge group.
d. Type **OPTIONAL PLAN PREMIUM RATES** and then press Ctrl + E to center-align the text in the cell. (The text you type will be italicized.)

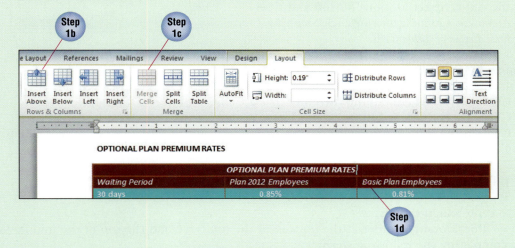

2. Select and then delete the text *OPTIONAL PLAN PREMIUM RATES* that displays above the bottom table.
3. Insert rows and text in the top table and merge cells by completing the following steps:
   a. Click in the cell containing the text *Maggie Rivera*.
   b. Click the Table Tools Layout tab.
   c. Click the Insert Above button twice. (This inserts two rows at the top of the table.)
   d. With the cells in the top row selected, click the Merge Cells button in the Merge group.
   e. Type **CONTACT INFORMATION, NORTH** and then press Ctrl + E to change the paragraph alignment to center.
   f. Type the following text in the four cells in the new second row.
       Name   **Title**   **Company**   **Telephone**

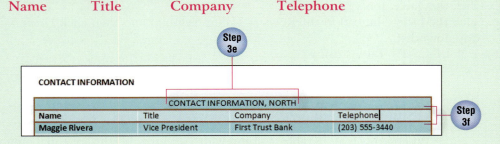

4. Apply heading formatting to the new top row by completing the following steps:
   a. Click the Table Tools Design tab.
   b. Click the *Header Row* check box in the Table Style Options dialog box.
5. Select and then delete the text *CONTACT INFORMATION* that displays above the top table.
6. Split a cell by completing the following steps:
   a. Click in the cell containing the telephone number *(301) 555-1221*.
   b. Click the Table Tools Layout tab.
   c. Click the Split Cells button in the Merge group.
   d. At the Split Cells dialog box, click OK. (The telephone number will wrap to a new line. You will change this in the next project.)

Chapter 7 ■ Creating Tables and SmartArt

e. Click in the new cell.
   f. Type **x453** in the new cell. If AutoCorrect automatically capitalizes the *x*, hover the mouse pointer over the *X* until the AutoCorrect Options button displays. Click the AutoCorrect Options button and then click *Undo Automatic Capitalization* or click *Stop Auto-capitalizing First Letter of Table Cells*.

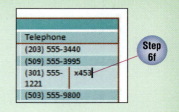

7. Split the cell containing the telephone number *(206) 555-6788* and then type **x2310** in the new cell. (If necessary, make the *x* lowercase.)
8. Split the top table into two tables by completing the following steps:
   a. Click in the cell containing the name *Teresa Getty*.
   b. Click the Split Table button in the Merge group.
   c. Click in the cell containing the name *Teresa Getty* (in the first row of the new table).
   d. Click the Insert Above button in the Rows and Columns group in the Table Tools Layout tab.
   e. With the new row selected, click the Merge Cells button.
   f. Type **CONTACT INFORMATION, SOUTH** in the new row and then press Ctrl + E to center-align the text.
9. Draw a dark orange border at the bottom of the top table and the top of the middle table by completing the following steps:
   a. Click the Table Tools Design tab.
   b. Click the Line Weight button arrow in the Draw Borders group and then click *1 ½ pt* at the drop-down list. (This activates the Draw Table button.)
   c. Using the mouse (mouse pointer displays as a pen), drag along the bottom border of the top table.
   d. Click the top border of the middle table.
   e. Click the Draw Table button to turn it off.
10. Save and then print **WL1-C7-P1-Tables.docx**.
11. Delete the middle table by completing the following steps:
    a. Click in any cell in the middle table.
    b. Click the Table Tools Layout tab.
    c. Click the Delete button in the Rows & Columns group and then click *Delete Table* at the drop-down list.
12. Save **WL1-C7-P1-Tables.docx**.

Customizing Cell Size

Distribute Rows

Distribute Columns

When you create a table, column width and row height are equal. You can customize the width of columns or height of rows with buttons in the Cell Size group in the Table Tools Layout tab. Use the *Table Row Height* measurement box to increase or decrease the height of rows and use the *Table Column Width* measurement box to increase or decrease the width of columns. The Distribute Rows button will distribute equally the height of selected rows and the Distribute Columns button will distribute equally the width of selected columns.

You can also change column width using the move table column markers on the horizontal ruler or by using the table gridlines. To change column width using the horizontal ruler, position the mouse pointer on a move table column marker until it turns into a left and right arrow, and then drag the marker to the desired position. Hold down the Shift key while dragging a table column marker and the horizontal ruler remains stationary while the table column marker moves. Hold down the Alt key while dragging a table column marker and measurements display on the horizontal ruler. To change column width using gridlines, position the arrow pointer on the gridline separating columns until the insertion point turns into a left and right arrow with a vertical line between and then drag the gridline to the desired position. If you want to see the column measurements on the horizontal ruler as you drag a gridline, hold down the Alt key.

Adjust row height in a manner similar to adjusting column width. You can drag the adjust table row marker on the vertical ruler or drag the gridline separating rows. Hold down the Alt key while dragging the adjust table row marker or the row gridline and measurements display on the vertical ruler.

AutoFit

Use the AutoFit button in the Cell Size group to make the column widths in a table automatically fit the contents. To do this, position the insertion point in any cell in the table, click the AutoFit button in the Cell Size group, and then click *AutoFit Contents* at the drop-down list.

Project 1g Changing Column Width and Row Height   Part 7 of 9

1. With **WL1-C7-P1-Tables.docx** open, change the width of the first column in the top table by completing the following steps:
    a. Click in the cell containing the name *Maggie Rivera*.
    b. Position the mouse pointer on the move table column marker that displays just right of the 1.5-inch marker on the horizontal ruler until the pointer turns into an arrow pointing left and right.
    c. Hold down the Shift key and then the left mouse button.
    d. Drag the marker to the 1.25-inch mark, release the mouse button, and then release the Shift key.
2. Complete steps similar to those in Step 1 to drag the move table column marker that displays just right of the 3-inch mark on the horizontal ruler to the 2.75-inch mark. (Make sure the text *Account Manager* in the second column does not wrap to the next line. If it does, slightly increase the width of the button.)
3. Change the width of the third column in the top table by completing the following steps:
    a. Position the mouse pointer on the gridline separating the third and fourth columns until the pointer turns into a left- and right-pointing arrow with a vertical double line between.
    b. Hold down the Alt key and then the left mouse button, drag the gridline to the left until the measurement for the third column on the horizontal ruler displays as *1.3"*, and then release the Alt key and then the mouse button.
4. Position the mouse pointer on the gridline that separates the telephone number *(301) 555-1221* from the extension *x453* and then drag the gridline to the 5.25-inch mark on the horizontal ruler.
5. Drag the right border of the top table to the 5.75-inch marker on the horizontal ruler.

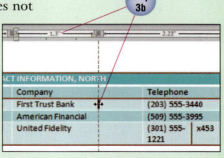
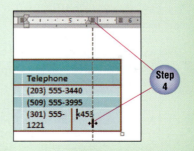

6. Automatically fit the columns in the bottom table by completing the following steps:
   a. Click in any cell in the bottom table.
   b. Click the AutoFit button in the Cell Size group in the Table Tools Layout tab and then click *AutoFit Contents* at the drop-down list.

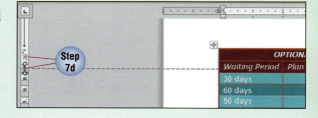

7. Increase the height of the first row in the bottom table by completing the following steps:
   a. Make sure the insertion point is located in one of the cells in the bottom table.
   b. Position the mouse pointer on the top adjust table row marker on the vertical ruler.
   c. Hold down the left mouse button and hold down the Alt key.
   d. Drag the adjust table row marker down until the first row measurement on the vertical ruler displays as *0.36"*, release the mouse button and then the Alt key.

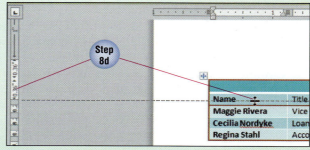

8. Increase the height of the first row in the top table by completing the following steps:
   a. Click in any cell in the top table.
   b. Position the arrow pointer on the gridline that displays at the bottom of the top row until the arrow pointer turns into an up- and down-pointing arrow with a vertical double line between.
   c. Hold down the left mouse button and then hold down the Alt key.
   d. Drag the gridline down until the first row measurement on the vertical ruler displays as *0.36"* and release the mouse button and then the Alt key.
9. Save **WL1-C7-P1-Tables.docx**.

Changing Cell Alignment

The Alignment group in the Table Tools Layout tab contains a number of buttons for specifying the horizontal and vertical alignment of text in cells. The buttons contain a visual representation of the alignment and you can also hover the mouse pointer over a button to determine the alignment.

Repeating a Header Row

▼ **Quick Steps**

Repeat Header Row(s)
1. Click in header row or select rows.
2. Click Table Tools Layout tab.
3. Click Repeat Header Rows button.

Repeat Header Rows

If a table is divided between pages, consider adding the header row at the beginning of the table that extends to the next page. This helps the reader understand the data that displays in each column. To repeat a header row, click in the header row, and then click the Repeat Header Rows button in the Data group in the Table Tools Layout tab. If you want to repeat more than one header row, select the rows and then click the Repeat Header Rows button.

258   Word Level 1 ■ Unit 2

Project 1h   Aligning Text in Cells and Repeating Header Rows   Part 8 of 9

1. With **WL1-C7-P1-Tables.docx** open, click in the top cell in the top table (the cell containing the title *CONTACT INFORMATION, NORTH*).
2. Click the Align Center button in the Alignment group in the Table Tools Layout tab.

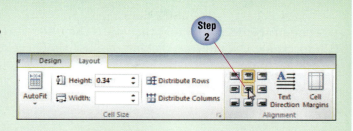

3. Format and align text in the second row in the top table by completing the following steps:
   a. Select the second row.
   b. Press Ctrl + B (this turns off bold for the entry in the first cell) and then press Ctrl + B again (this turns on bold for all entries in the second row).
   c. Click the Align Top Center button in the Alignment group.
4. Click in the top cell in the bottom table and then click the Align Center button in the Alignment group.
5. Press Ctrl + End to move the insertion point to the end of the document, press the Enter key six times, and then insert a table into the current document by completing the following steps:
   a. Click the Insert tab.
   b. Click the Object button arrow in the Text group and then click *Text from File* at the drop-down list.
   c. At the Insert File dialog box, navigate to the Word2010L1C7 folder on your storage medium and then double-click *ContactsWest.docx*.
6. Repeat the header row by completing the following steps:
   a. Select the first two rows in the table you just inserted.
   b. Click the Table Tools Layout tab.
   c. Click the Repeat Header Rows button in the Data group.
7. Save **WL1-C7-P1-Tables.docx**.

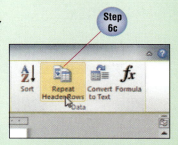

Inserting a Quick Table

Word includes a Quick Tables feature you can use to insert predesigned tables in a document. To insert a quick table, click the Insert tab, click the Table button, point to *Quick Tables*, and then click the desired table at the side menu. A quick table has formatting applied but you can further format the table with options at the Table Tools Design tab and the Table Tools Layout tab.

▼ **Quick Steps**
Insert Quick Table
1. Click Insert tab.
2. Click Table button.
3. Point to *Quick Tables*.
4. Click desired table.

Chapter 7 ■ Creating Tables and SmartArt   259

Project 1i Inserting a Quick Table — Part 9 of 9

1. With **WL1-C7-P1-Tables.docx** open, press Ctrl + End to move the insertion point to the end of the document and then press the Enter key.
2. Insert a quick table by clicking the Insert tab, clicking the Table button, pointing to *Quick Tables*, and then clicking the *Calendar 3* option at the side menu.

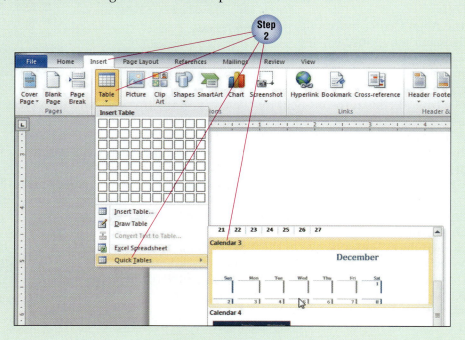

3. Edit text in each of the cells so the calendar reflects the current month.
4. Save, print, and then close **WL1-C7-P1-Tables.docx**.

Project 2 Create and Format Tables with Employee Information — 5 Parts

You will create and format a table containing information on the names and departments of employees of Tri-State Products and also insert a table containing additional information on employees and then format the table.

Changing Cell Margin Measurements

Cell Margins

By default, cells in a table contain specific margin settings. Top and bottom margins in a cell have a default measurement of *0"* and left and right margins have a default setting of *0.08"*. Change these default settings with options at the Table Options dialog box shown in Figure 7.7. Display this dialog box by clicking the Cell Margins button in the Alignment group in the Table Tools Layout tab. Use the options in the *Default cell margins* section to change the top, bottom, left, and/or right cell margin measurements.

Figure 7.7 Table Options Dialog Box

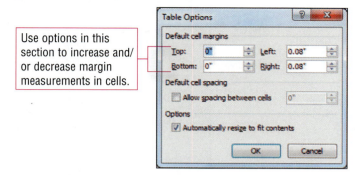

Changes to cell margins will affect all cells in a table. If you want to change the cell margin measurements for one cell or for selected cells, position the insertion point in the cell or select the desired cells and then click the Properties button in the Table group in the Table Tools Layout tab. (You can also click the Cell Size group dialog box launcher.) At the Table Properties dialog box that displays, click the Cell tab and then the Options button that displays in the lower right corner of the dialog box. This displays the Cell Options dialog box shown in Figure 7.8.

Properties

Before setting the new cell margin measurements, remove the check mark from the *Same as the whole table* option. With the check mark removed from this option, the cell margin options become available. Specify the new cell margin measurements and then click OK to close the dialog box.

Figure 7.8 Cell Options Dialog Box

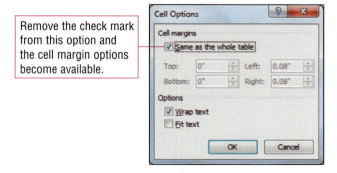

Project 2a — Changing Cell Margin Measurements — Part 1 of 5

1. Open **TSPTables.docx** and then save the document with Save As and name it **WL1-C7-P2-TSPTables**.
2. Change the top and bottom margins for all cells in the table by completing the following steps:
   a. Position the insertion point in any cell in the table and then click the Table Tools Layout tab.

Chapter 7 ■ Creating Tables and SmartArt   **261**

b. Click the Cell Margins button in the Alignment group.
c. At the Table Options dialog box, change the *Top* and *Bottom* measurements to *0.05"*.
d. Click OK to close the Table Options dialog box.
3. Change the top and bottom cell margin measurements for the first row of cells by completing the following steps:
   a. Select the first row of cells (the cells containing *Name* and *Department*).
   b. Click the Properties button in the Table group.
   c. At the Table Properties dialog box, click the Cell tab.
   d. Click the Options button.
   e. At the Cell Options dialog box, remove the check mark from the *Same as the whole table* option.
   f. Change the *Top* and *Bottom* measurements to *0.1"*.
   g. Click OK to close the Cell Options dialog box.
   h. Click OK to close the Table Properties dialog box.
4. Change the left cell margin measurement for specific cells by completing the following steps:
   a. Select all rows in the table *except* the top row.
   b. Click the Cell Size group dialog box launcher.
   c. At the Table Properties dialog box, make sure the Cell tab is active.
   d. Click the Options button.
   e. At the Cell Options dialog box, remove the check mark from the *Same as the whole table* option.
   f. Change the *Left* measurement to *0.3"*.
   g. Click OK to close the Cell Options dialog box.
   h. Click OK to close the Table Properties dialog box.
5. Save **WL1-C7-P2-TSPTables.docx**.

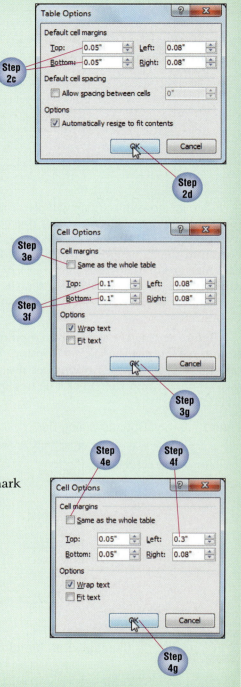

Changing Cell Direction

Text Direction

Change the direction of text in a cell using the Text Direction button in the Alignment group in the Table Tools Layout tab. Each time you click the Text Direction button, the text rotates in the cell 90 degrees.

Changing Table Alignment

By default, a table aligns at the left margin. Change this alignment with options at the Table Properties dialog box with the Table tab selected as shown in Figure 7.9. To change the alignment, click the desired alignment option in the *Alignment* section of the dialog box.

Figure 7.9 Table Properties Dialog Box with Table Tab Selected

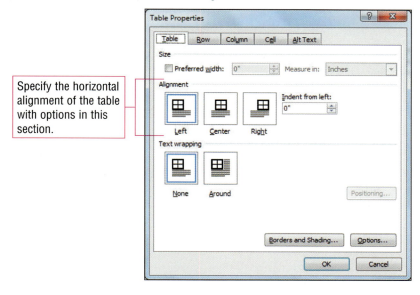

Specify the horizontal alignment of the table with options in this section.

Project 2b — Changing Table Alignment — Part 2 of 5

1. With **WL1-C7-P2-TSPTables.docx** open, insert a new column and change text direction by completing the following steps:
   a. Click in any cell in the first column.
   b. Click the Insert Left button in the Rows & Columns group.
   c. With the cells in the new column selected, click the Merge Cells button in the Merge group.
   d. Type **Tri-State Products**.
   e. Click the Align Center button in the Alignment group.
   f. Click twice on the Text Direction button in the Alignment group.
   g. With *Tri-State Products* selected, click the Home tab, and then increase the font size to *16*.

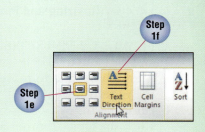

2. Automatically fit the contents by completing the following steps:
   a. Click in any cell in the table.
   b. Click the Table Tools Layout tab.
   c. Click the AutoFit button in the Cell Size group and then click the *AutoFit Contents* at the drop-down list.
3. Change the table alignment by completing the following steps:
   a. Click the Properties button in the Table group in the Table Tools Layout tab.

Chapter 7 ■ Creating Tables and SmartArt

b. At the Table Properties dialog box, click the Table tab.
c. Click the *Center* option in the *Alignment* section.
d. Click OK.
4. Select the two cells containing the text *Name* and *Department* and then click the Align Center button in the Alignment group.
5. Save **WL1-C7-P2-TSPTables.docx**.

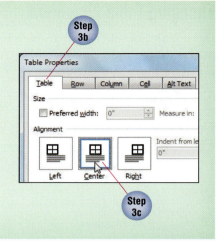

Changing Table Size with the Resize Handle

Quick Steps
Move a Table
1. Position mouse pointer on table move handle until pointer displays as a four-headed arrow.
2. Hold down left mouse button.
3. Drag table to desired position.
4. Release mouse button.

When you hover the mouse pointer over a table, a resize handle displays in the lower right corner of the table. The resize handle displays as a small, white square. Drag this resize handle to increase and/or decrease the size and proportion of the table.

Moving a Table

Position the mouse pointer in a table and a table move handle displays in the upper left corner. Use this handle to move the table in the document. To move a table, position the mouse pointer on the table move handle until the pointer turns into a four-headed arrow, hold down the left mouse button, drag the table to the desired position, and then release the mouse button.

Project 2c Resizing and Moving Tables   Part 3 of 5

1. With **WL1-C7-P2-TSPTables.docx** open, insert a table into the current document by completing the following steps:
    a. Press Ctrl + End to move the insertion point to the end of the document and then press the Enter key.
    b. Click the Insert tab.
    c. Click the Object button arrow in the Text group and then click *Text from File* at the drop-down list.
    d. At the Insert File dialog box, navigate to the Word2010L1C7 folder and then double-click **TSPEmps.docx**.
2. Automatically fit the bottom table by completing the following steps:
    a. Click in any cell in the bottom table.
    b. Click the Table Tools Layout tab.
    c. Click the AutoFit button in the Cell Size group and then click *AutoFit Contents* at the drop-down list.
3. Format the bottom table by completing the following steps:
    a. Click the Table Tools Design tab.

b. Click the More button that displays at the right side of the styles thumbnails in the Table Styles group and then click the *Medium Shading 1 - Accent 2* style (third style from the left in the fourth row of the *Built-In* section).
c. Click the *First Column* check box in the Table Style Options group to remove the check mark.
d. Select the first and second rows, click the Table Tools Layout tab, and then click the Align Center button in the Alignment group.
e. Select the second row and then press Ctrl + B to turn on bold.

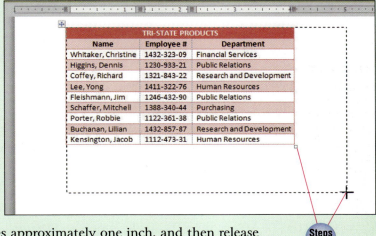

4. Resize the bottom table by completing the following steps:
   a. Position the mouse pointer on the resize handle located in the lower right corner of the bottom table.
   b. Hold down the left mouse button, drag down and to the right until the width and height of the table increases approximately one inch, and then release the mouse button.
5. Move the bottom table by completing the following steps:
   a. Hover the mouse pointer over the bottom table.
   b. Position the mouse pointer on the table move handle until the pointer displays with a four-headed arrow attached.
   c. Hold down the left mouse button, drag the table so it is positioned equally between the left and right margins, and then release the mouse button.

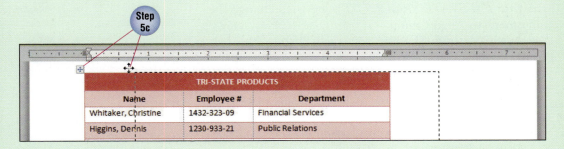

6. Select the cells in the column below the heading *Employee #* and then click the Align Top Center button in the Alignment group.
7. Save **WL1-C7-P2-TSPTables.docx**.

Quick Steps

Convert Text to Table
1. Select text.
2. Click Insert tab.
3. Click Table button.
4. Click *Convert Text to Table*.

Convert Table to Text
1. Position insertion point in any cell of table.
2. Click Table Tools Layout tab.
3. Click *Convert to Text*.
4. Specify desired separator at Convert Table to Text dialog box.
5. Click OK.

Converting Text to a Table

You can create a table and then enter data in the cells or you can create the data and then convert it to a table. To convert text to a table, type the text and separate it with a separator character such as a comma or tab. The separator character identifies where you want text divided into columns. To convert text, select the text, click the Insert tab, click the Table button in the Tables group, and then click *Convert Text to Table* at the drop-down list.

Converting a Table to Text

You can convert a table to text by positioning the insertion point in any cell of the table, clicking the Table Tools Layout tab, and then clicking the Convert to Text button in the Data group. At the Convert Table to Text dialog box, specify the desired separator and then click OK.

Convert to Text

Project 2d — Converting Text to a Table — Part 4 of 5

1. With **WL1-C7-P2-TSPTables.docx** open, press Ctrl + End to move the insertion point to the end of the document and then press the Enter key until the insertion point is positioned approximately a double space below the bottom table.
2. Insert the document named **TSPExecs.docx** into the current document.
3. Convert the text to a table by completing the following steps:
    a. Select the text you just inserted.
    b. Make sure the Insert tab is active.
    c. Click the Table button in the Tables group and then click *Convert Text to Table* at the drop-down list.
    d. At the Convert Text to Table dialog box, type 2 in the *Number of columns* text box.
    e. Click the *AutoFit to contents* option in the *AutoFit behavior* section.
    f. Click the *Commas* option in the *Separate text at* section.
    g. Click OK.
4. Select and merge the cells in the top row (the row containing the title *TRI-STATE PRODUCTS*) and then change the alignment to Align Center.
5. Apply the Medium Shading 1 - Accent 2 style (third style from the left in the fourth row of the *Built-In* section) and remove the check mark from the *First Column* check box in the Table Style Options group in the Table Tools Design tab.
6. Drag the table so it is centered and positioned below the table above.
7. Apply the Medium Shading 1 - Accent 2 style to the top table. Increase the width of the columns so the text *TRI-STATE PRODUCTS* is visible and the text in the second and third columns displays on one line.
8. Drag the table so it is centered and positioned above the middle table. Make sure the three tables fit on one page.
9. Save **WL1-C7-P2-TSPTables.docx**.

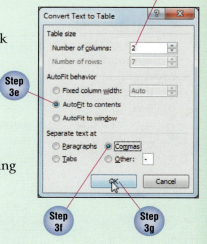

Drawing a Table

In Project 1 you used options in the Draw Borders group in the Table Tools Design tab to draw borders around an existing table. You can also use these options to draw an entire table. To draw a table, click the Insert tab, click the Table button in the Tables group, and then click *Draw Table* at the drop-down list. This turns the mouse pointer into a pen. Drag the pen pointer in the document to create the table. The first time you release the mouse button when drawing a table, the Table Tools Design tab becomes active. Use buttons in this table to customize the table. If you make a mistake while drawing a table, click the Eraser button in the Draw Borders group (this changes the mouse pointer to an eraser) and then drag over any border lines you want to erase. You can also click the Undo button to undo your most recent action.

Eraser

Project 2e — Drawing and Formatting a Table — Part 5 of 5

1. With **WL1-C7-P2-TSPTables.docx** open, select and then delete three rows in the middle table from the row that begins with the name *Lee, Yong* through the row that begins with the name *Schaffer, Mitchell*.
2. Move the insertion point to the end of the document (outside of any table) and then press the Enter key.
3. Click the Insert tab, click the Table button, and then click the *Draw Table* option at the drop-down list. (This turns the insertion point into a pen.)
4. Using the mouse, drag in the document (below the bottom table) to create the table shown at the right. If you make a mistake, click the Undo button. You can also click the Erase button and drag over a border line to erase it. Click the Draw Table button to turn it off.

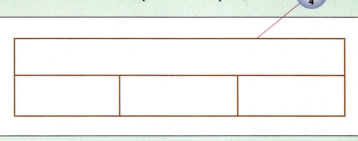

5. After drawing the table, type **Tri-State Products** in the top cell, **Washington Division** in the cell at the left, **Oregon Division** in the middle bottom cell, and **California Division** in the cell at the right.
6. Apply the Light Grid - Accent 2 style to the table.
7. Select the table, change the font size to 12, turn on bold, and then center-align the text in the cells.
8. Make any adjustments needed to border lines so text displays on one line in each cell.
9. Drag the table so it is centered and positioned below the bottom table.
10. Save, print, and then close **WL1-C7-P2-TSPTables.docx**.

Project 3 — Sort and Calculate Sales Data — 2 Parts

You will sort data in tables on Tri-State Products sales and then insert formulas to calculate total sales, average sales, and top sales.

▼ **Quick Steps**

Sort Text in Tables
1. Select desired rows in table.
2. Click Sort button in Table Tools Layout tab.
3. Specify the column containing text to sort.
4. Click OK.

Sort

Sorting Text in a Table

With the Sort button in the Data group in the Table Tools Layout tab, you can sort text in selected cells in a table in ascending alphabetic or numeric order. To sort text, select the desired rows in the table and then click the Sort button in the Data group. At the Sort dialog box, specify the column containing the text on which you want to sort, and then click OK.

Project 3a   Sorting Text in a Table   Part 1 of 2

1. Open **TSPSalesTables.docx** and then save the document with Save As and name it **WL1-C7-P3-TSPSalesTables**.
2. Sort text in the top table by completing the following steps:
   a. Select all of the rows containing names (from *Novak, Diana* through *Sogura, Jeffrey*).
   b. Click Table Tools Layout tab.
   c. Click the Sort button in the Data group.
   d. At the Sort dialog box, click OK. (This sorts the last names in the first column in alphabetical order.)
3. After looking at the table, you decide to sort by 2010 Sales. To do this, complete the following steps:
   a. With the rows still selected, click the Sort button in the Data group.
   b. At the Sort dialog box, click the down-pointing arrow at the right side of the *Sort by* option box and then click *Column 2* at the drop-down list.
   c. Click OK.
   d. Deselect the rows.
4. Save **WL1-C7-P3-TSPSalesTables.docx**.

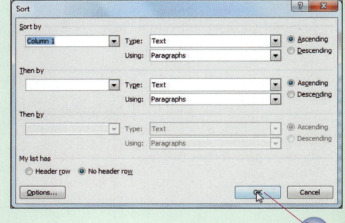

Step 2d

Performing Calculations in a Table

Formula

You can use the Formula button in the Data group in the Table Tools Layout tab to insert formulas that calculate data in a table. Numbers in cells in a table can be added, subtracted, multiplied, and divided. In addition, you can calculate averages, percentages, and minimum and maximum values. You can calculate data in a Word table, but for complex calculations use an Excel worksheet.

To perform a calculation on data in a table, position the insertion point in the cell where you want the result of the calculation inserted and then click the Formula button in the Data group in the Table Tools Layout tab. This displays the Formula dialog box shown in Figure 7.10. At this dialog box, accept the default formula that displays in the *Formula* text box or type the desired calculation, and then click OK.

Figure 7.10 Formula Dialog Box

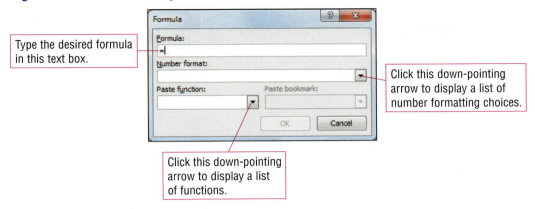

You can use four basic operators when writing a formula including the plus sign (+) for addition, the minus sign (hyphen) for subtraction, the asterisk (*) for multiplication, and the forward slash (/) for division. If a calculation contains two or more operators, Word calculates from left to right. If you want to change the order of calculation, use parentheses around the part of the calculation to be performed first.

In the default formula, the **SUM** part of the formula is called a *function*. Word provides other functions you can use to write a formula. These functions are available with the *Paste function* option in the Formula dialog box. For example, you can use the AVERAGE function to average numbers in cells.

Specify the numbering format with the *Number format* option at the Formula dialog box. For example, if you are calculating money amounts, you can specify that the calculated numbers display with no numbers or two numbers following the decimal point.

Project 3b Inserting Formulas   Part 2 of 2

1. With **WL1-C7-P3-TSPSalesTables.docx** open, insert a formula by completing the following steps:
   a. Click in cell B9 (the empty cell located immediately below the cell containing the amount *$623,214*).
   b. Click the Table Tools Layout tab.
   c. Click the Formula button in the Data group.
   d. At the Formula dialog box, make sure *=SUM(ABOVE)* displays in the *Formula* option box.
   e. Click the down-pointing arrow at the right side of the *Number format* option box and then click *#,##0* at the drop-down list (top option in the list).
   f. Click OK to close the Formula dialog box.
   g. At the table, type a dollar sign ($) before the number just inserted in cell B9.
2. Complete steps similar to those in Steps 1c through 1g to insert a formula in cell C9 (the empty cell located immediately below the cell containing the amount *$635,099*).

Chapter 7 ■ Creating Tables and SmartArt

3. Complete steps similar to those in Steps 1c through 1g to insert in the bottom table formulas that calculate totals. Insert formulas in the cells in the *Total* row and *Total* column. When inserting formulas in cells F3 through F6, you will need to change the formula to =*SUM(LEFT)*.
4. Insert a formula that calculates the average of amounts by completing the following steps:
   a. Click in cell B10 in the top table. (Cell B10 is the empty cell immediately right of the cell containing the word *Average*.)
   b. Click the Formula button in the Data group.
   c. At the Formula dialog box, delete the formula in the *Formula* text box *except* the equals sign.
   d. With the insertion point positioned immediately right of the equals sign, click the down-pointing arrow at the right side of the *Paste function* option box and then click *AVERAGE* at the drop-down list.
   e. With the insertion point positioned between the left and right parentheses, type **B2:B8**. (When typing cell designations in a formula, you can type either uppercase or lowercase letters.)
   f. Click the down-pointing arrow at the right side of the *Number format* option box and then click *#,##0* at the drop-down list (top option in the list).
   g. Click OK to close the Formula dialog box.
   h. Type a dollar sign (**$**) before the number just inserted in cell B10.
5. Complete steps similar to those in Steps 4b through 4h to insert a formula in cell C10 in the top table that calculates the average of cells C2 through C8.
6. Complete steps similar to those in Steps 4b through 4h to insert a formula in cell B7 in the bottom table that calculates the average of cells B2 through B5. Complete similar steps to insert in cell C7 the average of cells C2 through C5; insert in cell D7 the average of cells D2 through D5; insert in cell E7 the average of cells E2 through E5; and insert in cell F7 the average of cells F2 through F5.
7. Insert a formula that calculates the maximum number by completing the following steps:
   a. Click in cell B11 in the top table. (Cell B11 is the empty cell immediately right of the cell containing the words *Top Sales*.)
   b. Click the Formula button in the Data group.
   c. At the Formula dialog box, delete the formula in the *Formula* text box *except* the equals sign.
   d. With the insertion point positioned immediately right of the equals sign, click the down-pointing arrow at the right side of the *Paste function* option box and then click *MAX* at the drop-down list. (You will need to scroll down the list to display the *MAX* option.)
   e. With the insertion point positioned between the left and right parentheses, type **B2:B8**.
   f. Click the down-pointing arrow at the right side of the *Number format* option box and then click *#,##0* at the drop-down list (top option in the list).
   g. Click OK to close the Formula dialog box.
   h. Type a dollar sign (**$**) before the number just inserted in cell B11.
8. Complete steps similar to those in Steps 7b through 7h to insert the maximum number in cell C11.
9. Apply formatting to each table to enhance the visual appeal of the tables.
10. Save, print, and then close **WL1-C7-P3-TSPSalesTables.docx**.

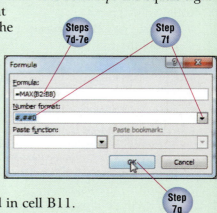

> **Project 4 Prepare and Format a Diagram** 2 Parts
>
> You will prepare a process diagram identifying steps in the production process and then apply formatting to enhance the diagram.

Creating SmartArt

With Word's SmartArt feature you can insert diagrams and organizational charts in a document. SmartArt offers a variety of predesigned diagrams and organizational charts that are available at the Choose a SmartArt Graphic dialog box shown in Figure 7.11. At this dialog box, *All* is selected in the left panel and all available predesigned diagrams display in the middle panel.

Use SmartArt to communicate your message and ideas in a visual manner.

SmartArt

Figure 7.11 Choose a SmartArt Graphic Dialog Box

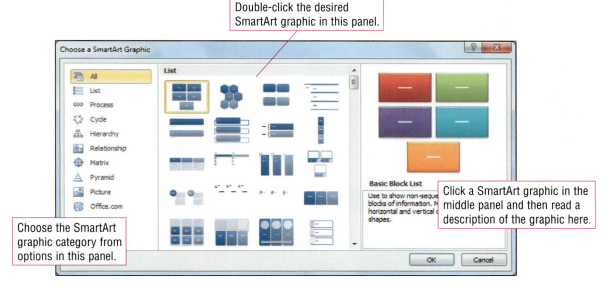

Inserting and Formatting a SmartArt Diagram

Predesigned diagrams display in the middle panel of the Choose a SmartArt Graphic dialog box. Use the scroll bar at the right side of the middle panel to scroll down the list of diagram choices. Click a diagram in the middle panel and the name of the diagram displays in the right panel along with a description of the diagram type. SmartArt includes diagrams for presenting a list of data; showing data processes, cycles, and relationships; and presenting data in a matrix or pyramid. Double-click a diagram in the middle panel of the dialog box and the diagram is inserted in the document.

When you double-click a diagram at the dialog box, the diagram is inserted in the document and a text pane displays at the left side of the diagram. You can type text in the diagram in the text pane or directly in the diagram. Apply design formatting to a diagram with options at the SmartArt Tools Design tab. This tab

▼ **Quick Steps**

Insert a SmartArt Diagram
1. Click Insert tab.
2. Click SmartArt button.
3. Double-click desired diagram.

Limit the number of shapes and the amount of text to key points.

is active when the diagram is inserted in the document. With options and buttons in this tab you add objects, change the diagram layout, apply a style to the diagram, and reset the diagram back to the original formatting.

Apply formatting to a diagram with options at the SmartArt Tools Format tab. With options and buttons in this tab you can change the size and shape of objects in the diagram; apply shape styles and WordArt styles; change the shape fill, outline, and effects; and arrange and size the diagram.

Project 4a — Inserting and Formatting a Diagram — Part 1 of 2

1. At a blank document, insert the diagram shown in Figure 7.12 by completing the following steps:
    a. Click the Insert tab.
    b. Click the SmartArt button in the Illustrations group.
    c. At the Choose a SmartArt Graphic dialog box, click *Process* in the left panel and then double-click the *Alternating Flow* diagram (see image at the right).
    d. If a *Type your text here* text pane does not display at the left side of the diagram, click the Text Pane button in the Create Graphic group to display the pane.
    e. With the insertion point positioned after the top bullet in the *Type your text here* text pane, type **Design**.
    f. Click *[Text]* that displays below *Design* and then type **Mock-up**.
    g. Continue clicking occurrences of *[Text]* and typing text so the text pane displays as shown at the right.
    h. Close the text pane by clicking the Close button (contains an X) that displays in the upper right corner of the pane. (You can also click the Text Pane button in the Create Graphic group.)

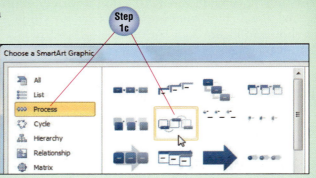

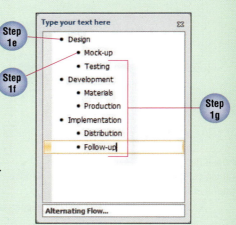

2. Change the diagram colors by clicking the Change Colors button in the SmartArt Styles group and then clicking the first option in the *Colorful* section (*Colorful - Accent Colors*).

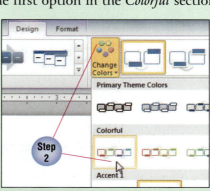

3. Apply a style by clicking the More button that displays at the right side of the thumbnails in the SmartArt Styles group and then clicking the second option from the left in the top row of the *3-D* section (*Inset*).

4. Copy the diagram and then change the layout by completing the following steps:
   a. Click inside the diagram border but outside of any shapes.
   b. Click the Home tab and then click the Copy button in the Clipboard group.
   c. Press Ctrl + End, press the Enter key once, and then press Ctrl + Enter to insert a page break.
   d. Click the Paste button in the Clipboard group.
   e. Click the bottom diagram in the document.
   f. Click the SmartArt Tools Design tab.
   g. Click the More button that displays at the right side of the thumbnails in the Layouts group and then click the Continuous Block Process layout (see image at the right).
   h. Click outside the diagram to deselect it.

5. Save the document and name it **WL1-C7-P4-Diagrams**.

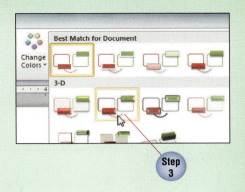

Step 3

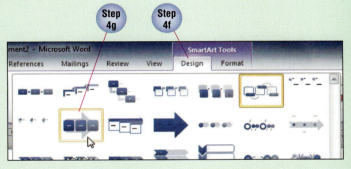

Step 4g   Step 4f

Figure 7.12 Project 4a

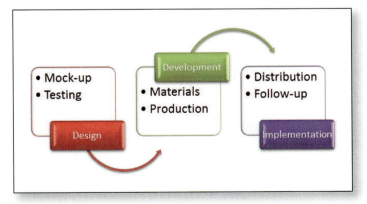

Arranging and Moving a SmartArt Diagram

Before moving a SmartArt diagram, you must select a text wrapping style. Select a text wrapping style with the Arrange button in the SmartArt Tools Format tab. Click the Position button, and then click the desired position at the drop-down gallery. You can also choose a text wrapping style by clicking the Wrap Text button

Chapter 7 ■ Creating Tables and SmartArt   **273**

Position

Text Wrap

and then clicking the desired wrapping style at the drop-down list. Move the diagram by positioning the arrow pointer on the diagram border until the pointer turns into a four-headed arrow, holding down the left mouse button, and then dragging the diagram to the desired location. Nudge selected shape(s) with the up, down, left, or right arrow keys on the keyboard.

Project 4b Formatting Diagrams   Part 2 of 2

1. With **WL1-C7-P4-Diagrams.docx** open, format shapes by completing the following steps:
    a. Click the diagram on the first page to select it (light gray border surrounds the diagram).
    b. Click the SmartArt Tools Format tab.
    c. In the diagram, click the rectangle shape containing the word *Design*.
    d. Hold down the Shift key and then click the shape containing the word *Development*.
    e. With the Shift key still down, click the shape containing the word *Implementation*. (All three shapes should now be selected.)
    f. Click the Change Shape button in the Shapes group.
    g. Click the seventh shape from the left in the second row of the *Block Arrows* section (the Pentagon shape).
    h. With the shapes still selected, click the Larger button in the Shapes group.
    i. With the shapes still selected, click the Shape Outline button arrow in the Shape Styles group and then click the red color *Red, Accent 2*.
    j. Click inside the diagram border but outside any shape. (This deselects the shapes but keeps the diagram selected.)

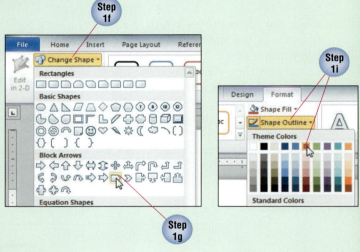

2. Change the size of the diagram by completing the following steps:
    a. Click the Size button located at the right side of the SmartArt Tools Format tab.
    b. Click in the *Height* measurement box, type **4**, and then press Enter.
3. Position the diagram by completing the following steps:
    a. Click the Position button in the Arrange group in the SmartArt Tools Format tab.
    b. Click the middle option in the second row of the *With Text Wrapping* section (the *Position in Middle Center with Square Text Wrapping* option).

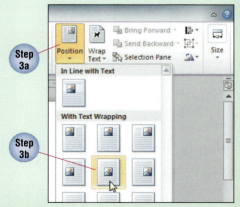

4. Format the bottom diagram by completing the following steps:
   a. Press Ctrl + End to move to the end of the document and then click in the bottom diagram to select it.
   b. Hold down the Shift key and then click each of the three shapes.
   c. Click the More button at the right side of the style thumbnail in the WordArt Styles group in the SmartArt Tools Format tab.
   d. Click the last WordArt style in the lower right corner of the drop-down gallery (*Fill - Blue, Accent 1, Metal Bevel, Reflection*).
   e. Click the Text Outline button arrow in the WordArt Styles group and then click the light blue color in the *Standard Colors* section (the seventh color from the left).
   f. Click the Text Effects button in the WordArt Styles group, point to *Glow* at the drop-down list, and then click the last option in the top row (*Orange, 5 pt glow, Accent color 6*).
   g. Click inside the diagram border but outside any shape.
5. Arrange the diagram by clicking the Position button in the Arrange group and then clicking the middle option in the second row of the *With Text Wrapping* section (the *Position in Middle Center with Square Text Wrapping* option).
6. Save, print, and then close **WL1-C7-P4-Diagrams.docx**.

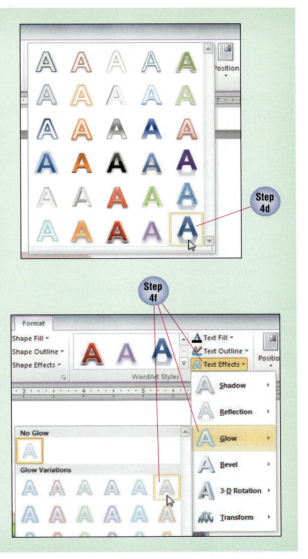

Project 5 Prepare and Format a Company Organizational Chart 1 Part

You will prepare an organizational chart for a company and then apply formatting to enhance the visual appeal of the organizational chart.

Creating an Organizational Chart with SmartArt

If you need to visually illustrate hierarchical data, consider creating an organizational chart with a SmartArt option. To display organizational chart SmartArt options, click the Insert tab and then click the SmartArt button in the Illustrations group. At the Choose a SmartArt Graphic dialog box, click *Hierarchy* in the left panel. Organizational chart options display in the middle panel of the dialog box. Double-click the desired organizational chart and the chart is inserted

Quick Steps

Insert an Organizational Chart
1. Click Insert tab.
2. Click SmartArt button.
3. Click *Hierarchy*.
4. Double-click desired organizational chart.

in the document. Type text in a diagram by selecting the shape and then typing text in the shape or you can type text in the *Type your text here* window that displays at the left side of the diagram. Format a SmartArt organizational chart with options and buttons in the SmartArt Tools Design tab and the SmartArt Tools Format tab.

Project 5 Creating and Formatting an Organizational Chart   Part 1 of 1

1. At a blank document, create the organizational chart shown in Figure 7.13. To begin, click the Insert tab.
2. Click the SmartArt button in the Illustrations group.
3. At the Choose a SmartArt Graphic dialog box, click *Hierarchy* in the left panel of the dialog box and then double-click the first option in the middle panel, *Organization Chart*.
4. If a *Type your text here* window displays at the left side of the organizational chart, close the pane by clicking the Text Pane button in the Create Graphic group.
5. Delete one of the boxes in the organizational chart by clicking the border of the box in the lower right corner to select it and then pressing the Delete key. (Make sure that the selection border that surrounds the box is a solid line and not a dashed line. If a dashed line displays, click the box border again. This should change it to a solid line.)
6. With the bottom right box selected, click the Add Shape button arrow in the Create Graphic group and then click the *Add Shape Below* option.
7. Click *[Text]* in the top box, type **Blaine Willis**, press Shift + Enter, and then type **President**. Click in each of the remaining boxes and type the text as shown in Figure 7.13. (Press Shift + Enter after typing the name.)
8. Click the More button located at the right side of the style thumbnails in the SmartArt Styles group and then click the *Inset* style in the *3-D* section (second option from the left in the top row of the *3-D* section).
9. Click the Change Colors button in the SmartArt Styles group and then click the *Colorful Range - Accent Colors 4 to 5* in the *Colorful* section (fourth option from the left in the *Colorful* row).
10. Click the SmartArt Tools Format tab.
11. Click the tab (displays with a right-pointing and a left-pointing triangle) that displays at the left side of the diagram border. (This displays the *Type your text here* window.)
12. Using the mouse, select the text that displays in the *Type your text here* window.

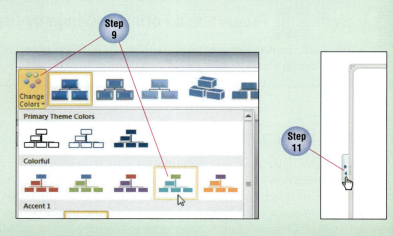

276 Word Level 1 ■ Unit 2

13. Click the Change Shape button in the Shapes group and then click the *Round Same Side Corner Rectangle* option (second option from the *right* in the top row).
14. Click the Shape Outline button arrow in the Shape Styles group and then click the dark blue color (second color from the *right* in the *Standard Colors* section).
15. Close the *Type your text here* window by clicking the Close button (marked with an X) located in the upper right corner of the window.
16. Click inside the organizational chart border but outside any shape.
17. Click the Size button located at the right side of the ribbon in the SmartArt Tools Format tab, click in the *Height* measurement box, and type **4**. Click in the *Width* measurement box, type **6.5**, and then press Enter.
18. Click outside the chart to deselect it.
19. Save the document and name it **WL1-C7-P5-OrgChart**.
20. Print and then close the document.

Figure 7.13 Project 5

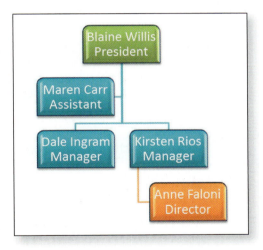

Chapter Summary

- Use the Tables feature to create columns and rows of information. Create a table with the Table button in the Tables group in the Insert tab or with options at the Insert Table dialog box.
- A cell is the intersection between a row and a column. The lines that form the cells of the table are called gridlines.
- Move the insertion point to cells in a document using the mouse by clicking in the desired cell or use the keyboard commands shown in Table 7.1.
- Change the table design with options and buttons in the Table Tools Design tab.
- Refer to Table 7.2 for a list of mouse commands for selecting specific cells in a table and Table 7.3 for a list of keyboard commands for selecting specific cells in a table.

- Change the layout of a table with options and buttons in the Table Tools Layout tab.
- You can select a table, column, row, or cell using the Select button in the Table group in the Table Tools Layout tab.
- Turn on and off the display of gridlines by clicking the Table Tools Layout tab and then clicking the View Gridlines button in the Table group.
- Insert and delete columns and rows with buttons in the Rows & Columns group in the Table Tools Layout tab.
- Merge selected cells with the Merge Cells button and split cells with the Split Cells button, both located in the Merge group in the Table Tools Layout tab.
- Change column width and row height using the height and width measurement boxes in the Cell Size group in the Table Tools Layout tab; by dragging move table column markers on the horizontal ruler, adjust table row markers on the vertical ruler, or gridlines in the table; or with the AutoFit button in the Cell Size group.
- Change alignment of text in cells with buttons in the Alignment group in the Table Tools Layout tab.
- If a table spans two pages, you can insert a header row at the beginning of the rows that extend to the next page. To do this, click in the header row, or select the desired header rows, and then click the Repeat Header Rows button in the Data group in the Table Tools Layout tab.
- Quick Tables are predesigned tables you can insert in a document by clicking the Insert tab, clicking the Table button, pointing to *Quick Tables*, and then clicking the desired table at the side menu.
- Change cell margins with options in the Table Options dialog box.
- Change text direction in a cell with the Text Direction button in the Alignment group.
- Change the table alignment at the Table Properties dialog box with the Table tab selected.
- You can use the resize handle to change the size of the table and the table move handle to move the table.
- Convert text to a table with the *Convert Text to Table* option at the Table button drop-down list. Convert a table to text with the Convert to Text button in the Data group in the Table Tools Layout tab.
- Draw a table in a document by clicking the Insert tab, clicking the Table button, and then clicking *Draw Table*. Using the mouse, drag in the document to create the table.
- Sort selected rows in a table with the Sort button in the Data group.
- Perform calculations on data in a table by clicking the Formula button in the Data group in the Table Tools Layout tab and then specifying the formula and number format at the Formula dialog box.
- Use the SmartArt feature to insert predesigned diagrams and organizational charts in a document. Click the SmartArt button in the Insert tab to display the Choose a SmartArt Graphic dialog box.
- Format a SmartArt diagram or organizational chart with options and buttons in the SmartArt Tools Design tab and the SmartArt Tools Format tab.
- To move a SmartArt diagram, first choose a position or a text wrapping style with the Arrange button in the SmartArt Tools Format tab.

Commands Review

FEATURE	RIBBON TAB, GROUP	BUTTON	OPTION
Table	Insert, Tables		
Insert Table dialog box	Insert, Tables		Insert Table
Draw table	Insert, Tables		Draw Table
View gridlines	Table Tools Layout, Table		
Insert column left	Table Tools Layout, Rows & Columns		
Insert column right	Table Tools Layout, Rows & Columns		
Insert row above	Table Tools Layout, Rows & Columns		
Insert row below	Table Tools Layout, Rows & Columns		
Delete table	Table Tools Layout, Rows & Columns		Delete Table
Delete row	Table Tools Layout, Rows & Columns		Delete Rows
Delete column	Table Tools Layout, Rows & Columns		Delete Columns
Merge cells	Table Tools Layout, Merge		
Split cells dialog box	Table Tools Layout, Merge		
AutoFit table contents	Table Tools Layout, Cell Size		
Cell alignment	Table Tools Layout, Alignment		
Repeat header row	Table Tools Layout, Data		
Insert Quick Table	Insert, Tables		Quick Tables
Table Options dialog box	Table Tools Layout, Alignment		
Text direction	Table Tools Layout, Alignment		
Convert text to table	Insert, Tables		Convert Text to Table
Convert table to text	Table Tools Layout, Data		
Sort text in table	Table Tools Layout, Data		
Formula dialog box	Table Tools Layout, Data		
Choose a SmartArt Graphic dialog box	Insert, Illustrations		

Concepts Check — Test Your Knowledge

Completion: In the space provided at the right, indicate the correct term, command, or number.

1. The Table button is located in this tab.

2. This is another name for the lines that form the cells of the table.

3. Use this keyboard shortcut to move the insertion point to the previous cell.

4. Use this keyboard shortcut to move the insertion point to a tab within a cell.

5. This tab contains table styles you can apply to a table.

6. Click this button in the Table Tools Layout tab to insert a column at the left side of the column containing the insertion point.

7. Insert and delete columns and rows with buttons in this group in the Table Tools Layout tab.

8. One method for changing column width is dragging this on the horizontal ruler.

9. Use this button in the Cell Size group to make the column widths in a table automatically fit the contents.

10. Change the table alignment at this dialog box with the Table tab selected.

11. Hover the mouse pointer over a table and this displays in the lower right corner of the table.

12. Position the mouse pointer in a table and this displays in the upper left corner.

13. Display the Formula dialog box by clicking the Formula button in this group in the Table Tools Layout tab.

14. A variety of predesigned diagrams and organizational charts are available at this dialog box.

15. The SmartArt button is located in this tab.

16. If you need to visually illustrate hierarchical data, consider creating this with the SmartArt feature.

Skills Check Assess Your Performance

Assessment

1 CREATE AND FORMAT A PROPERTY REPLACEMENT COSTS TABLE

1. At a blank document, create the table shown in Figure 7.14 with the following specifications:
   a. Create a table with two columns and eight rows.
   b. Merge the cells in the top row.
   c. Type the text in the cells as shown in Figure 7.14.
   d. Right-align the cells containing the money amounts as well as the blank line below the last amount (cells B2 through B8).
   e. Automatically fit the contents of the cells.
   f. Apply the *Light List - Accent 4* table style.
   g. Remove the check mark from the *First Column* check box.
   h. Draw a green (*Olive Green, Accent 3, Darker 25%*) 1½ pt border around the table.
   i. Change the font size to 14 for the text in cell A1 and change the alignment to Align Center.
   j. Use the resize handle located in the lower right corner of the table and increase the width and height of the table by approximately one inch.
2. Click in the *Accounts receivable* cell and insert a row below. Type **Equipment** in the new cell at the left and type **$83,560** in the new cell at the right.
3. Insert a formula in cell B9 that sums the amounts in cell B2 through B8. (Insert a dollar sign before the amount in cell B9.)
4. Save the document and name it **WL1-C7-A1-CostsTable**.
5. Print and then close **WL1-C7-A1-CostsTable.docx**.

Figure 7.14 Assessment 1

PROPERTY Replacement Costs	
Business personal property	$1,367,340
Earnings and expenses	$945,235
Domestic and foreign transit	$123,400
Accounts receivable	$95,460
Legal liability	$75,415
Computer coverage	$53,098
Total	

Assessment 2 FORMAT A TABLE CONTAINING TRANSPORTATION SERVICE INFORMATION

1. Open **ServicesTable.docx** and then save the document with Save As and name it **WL1-C7-A2-ServicesTable**.
2. Format the table so it appears as shown in Figure 7.15.
3. Position the table in the middle of the page.
4. Save, print, and then close **WL1-C7-A2-ServicesTable.docx**.

Figure 7.15 Assessment 2

	Service	Telephone
Metro Area Transportation Services	**Langley City Transit**	
	Subway and bus information	(507) 555-3049
	Service status hotline	(507) 555-4123
	Travel information	(507) 555-4993
	Valley Rail Road	
	Railway information	(202) 555-2300
	Status hotline	(202) 555-2343
	Travel information	(202) 555-2132
	Mainline Bus	
	Bus routes	(507) 555-6530
	Emergency hotline	(507) 555-6798
	Travel information	(507) 555-7542
	Village Travel Card	
	Village office	(507) 555-1232
	Card inquiries	(507) 555-1930

Assessment 3 CREATE AND FORMAT A COMPANY DIAGRAM

1. At a blank document, create the SmartArt diagram shown in Figure 7.16 with the following specifications:
   a. Use the Titled Matrix diagram.
   b. Apply the *Colorful - Accent Colors SmartArt* style.
   c. Type all of the text shown in Figure 7.16.
   d. Select all of the text and then apply the *Fill - Red, Accent 2, Matte Bevel WordArt* style.
2. Save the document and name it **WL1-C7-A3-SDCDiagram**.
3. Print and then close **WL1-C7-A3-SDCDiagram.docx**.

Figure 7.16 Assessment 3

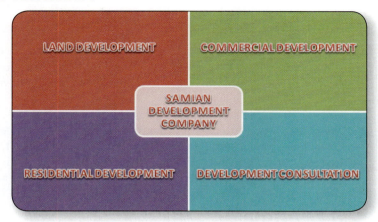

Assessment 4

CREATE AND FORMAT A COMPANY ORGANIZATIONAL CHART

1. At a blank document, create the organizational chart shown in Figure 7.17 with the following specifications:
   a. Use the Hierarchy chart.
   b. Select the top text box and insert a shape above.
   c. Select the top right text box and then add a shape below.
   d. Type the text shown in the organizational chart in Figure 7.17.
   e. Apply the *Colorful Range - Accent Colors 2 to 3* option.
   f. Increase the height to 4.5" and the width to 6.5".
   g. Position the organizational chart in the middle of the page.
2. Save the document and name it **WL1-C7-A4-OrgChart**.
3. Print and then close **WL1-C7-A4-OrgChart.docx**.

Figure 7.17 Assessment 4

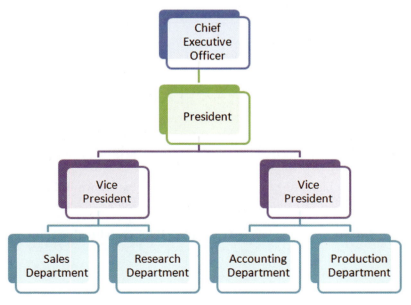

Assessment

5 INSERT FORMULAS IN A TABLE

1. In this chapter, you learned how to insert formulas in a table. Experiment with writing formulas (consider using the Help feature or other reference) and then open **FinAnalysis.docx**. Save the document with Save As and name it **WL1-C7-A5-FinAnalysis**.
2. Format the table so it appears as shown in Figure 7.18.
3. Insert a formula in cell B13 that sums the amounts in cells B6 through B12. Complete similar steps to insert a formula in cell C13, D13, and E13.
4. Insert a formula in cell B14 that subtracts the amount in B13 from the amount in B4. *Hint: The formula should look like this:* **=(B4-B13)**. Complete similar steps to insert a formula in cells C14, D14, and E14.
5. Save, print, and then close **WL1-C7-A5-FinAnalysis.docx**.

Figure 7.18 Assessment 5

TRI-STATE PRODUCTS

Financial Analysis

	2009	2010	2011	2012
Revenue	$1,450,348	$1,538,239	$1,634,235	$1,523,455
Expenses				
Facilities	$250,220	$323,780	$312,485	$322,655
Materials	$93,235	$102,390	$87,340	$115,320
Payroll	$354,390	$374,280	$380,120	$365,120
Benefits	$32,340	$35,039	$37,345	$36,545
Marketing	$29,575	$28,350	$30,310	$31,800
Transportation	$4,492	$5,489	$5,129	$6,349
Miscellaneous	$4,075	$3,976	$4,788	$5,120
Total				
Net Revenue				

Visual Benchmark — Demonstrate Your Proficiency

CREATE A COVER LETTER CONTAINING A TABLE

1. At a blank document, create the document shown in Figure 7.19. Create and format the table as shown in the figure. *Hint: Apply the* **Light Grid - Accent 5** *table style*.
2. Save the completed document and name it **WL1-C7-VB1-CoverLtr**.
3. Print and then close **WL1-C7-VB1-CoverLtr.docx**.

Figure 7.19 Visual Benchmark 1

10234 Larkspur Drive
Cheyenne, WY 82002
July 15, 2012

Dr. Theresa Solberg
Rocky Mountain News
100 Second Avenue
Cheyenne, WY 82001

Dear Dr. Solberg:

Your advertised opening for a corporate communications staff writer describes interesting challenges. As you can see from the table below, my skills and experience are excellent matches for the position.

QUALIFICATIONS AND SKILLS	
Your Requirements	**My Experience, Skills, and Value Offered**
Two years of business writing experience	Four years of experience creating diverse business messages, from corporate communications to feature articles and radio broadcast material.
Ability to complete projects on deadline	Proven project coordination skills and tight deadline focus. My current role as producer of a daily three-hour talk-radio program requires planning, coordination, and execution of many detailed tasks, always in the face of inflexible deadlines.
Oral presentation skills	Unusually broad experience, including high-profile roles as an on-air radio presence and "the voice" for an on-hold telephone message company.
Relevant education (BA or BS)	BA in Mass Communications; one year post-graduate study in Multimedia Communications.

As you will note from the enclosed résumé, my experience encompasses corporate, print media, and multimedia environments. I offer a diverse and proven skill set that can help your company create and deliver its message to various audiences to build image, market presence, and revenue. I look forward to meeting with you to discuss the value I can offer your company.

Sincerely,

Marcus Tolliver

Enclosure: Résumé

CREATE AND FORMAT A SMARTART DIAGRAM

1. At a blank document, create the document shown in Figure 7.20. Create and format the SmartArt diagram as shown in the figure. *Hint: Use the* **Step Up Process** *diagram*.
2. Save the completed document and name it **WL1-C7-VB2-SalesDiagram**.
3. Print and then close **WL1-C7-VB2-SalesDiagram.docx**.

Figure 7.20 Visual Benchmark 2

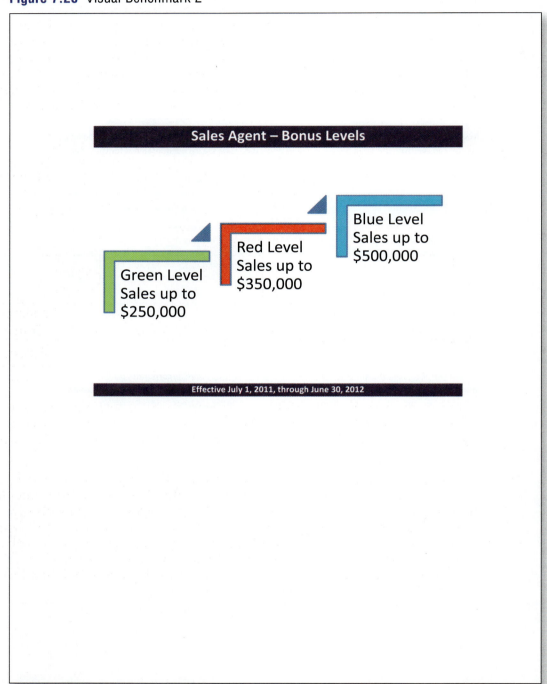

Case Study Apply Your Skills

Part 1

You have recently been hired as an accounting clerk for a landscaping business, Landmark Landscaping, which has two small offices in your city. The accounting clerk prior to you kept track of monthly sales using Word, and the manager would prefer that you continue using that application. Open the file named **LLMoSales.docx** and then save the document with Save As and name it **WL1-C7-CS-P1-LLMoSales**. After reviewing the information, you decide that a table would be a better way of maintaining and displaying the data. Convert the data to a table and modify its appearance so that it is easy to read and understand. Insert a total row at the bottom of the table and then insert formulas to sum the totals in the columns containing amounts. Apply formatting to the table to enhance the visual appeal. Determine a color theme for the table and then continue that same color theme when preparing other documents for Landmark Landscaping. Save, print, and then close the document.

Part 2

The president of Landmark Landscaping has asked you to prepare an organizational chart for the company that will become part of the company profile. Use a SmartArt organizational chart and create a chart with the following company titles (in the order shown below):

	President		
Westside Manager		Eastside Manager	
Landscape Architect	Landscape Director	Landscape Architect	Landscape Director
	Assistant		Assistant

Format the organizational chart to enhance the visual appeal and apply colors that match the color scheme you chose for the company in Part 1. Save the document and name it **WL1-C7-CS-P2-LLOrgChart**. Print and then close the document.

Part 3

As part of the company profile, the president of the company would like to include a diagram that represents the services offered by the company and use the diagram as a company marketing tool. Use SmartArt to create a diagram that contains the following services: Maintenance Contracts, Planting Services, Landscape Design, and Landscape Consultation. Format the diagram to enhance the visual appeal and apply colors that match the color scheme you chose for the company in Part 1. Save the document and name it **WL1-C7-CS-P3-LLServices**. Print and then close the document.

Part 4

The office manager has started a training document with information on using SmartArt. He has asked you to add information on keyboard shortcuts for working with shapes in a SmartArt graphic. Use the Help feature to learn about the keyboard shortcuts available for working with shapes and then create a table and insert the information in the table. Format the table to enhance the visual appeal and apply colors that match the color scheme you chose for the company in Part 1. Save the document and name it **WL1-C7-CS-P4-SAShortcuts**. Print and then close the document.

Part 5

One of the landscape architects has asked you to prepare a table containing information on trees that need to be ordered next month. She would also like to have you include the Latin name for the trees since this is important when ordering. Create a table that contains the common name of the tree, the Latin name, the number required, and the price per tree as shown in Figure 7.21. Use the Internet (or any other resource available to you) to find the Latin name of each tree listed in Figure 7.21. Create a column in the table that multiplies the number of trees required by the price and include this formula for each tree. Format and enhance the table so it is attractive and easy to read. Save the document and name it **WL1-C7-CS-P5-LLTrees**. Print and then close the document.

Figure 7.21 Case Study, Part 5

Douglas Fir, 15 required, $1.99 per tree
White Elm, 10 required, $2.49 per tree
Western Hemlock, 10 required, $1.89 per tree
Red Maple, 8 required, $6.99 per tree
Ponderosa Pine, 5 required, $2.69 per tree

Microsoft Word

CHAPTER 8

Merging Documents

PERFORMANCE OBJECTIVES

Upon successful completion of Chapter 8, you will be able to:
- Create and merge letters, envelopes, labels, and a directory
- Create custom fields for a merge
- Edit main documents and data source files
- Input text during a merge

Word includes a Mail Merge feature you can use to create customized letters, envelopes, labels, directories, e-mail messages, and faxes. The Mail Merge feature is useful for situations where you need to send the same letter to a number of people and create an envelope for each letter. Use Mail Merge to create a main document that contains a letter, envelope, or other data and then merge the main document with a data source. In this chapter, you will use Mail Merge to create letters, envelopes, labels, and directories. Model answers for this chapter's projects appear on the following pages.

Word2010L1C8

Note: Before beginning the projects, copy to your storage medium the Word2010L1C8 subfolder from the Word2010L1 folder in the CD that accompanies this textbook and then make Word2010L1C8 the active folder.

Project 1 Merge Letters to Customers

WL1-C8-P1-MFMD.docx

Page 1

February 23, 2012

Mr. Kenneth Porter
7645 Tenth Street
Apt. 314
New York, NY 10192

Dear Mr. Porter:

McCormack Funds is lowering its expense charges beginning May 1, 2012. The reductions in expense charges mean that more of your account investment performance in the Mutual Investment Fund is returned to you, Mr. Porter. The reductions are worth your attention because most of our competitors' fees have gone up.

Lowering expense charges is noteworthy because before the reduction, McCormack expense deductions were already among the lowest, far below most mutual funds and variable annuity accounts with similar objectives. At the same time, services for you, our client, will continue to expand. If you would like to discuss this change, please call us at (212) 555-2277. Your financial future is our main concern at McCormack.

Sincerely,

Jodie Langstrom
Director, Financial Services

xx
WL1-C8-P1-MFMD.docx

Page 2

February 23, 2012

Ms. Carolyn Renquist
13255 Meridian Street
New York, NY 10435

Dear Ms. Renquist:

McCormack Funds is lowering its expense charges beginning [...] charges mean that more of your account investment perf[...] to you, Ms. Renquist. The reductions are worth your atten[...] have gone up.

Lowering expense charges is noteworthy because before [...] were already among the lowest, far below most mutual fu[...] objectives. At the same time, services for you, our client, [...] discuss this change, please call us at (212) 555-2277. Your [...] McCormack.

Sincerely,

Jodie Langstrom
Director, Financial Services

xx
WL1-C8-P1-MFMD.docx

Page 3

February 23, 2012

Dr. Amil Ranna
433 South 17th
Apt. 17-D
New York, NY 10322

Dear Dr. Ranna:

McCormack Funds is lowering its expense charges beginn[...] charges mean that more of your account investment perfe[...] to you, Dr. Ranna. The reductions are worth your attentio[...] gone up.

Lowering expense charges is noteworthy because before [...] were already among the lowest, far below most mutual fu[...] objectives. At the same time, services for you, our client, [...] discuss this change, please call us at (212) 555-2277. Your [...] McCormack.

Sincerely,

Jodie Langstrom
Director, Financial Services

xx
WL1-C8-P1-MFMD.docx

Page 4

February 23, 2012

Mrs. Wanda Houston
566 North 22nd Avenue
New York, NY 10634

Dear Mrs. Houston:

McCormack Funds is lowering its expense charges beginning May 1, 2012. The reductions in expense charges mean that more of your account investment performance in the Quality Care Fund is returned to you, Mrs. Houston. The reductions are worth your attention because most of our competitors' fees have gone up.

Lowering expense charges is noteworthy because before the reduction, McCormack expense deductions were already among the lowest, far below most mutual funds and variable annuity accounts with similar objectives. At the same time, services for you, our client, will continue to expand. If you would like to discuss this change, please call us at (212) 555-2277. Your financial future is our main concern at McCormack.

Sincerely,

Jodie Langstrom
Director, Financial Services

xx
WL1-C8-P1-MFMD.docx

Project 2 Merge Envelopes

WL1-C8-P2-MFEnvs.docx

Project 3 Merge Mailing Labels

WL-C8-P3-LabelsMD.docx

Project 4 Merge a Directory

WL1-C8-P4-Directory.docx

Project 5 Select Records and Merge Mailing Labels

WL1-C8-P5-SFLabels.docx

Project 6 Edit Records in a Data Source File

WL1-C8-P6-Directory.docx

Chapter 8 ■ Merging Documents   291

Model Answers

Project 7 Add Fill-in Fields to a Main Document
WL1-C8-P7-MFMD.docx

Page 1, Page 2, Page 3, Page 4

Project 8 Use Mail Merge Wizard

Page 1, Page 2

WL1-C8-P8-SFLtrs.docx

Project 1 Merge Letters to Customers   3 Parts

You will create a data source file and a letter main document, and then merge the main document with the records in the data source file.

Completing a Merge

Use buttons and options in the Mailings tab to complete a merge. A merge generally takes two files — the ***data source*** file and the ***main document***. The main document contains the standard text along with fields identifying where variable information is inserted during the merge. The data source file contains the variable information that will be inserted in the main document.

Start Mail Merge

Use the Start Mail Merge button in the Mailings tab to identify the type of main document you want to create and use the Select Recipients button to create a data source file or to specify an existing data source file. You can also use the Mail Merge Wizard to guide you through the merge process. Start the wizard by clicking the Mailings tab, clicking the Start Mail Merge button, and then clicking *Step by Step Mail Merge Wizard*.

Select Recipients

Creating a Data Source File

Before creating a data source file, determine what type of correspondence you will be creating and the type of information you will need to insert in the correspondence. Word provides predetermined field names you can use when creating the data source file. Use these field names if they represent the data you are creating. Variable information in a data source file is saved as a *record*. A record contains all of the information for one unit (for example, a person, family, customer, client, or business). A series of fields makes one record, and a series of records makes a data source file.

Create a data source file by clicking the Select Recipients button in the Start Mail Merge group in the Mailings tab and then clicking *Type New List* at the drop-down list. At the New Address List dialog box shown in Figure 8.1, use the predesigned fields offered by Word or edit the fields by clicking the Customize

▼ **Quick Steps**

Create Data Source File
1. Click Mailings tab.
2. Click Select Recipients button.
3. Click *Type New List* at drop-down list.
4. Type data in predesigned or custom fields.
5. Click OK.

Figure 8.1 New Address List Dialog Box

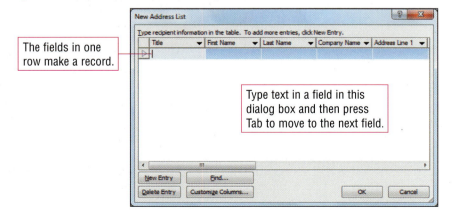

Chapter 8 ■ Merging Documents   293

Columns button. At the Customize Address List dialog box that displays, insert new fields or delete existing fields and then click OK. With the desired fields established, type the required data. Note that fields in the main document correspond to the column headings in the data source file. When all records have been entered, click OK. At the Save Address List dialog box, navigate to the desired folder, type a name for the data source file, and then click OK. Word saves a data source file as an Access database. You do not need Access on your computer to complete a merge with a data source file.

Project 1a Creating a Data Source File   Part 1 of 3

1. At a blank document, click the Mailings tab.
2. Click the Start Mail Merge button in the Start Mail Merge group and then click *Letters* at the drop-down list.
3. Click the Select Recipients button in the Start Mail Merge group and then click *Type New List* at the drop-down list.
4. At the New Address List dialog box, Word provides a number of predesigned fields. Delete the fields you do not need by completing the following steps:
    a. Click the Customize Columns button.
    b. At the Customize Address List dialog box, click *Company Name* to select it and then click the Delete button.
    c. At the message asking if you are sure you want to delete the field, click the Yes button.
    d. Complete steps similar to those in 4b and 4c to delete the following fields:
        Country or Region
        Home Phone
        Work Phone
        E-mail Address
5. Insert a custom field by completing the following steps:
    a. At the Customize Address List dialog box, click the Add button.
    b. At the Add Field dialog box, type **Fund** and then click OK.
    c. Click the OK button to close the Customize Address List dialog box.
6. At the New Address List dialog box, enter the information for the first client shown in Figure 8.2 by completing the following steps:
    a. Type **Mr.** in the Title field and then press the Tab key. (This moves the insertion point to the *First Name* field. You can also press Shift + Tab to move to the previous field.)
    b. Type **Kenneth** and then press the Tab key.
    c. Type **Porter** and then press the Tab key.
    d. Type **7645 Tenth Street** and then press the Tab key.

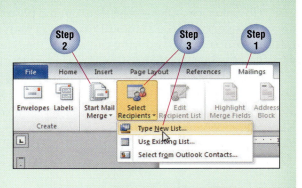
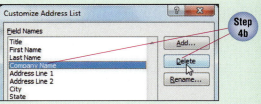
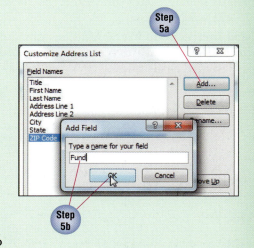

e. Type **Apt. 314** and then press the Tab key.
f. Type **New York** and then press the Tab key.
g. Type **NY** and then press the Tab key.
h. Type **10192** and then press the Tab key.
i. Type **Mutual Investment Fund** and then press the Tab key. (This makes the Title field active in the next row.)
j. With the insertion point positioned in the *Title* field, complete steps similar to those in 6a through 6i to enter the information for the three other clients shown in Figure 8.2.

7. After entering all of the information for the last client in Figure 8.2 (Mrs. Wanda Houston), click the OK button located in the bottom right corner of the New Address List dialog box.
8. At the Save Address List dialog box, navigate to the Word2010L1C8 folder on your storage medium, type **WL1-C8-P1-MFDS** in the *File name* text box, and then click the Save button.

Steps 6a-6i

Figure 8.2 Project 1a

Title	= Mr.		Title	= Ms.	
First Name	= Kenneth		First Name	= Carolyn	
Last Name	= Porter		Last Name	= Renquist	
Address Line 1	= 7645 Tenth Street		Address Line 1	= 13255 Meridian Street	
Address Line 2	= Apt. 314		Address Line 2	= (leave this blank)	
City	= New York		City	= New York	
State	= NY		State	= NY	
Zip Code	= 10192		Zip Code	= 10435	
Fund	= Mutual Investment Fund		Fund	= Quality Care Fund	
Title	= Dr.		Title	= Mrs.	
First Name	= Amil		First Name	= Wanda	
Last Name	= Ranna		Last Name	= Houston	
Address Line 1	= 433 South 17th		Address Line 1	= 566 North 22nd Avenue	
Address Line 2	= Apt. 17-D		Address Line 2	= (leave this blank)	
City	= New York		City	= New York	
State	= NY		State	= NY	
Zip Code	= 10322		Zip Code	= 10634	
Fund	= Priority One Fund		Fund	= Quality Care Fund	

Creating a Main Document

When you begin a mail merge, you specify the type of main document you are creating. After creating and typing the records in the data source file, type the main document. Insert in the main document fields identifying where you want the variable information inserted when the document is merged with the data source file. Use buttons in the Write & Insert Fields group to insert fields and field blocks in the main document.

▼ **Quick Steps**

Create Main Document
1. Click Mailings tab.
2. Click Start Mail Merge button.
3. Click desired document type at drop-down list.
4. Type main document text and insert fields as needed.

A field name is inserted in the main document surrounded by chevrons (« and »), which distinguish fields in the main document and do not display in the merged document.

Insert all of the fields required for the inside address of a letter with the Address Block button in the Write & Insert Fields group. Click this button and the Insert Address Block dialog box displays with a preview of how the fields will be inserted in the document to create the inside address; the dialog box also contains buttons and options for customizing the fields. Click OK and the «AddressBlock» field is inserted in the document. The «AddressBlock» field is an example of a composite field that groups a number of fields together.

Click the Greeting Line button and the Insert Greeting Line dialog box displays with options for customizing how the fields are inserted in the document to create the greeting line. When you click OK at the dialog box, the «GreetingLine» composite field is inserted in the document.

If you want to insert an individual field from the data source file, click the Insert Merge Field button. This displays the Insert Merge Field dialog box with a list of fields from the data source file. Click the Insert Merge Field button arrow and a drop-down list displays containing the fields in the data source file. If you want merged data formatted, you can format the merge fields at the main document.

Address Block   Greeting Line   Insert Merge Field

Project 1b — Creating a Main Document — Part 2 of 3

1. At the blank document, create the letter shown in Figure 8.3. Begin by clicking the No Spacing style in the Styles group in the Home tab.
2. Press the Enter key six times and then type **February 23, 2012**.
3. Press the Enter key four times and then insert the address fields by completing the following steps:
   a. Click the Mailings tab and then click the Address Block button in the Write & Insert Fields group.
   b. At the Insert Address Block dialog box, click the OK button.
   c. Press the Enter key twice.
4. Insert the greeting line fields by completing the following steps:
   a. Click the Greeting Line button in the Write & Insert Fields group.
   b. At the Insert Greeting Line dialog box, click the down-pointing arrow at the right of the option box containing the comma (the box to the right of the box containing *Mr. Randall*).
   c. At the drop-down list that displays, click the colon.
   d. Click OK to close the Insert Greeting Line dialog box.
   e. Press the Enter key twice.

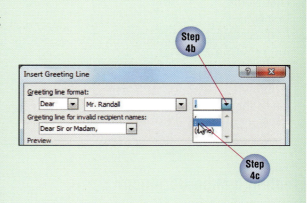

5. Type the letter to the point where «Fund» displays and then insert the «Fund» field by clicking the Insert Merge Field button arrow and then clicking *Fund* at the drop-down list.
6. Type the letter to the point where the «Title» field displays and then insert the «Title» field by clicking the Insert Merge Field button arrow and then clicking *Title* at the drop-down list.
7. Press the spacebar and then insert the «Last_Name» field by clicking the Insert Merge Field button arrow and then clicking *Last_Name* at the drop-down list.
8. Type the remainder of the letter shown in Figure 8.3. (Insert your initials instead of the *XX* at the end of the letter.)
9. Save the document and name it **WL1-C8-P1-MFMD**.

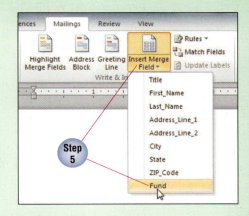

Figure 8.3 Project 1b

February 23, 2012

«AddressBlock»

«GreetingLine»

McCormack Funds is lowering its expense charges beginning May 1, 2012. The reductions in expense charges mean that more of your account investment performance in the «Fund» is returned to you, «Title» «Last_Name». The reductions are worth your attention because most of our competitors' fees have gone up.

Lowering expense charges is noteworthy because before the reduction, McCormack expense deductions were already among the lowest, far below most mutual funds and variable annuity accounts with similar objectives. At the same time, services for you, our client, will continue to expand. If you would like to discuss this change, please call us at (212) 555-2277. Your financial future is our main concern at McCormack.

Sincerely,

Jodie Langstrom
Director, Financial Services

XX
WL1-C8-P1-MFMD.docx

Chapter 8 ■ Merging Documents   297

Previewing a Merge

To view how the main document will appear when merged with the first record in the data source file, click the Preview Results button in the Mailings tab. You can view the main document merged with other records by using the navigation buttons in the Preview Results group. This group contains the First Record buttons, Previous Record, Go to Record, Next Record, and Last Record buttons. Click the button that will display the main document merged with the desired record. Viewing the merged document before printing is helpful to ensure that the merged data is correct. To use the Go to Record button, click the button, type the number of the desired record, and then press Enter. Turn off the preview feature by clicking the Preview Results button.

The Preview Results group in the Mailings tab also includes a Find Recipient button. If you want to search for and preview merged documents with specific entries, click the Preview Results button and then click the Find Recipient button. At the Find Entry dialog box that displays, type the specific field entry for which you are searching in the *Find* text box and then click the Find Next button. Continue clicking the Find Next button until Word displays a message telling you that there are no more entries that contain the text you typed.

Checking for Errors

Before merging documents, you can check for errors using the Auto Check for Errors button in the Preview Results group in the Mailings tab. Click this button and the Checking and Reporting Errors dialog box shown in Figure 8.4 displays containing three options. Click the first option, *Simulate the merge and report errors in a new document,* to tell Word to test the merge, not make any changes, and report errors in a new document. Choose the second option, *Complete the merge, pausing to report each error as it occurs,* and Word will merge the documents and display errors as they occur during the merge. Choose the third option, *Complete the merge without pausing. Report errors in a document,* and Word will complete the merge without pausing and insert any errors in a new document.

Merging Documents

To complete the merge, click the Finish & Merge button in the Finish group in the Mailings tab. At the drop-down list that displays, you can choose to merge the records and create a new document, send the merged documents directly to the printer, or send the merged documents by email.

Figure 8.4 Checking and Reporting Errors Dialog Box

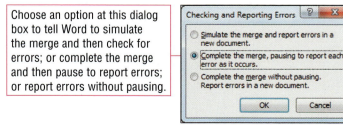

Choose an option at this dialog box to tell Word to simulate the merge and then check for errors; or complete the merge and then pause to report errors; or report errors without pausing.

To merge the documents and create a new document with the merged records, click the Finish & Merge button and then click *Edit Individual Documents* at the drop-down list. At the Merge to New Document dialog box, make sure *All* is selected in the *Merge records* section and then click OK. This merges the records in the data source file with the main document and inserts the merged documents in a new document. You can also display the Merge to New Document dialog box by pressing Alt + Shift + N. Press Alt + Shift + M to display the Merge to Printer dialog box.

You can identify specific records you want merged with options at the Merge to New Document dialog box. Display this dialog box by clicking the Finish & Merge button in the Mailings tab and then clicking the *Edit Individual Documents* option at the drop-down list. Click the *All* option in the Merge to New Document dialog box to merge all records in the data source and click the *Current record* option if you want to merge only the current record. If you want to merge specific adjacent records, click in the *From* text box, type the beginning record number, press the Tab key, and then type the ending record number in the *To* text box.

▼ **Quick Steps**

Merge Documents
1. Click Finish & Merge button.
2. Click *Edit Individual Documents* at drop-down list.
3. Make sure *All* is selected in Merge to New Document dialog box.
4. Click OK.

Project 1c Merging the Main Document with the Data Source File   Part 3 of 3

1. With **WL1-C8-P1-MFMD.docx** open, preview the main document merged with the first record in the data source file by clicking the Preview Results button in the Mailings tab.
2. Click the Next Record button to view the main document merged with the second record in the data source file.
3. Click the Preview Results button to turn it off.
4. Automatically check for errors by completing the following steps:
   a. Click the Auto Check for Errors button in the Preview Results group in the Mailings tab.
   b. At the Checking and Reporting Errors dialog box, click the first option, *Simulate the merge and report errors in a new document*.
   c. Click OK.
   d. If a new document displays with any errors, print the document and then close it without saving it. If a message displays telling you that no errors were found, click OK.
5. Click the Finish & Merge button in the Finish group and then click *Edit Individual Documents* at the drop-down list.
6. At the Merge to New Document dialog box, make sure *All* is selected and then click OK.
7. Save the merged letters and name the document **WL1-C8-P1-MFLtrs**.
8. Print **WL1-C8-P1-MFLtrs.docx**. (This document will print four letters.)
9. Close **WL1-C8-P1-MFLtrs.docx**.
10. Save and then close **WL1-C8-P1-MFMD.docx**.

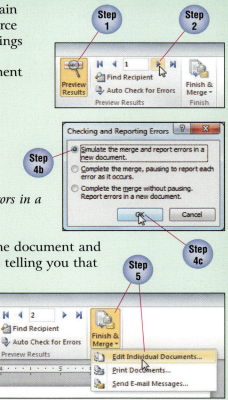

> **Project 2 Merge Envelopes** 1 Part
>
> You will use Mail Merge to prepare envelopes with customer names and addresses.

Merging Envelopes

If you create a letter as a main document and then merge it with a data source file, more than likely you will need properly addressed envelopes in which to send the letters. To prepare an envelope main document that is merged with a data source file, click the Mailings tab, click the Start Mail Merge button, and then click *Envelopes* at the drop-down list. This displays the Envelope Options dialog box as shown in Figure 8.5. At this dialog box, specify the desired envelope size, make any other changes, and then click OK.

The next step in the envelope merge process is to create the data source file or identify an existing data source file. To identify an existing data source file, click the Select Recipients button in the Start Mail Merge group and then click *Use Existing List* at the drop-down list. At the Select Data Source dialog box, navigate to the folder containing the desired data source file and then double-click the file.

With the data source file attached to the envelope main document, the next step is to insert the appropriate fields. Click in the envelope in the approximate location where the recipient's address will appear and a box with a dashed blue border displays. Click the Address Block button in the Write & Insert Fields group and then click OK at the Insert Address Block dialog box.

Figure 8.5 Envelope Options Dialog Box

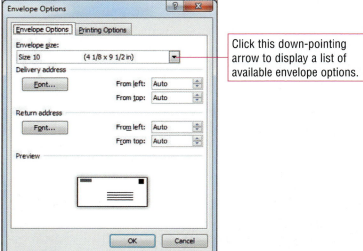

Click this down-pointing arrow to display a list of available envelope options.

300 Word Level 1 ■ Unit 2

Project 2 — Merging Envelopes — Part 1 of 1

1. At a blank document, click the Mailings tab.
2. Click the Start Mail Merge button in the Start Mail Merge group and then click *Envelopes* at the drop-down list.
3. At the Envelope Options dialog box, make sure the envelope size is 10 and then click OK.
4. Click the Select Recipients button in the Start Mail Merge group and then click *Use Existing List* at the drop-down list.
5. At the Select Data Source dialog box, navigate to the Word2010L1C8 folder on your storage medium and then double-click the data source file named *WL1-C8-P1-MFDS.mdb*.
6. Click in the approximate location in the envelope document where the recipient's address will appear. (This causes a box with a dashed blue border to display. If you do not see this box, try clicking in a different location on the envelope.)

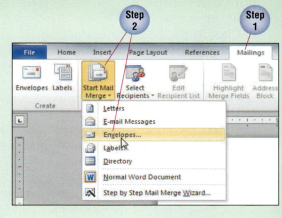

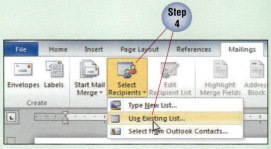

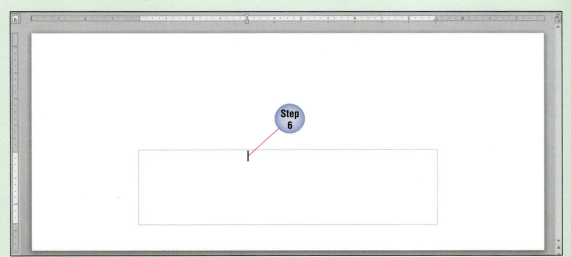

7. Click the Address Block button in the Write & Insert Fields group.
8. At the Insert Address Block dialog box, click the OK button.
9. Click the Preview Results button to see how the envelope appears merged with the first record in the data source file.
10. Click the Preview Results button to turn it off.
11. Click the Finish & Merge button in the Finish group and then click *Edit Individual Documents* at the drop-down list.

12. At the Merge to New Document dialog box, specify that you want only the first two records to merge by completing the following steps:
    a. Click in the *From* text box and then type **1**.
    b. Click in the *To* text box and then type **2**.
    c. Click OK. (This merges only the first two records and opens a document with two merged envelopes.)
13. Save the merged envelopes and name the document **WL1-C8-P2-MFEnvs**.
14. Print **WL1-C8-P2-MFEnvs.docx**. (This document will print two envelopes. Manual feed of the envelopes may be required. Please check with your instructor.)
15. Close **WL1-C8-P2-MFEnvs.docx**.
16. Save the envelope main document and name it **WL1-C8-P2-EnvMD**.
17. Close **WL1-C8-P2-EnvMD.docx**.

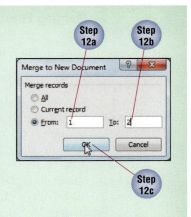

Project 3 Merge Mailing Labels   1 Part

You will use Mail Merge to prepare mailing labels with customer names and addresses.

Merging Labels

Create mailing labels for records in a data source file in much the same way that you create envelopes. Click the Start Mail Merge button and then click *Labels* at the drop-down list. This displays the Label Options dialog box as shown in Figure 8.6. Make sure the desired label is selected and then click OK to close the dialog box. The next step is to create the data source file or identify an existing data source file. With the data source file attached to the label main document, insert the appropriate fields and then complete the merge.

Figure 8.6 Label Options Dialog Box

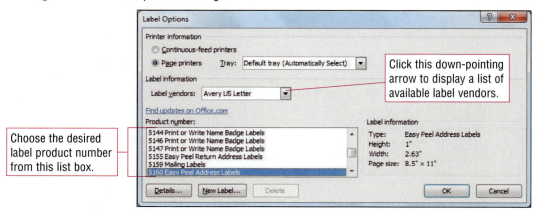

Word Level 1 ■ Unit 2

Project 3 Merging Mailing Labels   Part 1 of 1

1. At a blank document, click the Mailings tab.
2. Click the Start Mail Merge button in the Start Mail Merge group and then click *Labels* at the drop-down list.
3. At the Label Options dialog box, complete the following steps:
   a. If necessary, click the down-pointing arrow at the right side of the *Label vendors* option and then click *Avery US Letter* at the drop-down list. (If this product vendor is not available, choose a vendor name that offers labels that print on a full page.)
   b. Scroll in the *Product number* list box and then click *5160 Easy Peel Address Labels*. (If this option is not available, choose a label number that prints labels in two or three columns down a full page.)
   c. Click OK to close the dialog box.

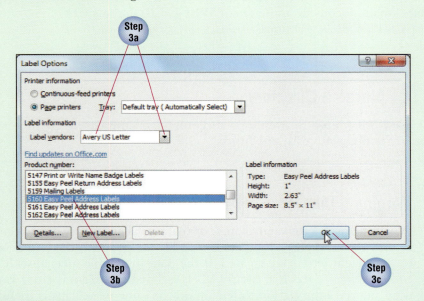

4. Click the Select Recipients button in the Start Mail Merge group and then click *Use Existing List* at the drop-down list.
5. At the Select Data Source dialog box, navigate to the Word2010L1C8 folder on your storage medium and then double-click the data source file named **WL1-C8-P1-MFDS.mdb**.
6. At the labels document, click the Address Block button in the Write & Insert Fields group.
7. At the Insert Address Block dialog box, click the OK button. (This inserts «AddressBlock» in the first label. The other labels contain the «Next Record» field.)
8. Click the Update Labels button in the Write & Insert Fields group. (This adds the «AddressBlock» field after each «Next Record» field in the second and subsequent labels.)
9. Click the Preview Results button to see how the labels appear merged with the records in the data source file.
10. Click the Preview Results button to turn it off.

11. Click the Finish & Merge button in the Finish group and then click *Edit Individual Documents* at the drop-down list.
12. At the Merge to New Document dialog box, make sure *All* is selected, and then click OK.
13. Format the labels by completing the following steps:
    a. Click the Table Tools Layout tab.
    b. Click the Select button in the Table group and then click *Select Table*.
    c. Click the Align Center Left button in the Alignment group.
    d. Click the Home tab and then click the Paragraph group dialog box launcher.
    e. At the Paragraph dialog box, click the up-pointing arrow at the right of *Before* and also at the right of *After* to change the measurement to 0 pt. Click the up-pointing arrow at the right of the *Inside* option to change the measurement to 0.3" and then click OK.
14. Save the merged labels and name the document **WL1-C8-P3-MFLabels**.
15. Print and then close **WL1-C8-P3-MFLabels.docx**.
16. Save the label main document and name it **WL1-C8-P3-LabelsMD**.
17. Close **WL1-C8-P3-LabelsMD.docx**.

Project 4 Merge a Directory   1 Part

You will use Mail Merge to prepare a directory list containing customer names and type of financial investment funds.

Merging a Directory

When merging letters, envelopes, or mailing labels, a new form is created for each record. For example, if the data source file merged with the letter contains eight records, eight letters are created. If the data source file merged with a mailing label contains twenty records, twenty labels are created. In some situations, you may want merged information to remain on the same page. This is useful, for example, when creating a list such as a directory or address list.

Begin creating a merged directory by clicking the Start Mail Merge button and then clicking *Directory* at the drop-down list. Create or identify an existing data source file and then insert the desired fields in the directory document. You may want to set tabs to insert text in columns.

Project 4 Merging a Directory

Part 1 of 1

1. At a blank document, click the Mailings tab.
2. Click the Start Mail Merge button in the Start Mail Merge group and then click *Directory* at the drop-down list.
3. Click the Select Recipients button in the Start Mail Merge group and then click *Use Existing List* at the drop-down list.
4. At the Select Data Source dialog box, navigate to the Word2010L1C8 folder on your storage medium and then double-click the data source file named **WL1-C8-P1-MFDS.mdb**.
5. At the document screen, set left tabs at the 1-inch mark, the 2.5-inch mark, and the 4-inch mark on the Ruler and then press the Tab key. (This moves the insertion point to the tab set at the 1-inch mark.)
6. Click the Insert Merge Field button arrow and then click *Last_Name* at the drop-down list.
7. Press the Tab key to move the insertion point to the 2.5-inch mark.
8. Click the Insert Merge Field button arrow and then click *First_Name* at the drop-down list.
9. Press the Tab key to move the insertion point to the 4-inch mark.
10. Click the Insert Merge Field button arrow and then click *Fund* at the drop-down list.
11. Press the Enter key once.
12. Click the Finish & Merge button in the Finish group and then click *Edit Individual Documents* at the drop-down list.
13. At the Merge to New Document dialog box, make sure *All* is selected and then click OK. (This merges the fields in the document.)
14. Press Ctrl + Home, press the Enter key once, and then press the Up Arrow key once.
15. Press the Tab key, turn on bold, and then type **Last Name**.
16. Press the Tab key and then type **First Name**.
17. Press the Tab key and then type **Fund**.

18. Save the directory document and name it **WL1-C8-P4-Directory**.
19. Print and then close the document.
20. Close the directory main document without saving it.

Chapter 8 ■ Merging Documents   305

Project 5 Select Records and Merge Mailing Labels 1 Part

You will use Mail Merge to prepare mailing labels with names and addresses of customers living in Baltimore.

Editing a Data Source File

Quick Steps

Edit Data Source File
1. Open main document.
2. Click Mailings tab.
3. Click Edit Recipient List button.
4. Make desired changes at Mail Merge Recipients dialog box.
5. Click OK.

Edit a main document in the normal manner. Open the document, make the required changes, and then save the document. Since a data source is actually an Access database file, you cannot open it in the normal manner. Open a data source file for editing using the Edit Recipient List button in the Start Mail Merge group in the Mailings tab. When you click the Edit Recipient List button, the Mail Merge Recipients dialog box displays as shown in Figure 8.7. Select or edit records at this dialog box.

Selecting Specific Records

All of the records in the Mail Merge Recipients dialog box contain a check mark before the first field. If you want to select specific records, remove the check mark from those records you do not want included in a merge. In this way you can select and then merge specific records in the data source file with the main document.

Figure 8.7 Mail Merge Recipients Dialog Box

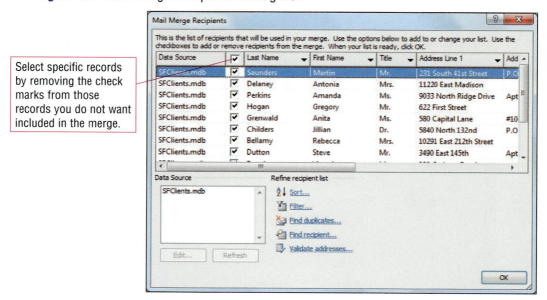

Select specific records by removing the check marks from those records you do not want included in the merge.

Project 5   **Selecting Records and Merging Mailing Labels**   Part 1 of 1

1. At a blank document, create mailing labels for customers living in Baltimore. Begin by clicking the Mailings tab.
2. Click the Start Mail Merge button in the Start Mail Merge group and then click *Labels* at the drop-down list.
3. At the Label Options dialog box, make sure *Avery US Letter* displays in the *Label products* option box, and *5160 Easy Peel Address Labels* displays in the *Product number* list box, and then click OK.
4. Click the Select Recipients button in the Start Mail Merge group and then click *Use Existing List* at the drop-down list.
5. At the Select Data Source dialog box, navigate to the Word2010L1C8 folder on your storage medium and then double-click the data source file named **SFClients.mdb**.
6. Click the Edit Recipient List button in the Start Mail Merge group.
7. At the Mail Merge Recipients dialog box, complete the following steps:
   a. Click the check box located immediately left of the *Last Name* field column heading to remove the check mark. (This removes all of the check marks from the check boxes.)
   b. Click the check box immediately left of each of the following last names: *Saunders, Perkins, Grenwald, Dutton, Fernandez,* and *Stahl*. (These are the customers who live in Baltimore.)
   c. Click OK to close the dialog box.

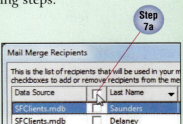

Step 7a

8. At the labels document, click the Address Block button in the Write & Insert Fields group.
9. At the Insert Address Block dialog box, click the OK button.
10. Click the Update Labels button in Write & Insert Fields group.
11. Click the Preview Results button and then click the Previous Record button to display each of the labels and make sure only those customers living in Baltimore display.
12. Click the Preview Results button to turn it off.
13. Click the Finish & Merge button in the Finish group and then click *Edit Individual Documents* at the drop-down list.
14. At the Merge to New Document dialog box, make sure *All* is selected, and then click OK.
15. Format the labels by completing the following steps:
    a. Click the Table Tools Layout tab.
    b. Click the Select button in the Table group and then click *Select Table*.
    c. Click the Align Center Left button in the Alignment group.
    d. Click the Home tab and then click the Paragraph group dialog box launcher.
    e. At the Paragraph dialog box, click the up-pointing arrow at the right of *Before* and also at the right of *After* to change the measurement to 0 pt. Click the up-pointing arrow at the right of the *Inside* option to change the measurement to 0.3" and then click OK.
16. Save the merged labels and name the document **WL1-C8-P5-SFLabels**.
17. Print and then close **WL1-C8-P5-SFLabels.docx**.
18. Close the main labels document without saving it.

Project 6 — Edit Records in a Data Source File — 1 Part

You will edit records in a data source file and then use Mail Merge to prepare a directory with the edited records that contains customer names, telephone numbers, and cell phone numbers.

Editing Records

A data source file may need editing on a periodic basis to add or delete customer names, update fields, insert new fields, or delete existing fields. To edit a data source file, click the Edit Recipient List button in the Start Mail Merge group. At the Mail Merge Recipients dialog box, click the data source file name in the *Data Source* list box and then click the Edit button that displays below the list box. This displays the Edit Data Source dialog box shown in Figure 8.8. At this dialog box you can add a new entry, delete an entry, find a particular entry, and customize columns.

Figure 8.8 Edit Data Source Dialog Box

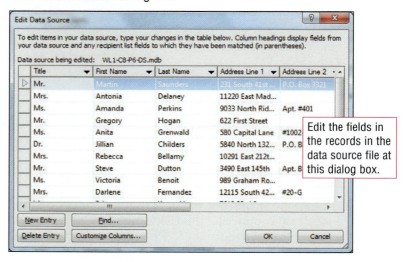

Edit the fields in the records in the data source file at this dialog box.

Project 6 — Editing Records in a Data Source File — Part 1 of 1

1. Make a copy of the **SFClients.mdb** file by completing the following steps:
   a. Display the Open dialog box and make Word2010L1C8 the active folder.
   b. If necessary, change the file type button to *All Files (*.*)*.
   c. Right-click on the **SFClients.mdb** file and then click *Copy* at the shortcut menu.
   d. Position the mouse pointer in a white portion of the Open dialog box Content pane (outside of any file name), click the right mouse button, and then click *Paste* at the shortcut menu. (This inserts a copy of the file in the dialog box Content pane and names the file **SFClients-Copy.mdb**.)
   e. Right-click on the file name **SFClients-Copy.mdb** and then click *Rename* at the shortcut menu.

f. Type **WL1-C8-P6-DS** and then press Enter.
g. Close the Open dialog box.
2. At a blank document, click the Mailings tab.
3. Click the Select Recipients button and then click *Use Existing List* from the drop-down list.
4. At the Select Data Source dialog box, navigate to the Word2010L1C8 folder on your storage medium and then double-click the data source file named **WL1-C8-P6-DS.mdb**.
5. Click the Edit Recipient List button in the Start Mail Merge group.
6. At the Mail Merge Recipients dialog box, click **WL1-C8-P6-DS.mdb** that displays in the *Data Source* list box and then click the Edit button.

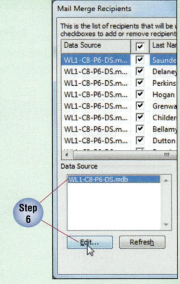

7. Delete the record for Steve Dutton by completing the following steps:
   a. Click the square that displays at the beginning of the row for *Mr. Steve Dutton*.
   b. Click the Delete Entry button.
   c. At the message asking if you want to delete the entry, click the Yes button.
8. Insert a new record by completing the following steps:
   a. Click the New Entry button in the dialog box.
   b. Type the following text in the new record in the specified fields:
      Title = **Ms.**
      First Name = **Jennae**
      Last Name = **Davis**
      Address Line 1 = **3120 South 21st**
      Address Line 2 = (none)
      City = **Rosedale**
      State = **MD**
      ZIP Code = **20389**

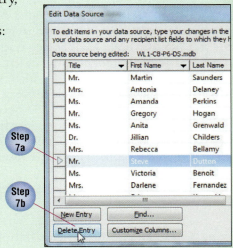

9. Insert a new field and type text in the field by completing the following steps:
   a. At the Edit Data Source dialog box, click the Customize Columns button.
   b. At the message asking if you want to save the changes made to the data source file, click Yes.
   c. At the Customize Address List dialog box, click *ZIP Code* in the *Field Names* list box. (A new field is inserted below the selected field.)
   d. Click the Add button.
   e. At the Add Field dialog box, type **Cell Phone** and then click OK.
   f. You decide that you want the *Cell Phone* field to display after the *Home Phone* field. To move the *Cell Phone* field, make sure it is selected and then click the Move Down button.
   g. Click OK to close the Customize Address List dialog box.

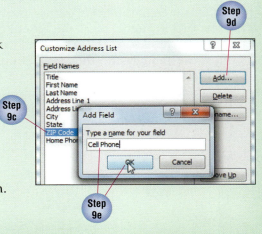

Chapter 8 ■ Merging Documents

h. At the Edit Data Source dialog box, scroll to the right to display the *Cell Phone* field (last field in the file) and then type the following cell phone numbers (after typing each cell phone number, except the last number, press the Down Arrow key to make the next cell below active):

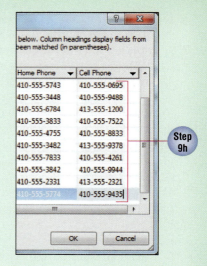

Step 9h

Record 1 = **410-555-1249**
Record 2 = **413-555-3492**
Record 3 = **410-555-0695**
Record 4 = **410-555-9488**
Record 5 = **413-555-1200**
Record 6 = **410-555-7522**
Record 7 = **410-555-8833**
Record 8 = **413-555-9378**
Record 9 = **410-555-4261**
Record 10 = **410-555-9944**
Record 11 = **413-555-2321**
Record 12 = **410-555-9435**

  i. Click OK to close the Edit Data Source dialog box.
  j. At the message asking if you want to update the recipient list and save changes, click Yes.
  k. At the Mail Merge Recipients dialog box, click OK.
10. Create a directory by completing the following steps:
  a. Click the Start Mail Merge button and then click *Directory* at the drop-down list.
  b. At the blank document, set left tabs on the horizontal ruler at the 1-inch mark, the 3-inch mark, and the 4.5-inch mark.
  c. Press the Tab key. (This moves the insertion point to the first tab set at the 1-inch mark.)
  d. Click the Insert Merge Field button arrow and then click *Last_Name* at the drop-down list.
  e. Type a comma and then press the spacebar.
  f. Click the Insert Merge Field button arrow and then click *First_Name* at the drop-down list.
  g. Press the Tab key, click the Insert Merge Field button arrow, and then click *Home_Phone* at the drop-down list.
  h. Press the Tab key, click the Insert Merge Field button arrow, and then click *Cell_Phone* at the drop-down list.
  i. Press the Enter key once.
  j. Click the Finish & Merge button in the Finish group and then click *Edit Individual Documents* at the drop-down list.
  k. At the Merge to New Document dialog box, make sure *All* is selected and then click OK. (This merges the fields in the document.)
11. Press Ctrl + Home, press the Enter key once, and then press the Up Arrow key once.
12. Press the Tab key, turn on bold, and then type **Name**.
13. Press the Tab key and then type **Home Phone**.
14. Press the Tab key and then type **Cell Phone**.

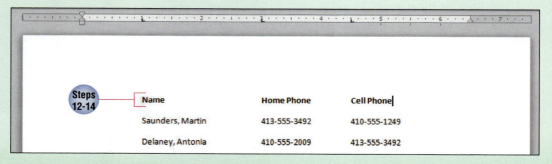

Steps 12-14

15. Save the directory document and name it **WL1-C8-P6-Directory**.
16. Print and then close the document.
17. Close the directory main document without saving it.

Project 7 Add Fill-in Fields to a Main Document   1 Part

You will edit a form letter and insert sales representative contact information during a merge.

Inputting Text during a Merge

Word's Merge feature contains a large number of Word fields you can insert in a main document. In this chapter, you will learn about the *Fill-in* field that is used for information input at the keyboard during a merge. For more information on the other Word fields, please refer to the on-screen help.

Situations may arise in which you do not need to keep all variable information in a data source file. For example, variable information that changes on a regular basis might include a customer's monthly balance, a product price, and so on. Word lets you input variable information into a document during the merge using the keyboard. A Fill-in field is inserted in a main document by clicking the Rules button in the Write & Insert Fields group in the Mailings tab and then clicking *Fill-in* at the drop-down list. This displays the Insert Word Field: Fill-in dialog box shown in Figure 8.9. At this dialog box, type a short message indicating what should be entered at the keyboard and then click OK. At the Microsoft Word dialog box with the message you entered displayed in the upper left corner, type text you want to display in the document and then click OK. When the Fill-in field or fields are added, save the main document in the normal manner. A document can contain any number of Fill-in fields.

When you merge the main document with the data source file, the first record is merged with the main document and the Microsoft Word dialog box displays with the message you entered displayed in the upper left corner. Type the required information for the first record in the data source file and then click the OK

▼ **Quick Steps**

Insert *Fill-in* Field in Main Document
1. Click Mailings tab.
2. Click Rules button.
3. Click *Fill-in* at drop-down list.
4. Type prompt text.
5. Click OK.
6. Type text to be inserted in document.
7. Click OK.

Rules

Figure 8.9 Insert Word Field: Fill-in Dialog Box

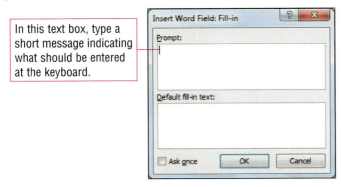

In this text box, type a short message indicating what should be entered at the keyboard.

Chapter 8 ■ Merging Documents   311

button. Word displays the dialog box again. Type the required information for the second record in the data source file and then click OK. Continue in this manner until the required information has been entered for each record in the data source file. Word then completes the merge.

Project 7 — Adding Fill-in Fields to a Main Document — Part 1 of 1

1. Open the document named **WL1-C8-P1-MFMD.docx** (at the message asking if you want to continue, click Yes) and then save the document with Save As and name it **WL1-C8-P7-MFMD**.
2. Change the second paragraph in the body of the letter to the paragraph shown in Figure 8.10. Insert the first Fill-in field (representative's name) by completing the following steps:
   a. Click the Mailings tab.
   b. Click the Rules button in the Write & Insert Fields group and then click *Fill-in* at the drop-down list.
   c. At the Insert Word Field: Fill-in dialog box, type **Insert rep name** in the *Prompt* text box and then click OK.
   d. At the Microsoft Word dialog box with *Insert rep name* displayed in the upper left corner, type **(representative's name)** and then click OK.

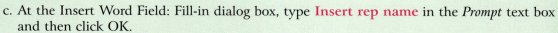
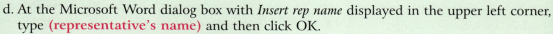

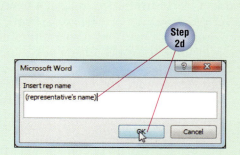

3. Complete steps similar to those in Step 2 to insert the second Fill-in field (phone number), except type **Insert phone number** in the *Prompt* text box at the Insert Word Field: Fill-in dialog box and type **(phone number)** at the Microsoft Word dialog box.
4. Save **WL1-C8-P7-MFMD.docx**.
5. Merge the main document with the data source file by completing the following steps:
   a. Click the Finish & Merge button and then click *Edit Individual Documents* at the drop-down list.
   b. At the Merge to New Document dialog box, make sure *All* is selected, and then click OK.
   c. When Word merges the main document with the first record, a dialog box displays with the message *Insert rep name* and the text *(representative's name)* selected. At this dialog box, type **Marilyn Smythe** and then click OK.
   d. At the dialog box with the message *Insert phone number* and *(phone number)* selected, type **(646) 555-8944** and then click OK.

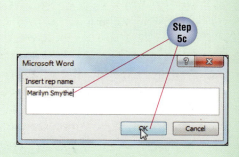

e. At the dialog box with the message *Insert rep name*, type **Anthony Mason** (over *Marilyn Smythe*) and then click OK.
f. At the dialog box with the message *Insert phone number*, type **(646) 555-8901** (over the previous number) and then click OK.
g. At the dialog box with the message *Insert rep name*, type **Faith Ostrom** (over *Anthony Mason*) and then click OK.
h. At the dialog box with the message *Insert phone number*, type **(646) 555-8967** (over the previous number) and then click OK.
i. At the dialog box with the message *Insert rep name*, type **Thomas Rivers** (over *Faith Ostrom*) and then click OK.
j. At the dialog box with the message *Insert phone number*, type **(646) 555-0793** (over the previous number) and then click OK.
6. Save the merged document and name it **WL1-C8-P7-MFLtrs**.
7. Print and then close **WL1-C8-P7-MFLtrs.docx**.
8. Save and then close **WL1-C8-P7-MFMD.docx**.

Figure 8.10 Project 7

Lowering expense charges is noteworthy because before the reduction, McCormack expense deductions were already among the lowest, far below most mutual funds and variable annuity accounts with similar objectives. At the same time, services for you, our client, will continue to expand. If you would like to discuss this change, please call our service representative, **(representative's name)**, at **(phone number)**.

Project 8 Use Mail Merge Wizard   1 Part

You will use the Mail Merge wizard to merge a main document with a data source file and create letters to clients of Sorenson Funds.

Merging Using the Mail Merge Wizard

The Mail Merge feature includes a Mail Merge wizard that guides you through the merge process. To access the Wizard, click the Mailings tab, click the Start Mail Merge button, and then click the *Step By Step Mail Merge Wizard* option at the drop-down list. The first of six Mail Merge task panes displays at the right side of the screen. Completing the tasks at one task pane displays the next task pane. The options in each task pane may vary depending on the type of merge you are performing. Generally, you complete one of the following steps at each task pane:

- Step 1: Select the type of document you want to create such as a letter, email message, envelope, label, or directory.
- Step 2: Specify whether you want to use the current document to create the main document, start from a template, or start from an existing document.
- Step 3: Specify whether you are typing a new list, using an existing list, or selecting from an Outlook contacts list.

- Step 4: Use the items in this task pane to help you prepare the main document such as inserting fields in the main document.
- Step 5: Preview the merged documents.
- Step 6: Complete the merge.

Project 8 Preparing Form Letters Using the Mail Merge Wizard   Part 1 of 1

1. At a blank document, click the Mailings tab, click the Start Mail Merge button in the Start Mail Merge group, and then click *Step by Step Mail Merge Wizard* at the drop-down list.
2. At the first Mail Merge task pane, make sure *Letters* is selected in the *Select document type* section and then click the Next: Starting document hyperlink located toward the bottom of the task pane.
3. At the second Mail Merge task pane, click the *Start from existing document* option in the *Select starting document* section.
4. Click the Open button in the *Start from existing* section of the task pane.
5. At the Open dialog box, navigate to the Word2010L1C8 folder on your storage medium and then double-click **SFLtrMD.docx**.
6. Click the Next: Select recipients hyperlink located toward the bottom of the task pane.
7. At the third Mail Merge task pane, click the Browse hyperlink that displays in the *Use an existing list* section of the task pane.
8. At the Select Data Source dialog box, navigate to the Word2010L1C8 folder on your storage medium and then double-click **SFClients.mdb**.
9. At the Mail Merge Recipients dialog box, click OK.
10. Click the Next: Write your letter hyperlink that displays toward the bottom of the task pane.
11. At the fourth Mail Merge task pane, enter fields in the form letter by completing the following steps:
    a. Position the insertion point a double space above the first paragraph of text in the letter.
    b. Click the Address block hyperlink located in the *Write your letter* section of the task pane.
    c. At the Insert Address Block dialog box, click the OK button.
    d. Press the Enter key twice and then click the Greeting line hyperlink located in the *Write your letter* section of the task pane.
    e. At the Insert Greeting Line dialog box, click the down-pointing arrow at the right of the option box containing the comma (the box to the right of the box containing *Mr. Randall*).
    f. At the drop-down list that displays, click the colon.
    g. Click OK to close the Insert Greeting Line dialog box.

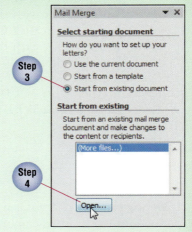
Step 3
Step 4

Step 7

Step 11b
Step 11d

12. Click the Next: Preview your letters hyperlink located toward the bottom of the task pane.
13. At the fifth Mail Merge task pane, look over the letter that displays in the document window and make sure the information merged properly. If you want to see the letters for the other recipients, click the button in the Mail Merge task pane containing the right-pointing arrow.
14. Click the Preview Results button in the Preview Results group to turn off the preview feature.
15. Click the Next: Complete the merge hyperlink that displays toward the bottom of the task pane.
16. At the sixth Mail Merge task pane, click the Edit individual letters hyperlink that displays in the *Merge* section of the task pane.
17. At the Merge to New Document dialog box, make sure *All* is selected and then click the OK button.
18. Save the merged letters documents with the name **WL1-C8-P8-SFLtrs**.
19. Print only the first two pages of **WL1-C8-P8-SFLtrs.docx**.
20. Close the document.
21. At the sixth Mail Merge task pane, close the letter main document without saving it.

Chapter Summary

- Use the Mail Merge feature to create letters, envelopes, labels, directories, email messages, and faxes, all with personalized information.
- Generally, a merge takes two documents — the data source file containing the variable information and the main document containing standard text along with fields identifying where variable information is inserted during the merge process.
- Variable information in a data source file is saved as a record. A record contains all of the information for one unit. A series of fields makes one record, and a series of records makes a data source file.
- A data source file is saved as an Access database but you do not need Access on your computer to complete a merge with a data source.
- You can use predesigned fields when creating a data source file or you can create your own custom field at the Customize Address List dialog box.
- Use the Address Block button in the Write & Insert Fields group in the Mailings tab to insert all of the fields required for the inside address of a letter. This inserts the «AddressBlock» field, which is considered a composite field because it groups a number of fields together.
- Click the Greeting Line button in the Write & Insert Fields group in the Mailings tab to insert the «GreetingLine» composite field in the document.
- Click the Insert Merge Field button arrow in the Write & Insert Fields group in the Mailings tab to display a drop-down list of fields contained in the data source file.

- Click the Preview Results button in the Mailings tab to view the main document merged with the first record in the data source. Use the navigation buttons in the Preview Results group in the Mailings tab to display the main document merged with the desired record.
- Before merging documents, check for errors by clicking the Auto Check for Errors button in the Preview Results group in the Mailings tab. This displays the Checking and Reporting Errors dialog box with three options for checking errors.
- Click the Finish & Merge button in the Mailings tab to complete the merge.
- Select specific records for merging by inserting or removing check marks from the desired records in the Mail Merge Recipients dialog box. Display this dialog box by clicking the Edit Recipient List button in the Mailings tab.
- Edit specific records in a data source file at the Edit Data Source dialog box. Display this dialog box by clicking the Edit Recipient List button in the Mailings tab, clicking the desired data source file name in the *Data Source* list box, and then clicking the Edit button.
- Use the Fill-in field in a main document to insert variable information at the keyboard during a merge.
- Word includes a Mail Merge wizard you can use to guide you through the process of creating letters, envelopes, labels, directories, and email messages with personalized information.

Commands Review

FEATURE	RIBBON TAB, GROUP	BUTTON	OPTION
New Address List dialog box	Mailings, Start Mail Merge		Type New List
Letter main document	Mailings, Start Mail Merge		Letters
Checking and Reporting Errors dialog box	Mailings, Preview Results		
Envelopes main document	Mailings, Start Mail Merge		Envelopes
Labels main document	Mailings, Start Mail Merge		Labels
Directory main document	Mailings, Start Mail Merge		Directory
Preview merge results	Mailings, Preview Results		
Mail Merge Recipients dialog box	Mailings, Start Mail Merge		
Address Block field	Mailings, Write & Insert Fields		
Greeting Line field	Mailings, Write & Insert Fields		
Insert merge fields	Mailings, Write & Insert Fields		

FEATURE	RIBBON TAB, GROUP	BUTTON	OPTION
Fill-in merge field	Mailings, Write & Insert Fields		Fill-in
Mail Merge wizard	Mailings, Start Mail Merge		Step by Step Mail Merge Wizard

Concepts Check Test Your Knowledge

Completion: In the space provided at the right, indicate the correct term, command, or number.

1. A merge generally takes two files — a data source file and this.

2. This term refers to all of the information for one unit in a data source file.

3. Create a data source file by clicking this button in the Mailings tab and then clicking *Type New List* at the drop-down list.

4. A data source file is saved as this type of file.

5. Create your own custom fields in a data source file with options at this dialog box.

6. Use this button in the Mailings tab to insert all of the required fields for the inside address in a letter.

7. The «GreetingLine» field is considered this type of field because it includes all of the fields required for the greeting line.

8. Click this button in the Mailings tab to display the first record merged with the main document.

9. Before merging a document, check for errors using this button in the Preview Results group in the Mailings tab.

10. To complete a merge, click this button in the Finish group in the Mailings tab.

11. When creating the envelope main document, click in the approximate location where the recipient's address will appear and then click this button in the Write & Insert Fields group.

12. Select specific records in a data source file by inserting or removing check marks from the records in this dialog box.

13. Use this field to insert variable information at the keyboard during a merge.

14. Click this option at the Start Mail Merge button drop-down list to begin the Mail Merge wizard.

Chapter 8 ■ Merging Documents   317

Skills Check Assess Your Performance

Assessment

1 PREPARE AND MERGE LETTERS, ENVELOPES, AND LABELS

1. Open **CCLtrhd.docx** and then save the document with Save As and name it **WL1-C8-A1-CCMD**.
2. Look at the information in Figure 8.11 and Figure 8.12 and then use the Mail Merge feature to prepare four letters. Create the data source file with the information in Figure 8.11 and then save the file and name it **WL1-C8-A1-CCDS**.
3. Merge the **WL1-C8-A1-CCMD** main document with the **WL1-C8-A1-CCDS.mdb** data source file and then save the merged letters document and name it **WL1-C8-A1-CCLtrs**.
4. Print and then close **WL1-C8-A1-CCLtrs.docx** and then save and close **WL1-C8-A1-CCMD.docx**.
5. Create an envelope main document and then merge it with the **WL1-C8-A1-CCDS.mdb** data source file.
6. Save the merged envelopes document and name it **WL1-C8-A1-CCEnvs**. Print and then close the envelopes document. (Check with your instructor before printing the envelopes.) Close the envelope main document without saving it.
7. Create a labels main document (use the Avery US Letter product number 5160 label) and then merge it with the **WL1-C8-A1-CCDS.mdb** data source file. When the labels are merged, press Ctrl + A to select the entire document, click the Home tab, and then click the No Spacing style in the Styles group.
8. Save the merged labels document and name it **WL1-C8-A1-CCLabels**. Print and then close the labels document and then close the labels main document without saving it.

Figure 8.11 Assessment 1

Mr. Tony Benedetti
1315 Cordova Road
Apt. 402
Santa Fe, NM 87505
Home Phone: 505-555-0489

Mrs. Mary Arguello
2554 Country Drive
#105
Santa Fe, NM 87504
Home Phone: 505-555-7663

Ms. Theresa Dusek
12044 Ridgway Drive
(leave this blank)
Santa Fe, NM 87505
Home Phone: 505-555-1120

Mr. Preston Miller
120 Second Street
(leave this blank)
Santa Fe, NM 87505
Home Phone: 505-555-3551

Figure 8.12 Assessment 1

May 8, 2012

«AddressBlock»

«GreetingLine»

The Cordova Children's Community Center is a nonprofit agency providing educational and recreational activities to children in the Cordova community. We are funded by donations from the community and rely on you and all of our volunteers to provide quality care and services to our children. As a member of our outstanding volunteer team, we are inviting you to attend our summer volunteer open house on Saturday, May 26, at the community center from 1:00 to 4:30 p.m. We want to honor you and our other volunteers for your commitment to children so please plan to attend so we can thank you in person.

The Center's summer volunteer session begins Friday, June 1, and continues through August 31. According to our volunteer roster, you have signed up to volunteer during the summer session. Throughout the summer we will be offering a variety of services to our children including tutoring, creative art classes, recreational activities, and a science camp. At the open house, you can sign up for the specific area or areas in which you want to volunteer. We look forward to seeing you at the open house and during the upcoming summer session.

Sincerely,

Andy Amura
Volunteer Coordinator

XX
WL1-C8-A1-CCMD.docx

Assessment 2 EDIT AND MERGE LETTERS

1. Open **WL1-C8-A1-CCMD.docx** (at the message asking if you want to continue, click Yes) and then save the main document with Save As and name it **WL1-C8-A2-CCMD**.
2. Edit the **WL1-C8-A1-CCDS.mdb** data source file by making the following changes:
    a. Display the record for Ms. Theresa Dusek and then change the address from *12044 Ridgway Drive* to *1390 Fourth Avenue*.
    b. Display the record for Mr. Preston Miller and change the home phone number from *505-555-3551* to *505-555-1289*.
    c. Delete the record for Mrs. Mary Arguello.
    d. Insert a new record with the following information:
       Mr. Cesar Rivera
       3201 East Third Street
       Santa Fe, NM 87505
       505-555-6675
3. At the main document, edit the second sentence of the second paragraph so it reads as follows (insert a *Fill-in* field for the *(number of hours)* shown in the sentence below):
    According to our volunteer roster, you have signed up to volunteer for *(number of hours)* during the summer session.
4. Merge the main document with the data source file and type the following text for each of the records:
    Record 1 = four hours a week
    Record 2 = six hours a week
    Record 3 = twelve hours a week
    Record 4 = four hours a week
5. Save the merged document and name it **WL1-C8-A2-CCLtrs**.
6. Print and then close **WL1-C8-A2-CCLtrs.docx**.
7. Save and then close **WL1-C8-A2-CCMD.docx**.

Assessment 3 CREATE A DIRECTORY

1. At a blank document, create a directory main document and specify **WL1-C8-A1-CCDS.mdb** as the data source file. Insert a left tab at the 1.5-inch mark and the 4-inch mark on the Ruler. Press the Tab key and then insert the «First_Name» field at the 1.5-inch tab. Press the spacebar and then insert the «Last_Name» field. Press the Tab key, insert the «Home_Phone» field at the second tab, and then press the Enter key.
2. Merge the directory main document with the data source.
3. Insert the heading *Volunteer* in bold above the first column and insert the heading *Telephone* in bold above the second column.
4. Save the directory document and name it **WL1-C8-A3-CCDir**.
5. Print and then close the document.
6. Close the directory main document without saving it.

Assessment

4 MERGE LETTERS AND ENVELOPES USING THE MAIL MERGE WIZARD

1. Open **TTSLtrMD.docx** from the Word2010L1C8 folder on your storage medium. Insert your initials in place of the *XX* that display toward the bottom of the letter.
2. Use the Mail Merge wizard to prepare letters using the **TTSLtrMD.docx** document as the main document and specify **TTSClients.mdb** as the data source file.
3. When the merge is complete save the merged letters document and name it **WL1-C8-A4-TTSLtrs**.
4. Print only the first two pages (letters) in the document.
5. Close **WL1-C8-A4-TTSLtrs.docx**.
6. Close **TTSLtrMD.docx** without saving the changes.

Visual Benchmark Demonstrate Your Proficiency

PREPARE AND MERGE LETTERS

1. Open **FPLtrhd.docx** and then save the document with Save As and name it **WL1-C8-VB-FPMD**.
2. Look at the information in Figure 8.13 and Figure 8.14 and then use Mail Merge to prepare four letters. (When creating the main document as shown in Figure 8.14, insert the appropriate fields where you see the text Title; First Name; Last Name; Street Address; and City, State ZIP. Insert the appropriate field where you see the text Title and Last Name in the first paragraph of text.) Create the data source file with the information in Figure 8.13 and then save the file and name it **WL1-C8-VB-FPDS**.
3. Merge the **WL1-C8-VB-FPMD.docx** main document with the **WL1-C8-VB-FPDS.mdb** data source file and then save the merged letters document and name it **WL1-C8-VB-FPLtrs**.
4. Print and then close **WL1-C8-VB-FPLtrs.docx**.
5. Save and then close **WL1-C8-VB-FPMD.docx**.

Figure 8.13 Visual Benchmark Data Source Records

Mr. and Mrs. Chris Gallagher 17034 234th Avenue Newport, VT 05855	Ms. Heather Segarra 4103 Thompson Drive Newport, VT 05855
Mr. Gene Goodrich 831 Cromwell Lane Newport, VT 05855	Mrs. Sonya Kraus 15933 Ninth Street Newport, VT 05855

Figure 8.14 Visual Benchmark

Frontline Photography Equipment and Supplies

(Current Date)

Title First Name Last Name
Street Address
City, State ZIP

Dear Title Last Name:

We have enjoyed being a part of the Newport community for the past two years. Our success in the community is directly related to you, Title Last Name, and all of our other loyal customers. Thank you for shopping at our store for all of your photography equipment and supply needs.

To show our appreciation for your loyalty and your business, we are enclosing a coupon for 20 percent off any item in our store, even our incredibly low-priced clearance items. Through the end of the month, all of our camera accessories are on sale. So, use your coupon and take advantage of additional savings on items such as camera lenses, tripods, cleaning supplies, and camera bags.

To accommodate our customers' schedules, we have increased our weekend hours. Our store will be open Saturdays until 7:00 p.m. and Sundays until 5:00 p.m. Come by and let our sales associates find just the right camera and camera accessories for you.

Sincerely,

(Student Name)

XX
WL1-C8-VB-FPMD.docx
Enclosure

559 Tenth Street, Suite A ◆ Newport, VT 05855 ◆ (802) 555-4411

Case Study — Apply Your Skills

Part 1

You are the office manager for Freestyle Extreme, a sporting goods store that specializes in snowboarding and snow skiing equipment and supplies. The store has two branches, one on the east side of town and the other on the west side. One of your job responsibilities is to send letters to customers letting them know about sales, new equipment, and upcoming events. Next month, both stores are having a sale and all snowboard and snow skiing supplies will be 15% off the regular price. Create a data source file that contains the following customer information: first name, last name, address, city, state, ZIP code, and branch. Add six customers to the data source file and indicate that three usually shop at the East branch and the other three usually shop at the West branch. Create a letter as a main document that includes information about the upcoming sale. The letter should contain at least two paragraphs and, in addition to the information on the sale, might include information about the store, snowboarding, and/or snow skiing. Save the data source file with the name **WL1-C8-CS-FEDS**, save the main document with the name **WL1-C8-CS-P1-FEMD**, and save the merged document with the name **WL1-C8-CS-P1-FELtrs**. Create envelopes for the six merged letters and name the merged envelope document **WL1-C8-CS-P1-FEEnvs**. Do not save the envelope main document. Print the merged letters document and the merged envelopes document.

Part 2

A well-known extreme snowboarder will be visiting both branches of the store to meet with customers and sign autographs. Use the Help feature to learn how to insert an If . . . Then . . . Else merge field in a document and then create a letter that includes the name of the extreme snowboarder (you determine the name), the time, which is 1:00 p.m. to 4:30 p.m., and any additional information that might interest the customer. Also include in the letter an If . . . Then . . . Else merge field that will insert *Wednesday, September 26* if the customer's Branch is *East* and will insert *Thursday, September 27* if the Branch is *West*. Add visual appeal to the letter by inserting a picture, clip art image, WordArt, or any other feature that will attract the reader's attention. Save the letter main document and name it **WL1-C8-CS-P2-MD**. Merge the letter main document with the **WL1-C8-CS-FEDS.mdb** data source. Save the merged letters document and name it **WL1-C8-CS-P2-AnnLtrs**. Print the merged letters document.

Part 3

The store owner wants to try selling shorter skis known as "snow blades" or "skiboards." He has asked you to research the shorter skis and identify one type and model to sell only at the West branch of the store. If the model sells well, he will consider selling it at the East branch at a future time. Prepare a main document letter that describes the new snow blade or skiboard that the West branch is selling. Include information about pricing and tell customers that the new item is being offered at a 40% discount if purchased within the next week. Merge the letter main document with the **WL1-C8-CS-FEDS.mdb** data source file and include only those customers that shop at the West branch. Save the merged letters document and name it **WL1-C8-CS-P3-SBLtrs**. Print the merged letters document. Save the letter main document and name it **WL1-C8-CS-P3-SBMD**. Print and then close the main document.

UNIT 2

Performance Assessment

Note: Before beginning unit assessments, copy to your storage medium the Word2010L1U2 subfolder from the Word2010L1 folder on the CD that accompanies this textbook and then make Word2010L1U2 the active folder.

Assessing Proficiency

In this unit, you have learned to format text into columns; insert, format, and customize objects to enhance the visual appeal of a document; manage files, print envelopes and labels, and create documents using templates; create and edit tables; visually represent data in SmartArt diagrams and organizational charts; and use Mail Merge to create letters, envelopes, labels, and directions.

Assessment 1 Format a Technology Occupations Document

1. Open **TechOccs.docx** and then save the document with Save As and name it **WL1-U2-A01-TechOccs**.
2. Move the insertion point to the beginning of the heading *Telecommuting* and then insert the file named **CommMedia.docx**.
3. Apply the Heading 1 style to the title and the Heading 2 style to the headings in the document.
4. Change the Quick Styles set to *Formal* and change the paragraph spacing to *Open*.
5. Insert a continuous section break at the beginning of the first paragraph of text (the paragraph that begins *The march of computer technology . . .*).
6. Format the text below the section break into two columns.
7. Balance the columns on the second page.
8. Insert a pull quote of your choosing on the first page of the document that includes the text *"As the future of wireless unfolds, many new jobs will emerge as well."*
9. Create a drop cap with the first letter of the first word *The* that begins the first paragraph of text and make the drop cap two lines in height.
10. Manually hyphenate words in the document.
11. Insert page numbering that prints at the bottom of each page (you determine the page number formatting).
12. Save, print, and then close **WL1-U2-A01-TechOccs.docx**.

Assessment 2 Create a Workshop Flyer

1. Create the flyer shown in Figure U2.1 with the following specifications:
   a. Create the WordArt with the following specifications:
      - Use the *Fill - Tan, Text 2, Outline - Background 2* option (first option from the left in the top row) at the WordArt button drop-down gallery.
      - Increase the width to 6.5 inches and the height to 1 inch.
      - Apply the *Deflate* text effect transform shape.
      - Change the text fill color to *Olive Green, Accent 3, Lighter 40%*.
   b. Type the text shown in the figure set in 22-point Calibri bold and center the text.
   c. Insert the clip art image shown in the figure (use the keyword *buildings* to find the clip art) and then change the wrapping style to *Square*. Position and size the image as shown in the figure.
2. Save the document and name it **WL1-U2-A02-TravelFlyer**.
3. Print and then close **WL1-U2-A02-TravelFlyer.docx**.

Figure U2.1 Assessment 2

Assessment 3 Create a Staff Meeting Announcement

1. Create the announcement shown in Figure U2.2 with the following specifications:
   a. Use the *Hexagon* shape in the *Basic Shapes* section of the Shapes drop-down list to create the shape.
   b. Apply the *Subtle Effect - Aqua, Accent 5* shape style.
   c. Apply the *Art Deco* bevel shape effect.
   d. Type the letter A (this makes active many of the tab options), click the Home tab, and then click the No Spacing style in the Styles group.
   e. Type the remaining text in the shape as shown in the figure. Insert the ñ as a symbol (in the *(normal text)* font and insert the clock as a symbol (in the *Wingdings* font). Set the text and clock symbol in larger font sizes.
2. Save the completed document and name it **WL1-U2-A03-MeetNotice**.
3. Print and then close **WL1-U2-A03-MeetNotice.docx**.

Figure U2.2 Assessment 3

Assessment 4 Create a River Rafting Flyer

1. At a blank document, insert the picture named **River.jpg**. (Insert the picture using the Picture button.)
2. Crop out a portion of the trees at the left and right and a portion of the hill at the top.
3. Correct the brightness and contrast to *Brightness: +20% Contrast: +40%*.
4. Specify that the picture should wrap behind text.
5. Insert the text *River Rafting Adventures* on one line, *Salmon River, Idaho* on the next line, and *1-888-555-3322* on the third line.
6. Increase the size of the picture so it is easier to see and the size of the text so it is easier to read. Center the text and position it on the picture on top of the river so the text is readable.
7. Save the document and name it **WL1-U2-A04-RaftingFlyer**.
8. Print and then close **WL1-U2-A04-RaftingFlyer.docx**.

Assessment 5 Create an Envelope

1. At a blank document, create an envelope with the text shown in Figure U2.3.
2. Save the envelope document and name it **WL1-U2-A05-Env**.
3. Print and then close **WL1-U2-A05-Env.docx**.

Figure U2.3 Assessment 5

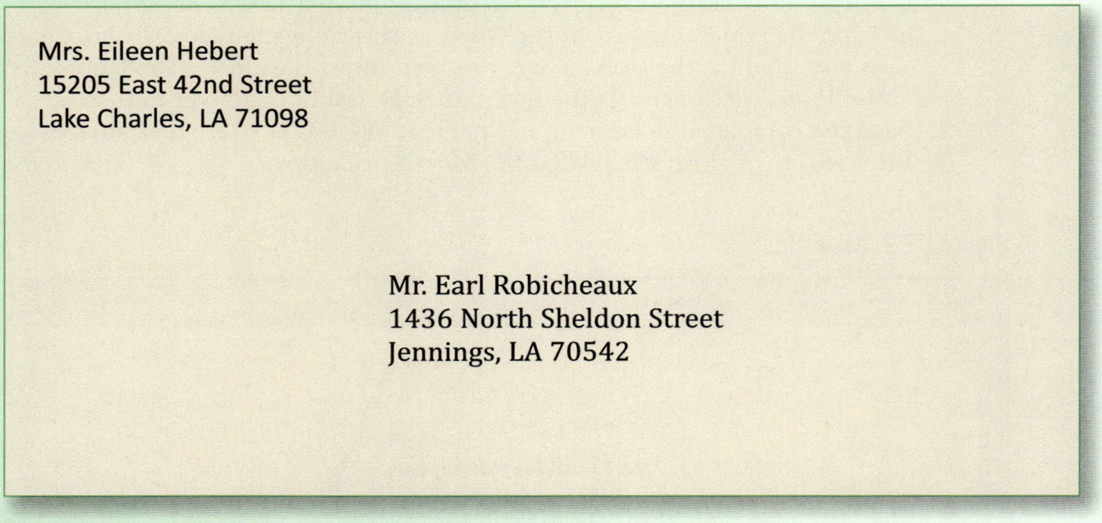

Mrs. Eileen Hebert
15205 East 42nd Street
Lake Charles, LA 71098

Mr. Earl Robicheaux
1436 North Sheldon Street
Jennings, LA 70542

Assessment 6 Create Mailing Labels

1. Create mailing labels with the name and address for Mrs. Eileen Hebert shown in Figure U2.3 using a label vendor and product of your choosing.
2. Save the document and name it **WL1-U2-A06-Labels**.
3. Print and then close **WL1-U2-A06-Labels.docx**.

Assessment 7 Create and Format a Table with Software Training Information

1. At a blank document, create the table shown in Figure U2.4. Format the table and the text in a manner similar to what is shown in Figure U2.4.
2. Insert a formula in B8 that totals the numbers in cells B4 through B7.
3. Insert a formula in C8 that totals the numbers in cells C4 through C7.
4. Save the document and name it **WL1-U2-A07-TechTraining**.
5. Print and then close **WL1-U2-A07-TechTraining.docx**.

Figure U2.4 Assessment 7

TRI-STATE PRODUCTS		
Computer Technology Department Microsoft® Office 2010 Training		
Application	# Enrolled	# Completed
Access 2010	20	15
Excel 2010	62	56
PowerPoint 2010	40	33
Word 2010	80	72
Total		

Assessment 8 Create and Format a Table Containing Training Scores

1. Open **TrainingScores.docx** and then save the document with Save As and name it **WL1-U2-A08-TrainingScores**.
2. Insert formulas that calculate the averages in the appropriate row and column. (When writing the formulas, change the *Number format* option to *0*.)
3. Autofit the contents of the table.
4. Apply a table style of your choosing to the table.
5. Appy any other formatting to improve the visual appeal of the table.
6. Save, print, and then close **WL1-U2-A08-TrainingScores.docx**.

Assessment 9 Create an Organizational Chart

1. Use SmartArt to create an organizational chart for the following text (in the order displayed). Change the colors to *Colorfutl Range - Accent Colors 2 to 3* and apply the *Metallic Scene* SmartArt style.
2. Save the completed document and name it **WL1-U2-A09-OrgChart**.
3. Print and then close **WL1-U2-A09-OrgChart.docx**.

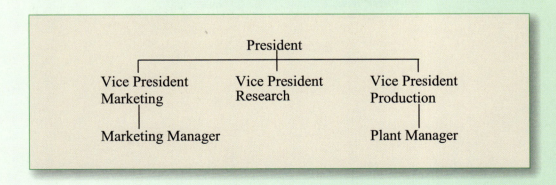

Assessment 10 Create a SmartArt Diagram

1. At a blank document, create the WordArt and diagram shown in Figure U2.5 with the following specifications:
    a. Insert the WordArt text with the *Gradient Fill - Blue, Accent 1, Outline - White* option. Change the shape height to 1 inch and the shape width to 6 inches and then apply the *Square* transform text effect.
    b. Create the diagram using the Vertical Picture Accent List diagram. Click the picture icon that displays in the top circle and then insert the picture named **Seagull.jpg** located in the Word2010L1U2 folder. Insert the same picture in the other two circles. Type the text in each rectangle shape as shown in Figure U2.5. Change the colors to *Colorful Range - Accent Colors 4 to 5* and apply the *Cartoon* SmartArt style.
2. Save the document and name it **WL1-U2-A10-SPDiagram**.
3. Print and then close **WL1-U2-A10-SPDiagram.docx**.

Figure U2.5 Assessment 10

Assessment 11 Merge and Print Letters

1. Look at the information shown in Figure U2.6 and Figure U2.7. Use the Mail Merge feature to prepare six letters using the information shown in the figures. When creating the letter main document, open **SMLtrhd.docx** and then save the document with Save As and name it **WL1-U2-A11-MD**. Insert Fill-in fields in the main document in place of the *(coordinator name)* and *(telephone number)* text. Create the data source file with the text shown in Figure U2.6 and name the file **WL1-U2-A11-DS**.
2. Type the text in the main document as shown in Figure U2.7 and then merge the document with the **WL1-U2-A11-DS.mdb** data source file. When merging, enter the first name and telephone number shown below for the first three records and enter the second name and telephone number shown below for the last three records.

    Jeff Greenswald   (813) 555-9886
    Grace Ramirez   (813) 555-9807
3. Save the merged letters document and name it **WL1-U2-A11-Ltrs**. Print and then close the document.
4. Save and then close the main document.

Figure U2.6 Assessment 11

Mrs. Antonio Mercado
3241 Court G
Tampa, FL 33623

Ms. Kristina Vukovich
1120 South Monroe
Tampa, FL 33655

Ms. Alexandria Remick
909 Wheeler South
Tampa, FL 33620

Mr. Minh Vu
9302 Lawndale Southwest
Tampa, FL 33623

Mr. Curtis Iverson
10139 93rd Court South
Tampa, FL 33654

Mrs. Holly Bernard
8904 Emerson Road
Tampa, FL 33620

Figure U2.7 Assessment 11

December 12, 2012

«AddressBlock»

«GreetingLine»

Sound Medical is switching hospital care in Tampa to St. Jude's Hospital beginning January 1, 2013. As mentioned in last month's letter, St. Jude's Hospital was selected because it meets our requirements for high-quality, customer-pleasing care that is also affordable and accessible. Our physicians look forward to caring for you in this new environment.

Over the past month, staff members at Sound Medical have been working to make this transition as smooth as possible. Surgeries planned after January 1 are being scheduled at St. Jude's Hospital. Mothers delivering babies any time after January 1 are receiving information about delivery room tours and prenatal classes available at St. Jude's. Your Sound Medical doctor will have privileges at St. Jude's and will continue to care for you if you need to be hospitalized.

You are a very important part of our patient family, «Title» «Last_Name», and we hope this information is helpful. If you have any additional questions or concerns, please call your Sound Medical health coordinator, (coordinator name), at (telephone number), between 8:00 a.m. and 4:30 p.m.

Sincerely,

Jody Tiemann
District Administrator

XX
WL1-U2-A11-MD.docx

Assessment 12 Merge and Print Envelopes

1. Use the Mail Merge feature to prepare envelopes for the letters created in Assessment 11.
2. Specify **WL1-U2-A11-DS.mdb** as the data source document.
3. Save the merged envelopes document and name the document **WL1-U2-A12-Envs**.
4. Print and then close **WL1-U2-A12-Envs.docx**.
5. Do not save the envelope main document.

Writing Activities

The following activities give you the opportunity to practice your writing skills along with demonstrating an understanding of some of the important Word features you have mastered in this unit. Use correct grammar, appropriate word choices, and clear sentence constructions.

Activity 1 Compose a Letter to Volunteers

You are an employee for the City of Greenwater and are responsible for coordinating volunteers for the city's Safe Night program. Compose a letter to the volunteers listed below and include the following information in the letter:

- Safe Night event scheduled for Saturday, June 16, 2012.
- Volunteer orientation scheduled for Thursday, May 17, 2012, at 7:30 p.m. At the orientation, participants will learn about the types of volunteer positions available and the work schedule.

Include any additional information in the letter, including a thank you to the volunteers. Use the Mail Merge feature to create a data source with the names and addresses shown below that is attached to the main document, which is the letter to the volunteers. Save the merged letters as **WL1-U2-Act01-Ltrs** and then print the letters.

Mrs. Laura Reston
376 Thompson Avenue
Greenwater, OR 99034

Mr. Matthew Klein
7408 Ryan Road
Greenwater, OR 99034

Ms. Cecilia Sykes
1430 Canyon Road
Greenwater, OR 99034

Mr. Brian McDonald
8980 Union Street
Greenwater, OR 99034

Mr. Ralph Emerson
1103 Highlands Avenue
Greenwater, OR 99034

Mrs. Nola Alverez
598 McBride Street
Greenwater, OR 99034

Activity 2 Create a Business Letterhead

You have just opened a new mailing and shipping business and need letterhead stationery. Create a letterhead for your company in a header and/or footer. Use Word's Help feature to learn about creating a header that only displays and prints on the first page. Create the letterhead in a header that displays and prints only on the first page and include *at least* one of the following: a clip art image, a picture, a shape, a text box, and/or WordArt. Include the following information in the header:

> Global Mailing
> 4300 Jackson Avenue
> Toronto, ON M4C 3X4
> (416) 555-0095
> www.emcp.net/globalmailing

Save the completed letterhead and name it **WL1-U2-Act02-Ltrhd**. Print and then close the document.

Internet Research

Create a Flyer on an Incentive Program

The owner of Terra Travel Services is offering an incentive to motivate travel consultants to increase travel bookings. The incentive is a sales contest with a grand prize of a one-week paid vacation to Cancun, Mexico. The owner has asked you to create a flyer that will be posted on the office bulletin board that includes information about the incentive program and some information about Cancun. Create this flyer using information about Cancun that you find on the Internet. Include a photo you find on a website (make sure it is not copyrighted) or include a clip art image representing travel. Include any other information or object to add visual appeal to the flyer. Save the completed flyer and name it **WL1-U2-InternetResearch**. Print and then close the document.

Job Study

Develop Recycling Program Communications

The Chief Operating Officer of Harrington Engineering has just approved your draft of the company's new recycling policy (see the file named **RecyclingPolicy.docx** located in the Word2010L1U2 folder). Edit the draft and prepare a final copy of the policy along with a memo to all employees describing the new guidelines. To support the company's energy resources conservation effort, you will send hard copies of the new policy to the Somerset Recycling Program president and to directors of Somerset Chamber of Commerce.

Using the concepts and techniques you learned in this unit, prepare the following documents:

- Format the recycling policy manual, including a cover page, appropriate headers and footers, and page numbers. Add at least one graphic and one diagram where appropriate. Format the document using a Quick Styles set and styles. Save the manual and name it **WL1-U2-JobStudyManual**. Print the manual.

- Download a memo template from Office.com Templates (at the New tab Backstage view) and then create a memo from Susan Gerhardt, Chief Operating Officer of Harrington Engineering to all employees introducing the new recycling program. Copy the *Procedure* section of the recycling policy manual into the memo where appropriate. Include a table listing five employees who will act as Recycling Coordinators at Harrington Engineering (make up the names). Add columns for the employees' department names and their telephone extensions. Save the memo and name it **WL1-U2-JobStudyMemo**. Print the memo.
- Write a letter to the President of the Somerset Recycling Program, William Elizondo, enclosing a copy of the recycling policy manual. Add a notation indicating copies with enclosures were sent to all members of the Somerset Chamber of Commerce. Save the letter and name it **WL1-U2-JobStudyLetter**. Print the letter.
- Create mailing labels (see Figure U2.8). Save the labels and name the file **WL1-U2-JobStudyLabels**. Print the file.

Figure U2.8 Mailing Labels

William Elizondo, President
Somerset Recycling Program
700 West Brighton Road
Somerset, NJ 55123

Paul Schwartz
Somerset Chamber of Commerce
45 Wallace Road
Somerset, NJ 55123

Ashley Crighton
Somerset Chamber of Commerce
45 Wallace Road
Somerset, NJ 55123

Carol Davis
Somerset Chamber of Commerce
45 Wallace Road
Somerset, NJ 55123

Robert Knight
Somerset Chamber of Commerce
45 Wallace Road
Somerset, NJ 55123

Index

* (asterisk)
    as excluded from file names, 9
    for round bullets, 78
- (hyphen), in indicating *through* in printing specific pages, 221
: (colon), as excluded from file names, 9
; (semicolon), as excluded from file names, 9
, (comma), in indicating *and* in printing specific pages, 221
" (quotation marks), as excluded from file names, 9
« » (chevrons), as indicating a field for entering text, 296
/ (forward slash), as excluded from file names, 9
< (less than sign), as excluded from file names, 9
> (greater than sign)
    for arrow bullets, 78
    as excluded from file names, 9
? (question mark), as excluded from file names, 9
\ (backslash), as excluded from file names, 9
| (pipe symbol), as excluded from file names, 9

A

active documents, 214
adding. *See also* inserting
    paragraph shading, 80–81
addresses, United States Postal Service (USPS) guidelines for, 224, 225
Adobe Reader, opening PDF files in, 213
alignment
    changing paragraph, 50–53
    vertical, of text, 167–168
Alignment button, 54, 85, 86
Align Text Left button, 51
Alt key
    in selecting text vertically, 19
    in setting tabs, 86
arrow bullets, 78
arrow keys, 16
arrow pointer, positioning, 15
arrow shapes, drawing, 178–179

asterisk (*)
    as excluded from file names, 9
    for round bullets, 78
attachments, sending documents as, 207
Auto Check for Errors button, 298
AutoComplete, 7
AutoCorrect, 5, 7, 76–77
AutoCorrect dialog box, 77
AutoFormat, 76, 78
automatic grammar checker, 5
automatic numbering, 75–76
automatic spell checker, 5

B

background color, 126
backslash (\), as excluded from file names, 9
backspace key
    in deleting page breaks, 117
    in deleting text, 91
Backstage view, 9
    getting help in, 27
    Help tab, 25, 26
    New tab, 11, 229–230
    Print tab, 9, 10, 127, 220–221
    Recent tab, 12
    Save & Send, 206, 207, 210, 212
balancing columns on page, 160
blank document, 5
Blank Page button, 118
blank pages, inserting, 118
blog posts, saving documents as, 208–209
book icon, 5
borders
    customizing, 82–84
    inserting page, 128–129
    inserting paragraph, 79–80
Borders and Shading dialog box, 82, 125, 127, 128
browsing in documents, 16
built-in text box, inserting, 177
bulleted lists, 78–79
bulleting
    automatic, 78
    paragraphs, 75–79
    turning off, 78
bullets, types of, 78
Bullets button, 75, 78

C

Center button, 51
Change Case button, 41
Change Styles button, 47
    changing paragraph spacing with, 61–62
changing
    margins, 113
    margins in the Page Setup dialog box, 115, 116
    page border options, 127–128
    page color, 126
    page orientation, 113
    page size, 114–115
    view, 109–110
character formatting, 37
    applying, while typing, 40–41
check box options, choosing, 133–134
chevrons (« »), as indicating a field for entering text, 296
Clear All button, 89
Clear Formatting button, 41
clearing, tabs, 89
click and type feature, using, 166–167
Clip Art, 169
    inserting, 173–176
Clip Art task pane, 169, 173–175
Clipboard, 91–92
    in cutting and pasting text, 91–92
    defined, 91
    in deleting selected text, 91
    inserting Print Screen file into, 200–201
    using, 95–96
Clipboard task pane, 95
Close button, 215
closing of document, 10
colon (:), as excluded from file names, 9
color
    background, 126
    page, 126
color formatting, 49
Colors dialog box, 80
color theme, 49
columns
    balancing, on page, 160
    creating, with Columns dialog box, 158

337

formatting, at the Columns dialog box, 159–160
formatting text into, 157–158
mandatory width of, 157
newspaper, 157
removing formatting, 159
Columns dialog box, 157
creating columns with, 158
formatting columns at, 159–160
comma (,), in indicating *and* in printing specific pages, 221
comparing formatting, 63–64
completing merges, 293–299
composite fields, 296
computer-related careers, 14
continuous section break, 153
inserting, 156–157
copying
shapes, 178
text, 94
Cover Page button, 118
cover pages, inserting, 118
creating
columns with the Columns dialog box, 158
data source files, 293–295, 300, 302
documents, 7–8
documents, using templates, 229–231
drop caps, 162–163
envelopes, 223–226
folders, 201–202
labels, 226–229
new documents, 11–12
screen clippings, 184–185
screenshots, 183–185
WordArt, 181–183
Ctrl key, in selecting documents, 202
Customize Address List dialog box, 294
Customize Columns button, 293–294
Customize Quick Access toolbar, 10, 12
customizing
borders and shading, 82–84
images, 169
pictures, 170–173
pull quotes, 176–177
Cut button, in deleting text, 91
cutting, text, 91–92

D

data, merging main document with, 299
data source files, 293
creating, 293–295, 300, 302
editing, 306–311
date, inserting, 165–166
Date and Time dialog box, 165
default formatting, 7, 35, 47
delete key, in deleting text, 91
deleting. *See also* removing
documents, 203–204
folders, 205, 206
page breaks, 117
section breaks, 156
selected text, 91
tabs, 88
text, 18
deletion commands, 18
Delivery Address text box, 223, 225
dialog box buttons, spelling and grammar, 23
dialog boxes, getting help in, 27
directories, merging, 304–305
documents
active, 214
blank, 5
browsing in, 16
closing, 10
creating, 7–8
creating envelope in existing, 226
creating new, 11–12
creating, using templates, 229–231
defined, 5
deleting, 203–204
determining open, 214
displaying, in Draft view, 109
displaying, in Full Screen Reading view, 109–110
editing, 15
grammar checking, 22–25
inserting Print Screen file into, 200–201
inserting WordArt in, 181
main, 293, 295–297
maintaining, 200–206
maximizing, 215
merging, 298–299
minimizing, 215
naming, 9
opening, 12
opening and printing multiple, 205–206
pinning, 13
previewing pages in, 219–220
printing, 9–10
printing pages in, 220–223
restoring, 215
saving, 8
saving, in different format, 210–212
saving, with Save As, 14
scrolling in, 15
selecting, 202
sending, by email, 207
sharing, 206–214
spell checking, 22–25
unpinning, 13
viewing, side by side, 217–218
Draft view
displaying documents in, 109
hard page break in, 117
dragging
scroll box, 15
text with mouse, 92
drawing
shapes, 178–181
text box, 180–181
Drawing Tools Format tab, 176, 181
drop cap, 162
creating, 162–163
Drop Cap dialog box, 162

E

Edit Data Source dialog box, 308
editing
data sources files, 306–311
documents, 15
predesigned headers and footers, 124–125
records, 308–311
effects theme, 49
email, sending document using, 207
enclosed objects, 178
Enter key
in AutoComplete, 7
in beginning new paragraph, 7, 16
pressing at end of each line, 5
in turning off automatic numbering, 75
Envelope Options dialog box, 300

envelopes
    creating and printing, 223–226
    merging, 300–301
Envelopes and Labels dialog box, 223–224, 228
errors, checking for, in merges, 298

F

F1, in assessing Help, 25
F3, in AutoComplete, 7
F4, in repeating last action, 57
F8, in turning on Selection Mode, 20
F9, for updating field, 165
fax service provider, 207
field name, 296
fields
    composite, 296
    Fill-in, 311
file management, print screen in, 200–201
file names, 9
    characters excluded from, 9
    length of, 9
files
    format of, 207
    inserting, 218
File tab, 6
Fill-in dialog box, 311–312
Fill-in field, 311
Find and Replace dialog box, 105, 132–133, 162
    check box options in, 133–134
    options at the expanded, 134
finding
    fonts, 136–137
    formatting, 135
    text, 130–133
Finish & Merge button, 298, 299
First Record button, 298
folders
    copying and moving documents to other, 204–205
    creating, 201–202
    deleting, 205, 206
    names for, 201
    renaming, 202
    root, 201
Font dialog box, 45
    changing fonts at, 45–46

font effect
    applying, 43–44
    choosing, 41–42
fonts
    changing, 37–40
    changing, at the Font dialog box, 45–46
    elements making up, 37
    finding and replacing, 136–137
    new, in Office 2007, 38
Font Size button, 38
font theme, 49
footers
    editing predesigned, 124–125
    inserting predesigned, 122–123
    removing, 122–123
format, defined, 35
    saving documents in different, 210–212
Format Painter, formatting with, 59
formatting
    character, 37
    color, 49
    columns at the Columns dialog box, 159–160
    comparing, 63–64
    default, 7, 35, 47
    finding and replacing, 135
    with Format Painter, 59
    images, 169
    with the Mini toolbar, 42
    page background, 125–129
    removing column, 159
    screen clippings, 184–185
    text box, 180–181
    text into columns, 157–158
forward slash (/), as excluded from file names, 9
Full Screen Reading view
    displaying document in, 109–110
    keyboard commands in, 110

G

Getting Started, 3
Go To option, 16
Go to Record button, 298
grammar
    automatic checker for, 5
    checking, in document, 22–25
grammar checker, 22–25

Grammar dialog box buttons, 23
greater than sign (>)
    for arrow bullets, 78
    as excluded from file names, 9
Greeting Line dialog box, 296

H

hanging indents, 78
hard copy, 9
hard page break, 16, 117
headers
    editing predesigned, 124–125
    inserting predesigned, 122–123
    removing, 122–123
Help, 25–27
Help tab Backstage view, 25, 26
Hide White Space icon, 112
hiding white space in Print Layout view, 112–113
horizontal ruler, 6
hyphen (-), in indicating *through* in printing specific pages, 221
hyphenation, 153
    automatic, 161
    canceling, 161
    manual, 161–162
Hyphenation dialog box, 161

I

I-beam pointer, 6
    positioning, 5, 15, 19
images
    customizing, 169
    formatting, 169
    moving, 169–170
    sizing, 169
indenting text in paragraphs, 54–57
inputting, text during merges, 311–313
Insert Address Block dialog box, 296
Insert File dialog box, 218
inserting. *See also* adding
    blank pages, 118
    built-in text box, 177
    Clip Art, 173–176
    cover pages, 118
    date and time, 165–166
    files, 218
    page borders, 127, 128–129

page breaks, 117–118
paragraph borders, 79–80
pictures, 170–173
predesigned headers and footers, 122–123
predesigned page numbering, 120–121
pull quotes, 176–177
screenshots, 183–185
section breaks, 156–157
symbols and special characters, 163–165
text, 18
watermark, 125
insertion point, 6
  movement between windows, 214
  movement commands for, 16–17
  moving, with keyboard, 16–17
  moving, to specific page, 16
  for split windows, 216
Insert Merge Field dialog box, 296
Insert Picture dialog box, 169, 170
Internet fax, sending email as, 207

K

keyboard
  moving insertion point with, 16–17
  Print Screen key on, 200–201
  selecting text with, 20, 21
keyboard commands in Full Screen Reading view, 110
keyboard shortcuts
  for automatic numbering, 75
  for closing documents, 10
  Font Group, 42
  for getting help, 25
  for line spacing, 60
  for paragraph alignment, 51
  for removing character formatting, 37
  using, 42

L

Label Options dialog box, 226, 302
labels
  changing options, 226, 228
  creating and printing, 226–229
  merging, 302–304
landscape orientation, 113, 221
last action, repeating, 57
Last Record button, 298
leader tabs, setting, 90
less than sign (<), as excluded from file names, 9
line drawings, 178
line spacing, 57
  changing, 60–61
  default, 60
lists
  automatic numbered, 77
  bulleted, 78–79
Live Preview, 38

M

mailing labels, creating, 226, 227–229
Mail Merge, 289
Mail Merge Recipients dialog box, 306
Mail Merge Wizard, 293
  merging using, 313–315
main document, 293
  creating, 295–297
maintaining documents, 200–206
manipulating tabs
  on the Ruler, 85–88
  at the Tabs dialog box, 88
Manual Hyphenation dialog box, 161
margins
  changing, 113
  changing, in the Page Setup dialog box, 115, 116
  default, 105
  printer requirements for, 113
Margins button, 105, 115
Maximize button, 215
maximizing documents, 215
Merge to New Document dialog box, 299
merging, 293–299
  checking for errors in, 298
  data source files in, 293–295, 306–311
  directories, 304–305
  documents, 298–299
  envelopes, 300–301
  inputting text during, 311–313
  labels, 302–304
Mail Merge Wizard in, 313–315
main document in, 295–297
previewing in, 298
Microsoft Word, opening, 5
Minimize button, 215
minimizing documents, 215
Mini toolbar, 18
  formatting with, 42
modifying WordArt, 181–183
monospaced typeface, 37–38
mouse
  moving text by dragging with, 92
  selecting text with, 19
moving
  images, 169–170
  selected text between split windows, 216–217
  tabs, 88
  text, by dragging with mouse, 92
multiple documents, opening and printing, 205–206

N

naming documents, 9
navigating using Navigation pane, 110–112
Navigation pane, navigating using, 110–112
New Address List dialog box, 293
New Line command, 7, 86
newspaper columns, 157
New tab Backstage view, 11, 229–230
Next Page button, 219
Next Record button, 298
numbering
  automatic, 75–76
  inserting predesigned page, 120–121
  paragraphs, 75–77
  turning off, 75
Numbering button, 75
numbers, ordinal, 5
Num Lock, 16

O

Open dialog box, 12, 200
  Address Bar in, 201
  copying and moving documents, 204
  deleting documents, 203
  opening and printing multiple documents, 205

Rename option in, 202, 205
renaming documents, 205
renaming folders, 202
saving in PDF/XPS format, 213
selecting documents in, 202
OpenDocument Text format, 210
opening
   documents, 12
   multiple documents, 205–206
   windows, 215
options buttons, 7
ordinal numbers, 5
Organize button, 203, 204

P

page
   balancing columns on, 160
   defined, 16
   moving insertion point to specific, 16
   previewing, in document, 219–220
   printing, in document, 220–223
page background, formatting, 125–129
page borders
   changing options, 127–128
   inserting, 127, 128–129
page breaks
   deleting, 117
   hard, 117
   inserting, 117–118
   soft, 117
page color, changing, 126
Page Color button, 126
Page Layout tab, Page Setup group in, 113
page numbering, inserting predesigned, 120–121
page orientation, 113, 221
   changing, 113
PageSetup, changing, 113–120
Page Setup dialog box
   changing margins in, 115, 116
   changing paper size at, 115
   Layout tab in, 167, 168
   vertical alignment option in, 168
page size
   changing, 114–115
   default, 114
panes, dividing window into, 216–218
paper size, changing, at Page Setup dialog box, 115
paragraph alignment, changing, 50–53
   at Paragraph dialog box, 52–53
paragraph borders, inserting, 79–80
paragraph dialog box, changing alignment at, 52–53
paragraphs
   bulleting, 75–79
   defined, 16, 35
   indenting text in, 54–57
   numbering, 75–77
   sorting text in, 84–85
   spacing before and after, 57, 58
paragraph shading, adding, 80–81
paragraph spacing, changing, with Change Styles button, 61–62
Paste Options button, 7, 93
pasting text, 91–92, 94
PDF (portable document format), 207
   saving document as, 213–214
pictures, inserting and customizing, 170–173
Picture Tools Format tab, 178, 183
pinning of document, 13
pipe symbol (|), as excluded from file names, 9
placeholder text, 118, 122
plain text, saving document in, 210
points, 38, 57
portrait orientation, 113, 221
predesigned headers and footers, inserting, 122–125
previewing
   merges, 298
   pages in a document, 219–220
Previous Page button, 219
Previous Record button, 298
printing
   documents, 9–10
   envelopes, 223–226
   labels, 226–229
   multiple documents, 205–206
   pages in a document, 220–223
Print Layout view, 109, 112
   hiding/showing white space in, 112–113
   visibility of headers and footers in, 122
Print Screen, using, 200–201
Print tab Backstage view, 9, 10, 127, 220–221
proportional typeface, 5, 7, 38
Publish as Blog Post option, 208
pull quote, 176
   inserting and customizing, 176–177
punctuation, spacing of, 5, 7

Q

question mark (?), as excluded from file names, 9
Quick Access toolbar, 6, 21
   Quick Print button on, 10
   Redo button on, 21–22
   Save As button on, 8
   Undo button on, 21–22
Quick Print button, 10
Quick Styles, 47
   changing sets, 47–48
quotation marks ("), as excluded from file names, 9
quote, pull, 176

R

readability, 157
Recent tab Backstage view, 12
records
   defined, 293
   editing, 308–311
   selecting specific, 306
Recycle Bin, 203
   displaying, 203
   emptying, 203
   restoring files from, 203
Redo button, 21–22
removing. *See also* deleting
   column formatting, 159
   footers, 122–123
   headers, 122–123
renaming
   documents, 205
   folders, 202
Repeat command, 57
replacing
   fonts, 136–137
   formatting, 135
   text, 130–133
Restore button, 215
restoring documents, 215

Return Address text box, 223
Reveal Formatting task pane, 63
ribbon, 6
Rich Text Format (rtf), saving document in, 210–211
root folders, 201
round bullets, 78
Ruler
    Alignment button on the, 54, 85, 86
    horizontal, 6
    manipulating tabs on the, 85–88
    vertical, 6

S

sans serif typeface, 38
Save Address List dialog box, 294
Save As dialog box, 8, 14, 200
    copying and moving documents, 204
    deleting documents, 203
    renaming folders, 202
    saving in PDF/XPS format, 213
    saving to SkyDrive, 208
Save as type options box, 212
Save & Send tab Backstage view, 206, 207, 212
    Change File Type option, 210
saving documents, 8
    as blog posts, 208–209
    in different formats, 210–212
    with Save As, 14
    to SharePoint, 208
    to SkyDrive, 208
screen clippings, creating and formatting, 184–185
screen features
    File tab, 6
    horizontal ruler, 6
    I-beam pointer, 6
    insertion point, 6
    Quick Access toolbar, 6
    ribbon, 6
    Status bar, 6
    tabs, 6
    Taskbar, 6
    Title bar, 6
    vertical ruler, 6
    vertical scroll bar, 6
Screenshot button, 183–184
screenshots, creating and inserting, 183–185

scroll bar, vertical, 6, 15
scrolling in documents, 15
section break, 153
    continuous, 153, 156–157
    deleting, 156
    inserting, 156–157
Select Data Source dialog box, 300
selecting
    documents, 202
    text, 18–21
Selection Mode, turning on, 20
Select Recipients button, 293
semicolon (:), as excluded from file names, 9
sending, documents using email, 207
serifs, 38
serif typeface, 38
setting, tabs, 89
    leader, 90
shading
    adding paragraph, 80–81
    customizing, 82–84
shapes, drawing, 178–181
SharePoint, saving documents to, 208
sharing documents, 206–214
shortcut menu, deleting document at, 203
Show/Hide ¶ button, 51
showing white space in Print Layout view, 112–113
Show White Space icon, 112
single page web document option, saving with, 211
sizing, images, 169
SkyDrive, saving documents to, 208
soft copy, 9
soft page break, 16, 117
sorting, text in paragraphs, 84–85
Sort Text dialog box, 84
spacing
    before and after paragraphs, 57, 58
    changing paragraph, with the Change Styles button, 61–62
    line, 57
    line, changing, 60–61
    of punctuation, 5, 7
special characters, inserting, 163–165
spelling
    automatic spell checker for, 5

    checking, in document, 22–25
spelling checker, 22–25
Spelling and Grammar dialog box buttons, 23
Spelling dialog box buttons, 23
Spelling dictionary, 5
split bar, 216
splitting windows, 216–218
split windows
    insertion point in, 216
    moving selected text between, 216–217
Start Mail Merge button, 293, 300, 302, 304
Status bar, 6
    book icon display in, 5
Strikethrough button, 42
Subscript button, 42
suffixes, finding and replacing, 134–135
superscript, 5
Superscript button, 42
Symbol dialog box, 163, 164
    with Symbols tab selected, 164
symbols, inserting, 163–165
Synchronous Scrolling button, 217

T

Tab alignment buttons, 85
tabs, 6
    clearing, 89
    deleting, 88
    manipulating, on the Ruler, 85–88
    manipulating, at Tabs dialog box, 88
    moving, 88
    setting, 86–87, 89
    setting leader, 90
Tabs dialog box
    clearing tabs at, 89
    manipulating tabs at, 88
    setting tabs at, 89
Taskbar, 6
    checking for open programs, 5
    Word button on, 214
templates
    creating documents using, 229–231
    default formatting in, 7, 35, 47
text
    copying, 94

cutting and pasting, 91–92
deleting, 18
deleting selected, 91
finding and replacing, 130–133
formatting, into columns, 157–158
indenting, in paragraphs, 54–57
inputting, during merges, 311–313
inserting, 18
line length of, 157
moving, by dragging with mouse, 92
moving selected, between split windows, 216–217
pasting, 94
placeholder, 118
sorting, in paragraphs, 84–85
vertically aligning, 167–168
vertically centering, 168
text box
   drawing and formatting, 180–181
   inserting, 177
Text Box Tools Format tab, 178, 179
Text Effects button, 42
Text Highlight Color button, 42
Theme Colors button, 49, 50
Theme Effects button, 49, 50
Theme Fonts button, 49, 50
themes
   applying, 49–50
   changing, 49–50
   defined, 49
this point forward option, 158

time, inserting, 165–166
Title bar, 6
typeface
   defined, 37
   monospaced, 37–38
   proportional, 5, 7, 38
   sans serif, 38
   serif, 38
type size, 38
type styles, 38
   choosing, 40–41

U

Undo button, 21–22, 92
United States Postal Service (USPS) guidelines for addresses, 224, 225
unpinning of document, 13

V

vertical alignment option, 153
vertically aligning text, 167–168
vertically centering text, 168
vertical ruler, 6
vertical scroll bar, 6, 15
view, changing, 109–110
View buttons, 109
viewing, documents side by side, 217–218
View Options button, 109
View Ruler button, 85
View Side by Side button, 217

W

watermark, 125
   inserting, 125
web browser, opening XPS files in, 213

white space
   at end of sentence, 7
   hiding/showing, in Print Layout view, 112–113
windows
   arranging, 215
   opening, 215
   splitting, 216–218
   working with, 214–217
Windows Live ID account, 208
Word, exiting, 14
WordArt, creating and modifying, 181–183
word forms, finding and replacing, 134–135
Word Options dialog box, 76
words
   automatically hyphenating, 161
   manually hyphenating, 161–162
word wrap, 5
Write & Insert Fields group, 295–296

X

XML (Extensible Markup Language), 207
XPS (XML paper specification) format, 207
   saving document as, 213–214

Z

Zoom In button, 109
Zoom Out button, 109
Zoom slider bar, 109, 219
Zoom to Page button, 219

Microsoft Excel Level 1

Unit 1 ■ Editing and Formatting Documents

Chapter 1 ■ Preparing an Excel Workbook

Chapter 2 ■ Inserting Formulas in a Worksheet

Chapter 3 ■ Formatting an Excel Worksheet

Chapter 4 ■ Enhancing a Worksheet

Preparing an Excel Workbook

CHAPTER 1

PERFORMANCE OBJECTIVES

Upon successful completion of Chapter 1, you will be able to:
- Identify the various elements of an Excel workbook
- Create, save, and print a workbook
- Enter data in a workbook
- Edit data in a workbook
- Insert a formula using the AutoSum button
- Apply basic formatting to cells in a workbook
- Use the Help feature

Many companies use a spreadsheet for numerical and financial data and to analyze and evaluate information. An Excel spreadsheet can be used for such activities as creating financial statements, preparing budgets, managing inventory, and analyzing cash flow. In addition, numbers and values can be easily manipulated to create "what if" situations. For example, using a spreadsheet, a person in a company can ask questions such as "What if the value in this category is decreased? How would that change affect the department budget?" Questions like these can be easily answered in an Excel spreadsheet. Change the value in a category and Excel will recalculate formulas for the other values. In this way, a spreadsheet can be used not only for creating financial statements or budgets, but also as a planning tool. Model answers for this chapter's projects appear on the following page.

Note: Before beginning the projects, copy to your storage medium the Excel2010L1C1 subfolder from the Excel2010L1 folder on the CD that accompanies this textbook. Steps on how to copy a folder are presented on the inside of the back cover of this textbook. Do this every time you start a chapter's projects.

Project 1 Prepare a Worksheet with Employee Information
EL1-C1-P1-EmpBene.xlsx

Project 2 Open and Format a Workbook and Insert Formulas
EL1-C1-P2-FillCells.xlsx

Project 3 Format a Worksheet
EL1-C1-P3-MoExps.xlsx

Project 1 — Prepare a Worksheet with Employee Information — 3 Parts

You will create a worksheet containing employee information, edit the contents, and then save and close the workbook.

Creating a Worksheet

Open Excel by clicking the Start button at the left side of the Taskbar, pointing to *All Programs*, clicking *Microsoft Office*, and then clicking *Microsoft Excel 2010*. (Depending on your operating system, these steps may vary.) When Excel is open, you are presented with a blank worksheet like the one shown in Figure 1.1. The elements of a blank Excel worksheet are described in Table 1.1.

Start

A file created in Excel is referred to as a **workbook**. An Excel workbook consists of individual worksheets (or *sheets*) like the sheets of paper in a notebook. Notice the tabs located toward the bottom of the Excel window that are named *Sheet1*, *Sheet2*, and so on. The area containing the gridlines in the Excel window is called the **worksheet area**. Figure 1.2 identifies the elements of the worksheet area. Create a worksheet in the worksheet area that will be saved as part of a workbook. Columns in a worksheet are labeled with letters of the alphabet and rows are numbered.

Figure 1.1 Blank Excel Worksheet

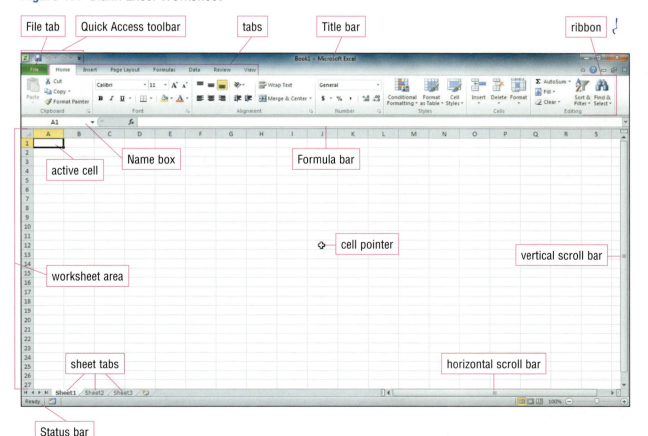

Table 1.1 Elements of an Excel Worksheet

Feature	Description
Quick Access toolbar	Contains buttons for commonly used commands
File tab	Click the File tab and the Backstage view displays containing buttons and tabs for working with and managing files
Title bar	Displays workbook name followed by program name
Tabs	Contain commands and features organized into groups
Ribbon	Area containing the tabs and commands divided into groups
Name box	Displays cell address (also called the cell reference) and includes the column letter and row number
Formula bar	Provides information about active cell; enter and edit formulas in this bar
Scroll bars	Use vertical and horizontal scroll bars to navigate within a worksheet
Sheet tab	Displays toward bottom of screen and identifies current worksheet
Status bar	Displays information about worksheet and active cell, view buttons, and Zoom slider bar

Figure 1.2 Elements of a Worksheet Area

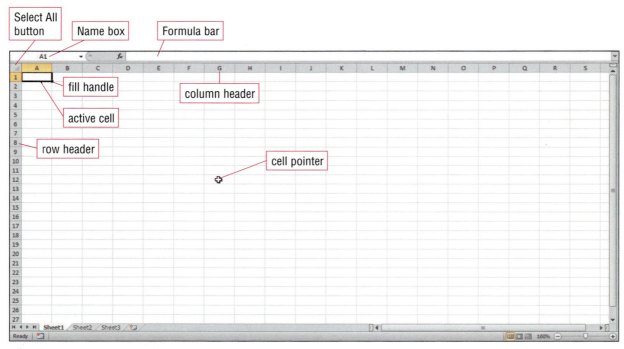

The horizontal and vertical lines that define the cells in the worksheet area are called *gridlines*. When a cell is active (displays with a black border), the **cell address**, also called the **cell reference**, displays in the **Name box**. The cell reference includes the column letter and row number. For example, if the first cell of the worksheet is active, the cell reference *A1* displays in the Name box. A thick black border surrounds the active cell.

Enter data such as text, a number, or a value in a cell. To enter data in a cell, make the desired cell active and then type the data. To make the next cell active, press the Tab key. Table 1.2 displays additional commands for making a specific cell active.

Another method for making a specific cell active is to use the Go To feature. To use this feature, click the Find & Select button in the Editing group in the Home tab and then click Go To. At the Go To dialog box, type the cell reference in the *Reference* text box, and then click OK.

When you are ready to type data into the active cell, check the Status bar. The word *Ready* should display at the left side. As you type data, the word *Ready* changes to *Enter*. Data you type in a cell displays in the cell as well as in the Formula bar. If the data you type is longer than the cell can accommodate, the data overlaps the next cell to the right. (It does not become a part of the next cell—it simply overlaps it.) You will learn how to change column widths to accommodate data later in this chapter.

To make a cell active, position the cell pointer in the cell and then click the left mouse button.

Ctrl + G is the keyboard command to display the Go To dialog box.

Find & Select

Table 1.2 Commands for Making a Specific Cell Active

To make this cell active	Press
Cell below current cell	Enter
Cell above current cell	Shift + Enter
Next cell	Tab
Previous cell	Shift + Tab
Cell at beginning of row	Home
Next cell in the direction of the arrow	Up, Down, Left, or Right Arrow keys
Last cell in worksheet	Ctrl + End
First cell in worksheet	Ctrl + Home
Cell in next window	Page Down
Cell in previous window	Page Up
Cell in window to right	Alt + Page Down
Cell in window to left	Alt + Page Up

If the data you enter in a cell consists of text and the text does not fit into the cell, it overlaps the next cell. If, however, you enter a number in a cell, specify it as a number (rather than text) and the number is too long to fit in the cell, Excel changes the display of the number to number symbols *(###)*. This is because Excel does not want you to be misled by a number when you see only a portion of it in the cell.

Along with the keyboard, you can use the mouse to make a specific cell active. To make a specific cell active with the mouse, position the mouse pointer, which displays as a white plus sign (called the ***cell pointer***), on the desired cell, and then click the left mouse button. The cell pointer displays as a white plus sign when positioned in a cell in the worksheet and displays as an arrow pointer when positioned on other elements of the Excel window such as options in tabs or scroll bars.

Scroll through a worksheet using the horizontal and/or vertical scroll bars. Scrolling shifts the display of cells in the worksheet area, but does not change the active cell. Scroll through a worksheet until the desired cell is visible and then click the desired cell.

Saving a Workbook

Quick Steps
Save a Workbook
1. Click Save button.
2. Type workbook name.
3. Press Enter.

Ctrl + S is the keyboard command to save a workbook.

Save

Save an Excel workbook, which may consist of a worksheet or several worksheets, by clicking the Save button on the Quick Access toolbar or by clicking the File tab and then clicking the Save button in the Quick commands area of the Backstage view. At the Save As dialog box, type a name for the workbook in the *File name* text box and then press Enter or click the Save button. A workbook file name can contain up to 255 characters, including drive letter and any folder names, and can include spaces. Note that you cannot give a workbook the same name in first uppercase and then lowercase letters. Also, some symbols cannot be used in a file name such as:

forward slash (/)	question mark (?)
backslash (\)	quotation mark (")
greater than sign (>)	colon (:)
less than sign (<)	semicolon (;)
asterisk (*)	pipe symbol (|)

To save an Excel workbook in the Excel2010L1C1 folder on your storage medium, display the Save As dialog box, click the drive representing your storage medium in the Navigation pane, and then double-click *Excel2010L1C1* in the Content pane.

Project 1a Creating and Saving a Document   Part 1 of 3

1. Open Excel by clicking the Start button on the Taskbar, pointing to *All Programs*, clicking *Microsoft Office*, and then clicking *Microsoft Excel 2010*. (Depending on your operating system, these steps may vary.)
2. At the Excel worksheet that displays, create the worksheet shown in Figure 1.3 by completing the following steps:
    a. Press the Enter key once to make cell A2 the active cell.
    b. With cell A2 active (displays with a thick black border), type **Employee**.
    c. Press the Tab key. (This makes cell B2 active.)
    d. Type **Location** and then press the Tab key. (This makes cell C2 active.)
    e. Type **Benefits** and then press the Enter key to move the insertion point to cell A3.
    f. With cell A3 active, type the name **Avery**.
    g. Continue typing the data shown in Figure 1.3. (For commands for making specific cells active, refer to Table 1.2.)
3. After typing the data shown in the cells in Figure 1.3, save the workbook by completing the following steps:
    a. Click the Save button on the Quick Access toolbar.
    b. At the Save As dialog box, click the drive representing your storage medium in the Navigation pane.
    c. Double-click the *Excel2010L1C1* folder that displays in the Content pane.
    d. Select the text in the *File name* text box and then type **EL1-C1-P1-EmpBene** (for Excel Level 1, Chapter 1, Project 1, and the workbook that contains information about employee benefits).
    e. Press the Enter key or click the Save button.

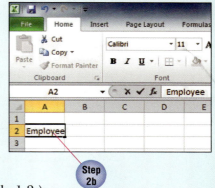

Step 2b

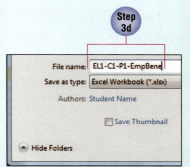

Step 3d

Figure 1.3 Project 1a

	A	B	C	D
1				
2	Employee	Location	Benefits	
3	Avery			
4	Connors			
5	Estrada			
6	Juergens			
7	Mikulich			
8	Talbot			
9				

Editing Data in a Cell

Edit data being typed in a cell by pressing the Backspace key to delete the character to the left of the insertion point or pressing the Delete key to delete the character to the right of the insertion point. To change the data in a cell, click the cell once to make it active and then type the new data. When a cell containing data is active, anything typed will take the place of the existing data.

If you want to edit only a portion of the data in a cell, double-click the cell. This makes the cell active, moves the insertion point inside the cell, and displays the word *Edit* at the left side of the Status bar. Move the insertion point using the arrow keys or the mouse and then make the needed corrections. If you are using the keyboard, you can press the Home key to move the insertion point to the first character in the cell or Formula bar, or press the End key to move the insertion point to the last character.

When you are finished editing the data in the cell, be sure to change out of the Edit mode. To do this, make another cell active. You can do this by pressing Enter, Tab, or Shift + Tab. You can also change out of the Edit mode and return to the Ready mode by clicking another cell or clicking the Enter button on the Formula bar.

Cancel

Enter

If the active cell does not contain data, the Formula bar displays only the cell reference (by column letter and row number). As you type data, the two buttons shown in Figure 1.4 display on the Formula bar to the right of the Name box. Click the Cancel button to delete the current cell entry. You can also delete the cell entry by pressing the Delete key. Click the Enter button to indicate that you are finished typing or editing the cell entry. When you click the Enter button on the Formula bar, the word *Enter* (or *Edit*) located at the left side of the Status bar changes to *Ready*.

Project 1b Editing Data in a Cell   Part 2 of 3

1. With **EL1-C1-P1-EmpBene.xlsx** open, double-click cell A7 (contains *Mikulich*).
2. Move the insertion point immediately left of the *k* and then type a **c**. (This changes the spelling to *Mickulich*.)
3. Click once in cell A4 (contains *Connors*), type **Bryant**, and then press the Tab key. (Clicking only once allows you to type over the existing data.)
4. Edit cell C2 by completing the following steps:
   a. Click the Find & Select button in the Editing group in the Home tab and then click *Go To* at the drop-down list.
   b. At the Go To dialog box, type **C2** in the *Reference* text box and then click OK.
   c. Type **Classification** (over *Benefits*).
5. Click once in any other cell.
6. Click the Save button on the Quick Access toolbar to save the workbook again.

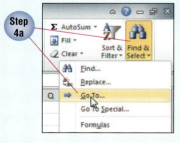

Figure 1.4 Buttons on the Formula Bar

Printing a Workbook

Click the File tab and the Backstage view displays as shown in Figure 1.5. Use buttons and tabs at this view to work with and manage workbooks such as opening, closing, saving, and printing a workbook. If you want to remove the Backstage view without completing an action, click the File tab, click any other tab in the ribbon, or press the Esc key on your keyboard.

Many of the computer projects you will be creating will need to be printed. Print a workbook from the Print tab of the Backstage view shown in Figure 1.6. To display this view, click the File tab and then click the Print tab. You can also display the Print tab Backstage view with the keyboard command Ctrl + P.

Figure 1.5 Backstage View

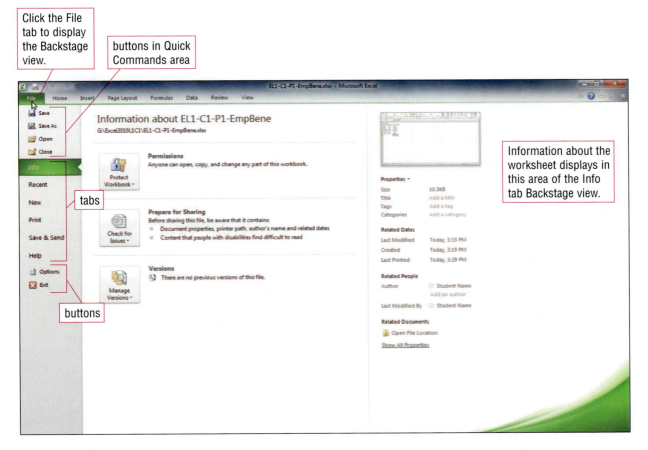

Figure 1.6 Print Tab Backstage View

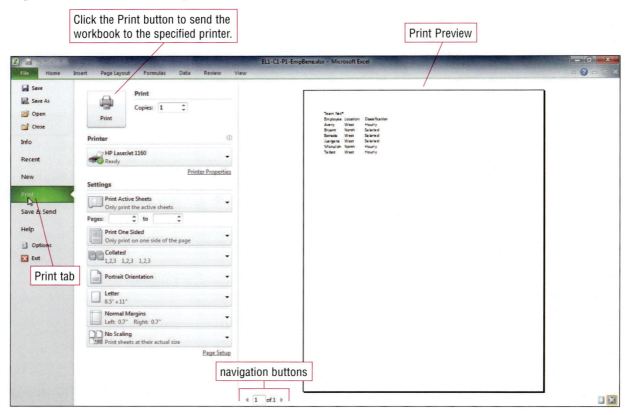

Quick Steps

Print a Workbook
1. Click File tab.
2. Click Print tab.
3. Click Print button.
OR
Click Quick Print button.

Close a Workbook
Click Close Window button.
OR
Click File tab, Close button.

Exit Excel
Click Close button.
OR
Click File tab, Exit button.

The left side of the Print tab Backstage view displays three categories—*Print*, *Printer*, and *Settings*. Click the Print button in the Print category to send the workbook to the printer and specify the number of copies you want printed in the *Copies* option text box. Use the gallery in the Printer category to specify the desired printer. The Settings category contains a number of galleries, each with options for specifying how you want your workbook printed. Use the galleries to specify whether or not you want the pages collated when printed; the orientation, page size, and margins of your workbook; and if you want the worksheet scaled to print all rows and columns of data on one page.

Another method for printing a workbook is to insert the Quick Print button on the Quick Access toolbar and then click the button. This sends the workbook directly to the printer without displaying the Print tab Backstage view. To insert the button on the Quick Access toolbar, click the Customize Quick Access Toolbar button that displays at the right side of the toolbar and then click *Quick Print* at the drop-down list. To remove the Quick Print button from the Quick Access toolbar, right-click the button and then click *Remove from Quick Access Toolbar* at the drop-down list.

Closing a Workbook

Close Window

To close an Excel workbook, click the File tab and then click the Close button. You can also close a workbook by clicking the Close Window button located toward the upper right corner of the screen. Position the mouse pointer on the button and a ScreenTip displays with the name *Close Window*.

Exiting Excel

To exit Excel, click the Close button that displays in the upper right corner of the screen. The Close button contains an X and if you position the mouse pointer on the button a ScreenTip displays with the name *Close*. You can also exit Excel by clicking the File tab and then clicking the Exit button.

Close

Using Automatic Entering Features

Excel contains several features that help you enter data into cells quickly and efficiently. These features include ***AutoComplete***, which automatically inserts data in a cell that begins the same as a previous entry; ***AutoCorrect***, which automatically corrects many common typographical errors; and ***AutoFill***, which will automatically insert words, numbers, or formulas in a series.

Using AutoComplete and AutoCorrect

The AutoComplete feature will automatically insert data in a cell that begins the same as a previous entry. If the data inserted by AutoComplete is the data you want in the cell, press Enter. If it is not the desired data, simply continue typing the correct data. This feature can be very useful in a worksheet that contains repetitive data entries. For example, consider a worksheet that repeats the word *Payroll*. The second and subsequent times this word is to be inserted in a cell, simply typing the letter *P* will cause AutoComplete to insert the entire word.

    The AutoCorrect feature automatically corrects many common typing errors. To see what symbols and words are in the AutoCorrect feature, click the File tab and then click the Options button located below the Help tab. At the Excel Options dialog box, click *Proofing* in the left panel and then click the AutoCorrect Options button located in the right panel. This displays the AutoCorrect dialog box with the AutoCorrect tab selected as shown in Figure 1.7 with a list box containing the replacement data.

Figure 1.7 AutoCorrect Dialog Box with AutoCorrect Tab Selected

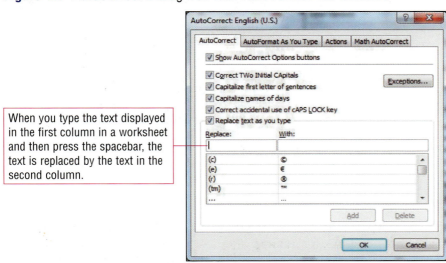

When you type the text displayed in the first column in a worksheet and then press the spacebar, the text is replaced by the text in the second column.

At the AutoCorrect dialog box, type the text shown in the first column in the list box and the text in the second column is inserted in the cell. Along with symbols, the AutoCorrect dialog box contains commonly misspelled words and common typographical errors.

Project 1c   Inserting Data in Cells with AutoComplete   Part 3 of 3

1. With **EL1-C1-P1-EmpBene.xlsx** open make cell A1 active.
2. Type the text in cell A1 as shown in Figure 1.8. Insert the ® symbol by typing **(r)**. [AutoCorrect will change (r) to ®.]
3. Type the remaining text in the cells. When you type the **W** in *West* in cell B5, the AutoComplete feature will insert *West*. Accept this by pressing the Enter key. (Pressing the Enter key accepts *West* and also makes the cell below active.) Use the AutoComplete feature to enter *West* in B6 and B8 and *North* in cell B7. Use AutoComplete to enter the second and subsequent occurrences of *Salaried* and *Hourly*.
4. Click the Save button on the Quick Access toolbar.
5. Print **EL1-C1-P1-EmpBene.xlsx** by clicking the File tab, clicking the Print tab, and then clicking the Print button at the Print tab Backstage view. (The gridlines will not print.)
6. Close the workbook by clicking the Close Window button (contains an X) that displays in the upper right corner of the screen. (Make sure you click the Close Window button and not the Close button.)

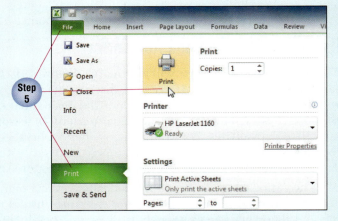

Figure 1.8 Project 1c

	A	B	C	D
1	Team Net®			
2	Employee	Location	Classification	
3	Avery	West	Hourly	
4	Bryant	North	Salaried	
5	Estrada	West	Salaried	
6	Juergens	West	Salaried	
7	Mickulich	North	Hourly	
8	Talbot	West	Hourly	
9				

> **Project 2 Open and Format a Workbook and Insert Formulas   3 Parts**
>
> You will open an existing workbook and insert formulas to find the sum and averages of numbers.

Using AutoFill

When a cell is active, a thick black border surrounds it and a small black square displays in the bottom right corner of the border. This black square is called the AutoFill *fill handle* (see Figure 1.2). With the fill handle, you can quickly fill a range of cells with the same data or with consecutive data. For example, suppose you need to insert the year 2012 in a row or column of cells. To do this quickly, type **2012** in the first cell, position the mouse pointer on the fill handle, hold down the left mouse button, drag across the cells in which you want the year inserted, and then release the mouse button.

You can also use the fill handle to insert a series in a row or column of cells. For example, suppose you are creating a worksheet with data for all of the months in the year. Type **January** in the first cell, position the mouse pointer on the fill handle, hold down the left mouse button, drag down or across to 11 more cells, and then release the mouse button. Excel automatically inserts the other 11 months in the year in the proper order. When using the fill handle, the cells must be adjacent. Table 1.3 identifies the sequence inserted in cells by Excel when specific data is entered.

Certain sequences, such as *2, 4* and *Jan 12, Jan 13*, require that both cells be selected before using the fill handle. If only the cell containing *2* is active, the fill handle will insert *2*s in the selected cells. The list in Table 1.3 is only a sampling of what the fill handle can do. You may find a variety of other sequences that can be inserted in a worksheet using the fill handle.

An Auto Fill Options button displays when you fill cells with the fill handle. Click this button and a list of options displays for filling the cells. By default, data and formatting are filled in each cell. You can choose to fill only the formatting in the cells or fill only the data without the formatting.

If you do not want a series to increment, hold down the Ctrl key while dragging the fill handle.

Auto Fill Options

Table 1.3 AutoFill Fill Handle Series

Enter this data (Commas represent data in separate cells.)	And the fill handle will insert this sequence in adjacent cells
January	February, March, April, and so on . . .
Jan	Feb, Mar, Apr, and so on . . .
Jan 12, Jan 13	14-Jan, 15-Jan, 16-Jan, and so on . . .
Monday	Tuesday, Wednesday, Thursday, and so on . . .
Product 1	Product 2, Product 3, Product 4, and so on . . .
Qtr 1	Qtr 2, Qtr 3, Qtr 4
2, 4	6, 8, 10, and so on . . .

Quick Steps

Open a Workbook
1. Click File tab.
2. Click Open button.
3. Display desired folder.
4. Double-click workbook name.

Opening a Workbook

Open an Excel workbook by displaying the Open dialog box and then double-clicking the desired workbook name. Display the Open dialog box by clicking the File tab and then clicking the Open button. You can also use the keyboard command Ctrl + O to display the Open dialog box.

Project 2a   **Inserting Data in Cells with the Fill Handle**   Part 1 of 3

1. Open **FillCells.xlsx**. (This workbook is located in the Excel2010L1C1 folder on your storage medium.)
2. Save the workbook with Save As and name it **EL1-C1-P2-FillCells**.
3. Add data to cells as shown in Figure 1.9. Begin by making cell B1 active and then typing **January**.
4. Position the mouse pointer on the fill handle for cell B1, hold down the left mouse button, drag across to cell G1, and then release the mouse button.
5. Type a sequence and then use the fill handle to fill the remaining cells by completing the following steps:
    a. Make cell A2 active and then type **Year 1**.
    b. Make cell A3 active and then type **Year 3**.
    c. Select cells A2 and A3 by positioning the mouse pointer in cell A2, holding down the left mouse button, dragging down to cell A3, and then releasing the mouse button.
    d. Drag the fill handle for cell A3 to cell A5. (This inserts *Year 5* in cell A4 and *Year 7* in cell A5.)
6. Use the fill handle to fill adjacent cells with a number but not the formatting by completing the following steps:
    a. Make cell B2 active. (This cell contains *100* with bold formatting.)
    b. Drag the fill handle for cell B2 to cell E2. (This inserts *100* in cells C2, D2, and E2.)
    c. Click the Auto Fill Options button that displays at the bottom right of the selected cells.
    d. Click the *Fill Without Formatting* option at the drop-down list.
7. Use the fill handle to apply formatting only by completing the following steps:
    a. Make cell B2 active.
    b. Drag the fill handle to cell B5.
    c. Click the Auto Fill Options button and then click *Fill Formatting Only* at the drop-down list.
8. Make cell A10 active and then type **Qtr 1**.
9. Drag the fill handle for cell A10 to cell A13.
10. Save **EL1-C1-P2-FillCells.xlsx**.

Figure 1.9 Project 2a

	A	B	C	D	E	F	G	H
1		January	February	March	April	May	June	
2	Year 1	100	100	100	100	125	125	
3	Year 3	150	150	150	150	175	175	
4	Year 5	200	200	200	150	150	150	
5	Year 7	250	250	250	250	250	250	
6								
7								
8								
9								
10	Qtr 1	$5,500	$6,250	$7,000	$8,500	$5,500	$4,500	
11	Qtr 2	$6,000	$7,250	$6,500	$9,000	$4,000	$5,000	
12	Qtr 3	$4,500	$8,000	$6,000	$7,500	$6,000	$5,000	
13	Qtr 4	$6,500	$8,500	$7,000	$8,000	$5,500	$6,000	
14								

Inserting Formulas

Excel is a powerful decision-making tool you can use to manipulate data to answer "what if" situations. Insert a formula in a worksheet and then manipulate the data to make projections, answer specific questions, and use as a planning tool. For example, the manager of a department might use an Excel worksheet to prepare a department budget and then determine the impact on the budget of hiring a new employee or increasing the volume of production.

Insert a *formula* in a worksheet to perform calculations on values. A formula contains a mathematical operator, value, cell reference, cell range, and a function. Formulas can be written that add, subtract, multiply, and/or divide values. Formulas can also be written that calculate averages, percentages, minimum and maximum values, and much more. Excel includes an AutoSum button in the Editing group in the Home tab that inserts a formula to calculate the total of a range of cells.

Using the AutoSum Button to Add Numbers

You can use the AutoSum button in the Editing group in the Home tab to insert a formula. The AutoSum button adds numbers automatically with the SUM function. Make active the cell in which you want to insert the formula (this cell should be empty) and then click the AutoSum button. Excel looks for a range of cells containing numbers above the active cell. If no cell above contains numbers, then Excel looks to the left of the active cell. Excel suggests the range of cells to be added. If the suggested range is not correct, drag through the desired range of cells with the mouse, and then press Enter. You can also just double-click the AutoSum button and this will insert the SUM function with the range Excel chooses.

▼ Quick Steps

Insert Formula Using Sum Button
1. Click in desired cell.
2. Click AutoSum button.
3. Check range identified and make changes if necessary.
4. Press Enter.

HINT
You can use the keyboard command Alt + = to insert the SUM function in the cell.

AutoSum

Chapter 1 ■ Preparing an Excel Workbook 17

 **Adding Values with the AutoSum Button**   Part 2 of 3

1. With **EL1-C1-P2-FillCells.xlsx** open, make cell A6 active and then type Total.
2. Make cell B6 active and then calculate the sum of cells by clicking the AutoSum button in the Editing group in the Home tab.
3. Excel inserts the formula *=SUM(B2:B5)* in cell B6. This is the correct range of cells, so press Enter.

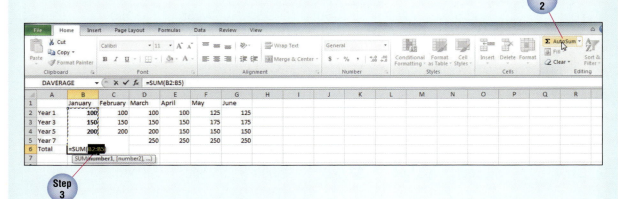

4. Make cell C6 active and then click the AutoSum button in the Editing group.
5. Excel inserts the formula *=SUM(C2:C5)* in cell C6. This is the correct range of cells, so press Enter.
6. Make cell D6 active.
7. Double-click the AutoSum button. [This inserts the formula *=SUM(D2:D5)* in cell D6 and inserts the sum *700*.]
8. Insert the sum in cells E6, F6, and G6.
9. Save **EL1-C1-P2-FillCells**.

Using the AutoSum Button to Average Numbers

▼ **Quick Steps**

Insert Average Formula Using Sum Button
1. Click in desired cell.
2. Click AutoSum button arrow.
3. Click *Average*.
4. Specify range.
5. Press Enter.

Copy Formula Using Fill Handle
1. Insert formula in cell.
2. Make active the cell containing formula.
3. Using fill handle, drag through cells you want to contain formula.

A common function in a formula is the AVERAGE function. With this function, a range of cells is added together and then divided by the number of cell entries. The AVERAGE function is available on the AutoSum button. Click the AutoSum button arrow and a drop-down list displays with a number of common functions.

Using the Fill Handle to Copy a Formula

In a worksheet, you may want to insert the same basic formula in other cells. In a situation where a formula is copied to other locations in a worksheet, use a ***relative cell reference***. Copy a formula containing relative cell references and the cell references change. For example, if you enter the formula *=SUM(A2:C2)* in cell D2 and then copy it relatively to cell D3, the formula in cell D3 displays as *=SUM(A3:C3)*. You can use the fill handle to copy a formula relatively in a worksheet. To do this, position the mouse pointer on the fill handle until the mouse pointer turns into a thin black cross, hold down the left mouse button, drag and select the desired cells, and then release the mouse button.

Project 2c Inserting the AVERAGE Function and Copying a Formula Relatively   Part 3 of 3

1. With **EL1-C1-P2-FillCells.xlsx** open, make cell A14 active, and then type *Average*.
2. Insert the average of cells B10 through B13 by completing the following steps:
    a. Make cell B14 active.
    b. Click the AutoSum button arrow in the Editing group and then click *Average* at the drop-down list.
    c. Excel inserts the formula *=AVERAGE(B10:B13)* in cell B14. This is the correct range of cells, so press Enter.
3. Copy the formula relatively to cells C14 through G14 by completing the following steps:
    a. Make cell B14 active.
    b. Position the mouse pointer on the fill handle, hold down the left mouse button, drag across to cell G14, and then release the mouse button.

	A	B	C	D	E	F	G
9							
10	Qtr 1	$5,500	$6,250	$7,000	$8,500	$5,500	$4,500
11	Qtr 2	$6,000	$7,250	$6,500	$9,000	$4,000	$5,000
12	Qtr 3	$4,500	$8,000	$6,000	$7,500	$6,000	$5,000
13	Qtr 4	$6,500	$8,500	$7,000	$8,000	$5,500	$6,000
14	Average	$5,625	$7,500	$6,625	$8,250	$5,250	$5,125
15							
16							

4. Save, print, and then close **EL1-C1-P2-FillCells.xlsx**.

Project 3 Format a Worksheet   2 Parts

You will open a monthly expenses workbook and then change column width, merge and center cells, and apply number formatting to numbers in cells.

Selecting Cells

You can use a variety of methods for formatting cells in a worksheet. For example, you can change the alignment of data in cells or rows or add character formatting. To identify the cells that are to be affected by the formatting, select the specific cells.

Selecting Cells Using the Mouse

Select specific cells in a worksheet using the mouse or select columns or rows. Table 1.4 displays the methods for selecting cells using the mouse.

Selected cells, except the active cell, display with a light blue background (this may vary) rather than a white background. The active cell is the first cell in the selection block and displays in the normal manner (white background with black data). Selected cells remain selected until you click a cell with the mouse or press an arrow key on the keyboard.

HINT The first cell in a range displays with a white background and is the active cell.

Table 1.4 Selecting with the Mouse

To select this	Do this
Column	Position the cell pointer on the column header (a letter) and then click the left mouse button.
Row	Position the cell pointer on the row header (a number) and then click the left mouse button.
Adjacent cells	Drag with mouse to select specific cells.
Nonadjacent cells	Hold down the Ctrl key while clicking column header, row header, or specific cells.
All cells in worksheet	Click Select All button (refer to Figure 1.2).

Selecting Cells Using the Keyboard

You can use the keyboard to select specific cells within a worksheet. Table 1.5 displays the commands for selecting specific cells. If a worksheet contains data, the last entry in Table 1.5 will select the cells containing data. If the worksheet contains groups of data separated by empty cells, Ctrl + A or Ctrl + Shift + spacebar will select a group of cells rather than all of the cells.

Selecting Data within Cells

Select nonadjacent columns or rows by holding down the Ctrl key while selecting cells.

The selection commands presented select the entire cell. You can also select specific characters within a cell. To do this with the mouse, position the cell pointer in the desired cell, and then double-click the left mouse button. Drag with the I-beam pointer through the data you want selected. Data selected within a cell displays in white with a black background. If you are using the keyboard to select data in a cell, hold down the Shift key, and then press the arrow key that moves the insertion point in the desired direction. Data the insertion point passes through will be selected. You can also press F8 to turn on the Extend Selection mode, move the insertion point in the desired direction to select the data, and then press F8 to turn off the Extend Selection mode. When the Extend Selection mode is on, the words *Extend Selection* display toward the left side of the Status bar.

Table 1.5 Selecting Cells Using the Keyboard

To select	Press
Cells in direction of arrow key	Shift + arrow key
From active cell to beginning of row	Shift + Home
From active cell to beginning of worksheet	Shift + Ctrl + Home
From active cell to last cell in worksheet containing data	Shift + Ctrl + End
An entire column	Ctrl + spacebar
An entire row	Shift + spacebar
An entire worksheet	Ctrl + A

Applying Basic Formatting

Excel provides a wide range of formatting options you can apply to cells in a worksheet. Some basic formatting options that are helpful when creating a worksheet include changing column width, merging and centering cells, and formatting numbers.

Changing Column Width

If data such as text or numbers overlaps in a cell, you can increase the width of the column to accommodate the data. To do this, position the mouse pointer on the blue boundary line between columns in the column header (Figure 1.2 identifies the column header) until the pointer turns into a double-headed arrow pointing left and right and then drag the boundary to the desired location. If the column contains data, you can double-click the column boundary at the right side of the column and the column will increase in size to accommodate the longest entry.

Merging and Centering Cells

As you learned earlier in this chapter, if text you type is longer than the cell can accommodate, the text overlaps the next cell to the right. You can merge cells to accommodate the text and also center the text within the merged cells. To merge cells and center text, select the desired cells and then click the Merge & Center button located in the Alignment group in the Home tab.

▼ Quick Steps

Change Column Width
Drag column boundary line.
OR
Double-click column boundary.

Merge and Center Cells
1. Select cells.
2. Click Merge & Center button.

Merge & Center

Project 3a   Changing Column Width and Merging and Centering Cells   Part 1 of 2

1. Open **MoExps.xlsx** from the Excel2010L1C1 folder on your storage medium.
2. Save the workbook with Save As and name it **EL1-C1-P3-MoExps**.
3. Change column width by completing the following steps:
   a. Position the mouse pointer in the column header on the boundary line between columns A and B until the pointer turns into a double-headed arrow pointing left and right.

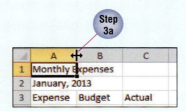
Step 3a

   b. Double-click the left mouse button.
   c. Position the mouse pointer in the column header on the boundary line between columns E and F and then double-click the left mouse button.
   d. Position the mouse pointer in the column header on the boundary line between columns F and G and then double-click the left mouse button.

Chapter 1 ■ Preparing an Excel Workbook   21

4. Merge and center cells by completing the following steps:
   a. Select cells A1 through C1.
   b. Click the Merge & Center button in the Alignment group in the Home tab.
   c. Select cells A2 through C2.
   d. Click the Merge & Center button.
   e. Select cells E1 and F1 and then click the Merge & Center button.
5. Save **EL1-C1-P3-MoExps.xlsx**.

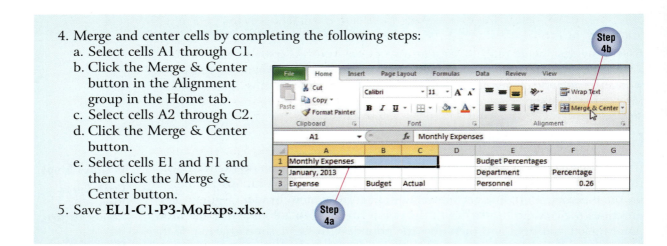

Formatting Numbers

Numbers in a cell, by default, are aligned at the right and decimals and commas do not display unless they are typed in the cell. You can change the format of numbers with buttons in the Number group in the Home tab. Symbols you can use to format numbers include a percent sign (%), a comma (,), and a dollar sign ($). For example, if you type the number *$45.50* in a cell, Excel automatically applies Currency formatting to the number. If you type *45%*, Excel automatically applies the Percent formatting to the number. The Number group in the Home tab contains five buttons you can use to format numbers in cells. The five buttons are shown and described in Table 1.6.

Table 1.6 Number Formatting Buttons

	Click this button	To do this
$ ▼	Accounting Number Format	Add a dollar sign, any necessary commas, and a decimal point followed by two decimal digits, if none are typed; right-align number in cell
%	Percent Style	Multiply cell value by 100 and display result with a percent symbol; right-align number in cell
,	Comma Style	Add any necessary commas and a decimal point followed by two decimal digits, if none are typed; right-align number in cell
←.0 .00	Increase Decimal	Increase number of decimal places displayed after decimal point in selected cell
.00 →.0	Decrease Decimal	Decrease number of decimal places displayed after decimal point in selected cell

Specify the formatting for numbers in cells in a worksheet before typing the numbers, or format existing numbers in a worksheet. The Increase Decimal and Decrease Decimal buttons in the Number group in the Home tab will change decimal places for existing numbers only. The Number group in the Home tab also contains the Number Format button. Click the Number Format button arrow and a drop-down list displays of common number formats. Click the desired format at the drop-down list to apply the number formatting to the cell or selected cells.

A general guideline in accounting is to insert a dollar sign before the first number amount in a column and before the total number amount but not before the number amounts in between. You can format a worksheet following this guideline by applying the Accounting Number Format to the first amount and total amount and apply the Comma Style formatting to the number amounts in between.

Project 3b Formatting Numbers   Part 2 of 2

1. With **EL1-C1-P3-MoExps.xlsx** open, make cell B13 active and then double-click the AutoSum button. (This inserts the total of the numbers in cells B4 through B12.)
2. Make cell C13 active and then double-click the AutoSum button.
3. Apply Accounting Number Format to cells by completing the following steps:
    a. Select cells B4 and C4.
    b. Click the Accounting Number Format button in the Number group in the Home tab.
    c. Decrease the decimals by clicking twice on the Decrease Decimal button in the Number group.

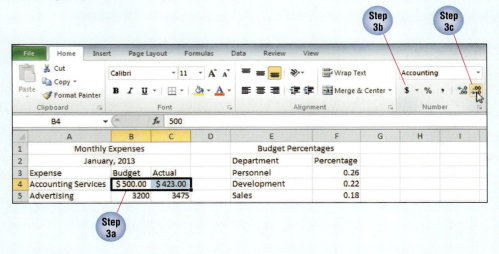

   d. Select cells B13 and C13.
   e. Click the Accounting Number Format button.
   f. Click twice on the Decrease Decimal button.

4. Apply Comma Style formatting to numbers by completing the following steps:
   a. Select cells B5 through C12.
   b. Click the Comma Style button in the Number group.
   c. Click twice on the Decrease Decimal button.

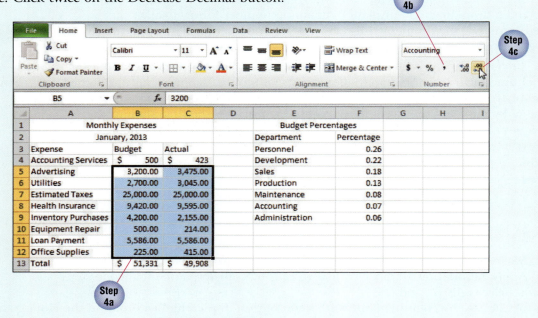

5. Apply Percent Style formatting to numbers by completing the following steps:
   a. Select cells F3 through F9.
   b. Click the Percent Style button in the Number group in the Home tab.
6. Click in cell A1.
7. Save, print, and then close **EL1-C1-P3-MoExps.xlsx**.

Project 4   Use the Help Feature   3 Parts

You will use the Help feature to learn more about entering data in cells and saving a workbook and use the ScreenTip to display information about a specific button. You will also learn about options available at the Help tab Backstage view and how to customize Help to search for information offline.

Using Help

▼ Quick Steps

Use the Help Feature
1. Click Microsoft Excel Help button.
2. Type topic or feature.
3. Press Enter.
4. Click desired topic.

Microsoft Excel includes a Help feature that contains information about Excel features and commands. This on-screen reference manual is similar to Windows Help and the Help features in Word, PowerPoint, and Access. Click the Microsoft Excel Help button (the circle with the question mark) located in the upper right corner of the screen or press the keyboard shortcut F1 to display the Excel Help window. In this window, type a topic, feature, or question in the search text box and then press the Enter key. Topics related to the search text display in the Excel Help window. Click a topic that interests you. If the topic window contains a

Show All hyperlink in the upper right corner, click this hyperlink and the topic options expand to show additional help information related to the topic. When you click the Show All hyperlink, it becomes the Hide All hyperlink.

Help

Getting Help at the Help Tab Backstage View

The Help tab Backstage view, shown in Figure 1.10, contains an option for displaying the Excel Help window as well as other options. Click the Microsoft Office Help button in the Support category to display the Excel Help window and click the Getting Started button to access the Microsoft website that displays information about getting started with Excel 2010. Click the Contact Us button in the Support category and the Microsoft Support website displays. Click the Options button in the Tools for Working With Office category and the Excel Options dialog box displays. You will learn about this dialog box in a later chapter. Click the Check for Updates button and the Microsoft Update website displays with information on available updates. The right side of the Help tab Backstage view displays information about Office and Excel.

▼ **Quick Steps**

Display Help Tab Backstage View
1. Click File tab.
2. Click Help button.

Getting Help on a Button

When you position the mouse pointer on a button, a ScreenTip displays with information about the button. Some button ScreenTips display with the message "Press F1 for more help" that is preceded by an image of the Help button. With the ScreenTip visible, press the F1 function key on your keyboard and the Excel Help window opens and displays information about the specific button.

Figure 1.10 Help Tab Backstage View

Project 4a Using the Help Feature   Part 1 of 3

1. At the blank screen, press Ctrl + N to display a blank workbook. (Ctrl + N is the keyboard command to open a blank workbook.)
2. Click the Microsoft Excel Help button located in the upper right corner of the screen.

3. At the Excel Help window, type **enter data** in the search text box and then press the Enter key. (Make sure that *Connected to Office.com* displays in the lower right corner of the window. If not, click the Search button arrow and then click *Content from Office.com* at the drop-down list.)
4. When the list of topics displays, click the Enter data manually in worksheet cells hyperlink.
5. Read the information about entering data in cells. (If you want a printing of the information, you can click the Print button located toward the top of the Excel Help window and then click the Print button at the Print dialog box.)

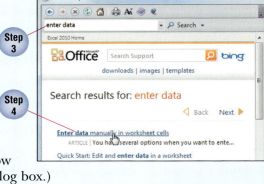

6. Close the Excel Help window by clicking the Close button located in the upper right corner of the window.
7. Click the File tab and then click the Help tab.
8. At the Help tab Backstage view, click the Getting Started button in the Support category. (You must be connected to the Internet to display the web page.)
9. Look at the information that displays at the website and then click the Close button located in the upper right corner of the web page.

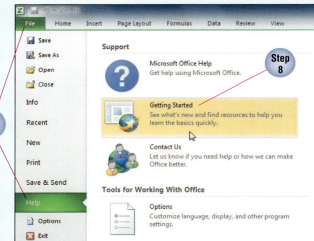

10. Click the File tab and then click the Help tab.
11. Click the Contact Us button, look at the information that displays at the website, and then close the web page.
12. Hover the mouse pointer over the Wrap Text button in the Alignment group in the Home tab until the ScreenTip displays and then press F1.
13. At the Excel Help window, read the information that displays and then close the window.

Getting Help in a Dialog Box or Backstage View

Some dialog boxes, as well as the Backstage view, contain a Help button you can click to display a help window with specific information about the dialog box or Backstage view. After reading and/or printing the information, close a dialog box by clicking the Close button located in the upper right corner of the dialog box or close the Backstage view by clicking the File tab or clicking any other tab in the ribbon.

Project 4b — Getting Help in a Dialog Box and Backstage View — Part 2 of 3

1. At the blank workbook, click the File tab and then click the Save As button.
2. At the Save As dialog box, click the Help button located near the upper right corner of the dialog box.
3. Read the information about saving files that displays in the Windows Help and Support window.
4. Close the window by clicking the Close button located in the upper right corner of the window.
5. Close the Save As dialog box.
6. Click the File tab.
7. At the Backstage view, click the Help button located near the upper right corner of the window.
8. At the Excel Help window, click a hyperlink that interests you.
9. Read the information and then close the Excel Help window by clicking the Close button located in the upper right corner of the window.
10. Click the File tab to return to the blank workbook.

Step 2

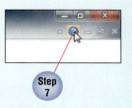

Step 7

Customizing Help

By default, the Excel Help feature will search for an Internet connection and, if one is found, display help resources from Office Online. If you are connected online to help resources, the message "Connected to Office.com" displays in the lower right corner of the Excel Help window. If you are not connected to the Internet, the message displays as "Offline."

Office Online provides additional help resources such as training and templates. To view the resources, display the Excel Help window and then click the down-pointing arrow at the right side of the Search button. This displays a drop-down list similar to the one shown in Figure 1.11. Generally, the *All Excel* option in the *Content from Office.com* section is selected. If you want to search only the Help resources available with your computer (offline), click the *Excel Help* option in the *Content from this computer* section. To access Office.com training, click the *Excel Training* option in the *Content from Office.com* section, type a training topic in the search text box, and then click OK.

Figure 1.11 Excel Help Search Drop-down List

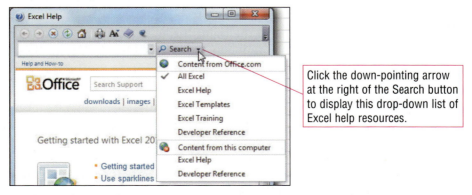

Click the down-pointing arrow at the right of the Search button to display this drop-down list of Excel help resources.

Chapter 1 ■ Preparing an Excel Workbook

Project 4c   **Customizing Help**   Part 3 of 3

1. At a blank worksheet, click the Microsoft Excel Help button located toward the upper right corner of the screen.
2. Click the down-pointing arrow at the right side of the Search button in the Excel Help window.
3. At the drop-down list that displays, click *Excel Help* in the *Content from this computer* section.
4. Click in the search text box, type **formulas**, and then press Enter.
5. Click a hyperlink that interests you and then read the information that displays.
6. Click the down-pointing arrow at the right side of the Search button and then click *Excel Training* in the *Content from Office.com* section.
7. Click in the search text box (this will select *FORMULAS*) and then press Enter.
8. Click the hyperlink of a training about formulas that interests you.
9. After completing the training, close Internet Explorer and then close the Excel Help window.

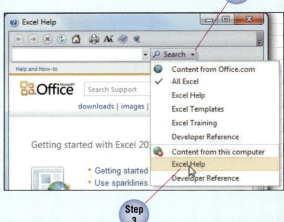

Chapter Summary

- A file created in Excel is called a workbook, which consists of individual worksheets. The intersection of columns and rows is referred to as a cell. Gridlines are the horizontal and vertical lines that define cells.
- An Excel window contains the following elements: Quick Access toolbar, File tab, Title bar, tabs, ribbon, Name box, Formula bar, scroll bars, sheet tabs, and Status bar.
- When the insertion point is positioned in a cell, the cell name (also called the cell reference) displays in the Name box located at the left side of the Formula bar. The cell name includes the column letter and row number.
- If data entered in a cell consists of text (letters) and it does not fit into the cell, it overlaps the cell to the right. If the data consists of numbers and it does not fit into the cell, the numbers are changed to number symbols (###).
- Save a workbook by clicking the Save button on the Quick Access toolbar or by clicking the File tab and then clicking the Save button.
- To replace data in a cell, click the cell once and then type the new data. To edit data within a cell, double-click the cell and then make necessary changes.
- Print a workbook by clicking the File tab, clicking the Print tab, and then clicking the Print button.

- Close a workbook by clicking the Close Window button located in the upper right corner of the screen or by clicking the File tab and then clicking the Close button.
- Exit Excel by clicking the Close button located in the upper right corner of the screen or by clicking the File tab and then clicking the Exit button.
- The AutoComplete feature will automatically insert a previous entry if the character or characters being typed in a cell match a previous entry. The AutoCorrect feature corrects many common typographical errors. Use the AutoFill fill handle to fill a range of cells with the same or consecutive data.
- Open a workbook by clicking the File tab and then clicking the Open button. At the Open dialog box, double-click the desired workbook.
- Use the AutoSum button in the Editing group in the Home tab to find the total or average of data in columns or rows.
- Select all cells in a column by clicking the column header. Select all cells in a row by clicking the row header. Select all cells in a worksheet by clicking the Select All button located immediately to the left of the column headers.
- Change column width by dragging the column boundary or double-clicking the column boundary.
- Merge and center cells by selecting the desired cells and then clicking the Merge & Center button in the Alignment group in the Home tab.
- Format numbers in cells with buttons in the Number group in the Home tab.
- Click the Microsoft Excel Help button or press F1 to display the Excel Help window. At this window, type a topic in the search text box and then press Enter.
- Some dialog boxes as well as the Backstage view contain a Help button you can click to display information specific to the dialog box or Backstage view.
- The ScreenTip for some buttons displays with a message telling you to press F1. Press F1 and the Excel Help window opens with information about the button.

Commands Review

FEATURE	RIBBON TAB, GROUP	BUTTON	FILE TAB	KEYBOARD SHORTCUT
Close workbook			Close	Ctrl + F4
Exit Excel			Exit	
Go To dialog box	Home, Editing			Ctrl + G
Excel Help window				F1
Open workbook			Open	Ctrl + O
Print tab Backstage view			Print	
Save workbook			Save	Ctrl + S

FEATURE	RIBBON TAB, GROUP	BUTTON	FILE TAB	KEYBOARD SHORTCUT
AutoSum button	Home, Editing	Σ		Alt + =
Merge & Center	Home, Alignment			
Accounting Number Format	Home, Number	$		
Comma Style	Home, Number	,		
Percent Style	Home, Number	%		Ctrl + Shift + %
Increase Decimal	Home, Number			
Decrease Decimal	Home, Number			

Concepts Check Test Your Knowledge

Completion: In the space provided at the right, indicate the correct term, symbol, or command.

1. The horizontal and vertical lines that define the cells in a worksheet area are referred to as this.

2. Columns in a worksheet are labeled with these.

3. Rows in a worksheet are labeled with these.

4. Press this key on the keyboard to move the insertion point to the next cell.

5. Press these keys on the keyboard to move the insertion point to the previous cell.

6. Data being typed in a cell displays in the cell as well as here.

7. If a number entered in a cell is too long to fit inside the cell, the number is changed to this.

8. This feature will automatically insert words, numbers, or formulas in a series.

9. This is the name of the small black square that displays in the bottom right corner of the active cell.

10. Use this button in the Editing group in the Home tab to insert a formula in a cell.

11. With this function, a range of cells is added together and then divided by the number of cell entries. _____

12. To select nonadjacent columns using the mouse, hold down this key on the keyboard while clicking the column headers. _____

13. Click this button in the worksheet area to select all of the cells in the table. _____

14. Click this button to merge selected cells and center data within the merged cells. _____

15. The Accounting Number Format button is located in this group in the Home tab. _____

16. Press this function key to display the Excel Help window. _____

Skills Check Assess Your Performance

Assessment

1 CREATE A WORKSHEET USING AUTOCOMPLETE

1. Create the worksheet shown in Figure 1.12 with the following specifications:
   a. To create the © symbols in cell A1, type (c).
   b. Type the misspelled words as shown and let the AutoCorrect feature correct the spelling. Use the AutoComplete feature to insert the second occurrence of *Category, Available,* and *Balance*.
   c. Merge and center cells A1 and B1.
2. Save the workbook and name it **EL1-C1-A1-Plan**.
3. Print and then close **EL1-C1-A1-Plan.xlsx**.

Figure 1.12 Assessment 1

	A	B	C
1	Premiere Plan©		
2	Plan A	Catagory	
3		Availalbe	
4		Balence	
5	Plan B	Category	
6		Available	
7		Balance	
8			

Assessment 2 CREATE AND FORMAT A WORKSHEET

1. Create the worksheet shown in Figure 1.13 with the following specifications:
   a. Merge and center cells A1 through C1.
   b. After typing the data, automatically adjust the width of column A.
   c. Insert in cell B8 the sum of cells B3 through B7 and insert in cell C8 the sum of cells C3 through C7.
   d. Apply the Accounting Number Format style and decrease the decimal point by two positions to cells B3, C3, B8, and C8.
   e. Apply the Comma Style and decrease the decimal point two times to cells B4 through C7.
   f. If any of the number amounts displays as number symbols (###), automatically adjust the width of the appropriate columns.
2. Save the workbook and name it **EL1-C1-A2-Exp**.
3. Print and then close **EL1-C1-A2-Exp.xlsx**.

Figure 1.13 Assessment 2

	A	B	C	D
1	Construction Project			
2	Expense	Original	Current	
3	Material	$129,000	$153,000	
4	Labor	97,000	98,500	
5	Equipmental rental	14,500	11,750	
6	Permits	1,200	1,350	
7	Tax	1,950	2,145	
8	Total	$243,650	$266,745	
9				

Assessment 3 CREATE A WORKSHEET USING THE FILL HANDLE

1. Type the worksheet data shown in Figure 1.14 with the following specifications:
   a. Type **Monday** in cell B2 and then use the fill handle to fill in the remaining days of the week.
   b. Type **350** in cell B3 and then use the fill handle to fill in the remaining numbers in the row.
   c. Merge and center cells A1 through G1.
2. Insert in cell G3 the sum of cells B3 through F3 and insert in cell G4 the sum of cells B4 through F4.
3. After typing the data, select cells B3 through G4 and then change to the accounting number format with two decimal points.
4. If necessary, adjust column widths.
5. Save the workbook and name it **EL1-C1-A3-Invest**.
6. Print and then close **EL1-C1-A3-Invest.xlsx**.

Figure 1.14 Assessment 3

	A	B	C	D	E	F	G	H
1		CAPITAL INVESTMENTS						
2		Monday	Tuesday	Wednesday	Thursday	Friday	Total	
3	Budget	350	350	350	350	350		
4	Actual	310	425	290	375	400		
5								

Assessment

4 INSERT FORMULAS IN A WORKSHEET

1. Open **DIAnalysis.xlsx** and then save the workbook with Save As and name it **EL1-C1-A4-DIAnalysis**.
2. Insert a formula in cell B15 that totals the amounts in cells B4 through B14.
3. Use the fill handle to copy relatively the formula in cell B15 to cell C15.
4. Insert a formula in cell D4 that finds the average of cells B4 and C4.
5. Use the fill handle to copy relatively the formula in cell D4 down to cells D5 through D14.
6. Select cells D5 through D14 and then apply the Comma Style with zero decimals.
7. Save, print, and then close **EL1-C1-A4-DIAnalysis.xlsx**.

Visual Benchmark Demonstrate Your Proficiency

CREATE, FORMAT, AND INSERT FORMULAS IN A WORKSHEET

1. At a blank workbook, create the worksheet shown in Figure 1.15 with the following specifications:
   a. Type the data in cells as shown in the figure. Use the fill handle when appropriate, merge and center the text *Personal Expenses – July through December*, and automatically adjust column widths.
   b. Insert formulas to determine averages and totals.
   c. Apply the Accounting Number Format style with zero decimal places to the amounts in cells B4 through H4 and cells B12 through H12.
   d. Apply the Comma Style with zero decimals to the amounts in cells B5 through G11.
2. Save the workbook and name it **EL1-C1-VB-PersExps**.
3. Print and then close **EL1-C1-VB-PersExps.xlsx**.

Figure 1.15 Visual Benchmark

	A	B	C	D	E	F	G	H	I
1									
2				Personal Expenses - July through December					
3	Expense	July	August	September	October	November	December	Average	
4	Rent	$ 850	$ 850	$ 850	$ 850	$ 850	$ 850		
5	Rental Insurance	55	55	55	55	55	55		
6	Health Insurance	120	120	120	120	120	120		
7	Electricity	129	135	110	151	168	173		
8	Utilities	53	62	49	32	55	61		
9	Telephone	73	81	67	80	82	75		
10	Groceries	143	137	126	150	147	173		
11	Gasoline	89	101	86	99	76	116		
12	Total								
13									

Case Study Apply Your Skills

Part 1

You are the office manager for Deering Industries. One of your responsibilities is creating a monthly calendar containing information on staff meetings, training, and due dates for time cards. Open **DICalendar.xlsx** and then insert the following information:

- Insert the text *October, 2012* in cell A2.
- Insert the days of the week (*Sunday*, *Monday*, *Tuesday*, *Wednesday*, *Thursday*, *Friday*, and *Saturday*) in cells A3 through G3. (Use the fill handle to fill in the days of the week and fill without formatting.)
- Insert the number *1* in cell B4, number *2* in cell C4, number *3* in cell D4, number *4* in cell E4, number *5* in cell F4, and number *6* in cell G4.
- Insert in the calendar the remaining numbers of the days (numbers *7* through *13* in cells A6 through G6, numbers *14* through *20* in cells A8 through G8, numbers *21* through *27* in cells A10 through G10, and numbers *28* through *31* in cells A12 through D12). If you use the fill handle, fill without formatting.
- Excel training will be held Thursday, October 4, from 9-11 a.m. Insert this information in cell E5. (Insert the text on two lines by typing **Excel Training**, pressing Alt + Enter to move the insertion point to the next line, and then typing **9-11 a.m.**)
- A staff meeting is held the second and fourth Monday of each month from 9-10 a.m. Insert this information in cell B7 and cell B11.
- Time cards are due the first and third Fridays of the month. Insert in cells F5 and F9 information indicating that time cards are due.
- A production team meeting is scheduled for Tuesday, October 23, from 1-3 p.m. Insert this information in cell C11.

Save the workbook and name it **EL1-C1-CS-DICalendar**. Print and then close the workbook.

Part 2

The manager of the Purchasing Department has asked you to prepare a worksheet containing information on quarterly purchases. Open **DIExpenditures.xlsx** and then insert the data as shown in Figure 1.16. After typing the data, insert in the appropriate cells formulas to calculate averages and totals. Save the workbook and name it **EL1-C1-CS-DIExpenditures**. Print and then close the workbook.

Figure 1.16 Case Study, Part 2

	A	B	C	D	E	F	G
1				DEERING INDUSTRIES			
2			PURCHASING DEPARTMENT - EXPENDITURES				
3	Category					Average	
4	Supplies	$ 645.75	$ 756.25	534.78	$ 78,950.00		
5	Equipment	4,520.55	10,789.35	3,825.00	12,890.72		
6	Furniture	458.94	2,490.72	851.75	743.20		
7	Training	1,000.00	250.00	1,200.00	800.00		
8	Software	249.00	1,574.30	155.45	3,458.70		
9	Total						
10							

Part 3

The manager of the Purchasing Department has asked you to prepare a note to the finances coordinator, Jennifer Strauss. In Word, type a note to Jennifer Strauss explaining that you have prepared an Excel worksheet with the Purchasing Department expenditures. You are including the cells from the worksheet containing the expenditure information. In Excel, open **EL1-C1-CS-DIExpenditures.xlsx**, copy cells A3 through F9, and then paste them in the Word document. Make any corrections to the table so the information is readable. Save the document and name it **EL1-C1-CS-DINotetoJS**. Print and then close the document. Close **EL1-C1-CS-DIExpenditures.xlsx**.

Part 4

You will be ordering copy machines for several departments in the company and decide to research prices. Using the Internet, find three companies that sell copiers and write down information on different copier models. Open **DICopiers.xlsx** and then type the company, model number, and price in the designated cells. Save the completed workbook and name it **EL1-C1-CS-DICopiers**. Print and then close **EL1-C1-CS-DICopiers.xlsx**.

Inserting Formulas in a Worksheet

CHAPTER 2

PERFORMANCE OBJECTIVES

Upon successful completion of Chapter 2, you will be able to:
- Write formulas with mathematical operators
- Type a formula in the Formula bar
- Copy a formula
- Use the Insert Function feature to insert a formula in a cell
- Write formulas with the AVERAGE, MAX, MIN, COUNT, PMT, FV, DATE, NOW, and IF functions
- Create an absolute and mixed cell reference

Excel is a powerful decision-making tool containing data that can be manipulated to answer "what if" situations. Insert a formula in a worksheet and then manipulate the data to make projections, answer specific questions, and use as a planning tool. For example, the owner of a company might prepare a worksheet on production costs and then determine the impact on company revenues if production is increased or decreased.

Insert a formula in a worksheet to perform calculations on values. A formula contains a mathematical operator, value, cell reference, cell range, and a function. Formulas can be written that add, subtract, multiply, and/or divide values. Formulas can also be written that calculate averages, percentages, minimum and maximum values, and much more. As you learned in Chapter 1, Excel includes an AutoSum button in the Editing group in the Home tab that inserts a formula to calculate the total of a range of cells and also includes some commonly used formulas. Along with the AutoSum button, Excel includes a Formulas tab that offers a variety of functions to create formulas. Model answers for this chapter's projects appear on the following pages.

Note: Before beginning the projects, copy to your storage medium the Excel2010L1C2 subfolder from the Excel2010L1 folder on the CD that accompanies this textbook and make Excel2010L1C2 the active folder.

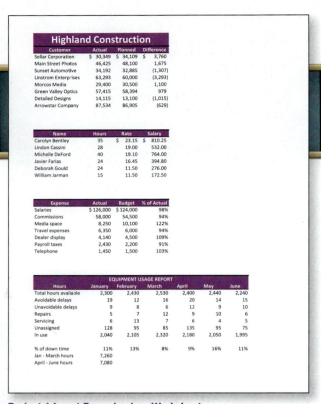

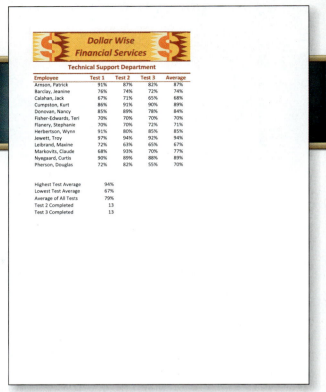

Project 1 Insert Formulas in a Worksheet

EL1-C2-P1-HCReports.xlsx

Project 2 Insert Formulas with Statistical Functions

EL1-C2-P2-DWTests.xlsx

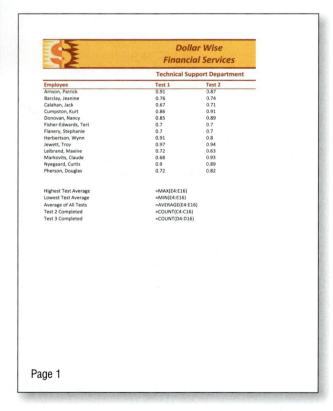

Page 1

Page 2

EL1-C2-P2-DWTests.xlsx, Formulas

EL1-C2-P2-DWTests.xlsx, Formulas

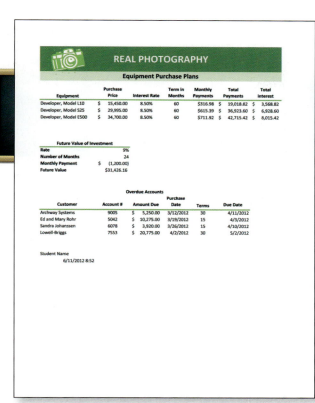

Project 3 Insert Formulas with Financial and Date and Time Functions
EL1-C2-P3-RPReports.xlsx

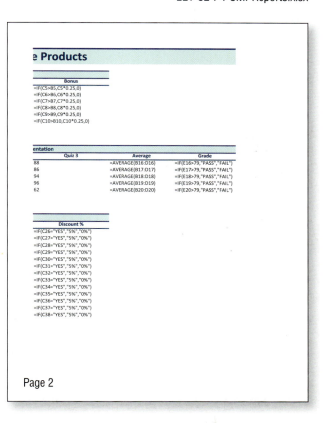

Project 4 Insert Formulas with the IF Logical Function
EL1-C2-P4-CMPReports.xlsx

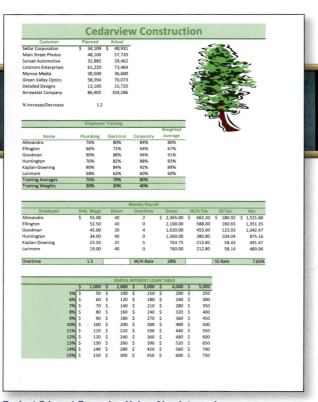

Project 5 Insert Formulas Using Absolute and Mixed Cell References   EL1-C2-P5-CCReports.xlsx

Project 1 — Insert Formulas in a Worksheet   4 Parts

You will open a worksheet containing data and then insert formulas to calculate differences, salaries, and percentages of budgets.

Writing Formulas with Mathematical Operators

After typing a formula in a cell, press the Enter key, the Tab key, Shift + Tab, or click the Enter button on the Formula bar.

As you learned in Chapter 1, the AutoSum button in the Editing group in the Home tab creates the formula for you. You can also write your own formulas using *mathematical operators*. Commonly used mathematical operators and their functions are displayed in Table 2.1. When writing your own formula, begin the formula with the equals sign (=). For example, to create a formula that divides the contents of cell B2 by the contents of cell C2 and inserts the result in cell D2, you would make D2 the active cell and then type =B2/C2.

If a formula contains two or more operators, Excel uses the same order of operations used in algebra. From left to right in a formula, this order, called the *order of operations*, is: negations (negative number — a number preceded by -) first, then percents (%), then exponentiations (^), followed by multiplications (*), divisions (/), additions (+), and finally subtractions (-). If you want to change the order of operations, use parentheses around the part of the formula you want calculated first.

Table 2.1 Mathematical Operators

Operator	Function
+	Addition
-	Subtraction
*	Multiplication
/	Division
%	Percent
^	Exponentiation

Copying a Formula with Relative Cell References

In many worksheets, the same basic formula is used repetitively. In a situation where a formula is copied to other locations in a worksheet, use a *relative cell reference*. Copy a formula containing relative cell references and the cell references change. For example, if you enter the formula *=SUM(A2:C2)* in cell D2 and then copy it relatively to cell D3, the formula in cell D3 displays as *=SUM(A3:C3)*. (Additional information on cell references is discussed later in this chapter in the "Using an Absolute Cell Reference in a Formula" section.)

To copy a formula relatively in a worksheet, use the Fill button or the fill handle. (You used the fill handle to copy a formula in Chapter 1.) To use the Fill button, select the cell containing the formula as well as the cells to which you want the formula copied and then click the Fill button in the Editing group in the Home tab. At the Fill button drop-down list, click the desired direction. For example, if you are copying the formula down cells, click the *Down* option.

▼ **Quick Steps**

Copy Relative Formula
1. Insert formula in cell.
2. Select cell containing formula and all cells you want to contain formula.
3. Click Fill button.
4. Click desired direction.

Fill

Project 1a — Finding Differences by Inserting and Copying a Formula — Part 1 of 4

1. Open **HCReports.xlsx**.
2. Save the workbook with Save As and name it **EL1-C2-P1-HCReports**.
3. Insert a formula by completing the following steps:
   a. Make cell D3 active.
   b. Type the formula **=C3-B3**.
   c. Press Enter.
4. Copy the formula to cells D4 through D10 by completing the following steps:
   a. Select cells D3 through D10.
   b. Click the Fill button in the Editing group in the Home tab and then click *Down* at the drop-down list.
5. Save **EL1-C2-P1-HCReports.xlsx**.
6. With the worksheet open, make the following changes to cell contents:
   B4: Change *48,290* to *46425*
   C6: Change *61,220* to *60000*
   B8: Change *55,309* to *57415*
   B9: Change *12,398* to *14115*

Step 4b

7. Make cell D3 active, apply the Accounting Number Format, and decrease the decimal point by two positions.
8. Save **EL1-C2-P1-HCReports.xlsx**.

Copying Formulas with the Fill Handle

Use the fill handle to copy a relative version of a formula.

Use the fill handle to copy a formula up, down, left, or right within a worksheet. To use the fill handle, insert the desired data in the cell (text, value, formula, etc.). With the cell active, position the mouse pointer on the fill handle until the mouse pointer turns into a thin, black cross. Hold down the left mouse button, drag and select the desired cells, and then release the mouse button. If you are dragging a cell containing a formula, a relative version of the formula is copied to the selected cells.

Project 1b — Calculating Salary by Inserting and Copying a Formula with the Fill Handle

Part 2 of 4

1. With **EL1-C2-P1-HCReports.xlsx** open, insert a formula by completing the following steps:
   a. Make cell D15 active.
   b. Click in the Formula bar text box and then type **=C15*B15**.
   c. Click the Enter button on the Formula bar.
2. Copy the formula to cells D16 through D20 by completing the following steps:
   a. Make sure cell D15 is the active cell.
   b. Position the mouse pointer on the fill handle that displays at the lower right corner of cell D15 until the pointer turns into a thin, black cross.
   c. Hold down the left mouse button, drag down to cell D20, and then release the mouse button.
3. Save **EL1-C2-P1-HCReports.xlsx**.
4. With the worksheet still open, make the following changes to cell contents:
   B16: Change *20* to *28*
   C17: Change *18.75* to *19.10*
   B19: Change *15* to *24*
5. Select cells D16 through D20 and then apply the Comma Style.
6. Save **EL1-C2-P1-HCReports.xlsx**.

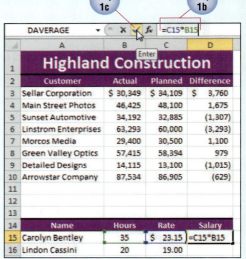

Writing a Formula by Pointing

In Project 1a and Project 1b, you wrote formulas using cell references such as =C3-B3. Another method for writing a formula is to "point" to the specific cells that are to be part of the formula. Creating a formula by pointing is more accurate than typing the cell reference since a mistake can happen when typing the cell reference.

To write a formula by pointing, click the cell that will contain the formula, type the equals sign to begin the formula, and then click the cell you want to reference in the formula. This inserts a moving border around the cell and also changes the mode from Enter to Point. (The word *Point* displays at the left side of the Status bar.) Type the desired mathematical operator and then click the next cell reference. Continue in this manner until all cell references are specified and then press the Enter key. This ends the formula and inserts the result of the calculation of the formula in the active cell. When writing a formula by pointing, you can also select a range of cells you want included in a formula.

▼ **Quick Steps**
Write Formula by Pointing
1. Click cell that will contain formula.
2. Type equals sign.
3. Click cell you want to reference in formula.
4. Type desired mathematical operator.
5. Click next cell reference.

Project 1c — Writing a Formula by Pointing that Calculates Percentage of Actual Budget

Part 3 of 4

1. With **EL1-C2-P1-HCReports.xlsx** open, enter a formula by pointing that calculates the percentage of actual budget by completing the following steps:
   a. Make cell D25 active.
   b. Type the equals sign.
   c. Click cell C25. (This inserts a moving border around the cell and the mode changes from Enter to Point.)
   d. Type the forward slash symbol (/).
   e. Click cell B25.
   f. Make sure the formula in D25 is =C25/B25 and then press Enter.
2. Make cell D25 active, position the mouse pointer on the fill handle, drag down to cell D31, and then release the mouse button.
3. Save **EL1-C2-P1-HCReports.xlsx**.

Using the Trace Error Button

As you are working in a worksheet, you may occasionally notice a button pop up near the active cell. The general term for this button is **smart tag**. The display of the smart tag button varies depending on the action performed. In Project 1d, you will insert a formula that will cause a smart tag button, named the Trace Error button, to appear. When the Trace Error button appears, a small dark green triangle also displays in the upper left corner of the cell. Click the Trace Error button and a drop-down list displays with options for updating the formula to include specific cells, getting help on the error, ignoring the error, editing the error in the Formula bar,

Trace Error

and completing an error check. In Project 1d, two of the formulas you insert return the desired results. You will click the Trace Error button, read information on what Excel perceives as the error, and then tell Excel to ignore the error.

Project 1d Writing a Formula by Pointing that Calculates Percentage of Down Time

Part 4 of 4

1. With **EL1-C2-P1-HCReports.xlsx** open, enter a formula by pointing that computes the percentage of equipment down time by completing the following steps:
   a. Make cell B45 active.
   b. Type the equals sign followed by the left parenthesis (=().
   c. Click cell B37. (This inserts a moving border around the cell and the mode changes from Enter to Point.)
   d. Type the minus symbol (-).
   e. Click cell B43.
   f. Type the right parenthesis followed by the forward slash ()/).
   g. Click cell B37.
   h. Make sure the formula in B45 is =(B37-B43)/B37 and then press Enter.

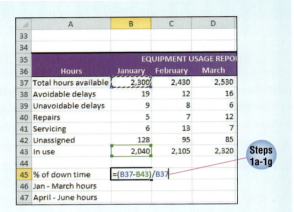

2. Make cell B45 active, position the mouse pointer on the fill handle, drag across to cell G45, and then release the mouse button.
3. Enter a formula by dragging through a range of cells by completing the following steps:
   a. Click in cell B46 and then click the AutoSum button in the Editing group in the Home tab.
   b. Select cells B37 through D37.
   c. Click the Enter button on the Formula bar. (This inserts *7,260* in cell B46.)
4. Click in cell B47 and then complete steps similar to those in Step 3 to create a formula that totals hours available from April through June (cells E37 through G37). (This inserts *7,080* in cell B47.)
5. Click in cell B46 and notice the Trace Error button that displays. Complete the following steps to read about the error and then tell Excel to ignore the error:
   a. Click the Trace Error button.
   b. At the drop-down list that displays, click the *Help on this error* option.
   c. Read the information that displays in the Excel Help window and then close the window.
   d. Click the Trace Error button again and then click *Ignore Error* at the drop-down list.

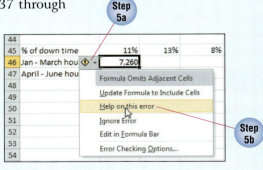

6. Remove the dark green triangle from cell B47 by completing the following steps:
   a. Click in cell B47.
   b. Click the Trace Error button and then click *Ignore Error* at the drop-down list.
7. Save, print, and then close **EL1-C2-P1-HCReports.xlsx**.

 **Insert Formulas with Statistical Functions** **4 Parts**

You will use the AVERAGE function to determine average test scores, use the MINIMUM and MAXIMUM functions to determine lowest and highest averages, use the COUNT function to count number of students taking a test, and display formulas in a cell rather than the result of the formula.

Inserting Formulas with Functions

In Project 2a in Chapter 1, you used the AutoSum button to insert the formula =SUM(B2:B5) in a cell. The beginning section of the formula, =SUM, is called a *function*, which is a built-in formula. Using a function takes fewer keystrokes when creating a formula. For example, the =SUM function saved you from having to type each cell to be included in the formula with the plus (+) symbol between cell entries.

Excel provides other functions for writing formulas. A function operates on what is referred to as an *argument*. An argument may consist of a constant, a cell reference, or another function. In the formula =SUM(B2:B5), the cell range (B2:B5) is an example of a cell reference argument. An argument may also contain a *constant*. A constant is a value entered directly into the formula. For example, if you enter the formula =SUM(B3:B9,100), the cell range B3:B9 is a cell reference argument and *100* is a constant. In this formula, 100 is always added to the sum of the cells.

When a value calculated by the formula is inserted in a cell, this process is referred to as *returning the result*. The term *returning* refers to the process of calculating the formula and the term *result* refers to inserting the value in the cell.

You can type a function in a cell in a worksheet or you can use the Insert Function button on the Formula bar or in the Formulas tab to help you write the formula. Figure 2.1 displays the Formulas tab. The Formulas tab provides the Insert Function button as well as other buttons for inserting functions in a worksheet. The Function Library group in the Formulas tab contains a number of buttons for inserting functions from a variety of categories such as Financial, Logical, Text, and Date & Time.

Insert Function

Click the Insert Function button on the Formula bar or in the Formulas tab and the Insert Function dialog box displays as shown in Figure 2.2. At the

Figure 2.1 Formulas Tab

Figure 2.2 Insert Function Dialog Box

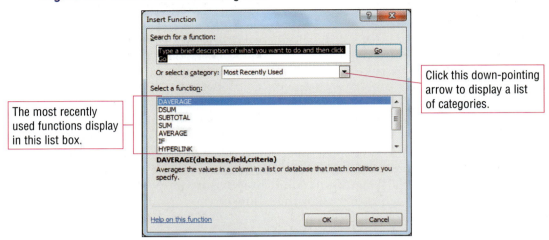

HINT
You can also display the Insert Function dialog box by clicking the down-pointing arrow at the right side of the AutoSum button and then clicking *More Functions*.

HINT
Click the AutoSum button arrow in the Formulas tab and common functions display in a drop-down list.

Insert Function dialog box, the most recently used functions display in the *Select a function* list box. You can choose a function category by clicking the down-pointing arrow at the right side of the *Or select a category* list box and then clicking the desired category at the drop-down list. Use the *Search for a function* option to locate a specific function.

With the desired function category selected, choose a function in the *Select a function* list box and then click OK. This displays a Function Arguments palette like the one shown in Figure 2.3. At this palette, enter in the *Number1* text box the range of cells you want included in the formula, enter any constants that are to be included as part of the formula, or enter another function. After entering a range of cells, a constant, or another function, click the OK button. You can include more than one argument in a function. If the function you are creating contains more than one argument, press the Tab key to move the insertion point to the *Number2* text box, and then enter the second argument. If you need to display a specific cell or cells behind the function palette, move the palette by clicking and dragging it.

Figure 2.3 Example Function Arguments Palette

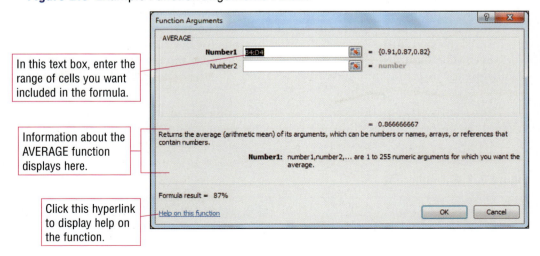

Excel includes over 200 functions that are divided into twelve different categories including *Financial, Date & Time, Math & Trig, Statistical, Lookup & Reference, Database, Text, Logical, Information, Engineering, Cube,* and *Compatibility*. Clicking the AutoSum button in the Function Library group in the Formulas tab or the Editing group in the Home tab automatically adds numbers with the SUM function. The SUM function is included in the *Math & Trig* category. In some projects in this chapter, you will write formulas with functions in other categories including *Statistical, Financial, Date & Time,* and *Logical*.

Excel includes the Formula AutoComplete feature that displays a drop-down list of functions. To use this feature, click in the desired cell or click in the Formula bar text box, type the equals sign (=), and then type the first letter of the desired function. This displays a drop-down list with functions that begin with the letter. Double-click the desired function, enter the cell references, and then press Enter.

Writing Formulas with Statistical Functions

In this section, you will learn to write formulas with the statistical functions AVERAGE, MAX, MIN, and COUNT. The AVERAGE function returns the average (arithmetic mean) of the arguments. The MAX function returns the largest value in a set of values and the MIN function returns the smallest value in a set of values. Use the COUNT function to count the number of cells that contain numbers within the list of arguments.

Finding Averages

A common function in a formula is the AVERAGE function. With this function, a range of cells is added together and then divided by the number of cell entries. In Project 2a you will use the AVERAGE function, which will add all of the test scores for a student and then divide that number by the total number of tests. You will use the Insert Function button to simplify the creation of the formula containing an AVERAGE function.

One of the advantages to using formulas in a worksheet is the ability to easily manipulate data to answer certain questions. In Project 2a you will learn the impact of retaking certain tests on the final average score.

Project 2a — Averaging Test Scores in a Worksheet — Part 1 of 4

1. Open **DWTests.xlsx**.
2. Save the workbook with Save As and name it **EL1-C2-P2-DWTests**.
3. Use the Insert Function button to find the average of test scores by completing the following steps:
    a. Make cell E4 active.
    b. Click the Insert Function button on the Formula bar.

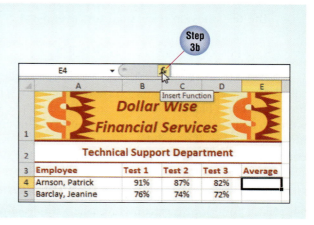

Step 3b

c. At the Insert Function dialog box, click the down-pointing arrow at the right side of the *Or select a category* list box and then click *Statistical* at the drop-down list.
d. Click *AVERAGE* in the *Select a function* list box.
e. Click OK.
f. At the Function Arguments palette, make sure *B4:D4* displays in the *Number1* text box. (If not, type **B4:D4** in the *Number1* text box.)
g. Click OK.

4. Copy the formula by completing the following steps:
   a. Make sure cell E4 is active.
   b. Position the mouse pointer on the fill handle until the pointer turns into a thin black cross.
   c. Hold down the left mouse button, drag down to cell E16, and then release the mouse button.

5. Save and then print **EL1-C2-P2-DWTests.xlsx**.

6. After viewing the averages of test scores, you notice that a couple of people have a low average. You decide to see what happens to the average score if students make up tests where they scored the lowest. You decide that a student can score a maximum of 70% on a retake of the test. Make the following changes to test scores to see how the changes will affect the test average.

   B9: Change *50* to *70*
   C9: Change *52* to *70*
   D9: Change *60* to *70*
   B10: Change *62* to *70*
   B14: Change *0* to *70*
   D14: Change *0* to *70*
   D16: Change *0* to *70*

7. Save and then print **EL1-C2-P2-DWTests.xlsx**. (Compare the test averages for Teri Fisher-Edwards, Stephanie Flanery, Claude Markovits, and Douglas Pherson to see what the effect of retaking the tests has on their final test averages.)

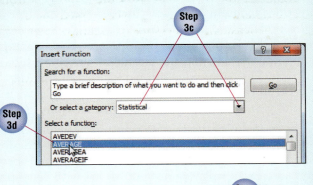
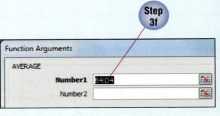
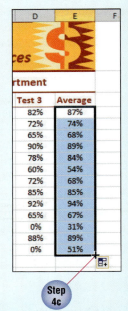

When a formula such as the AVERAGE formula you inserted in a cell in Project 2a calculates cell entries, it ignores certain cell entries. The AVERAGE function will ignore text in cells and blank cells (not zeros). For example, in the worksheet containing test scores, a couple of cells contained a *0%* entry. This entry was included in the averaging of the test scores. If you did not want that particular test to be included in the average, enter text in the cell such as *N/A* (for *not applicable*) or leave the cell blank.

Finding Maximum and Minimum Values

The MAX function in a formula returns the maximum value in a cell range and the MIN function returns the minimum value in a cell range. As an example, you could use the MAX and MIN functions in a worksheet containing employee hours to determine which employee worked the most number of hours and which worked the least. In a worksheet containing sales commissions, you could use the MAX and MIN functions to determine the salesperson who earned the most commission dollars and the one who earned the least.

Insert a MAX and MIN function into a formula in the same manner as an AVERAGE function. In Project 2b, you will use the Formula AutoComplete feature to insert the MAX function in cells to determine the highest test score average and the Insert Function button to insert the MIN function to determine the lowest test score average.

Project 2b Finding Maximum and Minimum Values in a Worksheet   Part 2 of 4

1. With **EL1-C2-P2-DWTests.xlsx** open, type the following in the specified cells:
   A19: Highest Test Average
   A20: Lowest Test Average
   A21: Average of All Tests
2. Insert a formula to identify the highest test score average by completing the following steps:
   a. Make cell B19 active.
   b. Type **=M**. (This displays the Formula AutoComplete list.)
   c. Double-click *MAX* in the Formula AutoComplete list.
   d. Type **E4:E16)** and then press Enter.

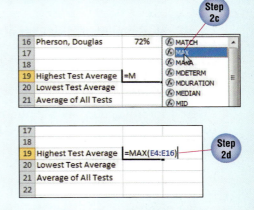

3. Insert a formula to identify the lowest test score average by completing the following steps:
   a. Make cell B20 active.
   b. Click the Insert Function button on the Formula bar.
   c. At the Insert Function dialog box, make sure *Statistical* is selected in the *Or select a category* list box, and then click *MIN* in the *Select a function* list box. (You will need to scroll down the list to display *MIN*.)
   d. Click OK.
   e. At the Function Arguments palette, type **E4:E16** in the *Number1* text box.
   f. Click OK.

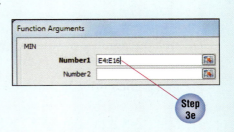

4. Insert a formula to determine the average of all test scores by completing the following steps:
   a. Make cell B21 active.
   b. Click the Formulas tab.
   c. Click the Insert Function button in the Function Library group.
   d. At the Insert Function dialog box, make sure *Statistical* is selected in the *Or select a category* list box and then click *AVERAGE* in the *Select a function* list box.
   e. Click OK.
   f. At the Function Arguments palette, type **E4:E16** in the *Number1* text box, and then click OK.

5. Save and then print **EL1-C2-P2-DWTests.xlsx**.
6. Change the *70%* values (which were previously *0%*) in cells B14, D14, and D16 to *N/A*. (This will cause the average of test scores for Claude Markovits and Douglas Pherson to increase and will change the minimum number and average of all test scores.)
7. Save and then print **EL1-C2-P2-DWTests.xlsx**.

Counting Numbers in a Range

Use the COUNT function to count the numeric values in a range. For example, in a range of cells containing cells with text and cells with numbers, you can count how many cells in the range contain numbers. In Project 2c, you will use the COUNT function to specify the number of students taking Test 2 and Test 3. In the worksheet, the cells containing the text N/A are not counted by the COUNT function.

Project 2c Counting the Number of Students Taking Tests   Part 3 of 4

1. With **EL1-C2-P2-DWTests.xlsx** open, make cell A22 active.
2. Type **Test 2 Completed**.
3. Make cell B22 active.
4. Insert a formula counting the number of students who have taken Test 2 by completing the following steps:
    a. With cell B22 active, click in the Formula bar text box.
    b. Type **=C**.
    c. At the Formula AutoComplete list that displays, scroll down the list until *COUNT* displays and then double-click *COUNT*.
    d. Type **C4:C16)** and then press Enter.

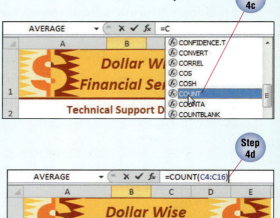

5. Count the number of students who have taken Test 3 by completing the following steps:
    a. Make cell A23 active.
    b. Type **Test 3 Completed**.
    c. Make cell B23 active.
    d. Click the Insert Function button on the Formula bar.
    e. At the Insert Function dialog box, make sure *Statistical* is selected in the *Or select a category* list box.
    f. Scroll down the list of functions in the *Select a function* list box until *COUNT* is visible and then double-click *COUNT*.
    g. At the formula palette, type **D4:D16** in the *Value1* text box and then click OK.
6. Save and then print **EL1-C2-P2-DWTests.xlsx**.
7. Add test scores by completing the following steps:
    a. Make cell B14 active and then type **68**.
    b. Make cell D14 active and then type **70**.
    c. Make cell D16 active and then type **55**.
    d. Press Enter.
8. Save and then print **EL1-C2-P2-DWTests.xlsx**.

Displaying Formulas

In some situations, you may need to display the formulas in a worksheet rather than the results of the formula. You may want to turn on formulas for auditing purposes or check formulas for accuracy. Display all formulas in a worksheet rather than the results by pressing Ctrl + ` (this is the grave accent, generally located to the left of the 1 key on the keyboard). Press Ctrl + ` to turn off the display of formulas.

Press Ctrl + ` to display formulas in a worksheet rather than the results.

 **Displaying Formulas**   Part 4 of 4

1. With **EL1-C2-P2-DWTests.xlsx** open, make cell A3 active.
2. Press Ctrl + ` to turn on the display of formulas.
3. Print the worksheet with the formulas. (The worksheet will print on two pages.)
4. Press Ctrl + ` to turn off the display of formulas.
5. Save and then close **EL1-C2-P2-DWTests.xlsx**.

 **Insert Formulas with Financial and Date and Time Functions**   3 Parts

You will use the PMT financial function to calculate payments and the FV function to find the future value of an investment. You will also use the DATE function to return the serial number for a date and the NOW function to insert the current date and time as a serial number.

Writing Formulas with Financial Functions

In this section, you will learn to write formulas with the financial functions PMT and FV. The PMT function calculates the payment for a loan based on constant payments and a constant interest rate. Use the FV function to return the future value of an investment.

Finding the Periodic Payments for a Loan

The PMT function finds the payment for a loan based on constant payments and a constant interest rate. The PMT function contains the arguments Rate, Nper, Pv, Fv, and Type. The Rate argument is the interest rate per period for a loan, the Nper is the number of payments that will be made to an investment or loan, Pv is the current value of amounts to be received or paid in the future, Fv is the value of a loan or investment at the end of all periods, and Type determines whether calculations will be based on payments made in arrears (at the end of each period) or in advance (at the beginning of each period).

Project 3a Calculating Payments   Part 1 of 3

1. Open **RPReports.xlsx**.
2. Save the workbook with Save As and name it **EL1-C2-P3-RPReports**.
3. The owner of Real Photography is interested in purchasing a new developer and needs to determine monthly payments on three different models. Insert a formula that calculates monthly payments and then copy that formula by completing the following steps:
   a. Make cell E5 active.
   b. Click the Formulas tab.
   c. Click the Financial button in the Function Library group, scroll down the drop-down list until *PMT* displays, and then click *PMT*.

   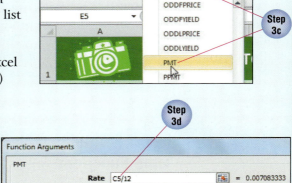

   d. At the Function Arguments palette, type **C5/12** in the *Rate* text box. (This tells Excel to divide the interest rate by 12 months.)
   e. Press the Tab key. (This moves the insertion point to the *Nper* text box.)
   f. Type **D5**. (This is the total number of months in the payment period.)
   g. Press the Tab key. (This moves the insertion point to the *Pv* text box.)
   h. Type **-B5**. (Excel displays the result of the PMT function as a negative number since the loan represents a negative cash flow to the borrower. Insert a minus sign before *B5* to show the monthly payment as a positive number rather than as a negative number.)

   i. Click OK. (This closes the palette and inserts the monthly payment of *$316.98* in cell E5.)
   j. Copy the formula in cell E5 down to cells E6 and E7.
4. Insert a formula in cell F5 that calculates the total amount of the payments by completing the following steps:
   a. Make cell F5 active.
   b. Type **=E5*D5** and then press Enter.
   c. Make cell F5 active and then copy the formula down to cells F6 and F7.
5. Insert a formula in cell G5 that calculates the total amount of interest paid by completing the following steps:
   a. Make cell G5 active.
   b. Type **=F5-B5** and then press Enter.
   c. Make cell G5 active and then copy the formula down to cells G6 and G7.

6. Save **EL1-C2-P3-RPReports.xlsx**.

Finding the Future Value of a Series of Payments

The FV function calculates the future value of a series of equal payments or an annuity. Use this function to determine information such as how much money can be earned in an investment account with a specific interest rate and over a specific period of time.

Project 3b — Finding the Future Value of an Investment — Part 2 of 3

1. Make sure **EL1-C2-P3-RPReports.xlsx** is open.
2. The owner of Real Photography has decided to save money to purchase a new developer and wants to compute how much money can be earned by investing the money in an investment account that returns 9% annual interest. The owner determines that $1,200 per month can be invested in the account for three years. Complete the following steps to determine the future value of the investment account by completing the following steps:
   a. Make cell B15 active.
   b. Click the Financial button in the Function Library group in the Formulas tab.
   c. At the drop-down list that displays, scroll down the list until *FV* is visible and then click *FV*.
   d. At the Function Arguments palette, type **B12/12** in the *Rate* text box.
   e. Press the Tab key.
   f. Type **B13** in the *Nper* text box.
   g. Press the Tab key.
   h. Type **B14** in the *Pmt* text box.
   i. Click OK. (This closes the palette and also inserts the future value of *$49,383.26* in cell B15.)
3. Save and then print **EL1-C2-P3-RPReports.xlsx**.
4. The owner decides to determine the future return after two years. To do this, change the amount in cell B13 from *36* to *24* and then press Enter. (This recalculates the future investment amount in cell B15.)
5. Save and then print **EL1-C2-P3-RPReports.xlsx**.

Writing Formulas with Date and Time Functions

In this section, you will learn to write formulas with the date and time functions NOW and DATE. The NOW function returns the serial number of the current date and time. The DATE function returns the serial number that represents a particular date. Excel can make calculations using dates because the dates are represented as serial numbers. To calculate a date's serial number, Excel counts the days since the beginning of the twentieth century. The date serial number for January 1, 1900, is 1. The date serial number for January 1, 2000, is 36,526. To access the DATE and NOW functions, click the Date & Time button in the Function Library group in the Formulas tab.

HINT
Ctrl + ; is the keyboard shortcut to insert the current date in the active cell.

Date & Time

Project 3c — Using the DATE and NOW Functions — Part 3 of 3

1. Make sure **EL1-C2-P3-RPReports.xlsx** is open.
2. Certain cells in this worksheet establish overdue dates for Real Photography accounts. Enter a formula in cell D20 that returns the serial number for the date March 12, 2012, by completing the following steps:

a. Make cell D20 active.
b. Click the Formulas tab.
c. Click the Date & Time button in the Function Library group.
d. At the drop-down list that displays, click *DATE*.
e. At the Function Arguments palette, type **2012** in the *Year* text box.
f. Press the Tab key and then type **03** in the *Month* text box.
g. Press the Tab key and then type **12** in the *Day* text box.
h. Click OK.

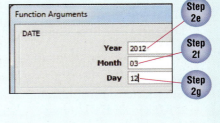

3. Complete steps similar to those in Step 2 to enter the following dates as serial numbers in the specified cells:
   D21 = March 19, 2012
   D22 = March 26, 2012
   D23 = April 2, 2012
4. Enter a formula in cell F20 that inserts the due date (the purchase date plus the number of days in the *Terms* column) by completing the following steps:
   a. Make cell F20 active.
   b. Type **=D20+E20** and then press Enter.
   c. Make cell F20 active and then copy the formula down to cells F21, F22, and F23.

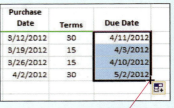

5. Make cell A26 active and then type your name.
6. Insert the current date and time as a serial number by completing the following steps:
   a. Make cell A27 active.
   b. Click the Date & Time button in the Function Library group in the Formulas tab and then click *NOW* at the drop-down list.
   c. At the Function Arguments palette telling you that the function takes no argument, click OK.
7. Save, print, and then close **EL1-C2-P3-RPReports.xlsx**.

Project 4 Insert Formulas with the IF Logical Function   2 Parts

You will use the IF logical function to calculate sales bonuses, determine letter grades based on test averages, and identify discounts and discount amounts.

Writing a Formula with the IF Logical Function

The IF function is considered a **conditional function**. With the IF function you can perform conditional tests on values and formulas. A question that can be answered with true or false is considered a **logical test**. The IF function makes a logical test and then performs a particular action if the answer is true and another action if the answer is false.

For example, an IF function can be used to write a formula that calculates a salesperson's bonus as 10% if the quota of $100,000 is met or exceeded, and zero if the quota is less than $100,000. That formula would look like this: =IF(quota=>100000,quota*0.1,0). The formula contains three parts—the condition or logical test, *IF(quota=>100000*, action taken if the condition or logical test is true, *quota*0.1*, and the action taken if the condition or logical test is false, *0*. Commas separate the condition and the actions. In the bonus formula, if the quota is equal to or greater than $100,000, then the quota is multiplied by 10%. If the quota is less than $100,000, then the bonus is zero.

In Project 4a, you will write a formula with cell references rather than cell data. The formula in Project 4a is *=IF(C5>B5,C5*0.15,0)*. In this formula the condition or logical test is whether or not the number in cell C5 is greater than the number in cell B5. If the condition is true and the number is greater, then the number in cell C5 is multiplied by 0.15 (providing a 15% bonus). If the condition is false and the number in cell C5 is less than the number in cell B5, then nothing happens (no bonus). Notice how commas are used to separate the logical test from the actions.

Editing a Formula

Edit a formula by making active the cell containing the formula and then editing the formula in the cell or in the Formula bar text box. After editing the formula, press Enter or click the Enter button on the Formula bar and Excel will recalculate the result of the formula.

Enter

Project 4a Writing a Formula with an IF Function and Editing the Formula   Part 1 of 2

1. Open **CMPReports.xlsx**.
2. Save the workbook with Save As and name it **EL1-C2-P4-CMPReports**.
3. Write a formula with the IF function by completing the following steps. (The formula will determine if the quota has been met and, if it has, will insert the bonus [15% of the actual sales]. If the quota has not been met, the formula will insert a zero.)
    a. Make cell D5 active.
    b. Type **=IF(C5>B5,C5*0.15,0)** and then press Enter.
    c. Make cell D5 active and then use the fill handle to copy the formula to cells D6 through D10.
4. Print the worksheet.
5. Revise the formula so it will insert a 25% bonus if the quota has been met by completing the following steps:
    a. Make cell D5 active.
    b. Click in the Formula bar, edit the formula so it displays as **=IF(C5>B5,C5*0.25,0)**, and then click the Enter button on the Formula bar.
    c. Copy the formula down to cells D6 through D10.
    d. Apply the Accounting Number Format to cell D5.
6. Save **EL1-C2-P4-CMPReports.xlsx**.

Step 3c

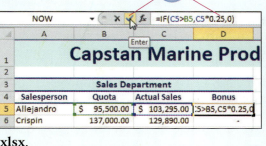

Step 5b

Step 5c

Writing IF Formulas Containing Text

If you write a formula with an IF function and you want text inserted in a cell rather than a value, you must insert quotation marks around the text. For example, in Project 4b, you will write a formula with an IF function that inserts the word *PASS* in a cell if the average of the new employee quizzes is greater than 79 and inserts the word *FAIL* if the condition is not met. To write this formula in Project 4b, you will type **=IF(E16>79,"PASS","FAIL")**. The quotation marks before and after PASS and FAIL identify the data as text rather than a value.

Project 4b — Writing IF Statements with Text — Part 2 of 2

1. With **EL1-C2-P4-CMPReports.xlsx** open, insert quiz averages by completing the following steps:
   a. Make E16 active and then insert a formula that calculates the average of the test scores in cells B16 through D16.
   b. Copy the formula in cell E16 down to cells E17 through E20.
2. Write a formula with an IF function that inserts the word *PASS* if the quiz average is greater than 79 and inserts the word *FAIL* if the quiz average is not greater than 79 by completing the following steps:
   a. Make cell F16 active.
   b. Type **=IF(E16>79,"PASS","FAIL")** and then press Enter.
   c. Copy the formula in cell F16 down to cells F17 through F20.
3. Write a formula with an IF function that inserts the word *YES* in the cell if the product price is greater than $599 and inserts the word *NO* if the price is not greater than $599 by completing the following steps:
   a. Make cell C26 active.
   b. Type **=IF(B26>599,"YES","NO")** and then press Enter.
   c. Copy the formula in cell C26 down to cells C27 through C38.
4. Write a formula with an IF function that inserts the text *5%* in the cell if the previous cell contains the text *YES* and inserts the text *0%* if the previous cell does not contain the text *YES* by completing the following steps:
   a. Make cell D26 active.
   b. Type **=IF(C26="YES","5%","0%")** and then press Enter.
   c. Copy the formula in cell D26 down to cells D27 through D38.
5. Save and then print **EL1-C2-P4-CMPReports.xlsx**.
6. Press Ctrl + ` to turn on the display of formulas.
7. Print the worksheet again (the worksheet will print on two pages).
8. Press Ctrl + ` to turn off the display of formulas.
9. Save and then close **EL1-C2-P4-CMPReports.xlsx**.

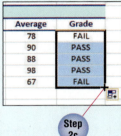

Step 2c

Step 4c

Project 5 Insert Formulas Using Absolute and Mixed Cell References
4 Parts

You will insert a formula containing an absolute cell reference that determines the effect on earnings with specific increases, insert a formula with multiple absolute cell references that determine the weighted average of scores, and use mixed cell references to determine simple interest.

Using Absolute and Mixed Cell References in Formulas

A reference identifies a cell or a range of cells in a worksheet and can be relative, absolute, or mixed. *Relative cell references* refer to cells relative to a position in a formula. *Absolute cell references* refer to cells in a specific location. When a formula is copied, a relative cell reference adjusts while an absolute cell reference remains constant. A *mixed cell reference* does both — either the column remains absolute and the row is relative or the column is relative and the row is absolute. Distinguish between relative, absolute, and mixed cell references using the dollar sign ($). Type a dollar sign before the column and/or row cell reference in a formula to specify that the column or row is an absolute cell reference.

Using an Absolute Cell Reference in a Formula

In this chapter you have learned to copy a relative formula. For example, if the formula =SUM(A2:C2) in cell D2 is copied relatively to cell D3, the formula changes to =SUM(A3:C3). In some situations, you may want a formula to contain an absolute cell reference, which always refers to a cell in a specific location. In Project 5a, you will add a column for projected job earnings and then perform "what if" situations using a formula with an absolute cell reference. To identify an absolute cell reference, insert a $ sign before the row and the column. For example, the absolute cell reference C12 would be typed as $C$12 in a formula.

Project 5a Inserting and Copying a Formula with an Absolute Cell Reference
Part 1 of 4

1. Open **CCReports.xlsx**.
2. Save the workbook with Save As and name it **EL1-C2-P5-CCReports**.
3. Determine the effect on actual job earnings with a 10% increase by completing the following steps:
   a. Make cell C3 active, type the formula =B3*$B$12, and then press Enter.
   b. Make cell C3 active and then use the fill handle to copy the formula to cells C4 through C10.

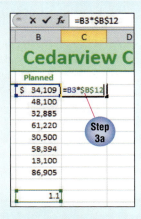
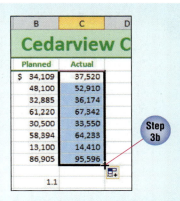

Chapter 2 ■ Inserting Formulas in a Worksheet   57

c. Make C3 active, click the Accounting Number Format button, and then click twice on the Decrease Decimal button.
4. Save and then print **EL1-C2-P5-CCReports.xlsx**.
5. With the worksheet still open, determine the effect on actual job earnings with a 10% decrease by completing the following steps:
   a. Make cell B12 active.
   b. Type **0.9** and then press Enter.
6. Save and then print the **EL1-C2-P5-CCReports.xlsx**.
7. Determine the effects on actual job earnings with a 20% increase. (To do this, type **1.2** in cell B12.)
8. Save and then print **EL1-C2-P5-CCReports.xlsx**.

In Project 5a, you created a formula with one absolute cell reference. You can also create a formula with multiple absolute cell references. For example, in Project 5b you will create a formula that contains both relative and absolute cell references to determine the average of training scores based on specific weight percentages.

Project 5b Inserting and Copying a Formula with Multiple Absolute Cell References — Part 2 of 4

1. With **EL1-C2-P5-CCReports.xlsx** open, insert the following formulas:
   a. Insert a formula in cell B23 that averages the percentages in cells B17 through B22.
   b. Copy the formula in cell B23 to the right to cells C23 and D23.
2. Insert a formula that determines the weighted average of training scores by completing the following steps:
   a. Make cell E17 active.
   b. Type the following formula:
      =$B$24*B17+$C$24*C17+$D$24*D17
   c. Press the Enter key.
   d. Copy the formula in cell E17 down to cells E18 through E22.
   e. With cells E17 through E22 selected, click the Decrease Decimal button three times.
3. Save and then print the **EL1-C2-P5-CCReports.xlsx**.
4. With the worksheet still open, determine the effect on weighted training scores if the weighted values change by completing the following steps:
   a. Make cell B24 active, type **30**, and then press Enter.
   b. Make cell D24 active, type **40**, and then press Enter.
5. Save and then print **EL1-C2-P5-CCReports.xlsx**.

Using a Mixed Cell Reference in a Formula

The formula you created in Step 3a in Project 5a contained a relative cell reference (B3) and an absolute cell reference ($B$12). A formula can also contain a mixed cell reference. In a mixed cell reference either the column remains absolute and the row is relative or the column is relative and the row is absolute. In Project 5c you will insert a number of formulas, two of which will contain mixed cell references. You will insert the formula =E29*E$26 to calculate withholding tax and =E29*H$36 to calculate Social Security tax. The dollar sign before the rows indicates that the row is an absolute cell reference.

Project 5c | **Determining Payroll Using Formulas with Absolute and Mixed Cell References** — Part 3 of 4

1. With **EL1-C2-P5-CCReports.xlsx** open, make cell E29 active and then type the following formula containing mixed cell references:
   =(B29*C29+(B29*$B$36*D29))
2. Copy the formula in cell E29 down to cells E30 through E34.
3. Make cell F29 active and then type the following formula that calculates the amount of withholding tax:
   =E29*E$36
4. Copy the formula in cell F29 down to cells F30 through F34.
5. Make cell G29 active and then type the following formula that calculates the amount of Social Security tax:
   =E29*H$36
6. Copy the formula in cell G29 down to cells G30 through G34.
7. Make cell H29 active and then type the following formula that calculates net pay:
   =E29-(F29+G29)
8. Copy the formula in cell H29 down to cells H30 through H34.
9. Select cells E29 through H29 and then click the Accounting Number Format button.
10. Save **EL1-C2-P5-CCReports.xlsx**.

As you learned in Project 5c, a formula can contain a mixed cell reference. In a mixed cell reference either the column remains absolute and the row is relative or the column is relative and the row is absolute. In Project 5d, you will create the formula =$A41*B$40. In the first cell reference in the formula, $A41, the column is absolute and the row is relative. In the second cell reference, B$40, the column is relative and the row is absolute. The formula containing the mixed cell references allows you to fill in the column and row data using only one formula.

Identify an absolute or mixed cell reference by typing a dollar sign before the column and/or row reference or press the F4 function key to cycle through the various cell references. For example, type =A41 in a cell, press F4, and the cell reference changes to =$A$41. Press F4 again and the cell reference changes to =A$41. The next time you press F4, the cell reference changes to =$A41 and press it again to change the cell reference back to =A41.

Project 5d — Determining Simple Interest Using a Formula with Mixed Cell References — Part 4 of 4

1. With **EL1-C2-P5-CCReports.xlsx** open, make cell B41 the active cell and then insert a formula containing mixed cell references by completing the following steps:
   a. Type **=A41** and then press the F4 function key three times. (This changes the cell reference to *$A41*.)
   b. Type ***B40** and then press the F4 function key twice. (This changes the cell reference to *B$40*.)
   c. Make sure the formula displays as *=$A41*B$40* and then press Enter.
2. Copy the formula to the right by completing the following steps:
   a. Make cell B41 active and then use the fill handle to copy the formula right to cell F41.
   b. With cells B41 through F41 selected, use the fill handle to copy the formula down to cell F51.
3. Save, print, and then close **EL1-C2-P5-CCReports.xlsx**.

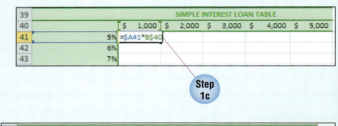

Chapter Summary

- Type a formula in a cell and the formula displays in the cell as well as in the Formula bar. If cell entries are changed, a formula will automatically recalculate the values and insert the result in the cell.
- Create your own formula with commonly used operators such as addition (+), subtraction (-), multiplication (*), division (/), percent (%), and exponentiation (^). When writing a formula, begin with the equals sign (=).
- Copy a formula to other cells in a row or column with the Fill button in the Editing group in the Home tab or with the fill handle that displays in the bottom right corner of the active cell.

- Another method for writing a formula is to point to specific cells that are part of the formula as the formula is being built.
- If Excel detects an error in a formula, a Trace Error button appears and a dark green triangle displays in the upper left corner of the cell containing the formula.
- Excel includes over 200 functions that are divided into twelve categories. Use the Insert Function feature to create formulas using built-in functions.
- A function operates on an argument, which may consist of a cell reference, a constant, or another function. When a value calculated by a formula is inserted in a cell, this is referred to as returning the result.
- The AVERAGE function returns the average (arithmetic mean) of the arguments. The MAX function returns the largest value in a set of values, and the MIN function returns the smallest value in a set of values. The COUNT function counts the number of cells containing numbers within the list of arguments.
- Use the keyboard shortcut, Ctrl + ` (grave accent) to turn on the display of formulas in a worksheet.
- The PMT function calculates the payment for a loan based on constant payments and a constant interest rate. The FV function returns the future value of an investment based on periodic, constant payments and a constant interest rate.
- The NOW function returns the serial number of the current date and time and the DATE function returns the serial number that represents a particular date.
- Use the IF function, considered a conditional function, to perform conditional tests on values and formulas. Use quotation marks around data in an IF statement to identify the data as text rather than a value.
- A reference identifies a cell or a range of cells in a worksheet and can be relative, absolute, or mixed. Identify an absolute cell reference by inserting a $ sign before the column and row. Cycle through the various cell reference options by typing the cell reference and then pressing F4.

Commands Review

FEATURE	RIBBON TAB, GROUP	BUTTON	KEYBOARD SHORTCUT
SUM function	Home, Editing OR Formulas, Function Library	Σ	Alt + =
Insert Function dialog box	Formulas, Function Library	f_x	Shift + F3
Display formulas			Ctrl + `

Concepts Check — Test Your Knowledge

Completion: In the space provided at the right, indicate the correct term, symbol, or command.

1. When typing a formula, begin the formula with this sign.

2. This is the operator for division that is used when writing a formula.

3. This is the operator for multiplication that is used when writing a formula.

4. As an alternative to the fill handle, use this button to copy a formula relatively in a worksheet.

5. A function operates on this, which may consist of a constant, a cell reference, or other function.

6. This function returns the largest value in a set of values.

7. This is the keyboard shortcut to display formulas in a worksheet.

8. This function finds the periodic payment for a loan based on constant payments and a constant interest rate.

9. This function returns the serial number of the current date and time.

10. This function is considered a conditional function.

11. Suppose cell B2 contains the total sales amount. Write a formula that would insert the word *BONUS* in cell C2 if the sales amount was greater than $99,999 and inserts the words *NO BONUS* if the sales amount is not greater than $99,999.

12. To identify an absolute cell reference, type this symbol before the column and row.

Skills Check Assess Your Performance

Assessment 1

INSERT AVERAGE, MAX, AND MIN FUNCTIONS

1. Open **DISalesAnalysis.xlsx**.
2. Save the workbook with Save As and name it **EL1-C2-A1-DISalesAnalysis**.
3. Use the AVERAGE function to determine the monthly sales (cells H4 through H9).
4. Format cell H4 with the Accounting Number Format with no decimal places.
5. Total each monthly column including the Average column (cells B10 through H10).
6. Use the MAX function to determine the highest monthly total (for cells B10 through G10) and insert the amount in cell B11.
7. Use the MIN function to determine the lowest monthly total (for cells B10 through G10) and insert the amount in cell B12.
8. Save, print, and then close **EL1-C2-A1-DISalesAnalysis.xlsx**.

Assessment 2

INSERT PMT FUNCTION

1. Open **CMRefiPlan.xlsx**.
2. Save the workbook with Save As and name it **EL1-C2-A2-CMRefiPlan**.
3. The manager of Clearline Manufacturing is interested in refinancing a loan for either $125,000 or $300,000 and wants to determine the monthly payments, total payments, and total interest paid. Insert a formula with the following specifications:
    a. Make cell E5 active.
    b. Use the Insert Function button on the Formula bar to insert a formula using the PMT function. At the formula palette, enter the following:

    Rate = C5/12
    Nper = D5
    Pv = -B5

    c. Copy the formula in cell E5 down to cells E6 through E8.
4. Insert a formula in cell F5 that multiplies the amount in E5 by the amount in D5.
5. Copy the formula in cell F5 down to cells F6 through F8.
6. Insert a formula in cell G5 that subtracts the amount in B5 from the amount in F5. (The formula is *=F5-B5*.)
7. Copy the formula in cell G5 down to cells G6 through G8.
8. Save, print, and then close **EL1-C2-A2-CMRefiPlan.xlsx**.

Assessment 3

INSERT FV FUNCTION

1. Open **RPInvest.xlsx**.
2. Save the workbook with Save As and name it **EL1-C2-A3-RPInvest**.
3. Make the following changes to the worksheet:
    a. Change the percentage in cell B3 from *9%* to *10%*.

b. Change the number in cell B4 from *36* to *60*.
c. Change the amount in cell B5 from *($1,200)* to *-500*.
d. Use the FV function to insert a formula that calculates the future value of the investment. ***Hint: For help with the formula, refer to Project 3b.***
4. Save, print, and then close **EL1-C2-A3-RPInvest.xlsx**.

Assessment 4   WRITE IF STATEMENT FORMULAS

1. Open **DISalesBonuses.xlsx**.
2. Save the workbook with Save As and name it **EL1-C2-A4-DISalesBonuses**.
3. Insert a formula in cell C4 that inserts the word *YES* if the amount in B4 is greater than 99999 and inserts *NO* if the amount is not greater than 99999. Copy the formula in cell C4 down to cells C5 through C14.
4. Make cell D4 active and then insert the formula **=IF(C4="YES",B4*0.05,0)**. If sales are over $99,000, this formula will multiply the amount of sales by 5 percent and then insert the product (result) of the formula in the cell. Copy the formula in cell D4 down to cells D5 through D14.
5. Format cell D4 with the accounting number format with no decimal places.
6. Save and then print **EL1-C2-A4-DISalesBonuses.xlsx**.
7. Display the formulas in the worksheet and then print the worksheet.
8. Turn off the display of formulas.
9. Save and then close **EL1-C2-A4-DISalesBonuses.xlsx**.

Assessment 5   WRITE FORMULAS WITH ABSOLUTE CELL REFERENCES

1. Open **CCQuotas.xlsx**.
2. Save the workbook with Save As and name it **EL1-C2-A5-CCQuotas**.
3. Make the following changes to the worksheet:
    a. Insert a formula using an absolute reference to determine the projected quotas with a 10% increase from the current quotas.
    b. Save and then print **EL1-C2-A5-CCQuotas.xlsx**.
    c. Determine the projected quotas with a 15% increase from the current quota by changing cell A15 to *15% Increase* and cell B15 to *1.15*.
    d. Save and then print **EL1-C2-A5-CCQuotas.xlsx**.
    e. Determine the projected quotas with a 20% increase from the current quota.
4. Format cell C4 with the Accounting Number Format with no decimal places.
5. Save, print, and then close **EL1-C2-A5-CCQuotas.xlsx**.

Assessment 6   USE HELP TO LEARN ABOUT EXCEL OPTIONS

1. Learn about specific options in the Excel Options dialog box by completing the following steps:
    a. At a blank workbook, display the Excel Options dialog box by clicking the File tab and then clicking the Options button.
    b. At the Excel Options dialog box, click the *Advanced* option located in the left panel.

c. Scroll down and look for the section *Display options for this workbook* and then read the information in the section. Read the information that displays in the *Display options for this worksheet* section.
d. Write down the check box options available in the *Display options for this workbook* section and the *Display options for this worksheet* section and identify whether or not the check box contains a check mark. (Record only check box options and ignore buttons and options preceded by circles.)
2. With the information you wrote down about the options, create an Excel spreadsheet with the following information:
   a. In column C, type each option you wrote down. (Include an appropriate heading.)
   b. In column B, insert an X in the cell that precedes any option that contains a check mark in the check box. (Include an appropriate heading.)
   c. In column A, write a formula with the IF function that inserts the word ON in the cell if the cell in column B contains an X and inserts the word OFF if it does not (the cell is blank). (Include an appropriate heading.)
   d. Apply formatting to improve the visual appeal of the worksheet.
3. Save the workbook and name it **EL1-C2-A6-DisplayOptions**.
4. Turn on the display of formulas.
5. Print the worksheet.
6. Turn off the display of formulas.
7. Save, print, and then close **EL1-C2-A6-DisplayOptions.xlsx**.

Visual Benchmark Demonstrate Your Proficiency

CREATE A WORKSHEET AND INSERT FORMULAS

1. At a blank workbook, type the data in the cells indicated in Figure 2.4 but **do not** type the data in the following cells—instead insert the formulas as indicated (the results of your formulas should match the results you see in the figure):
   - Cells D3 through D9: Insert a formula that calculates the salary.
   - Cells D14 through D19: Insert a formula that calculates the differences.
   - Cells D24 through D27: Insert the dates as serial numbers.
   - Cells F24 through F27: Insert a formula that calculates the due date.
   - Cells B37 through D37: Insert a formula that calculates the averages.
   - Cells E32 through E36: Insert a formula that calculates the weighted average of test scores.
2. Apply any other formatting so your worksheet looks similar to the worksheet shown in Figure 2.4.
3. Save the workbook and name it **EL1-C2-VB-Formulas**.
4. Print **EL1-C2-VB-Formulas.xlsx**.
5. Press Ctrl + ` to turn on the display of formulas and then print the worksheet again.
6. Turn off the display of formulas and then close the workbook.

Figure 2.4 Visual Benchmark

	A	B	C	D	E	F	G
1		Weekly Payroll					
2	Employee	Hours	Rate	Salary			
3	Alvarez, Rita	40	$ 22.50	$ 900.00			
4	Campbell, Owen	15	22.50	337.50			
5	Heitmann, Luanne	25	19.00	475.00			
6	Malina, Susan	40	18.75	750.00			
7	Parker, Kenneth	40	18.75	750.00			
8	Reitz, Collette	20	15.00	300.00			
9	Shepard, Gregory	15	12.00	180.00			
10							
11							
12		Construction Projects					
13	Project	Projected	Actual	Difference			
14	South Cascade	$ 145,000	$ 141,597	$ (3,403)			
15	Rogue River Park	120,000	124,670	4,670			
16	Meridian	120,500	99,450	(21,050)			
17	Lowell Ridge	95,250	98,455	3,205			
18	Walker Canyon	70,000	68,420	(1,580)			
19	Nettleson Creek	52,000	49,517	(2,483)			
20							
21							
22			Overdue Accounts				
23	Client	Account #	Amount Due	Pur. Date	Terms	Due Date	
24	Sunrise Marketing	120	$ 9,875	12/4/2012	15	12/19/2012	
25	National Systems	398	8,525	12/7/2012	30	1/6/2013	
26	First Street Signs	188	5,000	12/12/2012	15	12/27/2012	
27	Valley Services	286	3,250	12/19/2012	30	1/18/2013	
28							
29							
30			Test Scores				
31	Employee	Test No. 1	Test No. 2	Test No. 3	Wgt. Avg.		
32	Coffey, Annette	62%	64%	76%	70%		
33	Halverson, Ted	88%	96%	90%	91%		
34	Kohler, Jeremy	80%	76%	82%	80%		
35	McKnight, Carol	68%	72%	78%	74%		
36	Parkhurst, Jody	98%	96%	98%	98%		
37	Test Averages	79%	81%	85%			
38	Test Weights	25%	25%	50%			

Case Study   Apply Your Skills

Part 1

You are a loan officer for Dollar Wise Financial Services and work in the department that specializes in home loans. You have decided to prepare a sample home mortgage worksheet to show prospective clients. This sample home mortgage worksheet will show the monthly payments on variously priced homes with varying interest rates. Open the **DWMortgages.xlsx** worksheet and then complete the home mortgage worksheet by inserting the following formulas:

- Since many homes in your area sell for at least $400,000, you decide to add that amount to the worksheet with a 5%, 10%, 15%, and 20% down payment.
- In column C, insert a formula that determines the down payment amount.
- In column D, insert a formula that determines the loan amount.
- In column G, insert a formula using the PMT function. (The monthly payment will display as a negative number.)

Save the worksheet and name it **EL1-C2-CS-DWMortgages**.

Part 2

If home buyers put down less than 20 percent of the home's purchase price, mortgage insurance is required. With **EL1-C2-CS-DWMortgages.xlsx** open, insert an IF statement in the cells in column H that inserts the word "No" if the percentage in column B is equal to or greater than 20% or inserts the word "Yes" if the percentage in column B is less than 20%. Save and then print **EL1-C2-CS-DWMortgages.xlsx**.

Part 3

Interest rates fluctuate on a regular basis. Using the resources available to you, determine a current interest rate in your area. Delete the interest rate of 7% in the Dollar Wise worksheet and insert the interest rate for your area. Save and then print **EL1-C2-CS-DWMortgages.xlsx**.

Part 4

When a client is required to purchase mortgage insurance, you would like to provide information to the client concerning this insurance. Use the Help feature to learn about creating hyperlinks in Excel. Locate a helpful website that specializes in private mortgage insurance. Create a hyperlink in the worksheet that will display the website. Save, print, and then close **EL1-C2-CS-DWMortage.xlsx**.

Part 5

Once a loan has been approved and finalized, a letter is sent to the client explaining the details of the loan. Use a letter template in Word to create a letter that is sent to the client. Copy and link the information in the **EL1-C2-CS-DWMortage.xlsx** worksheet to the client letter. Save the letter document and name it **DWLetter**. Print and then close **DWLetter.docx**.

Microsoft Excel

Formatting an Excel Worksheet

CHAPTER 3

PERFORMANCE OBJECTIVES

Upon successful completion of Chapter 3, you will be able to:
- Change column widths
- Change row heights
- Insert rows and columns in a worksheet
- Delete cells, rows, and columns in a worksheet
- Clear data in cells
- Apply formatting to data in cells
- Apply formatting to selected data using the Mini toolbar
- Preview a worksheet
- Apply a theme and customize the theme font and color
- Format numbers
- Repeat the last action
- Automate formatting with Format Painter
- Hide and unhide rows and columns

The appearance of a worksheet on the screen and how it looks when printed is called the *format*. In Chapter 1, you learned how to apply basic formatting to cells in a worksheet. Additional types of formatting you may want to apply to a worksheet include changing column width and row height; applying character formatting such as bold, italics, and underlining; specifying number formatting; inserting and deleting rows and columns; and applying borders, shading, and patterns to cells. You can also apply formatting to a worksheet with a theme. A theme is a set of formatting choices that include colors and fonts. Model answers for this chapter's projects appear on the following page.

Excel2010L1C3

Note: Before beginning the projects, copy to your storage medium the Excel2010L1C3 subfolder from the Excel2010L1 folder on the CD that accompanies this textbook and then make Excel2010L1C3 the active folder.

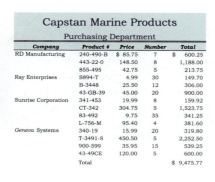

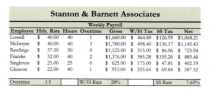

Project 1 Format a Product Pricing Worksheet

EL1-C3-P1-CMProducts.xlsx

Project 2 Apply a Theme to a Payroll Worksheet

EL1-C3-P2-SBAPayroll.xlsx

REAL PHOTOGRAPHY
Invoices

Invoice #	Client #	Service	Amount	Tax	Amount Due
2930	03-392	Family Portraits	$ 450.00	8.5%	$ 488.25
2942	02-498	Wedding Portraits	$ 1,075.00	8.8%	$ 1,169.60
2002	11-279	Development	$ 225.00	0.0%	$ 225.00
2007	04-325	Sports Portraits	$ 750.00	8.5%	$ 813.75
2376	03-392	Senior Portraits	$ 850.00	8.5%	$ 922.25
2129	11-279	Development	$ 350.00	0.0%	$ 350.00
2048	11-325	Wedding Portraits	$ 875.00	8.5%	$ 949.38
2054	04-325	Sports Portraits	$ 750.00	8.5%	$ 813.75
2064	05-665	Family Portraits	$ 560.00	8.8%	$ 609.28
2077	11-279	Development	$ 400.00	0.0%	$ 400.00
2079	04-325	Sports Portraits	$ 600.00	8.5%	$ 651.00
2908	55-340	Senior Portraits	$ 725.00	8.8%	$ 788.80
3001	11-279	Development	$ 310.00	8.8%	$ 337.28

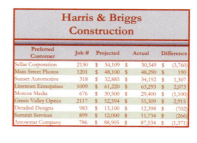

Project 3 Format an Invoices Worksheet

EL1-C3-P3-RPInvoices.xlsx

Project 4 Format a Company Budget Worksheet

EL1-C3-P4-HBCJobs.xlsx

Project 1 Format a Product Pricing Worksheet   7 Parts

You will open a workbook containing a worksheet with product pricing data, and then format the worksheet by changing column widths and row heights, inserting and deleting rows and columns, deleting rows and columns, and clearing data in cells. You will also apply font and alignment formatting to data in cells and then preview the worksheet.

Changing Column Width

Columns in a worksheet are the same width by default. In some worksheets you may want to change column widths to accommodate more or less data. You can change column width using the mouse on column boundaries or at a dialog box.

Changing Column Width Using Column Boundaries

As you learned in Chapter 1, you can adjust the width of a column by dragging the column boundary line or adjust a column width to the longest entry by double-clicking the boundary line. When you drag a column boundary, the column width displays in a box above the mouse pointer. The column width number that displays represents the average number of characters in the standard font that can fit in a cell.

HINT To change the width of all columns in a worksheet, click the Select All button and then drag a column boundary to the desired position.

You can change the width of selected adjacent columns at the same time. To do this, select the columns and then drag one of the column boundaries within the selected columns. As you drag the boundary the column width changes for all selected columns. To select adjacent columns, position the cell pointer on the first desired column header (the mouse pointer turns into a black, down-pointing arrow), hold down the left mouse button, drag the cell pointer to the last desired column header, and then release the mouse button.

Project 1a Changing Column Width Using a Column Boundary   Part 1 of 7

1. Open **CMProducts.xlsx**.
2. Save the workbook with Save As and name it **EL1-C3-P1-CMProducts**.
3. Insert a formula in cell D2 that multiplies the price in cell B2 with the number in cell C2. Copy the formula in cell D2 down to cells D3 through D14.
4. Change the width of column D by completing the following steps:
   a. Position the mouse pointer on the column boundary in the column header between columns D and E until it turns into a double-headed arrow pointing left and right.
   b. Hold down the left mouse button, drag the column boundary to the right until *Width: 11.00 (82 pixels)* displays in the box, and then release the mouse button.
5. Make cell D15 active and then insert the sum of cells D2 through D14.
6. Change the width of columns A and B by completing the following steps:
   a. Select columns A and B. To do this, position the cell pointer on the column A header, hold down the left mouse button, drag the cell pointer to the column B header, and then release the mouse button.

Chapter 3 ■ Formatting an Excel Worksheet   71

b. Position the cell pointer on the column boundary between columns A and B until it turns into a double-headed arrow pointing left and right.
c. Hold down the left mouse button, drag the column boundary to the right until *Width: 10.14 (76 pixels)* displays in the box, and then release the mouse button.
7. Adjust the width of column C to accommodate the longest entry by double-clicking on the column boundary between columns C and D.
8. Save **EL1-C3-P1-CMProducts.xlsx**.

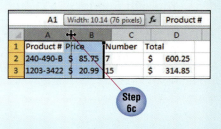

Step 6c

Changing Column Width at the Column Width Dialog Box

▼ **Quick Steps**

Change Column Width
Drag column boundary line.
OR
Double-click column boundary.
OR
1. Click Format button.
2. Click *Column Width* at drop-down list.
3. Type desired width.
4. Click OK.

At the Column Width dialog box shown in Figure 3.1, you can specify a column width number. Increase the column width number to make the column wider or decrease the column width number to make the column narrower.

To display the Column Width dialog box, click the Format button in the Cells group in the Home tab and then click *Column Width* at the drop-down list. At the Column Width dialog box, type the number representing the average number of characters in the standard font that you want to fit in the column and then press Enter or click OK.

Format

Figure 3.1 Column Width Dialog Box

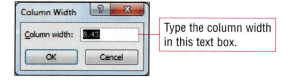

Type the column width in this text box.

Project 1b Changing Column Width at the Column Width Dialog Box   Part 2 of 7

1. With **EL1-C3-P1-CMProducts.xlsx** open, change the width of column A by completing the following steps:
   a. Make any cell in column A active.
   b. Click the Format button in the Cells group in the Home tab and then click *Column Width* at the drop-down list.
   c. At the Column Width dialog box, type **12.75** in the *Column width* text box.
   d. Click OK to close the dialog box.
2. Make any cell in column B active and then change the width of column B to *12.75* by completing steps similar to those in Step 1.
3. Make any cell in column C active and then change the width of column C to *8* by completing steps similar to those in Step 1.
4. Save **EL1-C3-P1-CMProducts.xlsx**.

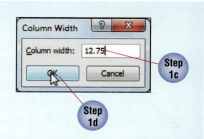

Step 1c

Step 1d

Changing Row Height

Row height can be changed in much the same manner as column width. For example, you can change the row height using the mouse on a row boundary, or at the Row Height dialog box. Change row height using a row boundary in the same manner as you learned to change column width. To do this, position the cell pointer on the boundary between rows in the row header until it turns into a double-headed arrow pointing up and down, hold down the left mouse button, drag up or down until the row is the desired height, and then release the mouse button.

The height of selected rows that are adjacent can be changed at the same time. (The height of nonadjacent rows will not all change at the same time.) To do this, select the rows and then drag one of the row boundaries within the selected rows. As the boundary is being dragged the row height changes for all selected rows.

As a row boundary is being dragged, the row height displays in a box above the mouse pointer. The row height number that displays represents a point measurement. A vertical inch contains approximately 72 points. Increase the point size to increase the row height; decrease the point size to decrease the row height.

At the Row Height dialog box shown in Figure 3.2, you can specify a row height number. To display the Row Height dialog box, click the Format button in the Cells group in the Home tab and then click *Row Height* at the drop-down list.

> ▼ **Quick Steps**
> **Change Row Height**
> Drag row boundary line.
> OR
> 1. Click Format button.
> 2. Click *Row Height* at drop-down list.
> 3. Type desired height.
> 4. Click OK.

> **HINT**
> To change the height of all rows in a worksheet, click the Select All button and then drag a row boundary to the desired position.

Figure 3.2 Row Height Dialog Box

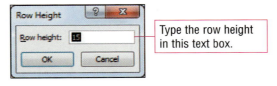

Project 1c Changing Row Height — Part 3 of 7

1. With **EL1-C3-P1-CMProducts.xlsx** open, change the height of row 1 by completing the following steps:
   a. Position the cell pointer in the row header on the row boundary between rows 1 and 2 until it turns into a double-headed arrow pointing up and down.
   b. Hold down the left mouse button, drag the row boundary down until *Height: 19.50 (26 pixels)* displays in the box, and then release the mouse button.
2. Change the height of rows 2 through 14 by completing the following steps:
   a. Select rows 2 through 14. To do this, position the cell pointer on the number 2 in the row header, hold down the left mouse button, drag the cell pointer to the number 14 in the row header, and then release the mouse button.
   b. Position the cell pointer on the row boundary between rows 2 and 3 until it turns into a double-headed arrow pointing up and down.

c. Hold down the left mouse button, drag the row boundary down until *Height: 16.50 (22 pixels)* displays in the box, and then release the mouse button.
3. Change the height of row 15 by completing the following steps:
   a. Make cell A15 active.
   b. Click the Format button in the Cells group in the Home tab and then click *Row Height* at the drop-down list.
   c. At the Row Height dialog box, type **20** in the *Row height* text box and then click OK.

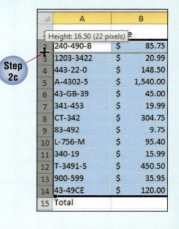

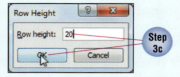

4. Save **EL1-C3-P1-CMProducts.xlsx**.

Inserting and Deleting Cells, Rows, and Columns

Quick Steps

Insert Row
Click Insert button.
OR
1. Click Insert button arrow.
2. Click *Insert Sheet Rows* at drop-down list.
OR
1. Click Insert button arrow.
2. Click *Insert Cells*.
3. Click *Entire row* in dialog box.
4. Click OK.

Insert

HINT
When you insert rows in a worksheet, all references affected by the insertion are automatically adjusted.

New data may need to be included in an existing worksheet. For example, a row or several rows of new data may need to be inserted into a worksheet or data may need to be removed from a worksheet.

Inserting Rows

After you create a worksheet, you can add (insert) rows to the worksheet. Insert a row with the Insert button in the Cells group in the Home tab or with options at the Insert dialog box. By default, a row is inserted above the row containing the active cell. To insert a row in a worksheet, select the row below where the row is to be inserted and then click the Insert button. If you want to insert more than one row, select the number of rows in the worksheet that you want inserted and then click the Insert button.

You can also insert a row by making a cell active in the row below where the row is to be inserted, clicking the Insert button arrow, and then clicking *Insert Sheet Rows*. Another method for inserting a row is to click the Insert button arrow and then click *Insert Cells*. This displays the Insert dialog box as shown in Figure 3.3. At the Insert dialog box, click *Entire row*. This inserts a row above the active cell.

Figure 3.3 Insert Dialog Box

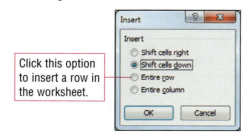

74   Excel Level 1 ■ Unit 1

Project 1d Inserting Rows Part 4 of 7

1. With **EL1-C3-P1-CMProducts.xlsx** open, insert two rows at the beginning of the worksheet by completing the following steps:
   a. Make cell A1 active.
   b. Click the Insert button arrow in the Cells group in the Home tab.
   c. At the drop-down list that displays, click *Insert Sheet Rows*.
   d. With cell A1 active, click the Insert button arrow and then click *Insert Sheet Rows* at the drop-down list.
2. Type the text **Capstan Marine Products** in cell A1.
3. Make cell A2 active and then type **Purchasing Department**.
4. Change the height of row 1 to *42.00 (56 pixels)*.
5. Change the height of row 2 to *21.00 (28 pixels)*.
6. Insert two rows by completing the following steps:
   a. Select rows 7 and 8 in the worksheet.
   b. Click the Insert button in the Cells group in the Home tab.
7. Type the following data in the specified cells: (You do not need to type the dollar sign in cells containing money amounts.)
   - A7 = **855-495**
   - B7 = **42.75**
   - C7 = **5**
   - A8 = **ST039**
   - B8 = **12.99**
   - C8 = **25**
8. Make D6 the active cell and then use the fill handle to copy the formula down to cells D7 and D8.
9. Save **EL1-C3-P1-CMProducts.xlsx**.

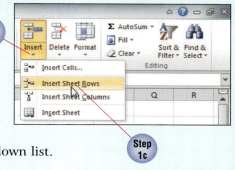

Inserting Columns

Insert columns in a worksheet in much the same way as rows. Insert a column with options from the Insert button drop-down list or with options at the Insert dialog box. By default, a column is inserted immediately to the left of the column containing the active cell. To insert a column in a worksheet, make a cell active in the column immediately to the right of where the new column is to be inserted, click the Insert button arrow, and then click *Insert Sheet Columns* at the drop-down list. If you want to insert more than one column, select the number of columns in the worksheet that you want inserted, click the Insert button arrow, and then click *Insert Sheet Columns*.

You also can insert a column by making a cell active in the column immediately to the right of where the new column is to be inserted, clicking the Insert button arrow, and then clicking *Insert Cells* at the drop-down list. This causes the Insert dialog box to display. At the Insert dialog box, click *Entire column*. This inserts an entire column immediately to the left of the active cell.

Excel includes an especially helpful and time-saving feature related to inserting columns. When you insert columns in a worksheet, all references affected by the insertion are automatically adjusted.

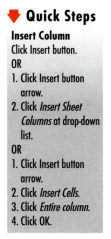

▼ **Quick Steps**

Insert Column
Click Insert button.
OR
1. Click Insert button arrow.
2. Click *Insert Sheet Columns* at drop-down list.
OR
1. Click Insert button arrow.
2. Click *Insert Cells*.
3. Click *Entire column*.
4. Click OK.

Chapter 3 ■ Formatting an Excel Worksheet   75

Project 1e Inserting a Column   Part 5 of 7

1. With **EL1-C3-P1-CMProducts.xlsx** open, insert a column by completing the following steps:
   a. Click in any cell in column A.
   b. Click the Insert button arrow in the Cells group in the Home tab and then click *Insert Sheet Columns* at the drop-down list.
2. Type the following data in the specified cell:
   - A3 = **Company**
   - A4 = **RD Manufacturing**
   - A8 = **Smithco, Inc.**
   - A11 = **Sunrise Corporation**
   - A15 = **Geneva Systems**
3. Make cell A1 active and then adjust the width of column A to accommodate the longest entry.
4. Insert another column by completing the following steps:
   a. Make cell B1 active.
   b. Click the Insert button arrow and then click *Insert Cells* at the drop-down list.
   c. At the Insert dialog box, click *Entire column*.
   d. Click OK.
5. Type **Date** in cell B3 and then press Enter.
6. Save **EL1-C3-P1-CMProducts.xlsx**.

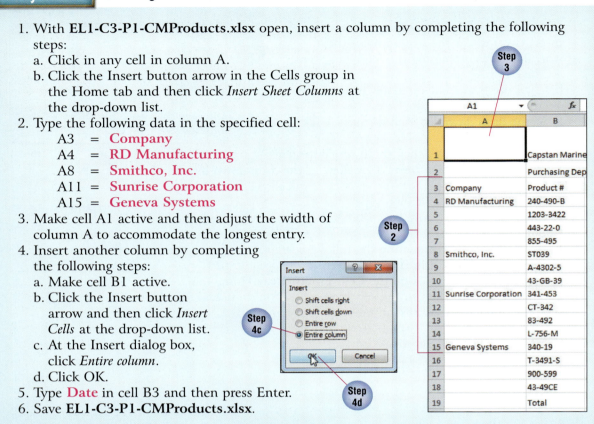

Deleting Cells, Rows, or Columns

HINT
Display the Delete dialog box by positioning the cell pointer in the worksheet, clicking the right mouse button, and then clicking *Delete* at the shortcut menu.

You can delete specific cells in a worksheet or rows or columns in a worksheet. To delete a row, select the row and then click the Delete button in the Cells group in the Home tab. To delete a column, select the column and then click the Delete button. Delete a specific cell by making the cell active, clicking the Delete button arrow, and then clicking *Delete Cells* at the drop-down list. This displays the Delete dialog box shown in Figure 3.4. At the Delete dialog box, specify what you want deleted and then click OK. You can also delete adjacent cells by selecting the cells and then displaying the Delete dialog box.

Delete

Figure 3.4 Delete Dialog Box

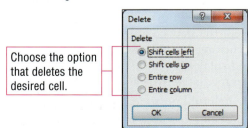

Choose the option that deletes the desired cell.

Clearing Data in Cells

If you want to delete cell contents but not the cell, make the cell active or select desired cells and then press the Delete key. A quick method for clearing the contents of a cell is to right-click the cell and then click *Clear Contents* at the shortcut menu. Another method for deleting cell contents is to make the cell active or select desired cells, click the Clear button in the Editing group in the Home tab, and then click *Clear Contents* at the drop-down list.

With the options at the Clear button drop-down list you can clear the contents of the cell or selected cells as well as formatting and comments. Click the *Clear Formats* option to remove formatting from cells or selected cells while leaving the data. You can also click the *Clear All* option to clear the contents of the cell or selected cells as well as the formatting.

Quick Steps

Clear Data in Cells
1. Select desired cells.
2. Press Delete key.
OR
1. Select desired cells.
2. Click Clear button.
3. Click *Clear Contents* at drop-down list.

Clear

Project 1f — Deleting and Clearing Rows in a Worksheet — Part 6 of 7

1. With **EL1-C3-P1-CMProducts.xlsx** open, delete column B in the worksheet by completing the following steps:
   a. Click in any cell in column B.
   b. Click the Delete button arrow in the Cells group in the Home tab and then click *Delete Sheet Columns* at the drop-down list.
2. Delete row 5 by completing the following steps:
   a. Select row 5.
   b. Click the Delete button in the Cells group.
3. Clear row contents by completing the following steps:
   a. Select rows 7 and 8.
   b. Click the Clear button in the Editing group in the Home tab and then click *Clear Contents* at the drop-down list.
4. Type the following data in the specified cell:
   A7 = **Ray Enterprises**
   B7 = **S894-T**
   C7 = **4.99**
   D7 = **30**
   B8 = **B-3448**
   C8 = **25.50**
   D8 = **12**
5. Make cell E6 active and then copy the formula down to cells E7 and E8.
6. Save **EL1-C3-P1-CMProducts.xlsx**.

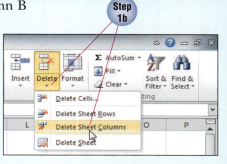

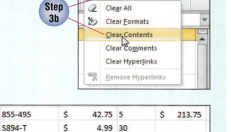

Applying Formatting

With many of the groups in the Home tab you can apply formatting to text in the active cells or selected cells. Use buttons in the Font group to apply font formatting to text and use buttons in the Alignment group to apply alignment formatting to text.

Figure 3.5 Font Group

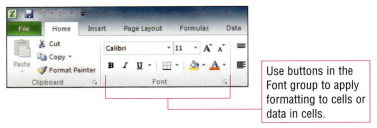

Use buttons in the Font group to apply formatting to cells or data in cells.

Applying Font Formatting

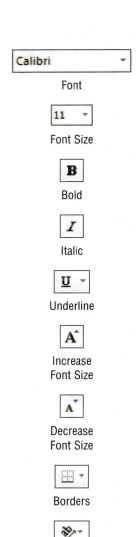

You can apply a variety of formatting to cells in a worksheet with buttons in the Font group in the Home tab. With buttons in the Font group shown in Figure 3.5, you can change the font, font size, and font color; bold, italicize, and underline data in cells; change the text color; and apply a border or add fill to cells.

Use the Font button in the Font group to change the font of text in a cell and use the Font Size button to specify size for the text. Apply bold formatting to text in a cell with the Bold button, italic formatting with the Italic button, and underlining with the Underline button.

Click the Increase Font Size button and the text in the active cell or selected cells increases from 11 points to 12 points. Click the Increase Font Size button again and the font size increases to 14. Each additional time you click the button, the font size increases by two points. Click the Decrease Font Size button and text in the active cell or selected cells decreases in point size.

With the Borders button in the Font group, you can insert a border on any or all sides of the active cell or any or all sides of selected cells. The name of the button changes depending on the most recent border applied to a cell or selected cells. Use the Fill Color button to insert color in the active cell or in selected cells. With the Font Color button, you can change the color of text within a cell.

Formatting with the Mini Toolbar

Double-click in a cell and then select data within the cell and the Mini toolbar displays in a dimmed fashion above the selected data. The Mini toolbar also displays when you right-click in any cell. Hover the mouse pointer over the Mini toolbar and it becomes active. The Mini toolbar contains buttons for applying font formatting such as font, font size, and font color as well as bold and italic formatting. Click a button on the Mini toolbar to apply formatting to selected text.

Applying Alignment Formatting

The alignment of data in cells depends on the type of data entered. Enter words or text combined with numbers in a cell and the text is aligned at the left edge of the cell. Enter numbers in a cell and the numbers are aligned at the right side of the cell. Use options in the Alignment group to align text at the left, center, or right side of the cell; align text at the top, center, or bottom of the cell; increase and/or decrease the indent of text; and change the orientation of text in a cell. As you learned in Chapter 1, you can merge selected cells by clicking the Merge & Center button. If you merged cells, you can split the merged cell into the original cells by selecting the cell and then clicking the Merge & Center button. If you click the Merge & Center button arrow, a drop-down list of options displays. Click the *Merge & Center* option to merge all of the selected cells and change to center cell alignment. Click the *Merge Across* to merge each row of the selected cells. For example, if you select three cells and two rows, clicking the *Merge Across* option will merge the three cells in the first row and merge the three cells in the second row so you end up with two cells. Click the *Merge Cells* option to merge all selected cells but not change to center cell alignment. Use the last option, *Unmerge Cells* to split cells that were previously merged. If you select and merge cells containing data, only the data in the upper-left cell will remain. Data in any other cells in the merged cells is deleted.

Orientation

Click the Orientation button to rotate data in a cell. Click the Orientation button and a drop-down list displays with options for rotating text in a cell. If data typed in a cell is longer than the cell, it overlaps the next cell to the right. If you want data to remain in a cell and wrap to the next line within the same cell, click the Wrap Text button in the Alignment group.

Wrap Text

Project 1g Applying Font and Alignment Formatting   Part 7 of 7

1. With **EL1-C3-P1-CMProducts.xlsx** open, make cell B1 active and then click the Wrap Text button in the Alignment group in the Home tab. (This wraps the company name within the cell.)
2. Make cell B2 active and then click the Wrap Text button.
3. Instead of wrapping text within cells, you decide to spread out the text over several cells and vertically align text in cells and change text in cell B2 by completing the following steps:
    a. Select cells A1 through E2.
    b. Click the Merge & Center button arrow in the Alignment group in the Home tab and then click the *Merge Across* option at the drop-down list.
    c. Click the Middle Align button in the Alignment group and then click the Center button.

4. Rotate text in the third row by completing the following steps:
    a. Select cells A3 through E3.
    b. Click the Orientation button in the Alignment group in the Home tab and then click *Angle Counterclockwise* at the drop-down list.
    c. After looking at the rotated text, you decide to return the orientation back to the horizontal by clicking the Undo button on the Quick Access toolbar.
5. Change the font, font size, and font color for text in specific cells by completing the following steps:
    a. Make cell A1 active.
    b. Click the Font button arrow in the Font group in the Home tab, scroll down the drop-down gallery, and then click *Bookman Old Style*.
    c. Click the Font Size button arrow in the Font group and then click *22* at the drop-down gallery.

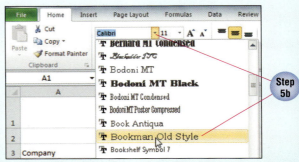

Chapter 3 ■ Formatting an Excel Worksheet   79

d. Click the Font Color button arrow and then click *Dark Blue* in the *Standard Colors* section of the drop-down color palette.

6. Make cell A2 active and then complete steps similar to those in Step 5 to change the font to Bookman Old Style, the font size to 16, and the font color to Dark Blue.

7. Select cells A3 through E3 and then click the Center button in the Alignment group.

8. With cells A3 through E3 still selected, click the Bold button in the Font group and then click the Italic button.

9. Select cells A3 through E18 and then change the font to Bookman Old Style.

10. Apply formatting to selected data using the Mini toolbar by completing the following steps:
    a. Double-click cell A4.
    b. Select the letters *RD*. (This displays the dimmed Mini toolbar above the selected word.)
    c. Click the Increase Font Size button on the Mini toolbar.
    d. Double-click cell A14.
    e. Select the word *Geneva* and then click the Italic button on the Mini toolbar.

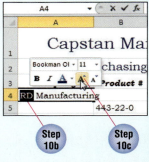

11. Adjust columns A through E to accommodate the longest entry in each column. To do this, select columns A through E and then double-click any selected column boundary.

12. Select cells D4 through D17 and then click the Center button in the Alignment group.

13. Add a double-line bottom border to cell A2 by completing the following steps:
    a. Make cell A2 active.
    b. Click the Borders button arrow in the Font group in the Home tab.
    c. Click the *Bottom Double Border* option at the drop-down list.

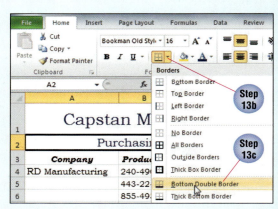

14. Add a single-line bottom border to cells A3 through E3 by completing the following steps:
    a. Select cells A3 through E3.
    b. Click the Borders button arrow and then click the *Bottom Border* option.

15. Apply fill color to specific cells by completing the following steps:
    a. Select cells A1 through E3.
    b. Click the Fill Color button arrow in the Font group.
    c. Click the *Aqua, Accent 5, Lighter 80%* color option.

16. Select cells C5 through C17 and then click the Comma Style button.
17. Select cells E5 through E17 and then click the Comma Style button.
18. Save, print, and then close **EL1-C3-P1-CMProducts.xlsx**.

Project 2 Apply a Theme to a Payroll Worksheet — 1 Part

You will open a workbook containing a worksheet with payroll information and then insert text, apply formatting to cells and cell contents, apply a theme, and then change the theme font and colors.

Applying a Theme

Excel provides a number of themes you can use to format text and cells in a worksheet. A theme is a set of formatting choices that include a color theme (a set of colors), a font theme (a set of heading and body text fonts), and an effects theme (a set of lines and fill effects). To apply a theme, click the Page Layout tab and then click the Themes button in the Themes group. At the drop-down gallery that displays, click the desired theme. Position the mouse pointer over a theme and the *live preview* feature will display the worksheet with the theme formatting applied. With the live preview feature you can see how the theme formatting affects your worksheet before you make your final choice.

Apply a theme to give your worksheet a professional look.

Themes

Project 2 Applying a Theme — Part 1 of 1

1. Open **SBAPayroll.xlsx** and then save it with Save As and name it **EL1-C3-P2-SBAPayroll**.
2. Make G4 the active cell and then insert a formula that calculates the amount of Social Security tax. (Multiply the gross pay amount in E4 with the Social Security rate in cell H11; you will need to use the mixed cell reference H$11 when writing the formula.)
3. Copy the formula in cell G4 down to cells G5 through G9.
4. Make H4 the active cell and then insert a formula that calculates the net pay (gross pay minus withholding and Social Security tax).
5. Copy the formula in H4 down to cells H5 through H9.
6. Increase the height of row 1 to 36.00.
7. Make A1 the active cell, click the Middle Align button in the Alignment group, click the Font Size button arrow, click *18* at the drop-down list, and then click the Bold button.
8. Type **Stanton & Barnett Associates** in cell A1.
9. Select cells A2 through H3 and then click the Bold button in the Font group.
10. Apply a theme and customize the font and colors by completing the following steps:
    a. Click the Page Layout tab.
    b. Click the Themes button in the Themes group and then click *Apothecary* at the drop-down gallery. (You might want to point the mouse to various themes to see how each theme's formatting affects the worksheet.)

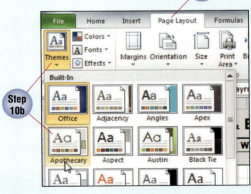

c. Click the Colors button in the Themes group and then click *Flow* at the drop-down gallery.
d. Click the Fonts button in the Themes group, scroll down the drop-down gallery, and then click *Black Tie*.

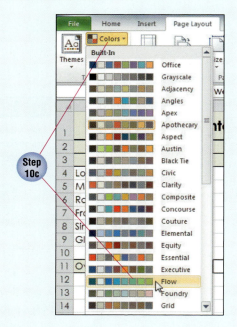
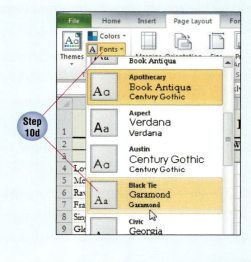

11. Select columns A through H and then adjust the width of the columns to accommodate the longest entries.
12. Save, print, and then close **EL1-C3-P2-SBAPayroll.xlsx**.

Project 3 Format an Invoices Worksheet   2 Parts

You will open a workbook containing an invoice worksheet and apply number formatting to numbers in cells.

Formatting Numbers

Numbers in a cell, by default, are aligned at the right and decimals and commas do not display unless they are typed in the cell. Change the format of numbers with buttons in the Number group in the Home tab or with options at the Format Cells dialog box with the Number tab selected.

Formatting Numbers Using Number Group Buttons

Format symbols you can use to format numbers include a percent sign (%), a comma (,), and a dollar sign ($). For example, if you type the number *$45.50* in a cell, Excel automatically applies Currency formatting to the number. If you type *45%*, Excel automatically applies the Percent formatting to the number.

The Number group in the Home tab contains five buttons you can use to format numbers in cells. You learned about these buttons in Chapter 1.

Specify the formatting for numbers in cells in a worksheet before typing the numbers, or format existing numbers in a worksheet. The Increase Decimal and Decrease Decimal buttons in the Number group in the Home tab will change decimal places for existing numbers only.

The Number group in the Home tab also contains the Number Format button. Click the Number Format button arrow and a drop-down list displays of common number formats. Click the desired format at the drop-down list to apply the number formatting to the cell or selected cells.

Number Format

Project 3a Formatting Numbers with Buttons in the Number Group   Part 1 of 2

1. Open **RPInvoices.xlsx**.
2. Save the workbook with Save As and name it **EL1-C3-P3-RPInvoices**.
3. Make the following changes to column widths:
    a. Change the width of column C to 17.00.
    b. Change the width of column D to 10.00.
    c. Change the width of column E to 7.00.
    d. Change the width of column F to 12.00.
4. Select row 1 and then click the Insert button in the Cells group.
5. Change the height of row 1 to 42.00.
6. Select cells A1 through F1 and then make the following changes:
    a. Click the Merge & Center button in the Alignment group in the Home tab.
    b. With cell A1 active, change the font size to 24 points.
    c. Click the Fill Color button arrow in the Font group and then click *Olive Green, Accent 3, Lighter 80%*.
    d. Click the Borders button arrow in the Font group and then click the *Top and Thick Bottom Border* option.
    e. With cell A1 active, type **REAL PHOTOGRAPHY** and then press Enter.
7. Change the height of row 2 to 24.00.
8. Select cells A2 through F2 and then make the following changes:
    a. Click the Merge & Center button in the Alignment group.
    b. With cell A2 active, change the font size to 18.
    c. Click the Fill Color button in the Font group. (This will fill the cell with light green color.)
    d. Click the Borders button arrow in the Font group and then click the *Bottom Border* option.
9. Make the following changes to row 3:
    a. Change the height of row 3 to 18.00.
    b. Select cells A3 through F3, click the Bold button in the Font group, and then click the Center button in the Alignment group.

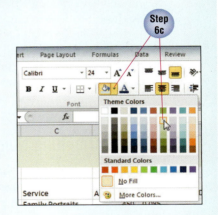

c. With the cells still selected, click the Borders button arrow and then click the *Bottom Border* option.
10. Make the following number formatting changes:
    a. Select cells E4 through E16 and then click the *Percent Style* button in the Number group in the Home tab.
    b. With the cells still selected, click once on the Increase Decimal button in the Number group. (The percent numbers should contain one decimal place.)

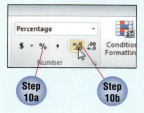

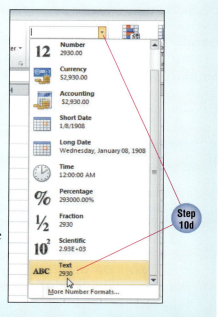

   c. Select cells A4 through B16.
   d. Click the Number Format button arrow, scroll down the drop-down list, and then click *Text*.
   e. With A4 through B16 still selected, click the Center button in the Alignment group.
11. Save **EL1-C3-P3-RPInvoices.xlsx**.

Formatting Numbers Using the Format Cells Dialog Box

Along with buttons in the Number group, you can format numbers with options at the Format Cells dialog box with the Number tab selected as shown in Figure 3.6. Display this dialog box by clicking the Number group dialog box

Figure 3.6 Format Cells Dialog Box with Number Tab Selected

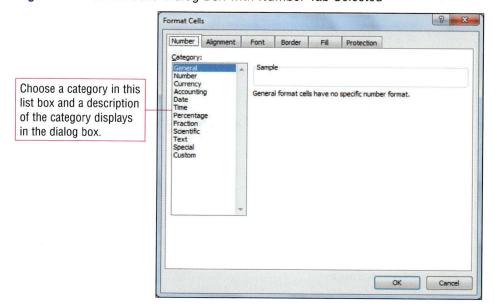

launcher or by clicking the Number Format button arrow and then clicking *More Number Formats* at the drop-down list. The left side of the dialog box displays number categories with a default category of *General*. At this setting no specific formatting is applied to numbers except right-aligning numbers in cells. The other number categories are described in Table 3.1.

Table 3.1 Number Categories at the Format Cells Dialog Box

Click this category	To apply this number formatting
Number	Specify number of decimal places and whether or not a thousand separator should be used; choose the display of negative numbers; right-align numbers in cell.
Currency	Apply general monetary values; dollar sign is added as well as commas and decimal points, if needed; right-align numbers in cell.
Accounting	Line up the currency symbol and decimal points in a column; add dollar sign and two digits after a decimal point; right-align numbers in cell.
Date	Display date as date value; specify the type of formatting desired by clicking an option in the *Type* list box; right-align date in cell.
Time	Display time as time value; specify the type of formatting desired by clicking an option in the *Type* list box; right-align time in cell.
Percentage	Multiply cell value by 100 and display result with a percent symbol; add decimal point followed by two digits by default; number of digits can be changed with the *Decimal places* option; right-align number in cell.
Fraction	Specify how fraction displays in cell by clicking an option in the *Type* list box; right-align fraction in cell.
Scientific	Use for very large or very small numbers. Use the letter *E* to tell Excel to move a decimal point a specified number of positions.
Text	Treat number in cell as text; number is displayed in cell exactly as typed.
Special	Choose a number type, such as *Zip Code*, *Phone Number*, or *Social Security Number* in the *Type* option list box; useful for tracking list and database values.
Custom	Specify a numbering type by choosing an option in the *Type* list box.

Project 3b   Formatting Numbers at the Format Cells Dialog Box   Part 2 of 2

1. With **EL1-C3-P3-PRInvoices.xlsx** open, make cell F4 active, insert the following formula: **=(D4*E4)+D4**, and then press Enter.
2. Make cell F4 active and then copy the formula down to cells F5 through F16.
3. Change number formatting by completing the following steps:
   a. Select cells D4 through D16.
   b. Click the Number group dialog box launcher.

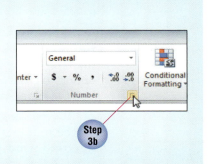

Step 3b

c. At the Format Cells dialog box with the Number tab selected, click *Accounting* in the *Category* section.

d. Make sure a *2* displays in the *Decimal places* option box and a dollar sign *$* displays in the *Symbol* option box.

e. Click OK.

4. Apply Accounting formatting to cells F4 through F16 by completing steps similar to those in Step 3.
5. Save, print, and then close **EL1-C3-P3-RPInvoices.xlsx**.

Project 4 Format a Company Budget Worksheet   6 Parts

You will open a workbook containing a company budget worksheet and then apply formatting to cells with options at the Format Cells dialog box, use the Format Painter to apply formatting, and hide and unhide rows and columns in the worksheet.

Formatting Cells Using the Format Cells Dialog Box

In the previous section, you learned how to format numbers with options at the Format Cells dialog box with the Number tab selected. This dialog box contains a number of other tabs you can select to format cells.

Aligning and Indenting Data

You can align and indent data in cells using buttons in the Alignment group in the Home tab or with options at the Format Cells dialog box with the Alignment tab selected as shown in Figure 3.7. Display this dialog box by clicking the Alignment group dialog box launcher.

In the *Orientation* section, you can choose to rotate data. A portion of the *Orientation* section shows points on an arc. Click a point on the arc to rotate the text along that point. You can also type a rotation degree in the *Degrees* text box. Type a positive number to rotate selected text from the lower left to the upper right of the cell. Type a negative number to rotate selected text from the upper left to the lower right of the cell.

If data typed in a cell is longer than the cell, it overlaps the next cell to the right. If you want data to remain in a cell and wrap to the next line within the same cell, click the *Wrap text* option in the *Text control* section of the dialog box. Click the *Shrink to fit* option to reduce the size of the text font so all selected data fits within the column. Use the *Merge cells* option to combine two or more selected cells into a single cell.

If you want to enter data on more than one line within a cell, enter the data on the first line and then press Alt + Enter. Pressing Alt + Enter moves the insertion point to the next line within the same cell.

Figure 3.7 Format Cells Dialog Box with Alignment Tab Selected

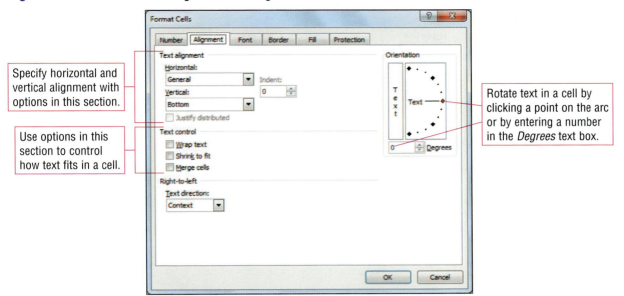

Project 4a — Aligning and Rotating Data in Cells — Part 1 of 6

1. Open **HBCJobs.xlsx**.
2. Save the workbook with Save As and name it **EL1-C3-P4-HBCJobs**.
3. Make the following changes to the worksheet:
   a. Insert a new row at the beginning of the worksheet.
   b. Change the height of row 1 to 66.00.
   c. Merge and center cells A1 through E1.
   d. Type **Harris & Briggs** in cell A1 and then press Alt + Enter. (This moves the insertion point down to the next line in the same cell.)
   e. Type **Construction** and then press Enter.
   f. With cell A2 active, type **Preferred**, press Alt + Enter, type **Customer**, and then press Enter.
   g. Change the width of column A to 20.00.
   h. Change the width of column B to 7.00.
   i. Change the width of columns C, D, and E to 10.00.
4. Change number formatting for specific cells by completing the following steps:
   a. Select cells C3 through E11.
   b. Click the Number group dialog box launcher.
   c. At the Format Cells dialog box with the Number tab selected, click *Accounting* in the *Category* section.
   d. Click the down-pointing arrow at the right side of the *Decimal places* option until *0* displays.
   e. Make sure a dollar sign $ displays in the *Symbol* option box.
   f. Click OK.
5. Make cell E3 active and then insert the formula **=D3-C3**. Copy this formula down to cells E4 through E11.

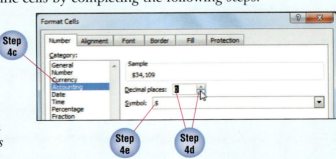

6. Change the orientation of data in cells by completing the following steps:
   a. Select cells B2 through E2.
   b. Click the Alignment group dialog box launcher.
   c. At the Format Cells dialog box with the Alignment tab selected, select *0* in the *Degrees* text box and then type **45**.
   d. Click OK.

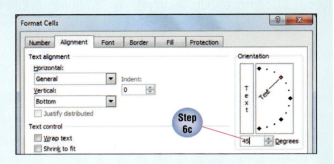

7. Change the vertical alignment of text in cells by completing the following steps:
   a. Select cells A1 through E2.
   b. Click the Alignment group dialog box launcher.
   c. At the Format Cells dialog box with the Alignment tab selected, click the down-pointing arrow at the right side of the *Vertical* alignment option.
   d. Click *Center* at the drop-down list.
   e. Click OK.

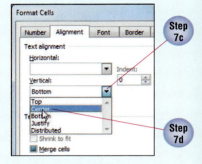

8. Change the horizontal alignment of text in cells by completing the following steps:
   a. Select cells A2 through E2.
   b. Click the Alignment group dialog box launcher.
   c. At the Format Cells dialog box with the Alignment tab selected, click the down-pointing arrow at the right side of the *Horizontal* alignment option.
   d. Click *Center* at the drop-down list.
   e. Click OK.

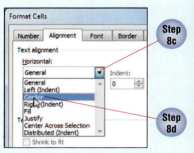

9. Change the horizontal alignment and indent of text in cells by completing the following steps:
   a. Select cells B3 through B11.
   b. Click the Alignment group dialog box launcher.
   c. At the Format Cells dialog box with the Alignment tab selected, click the down-pointing arrow at the right side of the *Horizontal* alignment option and then click *Right (Indent)* at the drop-down list.
   d. Click once on the up-pointing arrow at the right side of the *Indent* option box. (This displays *1* in the box.)
   e. Click OK.
10. Save **EL1-C3-P4-HBCJobs.xlsx**.

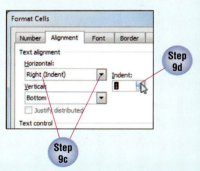

Changing the Font at the Format Cells Dialog Box

As you learned earlier in this chapter, the Font group in the Home tab contains buttons for applying font formatting to data in cells. You can also change the font for data in cells with options at the Format Cells dialog box with the Font tab selected as shown in Figure 3.8. At the Format Cells dialog box with the Font tab selected, you can change the font, font style, font size, and font color. You can also change the underlining method and add effects such as superscript and subscript. Click the Font group dialog box launcher to display this dialog box.

Figure 3.8 Format Cells Dialog Box with Font Tab Selected

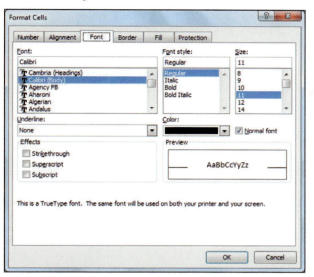

Project 4b   Applying Font Formatting at the Format Cells Dialog Box   Part 2 of 6

1. With **EL1-C3-P4-HBCJobs.xlsx** open, change the font and font color by completing the following steps:
   a. Select cells A1 through E11.
   b. Click the Font group dialog box launcher.
   c. At the Format Cells dialog box with the Font tab selected, click *Garamond* in the *Font* list box. (You will need to scroll down the list to make this font visible.)
   d. Click *12* in the *Size* list box.
   e. Click the down-pointing arrow at the right of the *Color* option box.
   f. At the palette of color choices that displays, click the *Dark Red* color (first color option from the left in the *Standard Colors* section).
   g. Click OK to close the dialog box.
2. Make cell A1 active and then change the font to 24-point Garamond bold.
3. Select cells A2 through E2 and then apply bold formatting.
4. Save and then print **EL1-C3-P4-HBCJobs.xlsx**.

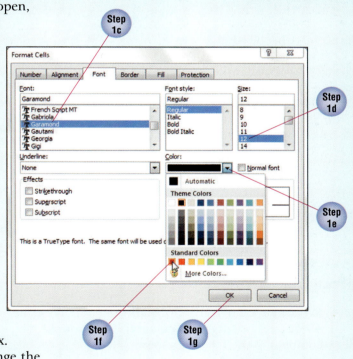

Chapter 3 ■ Formatting an Excel Worksheet   **89**

Adding Borders to Cells

▼ Quick Steps

Add Borders to Cells
1. Select cells.
2. Click Borders button arrow.
3. Click desired border.

OR
1. Select cells.
2. Click Borders button arrow.
3. Click *More Borders*.
4. Use options in dialog box to apply desired border.
5. Click OK.

The gridlines that display in a worksheet do not print. As you learned earlier in this chapter, you can use the Borders button in the Font group to add borders to cells that will print. You can also add borders to cells with options at the Format Cells dialog box with the Border tab selected as shown in Figure 3.9. Display this dialog box by clicking the Borders button arrow in the Font group and then clicking *More Borders* at the drop-down list.

With options in the *Presets* section, you can remove borders with the *None* option, add only outside borders with the *Outline* option, or click the *Inside* option to add borders to the inside of selected cells. In the *Border* section of the dialog box, specify the side of the cell or selected cells to which you want to apply a border. Choose the style of line desired for the border with the options that display in the *Style* list box. Add color to border lines with choices from the color palette that displays when you click the down-pointing arrow located at the right side of the *Color* option box.

Figure 3.9 Format Cells Dialog Box with Border Tab Selected

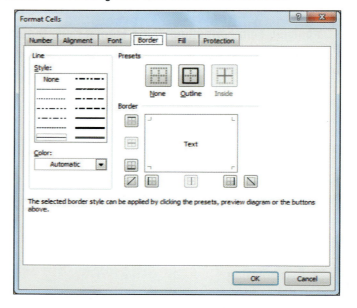

Project 4c Adding Borders to Cells   Part 3 of 6

1. With **EL1-C3-P4-HBCJobs.xlsx** open, remove the 45 degrees orientation you applied in Project 4a by completing the following steps:
   a. Select cells B2 through E2.
   b. Click the Alignment group dialog box launcher.
   c. At the Format Cells dialog box with the Alignment tab selected, select *45* in the *Degrees* text box and then type **0**.
   d. Click OK.

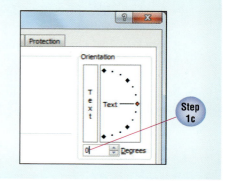

2. Change the height of row 2 to 33.00.
3. Add a thick, dark red border line to cells by completing the following steps:
   a. Select cells A1 through E11 (cells containing data).
   b. Click the Border button arrow in the Font group and then click the *More Borders* option at the drop-down list.
   c. At the Format Cells dialog box with the Border tab selected, click the down-pointing arrow at the right side of the *Color* option and then click *Dark Red* at the color palette (first color option from the left in the *Standard Colors* section).
   d. Click the thick single line option located in the second column (sixth option from the top) in the *Style* option box in the *Line* section.
   e. Click the *Outline* option in the *Presets* section.
   f. Click OK.

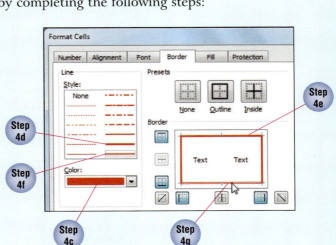

4. Add a border above and below cells by completing the following steps:
   a. Select cells A2 through E2.
   b. Click the Border button arrow in the Font group and then click *More Borders* at the drop-down list.
   c. At the Format Cells dialog box with the Border tab selected, make sure the color is Dark Red.
   d. Make sure the thick single line option (sixth option from the top in the second column) is selected in the *Style* option box in the *Line* section.
   e. Click the top border of the sample cell in the *Border* section of the dialog box.
   f. Click the double-line option (bottom option in the second column) in the *Style* option box.
   g. Click the bottom border of the sample cell in the *Border* section of the dialog box.
   h. Click OK.
5. Save **EL1-C3-P4-HBCJobs.xlsx**.

Adding Fill and Shading to Cells

▼ **Quick Steps**

Add Shading to Cells
1. Select cells.
2. Click Fill Color button arrow.
3. Click desired color.
OR
1. Select cells.
2. Click Format button.
3. Click *Format Cells* at drop-down list.
4. Click Fill tab.
5. Use options in dialog box to apply desired shading.
6. Click OK.

Repeat Last Action
1. Apply formatting.
2. Move to desired location.
3. Press F4 or Ctrl + Y.

To enhance the visual display of cells and data within cells, consider adding fill and/or shading to cells. As you learned earlier in this chapter, you can add fill color to cells with the Fill Color button in the Font group. You can also add fill color and/or shading to cells in a worksheet with options at the Format Cells dialog box with the Fill tab selected as shown in Figure 3.10. Display the Format Cells dialog box by clicking the Format button in the Cells group and then clicking *Format Cells* at the drop-down list. You can also display the dialog box by clicking the Font group, Alignment group, or Number group dialog box launcher. At the Format Cells dialog box, click the Fill tab or right-click in a cell and then click Format Cells at the shortcut menu.

Choose a fill color for a cell or selected cells by clicking a color choice in the Color palette. To add shading to a cell or selected cells, click the Fill Effects button and then click the desired shading style at the Fill Effects dialog box.

Repeating the Last Action

If you want to apply other types of formatting, such as number, border, or shading formatting to other cells in a worksheet, use the Repeat command by pressing F4 or Ctrl + Y. The Repeat command repeats the last action performed.

Figure 3.10 Format Cells Dialog Box with Fill Tab Selected

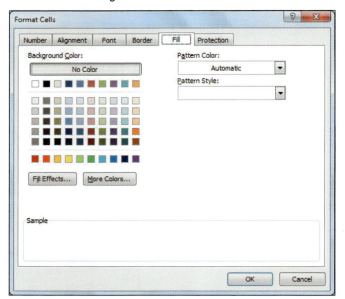

Project 4d Adding Fill Color and Shading to Cells Part 4 of 6

1. With **EL1-C3-P4-HBCJobs.xlsx** open, add fill color to cell A1 and repeat the formatting by completing the following steps:
   a. Make cell A1 active.
   b. Click the Format button in the Cells group and then click *Format Cells* at the drop-down list.
   c. At the Format Cells dialog box, click the Fill tab.
   d. Click a light purple color in the *Background Color* section. (Click the eighth color from the left in the second row.)

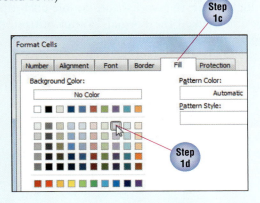
Step 1c

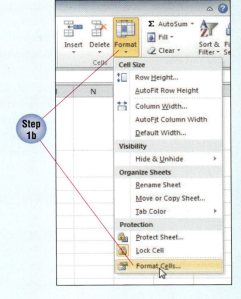
Step 1b

Step 1d

   e. Click OK.
   f. Select cells A2 through E2 and then press the F4 function key. (This repeats the light purple fill.)
2. Select row 2, insert a new row, and then change the height of the new row to 12.00.
3. Add shading to cells by completing the following steps:
   a. Select cells A2 through E2.
   b. Click the Format button in the Cells group and then click *Format Cells* at the drop-down list.
   c. At the Format Cells dialog box, if necessary, click the Fill tab.
   d. Click the Fill Effects button.
   e. At the Fill Effects dialog box, click the down-pointing arrow at the right side of the *Color 2* option box and then click *Purple, Accent 4* (eighth color from the left in the top row).
   f. Click OK to close the Fill Effects dialog box.
   g. Click OK to close the Format Cells dialog box.
4. Save **EL1-C3-P4-HBCJobs.xlsx**.

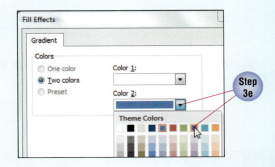
Step 3e

Chapter 3 ■ Formatting an Excel Worksheet

▼ **Quick Steps**

Format with Format Painter
1. Select cells with desired formatting.
2. Double-click Format Painter button.
3. Select cells.
4. Click Format Painter button.

Format Painter

Formatting with Format Painter

The Clipboard group in the Home tab contains a button you can use to copy formatting to different locations in the worksheet. This button is the Format Painter button and displays in the Clipboard group as a paintbrush. To use the Format Painter button, make a cell or selected cells active that contain the desired formatting, click the Format Painter button, and then click the cell or selected cells to which you want the formatting applied.

When you click the Format Painter button, the mouse pointer displays with a paintbrush attached. If you want to apply formatting a single time, click the Format Painter button once. If, however, you want to apply the character formatting in more than one location in the worksheet, double-click the Format Painter button. If you have double-clicked the Format Painter button, turn off the feature by clicking the Format Painter button once.

Project 4e Formatting with Format Painter   Part 5 of 6

1. With **EL1-C3-P4-HBCJobs.xlsx** open, select cells A5 through E5.
2. Click the Font group dialog box launcher.
3. At the Format Cells dialog box, click the Fill tab.
4. Click the light green color (seventh color from the left in the second row).
5. Click OK to close the dialog box.
6. Use Format Painter to "paint" formatting to rows by completing the following steps:
    a. With A5 through E5 selected, double-click the Format Painter button in the Clipboard group.
    b. Select cells A7 through E7.
    c. Select cells A9 through E9.
    d. Select cells A11 through E11.
    e. Turn off Format Painter by clicking the Format Painter button in the Clipboard group.
7. Save and then print **EL1-C3-P4-HBCJobs.xlsx**.

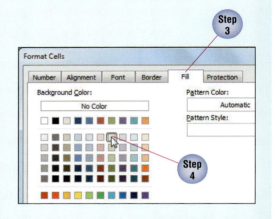

Hiding and Unhiding Columns and/or Rows

HINT
Set the column width to zero and the column is hidden. Set the row height to zero and the row is hidden.

If a worksheet contains columns and/or rows of sensitive data or data that you are not using or do not want to view, consider hiding the columns and/or rows. To hide columns in a worksheet, select the columns to be hidden, click the Format button in the Cells group in the Home tab, point to *Hide & Unhide*, and then click *Hide Columns*. To hide selected rows, click the Format button in the Cells group, point to *Hide & Unhide*, and then click *Hide Rows*. To make a hidden column visible, select the column to the left and the column to the right of the hidden column, click the Format button in the Cells group, point to *Hide & Unhide*, and then click *Unhide Columns*. To make a hidden row visible, select the row above and the row below the hidden row, click the Format button in the Cells group, point to *Hide & Unhide*, and then click *Unhide Rows*.

If the first row or column is hidden, use the Go To feature to make the row or column visible. To do this, click the Find & Select button in the Editing group in the Home tab and then click *Go To* at the drop-down list. At the Go To dialog box, type *A1* in the *Reference* text box and then click OK. At the worksheet, click the Format button in the Cells group, point to *Hide & Unhide*, and then click *Unhide Columns* or click *Unhide Rows*.

You can also unhide columns or rows using the mouse. If a column or row is hidden, the light blue boundary line in the column or row header displays as a slightly thicker blue line. To unhide a column, position the mouse pointer on the slightly thicker blue line that displays in the column header until the mouse pointer changes to left- and right-pointing arrows with a double line between. (Make sure the mouse pointer displays with two lines between the arrows. If a single line displays, you will simply change the size of the visible column.) Hold down the left mouse button, drag to the right until the column displays at the desired width, and then release the mouse button. Unhide a row in a similar manner. Position the mouse pointer on the slightly thicker blue line in the row header until the mouse pointer changes to up- and down-pointing arrows with a double line between. Drag down to display the row and then release the mouse button. If two or more adjacent columns or rows are hidden, you will need to unhide each column or row separately.

▼ Quick Steps

Hide Columns
1. Select columns.
2. Click Format button.
3. Point to *Hide & Unhide*.
4. Click *Hide Columns*.

Hide Rows
1. Select rows.
2. Click Format button.
3. Point to *Hide & Unhide*.
4. Click *Hide Rows*.

Project 4f Hiding and Unhiding Columns and Rows   Part 6 of 6

1. With **EL1-C3-P4-HBCJobs.xlsx** open, hide the row for Linstrom Enterprises and the row for Summit Services by completing the following steps:
   a. Click the row 7 header to select the entire row.
   b. Hold down the Ctrl key and then click the row 11 header to select the entire row.
   c. Click the Format button in the Cells group in the Home tab, point to *Hide & Unhide*, and then click *Hide Rows*.
2. Hide the column containing the actual amounts by completing the following steps:
   a. Click cell D3 to make it the active cell.
   b. Click the Format button in the Cells group, point to *Hide & Unhide*, and then click *Hide Columns*.
3. Save and then print **EL1-C3-P4-HBCJobs.xlsx**.
4. Unhide the rows by completing the following steps:
   a. Select rows 6 through 12.
   b. Click the Format button in the Cells group, point to *Hide & Unhide*, and then click *Unhide Rows*.
   c. Click in cell A4.
5. Unhide column D by completing the following steps:
   a. Position the mouse pointer on the thicker gray line that displays between columns C and E in the column header until the pointer turns into arrows pointing left and right with a double line between.

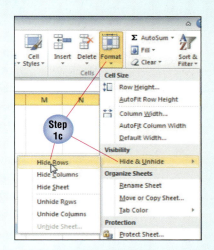

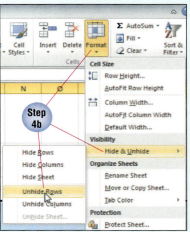

Chapter 3 ■ Formatting an Excel Worksheet   95

b. Hold down the left mouse button, drag to the right until *Width: 12.57 (93 pixels)* displays in a box above the mouse pointer, and then release the mouse button.

6. Save, print, and then close **EL1-C3-P4-HBCJobs.xlsx**.

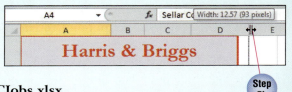

Step 5b

Chapter Summary

- Change column width using the mouse on column boundaries or with options at the Column Width dialog box.
- Change row height using the mouse on row boundaries or with options at the Row Height dialog box.
- Insert a row in a worksheet with the Insert button in the Cells group in the Home tab or with options at the Insert dialog box.
- Insert a column in a worksheet with the Insert button in the Cells group or with options at the Insert dialog box.
- Delete a specific cell by clicking the Delete button arrow and then clicking *Delete Cells* at the drop-down list. At the Delete dialog box, specify if you want to delete just the cell or an entire row or column.
- Delete a selected row(s) or column(s) by clicking the Delete button in the Cells group.
- Delete cell contents by pressing the Delete key or clicking the Clear button in the Editing group and then clicking *Clear Contents* at the drop-down list.
- Apply font formatting with buttons in the Font group in the Home tab.
- Use the Mini toolbar to apply font formatting to selected data in a cell.
- Apply alignment formatting with buttons in the Alignment group in the Home tab.
- Use the Themes button in the Themes group in the Page Layout tab to apply a theme to cells in a worksheet that applies formatting such as color, font, and effects. Use the other buttons in the Themes group to customize the theme.
- Format numbers in cells with buttons in the Number group in the Home tab. You can also apply number formatting with options at the Format Cells dialog box with the Number tab selected.
- Apply formatting to cells in a worksheet with options at the Format Cells dialog box. This dialog box includes the following tabs for formatting cells: Number, Alignment, Font, Border, and Fill.
- Press F4 or Ctrl + Y to repeat the last action performed.
- Use the Format Painter button in the Clipboard group in the Home tab to apply formatting to different locations in a worksheet.
- Hide selected columns or rows in a worksheet by clicking the Format button in the Cells group in the Home tab, pointing to *Hide & Unhide*, and then clicking *Hide Columns* or *Hide Rows*.

- To make a hidden column visible, select the column to the left and right, click the Format button in the Cells group, point to *Hide & Unhide*, and then click *Unhide Columns*.
- To make a hidden row visible, select the row above and below, click the Format button in the Cells group, point to *Hide & Unhide*, and then click *Unhide Rows*.

Commands Review

FEATURE	RIBBON TAB, GROUP	BUTTON	KEYBOARD SHORTCUT
Format	Home, Cells		
Insert cells, rows, columns	Home, Cells		
Delete cells, rows, columns	Home, Cells		
Clear cell or cell contents	Home, Editing	Clear	
Font	Home, Font	Calibri	
Font size	Home, Font	11	
Increase font size	Home, Font		
Decrease font size	Home, Font		
Bold	Home, Font	B	Ctrl + B
Italic	Home, Font	*I*	Ctrl + I
Underline	Home, Font	U	Ctrl + U
Borders	Home, Font		
Fill color	Home, Font		
Font color	Home, Font		
Top align	Home, Alignment		
Middle align	Home, Alignment		
Bottom align	Home, Alignment		
Orientation	Home, Alignment		

FEATURE	RIBBON TAB, GROUP	BUTTON	KEYBOARD SHORTCUT
Align text left	Home, Alignment		
Center	Home, Alignment		
Align text right	Home, Alignment		
Decrease indent	Home, Alignment		Ctrl + Alt + Shift + Tab
Increase indent	Home, Alignment		Ctrl + Alt + Tab
Wrap text	Home, Alignment		
Merge & Center	Home, Alignment		
Themes	Page Layout, Themes		
Number Format	Home, Number	General	
Format Painter	Home, Clipboard		
Repeat			F4 or Ctrl + Y

Concepts Check Test Your Knowledge

Completion: In the space provided at the right, indicate the correct term, symbol, or command.

1. By default, a column is inserted in this direction from the column containing the active cell.

2. To delete a row, select the row and then click the Delete button in this group in the Home tab.

3. With the options at this button's drop-down list, you can clear the contents of the cell or selected cells.

4. Use this button to insert color in the active cell or selected cells.

5. Select data in a cell and this displays in a dimmed fashion above the selected text.

6. By default, numbers are aligned at this side of a cell.

7. Click this button in the Alignment group in the Home tab to rotate data in a cell.

8. The Themes button is located in this tab. _____

9. If you type a number with a dollar sign, such as $50.25, Excel automatically applies this formatting to the number. _____

10. If you type a number with a percent sign, such as 25%, Excel automatically applies this formatting to the number. _____

11. Align and indent data in cells using buttons in the Alignment group in the Home tab or with options at this dialog box with the Alignment tab selected. _____

12. You can repeat the last action performed with the command Ctrl + Y or by pressing this function key. _____

13. The Format Painter button is located in this group in the Home tab. _____

14. To hide a column, select the column, click this button in the Cells group in the Home tab, point to *Hide & Unhide*, and then click *Hide Columns*. _____

Skills Check Assess Your Performance

Assessment

1 FORMAT A SALES AND BONUSES WORKSHEET

1. Open **NSPSales.xlsx**.
2. Save the workbook with Save As and name it **EL1-C3-A1-NSPSales**.
3. Change the width of columns as follows:
   - Column A = 14.00
   - Columns B – E = 10.00
   - Column F = 6.00
4. Select row 2 and then insert a new row.
5. Merge and center cells A2 through F2.
6. Type **Sales Department** in cell A2 and then press Enter.
7. Increase the height of row 1 to 33.00.
8. Increase the height of row 2 to 21.00.
9. Increase the height of row 3 to 18.00.
10. Make the following formatting changes to the worksheet:
    a. Make cell A1 active, change the font size to 18 points, and turn on bold.
    b. Make cell A2 active, change the font size to 14 points, and turn on bold.
    c. Select cells A3 through F3, click the Bold button in the Font group, and then click the Center button in the Alignment group.
    d. Select cells A1 through F3, change the vertical alignment to Middle Align.
11. Insert the following formulas in the worksheet:
    a. Insert a formula in D4 that adds the amounts in B4 and C4. Copy the formula down to cells D5 through D11.

b. Insert a formula in E4 that averages the amounts in B4 and C4. Copy the formula down to cells E5 through E11.
c. Insert an IF statement in cell F4 that says that if the amount in cell E4 is greater than 74999, then insert the word "Yes" and if the amount is not greater than 74999, then insert the word "No." Copy this formula down to cells F5 through F11.
12. Make the following changes to the worksheet:
   a. Select cells F4 through F11 and then click the Center button in the Alignment group.
   b. Select cells B4 through E4 and then change the number formatting to Accounting with 0 decimal places and a dollar sign.
   c. Select cells B5 through E11, click the Comma Style button, and then click twice on the Decrease Decimal button.
   d. Add a double-line border around cells A1 through F11.
   e. Select cells A1 and A2 and then apply a light orange fill color.
   f. Select cells A3 through F3 and then apply an orange fill color.
13. Save and then print the worksheet.
14. Apply the Verve theme to the worksheet.
15. Save, print, and then close **EL1-C3-A1-NSPSales.xlsx**.

Assessment 2

FORMAT AN OVERDUE ACCOUNTS WORKSHEET

1. Open **CCorpAccts.xlsx**.
2. Save the workbook with Save As and name it **EL1-C3-A2-CCorpAccts**.
3. Change the width of columns as follows:
   Column A = 21.00
   Column B = 10.00
   Column C = 10.00
   Column D = 12.00
   Column E = 7.00
   Column F = 12.00
4. Make cell A1 active and then insert a new row.
5. Merge and center cells A1 through F1.
6. Type **Compass Corporation** in cell A1 and then press Enter.
7. Increase the height of row 1 to 42.00.
8. Increase the height of row 2 to 24.00.
9. Make the following formatting changes to the worksheet:
   a. Select cells A1 through F11 and then change the font to 10-point Cambria.
   b. Make cell A1 active, change the font size to 24 points, and turn on bold.
   c. Make cell A2 active, change the font size to 18 points, and turn on bold.
   d. Select cells A3 through F3, click the Bold button in the Font group and then click the Center button in the Alignment group.
   e. Select cells A1 through F3, click the Middle Align button in the Alignment group.
   f. Select cells B4 through B11 and then click the Center button in the Alignment group.
   g. Select cells E4 through E11 and then click the Center button in the Alignment group.

10. Use the DATE function in the following cells to enter a formula that returns the serial number for the following dates:
    - D4 = October 1, 2012
    - D5 = October 3, 2012
    - D6 = October 8, 2012
    - D7 = October 10, 2012
    - D8 = October 15, 2012
    - D9 = October 30, 2012
    - D10 = November 6, 2012
    - D11 = November 13, 2012
11. Enter a formula in cell F4 that inserts the due date (the purchase date plus the number of days in the Terms column). Copy the formula down to cells F5 through F11.
12. Apply the following borders and fill color:
    a. Add a thick line border around cells A1 through F11.
    b. Make cell A2 active and then add a double-line border at the top and bottom of the cell.
    c. Select cells A3 through F3 and then add a single line border to the bottom of the cells.
    d. Select cells A1 and A2 and then apply a light blue fill color.
13. Save, print, and then close **EL1-C3-A2-CCorpAccts.xlsx**.

Assessment

3 FORMAT A SUPPLIES AND EQUIPMENT WORKSHEET

1. Open **OEBudget.xlsx**.
2. Save the workbook with Save As and name it **EL1-C3-A3-OEBudget**.
3. Select and then merge across cells A1 through D2. *Hint: Use the* **Merge Across** *option at the Merge & Center button drop-down list.*
4. With cells A1 and A2 selected, click the Middle Align button in the Alignment group and then click the Center button.
5. Make cell A1 active and then change the font size to 22 points and turn on bold.
6. Make cell A2 active and then change the font size to 12 points and turn on bold.
7. Change the height of row 1 to 36.00.
8. Change the height of row 2 to 21.00.
9. Change the width of column A to 15.00.
10. Select cells A3 through A17, turn on bold, and then click the Wrap Text button in the Alignment group.
11. Make cell B3 active and then change the number formatting to Currency with no decimal places.
12. Select cells C6 through C19 and then change the number formatting to Percentage with one decimal place.
13. Automatically adjust the width of column B.
14. Make cell D6 active and then type a formula that multiplies the absolute cell reference $B$3 with the percentage in cell C6. Copy the formula down to cells D7 through D19.
15. With cells D6 through D19 selected, change the number formatting to Currency with no decimal places.
16. Make cell D8 active and then clear the cell contents. Use the Repeat command, F4, to clear the contents from cells D11, D14, and D17.
17. Select cells A1 through D19, change the font to Constantia, and then change the font color to dark blue.

18. Add light green fill color to the following cells: A1, A2, A5–D5, A8–D8, A11–D11, A14–D14, and A17–D17.
19. Add borders and/or additional shading of your choosing to enhance the visual appeal of the worksheet.
20. Save, print, and then close **EL1-C3-A3-OEBudget.xlsx**.

Assessment

4 FORMAT A FINANCIAL ANALYSIS WORKSHEET

1. At a blank workbook, display the Format Cells dialog box with the Alignment tab selected and then experiment with the options in the *Text control* section.
2. Open **FinAnalysis.xlsx**.
3. Save the workbook with Save As and name it **EL1-C3-A4-FinAnalysis**.
4. Make cell B9 active and then insert a formula that averages the percentages in cells B3 through B8. Copy the formula to the right to cells C9 and D9.
5. Select cells B3 through D9, display the Format Cells dialog box with the Alignment tab selected, change the horizontal alignment to *Right (Indent)* and the indent to *2*, and then close the dialog box.
6. Select cells A1 through D9 and then change the font size to 14.
7. Select cells B2 through D2 and then change the orientation to 45 degrees.
8. With cells B2 through D2 still selected, shrink the font size to show all data in the cells.
9. Save, print, and then close **EL1-C3-A4-FinAnalysis.xlsx**.

Visual Benchmark   Demonstrate Your Proficiency

CREATE A WORKSHEET AND INSERT FORMULAS

1. At a blank workbook, type the data in the cells indicated in Figure 3.11 but **do not** type the data in the following cells—instead insert the formulas as indicated (the results of your formulas should match the results you see in the figure):
   - Cells C4 through C14: Insert a formula with an IF statement that inserts the word *Yes* if the sales amount is greater than $114,999 and inserts the word *No* if the sales amount is not greater than $114,999.
   - Cells D4 through D14: Insert a formula with an IF statement that if the content of the previous cell is *Yes*, then multiply the amount in the cell in column B by 0.05 and if the previous cell does not contain the word *Yes*, then insert a zero.
2. Apply formatting so your worksheet looks similar to the worksheet shown in Figure 3.11.
3. Save the workbook and name it **EL1-C3-VB-BonusAmounts**.
4. Print **EL1-C3-VB-BonusAmounts.xlsx**.
5. Press Ctrl + ` to turn on the display of formulas and then print the worksheet again.
6. Turn off the display of formulas and then close the workbook.

Figure 3.11 Visual Benchmark

	A	B	C	D	E
1	**Capstan Marine Products**				
2	*Sales Department Bonuses*				
3	Salesperson	Sales	Bonus	Amount	
4	Abrams, Warner	$ 130,490.00	Yes	$ 6,524.50	
5	Allejandro, Elaine	95,500.00	No	-	
6	Crispin, Nicolaus	137,000.00	Yes	6,850.00	
7	Frankel, Maria	124,000.00	Yes	6,200.00	
8	Hiesmann, Thomas	85,500.00	No	-	
9	Jarvis, Lawrence	159,000.00	Yes	7,950.00	
10	Littleman, Shirley	110,500.00	No	-	
11	McBride, Leah	78,420.00	No	-	
12	Ostlund, Sonya	101,435.00	No	-	
13	Ryckman, Graham	83,255.00	No	-	
14	Sharma, Anja	121,488.00	Yes	6,074.40	
15					

Case Study Apply Your Skills

Part 1

You are the office manager for HealthWise Fitness Center and you decide to prepare an Excel worksheet that displays the various plans offered by the health club. In this worksheet, you want to include yearly dues for each plan as well as quarterly and monthly payments. Open the **HFCDues.xlsx** workbook and then save it with Save As and name it **EL1-C3-CS-HFCDues-1**. Make the following changes to the worksheet:

- Select cells B3 through D8 and then change the number formatting to Accounting with two decimal places and a dollar sign.
- Make cell B3 active and then insert *500.00*.
- Make cell B4 active and then insert a formula that adds the amount in B3 with the product (multiplication) of B3 multiplied by 10%. (The formula should look like this: **=B3+(B3*10%)**. The Economy plan is the base plan and each additional plan costs 10% more than the previous plan.)
- Copy the formula in cell B4 down to cells B5 through B8.
- Insert a formula in cell C3 that divides the amount in cell B3 by 4 and then copy the formula down to cells C4 through C8.
- Insert a formula in cell D3 that divides the amount in cell B3 by 12 and then copy the formula down to cells D4 through D8.
- Apply formatting to enhance the visual display of the worksheet.

Save and print the completed worksheet.

With **EL1-C3-CS-HFCDues-1.xlsx** open, save the workbook with Save As and name it **EL1-C3-CS-HFCDues-2**, and then make the following changes:

- You have been informed that the base rate for yearly dues has increased from $500.00 to $600.00. Change this amount in cell B3 of the worksheet.
- If clients are late with their quarterly or monthly dues payments, a late fee is charged. You decide to add the late fee information to the worksheet. Insert a new column to the right of Column C. Type **Late Fees** in cell D2 and also in cell F2.
- Insert a formula in cell D3 that multiplies the amount in C3 by 5%. Copy this formula down to cells D4 through D8.
- Insert a formula in cell F3 that multiplies the amount in E3 by 7%. Copy this formula down to cells F4 through F8. If necessary, change the number formatting for cells F3 through F8 to Accounting with two decimal places and a dollar sign.
- Apply any additional formatting to enhance the visual display of the worksheet.

Save, print, and then close **EL1-C3-CS-HFCDues-2.xlsx**.

Part 2

Prepare a payroll sheet for the employees of the fitness center and include the following information:

HealthWise Fitness Center
Weekly Payroll

Employee	Hourly Wage	Hours	Weekly Salary	Benefits
Heaton, Kelly	$26.50	40		
Severson, Joel	$25.00	40		
Turney, Amanda	$20.00	15		
Walters, Leslie	$19.65	30		
Overmeyer, Jean	$18.00	20		
Haddon, Bonnie	$16.00	20		
Baker, Grant	$15.00	40		
Calveri, Shannon	$12.00	15		
Dugan, Emily	$10.50	10		
Joyner, Daniel	$10.50	10		
Lee, Alexander	$10.50	10		

Insert a formula in the *Weekly Salary* column that multiplies the hourly wage by the number of hours. Insert an IF statement in the *Benefits* column that states that if the number in the *Hours* column is greater than 19, then insert "Yes" and if not, then insert "No." Apply formatting to enhance the visual display of the worksheet. Save the workbook and name it **EL1-C3-CS-HFCPayroll**. Print **EL1-C3-CS-HFCPayroll.xlsx**. Press Ctrl + ` to turn on the display of formulas, print the worksheet, and then press Ctrl + ` to turn off the display of formulas.

Make the following changes to the worksheet:
- Change the hourly wage for Amanda Turney to *$22.00*.
- Increase the hours for Emily Dugan to *20*.
- Remove the row for Grant Baker.
- Insert a row between Jean Overmeyer and Bonnie Haddon and then type the following information in the cells in the new row: Employee: **Tonya McGuire**; Hourly Wage: **$17.50**; Hours: **15**.

Save and then print **EL1-C3-CS-HFCPayroll.xlsx**. Press Ctrl + ` to turn on the display of formulas and then print the worksheet. Press Ctrl + ` to turn off the display of formulas and then save and close **EL1-C3-CS-HFCPayroll.xlsx**.

Part 3

Your boss is interested in ordering new equipment for the health club. She is interested in ordering three elliptical machines, three recumbent bikes, and three upright bikes. She has asked you to use the Internet to research models and prices for this new equipment. She then wants you to prepare a worksheet with the information. Using the Internet, search for the following equipment:
- Search for elliptical machines for sale. Locate two different models and, if possible, find at least two companies that sell each model. Make a note of the company names, model numbers, and prices.
- Search for recumbent bikes for sale. Locate two different models and, if possible, find at least two companies that sell each model. Make a note of the company names, model numbers, and prices.
- Search for upright bikes for sale. Locate two different models and, if possible, find at least two companies that sell each model. Make a note of the company names, model numbers, and prices.

Using the information you found on the Internet, prepare an Excel worksheet with the following information:
- Equipment name
- Equipment model
- Price
- A column that multiplies the price by the number required (which is 3).

Include the fitness center name, HealthWise Fitness Center, and any other information you determine is necessary to the worksheet. Apply formatting to enhance the visual display of the worksheet. Save the workbook and name it **EL1-C3-CS-HFCEquip**. Print and then close **EL1-C3-CS-HFCEquip.xlsx**.

Part 4

When a prospective client contacts HealthWise about joining, you send a letter containing information about the fitness center, the plans offered, and the dues amounts. Use a letter template in Word to create a letter to send to a prospective client (you determine the client's name and address). Copy the cells in **EL1-C3-CS-HFCDues-02.xlsx** containing data and paste them into the body of the letter. Make any formatting changes to make the data readable. Save the document and name it **HFCLetter**. Print and then close **HFCLetter.docx**.

Microsoft Excel

Enhancing a Worksheet

CHAPTER 4

PERFORMANCE OBJECTIVES

Upon successful completion of Chapter 4, you will be able to:
- Change worksheet margins
- Center a worksheet horizontally and vertically on the page
- Insert a page break in a worksheet
- Print gridlines and row and column headings
- Set and clear a print area
- Insert headers and footers
- Customize print jobs
- Complete a spelling check on a worksheet
- Find and replace data and cell formatting in a worksheet
- Sort data in cells in ascending and descending order
- Filter a list using AutoFilter

Excel contains features you can use to enhance and control the formatting of a worksheet. In this chapter, you will learn how to change worksheet margins, orientation, size, and scale; print column and row titles; print gridlines; and center a worksheet horizontally and vertically on the page. You will also learn how to complete a spell check on text in a worksheet, find and replace specific data and formatting in a worksheet, sort and filter data, and plan and create a worksheet. Model answers for this chapter's projects appear on the following pages.

Excel2010L1C4

Note: Before beginning the projects, copy to your storage medium the Excel2010L1C4 subfolder from the Excel2010L1 folder on the CD that accompanies this textbook and make Excel2010L1C4 the active folder.

Page 1

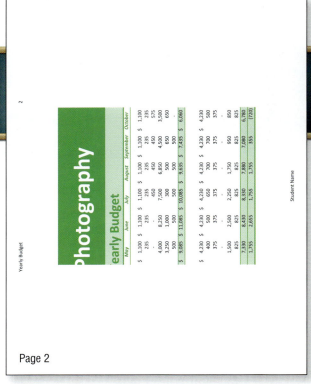

Page 2

Project 1 Format a Yearly Budget Worksheet

EL1-C4-P1-RPBudget.xlsx

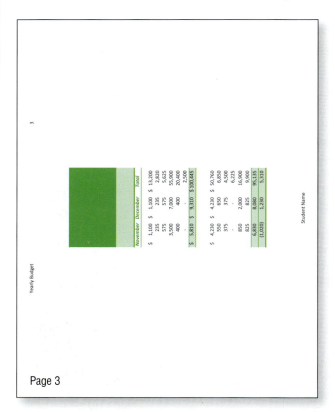

Page 3

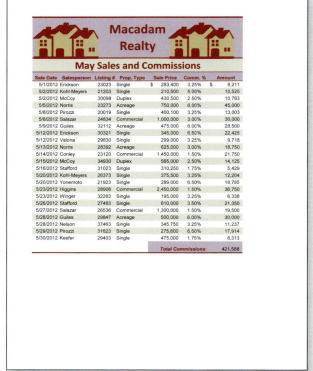

Project 2 Format a May Sales and Commissions Worksheet

EL1-C4-P2-MRSales.xlsx

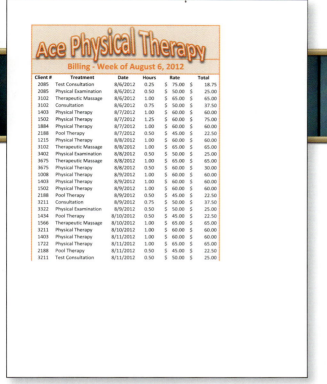

Project 3 Format a Billing Worksheet

EL1-C4-P3-APTBilling.xlsx

Project 1 Format a Yearly Budget Worksheet   12 Parts

You will format a yearly budget worksheet by inserting formulas; changing margins, page orientation, and page size; inserting a page break; printing column headings on multiple pages; scaling data to print on one page; inserting a background picture; inserting headers and footers; and identifying a print area and customizing print jobs.

Formatting a Worksheet Page

An Excel worksheet contains default page formatting. For example, a worksheet contains left and right margins of 0.7 inch and top and bottom margins of 0.75 inch, a worksheet prints in portrait orientation, and the worksheet page size is 8.5 inches by 11 inches. These default settings as well as additional options can be changed and/or controlled with options in the Page Layout tab.

Changing Margins

The Page Setup group in the Page Layout tab contains buttons for changing margins, the page orientation and size, as well as buttons for establishing a print area, inserting a page break, applying a picture background, and printing titles.

Change the worksheet margins by clicking the Margins button in the Page Setup group in the Page Layout tab. This displays a drop-down list of predesigned

▼ **Quick Steps**

Change Worksheet Margins
1. Click Page Layout tab.
2. Click Margins button.
3. Click desired predesigned margin.
OR
1. Click Page Layout tab.
2. Click Margins button.
3. Click *Custom Margins* at drop-down list.
4. Change the top, left, right, and/or bottom measurements.
5. Click OK.

Margins

Chapter 4 ■ Enhancing a Worksheet

margin choices. If one of the predesigned choices is what you want to apply to the worksheet, click the option. If you want to customize margins, click the *Custom Margins* option at the bottom of the Margins button drop-down list. This displays the Page Setup dialog box with the Margins tab selected as shown in Figure 4.1.

A worksheet page showing the cells and margins displays in the dialog box. As you increase or decrease the top, bottom, left, or right margin measurements, the sample worksheet page reflects the change. You can also increase or decrease the measurement from the top of the page to the header with the *Header* option or the measurement from the footer to the bottom of the page with the *Footer* option. (You will learn about headers and footers later in this chapter.)

Figure 4.1 Page Setup Dialog Box with Margins Tab Selected

Changes made to margin measurements are reflected in the sample worksheet page.

▼ Quick Steps

Center Worksheet Horizontally/ Vertically
1. Click Page Layout tab.
2. Click Margins button.
3. Click *Custom Margins* at drop-down list.
4. Click *Horizontally* option and/or click *Vertically* option.
5. Click OK.

Centering a Worksheet Horizontally and/or Vertically

By default, worksheets print in the upper left corner of the page. You can center a worksheet on the page by changing the margins; however, an easier method for centering a worksheet is to use the *Horizontally* and/or *Vertically* options that display in the Page Setup dialog box with the Margins tab selected. If you choose one or both of these options, the worksheet page in the preview section displays how the worksheet will print on the page.

Project 1a — Changing Margins and Horizontally and Vertically Centering a Worksheet

Part 1 of 12

1. Open **RPBudget.xlsx**.
2. Save the workbook with Save As and name it **EL1-C4-P1-RPBudget**.
3. Insert the following formulas in the worksheet:
    a. Insert formulas in column N, rows 5 through 10 that sum the totals for each income item.
    b. Insert formulas in row 11, columns B through N that sum the income as well as the total for all income items.

c. Insert formulas in column N, rows 14 through 19 that sum the totals for each expense item.
d. Insert formulas in row 20, columns B through N that sum the expenses as well as the total of expenses.
e. Insert formulas in row 21, columns B through N that subtract the total expenses from the income. (To begin the formula, make cell B21 active and then type the formula *=B11-B20*. Copy this formula to columns C through N.)
f. Apply the Accounting Number Format style with no decimal places to cells N5 and N14.

4. Click the Page Layout tab.
5. Click the Margins button in the Page Setup group and then click *Custom Margins* at the drop-down list.

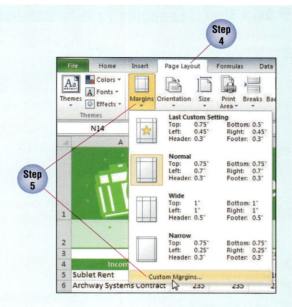

6. At the Page Setup dialog box with the Margins tab selected, click the up-pointing arrow at the right side of the *Top* text box until *3.5* displays.
7. Click the up-pointing arrow at the right side of the *Bottom* text box until *1.5* displays.
8. Preview the worksheet by clicking the Print Preview button located toward the bottom of the Page Setup dialog box. The worksheet appears to be a little low on the page so you decide to horizontally and vertically center it by completing the following steps:

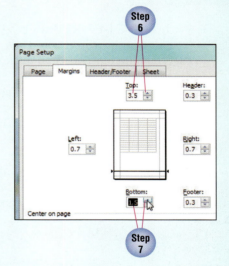

a. Click the Page Setup hyperlink that displays below the categories in the Print tab Backstage view.
b. Click the Margins tab at the Page Setup dialog box.
c. Change the *Top* and *Bottom* measurements to *1*.
d. Click the *Horizontally* option. (This inserts a check mark.)
e. Click the *Vertically* option. (This inserts a check mark.)
f. Click OK to close the dialog box.
g. Look at the preview of the worksheet and then click the File tab to return to the worksheet.
9. Save **EL1-C4-P1-RPBudget.xlsx**.

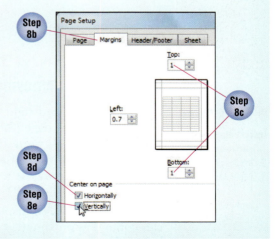

Chapter 4 ■ Enhancing a Worksheet   111

▼ Quick Steps

Change Page Orientation
1. Click Page Layout tab.
2. Click Orientation button.
3. Click desired orientation at drop-down list.

Change Page Size
1. Click Page Layout tab.
2. Click Size button.
3. Click desired size at drop-down list.

Orientation Size

Changing Page Orientation

Click the Orientation button in the Page Setup group and a drop-down list displays with two choices, *Portrait* and *Landscape*. The two choices are represented by sample pages. A sample page that is taller than it is wide shows how the default orientation (*Portrait*) prints data on the page. The other choice, *Landscape*, will rotate the data and print it on a page that is wider than it is tall.

Changing the Page Size

An Excel worksheet page size, by default, is set at 8.5 × 11 inches. You can change this default page size by clicking the Size button in the Page Setup group. At the drop-down list that displays, notice that the default setting is *Letter* and the measurement *8.5" × 11"* displays below *Letter*. This drop-down list also contains a number of page sizes such as *Executive*, *Legal*, and a number of envelope sizes.

Project 1b — Changing Page Orientation and Size — Part 2 of 12

1. With **EL1-C4-P1-RPBudget.xlsx** open, click the Orientation button in the Page Setup group in the Page Layout tab and then click *Landscape* at the drop-down list.
2. Click the Size button in the Page Setup group and then click *Legal* at the drop-down list.
3. Preview the worksheet by clicking the File tab and then clicking the Print tab. After viewing the worksheet in the Print tab Backstage view, click the File tab to return to the worksheet.
4. Save **EL1-C4-P1-RPBudget.xlsx**.

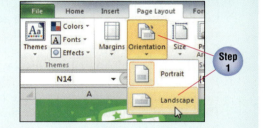
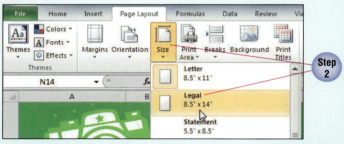

Inserting and Removing Page Breaks

▼ Quick Steps

Insert Page Break
1. Select column or row.
2. Click Page Layout tab.
3. Click Breaks button.
4. Click *Insert Page Break* at drop-down list.

The default left and right margins of 0.7 inch allow approximately 7 inches of cells across the page (8.5 inches minus 1.4 inches equals 7.1 inches). If a worksheet contains more than 7 inches of cells across the page, a page break is inserted in the worksheet and the remaining columns are moved to the next page. A page break displays as a broken line along cell borders. Figure 4.2 shows the page break in **EL1-C4-P1-RPBudget.xlsx**.

A page break also displays horizontally in a worksheet. By default, a worksheet can contain approximately 9.5 inches of cells vertically down the page. This is because the paper size is set by default at 11 inches. With the default top and bottom margins of 0.75 inch, this allows 9.5 inches of cells to print on one page.

Figure 4.2 Page Break

[Figure 4.2: Screenshot of Excel worksheet titled "Real Photography Yearly Budget" showing Income and Expenses by month, with a page break indicated between columns K and L.]

Excel automatically inserts a page break in a worksheet. You can insert your own if you would like more control over what cells print on a page. To insert your own page break, select the column or row, click the Breaks button in the Page Setup group in the Page Layout tab, and then click *Insert Page Break* at the drop-down list. A page break is inserted immediately left of the selected column or immediately above the selected row.

Breaks

If you want to insert both a horizontal and vertical page break at the same time, make a cell active, click the Breaks button in the Page Setup group and then click *Insert Page Break*. This causes a horizontal page break to be inserted immediately above the active cell, and a vertical page break to be inserted at the left side of the active cell. To remove a page break, select the column or row or make the desired cell active, click the Breaks button in the Page Setup group, and then click *Remove Page Break* at the drop-down list.

The page break automatically inserted by Excel may not be visible initially in a worksheet. One way to display the page break is to display the worksheet in the Print tab Backstage view. When you return to the worksheet, the page break will display in the worksheet.

Excel provides a page break view that displays worksheet pages and page breaks. To display this view, click the Page Break Preview button located in the view area at the right side of the Status bar or click the View tab and then click the Page Break Preview button in the Workbook Views group. This causes the worksheet to display similar to the worksheet shown in Figure 4.3. The word *Page* along with the page number is displayed in gray behind the cells in the worksheet. A solid blue line indicates a page break inserted by Excel and a dashed blue line indicates a page break inserted manually.

You can edit a worksheet in Page Break Preview.

Page Break Preview

You can move the page break by positioning the arrow pointer on the blue line, holding down the left mouse button, dragging the line to the desired location, and then releasing the mouse button. To return to the Normal view, click the Normal button in the view area on the Status bar or click the View tab and then click the Normal button in the Workbook Views group.

Normal

Figure 4.3 Worksheet in Page Break Preview

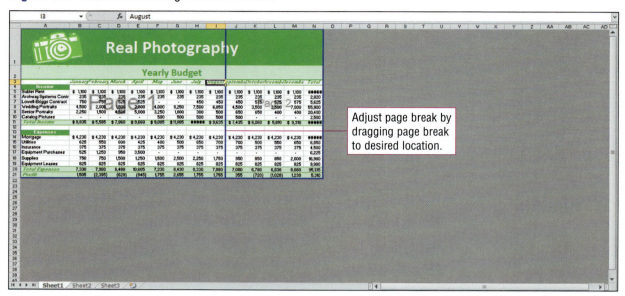

Project 1c Inserting a Page Break in a Worksheet   Part 3 of 12

1. With **EL1-C4-P1-RPBudget.xlsx** open, click the Size button in the Page Setup group in the Page Layout tab and then click *Letter* at the drop-down list.
2. Click the Margins button and then click *Custom Margins* at the drop-down list.
3. At the Page Setup dialog box with the Margins tab selected, click *Horizontally* to remove the check mark, click *Vertically* to remove the check mark, and then click OK to close the dialog box.
4. Insert a page break between columns I and J by completing the following steps:
   a. Select column J.
   b. Click the Breaks button in the Page Setup group and then click *Insert Page Break* at the drop-down list. Click in any cell in column I.

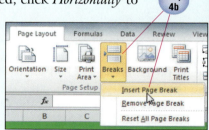

5. View the worksheet in Page Break Preview by completing the following steps:
   a. Click the Page Break Preview button located in the view area on the Status bar. (If a welcome message displays, click OK.)

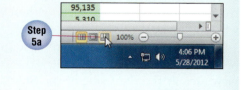

   b. View the pages and page breaks in the worksheet.
   c. You decide to include the first six months of the year on one page. To do this, position the arrow pointer on the vertical blue line, hold down the left mouse button, drag the line to the left so it is positioned between columns G and H, and then release the mouse button.

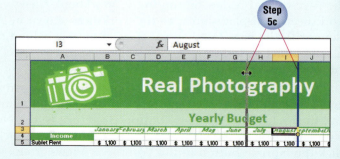

d. Click the Normal button located in the view area on the Status bar.
6. Save **EL1-C4-P1-RPBudget.xlsx**.

Printing Column and Row Titles on Multiple Pages

Columns and rows in a worksheet are usually titled. For example, in **EL1-C4-P1-RPBudget.xlsx**, column titles include *Income, Expenses, January, February, March*, and so on. Row titles include the income and expenses categories. If a worksheet prints on more than one page, having column and/or row titles printing on each page can be useful. To do this, click the Print Titles button in the Page Setup group in the Page Layout tab. This displays the Page Setup dialog box with the Sheet tab selected as shown in Figure 4.4.

At the Page Setup dialog box with the Sheet tab selected, specify the range of row cells you want to print on every page in the *Rows to repeat at top* text box. Type a cell range using a colon. For example, if you want cells A1 through J1 to print on every page, you would type *A1:J1* in the *Rows to repeat at top* text box. Type the range of column cells you want to print on every page in the *Columns to repeat at left* text box. To make rows and columns easier to identify on the printed page, specify that row and/or column headings print on each page.

▼ **Quick Steps**

Print Column and Row Titles
1. Click Page Layout tab.
2. Click Print Titles button.
3. Type row range in *Rows to repeat at top* option.
4. Type column range in *Columns to repeat at left* option.
5. Click OK.

Print Titles

Figure 4.4 Page Setup Dialog Box with Sheet Tab Selected

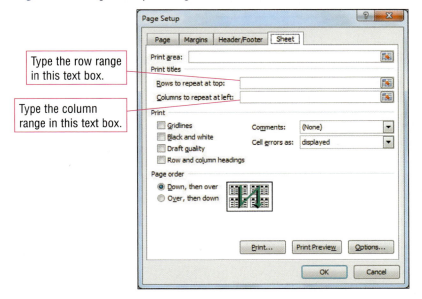

Chapter 4 ■ Enhancing a Worksheet   115

Project 1d   **Printing Column Titles on Each Page of a Worksheet**   Part 4 of 12

1. With **EL1-C4-P1-RPBudget.xlsx** open, click the Page Layout tab and then click the Print Titles button in the Page Setup group.
2. At the Page Setup dialog box with the Sheet tab selected, click in the *Columns to repeat at left* text box.
3. Type **A1:A21**.
4. Click OK to close the dialog box.
5. Save and then print **EL1-C4-P1-RPBudget.xlsx**.

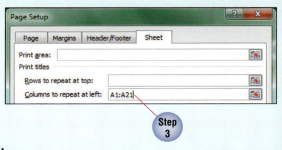

Step 3

Scaling Data

Width

With buttons in the Scale to Fit group in the Page Layout tab, you can adjust the printed output by a percentage to fit the number of pages specified. For example, if a worksheet contains too many columns to print on one page, click the down-pointing arrow at the right side of the *Width* box in the Scale to Fit group in the Page Layout tab and then click *1 page*. This causes the data to shrink so all columns display and print on one page.

Project 1e   **Scaling Data to Fit on One Page and Printing Row Titles on Each Page**   Part 5 of 12

1. With **EL1-C4-P1-RPBudget.xlsx** open, click the down-pointing arrow at the right side of the *Width* box in the Scale to Fit group in the Page Layout tab.
2. At the drop-down list that displays, click the *1 page* option.
3. Display the Print tab Backstage view, notice that all cells containing data display on one page in the worksheet, and then return to the worksheet.
4. Change margins by completing the following steps:
   a. Click the Page Layout tab.
   b. Click the Margins button in the Page Setup group and then click *Custom Margins* at the drop-down list.
   c. At the Page Setup dialog box with the Margins tab selected, select the current number in the *Top* text box and then type **3.5**.
   d. Select the current number in the *Left* text box and then type **0.3**.
   e. Select the current number in the *Right* text box and then type **0.3**.
   f. Click OK to close the Page Setup dialog box.
5. Specify that you want row titles to print on each page by completing the following steps:
   a. Click the Print Titles button in the Page Setup group in the Page Layout tab.
   b. At the Page Setup dialog box with the Sheet tab selected, select and then delete the text that displays in the *Columns to repeat at left* text box.

Step 1

Step 2

c. Click in the *Rows to repeat at top* text box and then type **A3:N3**.
   d. Click OK to close the dialog box.
6. Save and then print **EL1-C4-P1-RPBudget.xlsx**. (The worksheet will print on two pages with the row titles repeated on the second page.)
7. At the worksheet, return to the default margins by clicking the Page Layout tab, clicking the Margins button, and then clicking the *Normal* option at the drop-down list.
8. Remove titles from printing on second and subsequent pages by completing the following steps:
   a. Click the Print Titles button in the Page Setup group.
   b. At the Page Setup dialog box with the Sheet tab selected, select and then delete the text that displays in the *Rows to repeat at top* text box.
   c. Click OK to close the dialog box.
9. Change the scaling back to the default by completing the following steps:
   a. Click the down-pointing arrow at the right side of the *Width* box in the Scale to Fit group and then click *Automatic* at the drop-down list.
   b. Click the up-pointing arrow at the right side of the *Scale* measurement box until *100%* displays in the box.
10. Save **EL1-C4-P1-RPBudget.xlsx**.

Step 5c

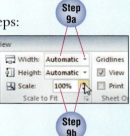
Step 9a
Step 9b

Inserting a Background Picture

With the Background button in the Page Setup group in the Page Layout tab you can insert a picture as a background to the worksheet. The picture displays only on the screen and does not print. To insert a picture, click the Background button in the Page Setup group. At the Sheet Background dialog box navigate to the folder containing the desired picture and then double-click the picture. To remove the picture from the worksheet, click the Delete Background button.

▼ **Quick Steps**

Insert Background Picture
1. Click Page Layout tab.
2. Click Background button.
3. Navigate to desired picture and double-click picture.

Background

Project 1f Inserting a Background Picture   Part 6 of 12

1. With **EL1-C4-P1-RPBudget.xlsx** open, insert a background picture by completing the following steps:
   a. Click the Background button in the Page Setup group in the Page Layout tab.
   b. At the Sheet Background dialog box, navigate to the Excel2010L1C4 folder, and then double-click **Ship.jpg**.
   c. Scroll down the worksheet to display the ship.
2. Display the Print tab Backstage view, notice that the picture does not display in the preview worksheet, and then return to the worksheet.
3. Remove the picture by clicking the Delete Background button in the Page Setup group in the Page Layout tab.
4. Save **EL1-C4-P1-RPBudget.xlsx**.

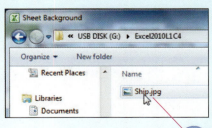
Step 1b

▼ **Quick Steps**

Print Gridlines
1. Click Page Layout tab.
2. Click *Print* check box in *Gridlines* section in Sheet Options group.
OR
1. Click Page Layout tab.
2. Click Sheet Options dialog box launcher.
3. Click *Gridlines* option.
4. Click OK.

Print Row and Column Headings
1. Click Page Layout tab.
2. Click *Print* check box in *Headings* section in Sheet Options group.
OR
1. Click Page Layout tab.
2. Click Sheet Options dialog box launcher.
3. Click *Row and column headings* option.
4. Click OK.

Printing Gridlines and Row and Column Headings

By default, the gridlines that create the cells in a worksheet and the row numbers and column letters do not print. The Sheet Options group in the Page Layout tab contain check boxes for gridlines and headings. The *View* check boxes for Gridlines and Headings contain check marks. At these settings, gridlines and row and column headings display on the screen but do not print. If you want them to print, insert check marks in the *Print* check boxes. Complex worksheets may be easier to read with the gridlines printed.

You can also control the display and printing of gridlines and headings with options at the Page Setup dialog box with the Sheet tab selected. Display this dialog box by clicking the Sheet Options dialog box launcher. To print gridlines and headings, insert check marks in the check boxes located in the *Print* section of the dialog box. The *Print* section contains two additional options — *Black and white* and *Draft quality*. If you are printing with a color printer, you can print the worksheet in black and white by inserting a check mark in the *Black and white* check box. Insert a check mark in the *Draft* option if you want to print a draft of the worksheet. With this option checked, some formatting such as shading and fill do not print.

Project 1g **Printing Gridlines and Row and Column Headings** Part 7 of 12

1. With **EL1-C4-P1-RPBudget.xlsx** open, click in the *Print* check box below Gridlines in the Sheet Options group in the Page Layout tab to insert a check mark.
2. Click in the *Print* check box below Headings in the Sheet Options group to insert a check mark.
3. Click the Margins button in the Page Setup group and then click *Custom Margins* at the drop-down list.
4. At the Page Setup dialog box with the Margins tab selected, click in the *Horizontally* check box to insert a check mark.
5. Click in the *Vertically* check box to insert a check mark.
6. Click OK to close the dialog box.
7. Save and then print **EL1-C4-P1-RPBudget.xlsx**.
8. Click in the *Print* check box below Headings in the Sheet Options group to remove the check mark.
9. Click in the *Print* check box below Gridlines in the Sheet Options group to remove the check mark.
10. Save **EL1-C4-P1-RPBudget.xlsx**.

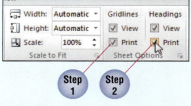

Printing a Specific Area of a Worksheet

Print Area

With the Print Area button in the Page Setup group in the Page Layout tab you can select and print specific areas in a worksheet. To do this, select the cells you want to print, click the Print Area button in the Page Setup group in the Page Layout tab, and then click *Set Print Area* at the drop-down list. This inserts a border around the selected cells. Display the Print tab Backstage view, click the Print button, and the cells within the border are printed.

You can specify more than one print area in a worksheet. To do this, select the first group of cells, click the Print Area button in the Page Setup group, and then click *Set Print Area*. Select the next group of cells, click the Print Area button, and then click *Add to Print Area*. Clear a print area by clicking the Print Area button in the Page Setup group and then clicking *Clear Print Area* at the drop-down list.

Each area specified as a print area will print on a separate page. If you want nonadjacent print areas to print on the same page, consider hiding columns and/or rows in the worksheet to bring the areas together.

Project 1h Printing Specific Areas

1. With **EL1-C4-P1-RPBudget.xlsx** open, print the first half of the year's income and expenses by completing the following steps:
   a. Select cells A3 through G21.
   b. Click the Print Area button in the Page Setup group in the Page Layout tab and then click *Set Print Area* at the drop-down list.
   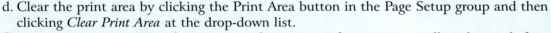
   c. With the border surrounding the cells A3 through G21, click the File tab, click the Print tab, and then click the Print button at the Print tab Backstage view.
   d. Clear the print area by clicking the Print Area button in the Page Setup group and then clicking *Clear Print Area* at the drop-down list.
2. Suppose you want to print the income and expenses information as well as the totals for the month of April. To do this, hide columns and select a print area by completing the following steps:
   a. Select columns B through D.
   b. Click the Home tab.
   c. Click the Format button in the Cells group, point to *Hide & Unhide*, and then click *Hide Columns*.
   d. Click the Page Layout tab.
   e. Select cells A3 through E21. (Columns A and E are now adjacent.)
   f. Click the Print Area button in the Page Setup group and then click *Set Print Area* at the drop-down list.
3. Click the File tab, click the Print tab, and then click the Print button.
4. Clear the print area by making sure cells A3 through E21 are selected, clicking the Print Area button in the Page Setup group, and then clicking *Clear Print Area* at the drop-down list.
5. Unhide the columns by completing the following steps:
   a. Click the Home tab.
   b. Select columns A and E. (These columns are adjacent.)
   c. Click the Format button in the Cells group, point to *Hide & Unhide*, and then click *Unhide Columns*.
   d. Deselect the text by clicking in any cell containing data in the worksheet.
6. Save **EL1-C4-P1-RPBudget.xlsx**.

Figure 4.5 Header & Footer Tools Design Tab

Inserting Headers and Footers

Quick Steps

Insert a Header or Footer
1. Click Insert tab.
2. Click Header & Footer button.
3. Click Header button and then click predesigned header or click Footer button and then click predesigned footer.

OR
1. Click Insert tab.
2. Click Header & Footer button.
3. Click desired header or footer elements.

HINT Close the header or footer pane by clicking in the worksheet or pressing Esc.

Header & Footer

Text that prints at the top of each worksheet page is called a ***header*** and text that prints at the bottom of each worksheet page is called a ***footer***. You can create a header and/or footer with the Header & Footer button in the Text group in the Insert tab, in Page Layout View, or with options at the Page Setup dialog box with the Header/Footer tab selected.

To create a header with the Header & Footer button, click the Insert tab and then click the Header & Footer button in the Text group. This displays the worksheet in Page Layout view and displays the Header & Footer Tools Design tab. Use buttons in this tab, shown in Figure 4.5, to insert predesigned headers and/or footers or insert header and footer elements such as the page number, date, time, path name, and file name. You can also create a different header or footer on the first page of the worksheet or create a header or footer for even pages and another for odd pages.

At the Print tab Backstage view, you can preview your headers and footers before printing. Click the File tab and then the Print tab to display the Print tab Backstage view. A preview of the worksheet displays at the right side of the Backstage view. If your worksheet will print on more than one page, you can view different pages by clicking the Next Page button or the Previous Page button. These buttons are located below and to the left of the preview worksheet at the Print tab Backstage view. Two buttons display in the bottom right corner of the Print tab Backstage view. Click the Show Margins button and margin guidelines display in the preview of the worksheet. Click the Zoom to Page button to zoom in or out of the preview of the worksheet.

Project 1i   Inserting a Header in a Worksheet   Part 9 of 12

1. With **EL1-C4-P1-RPBudget.xlsx** open, create a header by completing the following steps:
   a. Click the Insert tab.
   b. Click the Header & Footer button in the Text group.

c. Click the Header button located at the left side of the Header & Footer Tools Design tab and then click *Page 1, EL1-C4-P1-RPBudget.xlsx* at the drop-down list. (This inserts the page number in the middle header box and the workbook name in the right header box.)

2. Preview the worksheet by completing the following steps:
   a. Click the File tab and then click the Print tab.
   b. At the Print tab Backstage view look at the preview worksheet that displays at the right.
   c. View the next page of the worksheet by clicking the Next Page button that displays below and to the left of the preview worksheet.

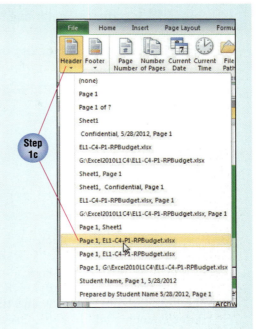

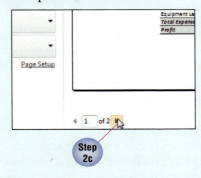

   d. View the first page by clicking the Previous Page button that displays left of the Next Page button.
   e. Click the File tab to return to the workbook.
3. Save **EL1-C4-P1-RPBudget.xlsx**.

You also can insert a header and/or footer by switching to Page Layout view. In Page Layout view, the top of the worksheet page displays with the text *Click to add header*. Click this text and the insertion point is positioned in the middle header box. Type the desired header in this box or click in the left box or the right box and then type the header. Create a footer in a similar manner. Scroll down the worksheet until the bottom of the page displays and then click the text *Click to add footer*. Type the footer in the center footer box or click the left or right box and then type the footer.

Project 1j Inserting a Footer and Modifying a Header in a Worksheet Part 10 of 12

1. With **EL1-C4-P1-RPBudget.xlsx** open, make sure the workbook displays in Page Layout view.
2. Scroll down the worksheet until the text *Click to add footer* displays and then click the text.

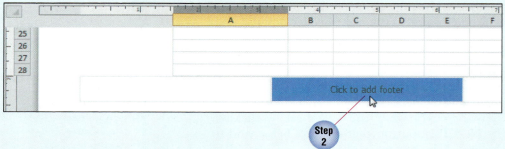

Step 2

3. Type your first and last names.
4. Click in the left footer box, click the Header & Footer Tools Design tab, and then click the Current Date button in the Header & Footer Elements group. (This inserts a date code. The date will display when you click outside the footer box.)
5. Click in the right footer box and then click the Current Time button in the Header & Footer Elements group. (This inserts the time as a code. The time will display when you click outside the footer box.)
6. View the headers and footers at the Print tab Backstage view and then return to the worksheet.
7. Modify the header by completing the following steps:
   a. Scroll to the beginning of the worksheet and display the header text.
   b. Click the page number in the middle header box. (This displays the Header & Footer Tools Design tab, changes the header to a field, and selects the field.)
   c. Press the Delete key to delete the header.
   d. Click the header text that displays in the right header box and then press the Delete key.
   e. With the insertion point positioned in the right header box, insert the page number by clicking the Header & Footer Tools Design tab and then clicking the Page Number button in the Header & Footer Elements group.
   f. Click in the left header box and then click the File Name button in the Header & Footer Elements group.

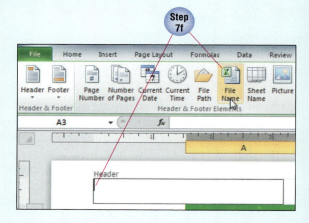

Step 7f

8. Click in any cell in the worksheet containing data.
9. View the headers and footers at the Print tab Backstage view and then return to the worksheet.
10. Save **EL1-C4-P1-RPBudget.xlsx**.

In addition to options in the Header & Footer Tools Design tab, you can insert and customize headers and footers with options at the Page Setup dialog box with the Header/Footer tab selected that displays in Figure 4.6. Display this dialog box by clicking the Page Layout tab and then clicking the Page Setup group dialog box launcher. At the Page Setup dialog box, click the Header/Footer tab. If your worksheet contains headers or footers, they will display in the dialog box.

Figure 4.6 Page Setup Dialog Box with Header/Footer Tab Selected

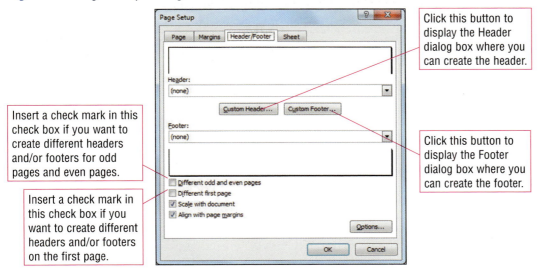

With the check box options that display in the lower left corner of the dialog box, you can specify that you want to insert a different odd and even page header or footer or insert a different first page header or footer. The bottom two check box options are active by default. These defaults scale the header and footer text with the worksheet text and align the header and footer with the page margins.

To create different odd and even page headers, click the *Different odd and even pages* check box to insert a check mark and then click the Custom Header button. This displays the Header dialog box with the Odd Page Header tab selected. Type or insert the desired odd page header data in the left, center, or right section boxes and then click the Even Page Header tab. Type or insert the desired even page header data in the section boxes and then click OK. Use the buttons that display above the section boxes to format the header text and insert information such as the page number, current date, current time, file name, worksheet name, and so on. Complete similar steps to create different odd and even page footers and different first page headers or footers.

Project 1k — **Creating Different Odd and Even Page Headers and Footers and a Different First Page Header and Footer** Part 11 of 12

1. With **EL1-C4-P1-RPBudget.xlsx** open, remove the page break by clicking the Page Layout tab, clicking the Breaks button in the Page Setup group, and then clicking *Reset All Page Breaks* at the drop-down list.
2. Change the margins by completing the following steps:
   a. Click the Margins button in the Page Setup group in the Page Layout tab and then click *Custom Margins* at the drop-down list.
   b. At the Page Setup dialog box with the Margins tab selected, select the current number in the *Left* text box and then type **3**.
   c. Select the current number in the *Right* text box and then type **3**.
   d. Click OK to close the dialog box.
3. Click the Page Layout tab and then click the Page Setup dialog box launcher.

4. At the Page Setup dialog box, click the Header/Footer tab.
5. At the Page Setup dialog box with the Header/Footer tab selected, click the *Different odd and even pages* check box to insert a check mark.
6. Click the Custom Header button.
7. At the Header dialog box with the Odd Page Header tab selected and the field selected in the left section box, type **Yearly Budget**.
8. Click the Even Page Header tab.
9. Click in the left section box and then click the Insert Page Number button.

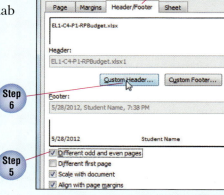
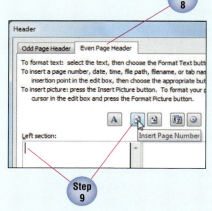
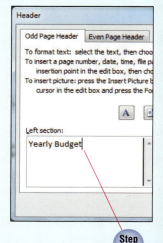

10. Click in the right section box, type **Yearly Budget**, and then click OK to close the Header dialog box.
11. Click the Custom Footer button.
12. At the Footer dialog box with the Odd Page Footer tab selected, select and then delete the data in the left section box and the right section box. (The footer should only contain your name.)
13. Click the Even Page Footer tab and then insert your name in the center section box.
14. Click OK to close the Footer dialog box and then click OK to close the Page Setup dialog box.
15. View the headers and footers in Print tab Backstage view and then return to the worksheet.
16. Click the Page Setup group dialog box launcher in the Page Layout tab.
17. At the Page Setup dialog box, click the Header/Footer tab.
18. At the Page Setup dialog box with the Header/Footer tab selected, click the *Different odd and even pages* check box to remove the check mark.
19. Click the *Different first page* check box to insert a check mark and then click the Custom Header button.
20. At the Header dialog box with the Header tab selected, click the First Page Header tab.
21. Click in the right section box and then click the Insert Page Number button located above the section boxes.

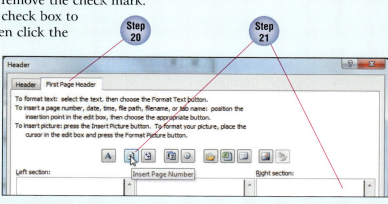

22. Click OK to close the Header dialog box and then click OK to close the Page Setup dialog box.
23. View the headers and footers in the Print tab Backstage view and then return to the worksheet.
24. Save **EL1-C4-P1-RPBudget.xlsx**.

Customizing Print Jobs

As you learned in this chapter, you can preview worksheets in the Print tab Backstage view. With options in the Settings category at the Print tab Backstage view, you can also specify what you want printed. By default, the active worksheet prints. You can change this by clicking the first gallery that displays in the Settings category. At the drop-down list that displays, you can specify that you want the entire workbook to print (this is useful when a workbook contains more than one worksheet) or print the selected cells. With the other galleries in the Settings category, you can specify if you want pages printed on one side or both sides (this is dependent on your printer) and collated. You can also specify the worksheet orientation, size, and margins as well as specify if you want the worksheet scaled to fit all columns or rows on one page.

With the *Pages* text boxes in the Settings category, you can specify the pages you want printed of your worksheet. For example, if you wanted to print pages 2 and 3 of your active worksheet, you would type **2** in the text box immediately right of the word *Pages* in the Settings category and then type **3** in the text box immediately right of the word *to*. You can also use the up- and down-pointing arrows to insert page numbers.

Project 1I Printing Specific Pages of a Worksheet   Part 12 of 12

1. With **EL1-C4-P1-RPBudget.xlsx** open, print the first two pages of the worksheet by completing the following steps:
   a. Click the File tab and then click the Print tab.
   b. At the Print tab Backstage view, click in the text box immediately right of *Pages* located below the first gallery in the Settings category and then type **1**.
   c. Click in the text box immediately right of *to* in the Settings category and then type **2**.
   d. Click the Print button.

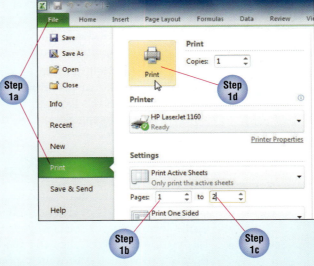

2. Print selected cells by completing the following steps:
   a. Display the worksheet in Normal view.
   b. Select cells A3 through D11.
   c. Click the File tab and then the Print tab.
   d. At the Print tab Backstage view, select and then delete the numbers in the *Pages* text boxes. (These are the numbers you inserted in Steps 1b and 1c.)
   e. Click the first gallery in the Settings category (displays with *Print Active Sheets*) and then click *Print Selection* at the drop-down list.
   f. Click the Print button.
3. Save and then close **EL1-C4-P1-RPBudget.xlsx**.

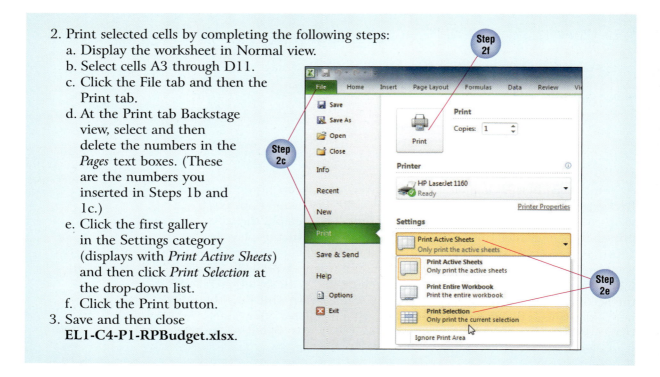

Project 2 Format a May Sales and Commissions Worksheet 3 Parts

You will format a sales commission worksheet by inserting a formula, completing a spelling check, and finding and replacing data and cell formatting.

Completing a Spelling Check

▼ **Quick Steps**

Complete a Spelling Check
1. Click Review tab.
2. Click Spelling button.
3. Replace or ignore selected words.

HINT Customize spell checking options at the Excel Options dialog box with *Proofing* selected.

Spelling

Excel includes a spelling checker you can use to check the spelling of text in a worksheet. Before checking the spelling in a worksheet, make the first cell active. The spell checker checks the worksheet from the active cell to the last cell in the worksheet that contains data.

To use the spelling checker, click the Review tab and then click the Spelling button. Figure 4.7 displays the Spelling dialog box. At this dialog box, you can click a button to tell Excel to ignore a word or you can replace a misspelled word with a word from the *Suggestions* list box.

Using Undo and Redo

Excel includes an Undo button on the Quick Access toolbar that will reverse certain commands or delete the last data typed in a cell. For example, if you apply formatting to selected cells in a worksheet and then decide you want the formatting removed, click the Undo button on the Quick Access toolbar. If you decide you want the formatting back again, click the Redo button on the Quick Access toolbar.

Figure 4.7 Excel Spelling Dialog Box

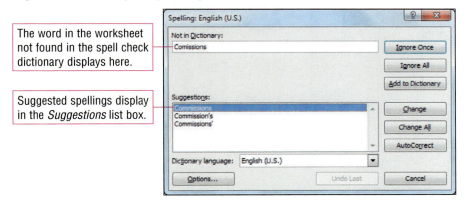

The word in the worksheet not found in the spell check dictionary displays here.

Suggested spellings display in the *Suggestions* list box.

HINT Ctrl + Z is the keyboard shortcut to undo a command.

Undo

Redo

Excel maintains actions in temporary memory. If you want to undo an action performed earlier, click the down-pointing arrow at the right side of the Undo button and a drop-down list displays containing the actions performed on the worksheet. Click the desired action at the drop-down list. Any actions preceding a chosen action are also undone. You can do the same with the Redo drop-down list. Multiple actions must be undone or redone in sequence.

Project 2a Spell Checking and Formatting a Worksheet   Part 1 of 3

1. Open **MRSales.xlsx**.
2. Save the workbook with Save As and name it **EL1-C4-P2-MRSales**.
3. Complete a spelling check on the worksheet by completing the following steps:
   a. Make cell A1 active.
   b. Click the Review tab.
   c. Click the Spelling button in the Proofing group.
   d. Click the Change button as needed to correct misspelled words in the worksheet. (When the spell checker stops at proper names *Pirozzi* and *Yonemoto*, click the Ignore All button.)
   e. At the message telling you the spelling check is completed, click OK.

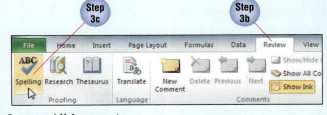

4. Insert a formula and then copy the formula without the formatting by completing the following steps:
   a. Make cell G4 active and then insert a formula that multiplies the sale price by the commission percentage.
   b. Copy the formula down to cells G5 through G26.
   c. Some of the cells contain shading that you do not want removed, so click the Auto Fill Options button that displays at the bottom right of the selected cells and then click the *Fill Without Formatting* option at the drop-down list.
5. Apply the Accounting Number Format style with no decimal places to cell G4.

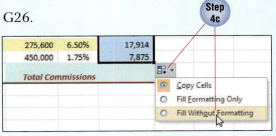

Chapter 4 ■ Enhancing a Worksheet   127

6. Make cell G27 active and then insert the sum of cells G4 through G26.
7. Apply a theme by clicking the Page Layout button, clicking the Themes button, and then clicking *Elemental* at the drop-down gallery.
8. After looking at the worksheet with the Elemental theme applied, you decide you want to return to the original formatting. To do this, click the Undo button on the Quick Access toolbar.

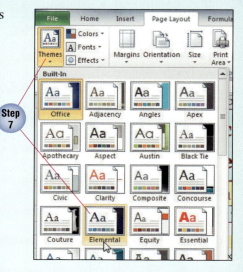

9. Save **EL1-C4-P2-MRSales.xlsx**.

Finding and Replacing Data and Cell Formatting in a Worksheet

Quick Steps

Find Data
1. Click Find & Select button.
2. Click *Find* at drop-down list.
3. Type data in *Find what* text box.
4. Click Find Next button.

Find & Select

Excel provides a Find feature you can use to look for specific data and either replace it with nothing or replace it with other data. This feature is particularly helpful in a large worksheet with data you want to find quickly. Excel also includes a find and replace feature. Use this to look for specific data in a worksheet and replace it with other data.

To find specific data in a worksheet, click the Find & Select button located in the Editing group in the Home tab and then click *Find* at the drop-down list. This displays the Find and Replace dialog box with the Find tab selected as shown in Figure 4.8. Type the data you want to find in the *Find what* text box and then click the Find Next button. Continue clicking the Find Next button to move to the next occurrence of the data. If the Find and Replace dialog box obstructs your view of the worksheet, use the mouse pointer on the title bar to drag the box to a different location.

Figure 4.8 Find and Replace Dialog Box with Find Tab Selected

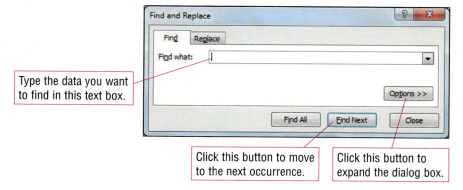

To find specific data in a worksheet and replace it with other data, click the Find & Select button in the Editing group in the Home tab and then click *Replace* at the drop-down list. This displays the Find and Replace dialog box with the Replace tab selected as shown in Figure 4.9. Enter the data for which you are looking in the *Find what* text box. Press the Tab key or click in the *Replace with* text box and then enter the data that is to replace the data in the *Find what* text box.

Click the Find Next button to tell Excel to find the next occurrence of the data. Click the Replace button to replace the data and find the next occurrence. If you know that you want all occurrences of the data in the *Find what* text box replaced with the data in the *Replace with* text box, click the Replace All button. Click the Close button to close the Replace dialog box.

Display additional find and replace options by clicking the Options button. This expands the dialog box as shown in Figure 4.10. By default, Excel will look for any data that contains the same characters as the data in the *Find what* text box, without concern for the characters before or after the entered data. For example, in Project 2b, you will be looking for sale prices of $450,000 and replacing with $475,000. If you do not specify to Excel that you want to find cells that contain only *450000*, Excel will stop at any cell containing *450000*. In this example, Excel would stop at a cell containing *$1,450,000* or a cell containing *$2,450,000*. To specify that the only data that should be contained in the cell is what is entered in the *Find what* text box, click the Options button to expand the dialog box and then insert a check mark in the *Match entire cell contents* check box.

▼ **Quick Steps**

Find and Replace Data
1. Click Find & Select button.
2. Click *Replace* at drop-down list.
3. Type data in *Find what* text box.
4. Type data in *Replace with* text box.
5. Click Replace button or Replace All button.

Figure 4.9 Find and Replace Dialog Box with Replace Tab Selected

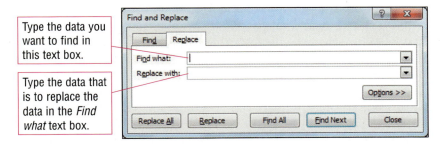

Figure 4.10 Expanded Find and Replace Dialog Box

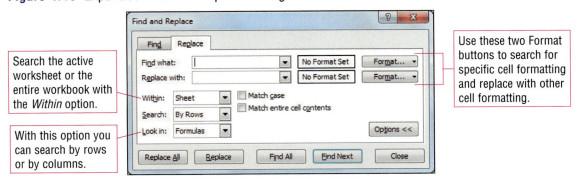

Chapter 4 ■ Enhancing a Worksheet   129

If the *Match case* option is active (contains a check mark), Excel will look for only that data that exactly matches the case of the data entered in the *Find what* text box. Remove the check mark from this check box if you do not want Excel to find exact case matches. Excel will search in the current worksheet. If you want Excel to search an entire workbook, change the *Within* option to *Workbook*. Excel, by default, searches by rows in a worksheet. You can change this to *By Columns* with the *Search* option.

Project 2b Finding and Replacing Data   Part 2 of 3

1. With **EL1-C4-P2-MRSales.xlsx** open, find all occurrences of *Land* in the worksheet and replace with *Acreage* by completing the following steps:
   a. Click the Find & Select button in the Editing group in the Home tab and then click *Replace* at the drop-down list.
   b. At the Find and Replace dialog box with the Replace tab selected, type **Land** in the *Find what* text box.
   c. Press the Tab key. (This moves the insertion point to the *Replace with* text box.)
   d. Type **Acreage**.
   e. Click the Replace All button.
   f. At the message telling you that four replacements were made, click OK.
   g. Click the Close button to close the Find and Replace dialog box.

2. Find all occurrences of *$450,000* and replace with *$475,000* by completing the following steps:
   a. Click the Find & Select button in the Editing group and then click *Replace* at the drop-down list.
   b. At the Find and Replace dialog box with the Replace tab selected, type **450000** in the *Find what* text box.
   c. Press the Tab key.
   d. Type **475000**.
   e. Click the Options button to display additional options. (If additional options already display, skip this step.)
   f. Click the *Match entire cell contents* option to insert a check mark in the check box.
   g. Click Replace All.
   h. At the message telling you that two replacements were made, click OK.
   i. At the Find and Replace dialog box, click the *Match entire cell contents* option to remove the check mark.
   j. Click the Close button to close the Find and Replace dialog box.
3. Save **EL1-C4-P2-MRSales.xlsx**.

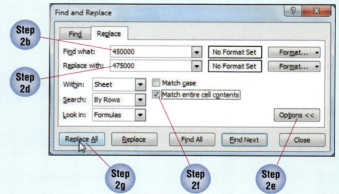

Use the Format buttons at the expanded Find and Replace dialog box (see Figure 4.10) to search for specific cell formatting and replace with other formatting. Click the down-pointing arrow at the right side of the Format button and a drop-down list displays. Click the *Format* option and the Find Format dialog box displays with the Number, Alignment, Font, Border, Fill, and Protection tabs. Specify formatting at this dialog box. Click the *Choose Format From Cell* option and the mouse pointer displays with a pointer tool attached. Click in the cell containing the desired formatting and the formatting displays in the *Preview* box to the left of the Format button. Click the *Clear Find Format* option and any formatting in the *Preview* box is removed.

Project 2c — Finding and Replacing Cell Formatting — Part 3 of 3

1. With **EL1-C4-P2-MRSales.xlsx** open, search for light turquoise fill color and replace with a purple fill color by completing the following steps:

    a. Click the Find & Select button in the Editing group in the Home tab and then click *Replace* at the drop-down list.

    b. At the Find and Replace dialog box with the Replace tab selected, make sure the dialog box is expanded. (If not, click the Options button.)

    c. Select and then delete any text that displays in the *Find what* text box.

    d. Select and then delete any text that displays in the *Replace with* text box.

    e. Make sure the boxes immediately preceding the two Format buttons display with the text *No Format Set*. (If not, click the down-pointing arrow at the right of the Format button, and then click the *Clear Find Format* option at the drop-down list. Do this for each Format button.)

    Step 1f

    f. Click the top Format button.

    g. At the Find Format dialog box, click the Fill tab.

    h. Click the More Colors button.

    i. At the Colors dialog box with the Standard tab selected, click the light turquoise color shown at the right.

    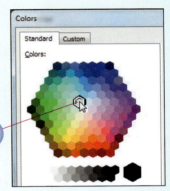
    Step 1i

    j. Click OK to close the Colors dialog box.

    k. Click OK to close the Find Format dialog box.

    l. Click the bottom Format button.

    m. At the Replace Format dialog box with the Fill tab selected, click the purple color shown at the right.

    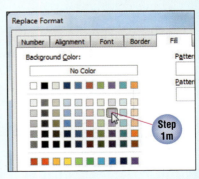
    Step 1m

    n. Click OK to close the dialog box.

    o. At the Find and Replace dialog box, click the Replace All button.

    p. At the message telling you that 10 replacements were made, click OK.

2. Search for yellow fill color and replace with a green fill color by completing the following steps:

    a. At the Find and Replace dialog box, click the top Format button.

    b. At the Find Format dialog box with the Fill tab selected, click the More Colors button.

Chapter 4 ■ Enhancing a Worksheet   **131**

c. At the Colors dialog box with the Standard tab selected, click the yellow color as shown at the right.
d. Click OK to close the Colors dialog box.
e. Click OK to close the Find Format dialog box.
f. Click the bottom Format button.
g. At the Replace Format dialog box with the Fill tab selected, click the green color shown below and to the right.
h. Click OK to close the dialog box.
i. At the Find and Replace dialog box, click the Replace All button.
j. At the message telling you that 78 replacements were made, click OK.

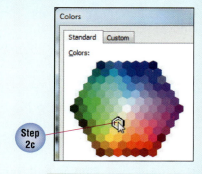

3. Search for 11-point Calibri formatting and replace with 10-point Arial formatting by completing the following steps:
   a. With the Find and Replace dialog box open, clear formatting from the top Format button by clicking the down-pointing arrow at the right side of the top Format button and then clicking the *Clear Find Format* option at the drop-down list.
   b. Clear formatting from the bottom Format button by clicking the down-pointing arrow at the right side of the bottom Format button and then clicking *Clear Replace Format*.
   c. Click the top Format button.
   d. At the Find Format dialog box, click the Font tab.
   e. Click *Calibri* in the *Font* list box. (You may need to scroll down the list to display this typeface.)
   f. Click *11* in the *Size* text box.
   g. Click OK to close the dialog box.
   h. Click the bottom Format button.
   i. At the Replace Format dialog box with the Font tab selected, click *Arial* in the *Font* list box (you may need to scroll down the list to display this typeface).
   j. Click *10* in the *Size* list box.
   k. Click OK to close the dialog box.
   l. At the Find and Replace dialog box, click the Replace All button.
   m. At the message telling you that 174 replacements were made, click OK.
   n. At the Find and Replace dialog box, remove formatting from both Format buttons.
   o. Click the Close button to close the Find and Replace dialog box.

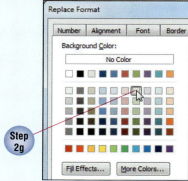

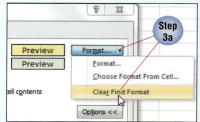

4. Save, print, and then close **EL1-C4-P2-MRSales.xlsx**.

Project Format a Billing Worksheet   4 Parts

You will insert a formula in a weekly billing worksheet and then sort and filter specific data in the worksheet.

Sorting Data

Excel is primarily a spreadsheet program, but it also includes some basic database functions. With a database program, you can alphabetize information or arrange numbers numerically. Data can be sorted by columns in a worksheet. Sort data in a worksheet with the Sort & Filter button in the Editing group in the Home tab.

To sort data in a worksheet, select the cells containing data you want to sort, click the Sort & Filter button in the Editing group and then click the option representing the desired sort. The sort option names vary depending on the data in selected cells. For example, if the first column of selected cells contains text, the sort options in the drop-down list display as *Sort A to Z* and *Sort Z to A*. If the selected cells contain dates, the sort options in the drop-down list display as *Sort Oldest to Newest* and *Sort Newest to Oldest* and if the cells contain numbers or values, the sort options display as *Sort Smallest to Largest* and *Sort Largest to Smallest*. If you select more than one column in a worksheet, Excel will sort the data in the first selected column.

▼ **Quick Steps**

Sort Data
1. Select cells.
2. Click Sort & Filter button.
3. Click desired sort option at drop-down list.

HINT
If you are not satisfied with the results of the sort, immediately click the Undo button.

Sort & Filter

Project 3a — Sorting Data — Part 1 of 4

1. Open **APTBilling.xlsx** and save it with Save As and name it **EL1-C4-P3-APTBilling**.
2. Insert a formula in cell F4 that multiplies the rate by the hours. Copy the formula down to cells F5 through F29.
3. Sort the data in the first column in descending order by completing the following steps:
   a. Make cell A4 active.
   b. Click the Sort & Filter button in the Editing group in the Home tab.
   c. Click the *Sort Largest to Smallest* option at the drop-down list.
4. Sort in ascending order by clicking the Sort & Filter button and then clicking *Sort Smallest to Largest* at the drop-down list.
5. Save **EL1-C4-P3-APTBilling.xlsx**.

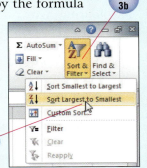

Completing a Custom Sort

If you want to sort data in a column other than the first column, use the Sort dialog box. If you select just one column in a worksheet, click the Sort & Filter button, and then click the desired sort option, only the data in that column is sorted. If this data is related to data to the left or right of the data in the sorted column, that relationship is broken. For example, if you sort cells C4 through C29 in EL1-C4-P3-APTBilling.xlsx, the client number, treatment, hours, and total would no longer match the date.

Use the Sort dialog box to sort data and maintain the relationship of all cells. To sort using the Sort dialog box, select the cells you want sorted, click the Sort & Filter button, and then click *Custom Sort*. This displays the Sort dialog box shown in Figure 4.11.

The data displayed in the *Sort by* option box will vary depending on what you have selected. Generally, the data that displays is the title of the first column

▼ **Quick Steps**

Complete Custom Sort
1. Select cells.
2. Click Sort & Filter button.
3. Click *Custom Sort* at drop-down list.
4. Specify options at Sort dialog box.
5. Click OK.

Figure 4.11 Sort Dialog Box

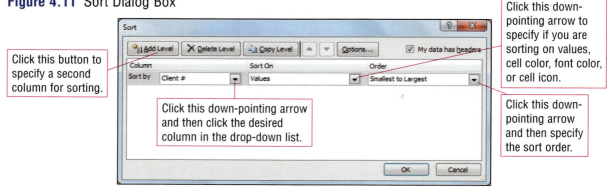

of selected cells. If the selected cells do not have a title, the data may display as *Column A*. Use this option to specify what column you want sorted. Using the Sort dialog box to sort data in a column maintains the relationship of the data.

Project 3b Sorting Data Using the Sort Dialog Box Part 2 of 4

1. With **EL1-C4-P3-APTBilling.xlsx** open, sort the rates in cells E4 through E29 in descending order and maintain the relationship to the other data by completing the following steps:
   a. Select cells A3 through F29.
   b. Click the Sort & Filter button and then click *Custom Sort*.
   c. At the Sort dialog box, click the down-pointing arrow at the right of the *Sort by* option box, and then click *Rate* at the drop-down list.
   d. Click the down-pointing arrow at the right of the *Order* option box and then click *Largest to Smallest* at the drop-down list.
   e. Click OK to close the Sort dialog box.
   f. Deselect the cells.

2. Sort the dates in ascending order (oldest to newest) by completing steps similar to those in Step 1.
3. Save and then print **EL1-C4-P3-APTBilling.xlsx**.

Sorting More Than One Column

When sorting data in cells, you can sort in more than one column. For example, in Project 3c you will be sorting the date from oldest to newest and then sorting client numbers from lowest to highest. In this sort, the dates are sorted first and then client numbers are sorted in ascending order within the same date.

To sort in more than one column, select all columns in the worksheet that need to remain relative and then display the Sort dialog box. At the Sort dialog box, specify the first column you want sorted in the *Sort by* option box, click the *Add Level* button, and then specify the second column in the first *Then by* option box. In Excel, you can sort on multiple columns. Add additional *Then by* option boxes by clicking the *Add Level* button.

Project 3c Sorting Data in Two Columns   Part 3 of 4

1. With **EL1-C4-P3-APTBilling.xlsx** open, select cells A3 through F29.
2. Click the Sort & Filter button and then click *Custom Sort*.
3. At the Sort dialog box, click the down-pointing arrow at the right side of the *Sort by* option box, and then click *Date* in the drop-down list. (Skip this step if Date already displays in the Sort by option box.)
4. Make sure *Oldest to Newest* displays in the *Order* option box.
5. Click the *Add Level* button.
6. Click the down-pointing arrow at the right of the *Then by* option box and then click *Client #* in the drop-down list.
7. Click OK to close the dialog box.
8. Deselect the cells.
9. Save and then print **EL1-C4-P3-APTBilling.xlsx**.

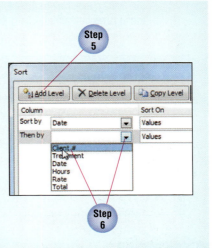

Filtering Data

You can place a restriction, called a *filter*, on data in a worksheet to temporarily isolate specific data. To turn on filtering, make a cell containing data active, click the Filter & Sort button in the Editing group in the Home tab, and then click *Filter* at the drop-down list. This turns on filtering and causes a filter arrow to appear in each column label in the worksheet as shown in Figure 4.12. You do not need to select before turning on filtering because Excel automatically searches for column labels in a worksheet.

To filter data in a worksheet, click the filter arrow in the heading you want to filter. This causes a drop-down list to display with options to filter all records, create a custom filter, or select an entry that appears in one or more of the cells in the column. When you filter data, the filter arrow changes to a funnel icon. The funnel icon indicates that rows in the worksheet have been filtered. To turn off filtering, click the Sort & Filter button and then click *Filter*.

If a column contains numbers, click the filter arrow, point to *Number Filters*, and a side menu displays with options for filtering numbers. For example, you can filter numbers that are equal to, greater than, or less than a number you specify; filter the top ten numbers; and filter numbers that are above or below a specified number.

▼ Quick Steps

Filter a List
1. Select cells.
2. Click Filter & Sort button.
3. Click *Filter* at drop-down list.
4. Click down-pointing arrow of heading to filter.
5. Click desired option at drop-down list.

Figure 4.12 Filtering Data

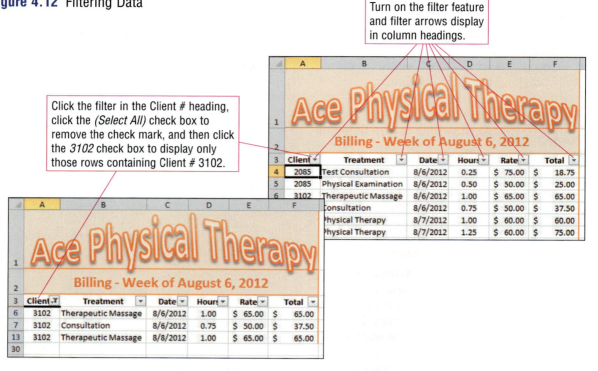

Project 3d   Filtering Data   Part 4 of 4

1. With **EL1-C4-P3-APTBilling.xlsx** open, click in cell A4.
2. Turn on filtering by clicking the Sort & Filter button in the Editing group in the Home tab and then clicking *Filter* at the drop-down list.
3. Filter rows for client number 3102 by completing the following steps:
   a. Click the filter arrow in the *Client #* heading.
   b. Click the *(Select All)* check box to remove the check mark.
   c. Scroll down the list box and then click *3102* to insert a check mark in the check box.
   d. Click OK.
4. Redisplay all rows containing data by completing the following steps:
   a. Click the funnel icon in the *Client #* heading.
   b. Click the *(Select All)* check box to insert a check mark. (This also inserts a check mark for all items in the list.)
   c. Click OK.
5. Filter a list of clients receiving physical therapy by completing the following steps:
   a. Click the filter arrow in the *Treatment* heading.
   b. Click the *(Select All)* check box.
   c. Click the *Physical Therapy* check box.
   d. Click OK.

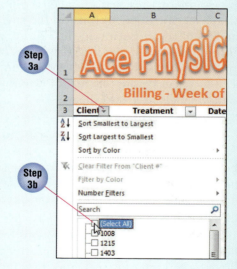

6. Redisplay all rows containing data by completing the following steps:
   a. Click the funnel icon in the *Treatment* heading.
   b. Click the *(Select All)* check box to insert a check mark. (This also inserts a check mark for all items in the list.)
   c. Click OK.
7. Display the top two highest rates by completing the following steps:
   a. Click the filter arrow in the *Rate* heading.
   b. Point to *Number Filters* and then click *Top 10* at the side menu.
   c. At the Top 10 AutoFilter dialog box, select the *10* that displays in the middle text box and then type **2**.
   d. Click OK to close the dialog box.

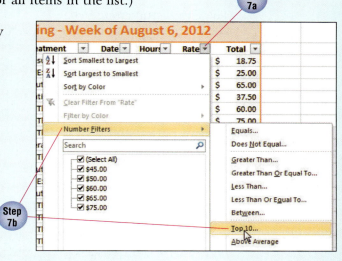

8. Redisplay all rows containing data by completing the following steps:
   a. Click the funnel icon in the *Rate* heading.
   b. Click the *(Select All)* check box to insert a check mark. (This also inserts a check mark for all items in the list.)
   c. Click OK.
9. Display totals greater than $60 by completing the following steps:
   a. Click the filter arrow in the *Total* heading.
   b. Point to *Number Filters* and then click *Greater Than*.
   c. At the Custom AutoFilter dialog box, type **60** and then click OK.
   d. Print the worksheet by clicking the File tab, clicking the Print tab, and then clicking the Print button.
10. Turn off the filtering feature by clicking the Sort & Filter button and then clicking *Filter* at the drop-down list.
11. Save, print, and then close **EL1-C4-P3-APTBilling.xlsx**.

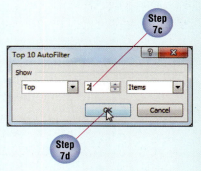

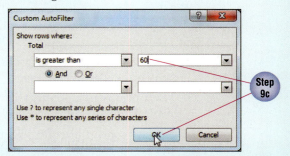

Chapter Summary

- The Page Setup group in the Page Layout tab contains buttons for changing margins, page orientation and size, and buttons for establishing a print area, inserting a page break, applying a picture background, and printing titles.
- The default left and right margins are 0.7 inch and the default top and bottom margins are 0.75 inch. Change these default margins with the Margins button in the Page Setup group in the Page Layout tab.
- Display the Page Setup dialog box with the Margins tab selected by clicking the Margins button and then clicking *Custom Margins* at the drop-down list.
- Center a worksheet on the page with the *Horizontally* and *Vertically* options at the Page Setup dialog box with the Margins tab selected.
- Click the Orientation button in the Page Setup group in the Page Layout tab to display the two orientation choices — *Portrait* and *Landscape*.
- Insert a page break by selecting the column or row, clicking the Breaks button in the Page Setup group in the Page Layout tab, and then clicking *Insert Page Break* at the drop-down list.
- To insert both a horizontal and vertical page break at the same time, make a cell active, click the Breaks button, and then click *Insert Page Break* at the drop-down list.
- Display a worksheet in page break preview by clicking the Page Break Preview button in the view area on the Status bar or clicking the View tab and then clicking the Page Break Preview button.
- Use options at the Page Setup dialog box with the Sheet tab selected to specify that you want column or row titles to print on each page. Display this dialog box by clicking the Print Titles button in the Page Setup group in the Page Layout tab.
- Use options in the Scale to Fit group in the Page Layout tab to scale data to fit on a specific number of pages.
- Use the Background button in the Page Setup group in the Page Layout tab to insert a worksheet background picture. A background picture displays on the screen but does not print.
- Use options in the Sheet Options group in the Page Layout tab to specify if you want gridlines and headings to view and/or print.
- Specify a print area by selecting the desired cells, clicking the Print Area button in the Page Setup group in the Page Layout tab, and then clicking *Set Print Area* at the drop-down list. Add another print area by selecting the desired cells, clicking the Print Area button, and then clicking *Add to Print Area* at the drop-down list.
- Create a header and/or footer with the Header & Footer button in the Text group in the Insert tab, in Page Layout view, or with options at the Page Setup dialog box with the Header/Footer tab selected.
- Customize print jobs with options at the Print tab Backstage view.
- To check spelling in a worksheet, click the Review tab and then click the Spelling button.

- Click the Undo button on the Quick Access toolbar to reverse the most recent action and click the Redo button to redo a previously reversed action.
- Use options at the Find and Replace dialog box with the Find tab selected to find specific data and/or formatting in a worksheet.
- Use options at the Find and Replace dialog box with the Replace tab selected to find specific data and/or formatting and replace with other data and/or formatting.
- Sort data in a worksheet with options from the Sort & Filter button in the Editing group in the Home tab.
- Create a custom sort with options at the Sort dialog box. Display this dialog box by clicking the Sort & Filter button and then clicking *Custom Sort* at the drop-down list.
- Use the filter feature to temporarily isolate specific data. Turn on the filter feature by clicking the Sort & Filter button in the Editing group in the Home tab and then clicking *Filter* at the drop-down list. This inserts filter arrows in each column label. Click a filter arrow and then use options at the drop-down list that displays to specify the filter data.

Commands Review

FEATURE	RIBBON TAB, GROUP	BUTTON, OPTION	KEYBOARD SHORTCUT
Margins	Page Layout, Page Setup		
Page Setup dialog box with Margins tab selected	Page Layout, Page Setup	, Custom Margins	
Orientation	Page Layout, Page Setup		
Size	Page Layout, Page Setup		
Insert page break	Page Layout, Page Setup	, Insert Page Break	
Remove page break	Page Layout, Page Setup	, Remove Page Break	
Page Break Preview	View, Workbook Views		
Page Setup dialog box with Sheet tab selected	Page Layout, Page Setup		
Scale width	Page Layout, Scale to Fit	Width: Automatic	
Scale height	Page Layout, Scale to Fit	Scale: 100%	
Scale	Page Layout, Scale to Fit	Height: Automatic	
Background picture	Page Layout, Page Setup		

FEATURE	RIBBON TAB, GROUP	BUTTON, OPTION	KEYBOARD SHORTCUT
Print Area	Page Layout, Page Setup		
Header and footer	Insert, Text		
Page Layout view	View, Workbook Views		
Spelling	Review, Proofing		F7
Find and Replace dialog box with Find tab selected	Home, Editing	, Find	Ctrl + F
Find and Replace dialog box with Replace tab selected	Home, Editing	, Replace	Ctrl + H
Sort data	Home, Editing		
Filter data	Home, Editing		

Concepts Check — Test Your Knowledge

Completion: In the space provided at the right, indicate the correct term, symbol, or command.

1. This is the default left and right margin measurement.

2. This is the default top and bottom margin measurement.

3. The Margins button is located in this tab.

4. By default, a worksheet prints in this orientation on a page.

5. Click the Print Titles button in the Page Setup group in the Page Layout tab and the Page Setup dialog box displays with this tab selected.

6. Use options in this group in the Page Layout tab to adjust the printed output by a percentage to fit the number of pages specified.

7. Use this button in the Page Setup group in the Page Layout tab to select and print specific areas in a worksheet.

8. Click the Header & Footer button in the Text group in the Insert tab and the worksheet displays in this view.

9. This tab contains options for formatting and customizing a header and/or footer. _____

10. Click this tab to display the Spelling button. _____

11. The Undo and Redo buttons are located on this toolbar. _____

12. Click this button in the Find and Replace dialog box to expand the dialog box. _____

13. Use these two buttons at the expanded Find and Replace dialog box to search for specific cell formatting and replace with other formatting. _____

14. Use this button in the Editing group in the Home tab to sort data in a worksheet. _____

15. Use this feature to temporarily isolate specific data in a worksheet. _____

Skills Check Assess Your Performance

Assessment

1 FORMAT A DATA ANALYSIS WORKSHEET

1. Open **DISemiSales.xlsx**.
2. Save the workbook with Save As and name it **EL1-C4-A1-DISemiSales**.
3. Make the following changes to the worksheet:
   a. Insert a formula in cell H4 that averages the amounts in cells B4 through G4.
   b. Copy the formula in cell H4 down to cells H5 through H9.
   c. Insert a formula in cell B10 that adds the amounts in cells B4 through B9.
   d. Copy the formula in cell B10 over to cells C10 through H10. (Click the Auto Fill Options button and then click *Fill Without Formatting* at the drop-down list.)
   e. Apply the Accounting Number Format style to cell H4.
   f. Change the orientation of the worksheet to landscape.
   g. Change the top margin to 3 inches and the left margin to 1.5 inches.
4. Save and then print **EL1-C4-A1-DISemiSales.xlsx**.
5. Make the following changes to the worksheet:
   a. Change the orientation back to portrait.
   b. Change the top margin to 1 inch and the left margin to 0.7 inch.
   c. Horizontally and vertically center the worksheet on the page.
   d. Scale the worksheet so it fits on one page.
6. Save, print, and then close **EL1-C4-A1-DISemiSales.xlsx**.

Assessment 2 FORMAT A TEST RESULTS WORKSHEET

1. Open **CMTests.xlsx**.
2. Save the workbook with Save As and name it **EL1-C4-A2-CMTests**.
3. Make the following changes to the worksheet.
    a. Insert a formula in cell N4 that averages the test scores in cells B4 through M4.
    b. Copy the formula in cell N4 down to cells N5 through N21.
    c. Type *Average* in cell A22.
    d. Insert a formula in cell B22 that averages the test scores in cells B4 through B21.
    e. Copy the formula in cell B22 across to cells C22 through N22.
    f. Insert a page break between columns G and H.
4. View the worksheet in Page Break Preview.
5. Change back to the Normal view.
6. Specify that the column titles (A3 through A22) are to print on each page.
7. Create a header that prints the page number at the right side of the page.
8. Create a footer that prints your name at the left side of the page and the workbook file name at the right side of the page.
9. Save and then print the worksheet.
10. Set a print area for cells N3 through N22 and then print the cells.
11. Clear the print area.
12. Save and then close **EL1-C4-A2-CMTests.xlsx**.

Assessment 3 FORMAT AN EQUIPMENT RENTAL WORKSHEET

1. Open **HERInvoices.xlsx**.
2. Save the workbook with Save As and name it **EL1-C4-A3-HERInvoices**.
3. Insert a formula in cell H3 that multiplies the rate in cell G3 by the hours in cell F3. Copy the formula in cell H3 down to cells H4 through H16.
4. Insert a formula in cell H17 that sums the amounts in cells H3 through H16.
5. Complete the following find and replaces:
    a. Find all occurrences of cells containing *75* and replace with *90*.
    b. Find all occurrences of cells containing *55* and replace with *60*.
    c. Find all occurrences of *Barrier Concrete* and replace with *Lee Sand and Gravel*.
    d. Find all occurrences of 11-point Calibri and replace with 10-point Cambria.
    e. After completing the find and replace, clear all formatting from the Format buttons.
6. Insert a header that prints the date at the left side of the page and the time at the right side of the page.
7. Insert a footer that prints your name at the left side of the page and the workbook file name at the right side of the page.
8. Print the worksheet horizontally and vertically centered on the page.
9. Save and then close **EL1-C4-A3-HERInvoices.xlsx**.

Assessment 4 — FORMAT AN INVOICES WORKSHEET

1. Open **RPInvoices.xlsx**.
2. Save the workbook with Save As and name it **EL1-C4-A4-RPInvoices**.
3. Insert a formula in G4 that multiplies the amount in E4 with the percentage in F4 and then adds the product to cell E4. (If you write the formula correctly, the result in G4 will display as *$488.25*.)
4. Copy the formula in cell G4 down to cells G5 through G17, click the Auto Fill Options button, and then click the *Fill Without Formatting* option.
5. Complete a spelling check on the worksheet.
6. Find all occurrences of *Picture* and replace with *Portrait*. (Do not type a space after *Picture* or *Portrait* because you want to find occurrences that end with an "s." Make sure the *Match entire cell contents* check box does not contain a check mark.)
7. Sort the records by invoice number in ascending order (smallest to largest).
8. Complete a new sort that sorts the records by client number in ascending order (A to Z).
9. Complete a new sort that sorts the date in ascending order (oldest to newest).
10. Insert a footer in the worksheet that prints your name at the left side of the page and the current date at the right side of the page.
11. Center the worksheet horizontally and vertically on the page.
12. Save and then print **EL1-C4-A4-RPInvoices.xlsx**.
13. Select cells A3 through G3 and then turn on the filter feature and complete the following filters:
    a. Filter and then print a list of rows containing client number 11-279 and then clear the filter.
    b. Filter and then print a list of rows containing the top three highest amounts due and then clear the filter.
    c. Filter and then print a list of rows containing amounts due that are less than $500 and then clear the filter.
14. Save and then close **EL1-C4-A4-RPInvoices.xlsx**.

Assessment 5 — CREATE A WORKSHEET CONTAINING KEYBOARD SHORTCUTS

1. Use Excel's Help feature and learn about keyboard shortcuts in Excel. After reading the information presented, create a worksheet with the following feature:
   - Create a title for the worksheet.
   - Include at least 10 keyboard shortcuts along with an explanation of the keyboard shortcut.
   - Set the data in cells in a typeface other than Calibri and change the data color.
   - Add borders to the cells. (You determine the border style.)
   - Add a color shading to cells. (You determine the color—make it complementary to the data color.)
   - Create a header that prints the date at the right margin and create a footer that prints your name at the left margin and the file name at the right margin.
2. Save the workbook and name it **EL1-C4-A5-KeyboardShortcuts**.
3. Print and then close **EL1-C4-A5-KeyboardShortcuts.xlsx**.

Visual Benchmark — Demonstrate Your Proficiency

CREATE AND FORMAT AN EXPENSE WORKSHEET

1. At a blank workbook, type the data in the cells indicated in Figure 4.13 but **do not** type the data in the following cells—instead insert the formulas as indicated (the results of your formulas should match the results you see in the figure):
   - Cells N3 through N8: Insert a formula that sums the monthly expenses for the year.
   - Cells B9 through N9: Insert a formula that sums the monthly expenses for each month and the entire year.
2. Change the left and right margins to *0.45* and change the top margin to *1.5*.
3. Apply formatting so your worksheet looks similar to the worksheet shown in Figure 4.13. (Set the heading in 26-point Cambria and set the remaining data in 10-point Cambria. Apply bold formatting as shown in the figure.)
4. Save the workbook and name it **EL1-C4-VB-HERExpenses**.
5. Look at the printing of the worksheet shown in Figure 4.14 and then make the following changes:
   - Insert a page break between columns G and H.
   - Insert the headers and footer as shown.
   - Specify that the column titles print on the second page as shown in Figure 4.14.
6. Save and then print **EL1-C4-VB-HERExpenses.xlsx**. (Your worksheet should print on two pages and appear as shown in Figure 4.14.)
7. Save and then close **EL1-C4-VB-HERExpenses.xlsx**.

Figure 4.13 Visual Benchmark Data

	A	B	C	D	E	F	G	H	I	J	K	L	M	N
1							**Hilltop Equipment Rental**							
2	Expenses	January	February	March	April	May	June	July	August	September	October	November	December	Total
3	Lease	$ 3,250	$ 3,250	$ 3,250	$ 3,250	$ 3,250	$ 3,250	$ 3,250	$ 3,250	$ 3,250	$ 3,250	$ 3,250	$ 3,250	$ 39,000
4	Utilities	3,209	2,994	2,987	2,500	2,057	1,988	1,845	1,555	1,890	2,451	2,899	3,005	29,380
5	Payroll	10,545	9,533	11,542	10,548	11,499	12,675	13,503	13,258	12,475	10,548	10,122	9,359	135,607
6	Insurance	895	895	895	895	895	895	895	895	895	895	895	895	10,740
7	Maintenance	2,439	1,856	2,455	5,410	3,498	3,110	2,479	3,100	1,870	6,105	4,220	3,544	40,086
8	Supplies	341	580	457	330	675	319	451	550	211	580	433	601	5,528
9	**Total Expenses**	$ 20,679	$ 19,108	$ 21,586	$ 22,933	$ 21,874	$ 22,237	$ 22,423	$ 22,608	$ 20,591	$ 23,829	$ 21,819	$ 20,654	$ 260,341
10														

Figure 4.14 Visual Benchmark Printed Pages

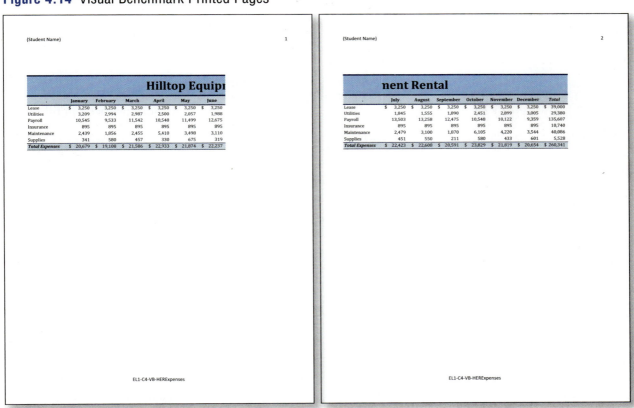

Case Study — Apply Your Skills

Part 1

You are the sales manager for Macadam Realty. You decide that you want to display sample mortgage worksheets in the reception area display rack. Open the **MRMortgages.xlsx** workbook, save it with Save As and name it **EL1-C4-CS-MRMortgages-01**, and then add the following information and make the following changes:

- In column C, insert a formula that determines the down payment amount.
- In column D, insert a formula that determines the loan amount.
- In column G, insert a formula using the PMT function. (Enter the *Pv* as a negative.)
- Insert the date and time as a header and your name and the workbook name (**EL1-C4-CS-MRMortgages-01.xlsx**) as a footer.
- Find 11-point Calibri formatting and replace with 11-point Candara formatting.
- Scale the worksheet so it prints on one page.

Save and then print **EL1-C4-CS-MRMortgages-01.xlsx**. After looking at the printed worksheet, you decide that you need to make the following changes:

- Sort the *Price of Home* column from smallest to largest.
- Change the percentage amount in column E from 6% to 7%.
- Shade the cells in row 4 in the light yellow color that matches the fill in cell A2. Copy this shading to every other row of cells in the worksheet (stopping at row 46).

Save the edited worksheet with Save As and name it **EL1-C4-CS-MRMortgages-02**. Edit the footer to reflect the workbook name change. Save, print, and then close **EL1-C4-CS-MRMortgages-02.xlsx**. (Make sure the worksheet prints on one page.)

Part 2

You are preparing for a quarterly sales meeting during which you will discuss retirement issues with the sales officers. You want to encourage them to consider opening an Individual Retirement Account (IRA) to supplement the retirement contributions made by Macadam Realty. You have begun an IRA worksheet but need to complete it. Open **MRIRA.xlsx** and then save it with Save As and name it **EL1-C4-CS-MRIRA-01**. Make the following changes to the worksheet:

- Insert in cell C6 a formula that calculates the future value of an investment. Use the FV function to write the formula. You must use absolute and mixed cell references for the formula. When entering the *Rate* (percentage), the column letter is variable but the row number is fixed; when entering the *Nper* (years), the column letter is fixed but the row number is variable; and when entering the *Pmt* (the contribution amount), both the column letter and row number are absolute.
- Copy the formula in cell C6 down to cells C7 through C19. Copy the formula in cell C6 across to cells D6 through K6. Continue in this manner until the amounts are entered in all the appropriate cells.

- Select and then merge and center cells A6 through A19. Type the text **Number of Years** and then rotate the text up. Make sure the text is centered in the merged cell. Apply 12-point Calibri bold formatting to the text.
- Adjust the column widths so all text is visible in the cells.
- Change the page orientation to landscape.
- Vertically and horizontally center the worksheet.
- Include a header that prints the page number and insert a footer that prints your name.

Save the worksheet and then print it so that the row titles print on both pages. After looking at the worksheet, you decide to make the following changes:

- Remove the header containing the page number.
- Edit the footer so the date prints at the left margin and your name prints at the right margin.
- Scale the worksheet so it prints on one page.

Save the workbook and name it **EL1-C4-CS-MRIRA-02** and then print the worksheet. Change the amount in cell D3 to *$3,000* and then print the worksheet again. Save and then close **EL1-C4-CS-MRIRA-02.xlsx**.

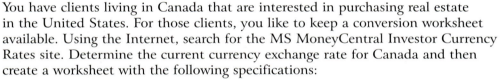

You have clients living in Canada that are interested in purchasing real estate in the United States. For those clients, you like to keep a conversion worksheet available. Using the Internet, search for the MS MoneyCentral Investor Currency Rates site. Determine the current currency exchange rate for Canada and then create a worksheet with the following specifications:

- Apply formatting that is similar to the formatting in the worksheets you worked with in the first two parts of the case study.
- Create the following columns:
  ◦ Column for home price in American dollars.
  ◦ Column for home price in Canadian dollars.
  ◦ Column for amount of down payment.
  ◦ Column for loan total.
  ◦ Column for monthly payment.
- In the column for home prices, insert home amounts beginning with $100,000, incrementing every $50,000, and ending with $1,000,000.
- Insert a formula in the home price in the Canadian dollars column that displays the home price in Canadian dollars.
- Insert a formula in the down payment column that multiplies the Canadian home price by 20%.
- Insert a formula in the loan total column that subtracts the down payment from the Canadian home price.
- Insert a formula in the monthly payment column that determines the monthly payment using the PMT function. Use 6% as the rate (be sure to divide by 12 months), 360 as the number of payments, and the loan amount as a negative as the present value.
- Apply any other formatting you feel necessary to improve the worksheet.

Save the completed workbook and name it **EL1-C4-CS-CanadaPrices**. Display formulas and then print the worksheet. Redisplay the formulas and then save and close the workbook.

UNIT 1

Performance Assessment

Note: Before beginning unit assessments, copy to your storage medium the Excel2010L1U1 subfolder from the Excel2010L1 folder on the CD that accompanies this textbook and then make Excel2010L1U1 the active folder.

Assessing Proficiency

In this unit, you have learned to create, save, print, edit, and format Excel worksheets; create and insert formulas; and enhance worksheets with features such as headers and footers, page numbering, sorting, and filtering.

Assessment 1 Create Sales Bonuses Workbook

1. Create the Excel worksheet shown in Figure U1.1. Format the cells as you see them in the figure.
2. Insert an IF statement in cell C4 that inserts *7%* if B4 is greater than 99999 and inserts *3%* if B4 is not greater than 99999.
3. Format the number in cell C4 so it displays as a percentage with no decimal places. Copy the formula in cell C4 down to cells C5 through C11. Center the percents in cells C4 through C11.
4. Insert a formula in cell D4 that multiplies the amount in B4 with the percentage in cell C4. Copy the formula in D4 down to cells D5 through D11.
5. Insert the sum of cells B4 through B11 in B12 and insert the sum of cells D4 through D11 in cell D12.
6. Apply the Accounting Number Format style with two decimal places to cells B4, B12, D4, and D12. Apply the Comma style with two decimal places to cells B5 through B11 and cells D5 through D11.
7. Insert a footer that contains your first and last names and the current date.
8. Print the worksheet horizontally and vertically centered on the page.
9. Save the workbook and name it **EL1-U1-A1-SBASales**.
10. Close **EL1-U1-A1-SBASales.xlsx**.

Figure U1.1 Assessment 1

	A	B	C	D	E
1	Stanton & Barnet Associates				
2	Sales Department				
3	Associate	Sales	Bonus	Bonus Amount	
4	Conway, Edward	$ 101,450.00			
5	Eckhart, Geneva	94,375.00			
6	Farris, Amanda	73,270.00			
7	Greenwood, Wayne	110,459.00			
8	Hagen, Chandra	120,485.00			
9	Logan, Courtney	97,520.00			
10	Pena, Geraldo	115,850.00			
11	Rubin, Alice	76,422.00			
12	Total				
13					

Assessment 2 Format Equipment Purchase Plan Workbook

1. Open **HERPurPlans.xlsx** and then save the workbook with Save As and name it **EL1-U1-A2-HERPurPlans**.
2. The owner of Hilltop Equipment Rental is interested in purchasing a new tractor and needs to determine monthly payments on three different models. Insert a formula in cell E4 that uses the PMT function to calculate monthly payments. Copy the formula down to cells E5 and E6.
3. Insert a formula in cell F4 that multiplies the amount in E4 by the amount in D4.
4. Copy the formula in cell F4 down to cells F5 and F6.
5. Insert a formula in cell G4 that subtracts the amount in B4 from the amount in F4. *Hint: The formula should return a positive number, not a negative number (a number surrounded by parentheses).*
6. Copy the formula in cell G4 down to cells G5 and G6.
7. Change the vertical alignment of cell A2 to Middle Align.
8. Change the vertical alignment of cells A3 through G3 to Bottom Align.
9. Save, print, and then close **EL1-U1-A2-HERPurPlans.xlsx**.

Assessment 3 Format Accounts Due Workbook

1. Open **RPAccts.xlsx** and then save the workbook with Save As and name it **EL1-U1-A3-RPAccts**.
2. Using the DATE function, enter a formula in each of the specified cells that returns the serial number for the specified date:
   - C4 = October 29, 2012
   - C5 = October 30, 2012
   - C6 = October 30, 2012
   - C7 = November 1, 2012
   - C8 = November 5, 2012
   - C9 = November 7, 2012
   - C10 = November 7, 2012
   - C11 = November 14, 2012
   - C12 = November 14, 2012
3. Enter a formula in cell E4 that inserts the due date (date of service plus the number of days in the *Terms* column).
4. Copy the formula in cell E4 down to cells E5 through E12.
5. Make cell A14 active and then type your name.
6. Make cell A15 active and then use the NOW function to insert the current date and time as a serial number.
7. Save, print, and then close **EL1-U1-A3-RPAccts.xlsx**.

Assessment 4 Format First Quarter Sales Workbook

1. Open **PSQtrlySales.xlsx** and then save the workbook with Save As and name it **EL1-U1-A4-PSQtrlySales**.
2. Insert a formula in cell E4 that totals the amounts in B4, C4, and D4. Copy the formula in cell E4 down to cells E5 through E18. Apply the Accounting Number Format style with no decimal places to cell E4.
3. Insert an IF statement in cell F4 that inserts 5% if E4 is greater than 74999 and inserts 0% if E4 is not greater than 74999.
4. Make sure the result of the IF formula displays in cell F4 as a percentage with no decimal points and then copy the formula down to cells F5 through F18. Center the percent amounts in cells F4 through F18.
5. Select cells A5 through F5 and then insert the same yellow fill as cell A2. Apply the same yellow fill to cells A7 through F7, A9 through F9, A11 through F11, A13 through F13, A15 through F15, and cells A17 through F17.
6. Insert a footer that prints your name at the left, the current date at the middle, and the current time at the right.
7. Print the worksheet horizontally and vertically centered on the page.
8. Save, print, and then close **EL1-U1-A4-PSQtrlySales.xlsx**.

Assessment 5 Format Weekly Payroll Workbook

1. Open **CCPayroll.xlsx** and then save the workbook with Save As and name it **EL1-U1-A5-CCPayroll**.
2. Insert a formula in cell E3 that multiplies the hourly rate by the hours and then adds that to the multiplication of the hourly rate by the overtime pay rate (1.5) and then overtime hours. (Use parentheses in the formula and use an absolute cell reference for the overtime pay rate (1.5). Refer to Chapter 2, Project 5c.) Copy the formula down to cells E4 through E16.

3. Insert a formula in cell F3 that multiplies the gross pay by the withholding tax rate (W/H Rate). (Use an absolute cell reference for the cell containing the withholding rate. Refer to Chapter 2, Project 5c.) Copy the formula down to cells F4 through F16.
4. Insert a formula in cell G3 that multiplies the gross pay by the Social Security rate (SS Rate). Use an absolute cell reference for the cell containing the Social Security rate. (Refer to Chapter 2, Project 5c.) Copy the formula down to cells G4 through G16.
5. Insert a formula in cell H4 that adds together the Social Security tax and the withholding tax and subtracts that from the gross pay. (Refer to Chapter 2, Project 5c.) Copy the formula down to cells H4 through H16.
6. Sort the employee last names alphabetically in ascending order (A to Z).
7. Center the worksheet horizontally and vertically on the page.
8. Insert a footer that prints your name at the left side of the page and the file name at the right side of the page.
9. Save, print, and then close **EL1-U1-A5-CCPayroll.xlsx**.

Assessment 6 Format Customer Sales Analysis Workbook

1. Open **DIAnnualSales.xlsx** and then save the workbook with Save As and name it **EL1-U1-A6-DIAnnualSales**.
2. Insert formulas and drag formulas to complete the worksheet. After dragging the total formula in row 10, specify that you want to fill without formatting. (This retains the right border in cell N10.) Do this with the AutoFill Options button.
3. Insert in cell B11 the highest total from cells B10 through M10. Insert in cell B12 the lowest total from cells B10 through M10.
4. Change the orientation to landscape.
5. Insert a header that prints the page number at the right side of the page.
6. Insert a footer that prints your name at the right side of the page.
7. Horizontally and vertically center the worksheet on the page.
8. Specify that the column headings in cells A3 through A12 print on both pages.
9. Save, print, and then close **EL1-U1-A6-DIAnnualSales.xlsx**.

Assessment 7 Format Invoices Workbook

1. Open **RPInvoices.xlsx** and then save the workbook with Save As and name it **EL1-U1-A7-RPInvoices**.
2. Insert a formula in cell G4 that multiplies the amount in E4 by the percentage in F4 and then adds that total to the amount in E4. (Use parentheses in this formula.)
3. Copy the formula in cell G4 down to cells G5 through G18.
4. Find all occurrences of cells containing *11-279* and replace with *10-005*.
5. Find all occurrences of cells containing *8.5* and replace with *9.0*.
6. Search for the Calibri font and replace with the Candara font. (Do not specify a type size so that Excel replaces all sizes of Calibri with Candara.)
7. Print **EL1-U1-A7-RPInvoices.xlsx**.
8. Filter and then print a list of rows containing only the client number *04-325*. (After printing, return the list to *(Select All)*.)
9. Filter and then print a list of rows containing only the service *Development*. (After printing, return the list to *(Select All)*.)
10. Filter and then print a list of rows containing the top three highest totals in the *Amount Due* column. (After printing, turn off the filter feature.)
11. Save and then close **EL1-U1-A7-RPInvoices.xlsx**.

Writing Activities

The following activities give you the opportunity to practice your writing skills along with demonstrating an understanding of some of the important Excel features you have mastered in this unit. Use correct grammar, appropriate word choices, and clear sentence construction.

Activity 1 Plan and Prepare Orders Summary Workbook

Plan and prepare a worksheet with the information shown in Figure U1.2. Apply formatting of your choosing to the worksheet. Save the completed worksheet and name it **EL1-U1-Act1-OrdersSumm**. Print and then close **EL1-U1-Act1-OrdersSumm.xlsx**.

Figure U1.2 Activity 1

> Prepare a weekly summary of orders taken that itemizes the products coming into the company and the average order size.
> The products and average order size include:
>
> Black and gold wall clock: $2,450 worth of orders, average order size of $125
> Traveling alarm clock: $l,358 worth of orders, average order size of $195
> Waterproof watch: $890 worth of orders, average order size of $90
> Dashboard clock: $2,135 worth of orders, average order size of $230
> Pyramid clock: $3,050 worth of orders, average order size of $375
> Gold chain watch: $755 worth of orders, average order size of $80
>
> In the worksheet, total the amount ordered and also calculate the average weekly order size. Sort the data in the worksheet by the order amount in descending order.

Activity 2 Prepare Depreciation Workbook

Assets within a company, such as equipment, can be depreciated over time. Several methods are available for determining the amount of depreciation such as the straight-line depreciation method, fixed-declining balance method, and the double-declining method. Use Excel's Help feature to learn about two depreciation methods — straight-line and double-declining depreciation. (The straight-line depreciation function, SNL, and the double-declining depreciation function, DDB, are located in the Financial category.) After reading about the two methods, create an Excel worksheet with the following information:

- An appropriate title
- A heading for straight-line depreciation
- The straight-line depreciation function
- The name and a description for each straight-line depreciation function argument category
- A heading for double-declining depreciation

- The double-declining depreciation function
- The name and a description for each double-declining depreciation function argument category

Apply formatting of your choosing to the worksheet. Save the completed workbook and name it **EL1-U1-Act2-DepMethods**. Print the worksheet horizontally and vertically centered on the page. Close **EL1-U1-Act2-DepMethods.xlsx**.

Activity 3 Insert Straight-Line Depreciation Formula

Open **RPDepreciation.xlsx** and then save the workbook and name it **EL1-U1-Act3-RPDepreciation**. Insert the function to determine straight-line depreciation in cell E3. Copy the formula down to cells E4 through E10. Apply formatting of your choosing to the worksheet. Print the worksheet horizontally and vertically centered on the page. Save and then close **EL1-U1-Act3-RPDepreciation.xlsx**.

Optional: Briefly research the topic of straight-line and double-declining depreciation to find out why businesses depreciate their assets. What purpose does it serve? Locate information about the topic on the Internet or in your school library. Then use Word 2010 to write a half-page, single-spaced report explaining the financial reasons for using depreciation methods. Save the document and name it **EL1-U1-Act3-DepReport**. Print and then close the document.

Internet Research

Activity 4 Create a Travel Planning Worksheet

Make sure you are connected to the Internet. Use a search engine of your choosing to look for information on traveling to a specific country that interests you. Find sites that provide cost information for airlines, hotels, meals, entertainment, and car rentals. Create a travel planning worksheet for the country that includes the following:

- appropriate title
- appropriate headings
- airline costs
- hotel costs (off-season and in-season rates if available)
- estimated meal costs
- entertainment costs
- car rental costs

Save the completed workbook and name it **EL1-U1-Act4-TrvlWksht**. Print and then close the workbook.

Microsoft® Excel® Level 1

Unit 2 ■ Enhancing the Display of Workbooks

Chapter 5 ■ Moving Data within and between Workbooks

Chapter 6 ■ Maintaining Workbooks

Chapter 7 ■ Creating a Chart in Excel

Chapter 8 ■ Adding Visual Interest to Workbooks

Microsoft® Excel®

Moving Data within and between Workbooks

CHAPTER 5

PERFORMANCE OBJECTIVES

Upon successful completion of Chapter 5, you will be able to:
- Create a workbook with multiple worksheets
- Move, copy, and paste cells within a worksheet
- Split a worksheet into windows and freeze panes
- Name a range of cells and use a range in a formula
- Open multiple workbooks
- Arrange, size, and move workbooks
- Copy and paste data between workbooks
- Link data between worksheets

Up to this point, the workbooks in which you have been working have consisted of only one worksheet. In this chapter, you will learn to create a workbook with several worksheets and complete tasks such as copying and pasting data within and between worksheets. Moving and pasting or copying and pasting selected cells in and between worksheets is useful for rearranging data or for saving time. You will also work with multiple workbooks and complete tasks such as arranging, sizing, and moving workbooks, and opening and closing multiple workbooks. Model answers for this chapter's projects appear on the following pages.

Note: Before beginning the projects, copy to your storage medium the Excel2010L1C5 subfolder from the Excel2010L1 folder on the CD that accompanies this textbook and then make Excel2010L1C5 the active folder.

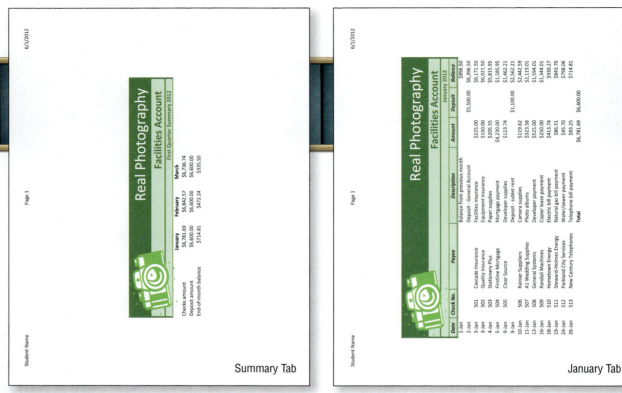

Project 1 Manage Data in a Multiple-Worksheet Account Workbook EL1-C5-P1-RPFacAccts.xlsx

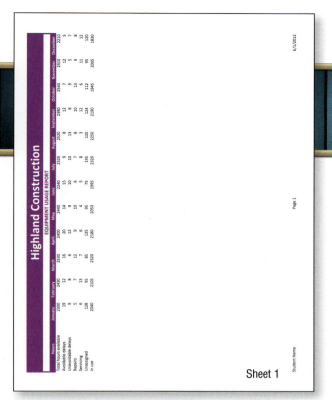

Project 2 Write Formulas Using Ranges in an Equipment Usage Workbook EL1-C5-P2-HCEqpRpt.xlsx

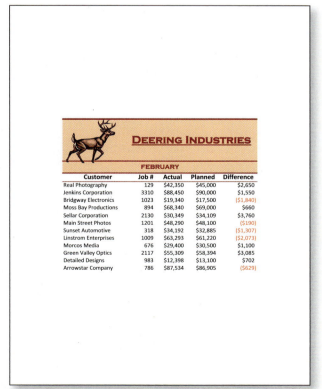

Project 3 Arrange, Size, and Copy Data between Workbooks EL1-C5-P3-DIFebJobs.xlsx

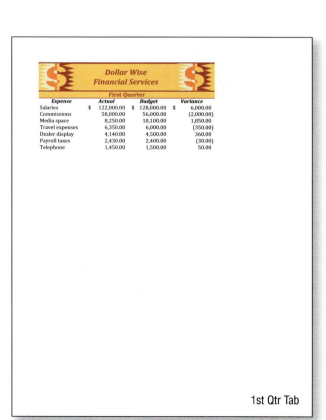

Project 4 Linking and Copying Data within and between Worksheets and Word EL1-C5-P4-DWQtrlyExp.xlsx

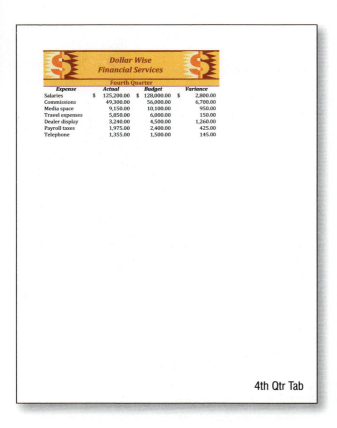

2nd Qtr Tab

3rd Qtr Tab

4th Qtr Tab

EL1-C5-P4-DWQtrlyRpt.docx

Project 1 — Manage Data in a Multiple-Worksheet Account Workbook — 9 Parts

You will open an account workbook containing three worksheets and then move, copy, and paste data between the worksheets. You will also hide and unhide worksheets, and format and print multiple worksheets in the workbook.

Creating a Workbook with Multiple Worksheets

An Excel workbook can contain multiple worksheets. You can create a variety of worksheets within a workbook for related data. For example, a workbook may contain a worksheet for the expenses for each salesperson in a company and another worksheet for the monthly payroll for each department within the company. Another example is recording sales statistics for each quarter in individual worksheets within a workbook.

By default, a workbook contains three worksheets named *Sheet1*, *Sheet2*, and *Sheet3*. (Later in this chapter, you will learn how to change these default names.) Display various worksheets in the workbook by clicking the desired tab.

HINT Worksheets in a workbook are helpful for saving related data.

Project 1a — Displaying Worksheets in a Workbook — Part 1 of 9

1. Open **RPFacAccts.xlsx** and then save the workbook with Save As and name it **EL1-C5-P1-RPFacAccts**.
2. This workbook contains three worksheets. Display the various worksheets by completing the following steps:
   a. Display the second worksheet by clicking the Sheet2 tab that displays immediately above the Status bar.
   b. Display the third worksheet by clicking the Sheet3 tab that displays immediately above the Status bar.
   c. Return to the first worksheet by clicking the Sheet1 tab.

Step 2a

3. Make the following changes to worksheets in the workbook:
   a. Click the Sheet2 tab and then change the column width for columns E, F, and G to 10.00.
   b. Click the Sheet3 tab and then change the column width for columns E, F, and G to 10.00.
   c. Click the Sheet1 tab to display the first worksheet.
4. Save **EL1-C5-P1-RPFacAccts.xlsx**.

Cutting, Copying, and Pasting Selected Cells

Situations may arise where you need to move cells to a different location within a worksheet, or you may need to copy repetitive data in a worksheet. You can perform these actions by selecting cells and then using the Cut, Copy, and/or Paste buttons in the Clipboard group in the Home tab. You can also perform these actions with the mouse.

▼ Quick Steps

Move and Paste Cells
1. Select cells.
2. Click Cut button.
3. Click desired cell.
4. Click Paste button.

Ctrl + X is the keyboard shortcut to cut selected data. Ctrl + V is the keyboard shortcut to paste data.

Cut   Paste

Moving Selected Cells

You can move selected cells and cell contents in a worksheet and between worksheets. Move selected cells with the Cut and Paste buttons in the Clipboard group in the Home tab or by dragging with the mouse.

To move selected cells with buttons in the Home tab, select the cells and then click the Cut button in the Clipboard group. This causes a moving dashed line border (called a *marquee*) to display around the selected cells. Click the cell where you want the first selected cell inserted and then click the Paste button in the Clipboard group. If you change your mind and do not want to move the selected cells, press the Esc key to remove the moving dashed line border or double-click in any cell.

To move selected cells with the mouse, select the cells and then position the mouse pointer on any border of the selected cells until the pointer turns into an arrow pointer with a four-headed arrow attached. Hold down the left mouse button, drag the outline of the selected cells to the desired location, and then release the mouse button.

Project 1b Moving Selected Cells   Part 2 of 9

1. With **EL1-C5-P1-RPFacAccts.xlsx** open, you realize that the sublet rent deposit was recorded on the wrong day. The correct day is January 9. To move the cells containing information on the deposit, complete the following steps:
   a. Make cell A13 active and then insert a row. (The new row should display above the row containing information on *Rainer Suppliers*.)
   b. Select cells A7 through F7.
   c. Click the Cut button in the Clipboard group in the Home tab.

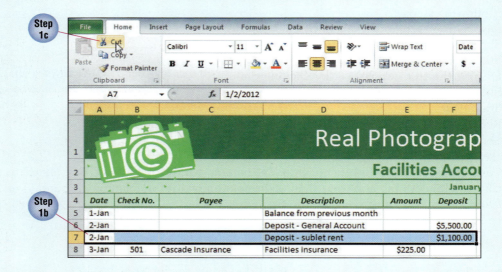

   d. Click cell A13 to make it active.
   e. Click the Paste button in the Clipboard group.
   f. Change the date of the deposit from January 2 to January 9.
   g. Select row 7 and then delete it.

2. Click the Sheet2 tab and then complete steps similar to those in Step 1 to move the sublet deposit row so it is positioned above the *Rainier Suppliers* row and below the *Clear Source* row. Change the date of the deposit to February 12 and make sure you delete row 7.
3. Move cells using the mouse by completing the following steps:
   a. Click the Sheet3 tab.
   b. Make cell A13 active and then insert a new row.
   c. Using the mouse, select cells A7 through F7.
   d. Position the mouse pointer on any boundary of the selected cells until it turns into an arrow pointer with a four-headed arrow attached.
   e. Hold down the left mouse button, drag the outline of the selected cells to row 13, and then release the mouse button.

4	Date	Check No.	Payee	Description	Amount	Deposit
5	1-Mar			Balance from previous month		
6	1-Mar			Deposit - General Account		$5,500.00
7	1-Mar			Deposit - sublet rent		$1,100.00
8	2-Mar	527				
9	5-Mar	528				
10	5-Mar	529				
11	6-Mar	530	Stationery Plus	Paper supplies	$113.76	
12	7-Mar	531	Clear Source	Developer supplies	$251.90	
13						
14	8-Mar	532	Rainier Suppliers	Camera supplies	$119.62	
15	9-Mar	533	A1 Wedding Supplies	Photo albums	$323.58	

   f. Change the date of the deposit to March 7.
   g. Delete row 7.
4. Save **EL1-C5-P1-RPFacAccts.xlsx**.

Copying Selected Cells

Copying selected cells can be useful in worksheets that contain repetitive data. To copy cells, select the cells and then click the Copy button in the Clipboard group in the Home tab. Click the cell where you want the first selected cell copied and then click the Paste button in the Clipboard group.

You can also copy selected cells using the mouse and the Ctrl key. To do this, select the cells you want to copy and then position the mouse pointer on any border around the selected cells until it turns into an arrow pointer. Hold down the Ctrl key and the left mouse button, drag the outline of the selected cells to the desired location, release the left mouse button, and then release the Ctrl key.

Using the Paste Options Button

The Paste Options button displays in the lower right corner of the pasted cell(s) when you paste a cell or cells. Display a list of paste options by hovering the mouse pointer over the button and then clicking the button or by pressing the Ctrl key. This causes a drop-down list to display as shown in Figure 5.1. Hover your mouse over a button in the drop-down list and the descriptive name of the button displays along with the keyboard shortcut. With buttons in this drop-down list, you can specify what you want pasted.

▼ **Quick Steps**

Copy and Paste Cells
1. Select cells.
2. Click Copy button.
3. Click desired cell.
4. Click Paste button.

Ctrl + C is the keyboard shortcut to copy selected data.

Copy

Paste Options

Figure 5.1 Paste Options Button Drop-down List

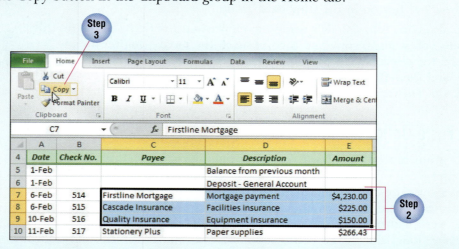

Click the button that specifies the formatting you desire for the pasted data.

Project 1c Copying Selected Cells in a Worksheet Part 3 of 9

1. With **EL1-C5-P1-RPFacAccts.xlsx** open, make Sheet2 active.
2. Select cells C7 through E9.
3. Click the Copy button in the Clipboard group in the Home tab.

4. Make Sheet3 active.
5. Make cell C7 active.
6. Click the Paste button in the Clipboard group.
7. Click the Paste Options button that displays in the lower right corner of the pasted cells and then click the Keep Source Column Widths button at the drop-down list.
8. Make Sheet2 active and then press the Esc key to remove the moving marquee.
9. Save **EL1-C5-P1-RPFacAccts.xlsx**.

Step 7

Using the Office Clipboard

Use the Office Clipboard feature to collect and paste multiple items. To use the Office Clipboard, display the Clipboard task pane by clicking the Clipboard group dialog box launcher. This button is located in the lower right corner of the Clipboard group in the Home tab. The Clipboard task pane displays at the left side of the screen in a manner similar to what you see in Figure 5.2.

▼ **Quick Steps**

Copy and Paste Multiple Items
1. Click Clipboard group dialog box launcher.
2. Select desired cells.
3. Click Copy button.
4. Continue selecting desired cells and then clicking the Copy button.
5. Make desired cell active.
6. Click item in Clipboard task pane that you want inserted in the worksheet.
7. Continue pasting desired items from the Clipboard task pane.

Figure 5.2 Clipboard Task Pane

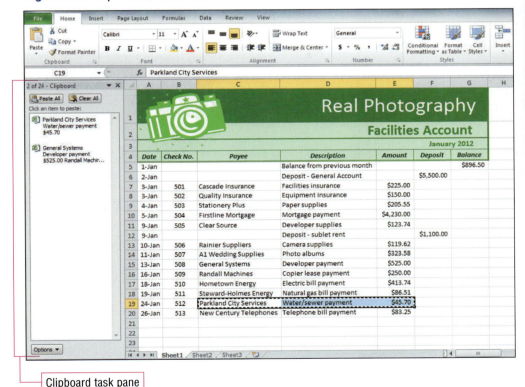

Clipboard task pane

Chapter 5 ■ Moving Data within and between Workbooks

Select data or an object you want to copy and then click the Copy button in the Clipboard group. Continue selecting text or items and clicking the Copy button. To insert an item, position the insertion point in the desired location and then click the item in the Clipboard task pane. If the copied item is text, the first 50 characters display. When all desired items are inserted, click the Clear All button to remove any remaining items. Sometimes, you may have a situation in which you want to copy all of the selected items to a single location. If so, position the insertion point in the desired location and then click the Paste All button in the Clipboard task pane.

Project 1d — Copying and Pasting Cells Using the Office Clipboard Part 4 of 9

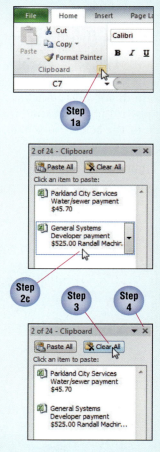

1. With **EL1-C5-P1-RPFacAccts.xlsx** open, select cells for copying by completing the following steps:
   a. Display the Clipboard task pane by clicking the Clipboard group dialog box launcher. (If the Clipboard contains any copied data, click the Clear All button.)
   b. Click the Sheet1 tab.
   c. Select cells C15 through E16.
   d. Click the Copy button in the Clipboard group.
   e. Select cells C19 through E19.
   f. Click the Copy button in the Clipboard group.
2. Paste the copied cells by completing the following steps:
   a. Click the Sheet2 tab.
   b. Make cell C15 active.
   c. Click the item in the Clipboard task pane representing *General Systems Developer*.
   d. Click the Sheet3 tab.
   e. Make C15 active.
   f. Click the item in the Clipboard task pane representing *General Systems Developer*.
   g. Make cell C19 active.
   h. Click the item in the Clipboard task pane representing *Parkland City Services*.
3. Click the Clear All button located toward the top of the Clipboard task pane.
4. Close the Clipboard task pane by clicking the Close button (contains an X) located in the upper right corner of the task pane.
5. Save **EL1-C5-P1-RPFacAccts.xlsx**.

Pasting Values Only

When you copy and then paste a cell containing a value as well as a formula, you can use buttons in the Paste Options button drop-down list to specify what you want pasted. With the buttons in the *Paste Values* section of the Paste Options button drop-down list, you can choose to insert the value only, the value with numbering formatting, or the value with the source formatting.

Project 1e Copying and Pasting Values   Part 5 of 9

1. With **EL1-C5-P1-RPFacAccts.xlsx** open, make Sheet1 active.
2. Make cell G6 active, insert the formula **=(F6-E6)+G5**, and then press Enter.
3. Copy the formula in cell G6 down to cells G7 through G20.
4. Copy the final balance amount from Sheet1 to Sheet2 by completing the following steps:
   a. Make cell G20 active.
   b. Click the Copy button in the Clipboard group.
   c. Click the Sheet2 tab.
   d. Make cell G5 active and then click the Paste button in the Clipboard group.
   e. Click the Paste Options button.
   f. At the drop-down list, click the Values button in the *Paste Values* section of the drop-down list. (This inserts the value and not the formula.)
5. Make cell G6 active, insert a formula that determines the balance (see Step 2), and then copy the formula down to cells G7 through G20.
6. Copy the amount in cell G20 and then paste the value only into cell G5 in Sheet3.
7. With Sheet3 active, make cell G6 active, insert a formula that determines the balance (see Step 2), and then copy the formula down to cells G7 through G20.
8. Save **EL1-C5-P1-RPFacAccts.xlsx**.

Inserting a Worksheet

A workbook, by default, contains three worksheets. You can insert additional worksheets in a workbook. To do this, click the Insert Worksheet tab located to the right of the Sheet3 tab. This inserts a new worksheet labeled *Sheet4* at the right of the Sheet3 tab. You can also press Shift + F11 to insert a new worksheet. Or, you can insert a worksheet by clicking the Insert button arrow in the Cells group in the Home tab and then clicking *Insert Sheet*.

▼ **Quick Steps**

Insert Worksheet
Click Insert Worksheet tab.
OR
Press Shift + F11.

Insert

Project 1f Inserting a Worksheet   Part 6 of 9

1. With **EL1-C5-P1-RPFacAccts.xlsx** open, make the following changes:
   a. Make Sheet1 active.
   b. Make cell D21 active, turn on bold, and then type **Total**.
   c. Make cell E21 active and then click once on the AutoSum button located in the Editing group in the Home tab. (This inserts the formula *=SUM(E13:E20)*.)
   d. Change the formula to *=SUM(E7:E20)* and then press Enter.
   e. Make cell F21 active and then click once on the AutoSum button in the Editing group. (This inserts the formula *=SUM(F12:F20)*.)
   f. Change the formula to *=SUM(F6:F20)* and then press Enter.

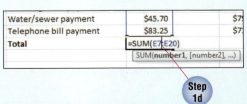

2. Make Sheet2 active and then complete the steps in Step 1 to insert the totals of the *Amount* and *Deposit* columns.
3. Make Sheet3 active and then complete the steps in Step 1 to insert the totals of the *Amount* and *Deposit* columns.
4. Insert a new worksheet by clicking the Insert Worksheet tab located to the right of the Sheet3 tab.

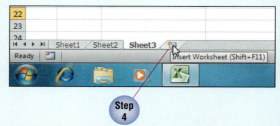

Step 4

5. Make Sheet1 active, copy cells A1 through G3, make Sheet4 active (with cell A1 active), and then paste the cells. (When copying the cells, position the cell pointer to the right of the image, make sure the pointer displays as a white plus symbol, and then drag to select the cells.)
6. Make the following changes to the worksheet:
   a. Make cell A3 active and then type **First Quarter Summary 2012**.
   b. Change the width of column A to 20.00.
   c. Change the width of columns B, C, and D to 12.00.
   d. Select cells B4 through D4, click the Bold button in the Font group in the Home tab, and then click the Center button in the Alignment group.
   e. Select cells B5 through D7 and then change the number formatting to Currency with two decimal places and include the dollar sign symbol.
   f. Type the following text in the specified cells:
      B4 = **January**
      C4 = **February**
      D4 = **March**
      A5 = **Checks amount**
      A6 = **Deposit amount**
      A7 = **End-of-month balance**

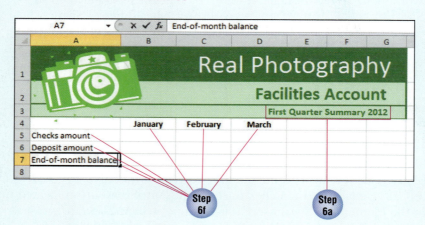

Step 6f   Step 6a

7. Copy a value by completing the following steps:
   a. Make Sheet1 active.
   b. Make cell E21 active and then click the Copy button in the Clipboard group in the Home tab.
   c. Make Sheet4 active.
   d. Make cell B5 active and then click the Paste button in the Clipboard group.

e. Click the Paste Options button and then click the Values button in the *Paste Values* section of the drop-down list.
f. Make Sheet1 active.
g. Press the Esc key to remove the moving marquee.
h. Make cell F21 active and then click the Copy button.
i. Make Sheet4 active.
j. Make cell B6 active and then click the Paste button.
k. Click the Paste Options button and then click the Values button at the drop-down list.
l. Make Sheet1 active.
m. Press the Esc key to remove the moving marquee.
n. Make cell G20 active and then click the Copy button.
o. Make Sheet4 active.
p. Make cell B7 active and then click the Paste button.
q. Click the Paste Options button and then click the Values button at the drop-down list.

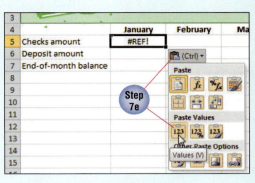

8. Complete steps similar to those in Step 7 to insert amounts and balances for February and March.
9. Save **EL1-C5-P1-RPFacAccts.xlsx**.

Managing Worksheets

Right-click a sheet tab and a shortcut menu displays as shown in Figure 5.3 with the options for managing worksheets. For example, remove a worksheet by clicking the *Delete* option. Move or copy a worksheet by clicking the *Move or Copy* option. Clicking this option causes a Move or Copy dialog box to display where you specify before what sheet you want to move or copy the selected sheet. By default, Excel names worksheets in a workbook *Sheet1, Sheet2, Sheet3,* and so on. To rename a worksheet, click the *Rename* option (this selects the default sheet name) and then type the desired name.

Quick Steps

Move or Copy a Worksheet
1. Right-click sheet tab.
2. Click *Move or Copy*.
3. At Move or Copy dialog box, click desired worksheet name in *Before sheet* list box.
4. Click OK.
OR
Drag worksheet tab to the desired position. (To copy, hold down Ctrl key while dragging.)

Figure 5.3 Sheet Tab Shortcut Menu

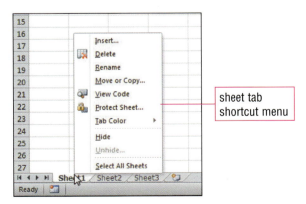

sheet tab shortcut menu

HINT

Use the tab scroll buttons, located to the left of the sheet tabs, to bring into view any worksheet tabs not currently visible.

Chapter 5 ■ Moving Data within and between Workbooks

In addition to the shortcut menu options, you can use the mouse to move or copy worksheets. To move a worksheet, position the mouse pointer on the worksheet tab, hold down the left mouse button (a page icon displays next to the mouse pointer), drag the page icon to the desired position, and then release the mouse button. For example, to move the Sheet2 tab after the Sheet3 tab you would position the mouse pointer on the Sheet2 tab, hold down the left mouse button, drag the page icon so it is positioned after the Sheet3 tab, and then release the mouse button. To copy a worksheet, hold down the Ctrl key while dragging the sheet tab.

Use the *Tab Color* option at the shortcut menu to apply a color to a worksheet tab. Right-click a worksheet tab, point to *Tab Color* at the shortcut menu, and then click the desired color at the color palette.

Quick Steps

Recolor Sheet Tab
1. Right-click sheet tab.
2. Point to *Tab Color*.
3. Click desired color at color palette.

Project 1g   Selecting, Moving, Renaming, and Changing the Color of Worksheet Tabs   Part 7 of 9

1. With **EL1-C5-P1-RPFacAccts.xlsx** open, move Sheet4 by completing the following steps:
   a. Right-click Sheet4 and then click *Move or Copy* at the shortcut menu.

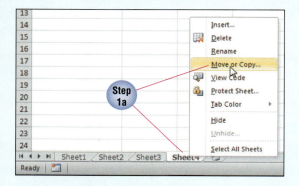

   b. At the Move or Copy dialog box, make sure *Sheet1* is selected in the *Before sheet* section, and then click OK.

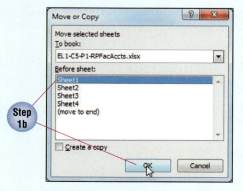

2. Rename Sheet4 by completing the following steps:
   a. Right-click the Sheet4 tab and then click *Rename*.
   b. Type **Summary** and then press Enter.

3. Complete steps similar to those in Step 2 to rename Sheet1 to January, Sheet2 to February, and Sheet3 to March.
4. Change the color of the Summary sheet tab by completing the following steps:
   a. Right-click the Summary sheet tab.
   b. Point to *Tab Color* at the shortcut menu.
   c. Click a red color of your choosing at the color palette.
5. Follow steps similar to those in Step 4 to change the January sheet tab to a blue color, the February sheet tab to a purple color, and the March sheet tab to a green color.
6. Save **EL1-C5-P1-RPFacAccts.xlsx**.

Hiding a Worksheet in a Workbook

In a workbook containing multiple worksheets, you can hide a worksheet that may contain sensitive data or data you do not want to display or print with the workbook. To hide a worksheet in a workbook, click the Format button in the Cells group in the Home tab, point to *Hide & Unhide*, and then click *Hide Sheet*. You can also hide a worksheet by right-clicking a worksheet tab and then clicking the *Hide* option at the shortcut menu. To make a hidden worksheet visible, click the Format button in the Cells group, point to *Hide & Unhide*, and then click *Unhide Sheet*, or right-click a worksheet tab and then click *Unhide* at the shortcut menu. At the Unhide dialog box shown in Figure 5.4, double-click the name of the hidden worksheet you want to display.

Formatting Multiple Worksheets

When you apply formatting to a worksheet, such as changing margins, orientation, or inserting a header or footer, and so on, the formatting is applied only to the active worksheet. If you want formatting to apply to multiple worksheets in a workbook, select the tabs of the desired worksheets and then apply the formatting. For example, if a workbook contains three worksheets and you want to apply formatting to the first and second worksheets only, select the tabs for the first and second worksheets and then apply the formatting.

To select adjacent worksheet tabs, click the first tab, hold down the Shift key, and then click the last tab. To select nonadjacent worksheet tabs, click the first tab, hold down the Ctrl key, and then click any other tabs you want selected.

▼ **Quick Steps**

Hide a Worksheet
1. Click Format button.
2. Point to *Hide & Unhide*.
3. Click *Hide Sheet*.
OR
1. Right-click worksheet tab.
2. Click *Hide* at shortcut menu.

Unhide a Worksheet
1. Click Format button.
2. Point to *Hide & Unhide*.
3. Click *Unhide Sheet*.
4. Double-click desired hidden worksheet in Unhide dialog box.
OR
1. Right-click worksheet tab.
2. Click *Unhide* at shortcut menu.
3. Double-click desired hidden worksheet in Unhide dialog box.

HINT If the *Hide* option is unavailable, the workbook is protected from change.

Format

Figure 5.4 Unhide Dialog Box

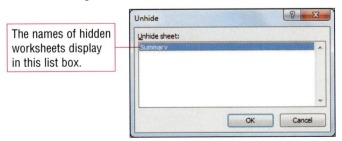

The names of hidden worksheets display in this list box.

 **Project 1h** Hiding a Worksheet and Formatting Multiple Worksheets   Part 8 of 9

1. With **EL1-C5-P1-RPFacAccts.xlsx** open, hide the Summary worksheet by completing the following steps:
   a. Click the Summary tab.
   b. Click the Format button in the Cells group in the Home tab, point to *Hide & Unhide*, and then click *Hide Sheet*.

2. Unhide the worksheet by completing the following steps:
   a. Click the Format button in the Cells group, point to *Hide & Unhide*, and then click *Unhide Sheet*.
   b. At the Unhide dialog box, make sure *Summary* is selected and then click OK.
3. Insert a header for each worksheet by completing the following steps:
   a. Click the Summary tab.
   b. Hold down the Shift key and then click the March tab. (This selects all four tabs.)
   c. Click the Insert tab.
   d. Click the Header & Footer button in the Text group.
   e. Click the Header button in the Header & Footer group in the Header & Footer Tools Design tab and then click the option at the drop-down list that prints your name at the left side of the page, the page number in the middle, and the date at the right side of the page.
4. With all the sheet tabs selected, horizontally and vertically center each worksheet on the page. *Hint: Do this at the Page Setup dialog box with the Margins tab selected.*
5. With all of the sheet tabs still selected, change the page orientation to landscape. *Hint: Do this with the Orientation button in the Page Layout tab.*
6. Save **EL1-C5-P1-RPFacAccts.xlsx**.

Printing a Workbook Containing Multiple Worksheets

By default, Excel prints the currently displayed worksheet. If you want to print all worksheets in a workbook, display the Print tab Backstage view, click the first gallery in the Settings category, click *Print Entire Workbook* at the drop-down list, and then click the Print button. You can also print specific worksheets in a workbook by selecting the tabs of the worksheets you want printed. With the desired worksheet tabs selected, display the Print tab Backstage view and then click the Print button.

▼ Quick Steps

Print All Worksheets in Workbook
1. Click File tab.
2. Click Print tab.
3. Click first gallery in Settings category.
4. Click *Print Entire Workbook*.
5. Click Print button.

Project 1i — Printing All Worksheets in a Workbook — Part 9 of 9

1. With **EL1-C5-P1-RPFacAccts.xlsx** open, click the File tab and then click the Print tab.
2. At the Print tab Backstage view, click the first gallery in the Settings category and then click *Print Entire Workbook* at the drop-down list.
3. Click the Print button.

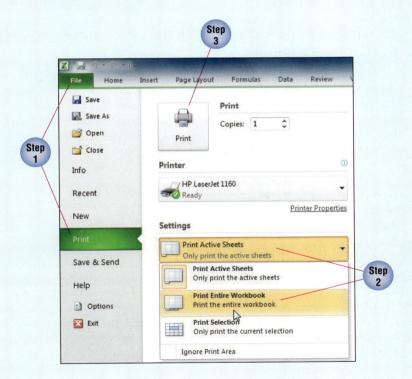

4. Save and then close **EL1-C5-P1-RPFacAccts.xlsx**.

Project 2 Write Formulas Using Ranges in an Equipment Usage Workbook **2 Parts**

You will open an equipment usage workbook and then split the window and edit cells. You will also name ranges and then use the range names to write formulas in the workbook.

Splitting a Worksheet into Windows and Freezing and Unfreezing Panes

▼ Quick Steps

Split a Worksheet
1. Click View tab.
2. Click Split button.
OR
Drag horizontal and/or vertical split bars.

In some worksheets, not all cells display at one time in the worksheet area (such as EL1-C5-P2-HCEqpRpt.xlsx). When working in worksheets with more cells than can display at one time, you may find splitting the worksheet window into panes helpful. Split the worksheet window into panes with the Split button in the Window group in the View tab or with the split bars that display at the top of the vertical scroll bar and at the right side of the horizontal scroll bar. Figure 5.5 identifies these split bars.

HINT Restore a split window by double-clicking anywhere on the split bar that divides the panes.

To split a window with the split bar located at the top of the vertical scroll bar, position the mouse pointer on the split bar until it turns into a double-headed arrow with a short double line in the middle. Hold down the left mouse button, drag down the thick gray line that displays until the pane is the desired size, and then release the mouse button. Split the window vertically with the split bar at the right side of the horizontal scroll bar.

Split

Figure 5.5 Split Bars

174   Excel Level 1 ■ Unit 2

Figure 5.6 Split Window

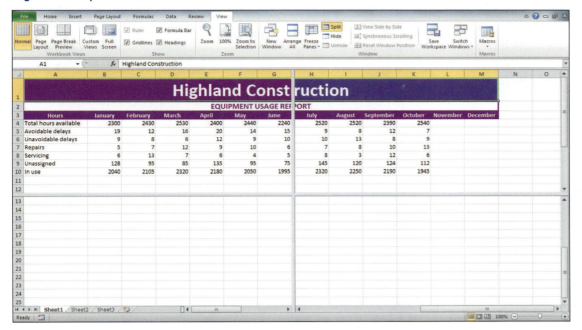

To split a worksheet window with the Split button, click the View tab and then click the Split button. This causes the worksheet to split into four window panes as shown in Figure 5.6. The windows are split by thick, light blue lines (with a three-dimensional look). To remove a split from a worksheet click the Split button to deactivate it or drag the split bars to the upper left corner of the worksheet.

A window pane will display the active cell. As the insertion point is moved through the pane, another active cell with a blue background may display. This additional active cell displays when the insertion point passes over one of the light blue lines that creates the pane. As you move through a worksheet, you may see both active cells — one with a normal background and one with a blue background. If you make a change to the active cell, the change is made in both. If you want only one active cell to display, freeze the window panes by clicking the Freeze Panes button in the Window group in the View tab and then clicking *Freeze Panes* at the drop-down list. You can maintain the display of column headings while editing or typing text in cells by clicking the Freeze Panes button and then clicking *Freeze Top Row*. Maintain the display of row headings by clicking the Freeze Panes button and then clicking *Freeze First Column*. Unfreeze window panes by clicking the Freeze Panes button and then clicking *Unfreeze Panes* at the drop-down list.

Freeze Panes

Using the mouse, you can move the thick, light blue lines that divide the window into panes. To do this, position the mouse pointer on the line until the pointer turns into a double-headed arrow with a double line in the middle. Hold down the left mouse button, drag the outline of the light blue line to the desired location, and then release the mouse button. If you want to move both the horizontal and vertical lines at the same time, position the mouse pointer on the intersection of the thick, light blue lines until it turns into a four-headed arrow. Hold down the left mouse button, drag the thick, light blue lines in the desired direction, and then release the mouse button.

Project 2a **Splitting Windows and Editing Cells** Part 1 of 2

1. Open **HCEqpRpt.xlsx** and then save the workbook with Save As and name it **EL1-C5-P2-HCEqpRpt**.
2. Make sure cell A1 is active and then split the window by clicking the View tab and then clicking the Split button in the Window group. (This splits the window into four panes.)
3. Drag the vertical light gray line by completing the following steps:
   a. Position the mouse pointer on the vertical split line until the pointer turns into a double-headed arrow pointing left and right with a double-line between.
   b. Hold down the left mouse button, drag to the left until the vertical light gray line is immediately to the right of the first column, and then release the mouse button.

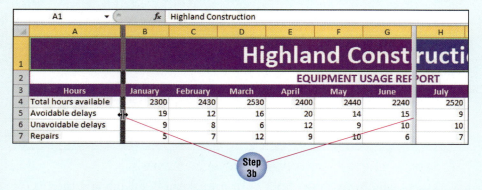

Step 3b

4. Freeze the window panes by clicking the Freeze Panes button in the Window group in the View tab and then clicking *Freeze Panes* at the drop-down list.

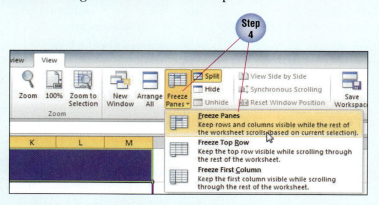

Step 4

5. Make cell L4 active and then type the following data in the specified cells:

   L4 = 2310   M4 = 2210
   L5 = 12   M5 = 5
   L6 = 5   M6 = 7
   L7 = 9   M7 = 8
   L8 = 11   M8 = 12
   L9 = 95   M9 = 120
   L10 = 2005   M10 = 1830

6. Unfreeze the window panes by clicking the Freeze Panes button and then clicking *Unfreeze Panes* at the drop-down list.
7. Remove the panes by clicking the Split button in the Window group to deactivate it.
8. Save **EL1-C5-P2-HCEqpRpt.xlsx**.

Working with Ranges

A selected group of cells is referred to as a *range*. A range of cells can be formatted, moved, copied, or deleted. You can also name a range of cells and then move the insertion point to the range or use a named range as part of a formula.

To name a range, select the cells and then click in the Name Box located at the left of the Formula bar. Type a name for the range (do not use a space) and then press Enter. To move the insertion point to a specific range and select the range, click the down-pointing arrow at the right side of the Name Box and then click the range name.

You can also name a range using the Define Name button in the Formulas tab. To do this, click the Formulas tab and then click the Define Name button in the Defined Names group. At the New Name dialog box, type a name for the range and then click OK.

You can use a range name in a formula. For example, if a range is named *Profit* and you want to insert the average of all cells in the *Profit* range, you would make the desired cell active and then type *=AVERAGE(Profit)*. You can use a named range in the current worksheet or in another worksheet within the workbook.

Quick Steps
Name a Range
1. Select cells.
2. Click in Name Box.
3. Type range name.
4. Press Enter.

HINT
Another method for moving to a range is to click the Find & Select button in the Editing group in the Home tab and then click *Go To*. At the Go To dialog box, double-click the range name.

Define Name

Project 2b — Naming a Range and Using a Range in a Formula — Part 2 of 2

1. With **EL1-C5-P2-HCEqpRpt.xlsx** open, click the Sheet2 tab and then type the following text in the specified cells:
   - A1 = **EQUIPMENT USAGE REPORT**
   - A2 = **Yearly hours**
   - A3 = **Avoidable delays**
   - A4 = **Unavoidable delays**
   - A5 = **Total delay hours**
   - A6 = (leave blank)
   - A7 = **Repairs**
   - A8 = **Servicing**
   - A9 = **Total repair/servicing hours**

2. Make the following formatting changes to the worksheet:
   a. Automatically adjust the width of column A.
   b. Center and bold the text in cells A1 and A2.

3. Select a range of cells in worksheet 1, name the range, and use it in a formula in worksheet 2 by completing the following steps:
   a. Click the Sheet1 tab.
   b. Select cells B5 through M5.
   c. Click in the Name Box located to the left of the Formula bar.
   d. Type **adhours** (for Avoidable Delays Hours) and then press Enter.
   e. Click the Sheet2 tab.
   f. Make cell B3 active.
   g. Type the equation **=SUM(adhours)** and then press Enter.

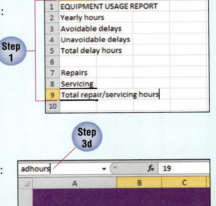

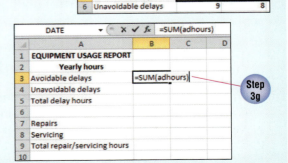

Chapter 5 ■ Moving Data within and between Workbooks 177

4. Click the Sheet1 tab and then complete the following steps:
    a. Select cells B6 through M6.
    b. Click the Formulas tab.
    c. Click the Define Name button in the Defined Names group.
    d. At the New Name dialog box, type **udhours** and then click OK.
    e. Make worksheet 2 active, make cell B4 active, and then type the equation **=SUM(udhours)**.

Step 4d

5. Make worksheet 1 active and then complete the following steps:
    a. Select cells B7 through M7 and then name the range *rhours*.
    b. Make worksheet 2 active, make cell B7 active, and then type the equation **=SUM(rhours)**.
    c. Make worksheet 1 active.
    d. Select cells B8 through M8 and then name the range *shours*.
    e. Make worksheet 2 active, make cell B8 active, and then type the equation **=SUM(shours)**.
6. With worksheet 2 still active, make the following changes:
    a. Make cell B5 active.
    b. Double-click the AutoSum button in the Editing group in the Home tab.
    c. Make cell B9 active.
    d. Double-click the AutoSum button in the Editing group in the Home tab.
7. Make worksheet 1 active and then move to the range *adhours* by clicking the down-pointing arrow at the right side of the Name Box and then clicking *adhours* at the drop-down list.
8. Select both sheet tabs, change the orientation to landscape, scale the contents to fit on one page (in Page Layout tab, change width to *1 page*), and insert a custom footer with your name, page number, and date.
9. Print both worksheets in the workbook.
10. Save and then close **EL1-C5-P2-HCEqpRpt.xlsx**.

Step 7

Arrange, Size, and Copy Data between Workbooks   3 Parts

You will open, arrange, hide, unhide, size, and move multiple workbooks. You will also copy cells from one workbook and paste in another workbook.

Working with Windows

You can open multiple workbooks in Excel and arrange the open workbooks in the Excel window. With multiple workbooks open, you can cut and paste or copy and paste cell entries from one workbook to another using the same techniques discussed earlier in this chapter with the exception that you activate the destination workbook before executing the Paste command.

Opening Multiple Workbooks

With multiple workbooks open, you can move or copy information between workbooks or compare the contents of several workbooks. When you open a new workbook, it is placed on top of the original workbook. Once multiple workbooks are opened, you can resize the workbooks to see all or a portion of them on the screen.

Open multiple workbooks at one time at the Open dialog box. If workbooks are adjacent, display the Open dialog box, click the first workbook name to be opened, hold down the Shift key, and then click the last workbook name to be opened. If the workbooks are nonadjacent, click the first workbook name to be opened and then hold down the Ctrl key while clicking the remaining desired workbook names. Release the Shift key or the Ctrl key and then click the Open button.

To see what workbooks are currently open, click the View tab and then click the Switch Windows button in the Window group. The names of the open workbooks display in a drop-down list and the workbook name preceded by a check mark is the active workbook. To make one of the other workbooks active, click the desired workbook name at the drop-down list.

Switch Windows

Another method for determining which workbooks are open is to hover your mouse over the Excel icon button that displays on the Taskbar. This causes a thumbnail to display of each open workbook. If you have more than one workbook open, the Excel button on the Taskbar displays another layer in a cascaded manner. The layer behind the Excel button displays only a portion of the edge at the right side of the button. If you have multiple workbooks open, hovering the mouse over the Excel button on the Taskbar will cause thumbnails of all of the workbooks to display above the button. (This is dependent on your monitor size.) To change to the desired workbook, click the thumbnail that represents the workbook.

Arranging Workbooks

If you have more than one workbook open, you can arrange the workbooks at the Arrange Windows dialog box shown in Figure 5.7. To display this dialog box, open several workbooks and then click the Arrange All button in the Window group in the View tab. At the Arrange Windows dialog box, click *Tiled* to display a portion of each open workbook. Figure 5.8 displays four tiled workbooks.

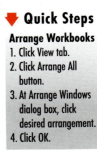

▼ **Quick Steps**

Arrange Workbooks
1. Click View tab.
2. Click Arrange All button.
3. At Arrange Windows dialog box, click desired arrangement.
4. Click OK.

Figure 5.7 Arrange Windows Dialog Box

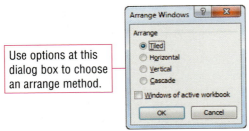

Arrange All

Figure 5.8 Tiled Workbooks

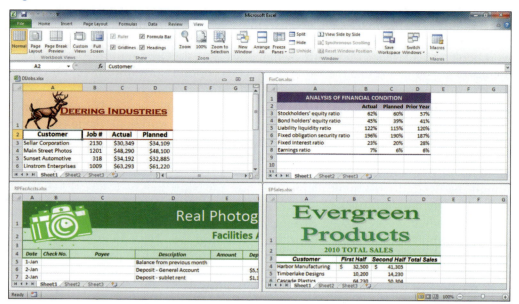

Choose the *Horizontal* option at the Arrange Windows dialog box and the open workbooks display across the screen. The *Vertical* option displays the open workbooks up and down the screen. The last option, *Cascade*, displays the Title bar of each open workbook. Figure 5.9 shows four cascaded workbooks.

The option you select for displaying multiple workbooks depends on which part of the workbooks is most important to view simultaneously. For example, the tiled workbooks in Figure 5.8 allow you to view the company logos and the first few rows and columns of each workbook.

Figure 5.9 Cascaded Workbooks

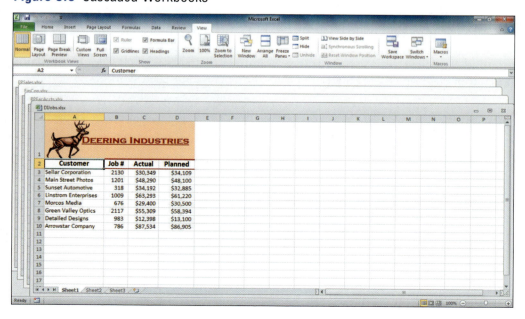

Hiding/Unhiding Workbooks

With the Hide button in the Window group in the View tab, you can hide the active workbook. If a workbook has been hidden, redisplay the workbook by clicking the Unhide button in the Window group in the View tab. At the Unhide dialog box, make sure the desired workbook is selected in the list box and then click OK.

Hide

Unhide

Project 3a   **Opening, Arranging, and Hiding/Unhiding Workbooks**   Part 1 of 3

1. Open several workbooks at the same time by completing the following steps:
   a. Display the Open dialog box.
   b. Click the workbook named ***DIJobs.xlsx***.
   c. Hold down the Ctrl key, click ***EPSales.xlsx***, click ***FinCon.xlsx***, and click ***RPFacAccts.xlsx***.
   d. Release the Ctrl key and then click the Open button in the dialog box.
2. Make **DIJobs.xlsx** the active workbook by clicking the View tab, clicking the Switch Windows button, and then clicking ***DIJobs.xlsx*** at the drop-down list.

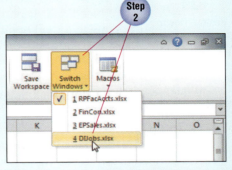

3. Tile the workbooks by completing the following steps:
   a. Click the Arrange All button in the Window group in the View tab.
   b. At the Arrange Windows dialog box, make sure *Tiled* is selected and then click OK.
4. Tile the workbooks horizontally by completing the following steps:
   a. Click the Arrange All button.
   b. At the Arrange Windows dialog box, click *Horizontal*.
   c. Click OK.

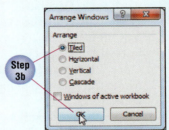

5. Cascade the workbooks by completing the following steps:
   a. Click the Arrange All button.
   b. At the Arrange Windows dialog box, click *Cascade*.
   c. Click OK.
6. Hide and unhide workbooks by completing the following steps:
   a. Make sure **DIJobs.xlsx** is the active workbook (displays on top of the other workbooks).
   b. Click the Hide button in the Window group in the View tab.
   c. Make sure **RPFacAccts.xlsx** is the active workbook (displays on top of the other workbooks).
   d. Click the Hide button.
   e. Click the Unhide button.
   f. At the Unhide dialog box, click ***RPFacAccts.xlsx*** in the list box, and then click OK.
   g. Click the Unhide button.
   h. At the Unhide dialog box, make sure **DIJobs.xlsx** is selected in the list box and then click OK.
7. Close all of the open workbooks without saving changes.

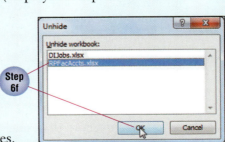

Sizing and Moving Workbooks

Maximize

Minimize

Close

Restore Down

You can use the Maximize and Minimize buttons located in the upper right corner of the active workbook to change the size of the window. The Maximize button is the button in the upper right corner of the active workbook immediately to the left of the Close button. (The Close button is the button containing the *X*.) The Minimize button is located immediately to the left of the Maximize button.

If you arrange all open workbooks and then click the Maximize button in the active workbook, the active workbook expands to fill the screen. In addition, the Maximize button changes to the Restore Down button. To return the active workbook back to its size before it was maximized, click the Restore Down button.

If you click the Minimize button in the active workbook, the workbook is reduced and displays as a layer behind the Excel button on the Taskbar. To maximize a workbook that has been minimized, click the Excel button on the Taskbar and then click the thumbnail representing the workbook.

Project 3b Minimizing, Maximizing, and Restoring Workbooks   Part 2 of 3

1. Open **DIJobs.xlsx**.
2. Maximize **DIJobs.xlsx** by clicking the Maximize button at the right side of the workbook Title bar. (The Maximize button is the button at the right side of the Title bar, immediately to the left of the Close button.)
3. Open **EPSales.xlsx** and **FinCon.xlsx**.
4. Make the following changes to the open workbooks:
   a. Tile the workbooks.
   b. Make **DIJobs.xlsx** the active workbook. (Title bar displays with a light gray background [the background color may vary depending on how Windows is customized]).
   c. Minimize **DIJobs.xlsx** by clicking the Minimize button that displays at the right side of the Title bar.
   d. Make **EPSales.xlsx** the active workbook and then minimize it.
   e. Minimize **FinCon.xlsx**.
5. Close all workbooks.

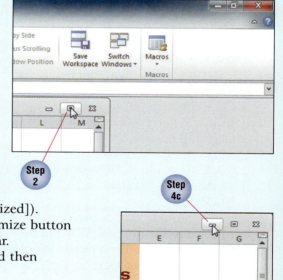

Moving, Copying, and Pasting Data

With more than one workbook open, you can move, copy, and/or paste data from one workbook to another. To move, copy, and/or paste data between workbooks, use the cutting and pasting options you learned earlier in this chapter, together with the information about windows in this chapter.

Project 3c — Copying Selected Cells from One Open Worksheet to Another   Part 3 of 3

1. Open **DIFebJobs.xlsx**.
2. If you just completed Project 3b, click the Maximize button so the worksheet fills the entire worksheet window.
3. Save the workbook with Save As and name it **EL1-C5-P3-DIFebJobs**.
4. With **EL1-C5-P3-DIFebJobs.xlsx** open, open **DIJobs.xlsx**.
5. Select and then copy text from **DIJobs.xlsx** to **EL1-C5-P3-DIFebJobs.xlsx** by completing the following steps:
   a. With **DIJobs.xlsx** the active workbook, select cells A3 through D10.
   b. Click the Copy button in the Clipboard group in the Home tab.
   c. Click the Excel button on the Taskbar and then click the **EL1-C5-P3-DIFebJobs.xlsx** thumbnail.

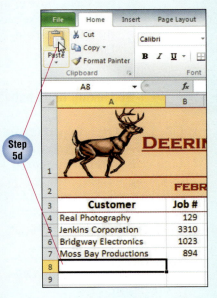

   d. Make cell A8 the active cell and then click the Paste button in the Clipboard group in the Home tab.
   e. Make cell E7 active and then drag the fill handle down to cell E15.
6. Print **EL1-C5-P3-DIFebJobs.xlsx** horizontally and vertically centered on the page.
7. Save and then close **EL1-C5-P3-DIFebJobs.xlsx**.
8. Close **DIJobs.xlsx**.

Project 4 — Linking and Copying Data within and between Worksheets and Word   2 Parts

You will open a workbook containing four worksheets with quarterly expenses data, copy and then link cells between the worksheets, and then copy and paste the worksheets into Word as picture objects.

Moving Data

You can move or copy data within a worksheet, between worksheets, and also between workbooks and other programs such as Word, PowerPoint, or Access. The Paste Options button provides a variety of options for pasting data in a worksheet, another workbook, or another program. In addition to pasting data, you can also link data and paste data as an object or a picture object.

Linking Data

In some situations, you may want to copy and link data within or between worksheets or workbooks rather than copy and paste data. Linking data is useful in worksheets or workbooks where you need to maintain consistency and control over critical data. When data is linked, a change made in a linked cell is automatically made to the other cells in the link. You can make links with individual cells or with a range of cells. When linking data, the worksheet that contains the original data is called the *source worksheet* and the worksheet relying on the source worksheet for the data in the link is called the *dependent worksheet*.

To create a link, make active the cell containing the data to be linked (or select the cells) and then click the Copy button in the Clipboard group in the Home tab. Make active the worksheet where you want to paste the cells, click the Paste button arrow, and then click the Paste Link button located in the *Other Paste Options* section in the drop-down list. You can also create a link by clicking the Paste button, clicking the Paste Options button, and then clicking the Paste Link button.

▼ Quick Steps

Link Data between Worksheets
1. Select cells.
2. Click Copy button.
3. Click desired worksheet tab.
4. Click in desired cell.
5. Click Paste button arrow.
6. Click *Paste Link* at drop-down list.

Project 4a Linking Cells between Worksheets   Part 1 of 2

1. Open **DWQtrlyExp.xlsx** and then save the workbook with Save As and name it **EL1-C5-P4-DWQtrlyExp**.
2. Link cells in the first quarter worksheet to the other three worksheets by completing the following steps:
   a. Select cells C4 through C10.
   b. Click the Copy button in the Clipboard group in the Home tab.
   c. Click the 2nd Qtr tab.
   d. Make cell C4 active.
   e. Click the Paste button arrow and then click the Paste Link button located in the *Other Paste Options* section in the drop-down list.
   f. Click the 3rd Qtr tab and then make cell C4 active.
   g. Click the Paste button arrow and then click the Paste Link button.
   h. Click the 4th Qtr tab and then make cell C4 active.
   i. Click the Paste button.
   j. Click the Paste Options button and then click the Paste Link button in the *Other Paste Options* section in the drop-down list.

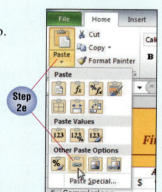

Step 2e

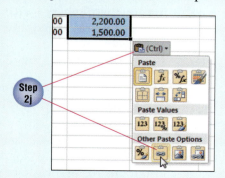

Step 2j

3. Click the 1st Qtr tab and then press the Esc key to remove the moving marquee.
4. Insert a formula in all worksheets that subtracts the Budget amount from the Variance amount by completing the following steps:
   a. Make sure the first quarter worksheet displays.
   b. Hold down the Shift key and then click the 4th Qtr tab. (This selects all four tabs.)
   c. Make cell D4 active and then type the formula =**C4-B4** and press Enter.
   d. Copy the formula in cell D4 down to cells D5 through D10.
   e. Make cell D4 active and then click the Accounting Number Format button.
   f. Click the 2nd Qtr tab and notice that the formula was inserted and copied in this worksheet.
   g. Click the other worksheet tabs and notice the amounts in column D.
   h. Click the 1st Qtr tab.
5. With the first quarter worksheet active, make the following changes to some of the linked cells:
   C4: Change *$126,000* to *$128,000*
   C5: Change *54,500* to *56,000*
   C9: Change *2,200* to *2,400*
6. Click the 2nd Qtr tab and notice that the values in cells C4, C5, and C9 automatically changed (because they were linked to the first quarter worksheet).
7. Click the other tabs and notice that the values changed.
8. Save **EL1-C5-P4-DWQtrlyExp.xlsx** and then print all four worksheets in the workbook.

Copying and Pasting Data between Programs

Microsoft Office is a suite that allows integration, which is the combining of data from two or more programs into one file. Integration can occur by copying and pasting data between programs. For example, you can create a worksheet in Excel, select specific data in the worksheet, and then copy it to a Word document. When pasting Excel data in a Word document, you can choose to keep the source formatting, use destination styles, link the data, insert the data as a picture, or keep the text only.

Project 4b   Copying and Pasting Excel Data into a Word Document   Part 2 of 2

1. With **EL1-C5-P4-DWQtrlyExp.xlsx** open, open the Word program.
2. In Word, open the document named **DWQtrlyRpt.docx** located in the Excel2010L1C5 folder on your storage medium.
3. Save the Word document with Save As and name it **EL1-C5-P4-DWQtrlyRpt**.
4. Click the Excel button on the Taskbar.
5. Copy the first quarter data into the Word document by completing the following steps:
   a. Click the 1st Qtr tab.
   b. Select cells A2 through D10.
   c. Click the Copy button in the Clipboard group in the Home tab.
   d. Click the Word button on the Taskbar.

e. In the **EL1-C5-P4-DWQtrlyRpt.docx** document, press Ctrl + End to move the insertion point below the heading.
  f. Click the Paste button arrow. (This displays a drop-down list of paste option buttons.)
  g. Move your mouse over the various buttons in the drop-down list to see how each option will insert the data in the document.
  h. Click the Picture button. (This inserts the data as a picture object.)
  i. Press the Enter key twice. (This moves the insertion point below the data.)
  j. Click the Excel button on the Taskbar.
6. Click the 2nd Qtr tab and then complete steps similar to those in Step 5 to copy and paste the second quarter data to the Word document.
7. Click the 3rd Qtr tab and then complete steps similar to those in Step 5 to copy and paste the third quarter data to the Word document.
8. Click the 4th Qtr tab and then complete steps similar to those in Step 5 to copy and paste the fourth quarter data to the Word document. (The data should fit on one page.)
9. Print the document by clicking the File tab, clicking the Print tab, and then clicking the Print button at the Print tab Backstage view.
10. Save and then close **EL1-C5-P4-DWQtrlyRpt.docx** and then exit Word.
11. In Excel, press the Esc key to remove the moving marquee and then make cell A1 active.
12. Save and then close **EL1-C5-P4-DWQtrlyExp.xlsx**.

Chapter Summary

- An Excel workbook, by default, contains three worksheets. Click a worksheet tab to display the worksheet.
- Move selected cells and cell contents in and between worksheets using the Cut, Copy, and Paste buttons in the Clipboard group in the Home tab or by dragging with the mouse.
- Move selected cells with the mouse by dragging the outline of the selected cells to the desired position.
- Copy selected cells with the mouse by holding down the Ctrl key and the left mouse button, dragging the outline of the selected cells to the desired location, releasing the left mouse button, and then releasing the Ctrl key.
- When pasting data, use the Paste Options button to specify what you want pasted. Click the Paste Options button and a drop-down list of buttons displays with options to specify how you want the data posted.
- Use the Clipboard task pane to collect and paste data within and between worksheets and workbooks. Display the Clipboard task pane by clicking the Clipboard group dialog box launcher.
- Insert a worksheet in a workbook by clicking the Insert Worksheet tab located to the right of the Sheet3 tab or pressing Shift + F11.

- Perform maintenance activities, such as deleting and renaming, on worksheets within a workbook by clicking the right mouse button on a sheet tab and then clicking the desired option at the shortcut menu.
- You can use the mouse to move or copy worksheets. To move a worksheet, drag the worksheet tab with the mouse. To copy a worksheet hold down the Ctrl key and then drag the worksheet tab with the mouse.
- Use the *Tab Color* option at the sheet tab shortcut menu to apply a color to a worksheet tab.
- Hide and unhide a worksheet by clicking the Format button in the Cells group and then clicking the desired option at the drop-down list or by right-clicking the worksheet tab and then clicking the desired option at the shortcut menu.
- Manage more than one worksheet at a time by first selecting the worksheets. Use the mouse together with the Shift key to select adjacent worksheet tabs and use the mouse together with the Ctrl key to select nonadjacent worksheet tabs.
- If you want formatting to apply to multiple worksheets in a workbook, select the tabs of the desired worksheets and then apply the formatting.
- To print all worksheets in a workbook, display the Print tab Backstage view, click the first gallery in the Settings category, and then click *Print Entire Workbook* at the drop-down list. You can also print specific worksheets by selecting the tabs of the worksheets you want to print.
- Split the worksheet window into panes with the Split button in the Window group in the View tab or with the split bars on the horizontal and vertical scroll bars.
- To remove a split from a worksheet, click the Split button to deactivate it or drag the split bars to the upper left corner of the worksheet.
- Freeze window panes by clicking the Freeze Panes button in the Window group in the View tab and then clicking *Freeze Panes* at the drop-down list. Unfreeze window panes by clicking the Freeze Panes button and then clicking *Unfreeze Panes* at the drop-down list.
- A selected group of cells is referred to as a range. A range can be named and used in a formula. Name a range by typing the name in the Name Box located to the left of the Formula bar or at the New Name dialog box.
- To open multiple workbooks that are adjacent, display the Open dialog box, click the first workbook, hold down the Shift key, click the last workbook, and then click the Open button. If workbooks are nonadjacent, click the first workbook, hold down the Ctrl key, click the desired workbooks, and then click the Open button.
- To see a list of open workbooks, click the View tab and then click the Switch Windows button in the Window group.
- Arrange multiple workbooks in a window with options at the Arrange Windows dialog box.
- Hide the active workbook by clicking the Hide button and unhide a workbook by clicking the Unhide button in the Window group in the View tab.
- Click the Maximize button located in the upper right corner of the active workbook to make the workbook fill the entire window area. Click the Minimize button to shrink the active workbook to a button on the Taskbar. Click the Restore Down button to return the workbook to its previous size.
- You can move, copy, and/or paste data between workbooks.

Commands Review

FEATURE	RIBBON TAB, GROUP	BUTTON, OPTION	KEYBOARD SHORTCUT
Cut selected cells	Home, Clipboard	✂	Ctrl + X
Copy selected cells	Home, Clipboard		Ctrl + C
Paste selected cells	Home, Clipboard		Ctrl + V
Clipboard task pane	Home, Clipboard		
Insert worksheet			Shift + F11
Hide worksheet	Home, Cells	, Hide & Unhide, Hide Sheet	
Unhide worksheet	Home, Cells	, Hide & Unhide, Unhide Sheet	
Split window into pane	View, Window		
Freeze window panes	View, Window	, Freeze Panes	
Unfreeze window panes	View, Window	, Unfreeze Panes	
New Name dialog box	Formulas, Defined Names		
Arrange Windows dialog box	View, Window		
Maximize window			
Restore Down			
Minimize window			

Concepts Check Test Your Knowledge

Completion: In the space provided at the right, indicate the correct term, symbol, or command.

1. By default, a workbook contains this number of worksheets. _____

2. The Cut, Copy, and Paste buttons are located in this group in the Home tab. _____

3. To copy selected cells with the mouse, hold down this key while dragging the outline of the selected cells to the desired location. _____

4. This button displays in the lower right corner of pasted cells. _____

5. Use this task pane to collect and paste multiple items. _____

6. Click this tab to insert a new worksheet. _____

7. Click this option at the sheet tab shortcut menu to apply a color to a worksheet tab. _____

8. To select adjacent worksheet tabs, click the first tab, hold down this key, and then click the last tab. _____

9. To select nonadjacent worksheet tabs, click the first tab, hold down this key, and then click any other tabs you want selected. _____

10. To print all worksheets in a workbook, display the Print tab Backstage view, click the first gallery in the Settings category, and then click this option at the drop-down list. _____

11. The Split button is located in this tab. _____

12. Display the Arrange Windows dialog box by clicking this button in the Window group in the View tab. _____

13. Click this button to make the active workbook expand to fill the screen. _____

14. Click this button to reduce the active workbook to a layer behind the Excel button on the Taskbar. _____

15. When linking data between worksheets, the worksheet containing the original data is called this. _____

Skills Check   Assess Your Performance

Assessment

1 COPY AND PASTE DATA BETWEEN WORKSHEETS IN A SALES WORKBOOK

1. Open **EPSales.xlsx** and then save the workbook with Save As and name it **EL1-C5-A1-EPSales**.
2. Turn on the display of the Clipboard task pane, click the Clear All button to clear any content, and then complete the following steps:
    a. Select and copy cells A7 through C7.
    b. Select and copy cells A10 through C10.
    c. Select and copy cells A13 through C13.
    d. Display the second worksheet, make cell A7 active, and then paste the *Avalon Clinic* cells.
    e. Make cell A10 active and then paste the *Stealth Media* cells.

f. Make A13 active and then paste the *Danmark Contracting* cells.
   g. Make the third worksheet active and then complete similar steps to paste the cells in the same location as the second worksheet.
   h. Clear the contents of the Clipboard task pane and then close the task pane.
3. Change the name of the Sheet1 tab to *2010 Sales*, the name of the Sheet2 tab to *2011 Sales*, and the name of the Sheet3 tab to *2012 Sales*.
4. Change the color of the 2010 Sales tab to blue, the color of the 2011 Sales tab to green, and the color of the 2012 Sales tab to yellow.
5. Display the 2010 Sales worksheet, select all three tabs, and then insert a formula in cell D4 that sums the amounts in cells B4 and C4. Copy the formula in cell D4 down to cells D5 through D14.
6. Make cell D15 active and then insert a formula that sums the amounts in cells D4 through D14.
7. Apply the Accounting Number Format style with no decimal places to cell D4 (on all three worksheets).
8. Insert a footer on all three worksheets that prints your name at the left side and the current date at the right.
9. Save **EL1-C5-A1-EPSales.xlsx**.
10. Print all three worksheets and then close **EL1-C5-A1-EPSales.xlsx**.

Assessment

2 COPY, PASTE, AND FORMAT WORKSHEETS IN AN INCOME STATEMENT WORKBOOK

1. Open **CMJanIncome.xlsx** and then save the workbook with Save As and name it **EL1-C5-A2-CMJanIncome**.
2. Copy cells A1 through B17 in Sheet1 and paste them into Sheet2. (Click the Paste Options button and then click the Keep Source Column Widths button at the drop-down list.)
3. Make the following changes to the Sheet2 worksheet:
   a. Adjust the row heights so they match the heights in the Sheet1 worksheet.
   b. Change the month from *January* to *February*.
   c. Change the amount in B4 to *97,655*.
   d. Change the amount in B5 to *39,558*.
   e. Change the amount in B11 to *1,105*.
4. Select both sheet tabs and then insert the following formulas:
   a. Insert a formula in B6 that subtracts the *Cost of Sales* from the *Sales Revenue* (=B4-B5).
   b. Insert a formula in B16 that sums the amounts in B8 through B15.
   c. Insert a formula in B17 that subtracts the *Total Expenses* from the *Gross Profit* (=B6-B16).
5. Change the name of the Sheet1 tab to *January* and the name of the Sheet2 tab to *February*.
6. Change the color of the January tab to blue and the color of the February tab to red.
7. Insert a custom header on both worksheets that prints your name at the left side, the date in the middle, and the file name at the right side.
8. Save, print, and then close **EL1-C5-A2-CMJanIncome.xlsx**.

Assessment

3 FREEZE AND UNFREEZE WINDOW PANES IN A TEST SCORES WORKBOOK

1. Open **CMCertTests.xlsx** and then save the workbook with Save As and name it **EL1-C5-A3-CertTests**.
2. Make cell A1 active and then split the window by clicking the View tab and then clicking the Split button in the Window group. (This causes the window to split into four panes.)
3. Drag both the horizontal and vertical gray lines up and to the left until the horizontal gray line is immediately below the second row and the vertical gray line is immediately to the right of the first column.
4. Freeze the window panes.
5. Add two rows immediately above row 18 and then type the following text in the specified cells:

A18	=	Nauer, Sheryl		A19	=	Nunez, James
B18	=	75		B19	=	98
C18	=	83		C19	=	96
D18	=	85		D19	=	100
E18	=	78		E19	=	90
F18	=	82		F19	=	95
G18	=	80		G19	=	93
H18	=	79		H19	=	88
I18	=	82		I19	=	91
J18	=	92		J19	=	89
K18	=	90		K19	=	100
L18	=	86		L19	=	96
M18	=	84		M19	=	98

6. Insert a formula in cell N3 that averages the percentages in cells B3 through M3 and then copy the formula down to cells N4 through N22.
7. Unfreeze the window panes.
8. Remove the split.
9. Change the orientation to *Landscape* and then scale the worksheet to print on one page. *Hint: Do this with the* **Width** *option in the Scale to Fit group in the Page Layout tab.*
10. Save, print, and then close **EL1-C5-A3-CertTests.xlsx**.

Assessment

4 CREATE, COPY, PASTE, AND FORMAT CELLS IN AN EQUIPMENT USAGE WORKBOOK

1. Create the worksheet shown in Figure 5.10. (Change the width of column A to 21.00.)
2. Save the workbook and name it **EL1-C5-A4-HCMachRpt**.
3. With **EL1-C5-A4-HCMachRpt.xlsx** open, open **HCEqpRpt.xlsx**.
4. Select and copy the following cells from **HCEqpRpt.xlsx** to **EL1-C5-A4-HCMachRpt.xlsx**:
   a. Copy cells A4 through G4 in **HCEqpRpt.xlsx** and paste them into **EL1-C5-A4-HCMachRpt.xlsx** beginning with cell A12.

    b. Copy cells A10 through G10 in **HCEqpRpt.xlsx** and paste them into **EL1-C5-A4-HCMachRpt.xlsx** beginning with cell A13.
 5. With **EL1-C5-A4-HCMachRpt.xlsx** the active workbook, make cell A1 active and then apply the following formatting:
    a. Change the height of row 1 to 25.50.
    b. Change the font size of the text in cell A1 to 14 points.
    c. Insert Olive Green, Accent 3, Lighter 60% fill color to cell A1.
 6. Select cells A2 through G2 and then insert Olive Green, Accent 3, Darker 50% fill color.
 7. Select cells B2 through G2, change the text color to white, and turn on italics. (Make sure the text in the cells is right aligned.)
 8. Select cells A3 through G3 and then insert Olive Green, Accent 3, Lighter 80% fill color.
 9. Select cells A7 through G7 and then insert Olive Green, Accent 3, Lighter 80% fill color.
 10. Select cells A11 through G11 and then insert Olive Green, Accent 3, Lighter 80% fill color.
 11. Print the worksheet centered horizontally and vertically on the page.
 12. Save and then close **EL1-C5-A4-HCMachRpt.xlsx**.
 13. Close **HCEqpRpt.xlsx** without saving the changes.

Figure 5.10 Assessment 4

	A	B	C	D	E	F	G	H
1		\multicolumn{6}{c}{EQUIPMENT USAGE REPORT}		
2		January	February	March	April	May	June	
3	Machine #12							
4	Total hours available	2300	2430	2530	2400	2440	2240	
5	In use	2040	2105	2320	2180	2050	1995	
6								
7	Machine #25							
8	Total hours available	2100	2240	2450	2105	2390	1950	
9	In use	1800	1935	2110	1750	2215	1645	
10								
11	Machine #30							
12								

Assessment 5 COPYING AND LINKING DATA IN A WORD DOCUMENT

 1. In this chapter you learned how to link data in cells between worksheets. You can also copy data in an Excel worksheet and then paste and link the data in a file in another program such as Word. Use buttons in the Paste Options button drop-down list to link data or use options at the Paste Special dialog box. Open Word and then open the document named **DWLtr.docx** located in the Excel2010L1C5 folder on your storage medium. Save the document with Save As and name it **EL1-C5-A5-DWLtr**.
 2. Click the Excel button on the Taskbar, open **DWMortgages.xlsx** and then save the workbook with Save As and name it **EL1-C5-A5-DWMortgages**.
 3. In column G, insert a formula using the PMT function. Automatically adjust the width of column G.

4. Select cells A2 through G10 and then click the Copy button.
5. Click the Word button on the Taskbar. (This displays **EL1-C5-A5-DWLtr.docx**.)
6. Move the insertion point between the two paragraphs of text.
7. Click the Paste button arrow and then click *Paste Special* at the drop-down list.
8. At the Paste Special dialog box, look at the options available and then click the *Paste link* option, click *Microsoft Excel Worksheet Object* in the *As* list box, and then click OK.
9. Click the Center button in the Paragraph group in the Home tab. (This centers the cells between the left and right margins.)
10. Save, print, and then close **EL1-C5-A5-DWLtr.docx**.
11. Click the Excel button on the Taskbar.
12. Make cell A3 active and then change the number from $300,000 to $400,000. Copy the number in cell A3 down to cells A4 through A10. (Cells A3 through A10 should now contain the amount $400,000.)
13. Save, print, and then close **EL1-C5-A5-DWMortgages.xlsx**.
14. Click the Word button on the Taskbar.
15. Open **EL1-C5-A5-DWLtr.docx**. At the message that displays asking if you want to update the data from the linked files, click Yes.
16. Save, print, and then close **EL1-C5-A5-DWLtr.docx**.
17. Exit Word.

Visual Benchmark — Demonstrate Your Proficiency

CREATE AND FORMAT A SALES WORKSHEET USING FORMULAS

1. At a blank workbook, create the worksheet shown in Figure 5.11 with the following specifications:
   - Do not type the data in cells D4 through D9; instead enter a formula that totals the first-half and second-half yearly sales.
   - Apply the formatting shown in the figure including changing font sizes, column widths, and row heights; and inserting shading and border lines.
   - Rename the sheet tab and change the tab color as shown in the figure.
2. Copy cells A1 through D9 and then paste the cells in Sheet2.
3. Edit the cells and apply formatting so your worksheet matches the worksheet shown in Figure 5.12. Rename the sheet tab and change the tab color as shown in the figure.
4. Save the completed workbook and name it **EL1-C5-VB-CMSemiSales**.
5. Print both worksheets.
6. Close **EL1-C5-VB-CMSemiSales.xlsx**.

Figure 5.11 Sales 2011 Worksheet

	A	B	C	D	E
1	Clearline Manufacturing				
2	SEMIANNUAL SALES - 2011				
3	Customer	1st Half	2nd Half	Total	
4	Lakeside Trucking	$ 84,300	$ 73,500	$ 157,800	
5	Gresham Machines	33,000	40,500	73,500	
6	Real Photography	30,890	35,465	66,355	
7	Genesis Productions	72,190	75,390	147,580	
8	Landower Company	22,000	15,000	37,000	
9	Jewell Enterprises	19,764	50,801	70,565	

Figure 5.12 Sales 2012 Worksheet

	A	B	C	D	E
1	Clearline Manufacturing				
2	SEMIANNUAL SALES - 2012				
3	Customer	1st Half	2nd Half	Total	
4	Lakeside Trucking	$ 84,300	$ 73,500	$ 157,800	
5	Gresham Machines	33,000	40,500	73,500	
6	Real Photography	20,750	15,790	36,540	
7	Genesis Productions	51,270	68,195	119,465	
8	Landower Company	22,000	15,000	37,000	
9	Jewell Enterprises	14,470	33,770	48,240	

Case Study Apply Your Skills

Part 1

You are an administrator for Gateway Global, an electronics manufacturing corporation. You are gathering information on money spent on supplies and equipment purchases. You have gathered information for the first quarter of the year and decide to create a workbook containing worksheets for monthly information. To do this, create a worksheet that contains the following information:

- Company name is Gateway Global.
- Create the title *January Expenditures*.
- Create the following columns:

Department	Supplies	Equipment	Total
Production	$25,425	$135,500	
Research and Development	$50,000	$125,000	
Technical Support	$14,500	$65,000	
Finance	$5,790	$22,000	
Sales and Marketing	$35,425	$8,525	
Facilities	$6,000	$1,200	
Total			

- Insert a formula in the *Total* column that sums the amounts in the *supplies* and *equipment* columns and insert a formula in the *total* row that sums the supplies amounts, equipment amounts, and total amounts.
- Apply formatting such as fill color, borders, font color, and shading to enhance the visual appeal of the worksheet.

After creating and formatting the worksheet, complete the following:
- Copy the worksheet data to Sheet2 and then to Sheet3.
- Make the following changes to data in Sheet2:
  - Change *January Expenditures* to *February Expenditures*.
  - Change the Production department supplies amount to *$38,550* and the equipment amount to *$88,500*.
  - Change the Technical Support department equipment amount to *$44,250*.
  - Change the Finance department supplies amount to *$7,500*.
- Make the following changes to data in Sheet3:
  - Change *January Expenditures* to *March Expenditures*.
  - Change the Research and Development department supplies amount to *$65,000* and the equipment amount to *$150,000*.
  - Change the Technical Support department supplies amount to *$21,750* and the equipment amount to *$43,525*.
  - Change the Facilities department equipment amount to *$18,450*.

Create a new worksheet that summarizes the supplies and equipment totals for January, February, and March. Apply the same formatting to the worksheet as applied to the other three. Change the tab name for Sheet1 to *Jan. Expenditures*, the tab name for Sheet2 to *Feb. Expenditures*, the tab name for Sheet3 to *Mar. Expenditures*, and the tab name for Sheet4 to *Qtr. Summary*. Change the color of each tab. (You determine the colors.)

Insert a header that prints your name at the left side of each worksheet and the current date at the right side of each worksheet. Save the workbook and name it **EL1-C5-CS-GGExp**. Print all the worksheets in the workbook and then close the workbook.

Part 2

Help

Employees of Gateway Global have formed two intramural co-ed softball teams and you have volunteered to keep statistics for the players. Open **GGStats.xlsx** and then make the following changes to both worksheets in the workbook:
- Insert a formula that calculates a player's batting average (Hits ÷ At Bats).
- Insert a formula that calculates a player's on-base percentage: (Walks + Hits) ÷ (At Bats + Walks). Select E5 through F15 and then specify that you want three decimal places displayed.
- Insert the company name.
- Apply formatting to enhance the visual appeal of the worksheets.
- Horizontally and vertically center the worksheets.
- Insert a footer that prints on both worksheets and prints your name at the left side of the worksheet and the date at the right of the worksheet.

Use the Help feature to learn about applying cell styles or click the Cells Styles button in the Styles group in the Home tab and then experiment with applying different styles. Apply the *Good* cell style to any cell in the *Batting Average* column with an average over .400. Apply this style to cells in both worksheets. Save the workbook and name it **EL1-C5-CS-GGStats**. Print both worksheets and then close **EL1-C5-CS-GGStats.xlsx**.

Part 3

Many of the suppliers for Gateway Global are international and use different length, weight, and volume measurements. The purchasing manager has asked you to prepare a conversion chart in Excel that displays conversion tables for length, weight, volume, and temperature. Use the Internet to locate conversion tables for length, weight, and volume. When preparing the workbook, create a worksheet with the following information:

- Include the following length conversions:
  - 1 inch to centimeters
  - 1 foot to centimeters
  - 1 yard to meters
  - 1 mile to kilometers
- Include the following weight conversions:
  - 1 ounce to grams
  - 1 pound to kilograms
  - 1 ton to metric tons
- Include the following volume conversions:
  - 1 fluid ounce to milliliters
  - 1 pint to liters
  - 1 quart to liters
  - 1 gallon to liters

Locate a site on the Internet that provides the formula for converting Fahrenheit temperatures to Celsius temperatures and then create another worksheet in the workbook with the following information:

- Insert Fahrenheit temperatures beginning with zero, continuing to 100, and incrementing by 5 (for example, 0, 5, 10, 15, and so on).
- Insert a formula that converts the Fahrenheit temperature to a Celsius temperature.

Include the company name, Gateway Global, in both worksheets. Apply additional formatting to improve the visual appeal of both worksheets. Rename both sheet names and apply a color to each tab (you determine the names and colors). Save the workbook and name it **EL1-C5-CS-GGConv**. Print both worksheets centered horizontally and vertically on the page and then close **EL1-C5-CS-GGConv.xlsx**.

Part 4

Open Microsoft Word and then create a letterhead document that contains the company name *Gateway Global*, the address (you decide the address including street address, city, state, and ZIP code or street address, city, province, and postal code), and the telephone number (you determine the telephone number). Apply formatting to improve the visual appeal of the letterhead. Save the document and name it **EL1-C5-CS-GGLtrhd**. Save the document again and name it **EL1-C5-CS-GGConvLtr**.

In Excel, open **EL1-C5-CS-GGConv.xlsx** (the workbook you created in Part 3). In the first worksheet, copy the cells containing data and then paste the cells in **EL1-C5-CS-GGConvLtr.docx** as a picture object. Center the cells (picture object) between the left and right margins. Save, print, and then close **EL1-C5-CS-GGConvLtr.docx**. Exit Microsoft Word and then, in Excel, close **EL1-C5-CS-GGConv.xlsx**.

Microsoft Excel

Maintaining Workbooks

CHAPTER 6

PERFORMANCE OBJECTIVES

Upon successful completion of Chapter 6, you will be able to:
- Create and rename a folder
- Delete workbooks and folders
- Copy and move workbooks within and between folders
- Copy, move, and rename worksheets within a workbook
- Maintain consistent formatting with styles
- Insert, modify, and remove hyperlinks
- Create financial forms using templates

Once you have been working with Excel for a period of time you will have accumulated several workbook files. Workbooks should be organized into folders to facilitate fast retrieval of information. Occasionally you should perform file maintenance activities such as copying, moving, renaming, and deleting workbooks to ensure the workbook list in your various folders is manageable. You will learn these file management tasks in this chapter along with creating and applying styles, inserting hyperlinks in a workbook, and using Excel templates to create a workbook. Model answers for this chapter's projects appear on the following pages.

Excel2010L1C6

Note: Before beginning the projects, copy to your storage medium the Excel2010L1C6 subfolder from the Excel2010L1 folder on the CD that accompanies this textbook and then make Excel2010L1C6 the active folder.

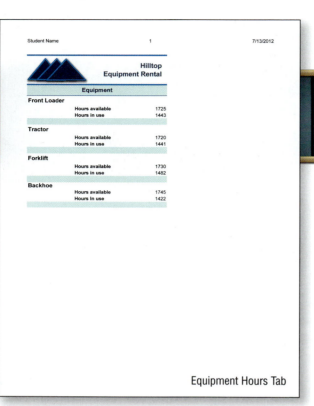

Equipment Hours Tab

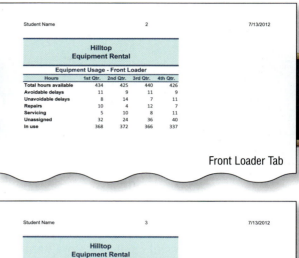

Front Loader Tab

Tractor Tab

Project 2 Copy and Move Worksheets into an Equipment Rental Workbook
EL1-C6-P2-HEREquip.xlsx

Forklift Tab

Backhoe Tab

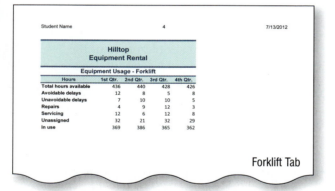

Weekly Payroll Tab

Invoices Tab

Project 3 Create and Apply Styles to a Payroll Workbook
EL1-C6-P3-OEPayroll.xlsx

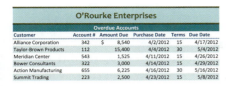
Overdue Accounts Tab

Summary Tab

Project 4 Insert, Modify, and Remove Hyperlinks

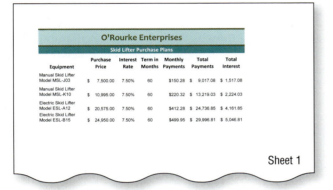
Sheet 1

EL1-C6-P4-PSAccts.xlsx

EL1-C6-P3-OEPlans.xlsx

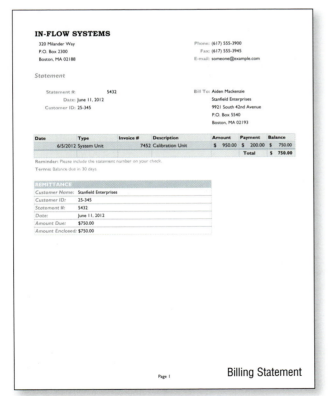
Billing Statement

Project 5 Create a Billing Statement Workbook Using a Template

EL1-C6-P5-Billing.xlsx

Chapter 6 ■ Maintaining Workbooks 199

Project 1 Manage Workbooks   8 Parts

You will perform a variety of file management tasks including creating and renaming a folder; selecting and then deleting, copying, cutting, pasting, and renaming workbooks; deleting a folder; and opening, printing, and closing a workbook.

Maintaining Workbooks

You can complete many workbook management tasks at the Open and Save As dialog boxes. These tasks can include copying, moving, printing, and renaming workbooks; opening multiple workbooks; and creating and renaming a new folder. You can perform some file maintenance tasks such as creating a folder and deleting files with options from the Organize button drop-down list or a shortcut menu and navigate to folders using the Address bar. The elements of the Open dialog box are identified in Figure 6.1.

Figure 6.1 Open Dialog Box

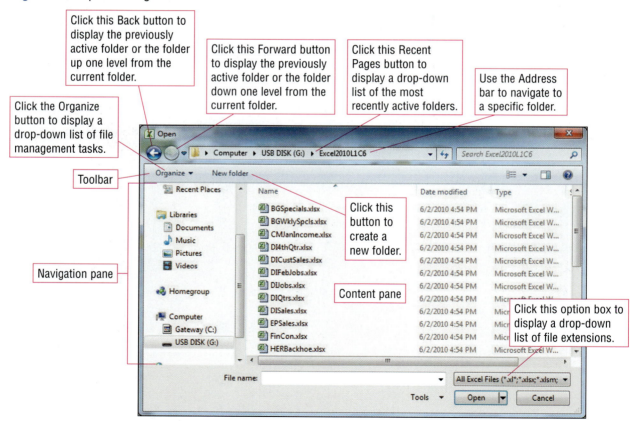

Creating a Folder

In Excel, you should logically group and store workbooks in folders. For example, you could store all of the workbooks related to one department in one folder with the department name being the folder name. You can create a folder within a folder (called a ***subfolder***). If you create workbooks for a department by individuals, each individual name could have a subfolder within the department folder. The main folder on a disk or drive is called the root folder. You create additional folders as branches of this root folder.

At the Open or Save As dialog boxes, workbook file names display in the Content pane preceded by a workbook icon and a folder name displays preceded by a folder icon. Create a new folder by clicking the New folder button located in the toolbar at the Open dialog box or Save As dialog box. This inserts a new folder in the Content pane. Type the name for the folder and then press Enter.

A folder name can contain a maximum of 255 characters. Numbers, spaces, and symbols can be used in the folder name, except those symbols explained in Chapter 1 in the "Saving a Workbook" section.

▼ **Quick Steps**

Create a Folder
1. Click File tab, Open button.
2. Click New folder button.
3. Type folder name.
4. Press Enter.

HINT
Change the default folder with the *Default file location* option at the Excel Options dialog box with *Save* selected.

New Folder

Project 1a — Creating a Folder — Part 1 of 8

1. Create a folder named *Payroll* on your storage medium. To begin, display the Open dialog box.
2. Double-click the *Excel2010L1C6* folder name to make it the active folder.
3. Click the New folder button on the toolbar.
4. Type **Payroll** and then press Enter.
5. Close the Open dialog box.

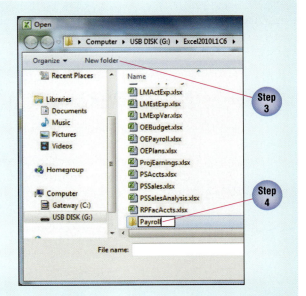

Chapter 6 ■ Maintaining Workbooks   201

Quick Steps

Rename a Folder
1. Click File tab, Open button.
2. Click desired folder.
3. Click Organize button, *Rename*.
4. Type new name.
5. Press Enter.

OR
1. Click File tab, Open button.
2. Right-click folder name.
3. Click *Rename*.
4. Type new name.
5. Press Enter.

Renaming a Folder

As you organize your files and folders, you may decide to rename a folder. Rename a folder using the Organize button in the Open dialog box or using a shortcut menu. To rename a folder using the Organize button, display the Open dialog box, click in the Content pane the folder you want to rename, click the Organize button located on the toolbar, and then click *Rename* at the drop-down list. This selects the folder name and inserts a border around the name. Type the new name for the folder and then press Enter. To rename a folder using a shortcut menu, display the Open dialog box, right-click the folder name in the Content pane, and then click *Rename* at the shortcut menu. Type a new name for the folder and then press Enter.

A tip to remember when you are organizing files and folders is to be sure that your system is set up to display all of the files in a particular folder and not just the Excel files, for example. You can display all files in a folder by clicking the button to the right of the *File name* text box and then clicking *All Files (*.*)* at the drop-down list.

Project 1b Renaming a Folder   Part 2 of 8

1. Display the Open dialog box.
2. Right-click the *Payroll* folder name in the Content pane.
3. Click *Rename* at the shortcut menu.
4. Type **Finances** and then press Enter.

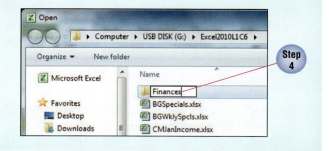

Selecting Workbooks

You can complete workbook management tasks on one workbook or selected workbooks. To select one workbook, display the Open dialog box and then click the desired workbook. To select several adjacent workbooks (workbooks that display next to each other), click the first workbook, hold down the Shift key, and then click the last workbook. To select workbooks that are not adjacent, click the first workbook, hold down the Ctrl key, click any other desired workbooks, and then release the Ctrl key.

Deleting Workbooks and Folders

At some point, you may want to delete certain workbooks from your storage medium or any other drive or folder in which you may be working. To delete a workbook, display the Open or Save As dialog box, click the workbook in the Content pane, click the Organize button, and then click *Delete* at the drop-down list. At the dialog box asking you to confirm the deletion, click Yes. To delete a workbook using a shortcut menu, display the Open dialog box, right-click the workbook name in the Content pane, and then click *Delete* at the shortcut menu. Click Yes at the confirmation dialog box.

▼ **Quick Steps**

Delete Workbook/ Folder
1. Click File tab, Open button.
2. Right-click workbook or folder name.
3. Click *Delete*.
4. Click Yes.

Deleting to the Recycle Bin

Workbooks deleted from the hard drive are automatically sent to the Windows Recycle Bin. You can easily restore a deleted workbook from the Recycle Bin. To free space on the drive, empty the Recycle Bin on a periodic basis. Restoring a workbook from or emptying the contents of the Recycle Bin is completed at the Windows desktop (not in Excel). To display the Recycle Bin, minimize the Excel window and then double-click the Recycle Bin icon located on the Windows desktop. At the Recycle Bin, you can restore file(s) and empty the Recycle Bin.

Project 1c Selecting and Deleting Workbooks Part 3 of 8

1. At the Open dialog box, open **RPFacAccts.xlsx** (located in the Excel2010L1C6 folder).
2. Save the workbook with Save As and name it **EL1-C6-P1-RPFacAccts**.
3. Close **EL1-C6-P1-RPFacAccts.xlsx**.
4. Delete **EL1-C6-P1-RPFacAccts.xlsx** by completing the following steps:
   a. Display the Open dialog box with Excel2010L1C6 the active folder.
   b. Click *EL1-C6-P1-RPFacAccts.xlsx* to select it.
   c. Click the Organize button and then click *Delete* at the drop-down list.
   d. At the question asking if you are sure you want to delete the worksheet, click Yes.

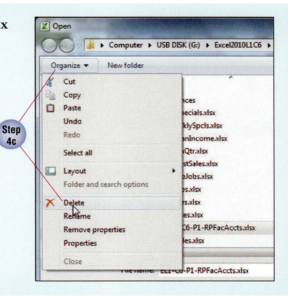

Step 4c

Chapter 6 ■ Maintaining Workbooks 203

5. Delete selected workbooks by completing the following steps:
    a. Click **DICustSales.xlsx** in the Content pane.
    b. Hold down the Shift key and then click **DIJobs.xlsx**.
    c. Position the mouse pointer on one of the selected workbooks and then click the right mouse button.
    d. At the shortcut menu that displays, click *Delete*.
    e. At the question asking if you are sure you want to delete the items, click Yes.
6. Close the Open dialog box.

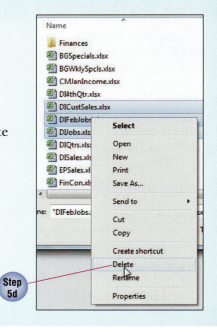

Step 5d

Copying Workbooks

In previous chapters, you have been opening a workbook from your storage medium and saving it with a new name in the same location. This process makes an exact copy of the workbook, leaving the original on your storage medium. You have been copying workbooks and saving the new workbook in the same folder as the original workbook. You can also copy a workbook into another folder.

Project 1d Saving a Copy of an Open Workbook   Part 4 of 8

1. Open **EPSales.xlsx**.
2. Save the workbook with Save As and name it **TotalSales**. (Make sure Excel2010L1C6 is the active folder.)
3. Save a copy of the **TotalSales.xlsx** workbook in the Finances folder you created in Project 1a (and renamed in Project 1b) by completing the following steps:
    a. With **TotalSales.xlsx** open, display the Save As dialog box.
    b. At the Save As dialog box, change to the Finances folder. To do this, double-click *Finances* at the beginning of the Content pane. (Folders are listed before workbooks.)
    c. Click the Save button located in the lower right corner of the dialog box.
4. Close **TotalSales.xlsx**.
5. Change back to the Excel2010L1C6 folder by completing the following steps:
    a. Display the Open dialog box.
    b. Click *Excel2010L1C6* that displays in the Address bar.
6. Close the Open dialog box.

Step 5b

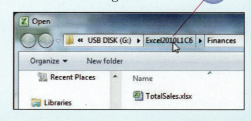

You can copy a workbook to another folder without opening the workbook first. To do this, use the *Copy* and *Paste* options from a shortcut menu at the Open (or Save As) dialog box. You can also copy a workbook or selected workbooks into the same folder. When you do this, Excel adds a hyphen followed by the word *Copy* to the end of the document name. You can copy one workbook or selected workbooks into the same folder.

▼ **Quick Steps**
Copy a Workbook
1. Click File tab, Open button.
2. Right-click workbook name.
3. Click *Copy*.
4. Navigate to desired folder.
5. Right-click blank area in Content pane.
6. Click *Paste*.

Project 1e Copying a Workbook at the Open Dialog Box   Part 5 of 8

1. Copy **CMJanIncome.xlsx** to the Finances folder. To begin, display the Open dialog box with the Excel2010L1C6 folder active.
2. Position the arrow pointer on **CMJanIncome.xlsx**, click the right mouse button, and then click *Copy* at the shortcut menu.
3. Change to the Finances folder by double-clicking *Finances* at the beginning of the Content pane.
4. Position the arrow pointer in any blank area in the Content pane, click the right mouse button, and then click *Paste* at the shortcut menu.
5. Change back to the Excel2010L1C6 folder by clicking *Excel2010L1C6* that displays in the Address bar.
6. Close the Open dialog box.

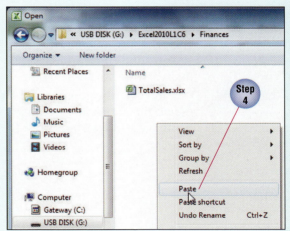

Step 4

Sending Workbooks to a Different Drive or Folder

Copy workbooks to another folder or drive with the *Copy* and *Paste* options from the shortcut menu at the Open or Save As dialog box. With the *Send To* option, you can send a copy of a workbook to another drive or folder. To use this option, position the arrow pointer on the workbook you want copied, click the right mouse button, point to *Send To* (this causes a side menu to display), and then click the desired drive or folder.

▼ **Quick Steps**
Move a Workbook
1. Click File tab, Open button.
2. Right-click workbook name.
3. Click *Cut*.
4. Navigate to desired folder.
5. Right-click blank area in Content pane.
6. Click *Paste*.

Cutting and Pasting a Workbook

You can remove a workbook from one folder and insert it in another folder using the *Cut* and *Paste* options from the shortcut menu at the Open dialog box. To do this, display the Open dialog box, position the arrow pointer on the workbook to be removed (cut), click the right mouse button, and then click *Cut* at the shortcut menu. Change to the desired folder or drive, position the arrow pointer in any blank area in the Content pane, click the right mouse button, and then click *Paste* at the shortcut menu.

Project 1f — Cutting and Pasting a Workbook — Part 6 of 8

1. Move a workbook to a different folder. To begin, display the Open dialog box with the Excel2010L1C6 folder active.
2. Position the arrow pointer on **FinCon.xlsx**, click the right mouse button, and then click *Cut* at the shortcut menu.
3. Double-click *Finances* to make it the active folder.
4. Position the arrow pointer in any blank area in the Content pane, click the right mouse button, and then click *Paste* at the shortcut menu.
5. Click *Excel2010L1C6* that displays in the Address bar.

▼ Quick Steps

Rename Workbook
1. Click File tab, Open button.
2. Click desired workbook.
3. Click Organize button, *Rename*.
4. Type new name.
5. Press Enter.
OR
1. Click File tab, Open button.
2. Right-click workbook name.
3. Click *Rename*.
4. Type new name.
5. Press Enter.

Renaming Workbooks

At the Open dialog box, use the *Rename* option from the Organize button drop-down list or the shortcut menu to give a workbook a different name. The *Rename* option changes the name of the workbook and keeps it in the same folder. To use *Rename*, display the Open dialog box, click once on the workbook to be renamed, click the Organize button, and then click *Rename*. This causes a thin black border to surround the workbook name and the name to be selected. Type the new name and then press Enter.

You can also rename a workbook by right-clicking the workbook name at the Open dialog box and then clicking *Rename* at the shortcut menu. Type the new name for the workbook and then press the Enter key.

Project 1g — Renaming a Workbook — Part 7 of 8

1. Rename a workbook located in the Finances folder. To begin, make sure the Open dialog box displays with Excel2010L1C6 the active folder.
2. Double-click *Finances* to make it the active folder.
3. Click once on **FinCon.xlsx** to select it.
4. Click the Organize button on the toolbar.
5. Click *Rename* at the drop-down list.
6. Type **Analysis** and then press the Enter key.
7. Complete steps similar to those in Steps 3 through 6 to rename **CMJanIncome.xlsx** to *CMJanProfits*.

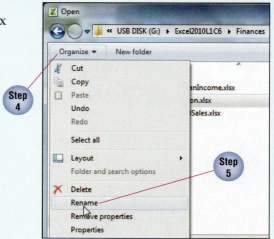

8. Click the Back button (displays as *Back to Excel2010L1C6*) at the left side of the Address bar.

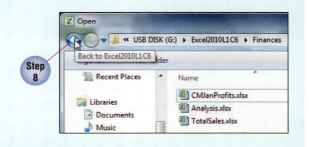

Step 8

Deleting a Folder and Its Contents

As you learned earlier in this chapter, you can delete a workbook or selected workbooks. In addition to workbooks, you can delete a folder and all of its contents. Delete a folder in the same manner as you delete a workbook.

 **Deleting a Folder and Its Contents** Part 8 of 8

1. Delete the Finances folder and its contents. To begin, make sure the Open dialog box displays with the Excel2010L1C6 folder active.
2. Right-click on the *Finances* folder.
3. Click *Delete* at the shortcut menu.
4. At the Delete Folder dialog box, click Yes.
5. Close the Open dialog box.

 **Copy and Move Worksheets into an Equipment Rental Workbook** 3 Parts

You will manage workbooks at the Recent tab Backstage view and then open multiple workbooks and copy and move worksheets between the workbooks.

Managing the Recent List

When you open and close workbooks, Excel keeps a list of the most recently opened workbooks. To view this list, click the File tab and then click the Recent tab. This displays the Recent tab Backstage view similar to what you see in Figure 6.2. (Your workbook names and recent places may vary from what you see in the figure.) The most recently opened workbook names display in the *Recent Workbooks* list and the most recently accessed folder names display in the *Recent Places* list. Generally, the 20 most recently opened workbook names display in the *Recent Workbooks* list. To open a workbook, scroll down the list and then click the desired workbook name.

Chapter 6 ■ Maintaining Workbooks   **207**

Figure 6.2 Recent Tab Backstage View

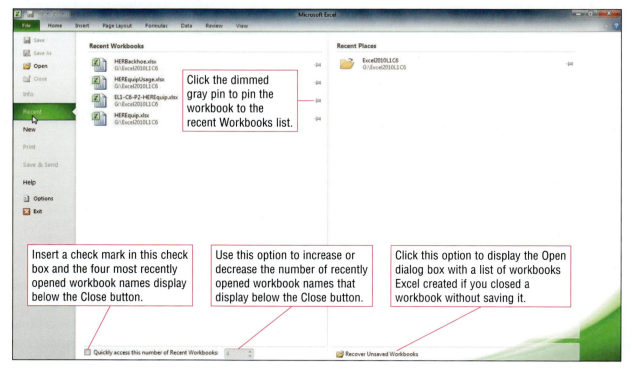

Displaying a Quick List

The Recent tab Backstage view contains the option *Quickly access this number of Recent Workbooks* located below the *Recent Workbooks* list. Insert a check mark in this option and the names of the four most recently opened workbooks display in the Backstage navigation bar (the panel at the left) below the Close button. You can increase or decrease the number of displayed workbook names by increasing or decreasing the number that displays at the right side of the *Quickly access this number of Recent Workbooks* option. To remove the list of most recently opened workbooks from the navigation bar, click the *Quickly access this number of Recent Workbooks* option to remove the check mark.

Pinning a Workbook

If you want a workbook name to remain at the top of the *Recent Workbooks* list, pin the workbook name. To do this, click the dimmed, gray pin that displays at the right side of the workbook name. This changes the dimmed, gray pin to a blue pin. The next time you display the Recent tab Backstage view, the workbook name you pinned displays at the top of the list. To unpin a workbook name, click the blue pin to change it to a dimmed, gray pin. You can also pin a workbook name to the Recent Workbooks list by right-clicking the workbook name and then clicking *Pin to list* at the shortcut menu. To unpin the workbook name, right-click the workbook name and then click *Unpin from list* at the shortcut menu.

Recovering an Unsaved Workbook

If you close a workbook without saving it, you can recover it with the *Recover Unsaved Workbooks* option located below the *Recent Places* list. Click this option and the Open dialog box displays with workbook names that Excel automatically saved. At this dialog box, double-click the desired workbook name to open the workbook.

Clearing the Recent Workbooks List

You can clear the contents (except pinned workbooks) of the *Recent Workbooks* list by right-clicking a workbook name in the list and then clicking *Clear unpinned Workbooks* at the shortcut menu. At the message asking if you are sure you want to remove the items, click the Yes button. To clear the *Recent Places* list, right-click a folder in the list and then click *Clear unpinned Places* at the shortcut menu. Click Yes at the message asking if you are sure you want to remove the items.

Project 2a — Managing Workbooks at the Recent Tab Backstage View — Part 1 of 3

1. Close any open workbooks.
2. Click the File tab. (This displays the Recent tab Backstage view.)
3. Notice the workbook names that display in the *Recent Workbooks* list and the folders that display in the *Recent Places* list.
4. Open **HEREquip.xlsx** and then save the workbook with Save As and name it **EL1-C6-P2-HEREquip**.
5. Close **EL1-C6-P2-HEREquip.xlsx**.
6. Open **HEREquipUsage.xlsx** and then close it.
7. Open **HERBackhoe.xlsx** and then close it.
8. You will use the three workbooks you just opened in Project 2b, so you decide to pin them to the *Recent Workbooks* list and display the three most recently opened workbook names below the Close button. To do this, complete the following steps:
    a. Click the File tab. (This should display the Recent tab Backstage view. If it does not display, click the Recent tab.)
    b. Click the dimmed gray pin that displays at the right side of **EL1-C6-P2-HEREquip.xlsx**. (This changes the gray pin to a blue pin.)

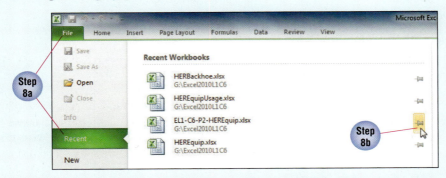

    c. Click the dimmed gray pin that displays at the right side of **HEREquipUsage.xlsx**.

Chapter 6 ■ Maintaining Workbooks 209

d. Right-click **HERBackhoe.xlsx** and then click *Pin to list* at the shortcut menu.
e. Click the *Quickly access this number of Recent Workbooks* option located at the bottom of the Recent tab Backstage view to insert a check mark.
f. Click the down-pointing arrow at the right side of the number *4*. (This changes *4* to *3*.)
g. Click the File tab to remove the Recent tab Backstage view.

9. Open **EL1-C6-P2-HEREquip.xlsx** by clicking the File tab (this displays the Recent tab Backstage view) and then clicking **EL1-C6-P2-HEREquip.xlsx** in the *Recent Workbooks* list.

Managing Worksheets

Quick Steps

Copy a Worksheet to Another Workbook
1. Right-click desired sheet tab.
2. Click *Move or Copy*.
3. Select desired destination workbook.
4. Select desired worksheet location.
5. Click *Create a copy* check box.
6. Click OK.

You can move or copy individual worksheets within the same workbook or to another existing workbook. Exercise caution when moving sheets since calculations or charts based on data on a worksheet might become inaccurate if you move the worksheet. To make a duplicate of a worksheet in the same workbook, hold down the Ctrl key and then drag the worksheet tab to the desired position.

Copying a Worksheet to Another Workbook

To copy a worksheet to another existing workbook, open both the source and the destination workbooks. Right-click the sheet tab and then click *Move or Copy* at the shortcut menu. At the Move or Copy dialog box shown in Figure 6.3, select the destination workbook name from the *To book* drop-down list, select the worksheet that you want the copied worksheet placed before in the *Before sheet* list box, click the *Create a copy* check box, and then click OK.

Figure 6.3 Move or Copy Dialog Box

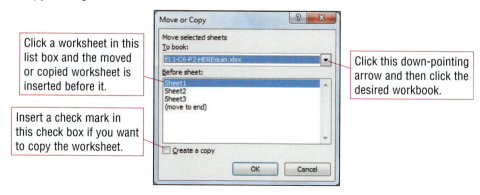

Project 2b Copying a Worksheet to Another Workbook   Part 2 of 3

1. With **EL1-C6-P2-HEREquip.xlsx** open, open **HEREquipUsage.xlsx**.
2. Copy the Front Loader worksheet by completing the following steps:
   a. With **HEREquipUsage.xlsx** the active workbook, right-click the Front Loader tab and then click *Move or Copy* at the shortcut menu.
   b. Click the down-pointing arrow next to the *To book* option box and then click *EL1-C6-P2-HEREqip.xlsx* at the drop-down list.
   c. Click *Sheet2* in the *Before sheet* list box.
   d. Click the *Create a copy* check box to insert a check mark.
   e. Click OK. (Excel switches to the **EL1-C6-P2-HEREquip.xlsx** workbook and inserts the copied Front Loader worksheet between Sheet1 and Sheet2.)
3. Complete steps similar to those in Step 2 to copy the Tractor worksheet to the **EL1-C6-P2-HEREquip.xlsx** workbook. (Insert the Tractor worksheet between Front Loader and Sheet2.)
4. Complete steps similar to those in Step 2 to copy the Forklift worksheet to the **EL1-C6-P2-HEREquip.xlsx** workbook. (Insert the Forklift worksheet between Tractor and Sheet2.)
5. Save **EL1-C6-P2-HEREquip.xlsx**.
6. Make **HEREquipUsage.xlsx** the active workbook and then close it.

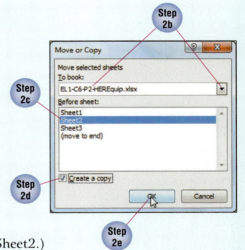

Moving a Worksheet to Another Workbook

To move a worksheet to another existing workbook, open both the source and the destination workbooks. Make active the sheet you want to move in the source workbook, right-click the sheet tab and then click *Move or Copy* at the shortcut menu. At the Move or Copy dialog box shown in Figure 6.3, select the destination workbook name from the *To book* drop-down list, select the worksheet that you want the worksheet placed before in the *Before sheet* list box, and then click OK. If you need to reposition a worksheet tab, drag the tab to the desired position.

Be careful when moving a worksheet to another workbook file. If formulas exist in the workbook that depend on the contents of the cells in the worksheet that is moved, they will no longer calculate properly.

▼ Quick Steps

Move a Worksheet to Another Workbook
1. Right-click desired sheet tab.
2. Click *Move or Copy*.
3. Select desired destination workbook.
4. Select desired worksheet location.
5. Click OK.

Project 2c Moving a Worksheet to Another Workbook — Part 3 of 3

1. With **EL1-C6-P2-HEREquip.xlsx** open, open **HERBackhoe.xlsx**.
2. Move Sheet1 from **HERBackhoe.xlsx** to **EL1-C6-P2-HEREquip.xlsx** by completing the following steps:
   a. With **HERBackhoe.xlsx** the active workbook, right-click the Sheet1 tab and then click *Move or Copy* at the shortcut menu.
   b. Click the down-pointing arrow next to the *To book* option box and then click **EL1-C6-P2-HEREquip.xlsx** at the drop-down list.
   c. Click *Sheet2* in the *Before sheet* list box.
   d. Click OK.
3. Make **HERBackhoe.xlsx** the active workbook and then close it without saving the changes.
4. With **EL1-C6-P2-HEREquip.xlsx** open, make the following changes:
   a. Delete the Sheet2 and Sheet3 tabs. (These worksheets are blank.)
   b. Rename Sheet1 to *Equipment Hours*.
   c. Rename Sheet1 (2) to *Backhoe*.
5. Create a range for the front loader total hours available by completing the following steps:
   a. Click the Front Loader tab.
   b. Select cells B4 through E4.
   c. Click in the Name Box.
   d. Type **FrontLoaderHours**.
   e. Press Enter.
6. Complete steps similar to those in Step 5 to create the following ranges:
   a. In the Front Loader worksheet, create a range with cells B10 through E10 and name it *FrontLoaderHoursInUse*.
   b. Click the Tractor tab and then create a range with cells B4 through E4 and name it *TractorHours* and create a range with cells B10 through E10 and name it *TractorHoursInUse*.
   c. Click the Forklift tab and then create a range with cells B4 through E4 and name it *ForkliftHours* and create a range with cells B10 through E10 and name it *ForkliftHoursInUse*.
   d. Click the Backhoe tab and then create a range with cells B4 through E4 and name it *BackhoeHours* and create a range with cells B10 through E10 and name it *BackhoeHoursInUse*.
7. Click the EquipmentHours tab to make it the active worksheet and then insert a formula that inserts the total hours for the front loader by completing the following steps:
   a. Make cell C4 active.
   b. Type **=SUM(Fr**.
   c. When you type *Fr* a drop-down list displays with the front loader ranges. Double-click *FrontLoaderHours*.

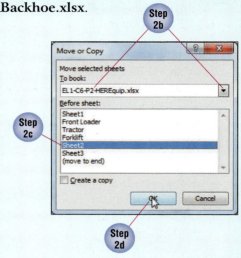

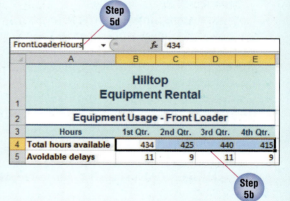

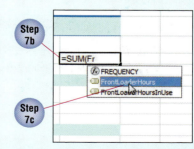

d. Type **)** (the closing parenthesis).
e. Press Enter.
8. Complete steps similar to those in Step 7 to insert ranges in the following cells:

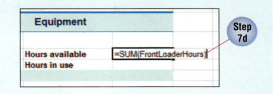

Step 7d

   a. Make cell C5 active and then insert a formula that inserts the total in-use hours for the front loader.
   b. Make cell C8 active and then insert a formula that inserts the total hours available for the tractor.
   c. Make cell C9 active and then insert a formula that inserts the total in-use hours for the tractor.
   d. Make cell C12 active and then insert a formula that inserts the total hours available for the forklift.
   e. Make cell C13 active and then insert a formula that inserts the total in-use hours for the forklift.
   f. Make cell C16 active and then insert a formula that inserts the total hours available for the backhoe.
   g. Make cell C17 active and then insert a formula that inserts the total in-use hours for the backhoe.
9. Make the following changes to specific worksheets:
   a. Click the Front Loader tab and then change the number in cell E4 from *415* to *426* and change the number in cell C6 from *6* to *14*.
   b. Click the Forklift tab and then change the number in cells E4 from *415* to *426* and change the number in cell D8 from *4* to *12*.
10. Select all of the worksheet tabs and then create a header that prints your name at the left side of each worksheet, the page number in the middle, and the current date at the right side of each worksheet.
11. Save and then print all of the worksheets in **EL1-C6-P2-HEREquip.xlsx**.
12. Close the workbook.
13. Make the following changes to the Recent tab Backstage view.
    a. Click the File tab.
    b. Change the number to the right of *Quickly access this number of Recent Workbooks* from *3* to *4*.
    c. Click the *Quickly access this number of Recent Workbooks* option to remove the check mark.
    d. Unpin the **EL1-C6-P2-HEREquip.xlsx** workbook name from the *Recent Workbooks* list by clicking the blue pin that displays at the right side of **EL1-C6-P2-HEREquip.xlsx**. (This changes the blue pin to a dimmed, gray pin and moves the file down the list.)
    e. Unpin the **HERBackhoe.xlsx** workbook and the **HEREquip.xlsx** workbook.
    f. Click the File tab to remove the Recent tab Backstage view.

Project 3 Create and Apply Styles to a Payroll Workbook   5 Parts

You will open a payroll workbook, define and apply styles, and then modify the styles. You will also copy the styles to another workbook and then apply the styles in the new workbook.

Formatting with Cell Styles

Quick Steps

Apply Cell Style
1. Select desired cell(s).
2. Click Cell Styles button.
3. Click desired style option.

Cell Styles

In some worksheets, you may want to apply formatting to highlight or accentuate certain cells. You can apply formatting to a cell or selected cells with a cell style. A *style* is a predefined set of formatting attributes such as font, font size, alignment, borders, shading, and so forth. You can use one of the predesigned styles from the Cell Styles drop-down gallery or create your own style.

Applying a Style

To apply a style, select the desired cell(s), click the Cell Styles button in the Styles group in the Home tab and then click the desired option at the drop-down gallery shown in Figure 6.4. If you hover your mouse pointer over a style option in the drop-down gallery, the cell or selected cells display with the formatting applied.

Figure 6.4 Cell Styles Drop-Down Gallery

Choose an option at this drop-down gallery to apply a predesigned style to a cell or selected cells in a worksheet.

Project 3a — Formatting with Cell Styles — Part 1 of 5

1. Open **OEPayroll.xlsx** and then save the workbook with Save As and name it **EL1-C6-P3-OEPayroll**.
2. With Sheet1 the active worksheet, insert the necessary formulas to calculate gross pay, withholding tax amount, Social Security tax amount, and net pay. *Hint: Refer to Project 5c in Chapter 2 for assistance.* Apply the Accounting Number Format style to cells D4 through G4.
3. Make Sheet2 active and then insert a formula that calculates the amount due. Apply the Accounting Number Format style to cell F4.

4. Make Sheet3 active and then insert a formula in the *Due Date* column that calculates the purchase date plus the number of days in the *Terms* column. **Hint: Refer to Project 3c in Chapter 2 for assistance**.
5. Apply cell styles to cells by completing the following steps:
   a. Make Sheet1 active and then select cells A11 and A12.
   b. Click the Cell Styles button in the Styles group in the Home tab.
   c. At the drop-down gallery, hover your mouse over style options to see how the style formatting affects the selected cells.
   d. Click the *Check Cell* option in the *Data and Model* section.
6. Select cells B11 and B12, click the Cell Styles button, and then click the *Output* option in the *Data and Model* section (first option from the left in the second row in the *Data and Model* section).

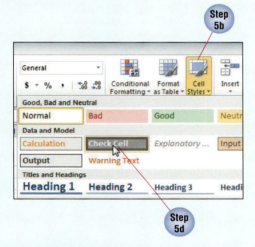

Step 5b

Step 5d

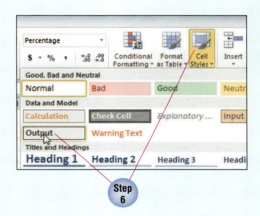

Step 6

7. Save **EL1-C6-P3-OEPayroll.xlsx**.

Defining a Cell Style

You can apply styles from the Cell Styles drop-down gallery or you can create your own style. Using a style to apply formatting has several advantages. A style helps to ensure consistent formatting from one worksheet to another. Once you define all attributes for a particular style, you do not have to redefine them again. If you need to change the formatting, change the style and all cells formatted with that style automatically reflect the change.

Two basic methods are available for defining your own cell style. You can define a style with formats already applied to a cell or you can display the Style dialog box, click the Format button, and then choose formatting options at the Format Cells dialog box. Styles you create are only available in the workbook in which they are created. To define a style with existing formatting, select the cell or cells containing the desired formatting, click the Cell Styles button in the Styles group in the Home tab, and then click the *New Cell Style* option located toward the bottom of the drop-down gallery. At the Style dialog box, shown in Figure 6.5, type a name for the new style in the *Style name* text box and then click OK to close the dialog box. The styles you create display at the top of the drop-down gallery in the *Custom* section when you click the Cell Styles button.

▼ **Quick Steps**

Define a Cell Style with Existing Formatting
1. Select cell containing formatting.
2. Click Cell Styles button.
3. Click *New Cell Style*.
4. Type name for new style.
5. Click OK.

Cell styles are based on the workbook theme.

▼ **Quick Steps**

Define a Style
1. Click in a blank cell.
2. Click Cell Styles button.
3. Click *New Cell Style*.
4. Type name for new style.
5. Click Format button.
6. Choose formatting options.
7. Click OK to close Format Cells dialog box.
8. Click OK to close Style dialog box.

Figure 6.5 Style Dialog Box

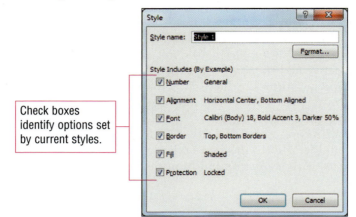

Check boxes identify options set by current styles.

Project 3b   Defining and Applying a Style   Part 2 of 5

1. With **EL1-C6-P3-OEPayroll.xlsx** open, define a style named *C06Title* with the formatting in cell A1 by completing the following steps:
    a. Make Sheet 1 active and then make cell A1 active.
    b. Click the Cell Styles button in the Styles group in the Home tab and then click the *New Cell Style* option located toward the bottom of the drop-down gallery.
    c. At the Style dialog box, type **C06Title** in the *Style name* text box.
    d. Click OK.

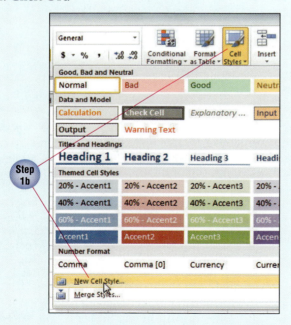
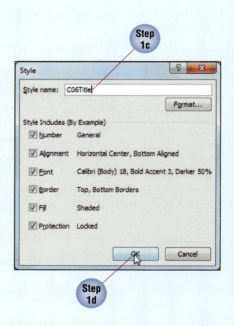

2. Even though cell A1 is already formatted, the style has not been applied to it. Later, you will modify the style and the style must be applied to the cell for the change to affect it. Apply the C06Title style to cell A1 by completing the following steps:
    a. Make sure cell A1 is the active cell.

b. Click the Cell Styles button in the Styles group in the Home tab.
c. Click the *C06Title* style in the *Custom* section located toward the top of the drop-down gallery.

3. Apply the C06Title style to other cells by completing the following steps:
   a. Click the Sheet2 tab.
   b. Make cell A1 active.
   c. Click the Cell Styles button in the Styles group and then click the *C06Title* style at the drop-down gallery. (Notice that the style did not apply the row height formatting. The style applies only cell formatting.)
   d. Click the Sheet3 tab.
   e. Make cell A1 active.
   f. Click the Cell Styles button and then click the *C06Title* style at the drop-down gallery.
   g. Click the Sheet1 tab.

4. Save **EL1-C6-P3-OEPayroll.xlsx**.

In addition to defining a style based on cell formatting, you can also define a new style without first applying the formatting. To do this, you would display the Style dialog box, type a name for the new style, and then click the Format button. At the Format Cells dialog box, apply any desired formatting and then click OK to close the dialog box. At the Style dialog box, remove the check mark from any formatting that you do not want included in the style and then click OK to close the Style dialog box.

Project 3c Defining a Style without First Applying Formatting   Part 3 of 5

1. With **EL1-C6-P3-OEPayroll.xlsx** open, define a new style named *C06Subtitle* without first applying the formatting by completing the following steps:
   a. With Sheet1 active, click in any empty cell.
   b. Click the Cell Styles button in the Styles group and then click *New Cell Style* at the drop-down gallery.
   c. At the Style dialog box, type **C06Subtitle** in the *Style name* text box.
   d. Click the Format button in the Style dialog box.
   e. At the Format Cells dialog box, click the Font tab.
   f. At the Format Cells dialog box with the Font tab selected, change the font to Candara, the font style to bold, the size to 12, and the color to white.

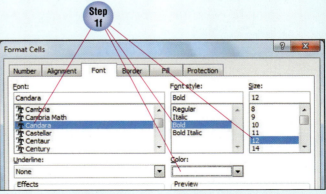

Chapter 6 ■ Maintaining Workbooks   217

g. Click the Fill tab.
h. Click the bottom color in the green column as shown at the right.
i. Click the Alignment tab.
j. Change the Horizontal alignment to Center.
k. Click OK to close the Format Cells dialog box.
l. Click OK to close the Style dialog box.

2. Apply the C06Subtitle style by completing the following steps:
   a. Make cell A2 active.
   b. Click the Cell Styles button and then click the C06Subtitle style located toward the top of the drop-down gallery in the *Custom* section.
   c. Click the Sheet2 tab.
   d. Make cell A2 active.
   e. Click the Cell Styles button and then click the C06Subtitle style.
   f. Click the Sheet3 tab.
   g. Make cell A2 active.
   h. Click the Cell Styles button and then click the C06Subtitle style.
   i. Click the Sheet1 tab.

3. Apply the following predesigned cell styles:
   a. Select cells A3 through G3.
   b. Click the Cell Styles button and then click the Heading 3 style at the drop-down gallery.
   c. Select cells A5 through G5.
   d. Click the Cell Styles button and then click the 20% - Accent3 style.
   e. Apply the 20% - Accent3 style to cells A7 through G7 and cells A9 through G9.
   f. Click the Sheet2 tab.
   g. Select cells A3 through F3 and then apply the Heading 3 style.
   h. Select cells A5 through F5 and then apply the 20% - Accent3 style.
   i. Apply the 20% - Accent3 style to every other row of cells (A7 through F7, A9 through F9, and so on, finishing with A17 through F17).
   j. Click the Sheet3 tab.
   k. Select cells A3 through F3 and then apply the Heading 3 style.
   l. Apply the 20% - Accent3 style to A5 through F5, A7 through F7, and A9 through F9.

4. With Sheet3 active, change the height of row 1 to 36.00 (48 pixels).
5. Make Sheet2 active and then change the height of row 1 to 36.00 (48 pixels).
6. Make Sheet1 active.
7. Save **EL1-C6-P3-OEPayroll.xlsx** and then print only the first worksheet.

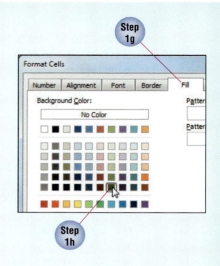

Modifying a Style

One of the advantages to formatting with a style is that you can modify the formatting of the style and all cells formatted with that style automatically reflect the change. You can modify a style you create or one of the predesigned styles provided by Word. When you modify a predesigned style, only the style in the current workbook is affected. If you open a blank workbook, the cell styles available are the default styles.

To modify a style, click the Cell Styles button in the Styles group in the Home tab and then right-click the desired style at the drop-down gallery. At the shortcut menu that displays, click *Modify*. At the Style dialog box, click the Format button. Make the desired formatting changes at the Format Cells dialog box and then click OK. Click OK to close the Style dialog box and any cells formatted with the specific style are automatically updated.

▼ **Quick Steps**

Modify a Style
1. Click Cell Styles button.
2. Right-click desired style at drop-down gallery.
3. Click *Modify*.
4. Click Format button.
5. Make desired formatting changes.
6. Click OK to close Format Cells dialog box.
7. Click OK to close Style dialog box.

Project 3d Modifying Styles   Part 4 of 5

1. With **EL1-C6-P3-OEPayroll.xlsx** open, modify the C06Title style by completing the following steps:
   a. Click in any empty cell.
   b. Click the Cell Styles button in the Styles group.
   c. At the drop-down gallery, right-click on the C06Title style located toward the top of the gallery in the *Custom* section, and then click *Modify*.
   d. At the Style dialog box, click the Format button.
   e. At the Format Cells dialog box, click the Font tab, and then change the font to Candara.
   f. Click the Alignment tab.
   g. Click the down-pointing arrow to the right of the *Vertical* option box, and then click *Center* at the drop-down list.
   h. Click the Fill tab.
   i. Click the light turquoise fill color as shown at the right.
   j. Click OK to close the Format Cells dialog box.
   k. Click OK to close the Style dialog box.

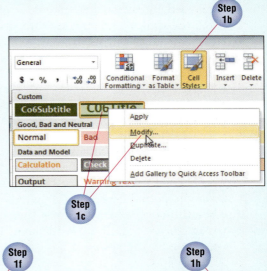
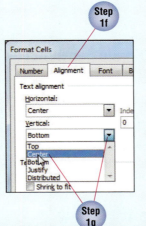
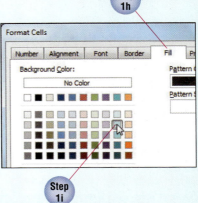

Chapter 6 ■ Maintaining Workbooks

2. Modify the C06Subtitle style by completing the following steps:
   a. Click in any empty cell.
   b. Click the Cell Styles button in the Styles group.
   c. At the drop-down gallery, right-click on the C06Subtitle style located toward the top of the gallery in the *Custom* section, and then click *Modify*.
   d. At the Style dialog box, click the Format button.
   e. At the Format Cells dialog box, click the Font tab, and then change the font to Calibri.
   f. Click the Fill tab.
   g. Click the dark turquoise fill color as shown at the right.
   h. Click OK to close the Format Cells dialog box.
   i. Click OK to close the Style dialog box.
3. Modify the predefined 20% - Accent3 style by completing the following steps:
   a. Click the Cell Styles button in the Styles group.
   b. At the drop-down gallery, right-click on the 20% - Accent3 style and then click *Modify*.
   c. At the Style dialog box, click the Format button.
   d. At the Format Cells dialog box, make sure the Fill tab is active.
   e. Click the light turquoise fill color as shown at the right.
   f. Click OK to close the Format Cells dialog box.
   g. Click OK to close the Style dialog box.
4. Click each sheet tab and notice the formatting changes made by the modified styles.
5. Change the name of Sheet1 to *Weekly Payroll*, the name of Sheet2 to *Invoices*, and the name of Sheet3 to *Overdue Accounts*.
6. Apply a different color to each of the three worksheet tabs.
7. Save and then print all the worksheets in **EL1-C6-P3-OEPayroll.xlsx**.

Quick Steps

Copy Styles to Another Workbook
1. Open workbook containing desired styles.
2. Open workbook you want to modify.
3. Click Cell Styles button.
4. Click *Merge Styles* option.
5. Double-click name of workbook that contains styles you want to copy.

Copying Styles to Another Workbook

Styles you define are saved with the workbook in which they are created. You can, however, copy styles from one workbook to another. To do this, open the workbook containing the styles you want to copy and open the workbook into which you want to copy the styles. Click the Cell Styles button in the Styles group in the Home tab and then click the *Merge Styles* option located at the bottom of the drop-down gallery. At the Merge Styles dialog box shown in Figure 6.6, double-click the name of the workbook that contains the styles you want to copy and then click OK.

Removing a Style

If you apply a style to text and then decide you do not want the formatting applied, return the formatting to Normal, which is the default formatting. To do this, select the cells formatted with the style you want to remove, click the Cell Styles button, and then click *Normal* at the drop-down gallery.

Figure 6.6 Merge Styles Dialog Box

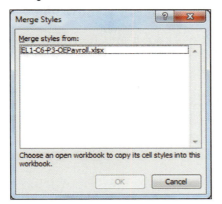

Deleting a Style

To delete a style, click the Cell Styles button in the Styles group in the Home tab. At the drop-down gallery that displays, right-click the style you want to delete and then click *Delete* at the shortcut menu. Formatting applied by the deleted style is removed from cells in the workbook.

▼ **Quick Steps**

Remove a Style
1. Select cells formatted with style you want removed.
2. Click Cell Styles button.
3. Click *Normal* at drop-down gallery.

Delete a Style
1. Click Cell Styles button.
2. Right-click desired style to delete.
3. Click *Delete* at shortcut menu.

HINT
You cannot delete the Normal style.

HINT
The Undo command will not reverse the effects of the Merge Styles dialog box.

Project 3e — **Copying Styles** — Part 5 of 5

1. With **EL1-C6-P3-OEPayroll.xlsx** open, open **OEPlans.xlsx**.
2. Save the workbook with Save As and name it **EL1-C6-P3-OEPlans**.
3. Copy the styles in **EL1-C6-P3-Payroll.xlsx** into **EL1-C6-P3-OEPlans.xlsx** by completing the following steps:
   a. Click the Cell Styles button in the Styles group in the Home tab.
   b. Click the *Merge Styles* option located toward the bottom of the drop-down gallery.
   c. At the Merge Styles dialog box, double-click **EL1-C6-P3-OEPayroll.xlsx** in the *Merge styles from* list box.
   d. At the message that displays asking if you want to merge styles that have the same names, click Yes.
4. Apply the C06Title style to cell A1 and the C06Subtitle style to cell A2.
5. Increase the height of row 1 to 36.00 (48 pixels).
6. Insert the required formulas in the workbook. **Hint: Refer to Project 3a in Chapter 2 for assistance.**
7. If neccessary, adjust column widths so all text is visible in cells.
8. Save, print, and then close **EL1-C6-P3-OEPlans.xlsx**.
9. Close **EL1-C6-P3-OEPayroll.xlsx**.

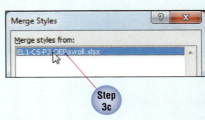

Step 3c

Project 4 Insert, Modify, and Remove Hyperlinks 3 Parts

You will open a facilities account workbook and then insert hyperlinks to a website, to cells in other worksheets in the workbook, and to another workbook. You will modify and edit hyperlinks and then remove a hyperlink from the workbook.

Inserting Hyperlinks

Quick Steps

Insert Hyperlink
1. Click Insert tab.
2. Click Hyperlink button.
3. Make desired changes at Insert Hyperlink dialog box.
4. Click OK.

Hyperlink

A hyperlink in a workbook can serve a number of purposes: Click it to navigate to a web page on the Internet or a specific location in the workbook, to display a different workbook, to open a file in a different program, to create a new document, or to link to an email address. You can create a customized hyperlink by clicking the desired cell in a workbook, clicking the Insert tab, and then clicking the Hyperlink button in the Links group. This displays the Insert Hyperlink dialog box, shown in Figure 6.7. At this dialog box, identify what you want to link to and the location of the link. Click the ScreenTip button to customize the hyperlink ScreenTip.

Linking to an Existing Web Page or File

You can link to a web page on the Internet by typing a web address or with the Existing File or Web Page button in the *Link to* group. To link to an existing web page, type the address of the web page such as *www.emcp.com*. By default, the automatic formatting of hyperlinks is turned on and the web address is formatted as a hyperlink (text is underlined and the color changes to blue). You can turn off the automatic formatting of hyperlinks at the AutoCorrect dialog box. Display this dialog box by clicking the File tab, clicking the Options button, and then clicking *Proofing* in the left panel of the Excel Options dialog box. Click the AutoCorrect Options button to display the AutoCorrect dialog box. At this dialog

Figure 6.7 Insert Hyperlink Dialog Box

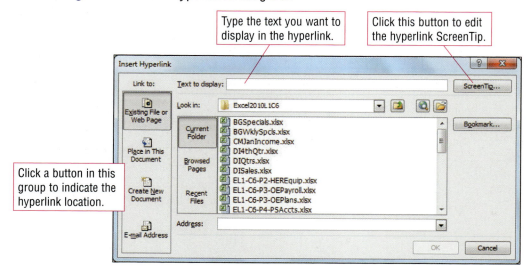

box, click the AutoFormat As You Type tab and then remove the check mark from the *Internet and network paths with hyperlinks* check box. To link to a web page at the Insert Hyperlink dialog box, display the dialog box, click the Existing File or Web Page button in the *Link to* group and then type the web address in the *Address* text box.

In some situations, you may want to provide information to your readers from a variety of sources. You may want to provide additional information in an Excel workbook, a Word document, or a PowerPoint presentation. To link an Excel workbook to a workbook or a file in another application, display the Insert Hyperlink dialog box and then click the Existing File or Web Page button in the *Link to* group. Use the *Look in* option to navigate to the folder containing the desired file and then click the file. Make other changes in the Insert Hyperlink dialog box as needed and then click OK.

Navigating Using Hyperlinks

Navigate to a hyperlink by clicking the hyperlink in the worksheet. Hover the mouse over the hyperlink and a ScreenTip displays with the hyperlink. If you want specific information to display in the ScreenTip, click the ScreenTip button in the Insert Hyperlink dialog box, type the desired text in the Set Hyperlink ScreenTip dialog box, and then click OK.

Project 4a Linking to a Website and Another Workbook   Part 1 of 3

1. Open **PSAccts.xlsx** and then save the workbook with Save As and name it **EL1-C6-P4-PSAccts**.
2. Insert a hyperlink to company information (since Pyramid Sales is a fictitious company, you will hyperlink to the publishing company website) by completing the following steps:
   a. Make cell A13 active.
   b. Click the Insert tab and then click the Hyperlink button in the Links group.
   c. At the Insert Hyperlink dialog box, if necessary, click the Existing File or Web Page button in the *Link to* group.
   d. Type **www.emcp.com** in the *Address* text box.
   e. Select the text that displays in the *Text to display* text box and then type **Company information**.
   f. Click the ScreenTip button located in the upper right corner of the dialog box.

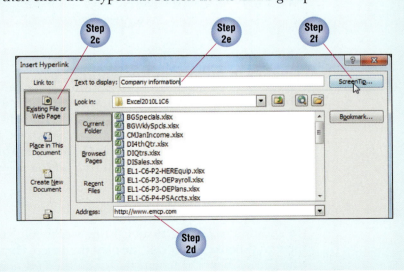

Chapter 6 ■ Maintaining Workbooks   223

g. At the Set Hyperlink ScreenTip dialog box, type **View the company website.** and then click OK.
h. Click OK to close the Insert Hyperlink dialog box.
3. Navigate to the company website (in this case, the publishing company website) by clicking the Company information hyperlink in cell A13.
4. Close the Web browser.
5. Create a link to another workbook by completing the following steps:
   a. Make cell A11 active, type **Semiannual sales**, and then press the Enter key.
   b. Make cell A11 active and then click the Hyperlink button in the Links group in the Insert tab.
   c. At the Insert Hyperlink dialog box, make sure the Existing File or Web Page button is selected.
   d. If necessary, click the down-pointing arrow at the right side of the *Look in* option and then navigate to the Excel2010L1C6 folder on your storage medium.
   e. Double-click **PSSalesAnalysis.xlsx**.
6. Click the Semiannual sales hyperlink to open the **PSSalesAnalysis.xlsx** workbook.
7. Look at the information in the workbook and then close the workbook.
8. Save **EL1-C6-P4-PSAccts.xlsx**.

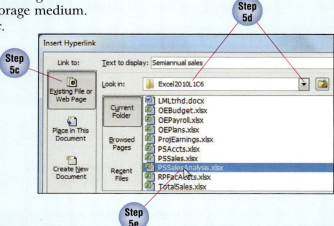

Linking to a Place in the Workbook

To create a hyperlink to another location in the workbook, click the Place in This Document button in the *Link to* group in the Edit Hyperlink dialog box. If you are linking to a cell within the same worksheet, type the cell name in the *Type the cell reference* text box. If you are linking to another worksheet in the workbook, click the desired worksheet name in the *Or select a place in this document* list box.

Linking to a New Workbook

In addition to linking to an existing workbook, you can create a hyperlink to a new workbook. To do this, display the Insert Hyperlink dialog box and then click the Create New Document button in the *Link to* group. Type a name for the new workbook in the *Name of new document* text box and then specify if you want to edit the workbook now or later.

Linking Using a Graphic

You can use a graphic such as a clip art image, picture, or text box to hyperlink to a file or website. To hyperlink with a graphic, select the graphic, click the Insert tab, and then click the Hyperlink button. You can also right-click the graphic and then click *Hyperlink* at the shortcut menu. At the Insert Hyperlink dialog box, specify where you want to link to and text you want to display in the hyperlink.

Linking to an Email Address

You can insert a hyperlink to an email address at the Insert Hyperlink dialog box. To do this, click the E-Mail Address button in the *Link to* group, type the desired address in the *E-mail address* text box, and type a subject for the email in the *Subject* text box. Click in the *Text to display* text box and then type the text you want to display in the document. To use this feature, the email address you use must be set up in Outlook 2010.

Project 4b — Linking to Place in a Workbook, to Another Workbook, and Using a Graphic — Part 2 of 3

1. With **EL1-C6-P4-PSAccts.xlsx** open, create a link from the checks amount in cell B6 to the check amount in cell G20 in the January worksheet by completing the following steps:
   a. Make cell B6 active.
   b. Click the Insert tab and then click the Hyperlink button in the Links group.
   c. At the Insert Hyperlink dialog box, click the Place in This Document button in the *Link to* group.
   d. Select the text in the *Type the cell reference* text box and then type **G20**.
   e. Click *January* in the *Or select a place in this document* list box.
   f. Click OK to close the Insert Hyperlink dialog box.
2. Make cell C6 active and then complete steps similar to those in Steps 1b through 1f except click *February* in the *Or select a place in this document* list box.
3. Make cell D6 active and then complete steps similar to those in Steps 1b through 1f except click *March* in the *Or select a place in this document* list box.
4. Click the hyperlinked amount in cell B6. (This makes cell G20 active in the January worksheet.)
5. Click the Summary worksheet tab.
6. Click the hyperlinked amount in cell C6. (This makes cell G20 active in the February worksheet.)
7. Click the Summary worksheet tab.
8. Click the hyperlinked amount in cell D6. (This makes cell G20 active in the March worksheet.)
9. Click the Summary worksheet tab.

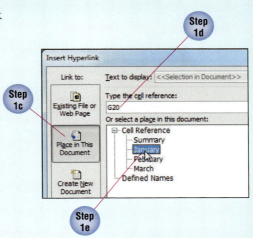

10. Use the first pyramid graphic image in cell A1 to create a link to the company web page by completing the following steps:
    a. Right-click the first pyramid graphic image in cell A1 and then click *Hyperlink* at the shortcut menu.
    b. At the Insert Hyperlink dialog box, if necessary, click the Existing File or Web Page button in the *Link to* group.
    c. Type **www.emcp.com** in the *Address* text box.
    d. Click the ScreenTip button located in the upper right corner of the dialog box.
    e. At the Set Hyperlink ScreenTip dialog box, type **View the company website.** and then click OK.
    f. Click OK to close the Insert Hyperlink dialog box.
11. Make cell A5 active.
12. Navigate to the company website (the publishing company website) by clicking the first pyramid graphic image.
13. Close the Web browser.
14. Save **EL1-C6-P4-PSAccts.xlsx**.

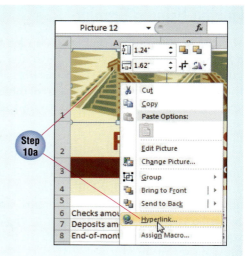

Modifying, Editing, and Removing a Hyperlink

You can modify or change hyperlink text or the hyperlink destination. To do this, right-click the hyperlink and then click *Edit Hyperlink* at the shortcut menu. At the Edit Hyperlink dialog box, make any desired changes and then close the dialog box. The Edit Hyperlink dialog box contains the same options as the Insert Hyperlink dialog box.

In addition to modifying the hyperlink, you can edit hyperlink text in a cell. To do this, make the cell active and then make the desired editing changes. For example, you can apply a different font or font size, change the text color, and apply a text effect. Remove a hyperlink from a workbook by right-clicking the cell containing the hyperlink and then clicking *Remove Hyperlink* at the shortcut menu.

Project 4c   **Modifying, Editing, and Removing a Hyperlink**   Part 3 of 3

1. With **EL1-C6-P4-PSAccts.xlsx** open, modify the Semiannual sales hyperlink by completing the following steps:
   a. Position the mouse pointer on the Semiannual sales hyperlink in cell A11, click the right mouse button, and then click *Edit Hyperlink* at the shortcut menu.
   b. At the Edit Hyperlink dialog box, select the text *Semiannual sales* in the *Text to display* text box and then type **Customer sales analysis**.
   c. Click the ScreenTip button located in the upper right corner of the dialog box.
   d. At the Set Hyperlink ScreenTip dialog box, type **Click this hyperlink to display workbook containing customer sales analysis.**

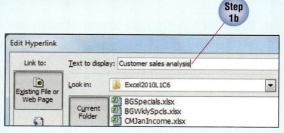

e. Click OK to close the Set Hyperlink ScreenTip dialog box.
   f. Click OK to close the Edit Hyperlink dialog box.
2. Click the Customer sales analysis hyperlink.
3. After looking at the **PSSalesAnalysis.xlsx** workbook, close the workbook.
4. With cell A11 active, edit the Customer sales analysis hyperlink text by completing the following steps:
   a. Click the Home tab.
   b. Click the Font Color button arrow in the Font group and then click the *Red, Accent 2, Darker 50%* color (located toward the bottom of the sixth column).
   c. Click the Bold button.
   d. Click the Underline button. (This removes underlining from the text.)
5. Remove the Company information hyperlink by right-clicking in cell A13 and then clicking *Remove Hyperlink* at the shortcut menu.
6. Press the Delete key to remove the contents of cell A13.
7. Save, print only the first worksheet (the Summary worksheet), and then close **EL1-C6-P4-PSAccts.xlsx**.

Project 5   Create a Billing Statement Workbook   1 Part
Using a Template

You will open a Billing Statement template provided by Excel, add data, save it as an Excel workbook, and then print the workbook.

Using Excel Templates

Excel includes a number of template worksheet forms formatted for specific uses. With Excel templates you can create a variety of worksheets with specialized formatting such as balance sheets, billing statements, loan amortizations, sales invoices, and time cards. Display installed templates by clicking the File tab and then clicking the New tab. This displays the New tab Backstage view as shown in Figure 6.8.

Click the Sample templates button in the *Available Templates* category and installed templates display. Click the desired template in the Sample templates list box and a preview of the template displays at the right side of the screen. Click the Create button that displays below the template preview and the template opens and displays on the screen. Locations for personalized text display in placeholders in the template worksheet. To enter information in the worksheet, position the mouse pointer (white plus sign) in the location where you want to type data and then click the left mouse button. After typing the data, click the next location. You can also move the insertion point to another cell using the commands learned in Chapter 1. For example, press the Tab key to make the next cell active or press Shift + Tab to make the previous cell active.

If you are connected to the Internet, you can download a number of predesigned templates that Microsoft offers. Templates are grouped into categories and the category names display in the *Office.com Templates* section of the New tab Backstage view. Click the desired template category and available templates display. Click the desired template and then click the Download button.

▼ Quick Steps

Use an Excel Template
1. Click File tab.
2. Click New tab.
3. Click Sample templates button.
4. Double-click desired template.

Figure 6.8 New Tab Backstage View

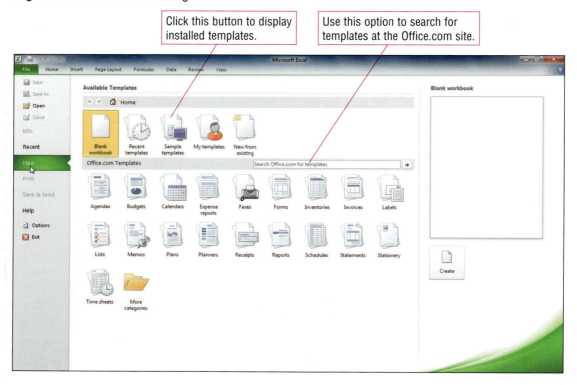

Project 5 — Preparing a Billing Statement Using a Template

1 Part

1. Click the File tab and then click the New tab.
2. At the New tab Backstage view, click the Sample templates button in the *Available Templates* category.
3. Double-click the *Billing Statement* template in the *Available Templates* category of the dialog box.
4. Click the Normal button in the view area on the Status bar.
5. With cell B1 active, type **IN-FLOW SYSTEMS**.
6. Click the text *Street Address* (cell B2) and then type **320 Milander Way**.

228   Excel Level 1 ■ Unit 2

7. Click in the specified location (cell) and then type the text indicated:
   Address 2 (cell B3) = **P.O. Box 2300**
   City, ST ZIP Code (cell B4) = **Boston, MA 02188**
   Phone (cell F2) = **(617) 555-3900**
   Fax (cell F3) = **(617) 555-3945**
   Statement # (cell C8) = **5432**
   Customer ID (cell C10) = **25-345**
   Name (cell F8) = **Aidan Mackenzie**
   Company Name (cell F9) = **Stanfield Enterprises**
   Street Address (cell F10) = **9921 South 42nd Avenue**
   Address 2 (cell F11) = **P.O. Box 5540**
   City, ST ZIP Code (cell F12) = **Boston, MA 02193**
   Date (cell B15) = (insert current date in numbers as ##/##/####)
   Type (cell C15) = **System Unit**
   Invoice # (cell D15) = **7452**
   Description (cell E15) = **Calibration Unit**
   Amount (cell F15) = **950**
   Payment (cell G15) = **200**
   Customer Name (cell C21) = **Stanfield Enterprises**
   Amount Enclosed (C26) = **750**

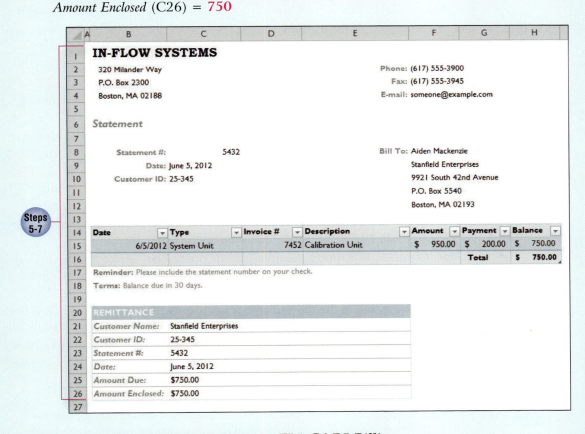

8. Save the completed invoice and name it **EL1-C6-P5-Billing**.
9. Print and then close **EL1-C6-P5-Billing.xlsx**.

Chapter Summary

- Perform file management tasks such as copying, moving, printing, and renaming workbooks and creating a new folder and renaming a folder at the Open or Save As dialog boxes.

- Create a new folder by clicking the New folder button located on the toolbar at the Open dialog box or Save As dialog box.

- Rename a folder with the *Rename* option from the Organize button drop-down list or with a shortcut menu.

- Use the Shift key to select adjacent workbooks in the Open dialog box and use the Ctrl key to select nonadjacent workbooks.

- To delete a workbook, use the *Delete* option from the Organize button drop-down list or with a shortcut menu option. Workbooks deleted from the hard drive are automatically sent to the Windows Recycle Bin where they can be restored or permanently deleted.

- Use the *Copy* and *Paste* options from the shortcut menu at the Open (or Save As) dialog box to copy a workbook from one folder to another folder or drive.

- Use the *Send To* option from the shortcut menu to send a copy of a workbook to another drive or folder.

- Remove a workbook from a folder or drive and insert it in another folder or drive using the *Cut* and *Paste* options from the shortcut menu.

- Use the *Rename* option from the Organize button drop-down list or the shortcut menu to give a workbook a different name.

- To move or copy a worksheet to another existing workbook, open both the source and the destination workbook and then open the Move or Copy dialog box.

- Use options from the Cell Styles button drop-down gallery to apply predesigned styles to a cell or selected cells.

- Automate the formatting of cells in a workbook by defining and then applying styles. A style is a predefined set of formatting attributes.

- Define a style with formats already applied to a cell or display the Style dialog box by clicking the Format button and then choosing formatting options at the Format Cells dialog box.

- To apply a style, select the desired cells, click the Cell Styles button in the Styles group in the Home tab, and then click the desired style at the drop-down gallery.

- Modify a style and all cells to which the style is applied automatically reflect the change. To modify a style, click the Cell Styles button in the Styles group in the Home tab, right-click the desired style, and then click *Modify* at the shortcut menu.

- Styles are saved in the workbook in which they are created. Styles can be copied, however, to another workbook. Do this with options at the Merge Styles dialog box.

- With options at the Insert Hyperlink dialog box, you can create a hyperlink to a web page, another workbook, a location within a workbook, a new workbook, or to an email. You can also create a hyperlink using a graphic.

- You can modify, edit, and remove hyperlinks.
- Excel provides preformatted templates for creating forms. Display the available templates by clicking the Sample templates button in the New tab Backstage view.
- Templates contain unique areas where information is entered at the keyboard. These areas vary depending on the template.

Commands Review

FEATURE	RIBBON TAB, GROUP	BUTTON, OPTION	KEYBOARD SHORTCUT
Open dialog box	File	Open	Ctrl + O
Save As dialog box	File	Save As	Ctrl + S
Cell Styles drop-down gallery	Home, Styles	🎨	
Style dialog box	Home, Styles	🎨, New Cell Style	
Merge Styles dialog box	Home, Styles	🎨, Merge Styles	
Insert Hyperlink dialog box	Insert, Links	🌐	
New tab Backstage view	File	New	
New folder	File	Open, New folder	

Concepts Check Test Your Knowledge

Completion: In the space provided at the right, indicate the correct term, symbol, or command.

1. Perform file management tasks such as copying, moving, or deleting workbooks with options at the Open dialog box or this dialog box. _____

2. At the Open dialog box, a list of folders and files displays in this pane. _____

3. Rename a folder or file at the Open dialog box using a shortcut menu or this button. _____

4. At the Open dialog box, hold down this key while selecting nonadjacent workbooks. _____

5. Workbooks deleted from the hard drive are automatically sent to this location. _____

6. Insert a check mark in this check box at the Recent tab Backstage view and the four most recently opened workbook names display in the Backstage navigation bar. _____

7. Do this to a workbook name you want to remain at the top of the *Recent Workbooks* list at the Recent tab Backstage view. _____

8. If you close a workbook without saving it, you can recover it with this option at the Recent tab Backstage view. _____

9. The Cell Styles button is located in this group in the Home tab. _____

10. Click the *New Cell Style* option at the Cell Styles button drop-down gallery and this dialog box displays. _____

11. A style you create displays in this section of the Cell Styles button drop-down gallery. _____

12. Copy styles from one workbook to another with options at this dialog box. _____

13. To link a workbook to another workbook, click this button in the Link to group in the Insert Hyperlink dialog box. _____

14. Display installed templates by clicking this button in the Available Templates category at the New tab Backstage view. _____

Skills Check Assess Your Performance

Assessment

1 MANAGE WORKBOOKS

1. Display the Open dialog box with Excel2010L1C6 the active folder.
2. Create a new folder named *O'Rourke* in the Excel2010L1C6 folder.
3. Copy **OEBudget.xlsx**, **OEPayroll.xlsx**, and **OEPlans.xlsx** to the O'Rourke folder.
4. Display the contents of the O'Rourke folder and then rename **OEBudget.xlsx** to **OEEquipBudget.xlsx**.
5. Rename **OEPlans.xlsx** to **OEPurchasePlans.xlsx** in the O'Rourke folder.
6. Change the active folder back to Excel2010L1C6.
7. Close the Open dialog box.

Assessment

2 MOVE AND COPY WORKSHEETS BETWEEN SALES ANALYSIS WORKBOOKS

1. Open **DISales.xlsx** and then save the workbook with Save As and name it **EL1-C6-A2-DISales**.
2. Rename Sheet1 to *1st Qtr*.
3. Open **DIQtrs.xlsx**.
4. Rename Sheet1 to *2nd Qtr* and then copy it to **EL1-C6-A2-DISales.xlsx** following the 1st Qtr worksheet. (When copying the worksheet, make sure you insert a check mark in the *Create a copy* check box in the Move or Copy dialog box.)
5. Make **DIQtrs.xlsx** active, rename Sheet 2 to *3rd Qtr* and then copy it to **EL1-C6-A2-DISales.xlsx** following the 2nd Qtr tab. (Make sure you insert a check mark in the *Create a copy* check box.)
6. Make **DIQtrs.xlsx** active and then close it without saving the changes.
7. Open **DI4thQtr.xlsx**.
8. Rename Sheet1 to *4th Qtr* and then move it to **EL1-C6-A2-DISales.xlsx** following the 3rd Qtr worksheet.
9. Make **DI4thQtr.xlsx** active and then close it without saving the changes.
10. With **EL1-C6-A2-DISales.xlsx** open, make the following changes to all four quarterly worksheets at the same time:
    a. Make 1st Qtr the active worksheet.
    b. Hold down the Shift key and then click the 4th Qtr tab. (This selects the four quarterly worksheet tabs.)
    c. Insert in cell E4 a formula to calculate average of cells B4 through D4 and then copy the formula down to cells E5 through E9.
    d. Insert in cell B10 a formula to calculate the sum of cells B4 through B9 and then copy the formula across to cells C10 through E10.
    e. Make cell E4 active and apply the Accounting Number Format with no decimal places.
11. Insert a footer on all worksheets that prints your name at the left, the page number in the middle, and the current date at the right.
12. Horizontally and vertically center all of the worksheets.
13. Click the Sheet2 tab and then delete it. Click the Sheet3 tab and then delete it.
14. Save and then print all four worksheets.
15. Close **EL1-C6-A2-DISales.xlsx**.

Assessment

3 DEFINE AND APPLY STYLES TO A PROJECTED EARNINGS WORKBOOK

1. At a blank worksheet, define a style named *C06Heading* that contains the following formatting:
   a. 14-point Cambria bold in dark blue color
   b. Horizontal alignment of Center
   c. Top and bottom border in a dark red color
   d. Light purple fill
2. Define a style named *C06Subheading* that contains the following formatting:
   a. 12-point Cambria bold in dark blue color
   b. Horizontal alignment of Center
   c. Top and bottom border in dark red color
   d. Light purple fill

3. Define a style named *C06Column* that contains the following formatting:
   a. At the Style dialog box, click the *Number* check box to remove the check mark.
   b. 12-point Cambria in dark blue color
   c. Light purple fill
4. Save the workbook and name it **EL1-C6-A3-Styles**.
5. With **EL1-C6-A3-Styles.xlsx** open, open **ProjEarnings.xlsx**.
6. Save the workbook with Save As and name it **EL1-C6-A3-ProjEarnings**.
7. Make cell C6 active and then insert a formula that multiplies the content of cell B6 with the amount in cell B3. (When writing the formula, identify cell B3 as an absolute reference.) Copy the formula down to cells C7 through C17.
8. Make cell C6 active and then click the Accounting Number Format button.
9. Copy the styles from **EL1-C6-A3-Styles.xlsx** into **EL1-C6-A3-ProjEarnings.xlsx**. *Hint: Do this at the Merge Styles dialog box.*
10. Apply the following styles:
    a. Select cells A1 and A2 and then apply the C06Heading style.
    b. Select cells A5 through C5 and then apply the C06Subheading style.
    c. Select cells A6 through A17 and then apply the C06Column style.
11. Save the workbook again and then print **EL1-C6-A3-ProjEarnings.xlsx**.
12. With **EL1-C6-A3-ProjEarnings.xlsx** open, modify the following styles:
    a. Modify the C06Heading style so it changes the font color to dark purple (instead of dark blue), changes the vertical alignment to Center, and inserts a top and bottom border in dark purple (instead of dark red).
    b. Modify the C06Subheading style so it changes the font color to dark purple (instead of dark blue) and inserts a top and bottom border in dark purple (instead of dark red).
    c. Modify the C06Column style so it changes the font color to dark purple (instead of dark blue). Leave all of the other formatting attributes.
13. Save and then print the workbook.
14. Close **EL1-C6-A3-ProjEarnings.xlsx** and then close **EL1-C6-A3-Styles.xlsx** without saving the changes.

Assessment

4 INSERT HYPERLINKS IN A BOOK STORE WORKBOOK

1. Open **BGSpecials.xlsx** and then save the workbook with Save As and name it **EL1-C6-A4-BGSpecials.xlsx**.
2. Make cell E3 active and then hyperlink it to the www.microsoft.com website.
3. Make cell E4 active and then hyperlink it to the www.symantec.com website.
4. Make cell E5 active and then hyperlink it to the www.nasa.gov website.
5. Make cell E6 active and then hyperlink it to the www.cnn.com website.
6. Make cell A8 active, type **Weekly specials!**, and then create a hyperlink to the workbook named **BGWklySpcls.xlsx**.
7. Click the hyperlink to the Microsoft website, explore the site, and then close the web browser.
8. Click the hyperlink to the NASA website, explore the site, and then close the web browser.
9. Click the Weekly specials! hyperlink, view the workbook, and then close the workbook.
10. Save, print, and then close **EL1-C6-A4-BGSpecials.xlsx**.

Assessment

5 APPLY CONDITIONAL FORMATTING TO A SALES WORKBOOK

1. Use Excel Help files or experiment with the options at the Conditional Formatting button drop-down gallery to learn about conditional formatting.
2. Open **PSSales.xlsx** and then save the workbook with Save As and name it **EL1-C6-A5-PSSales**.
3. Select cells D5 through D19 and then use conditional formatting to display the amounts as data bars.
4. Insert a header that prints your name, a page number, and the current date.
5. Save, print, and then close **EL1-C6-A5-PSSales.xlsx**.

Visual Benchmark Demonstrate Your Proficiency

FILL IN AN EXPENSE REPORT FORM

1. Display the New tab Backstage view, click the Sample templates button, and then double-click the *Expense Report* template.
2. With the expense report open, apply the Paper theme.
3. Select cells J1 through L1 and then apply the Note cell style.
4. Type the information in the cells as indicated in Figure 6.9.
5. Make cell L18 active and apply the Bad cell style.
6. Save the completed workbook and name it **EL1-C6-VB-OEExpRpt**.
7. Print and then close **EL1-C6-VB-OEExpRpt.xlsx**.

Figure 6.9 Visual Benchmark

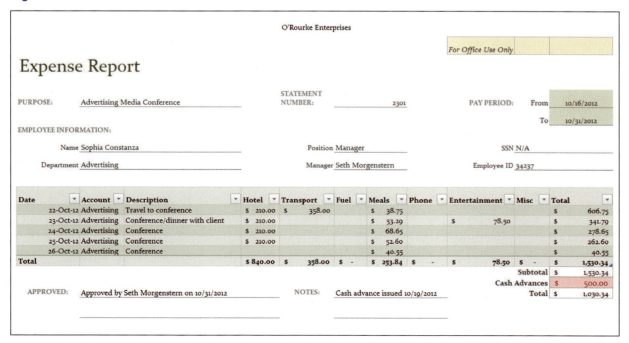

Case Study   Apply Your Skills

Part 1

You are the office manager for Leeward Marine and you decide to consolidate into one workbook worksheets containing information on expenses. Open **LMEstExp.xlsx** and then save the workbook and name it **EL1-C6-CS-LMExpSummary**. Open **LMActExp.xlsx**, copy the worksheet into **EL1-C6-CS-LMExpSummary.xlsx**, make **LMActExp.xlsx** the active workbook, and then close it. Apply appropriate formatting to numbers and insert necessary formulas in each worksheet. (Use the Clear button in the Home tab to clear the contents of cells N8, N9, M13, and M14 in both worksheets.) Include the company name, Leeward Marine, in each worksheet. Create styles and apply the styles to cells in each worksheet to maintain consistent formatting. Automatically adjust the widths of the columns to accommodate the longest entry. Save **EL1-C6-CS-LMExpSummary.xlsx**.

Part 2

You decide that you want to include another worksheet that displays the yearly estimated expenses, the actual expenses, and the variances (differences) between the expenses. With **EL1-C6-CS-LMExpSummary.xlsx** open, open **LMExpVar.xlsx**. Copy the worksheet into **EL1-C6-CS-LMExpSummary.xlsx**, make **LMExpVar.xlsx** the active workbook, and then close it. Rename the sheet tab containing the estimated expenses to *Estimated Exp*, rename the sheet tab containing the actual expenses to *Actual Exp*, and rename the sheet tab containing the variances to *Summary*. Recolor the three sheet tabs you just renamed.

Select the yearly estimated expense amounts (column N) in the Estimated Exp worksheet and then paste the amounts in the appropriate cells in the Summary worksheet. Click the Paste Options button and then click the Values & Number Formatting button in the *Paste Values* section of the drop-down list. (This pastes the value and the cell formatting rather than the formula.) Select the yearly actual expense amounts (column N) in the Actual Exp worksheet and then paste the amounts in the appropriate cells in the Summary worksheet. Click the Paste Options button and then click the Values & Number Formatting button in the *Paste Values* section of the drop-down list. Apply appropriate formatting to numbers and insert a formula to insert the variances (differences) of estimated and actual expenses. Clear the contents of cells D8, D9, D13, and D14. Apply styles to the Summary worksheet so it appears with formatting similar to the Estimated Exp and Actual Exp worksheets.

Insert an appropriate header or footer in each worksheet. Scale the worksheets so each prints on one page. Save, print all of the worksheets, and then close **EL1-C6-CS-LMExpSummary.xlsx**.

Part 3

You are not happy with the current product list form, so you decide to look at template forms available at Office.com. Display the New tab Backstage view, click the *Lists* option in the *Office.com Templates* section, click the *Business* folder, and then double-click the *Product price list* template. (These steps may vary.) Use the information below to fill in the form in the appropriate locations:

Leeward Marine
4500 Shoreline Drive
Ketchikan, AK 99901
(907) 555-2200
(907) 555-2595 (fax)
www.emcp.com/lmarine

Insert the following information in the appropriate columns:

Product Number	Name	Description	Retail Price Per Unit	Bulk Price Per Unit*
210-19	Ring Buoy	19-inch, white, solid plastic	$49.95	$42.00
210-20	Ring Buoy	20-inch, white, solid plastic	$52.95	$49.50
210-24	Ring Buoy	24-inch, white, solid plastic	$59.95	$52.00
320-05	Horseshoe Buoy	Vinyl fabric over plastic core	$83.95	$78.50
225-01	Ring Buoy Holder	Aluminum holder	$6.50	$5.75
234-24	Ring Buoy Bracket	Stainless steel bracket	$7.25	$6.50

Save the completed products list form and name it **EL1-C6-CS-LMProdList**. Print and then close the workbook.

Part 4

You need to print a number of copies of the product list and you want the company letterhead to print at the top of the page. You decide to use the letterhead you created in Word and copy the product list information from Excel into the Word letterhead document. To do this, open Word and then open the document named **LMLtrd.docx**. Press the Enter key four times. Make Excel the active program and then open **EL1-C6-CS-LMProdList.xlsx**. Copy cells A2 through E11 and then paste them into the **LMLtrhd.docx** Word document as a picture object (click the Paste Options button and then click the Picture button). Save the document with Save As and name it **EL1-C6-CS-LMProducts**. Print and then close **EL1-C6-CS-LMProducts.docx** and then exit Word. In Excel, close **EL1-C6-CS-ProdList.xlsx**.

Microsoft Excel
Creating a Chart in Excel

CHAPTER 7

PERFORMANCE OBJECTIVES

Upon successful completion of Chapter 7, you will be able to:
- Create a chart with data in an Excel worksheet
- Size, move, and delete charts
- Print a selected chart and print a worksheet containing a chart
- Choose a chart style, layout, and formatting
- Change chart location
- Insert, move, size, and delete chart labels, shapes, and pictures

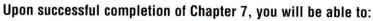

In the previous Excel chapters, you learned to create data in worksheets. While a worksheet does an adequate job of representing data, you can present some data more visually by charting the data. A *chart* is sometimes referred to as a *graph* and is a picture of numeric data. In this chapter, you will learn to create and customize charts in Excel. Model answers for this chapter's projects appear on the following pages.

Excel2010L1C7

Note: Before beginning the projects, copy to your storage medium the Excel2010L1C7 subfolder from the Excel2010L1 folder on the CD that accompanies this textbook and then make Excel2010L1C7 the active folder.

Model Answers

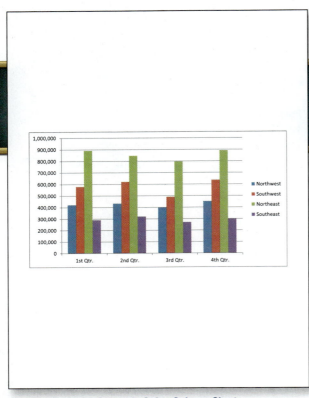

Project 1 Create a Quarterly Sales Column Chart
EL1-C7-P1-SalesChart.xlsx

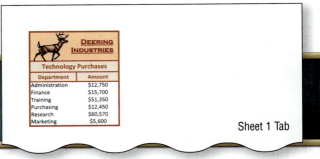

Sheet 1 Tab

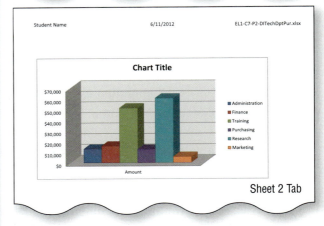

Sheet 2 Tab

Project 2 Create a Technology Purchases Bar Chart and Column Chart
EL1-C7-P2-DITechDptPur.xlsx

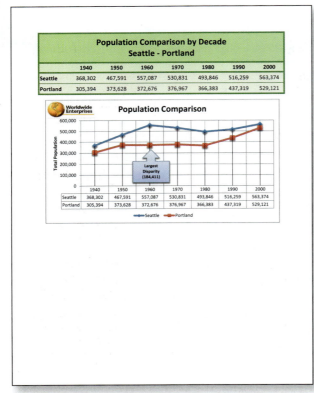

Project 3 Create a Population Comparison Bar Chart
EL1-C7-P3-PopComp.xlsx

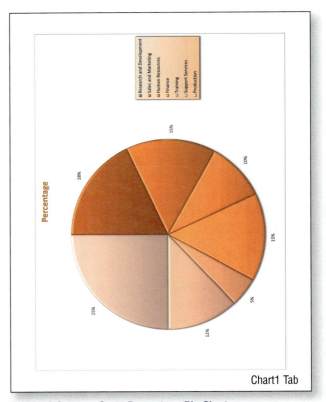

Chart1 Tab

Project 4 Create a Costs Percentage Pie Chart
EL1-C7-P4-DIDptCosts.xlsx

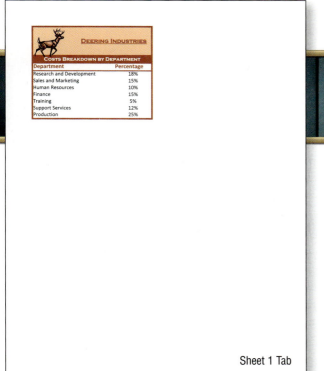

Sheet 1 Tab

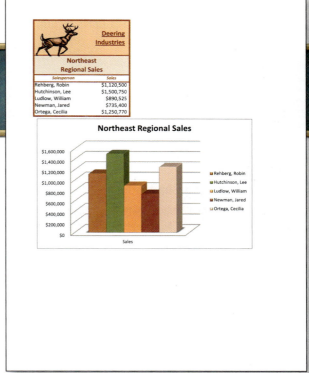

Project 5 Create a Regional Sales Column Chart
EL1-C7-P5-DIRegSales.xlsx

Project 1 Create a Quarterly Sales Column Chart   2 Parts

You will open a workbook containing quarterly sales data and then use the data to create a column chart. You will decrease the size of the chart, move it to a different location in the worksheet, and then make changes to sales numbers.

Creating a Chart

In Excel, create a chart with buttons in the Charts group in the Insert tab as shown in Figure 7.1. With buttons in the Charts group you can create a variety of charts such as a column chart, line chart, pie chart, and much more. Excel provides 11 basic chart types as described in Table 7.1. To create a chart, select cells in a worksheet that you want to chart, click the Insert tab, and then click the desired chart button in the Charts group. At the drop-down gallery that displays, click the desired chart style. You can also create a chart by selecting the desired cells and then pressing Alt + F1. This keyboard shortcut, by default, inserts the data in a 2-D column chart (unless the default chart type has been changed).

▼ Quick Steps

Create a Chart
1. Select cells.
2. Click Insert tab.
3. Click desired chart button.
4. Click desired chart style at drop-down list.

Create Chart as Default Chart Type
1. Select cells.
2. Press Alt + F1.

Chapter 7 ■ Creating a Chart in Excel   241

Figure 7.1 Charts Group Buttons

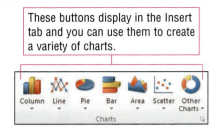

These buttons display in the Insert tab and you can use them to create a variety of charts.

Table 7.1 Type of Charts

Chart	Description
Area	Emphasizes the magnitude of change, rather than time and the rate of change. It also shows the relationship of parts to a whole by displaying the sum of the plotted values.
Bar	Shows individual figures at a specific time, or shows variations between components but not in relationship to the whole.
Bubble	Compares sets of three values in a manner similar to a scatter chart, with the third value displayed as the size of the bubble marker.
Column	Compares separate (noncontinuous) items as they vary over time.
Doughnut	Shows the relationship of parts of the whole.
Line	Shows trends and change over time at even intervals. It emphasizes the rate of change over time rather than the magnitude of change.
Pie	Shows proportions and relationships of parts to the whole.
Radar	Emphasizes differences and amounts of change over time and variations and trends. Each category has its own value axis radiating from the center point. Lines connect all values in the same series.
Stock	Shows four values for a stock — open, high, low, and close.
Surface	Shows trends in values across two dimensions in a continuous curve.
XY (Scatter)	Shows the relationships among numeric values in several data series or plots the interception points between *x* and *y* values. It shows uneven intervals of data and is commonly used in scientific data.

Sizing, Moving, and Deleting a Chart

When you create a chart, the chart is inserted in the same worksheet as the selected cells. Figure 7.2 displays the worksheet and chart you will create in Project 1a. The chart is inserted in a box which you can size and/or move in the worksheet.

To size the worksheet, position the mouse pointer on the four dots located in the middle of the border you want to size until the pointer turns into a two-headed arrow, hold down the left mouse button, and then drag to increase or decrease the size of the chart. To increase or decrease the height and width of

Figure 7.2 Project 1a Chart

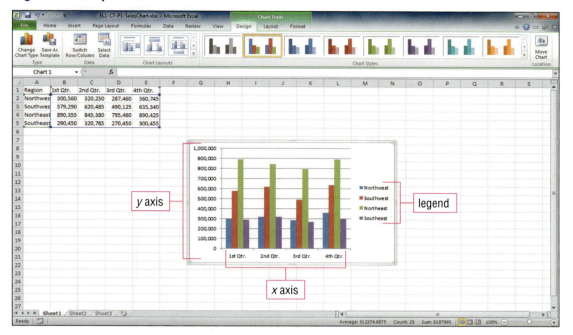

the chart at the same time, position the mouse pointer on the three dots that display in a chart border corner until the pointer displays as a two-headed arrow, hold down the left mouse button, and then drag to the desired size. To increase or decrease the size of the chart and maintain the proportions of the chart, hold down the Shift key while dragging a chart corner border.

To move the chart, make sure the chart is selected (light gray border displays around the chart), position the mouse pointer on a border until it turns into a four-headed arrow, hold down the left mouse button, and then drag to the desired position.

Editing Data

The cells you select to create the chart are linked to the chart. If you need to change data for a chart, edit the data in the desired cell and the corresponding section of the chart is automatically updated.

HINT Hide rows or columns that you do not want to chart.

Project 1a Creating a Chart   Part 1 of 2

1. Open **SalesChart.xlsx** and then save the workbook with Save As and name it **EL1-C7-P1-SalesChart**.
2. Select cells A1 through E5.
3. Press Alt + F1.
4. Slightly increase the size of the chart and maintain the proportions of the chart by completing the following steps:
   a. Position the mouse pointer on the bottom right corner of the chart border until the pointer turns into a two-headed arrow pointing diagonally.
   b. Hold down the Shift key and then hold down the left mouse button.

Chapter 7 ■ Creating a Chart in Excel

c. Drag out approximately one-half inch and then release the mouse button and then the Shift key.

Step 4c

5. Move the chart below the cells containing data by completing the following steps:
   a. Make sure the chart is selected (light gray border surrounds the chart).
   b. Position the mouse pointer on the chart border until the pointer turns into a four-headed arrow.
   c. Hold down the left mouse button, drag the chart so it is positioned below the cells containing data, and then release the mouse button.

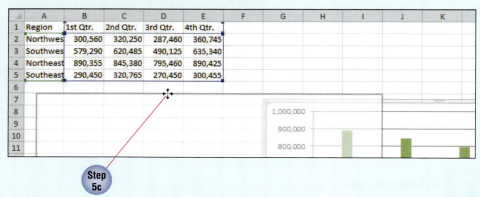

Step 5c

6. Make the following changes to the specified cells:
   a. Make cell B2 active and then change *300,560* to *421,720*.
   b. Make cell C2 active and then change *320,250* to *433,050*.
   c. Make cell D2 active and then change *287,460* to *397,460*.
   d. Make cell E2 active and then change *360,745* to *451,390*.
7. Save **EL1-C7-P1-SalesChart.xlsx**.

Printing a Chart

In a worksheet containing data in cells as well as a chart, you can print only the chart. To do this, select the chart, display the Print tab Backstage view, and then click the Print button. With a chart selected, the first gallery in the *Settings* category is automatically changed to *Print Selected Chart*. A preview of the chart displays at the right side of the Print tab Backstage view.

Project 1b Printing the Chart   Part 2 of 2

1. With **EL1-C7-P1-SalesChart.xlsx** open, make sure the chart is selected.
2. Click the File tab and then the Print tab.
3. At the Print tab Backstage view, look at the preview of the chart that displays at the right side and notice that the first gallery in the *Settings* category is set at *Print Selected Chart*.
4. Click the Print button.
5. Save and then close **EL1-C7-P1-SalesChart.xlsx**.

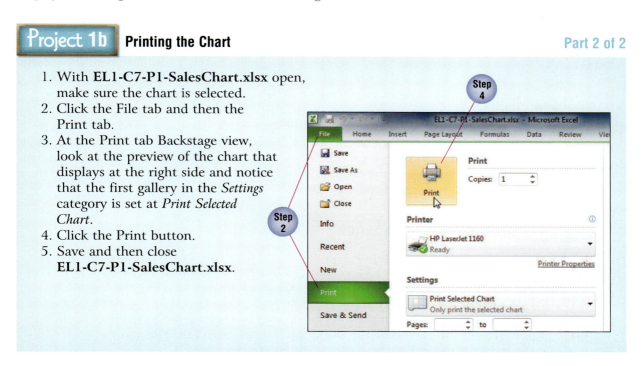

Project 2 Create a Technology Purchases Bar Chart and Column Chart   2 Parts

You will open a workbook containing technology purchases data by department and then create a bar chart with the data. You will then change the chart type, layout, and style and move the chart to a new sheet.

Changing the Chart Design

When you insert a chart in a worksheet, the Chart Tools Design tab displays as shown in Figure 7.3. With options in this tab, you can change the chart type, specify a different layout or style for the chart, and change the location of the chart so it displays in a separate worksheet.

Chapter 7 ■ Creating a Chart in Excel   **245**

Figure 7.3 Chart Tools Design Tab

Quick Steps

Change Chart Type and Style
1. Make the chart active.
2. Click Chart Tools Design tab.
3. Click Change Chart Type button.
4. Click desired chart type.
5. Click desired chart style.
6. Click OK.

Change Chart Data Series
1. Make the chart active.
2. Click Chart Tools Design tab.
3. Click Switch Row/Column button.

Change Chart Type

Switch Row/Column

Choosing a Custom Chart Style

The chart feature offers a variety of preformatted custom charts and offers varying styles for each chart type. You can choose a chart style with buttons in the Charts group by clicking a chart button and then choosing from the styles offered at the drop-down list. You can also choose a chart style with the Change Chart Type button in the Chart Tools Design tab. Click this button and the Change Chart Type dialog box displays as shown in Figure 7.4. Click the desired chart type in the panel at the left side of the dialog box and then click the desired chart style at the right. If you create a particular chart type on a regular basis, you may want to set that chart type as the default. To do this, click the Set as Default Chart button in the Change Chart Type dialog box.

Changing the Data Series

A data series is information represented on the chart by bars, lines, columns, pie slices, and so on. When Excel creates a chart, the data in the first column (except the first cell) is used to create the x axis (the information along the bottom of the chart) and the data in the first row (except the first cell) is used to create the legend. You can switch the data in the axes by clicking the Switch Row/Column button in the Data group in the Chart Tools Design tab. This moves the data on the x axis to the y axis and the y axis data to the x axis.

Figure 7.4 Change Chart Type Dialog Box

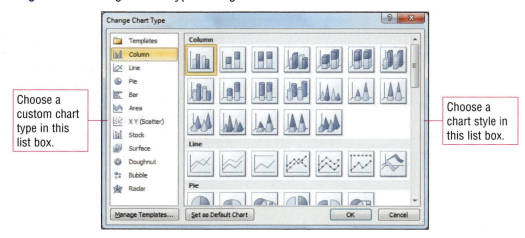

Choose a custom chart type in this list box.

Choose a chart style in this list box.

Excel Level 1 ■ Unit 2

Project 2a Creating a Chart and Changing the Design — Part 1 of 2

1. Open **DITechDptPur.xlsx** and then save the workbook with Save As and name it **EL1-C7-P2-DITechDptPur**.
2. Create a bar chart by completing the following steps:
    a. Select cells A3 through B9.
    b. Click the Insert tab.
    c. Click the Bar button in the Charts group.
    d. Click the first option from the left in the *Cylinder* section (*Clustered Horizontal Cylinder*).
3. With the chart selected and the Chart Tools Design tab displayed, change the data series by clicking the Switch Row/Column button located in the Data group.

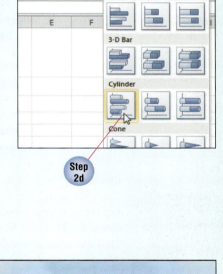

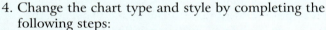

4. Change the chart type and style by completing the following steps:
    a. Click the Change Chart Type button located in the Type group.
    b. At the Change Chart Type dialog box, click the *Column* option in the left panel.
    c. Click the *3-D Cylinder* option in the *Column* section (fourth chart style from the left in the second row of the *Column* section).
    d. Click OK to close the Change Chart Type dialog box.
5. Save **EL1-C7-P2-DITechDptPur.xlsx**.

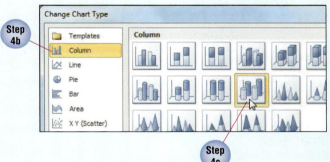

Changing Chart Layout and Style

The Chart Tools Design tab contains options for changing the chart layout and style. The Chart Layouts group in the tab contains preformatted chart layout options. Click the More button (contains an underline and a down-pointing arrow) to display a drop-down list of layout options. Hover the mouse pointer over an option and a ScreenTip displays with the option name. You can also scroll through layout options by clicking the up-pointing arrow or the down-pointing arrow located at the right side of the Chart Layouts group.

HINT Click the Save As Template button in the Type group in the Chart Tools Design tab to save the formatting and layout of the current chart as a template you can use to create future charts.

Use options in the Chart Styles group to apply a particular style of formatting to a chart. Click the More button located at the right side of the Chart Styles group to display a drop-down list with all the style options or click the up-pointing or down-pointing arrow at the right of the group to scroll through the options.

Changing Chart Location

▼ **Quick Steps**

Change Chart Location
1. Make the chart active.
2. Click Chart Tools Design tab.
3. Click Move Chart button.
4. Click *New Sheet* option.
5. Click OK.

Move Chart

Create a chart and the chart is inserted in the currently open worksheet as an embedded object. You can change the location of a chart with the Move Chart button in the Location group. Click this button and the Move Chart dialog box displays as shown in Figure 7.5. Click the *New sheet* option to move the chart to a new sheet within the workbook. Excel automatically names the sheet *Chart1*. Click the down-pointing arrow at the right side of the *Object in* option box and then click the desired location. The drop-down list will generally display the names of the worksheets within the open workbook. You can use the keyboard shortcut, F11, to create a default chart type (usually a column chart) and Excel automatically inserts the chart in a separate sheet.

If you have moved a chart to a separate sheet, you can move it back to the original sheet or move it to a different sheet within the workbook. To move a chart to a sheet, click the Move Chart button in the Location group in the Chart Tools Design tab. At the Move Chart dialog box, click the down-pointing arrow at the right side of the *Object in* option and then click the desired sheet at the drop-down list. Click OK and the chart is inserted in the specified sheet as an object that you can move, size, and format.

Deleting a Chart

▼ **Quick Steps**

Delete a Chart
1. Click once in chart.
2. Press Delete key.
OR
1. Right-click chart tab.
2. Click Cut.

Delete a chart created in Excel by clicking once in the chart to select it and then pressing the Delete key. If you move a chart to a different worksheet in the workbook and then delete the chart, the chart is deleted but not the worksheet. To delete the chart as well as the worksheet, position the mouse pointer on the Chart1 tab, click the right mouse button, and then click *Delete* at the shortcut menu. At the message box telling you that selected sheets will be permanently deleted, click Delete.

Figure 7.5 Move Chart Dialog Box

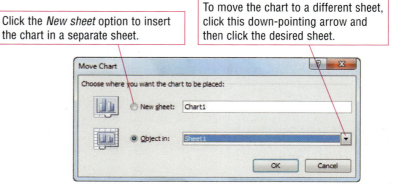

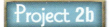 **Project 2b** **Changing Chart Layout, Style, and Location** Part 2 of 2

1. With **EL1-C7-P2-DITechDeptPur.xlsx** open, make sure the Chart Tools Design tab displays. (If it does not, make sure the chart is selected and then click the Chart Tools Design tab.)
2. Change the chart type by completing the following steps:
    a. Click the Change Chart Type button in the Type tab.
    b. Click *3-D Clustered Column* (fourth column style from the left in the top row).
    c. Click OK to close the dialog box.

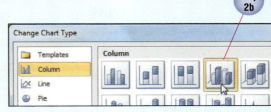

3. Change the chart layout by clicking the *Layout 1* option in the Chart Layouts group (first option from the left). This layout inserts the words *Chart Title* at the top of the chart.
4. Change the chart style by clicking the More button located at the right side of the Chart Styles group and then clicking *Style 34* (second option from the left in the fifth row).

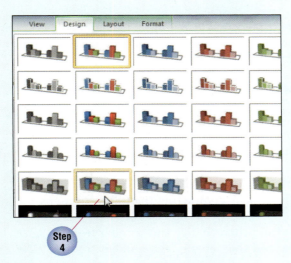

5. Move the chart to a new location by completing the following steps:
    a. Click the Move Chart button in the Location group.
    b. At the Move Chart dialog box, click the *New sheet* option and then click OK. (The chart is inserted in a worksheet named *Chart1*.)
6. Save **EL1-C7-P2-DITechDptPur.xlsx**.
7. Print the Chart1 worksheet containing the chart.

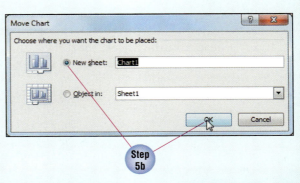

8. Move the chart from Chart1 to Sheet2 by completing the following steps:
   a. Make sure Chart1 is the active sheet and that the chart is selected (not an element in the chart).
   b. Make sure the Chart Tools Design tab is active.
   c. Click the Move Chart button in the Location group.
   d. At the Move Chart dialog box, click the down-pointing arrow at the right side of the *Object in* option and then click *Sheet2* at the drop-down list.

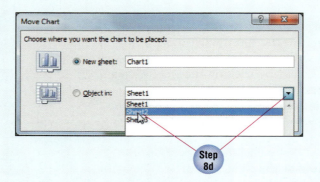

Step 8d

   e. Click OK.
9. Increase the size of the chart and maintain the proportions by completing the following steps:
   a. Click inside the chart but outside any chart elements. (This displays a light gray border around the chart. Make sure the entire chart is selected and not a specific chart element.)
   b. Hold down the Shift key.
   c. Position the mouse pointer on the upper left border corner until the pointer turns into a double-headed arrow pointing diagonally.
   d. Hold down the left mouse button, drag left approximately one inch and then release the mouse button and then the Shift key.
   e. Click outside the chart to deslect it.
   f. Display the Print tab Backstage view to determine if the chart will print on one page. If the chart does not fit on the page, return to the worksheet and then move and/or decrease the size of the chart until it fits on one page.
10. Change amounts in Sheet1 by completing the following steps:
    a. Click Sheet1.
    b. Make cell B4 active and then change the number from *$33,500* to *$12,750*.
    c. Make cell B9 active and then change the number from *$19,200* to *$5,600*.
    d. Make cell A2 active.
    e. Click the Sheet2 tab and notice that the chart displays the updated amounts.
11. Click outside the chart to deselect it.
12. Insert a header in the Sheet2 worksheet that prints your name at the left, the current date in the middle, and the workbook file name at the right.
13. Print the active worksheet (Sheet2).
14. Save and then close **EL1-C7-P2-DITechDptPur.xlsx**.

Project 3 Create a Population Comparison Bar Chart   3 Parts

You will open a workbook containing population comparison data for Seattle and Portland and then create a bar chart with the data. You will also add chart labels and shapes and move, size, and delete labels and shapes.

Changing the Chart Layout

Customize the layout of labels in a chart with options in the Chart Tools Layout tab as shown in Figure 7.6. With buttons in this tab, you can change the layout and/or insert additional chart labels. Certain chart labels are automatically inserted in a chart including a chart legend and labels for the *x* axis and *y* axis. Add chart labels to an existing chart with options in the Labels group in the Chart Tools Layout tab. In addition to chart labels, you can also insert shapes, pictures, and/or clip art and change the layout of 3-D chart labels.

Inserting, Moving, and Deleting Chart Labels

Certain chart labels are automatically inserted in a chart, including a chart legend and labels for the *x* axis and *y* axis. The legend identifies which data series is represented by which data marker. Insert additional chart labels with options in the Labels group in the Chart Tools Layout tab. For example, click the Chart Title button in the Labels group and a drop-down list displays with options for inserting a chart title in a specific location in the chart.

You can move and/or size a chart label. To move a chart label, click the label to select it and then move the mouse pointer over the border line until the pointer turns into a four-headed arrow. Hold down the left mouse button, drag the label to the desired location, and then release the mouse button. To size a chart label, use the sizing handles that display around the selected label to increase or decrease the size. To delete a chart label, click the label to select it and then press the Delete key. You can also delete a label by right-clicking the label and then clicking *Delete* at the shortcut menu.

▼ **Quick Steps**

Add Chart Labels
1. Make the chart active.
2. Click Chart Tools Layout tab.
3. Click desired chart labels button.
4. Choose desired option at drop-down list.

Chart Title

Figure 7.6 Chart Tools Layout Tab

Project 3a Creating a Chart and Changing Layout of Chart Labels   Part 1 of 3

1. Open **PopComp.xlsx** and then save the workbook with Save As and name it **EL1-C7-P3-PopComp**.
2. Create a Bar chart by completing the following steps:
   a. Select cells A2 through H4.
   b. Click the Insert tab.
   c. Click the Bar button in the Charts group and then click the *Clustered Horizontal Cylinder* option in the *Cylinder* section.
3. Change to a Line chart by completing the following steps:
   a. Click the Change Chart Type button in the Type group.
   b. At the Change Chart Type dialog box, click *Line* located at the left side of the dialog box.
   c. Click the *Line with Markers* option in the *Line* section (fourth option from the left).

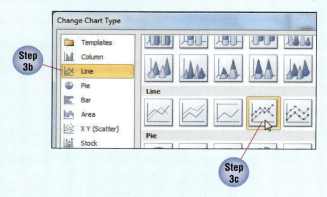

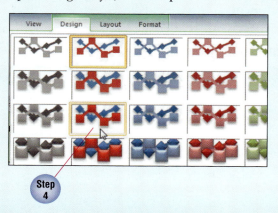

   d. Click OK to close the Change Chart Type dialog box.
4. Click the More button in the Chart Styles group in the Chart Tools Design tab and then click *Style 18* at the drop-down gallery (second option from left in the third row).

252   Excel Level 1 ■ Unit 2

5. Change the layout of the chart by completing the following steps:
   a. Click the Chart Tools Layout tab.
   b. Click the Legend button in the Labels group.
   c. At the drop-down list, click the *Show Legend at Bottom* option.
   d. Click the Chart Title button in the Labels group.
   e. At the drop-down list, click the *Above Chart* option.

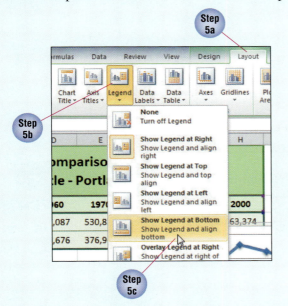
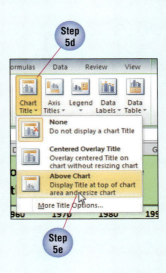

   f. Select the text *Chart Title* located in the chart title text box and then type **Population Comparison**.
6. Insert an *x*-axis title by completing the following steps:
   a. Click the Axis Titles button, point to the *Primary Horizontal Axis Title* option at the drop-down list, and then click *Title Below Axis* at the side menu.
   b. Select the text *Axis Title* located in the title text box and then type **Decades**.

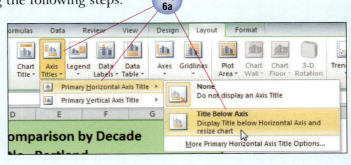

7. Insert a *y*-axis title by completing the following steps:
   a. Click the Axis Titles button, point to the *Primary Vertical Axis Title* option at the drop-down list, and then click *Rotated Title* at the side menu. (This inserts a rotated title at the left side of the chart containing the text *Axis Title*).
   b. Select the text *Axis Title* located in the axis title text box and then type **Total Population**.

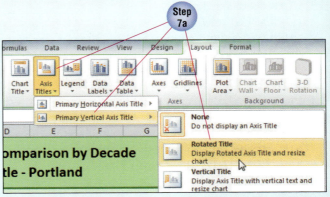

Chapter 7 ■ Creating a Chart in Excel 253

8. Click the Gridlines button in the Axes group, point to *Primary Vertical Gridlines*, and then click the *Major & Minor Gridlines* option at the side menu.

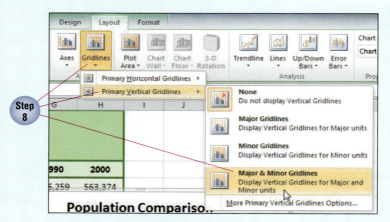

9. Click the Data Table button in the Labels group and then click the *Show Data Table* option. (This inserts cells toward the bottom of the chart containing cell data.)

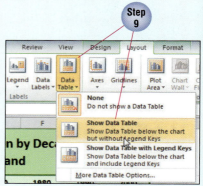

10. Click the Lines button in the Analysis group and then click *Drop Lines* at the drop-down list.

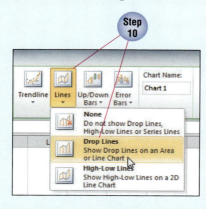

11. Drag the bottom right corner of the chart border to increase the size by approximately one inch.
12. Drag the chart so it is positioned below the data in cells but not overlapping the data.
13. Click the *x*-axis title (*Decades*) to select the title text box and then drag the box so it is positioned as shown at right.

14. Print only the selected chart.
15. Delete the horizontal axis title by clicking the axis title *Decades* and then pressing the Delete key.
16. Save **EL1-C7-P3-PopComp.xlsx**.

Inserting Shapes

The Insert group in the Chart Tools Layout tab contains three buttons with options for inserting shapes or images in a chart. Click the Shapes button in the Insert group and a drop-down list displays with a variety of shape options as shown in Figure 7.7. Click the desired shape at the drop-down list and the mouse pointer turns into a thin, black plus symbol. Drag with this pointer symbol to create the shape in the chart. The shape is inserted in the chart with default formatting. You can change this formatting with options in the Drawing Tools Format tab. This tab contains many of the same options as the Chart Tools Format tab. For example, you can insert a shape, apply a shape or WordArt style, and arrange and size the shape.

Moving, Sizing, and Deleting Shapes

Move, size, and delete shapes in the same manner as moving, sizing, and deleting chart elements. To move a shape, select the shape, position the mouse pointer over the border line until the pointer turns into a four-headed arrow. Hold down the left mouse button, drag the shape to the desired location, and then release the mouse button. To size a shape, select the shape and then use the sizing handles that display around the shape to increase or decrease the size. Delete a selected shape by clicking the Delete key or right-clicking the shape and then clicking *Cut* at the shortcut menu.

▼ Quick Steps
Insert Shape
1. Make the chart active.
2. Click Chart Tools Layout tab.
3. Click Shapes button.
4. Click desired shape at drop-down list.
5. Drag pointer symbol to create shape in chart.

Shapes

Chart elements can be repositioned for easier viewing.

Figure 7.7 Shapes Button Drop-down List

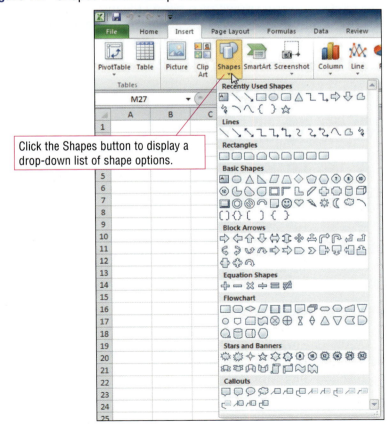

Click the Shapes button to display a drop-down list of shape options.

Chapter 7 ■ Creating a Chart in Excel   255

Project 3b | **Inserting and Customizing a Shape** | Part 2 of 3

1. With **EL1-C7-P3-PopComp.xlsx** open, make sure the Chart Tools Layout tab displays.
2. Create a shape similar to the shape shown in Figure 7.8. Begin by clicking the Shapes button in the Insert group.
3. Click the *Up Arrow Callout* shape in the *Block Arrows* section (last shape in the second row).

4. Drag in the chart to create the shape. To do this, position the mouse pointer in the chart, hold down the left mouse button, drag to create the shape, and then release the mouse button.
5. Click the More button located to the right of the shape style thumbnails in the Shapes Styles group and then click *Subtle Effect - Blue, Accent 1* at the drop-down gallery.

6. With the shape selected, use the sizing handles around the shape to increase and/or decrease the size so it displays as shown in Figure 7.8.
7. With the shape still selected, type **Largest Disparity** in the shape box, press Enter, and then type **(184,411)**.
8. Select the text you just typed and then complete the following steps:
   a. Click the Home tab.
   b. Click the Center button in the Alignment group.
   c. Click the Bold button in the Font group.
   d. Click the Font Size button arrow and then click 9.
9. With the shape selected, drag the shape so it is positioned as shown in Figure 7.8.
10. Save **EL1-C7-P3-PopComp.xlsx**.

Figure 7.8 Project 3b Chart

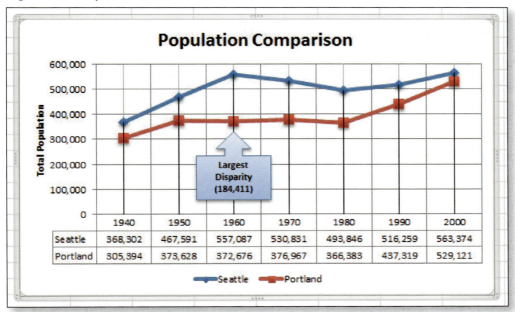

Inserting Images

Click the Picture button in the Insert group in the Chart Tools Layout tab and the Insert Picture dialog box displays. If you have a picture or image file saved in a folder, navigate to the desired folder and then double-click the file name. This inserts the picture or image in the chart. Drag the picture or image to the desired position in the chart and use the sizing handles to change the size.

▼ **Quick Steps**

Insert Image
1. Make the chart active.
2. Click Chart Tools Layout tab.
3. Click Picture button.
4. Double-click desired file name.

Project 3c Inserting a Picture in a Chart   Part 3 of 3

1. With **EL1-C7-P3-PopComp.xlsx** open, make sure the chart is selected and then click the Chart Tools Layout tab.
2. Insert the company logo by completing the following steps:
   a. Click the Picture button in the Insert group.
   b. At the Insert Picture dialog box, navigate to the Excel2010L1C7 folder on your storage medium and then double-click *WELogo.jpg* in the list box.
3. With the logo image inserted in the chart, use the sizing handles to decrease the size of the image and then move the image so it displays in the upper left corner of the chart area as shown in Figure 7.9.
4. Print only the selected chart.
5. Save and then close **EL1-C7-P3-PopComp.xlsx**.

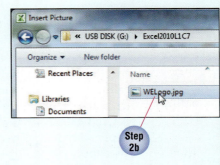

Step 2b

Chapter 7 ■ Creating a Chart in Excel   **257**

Figure 7.9 Project 3c Chart

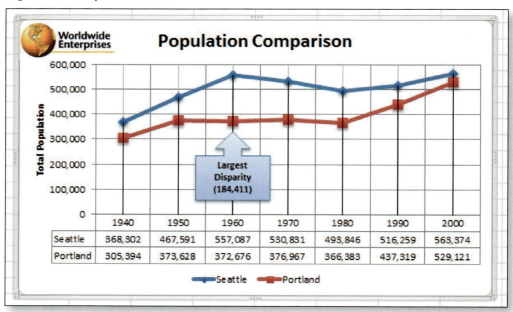

Project 4 Create a Costs Percentage Pie Chart 1 Part

You will open a workbook containing percentage of costs for company departments and then create a pie chart with the data. You will apply formatting to the chart and then move the chart to a new worksheet.

Reset to Match Style

Chart Elements

Apply a WordArt style to make numbers stand out.

Changing the Chart Formatting

Customize the format of the chart and chart elements with options in the Chart Tools Format tab as shown in Figure 7.10. With buttons in the Current Selection group you can identify a specific element in the chart and then apply formatting to that element. You can also click the Reset to Match Style button in the Current Selection group to return the formatting of the chart back to the original layout.

With options in the Shape Styles group, you can apply formatting styles to specific elements in a chart. Identify the desired element either by clicking the element to select it or by clicking the down-pointing arrow at the right side of the Chart Elements button in the Current Selection group and then clicking the desired element name at the drop-down list. With the chart element specified, apply formatting by clicking a style button in the Shape Styles group. You can also apply a style from a drop-down gallery. Display this gallery by clicking the

Figure 7.10 Chart Tools Format Tab

More button located at the right side of the shape styles. Click the up-pointing or the down-pointing arrow at the right of the shape styles to cycle through the available style options.

Project 4 — Creating and Formatting a Pie Chart — Part 1 of 1

1. Open **DIDptCosts.xlsx** and then save the workbook with Save As and name it **EL1-C7-P4-DIDptCosts**.
2. Create the pie chart as shown in Figure 7.11 by completing the following steps:
   a. Select cells A3 through B10.
   b. Click the Insert tab.
   c. Click the Pie button in the Charts group and then click the first pie option in the *2-D Pie* section.
3. Click the More button located at the right side of the Chart Styles group.
4. At the drop-down gallery, click the *Style 32* option (last option in the fourth row).

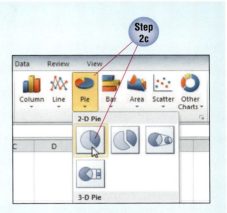

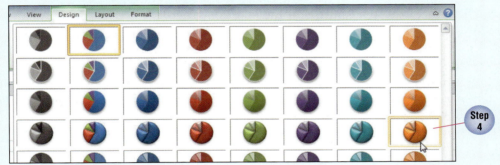

5. Click the Chart Tools Layout tab.
6. Insert data labels by clicking the Data Labels button in the Labels group and then clicking *Outside End* at the drop-down list.
7. Format chart elements by completing the following steps:
   a. Click the Chart Tools Format tab.
   b. Click the down-pointing arrow at the right side of the Chart Elements button in the Current Selection group and then click *Legend* at the drop-down list.
   c. Click the More button at the right of the shape style thumbnails in the Shape Styles group and then click the last option in the fourth row (*Subtle Effect - Orange, Accent 6*).
   d. Click the down-pointing arrow at the right side of the Chart Elements button in the Current Selection group and then click *Chart Title*.

Chapter 7 ■ Creating a Chart in Excel 259

e. Click the More button at the right side of the WordArt style thumbnails in the WordArt Styles group and then click the *Gradient Fill - Orange, Accent 6, Inner Shadow* (second option from the left in the fourth row).

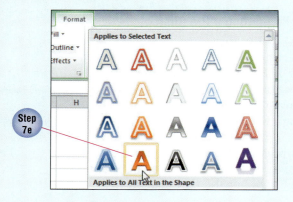

f. Deselect the chart title.
8. Insert the chart in a new sheet by completing the following steps:
   a. With the chart selected, click the Chart Tools Design tab.
   b. Click the Move Chart button in the Location group.
   c. At the Move Chart dialog box, click the *New sheet* option.
   d. Click OK.
9. Print only the worksheet containing the chart.
10. Save and then close **EL1-C7-P4-DIDptCosts.xlsx**.

Figure 7.11 Project 4

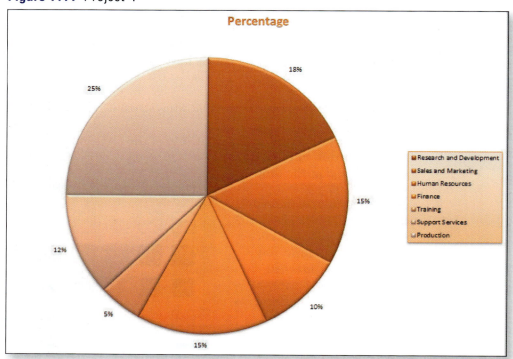

Project 5 Create a Regional Sales Column Chart — 1 Part

You will create a column chart using regional sales data, change the layout of the chart, apply formatting, and change the height and width of the chart.

Quick Steps

Change Chart Height and/or Width
1. Make the chart active.
2. Click Chart Tools Format tab.
3. Insert desired height and/or width with *Shape Height* and/or *Shape Width* text boxes.

You can size a chart by selecting the chart and then dragging a sizing handle. You can also size a chart to specific measurements with the *Shape Height* and *Shape Width* measurement boxes in the Size group in the Chart Tools Format tab. Change the height or width by clicking the up- or down-pointing arrows that display at the right side of the button or select the current measurement in the measurement box and then type a specific measurement.

Project 5 Changing the Height and Width of a Chart — Part 1 of 1

1. Open **DIRegSales.xlsx**.
2. Save the workbook with Save As and name it **EL1-C7-P5-DIRegSales**.
3. Create a Column chart by completing the following steps:
   a. Select cells A3 through B8.
   b. Click the Insert tab.
   c. Click the Column button in the Charts group.
   d. Click the *3-D Clustered Column* option (first option in the *3-D Column* section).
   e. Click the Switch Row/Column button located in the Data group to change the data series.
   f. Click the *Layout 1* option in the Chart Layouts group (first option from the left in the group).
   g. Select the text *Chart Title* and then type **Northeast Regional Sales**.
   h. Click the More button located at the right side of the thumbnails in the Chart Styles group and then click *Style 32* at the drop-down gallery (last option in fourth row).

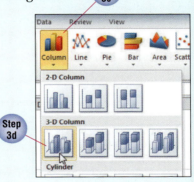

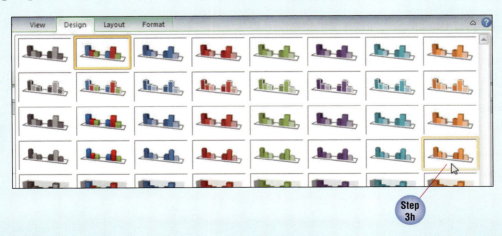

4. Change a series color by completing the following steps:
   a. Click the Chart Tools Format tab.
   b. Click the down-pointing arrow at the right side of the Chart Elements button in the Current Selection group and then click *Series "Newman, Jared"* at the drop-down list.

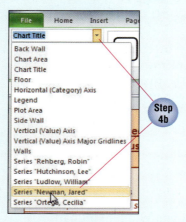

   c. Click the Shape Fill button arrow in the Shape Styles group and then click the dark red color *Red, Accent 2, Darker 25%*.

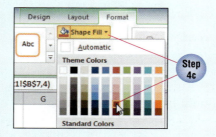

5. Change a series color by completing the following steps:
   a. With the Chart Tools Format tab active, click the down-pointing arrow at the right side of the Chart Elements button and then click *Series "Hutchinson, Lee"* at the drop-down list.
   b. Click the Shape Fill button arrow in the Shape Styles group and then click the dark green color *Olive Green, Accent 3, Darker 25%*.
6. Drag the chart down below the cells containing data.
7. Make sure the Chart Tools Format tab is selected.
8. Click in the *Shape Height* measurement box in the Size group and then type 3.8.
9. Click the up-pointing arrow at the right side of the *Shape Width* measurement box in the Size group until 5.5 displays in the text box.
10. Click outside the chart to deselect it.
11. Make sure the chart fits on one page and then print the worksheet (cells containing data and the chart).
12. Save and then close **EL1-C7-P5-DIRegSales.xlsx**.

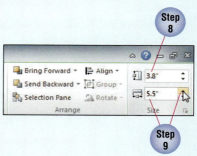

Chapter Summary

- A chart is a visual presentation of data. Excel provides 11 basic chart types: Area, Bar, Bubble, Column, Doughnut, Line, Pyramid, Radar, Stock, Surface, and XY (Scatter).
- To create a chart, select cells containing data you want to chart, click the Insert tab, and then click the desired chart button in the Charts group.
- A chart you create is inserted in the same worksheet as the selected cells.
- You can increase or decrease the size of a chart by positioning the mouse pointer on the four dots located in the middle of each border line or the three dots at each corner, and then dragging to the desired size.
- Move a chart by positioning the mouse pointer on the chart border until it turns into a four-headed arrow and then dragging with the mouse.
- Data in cells used to create the chart are linked to the chart. If you change the data in cells, the chart reflects the changes.
- Print by selecting the chart, displaying the Print tab Backstage view, and then clicking the Print button.
- When you insert a chart in a worksheet, the Chart Tools Design tab is active. Use options in this tab to change the chart type, specify a different layout or style, and change the location of the chart.
- Choose a chart style with buttons in the Charts group in the Insert tab or at the Change Chart Type dialog box.
- The Chart Layouts group in the Chart Tools Design tab contains preformatted chart layout options. Use options in the Chart Styles group to apply a particular style of formatting to a chart.
- By default, a chart is inserted in the active worksheet. You can move the chart to a new sheet within the workbook with the *New sheet* option at the Move Chart dialog box.
- To delete a chart in a worksheet, click the chart to select it, and then press the Delete key. To delete a chart created in a separate sheet, position the mouse pointer on the chart tab, click the right mouse button, and then click Delete.
- Use options in the Chart Tools Layout tab to change the layout and/or insert additional chart labels, shapes, pictures, or clip art images.
- Insert additional chart labels with options in the Labels group in the Chart Tools Layout tab.
- Use buttons in the Insert group in the Chart Tools Layout tab to insert shapes, pictures, or text boxes.
- To move a chart label, click the label to select it and then drag the label with the mouse. To delete a label, click the label and then press the Delete key.
- Use options in the Chart Tools Format tab to customize the format of the chart and chart elements.
- Change the chart size by dragging the chart sizing handles or by entering a measurement in the *Shape Height* and *Shape Width* measurement boxes in the Size group in the Chart Tools Format tab.

Commands Review

FEATURE	RIBBON TAB, GROUP	BUTTON, OPTION	KEYBOARD SHORTCUT
Default chart in worksheet			Alt + F1
Default chart in separate sheet			F11
Change Chart Type dialog box	Chart Tools Design, Type		
Move Chart dialog box	Chart Tools Design, Location		
Shapes button drop-down list	Chart Tools Layout, Insert		
Insert Picture dialog box	Chart Tools Layout, Insert		

Concepts Check Test Your Knowledge

Completion: In the space provided at the right, indicate the correct term, symbol, or command.

1. This is the keyboard shortcut to create a chart with the default chart type in the active worksheet.

2. The Charts group contains buttons for creating charts and is located in this tab.

3. This type of chart shows proportions and relationships of parts to the whole.

4. When you create a chart, the chart is inserted in this location by default.

5. Select a chart in a worksheet, display the Print tab Backstage view, and the first gallery in the Settings category is automatically changed to this option.

6. Use buttons in the Insert group in this tab to insert shapes or pictures.

7. When Excel creates a chart, the data in the first row (except the first cell) is used to create this.

8. Click this option at the Move Chart dialog box to move the chart to a separate sheet.

9. Click the Picture button in the Chart Tools Layout tab and this dialog box displays.

10. Change the chart size by entering measurements in these measurement boxes in the Size group in the Chart Tools Format tab.

Skills Check Assess Your Performance

Assessment 1   CREATE A COMPANY SALES COLUMN CHART

1. Open **CMSales.xlsx** and then save the workbook with Save As and name it **EL1-C7-A1-CMSales**.
2. Select cells A3 through C15 and then create a Column chart with the following specifications:
    a. Choose the *3-D Clustered Column* chart at the Chart button drop-down list.
    b. At the Chart Tools Design tab, click the *Layout 3* option in the Chart Layouts group.
    c. Change the chart style to *Style 26*.
    d. Select the text *Chart Title* and then type **Company Sales**.
    e. Move the location of the chart to a new sheet.
3. Print only the worksheet containing the chart.
4. Save and then close **EL1-C7-A1-CMSales.xlsx**.

Assessment 2   CREATE QUARTERLY DOMESTIC AND FOREIGN SALES BAR CHART

1. Open **CMPQtrlySales.xlsx** and then save the workbook with Save As and name it **EL1-C7-A2-CMPQtrlySales**.
2. Select cells A3 through E5 and then create a Bar chart with the following specifications:
    a. Click the *Clustered Bar in 3-D* option at the Bar button drop-down list.
    b. At the Chart Tools Design tab choose the *Layout 2* option in the Chart Layouts group.
    c. Choose the *Style 23* option in the Chart Styles group.
    d. Select the text *Chart Title*, type **Quarterly Sales**, and then click in the chart but outside any chart elements.
    e. Display the Chart Tools Layout tab and then insert primary vertical minor gridlines. (Do this with the Gridlines button.)
    f. Display the Chart Tools Format tab and then apply to the chart the *Subtle Effect - Olive Green, Accent 3* option in the Shape Styles group.
    g. Select the *Domestic* series (using the Chart Elements button) and then apply a purple fill (*Purple, Accent 4, Darker 25%*) using the Shape Fill button in the Shape Styles group.
    h. Select the Foreign series and then apply a dark aqua fill (*Aqua, Accent 5, Darker 25%*) using the Shape Fill button in the Shape Styles group.

i. Select the chart title and then apply the *Gradient Fill - Purple, Accent 4, Reflection* option with the WordArt Styles button.
j. Increase the height of the chart to 4 inches and the width to 6 inches.
k. Move the chart below the cells containing data and make sure the chart fits on the page with the data.
3. Print only the worksheet.
4. Save and then close **EL1-C7-A2-CMPQtrlySales.xlsx**.

Assessment 3 CREATE AND FORMAT A CORPORATE SALES COLUMN CHART

1. Open **CorpSales.xlsx** and then save the workbook with Save As and name it **EL1-C7-A3-CorpSales**.
2. Create a column chart and format the chart so it displays as shown in Figure 7.12.
3. Save, print, and then close **EL1-C7-A3-CorpSales.xlsx**.

Figure 7.12 Assessment 3

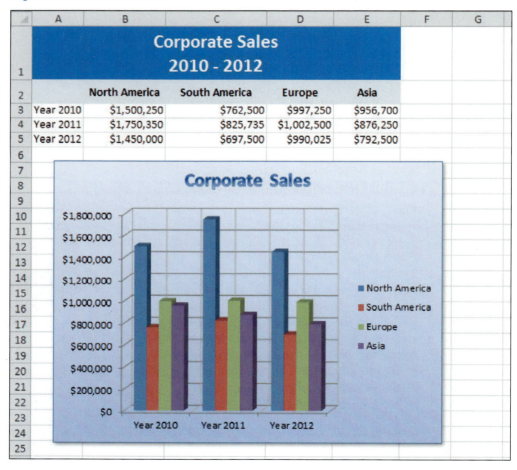

Assessment 4 CREATE A FUND ALLOCATIONS PIE CHART

1. At a blank worksheet, create a worksheet with the following data:

   Fund Allocations

Fund	Percentage
Annuities	23%
Stocks	42%
Bonds	15%
Money Market	20%

2. Using the data above, create a pie chart as a separate worksheet with the following specifications:
   a. Create a title for the pie chart.
   b. Add data labels to the chart.
   c. Add any other enhancements that will improve the visual presentation of the data.
3. Save the workbook and name it **EL1-C7-A4-Funds**.
4. Print only the worksheet containing the chart.
5. Close **EL1-C7-A4-Funds.xlsx**.

Assessment 5 CREATE AN ACTUAL AND PROJECTED SALES CHART

1. Open **StateSales.xlsx** and then save the workbook with Save As and name it **EL1-C7-A5-StateSales**.
2. Look at the data in the worksheet and then create a chart to represent the data. Add a title to the chart and add any other enhancements to improve the visual display of the chart.
3. Save the workbook and then print the chart.
4. Close **EL1-C7-A5-StateSales.xlsx**.

Assessment 6 CREATE A STACKED CYLINDER CHART

1. Use Excel's help feature to learn more about chart types and specifically about stacked 3-D column charts and then create a worksheet with the data shown in Figure 7.13. Create with the data a 100% stacked cylinder chart in a separate sheet. Create an appropriate title for the chart and apply any other formatting to enhance the appearance of the chart.
2. Save the completed workbook and name it **EL1-C7-A6-CMPerSales**.
3. Print both sheets of the workbook (the sheet containing the data in cells and the sheet containing the chart).
4. Close **EL1-C7-A6-CMPerSales.xlsx**.

Figure 7.13 Assessment 6

Clearline Manufacturing
Regional Sales Percentages

	Region 1	Region 2	Region 3	Region 4
Jan-June	12%	20%	41%	27%
July-Dec	16%	27%	35%	22%

Visual Benchmark Demonstrate Your Proficiency

CREATE AND FORMAT A PIE CHART

1. At a blank workbook, enter data and then create a pie chart in a separate sheet as shown in Figure 7.14. Use the information shown in the pie chart to create the data. Format the pie chart so it appears similar to what you see in Figure 7.14.
2. Save the completed workbook and name it **EL1-C7-VB-CMFebExp**.
3. Print both worksheets in the workbook.
4. Close **EL1-C7-VB-CMFebExp.xlsx**

Figure 7.14 Visual Benchmark

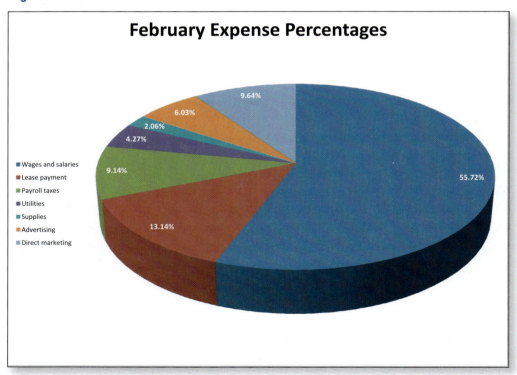

Case Study Apply Your Skills

Part 1

You are an administrator for Dollar Wise Financial Services and you need to prepare charts indicating home loan and commercial loan amounts for the past year. Use the information below to prepare a chart in Excel. You determine the type and style of chart and the layout and formatting of the chart. Insert a shape in the Commercial Loans chart that contains the text *All-time High* and points to the second quarter amount (*$6,785,250*).

Home Loans
- 1st Qtr. = $2,675,025
- 2nd Qtr. = $3,125,750
- 3rd Qtr. = $1,975,425
- 4th Qtr. = $875,650

Commercial Loans
- 1st Qtr. = $5,750,980
- 2nd Qtr. = $6,785,250
- 3rd Qtr. = $4,890,625
- 4th Qtr. = $2,975,900

Save the workbook and name it **EL1-C7-CS-DWQtrSales**. Print only the chart and then close **EL1-C7-CS-DWQtrSales.xlsx**.

Part 2

You need to present information on the budget for the company. You have the dollar amounts and need to convert the amounts to a percentage of the entire budget. Use the information below to calculate the percentage of the budget for each item and then create a pie chart with the information. You determine the chart style, layout, and formatting.

Total Budget: $6,000,000
- Building Costs = $720,000
- Salaries = $2,340,000
- Benefits = $480,000
- Advertising = $840,000
- Marketing = $600,000
- Client Expenses = $480,000
- Equipment = $420,000
- Supplies = $120,000

Save the workbook containing the pie chart and name it **EL1-C7-CS-DWBudgetPercentages**. Print only the chart and then close **EL1-C7-CS-DWBudgetPercentages.xlsx**.

Part 3

One of your clients owns a number of stocks and you would like to prepare a daily chart of the stocks' high, low, and close price. Use the Help feature to learn about stock charts and then create a stock chart with the following information (the company stock symbols are fictitious):

	IDE	POE	QRR
High	$23.75	$18.55	$34.30
Low	$18.45	$15.00	$31.70
Close	$19.65	$17.30	$33.50

Save the workbook containing the stock chart and name it **EL1-C7-CS-DWStocks**. Print only the chart and then close **EL1-C7-CS-DWStocks.xlsx**.

Part 4

You need to prepare information on mortgage rates for a community presentation. You decide to include the information on mortgage rates in a chart for easy viewing. Use the Internet to search for historical data on the national average for mortgage rates. Determine the average mortgage rate for a 30-year FRM (fixed-rate mortgage) for each January and July beginning with the year 2008 and continuing to the current year. Also include the current average rate. Use this information to create the chart. Save the workbook and name it **EL1-C7-CS-DWRates**. Print only the chart and then close **EL1-C7-CS-DWRates.xlsx**.

Microsoft Excel
Adding Visual Interest to Workbooks

CHAPTER 8

PERFORMANCE OBJECTIVES

Upon successful completion of Chapter 8, you will be able to:
- Insert symbols and special characters
- Insert, size, move, and format a clip art image
- Insert a screenshot
- Draw, format, and copy shapes
- Insert, size, move, and format a picture image
- Insert, format, and type text in a text box
- Insert a picture image as a watermark
- Insert and format SmartArt diagrams
- Insert and format WordArt

Microsoft Excel includes a variety of features that you can use to enhance the visual appeal of a workbook. Some methods for adding visual appeal that you will learn in this chapter include inserting and modifying clip art images, screenshots, shapes, pictures, text boxes, SmartArt, and WordArt. Model answers for this chapter's projects appear on the following pages.

Excel2010L1C8

Note: Before beginning the projects, copy to your storage medium the Excel2010L1C8 subfolder from the Excel2010L1 folder on the CD that accompanies this textbook and make Excel2010L1C8 the active folder.

Model Answers

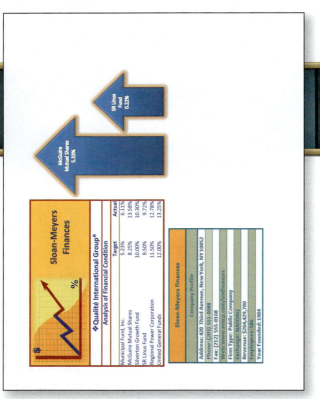

Project 1 Insert a Clip Art Image and Shapes in a Financial Analysis Workbook
EL1-C8-P1-SFFinCon.xlsx

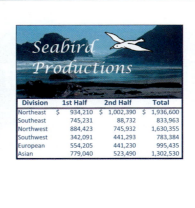

Project 2 Insert a Picture and Text Box in a Division Sales Workbook
EL1-C8-P2-SPDivSales.xlsx

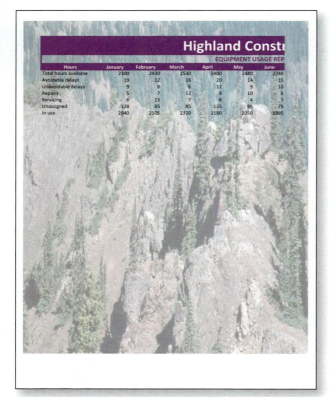

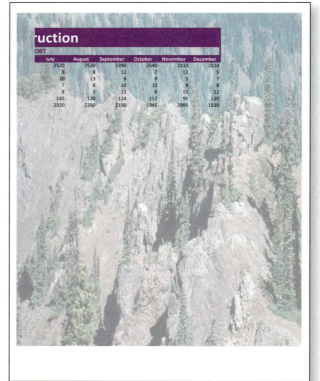

Project 3 Insert a Watermark in an Equipment Usage Workbook
EL1-C8-P3-HCEqpRpt.xlsx

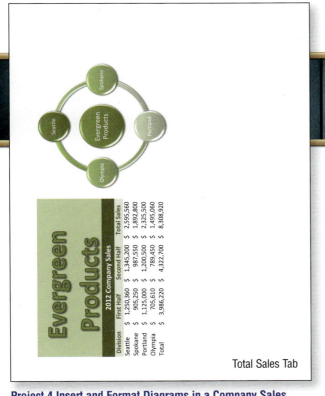
Total Sales Tab

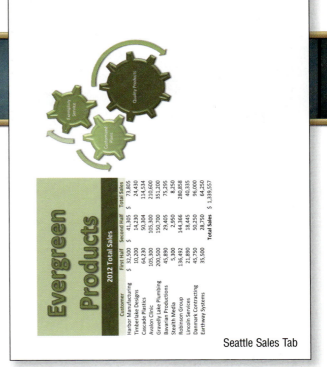
Seattle Sales Tab

Project 4 Insert and Format Diagrams in a Company Sales Workbook
EL1-C8-P4-EPSales.xlsx

 **1** **Insert a Clip Art Image and Shapes in a Financial Analysis Workbook** **5 Parts**

You will open a financial analysis workbook and then insert, move, size, and format a clip art image in the workbook. You will also insert an arrow shape, type and format text in the shape, and then copy the shape.

Inserting Symbols and Special Characters

You can use the Symbol button in the Insert tab to insert special symbols in a worksheet. Click the Symbol button in the Symbols group in the Insert tab and the Symbol dialog box displays as shown in Figure 8.1. At the Symbol dialog box, double-click the desired symbol and then click Close; or click the desired symbol, click the Insert button, and then click Close. At the Symbol dialog box with the Symbols tab selected, you can change the font with the *Font* option. When you change the font, different symbols display in the dialog box. Click the Special Characters tab at the Symbol dialog box and a list of special characters displays along with keyboard shortcuts to create the special character.

▼ **Quick Steps**

Insert Symbol
1. Click in desired cell.
2. Click the Insert tab.
3. Click Symbol button.
4. Double-click desired symbol.
5. Click Close.

Symbol

Chapter 8 ■ Adding Visual Interest to Workbooks

▼ **Quick Steps**

Insert Special Character
1. Click in desired cell.
2. Click Insert tab.
3. Click Symbol button.
4. Click Special Characters tab.
5. Double-click desired special character.
6. Click Close.

HINT

You can increase or decrease the size of the Symbol dialog box by positioning the mouse pointer on the lower right corner until the pointer displays as a two-headed arrow and then dragging with the mouse.

Figure 8.1 Symbol Dialog Box with Symbols Tab Selected

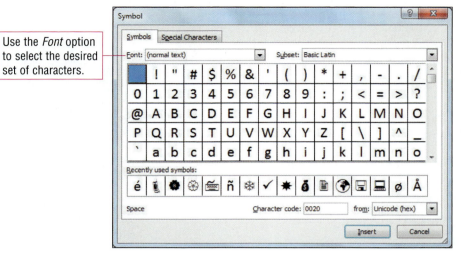

Use the *Font* option to select the desired set of characters.

Project 1a — Inserting Symbols and Special Characters — Part 1 of 5

1. Open **SFFinCon.xlsx** and then save the workbook with Save As and name it **EL1-C8-P1-SFFinCon**.
2. Insert a symbol by completing the following steps:
   a. Double-click cell A2.
   b. Delete the *e* that displays at the end of *Qualite*.
   c. With the insertion point positioned immediately right of the *t* in *Qualit*, click the Insert tab.
   d. Click the Symbol button in the Symbols group.
   e. At the Symbol dialog box, scroll down the list box and then click the *é* symbol (located in approximately the tenth or eleventh row).
   f. Click the Insert button and then click the Close button.

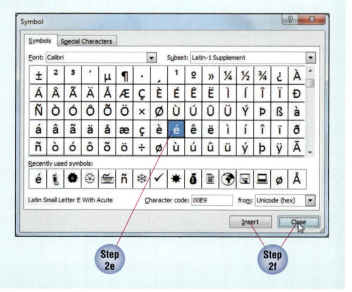

Step 2e

Step 2f

274   Excel Level 1 ■ Unit 2

3. Insert a special character by completing the following steps:
   a. With cell A2 selected and in Edit mode, move the insertion point so it is positioned immediately right of *Group*.
   b. Click the Symbol button in the Symbols group.
   c. At the Symbol dialog box, click the Special Characters tab.
   d. Double-click the ® symbol (tenth option from the top).
   e. Click the Close button.
4. Insert a symbol by completing the following steps:
   a. With cell A2 selected and in Edit mode, move the insertion point so it is positioned immediately left of the *Q* in *Qualité*.
   b. Click the Symbol button in the Symbols group.
   c. At the Symbol dialog box, click the down-pointing arrow at the right side of the *Font* option box and then click *Wingdings* at the drop-down list. (You will need to scroll down the list to display this option.)
   d. Click the ❖ symbol (located in approximately the sixth row).
   e. Click the Insert button and then click the Close button.
5. Click in cell A3.
6. Save **EL1-C8-P1-SFFinCon.xlsx**.

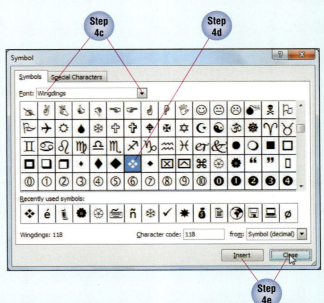

Inserting an Image

You can insert an image such as a picture or clip art in an Excel workbook with buttons in the Illustrations group in the Insert tab. Click the Picture button to display the Insert Picture dialog box where you can specify the desired picture file, or click the Clip Art button and then choose from a variety of images available at the Clip Art task pane. When you insert a picture or a clip art image in a worksheet, the Picture Tools Format tab displays as shown in Figure 8.2.

Picture

Figure 8.2 Picture Tools Format Tab

Chapter 8 ■ Adding Visual Interest to Workbooks

Customizing and Formatting an Image

With buttons in the Adjust group in the Picture Tools Format tab you can recolor the picture or clip art image, correct its brightness and contrast, and apply artistic effects. Use the Remove Background button to remove unwanted portions of the image. You can reset the picture or clip art back to its original color or change to a different image. You can also compress the size of the image file with the Compress Pictures button. Compressing the size of an image is a good idea because it reduces the amount of space the image requires on your storage medium.

Compress Pictures

Crop

With buttons in the Picture Styles group, you can apply a predesigned style to your image, change the image border, or apply other effects to the image. With options in the Arrange group, you can position the image in the worksheet, specify how text will wrap around it, align the image with other elements in the worksheet, and rotate the image. With the Crop button in the Size group, you can remove any unnecessary parts of the image and specify the image size with the *Shape Height* and *Shape Width* measurement boxes.

Sizing and Moving an Image

You can change the size of an image with the *Shape Height* and *Shape Width* measurement boxes in the Size group in the Picture Tools Format tab or with the sizing handles that display around the selected image. To change size with a sizing handle, position the mouse pointer on a sizing handle until the pointer turns into a double-headed arrow and then hold down the left mouse button. Drag the sizing handle in or out to decrease or increase the size of the image and then release the mouse button. Use the middle sizing handles at the left or right side of the image to make the image wider or thinner. Use the middle sizing handles at the top or bottom of the image to make the image taller or shorter. Use the sizing handles at the corners of the image to change both the width and height at the same time. Hold down the Shift key while dragging a sizing handle to maintain the proportions of the image.

HINT You can use arrow keys on the keyboard to move a selected object. To move the image in small increments, hold down the Ctrl key while pressing one of the arrow keys.

Move an image by positioning the mouse pointer on the image border until the pointer displays with a four-headed arrow attached. Hold down the left mouse button, drag the image to the desired position, and then release the mouse button. Rotate the image by positioning the mouse pointer on the green, round rotation handle until the pointer displays as a circular arrow. Hold down the left mouse button, drag in the desired direction, and then release the mouse button.

Project 1b Formatting an Image Part 2 of 5

1. With **EL1-C8-P1-SFFinCon.xlsx** open, scroll down the worksheet and then click the Wall Street image to select it. (This image is located below the cells containing data.)
2. Remove the yellow background from the image by completing the following steps:
   a. Click the Picture Tools Format tab.
   b. Click the Remove Background button in the Adjust group in the Picture Tools Format tab.

c. Position the mouse pointer on the middle sizing handle at the top of the image until the pointer displays as a two-headed arrow pointing up and down.
d. Hold down the left mouse button, drag the border up to the top of the image, and then release the mouse.
e. Position the mouse pointer on the middle sizing handle at the bottom of the image until the pointer displays as a two-headed arrow pointing up and down.
f. Hold down the left mouse button, drag the border down to the bottom of the image, and then release the mouse button.
g. Click the Keep Changes button in the Close group in the Background Removal tab.
3. Change the color by clicking the Color button in the Adjust group and then clicking the *Blue, Accent color 1 Light* color (second color from the left in the third row of the *Recolor* section).
4. Apply a correction by clicking the Corrections button and then clicking the *Brightness: +20% Contrast: +20%* option (fourth option from the left in the fourth row in the *Brightness and Contrast* section).

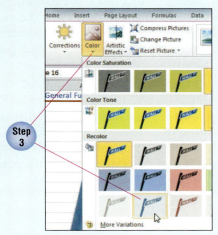
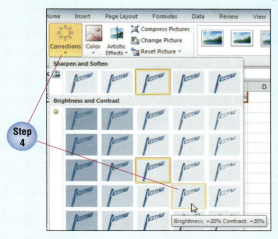

5. Apply an artistic effect by clicking the Artistic Effects button and then clicking the Glow Edges option (last option in the drop-down gallery).
6. Click in the *Height* measurement box in the Size group, type 2, and then press Enter.
7. Move the image by completing the following steps:
   a. Position the mouse pointer on the image (displays with a four-headed arrow attached).
   b. Hold down the left mouse button, drag the image to the upper left corner of the worksheet, and then release the mouse button.

8. Save and then print **EL1-C8-P1-SFFinCon.xlsx**.

Inserting a Clip Art Image

Quick Steps

Insert Clip Art Image
1. Click Insert tab.
2. Click Clip Art button.
3. Type desired word or topic in *Search for* text box.
4. Click Go button or press Enter.
5. Click desired image.

Clip Art

Microsoft Office includes a gallery of media images you can insert in a worksheet. The gallery includes clip art, photographs, and movie images, as well as sound clips. To insert an image, click the Insert tab and then click the Clip Art button in the Illustrations group. This displays the Clip Art task pane at the right side of the screen, as shown in Figure 8.3.

To view all picture, sound, and motion files available in the gallery, make sure the *Search for* text box in the Clip Art task pane does not contain any text and then click the Go button. Scroll through the images that display until you find one you want to use and then click the image to insert it in the worksheet. Use buttons in the Picture Tools Format tab (see Figure 8.2 on page 275) to format and customize the clip art image.

If you are searching for a specific type of image, click in the *Search for* text box, type a category and then click the Go button. For example, if you want to find images related to business, click in the *Search for* text box, type *business*, and then click the Go button. Clip art images related to business display in the viewing area of the task pane. If you are connected to the Internet, Word will search for images matching the word or topic at the Office.com website. You can drag a clip art image from the Clip Art task pane to your worksheet.

Unless the Clip Art task pane default setting has been customized, the task pane displays all illustrations, photographs, videos, and audio files. The *Results should be* option has a default setting of *Selected media file types*. Click the down-pointing arrow at the right of this option to display media types. To search for a specific media type, remove the check mark before all options at the drop-down list except for the desired type. For example, if you are searching only for photograph images, remove the check mark before *Illustrations*, *Videos*, and *Audio*.

Figure 8.3 Clip Art Task Pane

Project 1c   **Inserting and Formatting a Clip Art Image**   Part 3 of 5

1. With **EL1-C8-P1-SFFinCon.xlsx** open, delete the Wall Street sign image by clicking the image and then pressing the Delete key.
2. Insert a clip art image by completing the following steps:
    a. Make cell A1 active.
    b. Click the Insert tab and then click the Clip Art button in the Illustrations group.
    c. At the Clip Art task pane, click the down-pointing arrow at the right of the *Results should be* option box and then click in the *Photographs*, *Videos*, and *Audio* check boxes to remove the check marks. (The *Illustrations* check box should be the only one with a check mark.)

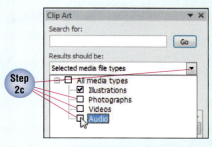
Step 2c

    d. Select any text that displays in the *Search for* text box, type **stock market**, and then press the Enter key.
    e. Click the image in the list box as shown at the right. (You will need to scroll down the list box to display the image. If this image is not available, click a similar image.)
    f. Click the down-pointing arrow at the right of the *Results should be* option box and then click in the *All media types* check box to insert check marks in all of the check boxes.
    g. Close the Clip Art task pane by clicking the Close button (contains an X) located in the upper right corner of the task pane.

Step 2d

Step 2e

3. Apply a correction by clicking the Corrections button in the Adjust group in the Picture Tools Format tab and then clicking the *Brightness: -20% Contrast: +40%* option (second option from the left in the bottom row of the drop-down gallery).
4. Apply a picture style by clicking the More button that displays at the right side of the thumbnails in the Picture Styles group and then clicking the *Soft Edge Rectangle* option.

Step 4

5. Increase the width of the image by completing the following steps:
    a. Position the mouse pointer on the middle sizing handle at the right side of the image until the pointer displays as a two-headed arrow pointing left and right.
    b. Hold down the left mouse button, drag to the right until the right edge of the image border aligns with the right edge of column A, and then release the mouse button.
6. Click outside the clip art image to deselect it.
7. Save **EL1-C8-P1-SFFinCon.xlsx**.

Creating Screenshots

The Illustrations group in the Insert tab contains a Screenshot button you can use to capture the contents of a screen as an image or capture a portion of a screen. This is useful for capturing information from a web page or from a file in

Screenshot

Chapter 8 ■ Adding Visual Interest to Workbooks   **279**

▼ **Quick Steps**

Insert Screenshot
1. Open workbook.
2. Open another file.
3. Display desired information.
4. Make workbook active.
5. Click Insert tab.
6. Click Screenshot button.
7. Click desired window at drop-down list.
OR
6. Click Screenshot button, Screen Clipping.
7. Drag to specify capture area.

another program. If you want to capture the entire screen, display the desired web page or open the desired file from a program, make Excel active, and then open a workbook or a blank workbook. Click the Insert tab, click the Screenshot button, and then click the desired screen thumbnail at the drop-down list. The currently active worksheet does not display as a thumbnail at the drop-down list, only any other file or program you have open. If you do not have another file or program open, the Windows desktop displays. When you click the desired thumbnail, the screenshot is inserted as an image in the open workbook, the image is selected, and the Picture Tools Format tab is active. Use buttons in this tab to customize the screenshot image.

In addition to making a screenshot of an entire screen, you can make a screenshot of a specific portion of the screen by clicking the *Screen Clipping* option at the Screenshot button drop-down list. When you click this option, the open web page, file, or Windows desktop displays in a dimmed manner and the mouse pointer displays as crosshairs. Using the mouse, draw a border around the specific area of the screen you want to capture. The specific area you identify is inserted in the workbook as an image, the image is selected, and the Picture Tools Format tab is active. If you have only one workbook or file open when you click the Screenshot tab, clicking the *Screen Clipping* option will cause the Windows desktop to display.

Project 1d Inserting and Formatting a Screenshot   Part 4 of 5

1. With **EL1-C8-P1-SFFinCon.xlsx** open, make sure that no other programs are open.
2. Open Word and then open the document named **SFCoProfile.docx** from the Excel2010L1C8 folder on your storage medium.
3. Click the Excel button on the Taskbar.
4. Insert a screenshot of the table in the Word document by completing the following steps:
   a. Click the Insert tab.
   b. Click the Screenshot button in the Illustrations group and then click *Screen Clipping* at the drop-down list.
   c. When the **SFCoProfile.docx** document displays in a dimmed manner, position the mouse crosshairs in the upper left corner of the table, hold down the left mouse button, drag down to the lower right corner of the table, and then release the mouse button. (See image at the right.)
5. With the screenshot image inserted in the **EL1-C8-P1-SFFinCon.xlsx** workbook, make the following changes:
   a. Click in the *Width* measurement box in the Size group in the Picture Tools Format tab, type 3.7, and then press Enter.

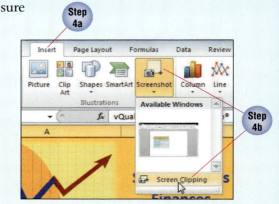

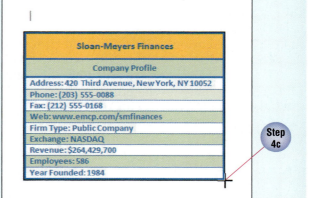

b. Click the Corrections button and then click the *Sharpen 25%* option (fourth option from the left in the *Sharpen and Soften* section).

c. Click the Corrections button and then click the *Brightness: 0% (Normal) Contrast: -40%* (third option from the left in the top row in the *Brightness and Contrast* section).

d. Using the mouse, drag the screenshot image one row below the data in row 10.

6. Make cell A4 active.
7. Save **EL1-C8-P1-SFFinCon.xlsx**.
8. Click the Word button, close **SFCoProfile.docx**, and then exit Word.

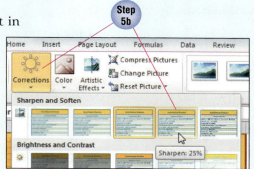

Step 5b

Inserting and Copying Shapes

In Chapter 7, you learned how to insert shapes in a chart. With the Shapes button in the Illustrations group in the Insert tab, you can also insert shapes in a worksheet. Use the Shapes button in the Insert tab to draw shapes in a worksheet including lines, basic shapes, block arrows, flow chart shapes, callouts, stars, and banners. Click a shape and the mouse pointer displays as crosshairs (plus sign). Position the crosshairs where you want the shape to begin, hold down the left mouse button, drag to create the shape, and then release the mouse button. This inserts the shape in the worksheet and also displays the Drawing Tools Format tab shown in Figure 8.4. Use buttons in this tab to change the shape, apply a style to the shape, arrange the shape, and change the size of the shape.

If you choose a shape in the *Lines* section of the Shapes button drop-down list, the shape you draw is considered a line drawing. If you choose an option in the other sections of the drop-down list, the shape you draw is considered an enclosed object. When drawing an enclosed object, you can maintain the proportions of the shape by holding down the Shift key while dragging with the mouse to create the shape. You can type text in an enclosed object and then use buttons in the WordArt Styles group to format the text.

If you have drawn or inserted a shape, you may want to copy it to other locations in the worksheet. To copy a shape, select the shape and then click the Copy button in the Clipboard group in the Home tab. Position the insertion point at the location where you want the copied image and then click the Paste button. You can also copy a selected shape by holding down the Ctrl key while dragging the shape to the desired location.

▼ **Quick Steps**

Insert Shape
1. Click Insert tab.
2. Click Shapes button.
3. Click desired shape at drop-down list.
4. Drag in worksheet to create shape.

Copy Shape
1. Select shape.
2. Click Copy button.
3. Position insertion point in desired location.
4. Click Paste button.
OR
1. Select shape.
2. Hold down Ctrl key.
3. Drag shape to desired location.

Shapes

Figure 8.4 Drawing Tools Format Tab

Chapter 8 ■ Adding Visual Interest to Workbooks   281

Project 1e **Drawing Arrow Shapes** Part 5 of 5

1. With **EL1-C8-P1-SFFinCon.xlsx** open, create the tallest arrow shown in Figure 8.5 on page 284 by completing the following steps:
   a. Click the Insert tab.
   b. Click the Shapes button and then click the *Up Arrow* shape (third option from the left in the top row of the *Block Arrows* section).

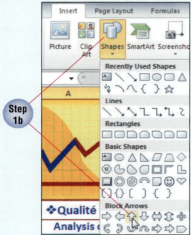

   c. Position the mouse pointer (displays as a thin, black cross) near the upper left corner of cell D1, hold down the left mouse button, drag down and to the right to create the shape as shown below, and then release the mouse button.
   d. Click in the *Shape Height* measurement box and then type **3.7**.
   e. Click in the *Shape Width* measurement box, type **2.1**, and then press Enter.
   f. If necessary, drag the arrow so it is positioned as shown in Figure 8.5. (To drag the arrow, position the mouse pointer on the border of the selected arrow until the pointer turns into a four-headed arrow, hold down the left mouse button, drag the arrow to the desired position, and then release the mouse button.)
   g. Click the More button at the right side of the thumbnails in the Shape Styles group in the Drawing Tools Format tab and then click the *Intense Effect - Blue, Accent 1* option (second option from the left in the bottom row).

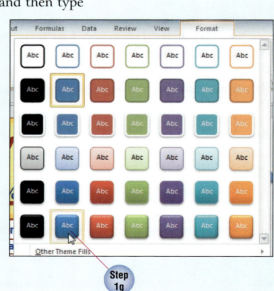

282 Excel Level 1 ■ Unit 2

h. Click the Shape Effects button in the Shape Styles group, point to *Glow*, and then click the last option in the third row in the *Glow Variations* section (*Orange, 11 pt glow, Accent color 6*).

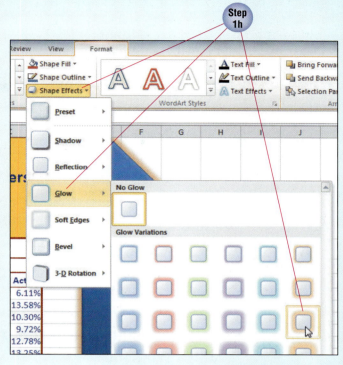

Step 1h

2. Insert text in the arrow shape by completing the following steps:
   a. With the arrow shape selected, type **McGuire Mutual Shares 5.33%**.
   b. Select the text you just typed (*McGuire Mutual Shares 5.33%*).
   c. Click the More button at the right side of the thumbnails in the WordArt Styles group and then click the third option from the left in the top row (*Fill - White, Drop Shadow*).
   d. Click the Home tab.
   e. Click the Center button in the Alignment group.

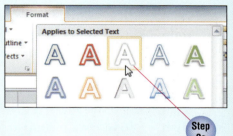

Step 2c

3. With the arrow selected, copy the arrow by completing the following steps:
   a. Hold down the Ctrl key.
   b. Position the mouse pointer on the arrow border until the pointer displays with a square box and plus symbol attached.
   c. Hold down the left mouse button and drag to the right so the outline of the arrow is positioned at the right side of the existing arrow.
   d. Release the mouse button and then release the Ctrl key.
4. Format the second arrow by completing the following steps:
   a. With the second arrow selected, click the Drawing Tools Format tab.
   b. Click in the *Shape Height* measurement box and then type **2**.
   c. Click in the *Shape Width* measurement box, type **1.6**, and then press Enter.
   d. Select the text *McGuire Mutual Shares 5.33%* and then type **SR Linus Fund 0.22%**.
   e. Drag the arrow so it is positioned as shown in Figure 8.5.
5. Change the orientation to landscape. (Make sure the cells containing data, the screenshot image, and the arrows will print on the same page.)
6. Save, print, and then close **EL1-C8-P1-SFFinCon.xlsx**.

Figure 8.5 Project 1e

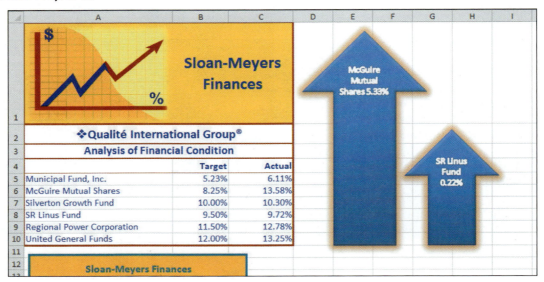

Project 2 — Insert a Picture and Text Box in a Division Sales Workbook   2 Parts

You will open a division sales workbook and then insert, move, and size a picture. You will also insert a text box and then format the text.

▼ **Quick Steps**

Insert Picture
1. Click Insert tab.
2. Click Picture button.
3. Navigate to desired folder.
4. Double-click desired picture.

Pictures

Inserting a Picture

To insert a picture in a worksheet, click the Insert tab and then click the Picture button in the Illustrations group. At the Insert Picture dialog box, navigate to the folder containing the desired picture and then double-click the picture. Use buttons in the Picture Tools Format tab to format and customize the picture.

Project 2a   Inserting and Customizing a Picture   Part 1 of 2

1. Open **SPDivSales.xlsx** and then save the workbook with Save As and name it **EL1-C8-P2-SPDivSales**.
2. Make the following changes to the bird clip art image:
   a. Click the bird clip art image to select it.
   b. Click the Picture Tools Format tab.
   c. Click the Rotate button in the Arrange group and then click *Flip Horizontal* at the drop-down list.

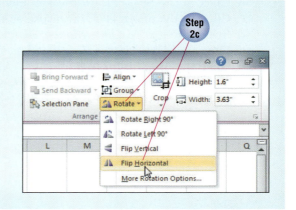

284   Excel Level 1 ■ Unit 2

d. Click the Color button in the Adjust group and then click the *Black and White: 75%* option in the *Recolor* section (last option in the top row).
e. Click in the *Shape Height* measurement box, type **0.6**, and then press Enter.

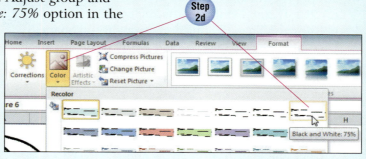

3. Insert and format a picture by completing the following steps:
   a. Click in cell A1 outside of the bird image.
   b. Click the Insert tab.
   c. Click the Picture button in the Illustrations group.
   d. At the Insert Picture dialog box, navigate to the Excel2010L1C8 folder on your storage medium and then double-click **Ocean.jpg**.
   e. With the picture selected, click the Send Backward button in the Arrange group in the Picture Tools Format tab.
   f. Use the sizing handles that display around the picture image to move and size it so it fills cell A1 as shown in Figure 8.6.
   g. Click the bird clip art image and then drag the image so it is positioned as shown in Figure 8.6.
4. Save **EL1-C8-P2-SPDivSales.xlsx**.

Drawing and Formatting a Text Box

Use the Text Box button in the Insert tab to draw a text box in a worksheet. To draw a text box, click the Insert tab and then click the Text Box button in the Text group. This causes the mouse pointer to display as a long, thin, cross-like pointer. Position the pointer in the worksheet and then drag to create the text box. When a text box is selected, the Drawing Tools Format tab displays with options for customizing the text box.

Click a text box to select it and a dashed border and sizing handles display around the text box. If you want to delete the text box, click the text box border again to change the dashed border lines to solid border lines and then press the Delete key.

▼ **Quick Steps**
Draw Text Box
1. Click Insert tab.
2. Click Text Box button.
3. Drag in worksheet to create text box.

Text Box

Project 2b   Inserting and Formatting a Text Box   Part 2 of 2

1. With **EL1-C8-P2-SPDivSales.xlsx** open, draw a text box by completing the following steps:
   a. Click the Insert tab.
   b. Click the Text Box button in the Text group.
   c. Drag in cell A1 to draw a text box the approximate size and shape shown at the right.

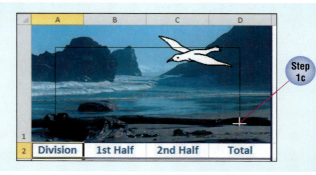

Chapter 8 ■ Adding Visual Interest to Workbooks   **285**

2. Format the text box by completing the following steps:
   a. Click the Drawing Tools Format tab.
   b. Click the Shape Fill button arrow in the Shape Styles group and then click *No Fill* at the drop-down gallery.
   c. Click the Shape Outline button arrow in the Shape Styles group and then click *No Outline* at the drop-down gallery.
3. Insert text in the text box by completing the following steps:
   a. With the text box selected, click the Home tab.
   b. Click the Font button arrow and then click *Lucida Calligraphy* at the drop-down gallery. (You will need to scroll down the gallery to display this font.)
   c. Click the Font Size button arrow and then click *32* at the drop-down gallery.
   d. Click the Font Color button arrow and then click *White, Background 1* (first option in the first row in the *Theme Colors* section).
   e. Type **Seabird Productions**.
4. Move the text box so the text is positioned in cell A1 as shown in Figure 8.6. If necessary, move the bird clip art image. (To move the bird image, you may need to move the text box so you can select the image. Move the text box back to the desired location after moving the bird image.)
5. Save, print, and then close **EL1-C8-P2-SPDivSales.xlsx**.

Figure 8.6 Projects 2a and 2b

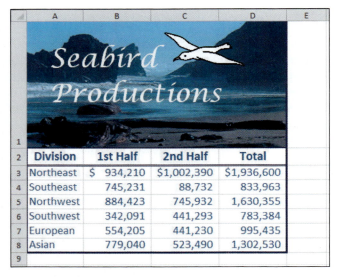

Project 3 Insert a Watermark in an Equipment Usage Workbook   1 Part

You will open an equipment usage report workbook and then insert a picture as a watermark that prints on both pages of the worksheet.

Inserting a Picture as a Watermark

A *watermark* is a lightened image that displays behind data in a file. You can create a watermark in a Word document but the watermark functionality is not available in Excel. You can, however, insert a picture in a header or footer and then resize and format the picture to display behind each page of the worksheet.

To create a picture watermark in a worksheet, click the Insert tab and then click the Header & Footer button in the Text group. With the worksheet in Print Layout view, click the Picture button in the Header & Footer Elements group in the Header & Footer Tools Design tab. At the Insert Picture dialog box, navigate to the desired folder and then double-click the desired picture. This inserts &*[Picture]* in the header. Resize and format the picture by clicking the Format Picture button in the Header & Footer Elements group. Use options at the Format Picture dialog box with the Size tab selected to specify the size of the picture and use options in the dialog box with the Picture tab selected to specify brightness and contrast.

▼ Quick Steps

Insert Picture as Watermark
1. Click Insert tab.
2. Click Header & Footer button.
3. Click Picture button.
4. Navigate to desired folder.
5. Double-click desired picture.

Format Picture

Project 3 — Inserting a Picture as a Watermark — Part 1 of 1

1. Open **HCEqpRpt.xlsx** and then save the workbook with Save As and name it **EL1-C8-P3-HCEqpRpt**.
2. Insert a picture as a watermark by completing the following steps:
   a. Click the Insert tab.
   b. Click the Header & Footer button in the Text group.
   c. Click the Picture button in the Header & Footer Elements group in the Header & Footer Tools Design tab.
   d. At the Insert Picture dialog box, navigate to the Excel2010L1C8 folder on your storage medium and then double-click **Olympics.jpg**.
   e. Click the Format Picture button in the Header & Footer Elements group.
   f. At the Format Picture dialog box with the Size tab selected, click the *Lock aspect ratio* check box in the *Scale* section to remove the check mark.
   g. Select the current measurement in the *Height* measurement box in the *Size and rotate* section and then type **10**.
   h. Select the current measurement in the *Width* measurement box in the *Size and rotate* section and then type **7.5**.
   i. Click the Picture tab.
   j. At the Format Picture dialog box with the Picture tab selected, select the current percentage number in the *Brightness* option box in the *Image control* section and then type **75**.
   k. Select the current percentage number in the *Contrast* option box and then type **25**.
   l. Click OK to close the Format Picture dialog box.

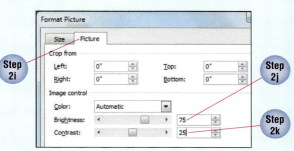

3. Click in the worksheet.
4. Display the worksheet in the Print tab Backstage view to view how the image will print on page 1 and page 2 and then print the worksheet.
5. Save and then close **EL1-C8-P3-HCEqpRpt.xlsx**.

Project 4 Insert and Format Diagrams in a Company Sales Workbook
4 Parts

You will open a workbook that contains two company sales worksheets. You will insert and format a cycle diagram in one worksheet and insert and format a relationship diagram in the other. You will also create and format WordArt text.

▼ **Quick Steps**

Insert SmartArt Diagram
1. Click Insert tab.
2. Click SmartArt button.
3. Double-click desired diagram.

SmartArt

Generally, you would use a SmartArt diagram to represent text and a chart to represent numbers.

Inserting a SmartArt Diagram

Excel includes the SmartArt feature you can use to insert diagrams and organizational charts in a worksheet. SmartArt offers a variety of predesigned diagrams and organizational charts that are available at the Choose a SmartArt Graphic dialog box shown in Figure 8.7. Display this dialog box by clicking the Insert tab and then clicking the SmartArt button in the Illustrations group. At the dialog box, *All* is selected in the left panel and all available predesigned diagrams display in the middle panel. Use the scroll bar at the right side of the middle panel to scroll down the list of diagram choices. Click a diagram in the middle panel and the name of the diagram displays in the right panel along with a description of the diagram type. SmartArt includes diagrams for presenting a list of data; showing data processes, cycles, and relationships; and presenting data in a matrix or pyramid. Double-click a diagram in the middle panel of the dialog box and the diagram is inserted in the worksheet.

Figure 8.7 Choose a SmartArt Graphic Dialog Box

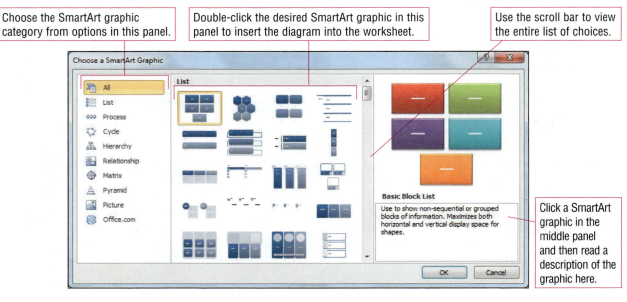

288 Excel Level 1 ■ Unit 2

Entering Data in a Diagram

Some diagrams are designed to include text. You can type text in a diagram by selecting the shape and then typing text in the shape or you can display a text pane and then type text in the pane. Display the text pane by clicking the Text Pane button in the Create Graphic group in the SmartArt Tools Design tab. Turn off the display of the pane by clicking the Text Pane button or by clicking the Close button that displays in the upper right corner of the text pane.

Text Pane

Sizing, Moving, and Deleting a Diagram

Increase or decrease the size of a diagram by dragging the diagram border. Increase or decrease the width of the diagram by positioning the mouse pointer on the set of four dots that displays in the middle of the left and right borders until the pointer turns into a left- and right-pointing arrow, hold down the left mouse button and then drag the border to the desired size. Increase or decrease the height of the diagram in a similar manner using the set of four dots that displays in the middle of the top and bottom borders. To increase or decrease both the height and the width of the diagram, drag one of the sets of three dots that displays in each corner of the border.

To move a diagram, select the diagram and then position the mouse pointer on the diagram border until the pointer turns into a four-headed arrow. Hold down the left mouse button, drag the diagram to the desired position, and then release the mouse button. Delete a diagram by selecting the diagram and then pressing the Delete key.

Project 4a — Inserting a Diagram in a Worksheet — Part 1 of 4

1. Open **EPSales.xlsx** and then save the workbook with Save As and name it **EL1-C8-P4-EPSales**.
2. Create the diagram shown in Figure 8.8 on page 291. To begin, click the Insert tab.
3. Click the SmartArt button in the Illustrations group.
4. At the Choose a SmartArt Graphic dialog box, click *Cycle* in the left panel.
5. Double-click *Radial Cycle* as shown at the right.
6. If the text pane is not open, click the Text Pane button in the Create Graphic group. (The text pane will display at the left side of the diagram.)
7. With the insertion point positioned after the top bullet in the text pane, type **Evergreen Products**.
8. Click the *[Text]* box below *Evergreen Products* and then type **Seattle**.
9. Click the next *[Text]* box and then type **Olympia**.

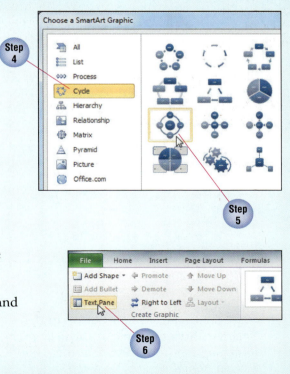

Chapter 8 ■ Adding Visual Interest to Workbooks

10. Click the next *[Text]* box and then type **Portland**.
11. Click the next *[Text]* box and then type **Spokane**.
12. Click the Text Pane button to turn off the display of the text pane.
13. Drag the diagram so it is positioned as shown in Figure 8.8. To drag the diagram, position the mouse pointer on the diagram border until the pointer turns into a four-headed arrow. Hold down the left mouse button, drag the diagram to the desired position, and then release the mouse button.
14. Increase or decrease the size of the diagram so it displays as shown in Figure 8.8. Use the sets of dots on the diagram border to drag the border to the desired size.
15. Save **EL1-C8-P4-EPSales.xlsx**.

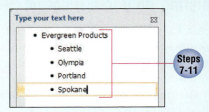

Steps 7-11

HINT Changing the Diagram Design

To restore the SmartArt default layout and color, click the Reset Graphic button in the Reset group in the SmartArt Tools Design tab.

When you double-click a diagram at the dialog box, the diagram is inserted in the worksheet and the SmartArt Tools Design tab is active. With options and buttons in this tab, you can add objects, change the diagram layout, apply a style to the diagram, and reset the diagram back to the original formatting.

Project 4b   Changing the Diagram Design   Part 2 of 4

1. With **EL1-C8-P4-EPSales.xlsx** open, make sure the SmartArt Tools Design tab is active and the *Spokane* circle shape is selected.
2. Click the Right to Left button in the Create Graphic group. (This switches *Olympia* and *Spokane*.)
3. Click the More button located at the right side of the SmartArt Styles group and then click the *Polished* option at the drop-down list (first option from the left in the top row of the *3-D* section).

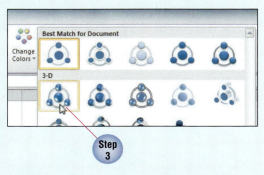

Step 3

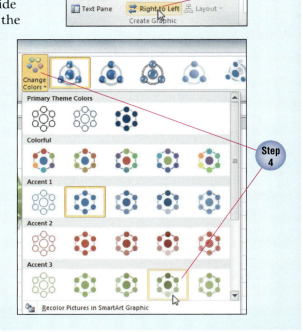

Step 2

Step 4

4. Click the Change Colors button in the SmartArt Styles group and then click the fourth option from the left in the *Accent 3* section (*Gradient Loop - Accent 3*).

5. Click outside the diagram to deselect it.
6. Change the orientation to landscape. (Make sure the diagram fits on the first page.)
7. Save **EL1-C8-P4-EPSales.xlsx** and then print the Total Sales worksheet.

Figure 8.8 Projects 4a and 4b

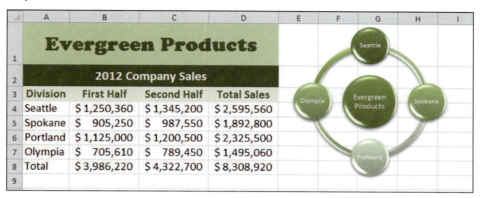

Changing the Diagram Formatting

Click the SmartArt Tools Format tab and options display for formatting a diagram. Use buttons in this tab to insert and customize shapes; apply a shape quick style; customize shapes; insert WordArt quick styles; and specify the position, alignment, rotation, wrapping style, height, and width of the diagram.

Project 4c Changing the Diagram Formatting Part 3 of 4

1. With **EL1-C8-P4-EPSales.xlsx** open, click the Seattle Sales worksheet tab.
2. Create the diagram shown in Figure 8.9. To begin, click the Insert tab and then click the SmartArt button in the Illustrations group.
3. At the Choose a SmartArt Graphic dialog box, click *Relationship* in the left panel and then double-click *Gear* in the middle panel.
4. Click *[Text]* that appears in the bottom gear and then type **Quality Products**.
5. Click *[Text]* that appears in the left gear and then type **Customized Plans**.
6. Click *[Text]* that appears in the top gear and then type **Exemplary Service**.
7. Click inside the diagram border but outside any diagram element.
8. Click the More button that displays at the right side of the SmartArt Styles group and then click the *Inset* option (second option from the left in the top row of the *3-D* section).

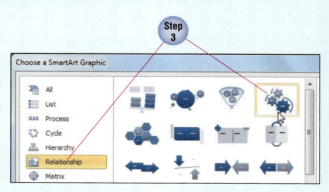

9. Click the Change Colors button in the SmartArt Styles group and then click the third option from the left in the *Accent 3* section (*Gradient Range - Accent 3*).
10. Click the SmartArt Tools Format tab.
11. Click in the *Height* text box in the Size group and then type **3.75**.
12. Click in the *Width* text box, type **5.25**, and then press Enter.

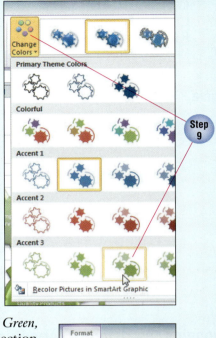

13. Click the bottom gear to select it.
14. Click the Shape Fill button arrow in the Shape Styles group and then click the bottom dark green color (*Olive Green, Accent 3, Darker 50%*) that displays in the *Theme Colors* section.
15. Click the top gear to select it.
16. Click the Shape Fill button arrow and then click the dark green color (*Olive Green, Accent 3, Darker 25%*) that displays in the *Theme Colors* section.
17. Change the orientation to landscape.
18. Move the diagram so it fits on the first page and displays as shown in Figure 8.9.
19. Click outside the chart to deselect it.
20. Save **EL1-C8-P4-EPSales.xlsx** and then print the Seattle Sales worksheet.

Figure 8.9 Project 4c

Creating WordArt

With the WordArt application, you can distort or modify text to conform to a variety of shapes. This is useful for creating company logos and headings. With WordArt, you can change the font, style, and alignment of text. You can also use different fill patterns and colors, customize border lines, and add shadow and three-dimensional effects.

To insert WordArt in an Excel worksheet, click the Insert tab, click the WordArt button in the Text group, and then click the desired option at the drop-down list. This displays *Your Text Here* inserted in the worksheet in the WordArt option you selected at the gallery. Type the desired text and then use the buttons on the Drawing Tools Format tab to format the WordArt.

Sizing and Moving WordArt

WordArt text inserted in a worksheet is surrounded by white sizing handles. Use the white sizing handles to change the height and width of the WordArt text. To move WordArt text, position the arrow pointer on the border of the WordArt until the pointer displays with a four-headed arrow attached. Hold down the left mouse button, drag the outline of the WordArt text box to the desired position, and then release the mouse button. When you change the shape of the WordArt text, the WordArt border displays with a purple diamond shape. Use this shape to change the slant of the WordArt text.

▼ Quick Steps
Create WordArt
1. Click Insert tab.
2. Click WordArt button.
3. Click desired WordArt style at drop-down list.
4. Type desired text.

HINT
To remove WordArt style from text and retain the text, click the More button in the WordArt Styles group in the Drawing Tools Format tab and then click *Clear WordArt*.

WordArt

Project 4d Inserting and Formatting WordArt Part 4 of 4

1. With **EL1-C8-P4-EPSales.xlsx** open, click the Total Sales worksheet tab.
2. Make cell A1 active and then press the Delete key. (This removes the text from the cell.)
3. Increase the height of row 1 to 136.50.
4. Click the Insert tab.
5. Click the WordArt button in the Text group and then click the last option in the top row (*Fill - Olive Green, Accent 3, Outline - Text 2*).
6. Type **Evergreen**, press the Enter key, and then type **Products**.
7. Position the mouse pointer on the WordArt border until the pointer displays with a four-headed arrow attached and then drag the WordArt inside cell A1.

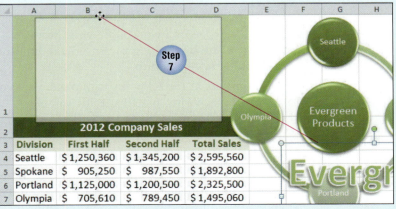

8. Click the Text Fill button arrow in the WordArt Styles group and then click the dark green color (*Olive Green, Accent 3, Darker 25%*).
9. Click the Text Outline button arrow in the WordArt Styles group and then click the dark green color (*Olive Green, Accent 3, Darker 50%*).
10. If necessary, resize the diagram and position it so it prints on one page with the data.
11. Click the Seattle Sales worksheet tab and then complete steps similar to those in Steps 2 through 9 to insert *Evergreen Products* as WordArt.
12. Make sure the SmartArt diagram fits on the page with the data. If necessary, decrease the size of the diagram.
13. Save **EL1-C8-P4-EPSales.xlsx** and then print both worksheets.
14. Close **EL1-C8-P4-EPSales.xlsx**.

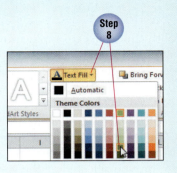

Step 8

Chapter Summary

- Insert symbols with options at the Symbol dialog box with the Symbols tab or the Special Characters tab selected.
- With buttons in the Illustrations group in the Insert tab, you can insert a picture, clip art image, shape, or a SmartArt diagram.
- When you insert a picture or clip art image in a worksheet, the Picture Tools Format tab is active and includes options for adjusting the image, applying preformatted styles, and arranging and sizing the image.
- Change the size of an image with the *Shape Height* and *Shape Width* measurement boxes in the Size group in the Picture Tools Format tab or with the sizing handles that display around the selected image.
- Move an image by positioning the mouse pointer on the image border until the pointer displays with a four-headed arrow attached and then drag the image to the desired location.
- Delete a selected image by pressing the Delete key.
- Insert an image in a workbook with options at the Clip Art task pane. Display this task pane by clicking the Insert tab and then clicking the Clip Art button in the Illustrations group.
- With options at the Clip Art task pane, you can narrow the search for images to specific locations and to specific images.
- Use the Screenshot button in the Illustrations group in the Insert tab to capture the contents of a screen or capture a portion of a screen.
- To draw shapes in a workbook, click the Insert tab, click the Shapes button in the Illustrations group, and then click the desired shape at the drop-down list. Drag in the worksheet to draw the shape. To maintain the proportions of the shape, hold down the Shift key while dragging in the worksheet.

- Copy a shape with the Copy and Paste buttons in the Clipboard group in the Home tab or by holding down the Ctrl key while dragging the shape.
- You can type text in an enclosed drawn object.
- To insert a picture in a worksheet, click the Insert tab and then click the Picture button in the Illustrations group. At the Insert Picture dialog box, navigate to the desired folder and then double-click the file name.
- Draw a text box in a worksheet by clicking the Insert tab, clicking the Text Box button in the Text group and then dragging in the worksheet. Use options at the Drawing Tools Format tab to format and customize the text box.
- A watermark is a lightened image that displays behind data in a file. You can create a picture watermark in a worksheet by inserting a picture in a header or footer and then changing the size and formatting of the picture.
- Insert a SmartArt diagram in a worksheet by clicking the Insert tab, clicking the SmartArt button in the Illustrations group, and then double-clicking the desired diagram at the Choose a SmartArt Graphic dialog box. Customize a diagram with options in the SmartArt Tools Design tab or the SmartArt Tools Format tab.
- Use WordArt to create, distort, modify, and/or conform text to a variety of shapes. Insert WordArt in a worksheet with the WordArt button in the Text group in the Insert tab. Customize WordArt text with options in the Drawing Tools Format tab.

Commands Review

FEATURE	RIBBON TAB, GROUP	BUTTON
Symbol dialog box	Insert, Symbols	Ω
Clip Art task pane	Insert, Illustrations	
Screenshot	Insert, Illustrations	
Shapes drop-down list	Insert, Illustrations	
Insert Picture dialog box	Insert, Illustrations	
Text box	Insert, Text	
Choose a SmartArt Graphic dialog box	Insert, Illustrations	
WordArt drop-down list	Insert, Text	

Concepts Check Test Your Knowledge

Completion: In the space provided at the right, indicate the correct term, symbol, or command.

1. The Symbol button is located in this tab.

2. The *Font* option is available at the Symbol dialog box with this tab selected.

3. Insert a picture, clip art image, screenshot, shape, or SmartArt diagram with buttons in this group in the Insert tab.

4. When you insert a picture or clip art image in a worksheet, this tab is active.

5. Maintain the proportions of the image by holding down this key while dragging a sizing handle.

6. To move an image, position the mouse pointer on the image border until the mouse pointer displays with this attached and then drag the image to the desired location.

7. To capture a portion of a screen, click the Screenshot button and then click this option at the drop-down list.

8. To copy a shape, hold down this key while dragging the shape.

9. When you draw a text box in a worksheet and then release the mouse button, this tab is active.

10. This term refers to a lightened image that displays behind data in a file.

11. Click the SmartArt button in the Illustrations group in the Insert tab and this dialog box displays.

Skills Check Assess Your Performance

Assessment

1 INSERT A CLIP ART IMAGE AND WORDART IN AN EQUIPMENT PURCHASE WORKBOOK

1. Open **ASPurPlans.xlsx** and then save the workbook with Save As and name it **EL1-C8-A1-ASPurPlans**.
2. Insert a formula in cell E4 using the PMT function that calculates monthly payments. *Hint: Refer to Chapter 2, Project 3a*.
3. Copy the formula in cell E4 down to cells E5 and E6.
4. Insert a formula in cell F4 that calculates the total amount of the payments. *Hint: Refer to Chapter 2, Project 3a*.
5. Copy the formula in cell F4 down to cells F5 and F6.
6. Insert a formula in cell G4 that calculates the total amount of interest paid. *Hint: Refer to Chapter 2, Project 3a*.
7. Copy the formula in cell G4 down to cells G5 and G6.
8. Insert the clip art image shown in Figure 8.10 with the following specifications:
   - Search for the clip art image using the search word *movies*. (The colors of the original clip art image are yellow and black.)
   - Change the clip art image color to *Blue, Accent color 1 Light*.
   - Apply the *Brightness: 0% (normal) Contrast: +40%* correction.
   - Apply the *Reflected Rounded Rectangle* picture style.
   - Size and move the image so it is positioned as shown in Figure 8.10.
9. Insert the company name *Azure Studios* in cell A1 as WordArt. Use the *Fill - Blue, Accent 1, Metal Bevel, Reflection* option to create the WordArt.
10. Change the worksheet orientation to landscape.
11. Save, print, and then close **EL1-C8-A1-ASPurPlans.xlsx**.

Figure 8.10 Assessment 1

	A	B	C	D	E	F	G
1				AZURE STUDIOS			
2				Equipment Purchase Plans			
3	Equipment	Purchase Price	Interest Rate	Term in Months	Monthly Payments	Total Payments	Total Interest
4	Photocopier, Model C120	$8,500.00	8.80%	60			
5	Photocopier, Model C150	$12,750.00	8.80%	60			
6	Photocopier, Model C280	$19,250.00	8.80%	60			
7							

Assessment 2 INSERT FORMULAS AND FORMAT A TRAVEL COMPANY WORKBOOK

1. Open **TSGEVacs.xlsx** and then save the workbook with Save As and name it **EL1-C8-A2-TSGEVacs**.
2. Apply the shading to data in cells as shown in Figure 8.11. (Use shading options in the Aqua column.)
3. Insert appropriate formulas to calculate the prices based on a 10 percent and 20 percent discount and apply the appropriate number formatting. *Hint: For the 10% discount column, multiply the price per person by .90 (this determines 90 percent of the price) and multiply the price per person by .80 for the 20% discount column.*
4. Format the image of the airplane and position as shown in Figure 8.11 with the following specifications:
   a. Use the Remove Background button in the Picture Tools Format tab to remove a portion of the yellow background so your image displays similar to what you see in the figure.
   b. Rotate the image.
   c. Apply the *Brightness: +20% Contrast: +20%* correction.
   d. Position the image as shown in the figure.
5. Open Word and then open the document named **TSAirfare.docx** located in the Excel2010L1C8 folder on your storage medium. Click the Excel button on the Taskbar and then use the Screenshot button (use the *Screen Clipping* option) to select and then insert the airfare information in **EL1-C8-A2-TSGEVacs.xlsx**. Position the information at the right side of the data in the worksheet.
6. Change the orientation to landscape.
7. Make sure the data and the airfare information display on one page and then print the worksheet.
8. Save and then close **EL1-C8-A2-TSGEVacs.xslx**.
9. Click the Word button on the Taskbar and then exit Word.

Figure 8.11 Assessment 2

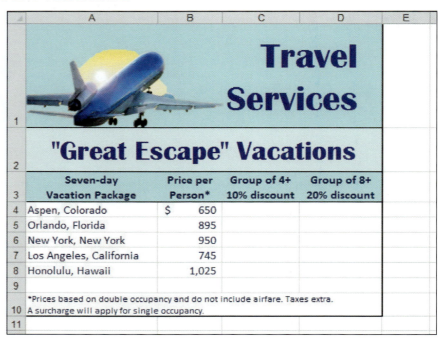

Assessment

3 INSERT AND FORMAT SHAPES IN A COMPANY SALES WORKBOOK

1. Open **MSSales.xlsx** and then save the workbook with Save As and name it **EL1-C8-A3-MSSales**.
2. In cell A1, type *Mountain*, press Alt + Enter, and then type *Systems*.
3. Select *Mountain Systems* and then change the font to 26-point Calibri bold.
4. Change the horizontal alignment of cell A1 to left and the vertical alignment to middle.
5. Display the Format Cells dialog box with the Alignment tab selected and then change the *Indent* measurement to 2. **Hint: Display the Format Cells dialog box by clicking the Alignment group dialog box launcher in the Home tab.**
6. Click outside cell A1.
7. Use the *Isosceles Triangle* shape located in the *Basic Shapes* section of the Shapes drop-down palette to draw a triangle as shown in Figure 8.12.
8. Copy the triangle three times. Add olive green fill and dark olive green outline color of your choosing to the triangles so they appear in a similar manner to the triangles in Figure 8.12. Position the triangles as shown in the figure.
9. Apply shading to cells as shown in the figure (use colors in the Olive Green column).
10. Insert the total amounts in cells B10 through D10.
11. Insert the arrow pointing to $97,549 using the left arrow shape. Apply olive green fill to the shape and remove the shape outline. Set the text in 10-point Calibri bold. Position the arrow as shown in the figure.
12. Save, print, and then close **EL1-C8-A3-MSSales.xlsx**.

Figure 8.12 Assessment 3

	A	B	C	D	E	F
1	Mountain Systems					
2	FIRST QUARTER SALES - 2012					
3	Customer	January	February	March		
4	Lakeside Trucking	$ 84,231	$ 73,455	$ 97,549	Largest Order	
5	Gresham Machines	33,199	40,390	50,112		
6	Real Photography	30,891	35,489	36,400		
7	Genesis Productions	72,190	75,390	83,219		
8	Landower Company	22,188	14,228	38,766		
9	Jewell Enterprises	19,764	50,801	32,188		
10	Total					
11						

Assessment 4

INSERT AND FORMAT A SMARTART DIAGRAM IN A SALES WORKBOOK

1. Open **PS2ndQtrSales.xlsx** and then save the workbook with Save As and name it **EL1-C8-A4-PS2ndQtrSales**.
2. Change the orientation to landscape.
3. Insert a pyramid shape at the right side of the worksheet data using the *Pyramid List* diagram with the following specifications:
   a. Change the color to *Gradient Loop - Accent 3*.
   b. Apply the *Cartoon* SmartArt style.
   c. In the bottom text box, type **Red Level**, press Enter, and then type **$25,000 to $49,999**.
   d. In the middle text box, type **Blue Level**, press Enter, and then type **$50,000 to $99,999**.
   e. In the top text box, type **Gold Level**, press Enter, and then type **$100,000+**.
   f. Apply fill to each of the text boxes to match the level color.
4. Size and/or move the diagram so it displays attractively at the right side of the worksheet data. (Make sure the entire diagram will print on the same page as the worksheet data.)
5. Save, print, and then close **EL1-C8-A4-PS2ndQtrSales.xlsx**.

Assessment 5

CREATE AND INSERT A SCREENSHOT

1. Open **RPRefiPlan.xlsx** and then display formulas by pressing Ctrl + `.
2. Insert the arrow shape shown in Figure 8.13. Add fill to the shape, remove the shape outline, bold the text in the shape, and then figure out how to rotate the shape using the rotation handle (green circle). Rotate, size, and position the arrow as shown in the figure.
3. Open Word.
4. At a blank document, press Ctrl + E to center the insertion point, press Ctrl + B to turn on bold, type **Excel Worksheet with PMT Formula**, and then press the Enter key twice.
5. Click the Insert tab, click the Screenshot button, and then click the thumbnail of the Excel worksheet.
6. Save the Word document and name it **EL1-C8-A5-PMTFormula**.
7. Print and then close the document and then exit Word.
8. In Excel, close **RPRefiPlan.xlsx** without saving the changes.

Figure 8.13 Assessment 5

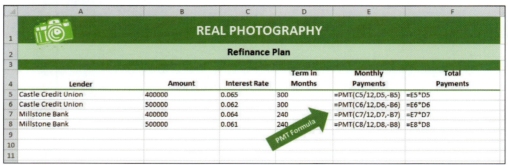

Visual Benchmark — Demonstrate Your Proficiency

INSERT FORMULAS, WORDART, AND CLIP ART IN A WORKSHEET

1. Open **TSYrlySales.xlsx** and then save the workbook with Save As and name it **EL1-C8-VB-TSYrlySales**.
2. Insert the following formulas in the worksheet shown in Figure 8.14: (***Do not*** type the data in the following cells—instead insert the formulas as indicated. The results of your formulas should match the results you see in the figure.)
   - Cells C4 through C14: Insert a formula with an IF function that inserts *5%* if the amount in the cell in column B is greater than $249,999 and inserts *2%* if the amount is not greater than $249,999.
   - Cells D4 through D14: Insert a formula that multiplies the amount in column B with the amount in column C.
3. Insert the company name *Target Supplies* as WordArt with the following specifications:
   - Use the *Gradient Fill - Black, Outline - White, Outer Shadow* WordArt option.
   - To type the WordArt text, press Ctrl + L (this changes to left text alignment), type **Target**, press Enter, and then type **Supplies**.
   - Change the text outline color to *Orange, Accent 6, Darker 25%*.
   - Move the WordArt so it is positioned as shown in Figure 8.14.
4. Insert the target clip art image (use the word *target* to search for this clip art image) with the following specifications:
   - Change the color to *Red, Accent color 2 Dark*.
   - Change the correction to *Brightness: 0% (Normal) Contrast: +40%*.
   - Apply the *Drop Shadow Rectangle* picture style.
   - Size and position the clip art image as shown in the figure.
5. Draw the shape that displays below the data with the following specifications:
   - Use the *Bevel* shape (located in the *Basic Shapes* section).
   - Type the text in the shape, apply bold formatting, and change to center and middle alignment.
   - Change the shape fill color to *Red, Accent 2, Darker 50%*.
   - Change the shape outline color to *Orange, Accent 6, Darker 25%*.
6. Save and then print the worksheet.
7. Press Ctrl + ` to turn on the display of formulas and then print the worksheet again.
8. Turn off the display of formulas and then close the workbook.

Figure 8.14 Visual Benchmark

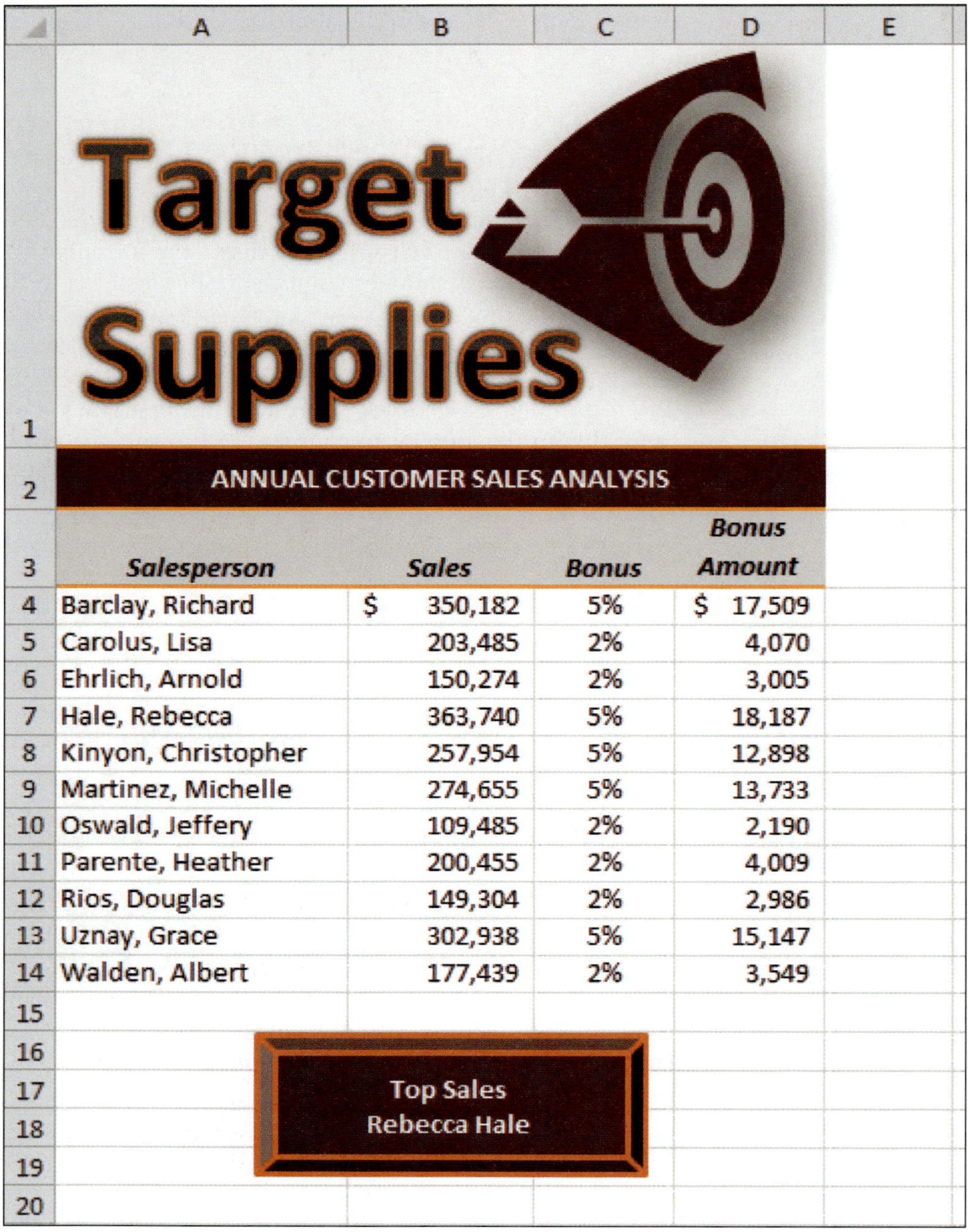

	A	B	C	D	E
1	Target Supplies				
2	ANNUAL CUSTOMER SALES ANALYSIS				
3	***Salesperson***	***Sales***	***Bonus***	***Bonus Amount***	
4	Barclay, Richard	$ 350,182	5%	$ 17,509	
5	Carolus, Lisa	203,485	2%	4,070	
6	Ehrlich, Arnold	150,274	2%	3,005	
7	Hale, Rebecca	363,740	5%	18,187	
8	Kinyon, Christopher	257,954	5%	12,898	
9	Martinez, Michelle	274,655	5%	13,733	
10	Oswald, Jeffery	109,485	2%	2,190	
11	Parente, Heather	200,455	2%	4,009	
12	Rios, Douglas	149,304	2%	2,986	
13	Uznay, Grace	302,938	5%	15,147	
14	Walden, Albert	177,439	2%	3,549	
15					
16					
17		Top Sales			
18		Rebecca Hale			
19					
20					

Case Study — Apply Your Skills

Part 1

You are the office manager for Ocean Truck Sales and are responsible for maintaining a spreadsheet of the truck and SUV inventory. Open **OTSales.xlsx** and then save the workbook and name it **EL1-C8-CS-OTSales**. Apply formatting to improve the appearance of the worksheet and insert at least one clip art image (related to "truck" or "ocean"). Save **EL1-C8-CS-OTSales.xlsx** and then print the worksheet.

Part 2

With **EL1-C8-CS-OTSales.xlsx** open, save the workbook with Save As and name it **EL1-C8-CS-OTSalesF&C**. You make the inventory workbook available to each salesperson at the beginning of the week. For easier viewing, you decide to divide the workbook into two worksheets with one worksheet containing all Ford vehicles and the other worksheet containing all Chevrolet vehicles. Rename the worksheet tabs to reflect the contents. Sort each worksheet by price from the most expensive to the least expensive. The owner offers incentives each week to help motivate the sales force. Insert in the first worksheet a SmartArt diagram of your choosing that contains the following information:

    Small-sized truck = $100

    2WD Regular Cab = $75

    SUV 4x4 = $50

Copy the diagram in the first worksheet and then paste it into the second worksheet. Change the orientation to landscape and then save, print, and close **EL1-C8-CS-OTSalesF&C.xlsx**.

Part 3

You have been asked to save the inventory worksheet as a web page for viewing online. Open **EL1-C8-CS-OTSales.xlsx**, display the Save As dialog box, click the *Save as type* option, and then determine how to save the workbook as a single file web page (*.mht, *.mhtml). Save the workbook as a single file web page with the name **EL1-CS-OTSales-WebPage**. Open your Internet browser and then open the web page. Look at the information in the file and then close the Internet browser.

Part 4

As part of your weekly duties, you need to post the incentive diagram in various locations throughout the company. You decide to insert the diagram in PowerPoint for easy printing. Open **EL1-C8-CS-OTSalesF&C.xlsx** and then open PowerPoint. Change the slide layout in PowerPoint to Blank. Copy the diagram in the first worksheet and paste it into the PowerPoint blank slide. Increase and/or move the diagram so it better fills the slide. Print the slide and then close PowerPoint without saving the presentation. Close **EL1-C8-CS-OTSalesF&C.xlsx**.

UNIT 2

Performance Assessment

Note: Before beginning unit assessments, copy to your storage medium the Excel2010L1U2 subfolder from the Excel2010L1 folder on the CD that accompanies this textbook and then make Excel2010L1U2 the active folder.

Assessing Proficiency

In this unit, you have learned how to work with multiple windows; move, copy, link, and paste data between workbooks and applications; create and customize charts with data in a worksheet; save a workbook as a web page; insert hyperlinks; and insert and customize pictures, clip art images, shapes, SmartArt diagrams, and WordArt.

Assessment 1 Copy and Paste Data and Insert WordArt in a Training Scores Workbook

1. Open **RLTraining.xlsx** and then save the workbook with Save As and name it **EL1-U2-A1-RLTraining**.
2. Delete row 15 (the row for *Kwieciak, Kathleen*).
3. Insert a formula in cell D4 that averages the percentages in cells B4 and C4.
4. Copy the formula in cell D4 down to cells D5 through D20.
5. Make cell A22 active, turn on bold, and then type **Highest Averages**.
6. Display the Clipboard task pane and make sure it is empty.
7. Select and then copy each of the following rows (individually): row 7, 10, 14, 16, and 18.
8. Make cell A23 active and then paste row 14 (the row for *Jewett, Troy*).
9. Make cell A24 active and then paste row 7 (the row for *Cumpston, Kurt*).
10. Make cell A25 active and then paste row 10 (the row for *Fisher-Edwards, Theresa*).
11. Make cell A26 active and then paste row 16 (the row for *Mathias, Caleb*).
12. Make cell A27 active and then paste row 18 (the row for *Nyegaard, Curtis*).
13. Click the Clear All button in the Clipboard task pane and then close the task pane.
14. Insert in cell A1 the text *Roseland* as WordArt. Format the WordArt text to add visual appeal to the worksheet.
15. Save, print, and then close **EL1-U2-A1-RLTraining.xlsx**.

Assessment 2 Manage Multiple Worksheets in a Projected Earnings Workbook

1. Open **RLProjEarnings.xlsx** and then save the workbook with Save As and name it **EL1-U2-A2-RLProjEarnings**.
2. Delete *Roseland* in cell A1. Open **EL1-U2-A1-RLTraining.xlsx** and then copy the *Roseland* WordArt text and paste it into cell A1 in **EL1-U2-A2-RLProjEarnings.xlsx**. If necessary, increase the height of row 1 to accommodate the WordArt text.
3. Notice the fill color in cells in **EL1-U2-A1-RLTraining.xlsx** and then apply the same fill color to cells of data in **EL1-U2-A2-RLProjEarnings.xlsx**. Close **EL1-U2-A1-RLTraining.xlsx**.
4. Select cells A1 through C11 and then copy and paste the cells to Sheet2 keeping the source column widths.
5. With Sheet2 displayed, make the following changes:
   a. Increase the height of row 1 to accommodate the WordArt text.
   b. Delete the contents of cell B2.
   c. Change the contents of the following cells:
      A6: Change *January* to *July*
      A7: Change *February* to *August*
      A8: Change *March* to *September*
      A9: Change *April* to *October*
      A10: Change *May* to *November*
      A11: Change *June* to *December*
      B6: Change *8.30%* to *8.10%*
      B8: Change *9.30%* to *8.70%*
6. Make Sheet1 active and then copy cell B2 and paste link it to cell B2 in Sheet2.
7. Rename Sheet1 to *First Half* and rename Sheet2 to *Second Half*.
8. Make the First Half worksheet active and then determine the effect on projected monthly earnings if the projected yearly income is increased by 10% by changing the number in cell B2 to *$1,480,380*.
9. Horizontally and vertically center both worksheets in the workbook and insert a custom header that prints your name at the left, the current date in the center, and the sheet name (click the Sheet Name button in the Header & Footer Elements group in the Header & Footer Tools Design tab) at the right.
10. Print both worksheets.
11. Determine the effect on projected monthly earnings if the projected yearly income is increased by 20% by changing the number in cell B2 to *$1,614,960*.
12. Save the workbook again and then print both worksheets.
13. Close **EL1-U2-A2-RLProjEarnings.xlsx**.

Assessment 3 Create Charts in Worksheets in a Sales Totals Workbook

1. Open **EPYrlySales.xlsx** and then save the workbook with Save As and name it **EL1-U2-A3-EPYrlySales**.
2. Rename Sheet1 to *2010 Sales*, rename Sheet2 to *2011 Sales*, and rename Sheet3 to *2012 Sales*.
3. Select all three sheet tabs, make cell A12 active, click the Bold button, and then type **Total**. Make cell B12 active and then insert a formula to total the amounts in cells B4 through B11. Make cell C12 active and then insert a formula to total the amounts in cells C4 through C11.
4. Make the 2010 Sales worksheet active, select cells A3 through C11 (make sure you do not select the totals in row 12) and create a column chart. Click the Switch Row/Column button at the Chart Tools Design tab. Apply formatting to increase the visual appeal of the chart. Drag the chart below the worksheet data. (Make sure the chart fits on the page.)
5. Make the 2011 Sales worksheet active and then create the same type of chart you created in Step 4.
6. Make the 2012 Sales worksheet active and then create the same type of chart you created in Step 4.
7. Save the workbook and then print the entire workbook.
8. Close **EL1-U2-A3-EPYrlySales.xlsx**.

Assessment 4 Create and Format a Line Chart

1. Type the following information in a worksheet:

Country	**Total Sales**
Denmark	$85,345
Finland	$71,450
Norway	$135,230
Sweden	$118,895

2. Using the data just entered in the worksheet, create a line chart with the following specifications:
   a. Apply a chart style of your choosing.
   b. Insert major and minor primary vertical gridlines.
   c. Insert drop lines. (Do this with the Lines button in the Analysis group in the Chart Tools Layout tab.)
   d. Apply any other formatting to improve the visual appeal of the chart.
   e. Move the chart to a new sheet.
3. Save the workbook and name it **EL1-U2-A4-CtrySales**.
4. Print only the sheet containing the chart.
5. Change the line chart to a bar chart of your choosing.
6. Save the workbook and then print only the sheet containing the chart.
7. Close **EL1-U2-A4-CtrySales.xlsx**.

Assessment 5 Create and Format a Pie Chart

1. Open **EPProdDept.xlsx** and then save the workbook with Save As and name it **EL1-U2-A5-EPProdDept**.
2. Create a pie chart as a separate sheet with the data in cells A3 through B10. You determine the type of pie. Include an appropriate title for the chart and include percentage labels.
3. Print only the sheet containing the chart.
4. Save and then close **EL1-U2-A5-EPProdDept.xlsx**.

Assessment 6 Insert a Text Box in and Save a Travel Workbook as a Web Page

1. Open **TravDest.xlsx** and then save the workbook with Save As and name it **EL1-U2-A6-TravDest**.
2. Insert a text box in the workbook with the following specifications:
   a. Draw the text box at the right side of the clip art image.
   b. Remove the fill in the text box and the outline around the text box.
   c. Type **Call 1-888-555-1288 for last-minute vacation specials!**
   d. Select the text and then change the font to 24-point Forte in a blue color.
   e. Size and position the text box so it appears visually balanced with the travel clip art image.
3. Make sure you are connected to the Internet and then search for sites that might be of interest to tourists for each of the cities in the worksheet. Write down the web address for the best web page you find for each city.
4. Create a hyperlink for each city to the web address you wrote down in Step 3. (Select the hyperlink text in each cell and change the font size to 18 points.)
5. Test the hyperlinks to make sure you entered the web addresses correctly by clicking each hyperlink and then closing the web browser.
6. Save, print, and then close **EL1-U2-A6-TravDest.xlsx**.

Assessment 7 Insert Clip Art Image and SmartArt Diagram in a Projected Quotas Workbook

1. Open **SalesQuotas.xlsx** and then save the workbook with Save As and name it **EL1-U2-A7-SalesQuotas**.
2. Insert a formula in cell C3 using an absolute reference to determine the projected quotas at a 10% increase of the current quotas.
3. Copy the formula in cell C3 down to cells C4 through C12. Apply the Accounting Number Format style to cell C3.
4. Insert a clip art image in row 1 related to money. You determine the size and position of the clip art image. If necessary, increase the height of the row.
5. Insert a SmartArt diagram at the right side of the data that contains three shapes. Insert the following quota ranges in the shapes and apply the specified fill color:
   $50,000 to $99,999 (apply green color)
   $100,000 to $149,999 (apply blue color)
   $150,000 to $200,000 (apply red color)
6. Apply formatting to the SmartArt diagram to improve the visual appeal.
7. Insert a custom header that prints your name at the left, the current date in the middle, and the file name at the right.
8. Change the orientation to landscape and make sure the diagram fits on the page.
9. Save, print, and then close **EL1-U2-A7-SalesQuotas.xlsx**.

Assessment 8 Insert Symbol, Clip Art, and Comments in a Sales Workbook

1. Open **CISales.xlsx** and then save the workbook with Save As and name it **EL1-U2-A8-CISales**.
2. Delete the text *Landower Company* in cell A7 and then type **Económico** in the cell. (Use the Symbol dialog box to insert *ó*.)
3. Insert a new row at the beginning of the worksheet.
4. Select and then merge cells A1 through D1.
5. Increase the height of row 1 to approximately 141.00.
6. Insert the text *Custom Interiors* as WordArt in cell A1. You determine the formatting of the WordArt. Move and size the WordArt so it fits in cell A1.
7. Open Word and then open **CICustomers.docx** located in the Excel2010L1U2 folder on your storage medium. Click the Excel button and with **EL1-U2-A8-CISales.xlsx** open, make a screenshot (use the *Screen Clipping* option) of the customer information in the Word document. Position the screenshot image below the data in the cells.
8. Insert a custom footer that prints your name at the left and the file name at the right.
9. Make sure the data in cells and the screenshot display on the same page and then print the worksheet.
10. Save and then close **EL1-U2-A8-CISales.xlsx**.

Assessment 9 Insert and Format a Shape in a Budget Workbook

1. Open **SEExpenses.xlsx** and then save the workbook with Save As and name it **EL1-U2-A9-SEExpenses**.
2. Make the following changes to the worksheet so it displays as shown in Figure U2.1:
   a. Select and then merge cells A1 through D1.
   b. Add fill to the cells as shown in Figure U2.1.
   c. Increase the height of row 1 to the approximate size shown in Figure U2.1.
   d. Type the text **SOLAR ENTERPRISES** in cell A1 set in 20-point Calibri bold, center and middle aligned, and set in aqua (*Aqua, Accent 5, Darker 25%*).
   e. Insert the sun shape (located in the *Basic Shapes* section of the Shapes button drop-down list). Apply orange shape fill and change the shape outline to aqua (*Aqua, Accent 5, Darker 25%*)
3. Save, print, and then close **EL1-U2-A9-SEExpenses.xlsx**.

Figure U2.1 Assessment 9

	A	B	C	D
1		SOLAR ENTERPRISES		
2	**Expense**	**Actual**	**Budget**	**% of Actual**
3	Salaries	$ 126,000.00	$ 124,000.00	98%
4	Benefits	25,345.00	28,000.00	110%
5	Commissions	58,000.00	54,500.00	94%
6	Media space	8,250.00	10,100.00	122%
7	Travel expenses	6,350.00	6,000.00	94%
8	Dealer display	4,140.00	4,500.00	109%
9	Payroll taxes	2,430.00	2,200.00	91%
10	Telephone	1,450.00	1,500.00	103%
11				

Writing Activities

The following activities give you the opportunity to practice your writing skills along with demonstrating an understanding of some of the important Excel features you have mastered in this unit. Use correct grammar, appropriate word choices, and clear sentence constructions.

Activity 1 Prepare a Projected Budget

You are the accounting assistant in the financial department of McCormack Funds and you have been asked to prepare a yearly proposed department budget. The total amount for the department is $1,450,000. You are given the percentages for the proposed budget items, which are: Salaries, 45%; Benefits, 12%; Training, 14%; Administrative Costs, 10%; Equipment, 11%; and Supplies, 8%. Create a worksheet with this information that shows the projected yearly budget, the budget items in the department, the percentage of the budget, and the amount for each item. After the worksheet is completed, save the workbook and name it **EL1-U2-Act1-MFBudget**. Print and then close the workbook.

Optional: Using Word 2010, write a memo to the McCormack Funds Finance Department explaining that the proposed annual department budget is attached for their review. Comments and suggestions are to be sent to you within one week. Save the file and name it **EL1-U2-Act1-MFMemo**. Print and then close the file.

Activity 2 Create a Travel Tours Bar Chart

Prepare a worksheet in Excel for Carefree Travels that includes the following information:

Scandinavian Tours

Country	Tours Booked
Norway	52
Sweden	62
Finland	29
Denmark	38

Use the information in the worksheet to create and format a bar chart as a separate sheet. Save the workbook and name it **EL1-U2-Act2-CTTours**. Print only the sheet containing the chart and then close **EL1-U2-Act2-CTTours.xlsx**.

Activity 3 Prepare a Ski Vacation Worksheet

Prepare a worksheet for Carefree Travels that advertises a snow skiing trip. Include the following information in the announcement:

- At the beginning of the worksheet, create a company logo that includes the company name *Carefree Travels* and a clip art image related to travel.
- Include the heading *Whistler Ski Vacation Package* in the worksheet.
- Include the following below the heading:
    - Round-trip air transportation: $395
    - Seven nights' hotel accommodations: $1,550
    - Four all-day ski passes: $425
    - Compact rental car with unlimited mileage: $250
    - Total price of the ski package: (calculate the total price)
- Include the following information somewhere in the worksheet:
    - Book your vacation today at special discount prices.
    - Two-for-one discount at many of the local ski resorts.

Save the workbook and name it **EL1-U2-Act3-CTSkiTrips**. Print and then close **EL1-U2-Act3-CTSkiTrips.xlsx**.

Internet Research

Find Information on Excel Books and Present the Data in a Worksheet

Locate two companies on the Internet that sell new books. At the first new book company site, locate three books on Microsoft Excel. Record the title, author, and price for each book. At the second new book company site, locate the same three books and record the prices. Create an Excel worksheet that includes the following information:

- Name of each new book company
- Title and author of the three books
- Prices for each book from the two book company sites

Create a hyperlink for each book company to the website on the Internet. Then save the completed workbook and name it **EL1-U2-DR-Books**. Print and then close the workbook.

Job Study

Create a Customized Time Card for a Landscaping Company

You are the manager of a landscaping company and are responsible for employee time cards. Locate the time card template that is available with *Sample templates* selected at the New tab Backstage view. Use the template to create a customized time card for your company. With the template open, insert additional blank rows to increase the spacing above the Employee row. Insert a clip art image related to landscaping or gardening and position and size it attractively in the form. Include a text box with the text Lawn and Landscaping Specialists inside the box. Format, size, and position the text attractively in the form. Fill in the form for the current week with the following employee information:

    Employee = Jonathan Holder
    Address = 12332 South 152nd Street, Baton Rouge, LA 70804
    Manager = (Your name)
    Employee phone = (225) 555-3092
    Employee email = None
    Regular hours = 8 hours for Monday, Tuesday, Wednesday, and Thursday
    Overtime = 2 hours on Wednesday
    Sick hours = None
    Vacation = 8 hours on Friday
    Rate per hour = $20.00
    Overtime pay = $30.00

Save the completed form and name it **EL1-U2-JS-TimeCard**. Print and then close **EL1-U2-JS-TimeCard.xlsx**.

Index

* (asterisk), as excluded from file name, 8
\ (backslash), as excluded from file names, 9
: (colon), as excluded from file name, 8
, (comma)
    in formatting numbers, 22, 82
    in separating condition and actions, 55
$ (dollar sign)
    in distinguishing between cell references, 57, 59
    in formatting numbers, 22, 82
/ (forward slash), as excluded from file name, 8
(number symbol), for exceeding space, 8
% (percent sign), in formatting numbers, 22, 82
| (pipe symbol), as excluded from file name, 8
? (question mark), as excluded from file name, 8
" (quotation marks), as excluded from file name, 8
; (semicolon), as excluded from file name, 8
< (less than sign), as excluded from file name, 8
= (equals sign), in writing formulas, 40, 47
> (greater than sign), as excluded from file name, 8

A

absolute cell references, 57
    in formulas, 57–58
accounting, as category in Format Cells dialog box, 85
Accounting Number Format, 22, 23
active cells, 19, 175
adding
    borders to cells, 90–91
    fill and shading to cells, 92, 93
addition, 41
    in order of operators, 40
aligning data, 86–88
alignment formatting, 78–80
Alignment tab, 86–88
area charts, 242

argument
    defined, 45
    in formulas, 51
Arrange Windows dialog box, 179–180
arrow shapes, drawing, 282–283
asterisk (*), as excluded from file name, 8
AutoComplete, 13
    inserting data in cells with, 14
AutoCorrect, 13–14
    in automatic formatting of hyperlinks, 222–223
AutoFill, 13, 15
automatic entering features, 13–15
automatic formatting of hyperlinks, 222
AutoSum button, 37, 47
    in adding numbers, 17–18
    in averaging numbers, 18
AVERAGE function, 18, 47–48
    inserting, 19
averages, finding, 47–48
averaging of numbers with AutoSum button, 18

B

background pictures, inserting, 117
backslash (\\), as excluded from file name, 8
backspace key, in editing data in cell, 6
Backstage view, 6, 10, 11
    getting help in, 26–27
    Help tab, 25
    Help tab, getting help at, 25
    New tab, 228
    Print tab, 12, 113, 245
    Recent tab, 207–210
bar charts, 242
billing statement, preparing, using template, 228–229
blank worksheets, 5
Bold button, 78
borders, adding to cells, 90–91
Borders button, 78, 90
bubble charts, 242
buttons, getting help on, 25

C

cell address, 6, 7
cell formatting, 128–132

cell pointers, 8
cell reference, 6, 7
    absolute, 57
    mixed, 57
    relative, 18, 57
cells
    active, 19, 175
    active commands for making, 7
    adding borders to, 90–91
    adding fill and shading to, 92, 93
    clearing data in, 77
    copying selected, 163
    deleting, 76
    editing data in, 10
    entering data in, 6–7
    entering data in, with AutoComplete, 14
    entering data in, with fill handle, 16–17
    formatting, using Format Cells dialog box, 86–93
    linking, between worksheets, 184–185
    merging and centering, 21–22
    moving selected, 162–163
    selecting, 19–20
    selecting data within, 20
    working with range of, 177–178
cell styles
    applying, 214
    copying, to another workbook, 220
    defining, 215–218
    deleting, 221
    formatting with, 214–222
    modifying, 219–220
    removing, 220
centering
    cells, 21–22
    worksheets, horizontally and/or vertically, 110–111
Change Chart Type dialog box, 246
changing
    chart height and width, 261–262
    margins, 109–110
    page orientation, 112
    page size, 112
character formatting, 69
charts
    area, 242

bar, 242
bubble, 242
changing data series for, 246–247
changing design, 245–248
changing formatting, 258–262
changing height and width, 261–262
changing layout, 251–258
changing layout and style of, 247–248
changing location, 248
choosing custom style, 246
column, 241, 242
creating, 241–245
defined, 239
deleting, 242–243, 248–250, 255
doughnut, 242
editing data in, 243–244
inserting, moving, and deleting labels for, 251–254
inserting images, 257–258
inserting shapes, 255, 256
line, 241, 242
moving, 242–243, 255
pie, 241, 242
printing, 245
radar, 242
sizing, 242–243, 255
stock, 242
surface, 242
2-D column, 241
XY (scatter), 242
Chart Tools Design tab, 245, 246
Chart Tools Format tab, 255, 258, 261
Chart Tools Layout tab, 251, 256, 257
clip art
inserting, 278–279
linking using, 225
Clip Art task pane, 275, 278
Clipboard task pane, 165–166
Close button, 182
closing workbooks, 12
colon (:), as excluded from file name, 8
color theme, 81
column charts, 241, 242
columns
changing column width using column boundaries, 71–72
changing width of, 21
deleting, 76
hiding and unhiding, 94–96
inserting, 75–76
printing headings for, 118
printing titles on multiple pages, 115–116
sorting more than one, 134–135
in worksheet, 5
column width, changing
at the Column Width dialog box, 72
using column boundaries, 71–72
Column Width dialog box, changing column width at, 72
comma (,)
in formatting numbers, 22, 82
in separating condition and actions, 55
Comma Style format, 22, 23
conditional functions, 54
constant, defined, 45
copying
cell styles to another workbook, 220
data, 182–183
data, between programs, 185–186
formula with fill handle, 18–19, 42
formula with relative cell references, 41–42
shapes, 281–283
workbooks, 204–205
worksheets to another workbook, 210–211
COUNT function, 47, 50
counting, numbers in range, 50
creating
charts, 241–245
screenshots, 279–284
WordArt, 293–294
workbooks, 9
workbooks, with multiple worksheets, 161
Ctrl key, in displaying options, 163
currency, as category in Format Cells dialog box, 85
currency formatting, 82
custom, as category in Format Cells dialog box, 85
custom chart style, choosing, 246
customizing
help, 27–28
images, 276–277
print jobs, 125–126
custom sort, completing, 133–134
cutting workbooks, 205–206

D

data
aligning and indenting, 86–88
clearing, in cells, 77
copying, 182–183
copying, between programs, 185–186
editing, in cell, 10
editing, on charts, 243–244
entering into cells, 6–7
entering into cells, with AutoComplete, 14
entering into cells, with fill handle, 16–17
entering into SmartArt diagram, 289
filtering, 135–137
finding and replacing, on worksheet, 128–132
linking, 184–185
moving, 182–183
pasting, 182–183
pasting, between programs, 185–186
scaling, 116–117
selecting, within cells, 20
sorting, 133–135
data series, changing, for charts, 246–247
date, as category in Format Cells dialog box, 85
DATE function, 51, 53–54
date functions, writing formulas with, 53–54
Decrease Decimal format, 22, 23, 83
Decrease Font Size button, 78
Delete dialog box, 76
Delete key
in deleting cell entry, 10
in deleting charts, 248
in editing data in cell, 6
deleting
cells, rows, or columns, 76
cell styles, 221

chart labels, 251
charts, 242–243, 248–250
chart shapes, 255
folders, 207
to Recycle Bin, 203
SmartArt diagrams, 289
dependent worksheet, 184
diagrams. *See* SmartArt diagrams
dialog boxes. *See also specific*
getting help in, 26–27
displaying
formulas, 51
quick list, 208
division, 41
in order of operators, 40
dollar sign ($)
in distinguishing between cell references, 57, 59
in formatting numbers, 22, 82
doughnut charts, 242
drawing, text boxes, 285–286
Drawing Tools Format tab, 285

E

Edit Hyperlink dialog box, 224, 226
editing
data in cell, 10
data on charts, 243–244
formulas, 55
hyperlinks, 226–227
effects theme, 81
email address, linking to, 225
enclosed objects, 281
End key, to move insertion point, 10
Enter button, to accept data in cell entry, 10
equals sign (=), in writing formulas, 40, 47
Esc key, in removing Backstage view, 10
Even Page Header tab, 123
Excel, exiting, 13
exponentiation, 41
in order of operators, 40

F

F4, for Repeat command, 92
F8, for Extend Selection mode, 20
F11, in creating default chart type, 248
file maintenance, 197
file names, characters in, 8

file name text box, 8
files, linking to existing, 222–223
file tab, 6, 11
fill, adding, to cells, 92, 93
Fill Color button, 78, 92
fill handle, 15
copying formula with, 18–19, 42
inserting data in cells with, 16–17
using, to copy formula, 18–19
filter, 135
number, 135
filtering data, 135–137
financial functions, writing formulas with, 51–53
Find and Replace dialog box, 128–132
finding and replacing data on worksheet, 128–132
Find & Select button, 7, 94–95
folder names, maximum number of characters in, 201
folders
creating, 201
deleting, 203, 207
renaming, 202
root, 201
font, changing, at Format Cells dialog box, 88–89
Font Color button, 78
font formatting, applying, 78, 79–80
Font Size button, 78
font theme, 81
footers, inserting, 120–125
format, defined, 69
Format Cells dialog box
adding fill and shading to cells, 92, 93
changing font at, 88–89
in defining cell style, 215–216, 217
formatting cells using, 86–93
formatting numbers with, 84–86
number categories in, 85
Format Painter, formatting with, 94
formatting
alignment, 78–80
basic, 21–24
with cell styles, 214–222

cells, using Format Cells dialog box, 86–93
changing chart, 258–262
changing SmartArt, 291–292
character, 69
currency, 82
font, 78–80
with Format Painter, 94
images, 276–277
with Mini toolbar, 78
multiple worksheets, 171–172
numbers, 22–24, 69
numbers, using Format Cells dialog box, 84–86
numbers, using Number group buttons, 82–84
percent, 82–83
text boxes, 285–286
worksheet pages, 109–119
Formula bar, 6, 10, 45
formulas, 37
absolute cell references in, 57–58
copying, with fill handle, 18–19, 42
copying, with relative cell references, 41–42
displaying, 51
editing, 55
inserting, 17–19
inserting, with functions, 45–57
mixed cell references in, 59–60
working with ranges in, 177–178
writing, with date and time functions, 53–54
writing, with financial functions, 51–53
writing, with IF function, 54–55, 56
writing, with mathematical operators, 40–45
writing, by pointing, 43, 44–45
writing, with statistical functions, 47–50
forward slash (/), as excluded from file name, 8
fractions, as category in Format Cells dialog box, 85
freezing panes, 174–176
Function Library group, 45

functions
    categories of, 47
    conditional, 54
    defined, 45
    inserting formulas with, 45–57
Functions Arguments palette, 45–46
future value, finding, for series of payments, 52–53
Fv argument in formula, 51
FV function, 51, 52–53

G

Go To, 7, 94
Go To dialog box, 7, 95
graphics, linking using, 225
graphs, 239. *See also* charts
greater than sign (>), as excluded from file name, 8
gridlines, 7
    printing, 118

H

headers, inserting, 120–125
help
    customizing, 27–28
    using, 24–28
Help tab Backstage view, 25
    getting help at, 25
hiding
    columns and rows, 94–96
    workbooks, 181
    worksheets in workbooks, 171, 172
horizontal scroll bars, 6, 174
Hyperlink button, 225
hyperlinks
    automatic formatting of, 222
    to email address, 225
    inserting, 222–227
    in linking to existing web page or file, 222–223
    in linking to new workbook, 224
    in linking to place in workbook, 224
    linking using graphics, 225
    modifying, editing, and removing, 226–227
    navigating using, 223–224
    purposes of, 222

I

I-beam pointer, dragging data with, 20
IF function, writing formulas with, 54–55, 56
images
    clip art, 278–279
    customizing, 276–277
    formatting, 276–277
    inserting, 275–279
    inserting, into charts, 257–258
    sizing and moving, 276
Increase Decimal format, 22, 23, 83
Increase Font Size button, 78
indenting data, 86–88
Insert Dialog box
    inserting columns with, 75–76
    inserting rows with, 74–75
Insert Function dialog box, 45–46
Insert Hyperlink dialog box, 222, 223, 224, 225
inserting
    background pictures, 117
    chart images, 257–258
    chart labels, 251
    chart shapes, 255, 256
    clip art, 278–279
    columns, 75–76
    data in cells, with AutoComplete, 14
    data in cells, with fill handle, 16–17
    formulas, 17–19
    formulas, with functions, 45–57
    headers and footers, 120–125
    hyperlinks, 222–227
    images, 275–279
    page breaks, 112–115
    pictures, 284–286
    rows, 74–75
    shapes, 281–283
    SmartArt diagrams, 288–292
    symbols and special characters, 273–275
    worksheets, 167–169
Insert Picture dialog box, 275
    inserting pictures with, 284
    inserting watermarks with, 287

integration between programs, 185–186
Italic button, 78

K

keyboard, selecting cells using, 20

L

landscape orientation, 112
last action, repeating, 92
less than sign (<), as excluded from file name, 8
line charts, 241, 242
linking data, 184–185
live preview feature, 81
loans, finding periodic payments for, 51–52
logical test, 54

M

margins, changing, 109–110
marquee, 162
mathematical operators, writing formulas with, 40–45
MAX function, 47, 48–50
Maximize button, 182
Merge & Center button, 78
Merge Styles dialog box, 220, 221
merging, cells, 21–22
MIN function, 47, 48–50
Minimize button, 182
Mini toolbar, formatting with, 78
mixed cell references, 57
    in formulas, 59–60
modifying
    cell styles, 219–220
    hyperlinks, 226–227
mouse, selecting cells using, 19–20
Move Chart dialog box, 248
Move or Copy dialog box, 169
    for copying worksheet to another workbook, 210, 211
moving
    chart labels, 251
    charts, 242–243
    chart shapes, 255
    data, 182–183
    images, 276
    selected cells, 162–163
    SmartArt diagrams, 289
    workbooks, 182

multiplication, 41
  in order of operators, 40

N

Name box, 6, 7
navigating, using hyperlinks, 223–224
negation, in order of operators, 40
New tab Backstage view, 228
NOW function, 51, 53–54
Nper argument, 51
number filter, 135
Number Format button, 83
number formatting, 69
  Format Cells dialog box in, 84–86
number formatting buttons, 22
Number group buttons, formatting numbers using, 82–84
numbers
  as category in Format Cells dialog box, 85
  counting, in range, 50
  formatting, 22–24
  formatting, using Number group buttons, 82–84
  using AutoSum button to add, 17–18
  using AutoSum button to average, 18
number symbols (###), for exceeding space in cell, 8

O

Odd Page Header tab, 123
Office Clipboard
  copying and pasting cells using, 166
  using, 165–166
Open dialog box
  for copying workbook, 205
  for creating folders, 200–201
  for deleting workbooks and folders, 203
  elements of, 200
  for opening multiple workbooks, 179
  for opening workbooks, 16
  for renaming folders, 202
  for renaming workbooks, 206
  for selecting workbooks, 202
order of operations, 40
Orientation button, 79

P

page breaks, inserting and removing, 112–115
page orientation, changing, 112
Page Setup dialog box, 110
  inserting headers and footers, 120–125
  printing column and row headings, 118
  printing column and row titles, 115–116
  printing gridlines, 118
page size, changing, 112
panes, freezing and unfreezing, 174–176
Paste command, 178
Paste Options button, 183
  using, 163–165
pasting
  data, 182–183
  data, between programs, 185–186
  workbooks, 205–206
payments, finding future value of series of, 52–53
percent formatting, 82–83
percents, 41
  as category in Format Cells dialog box, 85
  in order of operators, 40
percent sign (%), in formatting numbers, 22, 82
Percent Style format, 22
periodic payments, finding, for loans, 51–52
pictures
  inserting, 284–286
  inserting, into charts, 257
  inserting, as a watermark, 287–288
  inserting background, 117
  linking using, 225
Picture Tools Format tab, 275, 276
pie charts, 241, 242
  creating and formatting, 259–260
pinning workbooks, 208
pipe symbol (|), as excluded from file name, 8
PMT function, 51
portrait orientation, 112
printing
  charts, 245
  column and row titles on multiple pages, 115–116
  customizing, 125–126
  gridlines, 118
  row and column headings, 118
  specific areas of worksheets, 118–119
  workbooks, 11–12
  workbooks, containing multiple worksheets, 173
Print tab Backstage view, 12, 113
  for printing charts, 245
programs, copying and pasting data between, 185–186
Pv argument, in formula, 51

Q

question mark (?), as excluded from file name, 8
Quick Access toolbar, 8, 12
  Redo button on, 126–127
  Undo button on, 126–127
quick list, displaying, 208
quotation marks ("), as excluded from file name, 8

R

radar charts, 242
ranges
  counting numbers in, 50
  defined, 177
  working with, 177–178
Recent tab Backstage view, 207–210
recent workbook list
  clearing, 209
  managing, 207–210
Recycle Bin
  deleting workbooks to, 203
  displaying contents of, 203
  restoring workbooks from, 203
Redo button, 126–127
relative cell references, 18, 57
  copying formula with, 41–42
removing
  cell styles, 220
  hyperlinks, 226–227
  page breaks, 112–115
renaming
  folders, 202
  workbooks, 206–207
Repeat command, 92
repeating last action, 92
Restore Down button, 182
returning the result, 45
ribbon, 6

root folders, 201
Row Height dialog box, 73–74
rows
    changing height of, 73–74
    deleting, 76
    hiding and unhiding, 94–96
    inserting, 74–75
    printing headings for, 118
    printing titles, on multiple pages, 115–116

S

Save As dialog box, 8
    for creating folders, 201
    deleting workbooks and folders in, 203
    for saving workbook, 8
saving workbooks, 8–9
scaling data, 116–117
scatter charts, 242
scientific category, in Format Cells dialog box, 85
screenshots, creating, 279–284
scroll bars, 6
    horizontal, 6, 7, 174
    vertical, 6, 7, 174
selecting cells, 19–20
semicolon (;), as excluded from file name, 8
shading, adding to cells, 92, 93
shapes, inserting and copying, 281–283
sheet tab, 6
sheet tab shortcut menu, 169
sizing
    charts, 242–243
    chart shapes, 255
    images, 276
    SmartArt diagrams, 289
    workbooks, 182
SmartArt diagrams
    changing design, 290–291
    changing formatting, 291–292
    entering data into, 289
    inserting, 288–292
    sizing, moving, and deleting, 289
SmartArt Graphic dialog box, 288
SmartArt Tools Format tab, 291
smart tag, 43
Sort dialog box, sorting data using, 133–135
sorting data, 133–135
source worksheet, 184

special category in Format Cells dialog box, 85
special characters, inserting, 273–275
spell checking, 126, 127–128
split bar, 174
spreadsheets, using, 3
statistical functions, writing formulas with, 47–50
Status bar, 6, 7, 10
stock charts, 242
Style dialog box
    in defining cell style, 217
    in modifying cell style, 219
subfolders, 201
subscripts, 88
subtraction, 41
    in order of operators, 40
SUM function, 17, 47
superscripts, 88
surface charts, 242
Symbol dialog box, 273, 274
symbols, inserting, 273–275

T

tabs, 6
templates, using, 227–229
text
    as category in Format Cells dialog box, 85
    writing IF formulas containing, 56
text box
    drawing and formatting, 285–286
    linking using, 225
theme
    applying, 81–82
    color, 81
    defined, 69, 81
    effects, 81
    font, 81
time, as category in Format Cells dialog box, 85
time functions, writing formulas with, 53–54
Title bar, 6
Trace Error button, using, 43
2-D column chart, 241
type argument in formula, 51
typing errors, AutoCorrect in correcting, 12

U

Underline button, 78
Undo button, 126–127
unfreezing panes, 174–176

Unhide dialog box, 171, 181
unhiding
    columns and rows, 94–96
    workbooks, 181

V

values, pasting, 166–167
vertical scroll bars, 6, 7, 174

W

watermark
    defined, 287
    inserting pictures as, 287–288
web page, linking to existing, 222–223
"what if" situations, 3, 37, 57
windows, working with, 178–182
WordArt
    creating, 293–294
    sizing and moving, 293
Word document, copying and pasting data from Excel document to, 185–186
workbooks
    arranging, 179–180
    closing, 12
    copying, 204–205
    copying worksheets to another, 210–211
    creating, 5–8, 9
    creating, with multiple worksheets, 161
    cutting and pasting, 205–206
    defined, 5
    deleting, 203
    hiding/unhiding, 181
    hiding worksheets in, 171, 172
    inserting worksheets, 167–169
    linking to new, 224
    linking to place in, 224
    maintaining, 200–207
    moving, 182
    moving worksheets to, 211–213
    opening, 16–17
    opening, multiple, 179
    pinning, 208
    printing, 11–12
    printing, multiple worksheets, 173
    quick list of, 208
    recent list of, 207–210

recovering unsaved, 209
renaming, 206–207
saving, 8–9
selecting, 202
sending, to different drives or folders, 205
sizing, 182
worksheets included, by default, 161

worksheet areas, 5, 8
  printing specific, 118–119

worksheets
  blank, 5
  cell formatting on, 128–132
  centering horizontally and/or vertically, 110–111
  columns in, 5
  copying, to another workbook, 210–211
  creating workbooks with multiple, 161
  dependent, 184
  displaying formulas in, 51
  elements of, 6
  filtering data on, 135–137
  finding and replacing data on, 128–132
  finding averages in, 47–48
  finding maximum and minimum values in, 49–50
  formatting multiple, 171–172
  formatting pages, 109–119
  hiding, in workbook, 171, 172
  inserting, 167–169
  inserting and removing page breaks in, 112–115
  inserting headers and footers, 120–125
  inserting SmartArt diagram into, 289–290
  linking cells between, 184–185
  managing, 169–176, 210–213
  moving, to another workbook, 211–213
  printing column and row titles on multiple, 115–116
  printing specific areas of, 118–119
  printing workbooks containing multiple, 173
  scaling data for, 116–117
  sorting data on, 133–135
  source, 184
  splitting into windows, 174–176

writing
  formulas by pointing, 43, 44–45
  formulas with date and time functions, 53–54
  formulas with financial functions, 51–53
  formulas with IF function, 54–55
  formulas with statistical functions, 47–50
  IF formulas containing text, 56

X

x axis, 246, 251
XY charts, 242

Y

y axis, 246, 251

Microsoft Access Level 1

Unit 1 ■ Creating Tables and Queries

Chapter 1 ■ Managing and Creating Tables

Chapter 2 ■ Creating Relationships between Tables

Chapter 3 ■ Performing Queries

Chapter 4 ■ Creating and Modifying Tables in Design View

Microsoft Access
Managing and Creating Tables

CHAPTER 1

PERFORMANCE OBJECTIVES

Upon successful completion of Chapter 1, you will be able to:
- Open and close objects in a database
- Insert, delete, and move rows and columns in a table
- Adjust table column width
- Preview and print a table
- Design and create a table
- Rename column headings
- Insert a column name, caption, and description
- Insert Quick Start fields
- Assign a default value and field size

Managing information in a company is an integral part of operating a business. Information can come in a variety of forms, such as data about customers, including names, addresses, and telephone numbers; product data; purchasing and buying data; and much more. Most companies today manage data using a database management system software program. Microsoft Office Professional includes a database management system software program named *Access*. With Access, you can organize, store, maintain, retrieve, sort, and print all types of business data.

For example, the manager of a bookstore could use Access to maintain data on customers, such as names, addresses, types of books purchased, and types of books ordered. With this data in Access, the manager could use the information to determine what types of books have been ordered by customers in the past few months and determine what inventory to purchase. This chapter contains just a few ideas on how to manage data with Access. With a properly designed and maintained database management system, a company can operate smoothly with logical, organized, and useful information.

Model answers for this chapter's projects appear on the following pages.

Access2010L1C1

Note: Before beginning the projects, copy to your storage medium the Access2010L1C1 subfolder from the Access2010L1 folder on the CD that accompanies this textbook. Make sure you have copied the files from the CD to your storage medium. Open all database files from your removable storage device and not directly from the CD since Access database files on the CD are read-only. Steps on how to copy a folder are presented on the inside of the back cover of this textbook. Do this every time you start a chapter's projects.

Project 2 Manage Tables in a Database

AL1-C1-PacTrek.accdb

Suppliers Table

Supplier#	SupplierName	StreetAddress	City	Prov/State	PostalCode	Field1	EmailAddress
10	Hopewell, Inc.	5600 Carver Road	Port Moody	BC	V3H 1A4	(604) 555-3843	hopewell@emcp.net
25	Langley Corporation	805 First Avenue	Burnaby	BC	V3J 1C9	(604) 555-1200	langley@emcp.net
31	Sound Supplies	2104 Union Street	Seattle	WA	98105	(206) 555-4855	ssupplies@emcp.net
35	Emerald City Products	1059 Pike Street	Seattle	WA	98102	(206) 555-7728	ecproducts@emcp.net
38	Hadley Company	5845 Jefferson Street	Seattle	WA	98107	(206) 555-8003	hcompany@emcp.net
42	Fraser Valley Products	3894 Old Yale Road	Abbotsford	BC	V2S 1A9	(604) 555-1455	fvproducts@emcp.net
54	Manning, Inc.	1039 South 22nd	Vancouver	BC	V5K 1R1	(604) 555-0087	manning@emcp.net
68	Freedom Corporation	14 Fourth Avenue	Vancouver	BC	V5K 2C7	(604) 555-2155	freedom@emcp.net
70	Rosewood, Inc.	998 North 42nd Street	Vancouver	BC	V5K 2N8	(778) 555-6643	rosewood@emcp.net
84	Macadam, Inc.	675 Third Street	Vancouver	BC	V5K 2R9	(604) 555-5522	macadam@emcp.net
99	KL Distributions	402 Yukon Drive	Bellingham	WA	98435	(360) 555-3711	kldist@emcp.net

Products Table, Page 1

Product#	Product	Supplier#	UnitsInStock	UnitsOnOrder	ReorderLevel
101-S1B	SL 0-degrees down sleeping bag, black	54	16	0	15
101-S1R	SL 0-degrees down sleeping bag, red	54	17	0	15
101-S2B	SL 15-degrees synthetic sleeping bag, black	54	21	15	25
101-S2R	SL 15-degrees synthetic sleeping bag, red	54	12	15	25
101-S3B	SL 20-degrees synthetic sleeping bag, black	54	8	15	10
101-S3R	SL 20-degrees synthetic sleeping bag, red	54	4	25	10
209-L	Gordon wool ski hat, L	68	21	25	25
209-XL	Gordon wool ski hat, XL	68	14	25	25
209-XXL	Gordon wool ski hat, XXL	68	10	20	20
210-L	Tech-lite ski hat, L	68	17	25	25
210-M	Tech-lite ski hat, M	68	6	15	15
210-XL	Tech-lite ski hat, XL	68	22	0	20
299-M1	HT waterproof hiking boots, MS13	31	8	0	10
299-M2	HT waterproof hiking boots, MS12	31	2	10	10
299-M3	HT waterproof hiking boots, MS11	31	6	10	10
299-M4	HT waterproof hiking boots, MS10	31	7	0	10
299-M5	HT waterproof hiking boots, MS9	31	9	10	10
299-W1	HT waterproof hiking boots, W510	31	5	8	8
299-W2	HT waterproof hiking boots, W510	31	9	0	10
299-W3	HT waterproof hiking boots, W59	31	3	10	10
299-W4	HT waterproof hiking boots, W58	31	2	10	10
299-W5	HT waterproof hiking boots, W57	31	3	10	10
299-W6	HT waterproof hiking boots, W56	31	11	0	10
371-L	Lite-tech ski gloves, ML	68	3	10	10
371-M	Lite-tech ski gloves, MM	68	5	0	10
371-XL	Lite-tech ski gloves, MXXL	68	12	10	10
375-L	Lite-tech ski gloves, WL	68	22	0	20
375-M	Lite-tech ski gloves, WM	68	3	20	20
375-S	Lite-tech ski gloves, WS	68	6	20	20
442-1A	Polar backpack, 150BR	42	12	0	10
442-1B	Polar backpack, 150RW	42	9	10	10
443-1A	Polar backpack, 250BR	42	14	0	15
443-1B	Polar backpack, 250RW	42	6	15	15

Products Table, Page 2

Product#	Product	Supplier#	UnitsInStock	UnitsOnOrder	ReorderLevel
558-C	ICE snow goggles, clear	68	18	0	15
559-B	ICE snow goggles, bronze	68	22	0	20
602-XR	Binoculars, 8 x 42	35	3	5	5
602-XT	Binoculars, 10.5 x 45	35	5	5	5
602-XX	Binoculars, 10 x 50	35	7	0	5
647-1	Two-person dome tent	99	10	15	15
648-2	Three-person dome tent	99	5	0	10
651-1	K-2 one-person tent	99	8	0	10
652-2	K-2 two-person tent	99	12	0	10
804-50	AG freestyle snowboard, X50	70	7	0	5
804-60	AG freestyle snowboard, X60	70	8	0	5
897-L	Lang blunt snowboard	70	8	0	7
897-W	Lang blunt snowboard, wide	70	4	0	3
901-S	Solar battery pack	38	16	0	15
917-S	Silo portable power pack	38	8	0	10

Orders Table

Order#	Supplier Number	Product Number	UnitsOrdered	Order Amount	OrderDate
1	54	101-S3	10	$1,137.50	1/2/2012
2	68	209-L	25	$173.75	1/2/2012
3	68	209-XL	25	$180.00	1/2/2012
4	68	209-XXL	20	$145.80	1/2/2012
5	68	210-M	15	$97.35	1/2/2010
6	68	210-L	25	$162.25	1/2/2010
7	31	299-M2	10	$887.90	1/2/2012
8	31	299-M3	10	$887.90	1/16/2012
9	31	299-M5	10	$887.90	1/16/2012
10	31	299-W1	8	$602.32	1/16/2012
11	31	299-W3	10	$752.90	1/16/2012
12	31	299-W4	10	$752.90	1/16/2012
13	31	299-W5	10	$752.90	1/16/2012
14	35	602-XR	5	$2,145.00	1/16/2012

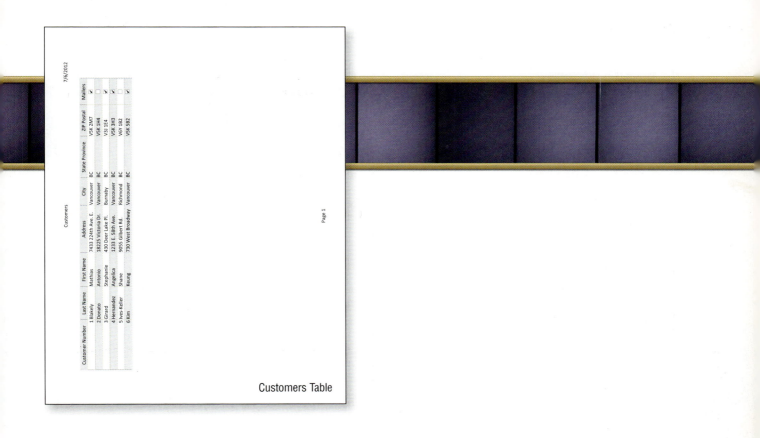

Customers Table

Project 1 — Explore an Access Database — 1 Part

You will open a database and open and close objects in the database including tables, queries, forms, and reports.

Exploring a Database

A ***database*** is comprised of a series of objects such as tables, queries, forms, and reports that you use to enter, manage, view, and print data. Data in a database is organized into tables, which contain information for related items such as customers, employees, orders, and products. To view the various objects in a database, you will open a previously created database and then navigate in the database and open objects.

To create a new database or open a previously created database, click the Start button on the Taskbar, point to *All Programs*, click *Microsoft Office*, and then click *Microsoft Access 2010*. (These steps may vary depending on your system configuration.) This displays the Access New tab Backstage view as shown in Figure 1.1. The Backstage view organizes database management tasks into tabs. Quick Command buttons such as Save, Save Object As, Save Database As, Open, and Close Database are located at the top left pane in the view. Below the Quick Command buttons the view is organized into tabs such as Info, Recent, New, Print, Save & Publish, and Help.

Start

Figure 1.1 New Tab Backstage View

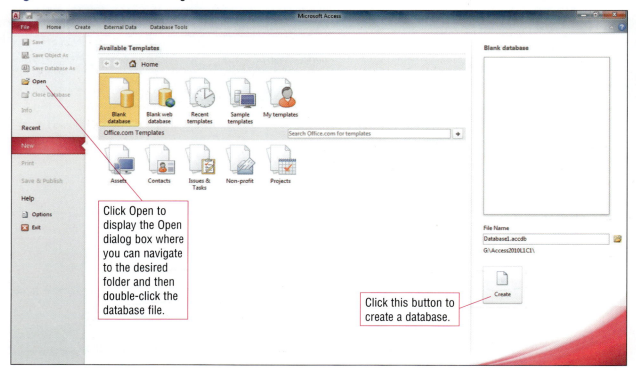

Create

▼ **Quick Steps**

Open a Database
1. Open Access.
2. Click Open button.
3. Navigate to desired location.
4. Double-click database.

HINT
Only one database can be open at a time.

HINT
The active database is saved automatically on a periodic basis and also when you make another record active, close the table, or close the database.

Close

To create a new database, click the folder icon that displays to the right of the file name at the right side of the screen, navigate to the location where you want to save your database, and then click the Create button.

Opening and Closing a Database

To open an existing Access database, click the Open button located at the left side of the New tab Backstage view. At the Open dialog box, navigate to the location where the database is located and then double-click the database name. You can also open a database that you previously opened by clicking the Recent tab at the New tab Backstage view. This displays the Recent tab Backstage view and a list of the most recently opened databases displays in the *Recent Databases* list box. To open a database, click the desired database in the list box.

When you open a database, the Access screen displays as shown in Figure 1.2. Refer to Table 1.1 for a description of the Access screen elements. To close a database, click the File tab and then click the Close Database button. To exit Access, click the Close button that displays in the upper right corner of the screen, or click the File tab and then click the Exit button that displays below the Help tab.

Only one Access database can be open at a time. If you open a new database in the current Access window, the existing database is closed. (You can however open multiple instances of Access and open a database in each.) In other applications in the Microsoft Office suite, you have to save a revised file after you edit data in the file. In an Access database, changes you make to data are saved automatically when you move to the next record.

Figure 1.2 Access Screen

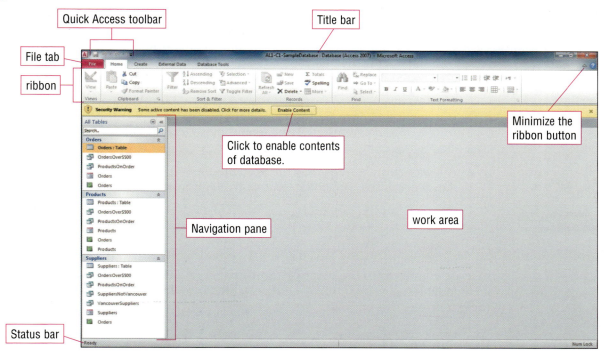

Table 1.1 Access Screen Elements

Feature	Description
Quick Access toolbar	Contains buttons for commonly used commands.
File tab	Click this tab and the Backstage view displays containing buttons and tabs for working with and managing databases.
Title bar	Displays database name followed by program name.
Tabs	Contain commands and features organized into groups.
Ribbon	Area containing the tabs and commands divided into groups.
Message bar	Displays security alerts if the database you open contains potentially unsafe content.
Navigation pane	Displays names of objects within database grouped by categories.
Work area	Area in screen where opened objects display.
Status bar	Displays number of pages and words, View buttons, and the Zoom slider bar.

A security warning message bar may appear below the ribbon if Access determines the file you are opening did not originate from a trusted location on your computer and may have viruses or other security hazards. This often occurs when you copy a file from another medium (such as a CD or the Web). Active content in the file is disabled until you click the Enable Content button. The message bar closes when you identify the database as a trusted source. Before making any changes to the database, you must click the Enable Content button.

Table 1.2 Database Objects

Object	Description
Table	Organizes data in fields (columns) and records (rows). A database must contain at least one table. The table is the base upon which other objects are created.
Query	Used to display data from a table or related tables that meets a conditional statement and/or to perform calculations. For example, display all records from a specific month or display only those records containing a specific city.
Form	Allows fields and records to be presented in a different layout than the datasheet. Used to facilitate data entry and maintenance.
Report	Prints data from tables or queries.

The Navigation pane at the left side of the Access screen displays the objects that are contained in the database. Some common objects found in a database include tables, queries, forms, and reports. Refer to Table 1.2 for a description of these four types of objects.

Opening and Closing Objects

Hide the Navigation pane by clicking the button in the upper right corner of the pane (called the Shutter Bar Open/Close Button) or by pressing F11.

Shutter

Database objects display in the Navigation pane. Control what displays in the pane by clicking the Menu bar at the top of the Navigation pane and then clicking the desired option at the drop-down list. For example, to display a list of all saved objects in the database, click the *Object Type* option at the drop-down list. This view displays the objects grouped by type—Tables, Queries, Forms, and Reports. To open an object, double-click the object in the Navigation pane. The object opens in the work area and a tab displays with the object name at the left side of the object.

To view more of an object, consider closing the Navigation pane by clicking the Shutter Bar Open/Close Button located in the upper right corner of the pane. Click the button again to open the Navigation pane. You can open more than one object in the work area. Each object opens with a visible tab. You can navigate to objects by clicking the object tab. To close an object, click the Close button that displays in the upper right corner of the work area.

Project 1   Opening and Closing a Database and Objects in a Database   Part 1 of 1

1. Open Access by clicking the Start button on the Taskbar, pointing to *All Programs*, clicking *Microsoft Office*, and then clicking *Microsoft Access 2010*. (These steps may vary.)
2. At the New tab Backstage view, click the Open button that displays at the left side of the screen.
3. At the Open dialog box, navigate to the Access2010L1C1 folder on your storage medium and then double-click the database ***AL1-C1-SampleDatabase.accdb***. (This database contains data on orders, products, and suppliers for a specialty hiking and backpacking outfitters store named Pacific Trek.)

4. Click the Enable Content button in the message bar if the security warning message appears. (The message bar will display immediately below the ribbon.)
5. With the database open, click the All Access Objects button (displays as a down-pointing arrow at the top of the Navigation pane) and then click *Object Type* at the drop-down list. (This option displays the objects grouped by type—Tables, Queries, Forms, and Reports.)
6. Double-click *Suppliers* in the *Tables* section of the Navigation pane. This opens the Suppliers table in the work area as shown in Figure 1.3.
7. Close the Suppliers table by clicking the Close button in the upper right corner of the work area.

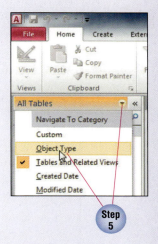

Step 5

Step 7

8. Double-click *OrdersOver$500* in the *Queries* section of the Navigation pane. A query displays data that meets a conditional statement and this query displays orders that meet the criterion of being more than $500.
9. Close the query by clicking the Close button in the upper right corner of the work area.
10. Double-click the *SuppliersNotVancouver* query in the Navigation pane and notice that the query displays information about suppliers except those located in Vancouver.
11. Click the Close button in the work area.
12. Double-click *Orders* in the *Forms* section of the Navigation pane. This displays an order form. A form is used to view and edit data in a table one record at a time.
13. Click the Close button in the work area.
14. Double-click *Orders* in the *Reports* section of the Navigation pane. This displays a report with information about orders and order amounts.
15. Close the Navigation pane by clicking the Shutter Bar Open/Close Button located in the upper right corner of the pane.
16. After viewing the report, click the button again to open the Navigation pane.
17. Click the Close button in the work area.
18. Close the database by clicking the File tab and then clicking the Close Database button.
19. Exit Access by clicking the Close button (contains an X) that displays in the upper right corner of the screen.

Step 15

Chapter 1 ■ Managing and Creating Tables 9

Figure 1.3 Open Suppliers Table

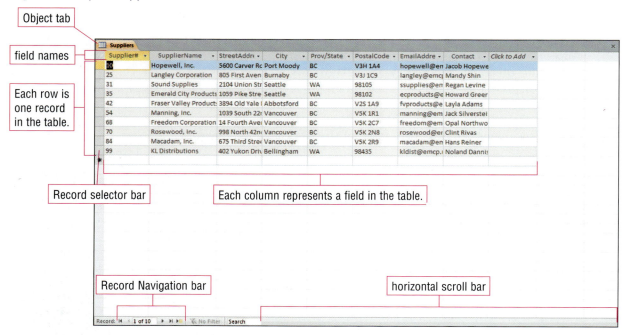

Project 2   Manage Tables in a Database   7 Parts

Pacific Trek is an outfitting store specializing in hiking and backpacking gear. Information about the store including suppliers and products are contained in a database. You will open the database and then insert and delete records; insert, move, and delete fields; preview and print tables; and create two new tables for the database.

Managing Tables

In a new database, tables are the first objects created since all other database objects rely on a table for the source of the data. Maintenance of the database and tables in the database is important to keep the database up to date. Managing tables in a database may include inserting or deleting records, inserting or deleting fields, renaming fields, and creating a hard copy of the table by printing the table.

Inserting and Deleting Records

When you open a table, it displays in Datasheet view in the work area. The Datasheet view displays the contents of a table in a column and row format similar to an Excel worksheet. Columns contain the field data, with the field names in the header row at the top of the table, and records are represented as rows. A Record Navigation bar displays at the bottom of the screen just above the Status bar and contains buttons to navigate in the table. Figure 1.4 identifies the buttons on the Record Navigation bar.

Figure 1.4 Record Navigation Bar

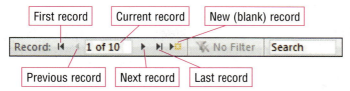

To add a new record to the open table, make sure the Home tab is selected and then click the New button in the Records group. This moves the insertion point to the first field in the blank row at the bottom of the table and the *Current Record* box on the Record Navigation bar indicates what record you are creating (or editing). In addition to clicking the New button in the Records group in the Home tab, you can create a new record by clicking the New (blank) record button on the Record Navigation bar.

When working in a table, press the Tab key to make the next field active or press Shift + Tab to make the previous field active. You can also click in the desired field using the mouse. When you begin typing data for the first field in the record, another row of cells is automatically inserted below the current row and a pencil icon displays in the record selector bar at the beginning of the current record. The pencil icon indicates that the record is being edited and that the changes to the data have not been saved. When you enter the data in the last field in the record and then move the insertion point out of the field, the pencil icon is removed, indicating that the data is saved.

When maintaining a table, you may need to delete a record when you no longer want the data in the record. One method for deleting a record is to click in one of the fields in the record, make sure the Home tab is selected, click the Delete button arrow, and then click *Delete Record* at the drop-down list. At the message that displays asking if you want to delete the record, click the Yes button. When you click in a field in a record, the Delete button displays in a dimmed manner unless specific data is selected.

When you are finished entering data in a record in a table, the data is automatically saved. Changes to the layout of a table, however, are not automatically saved. For example, if you delete a record in a table, when you close the table you will be asked if you are sure you want to delete the record.

▼ **Quick Steps**

Add New Record
1. Open table.
2. Click New button in Home tab.
3. Type data.
OR
1. Open table.
2. Click New (blank) record button on Record Navigation bar.
3. Type data.

Delete Record
1. Open table.
2. Click Delete button arrow in Home tab.
3. Click *Delete Record*.
4. Click Yes button.

New

Delete

Project 2a — Inserting and Deleting Records in a Table — Part 1 of 7

1. Open Access.
2. At the New tab Backstage view, click the Open button that displays at the left side of the screen.
3. At the Open dialog box, navigate to the Access2010L1C1 folder on your storage medium and then double-click the database *AL1-C1-PacTrek.accdb*.
4. Click the Enable Content button in the message bar if the security warning message appears. (The message bar will display immediately below the ribbon.)
5. With the database open, make sure the Navigation pane displays object types. (If it does not, click the All Access Objects button at the top of the Navigation pane and then click *Object Type* at the drop-down list.)

6. Double-click the *Suppliers* table in the Navigation pane. (This opens the table in Datasheet view.)
7. With the Suppliers table open and the Home tab active, type a new record by completing the following steps:
   a. Click the New button in the Records group in the Home tab. (This moves the insertion point to the first field in the blank record at the bottom of the table and the *Current Record* box in the Record Navigation bar indicates what record you are creating (or editing).
   b. Type **38**. (This inserts *38* in the field immediately below *99*.)
   c. Press the Tab key (this makes the next field active) and then type **Hadley Company**.
   d. Press the Tab key and then type **5845 Jefferson Street**.
   e. Press the Tab key and then type **Seattle**.
   f. Press the Tab key and then type **WA**.
   g. Press the Tab key and then type **98107**.
   h. Press the Tab key and then type **hcompany@emcp.net**.
   i. Press the Tab key and then type **Jurene Miller**.

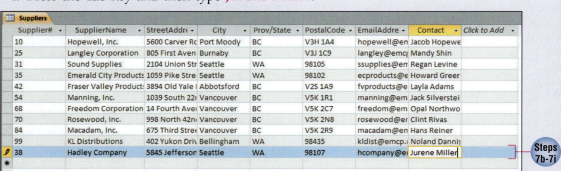

8. Close the Suppliers table by clicking the Close button in the work area.
9. Open the Products table by double-clicking *Products* in the *Tables* section of the Navigation pane. (This opens the table in Datasheet view.)
10. Insert two new records by completing the following steps:
    a. Click the New button in the Records group and then type data for a new record as shown in Figure 1.5 (the record that begins with *901-S*).
    b. When you type the last field entry in the record for product number 901-S, press the Tab key. This moves the insertion point to the blank field below *901-S*.
    c. Type the new record as shown in Figure 1.5 (the record that begins *917-S*).

11. With the Products table open, delete a record by completing the following steps:
    a. Click in the field containing the data *780-2*.
    b. Click the Delete button arrow in the Records group (the button will display in a dimmed manner) and then click *Delete Record* at the drop-down list.
    c. At the message asking if you want to delete the record, click the Yes button.
12. Click the Save button on the Quick Access toolbar.

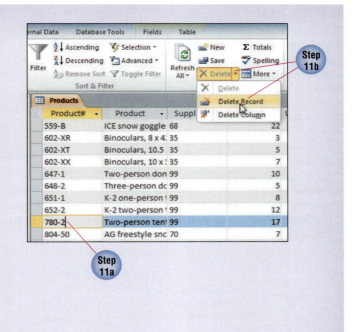

13. Close the Products table by clicking the Close button in the work area.

Figure 1.5 Project 2a, Step 10

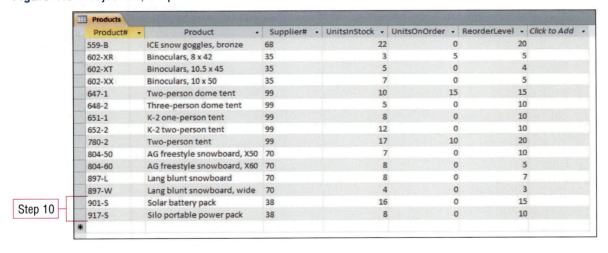

Inserting, Moving, and Deleting Fields

When managing a database, you may determine that you need to add additional information to a table. For example, you might decide that you want to insert a field for contact information, a field for cell phone numbers, or a field for the number of items in stock. To insert a new field in a table, open the table in Datasheet view and then click in the first field below the *Click to Add* heading. Type the desired data in the field for the first record, press the Down Arrow key

▼ **Quick Steps**

Insert New Field
1. Open table.
2. Click in first field below *Click to Add* heading.
3. Type desired data.

Chapter 1 ■ Managing and Creating Tables   13

▼ Quick Steps

Move Field Column
1. Select column.
2. Position mouse pointer on heading.
3. Hold down left mouse button.
4. Drag to desired location.
5. Release mouse button.

Delete Field
1. Click in field.
2. Click Delete button arrow in Home tab.
3. Click *Delete Column*.
4. Click Yes button.

to make the field below active, and then type the desired data for the second record. Continue in this manner until you have entered data in the new field for all records in the table. In addition to pressing the Down Arrow key to move the insertion point down to the next field, you can click in the desired field using the mouse. Or, you can press the Tab key until the desired field is active.

You add a new field to the right of the existing fields. In some situations you may want to change this location. Move a field by positioning the mouse pointer on the field heading until the pointer displays as a downward-pointing black arrow and then clicking the left mouse button. This selects the entire column. With the field column selected, position the mouse pointer on the heading (the mouse pointer should display as a white arrow pointing up and to the left), hold down the left mouse button, drag to the left until a thick, black vertical line displays in the desired location, and then release the mouse button. The thick, black vertical line indicates the position where the field column will be positioned when you release the mouse button. In addition, the pointer displays with the outline of a gray box attached to it, indicating that you are performing a move operation.

Delete a field column in a manner similar to deleting a row. Click in one of the fields in the column, make sure the Home tab is selected, click the Delete button arrow, and then click *Delete Column* at the drop-down list. At the message that displays asking if you want to delete the column, click the Yes button.

Project 2b — Inserting, Moving, and Deleting Fields — Part 2 of 7

1. With the **AL1-C1-PacTrek.accdb** database open, you decide that contacting suppliers by telephone is important so you decide to add a new field to the Suppliers table. Do this by completing the following steps:
    a. Double-click the *Suppliers* table in the Navigation pane.
    b. Click in the field immediately below the heading *Click to Add*.
    c. Type **(604) 555-3843** and then press the Down Arrow key on your keyboard.
    d. Type the remaining telephone numbers as shown at the right.

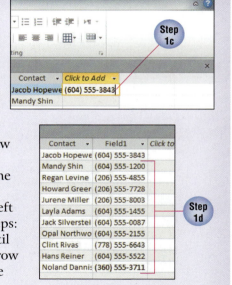

2. Move the field column so it is positioned immediately left of the *EmailAddress* field by completing the following steps:
    a. Position the mouse pointer on the heading *Field 1* until the pointer displays as a downward-pointing black arrow and then click the left mouse button. (This selects the column.)
    b. Position the mouse pointer on the heading (the pointer displays as the normal white arrow pointer), hold down the left mouse button, drag to the left until the thick, black vertical line displays immediately left of the *EmailAddress* field, and then release the mouse button.

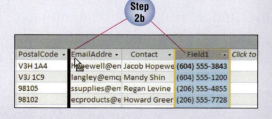

3. You realize that you no longer need the supplier contact information so you decide to delete the field. Do this by completing the following steps:
   a. Position the mouse pointer on the heading *Contact* until the pointer displays as a downward-pointing black arrow and then click the left mouse button. (This selects the column.)
   b. Click the Delete button arrow in the Records group and then click *Delete Column* at the drop-down list.
   c. At the message asking if you want to permanently delete the selected fields, click the Yes button.
4. Close the Suppliers table. At the message that displays asking if you want to save the changes to the layout of the table, click the Yes button.

Changing Column Width

When entering data in the Suppliers and Products table, did you notice that not all of the data was visible? To remedy this, you can adjust the widths of columns so that all data is visible. You can adjust the width of one column in a table to accommodate the longest entry in the column by positioning the arrow pointer on the column boundary at the right side of the column until it turns into a double-headed arrow pointing left and right with a line between and then double-clicking the left mouse button.

You can adjust the width of adjacent columns by selecting the columns first and then double-clicking on one of the selected column boundaries. To select adjacent columns, position the arrow pointer on the first column heading until the pointer turns into a down-pointing black arrow, hold down the left mouse button, drag to the last column you want to adjust, and then release the mouse button. With the columns selected, double-click one of the column boundaries.

You can also adjust the width of a column by dragging the boundary to the desired position. To do this, position the arrow pointer on the column boundary until it turns into a double-headed arrow pointing left and right with a line between, hold down the left mouse button, drag until the column is the desired width, and then release the mouse button.

▼ **Quick Steps**

Change Table Column Width
Double-click column boundary.
OR
Select columns, then double-click column boundary.
OR
Drag column boundary to desired position.

HINT
Automatically adjust column widths in an Access table in the same manner as adjusting column widths in an Excel worksheet.

Project 2c — Changing Table Column Widths — Part 3 of 7

1. With **AL1-C1-PacTrek.accdb** open, open the Suppliers table.
2. Adjust the width of the *Supplier#* column by positioning the arrow pointer on the column boundary at the right side of the *Supplier#* column until it turns into a double-headed arrow pointing left and right with a line between and then double-clicking the left mouse button.

   Step 2

3. Adjust the width of the remaining columns by completing the following steps:
   a. Position the arrow pointer on the *SupplierName* heading until the pointer turns into a down-pointing black arrow, hold down the left mouse button, drag to the *EmailAddress* heading, and then release the mouse button.
   b. With the columns selected, double-click one of the column boundaries.

4. Close the Suppliers table and click the Yes button at the message that asks if you want to save the changes to the layout.
5. Open the Products table and then complete steps similar to those in Step 3 to select and then adjust the column widths.
6. Close the Products table and click the Yes button at the message that asks if you want to save the changes to the layout.

▼ **Quick Steps**

Print a Table
1. Click File tab.
2. Click Print tab.
3. Click *Quick Print* option.
OR
1. Click File tab.
2. Click Print tab.
3. Click *Print* option.
4. Click OK.

Printing a Table

In some situations, you may want to print the data in a table. To do this, open the table, click the File tab, and then click the Print tab. This displays the Print tab Backstage view as shown in Figure 1.6. Click the *Quick Print* option to send the table directly to the printer without any changes to the printer setup or the table formatting. Click the *Print* option to display the Print dialog box where you can specify the printer, the page range, and specific records. Click OK to close the dialog box and send the table to the printer. By default, Access prints a table on letter-size paper in portrait orientation.

Figure 1.6 Print Tab Backstage View

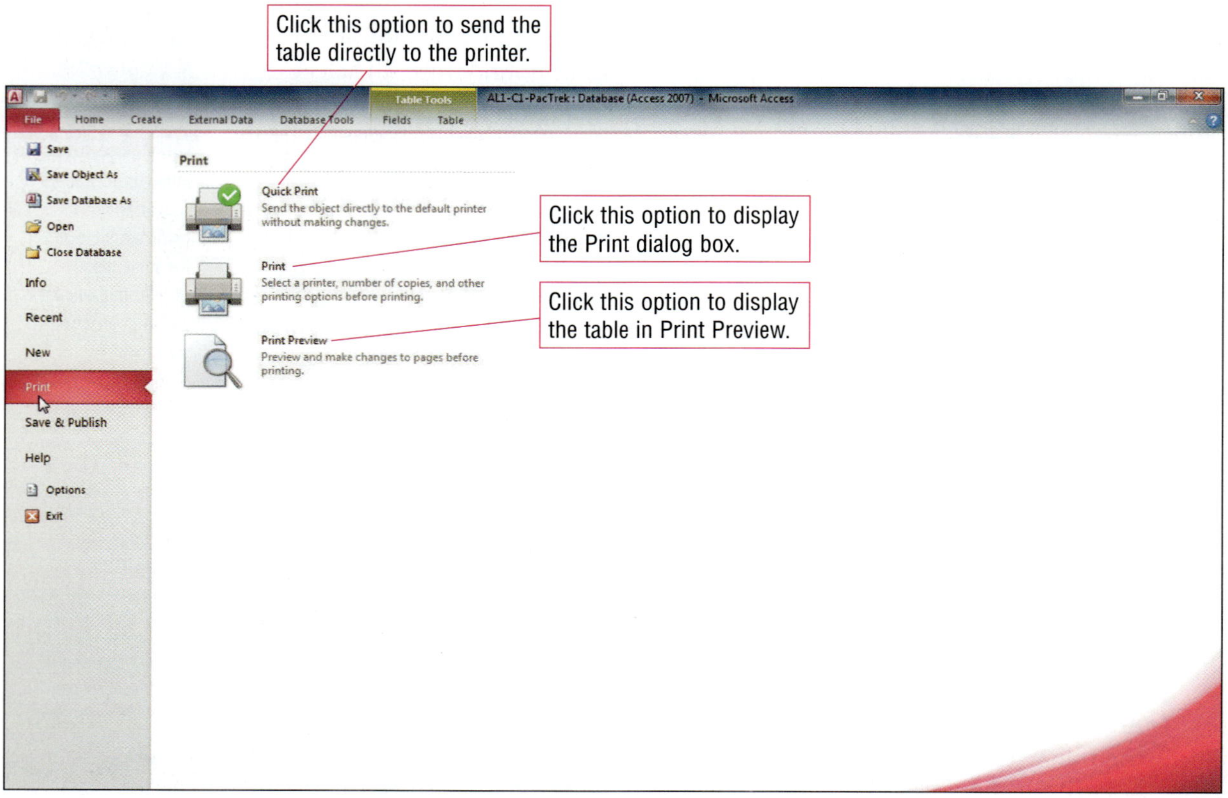

Previewing a Table

Before printing a table, you may want to display the table in Print Preview to determine how the table will print on the page. To display a table in Print Preview, as shown in Figure 1.7, click the *Print Preview* option at the Print tab Backstage view.

Use options in the Zoom group in the Print Preview tab to increase or decrease the size of the table display. You can also change the size of the table display using the Zoom slider bar located at the right side of the Status bar. If your table spans more than one page, you can use buttons on the Navigation bar to display the next or previous page in the table.

In Print Preview you can print the table by clicking the Print button located at the left side of the Print Preview tab. Click the Close Print Preview button if you want to close Print Preview and return to the table without printing the table.

Changing Page Size and Margins

By default, Access prints a table in standard page size that is 8.5 inches wide and 11 inches tall. Click the Size button in the Page Size group in the Print Preview tab and a drop-down list displays with options for changing the page size to legal size, executive size, envelope size, and so on. Access uses default top, bottom, left, and right margins of 1 inch. Change these default margins by clicking the Margins button in the Page Size group and then clicking one of the predesigned margin options.

▼ **Quick Steps**

Preview a Table
1. Click File tab.
2. Click Print tab.
3. Click *Print Preview* option.

Print Preview

Size

Margins

Figure 1.7 Print Preview

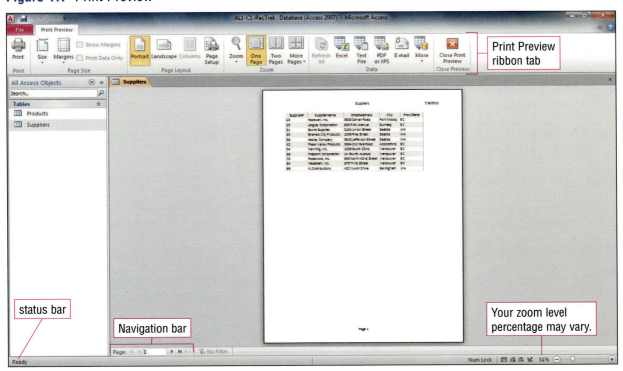

Chapter 1 ■ Managing and Creating Tables 17

Changing Page Layout

The Print Preview tab contains the Page Layout group with buttons for controlling how data is printed on the page. By default, Access prints a table in portrait orientation which prints the text on the page with the height taller than the width (like a page in this textbook). If a table contains a number of columns, changing to landscape orientation allows more columns to fit on a page. Landscape orientation rotates the printout to print wider than it is tall. To change from the default portrait orientation to landscape, click the Landscape button in the Page Layout group in the Print Preview tab.

Click the Page Setup button in the Page Layout group and the Page Setup dialog box displays as shown in Figure 1.8. At the Page Setup dialog box with the Print Options tab selected, notice that the default margins are 1 inch. Change these defaults by typing a different number in the desired margin text box. By default, the table name prints at the top center of the page along with the current date printed in the upper right side of the page. In addition, the word *Page* followed by the page number prints at the bottom of the page. If you do not want the name of the table and the date as well as the page number printed, remove the check mark from the *Print Headings* option at the Page Setup dialog box with the Print Options tab selected.

Click the Page tab at the Page Setup dialog box and the dialog box displays as shown in Figure 1.9. Change the orientation with options in the *Orientation* section, and change the paper size with options in the *Paper* section. Click the *Size* option button and a drop-down list displays with paper sizes similar to the options available at the *Size* button drop-down list in the Page Size group in the Print Preview tab. Specify the printer with options in the *Printer for (table name)* section of the dialog box.

▼ Quick Steps

Display Page Setup Dialog Box
1. Click File tab.
2. Click Print tab.
3. Click *Print Preview* option.
4. Click Page Setup button.

Landscape

Page Setup

Figure 1.8 Page Setup Dialog Box with Print Options Tab Selected

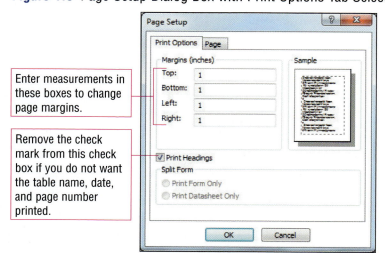

Enter measurements in these boxes to change page margins.

Remove the check mark from this check box if you do not want the table name, date, and page number printed.

Figure 1.9 Page Setup Dialog Box with Page Tab Selected

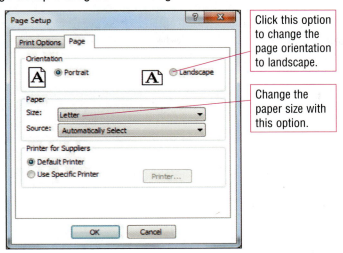

Project 2d Previewing, Changing Page Layout, and Printing Tables — Part 4 of 7

1. With **AL1-C1-PacTrek.accdb** open, open the Suppliers table.
2. Preview and then print the Suppliers table in landscape orientation by completing the following steps:
   a. Click the File tab and then click the Print tab.
   b. At the Print tab Backstage view, click the *Print Preview* option.
   c. In Print Preview, click the Two Pages button in the Zoom group in the Print Preview tab. (This displays two pages of the table.)
   d. Click the Zoom button arrow in the Zoom group in the Print Preview tab and then click *75%* at the drop-down list.

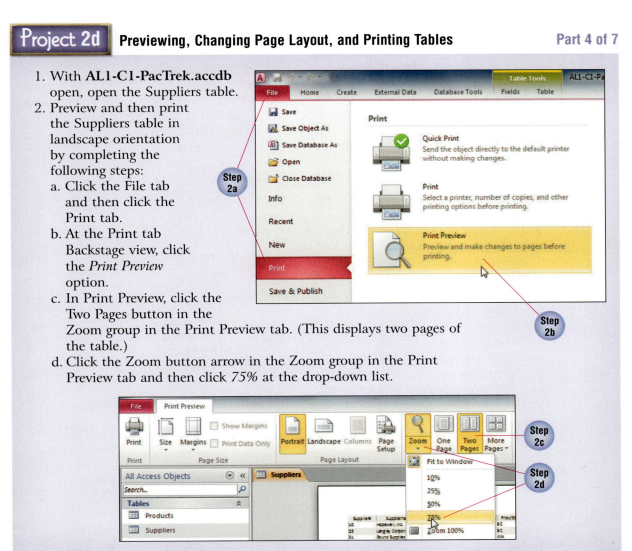

e. Position the arrow pointer on the Zoom slider bar button that displays at the right side of the Status bar, hold down the left mouse button, drag to the right until *100%* displays immediately left of the Zoom slider bar, and then release the mouse button.
f. Return the display to a full page by clicking the One Page button in the Zoom group in the Print Preview tab.
g. Click the Margins button in the Page Size group in the Print Preview tab and then click the *Narrow* option at the drop-down list. (Notice how the data will print on the page with the narrow margins.)
h. Change the margins back to the default by clicking the Margins button in the Page Size group and then clicking the *Normal* option at the drop-down list.
i. Change to landscape orientation by clicking the Landscape button in the Page Layout group. (Check the Next Page button on the Navigation pane and notice that it is dimmed. This indicates that the table will print on only one page.)
j. Print the table by clicking the Print button located at the left side of the Print Preview tab and then clicking the OK button at the Print dialog box.

3. Close the Suppliers table.
4. Open the Products table and then print the table by completing the following steps:
   a. Click the File tab and then click the Print tab.
   b. At the Print tab Backstage view, click the *Print Preview* option.
   c. Click the Page Setup button in the Page Layout group in the Print Preview tab. (This displays the Page Setup dialog box with the Print Options tab selected.)
   d. At the Page Setup dialog box, click the Page tab.
   e. Click the *Landscape* option.
   f. Click the Print Options tab.
   g. Select the current measurement in the *Top* measurement box and then type **0.5**.
   h. Select the current measurement in the *Bottom* measurement box and then type **0.5**.
   i. Select the current measurement in the *Left* measurement box and then type **1.5**.
   j. Click OK to close the dialog box.
   k. Click the Print button at the Print Preview tab and then click the OK button at the Print dialog box. (This table will print on two pages.)

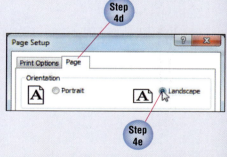

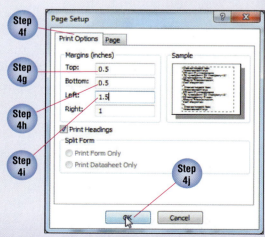

5. Close the Products table.

Designing a Table

Tables are the first objects created in a new database and all other objects in a database rely on a table for data. Designing a database involves planning the number of tables needed and the fields that will be included in each table. Each table in a database should contain information about one subject only. For example, the Suppliers table in the AL1-C1-PacTrek.accdb database contains data only about suppliers and the Products table contains data only about products.

Database designers often create a visual representation of the database's structure in a diagram similar to the one shown in Figure 1.10. Each table is represented by a box with the table name at the top of the box. Within each box, the fields that will be stored in the table are listed with the field names that will be used when the table is created. Notice that one field in each table has an asterisk next to the field name. The field with the asterisk is called a *primary key*. A primary key holds data that uniquely identifies each record in a table and is usually an identification number. The lines drawn between each table in Figure 1.10 are called *join lines* and represent links established between tables (called *relationships*) so that data can be extracted from one or more tables. Notice the join lines point to a common field name included in each table that is to be linked. (You will learn how to join [relate] tables in Chapter 2.) A database with related tables is called a *relational database*.

Notice the join line in the database diagram that connects the *Supplier#* field in the Suppliers table with the *Supplier#* field in the Products table and another join line that connects the *Supplier#* field in the Suppliers table with the *Supplier#* field in the Orders table. In the database diagram, a join line connects the *Product#* field in the Products table with the *Product#* field in the Orders table.

When designing a database, you need to consider certain design principles. The first principle is to reduce redundant (duplicate) data because redundant data increases the amount of data entry required, increases the chances for errors and inconsistencies, and takes up additional storage space. The Products table contains a *Supplier#* field and that field reduces the redundant data needed in the table. For example, rather than typing the supplier information in the Suppliers

HINT Organize data in tables to minimize or eliminate duplication.

Figure 1.10 Database Diagram

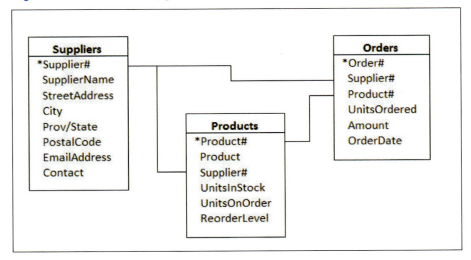

Chapter 1 ■ Managing and Creating Tables

table AND the Products table, you type the information once in the Suppliers table and then "join" the tables with the connecting field *Supplier#*. If you need information on suppliers as well as specific information about products, you can draw the information into one object such as a query or report using data from both tables. When you create the Orders table, you will use the *Supplier#* field and the *Product#* field rather than typing all of the information for the suppliers and the product description. Typing a two-letter unique identifier number for a supplier greatly reduces the amount of typing required to create the Orders table. Inserting the *Product#* field in the Orders table eliminates the need to type the product description for each order; instead, you type a unique five-, six-, or seven-digit identifier number.

Creating a Table

Creating a new table generally involves determining fields, assigning a data type to each field, modifying properties, designating the primary key, and naming the table. This process is referred to as **defining the table structure**.

The first step in creating a table is to determine the fields. A *field*, commonly called a column, is one piece of information about a person, a place, or an item. Each field contains data about one aspect of the table subject such as a company name or product number. All fields for one unit, such as a customer or product, are considered a *record*. For example, in the Suppliers table in the AL1-C1-PacTrek.accdb database, a record is all of the information pertaining to one supplier. A collection of records becomes a *table*.

A database table contains fields that describe a person, customer, client, object, place, idea, or event.

When designing a table, determine fields for information to be included on the basis of how you plan to use the data. When organizing fields, be sure to consider not only current needs for the data but also any future needs. For example, a company may need to keep track of customer names, addresses, and telephone numbers for current mailing lists. In the future, the company may want to promote a new product to customers who purchase a specific type of product. For this situation, a field that identifies product type must be included in the database. When organizing fields, consider all potential needs for the data but also try to keep the fields logical and manageable.

Table

You can create a table in Access in Datasheet view or in Design view. To create a table in Datasheet view, open the desired database (or create a new database), click the Create tab, and then click the Table button in the Tables group. This inserts a blank table in the work area with the tab labeled *Table1* as shown in Figure 1.11. Notice the column with the field name *ID* has been created automatically. Access creates *ID* as an AutoNumber field in which the field value is assigned automatically by Access as you enter each record. In many tables, you can use this AutoNumber field to create the unique identifier for the table. For example, in Project 2e you will create an Orders table and you will use the ID AutoNumber field to assign automatically a number to each order since each order must contain a unique number.

Assign a data type for each field that determines the values that can be entered for the field.

When creating a new field (column), determine the type of data you will insert in the field. For example, one field might contain text such as a name or product description, another field might contain an amount of money, and another might contain a date. The data type defines the type of information Access will allow to be entered into the field. For example, Access will not allow alphabetic characters to be entered into a field with a data type set to Date &

Figure 1.11 Blank Table

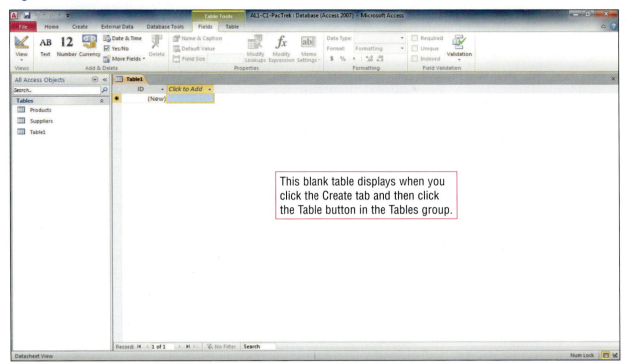

Time. The Add & Delete group in the Table Tools Fields tab contains five buttons for assigning data types plus a More Fields button. A description of the five data types assigned by the buttons is shown in Table 1.3.

More Fields

Table 1.3 Data Types

Data Type Button	Description
Text	Alphanumeric data up to 255 characters in length, such as a name, address, or value such as a telephone number or social security number that is used as an identifier and not for calculating.
Number	Positive or negative values that can be used in calculations; do not use for values that will calculate monetary amounts (see Currency).
Currency	Values that involve money; Access will not round off during calculations.
Date & Time	Use this data type to ensure dates and times are entered and sorted properly.
Yes/No	Data in the field will be either *Yes* or *No*; *True* or *False*, *On* or *Off*.

In Project 2e, you will create the Orders table as shown in Figure 1.10. Looking at the diagram in Figure 1.10, you will assign the following data types to the columns:

Order#	=	AutoNumber (Access automatically assigns this data type to the first column)
Supplier#	=	Text (the supplier numbers are identifiers, not numbers for calculating)
Product#	=	Text (the product numbers are identifiers, not numbers for calculating)
UnitsOrdered	=	Number (the unit numbers are values for calculating)
Amount	=	Currency
OrderDate	=	Date & Time

When you click a data type button, Access inserts a field to the right of the *ID* field and selects the field heading *Field1*. Type a name for the field, press the Enter key, and Access selects the next field column name *Click to Add* and inserts a drop-down list of data types. This drop-down list contains the same five data types as the buttons in the Add & Delete group as well as additional data types. Click the desired data type at the drop-down list, type the desired field name, and then press Enter. Continue in this manner until you have entered all field names for the table. When naming a field, consider the following naming guidelines:

- Each field must contain a unique name.
- The name should describe the contents of the field.
- A field name can contain up to 64 characters.
- A field name can contain letters and numbers. Some symbols are permitted but others are excluded, so you should avoid using symbols other than the underscore character that is used as a word separator and the number symbol to indicate an identifier number.
- Do not use a space in a field name. Although a space is an accepted character, most database designers avoid using spaces in field names and object names. Use field compound words for field names or the underscore character as a word separator. For example, a field name for a person's last name could be named *LastName*, *Last_Name*, or *LName*.
- Abbreviate field names so that the names are as short as possible but easily understood. For example, a field such as *CompanyName* could be shortened to *CoName* and a field such as *EmailAddress* could be shortened to *Email*.

Avoid using spaces in field names.

Project 2e Creating a Table and Entering Data   Part 5 of 7

1. With **AL1-C1-PacTrek.accdb** open, create a new table and specify data types and column headings by completing the following steps:
   a. Click the Create tab.
   b. Click the Table button in the Tables group.
   c. Click the Text button in the Add & Delete group.

Step 1c

d. With the *Field1* column heading selected, type **Supplier#**, and then press the Enter key. (This displays a drop-down list of data types below the *Click to Add* heading.)
e. Click the *Text* option at the drop-down list.
f. Type **Product#** and then press Enter.
g. Click *Number* at the drop-down list, type **UnitsOrdered**, and then press Enter.
h. Click *Currency* at the drop-down list, type **Amount**, and then press Enter.
i. Click *Date & Time* at the drop-down list and then type **OrderDate**. (Do not press the Enter key since this is the last column in the table.)

2. Enter the first record in the table as shown in Figure 1.12 by completing the following steps:
   a. Click twice in the first field below the *Supplier#* column heading. (The first time you click the mouse button, the row is selected. Clicking the second time makes active only the field below *Supplier#*.)
   b. Type the data in the fields as shown in Figure 1.12. Press the Tab key to move to the next field or press Shift + Tab to move to the previous field. Access will automatically insert the next number in the sequence in the first column (the *ID* column). When typing the money amounts in the *Amount* column, you do not need to type the dollar sign or the comma. Access will automatically insert them when you make the next field active.
3. When the 14 records have been entered, click the Save button on the Quick Access toolbar.
4. At the Save As dialog box, type **Orders** and then press the Enter key. (This saves the table with the name *Orders*.)
5. Close the Orders table by clicking the Close button located in the upper right corner of the work area.

Figure 1.12 Project 2e

ID	Supplier#	Product#	UnitsOrdere	Amount	OrderDate	Click to Add
1	54	101-S3	10	$1,137.50	1/2/2012	
2	68	209-L	25	$173.75	1/2/2012	
3	68	209-XL	25	$180.00	1/2/2010	
4	68	209-XXL	20	$145.80	1/2/2010	
5	68	210-M	15	$97.35	1/2/2010	
6	68	210-L	25	$162.25	1/2/2010	
7	31	299-M2	10	$887.90	1/16/2012	
8	31	299-M3	10	$887.90	1/16/2012	
9	31	299-M5	10	$887.90	1/16/2012	
10	31	299-W1	8	$602.32	1/16/2012	
11	31	299-W3	10	$752.90	1/16/2012	
12	31	299-W4	10	$752.90	1/16/2012	
13	31	299-W5	10	$752.90	1/16/2012	
14	35	602-XR	5	$2,145.00	1/16/2012	
(New)						

Renaming a Field Heading

When you click a data type button or click a data type at the data type drop-down list, the default heading such as *Field1* is automatically selected. You can type a name for the field heading that takes the place of the selected text. If you create a field heading and then decide to change the name, right-click the heading, click *Rename Field* at the shortcut menu (this selects the current column heading), and then type the new name.

Inserting a Name, Caption, and Description

Name & Caption

When you create a table that others will use, consider providing additional information so the user understands the fields in the table and what should be entered in each field in the table. Along with the field heading name, you can provide a caption and description for each field with options at the Enter Field Properties dialog box shown in Figure 1.13. Display this dialog by clicking the Name & Caption button in the Properties group in the Table Tools Fields tab.

At the Enter Field Properties dialog box, type the desired name for the field heading in the *Name* text box. If you want a more descriptive name for the field heading, type the heading in the *Caption* text box. The text you type will display as the field heading but the actual field name will still be part of the table structure. Creating a caption is useful if you abbreviate a field name or want to show spaces between words in a field name and a caption provides more information for others using the database. The name is what Access uses for the table and the caption is what displays to users.

The *Description* text box is another source for providing information about the field to someone using the database. Type information in the text box that specifies what should be entered in the field. The text you type in the *Description* text box displays at the left side of the Status bar when a field in the column is active. For example, if you type *Enter the total amount of the order* in the *Description* text box for the *Amount* field column, that text will display at the left side of the Status bar when a field in the column is active.

Figure 1.13 Enter Field Properties Dialog Box

Project 2f — Inserting a Name, Caption, and Description — Part 6 of 7

1. With **AL1-C1-PacTrek.accdb** open, open the Orders table.
2. Access automatically named the first field *ID*. You want to make the heading more descriptive so you decide to rename the heading. To do this, right-click the *ID* heading and then click *Rename Field* at the drop-down list.
3. Type **Order#**.
4. To provide more information for someone using the table, you decide to add information for the *Supplier#* field by creating a caption and a description. To do this, complete the following steps:
   a. Click the *Supplier#* field heading. (This selects the entire column.)
   b. Click the Table Tools Fields tab.
   c. Click the Name & Caption button in the Properties group. (At the Enter Field Properties dialog box, notice that *Supplier#* is already inserted in the *Name* text box.)
   d. At the Enter Field Properties dialog box, click in the *Caption* text box and then type **Supplier Number**.
   e. Click in the *Description* text box and then type **Supplier identification number**.
   f. Click OK to close the dialog box. (Notice that the field name now displays as *Supplier Number*. The field name is still *Supplier#* but what displays is *Supplier Number*.)
5. Click the *Product#* field heading and then complete steps similar to those in Steps 4c through 4f to create the caption *Product Number* and the description *Product identification number*.
6. Click the *Amount* field heading and then complete steps similar to those in Steps 4c through 4f to create the caption *Order Amount* and the description *Total amount of order*.
7. Click the Save button on the Quick Access toolbar to save the changes to the Orders table.
8. Close the Orders table.

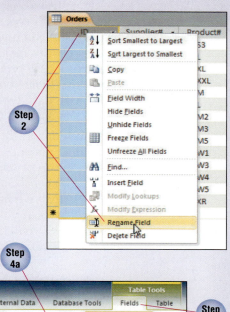
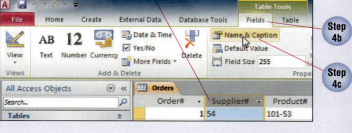
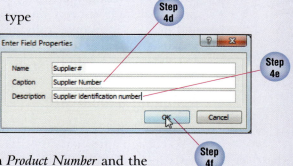

Inserting Quick Start Fields

Text

The Add & Delete group in the Table Tools Fields tab contains buttons for specifying a data type. You used the Text button to specify the data type for the *Supplier#* field when you created the Orders table. You also used the field heading drop-down list to choose a data type. In addition to these two methods, you can specify a data type by clicking the More Fields button in the Add & Delete group in the Table Tools Fields tab. When you click this button, a drop-down list displays with data types grouped into categories such as *Basic Types*, *Number*, *Date and Time*, *Yes/No*, and *Quick Start*.

The options in the *Quick Start* category not only define a data type but also assign a field name. Additionally, with options in the *Quick Start* category, you can add a group of related fields in one step. For example, if you click the *Name* option in the *Quick Start* category, Access inserts the *LastName* field in one column and the *FirstName* field in the next column. Both fields are automatically assigned a text data type. If you click the *Address* option in the *Quick Start* category, Access inserts five fields including *Address*, *City*, *StateProvince*, *ZIPPostal*, and *CountryRegion*, all with the text data type assigned.

Assigning a Default Value

Default Value

The Properties group in the Table Tools Fields tab contains additional buttons for defining field properties in a table. If most records in a table are likely to contain the same field value in a column, consider inserting that value by default. You can do this by clicking the Default Value button in the Properties group. At the Expression Builder dialog box that displays, type the default value you want to appear in the fields, and then click OK. For example, in Project 2g, you will create a new table in the AL1-C1-PacTrek.accdb database containing information on customers and most of the customers live in Vancouver, British Columbia. You will create a default value of *Vancouver* that is automatically inserted in the *City* field and *BC* that is automatically inserted in the *Prov/State* field. You can type different text over the value so if a customer lives in Abbotsford instead of Vancouver, you can type *Abbotsford* in the field.

Assigning a Field Size

Field Size

The default field size property varies depending on the data type. For example, if you assign a text data type to a field, the maximum length of the data you can enter in the field is 255 characters. You can decrease this number depending on what data will be entered in the field. You can also change the field size number to control how much data is entered and help reduce errors. For example, if you have a field for states and you want the two-letter state abbreviation inserted in each field in the column, you can assign a field size of 2. If someone entering data into the table tries to type more than two letters, Access will not accept the additional text. To change field size, click in the *Field Size* text box in the Properties group in the Table Tools Fields tab and then type the desired number.

Changing the AutoNumber Field

Access automatically applies the AutoNumber data type to the first field in a table and assigns a unique number to each record in the table. In many cases, letting

Access automatically assign a number to a record is a good idea. Some situations may arise, however, where you want the first field to contain a unique value for each record other than a number.

If you try to change the AutoNumber data type in the first column by clicking one of the data type buttons in the Add & Delete group in the Table Tools Fields tab, Access creates another field. To change the AutoNumber data type for the first field, you need to click the down-pointing arrow at the right side of the *Data Type* option box in the Formatting group in the Table Tools Fields tab and then click the desired data type at the drop-down list.

 Creating a Customers Table Part 7 of 7

1. The owners of Pacific Trek have decided to publish a semiannual product catalog and have asked customers who want to receive the catalog to fill out a form and include on the form whether or not they want to receive notices of upcoming sales as well as the catalog. Create a table to store the data for customers by completing the following steps:

    a. With the **AL1-C1-PacTrek.accdb** database open, click the Create tab.
    b. Click the Table button in the Tables group.
    c. With the *Click to Add* field heading active, click the More Fields button in the Add & Delete group in the Table Tools Fields tab.
    d. Scroll down the drop-down list and then click *Name* located in the *Quick Start* category. (This inserts the *Last Name* and *First Name* field headings in the table.)
    e. Click the *Click to Add* field heading that displays immediately right of the *First Name* field heading. (The data type drop-down list displays. You are going to use the More Fields button rather than the drop-down list to create the next fields.)

    f. Click the More Fields button, scroll down the drop-down list, and then click *Address* in the *Quick Start* category. (This inserts five more fields in the table.)
    g. Scroll to the right in the table to display the *Click to Add* field heading that follows the *Country Region* column heading. (You can scroll in the table using the horizontal scroll bar that displays to the right of the Navigation bar.)
    h. Click the *Click to Add* field heading and then click *Yes/No* at the drop-down list.

i. With the name *Field1* selected, type **Mailers**. (When you enter records in the table, you will insert a check mark in the field check box if a customer wants to receive sales promotion mailers. If a customer does not want to receive the mailers, you will leave the check box blank.)
2. Rename and create a caption and description for the *ID* column heading by completing the following steps:
    a. Scroll to the beginning of the table and then click the *ID* column heading. (You can scroll in the table using the horizontal scroll bar that displays to the right of the Navigation bar.)
    b. Click the Name & Caption button in the Properties group in the Table Tools Fields tab.
    c. At the Enter Field Properties dialog box, select the text *ID* that displays in the *Name* text box and then type **Customer#**.
    d. Press the Tab key and then type **Customer Number** in the *Caption* text box.
    e. Press the Tab key and then type **Access will automatically assign the record the next number in the sequence.**
    f. Click OK to close the Name & Caption dialog box. (Notice the description that displays at the left side of the Status bar.)

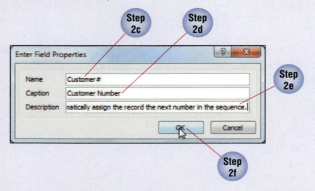

3. Add a description to the *Last Name* column by completing the following steps:
    a. Click the *Last Name* column heading.
    b. Click the Name & Caption button in the Properties group.
    c. At the Enter Field Properties dialog box notice that Access named the field *LastName* but provided the caption *Last Name*. You do not want to change the name and caption so press the Tab key twice to make the *Description* text box active and then type **Customer last name**.
    d. Click OK to close the dialog box.
4. You know that more than likely a customer's last name will not exceed 30 characters, so you decide to limit the field size. To do this, click in the *Field Size* text box in the Properties group (this selects *255*), type **30**, and then press the Enter key.
5. Click the *First Name* column heading and then complete steps similar to those in Steps 3 and 4 to create the description *Customer first name* and change the field size to *30*.
6. Since most of Pacific Trek's customers live in the city of Vancouver, you decide to make it the default field value. To do this, complete the following steps:
    a. Click the *City* column heading.
    b. Click the Default Value button in the Properties group.

c. At the Expression Builder dialog box, type **Vancouver**.
d. Click the OK button to close the dialog box.

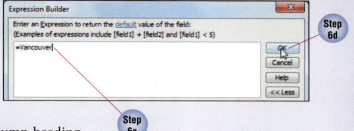

7. Change the name of the *State Province* field name and insert a default value by completing the following steps:
   a. Right-click the *State Province* column heading and then click *Rename Field* at the shortcut menu.
   b. Type **Province**.
   c. Click the Default Value button in the Properties group.
   d. Type **BC** in the Expression Builder dialog box and then click the OK button.
8. Click the *ZIP Postal* column heading and then limit the field size to 7 by clicking in the *Field Size* text box (this selects *255*), typing *7*, and then pressing the Enter key.
9. Since most of the customers want to be sent the sales promotional mailers, you decide to insert a check mark as the default value in the check boxes in the *Yes/No* column. To do this, complete the following steps:
   a. Click the *Mailers* field heading.
   b. Click the Default Value button in the Properties group.
   c. At the Expression Builder dialog box, press the Backspace key to delete the 0 and then type **1**. (The zero indicates a negative such as "no," "false," or "off" and the one indicates a positive such as "yes," "true," or "on.")
   d. Click OK to close the dialog box.
10. Delete the *Country Region* field by clicking the *Country Region* field heading and then clicking the Delete button in the Add & Delete group.
11. Save the table by completing the following steps:
    a. Click the Save button on the Quick Access toolbar.
    b. At the Save As dialog box, type **Customers**, and then press Enter.
12. Enter the six records in the table as shown in Figure 1.14. To remove a check mark in the *Mailers* column, press the spacebar.
13. Adjust the column widths to accommodate the longest entry in each column by completing the following steps:
    a. Position the arrow pointer on the *Customer Number* field heading until the pointer turns into a down-pointing black arrow, hold down the left mouse button, drag to the *Mailers* field heading, and then release the mouse button.
    b. With the columns selected, double-click one of the column boundaries.
14. Click the Save button to save the Customers table.
15. Print the Customers table by completing the following steps:
    a. Click the File tab and then click the Print tab.
    b. At the Print tab Backstage view, click the *Print Preview* option.
    c. Click the Landscape button in the Page Layout group in the Print Preview tab.
    d. Click the Print button that displays at the left side of the Print Preview tab.
    e. At the Print dialog box, click OK.
16. Close the Customers table.
17. Open the Orders table.
18. Automatically adjust the column widths to accommodate the longest entry in each column.
19. Click the Save button to save the Orders table.
20. Print the table in landscape orientation (refer to Step 15) and then close the table.
21. Close the **AL1-C1-PacTrek.accdb** database.

Figure 1.14 Project 2g

Customer Number	Last Name	First Name	Address	City	State Province	ZIP Postal	Mailers
1	Blakely	Mathias	7433 224th Ave. E.	Vancouver	BC	V5K 2M7	☑
2	Donato	Antonio	18225 Victoria Dr.	Vancouver	BC	V5K 1H4	☐
3	Girard	Stephanie	430 Deer Lake Pl.	Burnaby	BC	V3J 1E4	☑
4	Hernandez	Angelica	1233 E. 58th Ave.	Vancouver	BC	V5K 3H3	☑
5	Ives-Keller	Shane	9055 Gilbert Rd.	Richmond	BC	V6Y 1B2	☐
6	Kim	Keung	730 West Broadway	Vancouver	BC	V5K 5B2	☑
(New)				Vancouver	BC		☑

Chapter Summary

- Microsoft Access is a database management system software program that will organize, store, maintain, retrieve, sort, and print all types of business data.
- In Access, open an existing database by clicking the Open button at the New tab Backstage view. At the open dialog box, navigate to the location where the database is located, and then double-click the desired database.
- Only one database can be open at a time.
- Some common objects found in a database include tables, queries, forms, and reports.
- The Navigation pane displays at the left side of the Access screen and displays the objects that are contained in the database.
- Open a database object by double-clicking the object in the Navigation pane. Close an object by clicking the Close button that displays in the upper right corner of the work area.
- When a table is open, the Record Navigation bar displays at the bottom of the screen and contains a button for displaying records in the table.
- Insert a new record in a table by clicking the New button in the Records group in the Home tab or by clicking the New (blank) record button in the Record Navigation bar. Delete a record by clicking in a field in the record you want to delete, clicking the Delete button arrow in the Home tab, and then clicking *Delete Record* at the drop-down list.
- To add a column to a table, click the first field below the *Click to Add* column heading and then type the desired data. To move a column, select the column and then use the mouse to drag a thick, back vertical line (representing the column) to the desired location. To delete a column, click the column heading, click the Delete button arrow, and then click *Delete Column* at the drop-down list.
- Data you enter in a table is automatically saved while changes to the layout of a table are not automatically saved.
- Adjust the width of a column (or selected columns) to accommodate the longest entry by double-clicking the column boundary. You can also adjust the width of a column by dragging the column boundary.
- Print a table by clicking the File tab, clicking the Print tab, and then clicking the *Quick Print* option. You can also preview a table before printing by clicking the *Print Preview* option at the Print tab Backstage view.

- With buttons and option on the Print Preview tab, you can change the page size, orientation, and margins.
- The first principle in database design is to reduce redundant data because redundant data increases the amount of data entry required, increases the chances for errors, and takes up additional storage space.
- A data type defines the type of data Access will allow in the field. Assign a data type to a field with buttons in the Add & Delete group in the Table Tools Fields tab, by clicking an option from the column heading drop-down list, or with options at the More button drop-down list.
- Rename a column heading by right-clicking the heading, clicking *Rename Field* at the shortcut menu, and then typing the new name.
- Type a name, a caption, and a description for a column with options at the Enter Field Properties dialog box.
- Use options in the *Quick Start* category in the More Fields button drop-down list to define a data type and assign a field name to a group of related fields.
- Insert a default value in a column with the Default Value button and assign a field size with the *Field Size* text box in the Properties group in the Table Tools Fields tab.
- Use the *Data Type* option box in the Formatting group to change the AutoNumber data type for the first column in a table.

Commands Review

FEATURE	RIBBON TAB, GROUP	BUTTON, OPTION	KEYBOARD SHORTCUT
Open dialog box	File	Open	Ctrl + O
Close database	File	Close Database	
New record	Home, Records		Ctrl + +
Next field			Tab
Previous field			Shift + Tab
Delete record	Home, Records	, Delete Record	
Delete column	Home, Records	, Delete Column	
Print tab Backstage view	File	Print	
Print Preview	File	Print, Print Preview	
Print dialog box	File	Print, Print	Ctrl + P
Page size	File	Print, Print Preview,	
Page margins	File	Print, Print Preview,	
Page Setup dialog box	File	Print, Print Preview,	

FEATURE	RIBBON TAB, GROUP	BUTTON, OPTION	KEYBOARD SHORTCUT
Landscape orientation	File	Print, Print Preview,	
Portrait orientation	File	Print, Print Preview,	
Create table	Create, Tables		
Text data type	Table Tools Fields, Add & Delete		
Number data type	Table Tools Fields, Add & Delete		
Currency data type	Table Tools Fields, Add & Delete		
Date & Time data type	Table Tools Fields, Add & Delete		
Yes/No data type	Table Tools Fields, Add & Delete		
Enter Field Properties dialog box	Table Tools Fields, Properties		
Expression Builder dialog box	Table Tools Fields, Properties		

Concepts Check Test Your Knowledge

Completion: In the space provided at the right, indicate the correct term, symbol, or command.

1. This view displays when you open Access. _____

2. This toolbar contains buttons for commonly used commands. _____

3. This displays the names of objects within a database grouped by categories. _____

4. When you open a table, it displays in this view. _____

5. Use buttons on this bar to navigate in the table. _____

6. To add a new record, click the New button in this group in the Home tab. _____

7. At the Print tab Backstage view, click this option to send the table directly to the printer. _____

8. The Landscape button is located in this group in the Print Preview tab. _____

9. All fields for one unit, such as an employee or customer, are considered to be this. _____

10. Assign this data type to values that involve money. _____

11. Click this button in the Properties group in the Table Tools Fields tab to display the Enter Field Properties dialog box. _____

12. With options in this category in the More Fields button drop-down list, you can define a data type and also assign a field name. _____

13. If you want to assign the same field value to a column, click this button to display the Expression Builder dialog box and then type the desired value. _____

Skills Check   Assess Your Performance

The database designer for Griffin Technologies has created the database diagram, shown in Figure 1.15, to manage data about company employees. You will open the Griffin database and maintain and create tables that follow the diagram.

Figure 1.15 Griffin Technologies Database Diagram

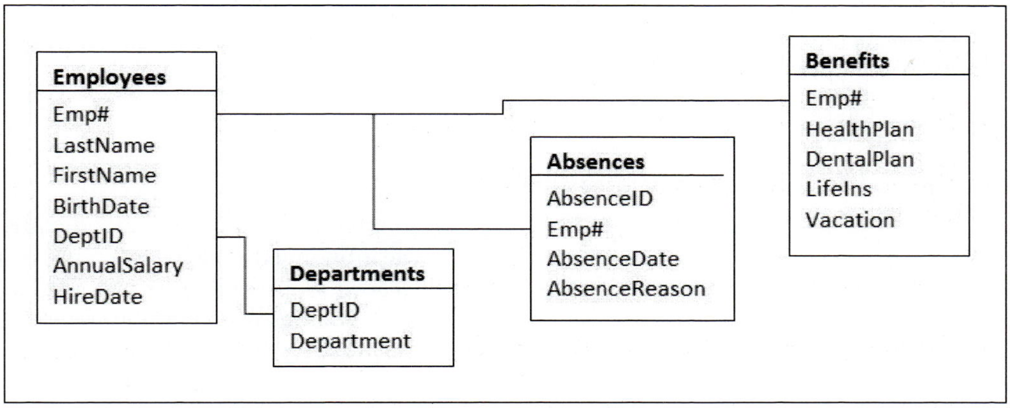

Employees
- Emp#
- LastName
- FirstName
- BirthDate
- DeptID
- AnnualSalary
- HireDate

Departments
- DeptID
- Department

Absences
- AbsenceID
- Emp#
- AbsenceDate
- AbsenceReason

Benefits
- Emp#
- HealthPlan
- DentalPlan
- LifeIns
- Vacation

Assessment

1 INSERTING AND DELETING ROWS AND COLUMNS

1. In Access, open the database named **AL1-C1-Griffin.accdb** located in the Access2010L1C1 folder on your storage medium and enable the contents.
2. Double-click the *Employees* table in the Navigation pane.
3. Delete the record for Scott Jorgensen (employee number 1025).
4. Delete the record for Leanne Taylor (employee number 1060).

5. Insert the following records:

   Emp#: **1010**
   LastName: **Harrington**
   FirstName: **Tyler**
   Birthdate: **9/7/1976**
   AnnualSalary: **$53,350**
   HireDate: **10/1/2005**

   Emp#: **1052**
   LastName: **Reeves**
   FirstName: **Carrie**
   Birthdate: **12/4/1978**
   AnnualSalary: **$38,550**
   HireDate: **10/1/2008**

6. Close the Employees table.
7. Looking at the database diagram in Figure 1.15, you realize that the Employees table includes a *DeptID* field. Open the Employees table, insert the new field in the Employees table and name it *DeptID*. Change the field size to 2 (since department abbreviations are only one or two letters in length). At the message telling you that some data may be lost, click the Yes button. Type the department identification for each record as shown below (the records are listed from left to right):

1001: HR	1002: RD	1003: IT	1005: DP	1010: DP
1013: RD	1015: HR	1020: A	1023: IT	1030: PR
1033: A	1040: DP	1043: HR	1045: RD	1050: IT
1052: PR	1053: HR	1063: DP	1065: DP	1080: IT
1083: HR	1085: PR	1090: RD	1093: A	1095: RD

8. Move the *DeptID* column so it is positioned between the *BirthDate* column and the *AnnualSalary* column.
9. Automatically adjust the widths of the columns.
10. Save the table.
11. Display the table in Print Preview, change the top margin to 1.5 inches, the left margin to 1.25 inches, and then print the table.
12. Close the Employees table.

Assessment

2 CREATE A DEPARTMENTS TABLE

1. You entered a one- or two-letter abbreviation representing a department within the company. Creating the abbreviations saved you from having to type the entire department name for each record. You need to create the Departments table that will provide the department names for each abbreviation. Create a new table in the **AL1-C1-Griffin.accdb** database with the column headings and data as shown in Figure 1.16 by completing the following steps:
   a. Click the Create tab and then click the Table button.
   b. Click the *ID* column heading, click the down-pointing arrow at the right side of the *Data Type* option box in the Formatting group, and then click *Text* at the drop-down list.
   c. Limit the field size to 2 and rename the heading to *DeptID*.
   d. Click the *Click to Add* column heading, click *Text* at the drop-down list, and then type **Department**.
   e. Type the data in the fields as shown in Figure 1.16.
   f. Automatically adjust the widths of the columns.
2. Save the table and name it *Departments*.
3. Print and then close the table.

Figure 1.16 Departments Table

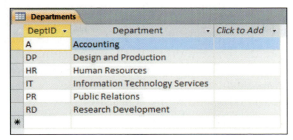

Assessment

3 CREATE A BENEFITS TABLE

1. Create a new table in the **AL1-C1-Griffin.accdb** database with the data shown in Figure 1.17 with the following specifications:
   a. Name the fields as shown in the Benefits table in the diagram in Figure 1.15 and create the caption names for the fields as shown in Figure 1.17. (For example, name the life insurance field *LifeIns* and create the caption *Life Insurance*.)
   b. For the first column (Employee number), click the *ID* column heading, click the down-pointing arrow at the right side of the *Data Type* option box in the Formatting group, and then click *Text* at the drop-down list. Limit the field size to 4 and rename the field to *Emp#*.
   c. Apply the Yes/No data type to the second column, make the default value a check mark (type a 1 at the Expression Builder dialog box), and provide the description *A check mark indicates the employee is signed up for the health plan*.

Figure 1.17 Benefits Table

Emp#	Health Plan	Dental Plan	Life Insurance	Vacation
1001	✓	✓	$100,000.00	4 weeks
1002	✓	✓	$200,000.00	4 weeks
1003	☐	✓	$150,000.00	3 weeks
1005	✓	✓	$200,000.00	3 weeks
1010	✓	✓	$185,000.00	4 weeks
1013	☐	✓	$200,000.00	3 weeks
1015	☐	☐	$100,000.00	3 weeks
1020	✓	✓	$200,000.00	4 weeks
1023	☐	☐	$75,000.00	2 weeks
1030	✓	✓	$125,000.00	3 weeks
1033	✓	✓	$200,000.00	3 weeks
1040	✓	✓	$200,000.00	3 weeks
1043	☐	☐	$50,000.00	2 weeks
1045	✓	☐	$125,000.00	2 weeks
1050	✓	✓	$85,000.00	3 weeks
1052	✓	✓	$175,000.00	3 weeks
1053	✓	☐	$100,000.00	2 weeks
1063	✓	✓	$150,000.00	2 weeks
1065	✓	✓	$200,000.00	2 weeks
1080	☐	✓	$150,000.00	1 week
1083	✓	☐	$75,000.00	1 week
1085	✓	✓	$125,000.00	1 week
1090	✓	☐	$150,000.00	1 week
1093	☐	✓	$185,000.00	1 week
1095	☐	☐	$200,000.00	1 week

d. Apply the Yes/No data type to the third column, make the default value a check mark (type a **1** at the Expression Builder dialog box), and provide the description *A check mark indicates the employee is signed up for the dental plan*.
e. Apply the Currency data type to the fourth column.
f. Apply the Text data type to the fifth column and limit the field size to 8.
g. Type the data in each record as shown in Figure 1.17.
h. Automatically adjust the column widths.
i. Save the table and name it *Benefits*.
2. Display the table in Print Preview, change the top and left margins to 1.5 inches, and then print the table.
3. Close the Benefits table.

Assessment

4 SORT DATA

1. With **AL1-C1-Griffin.accdb** open, open the Employees table.
2. Experiment with the buttons in the Sort & Filter group in the Home tab and figure out how to sort columns of data in ascending and descending order.
3. Sort the records in the Employees table in ascending order by last name.
4. Save, print, and then close the Employees table.
5. Open the Benefits table and then sort the records in descending order by life insurance amounts.
6. Save, print, and then close the Benefits table.

Visual Benchmark — Demonstrate Your Proficiency

CREATE AN ABSENCES TABLE

Note: The starting file for this activity is the file created after completing the previous Skills Check assessments.

1. With the **AL1-C1-Griffin.accdb** database open, create the Absences table shown in Figure 1.18 (using the field names as shown in Figure 1.15 on page 35) with the following specifications:
   a. Use the default AutoNumber data type for column 1. Apply the appropriate data type to the other columns.
   b. Create an appropriate caption and description for the *Emp#*, *AbsenceDate*, and *AbsenceReason* columns.
   c. Apply the default value of *Sick Day* to the *AbsenceReason* column. (You will need to type "Sick Day" in the Expression Builder dialog box.)
2. Save the table and name it *Absences*.
3. Print the table in landscape orientation with 1.5 inch top and left margins.
4. Close the Absences table and then close the **AL1-C1-Griffin.accdb** database.

Figure 1.18 Visual Benchmark

AbsenceID	Emp#	Absence Date	Absence Reason	Click to Add
1	1065	1/2/2012	Sick Day	
2	1065	1/3/2012	Sick Day	
3	1023	1/5/2012	Sick Day	
4	1023	1/6/2012	Sick Day	
5	1019	1/6/2012	Jury Duty	
6	1019	1/9/2012	Jury Duty	
7	1030	1/9/2012	Sick Day	
8	1052	1/20/2012	Bereavement	
9	1052	1/23/2012	Bereavement	
10	1013	1/23/2012	Sick Day	
11	1095	1/25/2012	Sick Day	
12	1095	1/26/2012	Sick Day	
13	1040	1/27/2012	Sick Day	
14	1083	1/27/2012	Sick Day	
15	1045	1/30/2012	Sick Day	
16	1010	1/30/2012	Sick Day	
17	1093	1/31/2012	Sick Day	
18	1007	1/31/2012	Sick Day	
(New)			Sick Day	

Case Study — Apply Your Skills

You are the office manager for Elite Limousines and your company is switching over to Access for managing company data. The database designer has provided you with the database diagram in Figure 1.19. She wants you to follow the diagram when creating the database.

Figure 1.19 Elite Limousines Database Diagram

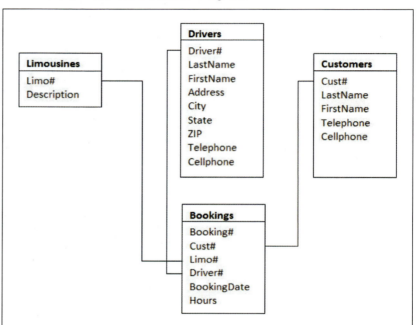

Part 1

Create a new database named **AL1-C1-Elite.accdb** and then create the Limousines table shown in the database diagram in Figure 1.19. The database designer has asked you to include an appropriate caption and description for both fields and change the field size for the *Limo#* field. Type the following records in the table:

Limo#: 01
Description: 2008 White stretch
Limo#: 04
Description: 2009 Black minibus
Limo#: 08
Description: 2011 Black SUV stretch

Limo#: 02
Description: 2008 Black stretch
Limo#: 06
Description: 2009 Black standard
Limo#: 10
Description: 2011 Black stretch

Part 2

With **AL1-C1-Elite.accdb** open, create the Drivers table shown in the database diagram shown in Figure 1.19 and include an appropriate caption and description for the fields and change the field size where appropriate. Type the following records in the table:

Driver#: 101
LastName: Brennan
FirstName: Andrea
Address: 4438 Gowan Rd.
City: Las Vegas
State: NV
ZIP: 89115
Telephone: (702) 555-3481
Cellphone: (702) 555-1322

Driver#: 114
LastName: Gould
FirstName: Randall
Address: 330 Aura Ave.
City: Las Vegas
State: NV
ZIP: 89052
Telephone: (702) 555-1239
Cellphone: (702) 555-7474

Driver#: 120
LastName: Martinelli
FirstName: Albert
Address: 107 Cameo Dr.
City: Las Vegas
State: NV
ZIP: 89138
Telephone: (702) 555-0349
Cellphone: (702) 555-6649

Driver#: 125
LastName: Nunez
FirstName: Frank
Address: 4832 Helena St.
City: Las Vegas
State: NV
ZIP: 89129
Telephone: (702) 555-3748
Cellphone: (702) 555-2210

Part 3

With **AL1-C1-Elite.accdb** open, create the Customers table shown in the database diagram shown in Figure 1.19 and include an appropriate caption and description for the fields and change the field size where appropriate. Type the following records in the table:

Cust#: 1001
LastName: Spencer
FirstName: Maureen
Telephone: (513) 555-3943
Cellphone: (513) 555-4884

Cust#: 1002
LastName: Tsang
FirstName: Lee
Telephone: (702) 555-4775
Cellphone: (702) 555-42116

Cust#: 1028
LastName: Gabriel
FirstName: Nicholas
Telephone: (612) 555-7885
Cellphone: (612) 555-7230

Cust#: 1031
LastName: Marshall
FirstName: Patricia
Telephone: (702) 555-6410
Cellphone: (702) 555-0137

Cust#: 1010
LastName: Chavez
FirstName: Blake
Telephone: (206) 555-3774
Cellphone: (206) 555-3006

Cust#: 1044
LastName: Vanderhage
FirstName: Vernon
Telephone: (213) 555-8846
Cellphone: (213) 555-4635

Part 4

With **AL1-C1-Elite.accdb** open, create the Bookings table shown in the database diagram and include an appropriate caption and description for the fields and change the field size where appropriate. Type the following records in the table:

Booking#: (AutoNumber)
Cust#: 1044
Limo#: 02
Driver#: 114
BookingDate: 07/01/2012
Hours: 6

Booking#: (AutoNumber)
Cust#: 1001
Limo#: 10
Driver#: 120
BookingDate: 07/01/2012
Hours: 8

Booking#: (AutoNumber)
Cust#: 1002
Limo#: 04
Driver#: 101
BookingDate: 07/06/2012
Hours: 8

Booking#: (AutoNumber)
Cust#: 1028
Limo#: 02
Driver#: 125
BookingDate: 07/06/2012
Hours: 4

Booking#: (AutoNumber)
Cust#: 1010
Limo#: 06
Driver#: 125
BookingDate: 07/03/2012
Hours: 3

Booking#: (AutoNumber)
Cust#: 1031
Limo#: 08
Driver#: 120
BookingDate: 07/07/2012
Hours: 5

Automatically adjust the column widths of each table to accommodate the longest entry in each column. Print each of the tables so all records fit on one page.

Access

Creating Relationships between Tables

CHAPTER

PERFORMANCE OBJECTIVES

Upon successful completion of Chapter 2, you will be able to:
- Define a primary key in a table
- Create a one-to-many relationship
- Specify referential integrity
- Print, edit, and delete relationships
- Create a one-to-one relationship
- View and edit a subdatasheet

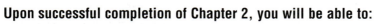

Access is a relational database program you can use to create tables that have a relation or connection to each other within the same database. When a relationship is established between tables, you can view and edit records in related tables with a subdatasheet. In this chapter, you will learn how to identify a primary key in a table that is unique to that table, how to join tables by creating a relationship between tables, and how to view and edit subdatasheets. Model answers for this chapter's projects appear on the following pages.

Note: Before beginning the projects, copy the Access2010L1C2 subfolder from the Access2010L1 folder on the CD that accompanies this textbook to your storage medium and make Access2010L1C2 the active folder.

Project 1 Establish Relationships between Tables

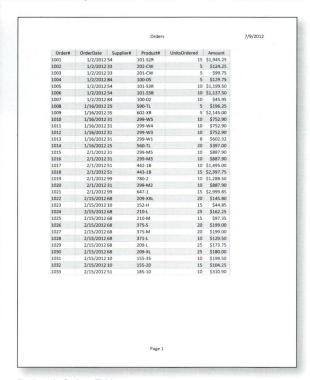

Project 1, Orders Table

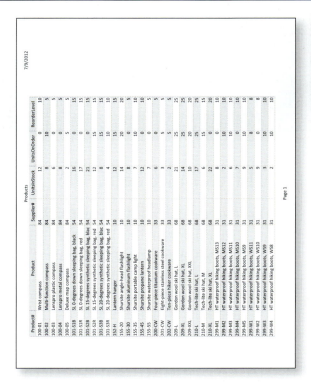

Project 1, Products Table, Page 1

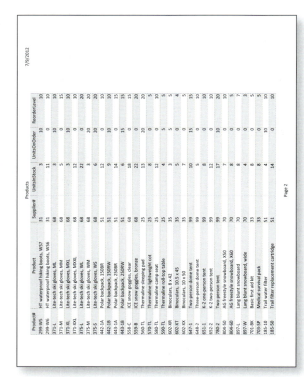

Project 1, Products Table, Page 2

Project 1, Suppliers Table

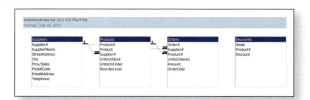

Project 1, Relationships Table

Project 2 Create Relationships and Display Subdatasheets in a Database

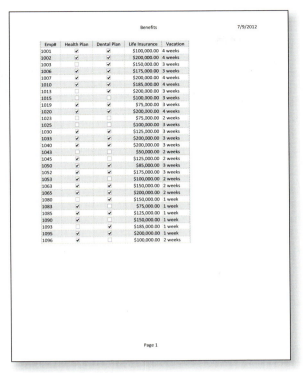

Project 2, Benefits Table

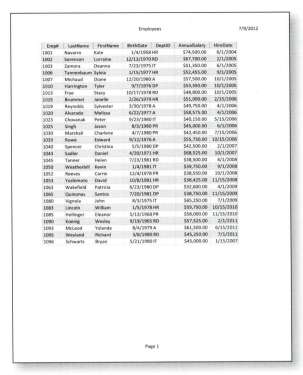

Project 2, Employees Table

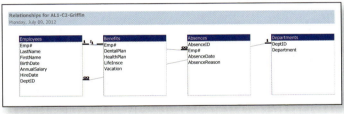

Project 2, Relationships

Project 1 Establish Relationships between Tables 4 Parts

You will specify primary keys in tables, establish one-to-many relationship between tables, specify referential integrity, and print the relationships. You will also edit and delete a relationship.

Creating Related Tables

Generally, a database management system fits into one of two categories—either a file management system (also sometimes referred to as a *flat file database*) or a relational database management system. A flat file management system stores all data in a single directory and cannot contain multiple tables. This type of management system is a simple way to store data but it becomes more inefficient as more data is added.

Chapter 2 ■ Creating Relationships between Tables 45

Defining a relationship between tables is one of the most powerful features of a relational database management system.

In a *relational database management system*, like Access, relationships are defined between sets of data allowing greater flexibility in manipulating data and eliminating data redundancy (entering the same data in more than one place).

In Project 1, you will define relationships between tables in the AL1-C2-PacTrek.accdb database. Because the tables in the database will be related, information on a product does not need to be repeated in a table on orders. If you used a flat file management system to maintain product information, you would need to repeat the product description for each order.

Determining Relationships

Taking time to plan a database is extremely important. Creating a database with related tables takes even more consideration. You need to determine how to break down the required data and what tables to create to eliminate redundancies. One idea to help you determine the necessary tables in a database is to think of the word "about." For example, the Pacific Trek store needs a table "about" products, another "about" suppliers, and another "about" orders. A table should be only about one subject such as products, suppliers, or orders.

Use the Table Analyzer Wizard to analyze your tables and restructure them to better conform to relational theory. Start the wizard by clicking the Database Tools tab and then clicking the Analyze Table button.

Along with deciding on the necessary tables for a database, you also need to determine the relationship between tables. The ability to relate, or "join," tables is what makes Access a relational database system. As you learned in Chapter 1, database designers often create a visual representation of the database's structure in a diagram. Figure 2.1 displays the database diagram for the AL1-C2-PacTrek.accdb database. (Some of the fields in the tables have been slightly modified from the database you used in Chapter 1.)

Defining the Primary Key

A database table can contain two different types of keys—a primary key and a foreign key. In the database diagram in Figure 2.1, notice that one field in each table contains an asterisk. The asterisk indicates a *primary key field*, which is a field that holds data that uniquely identifies each record in a table. For example,

Figure 2.1 AL1-C2-PacTrek.accdb Database Diagram

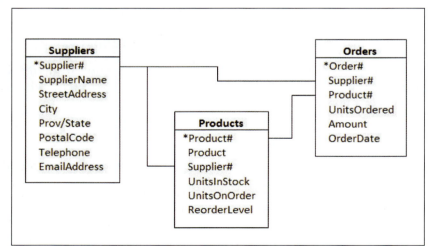

the *Supplier#* field in the Suppliers table contains a unique supplier number for each record in the table, and the *Product#* field in the Products table contains a unique product number for each product. A table can have only one primary key field and it is the field by which the table is sorted whenever the table is opened.

When a new record is added to a table, Access checks to ensure that there is no existing record with the same data in the primary key. If there is, Access displays an error message indicating there are duplicate values and will not allow the record to be saved. When adding a new record to a table, the primary key field cannot be left blank. Access expects a value in each record in the table and this is referred to as *entity integrity*. If a value is not entered in a field, Access actually enters a null value. A null value cannot be given to a primary key field. Access will not let you close a database containing a primary key field with a null value.

By default, Access includes the *ID* field as the first field in a table, assigns the AutoNumber data type, and identifies the field as the primary key. The AutoNumber data type assigns the first record a field value of *1* and each new record is assigned the next sequential number. You can use this default field as the primary key or define your own. To determine what field is the primary key or to define a primary key field, you must display the table in Design view. To do this, open the table and then click the View button located at the left side of the Home tab. You can also display the table in Design view by clicking the View button arrow and then clicking *Design View* at the drop-down list. To add or remove a primary key from a field, click the desired field in the *Field Name* column and then click the Primary Key button in the Tools group in the Table Tools Design tab. A key icon is inserted in the field selector bar (blank column to the left of the field names) for the desired field. Figure 2.2 displays the Products table in Design view with the *Product#* field identified as the primary key.

▼ **Quick Steps**

Define a Primary Key
1. Open table.
2. Click View button.
3. Click desired field.
4. Click Primary Key button.
5. Click Save button.

Primary Key

Figure 2.2 Products Table in Design View

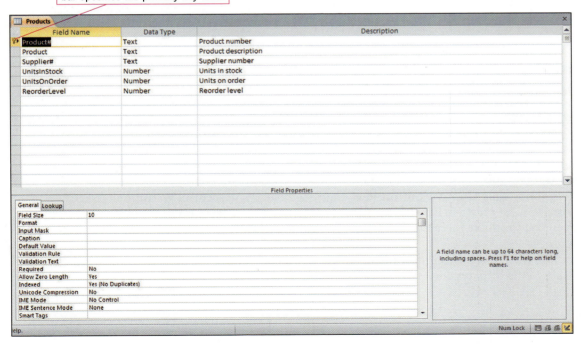

Access uses a primary key to associate data from multiple tables.

Typically, a primary key field in one table becomes the *foreign key field* in a related table. For example, the primary key field *Supplier#* in the Suppliers table is considered the foreign key field in the Orders table. In the Suppliers table, each entry in the *Supplier#* field must be unique since it is the primary key field, but the same supplier number may appear more than once in the *Supplier#* field in the Orders table (such as a situation where more than one product is ordered from the same supplier).

You must enter a value in the primary key in every record.

Data in the foreign key field must match data in the primary key field of the related table. For example, any supplier number you enter in the *Supplier#* field in the Orders table must be contained in the Suppliers table. In other words, you would not be making an order to a supplier that does not exist in the Suppliers table. Figure 2.3 identifies the primary and foreign keys in the tables in the AL1-C2-PacTrek.accdb database. Primary keys are identified with *(PK)* and the foreign keys are identified with *(FK)* in the figure.

Figure 2.3 AL1-C2-PacTrek.accdb Database Diagram with Primary and Foreign Keys Identified

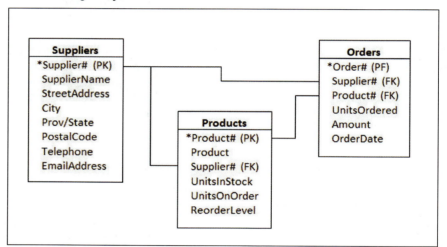

Project 1a Defining a Primary Key Field   Part 1 of 4

1. Open Access.
2. At the New tab Backstage view, click the Open button that displays at the left side of the screen.
3. At the Open dialog box, navigate to the Access2010L1C2 folder on your storage medium and then double-click the database **AL1-C2-PacTrek.accdb**.
4. Click the Enable Content button in the message bar if the security warning message appears. (The message bar will display immediately below the ribbon.)
5. Open the Products table and then view the primary key field by completing the following steps:
   a. Click the View button located at the left side of the Home tab. (This displays the table in Design view.)

b. In Design view, notice the *Field Name*, *Data Type*, and *Description* columns and notice the information that displays for each field. The first field, *Product#*, is the primary key field and is identified by the key icon that displays in the field selector bar.
  c. Click the View button to return to the Datasheet view.
  d. Close the Products table.
6. Open the Suppliers table, click the View button to display the table in Design view, and then notice the *Supplier#* field is defined as the primary key field.
7. Click the View button to return to Datasheet view and then close the table.
8. Open the Orders table. (The first field in the Orders table has been changed from the AutoNumber field automatically assigned by Access in the AL1-C2-PacTrek.accdb database to a Text data type field.)
9. Define the *Order#* field as the primary key field by completing the following steps:
  a. Click the View button located at the left side of the Home tab.
  b. With the table in Design view and the *Order#* field selected in the *Field Name* column, click the Primary Key button located in the Tools group in the Table Tools Design tab.

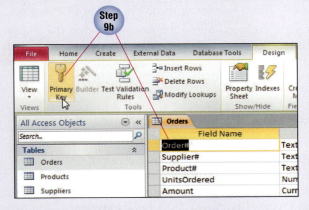

  c. Click the Save button on the Quick Access toolbar.
  d. Click the View button to return the table to Datasheet view.
10. Move the *OrderDate* field by completing the following steps:
  a. Click the *OrderDate* field heading. (This selects the column.)
  b. Position the mouse pointer on the heading, hold down the left mouse button, and then drag to the left until the thick, black vertical line displays immediately left of the *Supplier#* field, and then release the mouse button.

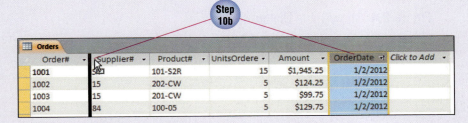

11. Automatically adjust the column widths.
12. Save and then close the Orders table.

Relating Tables in a One-to-Many Relationship

In Access, one table can be related to another, which is generally referred to as performing a *join*. When tables with a common field are joined, data can be extracted from both tables as if they were one large table. Relate tables to ensure the integrity of the data. For example, in Project 1b, you will create a relationship between the Suppliers table and the Products table. The relationship you establish will ensure that a supplier number cannot be entered in the Products table without first being entered in the Suppliers table. This type of relationship is called a *one-to-many relationship*, which means that one record in the Suppliers table will match zero, one, or many records in the Products table.

In a one-to-many relationship, the table containing the "one" is referred to as the *primary table* and the table containing the "many" is referred to as the *related table*. Access follows a set of rules known as *referential integrity*, which enforces consistency between related tables. These rules are enforced when data is updated in related tables. The referential integrity rules ensure that a record added to a related table has a matching record in the primary table.

Relationships

To create a one-to-many relationship, open the database containing the tables to be related. Click the Database Tools tab and then click the Relationships button in the Relationships group. This displays the Show Table dialog box, as shown in Figure 2.4. At the Show Table dialog box, each table that will be related must be added to the Relationships window. To do this, click the first table name to be included and then click Add (or double-click the desired table). Continue in this manner until all necessary table names have been added to the Relationships window and then click the Close button.

At the Relationships window, such as the one shown in Figure 2.5, use the mouse to drag the common field from the primary table (the "one") to the related table (the "many"). This causes the Edit Relationships dialog box to display as shown in Figure 2.6. At the Edit Relationships dialog box, check to make sure the correct field name displays in the *Table/Query* and *Related Table/Query* list boxes and the relationship type at the bottom of the dialog box displays as *One-To-Many*.

Specify the relationship options by choosing *Enforce Referential Integrity*, as well as *Cascade Update Related Fields* and/or *Cascade Delete Related Records*, and then click the Create button. This causes the Edit Relationships dialog box to close and the Relationships window to display showing the relationship between the tables.

Figure 2.4 Show Table Dialog Box

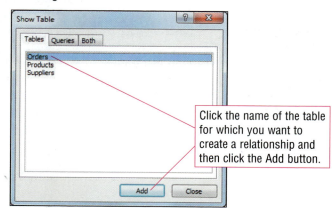

Figure 2.5 Relationships Window

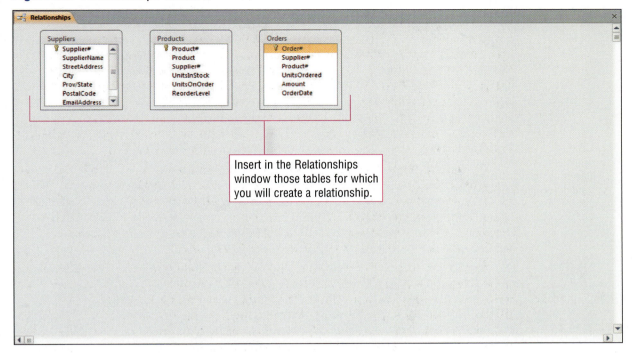

Figure 2.6 Edit Relationships Dialog Box

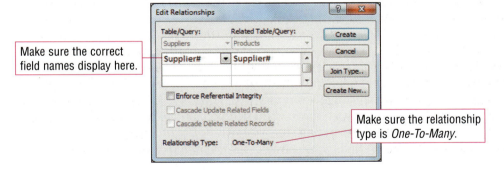

In Figure 2.7, the Suppliers table displays with a black line attached along with the number *1* (signifying the "one" side of the relationship). The black line is connected to the Products table along with the infinity symbol ∞ (signifying the "many" side of the relationship). The black line, called the ***join line***, is thick at both ends if the enforce referential integrity option has been chosen. If this option is not chosen, the line is thin at both ends. Click the Save button on the Quick Access toolbar to save the relationship. Close the Relationships window by clicking the Close button located in the upper right corner of the window.

Specifying Referential Integrity

Choose *Enforce Referential Integrity* at the Edit Relationships dialog box to ensure that the relationships between records in related tables are valid. Referential integrity can be set if the field from the primary table is a primary key and the

▼ **Quick Steps**

Create a One-to-Many Relationship
1. Click Database Tools tab.
2. Click Relationships button.
3. At Show Table dialog box, add tables.
4. In Relationships window, drag "one" field from primary table to "many" field in related table.
5. At Edit Relationships dialog box, enforce referential integrity.
6. Click Create button.
7. Click Save button.

Chapter 2 ■ Creating Relationships between Tables 51

Figure 2.7 One-to-Many Relationship

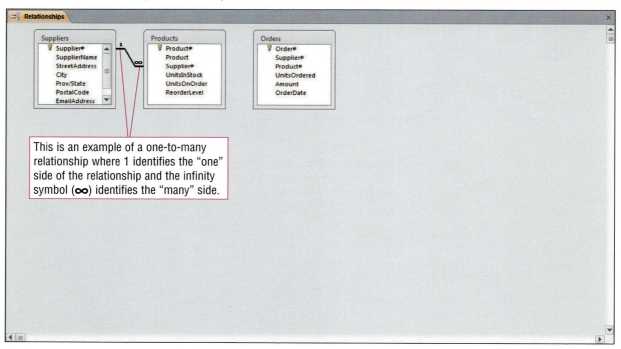

HINT

Referential integrity ensures that a record exists in the "one" table before the record can be entered in the "many" table.

related fields have the same data type. When referential integrity is established, a value for the primary key must first be entered in the primary table before it can be entered in the related table.

If you select only *Enforce Referential Integrity* and the related table contains a record, you will not be able to change a primary key field value in the primary table. You will not be able to delete a record in the primary table if its key value equals a foreign key in the related table. If you choose *Cascade Update Related Fields*, you will be able to change a primary key field value in the primary table and Access will automatically update the matching value in the related table. Choose *Cascade Delete Related Records* and you will be able to delete a record in the primary table and Access will delete any related records in the related table.

In Project 1b, you will be creating a one-to-many relationship between tables in the AL1-C2-PacTrek.accdb database. Figure 2.8 displays the Relationships window with the relationships identified that you will create in the project.

▼ **Quick Steps**

Print Relationships
1. Click Database Tools tab.
2. Click Relationships button.
3. Click Relationships Report button.
4. Click Print button.
5. Click OK.
6. Click Close button.

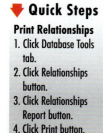

Relationship Report

Printing a Relationship

You can print a report displaying the relationships between tables. To do this, display the Relationships window and then click the Relationship Report button in the Tools group. This displays the Relationships report in Print Preview. Click the Print button in the Print group in the Print Preview tab and then click OK at the Print dialog box. After printing the relationships report, click the Close button to close the relationships report.

Figure 2.8 Relationships in the AL1-C2-PacTrek.accdb Database

One-to-many relationship with referential integrity and cascade updated and deleted records selected.

One-to-many relationship with referential integrity and cascade updated and deleted records selected.

One-to-many relationship with referential integrity selected. (Notice the join line is thick in the middle indicating that cascade updated and deleted records is not selected.)

Project 1b   Creating Relationships between Tables   Part 2 of 4

1. With the **AL1-C2-PacTrek.accdb** database open, click the Database Tools tab and then click the Relationships button in the Relationships group.
2. If the Show Table dialog box does not display, click the Show Table button in the Relationships group in the Relationship Tools Design tab. At the Show Table dialog box, add the Suppliers, Products, and Orders tables to the Relationships window by completing the following steps:
   a. Click *Suppliers* in the Show Table dialog box list box and then click the Add button.
   b. Click *Products* in the list box and then click the Add button.
   c. Click *Orders* in the list box and then click the Add button.
3. Click the Close button to close the Show Table dialog box.
4. At the Relationships window, drag the *Supplier#* field from the Suppliers table to the Products table by completing the following steps:
   a. Position the arrow pointer on the *Supplier#* field that displays in the Suppliers table.

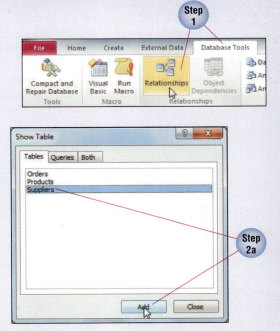

Chapter 2 ■ Creating Relationships between Tables   53

b. Hold down the left mouse button, drag the arrow pointer (with a field icon attached) to the *Supplier#* field in the Products table, and then release the mouse button. (This causes the Edit Relationships dialog box to display.)

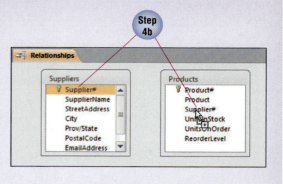

Step 4b

5. At the Edit Relationships dialog box, make sure *Supplier#* displays in the *Table/Query* and *Related Table/Query* list boxes and the relationship type at the bottom of the dialog box displays as *One-To-Many*.

6. Enforce the referential integrity of the relationship by completing the following steps:
   a. Click the *Enforce Referential Integrity* check box to insert a check mark. (This makes the other two options available.)
   b. Click the *Cascade Update Related Fields* check box.
   c. Click the *Cascade Delete Related Records* check box.

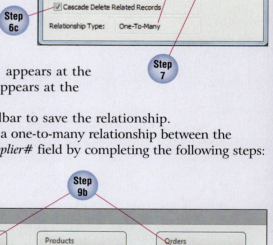

Step 5

Step 6a

Step 6b

Step 6c

Step 7

7. Click the Create button. (This causes the Edit Relationships dialog box to close and the Relationships window to display showing a thick black line connecting the *Supplier#* field in the Suppliers table to the *Supplier#* field in the Products table. A *1* appears at the Suppliers table side and an infinity symbol ∞ appears at the Products table side of the thick, black line.)

8. Click the Save button on the Quick Access toolbar to save the relationship.

9. With the Relationships window still open, create a one-to-many relationship between the Suppliers table and the Orders table with the *Supplier#* field by completing the following steps:
   a. Position the arrow pointer on the *Supplier#* field that displays in the Suppliers table.
   b. Hold down the left mouse button, drag the arrow pointer (with a field icon attached) to the *Supplier#* field in the Orders table, and then release the mouse button.

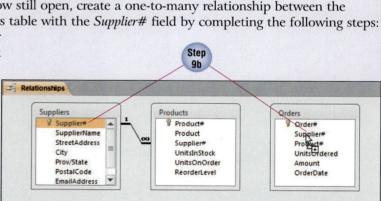

Step 9b

   c. At the Edit Relationships dialog box, make sure *Supplier#* displays in the *Table/Query* and *Related Table/Query* list boxes and the relationship type displays as *One-To-Many*.

d. Click the *Enforce Referential Integrity* check box. (This makes the other two options available.)
e. Click the *Cascade Update Related Fields* check box.
f. Click the *Cascade Delete Related Records* check box.
g. Click the Create button.

10. Create a one-to-many relationship between the Products table and the Orders table with the *Product#* field by completing the following steps:
    a. Position the arrow pointer on the *Product#* field that displays in the Products table.
    b. Hold down the left mouse button, drag the arrow pointer (with a field icon attached) to the *Product#* field in the Orders table, and then release the mouse button.
    c. At the Edit Relationships dialog box, make sure *Product#* displays in the *Table/Query* and *Related Table/Query* list boxes and the relationship type displays as *One-To-Many*.
    d. Click the *Enforce Referential Integrity* check box. (Do not insert check marks in the other two check boxes.)
    e. Click the Create button.
11. Click the Save button on the Quick Access toolbar to save the relationships.
12. Print the relationships by completing the following steps:
    a. At the Relationships window, click the Relationship Report button in the Tools group. This displays the Relationships report in Print Preview. (If a security notice displays, click the Open button.)
    b. Click the Print button in the Print group at the left side of the Print Preview tab.

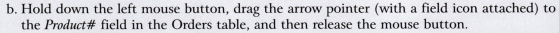

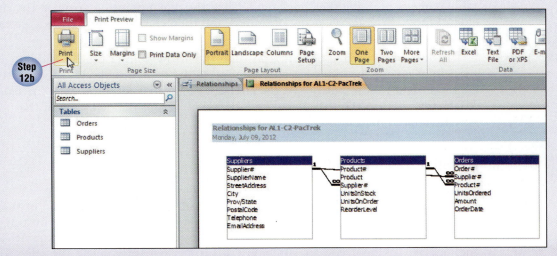

Chapter 2 ■ Creating Relationships between Tables   55

c. Click OK at the Print dialog box.
d. Close the report by clicking the Close button that displays in the upper right corner of the work area.
e. At the message asking if you want to save changes to the design of the report, click No.
13. Close the Relationships window by clicking the Close button that displays in the upper right corner of the work area.

Showing Tables

Show Table

Once a relationship has been established between tables and the Relationships window is closed, clicking the Relationships button causes the Relationships window to display without the Show Table dialog box. To display the Show Table dialog box, click the Show Table button in the Relationships group.

Pacific Trek offers a discount on one product each week. You want to keep track of this information so you decide to create a Discounts table that includes the discount item for each week of the first three months of the year. (You would add a new record to this field each week when the discount item is chosen.) In Project 1c, you will create the Discounts table shown in Figure 2.9 on page 59 and then relate the Products table with the Discounts table using the *Product#* field.

▼ **Quick Steps**

Edit a Relationship
1. Click Database Tools tab.
2. Click Relationships button.
3. Click Edit Relationships button.
4. Make desired changes at Edit Relationships dialog box.
5. Click OK.

Delete a Relationship
1. Click Database Tools tab.
2. Click Relationships button.
3. Right-click on black line connecting related tables.
4. Click *Delete*.
5. Click Yes.

Editing a Relationship

You can make changes to a relationship that has been established between tables or delete the relationship. To edit a relationship, open the database containing the tables with the relationship, click the Database Tools tab, and then click the Relationships button in the Relationships group. This displays the Relationships window with the related tables. Click the Edit Relationships button located in the Tools group to display the Edit Relationships dialog box similar to the one shown in Figure 2.5. Identify the relationship you want to edit by clicking the down-pointing arrow at the right side of the *Table/Query* option box and then clicking the table name containing the "one" field. Click the down-pointing arrow at the right side of the *Related Table/Query* option box and then click the table name containing the "many" field.

To edit a specific relationship, position the arrow pointer on the middle portion of one of the black lines that connects the related tables and then click the right mouse button. At the shortcut menu that displays, click the *Edit Relationship* option. This displays the Edit Relationships dialog box with the specific related field in both list boxes.

Edit Relationships

Deleting a Relationship

To delete a relationship between tables, display the related tables in the Relationships window. Position the arrow pointer on the middle portion of the black line connecting the related tables and then click the right mouse button. At the shortcut menu that displays, click the left mouse button on *Delete*. At the message asking if you are sure you want to permanently delete the selected relationship from your database, click Yes.

Project 1c Creating a Table and Creating and Editing Relationships   Part 3 of 4

1. With **AL1-C2-PacTrek.accdb** open, create the Discounts table shown in Figure 2.9 by completing the following steps:
   a. Click the Create tab.
   b. Click the Table button in Tables group.
   c. Click the Text button in the Add & Delete group. (This creates and then selects the *Field1* heading that displays to the right of the *ID* column.)
   d. Type **Product#** and then press Enter.
   e. Click the *Text* option at the drop-down list and then type **Discount**.
   f. Click the *ID* heading (the first column), click the down-pointing arrow at the right side of the *Data Type* option box in the Formatting group, and then click *Text* at the drop-down list.

   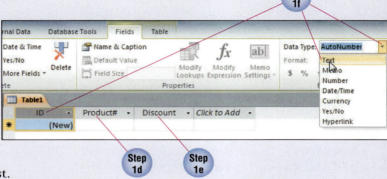

   g. Click in the *Field Size* text box in the Properties group (this selects *255*), type **5**, and then press the Enter key.
   h. Right-click the *ID* heading, click *Rename Field* at the shortcut menu, type **Week**, and then press Enter.
   i. Type the twelve records in the Discounts table as shown in Figure 2.9 on page 59.
2. After typing the records, save the table by completing the following steps:
   a. Click the Save button on the Quick Access toolbar.
   b. At the Save As dialog box, type **Discounts** and then press Enter.
3. Close the Discounts table.
4. Create a relationship from the Products table to the Discounts table by completing the following steps:
   a. Click the Database Tools tab and then click the Relationships button in the Relationships group.
   b. Display the Show Table dialog box by clicking the Show Table button in the Relationships group.

   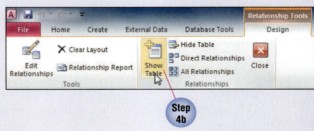

   c. At the Show Table dialog box, double-click the Discounts table.
   d. Click the Close button to close the Show Table dialog box.

Chapter 2 ■ Creating Relationships between Tables   57

5. At the Relationships window, create a one-to-many relationship between the Products table and the Discounts table with the *Product#* field by completing the following steps:
   a. Drag the *Product#* field from the Products table to the *Product#* field in the Discounts table.

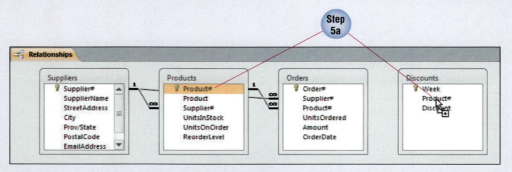

   b. At the Edit Relationships dialog box, make sure *Product#* displays in the *Table/Query* and *Related Table/Query* list boxes and the relationship type at the bottom of the dialog box displays as *One-To-Many*.
   c. Click the *Enforce Referential Integrity* check box.
   d. Click the *Cascade Update Related Fields* check box.
   e. Click the *Cascade Delete Related Records* check box.
   f. Click the Create button. (At the Relationships window, notice the join line that displays between the Products table and the Discounts table. If a message occurs telling you that the relationship cannot be created, click the Cancel button. Open the Discounts table, check to make sure the product numbers are entered correctly in the *Product#* field, and then close the Discounts table. Try again to create the relationship.)
6. Edit the one-to-many relationship between the *Product#* field in the Products table and the Orders table and specify that you want to cascade updated and related fields and cascade and delete related records by completing the following steps:
   a. Click the Edit Relationships button located in the Tools group in the Relationship Tools Design tab.
   b. At the Edit Relationships dialog box, click the down-pointing arrow at the right side of the *Table/Query* option box and then click *Products* at the drop-down list.
   c. Click the down-pointing arrow at the right side of the *Related Table/Query* option box and then click *Orders* at the drop-down list.
   d. Click the *Cascade Update Related Fields* check box.
   e. Click the *Cascade Delete Related Records* check box.
   f. Click the OK button.

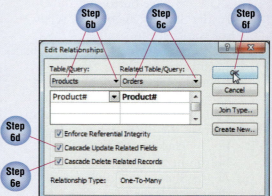

7. Click the Save button on the Quick Access toolbar to save the relationship.
8. Print the relationships by completing the following steps:
   a. Click the Relationship Report button in the Tools group.
   b. Click the Print button in the Print group.
   c. Click OK at the Print dialog box.
   d. Close the report by clicking the Close button that displays in the upper right corner of the work area.

e. At the message asking if you want to save changes to the design of the report, click No.
9. Delete the relationship between the Products table and the Discounts table by completing the following steps:
   a. Position the arrow pointer on the thin portion of the black line connecting the *Product#* field in the Products table with the *Product#* field in the Discounts table and then click the right mouse button.
   b. Click the *Delete* option at the shortcut menu.

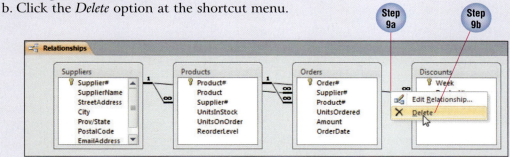

   c. At the message asking if you are sure you want to permanently delete the selected relationship from your database, click Yes.
10. Click the Save button on the Quick Access toolbar to save the relationship.
11. Print the relationships by completing the following steps:
    a. Click the Relationship Report button in the Tools group.
    b. Click the Print button in the Print group.
    c. Click OK at the Print dialog box.
    d. Close the report by clicking the Close button that displays in the upper right corner of the work area.
    e. At the message asking if you want to save changes to the design of the report, click No.
12. Close the Relationships window by clicking the Close button that displays in the upper right corner of the work area.

Figure 2.9 Discounts Table

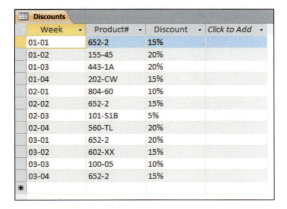

Inserting and Deleting Records in Related Tables

In the relationship established in Project 1b, a record must first be added to the Suppliers table before a related record can be added to the Products table. This is because you chose the *Enforce Referential Integrity* option at the Edit Relationships

Chapter 2 ■ Creating Relationships between Tables   59

dialog box. Because you chose the two options *Cascade Update Related Fields* and *Cascade Delete Related Records*, records in the Suppliers table (the primary table) can be updated and/or deleted and related records in the Products table (related table) will be automatically updated or deleted.

Project 1d Editing and Updating Records Part 4 of 4

1. With the **AL1-C2-PacTrek.accdb** database open, open the Suppliers table.
2. Change two supplier numbers in the Suppliers table (Access will automatically change the numbers in the Products table and the Orders table) by completing the following steps:
    a. Double-click the field value *15* that displays in the *Supplier#* field.
    b. Type **33**.
    c. Double-click the field value *42* that displays in the *Supplier#* field.
    d. Type **51**.
    e. Click the Save button on the Quick Access toolbar.
    f. Close the Suppliers table.
    g. Open the Products table and notice that the supplier number *15* changed to *33* and supplier number *42* changed to *51*.
    h. Close the Products table.
3. Open the Suppliers table and then add the following records:

    Supplier#: **16**
    SupplierName: **Olympic Suppliers**
    StreetAddress: **1773 50th Avenue**
    City: **Seattle**
    Prov/State: **WA**
    PostalCode: **98101**
    Telephone: **(206) 555-9488**
    EmailAddress: **olysuppliers@emcp.net**

    Supplier#: **28**
    SupplierName: **Gorman Company**
    StreetAddress: **543 26th Street**
    City: **Vancouver**
    Prov/State: **BC**
    PostalCode: **V5K 3C5**
    Telephone: **(778) 555-4550**
    EmailAddress: **gormanco@emcp.net**

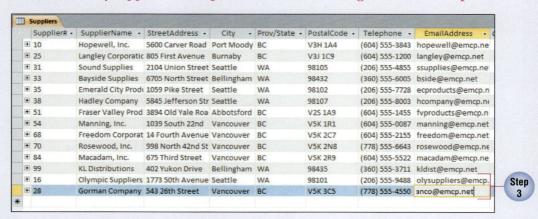

4. Delete the record for supplier number *38* (*Hadley Company*). At the message telling you that relationships that specify cascading deletes are about to cause records in this table and related tables to be deleted, click Yes.
5. Display the table in Print Preview, change to landscape orientation, and then print the table.

6. Close the Suppliers table.
7. Open the Products table and then add the following records to the table:

   Product#: **701-BK**
   Product: **Basic first aid kit**
   Supplier#: **33**
   UnitsInStock: **8**
   UnitsOnOrder: **0**
   ReorderLevel: **5**

   Product#: **703-SP**
   Product: **Medical survival pack**
   Supplier#: **33**
   UnitsInStock: **8**
   UnitsOnOrder: **0**
   ReorderLevel: **5**

   Product#: **185-10**
   Product: **Trail water filter**
   Supplier#: **51**
   UnitsInStock: **4**
   UnitsOnOrder: **10**
   ReorderLevel: **10**

   Product#: **185-50**
   Product: **Trail filter replacement cartridge**
   Supplier#: **51**
   UnitsInStock: **14**
   UnitsOnOrder: **0**
   ReorderLevel: **10**

8. Display the Products table in Print Preview, change to landscape orientation, change the top and bottom margins to 0.4 inches and then print the table. (The table will print on two pages.)
9. Close the Products table.
10. Open the Orders table and then add the following record:
    Order#: **1033**
    OrderDate: **2/15/2012**
    Supplier#: **51**
    Product#: **185-10**
    UnitsOrdered: **10**
    Amount: **$310.90**
11. Print and then close the Orders table.
12. Close the **AL1-C2-PacTrek.accdb** database.

Project 2 Create Relationships and Display Subdatasheets in a Database 2 Parts

You will open a company database and then create one-to-many relationships between tables as well as a one-to-one relationship. You will also display and edit subdatasheets.

Creating a One-to-One Relationship

You can create a *one-to-one relationship* between tables in which each record in the first table matches only one record in the second table and one record in the second table matches only one record in the first table. A one-to-one relationship is not as common as a one-to-many relationship since the type of information used to create the relationship can be stored in one table. A one-to-one relationship is generally used when you want to break a large table with many fields into two smaller tables.

In Project 2a, you will create a one-to-one relationship between the Employees table and the Benefits table. Each record in the Employees table and each record in the Benefits table pertains to one employee. These two tables could be

The Relationships window displays any relationship you have defined between tables.

merged into one but the data in each table is easier to manage when separated. Figure 2.10 shows the relationships you will define between the tables in the AL1-C2-Griffin.accdb database. The Benefits table and the Departments table have been moved down so you can more easily see the relationships.

Figure 2.10 AL1-C2-Griffin.accdb Table Relationships

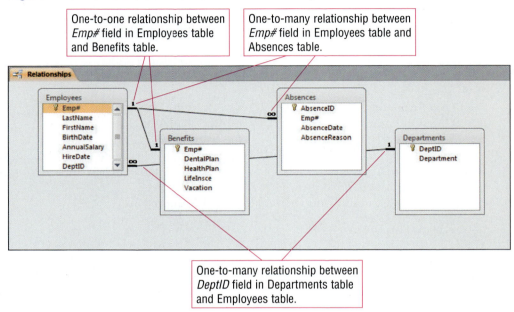

Project 2a — Creating One-to-Many and One-to-One Relationships — Part 1 of 2

1. Open **AL1-C2-Griffin.accdb** and enable the contents.
2. Click the Database Tools tab.
3. Click the Relationships button in the Relationships group.
4. At the Show Table dialog box, add all of the tables to the Relationships window by completing the following steps:
   a. Double-click *Employees* in the Show Table dialog box list box. (This inserts the table in the Relationships window.)
   b. Double-click *Benefits* in the list box.
   c. Double-click *Absences* in the list box.
   d. Double-click *Departments* in the list box.
   e. Click the Close button to close the Show Table dialog box.
5. At the Relationships window, create a one-to-many relationship with the *Emp#* field in the Employees table as the "one" and the *Emp#* field in the Absences table the "many" by completing the following steps:
   a. Position the arrow pointer on the *Emp#* field that displays in the Employees table.

b. Hold down the left mouse button, drag the arrow pointer (with a field icon attached) to the *Emp#* field in the Absences table, and then release the mouse button. (This causes the Edit Relationships dialog box to display.)

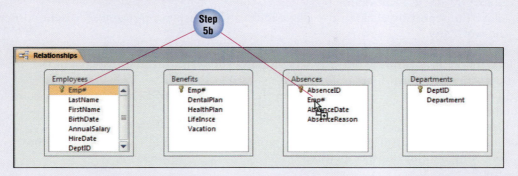

c. At the Edit Relationships dialog box, make sure *Emp#* displays in the *Table/Query* and *Related Table/Query* list boxes and the relationship type at the bottom of the dialog box displays as *One-To-Many*.
d. Click the *Enforce Referential Integrity* check box to insert a check mark.
e. Click the *Cascade Update Related Fields* check box.
f. Click the *Cascade Delete Related Records* check box.
g. Click the Create button. (A *1* appears at the Employees table side and an infinity symbol ∞ appears at the Absences table side of the thick, black line.)

6. Complete steps similar to those in Step 5 to create a one-to-many relationship with the *DeptID* field in the Departments table the "one" and the *DeptID* field in the Employees table the "many."
7. Create a one-to-one relationship with the *Emp#* field in the Employees table and the *Emp#* field in the Benefits table by completing the following steps:
   a. Position the arrow pointer on the *Emp#* field in the Employees table.
   b. Hold down the left mouse button, drag the arrow pointer to the *Emp#* field in the Benefits table, and then release the mouse button. (This displays the Edit Relationships dialog box; notice at the bottom of the dialog box that the relationship type displays as *One-To-One*.)
   c. Click the *Enforce Referential Integrity* check box to insert a check mark.
   d. Click the *Cascade Update Related Fields* check box.
   e. Click the *Cascade Delete Related Records* check box.
   f. Click the Create button. (Notice that a *1* appears at the side of the Employees table and at the side of the Benefits table, indicating a one-to-one relationship.)
8. Click the Save button on the Quick Access toolbar to save the relationships.

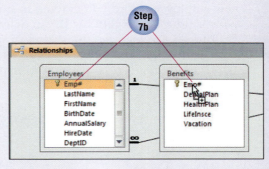

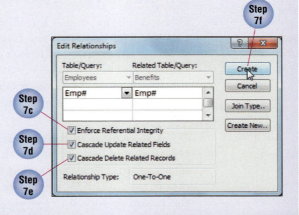

Chapter 2 ■ Creating Relationships between Tables

9. Print the relationships by completing the following steps:
   a. Click the Relationship Report button in the Tools group.
   b. Click the Print button in the Print group.
   c. Click OK at the Print dialog box.
   d. Close the report by clicking the Close button that displays in the upper right corner of the work area.
   e. At the message asking if you want to save changes to the design of the report, click No.
10. Close the Relationships window by clicking the Close button that displays in the upper right corner of the work area.
11. Add a record to and delete a record from the Employees and Benefits tables by completing the following steps:
    a. Open the Employees table.
    b. Click the New button in the Records group in the Home tab and then type the following data in the specified field:
       Emp#: 1096
       LastName: Schwartz
       FirstName: Bryan
       BirthDate: 5/21/1980
       DeptID: IT
       AnnualSalary: $45,000.00
       HireDate: 1/15/2007
    c. Delete the record for Trevor Sargent (employee number 1005). At the message telling you that relationships that specify cascading deletes are about to cause records in this table and related tables to be deleted, click Yes.
    d. Save, print, and then close the Employees table.
12. Open the Benefits table and notice that the record for Trevor Sargent was deleted but the new employee record you entered in the Employees table is not reflected in the Benefits table. Add a new record for Bryan Schwartz with the following information:
    Emp#: 1096
    Health Plan: (Leave check mark.)
    Dental Plan: (Press spacebar to remove check mark.)
    Life Insurance: $100,000.00
    Vacation: 2 weeks
13. Print and then close the Benefits table.

Displaying Related Records in a Subdatasheet

When a relationship is established between tables, you can view and edit records in related tables with a ***subdatasheet***. Figure 2.11 displays the Employees table with the subdatasheet displayed for the employee Kate Navarro. The subdatasheet displays the fields in the Benefits table related to Kate Navarro. Use this subdatasheet to view information and also to edit information in the Employees table as well as the Absences table. Changes made to fields in a subdatasheet affect the table and any related table.

Access automatically inserts plus symbols (referred to as ***expand indicators***) before each record in a table that is joined to another table by a one-to-many relationship. Click the expand indicator and, if the table is related to only one other table, a subdatasheet containing fields from the related table displays below the record as shown in Figure 2.11. To remove the subdatasheet, click the minus sign (referred to as the ***collapse indicator***) preceding the record. (The plus symbol turns into the minus symbol when a subdatasheet displays.)

Figure 2.11 Table with Subdatasheet Displayed

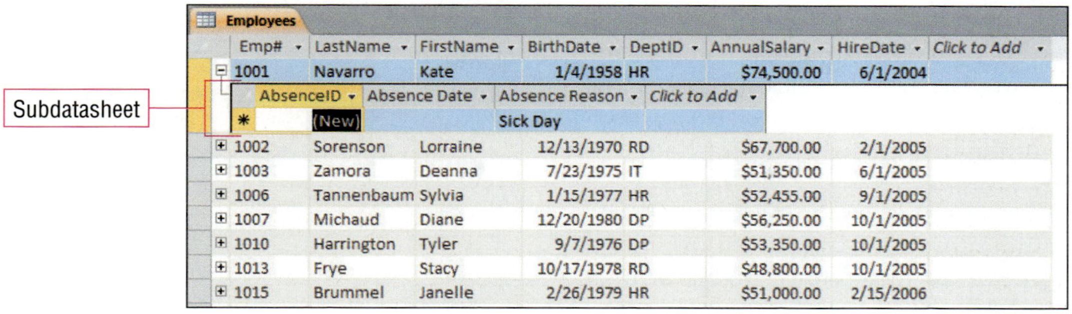

If a table has more than one relationship defined, clicking the expand indicator will display the Insert Subdatasheet dialog box shown in Figure 2.12. At this dialog box, click the desired table in the Tables list box and then click OK. You can also display the Insert Subdatasheet dialog box by clicking the More button in the Records group in the Home tab, pointing to *Subdatasheet*, and then clicking *Subdatasheet*. You can display subdatasheets for all records by clicking the More button, pointing to *Subdatasheet*, and then clicking *Expand All*. Remove all subdatasheets by clicking the More button, pointing to *Subdatasheet*, and then clicking *Collapse All*.

If a table is related to two or more tables, specify the desired subdatasheet at the Subdatasheet dialog box. If you decide to display a different subdatasheet, remove the subdatasheet first before selecting the next subdatasheet. Do this by clicking the More button, pointing to *Subdatasheet*, and then clicking *Remove*.

▼ **Quick Steps**

Display Subdatasheet
1. Open table.
2. Click expand indicator at left side of desired record.
3. Click desired table at Insert Subdatasheet dialog box.
4. Click OK.

Figure 2.12 Insert Subdatasheet Dialog Box

Chapter 2 ■ Creating Relationships between Tables   65

Project 2b Viewing and Editing a Subdatasheet Part 2 of 2

1. With the **AL1-C2-Griffin.accdb** database open, open the Employees table.
2. Display a subdatasheet by clicking the expand indicator (plus symbol) that displays at the left side of the first row (the row for Kate Navarro).
3. Remove the subdatasheet by clicking the collapse indicator (minus sign) that displays at the left side of the record for Kate Navarro.
4. Display subdatasheets for all of the records by clicking the More button in the Records group, pointing to *Subdatasheet*, and then clicking *Expand All*.

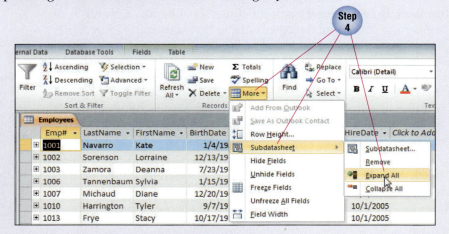

5. Remove the display of all subdatasheets by clicking the More button, pointing to *Subdatasheet*, and then clicking *Collapse All*.
6. Remove the connection between the Employees and Absences table by clicking the More button, pointing to *Subdatasheet*, and then clicking *Remove*. (Notice that the expand indicators [plus symbols] no longer display before each record.)
7. Suppose that the employee, Diane Michaud, has moved to a different department and has had an increase in salary. Display the Benefits subdatasheet and make changes to fields in the Employees table and the Benefits table by completing the following steps:

    a. Click the More button in the Records group, point to *Subdatasheet*, and then click *Subdatasheet* at the side menu.

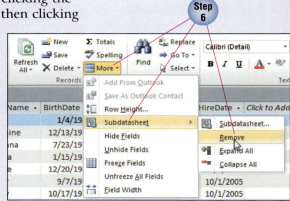

b. At the Insert Subdatasheet dialog box, click *Benefits* in the list box and then click OK.
c. Change the department ID for the *Diane Michaud* record from *DP* to *A*.
d. Change the salary from *$56,250.00* to *$57,500.00*.
e. Click the expand indicator (plus symbol) that displays at the left side of the *Diane Michaud* record.
f. Insert a check mark in the *Dental Plan* check box and change her vacation from 3 weeks to 4 weeks.

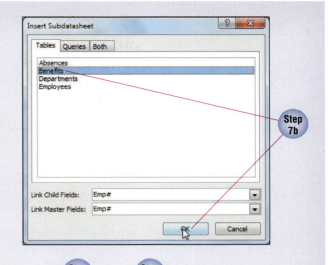

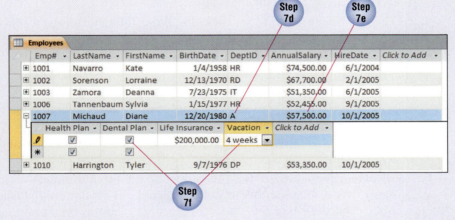

g. Click the collapse indicator (minus symbol) that displays at the left side of the *Diane Michaud* record.
8. Click the Save button on the Quick Access toolbar.
9. Print and then close the Employees table.
10. Open, print, and then close the Benefits table.
11. Close the **AL1-C2-Griffin.accdb** database.

Chapter Summary

- Access is a relational database software program in which you can create tables that have a relation or connection to one another.
- When planning a table, take time to determine how to break down the required data and what relationships will need to be defined to eliminate data redundancies.
- Generally, one field in a table must be unique so that one record can be distinguished from another. A field with a unique value is considered a primary key field.

- A table can have only one primary key field and it is the field by which the table is sorted whenever the table is opened.
- In a field defined as a primary key field, duplicate values are not allowed in the field and Access also expects a value in each record in the primary key field.
- Typically, a primary key field in one table becomes the foreign key field in a related table. Data in a foreign key field must match data in the primary key field of the related tables.
- In Access, you can relate a table to another by performing a join. When tables that have a common field are joined, you can extract data from both tables as if they were one large table.
- You can create a one-to-many relationship between tables. In this relationship, a record must be added to the "one" table before it can be added to the "many" table.
- To print table relationships, display the Relationships window, click the Relationship Report button, click the Print button in the Print Preview tab, and then click OK at the Print dialog box.
- At the Relationships window, click the Show Table button to display the Show Table dialog box.
- You can edit or delete a relationship between tables.
- You can create a one-to-one relationship between tables in which each record in the first table matches only one record in the related table. This type of relationship is generally used when you want to break a large table with many fields into two smaller tables.
- When a relationship is established between tables, you can view and edit fields in related tables with a subdatasheet.
- To display a subdatasheet for a record, click the expand indicator (plus symbol) that displays to the left of the record. To display subdatasheets for all records, click the More button in the Records group in the Home tab, point to *Subdatasheet*, and then click *Expand All*.
- Display the Insert Subdatasheet dialog box by clicking the More button in the Reports group in the Home tab, pointing to *Subdatasheet*, and then clicking *Subdatasheet*.
- Turn off the display of a subdatasheet by clicking the collapse indicator (minus symbol) at the beginning of the record. To turn off the display of subdatasheets for all records, click the More button, point to *Subdatasheet*, and then click *Collapse All*.

Commands Review

FEATURE	RIBBON, GROUP	BUTTON	OPTION
Primary key	Table Tools Design, Tools		
Relationships window	Database Tools, Relationships		
Relationships report window	Relationship Tools Design, Relationships		
Show Table dialog box	Relationship Tools Design, Relationships		
Edit Relationships dialog box	Relationship Tools Design, Tools		
Insert Subdatasheet dialog box	Home, Records		Subdatasheet, Subdatasheet

Concepts Check Test Your Knowledge

Completion: In the space provided at the right, indicate the correct term, symbol, or command.

1. A database table can contain a foreign key field and this type of key field. _____

2. In Access, one table can be related to another, which is generally referred to as performing this. _____

3. Open a table, click the View button in the Home tab, and the table displays in this view. _____

4. In a one-to-many relationship, the table containing the "one" is referred to as this. _____

5. In a one-to-many relationship, the table containing the "many" is referred to as this. _____

6. In a one-to-many relationship, Access follows a set of rules that enforces consistency between related tables and is referred to as this. _____

7. In related tables, this symbol displays near the black line next to the related table. _____

8. The black line that connects related tables is referred to as this. _____

9. Establish this type of relationship between tables in which each record in the first table matches only one record in the second table and one record in the second table matches only one record in the first table. _____

10. The plus symbol that displays at the beginning of a record in a related table is referred to as this. _____

11. The minus symbol that displays at the beginning of a record in a related table with a subdatasheet displayed is referred to as this. _____

12. Display subdatasheets for all records by clicking the More button, pointing to *Subdatasheet*, and then clicking this option. _____

Skills Check   Assess Your Performance

The database designer for Copper State Insurance has created the database diagram, shown in Figure 2.13, to manage company data. You will open the Copper State Insurance database and maintain and create tables that follow the diagram.

Figure 2.13 Copper State Insurance Database Design

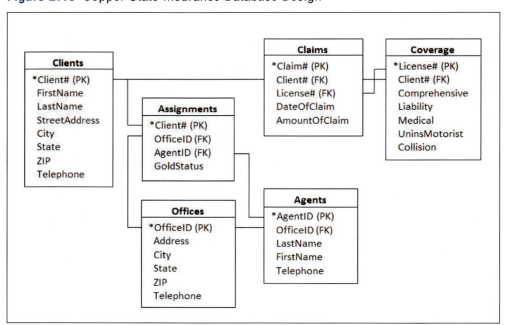

Assessment

1 CREATE RELATIONSHIPS IN AN INSURANCE COMPANY DATABASE

1. Open the **AL1-C2-CopperState.accdb** database and enable the contents.
2. Open the Claims table.
3. Display the table in Design view, define the *Claim#* field as the primary key field, click the Save button on the Quick Access toolbar, and then close the Claims table.
4. Display the Relationships window and then insert the Clients, Claims, and Coverage tables.
5. Create a one-to-many relationship with the *Client#* field in the Clients table the "one" and the *Client#* field in the Claims table the "many." Enforce referential integrity and cascade fields and records.
6. Create a one-to-many relationship with the *Client#* field in the Clients table the "one" and the *Client#* field in the Coverage table the "many." Enforce referential integrity and cascade fields and records.
7. Create a one-to-many relationship with the *License#* field in the Coverage table the "one" and the *License#* field in the Claims table the "many." Enforce referential integrity and cascade fields and records.
8. Save and then print the relationships.
9. Close the relationships report without saving it and close the Relationships window.

Assessment

2 CREATE A NEW TABLE AND RELATE THE TABLE

1. With **AL-C2-CopperState.accdb** open, create the Offices table shown in Figure 2.14. Change the data type of the first column to *Text*. (Do this with the *Data Type* option box in the Formatting group in the Table Tools Fields tab.) Change the field size to *2*. Change the default value for the *State* field to *AZ*.
2. After typing the records, adjust the column widths to accommodate the longest entry in each column and then save the Offices table.
3. Print and then close the Offices table.
4. Display the Relationships window and then add the Offices table and the Assignments table to the window.
5. Create a one-to-many relationship with the *OfficeID* field in the Offices table the "one" and the *OfficeID* field in the Assignments table the "many." Enforce referential integrity and cascade fields and records.
6. Create a one-to-one relationship with the *Client#* field in the Clients table and the *Client#* field in the Assignments table. Enforce referential integrity and cascade fields and records.
7. Save and then print the relationships in landscape orientation. To do this, click the Landscape button in the Page Layout group in Print Preview.
8. Close the relationships report without saving it and then close the Relationships window.

Figure 2.14 Assessment 2 Offices Table

OfficeID	Address	City	State	ZIP	Telephone	Click to Add
GN	North 51st Avenue	Glendale	AZ	85305	(623) 555-8800	
GW	West Bell Road	Glendale	AZ	85312	(623) 555-4300	
PG	Grant Street West	Phoenix	AZ	85003	(602) 555-6200	
PM	McDowell Road	Phoenix	AZ	85012	(602) 555-3800	
SE	East Thomas Road	Scottsdale	AZ	85251	(480) 555-5500	
SN	North 68th Street	Scottsdale	AZ	85257	(480) 555-9000	
*			AZ			

Assessment 3 — DELETE AND EDIT RECORDS IN TABLES

1. With **AL1-C2-CopperState.accdb** open, open the Clients table.
2. Delete the record for Harold McDougal (client number 9879). (At the message telling you that relationships that specify cascading deletes are about to cause records in this table and related tables to be deleted, click Yes.)
3. Delete the record for Vernon Cook (client number 7335). (At the message telling you that relationships that specify cascading deletes are about to cause records in this table and related tables to be deleted, click Yes.)
4. Change the client number for Paul Vuong from *4300* to *2560*.
5. Print the Clients table in landscape orientation and then close the table.
6. Open the Claims table, print the table, and then close the table. (The Claims table initially contained two entries for client number 9879 and one entry for 7335. These entries were deleted automatically when you deleted the records in the Clients table.)

Assessment 4 — DISPLAY AND EDIT RECORDS IN A SUBDATASHEET

1. With the **AL1-C2-CopperState.accdb** database open, open the Clients table.
2. Click the expand indicator (plus symbol) that displays at the left side of the record for Erin Hagedorn. At the Insert Subdatasheet dialog box, click *Claims* in the list box, and then click OK.
3. Change the amount of the claim from *$1,450.00* to *$1,797.00*, change Erin's street address from *4818 Oakes Boulevard* to *763 51st Avenue*, and change her ZIP code from *85018* to *85014*.
4. Click the collapse indicator (minus symbol) that displays at the left side of the record for Erin Hagedorn.
5. Remove the connection between the Clients and Claims tables by clicking the More button in the Records group in the Home tab, pointing to *Subdatasheet*, and then clicking *Remove*.
6. Click the More button in the Records group, point to *Subdatasheet*, and then click *Subdatasheet*.
7. At the Insert Subdatasheet dialog box, click *Coverage* in the list box and then click OK.
8. Expand all records by clicking the More button, pointing to *Subdatasheet*, and then clicking *Expand All*.
9. Change the telephone number for Claire Azevedo (client number 1379) from *480-555-2154* to *480-555-2143* and insert check marks in the *Medical* field and the *UninsMotorist* field.
10. Change the last name of Joanne Donnelly (client number 1574) to *Marquez* and remove the check mark from the *Collision* field.
11. Display the record for Brenda Lazzuri (client number 3156) and then insert a check mark in the *UninsMotorist* field and the *Collision* field for both vehicles.
12. Click in any field heading and then collapse all records.
13. Remove the connection between the Clients and Coverage tables.
14. Save, print, and then close the Clients table. (Make sure the table displays in landscape orientation.)
15. Open the Coverage table, print the table, and then close the table.

Visual Benchmark — Demonstrate Your Proficiency

CREATE AN AGENTS TABLE

Note: The starting file for this activity is the file created after completing the previous Skills Check assessments.

1. With the **AL1-C2-CopperState.accdb** database open, create the Agents table shown in Figure 2.15. You determine the data types and field sizes. Create a more descriptive caption for each field name and create a description for each field.
2. Save, print, and then close the Agents table.
3. Display the Relationships window, add the Agents table to the window, and then create the two additional relationships shown in the diagram in Figure 2.16. (You determine what table contains the "one" and what table contains the "many.")
4. Save and then print the relationships in landscape orientation and then close the Relationships window.
5. Open the Agents table.
6. Change the AgentID for Troy Bajema from *04* to *05*.
7. Change Joanna Logan's last name from *Logan* to *Janowski*.
8. Print and then close the Agents table.
9. Open the Assignments table, print the table, and then close the table. (Notice that the *04* AgentID in the Assignments table was changed to *05*. This is because the tables are related and the changes you make in the primary table are made automatically in the related table.)
10. Close the **AL1-C2-CopperState.accdb** database.

Figure 2.15 Visual Benchmark Agents Table

AgentID	OfficeID	FirstName	LastName	Telephone
02	PM	Marsha	Brundage	(602) 555-3805
03	PM	Greg	Dunlap	(602) 555-3811
04	PM	Troy	Bajema	(602) 555-3815
11	PG	Joanna	Logan	(480) 555-6255
12	PG	Dana	Rosario	(480) 555-6243
14	PG	Dennis	Stansbury	(480) 555-6218
21	GW	Kerri	Watanabe	(623) 555-4300
23	GW	Roland	Linderman	(623) 555-4328
25	GW	Marian	Monaghan	(623) 555-4317
32	GN	Eugene	Kessler	(623) 555-8803
34	GN	Bruce	Neville	(623) 555-8823
35	GN	Cheryl	Rhoades	(623) 555-8811
41	SE	Nina	Chesheva	(480) 555-5502
42	SE	Steven	Gabrielson	(480) 555-5510
45	SE	Laura	Mellema	(480) 555-5528
51	SN	Michael	Tan	(480) 555-9002
52	SN	Angie	Santagelo	(480) 555-9006
53	SN	Martin	Osborne	(480) 555-9010

Figure 2.16 Visual Benchmark Table Relationships Diagram

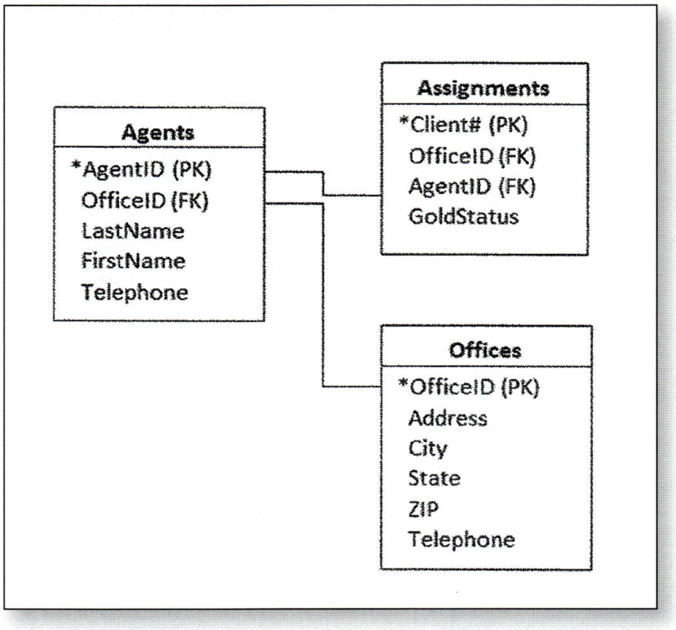

Agents
*AgentID (PK)
OfficeID (FK)
LastName
FirstName
Telephone

Assignments
*Client# (PK)
OfficeID (FK)
AgentID (FK)
GoldStatus

Offices
*OfficeID (PK)
Address
City
State
ZIP
Telephone

Case Study Apply Your Skills

You are the manager for Gold Star Cleaning Services and your company is switching over to Access for managing company data. The database designer has provided you with the database diagram in Figure 2.17. He wants you to follow the diagram when creating the database.

Figure 2.17 Gold Star Cleaning Services Database Diagram

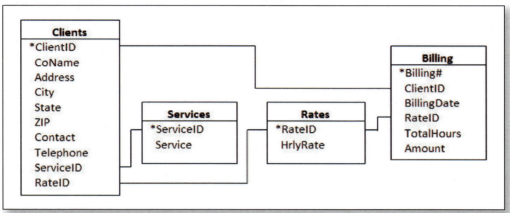

Part 1

Create a new database named **AL1-C2-GoldStar.accdb** and then create the Clients table shown in the database diagram. The database designer has asked you to include an appropriate caption and description for the fields. Specify a field size of *3* for the *ClientID* field, *4* for the *ServiceID* field, and *1* for the *RateID* field. You determine the field size for the *State*, *ZIP*, and *Telephone* fields. He also wants you to set the default value for the *City* field to *St. Louis* and the *State* field to *MO*. Type the following records in the table:

ClientID: **101**
CoName: **Smithson Realty**
Address: **492 Papin Street**
City: (default value)
State: (default value)
ZIP: **63108**
Contact: **Danielle Snowden**
Telephone: **(314) 555-3588**
ServiceID: **GS-1**
RateID: **B**

ClientID: **102**
CoName: **Air-Flow Systems**
Address: **1058 Pine Street**
City: (default value)
State: (default value)
ZIP: **63186**
Contact: **Nick Cline**
Telephone: **(314) 555-9452**
ServiceID: **GS-3**
RateID: **A**

ClientID: 107
CoName: Mainstreet Mortgage
Address: North 22nd Street
City: (default value)
State: (default value)
ZIP: 63134
Contact: Ted Farrell
Telephone: (314) 555-7744
ServiceID: GS-1
RateID: D

ClientID: 110
CoName: Firstline Finances
Address: 104 Scott Avenue
City: (default value)
State: (default value)
ZIP: 63126
Contact: Robert Styer
Telephone: (314) 555-8343
ServiceID: GS-2
RateID: A

ClientID: 112
CoName: GB Construction
Address: 988 Lucas Avenue
City: (default value)
State: (default value)
ZIP: 63175
Contact: Joy Ewing
Telephone: (314) 555-0036
ServiceID: GS-1
RateID: C

ClientID: 115
CoName: Simko Equipment
Address: 1200 Market Street
City: (default value)
State: (default value)
ZIP: 63140
ZIP: Dale Aldrich
Telephone: (314) 555-3315
ServiceID: GS-3
RateID: C

Create the Services table shown in the database diagram. Change the *ServiceID* field size to 4. Type the following records in the table:

ServiceID: GS-1
Service: Deep cleaning all rooms and surfaces, garbage removal, recycling, carpet cleaning, disinfecting

ServiceID: GS-2
Service: Deep cleaning all rooms, all surfaces, garbage removal, disinfecting

ServiceID: GS-3
Service: Deep cleaning all rooms and surfaces, disinfecting

Create the Rates table shown in the database diagram. Change the *RateID* field size to 1. Type the following records in the table:

RateID: A
HrlyRate: $75.50

RateID: B
HrlyRate: $65.00

RateID: C
HrlyRate: $59.75

RateID: D
HrlyRate: $50.50

Create the Billing table shown in the database diagram. Change the *Billing#* field size to 2, the *ClientID* field size to 3, and the *RateID* field size to 1. Apply the appropriate data types to the fields. Type the following records in the table:

Billing#: 40
ClientID: 101
BillingDate: 4/2/2012
RateID: B
TotalHours: 26
Amount: $1,690.00

Billing#: 41
ClientID: 102
BillingDate: 4/2/2012
RateID: A
TotalHours: 32
Amount: $2,416.00

Billing#: 42
ClientID: 107
BillingDate: 4/2/2012
RateID: D
TotalHours: 15
Amount: $747.50

Billing#: 43
ClientID: 110
BillingDate: 4/2/2012
RateID: A
TotalHours: 30
Amount: $2,265.00

Billing#: 44
ClientID: 112
BillingDate: 4/2/2012
RateID: C
TotalHours: 20
Amount: $1,195.00

Billing#: 45
ClientID: 115
BillingDate: 4/2/2012
RateID: C
TotalHours: 22
Amount: $1,314.50

Automatically adjust the column widths of each table to accommodate the longest entry in each column and then print each table on one page. *Hint: Check the table in Print Preview and, if necessary, change to landscape orientation and change the margins*.

Part 2

With **AL1-C2-GoldStar.accdb** open, create the one-to-many relationships required to connect the tables. (Refer to Figure 2.17 as a guide.) You will need to increase the size of the Clients table to view all of the fields. To do this, position the mouse pointer on the bottom border of the Clients table in the Relationships window until the pointer turns into a white arrow pointing up and down. Hold down the left mouse button, drag down to the desired position, and then release the mouse button. Print the relationships report.

Part 3

Open the Services table and then make the following changes to the field values in the *ServiceID* field:

Change *GS-1* to *GS-A*
Change *GS-2* to *GS-B*
Change *GS-3* to *GS-C*

Save, print, and then close the Services table. Open the Clients table, delete the record for client number 112 and then insert the following record:

ClientID: 108
Name: Cedar Ridge Products
Address: 6400 Olive Street
City: (default value)
State: (default value)
ZIP: 63114
Contact: Penny Childers
Telephone: (314) 555-7660
ServiceID: GS-B
RateID: B

Save, print, and then close the Clients table. Open the Billing table, print the table, and then close the table. Close the **AL1-C2-GoldStar.accdb** database.

Access

CHAPTER 3

Performing Queries

PERFORMANCE OBJECTIVES

Upon successful completion of Chapter 3, you will be able to:
- Design queries to extract specific data from tables
- Use the Simple Query Wizard to create queries
- Modify queries
- Design queries with *Or* and *And* criteria
- Create a calculated field
- Use aggregate functions in queries
- Create crosstab, duplicate, and unmatched queries

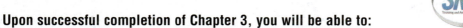

One of the primary uses of a database is to extract specific information from the database. A company might need to know such information as: How much inventory is currently on hand? What products have been ordered? What accounts are past due? What customers live in a particular city? You can extract this type of information from a table or multiple tables by completing a query. You will learn how to perform a variety of queries on information in tables in this chapter. Model answers for this chapter's projects appear on the following pages.

Access2010L1C3

Note: Before beginning the projects, copy the Access2010L1C3 subfolder from the Access2010L1 folder on the CD that accompanies this textbook to your storage medium and make Access2010L1C3 the active folder.

Project 1 Design Queries

Project 1a

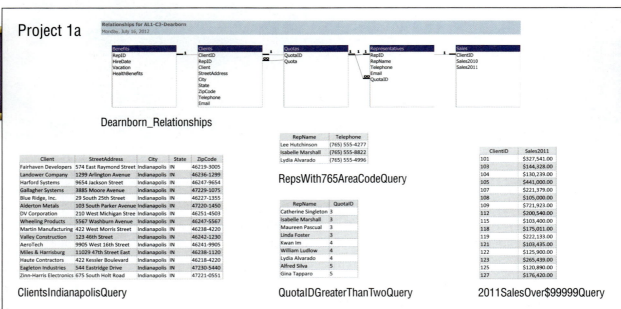

Project 1b

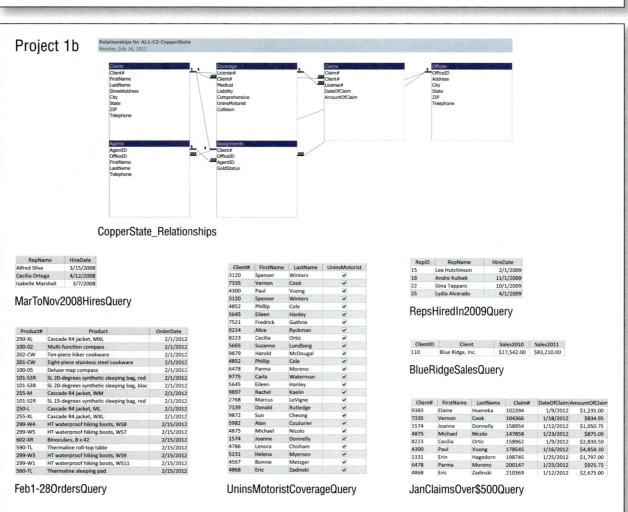

Project 1c

Product#	Supplier#	UnitsOrdered	Amount
442-1B	42	10	$1,495.00
780-2	99	10	$1,288.50
250-L	60	10	$1,285.00
250-XL	60	10	$1,285.00
101-S3R	54	10	$1,199.50
101-S3B	54	10	$1,137.50
299-M3	31	10	$887.90
299-M5	31	10	$887.90
299-M2	31	10	$887.90
299-W5	31	10	$752.90
299-W4	31	10	$752.90
299-W3	31	10	$752.90
299-W1	31	8	$602.32
255-M	60	5	$599.50
255-XL	60	5	$599.50
560-TL	25	20	$397.00
155-35	10	10	$199.50
375-S	68	20	$199.00
375-M	68	20	$199.00
590-TL	25	5	$196.25
209-XL	68	25	$180.00
209-L	68	25	$173.75
210-L	68	25	$162.25
209-XXL	68	20	$145.80
100-05	84	5	$129.75
371-L	68	10	$129.50
202-CW	15	5	$124.25
155-20	10	15	$104.25
201-CW	15	5	$99.75
210-M	68	15	$97.35
100-02	84	10	$45.95
152-H	10	15	$44.85

OrdersLessThan$1500Query

OfficeID	AgentID	FirstName	LastName
GW	23	Carlos	Alvarez
GW	25	Joanne	Donnelly
GW	25	Cecilia	Ortiz
GW	25	Donald	Rutledge
GW	21	Paul	Vuong

GWClientsQuery

Client	Sales2010	RepName
Madison Electrics	$99,450.00	William Ludlow
Landower Company	$97,653.00	Robin Rehberg
Providence, Inc.	$85,628.00	Isabelle Marshall
Karris Supplies	$61,349.00	Edward Harris
Paragon Corporation	$51,237.00	Jaren Newman
Martin Manufacturing	$35,679.00	Lydia Alvarado
Hoosier Corporation	$24,880.00	Craig Johnson
Blue Ridge, Inc.	$17,542.00	Maureen Pascual
Valley Construction	$15,248.00	Lee Hutchinson
Alderton Metals	$9,547.00	Alfred Silva
Northstar Services	$9,457.00	Alfred Silva
Milltown Contractors	$2,356.00	Kwan Im

2010SalesLessThan$100000Query

Project 1d

Client	Sales2011	RepName
Fairhaven Developers	$95,630.00	Kwan Im
Blue Ridge, Inc.	$83,210.00	Maureen Pascual
Providence, Inc.	$75,462.00	Isabelle Marshall
Franklin Services	$65,411.00	Catherine Singleton
Martin Manufacturing	$61,539.00	Lydia Alvarado
Alderton Metals	$45,230.00	Alfred Silva
Hoosier Corporation	$31,935.00	Craig Johnson
Milltown Contractors	$31,230.00	Kwan Im
Valley Construction	$22,478.00	Lee Hutchinson
Paragon Corporation	$20,137.00	Jaren Newman
Northstar Services	$15,094.00	Alfred Silva

2011SalesLessThan$100000Query

RepName	Vacation
Alfred Silva	3 weeks
Cecilia Ortega	3 weeks
Isabelle Marshall	3 weeks
Craig Johnson	3 weeks
Gina Tapparo	3 weeks
Edward Harris	3 weeks

RepsWith3WeekVacationsQuery

Project 1e

RepName	Vacation
William Ludlow	4 weeks
Alfred Silva	3 weeks
Cecilia Ortega	3 weeks
Robin Rehberg	4 weeks
Isabelle Marshall	3 weeks
Craig Johnson	3 weeks
Gina Tapparo	3 weeks
Edward Harris	3 weeks

RepsWith3Or4WeekVacationsQuery

Client	City	Sales2010	Sales2011
Harford Systems	Indianapolis	$215,420.00	$441,000.00
Gallagher Systems	Indianapolis	$199,346.00	$221,379.00
DV Corporation	Indianapolis	$138,560.00	$200,540.00
Wheeling Products	Indianapolis	$115,423.00	$103,400.00
AeroTech	Indianapolis	$156,439.00	$175,011.00
Miles & Harrisburg	Indianapolis	$201,430.00	$222,133.00
Haute Contractors	Indianapolis	$174,319.00	$125,900.00
Eagleton Industries	Indianapolis	$300,137.00	$265,439.00
Zinn-Harris Electronics	Indianapolis	$214,000.00	$176,420.00

SalesOver$100000IndianapolisQuery

Supplier#	SupplierName	Product
25	Langley Corporation	Thermaline sleeping pad
25	Langley Corporation	Thermaline light-weight cot
25	Langley Corporation	Thermaline camp seat
25	Langley Corporation	Thermaline roll-top table
31	Sound Supplies	HT waterproof hiking boots, MS13
31	Sound Supplies	HT waterproof hiking boots, MS12
31	Sound Supplies	HT waterproof hiking boots, MS11
31	Sound Supplies	HT waterproof hiking boots, MS10
31	Sound Supplies	HT waterproof hiking boots, MS9
31	Sound Supplies	HT waterproof hiking boots, WS11
31	Sound Supplies	HT waterproof hiking boots, WS10
31	Sound Supplies	HT waterproof hiking boots, WS9
31	Sound Supplies	HT waterproof hiking boots, WS8
31	Sound Supplies	HT waterproof hiking boots, WS7
31	Sound Supplies	HT waterproof hiking boots, WS6
42	Fraser Valley Product	Polar backpack, 250RW
42	Fraser Valley Product	Polar backpack, 150BR
42	Fraser Valley Product	Polar backpack, 150RW
42	Fraser Valley Product	Polar backpack, 250BR

Suppliers25-31-42Query

Order#	SupplierName	Product	UnitsOrdered
1017	Freedom Corporation	Gordon wool ski hat, L	25
1009	Freedom Corporation	Gordon wool ski hat, XL	25
1008	Freedom Corporation	Gordon wool ski hat, XXL	20
1012	Freedom Corporation	Tech-lite ski hat, L	25
1013	Freedom Corporation	Tech-lite ski hat, M	15
1016	Freedom Corporation	Lite-tech ski gloves, ML	10
1015	Freedom Corporation	Lite-tech ski gloves, WM	20
1014	Freedom Corporation	Lite-tech ski gloves, WS	20

SkiHatsGlovesOnOrderQuery

Client#	FirstName	LastName	Medical	Liability	Comprehensive	UninsMotorist	Collision
3156	Brenda	Lazzuri		✓			
8854	Edward	Bakalarski		✓			
3156	Brenda	Lazzuri		✓			
3164	Bret	Mardock		✓			
9746	Carlos	Alvarez		✓			

ClientsWithOnlyLiabilityQuery

Product#	Product	SupplierName
443-1B	Polar backpack, 250RW	Fraser Valley Product
101-S1B	SL 0-degrees down sleeping bag, black	Manning, Inc.
101-S1R	SL 0-degrees down sleeping bag, red	Manning, Inc.
101-S2B	SL 15-degrees synthetic sleeping bag, blac	Manning, Inc.
101-S2R	SL 15-degrees synthetic sleeping bag, red	Manning, Inc.
101-S3B	SL 20-degrees synthetic sleeping bag, blac	Manning, Inc.
101-S3R	SL 20-degrees synthetic sleeping bag, red	Manning, Inc.
299-M1	HT waterproof hiking boots, MS13	Sound Supplies
299-M2	HT waterproof hiking boots, MS12	Sound Supplies
299-M3	HT waterproof hiking boots, MS11	Sound Supplies
299-M4	HT waterproof hiking boots, MS10	Sound Supplies
299-M5	HT waterproof hiking boots, MS9	Sound Supplies
299-W1	HT waterproof hiking boots, WS11	Sound Supplies
299-W2	HT waterproof hiking boots, WS10	Sound Supplies
299-W3	HT waterproof hiking boots, WS9	Sound Supplies
299-W4	HT waterproof hiking boots, WS8	Sound Supplies
299-W5	HT waterproof hiking boots, WS7	Sound Supplies
299-W6	HT waterproof hiking boots, WS6	Sound Supplies
442-1A	Polar backpack, 150BR	Fraser Valley Product
442-1B	Polar backpack, 150RW	Fraser Valley Product
443-1A	Polar backpack, 250BR	Fraser Valley Product

BootsSleepingBagsBackpacksQuery

Project 1f

Client2010-2011SalesQuery

ClientID	Client	Sales2010	Sales2011
101	Bering Company	$289,563.00	$327,541.00
102	Fairhaven Developers	$101,210.00	$95,630.00
103	Clearwater Service	$125,436.00	$144,328.00
104	Landower Company	$97,653.00	$130,239.00
105	Harford Systems	$215,420.00	$441,000.00
106	Providence, Inc.	$85,628.00	$75,462.00
107	Gallagher Systems	$199,346.00	$221,379.00
108	Karris Supplies	$61,349.00	$105,000.00
109	HE Systems	$554,120.00	$721,923.00
110	Blue Ridge, Inc.	$17,542.00	$83,210.00
111	Alderton Metals	$9,547.00	$45,230.00
112	DV Corporation	$138,560.00	$200,540.00
113	Franklin Services	$141,670.00	$65,411.00
114	Milltown Contractors	$2,356.00	$31,230.00
115	Wheeling Products	$115,423.00	$103,400.00
116	Martin Manufacturing	$35,679.00	$61,539.00
117	Valley Construction	$15,248.00	$22,478.00
118	AeroTech	$156,439.00	$175,011.00
119	Miles & Harrisburg	$201,430.00	$222,133.00
120	Paragon Corporation	$51,237.00	$20,137.00
121	Madison Electrics	$99,450.00	$103,435.00
122	Haute Contractors	$174,319.00	$125,900.00
123	Eagleton Industries	$300,137.00	$265,439.00
124	Hoosier Corporation	$24,880.00	$31,935.00
125	Dover Industries	$151,003.00	$120,890.00
126	Northstar Services	$9,457.00	$15,094.00
127	Zinn-Harris Electronics	$214,000.00	$176,420.00

ProductOrderAmountsQuery

Supplier#	SupplierName	Product#	Amount
10	Hopewell, Inc.	155-35	$199.50
10	Hopewell, Inc.	152-H	$44.85
10	Hopewell, Inc.	155-20	$104.25
15	Bayside Supplies	202-CW	$124.25
15	Bayside Supplies	201-CW	$99.75
25	Langley Corporation	590-TL	$196.25
25	Langley Corporation	560-TL	$397.00
31	Sound Supplies	299-M5	$887.90
31	Sound Supplies	299-M3	$887.90
31	Sound Supplies	299-M2	$887.90
31	Sound Supplies	299-W4	$752.90
31	Sound Supplies	299-W5	$752.90
31	Sound Supplies	299-W3	$752.90
31	Sound Supplies	299-W1	$602.32
35	Emerald City Products	602-XR	$2,145.00
42	Fraser Valley Product	443-1B	$2,397.75
42	Fraser Valley Product	442-1B	$1,495.00
54	Manning, Inc.	101-S3R	$1,199.50
54	Manning, Inc.	101-S3B	$1,137.50
54	Manning, Inc.	101-S2R	$1,945.25
60	Cascade Gear	250-XL	$1,285.00
60	Cascade Gear	255-M	$599.50
60	Cascade Gear	250-L	$1,285.00
60	Cascade Gear	255-XL	$599.50
68	Freedom Corporation	209-XXL	$145.80
68	Freedom Corporation	209-XL	$180.00
68	Freedom Corporation	210-L	$162.25
68	Freedom Corporation	210-M	$97.35
68	Freedom Corporation	375-S	$199.00
68	Freedom Corporation	375-M	$199.00
68	Freedom Corporation	371-L	$129.50
68	Freedom Corporation	209-L	$173.75
84	Macadam, Inc.	100-02	$45.95
84	Macadam, Inc.	100-05	$129.75
99	KL Distributions	780-2	$1,288.50
99	KL Distributions	647-1	$2,999.85

Project 1h

SalesTotalQuery

Client	Sales2010	Sales2011	Total
Bering Company	$289,563.00	$327,541.00	$617,104.00
Fairhaven Developers	$101,210.00	$95,630.00	$196,840.00
Clearwater Service	$125,436.00	$144,328.00	$269,764.00
Landower Company	$97,653.00	$130,239.00	$227,892.00
Harford Systems	$215,420.00	$441,000.00	$656,420.00
Providence, Inc.	$85,628.00	$75,462.00	$161,090.00
Gallagher Systems	$199,346.00	$221,379.00	$420,725.00
Karris Supplies	$61,349.00	$105,000.00	$166,349.00
HE Systems	$554,120.00	$721,923.00	$1,276,043.00
Blue Ridge, Inc.	$17,542.00	$83,210.00	$100,752.00
Alderton Metals	$9,547.00	$45,230.00	$54,777.00
DV Corporation	$138,560.00	$200,540.00	$339,100.00
Franklin Services	$141,670.00	$65,411.00	$207,081.00
Milltown Contractors	$2,356.00	$31,230.00	$33,586.00
Wheeling Products	$115,423.00	$103,400.00	$218,823.00
Martin Manufacturing	$35,679.00	$61,539.00	$97,218.00
Valley Construction	$15,248.00	$22,478.00	$37,726.00
AeroTech	$156,439.00	$175,011.00	$331,450.00
Miles & Harrisburg	$201,430.00	$222,133.00	$423,563.00
Paragon Corporation	$51,237.00	$20,137.00	$71,374.00
Madison Electrics	$99,450.00	$103,435.00	$202,885.00
Haute Contractors	$174,319.00	$125,900.00	$300,219.00
Eagleton Industries	$300,137.00	$265,439.00	$565,576.00
Hoosier Corporation	$24,880.00	$31,935.00	$56,815.00
Dover Industries	$151,003.00	$120,890.00	$271,893.00
Northstar Services	$9,457.00	$15,094.00	$24,551.00
Zinn-Harris Electronics	$214,000.00	$176,420.00	$390,420.00

UnitsOrderedTotalQuery

SupplierName	Order#	UnitsOrdered	Amount	Total
Hopewell, Inc.	1010	10	$199.50	$1,995.00
Hopewell, Inc.	1011	15	$44.85	$672.75
Hopewell, Inc.	1018	15	$104.25	$1,563.75
Bayside Supplies	1021	5	$124.25	$621.25
Bayside Supplies	1022	5	$99.75	$498.75
Langley Corporation	1033	5	$196.25	$981.25
Langley Corporation	1036	20	$397.00	$7,940.00
Sound Supplies	1002	10	$887.90	$8,879.00
Sound Supplies	1003	10	$887.90	$8,879.00
Sound Supplies	1005	10	$887.90	$8,879.00
Sound Supplies	1030	10	$752.90	$7,529.00
Sound Supplies	1031	10	$752.90	$7,529.00
Sound Supplies	1034	10	$752.90	$7,529.00
Sound Supplies	1035	8	$602.32	$4,818.56
Emerald City Products	1032	5	$2,145.00	$10,725.00
Fraser Valley Product	1004	15	$2,397.75	$35,966.25
Fraser Valley Product	1007	10	$1,495.00	$14,950.00
Manning, Inc.	1024	10	$1,199.50	$11,995.00
Manning, Inc.	1025	10	$1,137.50	$11,375.00
Manning, Inc.	1027	15	$1,945.25	$29,178.75
Cascade Gear	1019	10	$1,285.00	$12,850.00
Cascade Gear	1026	5	$599.50	$2,997.50
Cascade Gear	1028	10	$1,285.00	$12,850.00
Cascade Gear	1029	5	$599.50	$2,997.50
Freedom Corporation	1008	20	$145.80	$2,916.00
Freedom Corporation	1009	25	$180.00	$4,500.00
Freedom Corporation	1012	25	$162.25	$4,056.25
Freedom Corporation	1013	15	$97.35	$1,460.25
Freedom Corporation	1014	20	$199.00	$3,980.00
Freedom Corporation	1015	20	$199.00	$3,980.00
Freedom Corporation	1016	10	$129.50	$1,295.00
Freedom Corporation	1017	25	$173.75	$4,343.75
Macadam, Inc.	1020	10	$45.95	$459.50
Macadam, Inc.	1023	5	$129.75	$648.75
KL Distributions	1001	10	$1,288.50	$12,885.00
KL Distributions	1006	15	$2,999.85	$44,997.75

Project 1g

SuppliersNotBCQuery

SupplierName	StreetAddress	City	Prov/State	PostalCode
Bayside Supplies	6705 North Street	Bellingham	WA	98432
Hadley Company	5845 Jefferson Street	Seattle	WA	98107
Cascade Gear	540 Broadway	Seattle	WA	98106
Sound Supplies	2104 Union Street	Seattle	WA	98105
Emerald City Products	1059 Pike Street	Seattle	WA	98102
KL Distributions	402 Yukon Drive	Bellingham	WA	96435

ClientsMuncieQuery

Client	StreetAddress	City	State	ZipCode
Bering Company	4521 East Sixth Street	Muncie	IN	47310-5500
Clearwater Service	10385 North Gavin Stree	Muncie	IN	47308-1236
Providence, Inc.	12490 141st Street	Muncie	IN	47306-3410
Paragon Corporation	4500 Meridian Street	Muncie	IN	47302-4338
Dover Industries	4839 Huchins Road	Muncie	IN	47306-4839
Northstar Services	5135 West Second Street	Muncie	IN	47301-7774

PhoenixClientClaimsOver$500Query

Client#	FirstName	LastName	StreetAddress	City	State	ZIP	Claim#	AmountOfClaim
7335	Vernon	Cook	1230 South Mesa	Phoenix	AZ	85018	104366	$834.95
1331	Erin	Hagedorn	4818 Oakes Boulevard	Phoenix	AZ	85018	198745	$1,797.00
9879	Harold	McDougal	7115 Elizabeth Lane	Phoenix	AZ	85009	174589	$752.45
9775	Carla	Waterman	3979 19th Avenue	Phoenix	AZ	85031	241485	$4,500.00
6478	Parma	Moreno	610 Sheridan Avenue	Phoenix	AZ	85031	200147	$925.75
4868	Eric	Zadinski	1301 North Meridian	Phoenix	AZ	85031	210369	$2,675.00
9879	Harold	McDougal	7115 Elizabeth Lane	Phoenix	AZ	85009	247823	$775.75

Project 2 Create Aggregate Functions, Crosstab, Find Duplicates, and Fund Unmatched Queries

Project 2a

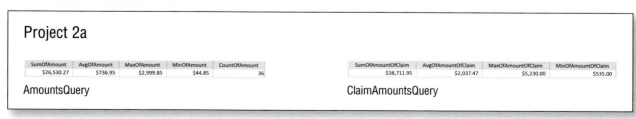

AmountsQuery

SumOfAmount	AvgOfAmount	MaxOfAmount	MinOfAmount	CountOfAmount
$26,530.27	$736.95	$2,999.85	$44.85	36

ClaimAmountsQuery

SumOfAmountOfClaim	AvgOfAmountOfClaim	MaxOfAmountOfClaim	MinOfAmountOfClaim
$38,711.95	$2,037.47	$5,230.00	$535.00

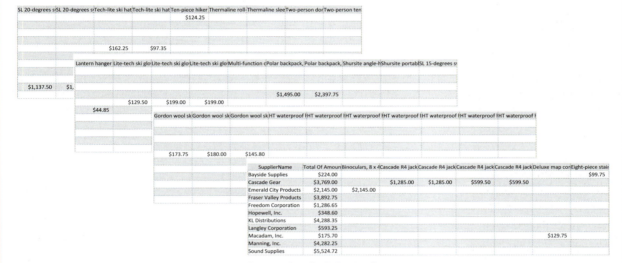

Project 2e

Supplier#	Order#	SupplierName	Product#	UnitsOrdered	Amount	OrderDate
10	1018	Hopewell, Inc.	155-20	15	$104.25	1/16/2012
10	1011	Hopewell, Inc.	152-H	15	$44.85	1/16/2012
10	1010	Hopewell, Inc.	155-35	10	$199.50	1/16/2012
15	1022	Bayside Supplies	201-CW	5	$99.75	2/1/2012
15	1021	Bayside Supplies	202-CW	5	$124.25	2/1/2012
25	1033	Langley Corporation	590-TL	5	$196.25	2/15/2012
25	1036	Langley Corporation	560-TL	20	$397.00	2/15/2012
31	1031	Sound Supplies	299-W5	10	$752.90	2/15/2012
31	1030	Sound Supplies	299-W4	10	$752.90	2/15/2012
31	1002	Sound Supplies	299-M5	10	$887.90	1/2/2012
31	1034	Sound Supplies	299-W3	10	$752.90	2/15/2012
31	1035	Sound Supplies	299-W1	8	$602.32	2/15/2012
31	1005	Sound Supplies	299-M2	10	$887.90	1/2/2012
31	1003	Sound Supplies	299-M3	10	$887.90	1/2/2012
42	1004	Fraser Valley Product	443-1B	15	$2,397.75	1/2/2012
42	1007	Fraser Valley Product	442-1B	10	$1,495.00	1/2/2012
54	1024	Manning, Inc.	101-S3R	10	$1,199.50	2/1/2012
54	1027	Manning, Inc.	101-S2R	15	$1,945.25	2/1/2012
54	1025	Manning, Inc.	101-S3B	10	$1,137.50	2/1/2012
60	1029	Cascade Gear	255-XL	5	$599.50	2/1/2012
60	1028	Cascade Gear	250-L	10	$1,285.00	2/1/2012
60	1026	Cascade Gear	255-M	5	$599.50	2/1/2012
60	1019	Cascade Gear	250-XL	10	$1,285.00	2/1/2012
68	1009	Freedom Corporation	209-XL	25	$180.00	1/16/2012
68	1017	Freedom Corporation	209-L	25	$173.75	1/16/2012
68	1008	Freedom Corporation	209-XXL	20	$145.80	1/16/2012
68	1016	Freedom Corporation	371-L	10	$129.50	1/16/2012
68	1012	Freedom Corporation	210-L	25	$162.25	1/16/2012
68	1013	Freedom Corporation	210-M	15	$97.35	1/16/2012
68	1014	Freedom Corporation	375-S	15	$199.00	1/16/2012
68	1015	Freedom Corporation	375-M	20	$199.00	1/16/2012
84	1023	Macadam, Inc.	100-05	5	$129.75	2/1/2012
84	1020	Macadam, Inc.	100-02	10	$45.95	2/1/2012
99	1001	KL Distributions	780-2	10	$1,288.50	1/2/2012
99	1006	KL Distributions	647-1	15	$2,999.85	1/2/2012

DuplicateSuppliersOrdersQuery

Project 2f

Product#	Product	Supplier#	UnitsInStock	UnitsOnOrder	ReorderLevel
558-C	ICE snow goggles, clear	68	18	0	15
559-B	ICE snow goggles, bronze	68	22	0	20
570-TL	Thermaline light-weight cot	25	8	0	5
580-TL	Thermaline camp seat	25	12	0	10
602-XT	Binoculars, 10.5 x 45	35	5	0	4
602-XX	Binoculars, 10 x 50	35	7	0	5
648-2	Three-person dome tent	99	5	0	10
651-1	K-2 one-person tent	99	8	0	10
652-2	K-2 two-person tent	99	12	0	10
804-50	AG freestyle snowboard, X50	70	7	0	10
804-60	AG freestyle snowboard, X60	70	8	0	5
897-L	Lang blunt snowboard	70	8	0	7
897-W	Lang blunt snowboard, wide	70	4	0	3
901-S	Solar battery pack	38	16	0	15
917-S	Silo portable power pack	38	8	0	10
100-01	Wrist compass	84	12	0	10
100-03	Lenspro plastic compass	84	6	0	5
100-04	Lenspro metal compass	84	8	0	5
101-51B	SL 0-degrees down sleeping bag, black	54	16	0	15
101-51R	SL 0-degrees down sleeping bag, red	54	17	0	15
101-52B	SL 15-degrees synthetic sleeping bag, blac	54	21	0	15
155-30	Shursite aluminum flashlight	10	8	0	5
155-45	Shursite propane lantern	10	12	0	10
155-55	Shursite waterproof headlamp	10	7	0	5
200-CW	Four-piece titanium cookware	15	6	0	5
210-XL	Tech-lite ski hat, XL	68	22	0	20
250-M	Cascade R4 jacket, MM	60	6	0	5
250-XXL	Cascade R4 jacket, MXXL	60	5	0	0
255-L	Cascade R4 jacket, WL	60	6	0	5
299-M1	HT waterproof hiking boots, MS13	31	8	0	10
299-M4	HT waterproof hiking boots, MS10	31	7	0	10
299-W2	HT waterproof hiking boots, WS10	31	9	0	8
299-W6	HT waterproof hiking boots, WS6	31	11	0	10
371-M	Lite-tech ski gloves, MM	68	5	0	15
371-XL	Lite-tech ski gloves, MXL	68	13	0	10
371-XXL	Lite-tech ski gloves, MXXL	68	12	0	10
375-L	Lite-tech ski gloves, WL	68	22	0	20
442-1A	Polar backpack, 150BR	42	12	0	10
443-1A	Polar backpack, 250BR	42	14	0	15

Products Without Matching Orders

Model Answers

Project 1   Design Queries   8 Parts

You will design and run a number of queries including queries with fields from one table and queries with fields from more than one table. You will also use the Simple Query Wizard to design queries.

Performing Queries

Being able to extract (pull out) specific data from a table is one of the most important functions of a database. Extracting data in Access is referred to as performing a query. The word *query* means to ask a question. Access provides several methods for performing a query. You can design your own query, use a simple query wizard, or use complex query wizards. In this chapter, you will learn to design your own query; use the Simple Query Wizard; use aggregate functions in a query; and use the Crosstab, Find Duplicates, and Unmatched Query wizards.

HINT The first step in building a query is to choose the fields that you wish to display in the query results datasheet.

Designing a Query

Designing a query consists of identifying the table from which you are gathering data, the field or fields from which the data will be drawn, and the criteria for selecting the data. To design a query and perform the query, open a database, click the Create tab, and then click the Query Design button in the Queries group. This displays a query window in the work area and also displays the Show Table dialog box as shown in Figure 3.1.

Query Design

Figure 3.1 Query Window with Show Table Dialog Box

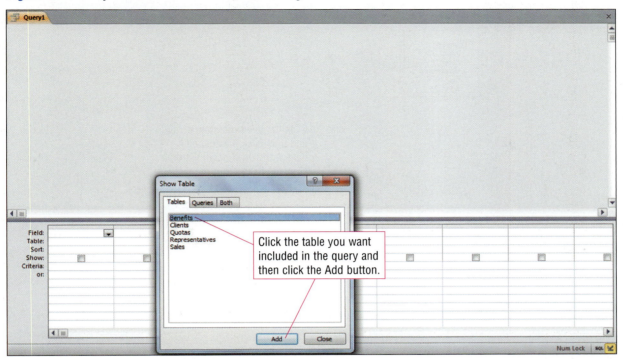

Click the table in the Show Table list box that you want included in the query and then click the Add button or double-click the desired table. Add any other tables required for the query. When all tables have been added, click the Close button. In the query window, click the down-pointing arrow at the right of the first *Field* row field in the query design grid and then click the desired field from the drop-down list. Figure 3.2 displays a sample query window.

To establish a criterion, click inside the *Criteria* row field in the column containing the desired field name in the query design grid and then type the criterion. With the fields and criteria established, click the Run button in the Results group in the Query Tools Design tab. Access searches the specified tables for records that match the criteria and then displays those records in the query results datasheet. If you plan to use the query in the future, save the query and name it. If you do not need the query again, close the query results datasheet without saving it.

You can click the down-pointing arrow at the right side of a *Field* row field and then click the desired field at the drop-down list. You can also double-click a field in a table and it is inserted in the first available *Field* row field in the query design grid. As an example, suppose you wanted to find out how many purchase orders were issued on a specific date. To do this, you would double-click *PurchaseOrderID* in the table (this inserts *PurchaseOrderID* in the first *Field* row field in the query design grid) and then double-click *OrderDate* in the table (this inserts *OrderDate* in the second *Field* row field in the query design grid). In this example, both fields are needed so the purchase order ID is displayed along with the specific order date. After inserting fields, you would then insert the criterion. The criterion for this example would be something like *#1/15/2012#*. After you insert the criterion, click the Run button in the Results group and the results of the query display in the query results datasheet.

▼ **Quick Steps**

Design a Query
1. Click Create tab.
2. Click Query Design button.
3. At Show Table dialog box, click desired table, click Add button.
4. Add any additional tables.
5. In query design grid, click down-pointing arrow in *Field* row field and click desired field from drop-down list.
6. Insert criterion.
7. Click Run button.
8. Save query.

Run

Figure 3.2 Query Window

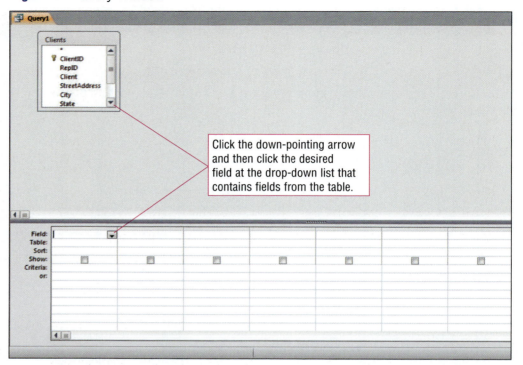

Insert fields in the *Field* row fields in the query design grid in the order in which you want the fields to display in the query results datasheet.

▼ **Quick Steps**

Establish Query Criterion
1. At query window, click in desired *Criteria* row field in query design grid.
2. Type criterion and then press Enter.
3. Click Run button.

A third method for inserting a field in the query design grid is to drag a field from the table to the desired field in the query design grid. To do this, position the mouse pointer on the desired field in the table, hold down the left mouse button, drag to the desired *Field* row field in the query design grid, and then release the mouse button.

Establishing Query Criteria

A query does not require that specific criteria are established. In the example described on the previous page, if the criterion for the date was not included, the query would "return" (*return* is the term used for the results of the query) all Purchase Order numbers with the dates. While this information may be helpful, you could easily find this information in the table. The value of performing a query is to extract specific information from a table. To do this, you must insert a criterion like the one described in the example.

Access makes writing a criterion fairly simple because it inserts the necessary symbols in the criterion. If you type a city such as *Indianapolis* in the *Criteria* row field and then press Enter, Access changes the criterion to *"Indianapolis"*. The quotation marks are inserted by Access and are necessary for the query to run properly. You can either let Access put the proper symbols in the *Criteria* row field, or you can type the criterion with the symbols. Table 3.1 shows some criteria examples including what is typed and what is returned.

In Table 3.1, notice the quotation marks surrounding field values (such as "Smith"). If you do not type the quotation marks when typing the criterion, Access will automatically insert them. The same is true for the pound symbol (#). If you do not type the pound symbol around a date, Access will automatically

Table 3.1 Criteria Examples

Typing this criteria	Returns this
"Smith"	Field value matching *Smith*
"Smith" or "Larson"	Field value matching either *Smith* or *Larson*
Not "Smith"	Field value that is not *Smith* (the opposite of "Smith")
"S*"	Field value that begins with *S* and ends in anything
"*s"	Field value that begins with anything and ends in *s*
"[A-D]*"	Field value that begins with *A* through *D* and ends in anything
#01/01/2012#	Field value matching the date 01/01/2012
<#04/01/2012#	Field value less than (before) 04/01/2012
>#04/01/2012#	Field value greater than (after) 04/01/2012
Between #01/01/2012# And #03/31/2012#	Any date between 01/01/2012 and 03/31/2012

insert the symbols. Access automatically inserts the correct symbol when you press the Enter key after typing the query criteria.

In the criteria examples, the asterisk is used as a wild card indicating any character. This is consistent with many other software applications where the asterisk is used as a wildcard character. Two of the criteria examples in Table 3.1 use the less than and greater than symbols. You can use these symbols for fields containing numbers, values, dates, amounts, and so forth. In the next several projects, you will be designing queries to extract specific information from different tables in databases.

HINT Access inserts quotation marks around text criteria and the pound symbol around date criteria.

Project 1a Performing Queries on Tables Part 1 of 8

1. Display the Open dialog box with Access2010L1C3 on your storage medium the active folder.
2. Open the **AL1-C3-Dearborn.accdb** database and enable the contents.
3. Create the following relationships and enforce referential integrity (and cascade fields and records) for each relationship:
   a. Create a one-to-one relationship where the *ClientID* field in the Clients table is the "one" and the *ClientID* field in the Sales table is the "one."
   b. Create a one-to-one relationship where the *RepID* field in the Representatives table is the "one" and the *RepID* field in the Benefits table is the "one."
   c. Create a one-to-many relationship where the *RepID* field in the Representatives table is the "one" and the *RepID* field in the Clients table is the "many."
   d. Create a one-to-many relationship where the *QuotaID* field in the Quotas table is the "one" and the *QuotaID* field in the Representatives table is the "many."
4. Click the Save button on the Quick Access toolbar.
5. Print the relationships by completing the following steps:
   a. Click the Relationship Report button in the Tools group in the Relationship Tools Design tab.

b. At the relationship report window, click the Landscape button in the Page Layout group in the Print Preview tab.
c. Click the Print button that displays at the left side of the Print Preview tab.
d. At the Print dialog box, click OK.
6. Close the relationships report window without saving the report.
7. Close the Relationships window.
8. Extract records of those clients located in Indianapolis by completing the following steps:
   a. Click the Create tab.
   b. Click the Query Design button in the Queries group.
   c. At the Show Table dialog box with the Tables tab selected (see Figure 3.1), click *Clients* in the list box, click the Add button, and then click the Close button.
   d. Insert fields from the table to *Field* row fields in the query design grid by completing the following steps:
      1) Click the down-pointing arrow located at the right of the first *Field* row field in the query design grid and then click *Client* in the drop-down list.
      2) Click inside the next *Field* row field (to the right of *Client*) in the query design grid, click the down-pointing arrow, and then click *StreetAddress* in the drop-down list.
      3) Click inside the next *Field* row field (to the right of *StreetAddress*), click the down-pointing arrow, and then click *City* in the drop-down list.
      4) Click inside the next *Field* row field (to the right of *City*), click the down-pointing arrow, and then click *State* in the drop-down list.
      5) Click inside the next *Field* row field (to the right of *State*), click the down-pointing arrow, and then select *ZipCode* in the drop-down list.

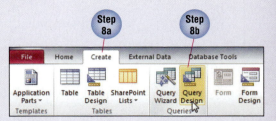
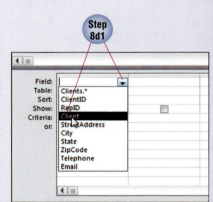
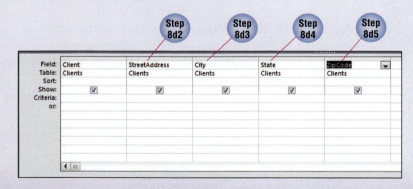

e. Insert the criterion text telling Access to display only those suppliers located in Indianapolis by completing the following steps:
   1) Click in the *Criteria* row field in the *City* column in the query design grid. (This positions the insertion point in the field.)
   2) Type **Indianapolis** and then press Enter. (This changes the criterion to "Indianapolis".)

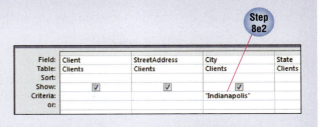

f. Return the results of the query by clicking the Run button in the Results group. (This displays the results in the query results datasheet.)

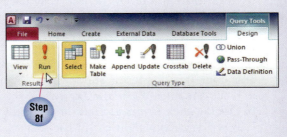

g. Save the results of the query by completing the following steps:
   1) Click the Save button on the Quick Access toolbar.
   2) At the Save As dialog box, type **ClientsIndianapolisQuery** and then press Enter or click OK. (See Project 1a query results on page 80.)
h. Print the query results datasheet by clicking the File tab, clicking the Print tab, and then clicking the *Quick Print* option.
i. Close ClientsIndianapolisQuery.

9. Extract those records with quota identification numbers higher than 2 by completing the following steps:
   a. Click the Create tab and then click the Query Design button in the Queries group.
   b. Double-click *Representatives* in the Show Table list box and then click the Close button.
   c. In the query window, double-click *RepName*. (This inserts the field in the first *Field* row field in the query design grid.)
   d. Double-click *QuotaID*. (This inserts the field in the second *Field* row field in the query design grid.)
   e. Insert the query criterion by completing the following steps:
      1) Click in the *Criteria* row field in the *QuotaID* column in the query design grid.
      2) Type **>2** and then press Enter. (Access will automatically insert quotation marks around *2* since the data type for the field is set at *Text* [rather than *Number*].)
   f. Return the results of the query by clicking the Run button in the Results group.
   g. Save the query and name it *QuotaIDGreaterThanTwoQuery*. (See Project 1a query results on page 80.)
   h. Print and then close the query.

10. Extract those 2011 sales greater than $99,999 by completing the following steps:
    a. Click the Create tab and then click the Query Design button.
    b. Double-click *Sales* in the Show Table dialog box and then click the Close button.
    c. At the query window, double-click *ClientID*. (This inserts the field in the first *Field* row field in the query design grid.)
    d. Insert the *Sales2011* field in the second *Field* row field.

e. Insert the query criterion by completing the following steps:
   1) Click in the *Criteria* row field in the *Sales2011* column in the query design grid.
   2) Type **>99999** and then press Enter. (Access will not insert quotation marks around *99999* since the field is identified as *Currency*.)

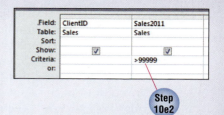

Step 10e2

f. Return the results of the query by clicking the Run button in the Results group.
g. Save the query and name it *2011SalesOver$99999Query*. (See Project 1a query results on page 80.)
h. Print and then close the query.

11. Extract records of those representatives with a telephone number that begins with the 765 area code by completing the following steps:
    a. Click the Create tab and then click the Query Design button.
    b. Double-click *Representatives* in the Show Table dialog box and then click the Close button.
    c. Insert the *RepName* field in the first *Field* row field.
    d. Insert the *Telephone* field in the second *Field* row field.
    e. Insert the query criterion by completing the following steps:
       1) Click in the *Criteria* row field in the *Telephone* column.
       2) Type ***765*** and then press Enter.

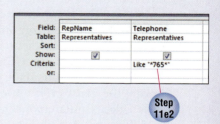

Step 11e2

    f. Return the results of the query by clicking the Run button in the Results group.
    g. Save the query and name it *RepsWith765AreaCodeQuery*. (See Project 1a query results on page 80.)
    h. Print and then close the query.

In Project 1a, you performed several queries on specific tables. A query can also be performed on fields from more than one table. In Project 1b, you will perform queries on related tables.

When completing steps in Project 1b you will be instructed to open the AL1-C3-CopperState.accdb database. Two of the tables in the database contain yes/no check boxes. When designing a query, you can extract records containing a check mark or records that do not contain a check mark. If you want to extract records that contain a check mark, you would click in the *Criteria* row field in the desired column in the query design grid, type a *1*, and then press Enter. When you press the Enter key, Access changes the *1* to *True*. If you want to extract records that do not contain a check mark, you would type *0* in the *Criteria* row field and then press Enter. Access changes the 0 to *False*.

Project 1b Performing a Query on Related Tables   Part 2 of 8

1. With the **AL1-C3-Dearborn.accdb** database open, extract information on representatives hired between March of 2008 and November of 2008 and include the representative's name by completing the following steps:

    a. Click the Create tab and then click the Query Design button.
    b. Double-click *Representatives* in the Show Table dialog box.
    c. Double-click *Benefits* in the Show Table dialog box list box and then click the Close button.
    d. At the query window, double-click *RepName* in the Representatives table.
    e. Double-click *HireDate* in the Benefits table.
    f. Insert the query criterion by completing the following steps:
       1) Click in the *Criteria* row field in the *HireDate* column.
       2) Type **Between 3/1/2008 And 11/30/2008** and then press Enter. (Make sure you type zeros and not capital *O*s.)
    g. Return the results of the query by clicking the Run button in the Results group.
    h. Save the query and name it *MarToNov2008HiresQuery*. (See Project 1b query results on page 80.)
    i. Print and then close the query.

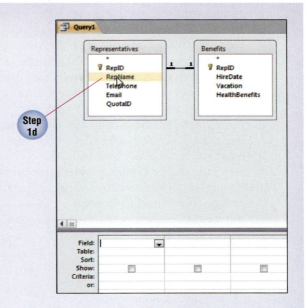

2. Extract records of those representatives who were hired in 2009 by completing the following steps:

    a. Click the Create tab and then click the Query Design button.
    b. Double-click *Representatives* in the Show Table dialog box.
    c. Double-click *Benefits* in the Show Table dialog box and then click the Close button.
    d. At the query window, double-click *RepID* field in the Representatives table.
    e. Double-click *RepName* in the Representatives table.
    f. Double-click *HireDate* in the Benefits table.
    g. Insert the query criterion by completing the following steps:
       1) Click in the *Criteria* row field in the *HireDate* column.
       2) Type ***2009** and then press Enter.
    h. Return the results of the query by clicking the Run button in the Results group.
    i. Save the query and name it *RepsHiredIn2009Query*. (See Project 1b query results on page 80.)
    j. Print and then close the query.

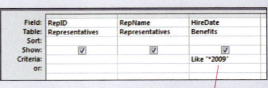

3. Suppose you need to determine 2010 and 2011 sales for a company but you can only remember that the company name begins with *Blue*. Create a query that finds the company and identifies the sales by completing the following steps:
   a. Click the Create tab and then click the Query Design button.
   b. Double-click *Clients* in the Show Table dialog box.
   c. Double-click *Sales* in the Show Table dialog box and then click the Close button.
   d. At the query window, insert the *ClientID* field from the Clients table in the first *Field* row field in the query design grid.
   e. Insert the *Client* field from the Clients table in the second *Field* row field.
   f. Insert the *Sales2010* field from the Sales table in the third *Field* row field.
   g. Insert the *Sales2011* field from the Sales table in the fourth *Field* row field.
   h. Insert the query criterion by completing the following steps:
      1) Click in the *Criteria* row field in the *Client* column.
      2) Type **Blue*** and then press Enter.
   i. Return the results of the query by clicking the Run button in the Results group.
   j. Save the query and name it *BlueRidgeSalesQuery*. (See Project 1b query results on page 80.)
   k. Print and then close the query.

Step 3h2

4. Close the **AL1-C3-Dearborn.accdb** database.
5. Display the Open dialog box with Access2010L1C3 on your storage medium the active folder.
6. Open the **AL1-C3-PacTrek.accdb** database and enable the contents.
7. Extract information on products ordered between February 1 and February 28, 2012, and include the supplier's name by completing the following steps:
   a. Click the Create tab and then click the Query Design button.
   b. Double-click *Products* in the Show Table dialog box.
   c. Double-click *Orders* in the Show Table dialog box and then click the Close button.
   d. At the query window, insert the *Product#* field from the Products table in the first *Field* row field.
   e. Insert the *Product* field from the Products table in the second *Field* row field.
   f. Insert the *OrderDate* field from the Orders table in the third *Field* row field.
   g. Insert the query criterion by completing the following steps:
      1) Click in the *Criteria* row field in the *OrderDate* column.
      2) Type **Between 2/1/2012 And 2/28/2012** and then press Enter. (Make sure you type zeros and not capital *O*s.)
   h. Return the results of the query by clicking the Run button in the Results group.
   i. Save the query and name it *Feb1-28OrdersQuery*. (See Project 1b query results on page 80.)
   j. Print and then close the query.

Step 7g2

8. Close the **AL1-C3-PacTrek.accdb** database.
9. Open the **AL1-C3-CopperState.accdb** database and enable the contents.
10. Display the Relationships window and create the following additional relationships (enforced referential integrity and cascade fields and records):
    a. Create a one-to-many relationships with the *AgentID* field in the Agents table the "one" and the *AgentID* field in the Assignments table the "many."

b. Create a one-to-many relationship with the *OfficeID* field in the Offices table the "one" and the *OfficeID* field in the Assignments table the "many."
c. Create a one-to-many relationship with the *OfficeID* field in the Offices table the "one" and the *OfficeID* field in the Agents table the "many."

11. Save and then print the relationships in landscape orientation.
12. Close the relationships report without saving it and then close the Relationships window.
13. Extract records of clients that have uninsured motorist coverage by completing the following steps:
    a. Click the Create tab and then click the Query Design button.
    b. Double-click *Clients* in the Show Table dialog box.
    c. Double-click *Coverage* in the Show Table dialog box and then click the Close button.
    d. At the query window, insert the *Client#* field from the Clients table in the first *Field* row field.
    e. Insert the *FirstName* field from the Clients table in the second *Field* row field.
    f. Insert the *LastName* field from the Clients table in the third *Field* row field.
    g. Insert the *UninsMotorist* field from the Coverage table in the fourth *Field* row field.
    h. Insert the query criterion by clicking in the *Criteria* row field in the *UninsMotorist* column, typing **1**, and then pressing the Enter. (Access changes the *1* to *True*.)
    i. Click the Run button in the Results group.
    j. Save the query and name it *UninsMotoristCoverageQuery*. (See Project 1b query results on page 80.)
    k. Print and then close the query.
14. Extract records of claims in January over $500 by completing the following steps:
    a. Click the Create tab and then click the Query Design button.
    b. Double-click *Clients* in the Show Table dialog box.
    c. Double-click *Claims* in the Show Table dialog box and then click the Close button.
    d. At the query window, insert the *Client#* field from the Clients table in the first *Field* row field.
    e. Insert the *FirstName* field from the Clients table in the second *Field* row field.
    f. Insert the *LastName* field from the Clients table in the third *Field* row field.
    g. Insert the *Claim#* field from the Claims table in the fourth *Field* row field.
    h. Insert the *DateOfClaim* field from the Claims table in the fifth *Field* row field.
    i. Insert the *AmountOfClaim* field from the Claims table in the sixth *Field* row field.
    j. Click in the *Criteria* row field in the *DateOfClaim* column, type **Between 1/1/2012 And 1/31/2012**, and then press Enter.
    k. With the insertion point positioned in the *Criteria* row field in the *AmountOfClaim* column, type **>500** and then press Enter.
    l. Click the Run button in the Results group.
    m. Save the query and name it *JanClaimsOver$500Query*. (See Project 1b query results on page 80.)
    n. Print and then close the query.

▼ **Quick Steps**

Sort Fields in Query
1. At query window, click in *Sort* row field in query design grid.
2. Click down arrow in *Sort* row field.
3. Click *Ascending* or *Descending*.

Sorting Fields in a Query

When designing a query, you can specify the sort order of a field or fields. Click inside one of the columns in the *Sort* row field and a down-pointing arrow displays at the right of the field. Click this down-pointing arrow and a drop-down list displays with the choices *Ascending*, *Descending*, and *(not sorted)*. Click *Ascending* to sort from lowest to highest or click *Descending* to sort from highest to lowest.

Project 1c Performing a Query on Related Tables and Sorting in Field Values   Part 3 of 8

1. With the **AL1-C3-CopperState.accdb** database open, extract information on clients with agents from the West Bell Road Glendale office and sort the information alphabetically by client last name by completing the following steps:
    a. Click the Create tab and then click the Query Design button.
    b. Double-click *Assignments* in the Show Table dialog box.
    c. Double-click *Clients* in the Show Table dialog box and then click the Close button.
    d. At the query window, insert the *OfficeID* field from the Assignments table in the first *Field* row field.
    e. Insert the *AgentID* field from the Assignments table in the second *Field* row field.
    f. Insert the *FirstName* field from the Clients table in the third *Field* row field.
    g. Insert the *LastName* field from the Clients table in the fourth *Field* row field.
    h. Click in the *Criteria* row field in the *OfficeID* column, type **GW**, and then press the Enter.
    i. Sort the *LastName* field in ascending alphabetical order (A–Z) by completing the following steps:
        1) Click in the *Sort* row field in the *LastName* column. (This causes a down-pointing arrow to display at the right side of the field.)
        2) Click the down-pointing arrow at the right side of the *Sort* row field and then click *Ascending*.
    j. Click the Run button in the Results group.
    k. Save the query and name it *GWClientsQuery*. (See Project 1c query results on page 81.)
    l. Print and then close the query.
2. Close the **AL1-C3-CopperState.accdb** database.
3. Open the **AL1-C3-PacTrek.accdb** database.
4. Extract information on orders less than $1,500 by completing the following steps:
    a. Click the Create tab and then click the Query Design button.
    b. Double-click *Products* in the Show Table dialog box.
    c. Double-click *Orders* in the Show Table dialog box and then click the Close button.
    d. At the query window, insert the *Product#* field from the Products table in the first *Field* row field.
    e. Insert the *Supplier#* field from the Products table in the second *Field* row field.
    f. Insert the *UnitsOrdered* field from the Orders table in the third *Field* row field.
    g. Insert the *Amount* field from the Orders table in the fourth *Field* row field.

h. Insert the query criterion by completing the following steps:
  1) Click in the *Criteria* row field in the *Amount* column.
  2) Type **<1500** and then press Enter. (Make sure you type zeros and not capital Os.)
i. Sort the *Amount* field values from highest to lowest by completing the following steps:
  1) Click in the *Sort* row field in the *Amount* column. (This causes a down-pointing arrow to display at the right side of the field.)
  2) Click the down-pointing arrow at the right side of the *Sort* field and then click *Descending*.
j. Return the results of the query by clicking the Run button in the Results group.
k. Save the query and name it *OrdersLessThan$1500Query*. (See Project 1c query results on page 81.)
l. Print and then close the query.

5. Close the **AL1-C3-PacTrek.accdb** database.
6. Open the **AL1-C3-Dearborn.accdb** database.
7. Extract information on sales below $100,000 for 2010 by completing the following steps:
  a. Click the Create tab and then click the Query Design button.
  b. Double-click *Clients* in the Show Table dialog box.
  c. Double-click *Sales* in the Show Table dialog box.
  d. Double-click *Representatives* in the Show Table dialog box and then click the Close button.
  e. At the query window, insert the *Client* field from the Clients table in the first *Field* row field.
  f. Insert the *Sales2010* field from the Sales table in the second *Field* row field.
  g. Insert the *RepName* field from the Representatives table in the third *Field* row field.
  h. Insert the query criterion by completing the following steps:
    1) Click in the *Criteria* row field in the *Sales2010* column.
    2) Type **<100000** and then press Enter. (Make sure you type zeros and not capital Os.)
  i. Sort the *Sales2010* field values from highest to lowest by completing the following steps:
    1) Click in the *Sort* row field in the *Sales2010* column.
    2) Click the down-pointing arrow at the right side of the *Sort* row field and then click *Descending*.
  j. Return the results of the query by clicking the Run button in the Results group.
  k. Save the query and name it *2010SalesLessThan$100000Query*. (See Project 1c query results on page 81.)
  l. Print and then close the query.

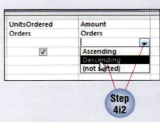

Modifying a Query

Quick Steps

Modify a Query
1. Double-click query in Navigation pane.
2. Click View button.
3. Make desired changes to query.
4. Click Run button.
5. Click Save button.

Save time designing a query by modifying an existing query.

You can modify a saved query. For example, suppose after designing the query that displays the 2010 sales that are less than $100,000, you decide that you want to find sales for 2011 that are less than $100,000. Rather than designing a new query, open the existing query, make any needed changes, and then run the query.

To modify an existing query, double-click the query in the Navigation pane. (This displays the query in Datasheet view.) Click the View button to display the query in Design view. Make the desired changes and then click the Run button in the Results group. Click the Save button on the Quick Access toolbar to save the query with the same name. If you want to save the query with a new name, click the File tab, and then click Save Object As. At the Save As dialog box, type a name for the query and then press Enter.

If your database contains a number of queries, you can group and display them in the Navigation pane. To do this, click the down-pointing arrow in the Navigation pane Menu bar and then click *Object Type* at the drop-down list. This displays objects grouped in categories such as *Tables* and *Queries*.

Project 1d Modifying Queries   Part 4 of 8

1. With the **AL1-C3-Dearborn.accdb** database open, find the sales less than $100,000 for 20011 by completing the following steps:
    a. Change the display of objects in the Navigation pane by clicking the down-pointing arrow in the Navigation pane Menu bar and then clicking *Object Type* at the drop-down list.
    b. Double-click the *2010SalesLessThan$100000Query* in the *Queries* section of the Navigation pane.
    c. Click the View button in the Views group to switch to Design view.
    d. Click in the *Field* row field containing the text *Sales2010*.
    e. Click the down-pointing arrow that displays at the right side of the *Field* row field and then click *Sales2011* at the drop-down list.

   f. Click the Run button in the Results group.
2. Save the query with a new name by completing the following steps:
    a. Click the File tab and then click Save Object As.

b. At the Save As dialog box, type **2011SalesLessThan$100000Query** and then press Enter. (See Project 1d query results on page 81.)
c. Click the File tab to return to the query.
d. Print and then close the query.
3. Modify an existing query and find employees with three weeks of vacation by completing the following steps:
   a. Double-click the *MarToNov2008HiresQuery*.
   b. Click the View button in the Views group to switch to Design view.
   c. Click in the *Field* row field containing the text *HireDate*.
   d. Click the down-pointing arrow that displays at the right side of the field and then click *Vacation* at the drop-down list.
   e. Select the current text in the *Criteria* row field in the *Vacation* column, type **3 weeks**, and then press Enter.

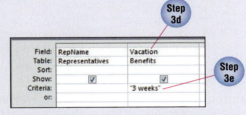

   f. Click the Run button in the Results group.
4. Save the query with a new name by completing the following steps:
   a. Click the File tab and then click Save Object As.
   b. At the Save As dialog box, type **RepsWith3WeekVacationsQuery** and then press Enter. (See Project 1d query results on page 81.)
   c. Click the File tab to return to the query.
   d. Print and then close the query.

Designing Queries with *Or* and *And* Criteria

The query design grid contains an *Or* row you can use to design a query that instructs Access to display records that match either of the two criteria. For example, to display a list of employees with three weeks of vacation *or* four weeks of vacation, you would type *3 weeks* in the *Criteria* row field for the *Vacation* column and then type *4 weeks* in the field immediately below *3 weeks* in the *Or* row. Other examples include finding clients that live in *Muncie* or *Lafayette* or finding representatives with a quota of *1* or *2*.

HINT You can design a query that combines *And* and *Or* statements.

You can also select records by entering criteria statements into more than one *Criteria* field. Multiple criteria all entered in the same row become an *And* statement where each criterion must be met for Access to select the record. For example, you could search for clients in the Indianapolis area with sales greater than $100,000.

Project 1e Designing Queries with *Or* and *And* Criteria   Part 5 of 8

1. With the **AL1-C3-Dearborn.accdb** database open, modify an existing query and find employees with three weeks or four weeks of vacation by completing the following steps:
   a. Double-click the *RepsWith3WeekVacationsQuery*.
   b. Click the View button in the Views group to switch to Design view.
   c. Click in the empty field below "*3 weeks*" in the *Or* row, type **4 weeks**, and then press Enter.
   d. Click the Run button in the Results group.
2. Save the query with a new name by completing the following steps:
   a. Click the File tab and then click Save Object As.
   b. At the Save As dialog box, type **RepsWith3Or4WeekVacationsQuery** and then press Enter. (See Project 1e query results on page 81.)
   c. Click the File tab to return to the query.
   d. Print and then close the query.
3. Design a query that finds records of clients in the Indianapolis area with sales over $100,000 for 2010 and 2011 by completing the following steps:
   a. Click the Create tab and then click the Query Design button.
   b. Double-click *Clients* in the Show Table dialog box.
   c. Double-click *Sales* in the Show Table dialog box and then click the Close button.
   d. At the query window, insert the *Client* field from the Clients table in the first *Field* row field.
   e. Insert the *City* field from the Clients table in the second *Field* row field.
   f. Insert the *Sales2010* field from the Sales table in the third *Field* row field.
   g. Insert the *Sales2011* field from the Sales table in the fourth *Field* row field.
   h. Insert the query criteria by completing the following steps:
      1) Click in the *Criteria* row field in the *City* column.
      2) Type **Indianapolis** and then press Enter.
      3) With the insertion point positioned in the *Criteria* row field in the *Sales2010* column, type **>100000** and then press Enter.
      4) With the insertion point positioned in the *Criteria* row field in the *Sales2011* column, type **>100000** and then press Enter.
   i. Click the Run button in the Results group.
   j. Save the query and name it *SalesOver$100000IndianapolisQuery*. (See Project 1e query results on page 81.)
   k. Print and then close the query.
4. Close the **AL1-C3-Dearborn.accdb** database.
5. Open the **AL1-C3-PacTrek.accdb** database.
6. Design a query that finds products available from supplier numbers 25, 31, and 42 by completing the following steps:
   a. Click the Create tab and then click the Query Design button.
   b. Double-click *Suppliers* in the Show Table dialog box.
   c. Double-click *Products* in the Show Table dialog box and then click the Close button.

d. At the query window, insert the *Supplier#* field from the Suppliers table in the first *Field* row field.
e. Insert the *SupplierName* field from the Suppliers table in the second *Field* row field.
f. Insert the *Product* field from the Products table in the third *Field* row field.
g. Insert the query criteria by completing the following steps:
   1) Click in the *Criteria* row field in the *Supplier#* column.
   2) Type **25** and then press the Down Arrow key on your keyboard. (This makes active the field below *25*.)
   3) Type **31** and then press the Down Arrow key on your keyboard. (This makes active the field below *31*.)
   4) Type **42** and then press Enter.

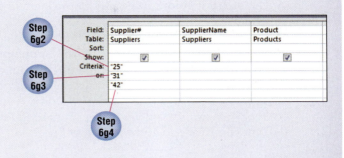

h. Click the Run button in the Results group.
i. Save the query and name it *Suppliers25-31-42Query*. (See Project 1e query results on page 81.)
j. Print and then close the query.

7. Design a query that finds ski hats and gloves on order and the number ordered by completing the following steps:
   a. Click the Create tab and then click the Query Design button.
   b. Double-click *Orders* in the Show Table dialog box.
   c. Double-click *Suppliers* in the Show Table dialog box.
   d. Double-click *Products* in the Show Table dialog box and then click the Close button.
   e. At the query window, insert the *Order#* field from the Orders table in the first *Field* row field.
   f. Insert the *SupplierName* field from the Suppliers table in the second *Field* row field.
   g. Insert the *Product* field from the Products table in the third *Field* row field.
   h. Insert the *UnitsOrdered* field from the Orders table in the fourth *Field* row field.
   i. Insert the query criteria by completing the following steps:
      1) Click in the *Criteria* row field in the *Product* column.
      2) Type ***ski hat*** and then press the Down Arrow key on your keyboard. (You need to type the asterisk before and after *ski hat* so the query will find any product that includes the words *ski hat* in the description no matter what text comes before or after the words.)
      3) Type ***gloves*** and then press Enter.
   j. Click the Run button in the Results group.
   k. Save the query and name it *SkiHatsGlovesOnOrderQuery*. (See Project 1e query results on page 81.)
   l. Print and then close the query.

8. Design a query that finds boots, sleeping bags, and backpacks and the suppliers that produce them by completing the following steps:
   a. Click the Create tab and then click the Query Design button.
   b. Double-click *Products* in the Show Table dialog box.
   c. Double-click *Suppliers* in the Show Table dialog box and then click the Close button.
   d. At the query window, insert the *Product#* field from the Products table in the first *Field* row field.
   e. Insert the *Product* field from the Products table in the second *Field* row field.
   f. Insert the *SupplierName* field from the Suppliers table in the third *Field* row field.
   g. Insert the query criteria by completing the following steps:
      1) Click in the *Criteria* row field in the *Product* column.
      2) Type **boots** and then press the Down Arrow key on your keyboard.
      3) Type ***sleeping bag*** and then press the Down Arrow key on your keyboard.
      4) Type ***backpack*** and then press Enter.

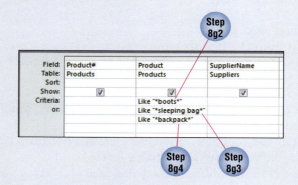

   h. Click the Run button in the Results group.
   i. Save the query and name it *BootsSleepingBagsBackpacksQuery*. (See Project 1e query results on page 81.)
   j. Print and then close the query.
9. Close the **AL1-C3-PacTrek.accdb** database.
10. Open the **AL1-C3-CopperState.accdb** database.
11. Design a query that finds clients that have only liability coverage by completing the following steps:
    a. Click the Create tab and then click the Query Design button.
    b. Double-click *Clients* in the Show Table dialog box.
    c. Double-click *Coverage* in the Show Table dialog box and then click the Close button.
    d. At the query window, insert the *Client#* field from the Clients table in the first *Field* row field.
    e. Insert the *FirstName* field from the Clients table in the second *Field* row field.
    f. Insert the *LastName* field from the Clients table in the third *Field* row field.
    g. Insert the *Medical* field from the Coverage table in the fourth *Field* row field.
    h. Insert the *Liability* field from the Coverage table in the fifth *Field* row field.
    i. Insert the *Comprehensive* field from the Coverage table in the sixth *Field* row field.
    j. Insert the *UninsMotorist* field from the Coverage table in the seventh *Field* row field.
    k. Insert the *Collision* field from the Coverage table in the eighth *Field* row field. (You will need to scroll down the Coverage table to display the *Collision* field.)

l. Insert the query criteria by completing the following steps:
   1) Click in the *Criteria* row field in the *Medical* column, type **0**, and then press Enter. (Access changes the *0* to *False*.)
   2) With the insertion point in the *Liability* column, type **1**, and then press Enter. (Access changes the *1* to *True*.)
   3) With the insertion point in the *Comprehensive* column, type **0**, and then press Enter.
   4) With the insertion point in the *UninsMotorist* column, type **0**, and then press Enter.
   5) With the insertion point in the *Collision* column, type **0**, and then press Enter.

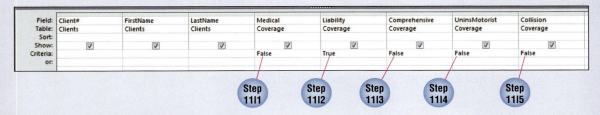

Steps 11l1, 11l2, 11l3, 11l4, 11l5

m. Click the Run button in the Results group.
n. Save the query and name it *ClientsWithOnlyLiabilityQuery*. (See Project 1e query results on page 81.)
o. Print the query in landscape orientation.
p. Close the query.

12. Close the **AL1-C3-CopperState.accdb** database.

Performing a Query with the Simple Query Wizard

The Simple Query Wizard provided by Access guides you through the steps for preparing a query. To use this wizard, open the database, click the Create tab, and then click the Query Wizard button in the Queries group. At the New Query dialog box, make sure *Simple Query Wizard* is selected in the list box and then click the OK button. At the first Simple Query Wizard dialog box, shown in Figure 3.3, specify the table(s) in the *Tables/Queries* option box. After specifying the table, insert the fields you want included in the query in the *Selected Fields* list box, and then click the Next button.

Query Wizard

Figure 3.3 First Simple Query Wizard Dialog Box

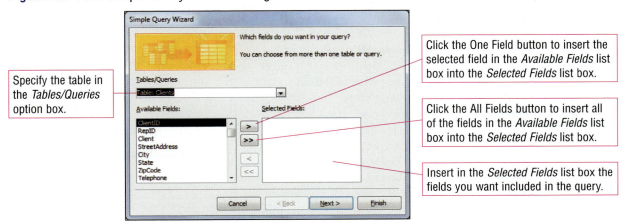

Specify the table in the *Tables/Queries* option box.

Click the One Field button to insert the selected field in the *Available Fields* list box into the *Selected Fields* list box.

Click the All Fields button to insert all of the fields in the *Available Fields* list box into the *Selected Fields* list box.

Insert in the *Selected Fields* list box the fields you want included in the query.

▼ **Quick Steps**

Create a Query with Simple Query Wizard
1. Click Create tab.
2. Click Query Wizard button.
3. Make sure *Simple Query Wizard* is selected in list box and then click OK.
4. Follow query steps.

At the second Simple Query Wizard dialog box, specify whether you want a detail or summary query, and then click the Next button. At the third (and last) Simple Query Wizard dialog box, shown in Figure 3.4, type a name for the completed query or accept the name provided by the wizard. At this dialog box, you can also specify that you want to open the query to view the information or modify the query design. If you want to extract specific information, be sure to choose the *Modify the query design* option. After making any necessary changes, click the Finish button.

If you do not modify the query design in the last Simple Query Wizard dialog box, the query displays all records for the fields identified in the first Simple Query Wizard dialog box. In Project 1f you will perform a query without modifying the design, and in Project 1g you will modify the query design.

Figure 3.4 Last Simple Query Wizard Dialog Box

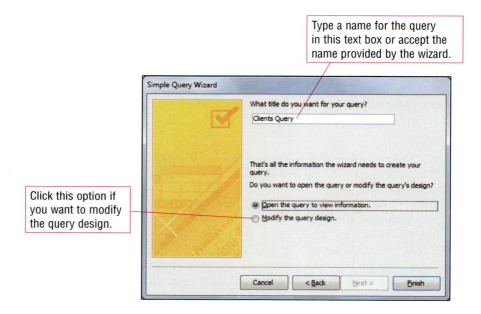

Project 1f Performing Queries with the Simple Query Wizard   Part 6 of 8

1. Open the **AL1-C3-Dearborn.accdb** database and then use the Simple Query Wizard to create a query that displays client names along with 2010 and 2011 sales by completing the following steps:
   a. Click the Create tab and then click the Query Wizard button in the Queries group.
   b. At the New Query dialog box, make sure *Simple Query Wizard* is selected in the list box and then click OK.
   c. At the first Simple Query Wizard dialog box, click the down-pointing arrow at the right of the *Tables/Queries* option box and then click *Table: Clients*. (You will need to scroll up the list to display this table.)

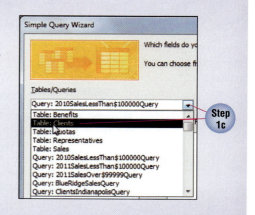

d. With *ClientID* selected in the *Available Fields* list box, click the One Field button (button containing the greater than symbol.) This inserts the *ClientID* field in the *Selected Fields* list box.
e. Click *Client* in the *Available Fields* list box and then click the One Field button.
f. Click the down-pointing arrow at the right of the *Tables/Queries* option box and then click *Table: Sales*.
g. Click *Sales2010* in the *Available Fields* list box and then click the One Field button.
h. With *Sales2011* selected in the *Available Fields* list box, click the One Field button.
i. Click the Next button.
j. At the second Simple Query Wizard dialog box, click the Next button.
k. At the last Simple Query Wizard dialog box, select the name in the *What title do you want for your query?* text box, type **Client2010-2011SalesQuery**, and then press Enter.

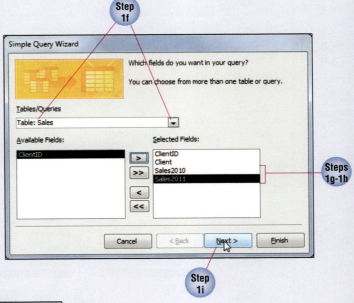

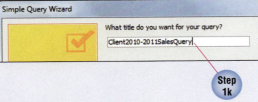

l. When the results of the query display, print the results. (See Project 1f query results on page 82.)
m. Close the query window.
2. Close the **AL1-C3-Dearborn.accdb** database.
3. Open the **AL1-C3-PacTrek.accdb** database.
4. Create a query that displays the products on order, the order amount, and the supplier name by completing the following steps:
   a. Click the Create tab and then click the Query Wizard button.
   b. At the New Query dialog box, make sure *Simple Query Wizard* is selected in the list box and then click OK.

Chapter 3 ■ Performing Queries   103

c. At the first Simple Query Wizard dialog box, click the down-pointing arrow at the right side of the *Tables/Queries* option box and then click *Table: Suppliers*.
d. With *Supplier#* selected in the *Available Fields* list box, click the One Field button. (This inserts the *Supplier#* field in the *Selected Fields* list box.)
e. With *SupplierName* selected in the *Available Fields* list box, click the One Field button.
f. Click the down-pointing arrow at the right of the *Tables/Queries* option box and then click *Table: Orders*.
g. Click *Product#* in the *Available Fields* list box and then click the One Field button.
h. Click *Amount* in the *Available Fields* list box and then click the One Field button.
i. Click the Next button.

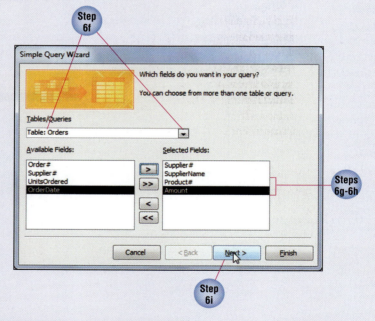

j. At the second Simple Query Wizard dialog box, click the Next button.
k. At the last Simple Query Wizard dialog box, select the text in the *What title do you want for your query?* text box, type **ProductOrderAmountsQuery**, and then press Enter.
l. When the results of the query display, print the results. (See Project 1f query results on page 82.)
m. Close the query window.

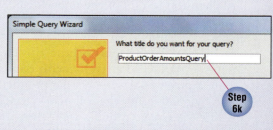

To extract specific information when using the Simple Query Wizard, tell the wizard that you want to modify the query design. This displays the query window with the query design grid where you can insert query criteria.

Project 1g — Performing and Modifying Queries with the Simple Query Wizard — Part 7 of 8

1. With the **AL1-C3-PacTrek.accdb** database open, use the Simple Query Wizard to create a query that displays suppliers outside of British Columbia by completing the following steps:
   a. Click the Create tab and then click the Query Wizard button.
   b. At the New Query dialog box, make sure *Simply Query Wizard* is selected and then click OK.
   c. At the first Simple Query Wizard dialog box, click the down-pointing arrow at the right side of the *Tables/Queries* option box and then click *Table: Suppliers*.
   d. Insert the following fields in the *Selected Fields* list box:
      SupplierName
      StreetAddress
      City
      Prov/State
      PostalCode
   e. Click the Next button.
   f. At the last Simple Query Wizard dialog box, select the current text in the *What title do you want for your query?* text box and then type **SuppliersNotBCQuery**.
   g. Click the *Modify the query design* option and then click the Finish button.
   h. At the query window, complete the following steps:
      1) Click in the *Criteria* row field in the *Prov/State* column in the query design grid.
      2) Type **Not BC** and then press Enter.
   i. Specify that the fields are to be sorted in descending order by postal code by completing the following steps:

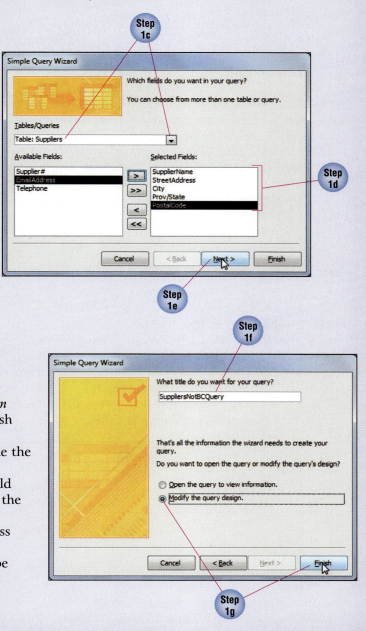

1) Click in the *Sort* row field in the *PostalCode* column.
2) Click the down-pointing arrow that displays at the right side of the field and then click *Descending*.

Step 1i2

j. Click the Run button in the Results group. (This displays suppliers that are not located in British Columbia and displays the records sorted by PostalCode in decending order. See Project 1g query results on page 82.)
k. Save, print, and then close the query.
2. Close the **AL1-C3-PacTrek.accdb** database.
3. Open the **AL1-C3-Dearborn.accdb** database.
4. Use the Simple Query Wizard to create a query that displays clients in Muncie by completing the following steps:
   a. Click the Create tab and then click the Query Wizard button.
   b. At the New Query dialog box, make sure *Simple Query Wizard* is selected and then click OK.
   c. At the first Simple Query Wizard dialog box, click the down-pointing arrow at the right of the *Tables/Queries* option box and then click *Table: Clients*. (You will need to scroll up the list to display this table.)
   d. Insert the following fields in the *Selected Fields* list box:
      Client
      StreetAddress
      City
      State
      ZipCode
   e. Click the Next button.
   f. At the last Simple Query Wizard dialog box, select the current text in the *What title do you want for your query?* text box and then type **ClientsMuncieQuery**.
   g. Click the *Modify the query design* option and then click the Finish button.
   h. At the query window, complete the following steps:
      1) Click in the *Criteria* row field in the *City* column.
      2) Type **Muncie** and then press Enter.

Step 4h2

   i. Click the Run button in the Results group. (This displays clients located in Muncie. See Project 1g query results on page 82.)
   j. Save, print, and then close the query.
5. Close the **AL1-C3-Dearborn.accdb** database.

6. Open the **AL1-C3-CopperState.accdb** database.
7. Use the Simple Query Wizard to display clients that live in Phoenix with claims over $500 by completing the following steps:
   a. Click the Create tab and then click the Query Wizard button in the Queries group.
   b. At the New Query dialog box, make sure *Simple Query Wizard* is selected in the list box and then click OK.
   c. At the first Simple Query Wizard dialog box, click the down-pointing arrow at the right of the *Tables/Queries* option box and then click *Table: Clients*.
   d. Insert the following fields in the *Selected Fields* list box:
      Client#
      FirstName
      LastName
      StreetAddress
      City
      State
      ZIP
   e. Click the down-pointing arrow at the right of the *Tables/Queries* option box and then click *Table: Claims*.
   f. With *Claim#* selected in the *Available Fields* list box, click the One Field button.
   g. Click *AmountOfClaim* in the *Available Fields* list box and then click the One Field button.
   h. Click the Next button.
   i. At the second Simple Query Wizard dialog box, click the Next button.
   j. At the last Simple Query Wizard dialog box, select the current text in the *What title do you want for your query?* text box and then type **PhoenixClientClaimsOver$500Query**.
   k. Click the *Modify the query design* option and then click the Finish button.
   l. At the query window, complete the following steps:
      1) Click in the *Criteria* row field in the *City* column.
      2) Type **"Phoenix"** and then press Enter. (Type the quotation marks to tell Access that this is a criterion rather than an Access built-in function.)
      3) Click in the *Criteria* row field in the *AmountOfClaim* column. (You will need to scroll to the right to display this field.)
      4) Type **>500** and then press Enter.

City	State	ZIP	Claim#	AmountOfClaim
Clients	Clients	Clients	Claims	Claims
✓	✓	✓	✓	✓
"Phoenix"				>500

   Step 7l2   Step 7l4

   m. Click the Run button in the Results group. (This displays clients located in Phoenix with a claim amount greater than $500. See Project 1g query results on page 82.)
   n. Save the query, print the query in landscape orientation, and then close the query.
8. Close the **AL1-C3-CopperState.accdb** database.

Creating a Calculated Field

In a query, you can calculate values from fields by inserting a *calculated field* in a *Field* row field in the query design grid. To insert a calculated field, click in the *Field* row field, type the desired field name followed by a colon, and then type the equation. For example, to add 2010 sales amounts with 2011 sales amounts, you would type *Total:[Sales2010]+[Sales2011]* in the *Field* row field. Use brackets to specify field names and use mathematical operators to perform the equation. Some basic operators include the plus symbol (+) for addition, the hyphen symbol (-) for subtraction, the asterisk (*) for multiplication, and the forward slash (/) for division.

Project 1h — Creating a Calculated Field in a Query — Part 8 of 8

1. Open the **AL1-C3-Dearborn.accdb** database.
2. Create a query that displays 2010 and 2011 sales and totals the sales by completing the following steps:
   a. Click the Create tab and then click the Query Design button.
   b. Double-click *Clients* in the Show Table dialog box.
   c. Double-click *Sales* in the Show Table dialog box and then click the Close button.
   d. At the query window, insert the *Client* field from the Clients table in the first *Field* row field.
   e. Insert the *Sales2010* field from the Sales table in the second *Field* row field.
   f. Insert the *Sales2011* field from the Sales table in the third *Field* row field.
   g. Click in the fourth *Field* row field.
   h. Type **Total:[Sales2010]+[Sales2011]** and then press Enter.

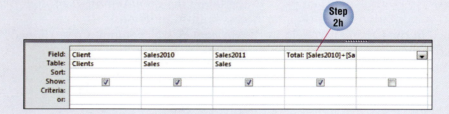

Step 2h

   i. Click the Run button in the Results group.
   j. Save the query and name it *SalesTotalQuery*. (See Project 1h query results on page 82.)
   k. Print and then close the query.
3. Close the **AL1-C3-Dearborn.accdb** database.
4. Open the **AL1-C3-PacTrek.accdb** database.
5. Create a query that displays order and total order amounts by completing the following steps:
   a. Click the Create tab and then click the Query Design button.
   b. Double-click *Suppliers* in the Show Table dialog box.
   c. Double-click *Orders* in the Show Table dialog box and then click the Close button.
   d. At the query window, insert the *SupplierName* field from the Suppliers table in the first *Field* row field.
   e. Insert the *Order#* field from the Orders table in the second *Field* row field.
   f. Insert the *UnitsOrdered* field from the Orders table in the third *Field* row field.

g. Insert the *Amount* field from the Orders table in the fourth *Field* row field.
h. Click in the fifth *Field* row field.
i. Type **Total:[Amount]*[UnitsOrdered]** and then press Enter.
j. Click the Run button in the Results group.

Step 5i

Field:	SupplierName	Order#	UnitsOrdered	Amount	Total: [Amount]*[Unit:
Table:	Suppliers	Orders	Orders	Orders	
Sort:					
Show:	☑	☑	☑	☑	☑
Criteria:					
or:					

k. Save the query and name it *UnitsOrderedTotalQuery*. (See Project 1h query results on page 82.)
l. Print and then close the query.

Project 2 — Create Aggregate Functions, Crosstab, Find Duplicates, and Find Unmatched Queries — 6 Parts

You will create an aggregate functions query that determines the total, average, minimum, and maximum order amounts and determine total and average order amounts grouped by supplier. You will also use the Crosstab, Find Duplicates, and Find Unmatched query wizards to design queries.

Designing Queries with Aggregate Functions

You can include an ***aggregate function*** such as Sum, Avg, Min, Max, or Count in a query to calculate statistics from numeric field values of all the records in the table. When an aggregate function is used, Access displays one row in the query results datasheet with the formula result for the function used. For example, in a table with a numeric field containing the annual salary amounts, you could use the Sum function to calculate the total of all salary amount values.

To display the aggregate function list, click the Totals button in the Show/Hide group in the Query Tools Design tab. Access adds a Total row to the design grid with a drop-down list from which you select the desired function. Access also inserts the words *Group By* in the *Total* row field. Click the down-pointing arrow and then click the desired aggregate function from the drop-down list. In Project 2a, Step 1, you will create a query in Design view and use aggregate functions to find the total of all sales, the average sales amount, the maximum and the minimum sales, and the total number of sales. The completed query will display as shown in Figure 3.5. Access automatically chooses the column heading names.

▼ Quick Steps

Design Query with Aggregate Function
1. At query window, click the Totals button.
2. Click the down-pointing arrow in *Total* row field.
3. Click desired aggregate function.

Totals

Figure 3.5 Query Results for Project 2a, Step 1

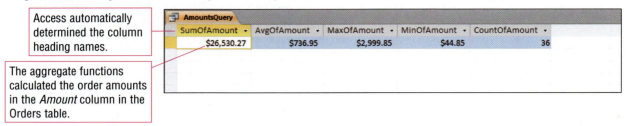

Access automatically determined the column heading names.

The aggregate functions calculated the order amounts in the *Amount* column in the Orders table.

Project 2a — Using Aggregate Functions in Queries — Part 1 of 6

1. With the **AL1-C3-PacTrek.accdb** database open, create a query with aggregate functions that determines total, average, minimum, and maximum order amounts as well as the total number of orders by completing the following steps:
   a. Click the Create tab and then click the Query Design button.
   b. At the Show Table dialog box, make sure *Orders* is selected in the list box, click the Add button, and then click the Close button.
   c. Insert the *Amount* field in the first, second, third, fourth, and fifth *Field* row fields.
   d. Click the Totals button in the Show/Hide group in the Query Tools Design tab. (This adds a *Total* row to the design grid between *Table* and *Sort* with the default option of *Group By*.)
   e. Specify a Sum function for the first *Total* row field by completing the following steps:
      1) Click in the first *Total* row field.
      2) Click the down-pointing arrow that displays at the right side of the field.
      3) Click *Sum* at the drop-down list.

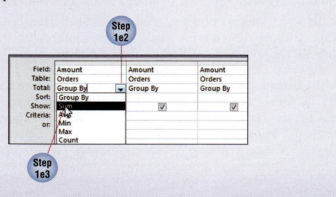

110 Access Level 1 ■ Unit 1

f. Complete steps similar to those in Step 1e to insert *Avg* in the second *Total* row field.
g. Complete steps similar to those in Step 1e to insert *Max* in the third *Total* row field.
h. Complete steps similar to those in Step 1e to insert *Min* in the fourth *Total* row field.
i. Complete steps similar to those in Step 1e to insert *Count* in the fifth *Total* row field.

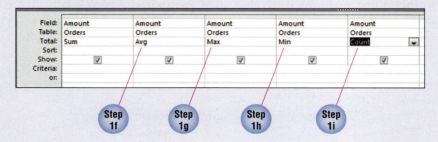

j. Click the Run button in the Results group. (Notice the headings that Access chooses for the columns.)
k. Automatically adjust the widths of the columns.
l. Save the query and name it *AmountsQuery*. (See Project 2a query results on page 82.)
m. Print and then close the query.
2. Close the **AL1-C3-PacTrek.accdb** database.
3. Open the **AL1-C3-CopperState.accdb** database.
4. Create a query with aggregate functions that determines total, average, minimum, and maximum claim amounts by completing the following steps:
   a. Click the Create tab and then click the Query Design button.
   b. At the Show Table dialog box, double-click *Claims*.
   c. Click the Close button to close the Show Table dialog box.
   d. Double-click the *AmountOfClaim* field. (This inserts the *AmountOfClaim* field in the first *Field* row field.)
   e. Double-click the *AmountOfClaim* field. (This inserts the *AmountOfClaim* field in the second *Field* row field.)
   f. Double-click the *AmountOfClaim* field. (This inserts the *AmountOfClaim* field in the third *Field* row field.)
   g. Double-click the *AmountOfClaim* field. (This inserts the *AmountOfClaim* field in the fourth *Field* row field.)
   h. Click the Totals button in the Show/Hide group.
   i. Click in the first *Total* row field, click the down-pointing arrow that displays at the right side of the field, and then click *Sum* at the drop-down list.

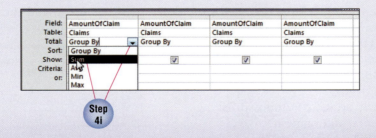

Chapter 3 ■ Performing Queries   111

j. Click in the second *Total* row field, click the down-pointing arrow, and then click *Avg* at the drop-down list.
k. Click in the third *Total* row field, click the down-pointing arrow, and then click *Max* at the drop-down list.
l. Click in the fourth *Total* row field, click the down-pointing arrow, and then click *Min* at the drop-down list.
m. Click the Run button in the Results group. (Notice the headings that Access chooses for the columns.)
n. Automatically adjust the widths of the columns.
o. Save the query and name it *ClaimAmountsQuery*. (See Project 2a query results on page 82.)
p. Print the query in landscape orientation and then close the query.

Using the *Group By* option in the *Total* field you can add a field to the query upon which you want Access to group records for statistical calculations. For example, to calculate the total of all orders for a specific supplier, add the *Supplier#* field to the design grid with the *Total* field set to *Group By*. In Project 2b, Step 1, you will create a query in Design view and use aggregate functions to find the total of all order amounts and the average order amounts grouped by the supplier number.

Project 2b Using Aggregate Functions and Grouping Records Part 2 of 6

1. With the **AL1-C3-CopperState.accdb** database open, determine the sum and average of client claims by completing the following steps:
   a. Click the Create tab and then click the Query Design button.
   b. At the Show Table dialog box, double-click *Clients* in the list box.
   c. Double-click *Claims* in the list box and then click the Close button.
   d. Insert the *Client#* field from the Clients table list box to the first *Field* row field.
   e. Insert the *AmountOfClaim* field from the Claims table list box to the second *Field* row field.
   f. Insert the *AmountOfClaim* field from the Claims table list box to the third *Field* row field.
   g. Click the Totals button in the Show/Hide group.
   h. Click in the second *Total* row field, click the down-pointing arrow, and then click *Sum* at the drop-down list.
   i. Click in the third *Total* row field, click the down-pointing arrow, and then click *Avg* at the drop-down list.
   j. Make sure *Group By* displays in the first *Total* row field.
   k. Click the Run button in the Results group.
   l. Automatically adjust column widths.
   m. Save the query and name it *SumAvgClaimAmountsQuery*. (See Project 2b query results on page 83.)
   n. Print and then close the query.
2. Close the **AL1-C3-CopperState.accdb** database.

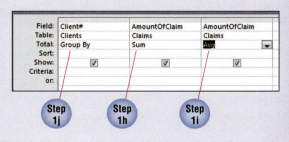

3. Open the **AL1-C3-PacTrek.accdb** database.
4. Determine the total and average order amounts for each supplier by completing the following steps:
   a. Click the Create tab and then click the Query Design button.
   b. At the Show Table dialog box, make sure *Orders* is selected in the list box and then click the Add button.
   c. Click *Suppliers* in the list box, click the Add button, and then click the Close button.
   d. Insert the *Amount* field from the Orders table list box to the first *Field* row field.
   e. Insert the *Amount* field from the Orders table list box to the second *Field* row field.
   f. Insert the *Supplier#* field from the Orders table list box to the third *Field* row field.
   g. Insert the *SupplierName* field from the Suppliers table to the fourth *Field* row field.
   h. Click the Totals button in the Show/Hide group.
   i. Click in the first *Total* row field, click the down-pointing arrow, and then click *Sum* at the drop-down list.
   j. Click in the second *Total* row field, click the down-pointing arrow, and then click *Avg* at the drop-down list.

   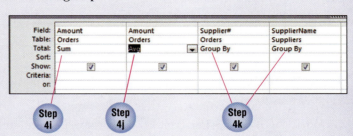

   k. Make sure *Group By* displays in the third and fourth *Total* row fields.
   l. Click the Run button in the Results group.
   m. Save the query and name it *SupplierAmountsQuery*. (See Project 2b query results on page 83.)
   n. Print and then close the query.

Creating a Crosstab Query

A *crosstab query* calculates aggregate functions such as Sum and Avg in which field values are grouped by two fields. A wizard is included that guides you through the steps to create the query. The first field selected causes one row to display in the query results datasheet for each group. The second field selected displays one column in the query results datasheet for each group. A third field is specified that is the numeric field to be summarized. The intersection of each row and column holds a value that is the result of the specified aggregate function for the designated row and column group.

Create a crosstab query from fields in one table. If you want to include fields from more than one table, you must first create a query containing the desired fields, and then create the crosstab query. For example, in Project 2c, Step 2, you will create a new query that contains fields from each of the three tables in the AL1-C3-PacTrek.accdb database. Using this query, you will use the Crosstab Query Wizard to create a query that summarizes the order amounts by supplier name and by product ordered. Figure 3.6 displays the results of that crosstab query. The first column displays the supplier names, the second column displays the total of amounts for each supplier, and the remaining columns display the amounts by suppliers for specific items.

Quick Steps

Create a Crosstab Query
1. Click Create tab.
2. Click Query Wizard button.
3. Double-click *Crosstab Query Wizard*.
4. Complete wizard steps.

Figure 3.6 Crosstab Query Results for Project 2c, Step 2

In this query, the order amounts are grouped by supplier name and by individual product.

SupplierName	Total Of Amt	Binoculars, E	Cascade R4 j	Cascade R4 j	Cascade R4 j	Cascade R4 j	Deluxe map	Eight-piece :
Bayside Supplies	$224.00							$99.75
Cascade Gear	$3,769.00		$1,285.00	$1,285.00	$599.50	$599.50		
Emerald City Products	$2,145.00	$2,145.00						
Fraser Valley Products	$3,892.75							
Freedom Corporation	$1,286.65							
Hopewell, Inc.	$348.60							
KL Distributions	$4,288.35							
Langley Corporation	$593.25							
Macadam, Inc.	$175.70						$129.75	
Manning, Inc.	$4,282.25							
Sound Supplies	$5,524.72							

Project 2c Creating a Crosstab Query Part 3 of 6

1. With the **AL1-C3-PacTrek.accdb** database open, create a query containing fields from the three tables by completing the following steps:
   a. Click the Create tab and then click the Query Design button.
   b. At the Show Table dialog box with *Orders* selected in the list box, click the Add button.
   c. Double-click *Products* in the Show Table dialog box.
   d. Double-click *Suppliers* in the list box and then click the Close button.
   e. Insert the following fields to the specified *Field* row fields:
      1) From the Orders table, insert the *Product#* field in the first *Field* row field.
      2) From the Products table, insert the *Product* field in the second *Field* row field.
      3) From the Orders table, insert the *UnitsOrdered* field in the third *Field* row field.
      4) From the Orders table, insert the *Amount* field in the fourth *Field* row field.
      5) From the Suppliers table, insert the *SupplierName* field in the fifth *Field* row field.
      6) From the Orders table, insert the *OrderDate* field in the sixth *Field* row field.

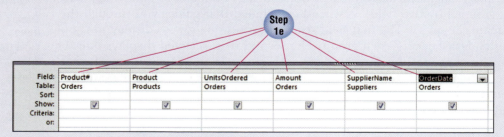

Step 1e

   f. Click the Run button to run the query.
   g. Save the query and name it *ItemsOrderedQuery*.
   h. Close the query.

2. Create a crosstab query that summarizes the orders by supplier name and by product ordered by completing the following steps:
   a. Click the Create tab and then click the Query Wizard button.
   b. At the New Query dialog box, double-click *Crosstab Query Wizard* in the list box.
   c. At the first Crosstab Query Wizard dialog box, click the *Queries* option in the *View* section and then click *Query: ItemsOrderedQuery* in the list box.
   d. Click the Next button.
   e. At the second Crosstab Query Wizard dialog box, click *SupplierName* in the *Available Fields* list box and then click the One Field button. (This inserts *SupplierName* in the *Selected Fields* list box and specifies that you want *SupplierName* for the row headings.)
   f. Click the Next button.
   g. At the third Crosstab Query Wizard dialog box, click *Product* in the list box. (This specifies that you want *Product* for the column headings.)
   h. Click the Next button.
   i. At the fourth Crosstab Query Wizard dialog box, click *Amount* in the *Fields* list box and click *Sum* in the *Functions* list box.
   j. Click the Next button.
   k. At the fifth Crosstab Query Wizard dialog box, select the current text in the *What do you want to name your query?* text box and then type **OrdersBySupplierByProductQuery**.
   l. Click the Finish button. (See Project 2c query results on page 83.)
3. Display the query in Print Preview, change the orientation to landscape, change the left and right margins to 0.5 inch, and then print the query. (The query will print on four pages.)
4. Close the query.

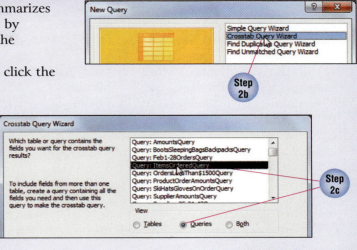

Step 2b

Step 2c

Step 2e

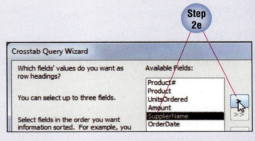

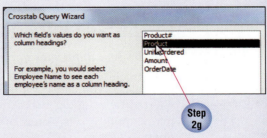

Step 2g

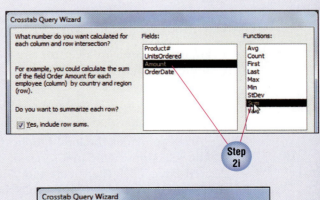

Step 2i

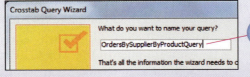

Step 2k

5. Close the **AL1-C3-PacTrek.accdb** database.
6. Open the **AL1-C3-CopperState.accdb** database.
7. Create a crosstab query from fields in one table that summarizes the claims by clients by completing the following steps:
    a. Click the Create tab and then click the Query Wizard button.
    b. At the New Query dialog box, double-click *Crosstab Query Wizard* in the list box.
    c. At the first Crosstab Query Wizard dialog box, click *Table: Claims* in the list box.
    d. Click the Next button.
    e. At the second Crosstab Query Wizard dialog box, click the One Field button. (This inserts the *Claim#* field in the *Selected Fields* list box.)
    f. Click the Next button.
    g. At the third Crosstab Query Wizard dialog, make sure *Client#* is selected in the list box and then click the Next button.
    h. At the fourth Crosstab Query Wizard dialog box, click *AmountOfClaim* in the *Fields* list box and click *Sum* in the *Functions* list box.
    i. Click the Next button.
    j. At the fifth Crosstab Query Wizard dialog box, select the current text in the *What do you want to name your query?* text box and then type **ClaimsByClaim#ByClient#Query**.
    k. Click the Finish button.
8. Change the orientation to landscape and then print the query. (The query will print on two pages. See Project 2c query results on page 83.)
9. Close the query.
10. Close the **AL1-C3-CopperState.accdb** database.

Creating a Find Duplicates Query

▼ **Quick Steps**

Create a Find Duplicates Query
1. Click Create tab.
2. Click Query Wizard button.
3. Double-click *Find Duplicates Query Wizard.*
4. Complete wizard steps.

Use the *find duplicates query* to search a specified table or query for duplicate field values within a designated field or fields. Create this type of query, for example, if you suspect a record, such as a product record, has inadvertently been entered twice under two different product numbers. A find duplicates query has many applications. A few other examples of how you can use a find duplicates query include:

- Find the records in an Orders table with the same customer number so that you can identify your loyal customers.
- Find the records in a Customers table with the same last name and mailing address so that you send only one mailing to a household to save on printing and postage costs.
- Find the records in an EmployeeExpenses table with the same employee number so that you can see which employee is submitting the most claims.

Access provides the Find Duplicates Query Wizard that builds the query based on the selections made in a series of dialog boxes. To use this wizard, open the desired table, click the Create tab, and then click the Query Wizard button. At the New Query dialog box, double-click *Find Duplicates Query Wizard* in the list box, and then complete the steps provided by the wizard.

In Project 2d, you will assume that you have been asked to update the address for a supplier in the AL1-C3-PacTrek.accdb database. Instead of updating the address, you create a new record. You will then use the Find Duplicates Query Wizard to find duplicate field values in the Suppliers table.

Project 2d Creating a Find Duplicates Query Part 4 of 6

1. Open the **AL1-C3-PacTrek.accdb** database and then open the Suppliers table.
2. Add the following record to the table:
   - *Supplier#* **29**
   - *SupplierName* **Langley Corporation**
   - *StreetAddress* **1248 Larson Avenue**
   - *City* **Burnaby**
   - *Prov/State* **BC**
   - *PostalCode* **V5V 9K2**
   - *EmailAddress* **lc@emcp.net**
   - *Telephone* **(604) 555-1200**
3. Close the Suppliers table.
4. Use the Find Duplicates Query Wizard to find any duplicate supplier names by completing the following steps:
   a. Click the Create tab and then click the Query Wizard button.
   b. At the New Query dialog box, double-click *Find Duplicates Query Wizard*.
   c. At the first wizard dialog box, click *Table: Suppliers* in the list box.

   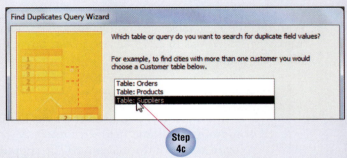

   d. Click the Next button.
   e. At the second wizard dialog box, click *SupplierName* in the *Available fields* list box and then click the One Field button. (This moves the *SupplierName* field to the *Duplicate-value fields* list box.)
   f. Click the Next button.
   g. At the third wizard dialog box, click the All Fields button (button containing the two greater than (>>) symbols). This moves all the fields to the *Additional query fields* list box. You are doing this because if you find a duplicate supplier name, you want to view all the fields to determine which record is accurate.

   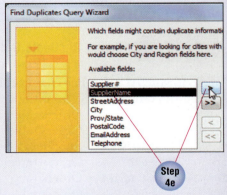

   h. Click the Next button.
   i. At the fourth (and last) wizard dialog box, type **DuplicateSuppliersQuery** in the *What do you want to name your query?* text box.

   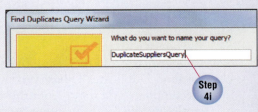

   j. Click the Finish button.
   k. Change the orientation to landscape and then print the query. (See Project 2d query results on page 83.)
5. As you look at the query results, you realize that an inaccurate record was entered for Langley so you decide to delete one of the records. To do this, complete the following steps:

a. With the query open, click in the record selector bar next to the second record (the one with a Supplier# of 29). (This selects the entire row.)
b. Click the Home tab and then click the Delete button in the Records group.
c. At the message asking you to confirm, click the Yes button.
d. Close the query.

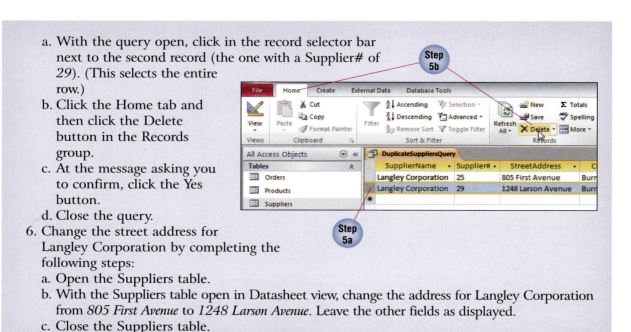

6. Change the street address for Langley Corporation by completing the following steps:
   a. Open the Suppliers table.
   b. With the Suppliers table open in Datasheet view, change the address for Langley Corporation from *805 First Avenue* to *1248 Larson Avenue*. Leave the other fields as displayed.
   c. Close the Suppliers table.

In Project 2d, you used the Find Duplicates Query Wizard to find records containing the same field. In Project 2e, you will use the Find Duplicates Query Wizard to find information on the suppliers you order from the most. You could use this information to negotiate for better prices or to ask for discounts.

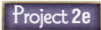 **Finding Duplicate Orders** — Part 5 of 6

1. With the **AL1-C3-PacTrek.accdb** database open, create a query with the following fields (in the order shown) from the specified tables:

Order#	Orders table
Supplier#	Orders table
SupplierName	Suppliers table
Product#	Orders table
UnitsOrdered	Orders table
Amount	Orders table
OrderDate	Orders table

2. Run the query.
3. Save the query with the name *SupplierOrdersQuery* and then close the query.
4. Use the Find Duplicates Query Wizard to find the suppliers you order from the most by completing the following steps:
   a. Click the Create tab and then click the Query Wizard button.
   b. At the New Query dialog box, double-click *Find Duplicates Query Wizard*.
   c. At the first wizard dialog box, click *Queries* in the *View* section, and then click *Query: SupplierOrdersQuery*. (You may need to scroll down the list to display this query.)

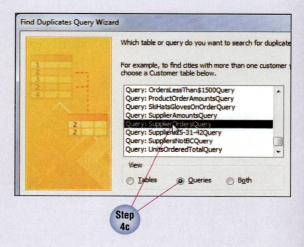

d. Click the Next button.
e. At the second wizard dialog box, click *Supplier#* in the *Available fields* list box and then click the One Field button.
f. Click the Next button.
g. At the third wizard dialog box, click the All Fields button. (This moves all the fields to the *Additional query fields* list box.)
h. Click the Next button.
i. At the fourth (and last) wizard dialog box, type **DuplicateSupplierOrdersQuery** in the *What do you want to name your query?* text box.
j. Click the Finish button.
k. Change the orientation to landscape and then print the query. (The query will print on two pages. See Project 2e query results on page 84.)
5. Close the query.

Step 4i

Creating a Find Unmatched Query

Create a ***find unmatched query*** to compare two tables and produce a list of the records in one table that have no matching record in the other related table. This type of query is useful to produce lists such as customers who have never placed an order or an invoice with no payment record. Access provides the Find Unmatched Query Wizard that builds the select query by guiding you through a series of dialog boxes.

In Project 2f, you will use the Find Unmatched Query Wizard to find all products that have no units on order. This information is helpful because it indicates which products are not selling and might need to be discontinued or returned. To use the Find Unmatched Query Wizard, click the Create tab and then click the Query Wizard button in the Queries group. At the New Query dialog box, double-click *Find Unmatched Query Wizard* in the list box and then follow the wizard steps.

▼ **Quick Steps**

Create a Find Unmatched Query
1. Click Create tab.
2. Click Query Wizard button.
3. Double-click *Find Unmatched Query Wizard*.
4. Complete wizard steps.

Project 2f Creating a Find Unmatched Query Part 6 of 6

1. With the **AL1-C3-PacTrek.accdb** database open, use the Find Unmatched Query Wizard to find all products that do not have any units on order by completing the following steps:
   a. Click the Create tab and then click the Query Wizard button.
   b. At the New Query dialog box, double-click *Find Unmatched Query Wizard*.
   c. At the first wizard dialog box, click *Table: Products* in the list box. (This is the table containing the fields you want to see in the query results.)
   d. Click the Next button.
   e. At the second wizard dialog box, make sure *Table: Orders* is selected in the list box. (This is the table containing the related records.)
   f. Click the Next button.

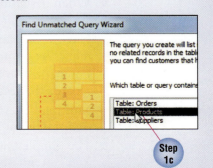
Step 1c

Chapter 3 ■ Performing Queries   119

g. At the third wizard dialog box, make sure *Product#* is selected in the *Fields in 'Products'* list box and in the *Fields in 'Orders'* list box.
h. Click the Next button.
i. At the fourth wizard dialog box, click the All Fields button to move all fields from the *Available fields* list box to the *Selected fields* list box.
j. Click the Next button.
k. At the fifth wizard dialog box, click the Finish button. (Let the wizard determine the query name: *Products Without Matching Orders*. See Project 2f query results on page 84.)

2. Print the query in landscape orientation and then close the query.
3. Close the **AL1-C3-PacTrek.accdb** database.

Step 1g

Chapter Summary

- Being able to extract specific information is one of the most important functions of a database. Data can be extracted from an Access database by performing a query, which can be accomplished by designing a query or using a query wizard.
- Designing a query consists of identifying the table, the field or fields from which the data will be drawn, and the criteria for selecting the data.
- During the designing of a query, write the criterion (or criteria) for extracting the specific data. Access inserts any necessary symbols in the criterion when the Enter key is pressed.
- In a criterion, quotation marks surround field values and pound symbols (#) surround dates. Use the asterisk (*) as a wildcard symbol.
- You can perform a query on fields within one table or on fields from related tables.
- When designing a query, you can specify the sort order of a field or fields.
- You can modify an existing query. To do this, double-click the query in the Navigation pane, click the View button to display the query in Design view, make the desired changes, and then click the Run button.
- Enter criterion in the *Or* row in the query design grid to instruct Access to display records that match either of the two criteria.
- Multiple criteria entered in the *Criteria* row in the query design grid become an *And* statement where each criterion must be met for Access to select the record.
- The Simple Query Wizard guides you through the steps for preparing a query. You can modify a query you create with the wizard.

- You can insert a calculated field in a *Field* row field when designing a query.
- Include an aggregate function such as Sum, Avg, Min, Max, or Count to calculate statistics from numeric field values. Click the Totals button in the Show/Hide group in the Query Tools Design tab to display the aggregate function list.
- Use the *Group By* option in the *Total* row field to add a field to a query upon which you want Access to group records for statistical calculations.
- Create a crosstab query to calculate aggregate functions such as Sum and Avg in which fields are grouped by two fields. Create a crosstab query from fields in one table. If you want to include fields from more than one table, create a query first, and then create the crosstab query.
- Use the find duplicates query to search a specified table or query for duplicate field values within a designated field or fields.
- Create a find unmatched query to compare two tables and produce a list of the records in one table that have no matching record in the other related table.

Commands Review

FEATURE	RIBBON TAB, GROUP	BUTTON, OPTION
Query design window	Create, Queries	
Run query	Query Tools Design, Results	
New Query dialog box	Create, Queries	
Simple Query Wizard	Create, Queries	, Simple Query Wizard
Add Total row to query design	Query Tools Design, Show/Hide	Σ
Crosstab Query Wizard	Create, Queries	, Crosstab Query Wizard
Find Duplicates Query Wizard	Create, Queries	, Find Duplicates Query Wizard
Find Unmatched Query Wizard	Create, Queries	, Find Unmatched Query Wizard

Concepts Check — Test Your Knowledge

Completion: For each description, indicate the correct term, symbol, or command.

1. The Query Design button is located in the Queries group in this tab.

2. Click the Query Design button and the query window displays with this dialog box open.

3. To establish a criterion for the query, click in this row in the column containing the desired field name and then type the criterion.

4. This is the term used for the results of the query.

5. This is the symbol Access automatically inserts around a date when writing a criterion for the query.

6. Use this symbol to indicate a wildcard character when writing a query criterion.

7. This is the criterion you would type to return field values greater than $500.

8. This is the criterion you would type to return field values that begin with the letter *L*.

9. This is the criterion you would type to return field values that are not in Oregon.

10. You can sort a field in a query in ascending order or this order.

11. Enter a criterion in this row in the query design grid to instruct Access to display records that match either of the two criteria.

12. This wizard guides you through the steps for preparing a query.

13. This type of query calculates aggregate functions in which field values are grouped by two fields.

14. Use this type of query to compare two tables and produce a list of the records in one table that have no matching record in the other related table.

Skills Check Assess Your Performance

Assessment

1 DESIGN QUERIES IN A LEGAL SERVICES DATABASE

1. Display the Open dialog box with Access2010L1C3 on your storage medium the active folder.
2. Open the **AL1-C3-WarrenLegal.accdb** database and enable the contents.
3. Design a query that extracts information from the Billing table with the following specifications:
   a. Include the fields *Billing#*, *ClientID*, and *CategoryID* in the query.
   b. Extract those records with the *SE* category. (Type **"SE"** in the *Criteria* row field in the *CategoryID* column. You need to type the quotation marks to tell Access that SE is a criterion and not an Access built-in function.)
   c. Save the query and name it *SECategoryBillingQuery*.
   d. Print and then close the query.
4. Design a query that extracts information from the Billing table with the following specifications:
   a. Include the fields *Billing#*, *ClientID*, and *Date*.
   b. Extract those records in the *Date* field with dates between 6/11/2012 and 6/15/2012.
   c. Save the query and name it *June11-15BillingQuery*.
   d. Print and then close the query.
5. Design a query that extracts information from the Clients table with the following specifications:
   a. Include the fields *FirstName*, *LastName*, and *City*.
   b. Extract those records with any city other than Kent in the *City* field.
   c. Save the query and name it *ClientsNotInKentQuery*.
   d. Print and then close the query.
6. Design a query that extracts information from two tables with the following specifications:
   a. Include the fields *Billing#*, *ClientID*, *Date*, and *Rate#* from the Billing table.
   b. Include the field *Rate* from the Rates table.
   c. Extract those records with a rate number greater than 2.
   d. Save the query and name it *RateGreaterThan2Query*.
   e. Print and then close the query.
7. Design a query that extracts information from three tables with the following specifications:
   a. Include the fields *AttorneyID, FName,* and *LName* from the Attorneys table.
   b. Include the fields *FirstName* and *LastName* from the Clients table.
   c. Include the fields *Date* and *Hours* from the Billing table.
   d. Extract those records with an AttorneyID of *12*.
   e. Save the query and name it Attorney12Query.
   f. Print and then close the query.
8. Design a query that extracts information from four tables with the following specifications:
   a. Include the fields *AttorneyID*, *FName*, and *LName* from the Attorneys table.
   b. Include the field *Category* from the Categories table.
   c. Include the fields *Rate#* and *Rate* from the Rates table.

d. Include the fields *Date* and *Hours* from the Billing table.
e. Extract those records with an AttorneyID of *17* and a Rate# of *4*.
f. Save the query and name it *Attorney17Rate4Query*.
g. Print the query in landscape orientation and then close the query.

9. Open the Attorney17Rate4Query query, click the View button in the Home tab to display the query in Design view, and then modify the query so it displays records with a Rate# of *4* with an AttorneyID of *17* and also *19* by making the following changes:
   a. Click below the field value "*17*" in the *AttorneyID* column and then type **19**.
   b. Click below the field value "*4*" in the *Rate#* column, type **4**, and then press Enter.
   c. Run the query.
   d. Save the query with the new name *Attorney17&19Rate4Query*. **Hint: Do this at the Save As dialog box. Display this dialog box by clicking the File tab and then clicking Save Object As.**
   e. Print the query in landscape orientation and then close the query.

Assessment

2 USE THE SIMPLE QUERY WIZARD AND DESIGN QUERIES

1. With **AL1-C3-WarrenLegal.accdb** database open, use the Simple Query Wizard to extract specific information from three tables with the following specifications:
   a. At the first Simple Query Wizard dialog box, include the following fields:
      From Attorneys table: *AttorneyID, FName,* and *LName*
      From Categories table: *Category*
      From Billing table: *Hours*
   b. At the second Simple Query Wizard dialog box, click Next.
   c. At the third Simple Query Wizard dialog box, click the *Modify the query design* option, and then click the Finish button.
   d. At the query window, insert *14* in the *Criteria* row field in the *AttorneyID* column.
   e. Run the query.
   f. Save the query with the default name.
   g. Print and then close the query.

2. Create a query in Design view with the Billing table with the following specifications:
   a. Insert the *Hours* field from the Billing table to the first, second, third, and fourth *Field* row fields.
   b. Click the Totals button in the Show/Hide group.
   c. Insert *Sum* in the first *Total* row field.
   d. Insert *Min* in the second *Total* row field.
   e. Insert *Max* in the third *Total* row field.
   f. Insert *Count* in the fourth *Total* row field.
   g. Run the query.
   h. Automatically adjust the widths of the columns.
   i. Save the query and name it *HoursAmountQuery*.
   j. Print and then close the query.

3. Create a query in Design view with the following specifications:
   a. Add the Attorneys table and the Billing table to the query window.
   b. Insert the *FName* field from the Attorneys table to the first *Field* row field.
   c. Insert the *LName* field from the Attorneys table to the second *Field* row field.

d. Insert the *AttorneyID* field from the Billing table to the third *Field* row field. (You will need to scroll down the Billing table list box to display the *AttorneyID* field.)
e. Insert the *Hours* field from the Billing table to the fourth *Field* row field.
f. Click the Totals button in the Show/Hide group.
g. Insert *Sum* in the fourth *Total* row field in the *Hours* column.
h. Run the query.
i. Save the query and name it *AttorneyHoursQuery*.
j. Print and then close the query.
4. Create a query in Design view with the following specifications:
a. Add the Attorneys, Clients, Categories, and Billing tables to the query window.
b. Insert the *AttorneyID* field from the Attorneys table to the first *Field* row field.
c. Insert the *ClientID* field from the Billing table to the second *Field* row field.
d. Insert the *Category* field from the Categories table to the third *Field* row field.
e. Insert the *Hours* field from the Billing table to the fourth *Field* row field.
f. Run the query.
g. Save the query and name it *AttorneyClientHours*.
h. Print and then close the query.

Assessment

3 CREATE A CROSSTAB QUERY AND USE THE FIND DUPLICATES AND FIND UNMATCHED QUERY WIZARDS

1. With the **AL1-C3-WarrenLegal.accdb** database open, create a crosstab query that summarizes the hours by attorney by category with the following specifications:
   a. At the first Crosstab Query Wizard dialog box, click the *Queries* option in the *View* section, and then click *Query: AttorneyClientHours* in the list box.
   b. At the second Crosstab Query Wizard dialog box with *AttorneyID* selected in the *Available Fields* list box, click the One Field button.
   c. At the third Crosstab Query Wizard dialog box, click *Category* in the list box.
   d. At the fourth Crosstab Query Wizard dialog box, click *Hours* in the *Fields* list box and click *Sum* in the *Functions* list box.
   e. At the fifth Crosstab Query Wizard dialog box, select the current name in the *What do you want to name your query?* text box and then type **HoursByAttorneyByCategory**.
   f. Display the query in Print Preview, change to landscape orientation, change the left and right margins to 0.5 inch, and then print the query.
   g. Close the query.
2. Use the Find Duplicates Query Wizard to find those clients with the same last name with the following specifications:
   a. At the first wizard dialog box, click *Table: Clients* in the list box.
   b. At the second wizard dialog box, click *LastName* in the *Available fields* list box and then click the One Field button.
   c. At the third wizard dialog box, click the All Fields button.
   d. At the fourth wizard dialog box, name the query *DuplicateLastNamesQuery*.
   e. Print the query in landscape orientation and then close the query.

3. Use the Find Unmatched Query Wizard to find all clients who do not have any billing hours with the following specifications:
   a. At the first wizard dialog box, click *Table: Clients* in the list box.
   b. At the second wizard dialog box, click *Table: Billing* in the list box.
   c. At the third wizard dialog box, make sure *ClientID* is selected in the *Fields in 'Clients'* list box and in the *Fields in 'Billing'* list box.
   d. At the fourth wizard dialog box, click the All Fields button to move all fields from the *Available fields* list box to the *Selected fields* list box.
   e. At the fifth wizard dialog box, click the Finish button. (Let the wizard determine the query name: *Clients Without Matching Billing*.)
4. Print the query in landscape orientation and then close the query.

Assessment

4 DESIGN AND HIDE FIELDS IN A QUERY

1. You can use the check boxes in the query design grid *Show* row to show or hide fields in the query. Experiment with these check boxes and then, with the **AL1-C3-WarrenLegal.accdb** database open, design the following query:
   a. At the Show Table dialog box, add the Clients table, the Billing table, and the Rates table.
   b. At the query window, insert the following fields in *Field* row fields:
      Clients table:
         FirstName
         LastName
      Billing table:
         Hours
      Rates table:
         Rate
   c. Insert in the fifth *Field* row field the calculated field *Total:[Hours]*[Rate]*.
   d. Hide the *Hours* and the *Rate* fields.
   e. Run the query.
   f. Save the query and name it *ClientBillingQuery*.
   g. Print and then close the query.
2. Close the **AL1-C3-WarrenLegal.accdb** database.

Visual Benchmark Demonstrate Your Proficiency

CREATING RELATIONSHIPS AND DESIGNING A QUERY

1. Open the **AL1-C3-MRInvestments.accdb** database from the Access2010L1C3 folder on your storage medium and enable the contents.
2. Display the Relationships window and then create the relationships shown in Figure 3.7. Enforce referential integrity and cascade fields and records. (The tables in Figure 3.7 have been rearranged in the Relationships window so you have a better view of the relationships.)
3. Save and then print the relationships.

4. Close the relationships report without saving it and then close the Relationships window.
5. Design the query shown in Figure 3.8.
6. Run the query.
7. Save the query with an appropriate name and then print the query.
8. Close the **AL1-C3-MRInvestments.accdb** database.

Figure 3.7 Visual Benchmark Relationships Window

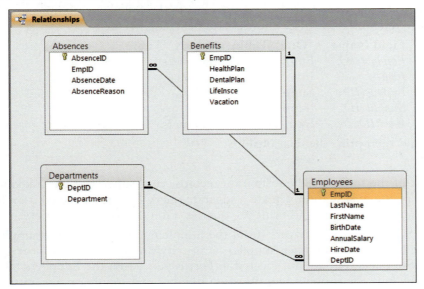

Figure 3.8 Visual Benchmark Query

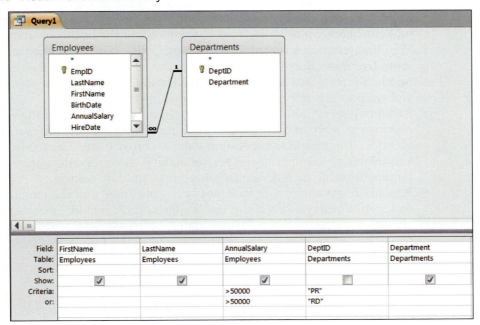

Case Study — Apply Your Skills

Part 1

You work for the Skyline Restaurant in Fort Myers, Florida. Your supervisor is reviewing the restaurant operations and has asked for a number of query reports. Before running queries, you realize that the tables in the restaurant database, **AL1-C3-Skyline.accdb**, are not related. Open the **AL1-C3-Skyline.accdb** database, enable the contents, and then create the following relationships (enforce referential integrity and cascade fields and records):

Field Name	"One" Table	"Many" Table
EmployeeID	Employees	Banquets
Item#	Inventory	Orders
SupplierID	Suppliers	Orders
SupplierID	Suppliers	Inventory
EventID	Events	Banquets

Save and then print the relationships.

Part 2

As part of the review of the restaurant records, your supervisor has asked you for the following information. Create a separate query for each bulleted item listed below and save, name, and print the queries. (You determine the query names.)

- Suppliers in Fort Myers (from the Suppliers table include the supplier identification number, supplier name, city, and telephone number)
- Suppliers that are not located in Fort Myers (from the Suppliers table include the supplier identification number and supplier name, city, and telephone number)
- Employees hired in 2009 (from the Employees table include the employee identification number, first and last names, and hire date)
- Employees that are signed up for health insurance (from the Employees table include employee first and last names and the health insurance field)
- Wedding receptions (event identification "WR") booked in the banquet room (from the Banquets table include the reservation identification number; reservation date; event identification; and first name, last name, and telephone number of the person making the reservation)
- Banquet reservations between 6/14/2012 and 6/30/2012 and the employees making the reservations (from the Banquets table include reservation identification number; reservation date; and first name, last name, and telephone number of the person making the reservation; from the Employees table include the employee first and last names)
- Banquet reservations that have not been confirmed and the employees making the reservations (from the Banquets table include reservation identification number; reservation date; confirmed field; and first and last names of person making the reservation; from the Employees table include the employee first and last names)
- Banquet room reserved by someone whose last name begins with "Wie" (from the Employees table include the first and last names of the employee who booked the reservation and from the Banquets table include the first and last names and telephone number of the person making the reservation)

- A query that inserts a calculated field that multiplies the number of units ordered by the unit price for all orders for supplier number 2 (from the Orders table include the order number, the supplier identification number, the units ordered, and the unit price; from the Inventory table include the item field)

Part 3

Use the Find Duplicates Query Wizard to find duplicate items in the Orders table with the following specifications:
- At the first wizard dialog box, specify the Orders table.
- At the second wizard dialog box, specify *Item#* as the duplicate-value field.
- At the third wizard dialog, specify that you want all of the fields in the query.
- At the fourth wizard dialog box, you determine the query name.
- Print and then close the query.

Use the Find Unmatched Query Wizard to find all employees who have not made a banquet reservation with the following specifications:
- At the first wizard dialog box, specify the Employees table.
- At the second wizard dialog box, specify the Banquets table.
- At the third wizard dialog box, specify the *EmployeeID* field in both list boxes.
- At the fourth wizard dialog box, specify that you want all of the fields in the query.
- At the fifth wizard dialog box, you determine the query name.
- Print the query in landscape orientation and then close the query.

Use the Crosstab Query Wizard to create a query that summarizes order amounts by supplier with the following specifications:
- At the first wizard dialog box, specify the Orders table.
- At the second wizard dialog box, specify the *SupplierID* field for row headings.
- At the third wizard dialog box, specify the *Item#* field for column headings.
- At the fourth wizard dialog box, click *UnitPrice* in the *Fields* list box and click *Sum* in the *Functions* list box.
- At the fifth wizard dialog box, you determine the query name.
- Automatically adjust the columns in the query. (You will need to scroll to the right to view and adjust all of the columns containing data.)
- Display the query in Print Preview, change to landscape orientation, and then change the left and right margins to 0.3 inch.
- Print and then close the crosstab query.

Part 4

Design at least three additional queries that require fields from at least two tables. Run the queries and then save and print the queries. In Microsoft Word, write the query information and include specific information about each query and format the document to enhance the visual appeal. Save the document and name it **AL1-C3-CS-Queries**. Print and then close **AL1-C3-CS-Queries.docx**.

Microsoft® Access®
Creating and Modifying Tables in Design View

CHAPTER 4

PERFORMANCE OBJECTIVES

Upon successful completion of Chapter 4, you will be able to:
- Create a table in Design view
- Assign a default value
- Use the Input Mask Wizard and the Lookup Wizard
- Validate field entries
- Insert a total row
- Sort records and print specific records in a table
- Complete a spelling check
- Find specific records in a table and find data and replace with other data
- Apply text formatting
- Use the Help feature

In Chapter 1 you learned how to create a table in Datasheet view. You can also create a table in Design view where you can establish the table's structure and properties before entering data. In this chapter, you will learn how to create a table in Design view and use the Input Mask Wizard and Lookup Wizards; insert, move, and delete fields in Design view; sort records; check spelling in a table; find and replace data; apply text formatting to a table; and use the Access Help feature. Model answers for this chapter's projects appear on the following pages.

Access2010L1C4

Note: Before beginning the projects, copy the Access2010L1C4 subfolder from the Access2010L1 folder on the CD that accompanies this textbook to your storage medium and make Access2010L1C4 the active folder.

Project 1 Create and Modify Tables in a Property Management Database

Project 1c

Step 11, Employees Table

EmpID	EmpCategory	FName	LName	Address	City	State	ZIP	Telephone	HealthIns	DentalIns	LifeIns
02-59	Hourly	Christina	Solomon	12241 East 51st	Citrus Heights	CA	95611	(916) 555-8844	✓	✓	$100,000.00
03-23	Salaried	Douglas	Ricci	903 Mission Road	Roseville	CA	95678	(916) 555-4125	✓		$25,000.00
03-55	Hourly	Tatiana	Kasadev	6558 Orchard Drive	Citrus Heights	CA	95610	(916) 555-8534	✓		$0.00
04-14	Salaried	Brian	West	12232 142nd Avenue East	Citrus Heights	CA	95611	(916) 555-0967	✓	✓	$50,000.00
04-32	Temporary	Kathleen	Addison	21229 19th Street	Citrus Heights	CA	95621	(916) 555-3408	✓	✓	$50,000.00
05-20	Hourly	Teresa	Villanueva	19453 North 42nd Street	Citrus Heights	CA	95611	(916) 555-2302	✓		$0.00
05-31	Salaried	Marcia	Griswold	211 Haven Road	North Highlands	CA	95660	(916) 555-1449			$100,000.00
06-24	Temporary	Tiffany	Gentry	12312 North 20th	Roseville	CA	95661	(916) 555-0043	✓	✓	$50,000.00
06-33	Hourly	Joanna	Gallegos	6850 York Street	Roseville	CA	95747	(916) 555-7446			$25,000.00
07-20	Salaried	Jesse	Scholtz	3412 South 21st Street	Fair Oaks	CA	95628	(916) 555-4204	✓		$0.00
07-23	Salaried	Eugene	Bond	530 Laurel Road	Orangevale	CA	95662	(916) 555-9412	✓		$100,000.00

Step 16, Employees Table

EmpID	FName	LName	Address	City	State	ZIP	Telephone	EmpCategory	HealthIns	LifeIns
02-59	Christina	Solomon	12241 East 51st	Citrus Heights	CA	95611	(916) 555-8844	Hourly	✓	$100,000.00
03-23	Douglas	Ricci	903 Mission Road	Roseville	CA	95678	(916) 555-4125	Salaried	✓	$25,000.00
03-55	Tatiana	Kasadev	6558 Orchard Drive	Citrus Heights	CA	95610	(916) 555-8534	Hourly	✓	$0.00
04-14	Brian	West	12232 142nd Avenue East	Citrus Heights	CA	95611	(916) 555-0967	Salaried	✓	$50,000.00
04-32	Kathleen	Addison	21229 19th Street	Citrus Heights	CA	95621	(916) 555-3408	Temporary	✓	$50,000.00
05-20	Teresa	Villanueva	19453 North 42nd Street	Citrus Heights	CA	95611	(916) 555-2302	Hourly	✓	$0.00
05-31	Marcia	Griswold	211 Haven Road	North Highlands	CA	95660	(916) 555-1449	Salaried		$100,000.00
06-24	Tiffany	Gentry	12312 North 20th	Roseville	CA	95661	(916) 555-0043	Temporary	✓	$50,000.00
06-33	Joanna	Gallegos	6850 York Street	Roseville	CA	95747	(916) 555-7446	Hourly		$25,000.00
07-20	Jesse	Scholtz	3412 South 21st Street	Fair Oaks	CA	95628	(916) 555-4204	Salaried	✓	$0.00
07-23	Eugene	Bond	530 Laurel Road	Orangevale	CA	95662	(916) 555-9412	Salaried	✓	$100,000.00

Payments Table

Pymnt#	RenterID	PymntDate	PymntAmount	LateFee
1	130	3/1/2012	$1,800.00	
2	111	3/1/2012	$1,900.00	
3	136	3/1/2012	$1,250.00	
4	110	3/1/2012	$1,300.00	
5	135	3/2/2012	$1,900.00	
6	123	3/2/2012	$1,000.00	
7	117	3/2/2012	$1,100.00	
8	134	3/3/2012	$1,400.00	
9	131	3/3/2012	$1,200.00	
10	118	3/3/2012	$900.00	
11	125	3/5/2012	$1,650.00	
12	119	3/5/2012	$1,500.00	
13	133	3/8/2012	$1,650.00	
14	129	3/9/2012	$1,650.00	
15	115	3/12/2012	$1,375.00	$25.00
16	121	3/12/2012	$950.00	$25.00
17	127	3/19/2012	$1,300.00	$50.00
Total			$23,825.00	$100.00

Project 1d

Step 2c, Renters Table

RenterID	FirstName	LastName	PropID	EmpID	CreditScore	LeaseBegDate	LeaseEndDate
118	Mason	Ahn	1004	07-23	538	3/1/2012	2/28/2013
119	Michelle	Bertram	1001	03-23	621	3/1/2012	2/28/2013
110	Greg	Hamilton	1029	04-14	624	1/1/2012	12/31/2012
121	Travis	Jorgenson	1010	04-14	590	3/1/2012	2/28/2013
135	Marty	Lobdell	1006	04-14	510	6/1/2012	5/31/2013
129	Susan	Lowrey	1002	04-14	634	4/1/2012	3/31/2013
130	Ross	Molaski	1027	03-23	688	5/1/2012	4/30/2013
136	Nadine	Paschal	1022	05-31	702	6/1/2012	5/31/2013
111	Julia	Perez	1013	07-20	711	1/1/2012	12/31/2012
115	Dana	Rozinski	1026	02-59	538	2/1/2012	1/31/2013
131	Danielle	Rubio	1020	07-20	722	5/1/2012	4/30/2013
133	Katie	Smith	1018	07-23	596	5/1/2012	4/30/2013
123	Richard	Terrell	1014	07-20	687	3/1/2012	2/28/2013
117	Miguel	Villegas	1007	07-20	695	2/1/2012	1/31/2013
125	Rose	Wagoner	1015	07-23	734	4/1/2012	3/31/2013
134	Carl	Weston	1009	03-23	655	6/1/2012	5/31/2013
127	William	Young	1023	05-31	478	4/1/2012	3/31/2013

Step 3c, Renters Table

RenterID	FirstName	LastName	PropID	EmpID	CreditScore	LeaseBegDate	LeaseEndDate
125	Rose	Wagoner	1015	07-23	734	4/1/2012	3/31/2013
131	Danielle	Rubio	1020	07-20	722	5/1/2012	4/30/2013
111	Julia	Perez	1013	07-20	711	1/1/2012	12/31/2012
136	Nadine	Paschal	1022	05-31	702	6/1/2012	5/31/2013
117	Miguel	Villegas	1007	07-20	695	2/1/2012	1/31/2013
130	Ross	Molaski	1027	03-23	688	5/1/2012	4/30/2013
123	Richard	Terrell	1014	07-20	687	3/1/2012	2/28/2013
134	Carl	Weston	1009	03-23	655	6/1/2012	5/31/2013
129	Susan	Lowrey	1002	04-14	634	4/1/2012	3/31/2013
110	Greg	Hamilton	1029	04-14	624	1/1/2012	12/31/2012
119	Michelle	Bertram	1001	03-23	621	3/1/2012	2/28/2013
133	Katie	Smith	1018	07-23	596	5/1/2012	4/30/2013
121	Travis	Jorgenson	1010	04-14	590	3/1/2012	2/28/2013
118	Mason	Ahn	1004	07-23	538	3/1/2012	2/28/2013
115	Dana	Rozinski	1026	02-59	538	2/1/2012	1/31/2013
135	Marty	Lobdell	1006	04-14	510	6/1/2012	5/31/2013
127	William	Young	1023	05-31	478	4/1/2012	3/31/2013

Step 6f, Properties Table

PropID	CatID	MoRent	Address	City	State	ZIP
1007	A	$1,100.00	904 Everson Road	Fair Oaks	CA	95628
1004	A	$900.00	1932 Oakville Drive	North Highlands	CA	95660
1010	A	$950.00	19334 140th East	Citrus Heights	CA	95621
1014	A	$1,000.00	9045 Valley Avenue	Citrus Heights	CA	95611

Step 7f, Properties Table

PropID	CatID	MoRent	Address	City	State	ZIP
1007	A	$1,100.00	904 Everson Road	Fair Oaks	CA	95628
1004	A	$900.00	1932 Oakville Drive	North Highlands	CA	95660
1010	A	$950.00	19334 140th East	Citrus Heights	CA	95621
1014	A	$1,000.00	9045 Valley Avenue	Citrus Heights	CA	95611
1029	C	$1,300.00	155 Aldrich Road	Roseville	CA	95678
1002	C	$1,650.00	2650 Crestline Drive	Citrus Heights	CA	95611
1001	C	$1,500.00	4102 Tenth Street	Citrus Heights	CA	95611
1026	C	$1,375.00	10057 128th Avenue	Citrus Heights	CA	95611
1023	C	$1,300.00	750 Birch Drive	Orangevale	CA	95662
1009	C	$1,400.00	159 Meridian Street	Orangevale	CA	95662
1019	C	$1,700.00	765 Chellis Street	Fair Oaks	CA	95628
1018	C	$1,650.00	9945 North 20th Road	North Highlands	CA	95660
1017	D	$1,300.00	4500 Maple Lane	Orangevale	CA	95662
1011	D	$1,350.00	348 Hampton Avenue	Citrus Heights	CA	95611
1008	D	$1,575.00	5009 North Garden	Roseville	CA	95661
1020	D	$1,200.00	23390 South 22nd Street	Citrus Heights	CA	95610
1006	S	$1,900.00	3412 Mango Street	Orangevale	CA	95662
1003	S	$1,800.00	10234 122nd Avenue	North Highlands	CA	95660
1012	S	$1,775.00	1212 Fairhaven Road	North Highlands	CA	95660
1013	S	$1,900.00	2606 30th Street	Citrus Heights	CA	95610
1016	S	$1,825.00	21388 South 42nd Street	Citrus Heights	CA	95621
1030	S	$1,950.00	5430 112th Southeast	Citrus Heights	CA	95611
1021	S	$1,875.00	652 Seventh Street	Fair Oaks	CA	95628
1024	S	$1,650.00	1195 24th Street	North Highlands	CA	95660
1027	S	$1,800.00	2203 Center Road	Orangevale	CA	95662
1028	S	$1,750.00	488 Franklin Drive	Fair Oaks	CA	95628
1022	T	$1,250.00	4572 152nd Avenue	Citrus Heights	CA	95611
1005	T	$1,350.00	12110 55th Southeast	Citrus Heights	CA	95611
1025	T	$1,200.00	3354 North 62nd Street	Citrus Heights	CA	95610
1015	T	$1,650.00	560 Tenth Street East	North Highlands	CA	95660

Project 1d–continued

Step 8g, Payments Table

Pymnt#	RenterID	PymntDate	PymntAmount	LateFee
1	130	3/1/2012	$1,800.00	
2	111	3/1/2012	$1,900.00	
3	136	3/1/2012	$1,250.00	
4	110	3/1/2012	$1,300.00	
5	135	3/2/2012	$1,900.00	
6	123	3/2/2012	$1,000.00	
7	117	3/2/2012	$1,100.00	
8	134	3/3/2012	$1,400.00	
9	131	3/3/2012	$1,200.00	
10	118	3/3/2012	$900.00	
11	125	3/5/2012	$1,650.00	
12	119	3/5/2012	$1,500.00	
13	133	3/8/2012	$1,650.00	
14	129	3/9/2012	$1,650.00	
15	115	3/12/2012	$1,375.00	$25.00
16	121	3/12/2012	$950.00	$25.00
17	127	3/19/2012	$1,300.00	$50.00
Total			$23,825.00	$100.00

Step 10j, Renters Table

RenterID	FirstName	LastName	PropID	EmpID	CreditScore	LeaseBegDate	LeaseEndDate
110	Greg	Hamilton	1029	04-14	624	1/1/2012	12/31/2012
111	Julia	Perez	1013	07-20	711	1/1/2012	12/31/2012
115	Dana	Rozinski	1026	02-59	538	2/1/2012	1/31/2013
117	Miguel	Villegas	1007	07-20	695	2/1/2012	1/31/2013
118	Mason	Ahn	1004	07-23	538	3/1/2012	2/28/2013
119	Michelle	Bertram	1001	03-23	621	3/1/2012	2/28/2013
121	Travis	Jorgenson	1010	04-14	590	3/1/2012	2/28/2013
123	Richard	Terrell	1014	07-20	687	3/1/2012	2/28/2013
125	Rose	Wagoner	1015	07-23	734	4/1/2012	3/31/2013
127	William	Young	1023	05-31	478	4/1/2012	3/31/2013
129	Susan	Lowrey	1002	04-14	634	4/1/2012	3/31/2013
130	Ross	Molaski	1027	03-23	688	5/1/2012	4/30/2013
131	Danielle	Rubio	1020	07-20	722	5/1/2012	4/30/2013
133	Katie	Smith	1018	07-23	596	5/1/2012	4/30/2013
134	Carl	Weston	1009	03-23	655	6/1/2012	5/31/2013
135	Marty	Lobdell	1006	04-14	510	6/1/2012	5/31/2013
136	Nadine	Paschal	1022	05-31	702	6/1/2012	5/31/2013

Project 1e

Employees Table

EmpID	FName	LName	Address	City	State	ZIP	Telephone	EmpCategory	HealthIns
02-59	Christina	Solomon	12241 East 51st	Citrus Heights	CA	95611	(916) 555-8844	Hourly	✓
03-23	Douglas	Ricci	903 Mission Road	Roseville	CA	95678	(916) 555-4125	Salaried	✓
03-55	Tatiana	Kasadev	6558 Orchard Drive	Citrus Heights	CA	95610	(916) 555-8534	Hourly	✓
04-14	Brian	West	12232 142nd Avenue East	Citrus Heights	CA	95611	(916) 555-0967	Salaried	✓
04-32	Kathleen	Addison	21229 19th Street	Citrus Heights	CA	95621	(916) 555-3408	Temporary	✓
05-20	Teresa	Villanueva	19453 North 42nd Street	Citrus Heights	CA	95611	(916) 555-2302	Hourly	✓
05-31	Marcia	Griswold	211 Haven Road	North Highlands	CA	95660	(916) 555-1449	Salaried	
06-24	Tiffany	Gentry	12312 North 20th	Roseville	CA	95611	(916) 555-0043	Temporary	✓
06-33	Joanna	Gallegos	6850 York Street	Roseville	CA	95747	(916) 555-7446	Hourly	
07-20	Jesse	Scholtz	3412 South 21st Street	Fair Oaks	CA	95628	(916) 555-4204	Salaried	✓
07-23	Eugene	Bond	530 Laurel Road	Orangevale	CA	95662	(916) 555-9412	Salaried	✓
02-72	Robin	Wilder	9945 Valley Avenue	Citrus Heights	CA	95610	(916) 555-6522	Salaried	

Project 1f

PropertiesTable

PropID	CatID	MoRent	Address	City	State	ZIP
1007	A	$1,100.00	904 Everson Road	Fair Oaks	CA	95628
1004	A	$900.00	1932 Oakville Drive	North Highlands	CA	95668
1010	A	$950.00	19334 140th East	Citrus Heights	CA	95621
1014	A	$1,000.00	9045 Valley Avenue	Citrus Heights	CA	95611
1029	C	$1,300.00	155 Aldrich Road	Roseville	CA	95678
1002	C	$1,650.00	2650 Crestline Drive	Citrus Heights	CA	95611
1001	C	$1,500.00	4102 Tenth Street	Citrus Heights	CA	95611
1026	C	$1,375.00	10057 128th Avenue	Citrus Heights	CA	95611
1023	C	$1,300.00	750 Birch Drive	Orangevale	CA	95662
1009	C	$1,400.00	159 Meridian Street	Orangevale	CA	95662
1019	C	$1,700.00	765 Chellis Street	Fair Oaks	CA	95628
1018	C	$1,650.00	9945 North 20th Road	North Highlands	CA	95660
1017	D	$1,300.00	4500 Maple Lane	Orangevale	CA	95662
1011	D	$1,350.00	348 Hampton Avenue	Citrus Heights	CA	95611
1008	D	$1,575.00	5009 North Garden	Roseville	CA	95611
1020	D	$1,200.00	23390 South 22nd Street	Citrus Heights	CA	95610
1006	S	$1,900.00	3412 Mango Street	Orangevale	CA	95662
1003	S	$1,800.00	10234 122nd Avenue	North Highlands	CA	95668
1012	S	$1,775.00	1212 Fairhaven Road	North Highlands	CA	95660
1013	S	$1,900.00	2606 30th Street	Citrus Heights	CA	95610
1016	S	$1,825.00	21388 South 42nd Street	Citrus Heights	CA	95621
1030	S	$1,950.00	5430 112th Southeast	Citrus Heights	CA	95611
1021	S	$1,875.00	652 Seventh Street	Fair Oaks	CA	95628
1024	S	$1,650.00	1195 24th Street	North Highlands	CA	95660
1027	S	$1,800.00	2203 Center Road	Orangevale	CA	95662
1028	S	$1,750.00	488 Franklin Drive	Fair Oaks	CA	95628
1022	T	$1,250.00	4572 152nd Avenue	Citrus Heights	CA	95621
1005	T	$1,350.00	12110 55th Southeast	Citrus Heights	CA	95611
1025	T	$1,200.00	3354 North 62nd Drive	Citrus Heights	CA	95610
1015	T	$1,650.00	560 Tenth Street East	North Highlands	CA	95668

Relationships Table

EmpsWithHealthInsQuery

FName	LName	HealthIns
Christina	Solomon	✓
Douglas	Ricci	✓
Tatiana	Kasadev	✓
Brian	West	✓
Kathleen	Addison	✓
Teresa	Villanueva	✓
Tiffany	Gentry	✓
Jesse	Scholtz	✓
Eugene	Bond	✓

CitrusHeightsPropsQuery

PropID	Category	Address	City	State	ZIP
1001	Condominium	4102 Tenth Street	Citrus Heights	CA	95611
1002	Condominium	2650 Crestline Drive	Citrus Heights	CA	95611
1005	Townhouse	12110 55th Southeast	Citrus Heights	CA	95611
1010	Apartment	19334 140th East	Citrus Heights	CA	95621
1011	Duplex	348 Hampton Avenue	Citrus Heights	CA	95611
1013	Single-family house	2606 30th Street	Citrus Heights	CA	95610
1014	Apartment	9045 Valley Avenue	Citrus Heights	CA	95611
1016	Single-family house	21388 South 42nd Street	Citrus Heights	CA	95621
1020	Duplex	23390 South 22nd Street	Citrus Heights	CA	95610
1022	Townhouse	4572 152nd Avenue	Citrus Heights	CA	95621
1025	Townhouse	3354 North 62nd Street	Citrus Heights	CA	95610
1026	Condominium	10057 128th Avenue	Citrus Heights	CA	95611
1030	Single-family house	5430 112th Southeast	Citrus Heights	CA	95611

Project 1f—continued

Pymnts3/1To3/5Query

RentLessThan$1501InCHAndOVQuery

Emp07-20CHPropsQuery

Project 1 — Create and Modify Tables in a Property Management Database

8 Parts

You will open the Sun Properties database, create two new tables in Design view, modify existing tables, and sort data in tables. You will also complete a spelling check on data in tables, find data in a table and replace with other data, create relationships and perform queries, and get help using the Access Help feature.

Creating a Table in Design View

In Datasheet view you can create a table by assigning each column a data type and typing the field name. Once the columns are defined, you enter the data into records. You can also create a table in Design view where you can set field properties before you begin entering data. To display a table in Design view, open the desired database, click the Create tab, and then click the Table button. This opens a new blank table in Datasheet view. Display the table in Design view by clicking the View button that displays at the left side of the Table Tools Design tab in the Views group. When you click the View button in a new table, Access displays the Save As dialog box where you type the table name and then press Enter or click OK. Figure 4.1 displays the Properties table in Design view in the AL1-C4-SunProperties.accdb database.

View

In Design view, each row in the top section represents one field in the table and is used to define the field name, the field's data type, and a description. The *Field Properties* section in the lower half of the work area displays the properties for the active field. The properties will vary depending on the active field. In the lower right corner of Design view, Help information displays about an option as you make an option active in the Design window. In Figure 4.1, the *PropID* field name is active in Design view, so Access displays information in the Help area on field names.

Figure 4.1 Properties Table in Design View

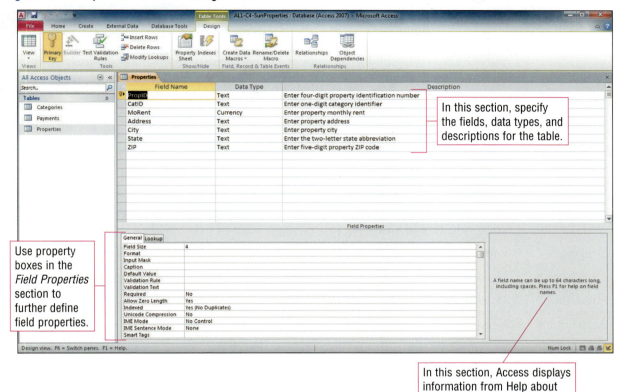

Define each field in the table in the rows in the top section of Design view. When you create a new table in Design view, Access automatically assigns the first field the name *ID* and assigns the AutoNumber data type. You can leave this field name or type a new name and you can also change the data type. To create a new field in the table, click in the field in the *Field Name* column, type the field name, and then press the Tab key or the Enter key. This makes active the *Data Type* field. Click the down-pointing arrow in the *Data Type* field and then click the desired data type at the drop-down list. In Chapter 1, you created tables in Datasheet view and assigned data types of Text, Date/Time, Currency, or Yes/No. The *Data Type* field drop-down list includes these data types as well as additional types as described in Table 4.1.

When you click the desired data type at the drop-down list and then press the Tab key, the *Description* field becomes active. Type a description in the field that provides useful information to someone entering data in the table. When typing a description, consider the field's purpose or contents, or provide instructional information for data entry. The description you type displays in the Status bar when the field is active in the table in Datasheet view.

When creating the table, continue typing field names, assigning a data type to each field, and typing field descriptions. When the table design is complete, save the table by clicking the Save button on the Quick Access toolbar. Return to Datasheet view by clicking the View button in the Views group in the Table Tools Design tab. In Datasheet view, type the records for the table.

▼ **Quick Steps**

Create Table in Design View
1. Open database.
2. Click Create tab.
3. Click Table button.
4. Click View button.
5. Type name for table.
6. Press Enter or click OK.
7. Type field names, specify data types, and include descriptions.
8. Click Save button.

Save

Chapter 4 ■ Creating and Modifying Tables in Design View   135

Table 4.1 Data Types

Data Type	Description
Text	Alphanumeric data up to 255 characters in length, such as a name, address, or value such as a telephone number or Social Security number that is used as an identifier and not for calculating.
Memo	Alphanumeric data up to 64,000 characters in length.
Number	Positive or negative values that can be used in calculations. Do not use for value that will calculate monetary amounts (see Currency).
Date/Time	Use this type to ensure dates and times are entered and sorted properly.
Currency	Values that involve money. Access will not round off during calculations.
AutoNumber	Access automatically numbers each record sequentially (incrementing by 1) when you begin typing a new record.
Yes/No	Data in the field will be either *Yes* or *No*, *True* or *False*, or *On* or *Off*.
OLE Object	Used to embed or link objects created in other Office applications.
Hyperlink	Field that will store a hyperlink such as a URL.
Attachment	Use this data type to add file attachments to a record such as a Word document or an Excel workbook.
Lookup Wizard	Use the Lookup Wizard to enter data in the field from another existing table or display a list of values in a drop-down list from which the user chooses.

Project 1a Creating a Table in Design View   Part 1 of 8

1. Open Access and then open the **AL1-C4-SunProperties.accdb** database located in the Access2010L1C4 folder on your storage medium.
2. Click the Enable Content button in the message bar. (The message bar will display immediately below the ribbon.)
3. View the Properties table in Design view by completing the following steps:
   a. Open the Properties table.
   b. Click the View button in the Views group in the Home tab. (This displays the table in Design view.)
   c. Click each of the field names and then look at the information that displays in the *Field Properties* section.

   Step 3b

   d. Click in various options and then read the information that displays in the Help area located in the lower right corner of Design view.
   e. Click the View button to return the table to Datasheet view.
   f. Close the Properties table.

4. Create a new table in Design view as shown in Figure 4.2 by completing the following steps:
   a. Click the Create tab and then click the Table button in the Tables group.
   b. Click the View button in the Views group in the Table Tools Fields tab.
   c. At the Save As dialog box, type **Renters** and then press Enter.
   d. Type **RenterID** in the *Field Name* column in the first row and then press the Tab key.
   e. Change the data type to Text by clicking the down-pointing arrow located in the *Data Type* column and then clicking *Text* at the drop-down list.
   f. Change the field size from the default of *255* to *3* by selecting *255* that displays in the *Field Size* property box in the *Field Properties* section and then typing *3*.
   g. Click in the *Description* column for the *RenterID* row, type **Enter three-digit renter identification number**, and then press the Tab key.

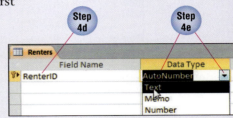
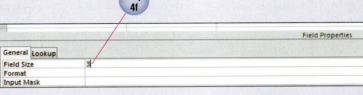
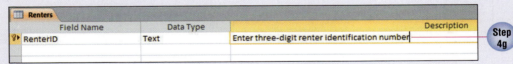

   h. Type **FirstName** in the *Field Name* column and then press the Tab key.
   i. Select *255* that displays in the *Field Size* property box in the *Field Properties* section and then type **20**.
   j. Click in the *Description* column for the *FirstName* row, type **Enter renter's first name**, and then press the Tab key.
   k. Type **LastName** in the *Field Name* column and then press the Tab key.
   l. Change the field size to *30* (at the *Field Size* property box).
   m. Click in the *Description* column for the *LastName* row, type **Enter renter's last name**, and then press the Tab key.
   n. Enter the remaining field names, data types, and descriptions as shown in Figure 4.2. (Change the field size to *4* for the *PropID* field, the field size to *5* for the *EmpID* field, and the field size to *3* for the *CreditScore* field.)
   o. When all fields are entered, click the Save button on the Quick Access toolbar.
   p. Make sure the *RenterID* field is identified as the primary key (a key icon displays in the *RenterID* field selector bar).
   q. Click the View button to return the table to Datasheet view.
5. Enter the records in the Renters table as shown in Figure 4.3.
6. After all records are entered, automatically adjust column widths.
7. Save and then close the Renters table.

Figure 4.2 Project 1a Renters Table in Design View

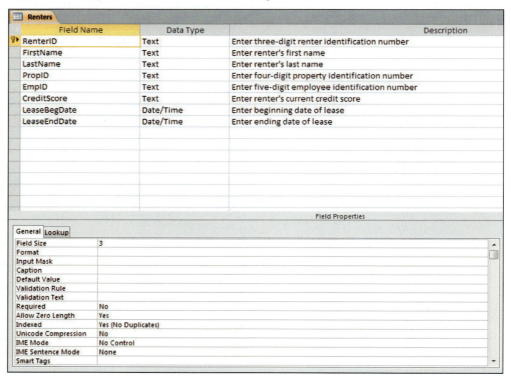

Figure 4.3 Project 1a Renters Table in Datasheet View

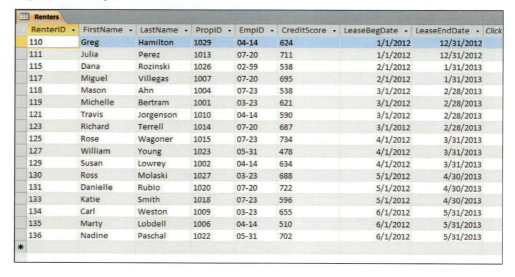

Assigning a Default Value

In Chapter 1, you learned how to specify a default value for a field in a table in Datasheet view using the Default Value button in the Properties group in the Table Tools Fields tab. In addition to this method, you can create a default value for a field in Design view with the *Default Value* property box in the *Field*

Properties section. Click in the *Default Value* property box and then type the desired field value. In Project 1b, you will create a health insurance field with a Yes/No data type. Since most of the agents of Sun Properties have signed up for health insurance benefits, you will set the default value for the field to *Yes*. If you add a new field that contains a default value to an existing table, the existing records will not reflect the default value, only new records entered in the table.

Using the Input Mask

For some fields, you may want to control the data entered in the field. For example, in a ZIP code field, you may want the nine-digit ZIP code entered (rather than the five-digit ZIP code); or you may want the three-digit area code included in a telephone number. Use the *Input Mask* field property to set a pattern for how data is entered in a field. An input mask ensures that data in records conforms to a standard format. Access includes an Input Mask Wizard that guides you through creating an input mask.

Use the Input Mask Wizard when assigning a data type to a field. In Design view, click in the Input Mask property box in the *Field Properties* section and then run the Input Mask Wizard by clicking the Build button (button containing three black dots) that appears at the right side of the Input Mask property box. This displays the first Input Mask Wizard dialog box as shown in Figure 4.4. In the *Input Mask* list box, choose which input mask you want your data to look like and then click the Next button. At the second Input Mask Wizard dialog box, as shown in Figure 4.5, specify the appearance of the input mask and the desired placeholder character and then click the Next button. At the third Input Mask Wizard dialog box, specify whether you want the data stored with or without the symbol in the mask and then click the Next button. At the fourth dialog box, click the Finish button.

▼ **Quick Steps**

Use Input Mask Wizard
1. Open table in Design view.
2. Type text in *Field Name* column.
3. Press Tab key.
4. Change data type to *Text*.
5. Click Save button.
6. Click in *Input Mask* property box.
7. Click Build button.
8. Complete wizard steps.

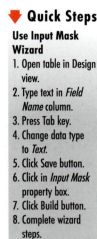

An input mask is a set of characters that control what you can and cannot enter in a field.

Build

Figure 4.4 First Input Mask Wizard Dialog Box

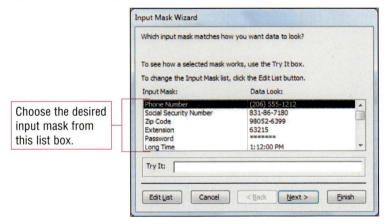

Choose the desired input mask from this list box.

Figure 4.5 Second Input Mask Wizard Dialog Box

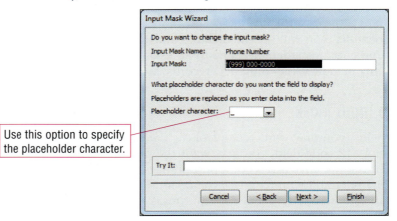

Use this option to specify the placeholder character.

Project 1b — Creating an Employees Table — Part 2 of 8

1. With the **AL1-C4-SunProperties.accdb** database open, create the Employees table in Design view as shown in Figure 4.6 on page 142. Begin by clicking the Create tab and then clicking the Table button.
2. Click the View button.
3. At the Save As dialog box, type **Employees** and then press Enter.
4. Type **EmpID** in the *Field Name* column in the first row and then press the Tab key.
5. Change the data type to Text by clicking the down-pointing arrow located in the *Data Type* column and then clicking *Text* at the drop-down list.
6. Change the field size from the default of *255* to *5* by selecting *255* that displays in the *Field Size* property box in the *Field Properties* section and then typing *5*.
7. Click in the *Description* column for the *EmpID* row, type **Enter five-digit employee identification number**, and then press the Tab key.

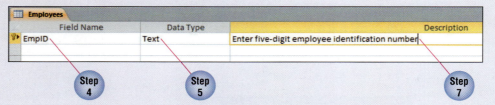

Step 4 | Step 5 | Step 7

8. Type **FName** in the *Field Name* column and then press the Tab key.
9. Select *255* that displays in the *Field Size* property box in the *Field Properties* section and then type **20**.
10. Click in the *Description* column for the *FName* row, type **Enter employee's first name**, and then press the Tab key.
11. Complete steps similar to those in Steps 8 through 10 to create the *LName*, *Address*, and *City* fields as shown in Figure 4.6. Change the field size for the *LName* field and *Address* field to *30* and change the *City* field to *20*.
12. Create the *State* field with a default value of *CA*, since all employees live in California, by completing the following steps:
    a. Type **State** in the *Field Name* column in the row below the *City* row and then press the Tab key.

b. Click in the *Default Value* property box in the *Field Properties* section and then type **CA**.

c. Click in the *Description* column for the *State* row, type **CA automatically entered as state**, and then press the Tab key.

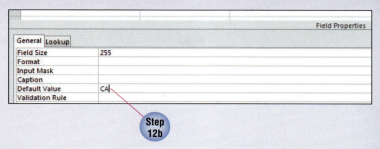

13. Type **ZIP** and then press the Tab key.
14. Select *255* that displays in the *Field Size* property box in the *Field Properties* section and then type **5**.
15. Click in the *Description* column for the ZIP row, type **Enter five-digit ZIP code**, and then press the Tab key.
16. Type **Telephone** and then press the Tab key.
17. Create an input mask for the telephone number by completing the following steps:
    a. Click the Save button to save the table. (You must save the table before using the Input Mask Wizard.)
    b. Click in the *Input Mask* property box in the *Field Properties* section.
    c. Click the Build button (button containing three black dots) that displays at the right side of the *Input Mask* property box.

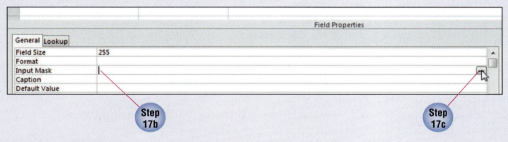

d. At the first *Input Mask* Wizard dialog box, make sure *Phone Number* is selected in the *Input Mask* list box and then click the Next button.

e. At the second Input Mask Wizard dialog box, click the down-pointing arrow at the right side of the *Placeholder character* box and then click **#** at the drop-down list.

Chapter 4 ■ Creating and Modifying Tables in Design View   141

f. Click the Next button.
g. At the third Input Mask Wizard dialog box, click the *With the symbols in the mask, like this* option.

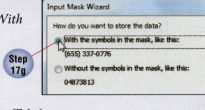

h. Click the Next button.
i. At the fourth Input Mask Wizard dialog box, click the Finish button.
18. Click in the *Description* column in the *Telephone* row, type **Enter employee's telephone number**, and then press the Tab key.
19. Type **HealthIns** and then press the Tab key.
20. Click the down-pointing arrow in the *Data Type* column and then click *Yes/No* at the drop-down list.
21. Click in the *Default Value* property box in the *Field Properties* section and then type **Yes**.
22. Click in the *Description* column for the *HealthIns* row, type **Leave check mark if employee is signed up for health insurance**, and then press the Tab key.
23. Type **DentalIns** and then press the Tab key.
24. Click the down-pointing arrow in the *Data Type* column and then click *Yes/No* at the drop-down list.
25. Click in the *Description* column for the *DentalIns* row, type **Insert check mark if employee is signed up for dental insurance**, and then press the Tab key.
26. When all fields are entered, click the Save button on the Quick Access toolbar.
27. Click the View button to return the table to Datasheet view.
28. Enter the records in the Employees table as shown in Figure 4.7.
29. After all records are entered, automatically adjust the widths of columns in the table.
30. Save and then close the Employees table.

Figure 4.6 Project 1b Employees Table in Design View

Field Name	Data Type	Description
EmpID	Text	Enter five-digit employee identification number
FName	Text	Enter employee's first name
LName	Text	Enter employee's last name
Address	Text	Enter employee's address
City	Text	Enter employee's city
State	Text	CA automatically entered as state
ZIP	Text	Enter five-digit ZIP code
Telephone	Text	Enter employee's telephone number
HealthIns	Yes/No	Leave check mark if employee is signed up for health insurance
DentalIns	Yes/No	Insert check mark if employee is signed up for dental insurance

Figure 4.7 Project 1b Employees Table in Datasheet View

EmpID	FName	LName	Address	City	State	ZIP	Telephone	HealthIns	DentalIns	Click
02-59	Christina	Solomon	12241 East 51st	Citrus Heights	CA	95611	(916) 555-8844	✓	✓	
03-23	Douglas	Ricci	903 Mission Road	Roseville	CA	95678	(916) 555-4125	✓	☐	
03-55	Tatiana	Kasadev	6558 Orchard Drive	Citrus Heights	CA	95610	(916) 555-8534	✓	☐	
04-14	Brian	West	12232 142nd Avenue East	Citrus Heights	CA	95611	(916) 555-0967	✓	✓	
04-32	Kathleen	Addison	21229 19th Street	Citrus Heights	CA	95621	(916) 555-3408	✓	✓	
05-20	Teresa	Villanueva	19453 North 42nd Street	Citrus Heights	CA	95611	(916) 555-2302	✓	✓	
05-31	Marcia	Griswold	211 Haven Road	North Highlands	CA	95660	(916) 555-1449	☐	☐	
06-24	Tiffany	Gentry	12312 North 20th	Roseville	CA	95661	(916) 555-0043	✓	✓	
06-33	Joanna	Gallegos	6850 York Street	Roseville	CA	95747	(916) 555-7446	☐	☐	
07-20	Jesse	Scholtz	3412 South 21st Street	Fair Oaks	CA	95628	(916) 555-4204	✓	☐	
07-23	Eugene	Bond	530 Laurel Road	Orangevale	CA	95662	(916) 555-9412	✓	☐	
*					CA			✓	☐	

Validating Field Entries

Use the *Validation Rule* property box in the *Field Properties* section in Design view to enter a statement containing a conditional test that is checked each time data is entered into a field. If you enter data that fails to satisfy the conditional test, Access does not accept the entry and displays an error message. By entering a conditional statement in the *Validation Rule* property box that checks each entry against the acceptable range, you can reduce errors. Enter in the *Validation Text* property box the content of the error message that you want to display.

Using the Lookup Wizard

Like the Input Mask Wizard, you can use the Lookup Wizard to control the data entered in a field. Use the Lookup Wizard to confine the data entered into a field to a specific list of items. For example, in Project 1c you will use the Lookup Wizard to restrict the new *EmpCategory* field to one of three choices—*Salaried*, *Hourly*, and *Temporary*. When the user clicks in the field in the datasheet, a down-pointing arrow displays. The user clicks this down-pointing arrow to display a drop-down list of available entries and then clicks the desired item.

Use the Lookup Wizard when assigning a data type to a field. Click in the desired field in the *Data Type* column and then click the down-pointing arrow that displays at the right side of the field. At the drop-down list that displays, click *Lookup Wizard*. This displays the first Lookup Wizard dialog box as shown in Figure 4.8. At this dialog box, indicate that you want to enter the field choices by clicking the *I will type in the values that I want* option and then click the Next button. At the second Lookup Wizard dialog box shown in Figure 4.9, click in the blank text box below *Col1* and then type the first choice. Press the Tab key and then type the second choice. Continue in this manner until all desired choices are entered and then click the Next button. At the third Lookup Wizard dialog box, make sure the proper name displays in the *What label would you like for your lookup column?* text box and then click the Finish button.

HINT
Enter a validation rule in a field to control what is entered in the field and to reduce errors. Create validation text that displays when someone enters invalid data in the field.

▼ **Quick Steps**
Use Lookup Wizard
1. Open table in Design view.
2. Type text in *Field Name* column.
3. Press Tab key.
4. Click down-pointing arrow.
5. Click *Lookup Wizard*.
6. Complete wizard steps.

Figure 4.8 First Lookup Wizard Dialog Box

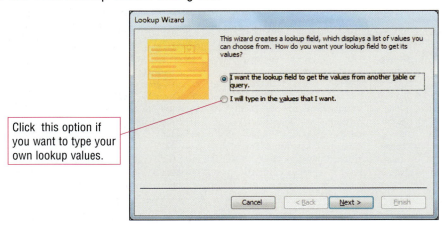

Figure 4.9 Second Lookup Wizard Dialog Box

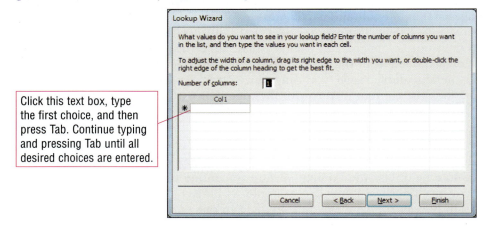

Quick Steps

Insert Field in Design View
1. Open table in Design view.
2. Click in row that will follow new field.
3. Click Insert Rows button.

Delete Field in Design View
1. Open table in Design view.
2. Click in row to be deleted.
3. Click Delete Rows button.
4. Click Yes.

Insert Rows

Inserting, Moving, and Deleting Fields in Design View

In Chapter 1, you learned how to insert, move, and delete fields in a table in Datasheet view. You can also perform these tasks in Design view. To insert a new field in a table in Design view, position the insertion point in a field in the row that will be located immediately *below* the new field and then click the Insert Rows button in the Tools group in the Table Tools Design tab. Or, position the insertion point on any text in the row that will display immediately *below* the new field, click the right mouse button, and then click *Insert Rows* at the shortcut menu. If you insert a row for a new field and then change your mind, immediately click the Undo button on the Quick Access toolbar. Remember that a *row* in the Design view creates a *field* in the table.

You can move a field in a table to a different location in Datasheet view or Design view. To move a field in Design view, click in the field selector bar at the left side of the row you want to move. With the row selected, position the arrow pointer in the field selector bar at the left side of the selected row, hold down the left mouse button, drag the arrow pointer with a gray square attached until a thick black line displays in the desired position, and then release the mouse button.

Delete a field in a table and all data entered in that field is also deleted. When you delete a field, it cannot be undone with the Undo button. Delete a field only if you are sure you really want it and the data associated with it completely removed from the table. To delete a field in Design view, click in the field selector bar at the left side of the row you want to delete and then click the Delete Rows button in the Tools group. At the message asking if you want to permanently delete the field and all of the data in the field, click Yes. You can also delete a row by positioning the mouse pointer in the row you want to delete, clicking the right mouse button, and then clicking *Delete Rows* at the shortcut menu.

Delete Rows

Inserting a Total Row

You can add a total row in a table in Datasheet view and then choose from a list of functions to find the sum, average, maximum, minimum, count, standard deviations, or variance result in a numeric column. To insert a total row, click the Totals button in the Records group in the Home tab. Access adds a row to the bottom of the table with the label *Total* at the left. Click in the *Total* row, click the down-pointing arrow that appears, and then click the desired function at the drop-down list.

Quick Steps
Insert a Total Row
1. Open table in Datasheet view.
2. Click Totals button.
3. Click in *Total* row.
4. Click down-pointing arrow.
5. Click desired function.

Totals

Project 1c — Validating Field Entries; Using the Lookup Wizard; and Inserting, Moving, and Deleting a Field — Part 3 of 8

1. With the **AL1-C4-SunProperties.accdb** database open, open the Employees table.
2. Insert in the Employees table a new field and apply a validation rule by completing the following steps:
   a. Click the View button to switch to Design view.
   b. Click in the empty field immediately below the *DentalIns* field in the *Field Name* column and then type **LifeIns**.
   c. Press the Tab key.
   d. Click the down-pointing arrow at the right side of the *Data Type* field and then click *Currency* at the drop-down list.
   e. Click in the *Validation Rule* property box, type **<=100000**, and then press Enter.
   f. With the insertion point positioned in the *Validation Text* property box, type **Enter a value that is equal to or less than $100,000.**
   g. Click in the field in the *Description* column for the *LifeIns* row and then type **Enter optional life insurance amount**.
   h. Click the Save button on the Quick Access toolbar. Since the validation rule was created *after* data was entered into the table, Access displays a warning message indicating that some data may not be valid. At this message, click No.
   i. Click the View button to switch to Datasheet view.
3. Click in the first empty field in the *LifeIns* column, type **200000**, and then press the Down Arrow key.

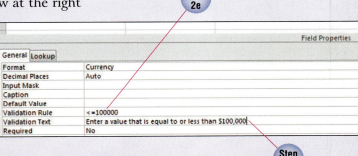

4. Access inserts the error message telling you to enter an amount that is equal to or less than $100,000. At this error message, click OK.
5. Edit the amount in the field so it displays as 100000 and then press the Down Arrow key.
6. Type the following entries in the remaining fields in the *LifeIns* column:

    25000
    0
    50000
    50000
    0
    100000
    50000
    25000
    0
    100000

7. Insert the field *EmpCategory* in the Employees table and use the Lookup Wizard to specify field choices by completing the following steps:
    a. Click the View button to change to Design view.
    b. Click on any character in the *FName* field entry in the *Field Name* column.
    c. Click the Insert Rows button in the Tools group.
    d. With the insertion point positioned in the new blank field in the *Field Name* column, type **EmpCategory**.
    e. Press the Tab key. (This moves the insertion point to the *Data Type* column.)
    f. Click the down-pointing arrow at the right side of the *Data Type* field and then click *Lookup Wizard* at the drop-down list.
    g. At the first Lookup Wizard dialog box, click the *I will type in the values that I want* option and then click the Next button.

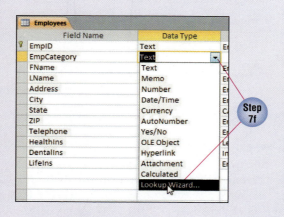

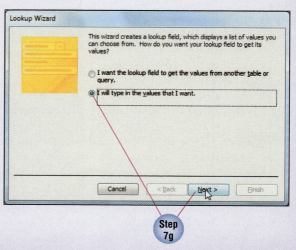

h. At the second Lookup Wizard dialog box, click in the blank text box below *Col1*, type **Salaried**, and then press the Tab key.
i. Type **Hourly** and then press the Tab key.
j. Type **Temporary**.
k. Click the Next button.
l. At the third Lookup Wizard dialog box, click the Finish button.
m. Press the Tab key and then type **Click down-pointing arrow and then click employee category** in the *Description* column.

8. Click the Save button on the Quick Access toolbar.
9. Click the View button to switch to Datasheet view.
10. Insert information in the *EmpCategory* column by completing the following steps:
    a. Click in the first blank field in the new *EmpCategory* field.
    b. Click the down-pointing arrow at the right side of the field and then click *Hourly* at the drop-down list.
    c. Click in the next blank field in the *EmpCategory* column, click the down-pointing arrow, and then click *Salaried* at the drop-down list.
    d. Continue entering information in the *EmpCategory* column by completing similar steps. Choose the following in the specified record:
       Third record: *Hourly*
       Fourth record: *Salaried*
       Fifth record: *Temporary*
       Sixth record: *Hourly*
       Seventh record: *Salaried*
       Eighth record: *Temporary*
       Ninth record: *Hourly*
       Tenth record: *Salaried*
       Eleventh record: *Salaried*

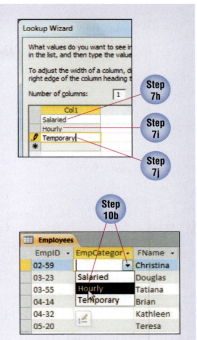

11. Print the Employees table. (The table will print on two pages.)
12. After looking at the printing of the table, you decide to move the *EmpCategory* field. You also need to delete the *DentalIns* field since Sun Properties no longer offers dental insurance benefits to employees. Move the *EmpCatgory* field and delete the *DentalIns* field in Design view by completing the following steps:
    a. With the Employees table open, click the View button to switch to Design view.
    b. Click in the field selector bar at the left side of the *EmpCategory* field to select the row.
    c. Position the arrow pointer in the *EmpCategory* field selector bar, hold down the left mouse button, drag down until a thick black line displays below the *Telephone* field, and then release the mouse button.

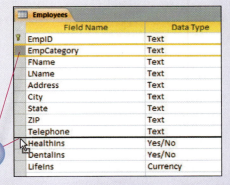

Chapter 4 ■ Creating and Modifying Tables in Design View   147

13. Delete the *DentalIns* field by completing the following steps:
    a. Click in the field selector bar at the left side of the *DentalIns* row. (This selects the row.)
    b. Click the Delete Rows button in the Tools group.
    c. At the message asking if you want to permanently delete the field and all of the data in the field, click Yes.
14. Click the Save button on the Quick Access toolbar.
15. Click the View button to switch to Datasheet view.
16. Print the Employees table. (The table will print on two pages.)
17. Close the Employees table.
18. Open the Payments table and then insert a new field and apply a validation rule by completing the following steps:

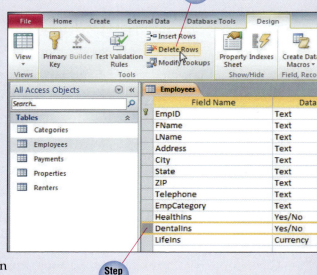

    a. Click the View button to switch to Design view.
    b. Click in the empty field immediately below the *PymntAmount* field in the *Field Name* column and then type **LateFee**.
    c. Press the Tab key.
    d. Click the down-pointing arrow at the right side of the *Text* box and then click *Currency* at the drop-down list.
    e. Click in the *Validation Rule* property box, type **<=50**, and then press Enter.
    f. With the insertion point positioned in the *Validation Text* property box, type **Late fee must be $50 or less**.
    g. Click in the box in the *Description* column for the *LateFee* field and then type **Enter a late fee amount if applicable**.
    h. Click the Save button on the Quick Access toolbar. Since the validation rule was created *after* data was entered into the table, Access displays a warning message indicating that some data may not be valid. At this message, click No.
    i. Click the View button to switch to Datasheet view.
19. Insert late fees for the last three records by completing the following steps:
    a. Click in the *LateFee* field for record 15, type **25**, and then press the Down Arrow key.
    b. With the *LateFee* field for record 16 active, type **25** and then press the Down Arrow key.
    c. With the *LateFee* field for record 17 active, type **50** and then press the Up Arrow key.

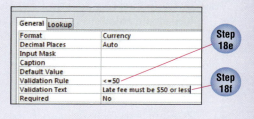

20. Insert a total row by completing the following steps:
    a. In Datasheet view, click the Totals button in the Records group in the Home tab.
    b. Click in the blank field in the *PymntAmount* column in the *Total* row.
    c. Click the down-pointing arrow at the left side of the field and then click *Sum* at the drop-down list.
    d. Click in the blank field in the *LateFee* column in the *Total* row.
    e. Click the down-pointing arrow at the left side of the field and then click *Sum* at the drop-down list.
    f. Click in any other field.
21. Save, print, and then close the Payments table.

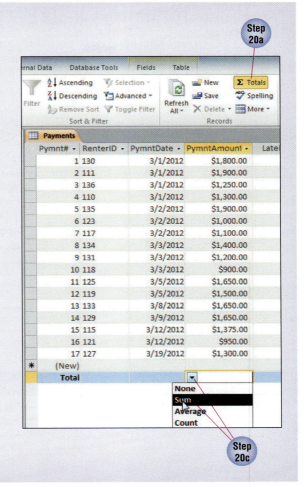

Sorting Records

The Sort & Filter group in the Home tab contains two buttons you can use to sort data in records. Click the Ascending button to sort data in the active field in alphabetic order from A to Z or numbers from lowest to highest, or click the Descending button to sort data in alphabetic order from Z to A or numbers from highest to lowest.

Printing Specific Records

If you want to print specific records in a table, select the records and then display the Print dialog box by clicking the File tab, clicking the Print tab, and then clicking the *Print* option. At the Print dialog box, click the *Selected Record(s)* option in the *Print Range* section and then click OK. To select specific records, display the table in Datasheet view, click the record selector of the first record and then drag to select the desired records. The record selector is the light blue square that displays at the left side of the record. When you position the mouse pointer on the record selector, the pointer turns into a right-pointing black arrow.

Quick Steps

Sort Records
1. Open table in Datasheet view.
2. Click in field in desired column.
3. Click Ascending button or Descending button.

Ascending

Descending

Chapter 4 ■ Creating and Modifying Tables in Design View   149

Formatting Table Data

Quick Steps

Print Selected Records
1. Open table and select records.
2. Click File tab.
3. Click Print tab.
4. Click *Print* option.
5. Click *Selected Record(s)*.
6. Click OK.

In Datasheet view, you can apply formatting to data in a table. Formatting options are available in the Text Formatting group in the Home tab as shown in Figure 4.10. To apply formatting, open a table in Datasheet view and then click the desired button in the Text Formatting group. The button formatting is applied to all of the data in the table. (Some of the buttons in the Text Formatting are dimmed and unavailable. These buttons are available for fields formatted as rich text.) The buttons available for formatting a table are shown in Table 4.2.

Click the Align Text Left, Center, or Align Text Right button and formatting is applied to text in the currently active column. Click one of the other buttons shown in Table 4.2 and formatting is applied to all columns and rows of data in

Figure 4.10 Home Tab Text Formatting Group

Table 4.2 Text Formatting Buttons

Button	Name	Description
Calibri (Detail)	Font	Change text font.
11	Font Size	Change text size.
B	Bold	Bold text.
I	Italic	Italicize text.
U	Underline	Underline text.
A	Font Color	Change text color.
	Background Color	Apply a background color to all fields.
	Align Text Left	Align all text in the currently active column at the left side of the fields.
	Center	Center all text in the currently active column in the center of the fields.
	Align Text Right	Align all text in the currently active column at the right side of the fields.
	Gridlines	Specify whether or not you want vertical and/or horizontal gridlines displayed.
	Alternate Row Color	Apply specified color to alternating rows in the table.

the table except the Background Color button that applies formatting to all fields in the table.

When creating a table, you specify a data type for a field such as the Text, Date, or Currency data type. If you want to format text in a field rather than all fields in a column or the entire table, you need to choose the Memo data type and then specify rich text formatting. For example, in Project 1d you will format specific credit scores in the *CreditScore* field column. To be able to format specific scores, you need to change the data type to Memo and then specify rich text formatting. Use the Memo data type only for fields containing text and not fields containing currency amounts, numbers, and dates.

To change the data type to Memo, open the table in Design view, click in the *Data Type* column for the desired field, click the down-pointing arrow, and then click *Memo* at the drop-down list. By default, the Memo data type uses plain text formatting. To change to rich text, click in the *Text Format* property box in the *Field Properties* section (displays with the text *Plain Text*), click the down-pointing arrow that displays at the right side of the property box, and then click *Rich Text* at the drop-down list.

Project 1d Sorting, Printing, and Formatting Records and Fields in Tables Part 4 of 8

1. With the **AL1-C4-SunProperties.accdb** database open, open the Renters table.
2. With the table in Datasheet view, sort records in ascending alphabetical order by last name by completing the following steps:
   a. Click any last name in the *LastName* field in the table.
   b. Click the Ascending button in the Sort & Filter group in the Home tab.
   c. Print the Renters table in landscape orientation.
3. Sort records in descending order (highest to lowest) by credit score number by completing the following steps:
   a. Click any number in the *CreditScore* field.
   b. Click the Descending button in the Sort & Filter group.
   c. Print the Renters table in landscape orientation.
4. Close the Renters table without saving the changes.
5. Open the Properties table.
6. Sort and then print selected records with the apartment property type by completing the following steps:
   a. Click any entry in the *CatID* field.
   b. Click the Ascending button in the Sort & Filter group.
   c. Position the mouse pointer on the record selector of the first record with *A* for a category ID, hold down the mouse button, and then drag to select the four records with a category ID of *A*.

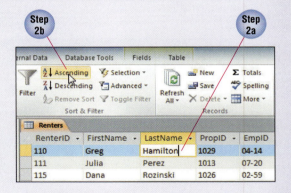

d. Click the File tab, click the Print tab, and then click the *Print* option.
e. At the Print dialog box, click the *Selected Record(s)* option in the *Print Range* section.

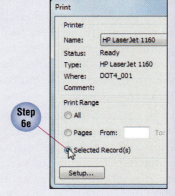

f. Click OK.
7. With the Properties table open, apply the following text formatting:
   a. Click in any field in the *CatID* column and then click the Center button in the Text Formatting group in the Home tab.

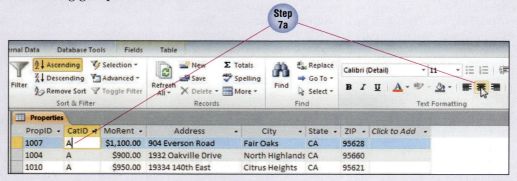

   b. Click in any field in the *PropID* column and then click the Center button in the Text Formatting group.
   c. Click the Bold button in the Text Formatting group. (This applies bold to all text in the table.)
   d. Click the Font Color button arrow and then click the *Dark Blue* color (located in the top row in the fourth column from the left in the *Standard Colors* section).
   e. Adjust the column widths.
   f. Save, print, and then close the Properties table.
8. Open the Payments table and apply the following text formatting:
   a. With the first field active in the *Pymnt#* column, click the Center button in the Text Formatting group in the Home tab.
   b. Click in any field in the *RenterID* column and then click the Center button in the Text Formatting group.

c. Click the Font button arrow, scroll down the drop-down list that displays, and then click *Candara*. (Fonts are listed in alphabetical order in the drop-down list.)
d. Click the Font Size button arrow and then click *12* at the drop-down list.
e. Click the Alternate Row Color button arrow and then click the *Green 2* color (located in the third row of the seventh column from the left in the *Standard Colors* section).

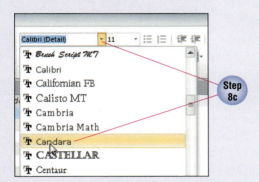

f. Adjust the column widths.
g. Save, print, and then close the Payments table.
9. Open the Renters table and then apply the following formatting to columns in the table:
a. With the first field active in the *RenterID* column, click the Center button in the Text Formatting group in the Home tab.
b. Click in any field in the *PropID* column and then click the Center button.
c. Click in any field in the *EmpID* column and then click the Center button
d. Click in any field in the *CreditScore* column and then click the Center button.
10. Change the data type for the *CreditScore* field to Memo with rich text formatting, and apply formatting by completing the following steps:
a. Click the View button to switch to Design view.
b. Click in the *Data Type* column in the *CreditScore* row, click the down-pointing arrow that displays in the field, and then click *Memo* at the drop-down list.
c. Click in the *Text Format* property box in the *Field Properties* section (displays with the words *Plain Text*), click the down-pointing arrow that displays at the right side of the property box, and then click *Rich Text* at the drop-down list.

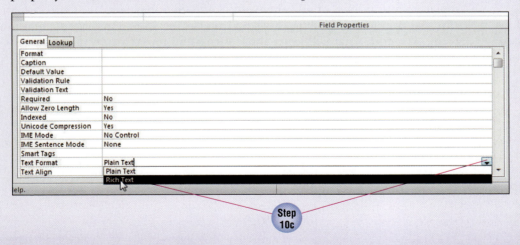

Chapter 4 ■ Creating and Modifying Tables in Design View   153

d. At the message that displays telling you that the field will be converted to rich text, click the Yes button.
e. Click the Save button on the Quick Access toolbar.
f. Click the View button to switch to Datasheet view.
g. Double-click on the field value *538* that displays in the *CreditScore* column in the row for Dana Rozinski. (Double-clicking in the field selects the field value *538*.)
h. With *538* selected, click the Font Color button in the Text Formatting group. (This changes the number to red. If the font color does not change to red, click the Font Color button arrow and then click the *Red* color in the bottom row of the *Standard Colors* section.)

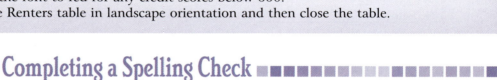

i. Change the font to red for any credit scores below 600.
j. Print the Renters table in landscape orientation and then close the table.

Completing a Spelling Check

Quick Steps

Complete a Spelling Check
1. Open table in Datasheet view.
2. Click Spelling button.
3. Change or ignore spelling as needed.
4. Click OK.

You can also begin spell checking with the keyboard shortcut F7.

Spelling

The spell checking feature in Access finds misspelled words and offers replacement words. It also finds duplicate words and irregular capitalizations. When you spell check an object in a database such as a table, the spelling checker compares the words in your table with the words in its dictionary. If a match is found, the word is passed over. If no match is found for the word, the spelling checker selects the word and offers replacement suggestions.

To complete a spelling check, open the desired table in Datasheet view and then click the Spelling button in the Records group in the Home tab. If the spelling checker does not find a match for a word in your table, the Spelling dialog box displays with replacement options. Figure 4.11 displays the Spelling dialog box with the word *Citruis* selected and possible replacements displayed in the *Suggestions* list box. At the Spelling dialog box, you can choose to ignore the word (for example, if the spelling checker has selected a proper name), change to one of the replacement options, or add the word to the dictionary or AutoCorrect feature. You can also complete a spelling check on other objects in a database such as a query, form, or report. (You will learn about forms and reports in future chapters.)

Figure 4.11 Spelling Dialog Box

The spelling checker selects this word in the table and offers suggestions in this list box.

Project 1e — Checking Spelling in a Table — Part 5 of 8

1. With the **AL1-C4-SunProperties.accdb** database open, open the Employees table.
2. Delete the *LifeIns* field by completing the following steps:
   a. Click the View button to switch to the Design view.
   b. Click in the field selector bar at the left side of the *LifeIns* row. (This selects the row.)
   c. Click the Delete Rows button in the Tools group.
   d. At the message asking if you want to permanently delete the field and all of the data in the field, click Yes.
   e. Click the Save button on the Quick Access toolbar.
   f. Click the View button to switch to Datasheet view.
3. Add the following record to the Employees table. (Type the misspelled words as shown below. You will correct the spelling in a later step.)
EmpID	=	02-72
FName	=	Roben
LName	=	Wildre
Address	=	9945 Valley Avenue
City	=	Citruis Heights
State	=	(CA automatically inserted)
ZIP	=	95610
Telephone	=	9165556522
EmpCategory	=	(choose *Salaried*)
HealthIns	=	No (Remove check mark)
4. Save the Employees table.
5. Click in the first entry in the *EmpID* column.
6. Click the Spelling button in the Records group in the Home tab.
7. The spelling checker selects the name *Kasadev*. This is a proper name, so click the Ignore button to tell the spelling checker to leave the name as written.

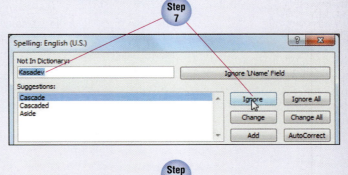

8. The spelling checker selects the name *Scholtz*. This is a proper name, so click the Ignore button to tell the spelling checker to leave the name as written.
9. The spelling checker selects *Roben*. The proper spelling *(Robin)* is selected in the *Suggestions* list box, so click the Change button.

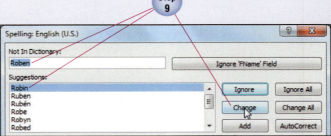

10. The spelling checker selects *Wildre*. The proper spelling *(Wilder)* is selected in the *Suggestions* list box, so click the Change button.
11. The spelling checker selects *Citruis*. The proper spelling *(Citrus)* is selected in the *Suggestions* list box, so click the Change button.
12. At the message telling you that the spelling check is complete, click the OK button.
13. Print the Employees table and then close the table.

Finding and Replacing Data

▼ **Quick Steps**

Find Data
1. Open table in Datasheet view.
2. Click Find button.
3. Type data in *Find What* text box.
4. Click Find Next button.

Find and Replace Data
1. Open table in Datasheet view.
2. Click Replace button.
3. Type find data in *Find What* text box.
4. Type replace data in *Replace With* text box.
5. Click Find Next button.
6. Click Replace button or Find Next button.

Press Ctrl + F to display the Find and Replace dialog box with the Find tab selected.

Press Ctrl + H to display the Find and Replace dialog box with the Replace tab selected.

Find

Replace

If you need to find a specific entry in a field in a table, consider using options at the Find and Replace dialog box with the Find tab selected as shown in Figure 4.12. Display this dialog box by clicking the Find button in the Find group in the Home tab. At the Find and Replace dialog box, enter the data for which you are searching in the *Find What* text box. By default, Access will look in the specific column where the insertion point is positioned. Click the Find Next button to find the next occurrence of the data or click the Cancel button to remove the Find and Replace dialog box.

The *Look In* option defaults to the column where the insertion point is positioned. You can choose to look in the entire table by clicking the down-pointing arrow at the right side of the option and then clicking the table name at the drop-down list. The *Match* option has a default setting of *Whole Field*. You can change this to *Any Part of Field* or *Start of Field*. The *Search* option has a default setting of *All*, which means that Access will search all data in a specific column. This can be changed to *Up* or *Down*. If you want to find data that contains specific uppercase and lowercase letters, insert a check mark in the *Match Case* check box. By default, Access will search fields as they are formatted.

You can use the Find and Replace dialog box with the Replace tab selected to search for specific data and replace with other data. Display this dialog box by clicking the Replace button in the Find group in the Home tab.

Figure 4.12 Find and Replace Dialog Box with Find Tab Selected

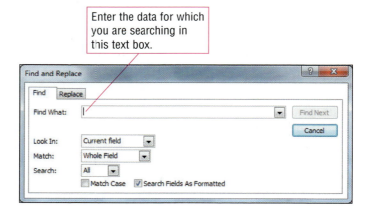

Project 1f Finding and Replacing Data, Creating Relationships, and Performing Queries — Part 6 of 8

1. With the **AL1-C4-SunProperties.accdb** database open, open the Properties table.
2. Find records containing the ZIP code *95610* by completing the following steps:
   a. Click in the first field in the *ZIP* column.
   b. Click the Find button in the Find group in the Home tab.
   c. At the Find and Replace dialog box with the Find tab selected, type **95610** in the *Find What* text box.
   d. Click the Find Next button. (Access finds and selects the first occurrence of *95610*. If the Find and Replace dialog box covers the data, drag the dialog box to a different location on the screen.)

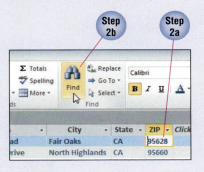
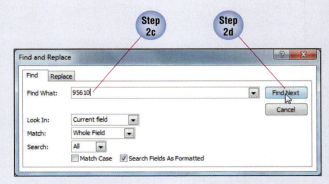

   e. Continue clicking the Find Next button until a message displays telling you that Access has finished searching the records. At this message, click OK.
   f. Click the Cancel button to close the Find and Replace dialog box.
3. Suppose a new ZIP code has been added to the city of North Highlands and you need to change to this new ZIP for some of the North Highlands properties. Complete the following steps to find *95660* and replace it with *95668*:
   a. Click in the first field in the *ZIP* column.
   b. Click the Replace button in the Find group.
   c. At the Find and Replace dialog box with the Replace tab selected, type **95660** in the *Find What* text box.
   d. Press the Tab key. (This moves the insertion point to the *Replace With* text box.)
   e. Type **95668** in the *Replace With* text box.
   f. Click the Find Next button.
   g. When Access selects the first occurrence of *95660*, click the Replace button.
   h. When Access selects the second occurrence of *95660*, click the Find Next button.
   i. When Access selects the third occurrence of *95660* click the Replace button.
   j. When Access selects the fourth occurrence of *95660*, click the Find Next button.
   k. When Access selects the fifth occurrence of *95660*, click the Find Next button.
   l. When Access selects the sixth occurrence of *95660*, click the Replace button.
   m. Access selects the first occurrence of *95660* (record 1018) in the table. Click the Cancel button to close the Find and Replace dialog box.
4. Print and then close the Properties table.

5. Display the Relationships window and then create the following relationships (enforce referential integrity and cascade fields and records):
   a. Create a one-to-many relationship with the *CatID* field in the Categories table the "one" and the *CatID* field in the Properties table the "many."
   b. Create a one-to-many relationship with the *EmpID* field in the Employees table the "one" and the *EmpID* field in the Renters table the "many."
   c. Create a one-to-many relationship with the *PropID* field in the Properties table the "one" and the *PropID* field in the Renters table the "many."
   d. Create a one-to-many relationship with the *RenterID* field in the Renters table the "one" and the *RenterID* field in the Payments table the "many."
   e. Save the relationships and then print the relationships in landscape orientation.
   f. Close the relationships report without saving it and then close the Relationships window.
6. Design a query that displays employees with health insurance benefits with the following specifications:
   a. Insert the Employees table in the query window.
   b. Insert the *EmpID* field in the first *Field* row field.
   c. Insert the *FName* field in the second *Field* row field.
   d. Insert the *LName* field in the third *Field* row field.
   e. Insert the *HealthIns* field in the fourth *Field* row field.
   f. Click in the check box in the *Show* row field in the *EmpID* column to remove the check mark. (This hides the EmpID numbers in the query results.)

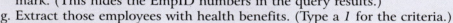

   g. Extract those employees with health benefits. (Type a *1* for the criteria.)
   h. Run the query.
   i. Save the query and name it *EmpsWithHealthInsQuery*.
   j. Print and then close the query.
7. Design a query that displays all properties in the city of Citrus Heights with the following specifications:
   a. Insert the Properties table and the Categories table in the query window.
   b. Insert the *PropID* field from the Properties table in the first *Field* row field.
   c. Insert the *Category* field from the Categories table in the second *Field* row field.
   d. Insert the *Address*, *City*, *State*, and *ZIP* fields from the Properties table to the third, fourth, fifth, and sixth *Field* row fields.
   e. Extract those properties in the city of Citrus Heights.
   f. Run the query.
   g. Save the query and name it *CitrusHeightsPropsQuery*.
   h. Print and then close the query.
8. Design a query that displays rent payments made between 3/1/2012 and 3/5/2012 with the following specifications:
   a. Insert the Payments table and the Renters table in the query window.
   b. Insert the *Pymnt#*, *PymntDate*, and *PymntAmount* fields from the Payments table in the first, second, and third *Field* row fields.
   c. Insert the *FirstName* and *LastName* fields from the Renters table in the fourth and fifth *Field* row fields.
   d. Extract those payments made between 3/1/2012 and 3/5/2012.

e. Run the query.
   f. Save the query and name it *Pymnts3/1To3/5Query*.
   g. Print and then close the query.
9. Design a query that displays properties in Citrus Heights or Orangevale that rent for less than $1,501 a month as well as the type of property with the following specifications:
   a. Insert the Categories table and the Properties table in the query window.
   b. Insert the *Category* field from the Categories table.
   c. Insert the *PropID*, *MoRent*, *Address*, *City*, *State*, and *ZIP* fields from the Properties table.
   d. Extract those properties in Citrus Heights and Orangevale that rent for less than $1,501.
   e. Run the query.
   f. Save the query and name it *RentLessThan$1501InCHAndOVQuery*.
   g. Print the query in landscape orientation and then close the query.
10. Design a query that displays properties in Citrus Heights assigned to employee identification number *07-20* with the following specifications:
    a. Insert the Employees table and the Properties table in the query window.
    b. Insert the *EmpID*, *FName*, and *LName* fields from the Employees table.
    c. Insert the *Address*, *City*, *State*, and *ZIP* fields from the Properties table.
    d. Extract those properties in Citrus Heights assigned to EmpID 07-20.
    e. Run the query.
    f. Save the query and name it *Emp07-20CHPropsQuery*.
    g. Print and then close the query.

Using Help

Microsoft Access includes a Help feature that contains information about Access features and commands. This on-screen reference manual is similar to Windows Help and the Help features in Word, PowerPoint, and Excel. Click the Microsoft Access Help button (the circle with the question mark) located in the upper right corner of the screen or press the keyboard shortcut F1 to display the Access Help window. In this window, type a topic, feature, or question in the search text box and then press the Enter key. Topics related to the search text display in the Access Help window. Click a topic that interests you. If the topic window contains a Show All hyperlink in the upper right corner, click this hyperlink and the topic options expand to show additional help information related to the topic. When you click the Show All hyperlink, it becomes the Hide All hyperlink.

Getting Help at the Help Tab Backstage View

The Help tab Backstage view, shown in Figure 4.13, contains an option for displaying the Access Help window as well as other options. Click the *Microsoft Office Help* option in the Support category to display the Access Help window and click the *Getting Started* option to access the Microsoft website that displays information about getting started with Access 2010. Click the *Contact Us* option in the Support category and the Microsoft Support website displays. Click *Options* in the Tools for Working With Office category and the Access Options dialog box displays. You will learn about this dialog box in a later chapter. Click the *Check for Updates* option and the Microsoft Update website displays with information on available updates. The right side of the Help tab Backstage view displays information about Office and Access.

▼ **Quick Steps**

Use the Help Feature
1. Click Microsoft Access Help button.
2. Type topic or feature.
3. Press Enter.
4. Click desired topic.

Display Help Tab Backstage View
1. Click File tab.
2. Click Help button.

Press F1 to display the Access Help window.

Help

Figure 4.13 Help Tab Backstage View

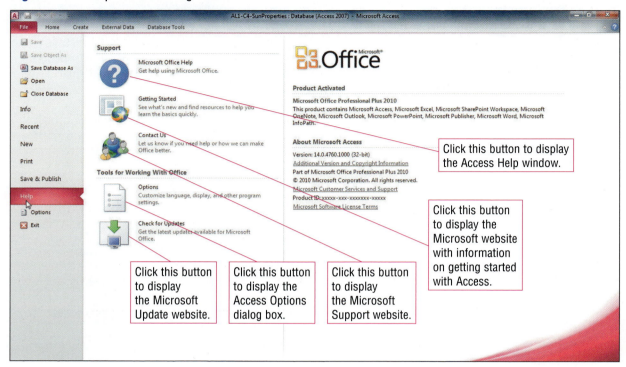

 **Using the Help Feature** Part 7 of 8

1. With the **AL1-C4-SunProperties.accdb** open, click the Microsoft Access Help button located in the upper right corner of the screen.
2. At the Access Help window, type **input mask** in the search text box and then press Enter. (Make sure that *Connected to Office.com* displays in the lower right corner of the window. If not, click the Search button arrow and then click *Content from Office.com* at the drop-down list.
3. When the list of topics displays, click the Control data entry formats with input masks hyperlink.
4. Read the information on creating an input mask. (If you want a printout of the information, you can click the Print button located toward the top of the Access Help window and then click the Print button at the Print dialog box.)
5. Close the Access Help window by clicking the Close button located in the upper right corner of the window.

6. Click the File tab and then click the Help tab.
7. At the Help tab Backstage view, click the *Getting Started* option in the Support category. (You must be connected to the Internet to display the web page.)
8. Look at the information that displays at the website and then click the Close button located in the upper right corner of the web page.
9. Click the File tab and then click the Help tab.
10. Click the *Contact Us* option, look at the information that displays at the website, and then close the web page.

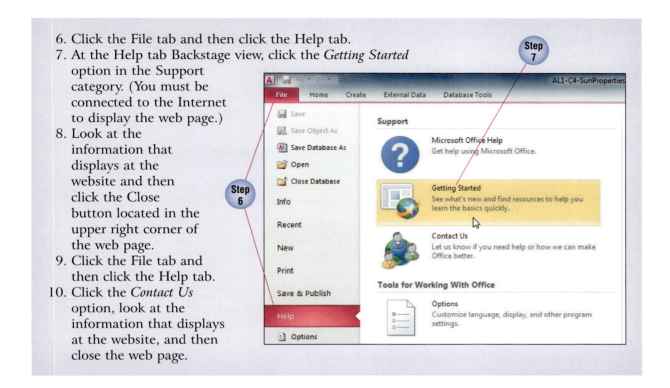

Getting Help on a Button

When you position the mouse pointer on a button, a ScreenTip displays with information about the button. Some button ScreenTips display with the message "Press F1 for more help" that is preceded by an image of the Help button. With the ScreenTip visible, press the F1 function key on your keyboard and the Access Help window opens and displays information about the specific button.

Getting Help in a Dialog Box or Backstage View

Some dialog boxes, as well as the Backstage view, contain a Help button you can click to display a help window with specific information about the dialog box or Backstage view. After reading and/or printing the information, close a dialog box by clicking the Close button located in the upper right corner of the dialog box or close the Backstage view by clicking the File tab or clicking any other tab in the ribbon.

Project 1h   Getting Help in a Dialog Box and Backstage View   Part 8 of 8

1. With the **AL1-C4-SunProperties.accdb** database open, click the Create tab.
2. Hover the mouse pointer over the Table button in the Tables group until the ScreenTip displays and then press F1.
3. At the Access Help window, look over the information that displays and then close the window.
4. Click the File tab and then click the Save Database As button.

5. At the Save As dialog box, click the Help button located near the upper right corner of the dialog box.
6. Read the information about saving files that displays in the Windows Help and Support window.
7. Close the window by clicking the Close button located in the upper right corner of the window.
8. Close the Save As dialog box.
9. Click the File tab.
10. At the Backstage view, click the Help button located near the upper right corner of the window.
11. At the Access Help window, click a hyperlink that interests you.
12. Read the information and then close the Access Help window by clicking the Close button located in the upper right corner of the window.
13. Click the File tab to return to the database.
14. Close the **AL1-C4-SunProperties.accdb** database.

Chapter Summary

- You can create a table in Datasheet view or Design view. Click the View button in the Table Tools Design tab or the Home tab to switch between Datasheet view and Design view.
- Define each field in a table in the rows in the top section of Design view. Access automatically assigns the first field the name *ID* and assigns the AutoNumber data type.
- In Design view, specify a field name, data type, and description for each field.
- Assign a data type in Design view by clicking in the *Data Type* field in the desired row, clicking the down-pointing arrow at the right side of the field, and then clicking the desired data type at the drop-down list.
- Create a default value for a field in Design view with the *Default Value* property box in the *Field Properties* section.
- Use the Input Mask Wizard to set a pattern for how data is entered in a field.
- Use the *Validation Rule* property box in the *Field Properties* section in Design view to enter a statement containing a conditional test. Enter in the *Validation Text* property box the error message you want to display if the data entered violates the validation rule.
- Use the Lookup Wizard to confine data entered in a field to a specific list of items.
- Insert a field in Design view by clicking in the row immediately below where you want the new field inserted and then clicking the Insert Rows button.

- Move a field in Design view by clicking in the field selector bar of the field you want to move and then dragging with the mouse to the desired position.
- Delete a field in Design view by clicking in the field selector bar at the left side of the row you want deleted and then clicking the Delete Rows button.
- Insert a total row in a table in Datasheet view by clicking the Totals button in the Records group in the Home tab. Click the down-pointing arrow in the *Total* row field and then click the desired function at the drop-down list.
- Click the Ascending button in the Sort & Filter group in the Home tab to sort records in ascending order and click the Descending button to sort records in descending order.
- To print specific records in a table, select the records, display the Print dialog box, make sure *Selected Record(s)* is selected, and then click OK.
- Apply formatting to a table in Datasheet view with buttons in the Text Formatting group in the Home tab. Depending on the button you click in the Text Formatting group, formatting is applied to all data in a table or data in a specific column in the table.
- If you want to format text in a specific field, change the data type to Memo and then specify rich text formatting. Do this in Design view with the *Text Format* property box in the *Field Properties* section.
- Use the spelling checker to find misspelled words in a table and offer replacement words.
- Use options at the Find and Replace dialog box with the Find tab selected to search for specific field entries in a table. Use options at the Find and Replace dialog box with the Replace tab selected to search for specific data and replace with other data.
- Click the Microsoft Access Help button or press F1 to display the Access Help window. At this window, type a topic in the search text box and then press Enter.
- Some dialog boxes as well as the Backstage view contain a Help button you can click to display information specific to the dialog box or Backstage view.
- The ScreenTip for some buttons displays with a message telling you to press F1. Press F1 and the Access Help window opens with information about the button.

Commands Review

FEATURE	RIBBON TAB, GROUP	BUTTON, OPTION	KEYBOARD SHORTCUT
Design view	Home, Views OR Table Tools Fields, Views		
Insert field	Table Tools Design, Tools		
Delete field	Table Tools Design, Tools		
Totals row	Home, Records	Σ	
Sort records ascending	Home, Sort & Filter		

FEATURE	RIBBON TAB, GROUP	BUTTON, OPTION	KEYBOARD SHORTCUT
Sort records descending	Home, Sort & Filter	Z↓A	
Font	Home, Text Formatting	Calibri (Detail)	
Font size	Home, Text Formatting	11	
Bold	Home, Text Formatting	B	
Italic	Home, Text Formatting	I	
Underline	Home, Text Formatting	U	
Font color	Home, Text Formatting	A	
Background color	Home, Text Formatting		
Align text left	Home, Text Formatting		
Center	Home, Text Formatting		
Align text right	Home, Text Formatting		
Gridlines	Home, Text Formatting		
Alternate row color	Home, Text Formatting		
Spelling check	Home, Records	ABC	F7
Find and Replace dialog box with Find tab selected	Home, Find		Ctrl + F
Find and Replace dialog box with Replace tab selected	Home, Find	ab/ac	Ctrl + H
Access Help window		?	F1

Concepts Check Test Your Knowledge

Completion: In the space provided at the right, indicate the correct term, symbol, or command.

1. The lower half of the work area in Design view that displays the properties for the active field is referred to as this. _____

2. When you create a new table in Design view, Access automatically assigns the first field the name *ID* and assigns this data type. _____

3. The description you type in the *Description* field displays in this location when the field is active in the table in Datasheet view. _____

4. Use this field property to set a pattern for how data is entered in a field. _____

5. Use this property box in Design view to enter a statement containing a conditional test that is checked each time data is entered into a field. _____

6. Use this wizard to confine the data entered in a field to a specific list of items. _____

7. To insert a new field in a table in Design view, click this button. _____

8. To insert a total row in a table, click the Totals button in this group in the Home tab. _____

9. The Ascending and Descending sort buttons are located in this group in the Home tab. _____

10. Click this button to change the text size of data in a table. _____

11. Click this button to align all text in the active column in the center of the fields. _____

12. Click this button to specify a color for alternating rows in a table. _____

13. Use options at the Find and Replace dialog box with this tab selected to search for specific data and replace with other data. _____

14. The ScreenTip for some buttons displays with a message telling you to press this key to display the Access Help window with information about the button. _____

Skills Check Assess Your Performance

Assessment

1 CREATE AN EMPLOYEES TABLE WITH THE INPUT MASK AND LOOKUP WIZARDS

1. Open Access and then create a new database by completing the following steps:
    a. At the New tab Backstage view, click in the *File Name* text box located at the right side of the screen.
    b. Type **AL1-C4-Hudson**.
    c. Click the Browse button that displays at the right side of the *File Name* text box.
    d. At the File New Database dialog box, navigate to the Access2010L1C4 folder on your storage medium and then click OK.

e. At the New tab Backstage view, click the Create button located below the *File Name* text box.
2. Create the Employees table in Design view as shown in Figure 4.14 with the following specifications:
    a. Limit the *EmpID* field size to *4*, the *FirstName* and *LastName* fields to *20*, and the *Address* field to *30*.
    b. Create a default value of *Pueblo* for the *City* field since most of the employees live in Pueblo.
    c. Create a default value of *CO* for the *State* field since all of the employees live in Colorado.
    d. Create an input mask for the telephone number.
    e. Use the Lookup Wizard to specify field choices for the *Status* field and include the following choices: *Full-time*, *Part-time*, *Temporary*, and *Contract*.
3. Save the table, switch to Datasheet view, and then enter the records as shown in Figure 4.15.
4. Adjust the column widths.
5. Save the table and then print the table in landscape orientation.
6. Switch to Design view and then add a row immediately above the *FirstName* row. Type **Title** in the *Field Name* field, limit the field size to *20*, and type the description **Enter employee job title**.
7. Delete the *HireDate* field.
8. Move the *Status* field so it is positioned between the *EmpID* row and the *Title* row.
9. Save the table and then switch to Datasheet view.
10. Enter the following information in the *Title* field:

Emp#	Title	Emp#	Title
1466	**Design Director**	2301	**Assistant**
1790	**Assistant**	2440	**Assistant**
1947	**Resources Director**	3035	**Clerk**
1955	**Accountant**	3129	**Clerk**
1994	**Assistant**	3239	**Assistant**
2013	**Production Director**	4002	**Contractor**
2120	**Assistant**	4884	**Contractor**

11. Apply the following text formatting to the table:
    a. Change the font to Arial and the font size to 10.
    b. Center the data in the *EmpID* field column and the *State* field column.
    c. Apply a light turquoise (you determine the specific color) alternating row color to the table.
12. Adjust the column widths.

Figure 4.14 Employees Table in Design View

Field Name	Data Type	Description
EmpID	Text	Enter four-digit employee identification number
FirstName	Text	Enter employee first name
LastName	Text	Enter employee last name
Address	Text	Enter employee street address
City	Text	Pueblo automatically inserted
State	Text	CO automatically inserted
ZIP	Text	Enter employee ZIP code
Telephone	Text	Enter employee telephone number
Status	Text	Click down-pointing arrow and then click employee status
HireDate	Date/Time	Enter employee hire date

Figure 4.15 Employees Table in Datasheet View

EmpID	FirstName	LastName	Address	City	State	ZIP	Telephone	Status	HireDate
1466	Samantha	O'Connell	9105 Pike Avenue	Pueblo	CO	81011	(719) 555-7658	Full-time	8/15/2010
1790	Edward	Sorrell	9958 Franklin Avenue	Pueblo	CO	81006	(719) 555-3724	Full-time	11/15/2006
1947	Brandon	Byrne	102 Hudson Avenue	Pueblo	CO	81012	(719) 555-1202	Full-time	8/1/2008
1955	Leland	Hughes	4883 Caledonia Road	Pueblo	CO	81005	(719) 555-1211	Full-time	3/1/2010
1994	Rosa	Martinez	310 Graham Avenue	Pueblo	CO	81004	(719) 555-8394	Part-time	8/15/2007
2013	Jean	Perrault	123 Chinook Lake	Pueblo	CO	82012	(719) 555-4027	Full-time	11/15/2006
2120	Michael	Turek	5503 East 27th Street	Boone	CO	81025	(719) 555-5423	Full-time	3/15/2008
2301	Gregory	Nitsche	12055 East 18th Street	Pueblo	CO	81007	(719) 555-6657	Part-time	3/15/2007
2440	Bethany	Rosario	858 West 27th Street	Pueblo	CO	81012	(719) 555-9481	Part-time	2/1/2011
3035	Alia	Shandra	7740 Second Street	Avondale	CO	81022	(719) 555-0059	Temporary	2/1/2010
3129	Gloria	Cushman	6590 East 14th Street	Pueblo	CO	81006	(719) 555-0332	Temporary	5/1/2012
3239	Rudolph	Powell	8874 Hood Avenue	Pueblo	CO	81008	(719) 555-2223	Temporary	4/1/2012
4002	Alice	Murray	4300 North 16th Street	Pueblo	CO	81003	(719) 555-4230	Contract	9/12/2006
4884	Simon	Banister	1022 Division Avenue	Boone	CO	81025	(719) 555-2378	Contract	5/15/2012
				Pueblo	CO				

13. Save the table and then print the table in landscape orientation.
14. Find all occurrences of *Director* and replace with *Manager*. **Hint: Position the insertion point in the first entry in the** Title **column and then display the Find and Replace dialog box. At the dialog box, change the** Match **option to** Any Part of Field.
15. Find all occurrences of *Assistant* and replace with *Associate*.
16. Save the table, print the table in landscape orientation with left and right margins of 0.5 inch, and then close the table.

Assessment

2 CREATE A PROJECTS TABLE

1. With the **AL1-C4-Hudson.accdb** database open, create a Projects table in Design view and include the following fields (make sure the *Proj#* field is identified as the primary key) and create an appropriate description for each field:

Field Name	Data Type
Proj#	Text (field size = 4)
EmpID	Text (field size = 4)
BegDate	Date/Time
EndDate	Date/Time
EstCosts	Currency

2. Save the table, switch to Datasheet view, and then type the following data or choose a field entry in the specified fields:

Proj#	08-A	*Proj#*	08-B
EmpID	2013	*EmpID*	1466
BegDate	08/01/2012	*BegDate*	08/15/2012
EndDate	10/31/2012	*EndDate*	12/15/2012
EstCosts	$5,250.00	*EstCosts*	$2,000.00

Proj#	10-A	*Proj#*	10-B
EmpID	1947	*EmpID*	2013
BegDate	10/01/2012	*BegDate*	10/01/2012
EndDate	01/15/2013	*EndDate*	12/15/2012
EstCosts	$10,000.00	*EstCosts*	$3,500.00

Proj#	11-A	*Proj#*	11-B
EmpID	1466	*EmpID*	1947
BegDate	11/01/2012	*BegDate*	11/01/2012
EndDate	02/01/2013	*EndDate*	03/31/2013
EstCosts	$8,000.00	*EstCosts*	$12,000.00

3. Adjust the column widths.
4. Save, print, and then close the Projects table.

Assessment

3 CREATE AN EXPENSES TABLE WITH A VALIDATION RULE AND INPUT MASK

1. With the **AL1-C4-Hudson.accdb** database open, create an Expenses table in Design view and include the following fields (make sure the *Item#* field is identified as the primary key) and include an appropriate description for each field:

Field Name	Data Type
Item#	AutoNumber
EmpID	Text (field size = 4)
Proj#	Text (field size = 4)
Amount	Currency (Type a condition in the *Validation Rule* property box that states the entry must be $500 or less. Type an error message in the *Validation Text* property box.)
DateSubmitted	Date/Time (Use the Input Mask to control the date so it is entered as a short date.)

2. Save the table, switch to Datasheet view, and then type the following data or choose a field entry in the specified fields (Access automatically inserts a number in the *Item#* field):

EmpID	1466	*EmpID*	2013
Proj#	08-B	*Proj#*	08-A
Amount	$245.79	*Amount*	$500.00
DateSubmitted	09/04/2012	*DateSubmitted*	09/10/2012
EmpID	4002	*EmpID*	1947
Proj#	08-B	*Proj#*	10-A
Amount	$150.00	*Amount*	$500.00
DateSubmitted	09/18/2012	*DateSubmitted*	10/03/2012
EmpID	2013	*EmpID*	1947
Proj#	10-B	*Proj#*	10-A
Amount	$487.25	*Amount*	$85.75
DateSubmitted	10/22/2012	*DateSubmitted*	10/24/2012
EmpID	1466	*EmpID*	1790
Proj#	08-B	*Proj#*	08-A
Amount	$175.00	*Amount*	$110.50
DateSubmitted	10/29/2012	*DateSubmitted*	10/30/2012
EmpID	2120	*EmpID*	1466
Proj#	10-A	*Proj#*	08-B
Amount	$75.00	*Amount*	$300.00
DateSubmitted	11/05/2012	*DateSubmitted*	11/07/2012
EmpID	1466	*EmpID*	2013
Proj#	11-A	*Proj#*	10-B
Amount	$75.00	*Amount*	$300.00
DateSubmitted	11/14/2012	*DateSubmitted*	11/19/2012

3. Adjust the column widths.
4. Insert a total row with the following specifications:
   a. Click the Totals button in the Records group in the Home tab.
   b. Click in the blank field in the *Amount* column in the *Total* row.
   c. Click the down-pointing arrow at the left side of the field and then click *Sum* at the drop-down list.
   d. Click in any other field.
5. Save, print, and then close the Expenses table.
6. Create a one-to-many relationship where *EmpID* in the Employees table is the "one" and *EmpID* in the Expenses table is the "many." (Enforce referential integrity and cascade fields and records.)
7. Create a one-to-many relationship where *EmpID* in the Employees table is the "one" and *EmpID* in the Projects table is the "many." (Enforce referential integrity and cascade fields and records.)
8. Create a one-to-many relationship where *Proj#* in the Projects table is the "one" and *Proj#* in the Expenses table is the "many." (Enforce referential integrity and cascade fields and records.)
9. Save the relationships, print the relationships, and then close the relationships report window and the relationships window.
10. Design and run a query that displays all full-time employees with the following specifications:
    a. Insert the Employees table in the query window.
    b. Insert the *EmpID*, *FirstName*, *LastName*, and *Status* fields.
    c. Click in the check box in the *Show* row field in the *EmpID* column to remove the check mark. (This hides the EmpID numbers in the query results.)
    d. Extract full-time employees.
    e. Save the query and name it *FTEmpsQuery*.
    f. Print and then close the query.
11. Design and run a query that displays projects managed by employee number 1947 with the following specifications:
    a. Insert the Employees table and the Projects table in the query window.
    b. Insert the *EmpID*, *FirstName*, and *LastName* fields from the Employees table.
    c. Insert the *Proj#* field from the Projects table.
    d. Extract those projects managed by employee number 1947.
    e. Save the query and name it *ProjsManagedByEmp1947Query*.
    f. Print and then close the query.
12. Design and run a query that displays expense amounts over $250.00 and the employee submitting the expense with the following specifications:
    a. Insert the Expenses table and the Employees table in the query window.
    b. Insert the *Item#*, *Amount*, and *DateSubmitted* fields from the Expenses table.
    c. Insert the *FirstName* and *LastName* fields from the Employees table.
    d. Hide the *Item#* field in the query results by clicking in the check box in the *Show* row field in the *Item#* column to remove the check mark.
    e. Extract those expense amounts over $250.
    f. Save the query and name it *ExpensesOver$250Query*.
    g. Print and then close the query.
13. Design and run a query that displays expenses submitted by employee number 1947 with the following specifications:
    a. Insert the Employees table and the Expenses table in the query window.
    b. Insert the *EmpID*, *FirstName*, and *LastName* fields from the Employees table.
    c. Insert the *Proj#*, *Amount*, and *DateSubmitted* from the Expenses table.

d. Click in the check box in the *Show* row field in the *EmpID* column to remove the check mark. (This hides the EmpID numbers in the query results.)
e. Extract those expenses submitted by employee number 1947.
f. Save the query and name it *ExpSubmittedBy1947Query*.
g. Print and then close the query.

Assessment

4 EDIT THE EMPLOYEES TABLE

1. With the **AL1-C4-Hudson.accdb** database open, open the Employees table.
2. Display the table in Design view, click in the *ZIP* field row *Data Type* column and then click in the *Input Mask* property box in the *Field Properties* section.
3. Use the Input Mask Wizard to create a nine-digit ZIP code input mask.
4. Save the table and then switch to Datasheet view.
5. Delete the record for employee number 3035 (Alia Shandra), employee number 3129 (Gloria Cushman), and employee number 4884 (Simon Banister).
6. Insert the following new records:

EmpID	2286	EmpID	2970
Status	Full-time	Status	Full-time
Title	Associate	Title	Associate
FirstName	Erica	FirstName	Daniel
LastName	Bonari	LastName	Ortiz
Address	4850 55th Street	Address	12021 Cedar Lane
City	(Pueblo automatically inserted)	City	(Pueblo automatically inserted)
State	(CO automatically inserted)	State	(CO automatically inserted)
ZIP	81005-5002	ZIP	81011-1255
Telephone	(719) 555-1293	Telephone	(719) 555-0790

7. Adjust the width of the *ZIP* column. (Only the two new records will contain the nine-digit ZIP code.)
8. Save the Employees table.
9. Display the table in Print Preview, change to landscape orientation, and then change the left and right margins to 0.5 inch. Print and then close the table.

Visual Benchmark Demonstrate Your Proficiency

EDIT THE EXPENSES TABLE

Note: The starting file for this activity is the file created after completing the previous Skills Check assessments.

1. With the **AL1-C4-Hudson.accdb** database open, open the Expenses table.
2. Insert fields, rearrange fields, insert new data, and apply text formatting as shown in Figure 4.16. Change the font of data in the table to Cambria and the font size to 12. Center align text as shown, add alternating row color, and adjust column widths.
3. Save the table, print the table in landscape orientation, and then close the Expenses table.

Figure 4.16 Visual Benchmark

Item#	Proj#	EmpID	Expense	Amount	DateSubmitted	Approved
1	08-B	1466	Design	$245.79	9/4/2012	✓
2	08-A	2013	Consultation	$500.00	9/10/2012	☐
3	08-B	4002	Supplies	$150.00	9/18/2012	✓
4	10-A	1947	Equipment	$500.00	10/3/2012	✓
5	10-B	2013	Printer	$487.25	10/22/2012	✓
6	10-A	1947	Supplies	$85.75	10/24/2012	✓
7	08-B	1466	Consultation	$175.00	10/29/2012	☐
8	08-A	1790	Design	$110.50	10/30/2012	✓
9	10-A	2120	Announcements	$75.00	11/5/2012	✓
10	08-B	1466	Brochures	$300.00	11/7/2012	☐
11	11-A	1466	Printing	$75.00	11/14/2012	☐
12	10-B	2013	Consultation	$300.00	11/19/2012	☐
(New)						☐
Total				$3,004.29		

Case Study Apply Your Skills

Part 1

You work for Blue Ridge Enterprises and your supervisor has asked you to create a database with information about representatives and clients. Create a new database named **AL1-C4-BlueRidge.accdb** and then create a Representatives table with the following fields:

- Create a field for the representative identification number, change the data type to Text, and limit the field size to 3. (This is the primary key field.)
- Create a field for the representative's first name and limit the field size to 20.
- Create a field for the representative's last name and limit the field size to 20.
- Create a field for the representative's telephone number and use the Input Mask Wizard.
- Create a field for the insurance plan and use the Lookup Wizard and include four options: *Platinum*, *Premium*, *Standard*, and *None*.
- Create a field for the yearly bonus amount and type a validation rule that states that the bonus must be less than $10,001 and include an error message (you determine the message).

In Datasheet view, enter six records in the table. When entering the data, make sure that at least two representatives will receive a yearly bonus over $5000 and that at least two representatives are signed up for the *Platinum* insurance plan. Insert a total row that sums the yearly bonus amounts. Change the font for the data in the table to Cambria, change the font size to 10, and apply a light green alternating row color. Center the data in the representative identification column. Adjust the column widths and then save the Representatives table. Print the table in landscape orientation and then close the table.

Part 2

With the **AL-C4-BlueRidge.accdb** database open, create a second table named Clients (table contains information on companies doing business with Blue Ridge Enterprises) with the following fields:

- Create a field for the client identification number and limit the field size to 2. (This is the primary key field.)
- Create a field for the representative identification number (use the same field name you used in Part 1 in the Representatives table) and limit the field size to 3.
- Create fields for the company name, address, city, state (or province), and ZIP (or postal code). Insert the city you live in as the default value for the city field and insert the two-letter state or province abbreviation where you live as the default value for the state or province field.
- Create a field for the client's telephone number and use the Input Mask.
- Create a field for the client's type of business and insert the word *Wholesaler* as the default value.

In Datasheet view, enter at least eight companies. Make sure you use the representative identification numbers in the Clients table that match numbers in the Representatives table. Identify at least one company as a *Retailer* rather than a *Wholesaler* and make at least one representative represent two or more companies. Change the font for the data in the table to Cambria, change the font size to 10, and apply a light green alternating row color (the same color you chose in Part 1). Center the data in the client identification column, the representative identification column, and the state (or province) column. Adjust the column widths and then save the Clients table. Print the table in landscape orientation and then close the table.

Part 3

Create a one-to-many relationship with the representative identification number in the Representatives table as the "one" and the representative identification number in the Clients table as the "many." Save the relationship, print the relationships report, and then close the report without saving it.

Part 4

Your supervisor has asked you for specific information about representatives and clients. To provide answers to your supervisor, create and print the following queries:

- Create a query that extracts records of representatives earning a yearly bonus over $5000. (You determine the fields to insert in the query window.) Save, print, and then close the query.
- Create a query that extracts records of representatives signed up for the Platinum insurance plan. (You determine the fields to insert in the query window.) Save, print, and then close the query.
- Create a query that extracts records of wholesale clients. (You determine the fields to insert in the query window.) Save, print, and then close the query.
- Create a query that extracts records of companies represented by a specific representative. (Use the representative identification number you entered in Part 2 that represents two or more companies.) Save, print, and then close the query.

UNIT 1

Performance Assessment

Note: The Student Resources CD does not include an Access Level 1, Unit 1 subfolder of files because no data files are required for the Unit 1 assessments. You will create all of the files yourself. Before beginning the assessments, create a folder for the new files called Access2010L1U1.

Assessing Proficiency

In this unit, you have learned to design, create, and modify tables and to create one-to-many relationships and one-to-one relationships between tables. You also learned how to perform queries on data in tables.

Assessment 1 Create Tables in a Cornerstone Catering Database

1. Use Access to create tables for Cornerstone Catering. Name the database **AL1-U1-Cornerstone**. Create a table named *Employees* that includes the following fields. If no data type is specified for a field, use the *Text* data type. You determine the field size and specify the same field size for a field that is contained in different tables. For example, if you specify a field size of *2* for the *Employee#* field in the Employees table, specify a field size of *2* for the *Employee#* field in the Events table. Provide a description for each field.

    Employee# (primary key)
    FirstName
    LastName
    CellPhone (Use the Input Mask Wizard for this field.)

2. After creating the table, switch to Datasheet view and then enter the following data in the appropriate fields:

    Employee#: **10**   Employee#: **14**
    FirstName: **Erin**   FirstName: **Mikio**
    LastName: **Jergens**   LastName: **Ogami**
    CellPhone: **(505) 555-3193**   CellPhone: **(505) 555-1087**

    Employee#: **19**   Employee#: **21**
    FirstName: **Martin**   FirstName: **Isabelle**
    LastName: **Vaughn**   LastName: **Baptista**
    CellPhone: **(505) 555-4461**   CellPhone: **(505) 555-4425**

173

Employee#: **24**
FirstName: **Shawn**
LastName: **Kettering**
CellPhone: **(505) 555-3885**

Employee#: **26**
FirstName: **Madison**
LastName: **Harris**
CellPhone: **(505) 555-2256**

Employee#: **28**
FirstName: **Victoria**
LastName: **Lamesa**
CellPhone: **(505) 555-6650**

Employee#: **30**
FirstName: **Isaac**
LastName: **Hobart**
CellPhone: **(505) 555-7430**

Employee#: **32**
FirstName: **Lester**
LastName: **Franklin**
CellPhone: **(505) 555-0440**

Employee#: **35**
FirstName: **Manuela**
LastName: **Harte**
CellPhone: **(505) 555-1221**

3. Change the font for data in the table to Cambria, the font size to 10, and apply a light blue alternating row color. Center-align the data in the *Employee#* column.
4. Adjust the column widths.
5. Save, print, and then close the Employees table.
6. Create a table named *Plans* that includes the following fields:

   PlanCode (primary key)
   Plan

7. After creating the table, switch to Datasheet view and then enter the following data in the appropriate fields:

   PlanCode: **A**
   Plan: **Sandwich Buffet**

   PlanCode: **B**
   Plan: **Cold Luncheon Buffet**

   PlanCode: **C**
   Plan: **Hot Luncheon Buffet**

   PlanCode: **D**
   Plan: **Combination Dinner**

   PlanCode: **E**
   Plan: **Vegetarian Luncheon Buffet**

   PlanCode: **F**
   Plan: **Vegetarian Dinner Buffet**

   PlanCode: **G**
   Plan: **Seafood Luncheon Buffet**

   PlanCode: **H**
   Plan: **Seafood Dinner Buffet**

8. Change the font for data in the table to Cambria, the font size to 10, and apply a light blue alternating row color. Center-align the data in the *PlanCode* column.
9. Adjust the column widths.
10. Save, print, and then close the Plans table.
11. Create a table named *Prices* that includes the following fields:

    PriceCode (primary key)
    PricePerPerson (identify this data type as Currency)

12. After creating the table, switch to Datasheet view and then enter the following data in the appropriate fields:

   PriceCode: 1
   PricePerPerson: $11.50

   PriceCode: 2
   PricePerPerson: $12.75

   PriceCode: 3
   PricePerPerson: $14.50

   PriceCode: 4
   PricePerPerson: $16.00

   PriceCode: 5
   PricePerPerson: $18.50

   PriceCode: 6
   PricePerPerson: $21.95

13. Change the font for data in the table to Cambria, the font size to 10, and apply a light blue alternating row color. Center-align the data in both columns.
14. Adjust the column widths.
15. Save, print, and then close the Prices table.
16. Create a table named *Clients* that includes the following fields:

   Client# (primary key)
   ClientName
   StreetAddress
   City
   State (Insert *NM* as the default value.)
   ZIP
   Telephone (Use the Input Mask Wizard for this field.)

17. After creating the table, switch to Datasheet view and then enter the following data in the appropriate fields:

   Client#: 104
   ClientName: Sarco Corporation
   StreetAddress: 340 Cordova Road
   City: Santa Fe
   State: NM
   ZIP: 87510
   Telephone: (505) 555-3880

   Client#: 155
   ClientName: Creative Concepts
   StreetAddress: 1026 Market Street
   City: Los Alamos
   State: NM
   ZIP: 87547
   Telephone: (505) 555-1200

   Client#: 218
   ClientName: Allenmore Systems
   StreetAddress: 7866 Second Street
   City: Espanola
   State: NM
   ZIP: 87535
   Telephone: (505) 555-3455

   Client#: 286
   ClientName: Sol Enterprises
   StreetAddress: 120 Cerrillos Road
   City: Santa Fe
   State: NM
   ZIP: 87560
   Telephone: (505) 555-7700

   Client#: 295
   ClientName: Benson Productions
   StreetAddress: 555 Junction Road
   City: Santa Fe
   State: NM
   ZIP: 87558
   Telephone: (505) 555-8866

   Client#: 300
   ClientName: Old Town Corporation
   StreetAddress: 1035 East Adams Way
   City: Santa Fe
   State: NM
   ZIP: 87561
   Telephone: (505) 555-2125

Client#: 305
ClientName: **Cromwell Company**
StreetAddress: **752 Rialto Way**
City: **Santa Fe**
State: **NM**
ZIP: **87512**
Telephone: **(505) 555-7500**

Client#: 320
ClientName: **GH Manufacturing**
StreetAddress: **9550 Stone Road**
City: **Los Alamos**
State: **NM**
ZIP: **87547**
Telephone: **(505) 555-3388**

18. Change the font for data in the table to Cambria, the font size to 10, and apply a light blue alternating row color. Center-align the data in the *Client#* column.
19. Adjust the column widths.
20. Save the table and then print the table in landscape orientation.
21. Close the Clients table.
22. Create a table named *Events* that includes the following fields:

    Event# (primary key; identify this data type as AutoNumber)
    Client#
    Employee#
    DateOfEvent (identify this data type as Date/Time)
    PlanCode
    PriceCode
    NumberOfPeople (identify this data type as Number)

23. After creating the table, switch to Datasheet view and then enter the following data in the appropriate fields:

    Event#: (AutoNumber)
    Client#: **218**
    Employee#: **14**
    DateOfEvent: **7/7/2012**
    PlanCode: **B**
    PriceCode: **3**
    NumberOfPeople: **250**

    Event#: (AutoNumber)
    Client#: **104**
    Employee#: **19**
    DateOfEvent: **7/8/2012**
    PlanCode: **D**
    PriceCode: **5**
    NumberOfPeople: **120**

    Event#: (AutoNumber)
    Client#: **155**
    Employee#: **24**
    DateOfEvent: **7/14/2012**
    PlanCode: **A**
    PriceCode: **1**
    NumberOfPeople: **300**

    Event#: (AutoNumber)
    Client#: **286**
    Employee#: **10**
    DateOfEvent: **7/15/2012**
    PlanCode: **C**
    PriceCode: **4**
    NumberOfPeople: **75**

    Event#: (AutoNumber)
    Client#: **218**
    Employee#: **14**
    DateOfEvent: **7/18/2012**
    PlanCode: **C**
    PriceCode: **4**
    NumberOfPeople: **50**

    Event#: (AutoNumber)
    Client#: **104**
    Employee#: **10**
    DateOfEvent: **7/20/2012**
    PlanCode: **B**
    PriceCode: **3**
    NumberOfPeople: **30**

Event#: (AutoNumber)
Client#: 305
Employee#: 30
DateOfEvent: 7/21/2012
PlanCode: H
PriceCode: 6
NumberOfPeople: 150

Event#: (AutoNumber)
Client#: 295
Employee#: 35
DateOfEvent: 7/22/2012
PlanCode: E
PriceCode: 4
NumberOfPeople: 75

Event#: (AutoNumber)
Client#: 300
Employee#: 32
DateOfEvent: 7/27/2012
PlanCode: B
PriceCode: 3
NumberOfPeople: 200

Event#: (AutoNumber)
Client#: 350
Employee#: 28
DateOfEvent: 7/28/2012
PlanCode: D
PriceCode: 6
NumberOfPeople: 100

24. Change the font for data in the table to Cambria, the font size to 10, and apply a light blue alternating row color. Center-align in all of the columns except the *DateOfEvent* column.
25. Adjust the column widths.
26. Save, print, and then close the Events table.

Assessment 2 Create Relationships between Tables

1. With the **AL1-U1-Cornerstone.accdb** database open, create the following one-to-many relationships and enforce referential integrity:
   a. *Client#* in the Clients table is the "one" and *Client#* in the Events table is the "many."
   b. *Employee#* in the Employees table is the "one" and *Employee#* in the Events table is the "many."
   c. *PlanCode* in the Plans table is the "one" and *PlanCode* in the Events table is the "many."
   d. *PriceCode* in the Prices table is the "one" and *PriceCode* in the Events table is the "many."
2. Save and then print the relationships in landscape orientation.

Assessment 3 Modify Tables

1. With the **AL1-U1-Cornerstone.accdb** database open, open the Plans table in Datasheet view and then add the following record at the end of the table:

   PlanCode: I
   Plan: Hawaiian Luau Dinner Buffet

2. Adjust the column widths.
3. Save, print, and then close the Plans table.
4. Open the Events table in Datasheet view and then add the following record at the end of the table:

   Event#: (AutoNumber)
   Client#: 104
   Employee#: 21
   Date: 7/29/2012
   PlanCode: I
   PriceCode: 5
   NumberOfPeople: 125

5. Save, print (in landscape orientation), and then close the Events table.

Assessment 4 Design Queries

1. With the **AL1-U1-Cornerstone.accdb** database open, create a query to extract records from the Events table with the following specifications:
    a. Include the fields *Client#*, *DateOfEvent*, and *PlanCode*.
    b. Extract those records with a PlanCode of C.
    c. Run the query.
    d. Save the query and name it *PlanCodeCQuery*.
    e. Print and then close the query.
2. Extract records from the Clients table with the following specifications:
    a. Include the fields *ClientName*, *City*, and *Telephone*.
    b. Extract those records with a city of Santa Fe.
    c. Run the query.
    d. Save the query and name it *SantaFeClientsQuery*.
    e. Print and then close the query.
3. Extract information from two tables with the following specifications:
    a. From the Clients table, include the fields *ClientName* and *Telephone*.
    b. From the Events table, include the fields *DateOfEvent*, *PlanCode*, and *NumberOfPeople*.
    c. Extract those records with a date between July 1 and July 15, 2012.
    d. Run the query.
    e. Save the query and name it *July1-15EventsQuery*.
    f. Print and then close the query.

Assessment 5 Design a Query with a Calculated Field Entry

1. With the **AL1-U1-Cornerstone.accdb** database open, create a query in Design view with the Events table and the Prices table and insert the following fields in the specified locations:
    a. Insert *Event#* from the Events table to the first *Field* row field.
    b. Insert *DateOfEvent* from the Events table to the second *Field* row field.
    c. Insert *NumberOfPeople* from the Events table to the third *Field* row field.
    d. Insert *PricePerPerson* from the Prices table to the fourth *Field* row field.
2. Insert the following calculated field entry in the fifth *Field* row field: Amount: [NumberOfPeople]*[PricePerPerson].
3. Run the query.
4. Save the query and name it *EventAmountsQuery*.
5. Print and then close the query.

Assessment 6 Design a Query with Aggregate Functions

1. With the **AL1-U1-Cornerstone.accdb** database open, create a query in Design view using EventAmountsQuery with the following specifications:
    a. Click the Create tab and then click the Query Design button.
    b. At the Show Tables dialog box, click the Queries tab.
    c. Double-click *EventAmountsQuery* in the list box and then click the Close button.
    d. Insert the *Amount* field to the first, second, third, and fourth *Field* text boxes.
    e. Click the Totals button in the Show/Hide group.
    f. Insert *Sum* in the first *Total* row field.
    g. Insert *Avg* in the second *Total* row field.
    h. Insert *Min* in the third *Total* row field.
    i. Insert *Max* in the fourth *Total* row field.

2. Run the query.
3. Automatically adjust the column widths.
4. Save the query and name it *AmountTotalsQuery*.
5. Print and then close the query.

Assessment 7 Design a Query Using Fields from Tables and a Query

1. With the **AL1-U1-Cornerstone.accdb** database open, create a query in Design view using the Employees table, the Clients table, the Events table, and EventAmountsQuery with the following specifications:
   a. Click the Create tab and then click the Query Design button.
   b. At the Show Tables dialog box, double-click *Employees*.
   c. Double-click *Clients*.
   d. Double-click *Events*.
   e. Click the Queries tab, double-click *EventAmountsQuery* in the list box, and then click the Close button.
   f. Insert the *LastName* field from the Employees table to the first *Field* row field.
   g. Insert the *ClientName* field from the Clients table to the second *Field* row field.
   h. Insert the *Amount* field from EventAmountsQuery to the third *Field* row field.
   i. Insert the *DateOfEvent* field from the Events table to the fourth *Field* row field.
2. Run the query.
3. Save the query and name it *EmployeeEventsQuery*.
4. Close the query.
5. Using the Crosstab Query Wizard, create a query that summarizes the total amount of events by employee by client using the following specifications:
   a. At the first Crosstab Query Wizard dialog box, click the *Queries* option in the *View* section, and then click *Query: EmployeeEventsQuery* in the list box.
   b. At the second Crosstab Query Wizard dialog box, click *LastName* in the *Available Fields* list box and then click the One Field button.
   c. At the third Crosstab Query Wizard dialog box, make sure *ClientName* is selected in the list box.
   d. At the fourth Crosstab Query Wizard dialog box, make sure *Amount* is selected in the *Fields* list box, and then click *Sum* in the *Functions* list box.
   e. At the fifth Crosstab Query Wizard dialog box, type **AmountsByEmployeeByClientQuery** in the *What do you want to name your query?* text box.
6. Automatically adjust the column widths.
7. Print the query in landscape orientation and then close the query.

Assessment 8 Use the Find Duplicates Query Wizard

1. With the **AL1-U1-Cornerstone.accdb** database open, use the Find Duplicates Query Wizard to find employees who are responsible for at least two events with the following specifications:
   a. At the first wizard dialog box, double-click *Table: Events* in the list box.
   b. At the second wizard dialog box, click *Employee#* in the *Available fields* list box and then click the One Field button.
   c. At the third wizard dialog box, move the *DateOfEvent* field and the *NumberOfPeople* field from the *Available fields* list box to the *Additional query fields* list box.
   d. At the fourth wizard dialog box, name the query *DuplicateEventsQuery*.
2. Print and then close the query.

Assessment 9 Use the Find Unmatched Query Wizard

1. With the **AL1-U1-Cornerstone.accdb** database open, use the Find Unmatched Query Wizard to find any employees who do not have an upcoming event scheduled with the following specifications:
   a. At the first wizard dialog box, click *Table: Employees* in the list box.
   b. At the second wizard dialog box, click *Table: Events* in the list box.
   c. At the third wizard dialog box, make sure *Employee#* is selected in the *Fields in 'Employees'* list box and in the *Fields in 'Events'* list box.
   d. At the fourth wizard dialog box, click the All Fields button to move all fields from the *Available fields* list box to the *Selected fields* list box.
   e. At the fifth wizard dialog box, click the Finish button. (Let the wizard determine the query name: *Employees Without Matching Events*.)
2. Print and then close the *Employees Without Matching Events* query.

Writing Activities

The following activity gives you the opportunity to practice your writing skills along with demonstrating an understanding of some of the important Access features you have mastered in this unit. Use correct grammar, appropriate word choices, and clear sentence constructions.

Create a Payroll Table and Word Report

The manager of Cornerstone Catering has asked you to add information to the **AL1-U1-Cornerstone.accdb** database on employee payroll. You need to create another table that will contain information on payroll. The manager wants the table to include the following (you determine the appropriate field name, data type, field size, and description):

Employee Number: **10**
Status: **Full-time**
Monthly Salary: **$2,850**

Employee Number: **14**
Status: **Part-time**
Monthly Salary: **$1,500**

Employee Number: **19**
Status: **Part-time**
Monthly Salary: **$1,400**

Employee Number: **21**
Status: **Full-time**
Monthly Salary: **$2,500**

Employee Number: **24**
Status: **Part-time**
Monthly Salary: **$1,250**

Employee Number: **26**
Status: **Part-time**
Monthly Salary: **$1,000**

Employee number: **28**
Status: **Full-time**
Monthly salary: **$2,500**

Employee number: **30**
Status: **Part-time**
Monthly salary: **$3,000**

Employee number: **32**
Status: **Full-time**
Monthly salary: **$2,300**

Employee number: **35**
Status: **Full-time**
Monthly salary: **$2,750**

Print and then close the payroll table. Open Word and then write a report to the manager detailing how you created the table. Include a title for the report, steps on how the table was created, and any other pertinent information. Save the completed report and name it **AL1-U1-Act01-TableRpt**. Print and then close **AL1-U1-Act01-TableRpt.docx**.

Internet Research

Vehicle Search

In this activity you will search the Internet for information on different vehicles before doing actual test drives. Learning about a major product, such as a vehicle, can increase your chances of finding a good buy, can potentially guide you away from a poor purchase, and can help speed up the process of narrowing the search to the type of vehicle that will meet your needs. Before you begin, list the top five criteria you would look for in a vehicle. For example, it must be a four-door vehicle, needs to be four-wheel drive, etc.

Using key search words, find at least two websites that list vehicle reviews. Use the search engines provided within the different review sites to find vehicles that fulfill the criteria you listed to meet your particular needs. Create a database in Access and create a table in that database that will contain the results from your vehicle search. Design the table keeping in mind what type of data you need to record for each vehicle that meets your requirements. Include at least the make, model, year, price, description, and special problems in the table. Also, include the ability to rate the vehicle as poor, fair, good, or excellent. You will decide on the rating of each vehicle depending on your findings.

Microsoft® Access® Level 1

Unit 2 ■ Creating Forms and Reports

Chapter 5 ■ Creating Forms

Chapter 6 ■ Creating Reports and Mailing Labels

Chapter 7 ■ Modifying, Filtering, and Viewing Data

Chapter 8 ■ Importing and Exporting Data

Creating Forms

CHAPTER 5

PERFORMANCE OBJECTIVES

Upon successful completion of Chapter 5, you will be able to:
- Create a form using the Form button
- Change views in a form
- Print and navigate in a form
- Add records to and delete records from a form
- Create a form with a related table
- Customize a form with options at the Form Layout Tools tab
- Create a split form and multiple items form
- Create a form using the Form Wizard

In this chapter, you will learn how to create forms from database tables, improving the data display and making data entry easier. Access offers several methods for presenting data on the screen for easier data entry. You will create a form using the Form button, create a split and multiple items form, and use the Form Wizard to create a form. You will also learn how to customize control objects in a form and insert control objects and fields in a form. Model answers for this chapter's projects appear on the following pages.

Access2010L1C5

Note: Before beginning the projects, copy to your storage medium the Access2010L1C5 subfolder from the Access2010L1 folder on the CD that accompanies this textbook and make Access2010L1C5 the active folder.

Project 1 Create Forms with the Form Button

Project 1a, Dearborn Clients Form

Project 1b, Dearborn Clients Form

Project 1c, Dearborn Representatives Form

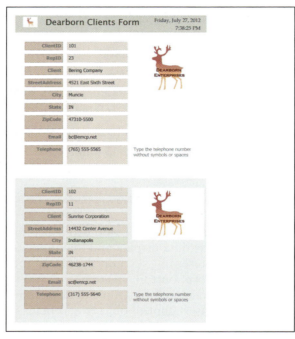

Project 1g, Dearborn Clients Form

Project 1g, Dearborn Sales Form

Project 2 Add Fields, Create a Split and Multiple Item Form, and Use the Form Wizard

Project 2a, Skyline Inventory Form

Project 2b, Skyline Suppliers Form

Project 2c, Skyline Orders Form

Project 2d, Skyline Employees Form, Carol Thompson

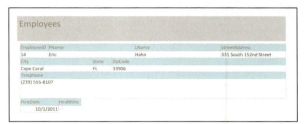

Project 2d, Skyline Employees Form, Eric Hahn

Project 2e, Skyline Upcoming Banquets Form

> **Project 1 Create Forms with the Form Button** **7 Parts**
>
> You will use the Form button to create forms with fields in the Clients, Representatives, and Sales tables. You will also add, delete, and print records and use buttons in the Form Layout Tools Format tab to apply formatting to control objects in the forms.

Creating a Form

▼ Quick Steps

Create a Form with Form Button
1. Click desired table.
2. Click Create tab.
3. Click Form button.

Access offers a variety of options for presenting data in a more easily read and attractive format. When entering data in a table in Datasheet view, multiple records display at the same time. If a record contains several fields, you may not be able to view all fields within a record at the same time. If you create a form, generally all fields for a record are visible on the screen. Several methods are available for creating a form. In this section, you will learn how to create a form using the Form, Split Form, and Multiple Items buttons as well as the Form Wizard.

HINT
A form allows you to focus on a single record at a time.

Creating a Form with the Form Button

You can view, add, or edit data in a table in Datasheet view. You can also perform these functions on data inserted in a form. A *form* is an object you can use to enter and edit data in a table or query and is a user-friendly interface for viewing, adding, editing, and deleting records. A form is also useful in helping prevent incorrect data from being entered and it can be used to control access to specific data.

HINT
Save a form before making changes or applying formatting to the form.

You can use a variety of methods to create a form. The simplest method to create a form is to click the Create tab and then click the Form button in the Forms groups. Figure 5.1 displays the form you will create in Project 1a with the Clients table in the AL1-C5-Dearborn.accdb database. Access creates the form using all fields in the table in a vertical layout and displays the form in Layout view with the Form Layout Tools Design tab active.

Form

Changing Views

View

When you click the Form button to create a form, the form displays in Layout view. This is one of three views you can use when working with forms. Use the Form view to enter and manage records. Use the Layout view to view the data as well as modify the appearance and contents of the form and use the Design view to view the structure of the form and modify the form. Change views with the View button in the Views group in the Form Layout Tools Design tab or with buttons in the view area located at the right side of the Status bar.

You can open an existing form in Layout view. To do this, right-click the form name in the Navigation pane and then click *Layout View* at the shortcut menu.

▼ Quick Steps

Print Specific Record
1. Display form.
2. Click File tab, Print tab.
3. Click *Print* option.
4. Click *Selected Record(s)*.
5. Click OK.

Printing a Form

Print all records in the form by clicking the File tab, clicking the Print tab, and then clicking the *Quick Print* option. If you want to print a specific record in a form, click the File tab, click the Print tab, and then click the *Print* option. At the Print dialog box that displays, click the *Selected Record(s)* option and then click OK.

Figure 5.1 Form Created from Data in the Clients Table

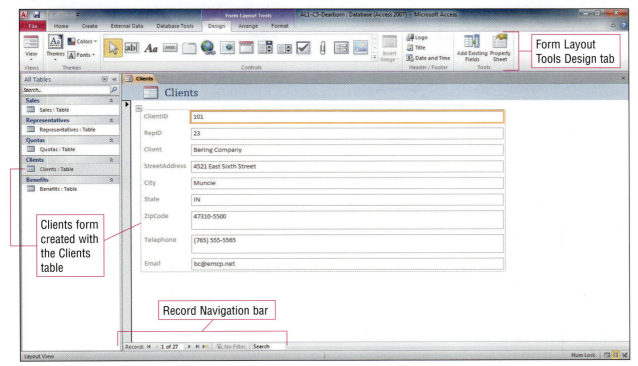

You can also print a range of records by clicking the *Pages* option in the *Print Range* section of the Print dialog box and then entering the beginning record number in the *From* text box and the ending record number in the *To* text box.

Navigating in a Form

When a form displays in either Form view or Layout view, navigation buttons display along the bottom of the form in the Record Navigation bar as identified in Figure 5.1. Using these navigation buttons, you can display the first record in the form, the previous record, the next record, the last record, and a new record.

Along with the Record Navigation bar, you can display records in a form using the keyboard. Press the Page Down key to move forward a single record or press the Page Up key to move back a single record. Press Ctrl + Home to display the first record or Press Ctrl + End to display the last record.

First Record

Previous Record

Next Record

Last Record

Project 1a   **Creating a Form with the Clients Table**   Part 1 of 7

1. Display the Open dialog box with Access2010L1C5 on your storage medium the active folder.
2. Open the **AL1-C5-Dearborn.accdb** database and enable the contents.
3. Display the Relationships window, insert all of the tables in the window, and then create the following relationships and enforce referential integrity and cascade fields and records:
    a. Create a one-to-many relationship with the *RepID* field in the Benefits table the "one" and the *RepID* field in the Clients table the "many."
    b. Create a one-to-one relationship with the *ClientID* field in the Clients table the "one" and the *ClientID* field in the Sales table the "one."

c. Create a one-to-many relationship with the *QuotaID* field in the Quotas table the "one" and the *QuotaID* in the Representatives table the "many."
d. Create a one-to-many relationship with the *RepID* field in the Representatives table the "one" and the *RepID* field in the Clients table the "many."
e. Create a one-to-one relationship with the *RepID* field in the Representatives table the "one" and the *RepID* field in the Benefits table the "one."
f. Save and then close the Relationships window.

4. Create a form with the Clients table by completing the following steps:
   a. Click the Clients table in the Navigation pane.
   b. Click the Create tab.
   c. Click the Form button in the Forms group.

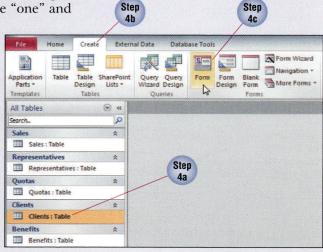

5. Switch to the Form view by clicking the View button in the Views group in the Form Layout Tools Design tab.

6. Navigate in the form by completing the following steps:
   a. Click the Next Record button in the Record Navigation bar to display the next record.
   b. Click the Last Record button in the Record Navigation bar to display the last record.
   c. Click the First Record button in the Record Navigation bar to display the first record.

7. Save the form by completing the following steps:
   a. Click the Save button on the Quick Access toolbar.
   b. At the Save As dialog box, with *Clients* inserted in the *Form Name* text box, click OK.

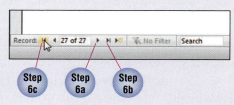

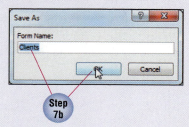

8. Print the current record in the form by completing the following steps:
   a. Click the File tab and then click the Print tab.
   b. Click the *Print* option.
   c. At the Print dialog box, click the *Selected Record(s)* option in the *Print Range* section, and then click OK.

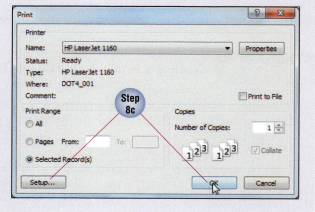

Adding and Deleting Records

Add a new record to the form by clicking the New (blank) Record button (contains a right arrow followed by a yellow asterisk) that displays in the Record Navigation bar along the bottom of the form. You can also add a new record to a form by clicking the Home tab and then clicking the New button in the Records group. To delete a record, display the record, click the Home tab, click the Delete button arrow in the Records group, and then click *Delete Record* at the drop-down list. At the message telling you that the record will be deleted permanently, click Yes.

Sorting Records

You can sort data in a form by clicking in the field containing data on which you want to sort and then clicking the Ascending button or Descending button in the Sort & Filter group in the Home tab. Click the Ascending button to sort text in alphabetic order from A to Z or numbers from lowest to highest or click the Descending button to sort text in alphabetic order from Z to A or numbers from highest to lowest.

▼ Quick Steps

Add a Record
Click New (blank) Record button in Record Navigation bar.
OR
1. Click Home tab.
2. Click New button.

Delete a Record
1. Click Home tab.
2. Click Delete button arrow.
3. Click *Delete Record*.
4. Click Yes.

New Record

Delete

Project 1b   Adding and Deleting Records in a Form   Part 2 of 7

1. With the Clients form open and the first record displayed, add a new record by completing the following steps:
   a. Click the New (blank) Record button located in the Record Navigation bar.
   b. At the new blank record, type the following information in the specified fields (move to the next field by pressing Tab or Enter; move to the previous field by pressing Shift + Tab):

ClientID	=	128
RepID	=	14
Client	=	Gen-Erin Productions
StreetAddress	=	1099 15th Street
City	=	Muncie
State	=	IN
ZipCode	=	473067963
Telephone	=	7655553120
Email	=	gep@emcp.net

2. Print the current record in the form by completing the following steps:
   a. Click the File tab and then click the Print tab.
   b. Click the *Print* option.
   c. At the Print dialog box, click the *Selected Record(s)* option in the *Print Range* section, and then click OK.
3. Delete the second record (ClientID 102) by completing the following steps:
   a. Click the First Record button in the Record Navigation bar.
   b. Click the Next Record button in the Record Navigation bar.

Step 1a

Step 1b

c. With Record 2 active, click the Home tab.
d. Click the Delete button arrow and then click *Delete Record* at the drop-down list.

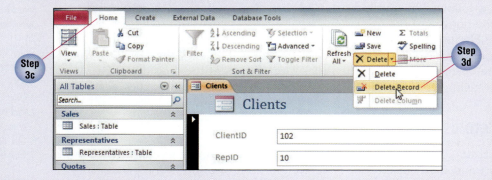

e. At the message that displays telling you that relationships that specify cascading deletes will cause records in the table to be deleted along with records in related tables, click the Yes button.
4. Click the New (blank) Record button in the Record Navigation bar and then type the following information in the specified fields.

> *ClientID* = 102
> *RepID* = 11
> *Client* = Sunrise Corporation
> *StreetAddress* = 14432 Center Avenue
> *City* = Indianapolis
> *State* = IN
> *ZipCode* = 462381744
> *Telephone* = 3175555640
> *Email* = sc@emcp.net

5. Sort the records in the form by completing the following steps:
   a. Click in the field containing the data *Sunrise Corporation* and then click the Ascending button in the Sort & Filter group in the Home tab.
   b. Click in the field containing the data *Indianapolis* and then click the Descending button in the Sort & Filter group.
   c. Click in the field containing the data *47310-5500* and then click the Ascending button in the Sort & Filter group.
   d. Click in the field containing the data *114* and then click the Ascending button in the Sort & Filter group.
6. Close the Clients form by clicking the Close button located in the upper right corner of the work area.

Creating a Form with a Related Table

When you created the form with the Clients table, only the Clients table fields displayed in the form. If you create a form with a table that has a one-to-many relationship established, Access adds a datasheet to the form that is based on the related table. For example, in Project 1c, you will create a form with the Representatives table and, since it is related to the Clients table by a one-to-many relationship, Access inserts a datasheet at the bottom of the form containing all of the records in the Clients table. Figure 5.2 displays the form you will create in Project 1c. Notice the datasheet that displays at the bottom of the form.

Figure 5.2 Representatives Form with Clients Datasheet

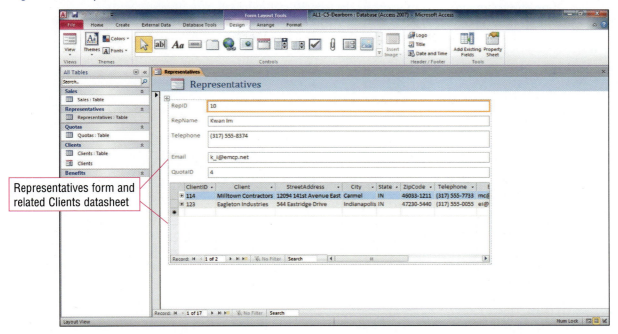

Representatives form and related Clients datasheet

If you have created only a single one-to-many relationship, the datasheet for the related table displays in the form. If you have created more than a single one-to-many relationship in a table, Access will not display any datasheets when you create a form with the table.

Project 1c   Creating a Form with a Related Table   Part 3 of 7

1. With the **AL1-C5-Dearborn.accdb** database open, create a form with the Representatives table by completing the following steps:
   a. Click the Representatives table in the Navigation pane.
   b. Click the Create tab.
   c. Click the Form button in the Forms group.
2. Insert a new record in the Clients table for representative 12 (Catherine Singleton) by completing the following steps:
   a. Click twice on the Next Record button in the Record Navigation bar at the bottom of the form window (not the Record Navigation bar in the Clients datasheet) to display the record for Catherine Singleton.
   b. Click in the cell immediately below *127* in the *ClientID* field in the Clients datasheet.

c. Type the following information in the specified fields:
   ClientID   =   129
   Client   =   Dan-Built Construction
   StreetAddress =   903 James Street
   City   =   Carmel
   State   =   IN
   ZipCode   =   460339050
   Telephone   =   3175551122
   Email   =   dc@emcp.net

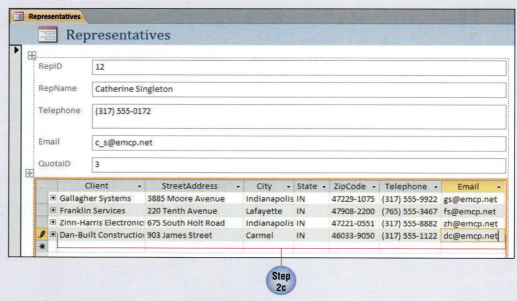

Step 2c

3. Click the Save button on the Quick Access toolbar and at the Save As dialog box with *Representatives* in the *Form Name* text box, click OK.
4. Print the current record in the form by completing the following steps:
   a. Click the File tab and then click the Print tab.
   b. Click the *Print* option.
   c. At the Print dialog box, click the *Select Record(s)* option in the *Print Range* section, and then click OK.
5. Close the Representatives form.

Customizing a Form

You can make almost all changes to a form in Layout view.

A form is comprised of a series of **control objects**, which are objects that display titles or descriptions, accept data, or perform actions. The area containing the control objects is called the *Detail* section and the area above the *Detail* section is the *Form Header* section.

You can customize control objects in the *Detail* section and data in the *Form Header* section with buttons in the Form Layout Tools ribbon with the Design tab, Arrange tab, or Format tab selected. When you open a form in Layout view, the Form Layout Tools Design tab is active. This tab contains options for applying a theme, inserting controls, inserting header or footer data, and adding existing fields.

Applying Themes

Access provides a number of themes you can use to format objects in a database. A *theme* is a set of formatting choices that include a color theme (a set of colors) and a font theme (a set of heading and body text fonts). To apply a theme, click the Themes button in the Themes group in the Form Layout Tools Design tab. At the drop-down gallery that displays, click the desired theme. Position the mouse pointer over a theme and the *live preview feature* will display the form with the theme formatting applied. With the live preview feature you can see how the theme formatting affects your form before you make your final choice. When you apply a theme, any new objects you create in the database will be formatted with the theme.

Themes

Colors

Font

You can further customize the formatting of a form with the Colors button and the Fonts button in the Themes group in the Form Layout Tools Design tab. If you want to customize the theme colors, click the Colors button in the Themes group, and then click the desired option at the drop-down list. Change the theme fonts by clicking the Themes button and then clicking the desired option at the drop-down list.

Themes available in Access are the same as the themes available in Word, Excel, and PowerPoint.

Inserting Data in the Form Header

Use buttons in the Header/Footer group in the Form Layout Tools Design tab to insert a logo, a form title, or the date and time. Click the Logo button and the Insert Picture dialog box displays. Browse to the folder containing the desired image and then double-click the image file. Click the Title button and the current title is selected. Type the new title and then press the Enter key. Click the Date and Time button in the Header/Footer group and the Date and Time dialog box displays. At this dialog box, choose the desired date and time format and then click OK. The date and time are inserted at the right side of the *Header* section.

Logo

Title

Date and Time

You can resize and move control objects in the Form *Header section*. To resize an object, click the object to select it and then drag a left or right border to increase or decrease the width. Drag a top or bottom border to increase or decrease the height of the object as well as the *Form Header* section. To move a selected object in the *Form Header* section, position the mouse pointer over the selected object until the pointer displays with a four-headed arrow attached. Hold down the left mouse button, drag the object to the desired position, and then release the mouse button.

Modifying a Control Object

When Access creates a form from a table, the first column in the form contains the label control objects and displays the field names from the table. The second column contains the text box control objects that display the field values you entered in the table. You can resize the width of either column. To do this, click in any control object in the desired column, position the mouse pointer on the right or left border of the selected control object until the pointer displays as a black, two-headed arrow pointing left and right. Hold down the left mouse button, drag left or right to change the width of the column, and then release the mouse button. Complete similar steps to change the height of the row containing the selected control object.

To delete a control object from the form, click the desired object and then press the Delete key. You can also right-click the object and then click *Delete* at the shortcut menu. If you want to delete a form row, right-click an object in the row you want to delete and then click *Delete Row* at the shortcut menu. To delete a column, right-click in one of the objects in the column you want to delete and then click *Delete Column* at the shortcut menu. In addition to the label and text box control objects, you can modify the size and position of objects in the *Form Header* section such as the logo and title.

Inserting a Control

The Controls group in the Form Layout Tools Design tab contains a number of control objects you can insert in a form. By default, the Select button is active. With this button active, use the mouse pointer to select control objects. You can insert a new label control and text box control object in your form by clicking the Text Box button in the Controls group and then clicking in the desired position in the form. Click in the label control object, select the default text, and then type the label text. You can enter text in a label control object in Layout view but you cannot enter data in a text box control object. In Form view, you can enter data in a text box control object but you cannot edit text in a label control object. The Controls group contains a number of additional buttons for inserting control objects in a form such as a hyperlink, combo box, or image.

Select

Text Box

Button

You can enter navigation control objects in a form by clicking the Button button in the Controls group and then clicking in the desired position in the form. This activates the Command Button Wizard. At the first Command Button Wizard dialog box, choose a category in the *Categories* list box and then choose the desired action in the *Actions* list box. The options in the *Actions* list box vary depending on the category you choose. Click the Next button and the second Command Button Wizard dialog box displays, choose whether you want text to display on the button or an image, and then click the Finish button.

Project 1d Customizing the Design of a Form Part 4 of 7

1. With the **AL1-C5-Dearborn.accdb** database open, open the Clients form you created in Project 1a by right-clicking the *Clients* form in the Navigation pane and then clicking *Layout View* at the shortcut menu.

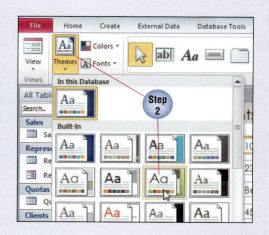

2. Apply a theme to the form by clicking the Themes button in the Themes group and then clicking *Austin* at the drop-down gallery.

3. Change the theme fonts by clicking the Fonts button in the Themes group and then clicking *Apex* at the drop-down gallery. (You may need to scroll down the list to display *Apex*.)
4. Insert a logo image in the *Form Header* section by completing the following steps:
   a. Right-click the logo object that displays in the *Form Header* section (located to the left of the title *Clients*) and then click *Delete* at the shortcut menu.

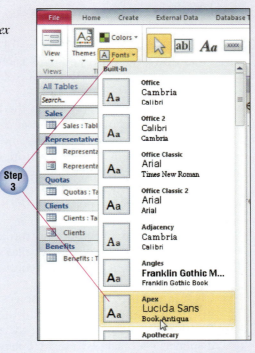

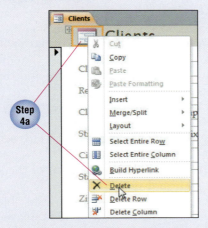

   b. Click the Logo button in the Header/Footer group.
   c. At the Insert Picture dialog box, navigate to the Access2010L1C5 folder on your storage medium and then double-click the file named **DearbornLogo.jpg**.
5. Change the title by completing the following steps:
   a. Click the Title button in the Header/Footer group. (This selects *Clients* in the *Form Header* section.)
   b. Type **Dearborn Clients Form** and then press Enter.

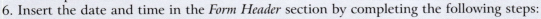

6. Insert the date and time in the *Form Header* section by completing the following steps:
   a. Click the Date and Time button in the Header/Footer group.
   b. At the Date and Time dialog box, click OK.
7. Size the control object containing the title by completing the following steps:
   a. Click in any field outside the title and then click the title to select the control object.
   b. Position the mouse pointer on the right border of the selected object until the pointer displays as a black, two-headed arrow pointing left and right.
   c. Hold down the left mouse button, drag to the left until the right border is immediately right of the title, and then release the mouse button.

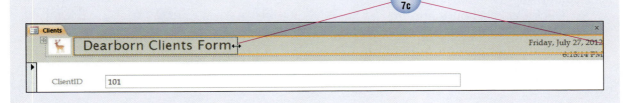

Chapter 5 ■ Creating Forms   197

8. Size and move the control objects containing the date and time by completing the following steps:
   a. Click the date to select the control object.
   b. Hold down the Shift key, click the time, and then release the Shift key. (Both control objects should be selected.)
   c. Position the mouse pointer on the left border of the selected objects until the pointer displays as a black, two-headed arrow pointing left and right.
   d. Hold down the left mouse button, drag to the right until the border displays immediately left of the date and time, and then release the mouse button.
   e. Position the mouse pointer in the selected objects until the pointer displays with a four-headed arrow attached.
   f. Hold down the left mouse button and then drag the outline of the date and time objects to the left until the outline displays near the title.

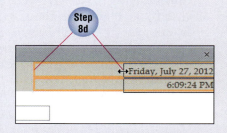

Step 8d

9. Decrease the size of the second column of control objects in the *Detail* section by completing the following steps:
   a. Click in the text box control object containing the client number *101*. (This selects and inserts an orange border around the object.)
   b. Position the mouse pointer on the right border of the selected object until the pointer displays as a black, two-headed arrow pointing left and right.
   c. Hold down the left mouse button, drag to the left until the text box control objects are just slightly wider than the text, and then release the mouse button. (See image below.)

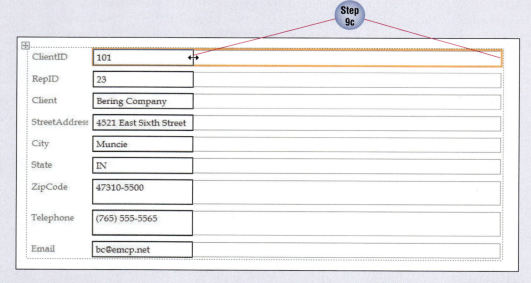

Step 9c

10. Insert a label control object by completing the following steps:
    a. Click the Label button in the Controls group.

Step 10a

b. Click immediately right of the text box containing the telephone number *(765) 555-5565*. (This inserts the label to the right of the *telephone number* text box.)
   c. With the insertion point positioned inside the label, type **Type the telephone number without symbols or spaces** and then press the Enter key.
11. Change the size of the new label control object by completing the following steps:
   a. Position the arrow pointer on the right border of the new label control object until the pointer displays as a black, two-headed arrow pointing left and right.
   b. Hold down the left mouse button, drag the border to the right approximately an inch, and then release the mouse button. The text line in the label should break after the word *number*.
   c. Decrease the height of the new label control object by dragging the bottom border up so it is positioned just below the second line of text. (See image at right.)
12. Click the Save button on the Quick Access toolbar to save the changes you made to the form.

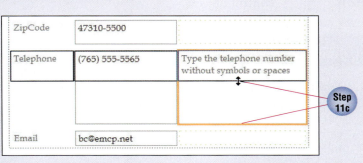

Arranging Objects

With options in the Form Layout Tools Arrange tab, you can select, insert, delete, arrange, merge, and split cells. When you inserted a label control object to the right of the *Telephone* text box control in Project 1d, empty cells were inserted in the form above and below the new label control object. You can select a control object or cell by clicking in the desired object or cell. You can select adjacent objects or cells by holding down the Shift key while clicking in the desired objects or cells. To select nonadjacent objects or cells, hold down the Ctrl key while clicking in the desired objects or cells.

Select a row of control objects and cells by clicking the Select Row button in the Rows & Columns group or by right-clicking in an object or cell and then clicking *Select Entire Row* at the shortcut menu. To select a column of control objects and cells, click the Select Column button in the Rows & Columns group, or right-click an object or cell and then click *Select Entire Column* at the shortcut menu. You can also select a column by positioning the mouse pointer at the top of the column until the pointer displays as a small, down-pointing black arrow and then clicking the left mouse button.

Select Row

Select Column

Insert Above

Insert Below

Merge

Chapter 5 ■ Creating Forms

Split Vertically

Split Horizontally

Control Margins

Control Padding

HINT You can move a control object by dragging it to the desired location.

The Rows & Columns group contains buttons for inserting a row or column of blank cells. To insert a new row, select a cell or object in a row and then click the Insert Above button to insert a row of blank cells above the current row or click the Insert Below button to insert a row below. Complete similar steps to insert a new column of blank cells either left or right of the current column.

You can merge adjacent selected cells by clicking the Merge button in the Merge/Split group in the Form Layout Tools Arrange tab. You can split a control object or a cell by clicking the object or cell to make it active and then clicking the Split Vertically button or Split Horizontally button in the Merge/Split group. When you split a control object, an empty cell is created to the right of the control object.

You can move up or down a row of control objects. To do this, select the desired row and then click the Move Up button in the Move group to move the row above the current row or click the Move Down button to move the row below the current row. Use the Control Margins button in the Position group to increase or decrease margins within control objects. The Position group also contains a Control Padding button you can use to increase or decrease spacing between control objects.

Project 1e Arranging Objects in a Form   Part 5 of 7

1. With the Clients form open in Layout view in the **AL1-C5-Dearborn.accdb** database, select and merge cells by completing the following steps:
   a. Click to the right of the text box control object containing the text *101*. (This selects the empty cell.)
   b. Hold down the Shift key and then click to the right of the text box control containing the text *Muncie*. (This selects five adjacent cells.)
   c. Click the Form Layout Tools Arrange tab.
   d. Click the Merge button in the Merge/Split group.
2. With the cells merged, insert an image control object and then insert an image by completing the following steps:
   a. Click the Form Layout Tools Design tab.
   b. Click the Image button in the Controls group.

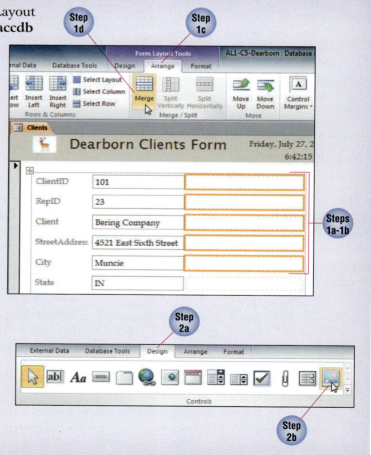

c. Move the mouse pointer (pointer displays as a plus symbol next to an image icon) to the location of the merged cell until the cell displays with yellow fill color and then click the left mouse button.

d. At the Insert Picture dialog box, navigate to the Access2010L1C5 folder on your storage medium and then double-click *Dearborn.jpg*.

3. Insert a row by completing the following steps:
   a. Click in the control object containing the field name *Email*.
   b. Click the Form Layout Tools Arrange tab.
   c. Click the Insert Below button in the Rows & Columns group. (This inserts a row of blank cells at the bottom of the form.)

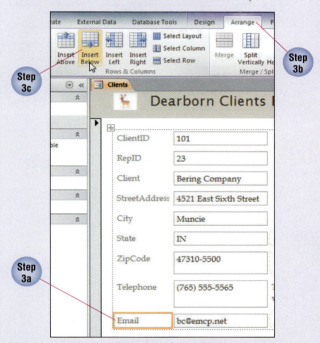

4. Split cells horizontally by completing the following steps:
   a. Click below the text box control object containing the text *bc@emcp.net*. (This selects the empty cell.)
   b. Click the Split Horizontally button in the Merge/Split group.
5. Insert a Previous button in the selected cell (the left empty cell below the text *bc@emcp.net*) by completing the following steps:
   a. Click the Form Layout Tools Design tab.
   b. Click the Button button in the Controls group.
   c. Move the mouse pointer to the left empty cell below the text *bc@emcp.net* until the cell displays with yellow fill color and then click the left mouse button.

d. At the Command Button Wizard dialog box that displays, click the *Go To Previous Record* option in the *Actions* list box and then click the Finish button.

6. Insert a Next button in the cell immediately right of the Previous button by completing the following steps:
   a. Click the Button button in the Controls group.
   b. Move the mouse pointer to the cell to the right of the Previous button in the bottom row until the cell displays with yellow fill color and then click the left mouse button.
   c. At the Command Button Wizard dialog box, click the *Go To Next Record* option in the *Actions* list box and then click the Finish button.
7. Move down the telephone row by completing the following steps:
   a. Click the Form Layout Tools Arrange tab.
   b. Click in the control object containing the text *Telephone*.
   c. Click the Select Row button in the Rows & Columns group.
   d. Click the Move Down button in the Move group.
8. Increase the spacing (padding) between all objects and cells in the form by completing the following steps:
   a. Click the Form Layout Tools Arrange tab.
   b. Click the Select Layout button in the Rows & Columns group. (This selects all objects and cells in the form.)
   c. Click the Control Padding button in the Position group and then click *Medium* at the drop-down list.
9. Click in the control object containing the field name *ClientID*.
10. Save the Clients form.

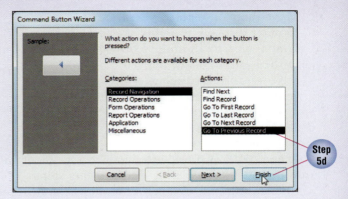

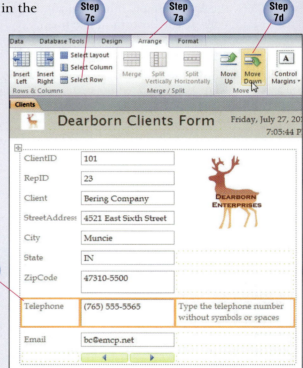

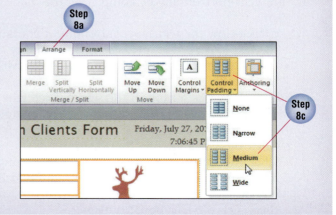

Formatting a Form

Click the Form Layout Tools Format tab and buttons and options display for applying formatting to a form or specific objects in a form. If you want to apply formatting to a specific object, click the object in the form, or click the Object button arrow in the Selection group and then click the desired object at the drop-down list. To format all objects in the form, click the Select All button in the Selection group. This selects all objects in the form including objects in the *Form Header* section. If you want to select all of the objects in the *Detail* section (and not the *Form Header* section), click the selector button that displays in the upper left corner of form objects in the *Detail* section. Click an object in the *Detail* section to display the selector button, which displays as a small square with a four-headed arrow inside. You can also click the selector button and then drag the button to move the objects in the form.

Object

Select All

With buttons in the Font, Number, Background, and Control Formatting groups, you can apply formatting to a control object or cell and to selected objects cells in a form. Use buttons in the Font group to change the font, apply a different font size, apply text effects such as bold and underline, and change the alignment of data in objects. If the form contains data with a data type of Number or Currency, use buttons in the Number group to apply specific formatting to numbers. Insert a background image in the form using the Background button and apply formatting to objects or cells with buttons in the Control Formatting group. Depending on what is selected in the form, some of the buttons may not be active.

Project 1f   Formatting a Form   Part 6 of 7

1. With the Clients form open in the **AL1-C5-Dearborn.accdb** database, change the font and font size of text in the form by completing the following steps:
   a. Click in any control object in the form.
   b. Select all control objects and cells in the form by clicking the selector button that displays in the upper left corner of the *Detail* section. (See the image below.)
   c. Click the Form Layout Tools Format tab.
   d. Click the Font button arrow, scroll down the drop-down list, and then click *Tahoma*. (Fonts are alphabetized in the drop-down list.)
   e. Click the Font Size button arrow and then click *10* at the drop-down list.

2. Apply formatting and change the alignment of the first column by completing the following steps:
   a. Click the control object containing the field name *ClientID*, hold down the Shift key, click the bottom control object containing field name *Telephone*, and then release the Shift key.

b. Click the Bold button in the Font group.
   c. Click the Shape Fill button in the Control Formatting group and then click the *Brown, Accent 5, Lighter 60%* color option (located in the ninth column from the left in the *Theme Colors* section).
   d. Click the Shape Outline button in the Control Formatting group and then click the *Brown, Accent 5, Darker 50%* option (last option in the ninth column in the *Theme Colors* section).
   e. Click the Align Text Right button in the Font group.
3. Apply shape fill to the second column by completing the following steps:
   a. Click the text box control object containing the text *101*.
   b. Position the mouse pointer at the top border of the selected object until the pointer displays as a small, black, down-pointing arrow and then click the left mouse button. (Make sure all of the objects in the second column are selected.)
   c. Click the Shape Fill button in the Control Formatting group and then click the *Brown, Accent 5, Lighter 80%* color option (located in the ninth column in the *Theme Colors* section).
4. Apply quick styles and change the shape of the Previous Record button by completing the following steps:
   a. Click the Previous Record button (the button on the left).
   b. Click the Quick Styles button in the Control Formatting group and then click the *Subtle Effect - Orange, Accent 6* option (last option in the fourth row).
   c. With the Previous Record button still selected, click the Change Shape button in the Control Formatting group and then click the *Rounded Rectangle* option (last option in the first row).

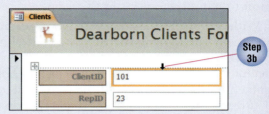
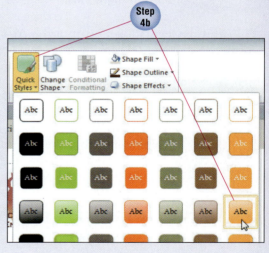
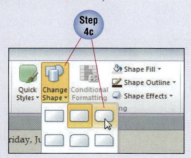

5. Select the Next Record button and then apply the same quick style and shape that you applied to the Previous Record button.
6. Save the Clients form.

Applying Conditional Formatting

With the Conditional Formatting button in the Control Formatting group, you can apply formatting to data that meets a specific criterion or apply conditional formatting to data in all records in a form. For example, you can apply conditional formatting to sales amounts in a form that displays amounts higher than a specified number in a different color or you can apply conditional formatting to states' names and specify a specific color for companies in a particular state. You can also include conditional formatting that inserts data bars that visually compare data among records. The data bars provide a visual representation of the comparison of data in records. For example, in Project 1g, you will insert data bars in the *Sales 2010* field that provide a visual representation of how the sales amount in one record compares to the sales amount in other records.

To apply conditional formatting, click the Conditional Formatting button in the Control Formatting group and the Conditional Formatting Rules Manager dialog box displays. At this dialog box, click the New Rule button and the New Formatting Rule dialog box displays as shown in Figure 5.3. In the *Select a rule type* option box, choose the *Check values in the current record or use an expression* option if the conditional formatting is applied to a field in the record that matches a specific condition. Click the *Compare to other records* option if you want to insert data bars in a field in all records that compare the data among the records.

If you want to apply conditional formatting to a field, specify the field and field condition with options in the *Edit the rule description* section of the dialog box. Specify the type of formatting you want applied to data in a field that meets the specific criterion. For example, in Project 1g, you will specify that you want to change the shape fill to light green for all *City* fields containing *Indianapolis*. When you have made all the desired changes to the dialog box, click OK to close the dialog box and then click OK to close the Conditional Formatting Rules Manager dialog box.

To insert data bars in a field, click the Conditional Formatting button, click the New Rule button at the Conditional Formatting Rules Manager dialog box, and then click the *Compare to other records* option in the *Select a rule type* section. This changes the options in the dialog box as shown in Figure 5.4. Make the desired changes in the *Edit the rule description* section.

Figure 5.3 New Formatting Rule Dialog Box

Figure 5.4 New Formatting Rule Dialog Box with Compare to Other Records Option Selected

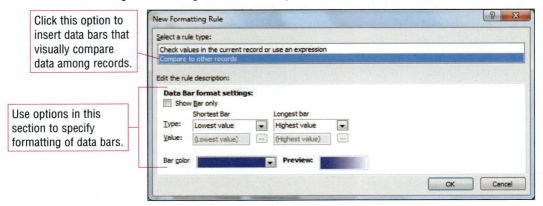

Click this option to insert data bars that visually compare data among records.

Use options in this section to specify formatting of data bars.

Project 1g Applying Conditional Formatting to Fields in Forms   Part 7 of 7

1. With the Clients form open in the **AL1-C5-Dearborn.accdb** database, apply conditional formatting so that the *City* field displays any Indianapolis entries with a light green shape fill by completing the following steps:
   a. Click in the text box control object containing the text *Muncie*.
   b. Click the Form Layout Tools Format tab.
   c. Click the Conditional Formatting button in the Control Formatting group.
   d. At the Conditional Formatting Rules Manager dialog box, click the New Rule button.
   e. At the New Formatting Rule dialog box, click the down-pointing arrow at the right side of the option box containing the word *between* and then click *equal to* at the drop-down list.
   f. Click in the text box to the right of the *equal to* option box and then type **Indianapolis**.
   g. Click the Background color button arrow and then click the *Green 2* color option (located in the seventh column).
   h. Click OK to close the New Formatting Rule dialog box.
   i. Click OK to close the Conditional Formatting Rules Manager dialog box.

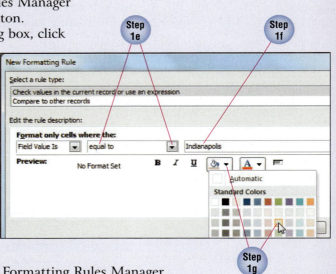

2. Click the Home tab and then click the View button to switch to Form view.
3. Click the Next Record button (one of the buttons you inserted) to display the next record in the form. Continue clicking the Next Record button to view records and notice that *Indianapolis* displays with light green shading fill.
4. Click the First Record button in the Navigation bar.
5. Click the Save button on the Quick Access toolbar.

6. Print page 1 of the form by completing the following steps:
   a. Click the File tab and then click the Print tab.
   b. Click the *Print* option.
   c. At the Print dialog box, click the *Pages* option in the *Print Range* section, type **1** in the *From* text box, press the Tab key, and then type **1** in the *To* text box.
   d. Click OK.
7. Close the Clients form.
8. Create a form with the Sales table by completing the following steps:
   a. Click once on the Sales table name in the Navigation pane.
   b. Click the Create tab.
   c. Click the Form button in the Forms group.
9. With the text box control object containing the text *101* selected, drag the right border to the left until the border is positioned as shown in the image below. (The right border should be positioned approximately one inch to the right of the sales amounts.)

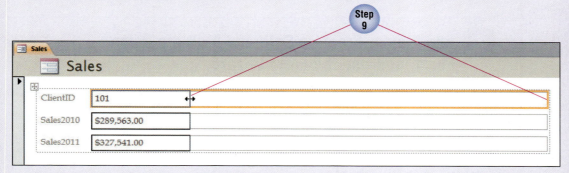

10. Change the alignment of text by completing the following steps:
    a. Right-click the selected text box control object (the object containing the text *101*) and then click *Select Entire Column* at the shortcut menu.
    b. Click the Form Layout Tools Format tab.
    c. Click the Align Text Right button in the Font group.
11. Apply data bars to the *Sales2010* field by completing the following steps:
    a. Click in the text box control object containing the text *$289,563.00*.
    b. Make sure the Form Layout Tools Format tab is active.
    c. Click the Conditional Formatting button.
    d. At the Conditional Formatting Rules Manager dialog box, click the New Rule button.
    e. At the New Formatting Rule dialog box, click the *Compare to other records* option in the *Select a rule type* section.
    f. Click the down-pointing arrow at the right side of the *Bar color* option box and then click the *Green 3* color option (located in the seventh column).
    g. Click OK to close the New Formatting Rule dialog box and then click OK to close the Conditional Formatting Rules Manager dialog box.

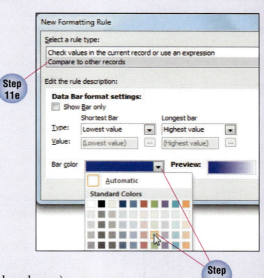

12. Click in the text box control object containing the text *$327,541.00* and then apply the same data bars that you applied to the *Sales2010* field.

13. Click the Next Record button in the Navigation bar to display the next record. Continue clicking the Next Record button and notice the data bars that display in the *Sales2010* and *Sales2011* fields.
14. Click the First Record button in the Navigation bar.
15. Click the Save button on the Quick Access toolbar. At the Save As dialog box with *Sales* inserted in the *Form Name* text box, click OK.
16. Print page 1 of the form by completing the following steps:
    a. Click the File tab and then click the Print tab.
    b. Click the *Print* option.
    c. At the Print dialog box, click the *Pages* option in the *Print Range* section, type 1 in the *From* text box, press the Tab key, type 1 in the *To* text box, and then click OK.
17. Close the Sales form.
18. Close the **AL1-C5-Dearborn.accdb** database.

Project 2 Add Fields, Create a Split and Multiple Items Form, and Use the Form Wizard   5 Parts

You will open the Skyline database, create a form and add related fields to the form, create a split and multiple items form, and create a form using the Form Wizard.

Adding Existing Fields

Alt + F8 is the keyboard shortcut to display the Field List pane.

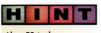

Use the Field List pane to add fields from a table or query to your form.

Add Existing Fields

If you create a form and then realize that you forgot a field or want to insert an existing field in the form, display the form in Layout view and then click the Add Existing Fields button located in the Tools group in the Form Layout Tools Design tab. When you click the Add Existing Fields button, the Field List pane opens and displays at the right side of the screen. This pane displays the fields available in the current view, fields available in related tables, and fields available in other tables. Figure 5.5 displays the Field List pane you will open in Project 2a.

In the *Fields available for this view* section, Access displays all fields in any tables used to create the form. So far, you have been creating a form with all fields in one table. In the *Fields available in related tables*, Access displays tables that are related to the table(s) used to create the form. To display the fields in the related table, click the plus symbol that displays before the table name in the Field List pane and the list expands to display all field names.

To add a field to the form, double-click the desired field in the Field List pane. This inserts the field below the existing fields in the form. You can also drag a field from the Field List pane into the form. To do this, position the mouse pointer on the desired field in the Field List window, hold down the left mouse button, drag into the form window, and then release the mouse button. A yellow insert indicator bar displays as you drag the field in the existing fields in the form. When you drag over a cell, the cell displays with yellow fill. When the insert indicator bar is in the desired position or the desired cell is selected, release the mouse button.

You can insert multiple fields in a form from the Field List pane. To do this, hold down the Ctrl key while clicking the desired fields and then drag the fields into the form. If you try to drag a field from a table in the *Fields available in other*

Figure 5.5 Field List Pane

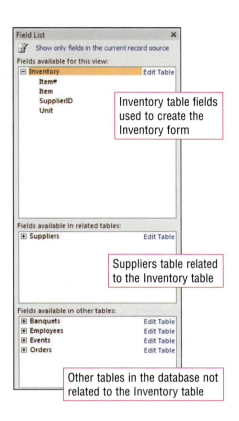

tables section, the Specify Relationship dialog box will display. To move a field from the Field List pane to the form, the field must be located in a table that is related to the table(s) used to create the form.

Project 2a Adding Existing Fields to a Form   Part 1 of 5

1. Display the Open dialog box with Access2010L1C5 on your storage medium the active folder, open the **AL1-C5-Skyline.accdb** database, and enable the contents.
2. Create a form with the Inventory table by clicking the Inventory table name in the Navigation pane, clicking the Create tab, and then clicking the Form button in the Forms group.
3. With the text box control object containing the text *001* selected, drag the right border to the left until the selected object is approximately one-half of the original width. (See the image below.)

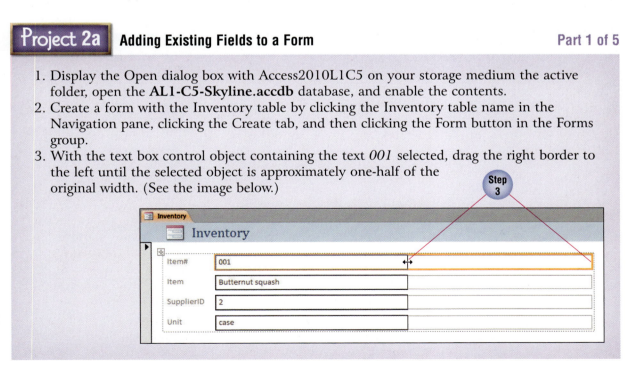

Chapter 5 ■ Creating Forms   209

4. With the text box control object still selected, click the Form Layout Tools Arrange tab and then click the Split Horizontally button in the Merge/Split group. (This splits the text box control object into one object and one empty cell.)
5. You decide that you want to add the supplier name to the form so the name displays when entering a form. Add the supplier name field by completing the following steps:
   a. Click the Form Layout Tools Design tab.
   b. Click the Add Existing Fields button in the Tools group in the Form Layout Tools Design tab.
   c. Click the Show all tables hyperlink that displays toward the top of the Field List pane.

   d. Click the plus symbol that displays immediately left of the Suppliers table name located in the *Fields available in related tables* section of the Field List window.
   e. Position the mouse pointer on the *SupplierName* field, hold down the left mouse button, drag into the form until the yellow insert indicator bar displays immediately right of the text box control containing *2* (the text box control that displays at the right side of the *SupplierID* label control), and then release the mouse button. Access inserts the field as a Lookup field (down-pointing arrow displays at right side of field).

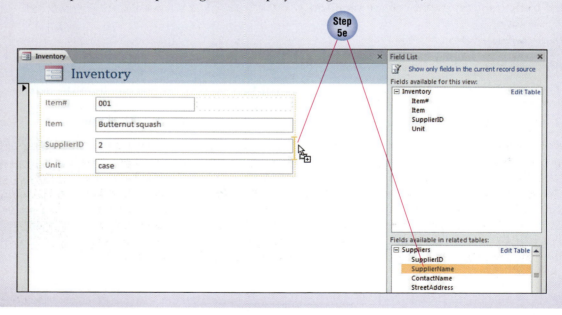

f. Change the *SupplierName* field from a Lookup field to a text box by clicking the Options button that displays below the field and then clicking *Change to Text Box* at the drop-down list. (This removes the down-pointing arrow at the right side of the field.)

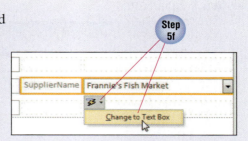

g. Close the Field List pane by clicking the Close button located in the upper right corner of the window.

6. Insert a logo image in the *Form Header* section by completing the following steps:
   a. Right-click the logo object that displays in the *Form Header* section (located to the left of the title *Inventory*) and then click *Delete* at the shortcut menu.
   b. Click the Logo button in the Header/Footer group.
   c. At the Insert Picture dialog box, navigate to the Access2010L1C5 folder on your storage medium and then double-click the file named ***Cityscape.jpg***.
7. Change the title by completing the following steps:
   a. Click the Title button in the Header/Footer group. (This selects *Inventory* in the *Form Header* section.)
   b. Type **Skyline Inventory Input Form** and then press Enter.
8. Insert the date and time in the *Form Header* section by clicking the Date and Time button in the Header/Footer group and then clicking OK at the Date and Time dialog box.
9. Click in any field outside the title, click the title to select the control object, and then drag the right border of the title control object to the left until the border displays near the title.
10. Select the date and time control objects, drag in the left border until the border displays near the date and time, and then drag the objects so they are positioned near the title.
11. Scroll through the records in the form.
    12. Click the First Record button in the Record Navigation bar.
13. Click the Save button on the Quick Access toolbar and save the form with the name *Inventory*.
14. Print the current record.
15. Close the Inventory form.

Creating a Split Form

You can create a form by choosing the *Split Form* option at the More Forms button drop-down list in the Forms group in the Create tab. When you use this option to create a form, Access splits the screen in the work area and provides two views for the form. The top half of the work area displays the form in Layout view and the bottom half of the work area displays the form in Datasheet view. The two views are connected and are **synchronous**, which means that displaying or modifying a specific field in the Form view portion will cause the same action to occur in the field in the Datasheet view portion. Figure 5.6 displays the split form you will create for Project 2b.

▼ **Quick Steps**

Create a Split Form
1. Click desired table.
2. Click Create tab.
3. Click More Forms button.
4. Click *Split Form*.

More Forms

Figure 5.6 Split Form

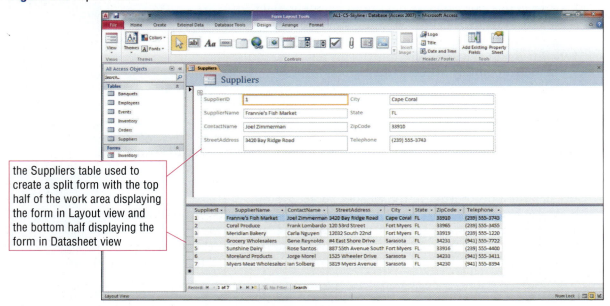

the Suppliers table used to create a split form with the top half of the work area displaying the form in Layout view and the bottom half displaying the form in Datasheet view

Project 2b Creating a Split Form   Part 2 of 5

1. With the **AL1-C5-Skyline.accdb** database open, create a split form with the Suppliers table by completing the following steps:
   a. Click the Suppliers table in the Navigation pane.
   b. Click the Create tab.
   c. Click the More Forms button in the Forms group and then click *Split Form* at the drop-down list.

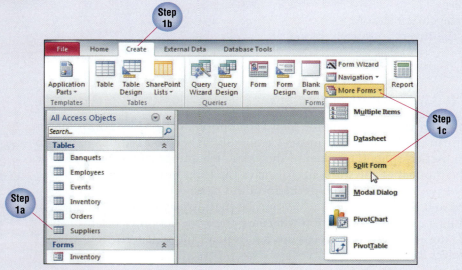

   d. Click several times on the Next Record button in the Navigation bar. (As you display records, notice that the current record in the Form view in the top portion of the window is the same record selected in Datasheet view in the lower portion of the window.)

2. Apply a theme by clicking the Themes button in the Themes group in the Form Layout Tools Design tab and then clicking *Adjacency* at the drop-down gallery.

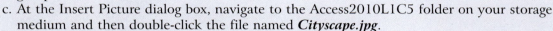

3. Insert a logo image in the *Form Header* section by completing the following steps:
   a. Right-click the logo object that displays in the *Form Header* section (located to the left of the title *Clients*) and then click *Delete* at the shortcut menu.
   b. Click the Logo button in the Header/Footer group.
   c. At the Insert Picture dialog box, navigate to the Access2010L1C5 folder on your storage medium and then double-click the file named ***Cityscape.jpg***.
4. Change the title by completing the following steps:
   a. Click the Title button in the Header/Footer group. (This selects *Suppliers* in the *Form Header* section.)
   b. Type **Skyline Suppliers Input Form** and then press Enter.
5. Insert the date and time in the *Form Header* section by clicking the Date and Time button in the Header/Footer group and then clicking OK at the Date and Time dialog box.
6. Click in any field outside the title, click the title to select the control object, and then drag the right border of the title control object to the left until the border displays near the title.
7. Select the date and time control objects, drag in the left border until the border displays near the date and time, and then drag the objects so they are positioned so the right border is aligned with the right side of the field value *Cape Coral*.
8. Insert a new record in the Suppliers form by completing the following steps:
   a. Click the View button to switch to Form view.
   b. Click the New (blank) Record button in the Record Navigation bar.
   c. Click in the *SupplierID* field in the Form view portion of the window and then type the following information in the specified fields:

SupplierID	=	**8**
SupplierName	=	**Jackson Produce**
ContactName	=	**Marshall Jackson**
StreetAddress	=	**5790 Cypress Avenue**
City	=	**Fort Myers**
State	=	**FL**
ZipCode	=	**33917**
Telephone	=	**2395555002**

9. Click the Save button on the Quick Access toolbar and save the form with the name *Suppliers*.

10. Print the current form by completing the following steps:
    a. Click the File tab and then click the Print tab.
    b. Click the *Print* option.
    c. At the Print dialog box, click the Setup button.
    d. At the Page Setup dialog box, click the *Print Form Only* option in the *Split Form* section of the dialog box and then click OK.
    e. At the Print dialog box, click the *Selected Record(s)* option and then click OK.
11. Close the Suppliers form.

Step 10d

▼ **Quick Steps**

Create a Multiple Items Form
1. Click desired table.
2. Click Create tab.
3. Click More Forms button.
4. Click *Multiple Items*.

Creating a Multiple Items Form

When you create a form with the Form button, a single record displays. You can use the *Multiple Items* option at the More Forms button drop-down list to create a form that displays multiple records. The advantage to creating a multiple items form over displaying the table in Datasheet view is that you can customize the form using buttons in the Form Layout Tools ribbon with the Design, Arrange, or Format tab selected.

Project 2c — Creating a Multiple Items Form — Part 3 of 5

1. With the **AL1-C5-Skyline.accdb** database open, create a multiple items form by completing the following steps:
   a. Click the Orders table in the Navigation pane.
   b. Click the Create tab.
   c. Click the More Forms button in the Forms group and then click *Multiple Items* at the drop-down list.
2. Insert the **Cityscape.jpg** image as the logo.
3. Insert the title *Skyline Orders*.
4. Insert the date and time in the *Form Header* section.
5. Decrease the border of the title control object and then size and move the date and time control objects so they display near the title.
6. Save the form with the name *Orders*.
7. Print the first record in the form by completing the following steps:
   a. Click the File tab and then click the Print tab.
   b. Click the *Print* option.
   c. At the Print dialog box, click the *Pages* option in the *Print Range* section.
   d. Type **1** in the *From* text box, press the Tab key, and then type **1** in the *To* text box.
   e. Click OK.
8. Close the Orders form.

Creating a Form Using the Form Wizard

Access offers a Form Wizard that guides you through the creation of a form. To create a form using the Form Wizard, click the Create tab and then click the Form Wizard button in the Forms group. At the first Form Wizard dialog box, shown in Figure 5.7, specify the table and then the fields you want included in the form. To select the table, click the down-pointing arrow at the right side of the *Table/Queries* option box and then click the desired table. Select the desired field in the *Available Fields* list box and then click the button containing the One Field button (the button containing the greater than symbol). This inserts the field in the *Selected Fields* list box. Continue in this manner until you have inserted all desired fields in the *Selected Fields* list box. If you want to insert all fields into the *Selected Fields* list box at one time, click the All Fields button (button containing two greater than symbols). After specifying fields, click the Next button.

At the second Form Wizard dialog box, specify the layout for the records. You can choose from *Columnar*, *Tabular*, *Datasheet*, and *Justified*. Click the Next button and the third and final Form Wizard dialog box displays and offers a title for the form and also provides the option *Open the form to view or enter information*. Make any necessary changes in this dialog box and then click the Finish button.

▼ **Quick Steps**

Create a Form Using Form Wizard
1. Click Create tab.
2. Click Form Wizard button.
3. Choose desired options at each Form Wizard dialog box.

HINT

With the Form Wizard, you can be more selective about what fields you insert in a form.

Form Wizard

Figure 5.7 First Form Wizard Dialog Box

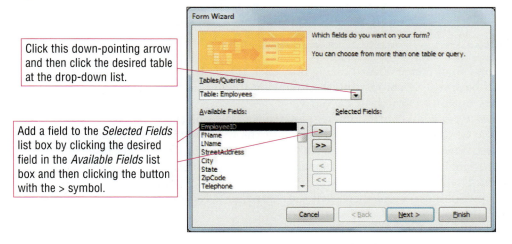

Project 2d **Creating a Form Using the Form Wizard** Part 4 of 5

1. With the **AL1-C5-Skyline.accdb** database open, create a form with the Form Wizard by completing the following steps:
   a. Click the Create tab.
   b. Click the Form Wizard button in the Forms group.

c. At the first Form Wizard dialog box, click the down-pointing arrow at the right side of the *Tables/Queries* option box and then click *Table: Employees* at the drop-down list.
d. Specify that you want all fields included in the form by clicking the All Fields button (button containing the two greater than symbols).
e. Click the Next button.
f. At the second Form Wizard dialog box, click the *Justified* option and then click the Next button.

Step 1c

Step 1d

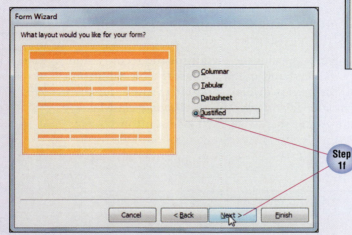

Step 1f

g. At the third and final Form Wizard dialog box, click the Finish button.
2. Format the field headings by completing the following steps:
   a. Click the View button to switch to Layout view.
   b. Click the *EmployeeID* label control object. (This selects the object.)
   c. Hold down the Ctrl key and then click on each of the following label control objects: *FName*, *LName*, *StreetAddress*, *City*, *State*, *ZipCode*, *Telephone*, *HireDate*, and *HealthIns*.
   d. With all of the label control objects selected, release the Ctrl key.
   e. Click the Form Layout Tools Format tab.
   f. Click the Shape Fill button and then click the *Aqua Blue 2* color option (located in the ninth column in the *Standard Colors* section).
   g. Click the Form Layout Tools Design tab and then click the View button to switch to Form view.
3. In Form view, click the New (blank) Record button and then add the following records:

EmployeeID	=	**13**
FirstName	=	**Carol**
LastName	=	**Thompson**
StreetAddress	=	**6554 Willow Drive, Apt. B**
City	=	**Fort Myers**
State	=	**FL**
ZipCode	=	**33915**
Telephone	=	**2395553719**
HireDate	=	**10/1/2011**
HealthIns	=	(Click in the check box to insert a check mark.)

```
EmployeeID     =   14
FirstName      =   Eric
LastName       =   Hahn
StreetAddress  =   331 South 152nd Street
City           =   Cape Coral
State          =   FL
ZipCode        =   33906
Telephone      =   2395558107
HireDate       =   10/1/2011
HealthIns      =   (Leave blank.)
```
4. Click the Save button on the Quick Access toolbar.
5. Print the record for Eric Hahn and then print the record for Carol Thompson.
6. Close the Employees form.

In Project 2d you used the Form Wizard to create a form with all of the fields in one table. If tables are related, you can create a form using fields from related tables. At the first Form Wizard dialog box, choose fields from the selected table and then choose fields from a related table. To change to the related table, click the down-pointing arrow at the right of the *Tables/Queries* option box and then click the name of the desired table.

Project 2e Creating a Form with Related Tables   Part 5 of 5

1. With the **AL1-C5-Skyline.accdb** database open, create a form with related tables by completing the following steps:
   a. Click the Create tab.
   b. Click the Form Wizard button in the Forms group.
   c. At the first Form Wizard dialog box, click the down-pointing arrow at the right of the *Tables/Queries* option box and then click *Table: Banquets*.
   d. Click *ResDate* in the *Available Fields* list box and then click the One Field button (button containing one greater than symbol). (This inserts *ResDate* in the *Selected Fields* list box.)
   e. Click *AmountTotal* in the *Available Fields* list box and then click the One Field button.
   f. Click *AmountPaid* in the *Available Fields* list box and then click the One Field button.
   g. Click the down-pointing arrow at the right side of the *Tables/Queries* option box and then click *Table: Events* at the drop-down list.
   h. Click *Event* in the *Available Fields* list box and then click the One Field button.
   i. Click the down-pointing arrow at the right side of the *Tables/Queries* option box and then click *Table: Employees* at the drop-down list.

j. Click *LName* in the *Available Fields* list box and then click the One Field button.
k. Click the Next button.
l. At the second Form Wizard dialog box, click the Next button.
m. At the third Form Wizard dialog box, click the Next button.
n. At the fourth Form Wizard dialog box, select the text in the *What title do you want for your form?* text box, type **Upcoming Banquets**, and then click the Finish button.

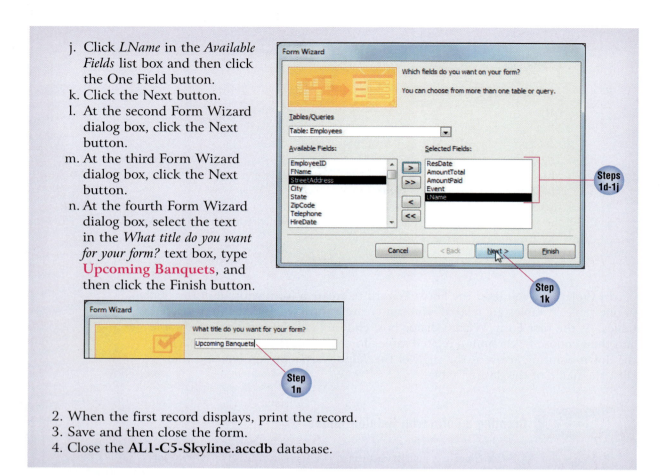

2. When the first record displays, print the record.
3. Save and then close the form.
4. Close the **AL1-C5-Skyline.accdb** database.

Chapter Summary

- A form generally improves the ease with which data is entered into a table. Some methods for creating a form include using the Form, Split Form, or Multiple Items buttons or the Form Wizard.
- A form is an object you can use to enter and edit data in a table or query and to help prevent incorrect data from being entered in a database.
- The simplest method for creating a form is to click a table in the Navigation pane, click the Create button, and then click the Form button in the Forms group.
- When you create a form, it displays in Layout view. Use this view to display data as well as modify the appearance and contents of the form. Other form views include Form view and Design view. Use Form view to enter and manage records and use Design view to view the structure of the form and modify the form.
- Open an existing form in Layout View by right-clicking the form in the Navigation pane and then clicking *Layout View* at the shortcut menu.
- Print a form with options at the Print dialog box. To print an individual record, display the Print dialog box, click the *Selected Record(s)* option, and then click OK.

- Navigate in a form with buttons in the Record Navigation bar.
- Add a new record to a form by clicking the New Record button in the Record Navigation bar or by clicking the Home tab and then clicking the New button in the Records group.
- Delete a record from a form by displaying the record, clicking the Home tab, clicking the Delete button arrow, and then clicking *Delete Record* at the drop-down list.
- If you create a form with a table that has a one-to-many relationship established, Access adds a datasheet at the bottom of the form.
- A form is comprised of a series of control objects and you can customize these control objects with buttons in the Form Layout Tools ribbon with the Design tab, Arrange tab, or Format tab. These tabs are active when you display a form in Layout view.
- Apply a theme to a form with the Themes button in the Themes group in the Form Layout Tools Design tab. Use the Colors and Fonts buttons in the Themes group to further customize a theme.
- With buttons in the Header/Footer group in the Form Layout Tools Design tab, you can insert a logo, form title, and the date and time.
- In Layout view, you can size, delete, and insert control objects.
- In the Rows & Columns group in the Form Layout Tools Arrange tab, you can use buttons to select or insert rows or columns.
- The Controls group in the Form Layout Tools Design tab contains control objects you can insert in a form.
- Merge cells in a form by selecting cells and then clicking the Merge button in the Merge/Split group in the Form Layout Tools Arrange tab. Split selected cells by clicking the Split Vertically or Split Horizontally button.
- Format control objects and cells in a form with buttons in the Form Layout Tools Format tab.
- Use the Conditional Formatting button in the Control Formatting group in the Form Layout Tools Format tab to apply specific formatting to data that matches a specific criterion.
- Click the Add Existing Fields button in the Tools group in the Form Layout Tools Design tab to display the Field List pane. Add fields to the form by double-clicking on or dragging the field from the pane.
- Create a split form by clicking the More Forms button and then clicking *Split Form* in the drop-down list. Access displays the form in Form view in the top portion of the work area and the form in Datasheet view in the bottom of the work area. The two views are connected and are synchronous.
- Create a Multiple Items form by clicking the More Forms button and then clicking *Multiple Items* in the drop-down list.
- The Form Wizard walks you through the steps for creating a form and lets you specify the fields you want included in the form, a layout for the records, and a name for the form.
- You can create a form with the Form Wizard that contains fields from tables connected by a one-to-many relationship.

Commands Review

FEATURE	RIBBON TAB, GROUP	BUTTON, OPTION
Form	Create, Forms	
Conditional Formatting Rules Manager dialog box	Form Layout Tools Format, Control Formatting	
Field List pane	Form Layout Tools Design, Tools	
Split Form	Create, Forms	, Split Form
Multiple Items form	Create, Forms	, Multiple Items
Form Wizard	Create, Forms	

Concepts Check Test Your Knowledge

Completion: In the space provided at the right, indicate the correct term, symbol, or command.

1. The simplest method to create a form is to click this tab and then click the Form button.

2. When you click the Form button to create a form, the form displays in this view.

3. To print the current record in a form, click this option at the Print dialog box and then click OK.

4. Navigate in a form using buttons in this bar.

5. Click this button to add a new record to a form.

6. The Form Layout Tools Design tab is active when a form displays in this view.

7. The Themes group in the Form Layout Tools Design tab contains three buttons—the Themes button, the Colors button, and this button.

8. Click the Logo button in the Form Layout Tools Design tab and this dialog box displays.

9. To select nonadjacent objects or cells, hold down this key on the keyboard while clicking the desired objects or cells.

10. This group in the Form Layout Tools Arrange tab contains buttons for selecting and inserting rows and columns in a form. _____

11. With this button in the Control Formatting group in the Form Layout Tools Format tab, you can apply formatting to data that meets a specific criterion. _____

12. Click the Add Existing Fields button in the Tools group in the Form Layout Tools Design tab and this pane displays. _____

13. When you create a form with the *Split Form* option, the form displays in this view in the top half of the work area. _____

14. Create a split form or a multiple items form with options in this button drop-down list. _____

Skills Check Assess Your Performance

Assessment

1 CREATE AND CUSTOMIZE A SALES FORM

1. Display the Open dialog box with Access2010L1C5 on your storage medium the active folder.
2. Open the **AL1-C5-PacTrek.accdb** database and enable the contents.
3. Use the Form button in the Forms group in the Create tab to create a form with the Suppliers table.
4. Switch to Form view and then add the following records to the Suppliers form:

    Supplier# = **12**
    SupplierName = **Seaside Suppliers**
    StreetAddress = **4120 Shoreline Drive**
    City = **Vancouver**
    Prov/State = **BC**
    PostalCode = **V2V 8K4**
    EmailAddress = **seaside@emcp.net**
    Telephone = **6045557945**

    Supplier# = **34**
    SupplierName = **Carson Company**
    StreetAddress = **120 Plaza Center**
    City = **Vancouver**
    Prov/State = **BC**
    PostalCode = **V2V 1K6**
    EmailAddress = **carson@emcp.net**
    Telephone = **6045551955**

5. Delete the record containing information on Manning, Inc.
6. Switch to Layout view and then apply the Civic theme to the form.

7. Select and delete the logo object in the *Form Header* section and then click the Logo button in the Header/Footer group. At the Insert Picture dialog box, navigate to the Access2010L1C5 folder on your storage medium and then double-click **River.jpg**.
8. Create the title *Pacific Trek Suppliers* for the form. Click in any field outside the title and then click in the title (selects the title). Drag the right border of the title control object to the left until the border displays near the title.
9. Insert the date and time in the *Form Header* section.
10. Select the date and time control objects, drag in the left border until the border displays near the date and time, and then drag the objects so they are positioned near the title.
11. Click the text box control object containing the supplier number and then drag the right border to the left until the border displays approximately one inch to the right of the longest entry in the record.
12. Select the bottom row (the row containing the *Telephone* label control object) and the text box control object containing the telephone number and then insert a new row below the current row.
13. Click in the empty cell below the telephone number and then split the cell horizontally.
14. Click in the empty cell at the left side of the bottom row and then insert a Button control that, when clicked, displays the previous record.
15. Click in the empty cell at the right side of the bottom row and then insert a Button control that, when clicked, displays the next record.
16. Select the fields in the first column (*Supplier#* through *Telephone*) and then apply the following formatting:
    a. Apply bold formatting.
    b. Change the font color to *Dark Blue* (last option in the ninth column in the *Standard Colors* section).
    c. Change the alignment to Align Text Right.
    d. Apply the *Light Blue 2* shape fill (located in the fifth column in the *Standard Colors* section).
    e. Change the shape outline color to *Dark Blue* (last option in the ninth column in the *Standard Colors* section).
17. Select the second column and then apply the following formatting:
    a. Apply the *Light Blue 1* shape fill (located in the fifth column in the *Standard Colors* section).
    b. Change the shape outline color to *Dark Blue* (last option in the ninth column in the *Standard Colors* section).
18. Select both navigation buttons you inserted in the form. **Hint: To select both buttons, click the first button, hold down the Ctrl key, and then click the second button.**
19. With both buttons selected, apply the *Subtle Effect - Teal, Accent 3* Quick Style.
20. Switch to Form view and then navigate in the form using the navigation buttons you inserted.
21. Save the form with the name *Suppliers*.
22. Make active the record for supplier number 12 (one of the new records you entered) and then print the record. (Make sure you only print the record for supplier number 12. The buttons do not print.)
23. Make active the record for supplier number 34 and then print the record.

24. Create a screen capture of the record, paste it in a Word file, and then print the file by completing the following steps:
    a. With the supplier number 34 record active, press the Print Screen button on your keyboard.
    b. Open Microsoft Word. (If necessary, check with your instructor to determine how to open Word.)
    c. Click the Paste button located in the Clipboard group in the Home tab. (This pastes the screen capture image in the Word document.)
    d. Click the File tab, click the Print tab, and then click the *Print* option at the Print tab Backstage view.
    e. Exit Word by clicking the Close button located in the upper right corner of the screen. At the message asking if you want to save the document, click the Don't Save button.
25. Close the Suppliers table.

Assessment

2 CREATE AND CUSTOMIZE AN ORDERS FORM AND A PRODUCTS FORM

1. With the **AL1-C5-PacTrek.accdb** database open, create a form with the Orders table using the Form button in the Create tab.
2. Insert a field from a related table by completing the following steps:
    a. Display the Field List pane and then, if necessary, click the <u>Show all tables</u> hyperlink.
    b. Expand the Suppliers table in the *Fields available in related tables* section.
    c. Drag the field named *SupplierName* into the form and position it between *Supplier#* and *Product#*.
    d. Change the *SupplierName* field from a Lookup field to a text box by clicking the Options button that displays below the field and then clicking *Change to Text Box* at the drop-down list.
    e. Close the Field List pane.
3. Click the text box control object containing the text *1010* and then drag the right border to the left until the border displays approximately one inch to the right of the longest entry in the record.
4. Select all of the objects in the *Detail* section by clicking an object in the *Detail* section and then clicking the selector button (small square button with a four-headed arrow inside). With the objects selected, apply the following formatting:
    a. Change the font to Cambria and the font size to 12.
    b. Change the alignment to Align Text Right.
5. Select the first column and then apply the following formatting:
    a. Apply the *Green 2* shape fill (located in the seventh column in the *Standard Colors* section).
    b. Apply bold formatting.
6. Apply conditional formatting that changes the font color to blue for any *Amount* field entry that contains an amount greater than $999. **Hint: Click the Conditional Formatting button, click the New Rule button, change the second option in the** Edit the rule description *section to* greater than, *and then enter 999 in the third option box [without the dollar sign].*
7. Save the form with the name *Orders*.
8. Print the fifteenth record in the form and then close the form.

Assessment 3: CREATE A SPLIT FORM WITH THE PRODUCTS TABLE

1. With the **AL1-C5-PacTrek.accdb** database open, create a form with the Products table using the *Split Form* option from the More Forms button drop-down list.
2. Decrease the width of the second column so the second column is approximately twice the width of the first column.
3. Select the first column and then apply the following formatting:
   a. Apply bold formatting.
   b. Apply the *Aqua Blue 1* shape fill (located in the ninth column in the *Standard Colors* section).
   c. Change the shape outline color to *Blue* (located in the bottom row in the *Standard Colors* section).
4. Click in the text box control object containing the number *0* (the UnitsOnOrder number) and then apply conditional formatting that displays the number in red in any field value equal to 0 (zero).
5. Change to Form view, create a new record, and then enter the following information in the specified fields:

Product#	=	205-CS
Product	=	Timberline solo cook set
Supplier#	=	15
UnitsInStock	=	8
UnitsOnOrder	=	0
ReorderLevel	=	5

6. Save the form with the name *Products*.
7. Print the current record (the record you just typed). **Hint: At the Print dialog box, click the Setup button. At the Page Setup dialog box, click the Print Form Only** *option.*
8. Close the Products form.
9. Close the **AL1-C5-PacTrek.accdb** database.

Assessment 4: CREATE AND CUSTOMIZE AN EMPLOYEES FORM

1. Open the **AL1-C5-Griffin.accdb** database from the Access2010L1C5 folder on your storage medium and enable the contents.
2. Suppose you want to create a form for entering employee information but you do not want to include the employee's salary since that is confidential information that only the account manager has access to. Use the Form Wizard to create an Employees form that includes all fields *except* the *AnnualSalary* field and name the form *Employees*.
3. Switch to Layout view and then apply the Slipstream theme to the form.
4. Switch to Form view and then type a new record with the following information in the specified fields:

Emp#	=	1099
LastName	=	Williamson
FirstName	=	Carrie
BirthDate	=	6/24/1983
HireDate	=	8/1/2011
DeptID	=	RD

5. Print the record you just typed.
6. Close the Employees form.

Assessment

5 CREATE AND CUSTOMIZE A BENEFITS FORM

1. With the **AL1-C5-Griffin.accdb** database open, create a form with the Benefits table using the Form button.
2. With the Benefits form in Layout view, decrease the width of the second column so it is approximately twice as wide as the first column.
3. Select the bottom row of control objects and then insert a row below. With the row still selected, insert another row below. (You should have two rows of empty cells at the bottom of the form.)
4. Click in the empty cell immediately below the text box control containing the text *4 weeks* and then split the cell horizontally.
5. Click in the empty cell immediately below the cell you just split and then split that cell horizontally.
6. Insert a button control by completing the following steps:
   a. Click the Form Layout Tools Design tab and then click the Button button.
   b. Click in the empty cell immediately below the label object control containing the label *Vacation*.
   c. At the first Command Button Wizard dialog box, click the *Go To Previous Record* in the *Actions* list box and then click the Next button.
   d. At the second Command Button Wizard dialog box, click the *Text* option and then click the Finish button.
7. Complete steps similar to those in Step 6 to insert in the cell at the right side of the first empty row of cells a Go To Next Record button that contains text on the button.
8. Complete steps similar to those in Step 6 to insert a button in the cell immediately below the Previous button that prints the current record. (To find this option, click the *Record Operations* option in the *Categories* list box. Specify that you want text on the button.)
9. Insert a button immediately below the Next Record button that closes the form. (To find this option, click the *Form Operations* option in the *Categories* list box. Specify that you want text on the button.)
10. Select each of the four new buttons and then change the font size to 10.
11. Save the form with the name *Benefits*.
12. Switch to Form view and then click the Print Record button you inserted. At the Print dialog box, make sure the *Selected Record(s)* option is selected and then click OK.
13. Create a screen capture of the record, paste it in a Word file, and then print the file by completing the following steps:
    a. With the current record displayed, press the Print Screen button on your keyboard.
    b. Open Microsoft Word.
    c. Click the Paste button located in the Clipboard group in the Home tab. (This pastes the screen capture image in the Word document.)
    d. Click the File tab, click the Print tab, and then click the *Print* option at the Print tab Backstage view.
    e. Exit Word by clicking the Close button located in the upper right corner of the screen. At the message asking if you want to save the document, click the Don't Save button.
14. Close the Benefits form.
15. Close the **AL1-C5-Griffin.accdb** database.

Visual Benchmark — Demonstrate Your Proficiency

CREATE AND FORMAT A PROPERTIES FORM

1. Open the **AL1-C5-SunProperties.accdb** database located in the Access2010L1C5 folder on your storage medium and enable the contents.
2. Create a form with the Properties table and format your form so it appears in a manner similar to the form in Figure 5.8 with the following specifications:
   a. Apply the Thatch theme.
   b. Insert the logo, title, date, and time in the *Form Header* section as shown in the figure. (Insert the file **SunPropLogo.jpg** for the logo. Adjust the size of the title control object and then move the date and time as shown in the figure.)
   c. Select all of the objects in the *Detail* section and then change the font color to *Maroon 5* (located in the *Standard Colors* section).
   d. Select the first column, apply bold formatting, apply *Yellow, Accent 2, Lighter 60%* shape fill (color is located in the *Theme Colors* section), change the shape outline color to *Yellow, Accent 2, Darker 50%*, and then change to align text right.
   e. Insert a new column to the right of the second column, merge cells in the new column to accommodate the sun image and then insert the image **SunProp.jpg** (as a control object). Adjust the width of the third column so the image displays as shown in Figure 5.8.

Figure 5.8 Visual Benchmark

f. Apply conditional formatting to the *MoRent* field that displays in green any rent amount greater than $999.
g. Insert a new row at the bottom of the form and then insert the buttons as shown in the figure. Apply the *Subtle Effect - Blue-Gray, Accent 1* Quick Style to each button. Slightly increase the height of the bottom row containing the buttons until the text on the buttons displays as shown in the figure.
3. Save the form with the name *PropertiesForm* and then print the current record.
4. Use the Print Screen button to make a screen capture image of the current record, insert the image in a Word document, print the document, and then exit Word without saving the document.
5. Close the form and then close the **AL1-C5-SunProperties.accdb** database.

Case Study Apply Your Skills

Part 1

You are the office manager at the Lewis Vision Care Center and your center is switching over to Access to manage files. You have already created four basic tables and now need to create relationships and enter data. Open the **AL1-C5-LewisCenter.accdb** database and then create the following relationships between tables:

Field Name	"One" Table	"Many" Table
Patient#	Patients	Billing
ServiceID	Services	Billing
Doctor#	Doctors	Billing

Save and then print the relationships.

Part 2

Before entering data in the tables, create a form for each table and apply a theme of your choosing. Enter data in the forms in the order in which data appears in Figure 5.10 on the next page. Apply any additional formatting to enhance the visual appeal of each form. After entering the information in the forms, print the first record of each form.

Part 3

Apply the following conditions to fields in forms:
- In the Patients form, apply the condition that the city *Tulsa* displays in red and the city *Broken Arrow* displays in blue in the *City* field.
- In the Billing form, apply the condition that amounts in the *Fee* field over $99 display in green.

Print the first record of the form. Close the Patients form and then close the **AL1-C5-LewisCenter.accdb** database.

Part 4

Your center has a procedures manual that describes processes and procedures in the center. Open Word and then create a document for the procedures manual that describes the formatting and conditions you applied to the forms in the **AL1-C5-LewisCenter.accdb** database. Save the completed document and name it **AL1-C5-CS-Manual**. Print and then close **AL1-C5-CS-Manual.docx**.

Figure 5.10 Case Study Part 2

Patients form		
Patient number-030 Rhonda J. Mahler 130 East 41st Street Tulsa, OK 74155 (918) 555-3107	Patient number-076 Patrick S. Robbins 3281 Aspen Avenue Tulsa, OK 74108 (918) 555-9672	Patient number-092 Oren L. Vargas 21320 Tenth Street Broken Arrow, OK 74012 (918) 555-1188
Patient number-085 Michael A. Dempsey 506 Houston Street Tulsa, OK 74142 (918) 555-5541	Patient number-074 Wendy L. Holloway 23849 22nd Street Broken Arrow, OK 74009 (918) 555-8842	Patient number-023 Maggie M. Winters 4422 South 121st Tulsa, OK 74142 (918) 555-8833

Doctors form		
Doctor number-1 Carolyn Joswick (918) 555-4772	Doctor number-2 Gerald Ingram (918) 555-9890	Doctor number-3 Kay Feather (918) 555-7762
Doctor number-4 Sean Granger (918) 555-1039	Doctor number-5 Jerome Deltoro (918) 555-8021	

Services form		
Co = Consultation C = Cataract Testing	V = Vision Screening S = Surgery	G = Glaucoma Testing E = Emergency

Billing form		
Patient number-076 Doctor number-2 Date of visit = 4/2/2012 Service ID = C Fee = $85	Patient number-076 Doctor number-3 Date of visit = 4/2/2012 Service ID = V Fee = $150	Patient number-085 Doctor number-1 Date of visit = 4/2/2012 Service ID = Co Fee = $0
Patient number-074 Doctor number-3 Date of visit = 4/2/2012 Service ID = V Fee = $150	Patient number-023 Doctor number-5 Date of visit = 4/2/2012 Service ID = S Fee = $750	Patient number-092 Doctor number-1 Date of visit = 4/2/2012 Service ID = G Fee = $85

Access

Creating Reports and Mailing Labels

CHAPTER 6

PERFORMANCE OBJECTIVES

Upon successful completion of Chapter 6, you will be able to:
- Create a report using the Report button
- Display a report in Print Preview
- Create a report with a query
- Format and customize a report
- Group and sort records in a report
- Create a report using the Report Wizard
- Create mailing labels using the Label Wizard

In this chapter, you will learn how to prepare reports from data in a table using the Report button in the Reports group in the Create tab and with the Report Wizard. You will also learn how to format and customize a report and create mailing labels using the Label Wizard. Model answers for this chapter's projects appear on the following pages.

Access2010L1C6

Note: Before beginning the projects, copy to your storage medium the Access2010L1C6 subfolder from the Access2010L1 folder on the CD that accompanies this textbook and make Access2010L1C6 the active folder.

229

Project 1 Create and Customize Reports Using Tables and Queries

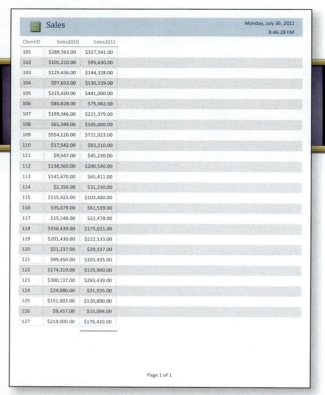

Project 1a, Dearborn Sales Report

Project 1b, Dearborn Sales Report

Project 1b, Dearborn Representatives Report

Project 1c, Dearborn InMun2010Sales Report

Project 1d, Dearborn Sales Report

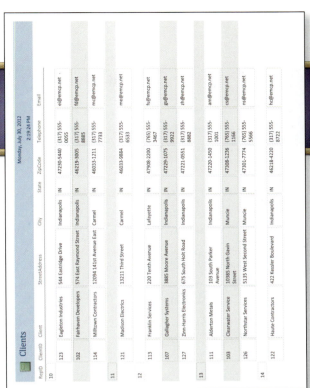

Project 1e, Dearborn ClientsGroupedRpt Report

Project 1e, Dearborn InMun2010Sales Report

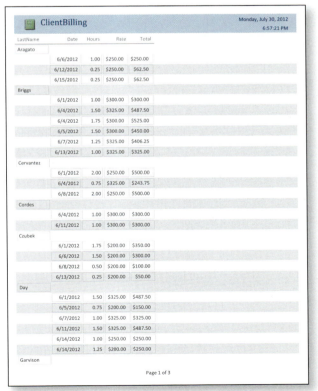

Project 1e, Dearborn ClientBillingRpt Report

Chapter 6 ■ Creating Reports and Mailing Labels   231

Project 1e, Dearborn ClientBillingRpt Report—*Continued*

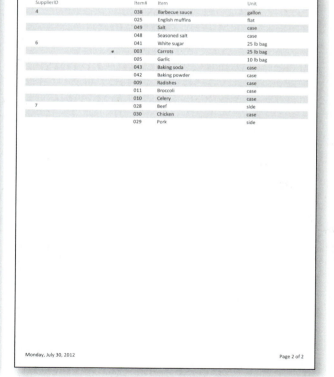

Project 2 Use Wizards to Create Reports and Labels

Project 2a, Skyline Inventory Report

Project 2b, Skyline BanquetEvents Report

BanquetEvents

Event	ResDate	FirstName	LastName	AmountTotal	AmountPaid
Birthday	6/9/2012	Joanne	Blair	$650.00	$200.00
	6/17/2012	Jason	Haley	$1,500.00	$400.00
	6/23/2012	Heidi	Thompson	$1,750.00	$750.00
Bar mitzvah	6/30/2012	Kirsten	Simpson	$1,750.00	$150.00
	6/25/2012	Robin	Gehring	$2,000.00	$700.00
Bat mitzvah	6/16/2012	Aaron	Williams	$2,000.00	$500.00
	6/9/2012	Tim	Drysdale	$1,000.00	$250.00
Other	6/15/2012	Tristan	Strauss	$1,400.00	$300.00
	6/10/2012	Gabrielle	Johnson	$500.00	$100.00
	6/8/2012	Bridget	Kohn	$800.00	$200.00
Wedding rehearsal dinner	6/29/2012	David	Fitzgerald	$500.00	$100.00
	6/19/2012	Lillian	Krakosky	$750.00	$250.00
	6/2/2012	Terrance	Schaefer	$800.00	$500.00
Wedding anniversary	6/13/2012	Cliff	Osborne	$2,000.00	$300.00
	6/23/2012	Anthony	Rozier	$900.00	$300.00
Wedding reception	6/7/2012	Shane	Wiegand	$800.00	$500.00
	6/3/2012	David	Hooper	$1,250.00	$1,000.00
	6/24/2012	Andrea	Wyatt	$3,000.00	$750.00
	6/22/2012	Mallory	Satter	$2,500.00	$500.00
Wedding shower	6/15/2012	Janis	Rivas	$750.00	$200.00
	6/16/2012	Willow	Semala	$575.00	$175.00
	6/3/2012	Luis	Earhart		
			Castillo		

Monday, July 30, 2012

Page 1 of 1

Project 2c, Warren Legal Mailing Labels

Page 1

Haley Brown
3219 North 33rd Street
Auburn, WA 98001

Margaret Kasper
40210 42nd Avenue
Auburn, WA 98001

Abigail Jefferson
1204 Meridian Road
Auburn, WA 98001

Doris Sturtevant
3713 Nelton Road
Auburn, WA 98001

Carlina McFadden
7809 52nd Street East
Auburn, WA 98001

Ewan Aragato
904 Marine View Drive
Auburn, WA 98002

Tricia O'Connor
3824 Sanders Court
Auburn, WA 98002

Carol Kendall
24 Ferris Parkway
Kent, WA 98003

James Weyland
2533 145th Street East
Kent, WA 98031

Janice Saunders
2757 179th Avenue East
Kent, WA 98032

Jeffrey Day
317 Meridian Street
Kent, WA 98033

Mindy Garvison
68 Queens Avenue
Kent, WA 98033

Kevin Stein
12034 South 22nd Avenue
Kent, WA 98035

Jean Briggs
2110 West Valley Avenue
Kent, WA 98036

Arthur Norheim
10533 Ashton Boulevard
Kent, WA 98036

Consuelo Day
13321 North Lake Drive
Kent, WA 98036

Christina Miles
13043 South 25th Avenue
Kent, WA 98036

Matthew Waide
18391 North 45th Street
Renton, WA 98055

Page 2

Karl Cordes
240 Mill Avenue
Renton, WA 98055

Mira Valencia
114 Springfield Avenue
Renton, WA 98056

Charles Hobart
11038 132nd Street
Renton, WA 98056

Taylor Reyes
201 Northwest Boulevard
Renton, WA 98056

Eric Rosenthal
1230 Maplewood Road
Auburn, WA 98071

Jennifer Czubek
8790 34th Avenue
Renton, WA 98228

Maddie Singh
450 Mill Avenue
Renton, WA 98228

Chris Cervantez
8722 Riverside Road
Renton, WA 98228

Arthur Jefferson
23110 North 33rd Street
Renton, WA 98230

 **Project 1 Create and Customize Reports Using Tables and Queries** **5 Parts**

You will create reports with the Report button using tables and queries. You will change the report views; select, move, and resize control objects; sort records; customize reports; apply conditional formatting; and group and sort fields in a report.

Creating a Report

▼ **Quick Steps**
Create a Report
1. Click desired table or query in Navigation pane.
2. Click Create tab.
3. Click Report button.

Create a report to control what data appears on the page when printed.

The primary purpose for inserting data in a form is to improve the display of the data and to make data entry easier. You can also insert data in a report. The purpose for this is to control what data appears on the page when printed. Reports generally answer specific questions (queries). For example, a report could answer the question *What customers have submitted claims?* or *What products do we currently have on order?* You can use the Report button in the Reports group in the Create tab to create a report based on a table or query. You can also use the Report Wizard that walks you through the process of creating a report.

Creating a Report with the Report Button

To create a report with the Report button, click the desired table or query in the Navigation pane, click the Create tab, and then click the Report button in the Reports group. This displays the report in columnar style in Layout view with the Report Layout Tools Design tab active as shown in Figure 6.1. Access creates the report using all of the fields in the table.

Figure 6.1 Report Created with Sales Table

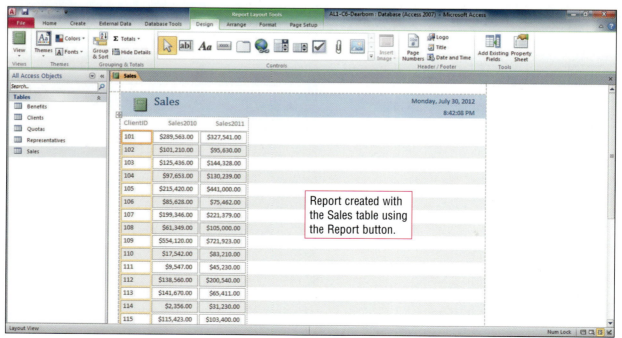

Project 1a   **Creating a Report with the Report Button**   Part 1 of 5

1. Display the Open dialog box with Access2010L1C6 on your storage medium the active folder.
2. Open the **AL1-C6-Dearborn.accdb** database and enable the contents.
3. Create a report by completing the following steps:
   a. Click the Sales table in the Navigation pane.
   b. Click the Create tab.
   c. Click the Report button in the Reports group.

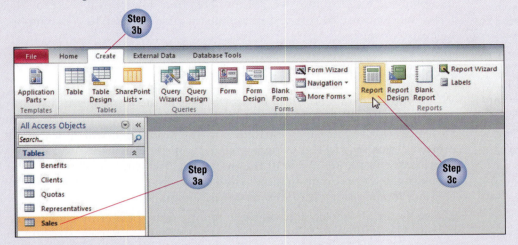

4. Access automatically inserted a total amount for the *Sales2011* column. Delete this amount by scrolling down to the bottom of the report, clicking the total amount at the bottom of the *Sales2011* column, and then pressing the Delete key. (This deletes the total amount but not the underline above the amount.)
5. Print the report by clicking the File tab, clicking the Print tab, and then clicking the *Quick Print* option.
6. Save the report by clicking the Save button on the Quick Access toolbar, making sure *Sales* displays in the *Report Name* text box in the Save As dialog box, and then clicking OK.

Modifying Control Objects

A report, like a form, is comprised of control objects such as a logo, title, labels, and text boxes. You can select an object in a report by clicking the object. A selected object displays with an orange border. If you click a data field in the report, Access selects all objects in the column except the column heading.

    Like a form, a report contains a *Header* section and a *Detail* section. You can select all control objects in the report in both the *Header* and *Detail* sections by pressing Ctrl + A. To select only objects in the *Detail* section, click the selector button (small square containing a four-headed arrow) that displays in the upper left corner of the *Detail* section.

    You can adjust column widths in a report by dragging the column border left or right. In addition to adjusting column width, you can change the order of a selected column. To do this, select the desired column, position the mouse pointer in the column heading until the pointer displays with a four-headed arrow

Chapter 6 ■ Creating Reports and Mailing Labels   **235**

attached, and then drag the column left or right to the desired position. As you drag the column, a vertical orange bar displays indicating the location where the column will be placed when you release the mouse button.

Sorting Records

Quick Steps

Sort Records
1. Click in field containing data.
2. Click Ascending button or click Descending button.

Sort data in a report by clicking in the field containing the data on which you want to sort and then clicking the Ascending button or Descending button in the Sort & Filter group in the Home tab. Click the Ascending button to sort text in alphabetic order from A to Z or numbers from lowest to highest, or click the Descending button to sort text in alphabetic order from Z to A or numbers from highest to lowest.

Ascending

Descending

Print Preview

View

Displaying a Report in Print Preview

When you create a report, the report displays in the work area in Layout view. This is one of four views available including Report view, Print Preview, and Design view. Use Print Preview to display the report as it will appear when printed. To change to Print Preview, click the Print Preview button in the view area located at the right side of the Status bar. You can also click the View button arrow in the Views group in either the Home tab or the Report Layout Tools Design tab and then click *Print Preview* at the drop-down list.

At the Print Preview tab, send the report to the printer by clicking the Print button. Use options in the Page Size group to change the page size and change margins. If you want to print only the report data and not the column headings, report title, shading, and gridlines, insert a check mark in the *Print Data Only* check box. Use options in the Page Layout group to specify the page orientation, specify columns, and display the Page Setup dialog box. Click the Page Setup button and the Page Setup dialog box displays with options for customizing margins, orientation, size, and columns.

Project 1b — Adjusting Control Objects, Sorting Data, and Displaying a Report in Print Preview

Part 2 of 5

1. With the Sales report open, reverse the order of the *Sales2010* and *Sales2011* columns by completing the following steps:
   a. Make sure the report displays in Layout view.
   b. Click the *Sales2011* column heading.
   c. Hold down the Shift key and then click in the last control object containing text ($176,420.00).
   d. Position the mouse pointer inside the *Sales2011* column heading until the pointer displays with a four-headed arrow attached.
   e. Hold down the left mouse button, drag to the left until the vertical orange bar displays between *ClientID* and *Sales2010*, and then release the mouse button.

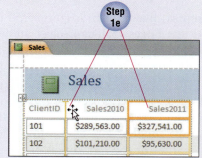

Step 1e

2. Sort the data in the *Sales2011* column in descending order by completing the following steps:
   a. Click the Home tab.
   b. Click in any field in the *Sales2011* column.
   c. Click the Descending button in the Sort & Filter group.
3. Display the report in Print Preview by clicking the Print Preview button in the view area at the right side of the Status bar.

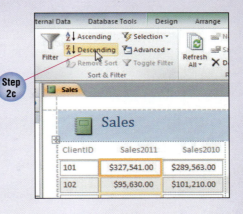

4. Click the Two Pages button in the Zoom group. (Since this report contains only one page, the page displays at the left side of the work area.)
5. Click the Zoom button arrow in the Zoom group and then click *50%* at the drop-down list.
6. Click the One Page button in the Zoom group.

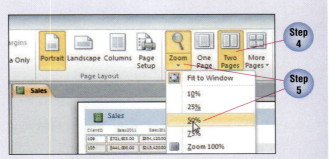

7. Print the report by clicking the Print button in the Print Preview tab and then clicking OK at the Print dialog box.
8. Close Print Preview by clicking the Close Print Preview button located at the right side of the Print Preview tab.
9. Save and then close the Sales report.
10. Create a report with the Representatives table by completing the following steps:
    a. Click the Representatives table in the Navigation pane.
    b. Click the Create tab.
    c. Click the Report button in the Reports group.
11. Adjust the width of the second column by completing the following steps:
    a. Click in the *RepName* column heading.
    b. Drag the right border of the selected column heading to the left until the border displays near the longest entry in the column.
12. Complete steps similar to those in Step 11 to decrease the width of the third column (*Telephone*) and the fourth column (*Email*).
13. Scroll down the report, click the control object at the bottom of the *RepID* column containing the number *17*, and then press the Delete key. (This does not delete the underline above the amount.)

14. Switch to Print Preview by clicking the View button arrow in the Views group in the Report Layout Tools Design tab and then clicking *Print Preview* at the drop-down list.
15. Click the Margins button in the Page Size group and then click *Normal* at the drop-down list.

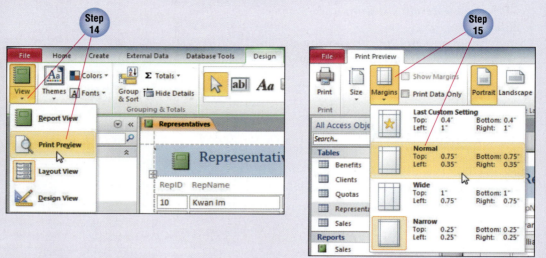

16. Print the report by clicking the Print button at the left side of the Print Preview tab and then clicking OK at the Print dialog box. (The report will print on three pages. The second and third pages contain only shading.)
17. Close Print Preview by clicking the Close Print Preview button.
18. Save the report with the name *Representatives*.
19. Close the Representatives report.

Creating a Report with a Query

Since one of the purposes of a report is to answer specific questions, design and run a query and then create a report based on that query. Create a report from a query in the same manner as creating a report from a table.

Project 1c Creating a Report with a Query   Part 3 of 5

1. With the **AL1-C6-Dearborn.accdb** database open, design a query that extracts records from two tables with the following specifications:
   a. Add the Clients and Sales tables to the query window.
   b. Insert the *Client* field from the Clients table to the first *Field* row field.
   c. Insert the *StreetAddress* field from the Clients table to the second *Field* row field.
   d. Insert the *City* field from the Clients table to the third *Field* row field.
   e. Insert the *State* field from the Clients table to the fourth *Field* row field.
   f. Insert the *ZipCode* field from the Clients table to the fifth *Field* row field.
   g. Insert the *Sales2010* field from the Sales table to the sixth *Field* row field.
   h. Insert the criterion *Indianapolis Or Muncie* in the *Criteria* row field in the *City* column.

i. Insert the criterion *>75000* in the *Criteria* row field in the *Sales2010* column.

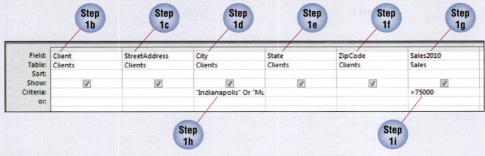

j. Run the query.
k. Save the query and name it *InMunSalesOver$75000*.
l. Close the query.
2. Create a report with the query by completing the following steps:
    a. Click the *InMunSalesOver$75000* query in the Navigation pane.
    b. Click the Create tab.
    c. Click the Report button in the Reports group.
    d. Click in the column heading *Client* and then drag the right border to the left until the border displays near the longest entry in the column.
    e. Click in each of the remaining column headings and reduce the column widths. (Make sure the longest entry in each column is visible.)
    f. Access automatically inserted a total amount for the *Sales2010* column. Scroll down the report to display the total amount, click the amount, and then increase the height and width of the object so the entire amount is visible.
3. Display the report in Print Preview by clicking the View button arrow in the Views group in the Report Layout Tools Design tab and then clicking *Print Preview* at the drop-down list.
4. Make sure that all columns of data display on the first page.
5. Change the top margin by completing the following steps:
    a. Click the Page Setup button in the Page Layout group.
    b. At the Page Setup dialog box, select the current measurement in the *Top* measurement box and then type **1**.
    c. Click OK.

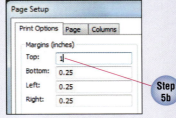

6. Print the first page of the report (the second page contains only shading) by completing the following steps:
    a. Click the Print button that displays at the left side of the Print Preview tab.
    b. At the Print dialog box, click the *Pages* option in the *Print Range* section.
    c. Type **1** in the *From* text box, press the Tab key, and then type **1** in the *To* text box.
    d. Click OK.
7. Close Print Preview.
8. Save the report and name it *InMun2010Sales*.
9. Close the report.

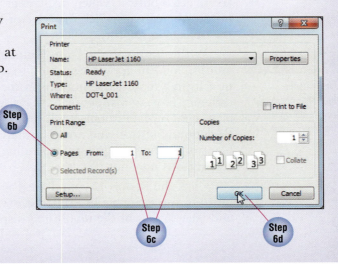

Chapter 6 ■ Creating Reports and Mailing Labels   239

Customizing a Report

You can customize a report in much the same manner as customizing a form. When you first create a report, the report displays in Layout view and the Report Layout Tools Design tab is active. You can customize control objects in the *Detail* section and the *Header* section with buttons in the Report Layout Tools ribbon with the Design tab, the Arrange tab, the Format tab, or the Page Setup tab selected.

The themes available in Access are the same as the themes available in Word, Excel, and PowerPoint.

The Report Layout Tools Design tab contains many of the same options at the Form Layout Tools Design tab. With options in this tab, you can apply a theme, insert controls, insert header or footer data, and add existing fields. The tab also contains the Grouping & Totals group, which you will learn about in the next section. Use the Totals button in the Grouping & Totals group to perform functions such as finding the sum, average, maximum, or minimum of the numbers in a column. To use the Totals button, click the column heading of the column containing data you want to total, click the Totals button, and then click the desired function at the drop-down list. Use the Page Number button in the Report Layout Tools Design tab to insert and format page numbers.

Totals

Click the Report Layout Tools Arrange tab and options display for inserting and selecting rows, splitting cells horizontally and vertically, moving data up or down, controlling margins, and changing the padding between objects and cells. The options in the Report Layout Tools Arrange tab are the same as the options in the Form Layout Tools Arrange tab.

Select and format data in a report with options at the Report Layout Tools Format tab. The options in this tab are the same as the options in the Form Layout Tools Format tab. You can apply formatting to a report or specific objects in a report. If you want to apply formatting to a specific object, click the object in the report or click the Object button arrow in the Selection group in the Report Layout Tools Format tab and then click the desired object at the drop-down list. To format all objects in the report, click the Select All button in the Selection group. This selects all objects in the report including objects in the *Header* section. If you want to select all of the objects in the *Detail* section (and not the *Header* section), click the selector button that displays in the upper left corner of the report objects in the *Detail* section. Click an object in the *Detail* section to display the selector button, which displays as a small square with a four-headed arrow inside. You can also click the selector button and then drag the button to move the objects in the form.

Customize the formatting of control objects with options at the Report Layout Tools Format tab.

With buttons in the Font, Number, Background, and Control Formatting groups, you can apply formatting to a control object or cell and to selected objects or cells in a report. Use buttons in the Font group to change the font, apply a different font size, apply text effects such as bold and underline, and change the alignment of data in objects. Insert a background image in the report using the Background button and apply formatting to objects or cells with buttons in the Control Formatting group. Depending on what is selected in the report, some of the buttons may not be active.

Click the Report Layout Tools Page Setup tab and the buttons that display are buttons also available in Print Preview. For example, you can change the page size and page layout of the report and display the Page Setup dialog box.

Project 1d Applying Formatting to a Report   Part 4 of 5

1. With the **AL1-C6-Dearborn.accdb** database open, open the Sales report in Layout view by right-clicking the report in the Navigation pane and then clicking *Layout View* at the shortcut menu.
2. Change the font for all control objects in the report by completing the following steps:
   a. Press Ctrl + A to select all control objects in the report. (An orange border displays around selected objects.)
   b. Click the Report Layout Tools Format tab.
   c. Click the Font button arrow in the Font group and then click *Cambria* at the drop-down list. (You may need to scroll down the list to display *Cambria*.)

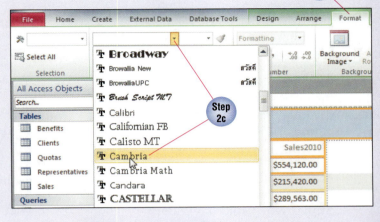

3. Apply bold formatting and change the alignment of the column headings by completing the following steps:
   a. Click *ClientID* to select the control object.
   b. Hold down the Shift key and then click *Sales2010*. (This selects the three column headings.)
   c. Click the Bold button in the Font group.
   d. Click the Center button in the Font group.

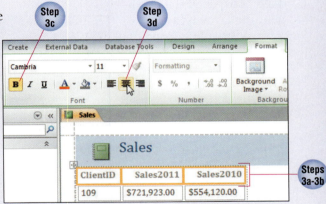

4. Change the alignment of data in the *ClientID* column by clicking the field value *109* (located below the *ClientID* column heading) and then clicking the Center button in the Font group.
5. Format amounts and apply conditional formatting to the amounts by completing the following steps:
   a. Click the first field value below the *Sales2011* column heading. (This selects all of the amounts in the column.)
   b. Hold down the Shift key and then click the first field value below the *Sales2010* column heading.
   c. Click twice on the Decrease Decimals button in the Number group.
   d. Click the Conditional Formatting button in the Control Formatting group.

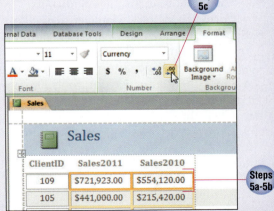

Chapter 6 ■ Creating Reports and Mailing Labels   241

e. At the Conditional Formatting Rules Manager dialog box, click the New Rule button.
f. At the New Formatting Rule dialog box, click the down-pointing arrow at the right side of the second option box in the *Edit the rule description* section and then click *greater than* at the drop-down list.
g. Click in the text box immediately right of the option box containing *greater than* and then type **199999**.
h. Click the Background color button arrow and then click the *Green 2* color option (located in the seventh column).
i. Click the OK button.
j. At the Conditional Formatting Rules Manager dialog box, click the New Rule button.
k. At the New Formatting Rule dialog box, click the down-pointing arrow at the right side of the second option box in the *Edit the rule description* section and then click *less than* at the drop-down list.
l. Click in the text box immediately right of the option containing *less than* and then type **200000**.
m. Click the Background color button arrow and then click the *Maroon 2* color option (located in the sixth column).
n. Click OK to close the New Formatting Rule dialog box.
o. Click OK to close the Conditional Formatting Rules Manager dialog box.

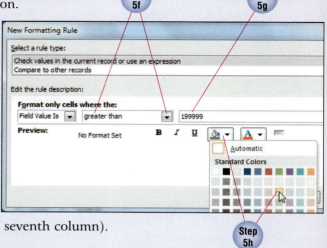

6. Sum the totals in the *Sales2011* column by completing the following steps:
   a. Click in the *Sales2011* column heading.
   b. Click the Report Layout Tools Design tab.
   c. Click the Totals button in the Grouping & Totals group and then click *Sum* at the drop-down list.

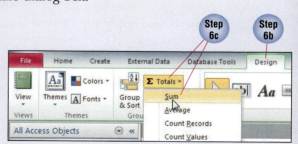

7. Sum the totals in the *Sales2010* column by clicking the *Sales2010* column heading, clicking the Totals button in the Grouping & Totals group, and then clicking *Sum* at the drop-down list.

8. Scroll down to the bottom of the report and check to see if the total amounts are visible in the bottom control objects in the *Sales2011* and *Sales2010* columns. If the amounts are not completely visible, click the amount to select it and then drag down the bottom border.
9. Insert a title by completing the following steps:
   a. Make sure the Report Layout Tools Design tab is active.
   b. Click the Title button in the Header/Footer group.
   c. Type **Dearborn Sales 2010-2011** and then press Enter.

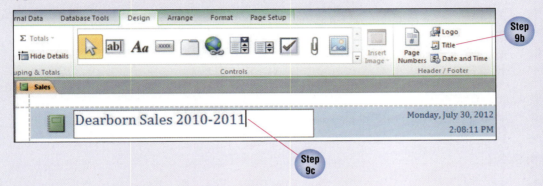

Step 9b

Step 9c

10. Change the top margin by completing the following steps:
    a. With the report in Layout view, click the Report Layout Tools Page Setup tab.
    b. Click the Page Setup button in the Page Layout group.
    c. At the Page Setup dialog box with the Print Options tab selected, select the current measurement in the *Top* measurement box and then type **0.5**.
    d. Click OK to close the Page Setup dialog box.
11. Print the report by clicking the File tab, clicking the Print tab, and then clicking the *Quick Print* option.
12. Save and then close the Sales report.

Grouping and Sorting Records

A report presents database information in a printed form and generally displays data that answers a specific question. To make the data in a report easy to understand, you can divide the data into groups. For example, you can divide data in a report by region, sales, dates, or any other division that helps identify the data to the reader. Access contains a powerful group and sort feature you can use in a report. In this section you will complete basic group and sort functions. For more detailed information on grouping and sorting, please refer to the Access help files.

Click the Group & Sort button in the Grouping & Totals group in the Report Layout Tools Design tab and the Group, Sort, and Total pane displays at the bottom of the work area as shown in Figure 6.2. Click the Add a group button in the Group, Sort, and Total pane and Access adds a new grouping level row to the pane along with a list of available fields. Click the field on which you want to group data in the report and Access adds the grouping level in the report. With options in the grouping level row, you can change the group, specify the sort order, and expand the row to display additional options.

When you specify a grouping level, Access automatically sorts that level in ascending order (from A to Z or from lowest to highest). You can then sort additional data within the report by clicking the Add a sort button in the Group,

▼ Quick Steps

Group and Sort Records
1. Open desired report in Layout view.
2. Click Group & Sort button.
3. Click Add a group button.
4. Click desired group field.

Group & Sort

Add a group

Add a sort

Figure 6.2 Group, Sort, and Total Pane

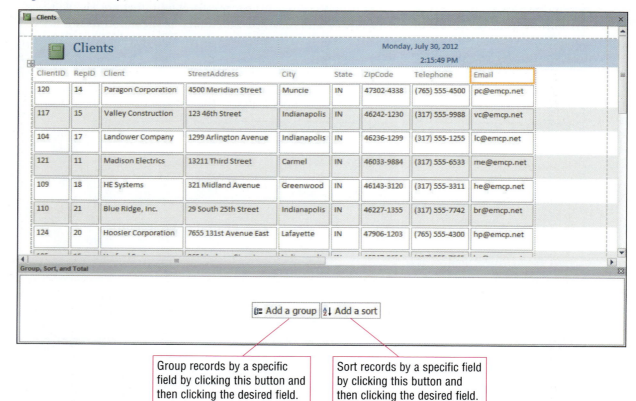

Sort, and Total pane. This inserts a sorting row in the pane below the grouping level row along with a list of available fields. At this list, click the field on which you want to sort. For example, in Project 1e you will specify that a report is grouped by city (which will display in ascending order) and then specify that the client names display in alphabetical order within the city.

HINT Grouping allows you to separate groups of records visually.

To delete a grouping or sorting level in the Group, Sort, and Total pane, click the Delete button that displays at the right side of the level row. After specifying the grouping and sorting levels, close the Group, Sort, and Total pane by clicking the close button located in the upper right corner of the pane.

Project 1e Grouping and Sorting Data Part 5 of 5

1. With the **AL1-C6-Dearborn.accdb** database open, create a report with the Clients table using the Report button in the Create tab.
2. Click each of the column headings individually and then decrease the size of each column so the right border of the column is just right of the longest entry in each column.
3. Change the orientation to landscape by completing the following steps:
   a. Click the Report Layout Tools Page Setup tab.
   b. Click the Landscape button in the Page Layout group.

4. Group the report by RepID and then sort by clients by completing the following steps:
   a. Click the Report Layout Tools Design tab.
   b. Click the Group & Sort button in the Grouping & Totals group.
   c. Click the Add a group button in the Group, Sort, and Total pane.

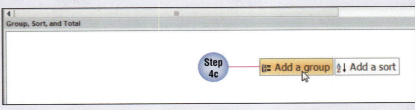

   d. Click the *RepID* field in the list box.
   e. Scroll through the report and notice that the records are grouped by the *RepID* field. Also, notice that the client names within each RepID group are not in alphabetic order.
   f. Click the Add a sort button in the Group, Sort, and Total pane.
   g. Click the *Client* field in the list box.
   h. Scroll through the report and notice that client names are now alphabetized within RepID groups.
   i. Close the Group, Sort, and Total pane by clicking the Close button located in the upper right corner of the pane.

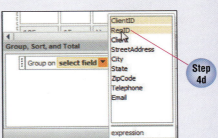

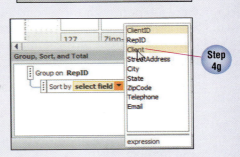

5. Save the report and name it *ClientsGroupedRpt*.
6. Print the first page of the report by completing the following steps:
   a. Click the File tab, click the Print tab, and then click the *Print* option.
   b. At the Print dialog box, click *Pages* option in the *Print Range* section.
   c. Type 1 in the *From* text box, press the Tab key, and then type 1 in the *To* text box.
   d. Click OK.
7. Close the *ClientsGroupedRpt* report.
8. Open the InMun2010Sales report in Layout view.
9. Group the report by city and then sort by clients by completing the following steps:
   a. Click the Group & Sort button in the Grouping & Totals group in the Report Layout Tools Design tab.
   b. Click the Add a group button in the Group, Sort, and Total pane.
   c. Click the *City* field in the list box.
   d. Click the Add a sort button in the Group, Sort, and Total pane and then click the *Client* field in the list box.
   e. Close the Group, Sort, and Total pane by clicking the Close button located in the upper right corner of the pane.
10. Print the first page of the report (refer to Step 6).
11. Save and then close the InMun2010Sales report.
12. Close the **AL1-C6-Dearborn.accdb** database.
13. Display the Open dialog box with Access2010L1C6 on your storage medium the active folder, open the **AL1-C6-WarrenLegal.accdb** database and enable the contents.

14. Design a query that extracts records from three tables with the following specifications:
    a. Add the Billing, Clients, and Rates tables to the query window.
    b. Insert the *LastName* field from the Clients table to the first *Field* row field.
    c. Insert the *Date* field from the Billings table to the second *Field* row field.
    d. Insert the *Hours* field from the Billings table to the third *Field* row field.
    e. Insert the *Rate* field from the Rates table to the fourth *Field* row field.
    f. Click in the fifth *Field* row field, type **Total: [Hours]*[Rate]**, and then press Enter.

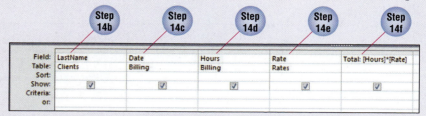

    g. Run the query.
    h. Save the query and name it *ClientBilling*.
    i. Close the query.
15. Create a report with the ClientBilling query using the Report button in the Create tab.
16. Click each of the column headings individually and then decrease the size of each column so the right border of the column is near the longest entry.
17. Apply Currency formatting to the numbers in the *Total* column by completing the following steps:
    a. Click the Report Layout Tools Format tab.
    b. Click in the first field below the *Total* column (the field containing the number *350*).
    c. Click the Apply Currency Format button in the Number group.

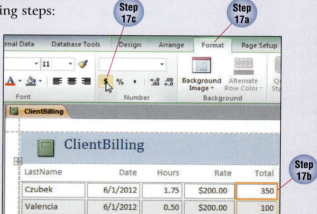

18. Group the report by last name by completing the following steps:
    a. Click the Report Layout Tools Design tab.
    b. Click the Group & Sort button in the Grouping & Totals group.
    c. Click the Add a group button in the Group, Sort, and Total pane.
    d. Click the *LastName* field in the list box.
    e. Click the Add a sort button in the Group, Sort, and Total pane.
    f. Click the *Date* field in the list box.
    g. Close the Group, Sort, and Total pane by clicking the Close button located in the upper right corner of the pane.
19. Save the report and name it *ClientBillingRpt*.
20. Print and then close the report. (The report will print on three pages.)
21. Close the **AL1-C6-WarrenLegal.accdb** database.

Project 2 Use Wizards to Create Reports and Labels   3 Parts

You will create reports using the Report Wizard and prepare mailing labels using the Label Wizard.

Creating a Report Using the Report Wizard

Access offers a Report Wizard that will guide you through the steps for creating a report. To create a report using the wizard, click the Create tab and then click the Report Wizard button in the Reports group. At the first wizard dialog box, shown in Figure 6.3, choose the desired table or query with options from the *Tables/Queries* option box. Specify the fields you want included in the report by inserting them in the *Selected Fields* list box and then clicking the Next button.

At the second Report Wizard dialog box, shown in Figure 6.4, you can specify the grouping level of data in the report. To group data by a specific field, click the field in the list box at the left side of the dialog box and then click the One Field button. Use the button containing the left-pointing arrow to remove an option as a grouping level. Use the up-pointing and down-pointing arrows to change the priority of the field.

Specify a sort order with options at the third Report Wizard dialog box shown in Figure 6.5. To specify a sort order, click the down-pointing arrow at the right of the option box preceded by a number 1 and then click the field name. The default sort order is ascending. You can change this to descending by clicking the button that displays at the right side of the text box. After identifying the sort order, click the Next button.

Quick Steps

Create a Report Using Report Wizard
1. Click Create tab.
2. Click Report Wizard button.
3. Choose desired options at each of the Report Wizard dialog boxes.

HINT
Use the Report Wizard to select specific fields and specify how data is grouped and sorted.

Report Wizard

Figure 6.3 First Report Wizard Dialog Box

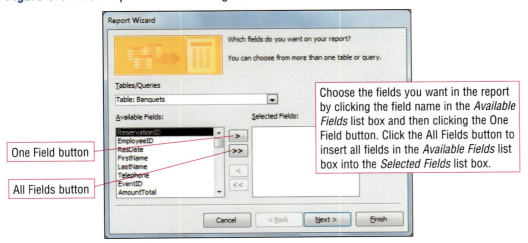

Chapter 6 ■ Creating Reports and Mailing Labels   247

Figure 6.4 Second Report Wizard Dialog Box

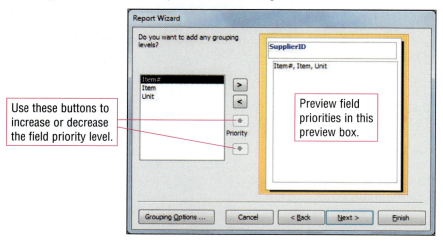

Figure 6.5 Third Report Wizard Dialog Box

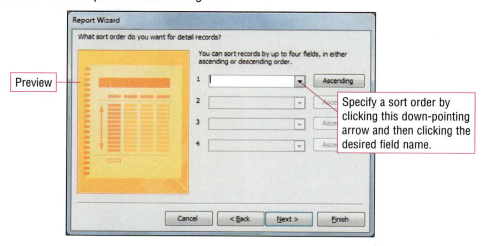

Use options at the fourth Report Wizard dialog box as shown in Figure 6.6 to specify the layout and orientation of the report. The *Layout* option has a default setting of *Stepped*. You can change this to *Block* or *Outline*. By default the report will print in *Portrait* orientation. You can change this to *Landscape* in the *Orientation* section of the dialog box. Access will adjust field widths in the report so all fields fit on one page. If you do not want Access to make the adjustment, remove the check mark from the *Adjust the field width so all fields fit on a page* option.

At the fifth and final Report Wizard dialog box, type a name for the report and then click the Finish button.

Figure 6.6 Fourth Report Wizard Dialog Box

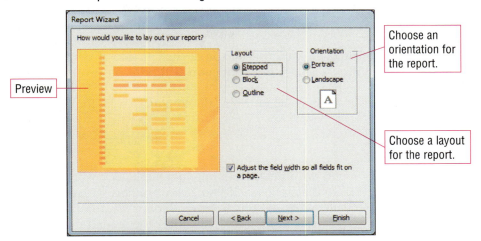

Project 2a — Using the Report Wizard to Prepare a Report — Part 1 of 3

1. Display the Open dialog box with Access2010L1C6 on your storage medium the active folder.
2. Open the **AL1-C6-Skyline.accdb** database and enable the contents.
3. Create a report using the Report Wizard by completing the following steps:
   a. Click the Create tab.
   b. Click the Report Wizard button in the Reports group.
   c. At the first Report Wizard dialog box, click the down-pointing arrow at the right side of the *Tables/Queries* option box and then click *Table: Inventory* at the drop-down list.
   d. Click the All Fields button to insert all Inventory fields in the *Selected Fields* list box.
   e. Click the Next button.
   f. At the second Report Wizard dialog box, make sure *Supplier ID* displays in blue at the top of the preview page at the right side of the dialog box and then click the Next button.
   g. At the third Report Wizard dialog box, click the Next button. (You want to use the sorting defaults.)
   h. At the fourth Report Wizard dialog box, click the *Block* option in the *Layout* section and then click the Next button.

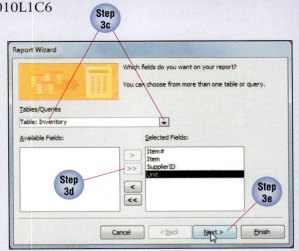

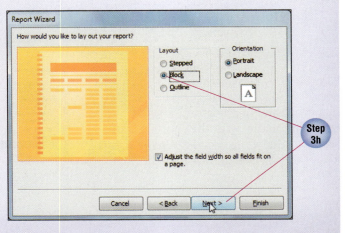

Chapter 6 ■ Creating Reports and Mailing Labels   **249**

i. At the fifth Report Wizard dialog box, make sure *Inventory* displays in the *What title do you want for your report?* text box and then click the Finish button. (The report displays in Print Preview.)
4. With the report in Print Preview, click the Print button at the left side of the Print Preview tab and then click OK at the Print dialog box. (The report will print on two pages.)
5. Close Print Preview.
6. Switch to Report view by clicking the View button in the Report Design Tools Design tab.
7. Close the Inventory report.

If you create a report with fields from only one table, you will choose options from five Report Wizard dialog boxes. If you create a report with fields from more than one table, you will choose options from six Report Wizard dialog boxes. After choosing the tables and fields at the first dialog box, the second dialog box that displays asks how you want to view the data. For example, if you specify fields from a Suppliers table and fields from an Orders table, the second Report Wizard dialog box will ask you if you want to view data "by Suppliers" or "by Orders."

Project 2b Creating a Report with Fields from Multiple Tables   Part 2 of 3

1. With the **AL1-C6-Skyline.accdb** database open, create a report with the Report Wizard by completing the following steps:
   a. Click the Create tab.
   b. Click the Report Wizard button in the Reports group.
   c. At the first Report Wizard dialog box, click the down-pointing arrow at the right side of the *Tables/Queries* option box and then click *Table: Events* at the drop-down list.
   d. Click the *Event* field in the *Available Fields* list box and then click the One Field button.
   e. Click the down-pointing arrow at the right side of the *Tables/Queries* option box and then click *Table: Banquets* at the drop-down list.
   f. Insert the following fields in the *Selected Fields* list box:
      ResDate
      FirstName
      LastName
      AmountTotal
      AmountPaid
   g. After inserting the fields, click the Next button.
   h. At the second Report Wizard dialog box, make sure *by Events* is selected and then click the Next button.

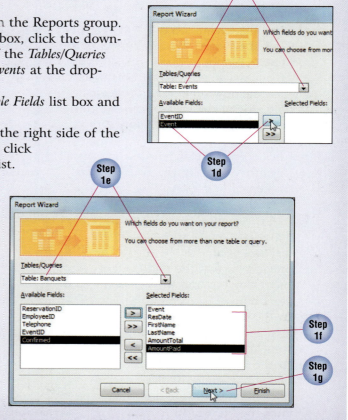

i. At the third Report Wizard dialog box, click the Next button. (The report preview shows that the report will be grouped by event.)
j. At the fourth Report Wizard dialog box, click the Next button. (You want to use the sorting defaults.)
k. At the fifth Report Wizard dialog box, click the *Block* option in the *Layout* section, click *Landscape* in the *Orientation* section, and then click the Next button.

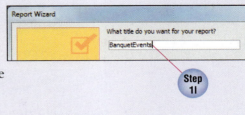

Step 1l

l. At the sixth Report Wizard dialog box, select the current name in the *What title do you want for your report?* text box, type **BanquetEvents**, and then click the Finish button.
2. Close Print Preview and then change to Layout view.
3. Print and then close the BanquetEvents report.
4. Close the **AL1-C6-Skyline.accdb** database.

Preparing Mailing Labels

Access includes a mailing label wizard that walks you through the steps for creating mailing labels with fields in a table. To create mailing labels, click the desired table, click the Create tab, and then click the Labels button in the Reports group. At the first Label Wizard dialog box shown in Figure 6.7, specify the label size, units of measure, and the label type, and then click the Next button.

At the second Label Wizard dialog box shown in Figure 6.8, specify the font name, size, weight, and color, and then click the Next button.

Specify the fields you want included in the mailing labels at the third Label Wizard dialog box shown in Figure 6.9. To do this, click the field in the *Available fields* list box, and then click the One Field button. This moves the field to the *Prototype label* box. Insert the fields in the *Prototype label* box as you want the text to display on the label. After inserting the fields in the *Prototype label* box, click the Next button.

▼ **Quick Steps**

Create Mailing Labels Using Label Wizard
1. Click the desired table.
2. Click Create tab.
3. Click Labels button.
4. Choose desired options at each of the Label Wizard dialog boxes.

Labels

Figure 6.7 First Label Wizard Dialog Box

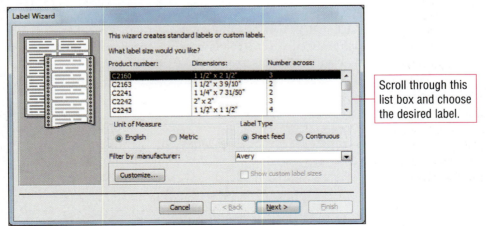

Scroll through this list box and choose the desired label.

Figure 6.8 Second Label Wizard Dialog Box

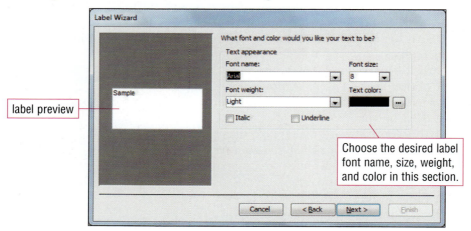

Figure 6.9 Third Label Wizard Dialog Box

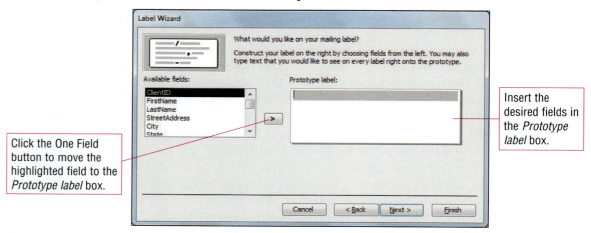

At the fourth Label Wizard dialog box, shown in Figure 6.10, you can specify a field from the database by which the labels are sorted. If you want the labels sorted (for example, by last name, postal code, etc.), insert the field by which you want the fields sorted in the *Sort by* list box and then click the Next button.

At the last Label Wizard dialog box, type a name for the label file, and then click the Finish button. After a few moments, the labels display on the screen in Print Preview. Print the labels and/or close Print Preview.

Figure 6.10 Fourth Label Wizard Dialog Box

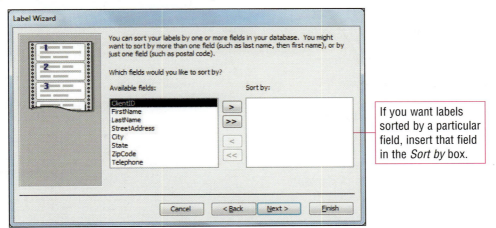

If you want labels sorted by a particular field, insert that field in the *Sort by* box.

Project 2c   Preparing Mailing Labels   Part 3 of 3

1. Open the **AL1-C6-WarrenLegal.accdb** database.
2. Click the Clients table in the Navigation pane.
3. Click the Create tab and then click the Labels button in the Reports group.
4. At the first Label Wizard dialog box, make sure *English* is selected in the *Unit of Measure* section, *Avery* is selected in the *Filter by manufacturer* list box, *Sheet feed* is selected in the *Label Type* section, *C2160* is selected in the *Product number* list box, and then click the Next button.
5. At the second Label Wizard dialog box, change the font size to 10, and then click the Next button.
6. At the third Label Wizard dialog box, complete the following steps to insert the fields in the *Prototype label* box:
    a. Click *FirstName* in the *Available fields* list box and then click the One Field button.
    b. Press the spacebar, make sure *LastName* is selected in the *Available fields* list box, and then click the One Field button.
    c. Press the Enter key. (This moves the insertion point down to the next line in the *Prototype label* box.)
    d. With *StreetAddress* selected in the *Available fields* list box, click the One Field button.
    e. Press the Enter key.
    f. With *City* selected in the *Available fields* list box, click the One Field button.
    g. Type a comma (,) and then press the spacebar.

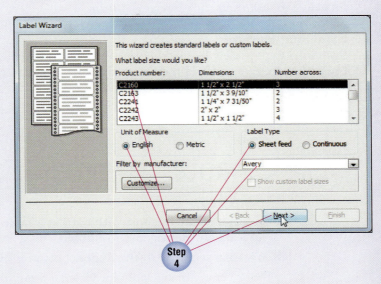

Step 4

h. With *State* selected in the *Available fields* list box, click the One Field button.
i. Press the spacebar.
j. With *ZipCode* selected in the *Available fields* list box, click the One Field button.
k. Click the Next button.

7. At the fourth Label Wizard dialog box, sort by ZIP code. To do this, click *ZipCode* in the *Available fields* list box and then click the One Field button.
8. Click the Next button.
9. At the last Label Wizard dialog box, click the Finish button. (The Label Wizard automatically names the label report *Labels Clients*.)
10. Print the labels by clicking the Print button that displays at the left side of the Print Preview tab and then click OK at the Print dialog box.
11. Close Print Preview.
12. Switch to Report view by clicking the View button in the Report Design Tools Design tab.
13. Close the labels report and then close the **AL1-C6-WarrenLegal.accdb** database.

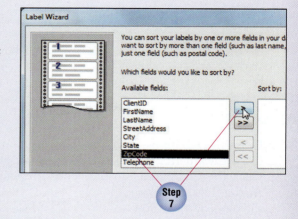

Chapter Summary

- You can create a report with data in a table or query to control how data appears on the page when printed.
- Create a report with the Report button in the Reports group in the Create tab.
- Four views are available for viewing a report — Report view, Print Preview, Layout view, and Design view.
- Use options in the Print Preview tab to specify how a report prints.
- In Layout view, you can select a report control object and then size or move the object. You can also change column width by clicking a column heading and then dragging the border to the desired width.
- Sort data in a record using the Ascending or Descending buttons in the Sort & Filter group in the Home tab.
- Customize a report with options in the Report Layout Tools ribbon with the Design tab, Arrange tab, Format tab, or Page Setup tab selected.

- You can customize control objects in the *Detail* section and the *Header* section with buttons in the Report Layout Tools ribbon with the Design tab, the Arrange tab, the Format tab, or the Page Setup tab selected.
- To make data in a report easier to understand, divide the data into groups using the Group, Sort, and Total pane. Display this pane by clicking the Group & Sort button in the Grouping & Totals group in the Report Layout Tools Design tab.
- Use the Report Wizard to guide you through the steps for creating a report. Begin the wizard by clicking the Create tab and then clicking the Report Wizard button in the Reports group.
- Create mailing labels with data in a table using the Label Wizard. Begin the wizard by clicking the desired table, clicking the Create tab, and then clicking the Labels button in the Reports group.

Commands Review

FEATURE	RIBBON TAB, GROUP	BUTTON
Report	Create, Reports	
Group, Sort, and Total pane	Report Layout Tools Design, Grouping & Totals	
Report Wizard	Create, Reports	
Labels Wizard	Create, Reports	

Concepts Check   Test Your Knowledge

Completion: In the space provided at the right, indicate the correct term, symbol, or command.

1. The Report button is located in the Reports group in this tab.   _____

2. Layout view is one of four views available in a report including Report view, Design view, and this.   _____

3. Press these keys to select all control objects in a report in Layout view.   _____

4. The Ascending button is located in this group in the Home tab.   _____

5. Click this button in the Grouping & Totals group in the Report Layout Tools Design tab to perform functions such as finding the sum, average, maximum, or minimum of the numbers in a column.   _____

6. With options in this tab, you can insert controls, insert headers or footers data, and add existing fields. _____

7. The Group & Sort button is located in this group in the Report Layout Tools Design tab. _____

8. Click the Group & Sort button and this pane displays. _____

9. Use this to guide you through the steps for creating a report. _____

10. To create mailing labels, click the desired table, click the Create tab, and then click the Labels button in this group. _____

Skills Check Assess Your Performance

Assessment

1 CREATE AND FORMAT REPORTS IN THE HILLTOP DATABASE

1. Open the **AL1-C6-Hilltop.accdb** database and enable the contents.
2. Create a report with the Inventory table using the Report button.
3. With the report in Layout view, apply the following formatting:
   a. Center the data below each of the following column headings: *Equipment#*, *AvailableHours*, *ServiceHours*, and *RepairHours*.
   b. Select all of the control objects and then change the font to Constantia.
   c. Select the money amounts below the *PurchasePrice* column heading and then decrease the decimal so the money amounts display without a decimal point.
   d. Click in the *$473,260.00* amount and then decrease the decimal so the amount displays without a decimal.
   e. Change the title of the report to *Inventory Report*.
4. Save the report and name it *InventoryReport*.
5. Print and then close InventoryReport.
6. Create a query in Design view with the following specifications:
   a. Add the Customers, Equipment, Invoices, and Rates tables to the query window.
   b. Insert the *Customer* field from the Customers table in the first *Field* row field.
   c. Insert the *Equipment* field from the Equipment table in the second *Field* row field.
   d. Insert the *Hours* field from the Invoices table in the third *Field* row field.
   e. Insert the *Rate* field from the Rates table in the fourth *Field* row field.
   f. Click in the fifth *Field* row field, type **Total: [Hours]*[Rate]**, and then press Enter.
   g. Run the query.
   h. Save the query and name it *CustomerRentals* and then close the query.

7. Create a report with the CustomerRentals query using the Report button.
8. With the report in Layout view, apply the following formatting:
   a. Decrease the width of columns so the right border of each column displays near the right side of the longest entry.
   b. Select the money amounts and then decrease the decimal so the amounts display with no decimal point.
   c. Click in the *Total* column and then total the amounts by clicking the Report Layout Tools Design tab, clicking the Totals button in the Grouping & Totals group, and then clicking *Sum* at the drop-down list.
   d. Click the total amount (located at the bottom of the *Total* column), click the Report Layout Tools Format tab, and then click the Apply Currency Format button.
   e. Increase the height of the total amount until the entire amount is visible.
   f. Select and then delete the amount that displays at the bottom of the *Rate* column.
   g. Display the Group, Sort, and Total pane, group the records by *Customer*, sort by *Equipment*, and then close the pane.
   h. Apply the Grid theme. (Do this with the Themes button in the Themes group in the Report Layout Tools Design tab.)
   i. Select the five column headings and change the font color to black.
   j. Change the title to *Rentals*.
9. Save the report and name it *RentalReport*.
10. Print and then close RentalReport.

Assessment

2 CREATE REPORTS USING THE REPORT WIZARD

1. With the **AL1-C6-Hilltop.accdb** database open, create a report using the Report Wizard with the following specifications:
   a. At the first Report Wizard dialog box, insert the following fields in the *Selected Fields* list box:
      From the Equipment table:
         Equipment
      From the Inventory table:
         PurchaseDate
         PurchasePrice
         AvailableHours
   b. Do not make any changes at the second Report Wizard dialog box.
   c. Do not make any changes at the third Report Wizard dialog box.
   d. At the fourth Report Wizard dialog box, choose the *Columnar* option.
   e. At the fifth and last Report Wizard dialog box, click the Finish button. (This accepts the default report name of *Equipment*.)
2. Print and then close the report.

3. Create a report using the Report Wizard with the following specifications:
   a. At the first Report Wizard dialog box, insert the following fields in the *Selected Fields* list box:
      From the Customers table:
         Customer
      From the Invoices table:
         BillingDate
         Hours
      From the Equipment table:
         Equipment
      From the Rates table:
         Rate
   b. Do not make any changes at the second Report Wizard dialog box.
   c. Do not make any changes at the third Report Wizard dialog box.
   d. Do not make any changes at the fourth Report Wizard dialog box.
   e. At the fifth Report Wizard dialog box, choose the *Block* option.
   f. At the sixth and last Report Wizard dialog box, name the report *Rentals*.
4. Print and then close the report.

Assessment

3 CREATE MAILING LABELS

1. With the **AL1-C6-Hilltop.accdb** database open, click the Customers table in the Navigation pane.
2. Use the Label Wizard to create mailing labels (you determine the label type) with the customer names and addresses and sorted by customer names. Name the mailing label report *CustomerMailingLabels*.
3. Print the mailing labels.
4. Close the mailing labels.

Assessment

4 ADD A FIELD TO A REPORT

1. In Chapter 5, you added a field list to an existing form using the Field List pane. Experiment with adding a field to an existing report and then complete the following:
   a. Open the report named RentalReport (created in Assessment 1) in Layout view.
   b. Display the Field List pane and display all tables.
   c. Drag the *BillingDate* field from the Invoices table so the field is positioned between the *Equipment* column and the *Hours* column.
   d. At the message indicating that Access will modify the RecordSource property and asking if you want to continue, click Yes.
   e. Close the Field List pane.
3. Save, print, and then close the report.
4. Close the **AL1-C6-Hilltop.accdb** database.

Visual Benchmark Demonstrate Your Proficiency

DESIGN A QUERY AND CREATE A REPORT WITH THE QUERY

1. Open the **AL1-C6-Skyline.accdb** database and then create and run the query shown in Figure 6.11.
2. Save the query and name it *Suppliers2&4Orders* and then close the query.
3. Use the Report button to create the report shown in Figure 6.12 using the *Suppliers2&4Orders* query with the following specifications:
   a. Apply the *Concourse* theme.
   b. Adjust column widths and change the alignment of data as shown in Figure 6.12.
   c. Change the title as shown in the figure.
   d. Select the column headings and then change the font color to black.
   e. Insert the sum total of the amounts in the *Total* column. Format the total amount as shown in the figure.
   f. Delete the sum amount at the bottom of the *UnitPrice* column.
4. Save the report and name it *Suppliers2&4OrdersRpt*.
5. Print the report, close the report, and then close the **AL1-C6-Skyline.accdb** database.

Figure 6.11 Visual Benchmark Query

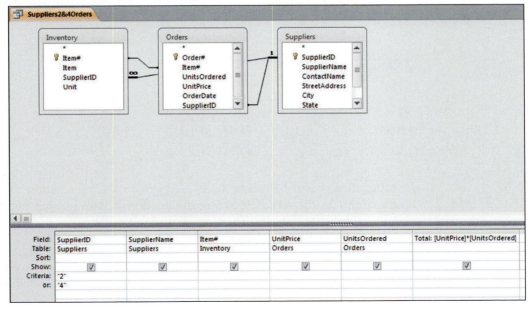

Figure 6.12 Visual Benchmark Report

SupplierID	SupplierName	Item#	UnitPrice	UnitsOrdered	Total
2	Coral Produce	002	$10.50	3	$31.50
2	Coral Produce	016	$24.00	1	$24.00
4	Grocery Wholesalers	020	$18.75	2	$37.50
2	Coral Produce	021	$31.00	1	$31.00
4	Grocery Wholesalers	026	$29.25	1	$29.25
4	Grocery Wholesalers	034	$13.75	2	$27.50
4	Grocery Wholesalers	035	$17.00	1	$17.00
4	Grocery Wholesalers	025	$28.50	1	$28.50
4	Grocery Wholesalers	013	$14.00	2	$28.00
4	Grocery Wholesalers	036	$17.00	2	$34.00
2	Coral Produce	014	$15.75	2	$31.50
4	Grocery Wholesalers	027	$22.00	1	$22.00
2	Coral Produce	004	$10.95	2	$21.90
4	Grocery Wholesalers	012	$30.25	1	$30.25
4	Grocery Wholesalers	018	$45.00	1	$45.00
2	Coral Produce	016	$39.40	2	$78.80
4	Grocery Wholesalers	035	$17.00	1	$17.00
2	Coral Produce	014	$15.75	2	$31.50
4	Grocery Wholesalers	020	$18.75	2	$37.50
					$603.70

Suppliers 2 and 4 Orders — Monday, July 30, 2012 9:00:15 PM

Case Study — Apply Your Skills

Part 1

As the office manager at Millstone Legal Services, you need to enter records for three new clients in the **AL1-C6-Millstone.accdb** database. Using the following information, enter the data in the appropriate tables:

Client number 42
Martin Costanzo
1002 Thomas Drive
Casper, WY 82602
(307) 555-5001
Mr. Costanzo saw Douglas Sheehan regarding divorce proceedings with a billing date of 3/15/2012 and a fee of $150.

Client number 43
Susan Nordyke
23193 Ridge Circle East
Mills, WY 82644
(307) 555-2719
Ms. Nordyke saw Loretta Ryder regarding support enforcement with a billing date of 3/15/2012 and a fee of $175.

Client number 44
Monica Sommers
1105 Riddell Avenue
Casper, WY 82609
(307) 555-1188
Ms. Sommers saw Anita Leland regarding a guardianship with a billing date of 3/15/2012 and a fee of $250.

Part 2

Create and print the following queries, reports, and labels:
- Create a report with the Clients table. Apply formatting to enhance the visual appeal of the report.
- Create a query that displays the client ID, first name, and last name; attorney last name; billing date; and fee. Name the query *ClientBilling*.
- Create a report with the ClientBilling query. Group the records in the report by attorney last name (the *LName* field in the drop-down list) and sort alphabetically in ascending order by client last name (the *LastName* field in the drop-down list). Apply formatting to enhance the visual appeal of the report.
- Create a telephone directory by creating a report that includes client last names, first names, and telephone numbers. Sort the records in the report alphabetically by last name and in ascending order.
- Edit the ClientBilling query so it includes a criterion that displays only billing dates between 3/12/2012 and 3/15/2012. Save the query with Save As and name it *ClientBilling12-15*.
- Create a report with the ClientBilling12-15 query. Apply formatting to enhance the visual appeal of the report.
- Create mailing labels for the clients.

Part 3

Apply the following conditions to fields in reports and then print the reports:
- In the Clients report, apply the condition that the city *Casper* displays in red and the city *Mills* displays in blue in the *City* field.
- In the ClientBilling report, apply the condition that fees over $199 display in green and fees less than $200 display in blue.

Part 4

Your center has a procedures manual that describes processes and procedures in the center. Open Word and then create a document for the procedures manual that describes the process for creating a report using the Report button, the Report Wizard, and the process for preparing mailing labels using the Label Wizard. Save the completed document and name it **A4-C6-CS-Manual**. Print and then close **A4-C6-CS-Manual.docx**.

Microsoft® Access®
Modifying, Filtering, and Viewing Data

CHAPTER 7

PERFORMANCE OBJECTIVES

Upon successful completion of Chapter 7, you will be able to:
- Filter data by selection and by form
- Remove a filter
- View object dependencies
- Compact and repair a database
- Encrypt a database with a password
- View and customize document properties
- Customize the Recent tab Backstage view
- Save a database in an earlier version of Access
- Save a database object in PDF format

You can filter data in a database object to view specific records without having to change the design of the object. In this chapter, you will learn how to filter data, filter by selection, and filter by form. You will also learn how to view object dependencies, manage a database with options at the Info tab and Recent tab Backstage views, save a database in an earlier version, and save a database object in PDF format. Model answers for this chapter's projects appear on the following pages.

Access2010L1C7

Note: Before beginning the projects, copy to your storage medium the Access2010L1C7 subfolder from the Access2010L1 folder on the CD that accompanies this textbook and make Access2010L1C7 the active folder.

Project 1 Filter Records

Project 1a

EmployeeID	FName	LName	StreetAddress	City	State	ZipCode
02	Wayne	Weber	17362 North Tenth	Fort Myers	FL	33994
03	Owen	Pasqual	4010 Shannon Drive	Fort Myers	FL	33910
04	Vadim	Sayenko	1328 St. Paul Avenue	Fort Myers	FL	33907
07	Donald	Sellars	23103 Summer Highway	Fort Myers	FL	33919
09	Elizabeth	Mohr	1818 Brookdale Road	Fort Myers	FL	33902
11	Nicole	Bateman	5001 150th Street	Fort Myers	FL	33908

Skyline Employees Filtered Records, Page 1

Telephone	HireDate	HealthIns
(239) 555-6041	4/1/2007	☐
(239) 555-3492	4/15/2006	☐
(239) 555-9487	6/15/2006	✔
(239) 555-4348	6/6/2008	✔
(239) 555-0430	5/1/2008	✔
(239) 555-2631	2/1/2010	☐

Skyline Employees Filtered Records, Page 2

Project 1b

ResDate	FirstName	LastName	Telephone	Event	EmployeeID
6/2/2012	Terrance	Schaefer	(239) 555-6239	Wedding rehearsal dinner	03
6/3/2012	Andrea	Wyatt	(239) 555-4282	Wedding reception	01
6/3/2012	Luis	Castillo	(239) 555-4001	Wedding shower	11
6/7/2012	David	Hooper	(941) 555-2338	Wedding anniversary	04
6/8/2012	Bridget	Kohn	(239) 551-1299	Other	02
6/9/2012	Joanne	Blair	(239) 555-7783	Birthday	03
6/9/2012	Tim	Drysdale	(941) 555-0098	Bat mitzvah	02
6/10/2012	Gabrielle	Johnson	(239) 555-1882	Other	05
6/13/2012	Cliff	Osborne	(239) 555-7823	Wedding rehearsal dinner	12
6/15/2012	Janis	Semala	(239) 555-0476	Wedding reception	06
6/15/2012	Tristan	Strauss	(941) 555-7746	Other	03

Skyline Banquet Reservations Query

ResDate	FirstName	LastName	Telephone	Event	EmployeeID
6/9/2012	Joanne	Blair	(239) 555-7783	Birthday	03
6/2/2012	Terrance	Schaefer	(239) 555-6239	Wedding rehearsal dinner	03

Skyline Banquet Report

Project 1c

Item#	Item	SupplierID	Unit
003	Carrots	6	25 lb bag
005	Garlic	6	10 lb bag
009	Radishes	6	case
010	Celery	6	case
011	Broccoli	6	case
041	White sugar	6	25 lb bag
042	Baking powder	6	case
043	Baking soda	6	case

Skyline Filtered Inventory Records, Step 2c

Item#	Item	SupplierID	Unit
006	Green peppers	2	case
007	Red peppers	2	case
008	Yellow peppers	2	case

Skyline Filtered Inventory Records, Step 3d

ResDate	FirstName	LastName	Telephone	Event	EmployeeID
6/16/2012	Aaron	Williams	(239) 555-3821	Bar mitzvah	04
6/25/2012	Robin	Gehring	(239) 555-0126	Bar mitzvah	06
6/9/2012	Tim	Drysdale	(941) 555-0098	Bat mitzvah	02

Skyline Filtered Banquet Reservations Records, Step 7d

ResDate	FirstName	LastName	Telephone	Event	EmployeeID
6/3/2012	Luis	Castillo	(239) 555-4001	Wedding shower	11
6/16/2012	Willow	Earhart	(239) 555-0034	Wedding shower	04
6/9/2012	Joanne	Blair	(239) 555-7783	Birthday	03
6/17/2012	Jason	Haley	(239) 555-6641	Birthday	06
6/23/2012	Heidi	Thompson	(941) 555-3215	Birthday	01
6/30/2012	Kirsten	Simpson	(941) 555-4425	Birthday	02
6/16/2012	Aaron	Williams	(239) 555-3821	Bar mitzvah	04
6/25/2012	Robin	Gehring	(239) 555-0126	Bar mitzvah	06
6/9/2012	Tim	Drysdale	(941) 555-0098	Bat mitzvah	02
6/8/2012	Bridget	Kohn	(239) 551-1299	Other	02
6/10/2012	Gabrielle	Johnson	(239) 555-1882	Other	05
6/15/2012	Tristan	Strauss	(941) 555-7746	Other	03
6/19/2012	Lillian	Krakosky	(239) 555-8890	Other	03
6/29/2012	David	Fitzgerald	(941) 555-3792	Other	01
6/2/2012	Terrance	Schaefer	(239) 555-6239	Wedding rehearsal dinner	03
6/13/2012	Cliff	Osborne	(239) 555-7823	Wedding rehearsal dinner	12
6/7/2012	David	Hooper	(941) 555-2338	Wedding anniversary	04
6/23/2012	Anthony	Wiegand	(239) 555-7853	Wedding anniversary	11
6/30/2012	Shane	Rozier	(941) 555-1033	Wedding anniversary	12

Skyline Filtered Banquet Reservations Records, Step 6c

Project 1d

ReservationID	EmployeeID	ResDate	FirstName	LastName	Telephone	EventID	AmountTotal	AmountPaid	Confirmed
1	03	6/2/2012	Terrance	Schaefer	(239) 555-6239	RD	$750.00	$250.00	✔
6	03	6/9/2012	Joanne	Blair	(239) 555-7783	BD	$650.00	$200.00	✔
11	03	6/15/2012	Tristan	Strauss	(941) 555-7746	OT	$1,400.00	$300.00	☐
15	03	6/19/2012	Lillian	Krakosky	(239) 555-8890	OT	$500.00	$100.00	☐

Skyline Filtered Banquet Records

Item#	Item	SupplierID	Unit
001	Butternut squash	2	case
002	Potatoes	2	50 lb bag
004	Onions	2	25 lb bag
006	Green peppers	2	case
007	Red peppers	2	case
008	Yellow peppers	2	case
014	Green beans	2	case
016	Iceberg lettuce	2	case
017	Romaine lettuce	2	case
021	Cantaloupes	2	case
028	Beef	7	side
029	Pork	7	side
030	Chicken	7	case
051	Watermelon	2	case
052	Kiwi	2	case

Skyline Filtered Inventory Records

Project 2 View Object Dependencies and Manage a Database with Options in the Info Tab and Recent Tab Backstage View

Project 2e, Skyline Orders Table

Project 1 Filter Records — 4 Parts

You will filter records in a table, query, and report in the Skyline database using the Filter button, Selection button, Toggle Filter button, and shortcut menu. You will also remove filters and filter by form.

Filtering Data

You can place a set of restrictions, called a *filter*, on records in a table, query, form, or report to isolate temporarily specific records. A filter, like a query, lets you view specific records without having to change the design of the table, query, form, or report. Access provides a number of buttons and options for filtering data. You can filter data using the Filter button in the Sort & Filter group in the Home tab, right-click specific data in a record and then specify a filter, and use the Selection and Advanced buttons in the Sort & Filter group.

Filtering Using the Filter Button

You can use the Filter button in the Sort & Filter group in the Home tab to filter records in an object (table, query, form or report). To use this button, open the desired object, click in any entry in the field column on which you want to filter, and then click the Filter button. This displays a drop-down list with sorting options and a listing of all of the field entries. In a table, you can also display this drop-

▼ Quick Steps
Filter Records
1. Open desired object.
2. Click in entry of desired field column to filter.
3. Click Filter button.
4. Select desired sorting option at drop-down list.

HINT Filters available depend on the type of data selected in a column.

Figure 7.1 *City* Field Drop-down List

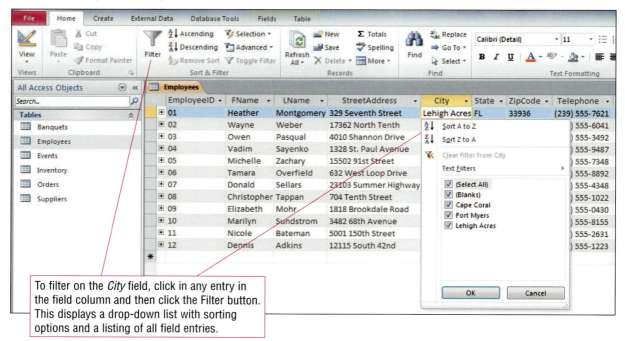

To filter on the *City* field, click in any entry in the field column and then click the Filter button. This displays a drop-down list with sorting options and a listing of all field entries.

Filter

down list by clicking the filter arrow that displays at the right side of a column heading. Figure 7.1 displays the drop-down list that displays when you click in the *City* field and then click the Filter button. To sort on a specific criterion, click the *(Select All)* check box to move all check marks from the list of field entries. Click the item in the list box on which you want to sort and then click OK.

When you open a table, query, or form, the Record Navigation bar contains the dimmed words *No Filter* preceded by a filter icon with a delete symbol (an X). If you filter records in one of these objects, *Filtered* displays in place of *No Filter*, the delete symbol is removed, and the text and filter icon display with an orange background. In a report, the word *Filtered* displays at the right side of the Record Navigation bar if you apply a filter to records.

Removing a Filter

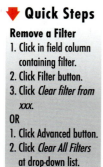

Quick Steps

Remove a Filter
1. Click in field column containing filter.
2. Click Filter button.
3. Click *Clear filter from xxx*.
OR
1. Click Advanced button.
2. Click *Clear All Filters* at drop-down list.

When you filter data, the underlying data in the object is not deleted. You can switch back and forth between the data and the filtered data by clicking the Toggle Filter button in the Sort & Filter group in the Home tab. If you click the Toggle Filter button and turn off the filter, all of the data in a table, query, or form displays and the message *Filtered* in the Record Navigation bar changes to *Unfiltered*.

Clicking the Toggle Filter button may redisplay all data in an object but it does not remove the filter. To remove the filter, click in the field column containing the filter and then click the Filter button in the Sort & Filter group in the Home tab. At the drop-down list that displays, click the *Clear filter from xxx* (where *xxx* is the name of the field). You can remove all filters from an object by clicking the Advanced button in the Sort & Filter group and then clicking the *Clear All Filters* option.

Project 1a   Filtering Records in a Table, Form, and Report   Part 1 of 4

1. Display the Open dialog box with Access2010L1C7 on your storage medium the active folder.
2. Open the **AL1-C7-Skyline.accdb** database and enable the contents.
3. Filter records in the Employees table by completing the following steps:
   a. Open the Employees table.
   b. Click in any entry in the *City* field.
   c. Click the Filter button in the Sort & Filter group in the Home tab. (This displays a drop-down list in the *City* field.)

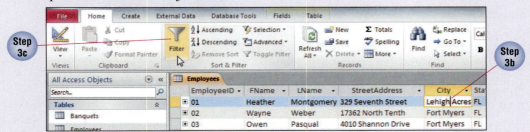

   d. Click the *(Select All)* check box in the filter drop-down list box. (This removes all check marks from the list options.)
   e. Click the *Fort Myers* check box in the list box. (This inserts a check mark in the check box.)
   f. Click OK. (Access displays only those records with a city field of *Fort Myers* and also displays *Filtered* and the filter icon with an orange background in the Record Navigation bar.)
   g. Print the filtered records by pressing Ctrl + P (the keyboard shortcut to display the print dialog box) and then clicking OK at the Print dialog box.
4. Toggle the display of filtered data by clicking the Toggle Filter button in the Sort & Filter group in the Home tab. (This redisplays all data in the table.)
5. Remove the filter by completing the following steps:
   a. Click in any entry in the *City* field.
   b. Click the Filter button in the Sort & Filter group.
   c. Click the *Clear filter from City* option at the drop-down list. (Notice that the message on the Record Navigation bar changes to *No Filter* and dims the words.)

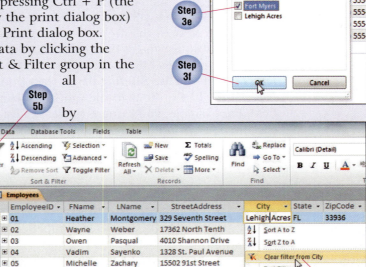

Chapter 7 ■ Modifying, Filtering, and Viewing Data   **267**

6. Save and then close the Employees table.
7. Create a form by completing the following steps:
   a. Click the Orders table in the Navigation pane.
   b. Click the Create tab and then click the Form button in the Forms group.
   c. Click the Form View button in the view area at the right side of the Status bar.
   d. Save the form with the name *Orders*.
8. Filter the records and display only those records with a supplier identification number of 2 by completing the following steps:
   a. Click in the *SupplierID* field containing the text *2*.
   b. Click the Filter button in the Sort & Filter group.
   c. At the filter drop-down list, click *(Select All)* to remove all of the check marks from the list options.
   d. Click the *2* option to insert a check mark.
   e. Click OK.
   f. Navigate through the records and notice that only the records with a supplier identification number of 2 display.
   g. Close the Orders form.

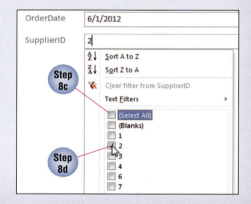

Filtering on Specific Values

Hover the mouse over a column heading to display a tip showing the filter criteria.

When you filter on a specific field, you can display a list of unique values for that field. If you click the Filter button for a field containing text, the drop-down list for the specific field will contain a *Text Filters* option. Click this option and a values list displays next to the drop-down list. The options in the values list will vary depending on the type of data in the field. If you click the Filter button for a field containing number values, the option in the drop-down list displays as *Number Filters* and if you are filtering dates, the option at the drop-down list displays as *Date Filters*. Use options in the values list to refine further a filter for a specific field. For example, you can use the values list to display money amounts within a specific range or order dates between certain dates. You can use the values list to find fields that are "equal to" or "not equal to" text in the current field.

Project 1b Filtering Records in a Query and a Report   Part 2 of 4

1. With the **AL1-C7-Skyline.accdb** database open, create a query in Design view with the following specifications:
   a. Add the Banquets and Events tables to the query window.
   b. Insert the *ResDate* field from the Banquets table to the first *Field* row field.
   c. Insert the *FirstName* field from the Banquets table to the third *Field* row field.
   d. Insert the *LastName* field from the Banquets table to the second *Field* row field.
   e. Insert the *Telephone* field from the Banquets table to the fourth *Field* row field.
   f. Insert the *Event* field from the Events table to the fifth *Field* row field.
   g. Insert the *EmployeeID* field from the Banquets table to the sixth *Field* row field.
   h. Run the query.
   i. Save the query and name it *BanquetReservations*.

2. Filter records of reservations on or before June 15, 2012 in the query by completing the following steps:
   a. With the BanquetReservations query open, make sure the first entry is selected in the *ResDate* field.
   b. Click the Filter button in the Sort & Filter group in the Home tab.
   c. Point to the *Date Filters* option in the drop-down list box.
   d. Click *Before* in the values list.
   e. At the Custom Filter dialog box, type **6/15/2012** and then click OK.

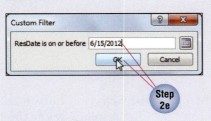

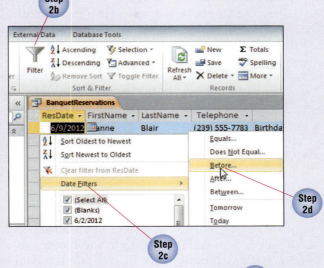

   f. Print the filtered query by pressing Ctrl + P and then clicking OK at the Print dialog box.
3. Remove the filter by clicking the filter icon that displays at the right side of the *ResDate* column heading and then clicking *Clear filter from ResDate* at the drop-down list.
4. Save and then close the BanquetReservations query.
5. Create a report by completing the following steps:
   a. Click the BanquetReservations query in the Navigation pane.
   b. Click the Create tab and then click the Report button in the Reports group.
   c. Delete the total amount at the bottom of the *ResDate* column.
   d. With the report in Layout view, decrease the column widths so the right column border displays near the longest entry in each column.
   e. Click the Report View button in the view area at the right side of the Status bar.
   f. Save the report and name it *BanquetReport*.
6. Filter the records and display all records of events except *Other* events by completing the following steps:
   a. Click in the first entry in the *Event* field.
   b. Click the Filter button in the Sort & Filter group.
   c. Point to the *Text Filters* option in the drop-down list box and then click *Does Not Equal* at the values list.
   d. At the Custom Filter dialog box, type **Other** and then click OK.

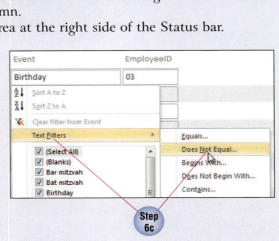

Chapter 7 ■ Modifying, Filtering, and Viewing Data   269

7. Further refine the filter by completing the following steps:
   a. Click in the first entry in the *EmployeeID* field.
   b. Click the Filter button.
   c. At the filter drop-down list, click the *(Select All)* check box to remove all of the check marks from the list options.
   d. Click the *03* check box to insert a check mark.
   e. Click OK.
8. Print only the first page of the report (the second page only contains shading) by completing the following steps:
   a. Press Ctrl + P to display the Print dialog box.
   b. Click the *Pages* option in the *Print Range* section.
   c. Type 1 in the *From* text box, press the Tab key, and then type 1 in the *To* text box.
   d. Click OK.
9. Save and then close the BanquetReport report.

Filtering by Selection

Selection

If you click in a field in an object and then click the Selection button in the Sort & Filter group in the Home tab, a drop-down list displays below the button with options for filtering on the data in the field. For example, if you click in a field containing the city name *Fort Myers*, clicking the Selection button will cause a drop-down list to display as shown in Figure 7.2. Click one of the options at the drop-down list to filter records. You can select specific text in a field entry and then filter based on the specific text. For example, in Project 1c you will select the word *peppers* in the entry *Green peppers* and then filter records containing the word *peppers*.

Figure 7.2 Selection Button Drop-down List

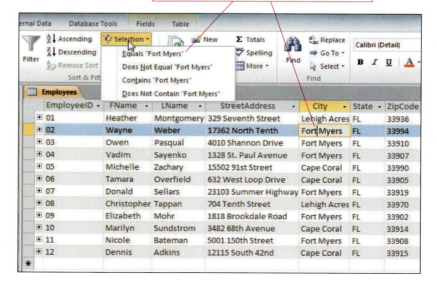

Filtering by Shortcut Menu

If you right-click on a field entry, a shortcut menu displays with options to sort the text, display a values list, or filter on a specific value. For example, if you right-click the field entry *Birthday* in the *Event* field, a shortcut menu displays as shown in Figure 7.3. Click a sort option to sort text in the field in ascending or descending order, point to the *Text Filters* option to display a values list, or click one of the values filters located toward the bottom of the menu. You can also select specific text within a field entry and then right-click the selection to display the shortcut menu.

Figure 7.3 Filtering Shortcut Menu

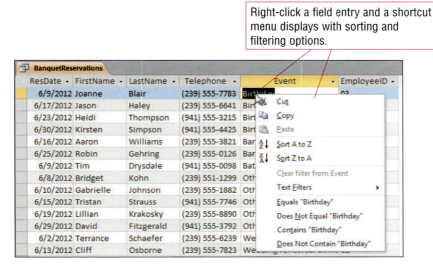

Project 1c   Filtering Records by Selection   Part 3 of 4

1. Open the Inventory table.
2. Filter only those records with a supplier number of 6 by completing the following steps:
   a. Click in the first entry containing *6* in the *SupplierID* field.
   b. Click the Selection button and then click *Equals "6"* at the drop-down list.
   c. Print the filtered table by pressing Ctrl + P and then clicking OK at the Print dialog box.
   d. Click the Toggle Filter button in the Sort & Filter group.

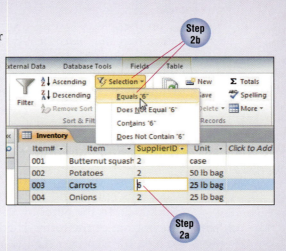

Chapter 7 ■ Modifying, Filtering, and Viewing Data   271

3. Filter any records in the *Item* field containing the word "pepper" by completing the following steps:
   a. Click in an entry in the *Item* field containing the entry *Green peppers*.
   b. Using the mouse, select the word *peppers*.
   c. Click the Selection button and then click *Contains "peppers"* at the drop-down list.
   d. Print the filtered table by pressing Ctrl + P and then clicking OK at the Print dialog box.
4. Close the Inventory table without saving the changes.
5. Open the BanquetReservations query.
6. Filter records in the *Event* field except *Wedding reception* by completing the following steps:
   a. Right-click in the first *Wedding reception* entry in the *Event* field.
   b. Click *Does Not Equal "Wedding reception"* at the shortcut menu.
   c. Print the filtered query.
   d. Click the Toggle Filter button in the Sort & Filter group.
7. Filter any records in the *Event* field containing the word *mitzvah* by completing the following steps:
   a. Click in an entry in the *Event* field containing the entry *Bar mitzvah*.
   b. Using the mouse, select the word *mitzvah*.
   c. Right-click on the selected word and then click *Contains "mitzvah"* at the shortcut menu.
   d. Print the filtered query.
8. Close the BanquetReservations query without saving the changes.

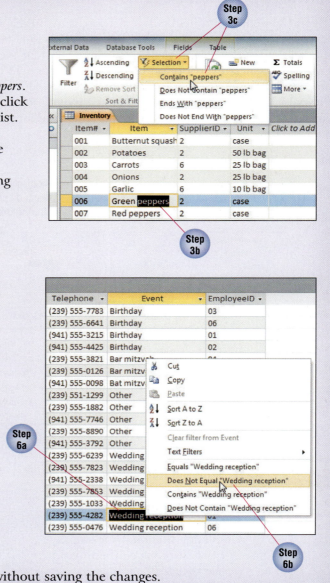

▼ **Quick Steps**

Use *Filter By Form*
1. Click Advanced button.
2. Click *Filter By Form* at drop-down list.
3. Click in empty field below desired column to filter.
4. Click down-pointing arrow.
5. Click on item to filter.

Using *Filter By Form*

One of the options from the Advanced button drop-down list is *Filter By Form*. Click this option and a blank record displays in a Filter by Form window in the work area. In the Filter by Form window, the *Look for* and *Or* tabs display toward the bottom of the form. The Look for tab is active by default and tells Access to look for whatever data you insert in a field. Click in the empty field below the desired column and a down-pointing arrow displays at the right side of the field. Click the down-pointing arrow and then click the item on which you want to filter. Click the Toggle Filter button to display the desired records. Add an additional value to a filter by clicking the Or tab at the bottom of the form.

Project 1d Using *Filter By Form* to Display Specific Records Part 4 of 4

1. With the **AL1-C7-Skyline.accdb** database open, open the Banquets table.
2. Filter records for a specific employee identification number by completing the following steps:
   a. Click the Advanced button in the Sort & Filter group in the Home tab and then click *Filter By Form* at the drop-down list.

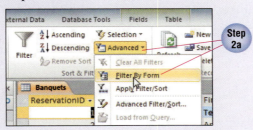

   b. At the Filter by Form window, click in the blank record below the *EmployeeID* field.
   c. Click the down-pointing arrow at the right side of the field and then click *03* at the drop-down list.
   d. Click the Toggle Filter button in the Sort & Filter group.

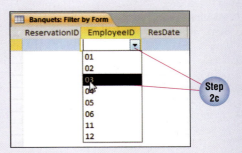

3. Print the filtered table by completing the following steps:
   a. Click the File tab, click the Print tab, and then click the *Print Preview* option.
   b. Click the Landscape button in the Page Layout group.
   c. Click the Print button and then click OK at the Print dialog box.
   d. Click the Close Print Preview button.
4. Close the Banquets table without saving the changes.
5. Open the Inventory table.
6. Filter records for supplier numbers 2 or 7 by completing the following steps:
   a. Click the Advanced button in the Sort & Filter group in the Home tab and then click *Filter By Form* at the drop-down list.
   b. At the Filter by Form window, click in the blank record below the *SupplierID* field.
   c. Click the down-pointing arrow at the right side of the field and then click *2* at the drop-down list.
   d. Click the Or tab located toward the bottom of the form.
   e. If necessary, click in the blank record below the *SupplierID* field.
   f. Click the down-pointing arrow at the right side of the field and then click *7* at the drop-down list.
   g. Click the Toggle Filter button in the Sort & Filter group.
   h. Print the filtered table.
   i. Click the Toggle Filter button to redisplay all records in the table.
   j. Click the Advanced button and then click *Clear All Filters* from the drop-down list.
7. Close the Inventory table without saving the changes.

Chapter 7 ■ Modifying, Filtering, and Viewing Data

> **Project 2** **View Object Dependencies and Manage a Database with Options in the Info Tab and Recent Tab Backstage View** — **4 Parts**
>
> You will display object dependencies in the Skyline database, compact and repair the database, encrypt it with a password, view and customize document properties, save an object in the database in the PDF file format, and save the database in a previous version of Word.

Viewing Object Dependencies

▼ Quick Steps

View Object Dependencies
1. Open desired database.
2. Click object in Navigation pane.
3. Click Database Tools tab.
4. Click Object Dependencies button.

Object Dependencies

The structure of a database is comprised of table, query, form, and report objects. Tables are related to other tables by creating relationships. Queries, forms, and reports draw the source data from records in the tables to which they have been associated and forms and reports can include subforms and subreports which further expand the associations between objects. A database with a large number of interdependent objects is more complex to work with. Viewing a list of the objects within a database and viewing the dependencies between objects can be beneficial to ensure an object is not deleted or otherwise modified causing an unforeseen effect on another object.

Display the structure of a database, including tables, queries, forms, and reports as well as relationships, at the Object Dependencies task pane. Display this task pane by opening the database, clicking the desired object in the Navigation pane, clicking the Database Tools tab, and then clicking the Object Dependencies button in the Relationships group. The Object Dependencies task pane in Figure 7.4 displays the objects in the AL1-C7-Skyline.accdb database that depend on the Banquets table.

Figure 7.4 Object Dependencies Task Pane

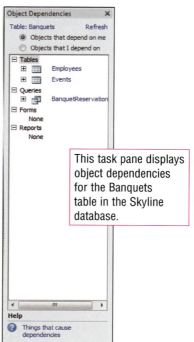

This task pane displays object dependencies for the Banquets table in the Skyline database.

By default, *Objects that depend on me* is selected in the Object Dependencies task pane and the list box displays the names of objects for which the selected object is the source. Next to each object in the task pane list is an expand button (plus symbol). Clicking the expand button will show objects dependent at the next level. For example, if a query is based upon the Banquets and Events tables and the query is used to generate a report, clicking the expand button next to the query name would show the report name. Clicking an object name in the Object Dependencies task pane opens the object in Design view.

Project 2a Viewing Object Dependencies Part 1 of 5

1. With the **AL1-C7-Skyline.accdb** database open, display the structure of the database by completing the following steps:
   a. Click the Banquets table in the Navigation pane.
   b. Click the Database Tools tab and then click the Object Dependencies button in the Relationships group. (This displays the Object Dependencies task pane. By default, *Objects that depend on me* is selected and the task pane lists the names of objects for which the Banquets table is the source.)

   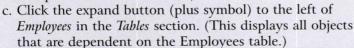
   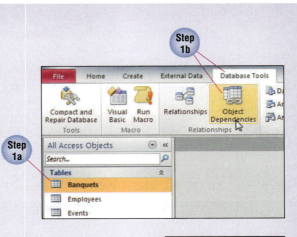

   c. Click the expand button (plus symbol) to the left of *Employees* in the *Tables* section. (This displays all objects that are dependent on the Employees table.)
   d. Click the *Objects that I depend on* option located toward the top of the Object Dependencies task pane.

   e. Click the Events table in the Navigation pane. (Click the Events table in the Navigation pane and not the Object Dependencies task pane.)
   f. Click the Refresh hyperlink located in the upper right corner of the Object Dependencies task pane.
   g. Click the *Objects that depend on me* option located toward the top of the Object Dependencies task pane.

   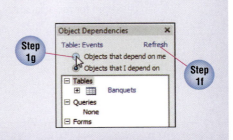

2. Close the Object Dependencies task pane.

Chapter 7 ■ Modifying, Filtering, and Viewing Data   275

▼ **Quick Steps**

Compact and Repair Database
1. Open database.
2. Click File tab.
3. Click Compact & Repair Database button.

Before compacting and repairing a database in a multi-user environment, make sure that no other user has the database open.

Compact & Repair Database

Using Options at the Info Tab Backstage View

The Info tab Backstage view contains options for compacting and repairing a database, encrypting a database with a password, and displaying and customizing database properties. Display the Info tab Backstage view as shown in Figure 7.5 by opening a database and then clicking the File tab.

Compacting and Repairing a Database

To optimize the performance of your database, compact and repair the database on a regular basis. As you work with a database, data in the database can become fragmented causing the amount of space the database takes on the storage medium or in the folder to be larger than necessary. To compact and repair a database, open the database, click the File tab and then click the Compact & Repair Database button.

You can tell Access to compact and repair a database each time you close the database. To do this, click the File tab and then click the Options button that displays below the Help tab. At the Access Options dialog box, click the *Current Database* option in the left panel. Click the *Compact on Close* option to insert a check mark and then click OK to close the dialog box.

Figure 7.5 Info Tab Backstage View

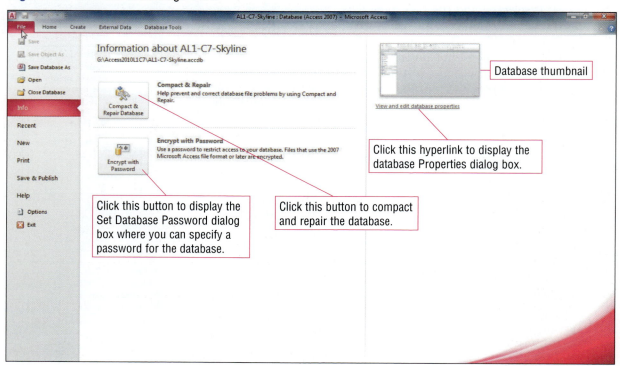

Encrypting a Database with a Password

If you want to prevent unauthorized access to a database, encrypt the database with a password to ensure that the database is opened only by someone who knows the password. Be careful when encrypting a database with a password because if you lose the password, you will be unable to use the database. You will not be able to remove a password from a database if you do not remember the password.

To encrypt a database with a password, you must open the database in Exclusive mode. To do this, display the Open dialog box, navigate to the desired folder, and then click the database to select it. Click the down-pointing arrow at the right side of the Open button located in the lower right corner of the dialog box, and then click *Open Exclusive* at the drop-down list. When the database opens, click the File tab and then click the Encrypt with Password button in the Info tab Backstage view. This displays the Set Database Password dialog box shown in Figure 7.6. At this dialog box, type a password in the *Password* text box, press the Tab key, and then type the password again. The text you type will display as asterisks. Click OK to close the Set Database Password dialog box. To remove a password from a database, open the database in Exclusive mode, click the File tab, and then click the Decrypt Database button. At the Unset Database Password dialog box, type the password and then click OK.

▼ Quick Steps

Open Database in Exclusive Mode
1. Display Open dialog box.
2. Click desired database.
3. Click down-pointing arrow at right of Open button.
4. Click *Open Exclusive*.

Encrypt Database with Password
1. Open database in Exclusive mode.
2. Click File tab.
3. Click Encrypt with Password button.
4. Type password, press Tab, type password again.
5. Click OK.

HINT When encrypting a database with a password, use passwords that combine uppercase and lowercase letters, numbers, and symbols.

Figure 7.6 Set Database Password Dialog Box

 Encrypt   Decrypt

Project 2b Compact and Repair and Encrypt a Database   Part 2 of 5

1. With the **AL1-C7-Skyline.accdb** database open, compact and repair the database by completing the following steps:
   a. Click the File tab. (This displays the Info tab Backstage view.)
   b. Click the Compact & Repair Database button.
2. Close the **AL1-C7-Skyline.accdb** database.

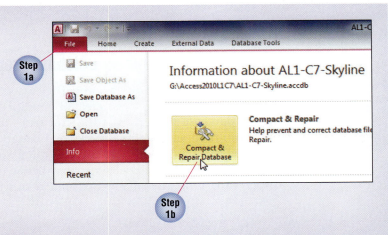

Chapter 7 ■ Modifying, Filtering, and Viewing Data   **277**

3. Open the database in Exclusive mode by completing the following steps:
   a. Display the Open dialog box.
   b. Click the **AL1-C7-Skyline.accdb** database in the Content pane to select it.
   c. Click the down-pointing arrow at the right side of the Open button that displays in the lower right corner of the dialog box and then click *Open Exclusive* at the drop-down list.

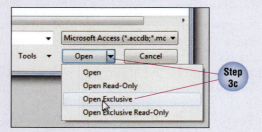

4. Encrypt the database with a password by completing the following steps:
   a. Click the File tab.
   b. At the Info tab Backstage view, click the Encrypt with Password button.
   c. At the Set Database Password dialog box, type your first and last names in all lowercase letters with no space, press the Tab key, and then type your first and last names again in lowercase letters.
   d. Click OK to close the dialog box.
   e. If a message displays with information about encrypting with a block cipher, click the OK button.

5. Close the **AL1-C7-Skyline.accdb** database.
6. Display the Open dialog box and then open the **AL1-C7-Skyline.accdb** database in Exclusive mode.
7. At the Password Required dialog box, type your password (first and last names) and then click OK.
8. Remove the password by completing the following steps:
   a. Click the File tab.
   b. Click the Decrypt Database button.
   c. At the Unset Database Password dialog box, type your first and last names in lowercase letters and then press the Enter key.

Viewing and Customizing Database Properties

Each database you create has properties associated with it such as the type of file, its location, and when it was created, modified, and accessed. You can view and modify database properties at the Properties dialog box. To view properties for the currently open database, click the File tab to display the Info tab Backstage view and then click the <u>View and edit database properties</u> hyperlink that displays at the right side of the Backstage view below the thumbnail of the database. This displays the Properties dialog box similar to what you see in Figure 7.7.

Figure 7.7 Properties Dialog Box

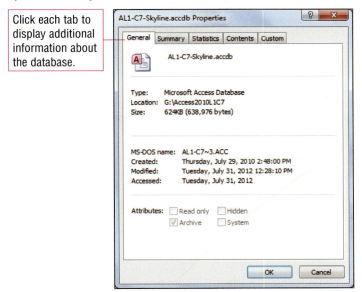

Click each tab to display additional information about the database.

The Properties dialog box for an open database contains tabs with information about the database. With the General tab selected, the dialog box displays information about the database type, size, and location. Click the Summary tab and fields display such as title, subject, author, category, keywords, and comments. Some fields may contain data and others may be blank. You can insert, edit, or delete text in the fields. Move the insertion point to a field by clicking in the field or by pressing the Tab key until the insertion point is positioned in the desired field.

Click the Statistics tab and information displays such as dates for when the database was created, modified, accessed, and printed. You can view the objects in the database by clicking the Contents tab. The *Document contents* section displays the objects in the database including tables, queries, forms, reports, macros, and modules.

Use options at the Properties dialog box with the Custom tab selected to add custom properties to the database. For example, you can add a property that displays the date the database was completed, information on the department in which the database was created, and much more. The list box below the *Name* option box displays the predesigned properties provided by Access. You can choose a predesigned property or create your own.

To choose a predesigned property, select the desired property in the list box, specify what type of property it is (value, date, number, yes/no), and then type a value. For example, to specify the department in which the database was created, you would click *Department* in the list box, make sure the *Type* displays as *Text*, click in the *Value* text box, and then type the name of the department.

Project 2c Viewing and Customizing Database Properties   Part 3 of 5

1. With the **AL1-C7-Skyline.accdb** database open, click the File tab and then click the <u>View and edit database properties</u> hyperlink that displays at the right side of the Backstage view below the database thumbnail.

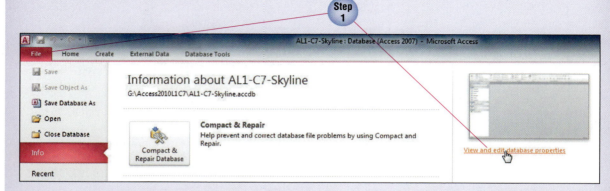

2. At the **AL1-C7-Skyline.accdb** Properties dialog box, click the General tab and then read the information that displays in the dialog box.
3. Click the Summary tab and then type the following text in the specified text boxes:

    Title   =   **AL1-C7-Skyline database**
    Subject   =   **Restaurant and banquet facilities**
    Author   =   *(type your first and last names)*
    Category   =   **restaurant**
    Keywords   =   **restaurant, banquet, event, Fort Myers**
    Comments   =   **This database contains information on Skyline Restaurant employees, banquets, inventory, and orders.**

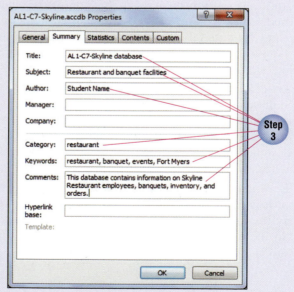

4. Click the Statistics tab and read the information that displays in the dialog box.
5. Click the Contents tab and notice that the *Document contents* section of the dialog box displays the objects in the database.

6. Click the Custom tab and then create custom properties by completing the following steps:

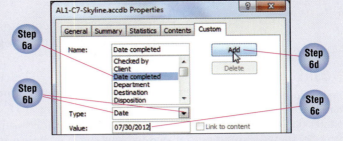

   a. Click the *Date completed* option in the *Name* list box.
   b. Click the down-pointing arrow at the right of the *Type* option box and then click *Date* at the drop-down list.
   c. Click in the *Value* text box and then type the current date in this format: *dd/mm/yyyy*.
   d. Click the Add button.
   e. With the insertion point positioned in the *Name* text box, type **Course**.
   f. Click the down-pointing arrow at the right of the *Type* option box and then click *Text* at the drop-down list.
   g. Click in the *Value* text box, type your current course number, and then press Enter.
   h. Click OK to close the dialog box.
7. Click the File tab to return to the database.

Customizing the Recent Tab Backstage View

When you open and close databases, Access keeps a list of the most recently opened databases. To view this list, click the File tab and then click the Recent tab. This displays the Recent tab Backstage view similar to what you see in Figure 7.8. (Your database file names may vary from what you see in the figure.) The most recently opened database names display in the *Recent Databases* list. Generally, the 20 most recently opened database names display in the list. To open a database, scroll down the list and then click the desired database name.

Figure 7.8 Recent Tab Backstage View

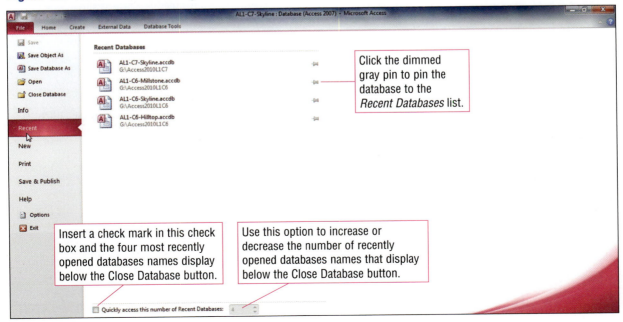

Chapter 7 ■ Modifying, Filtering, and Viewing Data

Displaying a Quick List

The Recent tab Backstage view contains the option *Quickly access this number of Recent Databases* located below the *Recent Databases* list. Insert a check mark in this option and the names of the four most recently opened databases display in the Backstage navigation bar (the panel at the left) below the Close Database button.

You can increase or decrease the number of displayed database names by increasing or decreasing the number that displays at the right side of the *Quickly access this number of Recent Databases* option. To remove the list of most recently opened databases from the navigation bar, click the *Quickly access this number of Recent Databases* option to remove the check mark.

Pinning a Database

If you want a database name to remain at the top of the *Recent Databases* list, pin the database name. To do this, click the dimmed gray pin that displays at the right side of the database name. This changes the dimmed gray pin to a blue pin. The next time you display the Recent tab Backstage view, the database name you pinned displays at the top of the list. To unpin a database name, click the blue pin to change it to a dimmed gray pin. You can also pin a database name to the *Recent Databases* list by right-clicking the database name and then clicking *Pin to list* at the shortcut menu. To unpin the database name, right-click the database name and then click *Unpin from list* at the shortcut menu.

Clearing the *Recent Databases* List

You can clear the contents (except pinned databases) of the *Recent Databases* list by right-clicking a database name in the list and then clicking *Clear unpinned items* at the shortcut menu. At the message asking if you are sure you want to remove the items, click the Yes button.

▼ Quick Steps

Display Recent Documents in Backstage Navigation Bar
1. Click File tab.
2. Click Recent tab.
3. Click *Quickly access this number of Recent Databases* check box.

Pin Database File Name
1. Click File tab.
2. Click Recent tab.
3. Click dimmed gray pin at right of desired database file name.

Project 2d — Managing Databases at the Recent Tab Backstage View — Part 4 of 5

1. Close the **AL1-C7-Skyline.accdb** database.
2. Click the Recent tab.
3. Notice the database names that display in the *Recent Databases* list.
4. Pin the **AL1-C7-Skyline.accdb** database to the *Recent Databases* list by clicking the dimmed gray pin that displays at the right side of the AL1-C7-Skyline.accdb database name in the *Recent Databases* list. (This changes the gray pin to a blue pin.)

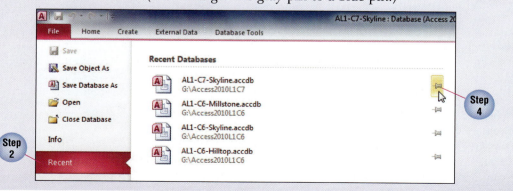

5. Click the *Quickly access this number of Recent Databases* check box located toward the bottom of the screen to insert a check mark. (With this option active, the four most recently opened database file names display in the Backstage navigation bar located below the Close Database button.)
6. Increase the number of database file names in the navigation bar by clicking twice on the up-pointing arrow in the option box located to the right of the *Quickly access this number of Recent Databases*. (This changes the number from *4* to *6*.)
7. Open the **AL1-C7-Skyline.accdb** database by clicking *AL1-C7-Skyline.accdb* that displays at the top of the *Recent Databases* list.
8. Click the File tab, click the Recent tab, and then make the following changes at the Recent tab Backstage view:
   a. Click the twice on the down-pointing arrow in the option box located to the right of the *Quickly access this number of Recent Databases*. (This changes the number from *6* to *4*.)
   b. Click the *Quickly access this number of Recent Databases* check box to remove the check mark.
   c. Unpin the **AL1-C7-Skyline.accdb** database by clicking the blue pin that displays at the right side of the database name. (This changes the blue pin to a gray pin.)
   d. Click the File tab to return to the database.

Saving a Database and Database Object

An Access 2010 or Access 2007 database is saved with the .accdb file extension. Earlier versions of Access such as 2003, 2002, or 2000 save a database with the .mdb file extension. To open an Access 2010 or 2007 database in an earlier version, you need to save the database in the .mdb file format.

To save an Access database in the 2002-2003 file format, open the database, click the File tab, and then click the Save & Publish tab. This displays the Save & Publish tab Backstage view as shown in Figure 7.9. Click the *Access 2002-2003 Database (*.mdb)* option in the *Save Database As* section and then click the Save As button that displays at the bottom of the *Save Database As* section. This displays the Save As dialog box with the *Save as type* option set to *Microsoft Access Database (2002-2003) (*.mdb)* and the current database file name with the *.mdb* file extension inserted in the *File name* text box. At this dialog box, click the Save button.

Click the *Save Object As* option in the File Types category of the Save & Publish tab Backstage view and options display for saving the currently selected object. Click the *Save Object As* option to save the selected object in the database or click the *PDF or XPS* option if you want to save the object in the PDF or XPS file format. The letters *PDF* stand for *portable document format*, which is a file format developed by Adobe Systems® that captures all of the elements of a file as an electronic image. An XPS file is a Microsoft file format for publishing content in an easily viewable format. The letters *XPS* stand for *XML paper specification* and the letters *XML* stand for *Extensible Markup Language*, which is a set of rules for encoding files electronically.

To save an object in the PDF or XPS file format, click the desired object in the database Navigation pane, click the File tab, and then click the Save & Publish tab. At the Save & Publish tab Backstage view, click the *Save Object As* option

▼ Quick Steps

Save Object in PDF Format
1. Click desired object in Navigation pane.
2. Click File tab.
3. Click Save & Publish tab.
4. Click *Save Object As* option.
5. Click *PDF or XPS* option.
6. Click Save As button.

Save a Database in an Earlier Version
1. Open database.
2. Click File tab.
3. Click Save & Publish tab.
4. Click desired version in Save Database As category.
5. Click Save As button.

Figure 7.9 Save & Publish Tab Backstage View

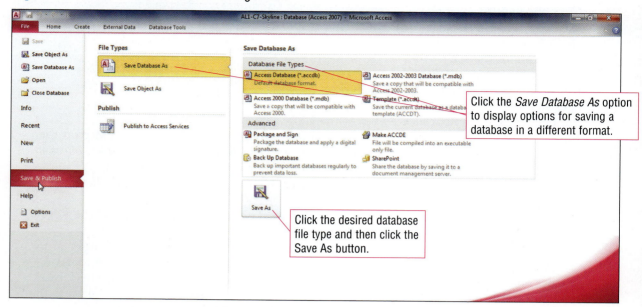

HINT An Access 2007 or 2010 database cannot be opened with an earlier version of Access.

in the File Types category, click the *PDF or XPS* option in the Save the current database object category, and then click the Save As button. This displays the Publish as PDF or XPS dialog box with the name of the object inserted in the *File name* text box followed by the file extension *.pdf*, and the *Save as type* option set at *PDF (*.pdf)*. Click the Publish button and the object is saved in PDF format and opens in Adobe Reader. Close Adobe Reader by clicking the Close button that displays in the upper right corner of the screen.

You can open a PDF file in Adobe Reader or in your web browser, and you can open an XPS file in your web browser. To open a PDF file or XPS file in your web browser, click the *File* option on the browser Menu bar and then click *Open* at the drop-down list. At the Open dialog box, click the Browse button. At the browser window Open dialog box, change the *Files of type* to *All Files (*.*)*, navigate to the desired folder, and then double-click the document.

Project 2e — Saving a Database in a Previous Version and Saving an Object in PDF Format
Part 5 of 5

1. With the **AL1-C7-Skyline.accdb** database open, save the Orders table in PDF file format by completing the following steps:
   a. Click the Orders table in the Navigation pane.
   b. Click the File tab and then click the Save & Publish tab.
   c. At the Save & Publish tab Backstage view, click the *Save Object As* option in the File Types category.
   d. Click the *PDF or XPS* option in the Save the current database object category.
   e. Click the Save As button.

284 Access Level 1 ■ Unit 2

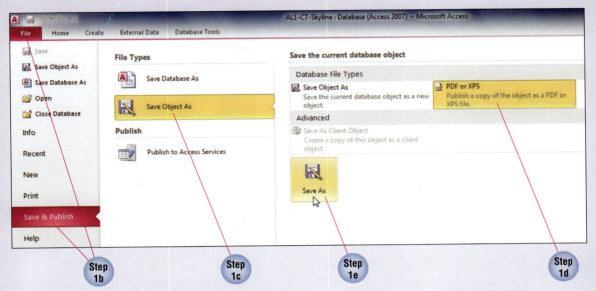

f. At the Publish as PDF or XPS dialog box, make sure the Access2010L1C7 folder on your storage medium is the active folder and then click the Publish button.
g. When the Orders table opens in Adobe Reader, scroll through the file, and then close the file by clicking the Close button located in the upper right corner of the screen.
2. Save the database in a previous version of Access by completing the following steps:
a. Click the File tab and then click the Save & Publish tab.
b. At the Save & Publish tab Backstage view, click the *Access 2002-2003 Database (*.mdb)* option in the Save Database As category.
c. Click the Save As button.

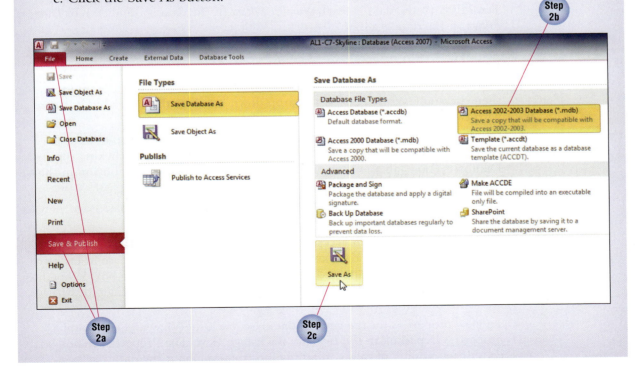

Chapter 7 ■ Modifying, Filtering, and Viewing Data   285

d. At the Save As dialog box, make sure the Access2010L1C7 folder on your storage medium is the active folder and then click the Save button. This saves the database with the same name (**AL1-C7-Skyline**) but with the *.mdb* file extension.

e. Notice that the Title bar displays the database file name *AL1-C7-Skyline : Database (Access 2002 - 2003 file format)*.

3. Close the database.

Chapter Summary

- A set of restrictions, called a filter, can be set on records in a table or form. A filter lets you select specific field values.
- You can filter records with the Filter button in the Sort & Filter group in the Home tab.
- Click the Toggle Filter button in the Sort & Filter group to switch back and forth between data and filtered data.
- Remove a filter by clicking the Filter button in the Sort & Filter group and then clicking the *Clear filter from xxx* (where *xxx* is the name of the field).
- Another method for removing a filter is to click the Advanced button in the Sort & Filter group and then click *Clear All Filters*.
- Display a list of filter values by clicking the Filter button and then pointing to *Text Filters* (if the data is text), *Number Filters* (if the data is numbers), or *Date Filters* (if the data is a date).
- Filter by selection by clicking the Selection button in the Sort & Filter group.
- Right-click a field entry to display a shortcut menu with filtering options.
- Filter by form by clicking the Advanced button in the Sort & Filter group and then clicking *Filter By Form* at the drop-down list. This displays a blank record with two tabs Look for and Or.
- Display the structure of a database and the relationship between objects at the Object Dependencies task pane. Display this task pane by clicking the Database Tools tab and then clicking the Object Dependencies button in the Relationships group.
- Click the Compact & Repair Database button in the Info tab Backstage view to optimize database performance.
- To prevent unauthorized access to a database, encrypt the database with a password. To encrypt a database, you must first open the database in Exclusive mode using the Open button drop-down list in the Open dialog box. While in Exclusive mode, encrypt a database with a password using the Encrypt with Password button in the Info tab Backstage view.
- To view properties for the current database, click the View and edit database properties hyperlink in the Info tab Backstage view. The Properties dialog box contains a number of tabs containing information about the database.

- The Recent tab Backstage view displays a list of the most recently opened databases. Insert a check mark in the *Quickly access this number of Recent Databases* check box to display the four most recently opened databases in the Backstage navigation bar.
- At the Recent tab Backstage view, click the gray pin to the right of the desired database in order to pin the database to the top of the *Recent Databases* list.
- Save a database in a previous version of Access using options in the Save Database As category of the Save & Publish tab Backstage view.
- To save a database object in PDF or XPS format, display the Save & Publish tab Backstage view, click the *Save Object As* option, and then click the *PDF or XPS* option.

Commands Review

FEATURE	RIBBON TAB, GROUP	BUTTON, OPTION
Filter	Home, Sort & Filter	
Toggle filter	Home, Sort & Filter	
Remove filter	Home, Sort & Filter	, *Clear filter from xxx* OR , Clear All Filters
Filter by selection	Home, Sort & Filter	
Filter by form	Home, Sort & Filter	, Filter By Form
Object Dependencies task pane	Database Tools, Relationships	
Info tab Backstage view	File, Info	
Recent tab Backstage view	File, Recent	

Chapter 7 ■ Modifying, Filtering, and Viewing Data

Concepts Check Test Your Knowledge

Completion: In the space provided at the right, indicate the correct term, symbol, or command.

1. The Filter button is located in this group in the Home tab.

2. If you filter data, you can switch between the data and the filtered data by clicking this button.

3. Remove all filtering from an object with the Filter button or by clicking this button and then clicking *Clear All Filters*.

4. In the Filter by Form window, these two tabs display toward the bottom of the form.

5. Display the structure of a database at this task pane.

6. Do this to a database to optimize database performance.

7. Before encrypting a database with a password, you have to open the database in this mode.

8. Display the Set Database Password dialog box by clicking this button in the Info tab Backstage view.

9. Data in this dialog box describes details about a database such as title, author name, and subject.

10. Insert a check mark in this option and the names of the four most recently opened databases display in the Backstage navigation bar.

11. Do this to a database file name if you want it to remain at the top of the *Recent Databases* list at the Recent tab Backstage view.

12. Save a database object in PDF file format with the *PDF or XPS* option in this Backstage view tab.

Skills Check   Assess Your Performance

Assessment 1 — FILTER RECORDS IN TABLES

1. Display the Open dialog box with Access2010L1C7 on your storage medium the active folder.
2. Open the **AL1-C7-WarrenLegal.accdb** database and enable the contents.
3. Open the Clients table and then filter the records to display the following records:
    a. Display only those records of clients who live in Renton. When the records of clients in Renton display, print the results in landscape orientation and then remove the filter. *Hint: Change to landscape orientation in Print Preview*.
    b. Display only those records of clients with the ZIP code of 98033. When the records of clients with the ZIP code 98033 display, print the results in landscape orientation and then remove the filter.
4. Close the Clients table without saving the changes.
5. Open the Billing table and then filter records by selection to display the following records:
    a. Display only those records with a Category of CC. Print the CC records and then remove the filter.
    b. Display only those records with an Attorney ID of 12. Print the records and then remove the filter.
    c. Display only those records between the dates 6/1/2012 and 6/10/2012. Print the records and then remove the filter.
6. Close the Billing table without saving the changes.
7. Open the Clients table and then use Filter By Form to display clients in Auburn or Renton. (Be sure to use the Or tab at the very bottom of the table.) Print the table in landscape orientation and then remove the filter.
8. Close the Clients table without saving the changes.
9. Open the Billing table and then use Filter By Form to display categories G or P. Print the table and then remove the filter.
10. Close the Billing table without saving the changes.
11. Close the **AL1-C7-WarrenLegal.accdb** database.

Assessment 2 — SAVE A TABLE AND DATABASE IN DIFFERENT FILE FORMATS

1. Open the **AL1-C7-Hilltop.accdb** database in Exclusive mode and enable the contents.
2. Create a password for the database and, with the Set Database Password dialog box open, create a screen capture of the screen with the dialog box by completing the following steps:
    a. Press the Print Screen button on your keyboard.
    b. Open Microsoft Word.
    c. Click the Paste button located in the Clipboard group in the Home tab. (This pastes the screen capture image in the Word document.)
    d. Click the File tab, click the Print tab, and then click the *Print* option at the Print tab Backstage view.

  e. Exit Word by clicking the Close button located in the upper right corner of the screen. At the message asking if you want to save the document, click the Don't Save button.
3. Click OK to close the Set Database Password dialog box.
4. At the message telling you that block cipher is incompatible with row level locking, click OK.
5. Close the database.
6. Open the **AL1-C7-Hilltop.accdb** database in Exclusive mode and enter the password when prompted.
7. Remove the password. *Hint: Do this with the Decrypt Database button in the Info tab Backstage view.*
8. Customize the Recent tab Backstage view by completing the following steps:
  a. Insert a check mark in the *Quickly access this number of Recent Databases* check box.
  b. Change the number of database files names that display to *6*.
  c. Pin the **AL1-C7-Hilltop.accdb** database to the *Recent Databases* list.
9. Use the Print Screen button on the keyboard to make a screen capture of the Recent tab Backstage view. Open Word and then paste the screen capture image in the Word document. Print the document containing the screen capture image and then exit Word without saving the document.
10. Change the Recent tab Backstage view options back by changing the number of database file names to display to *4*, removing the check mark from the *Quickly access this number of Recent Databases* check box, and unpinning the **AL1-C7-Hilltop.accdb** database.
11. Save the Invoices table in PDF format. When the table displays in Adobe Reader, print the table by clicking the Print button located toward the upper left side of the screen and then clicking OK at the Print dialog box. (If the Print button is not visible, click the File option, click *Print* at the drop-down list, and then click OK at the Print dialog box.)
12. Close Adobe Reader.
13. Save the **AL1-C7-Hilltop.accdb** database in the *Access 2002-2003 Database (*.mdb)* file format.
14. With the database open, make a screen capture using the Print Screen button on the keyboard. Open Word, paste the screen capture image in the Word document, print the document, and then exit Word without saving the document.
15. Close the database.

Assessment

3   DELETE AND RENAME OBJECTS

1. Open the **AL1-C7-Hilltop.accdb** database.
2. Right-click an object in the Navigation pane, experiment with options in the shortcut menu, and then complete these steps using the shortcut menu:
  a. Delete the Inventory form.
  b. Rename the form Equipment to *EquipForm*.
  c. Rename the report InvReport to *InventoryReport*.
  d. Export (using the shortcut menu) the *EquipmentQuery* to a Word RTF file. *Hint: Click the Browse button at the Export - RTF File dialog box and make Access2010L1C7 the active folder.*
  e. Open the *EquipmentQuery.rtf* file in Word, print the file, and then exit Word.
3. Close the **AL1-C7-Hilltop.accdb** database.

Visual Benchmark — Demonstrate Your Proficiency

DESIGN A QUERY AND FILTER THE QUERY

1. Open the **AL1-C7-PacTrek.accdb** database and enable the contents.
2. Create and run the query shown in Figure 7.10.
3. Save the query and name it *ProductsOnOrderQuery*.
4. Print the query.
5. Filter the query so the records display as shown in Figure 7.11. ***Hint: Filter the supplier names as shown in Figure 7.11 and then filter the UnitsOnOrder field to show records that do not equal 0.***
6. Print the filtered query.
7. Remove the filters and then close the query without saving the changes.
8. Close the **AL1-C7-PacTrek.accdb** database.

Figure 7.10 Visual Benchmark Query

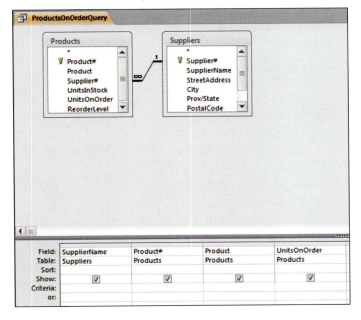

Figure 7.11 Visual Benchmark Filtered Query

SupplierName	Product#	Product	UnitsOnOrder
Hopewell, Inc.	152-H	Lantern hanger	15
Hopewell, Inc.	155-20	Shursite angle-head flashlight	20
Hopewell, Inc.	155-35	Shursite portable camp light	10
Cascade Gear	250-L	Cascade R4 jacket, ML	10
Cascade Gear	250-XL	Cascade R4 jacket, MXL	10
Cascade Gear	255-M	Cascade R4 jacket, WM	5
Cascade Gear	255-XL	Cascade R4 jacket, WXL	5

Case Study — Apply Your Skills

Part 1

As the office manager at Summit View Medical Services, you are responsible for maintaining clinic records. Open the **AL1-C7-SummitView.accdb** database, enable the contents, and then insert the following additional services into the appropriate table:

- Edit the *Doctor visit* entry in the Services table so it displays as *Clinic visit*.
- Add the entry *X-ray* with a service identification of *X*.
- Add the entry *Cholesterol screening* with a service identification of *CS*.

Add the following new patient information in the database in the appropriate tables:

Patient number 121
Brian M. Gould
2887 Nelson Street
Helena, MT 59604
(406) 555-3121
Mr. Gould saw Dr. Wallace for a clinic visit on 4/6/2012, which has a fee of $75.

Patient number 122
Ellen L. Augustine
12990 148th Street
East Helena, MT 59635
(406) 555-0722
Ms. Augustine saw Dr. Kennedy for cholesterol screening on 4/6/2012, which has a fee of $90.

Patient number 123
Jeff J. Masura
3218 Eldridge Avenue
Helena, MT 59624
(406) 555-6212
Mr. Masura saw Dr. Rowe for an x-ray on 4/6/2012, which has a fee of $75.

Add the following information to the Billing table:

- Patient 109 came for cholesterol screening with Dr. Kennedy on 4/6/2012 with a $90 fee.
- Patient 106 came for immunizations with Dr. Pena on 4/6/2012 with a $100 fee.
- Patient 114 came for an x-ray with Dr. Kennedy on 4/6/2012 with a $75 fee.

Part 2

Create the following filters and queries:
- Open the Billing table and then filter and print the records for the date 04/2/2012. Clear the filter and then filter and print the records with a doctor number of 18. Save and then close the table.
- Create a report that displays the patient's first name, last name, street address, city, state, and ZIP code. Apply formatting to enhance the visual appeal of the report. Filter and print the records of those patients living in Helena, remove the filter, and then filter and print the records of those patients living in East Helena. Close the report.
- Design a query that includes the doctor number, doctor last name, patient number, date of visit, and fee. Save the query with the name *DoctorBillingFees* and then print the query. Filter and print the records for Dr. Kennedy and Dr. Pena, remove the filter, and then filter and print the records for the dates 4/5/2012 and 4/6/2012. Save and then close the query.

Part 3

You want to make the Billing table available for viewing on computers without Access so you decide to save the table in PDF format. Save the Billing table in PDF format, print the table in Adobe Reader, and then close Adobe Reader. Close the **AL1-C7-SummitView.accdb** database.

Part 4

Your clinic has a procedures manual that describes processes and procedures in the center. Open Word and then create a document for the procedures manual that describes the steps you followed to create the *DoctorBillingFees* query and the steps you followed to create and print the two filters. Save the completed document and name it **AL1-C7-CS-Manual**. Print and then close **AL1-C7-CS-Manual.docx**.

Microsoft® Access®
Importing and Exporting Data

CHAPTER 8

PERFORMANCE OBJECTIVES

Upon successful completion of Chapter 8, you will be able to:
- Export Access data to Excel
- Export Access data to Word
- Merge Access data with a Word document
- Import data to a new table
- Link data to a new table
- Use the Office Clipboard

Microsoft Office 2010 is a suite of programs that allows easy data exchange between programs. In this chapter you will learn how to export data from Access to Excel and Word, merge Access data with a Word document, import and link data to a new table, and copy and paste data between programs. You will also learn how to copy and paste data between applications. Model answers for this chapter's projects appear on the following pages.

Access2012L1C8

Note: Before beginning the projects, copy to your storage medium the Access2010L1C8 subfolder from the Access2010L1 folder on the CD that accompanies this textbook and make Access2010L1C8 the active folder.

Project 1 Export Data to Excel and Export and Merge Data to Word

Project 1a

Equipment#	PurchaseDate	PurchasePrice	AvailableHours	ServiceHours	RepairHours
10	05-Feb-08	$65,540.00	120	15	10
11	01-Sep-09	$105,500.00	125	20	15
12	01-Jun-07	$55,345.00	140	10	10
13	05-May-10	$86,750.00	120	20	20
14	15-Jul-09	$4,500.00	160	5	5
15	01-Oct-07	$95,900.00	125	25	20
16	01-Dec-10	$3,450.00	150	10	5
17	10-Apr-09	$5,600.00	160	5	10
18	15-Jun-10	$8,000.00	150	5	5
19	30-Sep-11	$42,675.00	120	20	25

Hilltop Inventory

BillingDate	Customer	Hours	Rate	Total
01-May-12	Lakeside Trucking	8	$75.00	$600.00
01-May-12	Lakeside Trucking	8	$100.00	$800.00
01-May-12	Martin Plumbing	4	$50.00	$200.00
02-May-12	Country Electrical	16	$75.00	$1,200.00
02-May-12	Able Construction	5	$100.00	$500.00
03-May-12	Able Construction	5	$25.00	$125.00
03-May-12	Miles Contracting	10	$50.00	$500.00
04-May-12	Miles Contracting	10	$35.00	$350.00
04-May-12	Evergreen Painting	8	$25.00	$200.00
07-May-12	Barrier Concrete	8	$25.00	$200.00
07-May-12	Barrier Concrete	8	$25.00	$200.00
07-May-12	Cascade Enterprises	10	$100.00	$1,000.00
08-May-12	Cascade Enterprises	10	$75.00	$750.00
08-May-12	Allied Builders	6	$50.00	$300.00
08-May-12	Martin Plumbing	8	$35.00	$280.00
09-May-12	Evergreen Painting	8	$25.00	$200.00
09-May-12	Evergreen Painting	8	$25.00	$200.00
09-May-12	Able Construction	4	$75.00	$300.00
10-May-12	Able Construction	4	$100.00	$400.00
10-May-12	Miles Contracting	4	$50.00	$200.00
10-May-12	Ccuntry Electrical	6	$50.00	$300.00
11-May-12	Martin Plumbing	5	$75.00	$375.00
11-May-12	Lakeside Trucking	6	$100.00	$600.00
11-May-12	Cascade Enterprises	8	$25.00	$200.00
14-May-12	Miles Contracting	6	$25.00	$150.00
14-May-12	Evergreen Painting	6	$35.00	$210.00
14-May-12	Barrier Concrete	4	$100.00	$400.00
15-May-12	Allied Builders	4	$100.00	$400.00
15-May-12	Martin Plumbing	4	$50.00	$200.00
15-May-12	Miles Contracting	8	$25.00	$200.00

Hilltop Customer Invoices Query in Excel

Project 1b

Invoice#	BillingDate	Customer#	Equipment#	Hours	RateID
1	5/1/2012	310	10	8	D
2	5/1/2012	310	11	8	E
3	5/1/2012	267	12	4	C
4	5/2/2012	196	10	16	D
5	5/2/2012	305	13	5	E
6	5/3/2012	305	14	5	A
7	5/3/2012	106	15	10	C
8	5/4/2012	106	16	10	B
9	5/4/2012	275	17	8	A
10	5/7/2012	154	18	8	A
11	5/7/2012	154	17	8	A
12	5/7/2012	209	11	10	E
13	5/8/2012	209	19	10	D
14	5/8/2012	316	15	6	C
15	5/8/2012	267	16	8	B
16	5/9/2012	275	18	8	A
17	5/9/2012	275	17	8	A
18	5/9/2012	305	10	4	D
19	5/10/2012	305	13	4	E
20	5/10/2012	106	12	4	C
21	5/10/2012	196	15	6	C
22	5/11/2012	267	19	5	D
23	5/11/2012	310	11	6	E
24	5/11/2012	209	17	8	A
25	5/14/2012	106	14	6	A
26	5/14/2012	275	16	6	B
27	5/14/2012	154	13	4	E
28	5/15/2012	316	11	4	E
29	5/15/2012	267	15	4	C
30	5/15/2012	106	18	8	A

Hilltop Customer Invoices in Word

Project 1b, Hilltop Customer Report in Access

Project 1b, Hilltop Customer Report in Word

Model Answers

296 Access Level 1 ■ Unit 2

July 31, 2012

Miles Contracting
640 Smith Road
Aurora, CO 80041-6400

Ladies and Gentlemen:

Please join us June 1 for our annual equipment sales auction. Some of the choice items up for auction include three forklifts, two flatbed trucks, a front loader, and a bulldozer. We will also be auctioning painting equipment including pressure sprayers, ladders, and scaffolding.

The auction begins at 7:30 a.m. in the parking lot of our warehouse at 2605 Evans Avenue in Denver. For a listing of all equipment available for auction, stop by our store or call us at (303) 555-9066 and we will mail you the list.

Sincerely,

Lou Galloway
Manager
XX
HilltopLetter.docx

July 31, 2012

Barrier Concrete
220 Colorado Boulevard
Denver, CO 80125-2204

Ladies and Gentlemen:

Please join us June 1 for our annual equipment sales auction. Some of the choice items up for auction include three forklifts, two flatbed trucks, a front loader, and a bulldozer. We will also be auctioning painting equipment including pressure sprayers, ladders, and scaffolding.

The auction begins at 7:30 a.m. in the parking lot of our warehouse at 2605 Evans Avenue in Denver. For a listing of all equipment available for auction, stop by our store or call us at (303) 555-9066 and we will mail you the list.

Sincerely,

Lou Galloway
Manager
XX
HilltopLetter.docx

Project 1c, Hilltop Letters

July 31, 2012

Vernon Cook
1230 South Mesa
Phoenix, AZ 85018

Ladies and Gentlemen:

At the Grant Street West office of Copper State Insurance, we have hired two additional insurance representatives as well as one support staff member to ensure that we meet all your insurance needs. To accommodate the new staff, we have moved to a larger office just a few blocks away. Our new address is 3450 Grant Street West, Suite 110, Phoenix, AZ 85003. Our telephone number, (602) 555-6200, has remained the same.

If you have any questions or concerns about your insurance policies or want to discuss adding or changing current coverage, please stop by or give us a call. We are committed to providing our clients with the most comprehensive automobile insurance coverage in the country.

Sincerely,

Lou Galloway
Manager
XX
AL1-C8-CSLtrs.docx

July 31, 2012

Helena Myerson
9032 45th Street East
Phoenix, AZ 85009

Ladies and Gentlemen:

At the Grant Street West office of Copper State Insurance, we have hired two additional insurance representatives as well as one support staff member to ensure that we meet all your insurance needs. To accommodate the new staff, we have moved to a larger office just a few blocks away. Our new address is 3450 Grant Street West, Suite 110, Phoenix, AZ 85003. Our telephone number, (602) 555-6200, has remained the same.

If you have any questions or concerns about your insurance policies or want to discuss adding or changing current coverage, please stop by or give us a call. We are committed to providing our clients with the most comprehensive automobile insurance coverage in the country.

Sincerely,

Lou Galloway
Manager
XX
AL1-C8-CSLtrs.docx

Project 1d, Copper State Main Document

Project 2 Import and Link Excel Worksheets with an Access Table

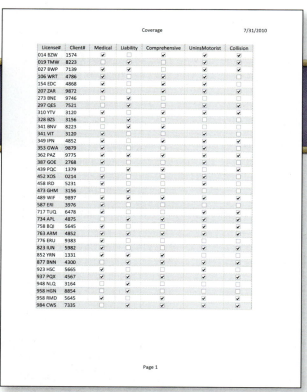

Project 1e, Copper State Coverage Table

Project 3 Collect Data in Word and Paste in an Access Table

Project 1 Export Data to Excel and Export and Merge Data to Word — 5 Parts

You will export a table and query to Excel and export a table and report to Word. You will also merge data in an Access table and query with a Word document.

Exporting Data

One of the advantages of a suite like Microsoft Office is the ability to exchange data between programs. Access, like other programs in the suite, offers a feature to export data from Access into Excel and/or Word. The Export group in the External Data tab contains buttons for exporting a table, query, form, or report to other programs such as Excel and Word.

Exporting Data to Excel

Use the Excel button in the Export group in the External Data tab to export data in a table, query, or form to an Excel worksheet. Click the object containing data you want to export to Excel, click the External Data tab, click the Excel button in the Export group and the first Export - Excel Spreadsheet wizard dialog box displays as shown in Figure 8.1.

Quick Steps

Export Data to Excel
1. Click the desired table, query, or form.
2. Click the External Data tab.
3. Click Excel button in Export group.
4. Make desired changes at Export - Excel Spreadsheet dialog box.
5. Click OK.

Excel

Figure 8.1 Export - Excel Spreadsheet Dialog Box

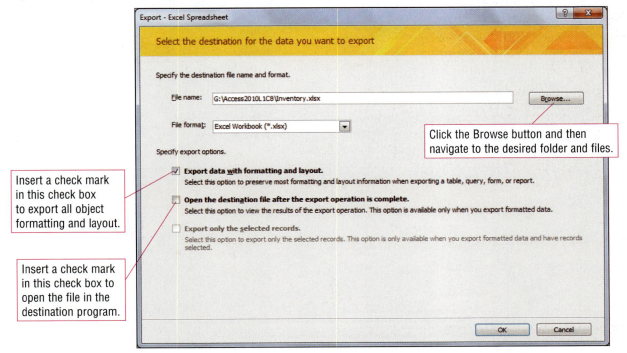

Chapter 8 ■ Importing and Exporting Data   299

HINT Data exported from Access to Excel is saved as an Excel workbook with the .xlsx file extension.

HINT You can export only one database object at a time, and you cannot export reports to Excel.

At the first wizard dialog box, Access uses the name of the object as the Excel workbook name. You can change this by selecting the current name and then typing a new name and you can specify the file format with the *File format* option. Click the *Export data with formatting and layout* check box to insert a check mark. This exports all data formatting to the Excel workbook. If you want Excel to open with the exported data, click the *Open the destination file after the export operation is complete* option to insert a check mark. When you have made all desired changes, click the OK button. This opens Excel with the data in a workbook. Make any desired changes to the workbook and then save, print, and close the workbook. Exit Excel and Access displays with a second wizard dialog box asking if you want to save the export steps. At this dialog box, insert a check mark in the *Save export steps* if you want to save the export steps, or leave the option blank and then click the Close button.

Project 1a Exporting a Table and Query to Excel   Part 1 of 5

1. Display the Open dialog box with Access2010L1C8 on your storage medium the active folder.
2. Open the **AL1-C8-Hilltop.accdb** database and enable the contents.
3. Save the Inventory table as an Excel worksheet by completing the following steps:
   a. Click the Inventory table in the Navigation pane.
   b. Click the External Data tab and then click the Excel button in the Export group.
   c. At the Export - Excel Spreadsheet dialog box, click the Browse button.
   d. At the File Save dialog box, navigate to the Access2010L1C8 folder on your storage medium and then click the Save button.

   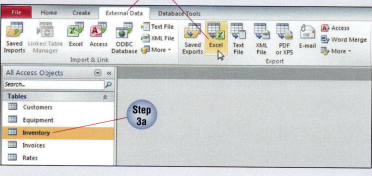

   e. Click the *Export data with formatting and layout* option to insert a check mark in the check box.
   f. Click the *Open the destination file after the export operation is complete* option to insert a check mark in the check box.

   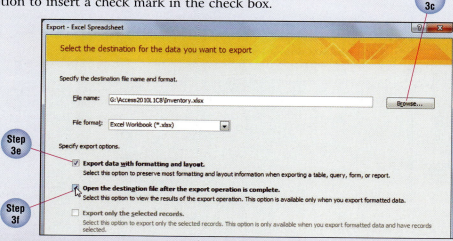

g. Click OK.
h. When the data displays on the screen in Excel as a worksheet, select cells A2 through A11 and then click the Center button in the Alignment group in the Home tab.
i. Select cells D2 through F11 and then click the Center button.
j. Click the Save button on the Quick Access toolbar.
k. Print the worksheet by pressing Ctrl + P and then clicking the *Print* option at the Print tab Backstage view.
l. Close the worksheet and then exit Excel.
4. In Access, click the Close button to close the second wizard dialog box.
5. Design a query that extracts records from three tables with the following specifications:
   a. Add the Invoices, Customers, and Rates tables to the query window.
   b. Insert the *BillingDate* field from the Invoices table to the first *Field* row field.
   c. Insert the *Customer* field from the Customers table to the second *Field* row field.
   d. Insert the *Hours* field from the Invoices table to the third *Field* row field.
   e. Insert the *Rate* field from the Rates table to the fourth *Field* row field.
   f. Click in the fifth *Field* row field, type **Total: [Hours]*[Rate]**, and then press Enter.
   g. Run the query.
   h. Automatically adjust the column width of the *Customer* field.
   i. Save the query and name it *CustomerInvoices*.
   j. Close the query.
6. Export the CustomerInvoices query to Excel by completing the following steps:
   a. Click the CustomerInvoices query in the Navigation pane.
   b. Click the External Data tab and then click the Excel button in the Export group.
   c. At the Export - Excel Spreadsheet dialog box, click the *Export data with formatting and layout* option to insert a check mark in the check box.
   d. Click the *Open the destination file after the export operation is complete* option to insert a check mark in the check box.
   e. Click OK.
   f. When the data displays on the screen in Excel as a worksheet, select cells C2 through C31 and then click the Center button in the Alignment group in the Home tab.
   g. Click the Save button on the Quick Access toolbar.

Chapter 8 ■ Importing and Exporting Data

h. Print the worksheet by pressing Ctrl + P and then clicking the *Print* option at the Print tab Backstage view.
i. Close the worksheet and then exit Excel.
7. In Access, click the Close button to close the second wizard dialog box.

▼ Quick Steps

Export Data to Word
1. Click the desired table, query, form, or report.
2. Click External Data tab.
3. Click More button in Export group.
4. Click Word.
5. Make desired changes at Export - RTF File dialog box.
6. Click OK.

Exporting Data to Word

Export data from Access to Word in a similar manner as exporting to Excel. To export data to Word, select the desired object in the Navigation pane, click the External Data tab, click the More button in the Export group, and then click *Word* at the drop-down list. At the Export - RTF File dialog box, make desired changes and then click OK. Word automatically opens and the data displays in a Word document that is saved automatically with the same name as the database object. The difference is that the file extension .rtf is added to the name. An RTF file is saved in "rich-text format," which preserves formatting such as fonts and styles. You can export a document saved with the .rtf extension in Word and other Windows word processing or desktop publishing programs.

HINT Data exported from Access to Word is saved with the .rtf file extension.

More

Project 1b   Exporting a Table and Report to Word   Part 2 of 5

1. With the **AL1-C8-Hilltop.accdb** database open, click the Invoices table in the Navigation pane.
2. Click the External Data tab, click the More button in the Export group, and then click *Word* at the drop-down list.

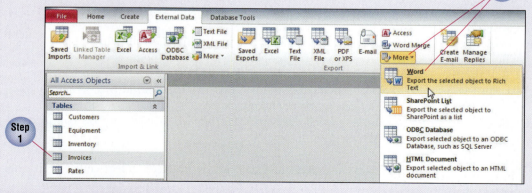

3. At the Export - RTF File wizard dialog box, click the Browse button.

302   Access Level 1 ■ Unit 2

4. At the File Save dialog box, navigate to the Access2010L1C8 folder on your storage medium and then click the Save button.
5. At the Export - RTF File wizard dialog box, click the *Open the destination file after the export operation is complete* check box to insert a check mark.

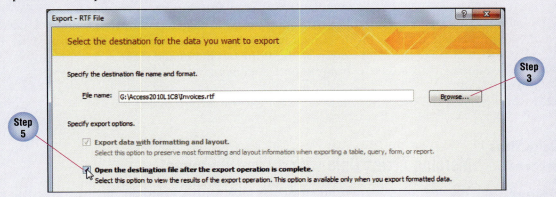

6. Click OK.
7. With the **Invoices.rtf** file open in Word, print the document by pressing Ctrl + P and then clicking the *Print* option at the Print tab Backstage view.
8. Close the **Invoices.rtf** file and then exit Word.
9. In Access click the Close button to close the wizard dialog box.
10. Create a report with the Report Wizard by completing the following steps:
    a. Click the Create tab and then click the Report Wizard button in the Reports group.
    b. At the first Report Wizard dialog box, insert the following fields in the *Selected Fields* list box:
       From the Customers table:
          Customer
       From the Equipment table:
          Equipment
       From the Invoices table:
          BillingDate
          Hours

    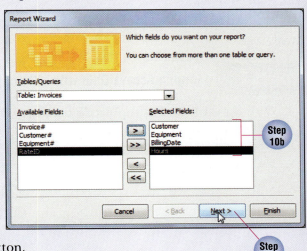

    c. After inserting the fields, click the Next button.
    d. At the second Report Wizard dialog box, make sure *by Customers* is selected in the list box in the upper left corner and then click the Next button.
    e. At the third Report Wizard dialog box, click the Next button.
    f. At the fourth Report Wizard dialog box, click the Next button.
    g. At the fifth Report Wizard dialog box, click *Block* in the *Layout* section and then click the Next button.
    h. At the sixth and final Report Wizard dialog box, select the current name in the *What title do you want for your report?* text box, type **CustomerReport**, and then click the Finish button.
    i. When the report displays in Print Preview, click the Print button at the left side of the Print Preview tab and then click OK at the Print dialog box.
    j. Save and then close the CustomerReport report.

11. Export the CustomerReport report to Word by completing the following steps:
    a. Click the CustomerReport report in the Navigation pane.
    b. Click the External Data tab, click the More button in the Export group, and then click *Word* at the drop-down list.
    c. At the Export - RTF File wizard dialog box, click the *Open the destination file after export operation is complete* option to insert a check mark in the check box and then click OK.
    d. When the data displays on the screen in Word, print the document by pressing Ctrl + P and then clicking the *Print* option at the Print tab Backstage view.
    e. Save and then close the CustomerReport document.
    f. Exit Word.
12. In Access, click the Close button to close the second wizard dialog box.

▼ **Quick Steps**

Merge Data with Word
1. Click the desired table or query.
2. Click External Data tab.
3. Click Word Merge button.
4. Make desired choices at each wizard dialog box.

Merging Access Data with a Word Document

You can merge data from an Access table with a Word document. When merging data, the data in the Access table is considered the data source and the Word document is considered the main document. When the merge is completed, the merged documents display in Word. To merge data, click the desired table in the Navigation pane, click the External Data tab, and then click the Word Merge button. When merging Access data, you can either type the text in the main document or merge Access data with an existing Word document.

Word Merge

Project 1c   **Merging Access Data with a Word Document**   Part 3 of 5

1. With the **AL1-C8-Hilltop.accdb** database open, click the Customers table in the Navigation pane.
2. Click the External Data tab.

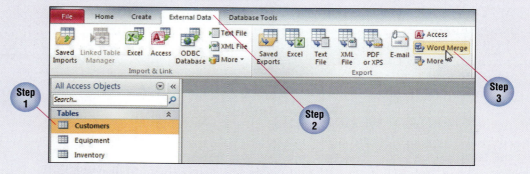

3. Click the Word Merge button in the Export group.
4. At the Microsoft Word Mail Merge Wizard dialog box, make sure *Link your data to an existing Microsoft Word document* is selected and then click OK.
5. At the Select Microsoft Word Document dialog box, make the Access2010L1C8 folder on your storage medium the active folder and then double-click the document named *HilltopLetter.docx*.

6. Click the Word button on the Taskbar.
7. Click the Maximize button located at the right side of the HilltopLetter.docx title bar and then close the Mail Merge task pane.
8. Press the down arrow key six times (not the Enter key) and then type the current date.
9. Press the down arrow key four times and then insert fields for merging from the Customers table by completing the following steps:
    a. Click the Insert Merge Field button arrow located in the Write & Insert Fields group and then click *Customer1* in the drop-down list. (This inserts the «*Customer1*» field in the document. The drop-down list contains a *Customer* and a *Customer1* option. The first *Customer* option is actually the *Customer#* field. Word dropped the # symbol from the field name and added the *1* to the second *Customer* field to differentiate the two fields.)

    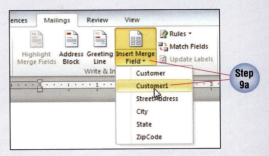

    b. Press Enter, click the Insert Merge Field button arrow, and then click *StreetAddress* in the drop-down list.
    c. Press Enter, click the Insert Merge Field button arrow, and then click *City* in the drop-down list.
    d. Type a comma (,) and then press the spacebar.
    e. Click the Insert Merge Field button arrow and then click *State* in the drop-down list.
    f. Press the spacebar, click the Insert Merge Field button arrow, and then click *ZipCode* in the drop-down list.

    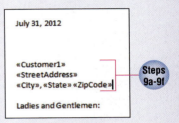

    g. Replace the letters *XX* that display toward the bottom of the letter with your initials.
    h. Click the Finish & Merge button in the Finish group and then click *Edit Individual Documents* in the drop-down list.

    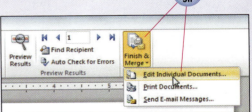

    i. At the Merge to New Document dialog box, make sure *All* is selected and then click OK.
    j. When the merge is completed, save the new document and name it **AL1-C8-HilltopLtrs** in the Access2010L1C8 folder on your storage medium.
10. Print just the first two pages (two letters) of **AL1-C8-HilltopLtrs.docx**.
11. Close **AL1-C8-HilltopLtrs.docx** and then close **HilltopLetter.docx** without saving the changes.
12. Exit Word.
13. Close the **AL1-C8-Hilltop.accdb** database.

Merging Query Data with a Word Document

You can perform a query in a database and then use the query to merge with a Word document. In Project 1c you merged a table with an existing Word document. You can also merge a table or query and then type the Word document. You will create a query in Project 1d and then merge data in the query with a new document in Word.

In Project 1c, you inserted a number of merge fields for the inside address of a letter. You can also insert a field that will insert all of the fields required for the inside address of a letter with the Address Block button in the Write & Insert

Chapter 8 ■ Importing and Exporting Data   305

Fields group in the Mailings tab. When you click the Insert the Address Block button, the Insert Address Block dialog box displays with a preview of how the fields will be inserted in the document to create the inside address; the dialog box also contains buttons and options for customizing the fields. Click OK and the *«AddressBlock»* field is inserted in the document. The *«AddressBlock»* field is an example of a composite field that groups a number of fields together.

In Project 1c you could not use the *«AddressBlock»* composite field because the *Customer1* field was not recognized by Word as a field for the inside address. In Project 1d you will create a query that contains the *FirstName* and *LastName* fields, which Word recognizes and uses for the *«AddressBlock»* composite field.

Project 1d Performing a Query and Then Merging with a Word Document Part 4 of 5

1. Display the Open dialog box with Access2010L1C8 on your storage medium the active folder.
2. Open the **AL1-C8-CopperState.accdb** database and enable the contents.
3. Perform a query with the Query Wizard and modify the query by completing the following steps:
   a. Click the Create tab and then click the Query Wizard button in the Queries group.
   b. At the New Query dialog box, make sure Simple Query Wizard is selected and then click OK.
   c. At the first Simple Query Wizard dialog box, click the down-pointing arrow at the right of the *Tables/Queries* option box and then click *Table: Clients*.
   d. Click the All Fields button to insert all of the fields in the *Selected Fields* list box.
   e. Click the Next button.
   f. At the second Simple Query Wizard dialog box, make the following changes:
      1) Select the current name in the *What title do you want for your query?* text box and then type **ClientsPhoenixQuery**.
      2) Click the *Modify the query design* option.
      3) Click the Finish button.
   g. At the query window, click in the *Criteria* field in the *City* column, type **Phoenix**, and then press Enter.
   h. Click the Run button in the Results group. (Only clients living in Phoenix will display.)
   i. Save and then close the query.
4. Click the ClientsPhoenixQuery query in the Navigation pane.
5. Click the External Data tab and then click the Word Merge button in the Export group.
6. At the Microsoft Word Mail Merge Wizard dialog box, click the *Create a new document and then link the data to it* option and then click OK.

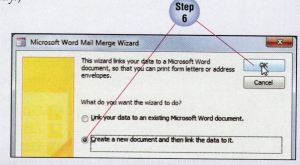

7. Click the Word button on the Taskbar.
8. Click the Maximize button located at the right side of the Document1 title bar and then close the Mail Merge task pane.
9. Complete the following steps to type text and insert the «AddressBlock» in the blank Word document:
   a. Click the Home tab and then click the No Spacing style in the Styles group.
   b. Press Enter six times.
   c. Type the current date.
   d. Press Enter four times.
   e. Click the Mailings tab.
   f. Insert the «AddressBlock» field by clicking the Address Block button in the Write & Insert Fields group in the Mailings tab and then clicking OK at the Insert Address Block dialog box. (This inserts the composite field «AddressBlock» in the document.)
   g. Press Enter twice and then type the salutation **Ladies and Gentlemen:**.
   h. Press Enter twice and then type the following paragraphs of text:

   At the Grant Street West office of Copper State Insurance, we have hired two additional insurance representatives as well as one support staff member to ensure that we meet all your insurance needs. To accommodate the new staff, we have moved to a larger office just a few blocks away. Our new address is 3450 Grant Street West, Suite 110, Phoenix AZ 85003. Our telephone number, (602) 555-6200, has remained the same.

   If you have any questions or concerns about your insurance policies or want to discuss adding or changing current coverage, please stop by or give us a call. We are committed to providing our clients with the most comprehensive automobile insurance coverage in the county.

   i. Press Enter twice and then type the following complimentary close (at the left margin):

   Sincerely,

   **Lou Galloway
   Manager**

   XX (Type your initials instead of XX.)
   AL1-C8-CSLtrs.docx
   j. Click the Finish & Merge button in the Finish group on the Mailings tab and then click *Edit Individual Documents* in the drop-down menu.
   k. At the Merge to New Document dialog box, make sure *All* is selected, and then click OK.
   l. When the merge is complete, save the new document and name it **AL1-C8-CSLtrs** in the Access2010L1C8 folder on your storage medium.
10. Print the first two pages (two letters) of **AL1-C8-CSLtrs.docx**.
11. Close **AL1-C8-CSLtrs.docx**.
12. Save the main document as **AL1-C8-CSMainDoc** in the Access2010L1C8 folder on your storage medium and then close the document.
13. Exit Word.

Exporting an Access Object to a PDF or XPS File

▼ **Quick Steps**

Export Access Object to PDF File
1. Click object in the Navigation pane.
2. Click External Data tab.
3. Click PDF or XPS button.
4. Navigate to desired folder.
5. Click Publish button.

PDF or XPS

With the PDF or XPS button in the Export group in the External Data tab, you can export an Access object to a PDF or XPS file. As you learned in Chapter 7, the letters *PDF* stand for *portable document format*, which is a file format that captures all of the elements of a file as an electronic image. The letters *XPS* stand for *XML paper specification* and the letters *XML* stand for *Extensible Markup Language*, which is a set of rules for encoding files electronically.

To export an Access object to the PDF or XPS file format, click the desired object, click the External Data tab, and then click the PDF or XPS button in the Export group. This displays the Publish as PDF or XPS dialog box with the *PDF (*.pdf)* option selected in the *Save as type* option box. If you want to save the Access object in XPS format, click in the *Save as type* option box and then click *XPS Document (*.xps)* at the drop-down list. At the Save As dialog box, type a name in the *File name* text box and then click the Publish button. If you save the Access object in PDF format, the Access object opens in Adobe Reader, and if you save the Access object in XPS format, the object opens in your browser window.

You can open a PDF file in Adobe Reader or in your web browser, and you can open an XPS file in your web browser. To open a PDF file or XPS file in your web browser, click File in the browser Menu bar and then click *Open* at the drop-down list. At the Open dialog box, click the Browse button. At the browser window Open dialog box, change the *Files of type* to *All Files (*.*)*, navigate to the desired folder, and then double-click the document.

Project 1e Exporting an Access Object to a PDF File   Part 5 of 5

1. With the **AL1-C8-CopperState.accdb** database open, export the Coverage table to a PDF format by completing the following steps:
   a. Click the Coverage table in the Navigation pane.
   b. Click the External Data tab.
   c. Click the PDF or XPS button in the Export group.
   d. At the Publish as PDF or XPS dialog box, navigate to the Access2010L1C8 folder on your storage medium and then click the Publish button.
   e. When the Coverage table data displays in Adobe Reader, scroll through the file and notice how it displays.
   f. Print the PDF file by clicking the Print button that displays at the left side of the toolbar and then clicking OK at the Print dialog box.
   g. Close Adobe Reader by clicking the Close button located in the upper right corner of the screen.
2. In Access, click the Close button to close the wizard dialog box.

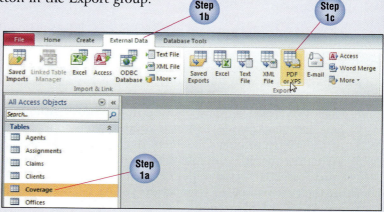

Project 2 Import and Link Excel Worksheets with an Access Table

2 Parts

You will import an Excel worksheet into an Access table. You will also link an Excel worksheet into an Access table and then add a new record to the Access table.

Importing and Linking Data to a New Table

In this chapter, you learned how to export Access data to Excel and Word. You can also import data from other programs into an Access table. For example, you can import data from an Excel worksheet and create a new table in a database using data from the worksheet. Data in the original program is not connected to the data imported into an Access table. If you make changes to the data in the original program, those changes are not reflected in the Access table. If you want the imported data connected to the original program, link the data.

Importing Data to a New Table

To import data, click the External Data tab and then determine where you would like to retrieve data with options in the Import & Link group. At the Import dialog box that displays, click Browse and then double-click the desired file name. This activates the Import Wizard and displays the first wizard dialog box. The appearance of the dialog box varies depending on the file selected. Complete the steps of the Import Wizard specifying information such as the range of data, whether or not the first row contains column headings, whether you want to store the data in a new table or store it in an existing table, the primary key, and the name of the table.

▼ Quick Steps

Import Data to a New Table
1. Click External Data tab.
2. Click desired application in Import & Link group.
3. Click Browse button.
4. Double-click desired file name.
5. Make desired choices at each wizard dialog box.

HINT
Store data in Access and use Excel to analyze data.

HINT
You can import and link data between Access databases.

Project 2a Importing an Excel Worksheet into an Access Table Part 1 of 2

1. With the **AL1-C8-CopperState.accdb** database open, import an Excel worksheet into a new table in the database by completing the following steps:
   a. Click the External Data tab and then click the Excel button in the Import & Link group.
   b. At the Get External Data - Excel Spreadsheet dialog box, click Browse and then make the Access2010L1C8 folder on your storage medium the active folder.
   c. Double-click **AL1-C8-Policies.xlsx** in the list box.
   d. Click OK at the Get External Data - Excel Spreadsheet dialog box.
   e. At the first Import Spreadsheet Wizard dialog box, click the Next button.

Chapter 8 ■ Importing and Exporting Data 309

f. At the second Import Spreadsheet Wizard dialog box, make sure the *First Row Contains Column Headings* option contains a check mark and then click the Next button.
g. At the third Import Spreadsheet Wizard dialog box, click the Next button.
h. At the fourth Import Spreadsheet Wizard dialog box, click the *Choose my own primary key* option (this inserts *Policy#* in the text box located to the right of the option) and then click the Next button.

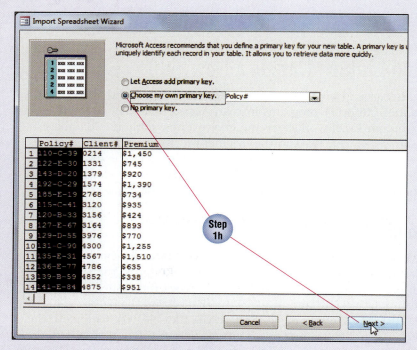

i. At the fifth Import Spreadsheet Wizard dialog box, type **Policies** in the *Import to Table* text box and then click the Finish button.

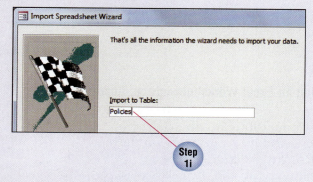

j. At the Get External Data - Excel Spreadsheet dialog box, click the Close button.
2. Open the new Policies table in Datasheet view.
3. Print and then close the Policies table.

Linking Data to an Excel Worksheet

Imported data is not connected to the source program. If you know that you will use your data only in Access, import it. However, if you want to update data in a program other than Access, link the data. Changes made to linked data in the source program file are reflected in the destination program file. For example, you can link an Excel worksheet with an Access table and when you make changes in the Excel worksheet, the changes are reflected in the Access table.

To link data to a new table, click the External Data tab and then click the Excel button in the Import group. At the Get External Data - Excel Spreadsheet dialog box, click the Browse button, double-click the desired file name, click the *Link to a data source by creating a linked table* option, and then click OK. This activates the Link Wizard and displays the first wizard dialog box. Complete the steps of the Link Wizard, specifying the same basic information as the Import Wizard.

▼ Quick Steps

Link Data to Excel Worksheet
1. Click External Data tab.
2. Click Excel button in Import & Link group.
3. Click Browse button.
4. Double-click desired file name.
5. Click *Link to a data source by creating a linked table*.
6. Make desired choices at each wizard dialog box.

Import Excel

Project 2b — Linking an Excel Worksheet with an Access Table — Part 2 of 2

1. With the **AL1-C8-CopperState.accdb** database open, click the External Data tab and then click the Excel button in the Import & Link group.
2. At the Get External Data - Excel Spreadsheet dialog box, click the Browse button, navigate to the Access2010L1C8 folder on your storage medium, and then double-click **AL1-C8-Policies.xlsx**.
3. At the Get External Data - Excel Spreadsheet dialog box, click the *Link to the data source by creating a linked table* option and then click OK.

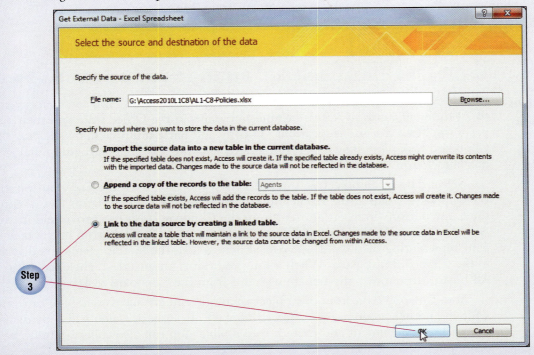

Chapter 8 ■ Importing and Exporting Data   311

4. At the first Link Spreadsheet Wizard dialog box, make sure *Show Worksheets* and *Sheet 1* are selected in the list box and then click the Next button.
5. At the second Link Spreadsheet Wizard dialog box, make sure the *First Row Contains Column Headings* option contains a check mark and then click the Next button.
6. At the third Link Spreadsheet Wizard dialog box, type **LinkedPolicies** in the *Linked Table Name* text box and then click the Finish button.
7. At the message stating the linking is finished, click OK.
8. Open the new LinkedPolicies table in Datasheet view.
9. Close the LinkedPolicies table.
10. Open Excel, open the **AL1-C8-Policies.xlsx** workbook, and then make the following changes:
    a. Change the amount *$745* in cell C3 to *$850*.
    b. Add the following information in the specified cells:
       A26 = **190-C-28**
       B26 = **3120**
       C26 = **$685**

Step 10b

11. Save, print, and then close **AL1-C8-Policies.xlsx**.
12. Exit Excel.
13. With Access the active program and the **AL1-C8-CopperState.accdb** database open, open the LinkedPolicies table. Notice the changes you made in Excel are reflected in the table.
14. Close the LinkedPolicies table.
15. Close the **AL1-C8-CopperState.accdb** database.

Project 3 Collect Data in Word and Paste in an Access Table 1 Part

You will open a Word document containing Hilltop customer names and addresses and then copy the data and paste it into an Access table.

Using the Office Clipboard

▼ **Quick Steps**

Display Clipboard Task Pane
Click Clipboard group dialog box launcher.

Use the Office Clipboard to collect and paste multiple items. You can collect up to 24 different items in Access or other programs in the Office suite and then paste the items in various locations. To copy and paste multiple items, display the Clipboard task pane shown in Figure 8.2 by clicking the Clipboard group dialog box launcher in the Home tab.

Select data or an object you want to copy and then click the Copy button in the Clipboard group in the Home tab. Continue selecting text or items and clicking the Copy button. To insert an item from the Clipboard task pane to a field in an Access table, make the desired field active and then click the button in the task pane representing the item. If the copied item is text, the first 50 characters display in the Clipboard task pane. When all desired items are inserted, click the Clear All button to remove any remaining items from the Clipboard task pane.

You can copy data from one object to another in an Access database or from a file in another program to an Access database. In Project 3, you will copy data from a Word document and paste it into a table. You can also collect data from other programs such as PowerPoint and Excel.

Figure 8.2 Office Clipboard Task Pane

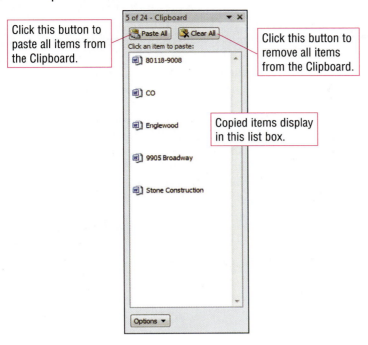

Project 3 — Collecting Data in Word and Pasting It in an Access Table — Part 1 of 1

1. Open the **AL1-C8-Hilltop.accdb** database.
2. Open the Customers table.
3. Copy data from Word and paste it into the Customers table by completing the following steps:
   a. Open Word, make the Access2010L1C8 folder active, and then open **HilltopCustomers.docx**.
   b. Make sure the Home tab is active.
   c. Click the Clipboard group dialog box launcher to display the Clipboard task pane.
   d. Select the first company name, *Stone Construction*, and then click the Copy button in the Clipboard group.

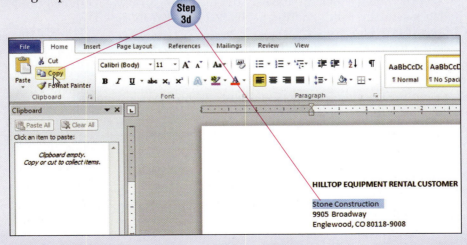

Chapter 8 ■ Importing and Exporting Data 313

e. Select the street address, *9905 Broadway*, and then click the Copy button.
f. Select the city, *Englewood*, and then click the Copy button.
g. Select the state, *CO* (select only the two letters and not the space after the letters), and then click the Copy button.
h. Select the ZIP code, *80118-9008*, and then click the Copy button.
i. Click the button on the Taskbar representing Access. (Make sure the Customer table is open and displays in Datasheet view.)
j. Click in the first empty cell in the *Customer#* field and then type 178.
k. Display the Clipboard task pane by clicking the Home tab and then clicking the Clipboard group dialog box launcher.
l. Close the Navigation pane by clicking the Shutter Bar Open/Close Button.
m. Click in the first empty cell in the *Customer* field and then click *Stone Construction* in the Clipboard task pane.

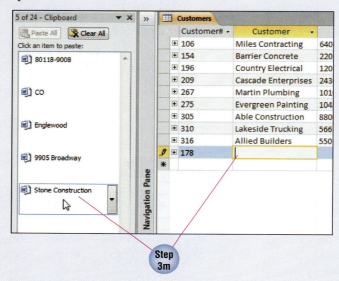

n. Click in the *StreetAddress* field and then click *9905 Broadway* in the Clipboard task pane.
o. Click in the *City* field and then click *Englewood* in the Clipboard task pane.
p. Click in the *State* field and then click *CO* in the Clipboard task pane.
q. Click in the *ZipCode* field, make sure the insertion point is positioned at the left side of the field, and then click *80118-9008* in the Clipboard task pane.
r. Click the Clear All button in the Clipboard task pane. (This removes all entries from the Clipboard.)
4. Complete steps similar to those in 3d through 3q to copy the information for Laughlin Products and paste it into the Customers table. (The Customer# is 225.)
5. Click the Clear All button in the Clipboard task pane.
6. Close the Clipboard task pane by clicking the Close button (contains an *X*) located in the upper right corner of the task pane.
7. Save, print, and then close the Customers table.
8. Open the Navigation pane by clicking the Shutter Bar Open/Close Button.
9. Make Word the active program, close **HilltopCustomers.docx** without saving changes, and then exit Word.
10. Close the **AL1-C8-Hilltop.accdb** database.

Chapter Summary

- Use the Excel button in the Export group in the External Data tab to export data in a table, query, or form to an Excel worksheet.
- Export data in a table, query, form, or report to a Word document by clicking the More button and then clicking *Word* at the drop-down list. Access exports the data to an RTF (rich-text format) file.
- Export an Access object to a PDF or XPS file with the PDF or XPS button in the Export group in the External Data tab.
- You can merge Access data with a Word document. The Access data is the data source and the Word document is the main document. To merge data, click the desired table or query, click the External Data tab, and then click the Word Merge button in the Export group.
- Use the Excel button in the Import group in the External Data tab to import Excel data to an Access table.
- You can link imported data. Changes made to the data in the source program file are reflected in the destination source file.
- If you want to link imported data, click the *Link to the data source by creating a linked table* option at the Get External Data dialog box.
- Use the Clipboard task pane to collect up to 24 different items in Access or other programs and paste them in various locations.
- Display the Clipboard task pane by clicking the Clipboard group dialog box launcher in the Home tab.

Commands Review

FEATURE	RIBBON TAB, GROUP	BUTTON
Export object to Excel	External Data, Export	
Export object to Word	External Data, Export	, Word
Merge Access data with Word	External Data, Export	
Export object to PDF or XPS	External Data, Export	
Import Excel data	External Data, Import & Link	
Clipboard task pane	Home, Clipboard	

Concepts Check — Test Your Knowledge

Completion: In the space provided at the right, indicate the correct term, symbol, or command.

1. Click this tab to display the Export group. _____

2. Click this button in the Export group to display the Export - Excel Spreadsheet wizard dialog box. _____

3. At the first Export - Excel Spreadsheet wizard dialog box, click this option if you want Excel to open with the exported data. _____

4. To export Access data to Word, click this button in the Export group in the External Data tab and then click *Word* at the drop-down list. _____

5. When you export Access data to Word, the document is saved in this file format. _____

6. When merging data, the data in the Access table is considered this. _____

7. To merge data, click this button in the Export group in the External Data tab. _____

8. You can export an Access object to the PDF file format and the letters PDF stand for this. _____

9. Import an Excel worksheet into an Access database with the Excel button in this group in the External Data tab. _____

10. If you want imported data connected to the original program, do this to the data. _____

11. Use this task pane to collect and paste multiple items. _____

Skills Check Assess Your Performance

Assessment

1 EXPORT A FORM TO EXCEL AND A REPORT TO WORD

1. Display the Open dialog box with Access2010L1C8 on your storage medium the active folder.
2. Open the **AL1-C8-WarrenLegal.accdb** database and enable the contents.
3. Create a form named *Billing* using the Form Wizard with the following fields:
    From the Billing table:
       Billing#
       ClientID
       BillingDate
       Hours
    From the Rates table:
       Rate
4. When the form displays, close it.
5. Create an Excel worksheet with the Billing form.
6. Make the following changes to the Excel Billing worksheet:
    a. Select columns A through E and then adjust the column widths.
    b. Select cells A2 through B42 and then click the Center button in the Alignment group in the Home tab.
    c. Save the Billing worksheet.
    d. Print and then close the Billing worksheet.
    e. Exit Excel.
7. In Access, close the Export Wizard.
8. Create a report named *ClientBilling* using the Report Wizard (at the fifth wizard dialog box, change the layout to *Block*) with the following fields:
    From the Clients table:
       FirstName
       LastName
    From the Billing table:
       BillingDate
       Hours
    From the Rates table:
       Rate
9. When the report displays, close Print Preview, change to Layout view, and then decrease the size of the columns so the right border of the column displays just right of the longest entry in the column.
10. Save and then close the report.
11. Create a Word document with the ClientBilling report and save it to the Access2010L1C8 folder on your storage medium with the default name. In the Word document, make the following changes:
    a. Press Ctrl + A to select the entire document, change the font color to black, and then deselect the text.
    b. Insert a space between *Client* and *Billing* in the title.
    c. Position the insertion point immediately right of the word *Billing*, press the spacebar, and then type **of Legal Services**.

12. Save and then print **ClientBilling.rtf**.
13. Close the document and then exit Word.
14. In Access, close the wizard dialog box.

Assessment

2 MERGE TABLE AND QUERY DATA WITH A WORD DOCUMENT

1. With the **AL1-C8-WarrenLegal.accdb** database open, merge data in the Clients table to a new Word document using the Word merge button.
2. Maximize the Word document, close the Mail Merge task pane, and then compose a letter with the following elements:
   a. Click the Home tab and then click the No Spacing style in the Styles group.
   b. Press Enter six times, type the current date, and then press Enter four times.
   c. Click the Mailings tab and then insert the «AddressBlock» composite field.
   d. Insert a proper salutation.
   e. Compose a letter to clients that includes the following information:

   > The last time you visited our offices, you may have noticed how crowded we were. To alleviate the overcrowding, we are leasing new offices in the Meridian Building and will be moving in at the beginning of next month.
   >
   > Stop by and see our new offices at our open house planned for the second Friday of next month. Drop by any time between 2:00 and 5:30 p.m. We look forward to seeing you.

   f. Include an appropriate complimentary close for the letter. Use the name and title *Marjorie Shaw, Senior Partner* for the signature and add your reference initials and the document name (**AL1-C8-WLLtrs.docx**).
3. Merge to a new document and then save the document with the name **AL1-C8-WLLtrs**.
4. Print only the first two letters in the document and then close **AL1-C8-WLLtrs.docx**.
5. Save the main document and name it **AL1-C8-WLLtrMD1**, close the document, and then exit Word.
6. With the **AL1-C8-WarrenLegal.accdb** database open, extract the records from the Clients table of those clients located in Kent and then name the query *ClientsKentQuery*. (Include all of the fields from the table in the query.)
7. Merge the ClientsKentQuery to a new Word document using the Word Merge Button.
8. Maximize the Word document, close the Mail Merge task pane, and then compose a letter with the following elements:
   a. Click the Home tab and then click the No Spacing style in the Styles group.
   b. Press Enter six times, type the current date, and then press Enter four times.
   c. Click the Mailings tab and then insert the «AddressBlock» composite field.
   d. Insert a proper salutation.
   e. Compose a letter to clients that includes the following information:

   > The City of Kent Municipal Court has moved from 1024 Meeker Street to a new building located at 3201 James Avenue. All court hearings after the end of this month will be held at the new address. If you need directions to the new building, please call our office.

f. Include an appropriate complimentary close for the letter. Use the name *Thomas Zeiger* and the title *Attorney* in the complimentary close and add your reference initials and the document name (**AL1-C8-WLKentLtrs.docx**).
9. Merge the letter to a new document and then save the document with the name **AL1-C8-WLKentLtrs**.
10. Print only the first two letters in the document and then close **AL1-C8-WLKentLtrs.docx**.
11. Save the main document and name it **AL1-C8-WLLtrMD2**, close the document, and then exit Word.

Assessment

3 LINK AN EXCEL WORKBOOK

1. With the **AL1-C8-WarrenLegal.accdb** database open, link **AL1-C8-Cases.xlsx** into a new table named *Cases*.
2. Open the Cases table in Datasheet view.
3. Print and then close the Cases table.
4. Open Excel, open the **AL1-C8-Cases.xlsx** workbook and then add the following data in the specified cell:

    A8 = 57-D
    B8 = 130
    C8 = $1,100

    A9 = 42-A
    B9 = 144
    C9 = $3,250

    A10 = 29-C
    B10 = 125
    C10 = $900

5. Save, print, and then close **AL1-C8-Cases.xlsx**.
6. Exit Excel.
7. In Access, open the Cases table in Datasheet view. (Notice the changes you made in Excel are reflected in the table.)
8. Print and then close the Cases table.
9. Close the **AL1-C8-WarrenLegal.accdb** database.

Visual Benchmark — Demonstrate Your Proficiency

CREATE A REPORT AND EXPORT THE REPORT TO WORD

1. Open the **AL1-C8-Dearborn.accdb** database and enable the contents.
2. Use the Report Wizard to create the report shown in Figure 8.3. (Use the Quotas table and the Representatives table when creating the report.) Save the report and name it *RepQuotas* and then print the report.
3. Use the RepQuotas report and export it to Word. Format the report in Word as shown in Figure 8.4. Print the Word document and then exit Word.
4. In Access, close the **AL1-C8-Dearborn.accdb** database.

Figure 8.3 Visual Benchmark Report

RepQuotas

Quota	RepName	Telephone
$100,000.00		
	Robin Rehberg	(317) 555-9812
	Andre Kulisek	(317) 555-2264
	Edward Harris	(317) 555-3894
	Cecilia Ortega	(317) 555-4810
$150,000.00		
	David DeBruler	(317) 555-8779
	Jaren Newman	(317) 555-6790
	Lee Hutchinson	(317) 555-4277
	Craig Johnson	(317) 555-4391
$200,000.00		
	Isabelle Marshall	(765) 555-8822
	Maureen Pascual	(317) 555-5513
	Linda Foster	(317) 555-2101
	Catherine Singleton	(317) 555-0172
$250,000.00		

Figure 8.4 Visual Benchmark Word Document

Representatives Quotas

Quota	RepName	Telephone
$100,000.00		
	Robin Rehberg	(317) 555-9812
	Andre Kulisek	(317) 555-2264
	Edward Harris	(317) 555-3894
	Cecilia Ortega	(317) 555-4810
$150,000.00		
	David DeBruler	(317) 555-8779
	Jaren Newman	(317) 555-6790
	Lee Hutchinson	(317) 555-4277
	Craig Johnson	(317) 555-4391
$200,000.00		
	Isabelle Marshall	(765) 555-8822
	Maureen Pascual	(317) 555-5513
	Linda Foster	(317) 555-2101
	Catherine Singleton	(317) 555-0172
$250,000.00		
	Kwan Im	(317) 555-8374
	William Ludlow	(317) 555-0991
	Lydia Alvarado	(317) 555-4996

Case Study Apply Your Skills

Part 1

As the office manager at Woodland Dermatology Center, you are responsible for managing the center database. In preparation for an upcoming meeting, open the **AL1-C8-Woodland.accdb** database and prepare the following with data in the database:

- Create a query that displays the patient number, first name, and last name; doctor last name; date of visit; and fee. Name the query *PatientBilling*.
- Export the PatientBilling query to an Excel worksheet. Apply formatting to enhance the appearance of the worksheet and then print the worksheet.
- Create mailing labels for the patients.
- Export the patient labels to a Word (.rtf) document and then print the document.
- Import and link the **AL1-C8-Payroll.xlsx** Excel worksheet to a new table named *WeeklyPayroll*. Print the WeeklyPayroll table.

You have been given some updated information about the weekly payroll and need to make the following changes to the **AL1-C8-Payroll.xlsx** worksheet: Change the hours for Irene Vaughn to *30*, change the wage for Monica Saunders to *$10.50*, and change the hours for Dale Jorgensen to *20*. After making the changes, open, print, and then close the WeeklyPayroll table.

Part 2

The center is expanding and will be offering cosmetic dermatology services at the beginning of next month to residents in the Altoona area. Design a query that extracts records of patients living in the city of Altoona and then merge the query with Word. At the Word document, write a letter describing the new services which include microdermabrasion, chemical peels, laser resurfacing, sclerotherapy, and photorejuvenation as well as an offer for a free facial and consultation. Insert the appropriate fields in the document and then complete the merge. Save the merged document and name it **AL1-C8-WLDLtr**. Print the first two letters of the document and then close the document. Close the main document without saving it and then exit Word.

Part 3

You need to save objects in the Woodland database in a format that can be read by employees that do not have Access available. You have researched the various file formats available and have determined that the PDF format is the most universal. Use the Access Help feature to learn how to save a database object in PDF format. Save the Patients table in PDF format and then print the PDF file. Save the Doctors table in PDF format and then print the PDF file.

Part 4

Since you are responsible for updating the clinic procedures manual, you decide to create a Word document that describes the steps for saving an object in PDF format. Save the completed document and name it **AL1-C8-CS-Manual**. Print and then close **AL1-C8-CS-Manual.docx**.

UNIT 2

Performance Assessment

Note: Before beginning unit assessments, copy to your storage medium the Access2010L1U2 subfolder from the Access2010L1 folder on the CD that accompanies this textbook and then make Access2010L1U2 the active folder.

Assessing Proficiency

In this unit, you have learned to create forms, reports, and mailing labels; and to filter data. You also learned how to modify document properties; view object dependencies; and export, import, and link data between programs.

Assessment 1 Create Tables in a Clinic Database

1. Use Access to create a database for clients of a mental health clinic. Name the database **AL1-U2-LancasterClinic**. Create a table named *Clients* that includes the following fields (you determine the field name, data type, field size, and description):

    ClientNumber (primary key)
    ClientName
    StreetAddress
    City
    State
    ZipCode
    Telephone
    DateOfBirth
    DiagnosisID

2. After creating the table, switch to Datasheet view and then enter the following data in the appropriate fields:

    ClientNumber: **1831**
    George Charoni
    3980 Broad Street
    Philadelphia, PA 19149
    (215) 555-3482
    DateOfBirth: **4/12/1958**
    DiagnosisID: **SC**

    ClientNumber: **3219**
    Marian Wilke
    12032 South 39th
    Jenkintown, PA 19209
    (215) 555-9083
    DateOfBirth: **10/23/1981**
    DiagnosisID: **OCD**

ClientNumber: **2874**
**Arthur Shroeder
3618 Fourth Avenue
Philadelphia, PA 19176
(215) 555-8311**
DateOfBirth: **3/23/1958**
DiagnosisID: **OCD**

ClientNumber: **5831**
**Roshawn Collins
12110 52nd Court East
Cheltenham, PA 19210
(215) 555-4779**
DateOfBirth: **11/3/1965**
DiagnosisID: **SC**

ClientNumber: **4419**
**Lorena Hearron
3112 96th Street East
Philadelphia, PA 19132
(215) 555-3281**
DateOfBirth: **7/2/1984**
DiagnosisID: **AD**

ClientNumber: **1103**
**Raymond Mandato
631 Garden Boulevard
Jenkintown, PA 19209
(215) 555-0957**
DateOfBirth: **9/20/1979**
DiagnosisID: **MDD**

3. Automatically adjust column widths.
4. Save, print, and then close the Clients table.
5. Create a table named *Diagnoses* that includes the following fields:

   DiagnosisID (primary key)
   Diagnosis

6. After creating the table, switch to Datasheet view and then enter the following data in the appropriate fields:

   DiagnosisID = **AD**
   Diagnosis   = **Adjustment Disorder**

   DiagnosisID = **MDD**
   Diagnosis   = **Manic-Depressive Disorder**

   DiagnosisID = **OCD**
   Diagnosis   = **Obsessive-Compulsive Disorder**

   DiagnosisID = **SC**
   Diagnosis   = **Schizophrenia**

7. Automatically adjust column widths.
8. Save, print, and then close the Diagnoses table.
9. Create a table named *Fees* that includes the following fields (you determine the field name, data type, field size, and description):

   FeeCode (primary key)
   HourlyFee

10. After creating the table, switch to Datasheet view and then enter the following data in the appropriate fields:

   FeeCode   =   A   FeeCode   =   E
   HourlyFee = $75.00   HourlyFee = $95.00

   FeeCode   =   B   FeeCode   =   F
   HourlyFee = $80.00   HourlyFee = $100.00

   FeeCode   =   C   FeeCode   =   G
   HourlyFee = $85.00   HourlyFee = $105.00

   FeeCode   =   D   FeeCode   =   H
   HourlyFee = $90.00   HourlyFee = $110.00

11. Automatically adjust column widths.
12. Save, print, and then close the Fees table.
13. Create a table named *Employees* that includes the following fields (you determine the field name, data type, field size, and description):

    ProviderNumber (primary key)
    ProviderName
    Title
    Extension

14. After creating the table, switch to Datasheet view and then enter the following data in the appropriate fields:

    ProviderNumber: 29   *ProviderNumber:* 15
    ProviderName: James Schouten   *ProviderName:* Lynn Yee
    Title: Psychologist   *Title:* Child Psychologist
    Extension: 399   *Extension:* 102

    ProviderNumber: 33   *ProviderNumber:* 18
    ProviderName: Janice Grisham   *ProviderName:* Craig Chilton
    Title: Psychiatrist   *Title:* Psychologist
    Extension: 11   *Extension:* 20

15. Automatically adjust column widths.
16. Save, print, and then close the Employees table.
17. Create a table named *Billing* that includes the following fields (you determine the field name, data type, field size, and description):

    BillingNumber   (primary key; identify the data type as AutoNumber)
    ClientNumber
    DateOfService   (apply the Date/Time data type)
    Insurer
    ProviderNumber
    Hours   (Change the data type to *Number*, the *Field Size* option in the *Field Properties* section to *Double*, and the *Decimal Places* option in the *Field Properties* section in Design view to *1*. Two of the records will contain a number requiring this format.)
    FeeCode

18. After creating the table, switch to Datasheet view and then enter the following data in the appropriate fields:

ClientNumber: 4419
DateOfService: 3/1/2012
Insurer: Health Plus
ProviderNumber: 15
Hours: 2
FeeCode: B

ClientNumber: 1831
DateOfService: 3/1/2012
Insurer: Self
ProviderNumber: 33
Hours: 1
FeeCode: H

ClientNumber: 3219
DateOfService: 3/2/2012
Insurer: Health Plus
ProviderNumber: 15
Hours: 1
FeeCode: D

ClientNumber: 5831
DateOfService: 3/2/2012
Insurer: Penn-State Health
ProviderNumber: 18
Hours: 2
FeeCode: C

ClientNumber: 4419
DateOfService: 3/5/2012
Insurer: Health Plus
ProviderNumber: 15
Hours: 1
FeeCode: A

ClientNumber: 1103
DateOfService: 3/5/2012
Insurer: Penn-State Health
ProviderNumber: 18
Hours: 0.5
FeeCode: A

ClientNumber: 1831
DateOfService: 3/6/2012
Insurer: Self
ProviderNumber: 33
Hours: 1
FeeCode: H

ClientNumber: 5831
DateOfService: 3/6/2012
Insurer: Penn-State Health
ProviderNumber: 18
Hours: 0.5
FeeCode: C

19. Automatically adjust column widths.
20. Save, print in landscape orientation, and then close the Billing table.

Assessment 2 Relate Tables and Create Forms in a Clinic Database

1. With the **AL1-U2-LancasterClinic.accdb** database open, create the following one-to-many relationships and enforce referential integrity and cascade fields and records:
   a. *ClientNumber* in the Clients table is the "one" and *ClientNumber* in the Billing table is the "many."
   b. *DiagnosisID* in the Diagnoses table is the "one" and *DiagnosisID* in the Clients table is the "many."
   c. *ProviderNumber* in the Employees table is the "one" and *ProviderNumber* in the Billing table is the "many."
   d. *FeeCode* in the Fees table is the "one" and *FeeCode* in the Billing table is the "many."
2. Create a form with the data in the Clients table.
3. After creating the form, add the following record to the Clients form:

   ClientNumber: 1179
   Timothy Fierro
   1133 Tenth Southwest

>
> Philadelphia, PA 19178
> (215) 555-5594
> *DateOfBirth:* 12/7/1987
> *DiagnosisID:* **AD**

4. Save the form, print the form in landscape orientation, and then close the form.
5. Add the following records to the Billing table:

   ClientNumber: **1179**   *ClientNumber:* **1831**
   DateOfService: **3/6/2012**   *DateOfService:* **3/6/2012**
   Insurer: **Health Plus**   *Insurer:* **Self**
   ProviderNumber: **15**   *ProviderNumber:* **33**
   Hours: **0.5**   *Hours:* **1**
   FeeCode: **C**   *FeeCode:* **H**

6. Save and then print the Billing table in landscape orientation.
7. Close the Billing table.

Assessment 3 Create Forms Using the Form Wizard

1. With the **AL1-U2-LancasterClinic.accdb** database open, create a form with fields from related tables using the Form Wizard with the following specifications:
   a. At the first Form Wizard dialog box, insert the following fields in the Selected Fields list box:

   From the Clients table: From the Billing table:
       ClientNumber   *Insurer*
       DateOfBirth   *ProviderNumber*
       DiagnosisID

   b. Do not make any changes at the second Form Wizard dialog box.
   c. Do not make any changes at the third Form Wizard dialog box.
   d. At the fourth Form Wizard dialog box, type the name **ProviderInformation** in the *Form* text box.
2. When the first record displays, print the first record.
3. Close the form.

Assessment 4 Create Labels with the Label Wizard

1. With the **AL1-U2-LancasterClinic.accdb** database open, use the Label Wizard to create mailing labels with the client names and addresses and sorted by ZIP code. Name the mailing label file **ClientMailingLabels**.
2. Print the mailing labels.
3. Close the mailing labels file.

Assessment 5 Filter Records in Tables

1. With the **AL1-U2-LancasterClinic.accdb** database open, open the Billing table and then filter the records to display the following records:
   a. Display only those records with the Health Plus insurer. Print the results and then remove the filter.
   b. Display only those records with the 4419 client number. Print the results and then remove the filter.
2. Filter records by selection to display the following records:
   a. Display only those records with a C fee code. Print the results and then remove the filter.

b. Display only those records between the dates of 3/1/2012 and 3/5/2012. Print the results and then remove the filter.
3. Close the Billing table without saving the changes.
4. Open the Clients table and then use Filter By Form to display clients in Jenkintown or Cheltenham. Print the results and then remove the filter.
5. Close the Clients table without saving the changes.

Assessment 6 Export a Table to Excel

1. With the **AL1-U2-LancasterClinic.accdb** database open, export the Billing table to an Excel workbook.
2. Apply formatting to the cells in the Excel workbook to enhance the appearance of the data.
3. Change the page orientation to landscape.
4. Save, print, and then close the workbook.
5. Exit Excel.

Assessment 7 Merge Records to Create Letters in Word

1. With the **AL1-U2-LancasterClinic.accdb** database open, merge data in the Clients table to a blank Word document. *Hint: Use the Word Merge button in the Export group in the External Data tab.* You determine the fields to use in the inside address and an appropriate salutation. Type **March 12, 2012** as the date of the letter and type the following text in the body of the document:

   > The building of a new wing for the Lancaster Clinic will begin April 1, 2012. We are excited about this new addition to our clinic. With the new facilities, we will be able to offer additional community and group services along with enhanced child-play therapy treatment.
   >
   > During the construction, the main entrance will be moved to the north end of the building. Please use this entrance until the construction of the wing is completed. We apologize in advance for any inconvenience this causes you.

   Include an appropriate complimentary close for the letter. Use the name and title *Marianne Lambert, Clinic Director* for the signature and add your reference initials and the document name (**AL1-U2-A7-LCLtrs.docx**).
2. Merge to a new document and then save the document with the name **AL1-U2-A7-LCLtrs**.
3. Print the first two letters of the document and then close **AL1-U2-A7-LCLtrs.docx**.
4. Save the main document as **AL1-U2-A7-ConstLtrMD** and then close the document.
5. Exit Word.

Assessment 8 Import and Link Excel Data to an Access Table

1. With the **AL1-U2-LancasterClinic.accdb** database open, import and link **AL1-U2-StaffHours.xlsx** into a new table named *StaffHours*.
2. Open the StaffHours table in Datasheet view.
3. Print and then close the StaffHours table.
4. Open **AL1-U2-StaffHours.xlsx** in Excel.

5. Insert a formula in cell D2 that multiplies B2 with C2 and then copy the formula down to cells D3 through D7.
6. Save and then close **AL1-U2-StaffHours.xlsx**.
7. Exit Excel.
8. In Access with the **AL1-U2-LancasterClinic.accdb** database open, open the StaffHours table.
9. Print and then close the StaffHours table.

Writing Activities

The following activities give you the opportunity to practice your writing skills along with demonstrating an understanding of some of the important Access features you have mastered in this unit. Use correct grammar, appropriate word choices, and clear sentence constructions.

Activity 1 Add a Table to the Clinic Database

The director at Lancaster Clinic has asked you to add information to the **AL1-U2-LancasterClinic.accdb** database on insurance companies contracted by the clinic. You need to create a table that will contain information on insurance companies. The director wants the table to include the insurance company name, address, city, state, and ZIP code along with a telephone number and the name of a representative. You determine the field names, data types, field sizes, and description for the table and then include the following information (in the appropriate fields):

Health Plus
4102 22nd Street
Philadelphia, PA 19166
(212) 555-0990
Representative: Byron Tolleson

Penn-State Health
5933 Lehigh Avenue
Philadelphia, PA 19148
(212) 555-3477
Representative: Tracey Pavone

Quality Medical
51 Cecil B. Moore Avenue
Philadelphia, PA 19168
(212) 555-4600
Representative: Lee Stafford

Delaware Health
4418 Front Street
Philadelphia, PA 19132
(212) 555-6770
Representative: Melanie Chon

Save, print, and then close the insurance company table. Open Word and then write a report to the clinic director detailing how you created the table. Include a title for the report, steps on how you created the table, and any other pertinent information. Save the completed report and name it **AL1-U2-Act1-LCRpt**. Print and then close **AL1-U2-Act1-LCRpt.docx**.

Activity 2 Merge Records to Create Letters to Insurance Companies

Merge data in the insurance company database to a blank Word document. You determine the fields to use in the inside address and an appropriate salutation. Compose a letter to the insurance companies informing them that Lancaster Clinic is providing mental health counseling services to people with health insurance through their company. You are sending an informational brochure about

Lancaster Clinic and are requesting information from the insurance companies on services and service limitations. Include an appropriate complimentary close for the letter. Use the name and title *Marianne Lambert, Clinic Director* for the signature and add your reference initials. When the merge is completed, name the document containing the merged letters **AL1-U2-Act2-LCIns**. Print the first two letters in the merged document and then close **AL1-U2-Act2-LCIns.docx**. Close the main document without saving it and then exit Word. Close the **AL1-U2-LancasterClinic.accdb** database.

Internet Research

Health Information Search

In this activity, you will search the Internet for information on a health concern or disease that interests you. You will be looking for specific organizations, interest groups, or individuals who are somehow connected to the topic you have chosen. Your topic may be an organization that raises money to support research, it may be a support group that posts information or answers questions, or you may find information about clinics or doctors who specialize in your topic. Try to find at least ten different groups that support the health concern you are researching.

Create a database in Access and create a table that includes information from your search. Design the table so that you can store the name, address, phone number, and web address of the organizations you find. You will also want to identify the connection the group has to your topic (supports research, interest group, treats patients, etc.). Create a report to summarize your findings. In Microsoft Word, create a letter that you can use to write for further information about the organization. Use the names and addresses in your database to merge with the letter. Select and then print the first two letters that result from the merge. Finally, write a paragraph describing information you learned about the health concern that you previously did not know.

Job Study

City Improvement Projects

In this activity, you are working with the city council in your area to keep the public informed of the progress being made on improvement projects throughout the city. These projects are paid for through tax dollars voted on by the public, and the city council feels that an informed public leads to good voter turnout when it is time to make more improvements.

Your job is to create a database and a table in the database that will store the following information for each project: a project ID number, a description of the project, the budgeted dollar amount to be spent, the amount spent so far, the amount of time allocated to the project, and the amount of time spent so far. Enter five city improvement projects into the table (sample data created by you). Create a query based on the table that calculates the percent of budgeted dollars spent so far and the percent of budgeted time spent so far. Print the table and the query.

Index

A

Access
    exporting object to PDF or XPS file, 309–310
    merging data in Word document, 305–306
    screen elements of, 7
Add & Delete group, 24
adding records in forms, 191
Adobe Reader, opening PDF file in, 284
aggregate functions, 109
    designing queries with, 109–113
alphanumeric data, 23
And criteria, designing queries with, 97–100
Ascending button, 149
Attachment as data type, 136
AutoNumber as data type, 47, 136
AutoNumber field, 22
    changing, in table, 28–32
Avg function, 109

B

Backstage view, 5, 6
    getting help in, 161–162
    New tab, 5, 6
    Recent tab, 6
buttons, getting help on, 161–162

C

calculated field, 108
    creating, 108–109
Caption text box, 26
    inserting, in table, 26–27
Cascade Delete Related Records, 52
Cascade Update Related Fields, 52
Close Database button, 6
Close Print Preview button, 17
closing database, 6–8
collapse indicator, 64
columns, 10, 22
    changing width in table, 15–16
Conditional Formatting, applying, in forms, 205–208
control, inserting, in forms, 196–199
control objects, 194
    modifying, in forms, 195–196
    modifying, in reports, 235–236
Count function, 109
crosstab query, 113
    creating, 113–116
Crosstab Query Wizard, 113
Currency as data type, 23, 135, 136
customizing
    form, 194–211
    Recent tab Backstage view, 281–283
    report, 240–243

D

data
    in databases, 5
    entering, 24–25
    exporting, to Excel, 300–303
    exporting, to Word, 303–305
    filtering, 265–274
    finding and replacing, 156–159
    in foreign key field, 48
    formatting table, 150–154
    importing, to new table, 310–311
    inserting, in Form Header, 195
    linking, to Excel worksheet, 312–313
    merging Access, with Word document, 305–306
    merging query, with Word document, 307–308
    in primary key, 21
    sorting, in records, 149
database diagram, 21–22
database objects, 8
    saving, 283–286
databases
    clearing recent list, 282–283
    compacting and repairing, 276
    creating table in, 22–25
    data in, 5
    defined, 5
    encrypting, with password, 277–278
    exploring, 5–6
    flat file, 45
    managing tables in, 10–16
    opening and closing, 6–10
    pinning, 282
    primary use of, 79
    printing table in, 16–20
    relational, 21
    saving, 283–286
    structure of, 274
    viewing and customizing properties, 278–280
Datasheet view, 10, 13, 22
    creating tables in, 22–25, 131

displaying specific records in, 149
entering data in table in, 188
inserting total row in, 145–149
Data Type field drop-down list, 135
data types, 22, 23, 136
Date & Time as data type, 22–23, 135, 136
Default Value, assigning
    in Design view, 138–139
    in table, 28
Default Value button, 28
defining table structure, 22
deleting
    fields, in Design view, 144–145
    fields, in table, 13–15
    records, in forms, 191
    records, in related tables, 59–61
    records, in table, 10–13
    relationship, 56
Descending button, 149
Description text box, 26
    inserting, in table, 26–27
Design view, 22
    assigning Default Value in, 138–139
    creating tables in, 131, 134–145
    Input Mask in, 139–140
    inserting, moving, and deleting fields in, 144–145
    Lookup Wizard in, 143–144
    validating field entries in, 143
dialog box, getting help in, 161–162
displaying Quick list, 282
Down Arrow key, 14

E

editing relationship, 56
Edit Relationships dialog box, 50
    specifying referential integrity at, 51–52
Enable Content button, 7
Enter Field Properties dialog box, 26
entity integrity, 47
Excel worksheet
    exporting data to, 300–303
    linking data to, 312–313
existing fields, adding, in forms, 208–211
expand indicators, 64
exporting
    Access object to PDF or XPS file, 309–310
    data to Excel, 300–303
    data to Word, 303–305
Expression Builder dialog box, 28

F

field names
    abbreviating, 24–25
    avoiding spaces in, 24
    letters and numbers in, 24
fields, 22
    creating calculated, 108–109
    inserting, moving, and deleting, 13–15
    inserting, moving, and deleting, in Design view, 144–145
    sorting, in query, 94–95
    validating entries in Design view, 143
field size, assigning, in table, 28
File tab, 7
filter, 265
    removing, 266–267
    using, by form, 272–273
Filter button, filtering using, 265–266
filtering
    by Filter button, 265–266
    by selection, 270
    by shortcut menu, 271–272
    on specific values, 268–270
find and replace data, 156–159
Find and Replace dialog box, 156
Find Duplicates Query Wizard, 116
find duplication query, 116
find unmatched query, creating, 119–120
Find Unmatched Query Wizard, 119
flat file database, 45
flat file management system, 45
foreign key field, 48
    data in, 48
formatting
    applying conditional, in forms, 205–207
    forms, 203–204
Form button, creating form with, 188
Form Header, inserting data in, 195
Form Layout Tools Design tab, 188, 240
forms, 188
    adding and deleting records, 191
    adding existing fields, 208–211
    applying conditional formatting, 205–208
    applying themes in, 195
    arranging objects, 199–202
    changing views, 188
    creating, with Form button, 188
    creating, multiple items, 214
    creating, with related table, 192–193
    creating, split, 211–214
    creating, using Form Wizard, 215–218
    customizing, 194–211

as database object, 8
filtering records in, 267–268
formatting, 203–204
inserting a control, 196–199
modifying control object, 195–196
navigating in, 189
printing, 188–189
sorting records, 191
using filter by, 272–273
Form Tools Layout Design tab, 195
Form view, in entering and managing records, 188
Form Wizard, creating form using, 215–218

H

help, using, 159–162
Help tab Backstage view, 159–160
Hide All hyperlink, 159
home tab, 11
Hyperlink as data type, 136

I

ID field, 47
importing data to new table, 310–311
information
　forms of, 3
　managing, 3
Info tab Backstage view, using options at, 276–281
Input Mask, using, in Design view, 139–140
Input Mask Wizard, 139
Input Mask Wizard dialog box, 139–140
inserting
　fields, in Design view, 144–145
　fields, in table, 13–15
　records, in related tables, 59–61
　records, in table, 10–13
　total row, 145–149

J

join, 50
　tables, 22
join lines, 21, 51

L

Label Wizard dialog box, 251, 252
landscape orientation, 18
Layout Tools Design tab, 240
Layout view, to view data, 188
linking data to Excel worksheet, 312–313
live preview feature, 195
Lookup Wizard
　as data type, 136
　in Design view, 143–144

M

mailing labels, preparing, 251–254
margins, changing, in table, 17
Max function, 109
Memo as data type, 136
merging
　Access data with Word document, 305–306
　query data with Word document, 307–308
Message bar, 7
Min function, 109
minus symbol as collapse indicator, 64
modifying queries, 96–97
moving fields
　in Design view, 144–145
　in tables, 13–15
multiple items form, creating, 214

N

name, inserting, in table, 26–27
Name text box, 26
navigating in forms, 189
Navigation pane, 7, 96
　hiding, 8
New Formatting Rule dialog box, 205
New Query dialog box, 101, 116, 119
New tab Backstage view, 5, 6
Number as data type, 23, 136

O

objects
　arranging, in forms, 199–202
　control, 194
　exporting Access, to PDF or XPS file, 309–310
　modifying control, in reports, 235–236
　opening and closing, 8–10
　viewing dependencies, 274–275
Office Clipboard, using, 313–315
OLE Object as data type, 136
one-to-many relationship, 50, 192–193
　relating tables in, 50–51
one-to-one relationship, creating, 61–64
opening database, 6–8
options, using, at Info tab Backstage view, 276–281
Or criteria, designing queries with, 97–100
orientation
　landscape, 18
　portrait, 16, 18

P

Page Layout, changing, 18–19
Page Setup dialog box, 18
Page Size, changing, in table, 17
password, encrypting database with, 277–278
PDF file
    exporting Access object to, 309–310
    opening in Adobe Reader, 284
pencil icon, 11
performing queries, 84–113
pinning database, 282
plus symbol as expand indicator, 64
portrait orientation, 16, 18
previewing, table, 17
primary key, 21
    defining, in related tables, 46–49
primary key field, 46
primary table, 50
Print dialog box, 149
printing
    forms, 189
    relationship, 52–56
    specific records, 149
    table, 16–20
Print Options tab, 18
Print Preview, 17
    displaying report in, 236–238
Print Preview button, 17
Print tab Backstage view, 16, 17
Properties dialog box, 279

Q

queries
    creating, calculated field, 108–109
    creating, crosstab, 113–116
    creating, find duplicates, 116–119
    creating, find unmatched, 119–120
    creating, report with, 238–239
    as database object, 8
    designing, 84–86
    designing, with aggregate functions, 109–113
    designing, with *Or* and *And* criteria, 97–100
    establishing criteria, 86–93
    fields in, 94–95
    modifying, 96–97
    performing, 84–113
    performing, with Simple Query Wizard, 101–107
query data, merging, with Word document, 307–308
Query Design button, 84

Query Tools Design tab, 85
Quick Access toolbar, 7
Quick Command buttons, 5
quick list, displaying, 282
Quick Start field, inserting, in table, 28

R

Recent tab Backstage view, 6
    customizing, 281–283
Record Navigation bar, 10, 11, 189
    buttons on, 10, 11
records, 22
    adding and deleting in forms, 191
    displaying related, in subdatasheet, 64–67
    filtering, in table, form, and report, 267–268
    grouping and sorting, 243–246
    inserting and deleting, 10–13
    inserting and deleting, in related tables, 59–61
    printing specific, 149
    sorting, 149, 236
    sorting, in forms, 191–192
referential integrity, 50
    specifying, 51–52
related records, displaying, in subdatasheet, 64–67
related tables, 50
    creating, 45–61
    creating, form with, 192–193
    defining primary key, 46–49
    determining relationships in, 46
    inserting and deleting records in, 59–61
    in one-to-many relationship, 50–51
relational database, 21
relational database management system, 46
relationships, 21
    creating, between tables, 43–67
    creating, one-to-one, 61–64
    deleting, 56
    determining, in related tables, 46
    editing, 56
    printing, 52–56
    relating tables in one-to-many, 50–51
renaming, field heading in table, 26
Report button, creating report with, 234–235
Report Layout Tools Design tab, 240
reports
    creating, with query, 238–239
    creating, with Report button, 234–235
    creating, using Report Wizard, 247–251
    customizing, 240–243
    as database object, 8

displaying, in Print Preview, 236–238
filtering records in, 267–268
grouping and sorting records, 243–246
modifying control objects, 235–236
preparing mailing labels, 251–254
printing relationships, 52–56
sorting, 236
sorting records in, 236
Report Wizard, creating report using, 247–251
return, 86
ribbon, 7

S

Save As dialog box, 96, 134
security warning message bar, 7
Selected Fields list box, 247–248
selection, filtering by, 270
Set Database Password dialog box, 277
shortcut menu, filtering by, 271–272
Show All hyperlink, 159
showing tables, 56
Show Table dialog box, 50, 56
Shutter Bar Open/Close button, 8
Simple Query Wizard, performing query with, 101–107
Simple Query Wizard dialog box, 101–102
sorting records, 149
spelling check, 154–155
Spelling dialog box, 154
Split Form, creating, 211–214
Status bar, 7
subdatasheet, 64
displaying related records in, 64
Sum function, 109
synchronous views, 211

T

tables, 192–193
assigning, Default Value, 28
assigning, field size, 28
changing, AutoNumber field, 28–32
changing, column width, 15–16
changing, margins in, 17
changing, page layout in, 18–19
changing, page size in, 17
creating, 22–25
creating, in Design view, 134–135
creating, a form with a related, 192–193
creating, related, 45–61
as database object, 8
designing, 21–22
filtering records in, 267–268
finding and replacing data in, 156–159
formatting data in, 150–154
importing data to new, 310–311
inserting, moving, and deleting, 13–15
inserting and deleting records in, 10–13
inserting name, caption, and description, 26–27
inserting Quick Start fields, 28
join, 22
managing, 10–16
performance objectives, 43–67
previewing, 17
primary, 50
printing, 16–20
related, 50
relating, in one-to-many relationship, 50–51
renaming of field heading, 26
showing, 56
spell checking, 154–155
tabs, 7
Text as data type, 23, 135, 136
Text Filters option, 268
Text Formatting buttons, 150
themes, 195
applying, in forms, 195
Title bar, 7
total row, inserting, 145–149

V

Validation Rule property box, 143
values
assigning default, in table, 28
filtering on specific, 268–270

W

Word document
exporting data to, 303–305
merging Access data with, 305–306
merging query data with, 307–308
work area, 7

X

XPS file, 284
exporting Access object to, 309–310

Y

Yes/No as data type, 23, 135, 136

Z

Zoom group, 17
Zoom slider bar, 17

Activity 12 Assess Your Work

Review the documents you developed and assess your own work in writing. In order to develop an objective perspective of your work, openly solicit constructive criticism from your teacher, peers, and contacts outside of school. Your self-assessment document should specify the weaknesses and strengths of each piece and your specific recommendations for revision and improvement.

Type the following data in the Products table:

Product# = 12A-0		Product# = 59R-1
Product = Premium blend		Product = Vanilla syrup
Supplier# = 24		Supplier# = 62
Product# = 12A-1		Product# = 59R-2
Product = Cappuccino blend		Product = Raspberry syrup
Supplier# = 24		Supplier# = 62
Product# = 12A-2		Product# = 59R-3
Product = Hazelnut blend		Product = Chocolate syrup
Supplier# = 24		Supplier# = 62
Product# = 21B-2		Product# = 89T-3
Product = 12-oz cup		Product = Napkins, 500 ct
Supplier# = 36		Supplier# = 41
Product# = 21B-3		Product# = 89T-4
Product = 16-oz cup		Product = 6-inch stir stick
Supplier# = 36		Supplier# = 41

Print both the Suppliers table and the Products table in landscape orientation. Prepare a report with the following information: supplier name, supplier #, supplier email, and product.

Merge the records of those suppliers that are located in Tacoma to a blank Word document. You determine the fields to use in the inside address and an appropriate salutation. Compose a business letter that you will send to the contacts in Tacoma that includes the following information:

- Explain that Classique Coffees is interested in selling protein smoothies in the greater Seattle/Tacoma area.
- Ask if the company offers any protein smoothie products.
- If the company does not currently offer any protein smoothie products, will these products be available in the future?
- Ask the company to send any materials on current products and specifically on protein smoothies.
- Ask someone at the company to contact you at the Classique Coffees address, by telephone at (206) 555-6690 or by email at ccoffees@emcp.net.
- Include any other information you think appropriate to the topic.

Merge to a new document and then save the document with the name **ProjectAct11**. Print and then close **ProjectAct11.docx**. Save the main document as **SmoothieLtrMD** and then close **SmoothieLtrMD.docx**.

When preparing the slide presentation, you determine the presentation design theme and the layouts. Include any clip art images that might be appropriate and apply an animation scheme to all slides. When the presentation is completed, save it and name it **ProjectAct10**. Run the presentation and then print the presentation with six slides horizontally per page.

Activity 11 Create a Database File and Organize Data

Use Access to create a database for Classique Coffees that contains information on suppliers and products. Include the following fields in the Suppliers table and the Products table (you determine the specific field names):

Suppliers table:
Supplier#
SupplierName
Address
City
State
ZipCode
Email

Products table:
Product#
Product
Supplier#

Type the following data in the Suppliers table:

Supplier#	=	24	*Supplier#*	=	62
SupplierName	=	Gourmet Blends	*SupplierName*	=	Sure Shot Supplies
Address	=	109 South Madison	*Address*	=	291 Pacific Avenue
City	=	Seattle	*City*	=	Tacoma
State	=	WA	*State*	=	WA
ZipCode	=	98032	*ZipCode*	=	98418
Email	=	gblends@emcp.net	*Email*	=	sssupplies@emcp.net
Supplier#	=	36	*Supplier#*	=	41
SupplierName	=	Jannsen Company	*SupplierName*	=	Bertolinos
Address	=	4122 South Sprague	*Address*	=	11711 Meridian East
City	=	Tacoma	*City*	=	Seattle
State	=	WA	*State*	=	WA
ZipCode	=	98402	*ZipCode*	=	98109
Email	=	jannsen@emcp.net	*Email*	=	bertolino@emcp.net

Activity 9 Build a Projected Sales Worksheet and Create a Chart

Using Excel, prepare a worksheet with the following information:

Type of Coffee	Percent of Sales
Regular blend	21%
Espresso blend	10%
Regular blend decaf	16%
Espresso blend decaf	8%
Flavored blend	24%
Flavored blend decaf	16%
Protein smoothie	5%

Create a pie chart as a new sheet with the data in the worksheet. Title the pie chart *Year 2013 Projected Percentage of Sales*. When the chart is completed, save the worksheet (two sheets) and name it **ProjectAct09**. Print and then close **ProjectAct09.xlsx**.

Analyze the sales data by comparing and contrasting the pie charts created in **ProjectAct08.xlsx** and **ProjectAct09.xlsx**. What areas in the projected sales percentages have changed? What do these changes indicate? Assume that the projected 2013 annual income for Classique Coffees is $2,200,000. What amount of that income will come from protein smoothies? Does this amount warrant marketing this new product? Prepare a memo in Word to Leslie Steiner that includes your analysis. Add any other interpretations you can make from analyzing the pie charts. Save the memo and name it **WordProject09**. Print and then close **WordProject09.docx**.

Activity 10 Design and Create a Presentation

Using PowerPoint, prepare a marketing slide presentation. Include the following information in the presentation:

- Classique Coffees 2013 Marketing Plan (title)
- Company reorganization (insert the organizational chart you created in Activity 4)
- 2012 sales percentages (insert into the slide the pie chart that is part of the **ProjectAct08.xlsx** worksheet)
- 2013 projected sales percentages (insert into the slide the pie chart that is part of the **ProjectAct09.xlsx** worksheet)
- Protein smoothie marketing strategy
    > target customer
    > analysis of competition
    > wholesale resources
    > pricing
    > volume
- Product placement
    > stocking strategies
    > shelf allocation
    > stock rotation schedule
    > seasonal display

Activity 7 Determine Sales Quota Increases

The Marketing Department for Classique Coffees employs seven employees who market the company products to customers. These employees are given a quota for yearly sales that they are to meet. You have determined that the quota needs to be raised for the upcoming year. You are not sure whether the quotas should be increased 5 percent or 10 percent. Using Excel, prepare a worksheet with the following information:

CLASSIQUE COFFEES
Sales Quotas

Employee	Current Quota	Projected Quota
Berenstein	$125,000	
Evans	$100,000	
Grayson	$110,000	
Lueke	$135,000	
Nasson	$125,000	
Phillips	$150,000	
Samuels	$175,000	

Insert a formula to determine the projected quotas at 5 percent more than the current quota. Save the worksheet, name it **ProjectAct07A,** and then print **ProjectAct07A.xlsx.** Determine the projected quotas at 10 percent more than the current quota. Save the worksheet and name it **ProjectAct07B.** Print and then close **ProjectAct07B.xlsx.**

Activity 8 Build a Sales Worksheet and Create a Chart

Using Excel, prepare a worksheet with the following information:

Type of Coffee	Percent of Sales
Regular blend	22%
Espresso blend	12%
Regular blend decaf	17%
Espresso blend decaf	10%
Flavored blend	25%
Flavored blend decaf	14%

Save the completed worksheet, name it **ProjectAct08,** and then print **ProjectAct08.xlsx.** With the worksheet still displayed, create a pie chart as a new sheet with the data in the worksheet. Title the pie chart *Year 2012 Percentage of Sales*. When the chart is completed, save the worksheet (now two sheets) with the same name (**ProjectAct08.xlsx**). Print only the sheet containing the pie chart and then close **ProjectAct08.xlsx.**

Activity 4 Create an Organizational Chart

In preparation for an upcoming meeting, you need to prepare an organizational chart for the organization of the leadership team at Classique Coffees. Using Word, create an organizational chart using a SmartArt graphic that includes the following:

President
Vice President

Marketing Manager	Sales Manager	Personnel Manager
Marketing Assistants	Sales Associates	Assistant Manager

Apply formatting to improve the visual appeal of the chart. Save the chart and name it **ProjectAct04**. Print and then close **ProjectAct04.docx**.

Activity 5 Create a SmartArt Graphic

In addition to the organizational chart, you also want to create a SmartArt graphic that illustrates the steps in a marketing plan. Those steps are:

- Planning
- Development
- Marketing
- Distribution

Apply formatting to improve the visual appeal of the graphic. Save the SmartArt graphic and name it **ProjectAct05**. Print and then close **ProjectAct05.docx**.

Activity 6 Build a Budget Worksheet

Using Excel, prepare a worksheet with the following information:

Annual Budget: $1,450,000

Department	Percent of Budget	Total
Administration	10%	
Purchasing	24%	
Sales	21%	
Marketing	23%	
Personnel	12%	
Training	10%	

Insert formulas that will calculate the total amount for each department based on the specified percentage of the annual budget. When the worksheet is completed, save it, name it **ProjectAct06**, and then print **ProjectAct06.xlsx**.

Determine the impact of a 10-percent increase in the annual budget on the total amount for each department. With the amounts displayed for a 10-percent increase, save, print, and then close **ProjectAct06.xlsx**.

Activity 2 Design a Letterhead

You are not satisfied with the current letterhead used by your company. Design a new letterhead for Classique Coffees using Word and include the following information:

- Use a clip art image in the letterhead. (Consider downloading a clip art image from Office.com.)
- Include the company name—Classique Coffees.
- Include the company address—355 Pioneer Square, Seattle, WA 98211.
- Include the company telephone number—(206) 555-6690.
- Include the company email address—ccoffees@emcp.net.
- Create a slogan that will help your business contacts remember your company.
- Add any other information or elements that you feel are appropriate.

When the letterhead is completed, save it and name it **ProjectAct02**. Print and then close **ProjectAct02.docx**.

Activity 3 Prepare a Notice

Using Word, prepare a notice about an upcoming marketing seminar. Include the following information in the notice:

- Name of the seminar—Marketing to the Coffee Gourmet
- Location of the seminar—Conference room at the corporate office, 355 Pioneer Square, Seattle, WA 98211
- Date and time of seminar—Friday, October 19, 2012, 9:00 a.m. to 2:30 p.m.
- Topics that will be covered at the seminar:
    - > identifying coffee-drinking trends
    - > assessing the current gourmet coffee market
    - > developing new products
    - > analyzing the typical Classique Coffees customer
    - > marketing a new product line
- Consider including a clip art image in the notice. (You determine an appropriate clip art image.)

When the notice is completed, save it and name it **ProjectAct03**. Print and then close **ProjectAct03.docx**.

Office 2010 Integrated Project

Now that you have completed the chapters in this textbook, you have learned to create documents in Word, build worksheets in Excel, organize data in Access, and design presentations in PowerPoint. To learn the various programs in the Microsoft Office 2010 suite, you have completed a variety of projects, assessments, and activities. This integrated project is a final assignment that allows you to apply the knowledge you have gained about the programs in the Office suite to produce a variety of documents and files.

Situation

You are the vice president of Classique Coffees, a gourmet coffee company. Your company operates two retail stores that sell gourmet coffee and related products to the public. One retail store is located in Seattle, Washington, the other in Tacoma. The company is three years old and has seen approximately 10- to 20-percent growth in profit each year. Your duties as the vice president of the company include researching the coffee market; studying coffee buying trends; designing and implementing new projects; and supervising the marketing, sales, and personnel managers.

Activity 1 Write Persuasively

Using Word, compose a memo to the president of Classique Coffees, Leslie Steiner, detailing your research and recommendations:

- Research has shown 10-percent growth in the protein smoothie market.
- The target population for protein smoothies is people from ages 18 to 35.
- Market analysis indicates that only three local retail companies sell protein smoothies in the greater Seattle-Tacoma area.
- The recommendation is that Classique Coffees develop a suite of protein smoothies for market consumption by early next year. (Be as persuasive as possible.)

Save the completed memo and name it **ProjectAct01**. Print and then close **ProjectAct01.docx**.

Microsoft® PowerPoint®

Unit 1 ■ Creating and Formatting PowerPoint Presentations

Chapter 1 ■ Preparing a PowerPoint Presentation

Chapter 2 ■ Modifying a Presentation and Using Help

Chapter 3 ■ Formatting Slides

Chapter 4 ■ Inserting Elements in Slides

Microsoft PowerPoint
Preparing a PowerPoint Presentation

CHAPTER 1

PERFORMANCE OBJECTIVES

Upon successful completion of Chapter 1, you will be able to:
- Create a PowerPoint presentation with an installed template
- Open, save, run, print, close, and delete a presentation
- Plan a presentation
- Create a presentation using a theme template
- Insert slides, insert text in slides, and choose slide layouts
- Change presentation views
- Navigate and edit slides
- Preview and print a presentation
- Create a presentation from an existing presentation
- Apply a design theme to slides in a presentation
- Prepare a presentation from a blank presentation
- Prepare a presentation in the Slides/Outline pane
- Add transitions and sounds to a presentation

During a presentation, the person doing the presenting may use visual aids to strengthen the impact of the message as well as help organize the information. Visual aids may include transparencies, slides, photographs, or an on-screen presentation. With Microsoft's PowerPoint program, you can easily create visual aids for a presentation and then print copies of the aids as well as run the presentation. PowerPoint is a presentation graphics program that you can use to organize and present information. Model answers for this chapter's projects appear on the following page.

Note: Before beginning the projects, copy to your storage medium the PowerPoint2010C1 subfolder from the PowerPoint2010 folder on the CD that accompanies this textbook. Steps on how to copy a folder are presented on the inside of the back cover of this textbook. Do this every time you start a chapter's projects.

Model Answers

Project 2 Create an Internet Presentation Using a Theme Template
P-C1-P2-Internet.pptx

Project 3 Create a Planning Presentation from an Existing Presentation
P-C1-P3-PlanningPres.pptx

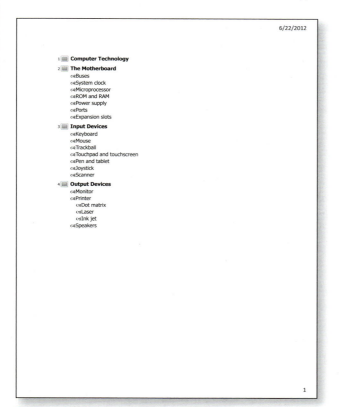

Project 4 Create a Technology Presentation in the Slides/Outline Pane
P-C1-P4-Computers.pptx

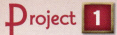

Project 1 Open and Run a Template Presentation   1 Part

You will open an installed template presentation, run the presentation, and then close the presentation.

Creating a PowerPoint Presentation

PowerPoint provides several methods for creating a presentation. You can create a presentation using an installed template or using a theme template and prepare a presentation from a blank presentation or from an existing presentation. The steps you follow to create a presentation will vary depending on the method you choose, but will probably follow these basic steps:

1. Open PowerPoint.
2. Choose the desired installed template or theme or open an existing presentation or start with a blank presentation.
3. Type the text for each slide, adding additional elements as needed such as graphic images.
4. If necessary, apply a design theme.
5. Save the presentation.
6. Print the presentation as slides, handouts, notes pages, or an outline.
7. Run the presentation.
8. Close the presentation.
9. Exit PowerPoint.

When you choose the specific type of presentation you want to create, you are presented with the PowerPoint window in the Normal view. What displays in the window will vary depending on the type of presentation you are creating. However, the PowerPoint window contains some consistent elements as shown in Figure 1.1. The PowerPoint window contains many elements that are similar to other Microsoft Office programs such as Word and Excel. For example, the PowerPoint window, like the Word window, contains a File tab, Quick Access toolbar, tabs, ribbon, vertical and horizontal scroll bars, and a Status bar. The PowerPoint window elements are described in Table 1.1.

PowerPoint, like other Microsoft Office programs, provides enhanced ScreenTips for buttons and options. Hover the mouse pointer on a button or option and, after approximately one second, an enhanced ScreenTip displays near the button or option. The enhanced ScreenTip displays the name of the button or option, any shortcut command if one is available, and a description of the button or option.

Figure 1.1 PowerPoint Window

Table 1.1 PowerPoint Window Elements

Feature	Description
Quick Access toolbar	Contains buttons for commonly used commands.
File tab	Click the File tab and the Backstage view displays containing tabs and buttons for working with and managing presentations.
Title bar	Displays presentation name followed by the program name.
Tabs	Contains commands and features organized into groups.
Ribbon	Area containing the tabs and commands divided into groups.
Slides/Outline pane	Displays at the left side of the window with two tabs — Slides and Outline. With the Slides tab selected, slide miniatures (thumbnails) display in the pane; with the Outline tab selected, presentation contents display in the pane.
Slide pane	Displays the slide and slide contents.
Notes pane	Add notes to a presentation in this pane.
Vertical scroll bar	Display specific slides using this scroll bar.
I-beam pointer	Used to move the insertion point or to select text.
Insertion point	Indicates the location of the next character entered at the keyboard.
View area	Located toward the right side of the Status bar and contains buttons for changing the presentation view.
Status bar	Displays the slide number and number of slides, name of the applied design theme, view buttons, and the Zoom slider bar.

Opening a Presentation

When you create and then save a presentation, you can open the presentation at the Open dialog box. Display this dialog box by clicking the File tab and then clicking the Open button at the Backstage view. You can also display the Open dialog box by using the keyboard shortcut, Ctrl + O, or by inserting an Open button on the Quick Access toolbar. To insert the button, click the Customize Quick Access toolbar button that displays at the right side of the toolbar and then click *Open* at the drop-down list. At the Open dialog box, navigate to the desired folder and then double-click the desired presentation in the Content pane.

By default, PowerPoint displays the recently opened presentations in the Recent Presentations list. To open one of these presentations, click the File tab, click the Recent tab, and then click the desired presentation in the *Recent Presentations* list. If you want a presentation to remain in the list, "pin" the presentation to the list by clicking the pin button that displays at the right side of the presentation name. This changes the dimmed gray stick pin to a blue stick pin. To "unpin" the presentation, click the pin button to change it from a blue pin to a gray pin.

Microsoft provides a number of predesigned presentation templates you can view and also use as a basis for preparing your own presentation. To display the installed templates, click the File tab and then click the New tab. This displays the New tab Backstage view as shown in Figure 1.2. In this view, available templates and themes display as well as online templates. To display available templates, click the *Sample templates* option in the Available Templates and Themes category of the Backstage view. To open a template presentation, double-click the desired presentation.

▼ Quick Steps

Open a Presentation
1. Click File tab, Open button.
2. Navigate to desired folder or drive.
3. Double-click presentation.

Open an Installed Template
1. Click File tab, New tab.
2. Click *Sample templates* option.
3. Double-click desired presentation.

Figure 1.2 New Tab Backstage View

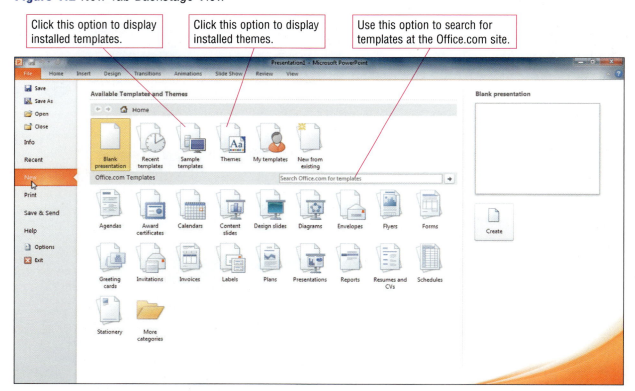

Chapter 1 ■ Preparing a PowerPoint Presentation

Starting a Presentation

▼ **Quick Steps**

Run a Presentation
1. Click Slide Show button in view area on Status bar.
2. Click left mouse button to advance slides.

Close a Presentation
1. Click File tab.
2. Click Close button.
OR
Press Ctrl + F4.

When you open a presentation, the presentation displays in Normal view. In this view, you can edit and customize the presentation. To run the presentation, click the Slide Show button in the view area on the Status bar or click the Slide Show tab and then click the From Beginning button in the Start Slide Show group. Navigate through slides in the presentation by clicking the left mouse button.

Closing a Presentation

To remove a presentation from the screen, close the presentation. You can close a presentation by clicking the File tab and then clicking the Close button. You can also close a presentation with the keyboard shortcut Ctrl + F4. To use this shortcut, hold down the Ctrl key on the keyboard, press the F4 function key located toward the top of the keyboard, and then release the Ctrl key. If you made any changes to the presentation, you will be asked if you want to save the presentation.

Project 1 Opening, Running, and Closing a Template Presentation   Part 1 of 1

1. Open PowerPoint by clicking the Start button on the Taskbar, pointing to *All Programs*, clicking *Microsoft Office*, and then clicking *Microsoft PowerPoint 2010*. (Depending on your operating system, these steps may vary.)
2. Click the File tab and then click the New tab.
3. At the New tab Backstage view, click the *Sample templates* option in the Available Templates and Themes category.
4. Double-click the *Introducing PowerPoint 2010* template.

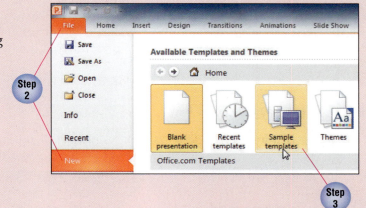

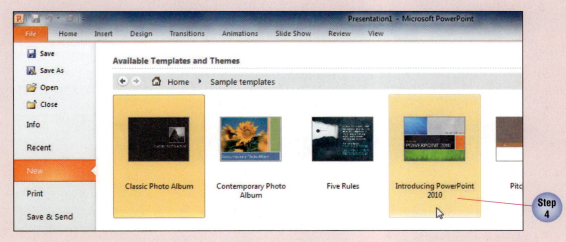

5. Run the presentation by completing the following steps:
   a. Click the Slide Show button in the view area on the Status bar.
   b. Read the information in the first slide in the presentation and then click the left mouse button.
   c. Continue reading information in slides and clicking the left mouse button to advance slides.
   d. At the black screen with the message *End of slide show, click to exit*, click the left mouse button. (This returns the presentation to Normal view.)
6. Close the presentation by clicking the File tab and then clicking the Close button.

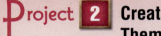
Step 5a

Project 2 — Create an Internet Presentation Using a Theme Template (3 Parts)

You will use a theme template to create a presentation, insert text in slides in the presentation, choose a slide layout, insert new slides, change views, navigate through the presentation, edit text in slides, and then print the presentation.

Planning a Presentation

With PowerPoint, you can create slides for an on-screen presentation and you can print handouts of the presentation, print an outline, or print the entire presentation. When planning a presentation, first define the purpose of the presentation. Is the intent to inform? educate? sell? motivate? and/or entertain? Additionally, consider the audience who will be listening to and watching the presentation. Determine the content of the presentation and also the medium that will be used to convey the message. Will a computer be used to display the slides of a presentation or will the presentation be projected onto a screen? Some basic guidelines to consider when preparing the content of the presentation include:

- **Determine the main purpose of the presentation.** Do not try to cover too many topics — this may strain the audience's attention or cause confusion. Identifying the main point of the presentation will help you stay focused and convey a clear message to the audience.
- **Determine the output.** Is the presentation going to be presented on a computer or will the slides be projected? To help decide the type of output needed, consider the availability of equipment, the size of the room where the presentation will be made, and the number of people who will be attending the presentation.
- **Show one idea per slide.** Each slide in a presentation should convey only one main idea. Too many thoughts or ideas on a slide may confuse the audience and cause you to stray from the purpose of the slide. Determine the specific message you want to convey to the audience and then outline the message to organize ideas.
- **Maintain a consistent layout.** A consistent layout and color scheme for slides in a presentation will create continuity and cohesiveness. Do not get carried away by using too many colors and too many pictures or other graphic elements.

- **Keep slides easy to read and uncluttered.** Keep slides simple and easy for the audience to read. Keep words and other items such as bullets to a minimum.
- **Determine the output needed.** Will you be providing audience members with handouts? If so, will these handouts consist of a printing of each slide? an outline of the presentation? a printing of each slide with space for taking notes?

Creating a Presentation Using a Theme Template

▼ **Quick Steps**

Create Presentation Using a Theme Template
1. Click File tab.
2. Click New tab.
3. Click *Themes* option.
4. Double-click desired theme template.

PowerPoint provides a variety of predesigned theme templates you can use when creating slides for a presentation. These *theme templates* include formatting such as color, background, fonts, and so on. You can choose a theme template in the Available Templates and Themes category in the New tab Backstage view. Display these options by clicking the File tab and then clicking the New tab. In the Available Templates and Themes category, click *Themes* and then double-click the desired theme template.

Inserting Text in Slides

When you choose a theme template at the New tab Backstage view or start with a blank presentation, click the Design tab and then click the desired theme in the Themes group, a slide displays in the Slide pane in Normal view. The slide displays with a default Title Slide layout. This layout contains placeholders for entering the slide title and the slide subtitle. To insert text in a placeholder, click the placeholder text. This moves the insertion point inside the placeholder, removes the default placeholder text, and selects the placeholder. A selected placeholder displays surrounded by a dashed border with sizing handles and a green rotation handle. Figure 1.3 displays a selected placeholder.

With the insertion point positioned in a placeholder, type the desired text. Edit text in a placeholder in the same manner as editing text in a Word document. Press the Backspace key to delete the character immediately left of the insertion point and press the Delete key to delete the character immediately right of the insertion point. Use the arrow keys on the keyboard to move the insertion point in the desired direction.

Figure 1.3 Selected Placeholder

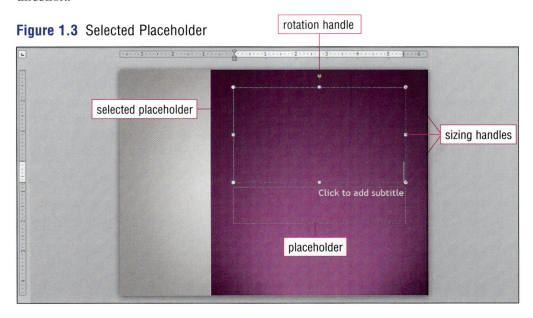

Choosing a Slide Layout

When you choose a theme template or a theme in a blank presentation, the slide displays in the Title Slide layout. This layout provides two placeholders for text — title text and subtitle text. You can change the slide layout with the Layout button in the Slides group in the Home tab. Click the Layout button and a drop-down list of layouts displays. Click the desired layout at the drop-down list and the layout is applied to the current slide.

Inserting a New Slide

Create a new slide in a presentation by clicking the New Slide button in the Slides group in the Home tab. By default, PowerPoint inserts a new slide with the Title and Content layout. You can choose a different slide layout for a new slide by clicking the New Slide button arrow and then clicking the desired layout at the drop-down list. You can also change the slide layout by clicking the Layout button in the Slides group in the Home tab and then clicking the desired layout at the drop-down list.

Saving a Presentation

After creating a presentation, save it by clicking the Save button on the Quick Access toolbar or by clicking the File tab and then the Save As button. This displays the Save As dialog box. At the Save As dialog box, type a name for the presentation in the *File name* text box, navigate to the desired folder, and then click the Save button.

▼ **Quick Steps**

Choose a Slide Layout
1. Click Layout button.
2. Click desired layout option in drop-down list.

Insert a New Slide
Click New Slide button.

Save a Presentation
1. Click Save button.
2. Type presentation name in *File name* text box.
3. Navigate to desired folder.
4. Click Save button.

PowerPoint includes nine built-in standard layouts.

Layout   New   Save
         Slide

Project 2a Creating a Presentation Using a Theme Template   Part 1 of 3

1. With PowerPoint open, click the File tab and then click the New tab.
2. At the New tab Backstage view, click the *Themes* option.
3. Scroll down the *Themes* list box and then double-click *Opulent*.
4. Click in the placeholder text *CLICK TO ADD TITLE* and then type **the internet**. (The design theme changes the text to uppercase letters.)
5. Click in the placeholder text *Click to add subtitle* and then type **A Global Network**.

Chapter 1 ■ Preparing a PowerPoint Presentation   11

6. Click the New Slide button in the Slides group in the Home tab (this inserts a slide with the Title and Content layout).
7. Click the placeholder text *CLICK TO ADD TITLE* and then type **communications**. (The design theme changes the text to uppercase letters.)
8. Click the placeholder text *Click to add text* and then type **Email**.
9. Press the Enter key (this moves the insertion point to the next line and inserts a bullet) and then type **Chat Rooms**.
10. Press the Enter key and then type **Instant Messaging**.
11. Press the Enter key and then type **Blogs**.
12. Press the Enter key and then type **Electronic Bulletin Boards**.

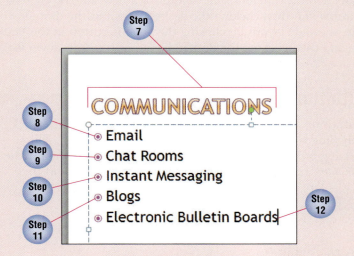

13. Click the New Slide button in the Slides group in the Home tab.
14. Click the placeholder text *CLICK TO ADD TITLE* and then type **entertainment**.
15. Click the placeholder text *Click to add text* and then type **Online Games**.
16. Press the Enter key and then type **Online Gambling**.
17. Press the Enter key and then type **Music**.
18. Press the Enter key and then type **Video**.

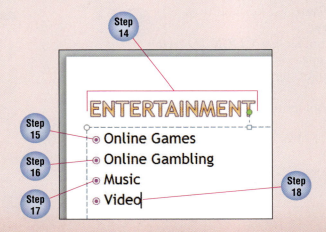

19. Click the New Slide button arrow and then click the *Title Slide* layout.
20. Click the placeholder text CLICK TO ADD TITLE and then type **internet issues**.
21. Click the placeholder text *Click to add subtitle* and then type **Community and Policy Issues**.
22. Click the New Slide button.
23. Click the placeholder text CLICK TO ADD TITLE and then type **community issues**.
24. Click the placeholder text *Click to add text* and then type **Flaming**.
25. Press the Enter key and then type **Netiquette**.
26. Press the Enter key and then type **Moderated Environments**.
27. Click the New Slide button in the Slides group in the Home tab.
28. Click the placeholder text CLICK TO ADD TITLE and then type **policy issues**.
29. Click the placeholder text *Click to add text* and then type **Privacy Issues**.
30. Press the Enter key and then type **Security Protection**.
31. Press the Enter key and then type **Viruses**.
32. Press the Enter key and then type **Copyright Infringement**.
33. Click in the Slide pane but outside the slide. (This deselects the placeholder.)
34. Save the presentation by completing the following steps:
    a. Click the Save button on the Quick Access toolbar.
    b. At the Save As dialog box type **P-C1-P2-Internet** (for PowerPoint, Chapter 1, Project 2, and the topic of the presentation).
    c. Navigate to the PowerPoint2010C1 folder on your storage medium.
    d. Click the Save button.

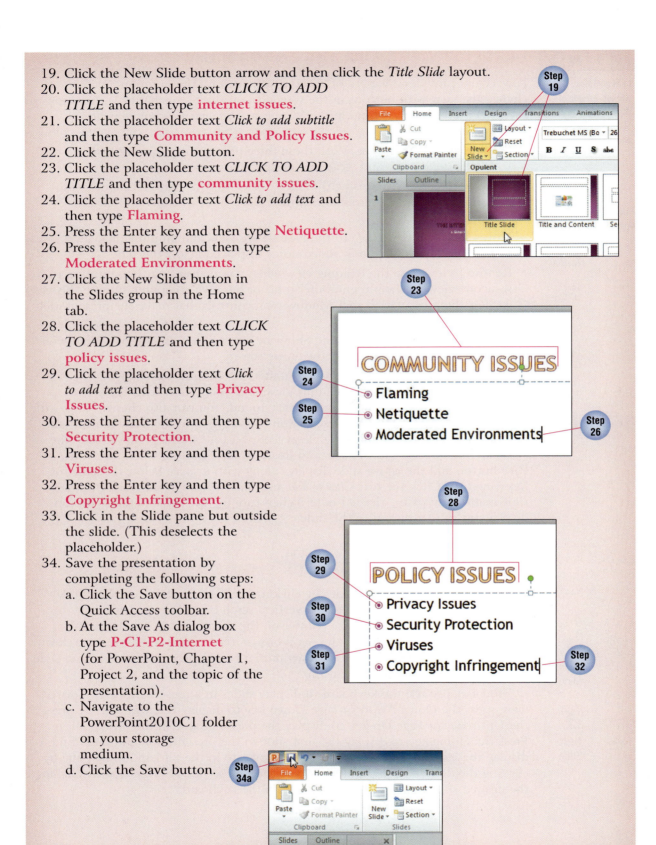

Chapter 1 ■ Preparing a PowerPoint Presentation

In Normal view, you can increase or decrease the size of the Slides/Outline pane and the Notes pane.

Changing Views

PowerPoint provides a variety of viewing options for a presentation. You can change the view with buttons in the view area on the Status bar or with options in the Presentation Views group in the View tab. The viewing choices include:

- **Normal view:** This is the default view and displays three panes — Slides/Outline, Slide, and Notes. With these three panes, you can work with all features in one place and write and design your presentation.
- **Slide Sorter view:** Choosing the Slide Sorter view displays all slides in the presentation in slide thumbnails. In this view, you can easily add, move, rearrange, and delete slides.
- **Notes Page view:** Change to the Notes Page view and an individual slide displays on a page with any added notes displayed below the slide.
- **Reading view:** Use the Reading view when you deliver your presentation to someone viewing the presentation on his or her own computer. Or, use this view to view the presentation in a window with controls that make the presentation easy to view.
- **Slide Show view:** Use the Slide Show view to run a presentation. When you choose this view, the slide fills the entire screen.

The view area on the Status bar contains four buttons for changing the view — Normal, Slide Sorter, Reading View, and Slide Show with the active button displaying with a light orange background. You can also change views with buttons in the View tab. The Presentation Views group in the View tab contains a number of buttons for changing views. Four buttons in the group include the Normal, Slide Sorter, Notes Page, and Reading View button. Click the Notes Page button and the active slide displays along with a space below the slide for inserting text. Click the text *Click to add text* that displays in the box below the slide and then type the desired note. When running the presentation, you can display any note attached to the slide.

Navigating in a Presentation

In the Normal view, change slides by clicking the Previous Slide or Next Slide buttons located at the bottom of the vertical scroll bar. You can also change to a different slide using the mouse pointer on the vertical scroll bar. To do this, position the mouse pointer on the scroll box on the vertical scroll bar, hold down the left mouse button, drag up or down until a box displays with the desired slide number, and then release the button.

Previous Slide

Next Slide

You can also use the keyboard to display slides in a presentation. In Normal view, press the Down Arrow or Page Down key to display the next slide or press the Up Arrow or Page Up key to display the previous slide in the presentation. Press the Home key to display the first slide in the presentation and press End to display the last slide in the presentation. Navigate in the Slides/Outline pane by clicking the desired slide thumbnail. Navigate in the Slide Sorter view by clicking the desired slide or using the arrow keys on the keyboard.

Project 2b Navigating and Editing Slides in a Presentation   Part 2 of 3

1. With **P-C1-P2-Internet.pptx** open, navigate in the presentation by completing the following steps:
   a. Make sure that a placeholder in the slide is not selected.
   b. Press the Home key to display Slide 1 in the Slide pane.
   c. Click the Next Slide button located toward the bottom of the vertical scroll bar.
   d. Press the End key to display the last slide in the Slide pane.
   e. Click the Slide Sorter button in the view area on the Status bar.

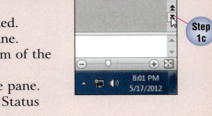

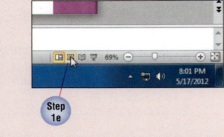

   f. Click Slide 1. (Notice that the active slide displays with an orange border.)
   g. Double-click Slide 5. (This closes Slide Sorter view and displays the presentation in Normal view with Slide 5 active.)
2. Insert text in slides by completing the following steps:
   a. Click on any character in the bulleted text. (This selects the placeholder.)
   b. Move the insertion point so it is positioned immediately right of *Flaming*.
   c. Press the Enter key and then type **Email Pointers**.

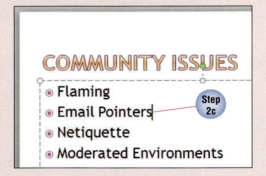

   d. Click Slide 3 in the Slides/Outline pane. (This displays Slide 3 in the Slide pane.)
   e. Click on any character in the bulleted text.
   f. Move the insertion point so it is positioned immediately right of *Video*.
   g. Press the Enter key and then type **Travel**.
3. Type a note in the Notes pane by completing the following steps:
   a. Click Slide 6 in the Slides/Outline pane.
   b. Click the text *Click to add notes* that displays in the Notes pane.

c. Type **Discuss the Digital Millennium Copyright Act of 1998.**

d. Display the slide in Notes Page view by clicking the View tab and then clicking the Notes Page button in the Presentation Views group. (Notice the note you typed displays below the slide in this view.)

e. Return to Normal view by clicking the Normal button in the view area on the Status bar.
f. Press the Home key to make Slide 1 the active slide.
4. Save the presentation by clicking the Save button on the Quick Access toolbar.

Printing and Previewing a Presentation

▼ Quick Steps

Print a Presentation
1. Click File tab.
2. Click Print tab.
3. Click Print button.

Printing a hard copy of your presentation and distributing it to your audience helps reinforce your message.

You can print a PowerPoint presentation in a variety of formats. You can print each slide on a separate piece of paper; print each slide at the top of the page, leaving the bottom of the page for notes; print a specific number of slides (up to nine slides) on a single piece of paper; or print the slide titles and topics in outline form. Use options in the Print tab in the Backstage view, shown in Figure 1.4, to specify what you want printed. To display options in the Print tab, click the File tab and then click the Print tab. You can also press Ctrl + P, which is the keyboard shortcut to display the Print tab Backstage view.

The left side of the Print tab Backstage view displays three categories—Print, Printer, and Settings. Click the Print button in the Print category to send the presentation to the printer and specify the number of copies you want printed with the *Copies* option. The two other categories contain galleries. For example, use the gallery in the Printer category to specify the desired printer. Click the first gallery in the Settings category and options display for specifying what you want printed such as all of the presentation or specific slides in the presentation. The Settings category also contains a number of galleries that describe how the slides will print.

In the Settings category, you can print a range of slides using the hyphen and print specific slides using a comma. For example, to print Slides 2 through 6, you would type *2-6* in the *Slides* text box. To print Slides 1, 3, and 7, you would type *1,3,7*. You can combine a hyphen and comma. For example, to print Slides 1 through 5 and Slide 8, you would type *1-5,8* in the *Slides* text box.

Figure 1.4 Print Tab Backstage View

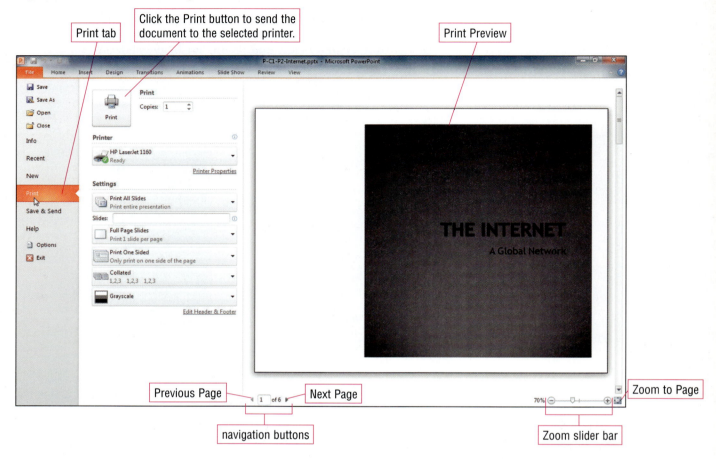

A preview of how a slide or slides will print displays at the right side of the Print tab Backstage view. If you have a color printer selected, the slide or slides that display at the right side of the Print tab Backstage view display in color, and if you have a black and white printer selected, the slide or slides will display in grayscale. Use the Next Page button (right-pointing arrow) located below and to the left of the page to view the next slide in the presentation, click the Previous Page button (left-pointing arrow) to display the previous slide in the presentation, use the Zoom slider bar to increase/decrease the size of the slide, and click the Zoom to Page button to fit the slide in the viewing area in the Print tab Backstage view.

You can choose to print a presentation as individual slides, handouts, notes pages, or an outline. If you print a presentation as handouts or an outline, PowerPoint will automatically print the current date in the upper right corner of the page and the page number in the lower right corner. If you print the presentation as notes pages, PowerPoint will automatically print the page number in the lower right corner. PowerPoint does not insert the date or page number when you print individual slides.

Project 2c — Printing a Presentation — Part 3 of 3

1. With **P-C1-P2-Internet.pptx** open, click the File tab and then click the Print tab.
2. Click twice on the Next Page button located below and to the left of the slide in the previewing area to display Slide 3 in the presentation.

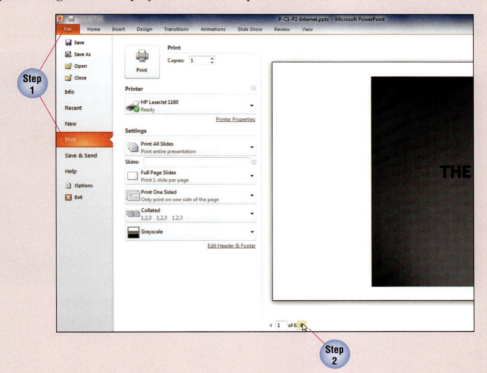

3. Click twice on the Previous Page button to display Slide 1.
4. Increase and decrease the zoom by completing the following steps:
    a. Position the mouse pointer on the Zoom slider bar button (located at the bottom right of the Print tab Backstage view), drag the button to the right to increase the size of the slide in the viewing area of the Print tab Backstage view, and then drag the slider bar to the left to decrease the size of the slide.
    b. Click the percentage number that displays at the left side of the Zoom slider bar. (This displays the Zoom dialog box.)
    c. Click the *50%* option in the Zoom dialog box and then click OK.
    d. Click the Zoom to Page button located to the right of the Zoom slider bar. (This increases the size of the slide to fill the viewing area in the Print tab Backstage view.)

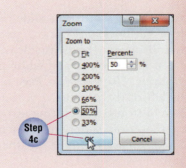

5. Print the presentation as a handout with six slides per page by completing the following steps:
   a. At the Print tab Backstage view, click the *Full Page Slides* option (the second gallery) in the Settings category and then click *6 Slides Horizontal* in the *Handouts* section.
   b. Click the Print button.

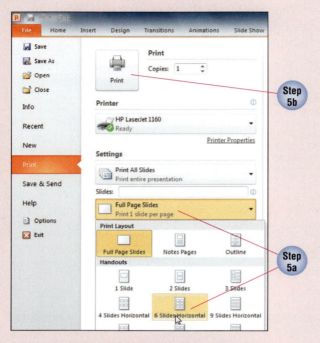

6. Print Slide 6 as a notes page by completing the following steps:
   a. Click the File tab and then click the Print tab at the Backstage view.
   b. At the Print tab Backstage view, click in the *Slides* text box located in the Settings category, and then type 6.
   c. Click the *6 Slides Horizontal* option in the Settings category and then click *Notes Pages* in the *Print Layout* section.
   d. Click the Print button.

Chapter 1 ■ Preparing a PowerPoint Presentation

7. Print Slides 1 through 3 and Slide 5 by completing the following steps:
   a. Click the File tab *and* then click the Print tab.
   b. At the Print tab Backstage view, click in the *Slides* text box located in the Settings category, and then type 1-3,5.
   c. Click the *Notes Pages* option in the Settings category and then click *4 Slides Horizontal* in the *Handouts* section.
   d. Click the Print button.

8. Close the presentation by clicking the File tab and then clicking the Close button.

Project 3   Create a Planning Presentation from an Existing Presentation   3 Parts

You will create a presentation from an existing presentation, apply a design theme to the presentation, run the presentation, and then delete the presentation.

Running a Slide Show

From Beginning

From Current Slide

As you learned earlier in this chapter, run a presentation by clicking the Slide Show button in the view area on the Status bar or by clicking the Slide Show tab and then clicking the From Beginning button in the Start Slide Show group. This group also contains a From Current Slide button. Use this button to begin running the slide show with the currently active slide rather than the first slide in the presentation.

PowerPoint offers a wide variety of options for navigating through slides in a presentation. You can click the left mouse button to advance slides in a presentation, right-click in a slide and then choose options from a shortcut menu, or use buttons on the Slide Show toolbar. The Slide Show toolbar displays in the lower left corner of a slide when you are running the presentation. Figure 1.5 identifies the Slide Show toolbar.

Figure 1.5 Slide Show Toolbar

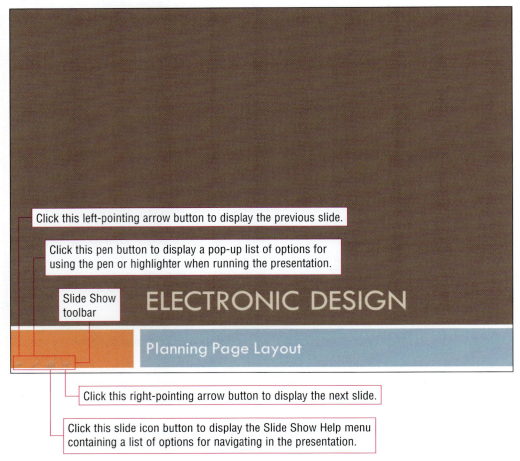

To display this toolbar, run the presentation and then move the mouse pointer over the buttons. Click the right arrow button on the toolbar to display the next slide and click the left arrow button to display the previous slide. Click the slide icon button and a pop-up list displays with the following options: *Next, Previous, Last Viewed, Go to Slide, Go to Section, Custom Show, Screen, Help, Pause*, and *End Show*. Use these options to navigate to a particular slide in the presentation, display the Slide Show Help window, and pause or end the show. If you click the *Help* option at the pop-up list, the Slide Show Help window displays as shown in Figure 1.6. This helpful window describes the various keyboard options available when running a presentation.

The Slide Show toolbar also contains a pen button. Click this button and a pop-up list displays with the following options: *Arrow, Pen, Highlighter, Ink Color, Eraser, Erase All Ink on Slide*, and *Arrow Options*. Click the desired option and then drag with the mouse in the slide to draw or erase content on the slide. For example, to draw in a slide with the mouse, click the pen button on the Slide Show toolbar and then click the *Pen* option at the pop-up list. This turns the arrow pointer into a small dot. Draw in the slide by dragging with the mouse.

▼ **Quick Steps**

Use Pen/Highlighter during Presentation
1. Run presentation.
2. Display desired slide.
3. Click pen button on Slide Show toolbar.
4. Click pen or highlighter option.
5. Drag to draw line or highlight text.

If you use the pen or highlighter on a slide when running a presentation, choose an ink color that the audience can see easily.

Figure 1.6 Slide Show Help Menu

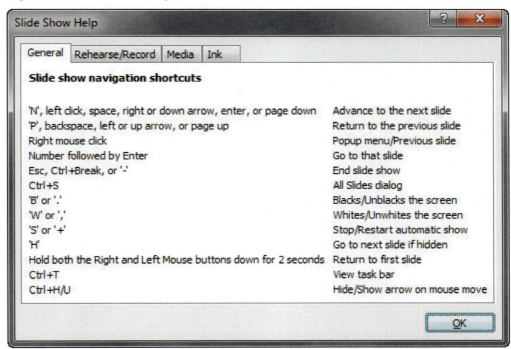

When running a presentation, the mouse pointer is set, by default, to be hidden automatically after three seconds of inactivity. The mouse pointer will appear again when you move the mouse. You can change this default setting by clicking the pen button on the Slide Show toolbar, pointing to *Arrow Options*, and then clicking *Visible* if you want the mouse pointer always visible or *Hidden* if you do not want the mouse to display at all as you run the presentation. The *Automatic* option is the default setting.

Creating a Presentation from an Existing Presentation

▼ **Quick Steps**

Create Presentation from an Existing Presentation
1. Click File tab, New tab.
2. Click *New from existing* option.
3. Double-click desired presentation.
4. Edit presentation.
5. Save presentation with new name.

You can create a presentation from an installed template, an installed theme, a blank presentation, or from an existing presentation. To create a presentation from an existing presentation, click the File tab and then click the New tab. At the New tab Backstage view, click the *New from existing* option in the Available Templates and Themes category. This displays the New from Existing Presentation dialog box with options similar to the Open dialog box. Double-click the desired presentation in the dialog box Content pane. This opens a new presentation based on the existing presentation and the Title bar displays *Presentation* followed by a number. Edit the presentation and then save the presentation with a new name.

Project 3a Creating and Running a Presentation from an Existing Presentation Part 1 of 3

1. Click the File tab and then click the New tab.
2. At the New tab Backstage view, click the *New from existing* option in the Available Templates and Themes category.
3. At the New from Existing Presentation dialog box, navigate to the PowerPoint2010C1 folder on your storage medium and then double-click ***PlanningPres.pptx***.
4. Save the presentation by completing the following steps:
   a. Click the Save button on the Quick Access toolbar.
   b. At the Save As dialog box, make sure the PowerPoint2010C1 folder on your storage medium is active and then type **P-C1-P3-PlanningPres** in the *File name* text box.
   c. Press Enter or click the Save button.
5. Run the presentation by completing the following steps:
   a. Click the Slide Show button in the view area on the Status bar.
   b. When Slide 1 fills the screen, move the mouse to display the Slide Show toolbar. (This toolbar displays in a dimmed manner in the lower left corner of the slide.)
   c. Click the button containing the right arrow. (This displays the next slide.)
   d. Continue clicking the button containing the right arrow until a black screen displays.
   e. Click the left mouse button. (This displays the presentation in Normal view.)
6. Run the presentation from the current slide and use the pen and highlighter to emphasize specific words by completing the following steps:
   a. Click Slide 2 in the Slides/Outline pane. (This makes Slide 2 active.)
   b. Click the Slide Show tab.
   c. Click the From Current Slide button in the Start Slide Show group.

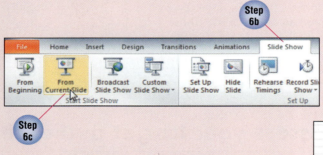

Step 5c

Step 6b

Step 6c

Step 6d2

   d. With Slide 2 active, use the pen to underline a word by completing the following steps:
   1) Move the mouse to display the Slide Show toolbar.
   2) Click the pen button on the Slide Show toolbar and then click *Pen* at the pop-up list. (This changes the mouse pointer to a small circle.)

Chapter 1 ■ Preparing a PowerPoint Presentation   23

3) Using the mouse, draw a circle around the text *STEP 1*.
4) Draw a line below the word *identify*.

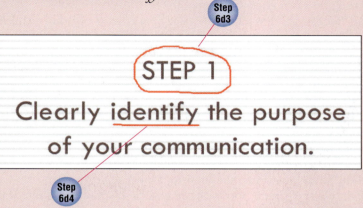

5) Click the pen button on the Slide Show toolbar and then click *Arrow* at the pop-up list. (This returns the mouse pointer to an arrow.)

e. Erase the pen markings by clicking the pen button on the Slide Show toolbar and then clicking *Erase All Ink on Slide* at the pop-up list.

f. Change the color of the pen ink by clicking the pen button, pointing to *Ink Color*, and then clicking the purple color (first option from the right in the bottom row).

g. Draw a circle around *STEP 1*.

h. Click the pen button on the Slide Show toolbar and then click *Arrow* at the pop-up list.

i. Click the left mouse button to display the next slide (Slide 3).

j. Click the pen button in the Slide Show toolbar and then click *Highlighter* at the pop-up list.

k. Drag through the word *target* to highlight it.

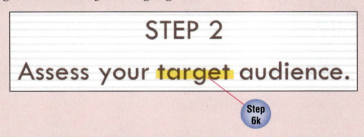

l. Click the button in the Slide Show toolbar containing the right arrow. (This displays Slide 4.)

m. Turn on the highlighter and then drag through the words *best format* to highlight them.

n. Click the pen button on the Slide Show toolbar and then click *Arrow* at the pop-up list.

7. Continue clicking the left mouse button to run the presentation.
8. At the black screen, click the left mouse button.
9. At the message asking if you want to keep your ink annotations, click the Discard button.
10. Save **P-C1-P3-PlanningPres.pptx**.

Applying a Design Theme

As you learned, PowerPoint provides a variety of predesigned theme templates you can use when creating slides for a presentation. You can choose a theme template at the New tab Backstage view or with options in the Themes group in the Design tab. Click the Design tab and theme thumbnails display in the Themes group. Click one of these themes to apply it to the current presentation. To display additional themes, click the More button that displays at the right side of the visible theme thumbnails. You can also click the up-pointing or down-pointing arrow at the right side of the theme thumbnails to scroll through the list. Hover your mouse pointer over a theme and the active slide in the presentation displays with the theme formatting applied. This is an example of the *live preview* feature, which allows you to see how theme formatting affects your presentation.

Themes similar to the ones available in PowerPoint are also available in Word, Excel, Access, and Outlook. When you hover the mouse pointer over a theme thumbnail, a ScreenTip displays (after approximately a second) containing the theme name. Theme names in PowerPoint are similar in Word, Excel, Access, and Outlook and apply similar formatting. With the availability of the themes across these applications, you can "brand" your business files such as documents, workbooks, and presentations with a consistent and uniform appearance.

▼ **Quick Steps**

Apply a Design Theme
1. Click Design tab.
2. Click desired theme in Themes group.

Design themes were designed by professional graphic artists who understand the use of color, space, and design.

More

Project 3b   Applying Design Themes   Part 2 of 3

1. With **P-C1-P3-PlanningPres.pptx** open, make Slide 1 active, and make sure the presentation displays in Normal view.
2. Apply a different design theme to the presentation by completing the following steps:
   a. Click the Design tab.
   b. Hover the mouse pointer over the third theme thumbnail in the Themes group and notice the theme formatting applied to the slide in the Slide pane.
   c. Click the More button located to the right of the theme thumbnails, hover the mouse pointer over the remaining visible theme thumbnails, and notice the formatting applied to the active slide.
   d. Click the *Civic* theme.

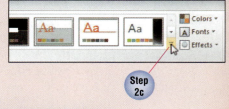
Step 2c

Step 2d

3. Run the presentation and notice the formatting applied by the theme.
4. With the presentation in Normal view, apply a different design theme by completing the following steps:
   a. Click the More button that displays at the right side of the theme thumbnails.
   b. Click *Verve* at the drop-down gallery.

5. Run the presentation.
6. Print the presentation as a handout by completing the following steps:
   a. Click the File tab and then click the Print tab.
   b. At the Print tab Backstage view, click the *Full Page Slides* option in the Settings category and then click *6 Slides Horizontal* in the *Handouts* section.
   c. Click the Print button.
7. Save and then close **P-C1-P3-PlanningPres.pptx**.

▼ Quick Steps

Delete Presentation
1. Click File tab.
2. Click Open button.
3. Navigate to desired folder or drive.
4. Click the presentation.
5. Click Organize button, *Delete*.
6. Click Yes.

Deleting a Presentation

File management tasks in PowerPoint can be performed at the Open or Save As dialog box. To delete a PowerPoint presentation, display the Open dialog box, click the presentation you want deleted, click the Organize button on the toolbar, and then click *Delete* at the drop-down list. At the message asking if you are sure you want to delete the presentation, click the Yes button. The presentation file must be closed to delete the file.

Project 3c — Deleting a PowerPoint Presentation — Part 3 of 3

1. Click the File tab and then click the Open button.
2. At the Open dialog box, make sure the PowerPoint2010C1 folder on your storage medium is the active folder, and then click **PlanningPres.pptx** in the Content pane.
3. Click the Organize button on the toolbar and then click *Delete* at the drop-down list.

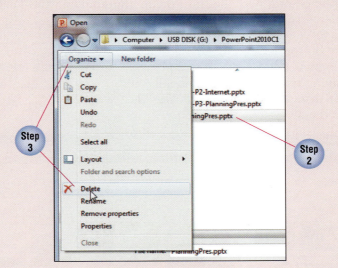

4. At the message asking if you are sure you want to delete the presentation, click Yes.
5. Click the Cancel button to close the Open dialog box.

Project 4 — Create a Technology Presentation in the Slides/Outline Pane

3 Parts

You will create a computer technology presentation in the Slides/Outline pane with the Outline tab selected, add and remove transitions and sounds to the presentation, and set up the presentation to advance slides automatically after a specified amount of time.

Preparing a Presentation from a Blank Presentation

When you first open PowerPoint, a blank presentation displays in which you can enter text in slides. You can also display a blank presentation by clicking the File tab and clicking the New tab. At the New tab Backstage view, click the *Blank presentation* option in the Available Templates and Themes category and then click the Create button that displays at the right side of the New tab Backstage view. You can also double-click *Blank presentation*.

▼ Quick Steps

Prepare a Presentation from a Blank Presentation
1. Click File tab.
2. Click New tab.
3. Click *Blank presentation* option.
4. Click Create button.

Create

Preparing a Presentation in the Slides/Outline Pane

In Normal view, you can enter text in a slide in the Slide pane and you can also enter text in a presentation in the Slides/Outline pane with the Outline tab selected. To create a slide in the Slides/Outline pane, click the Outline tab, click in the pane, and then type the text. Press the Tab key to move the insertion point to the next tab stop. This moves the insertion point and also changes the formatting. The formatting will vary depending on the theme you chose. Press Shift + Tab to move the insertion point to the previous tab stop and change the formatting. Moving the insertion point back to the left margin will begin another slide. Slides are numbered at the left side of the screen and are followed by a slide icon.

Project 4a — Preparing a Presentation in the Slides/Outline Pane

Part 1 of 3

1. At a blank screen, click the File tab and then click the New tab.
2. At the New tab Backstage view, double-click the *Blank presentation* option in the Available Templates and Themes category.
3. At the blank presentation, click the Outline tab in the Slides/Outline pane.

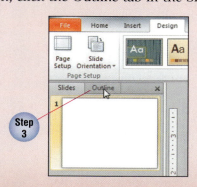

4. Click immediately right of the Slide 1 icon in the Slides/Outline pane, type the first slide title shown in Figure 1.7 *(Computer Technology)*, and then press Enter.
5. Type the second slide title shown in Figure 1.7 *(The Motherboard)* and then press Enter.
6. Press the Tab key, type the text after the first bullet in Figure 1.7 *(Buses)*, and then press Enter.
7. Continue typing the text as it displays in Figure 1.7. Press the Tab key to move the insertion point to the next tab stop or press Shift + Tab to move the insertion point back to a previous tab stop.

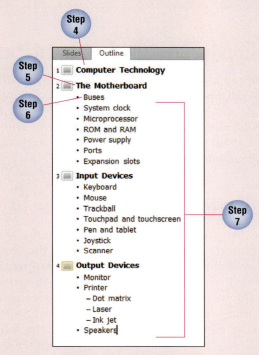

8. After typing all of the information as shown in Figure 1.7, click the Slides tab in the Slides/Outline tab.
9. Click Slide 1 in the Slides/Outline pane. (This displays Slide 1 in the Slide pane.)
10. Apply a design theme by completing the following steps:
    a. Click the Design tab.
    b. Click the More button that displays at the right side of the design theme thumbnails.
    c. Click *Hardcover* at the drop-down gallery.
11. Save the presentation with Save As and name it **P-C1-P4-Computers**.
12. Run the presentation.

Figure 1.7 Project 4a

```
1  Computer Technology
2  The Motherboard
     • Buses
     • System clock
     • Microprocessor
     • ROM and RAM
     • Power supply
     • Ports
     • Expansion slots
3  Input Devices
     • Keyboard
     • Mouse
     • Trackball
     • Touchpad and touchscreen
     • Pen and tablet
     • Joystick
     • Scanner
4  Output Devices
     • Monitor
     • Printer
         – Dot matrix
         – Laser
         – Ink jet
     • Speakers
```

Adding Transition and Sound Effects

You can apply interesting transitions and sounds to a presentation. A *transition* is how one slide is removed from the screen during a presentation and the next slide is displayed. You can apply transitions such as splits, fades, wipes, push, cover, reveal, and bar. To add transitions and sounds, open a presentation, and then click the Transitions tab. This displays transition buttons and options as shown in Figure 1.8.

Transitions and sounds apply by default to the active slide. If you want transitions and sound to affect all slides, click the Apply To All button in the Timing group. In Slide Sorter view, you can select all slides by pressing Ctrl + A (or by clicking the Home tab, clicking the Select button, and then clicking *Select All* at the drop-down list) and then apply the desired transition and/or sound.

Apply To All

Figure 1.8 Transitions Tab

Quick Steps

Apply Transition to Slides
1. Click Transitions tab.
2. Click desired transition in Transition to This Slide group.
3. Click Apply To All button.

Apply Sound to Slides
1. Click Transitions tab.
2. Click down-pointing arrow at right of *Sound* option.
3. Click desired sound.
4. Click Apply To All button.

Make a presentation more appealing by adding effects such as transitions and sounds.

Adding Transitions

To add a transition, click a transition thumbnail in the Transition to This Slide group in the Transitions tab. When you click a transition thumbnail, the transition displays in the slide in the Slide pane. Use the down-pointing and up-pointing arrows at the right side of the transition thumbnails to display additional transitions. Click the More button that displays at the right side of the visible transition thumbnails and a drop-down gallery displays with additional transition options. Use the *Duration* option to specify the duration slides transition when running the presentation. Click the up- or down-pointing arrow at the right side of the *Duration* option box to apply a duration time to slides. You can also select the current time in the text box and then type the desired time.

When you apply a transition to slides in a presentation, animation icons display below the slides in the Slides/Outline pane and in Slide Sorter view. Click an animation icon for a particular slide and the slide will display the transition effect.

Adding Sounds

As a slide is removed from the screen and another slide is displayed, you can add a sound. To add a sound, click the down-pointing arrow at the right side of the *Sound* option box and then click the desired sound at the drop-down gallery. If you have applied a transition to slides, you can hover your mouse pointer over a sound in the list box to hear the sound.

Removing Transitions and Sounds

You can remove a transition and sound from specific slides or from all slides in a presentation. To remove a transition, click the *None* transition thumbnail in the Transition to This Slide group. To remove transitions from all slides, click the Apply To All button in the Timing group. To remove sound from a slide, click the down-pointing arrow at the right side of the *Sound* option and then click *[No Sound]* at the drop-down gallery. To remove sound from all slides, click the Apply To All button.

Project 4b Adding Transitions and Sounds to a Presentation Part 2 of 3

1. With **P-C1-P4-Computers.pptx** open, click the Transitions tab.
2. Hover the mouse pointer over each of the transition thumbnails (except the first one) and notice how the transition displays in the slide in the Slide pane.
3. Apply transitions and sound to all slides in the presentation by completing the following steps:
   a. Click the More button at the right side of the transition thumbnails and then click the *Box* option in the *Exciting* section.

Step 3a

b. Click the Effect Options button in the Transition to This Slide group and then click *From Top* at the drop-down list.

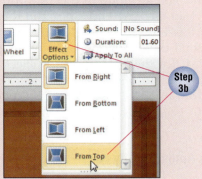

Step 3b

c. Click in the *Duration* option box in the Timing group, type 3, and then press Enter.
d. Click the down-pointing arrow at the right side of the *Sound* option box in the Timing group and then click *Chime* at the drop-down gallery.
e. Click the Apply To All button in the Timing group.

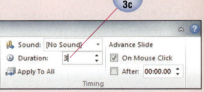

Step 3c

4. Run the presentation. (Notice the transitions and sounds as you move from slide to slide.)
5. With the presentation in Normal view and the Transitions tab active, remove the transitions and sound by completing the following steps:
   a. Click the More button at the right side of the transition thumbnails and then click the *None* option in the *Subtle* section.
   b. Click the down-pointing arrow at the right side of the *Sound* option box and then click *[No Sound]* at the drop-down gallery.
   c. Click the Apply To All button.

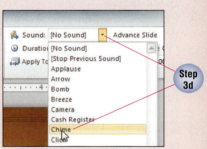

Step 3d

6. Apply transitions and sounds to specific slides by completing the following steps:
   a. Make sure the presentation displays in Normal view.
   b. Click Slide 1 in the Slides/Outline pane.
   c. Hold down the Shift key and then click Slide 2. (Slides 1 and 2 will display with orange backgrounds.)
   d. Click the More button at the right side of the transition thumbnails and then click a transition of your choosing.
   e. Click the down-pointing arrow at the right side of the *Sound* option box and then click a sound of your choosing.
   f. Click Slide 3 in the Slides/Outline pane.
   g. Hold down the Shift key and then click Slide 4.
   h. Click the More button at the right side of the transition thumbnails and then click a transition of your choosing.
   i. Click the down-pointing arrow at the right side of the *Sound* option box and then click a sound of your choosing.
7. Run the presentation from the beginning.
8. Remove the transitions and sounds from all slides. (Refer to Step 5.)
9. Save **P-C1-P4-Computers.pptx**.

▼ Quick Steps

Advance Slides Automatically
1. Click Transitions tab.
2. Click *After* check box.
3. Insert desired number of seconds in text box.
4. Click *On Mouse Click* check box.
5. Click Apply To All button.

Advancing Slides Automatically

You can advance slides in a slide show after a specific number of seconds with options in the Timing group in the Transitions tab. To advance slides automatically, click in the *After* check box and then insert the desired number of seconds in the text box. You can select the current time in the text box and then type the desired time or click the up- or down-pointing arrow to increase or decrease the time. Click the *On Mouse Click* check box to remove the check mark. If you want the transition time to affect all slides in the presentation, click the Apply To All button. In Slide Sorter view, the transition time displays below each affected slide.

Project 4c — Advancing Slides Automatically — Part 3 of 3

1. With **P-C1-P4-Computers.pptx** open, make sure the Transitions tab is active.
2. Click in the *After* check box in the Timing group to insert a check mark.
3. Click in the *On Mouse Click* check box to remove the check mark.
4. Click the up-pointing arrow at the right side of the *After* option box until *00:04.00* displays in the box.
5. Click the Apply To All button.
6. Run the presentation from the beginning. (Each slide will advance automatically after four seconds.)
7. At the black screen, click the left mouse button.
8. Print the presentation as an outline by completing the following steps:
   a. Click the File tab and then click the Print tab.
   b. At the Print tab Backstage view, click the *Full Page Slides* option in the Settings category and then click *Outline* in the *Print Layout* section.
   c. Click the Print button.
9. Save and then close **P-C1-P4-Computers.pptx**.

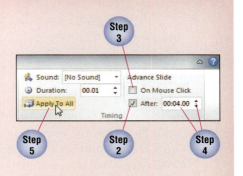

Chapter Summary

- PowerPoint is a software program you can use to create slides for an on-screen presentation.
- Open a presentation at the Open dialog box. Display this dialog box by clicking the File tab and then clicking the Open button.
- Predesigned presentation templates are available at the New tab Backstage view. Display this Backstage view by clicking the File tab and then clicking the New tab.
- Start running a presentation by clicking the Slide Show button in the view area on the Status bar or by clicking the View tab and then clicking the From Beginning button.

- Close a presentation by clicking the File tab and then clicking the Close button or with the keyboard shortcut, Ctrl + F4.
- Before creating a presentation in PowerPoint, plan the presentation by defining the purpose and determining the content and medium.
- You can use a predesigned theme template to create a presentation. A theme template provides slides with formatting such as color, background elements, and fonts.
- To insert text in a slide, click the desired placeholder and then type text.
- A slide layout provides placeholders for specific data in a slide. Choose a slide layout by clicking the Layout button in the Slides group in the Home tab.
- Insert a new slide in a presentation with the Title and Content layout by clicking the New Slide button in the Slides group in the Home tab. Insert a new slide with a specific layout by clicking the New Slide button arrow and then clicking the desired layout at the drop-down list.
- Save a presentation by clicking the Save button on the Quick Access toolbar or clicking the File tab and then clicking the Save As button. At the Save As dialog box, type a name for the presentation.
- View a presentation in one of the following five views: Normal view, which is the default and displays three panes — Slides/Outline, Slide, and Notes; Slide Sorter view, which displays all slides in the presentation in slide miniatures; Reading view when delivering a presentation to someone viewing it on his or her own computer; Notes Page view, which displays an individual slide with any added notes displayed below the slide; and Slide Show view, which runs the presentation.
- Navigate to various slides in a presentation using the mouse and/or keyboard. You can use the Previous Slide and Next Slide buttons located at the bottom of the vertical scroll bar, the scroll box on the vertical scroll bar, arrow keys on the keyboard, or the Page Up and Page Down buttons on the keyboard.
- Click the File tab and the Backstage view displays containing tabs and buttons for working with and managing presentations.
- With options at the Print tab Backstage view, you can print presentations with each slide on a separate piece of paper; each slide at the top of the page, leaving room for notes; all or a specific number of slides on a single piece of paper; or slide titles and topics in outline form.
- When running a presentation, the Slide Show toolbar displays in the lower left corner of the slide. This toolbar contains buttons and options for running a presentation. You can navigate to slides, make ink notations on slides, and display a Help menu. Click the slide show icon on the toolbar and then click *Help* and the Slide Show Help menu displays with options for using the keyboard to navigate in a presentation.
- Apply a design theme to a presentation by clicking the Design tab and then clicking the desired theme in the Themes group. Click the More button to display additional themes.
- Delete a presentation at the Open dialog box by clicking the presentation file name, clicking the Organize button on the toolbar, and then clicking *Delete* at the drop-down list.
- At the New tab Backstage view you can choose to prepare a presentation from an existing presentation or a blank presentation.

- You can type text in a slide in the Slide pane or in the Slides/Outline pane with the Outline tab selected.
- Enhance a presentation by adding transitions (how one slide is removed from the screen and replaced with the next slide) and sound. Add transitions and sound to a presentation with options in the Transitions tab.
- Advance slides automatically in a slide show by removing the check mark from the *On Mouse Click* check box in the Transitions tab, inserting a check mark in the *After* check box, and then specifying the desired time in the time option box.
- Click the Apply To All button to apply transitions, sounds, and/or time settings to all slides in a presentation.

Commands Review

FEATURE	RIBBON TAB, GROUP	BUTTON, OPTION	KEYBOARD SHORTCUT
Open dialog box	File	Open	Ctrl + O
New tab Backstage view	File	New	
Run presentation	Slide Show, Start Slide Show		F5
Close presentation	File	Close	Ctrl + F4
Slide layout	Home, Slides		
New slide	Home, Slides		Ctrl + M
Save As dialog box	File		Ctrl + S
Normal view	View, Presentation Views		
Slide Sorter view	View, Presentation Views		
Notes page	View, Presentation Views		
Print tab Backstage view	File	Print	Ctrl + P
Design theme	Design, Themes		
Transition	Transitions, Transition to This Slide		
Sound	Transitions, Timing		
Transition duration	Transitions, Timing		

Concepts Check Test Your Knowledge

Completion: In the space provided at the right, indicate the correct term, command, or number.

1. Click this tab to display tabs and buttons for working with presentations. _____

2. This toolbar contains buttons for commonly used commands. _____

3. This area contains the tabs and commands divided into groups. _____

4. Display installed templates in this Backstage view tab. _____

5. This is the keyboard shortcut to close a presentation. _____

6. Apply a theme template to a presentation by clicking this tab and then clicking the desired theme in the Themes group. _____

7. Insert a new slide by clicking the New Slide button in this group in the Home tab. _____

8. Change to this view to view displays of all slides in the presentation in slide thumbnails. _____

9. This is the default view and displays three panes. _____

10. The Previous Slide and Next Slide buttons display in this location. _____

11. To run a presentation beginning with Slide 1, click this button in the Slide Show tab. _____

12. In Normal view, you can enter text in a slide in this pane or in the Slides/Outline pane with the Outline tab selected. _____

13. To add a transition, click a transition thumbnail in the Transition to This Slide group in this tab. _____

14. When you apply a transition to slides in a presentation, these display below the slides in the Slides/Outline pane. _____

15. To advance slides automatically, remove the check mark from the *On Mouse Click* option, insert a check mark in this option, and then insert the desired number of seconds. _____

Skills Check Assess Your Performance

Assessment

1 CREATE A DEDUCTIBLE INCOME EXCEPTIONS PRESENTATION

1. Create a presentation with the text shown in Figure 1.9 by completing the following steps:
   a. With PowerPoint open, click the File tab and then click the New tab.
   b. At the New tab Backstage view, click the *Themes* option, and then double-click *Waveform* in the list box. (You may need to scroll down the list to display this theme.)
   c. Create slides with the text shown in Figure 1.9. Choose the *Title Slide* layout when inserting new slides.
2. Save the completed presentation in the PowerPoint2010C1 folder on your storage medium and name the presentation **P-C1-A1-Income**.
3. Apply the *Blinds* transition with a *Vertical* effect to all slides in the presentation.
4. Change the transition speed to *02.00*.
5. Apply the *Laser* sound to all slides in the presentation.
6. Run the presentation.
7. Print the presentation as a handout with six slides horizontally per page.
8. Save and then close **P-C1-A1-Income.pptx**.

Figure 1.9 Assessment 1

Slide 1	Title	=	DEDUCTIBLE INCOME
	Subtitle	=	Exceptions to Deductible Income
Slide 2	Title	=	EXCEPTION 1
	Subtitle	=	Any cost of living increase if increase becomes effective while disabled
Slide 3	Title	=	EXCEPTION 2
	Subtitle	=	Reimbursement for hospital, medical, or surgical expense
Slide 4	Title	=	EXCEPTION 3
	Subtitle	=	Reasonable attorney's fees incurred in connection with a claim for deductible income
Slide 5	Title	=	EXCEPTION 4
	Subtitle	=	Benefits from any individual disability insurance policy
Slide 6	Title	=	EXCEPTION 5
	Subtitle	=	Group credit or mortgage disability insurance benefits

Assessment

2 CREATE A PRESENTATION ON PREPARING A COMPANY NEWSLETTER

1. At the blank screen, click the File tab and then click the New tab.
2. At the New tab Backstage view, double-click the *Blank presentation* option in the Available Templates and Themes category.
3. Create slides with the text shown in Figure 1.10.
4. Apply a design theme of your choosing.
5. Run the presentation.
6. Print the presentation as a handout with six slides horizontally per page.
7. Make the following changes to the presentation:
   a. Apply a different design theme.
   b. Add a transition of your choosing to all slides.
   c. Add a sound of your choosing to all slides.
   d. Specify that all slides advance automatically after five seconds.
8. Run the presentation.
9. Save the presentation and name it **P-C1-A2-Newsletter**.
10. Close **P-C1-A2-Newsletter.pptx**.

Visual Benchmark — Demonstrate Your Proficiency

CREATE A PRESENTATION ON PREPARING A NEWSLETTER

1. Create the presentation shown in Figure 1.11 with the following specifications:
   a. At a blank presentation, apply the *Austin* theme.
   b. Create the slides as shown in the figure (reading from left to right).
   c. Apply a transition, sound, and transition duration time of your choosing to each slide in the presentation.
2. Save the completed presentation and name it **P-C1-VB-Interview**.
3. Run the presentation.
4. Print the presentation as a handout with all six slides printed horizontally on the page.
5. Close the presentation.

Figure 1.10 Assessment 2

| Slide 1 | Title | = | PREPARING A COMPANY NEWSLETTER |
| | Subtitle | = | Planning and Designing the Layout |

Slide 1   Title = PREPARING A COMPANY NEWSLETTER
              Subtitle = Planning and Designing the Layout

Slide 2   Title = Planning a Newsletter
              Bullets =
- If a scanner is available, use pictures of different people from your organization in each issue.
- Distribute contributor sheets soliciting information from employees.
- Keep the focus of the newsletter on issues of interest to employees.

Slide 3   Title = Planning a Newsletter
              Bullets =
- Make sure the focus is on various levels of employment; do not focus on top management only.
- Conduct regular surveys to see if your newsletter provides a needed source of information.

Slide 4   Title = Designing a Newsletter
              Bulllets =
- Maintain consistent elements from issue to issue such as:
  - Column layout
  - Nameplate formatting and location
  - Formatting of headlines
  - Use of color

Slide 5   Title = Designing a Newsletter
              Bullets =
- Consider the following elements when designing a newsletter:
  - Focus
  - Balance
  - White space
  - Directional flow

Slide 6   Title = Creating a Newsletter Layout
              Bullets =
- Choose paper size
- Choose paper weight
- Determine margins
- Specify column layout

Figure 1.11 Visual Benchmark

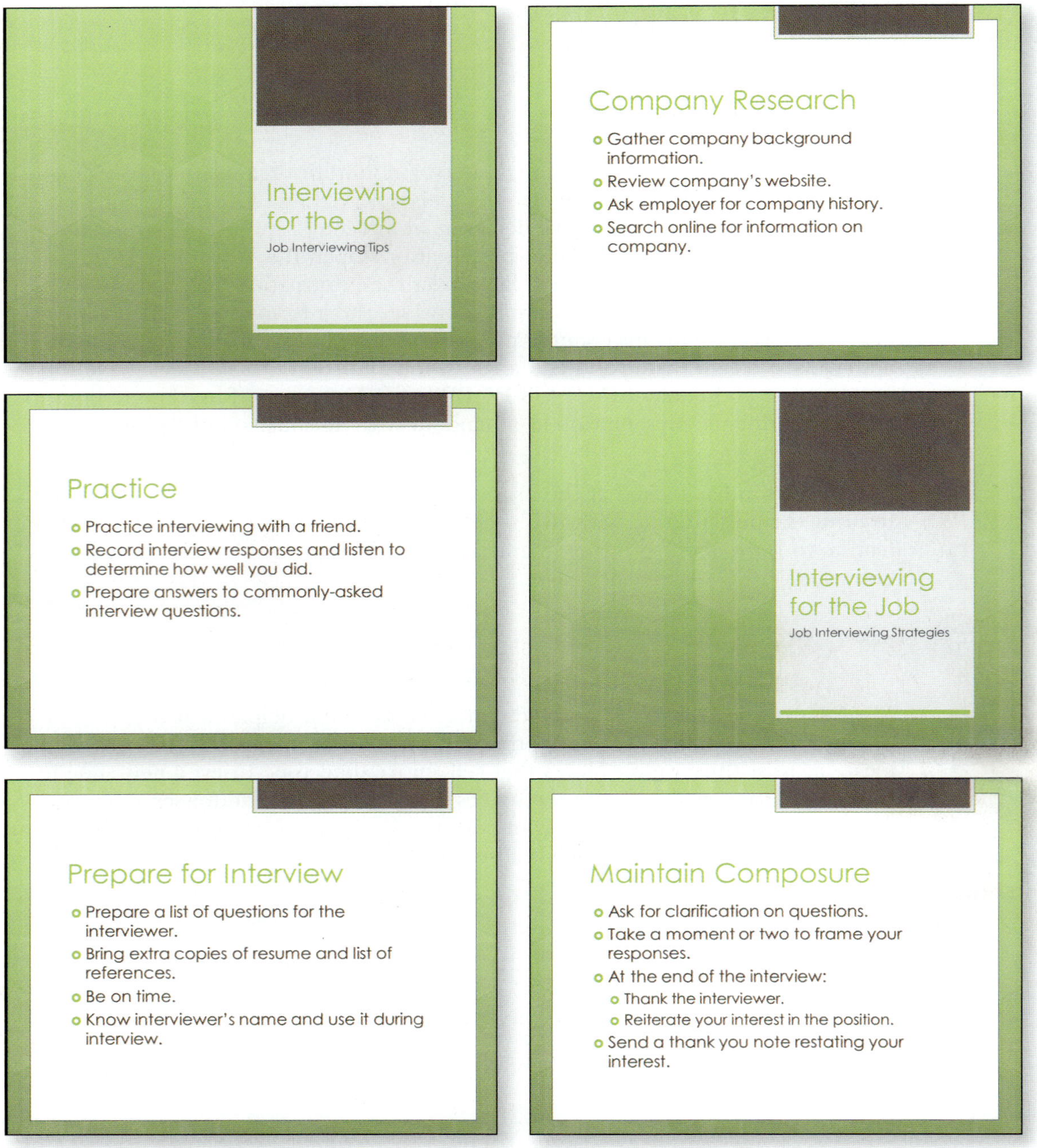

Case Study Apply Your Skills

Part 1

You work for Citizens for Consumer Safety, a nonprofit organization providing information on household safety. Your supervisor, Melinda Johansson, will be presenting information on smoke detectors at a community meeting and has asked you to prepare a PowerPoint presentation. Open the Word document named **PPSmokeDetectors.docx**. Read over the information and then use the information to prepare a presentation. Consider the information in the *Planning a Presentation* section of this chapter and then prepare at least five slides. Apply an appropriate design theme and add a transition and sound to all slides. Save the presentation and name it **P-C1-CS-P1-PPSmokeDetectors**. Run the presentation and then print the presentation as a handout with all slides on one page.

Part 2

Ms. Johansson has looked at the printout of the presentation and has asked you to print the presentation with two slides per page and in grayscale. Use the Help feature to learn about printing in grayscale and then print the presentation in grayscale with two slides per page.

Part 3

Ms. Johansson would like to provide information to participants at the presentation on online companies that sell smoke detectors. Using the Internet, locate at least three online stores that sell smoke detectors. Insert a new slide in the presentation that includes the names of the stores, web addresses, and any additional information you feel is important. Save the presentation and then print the presentation in Outline view. Close the presentation.

Microsoft® PowerPoint®

Modifying a Presentation and Using Help

CHAPTER 2

PERFORMANCE OBJECTIVES

Upon successful completion of Chapter 2, you will be able to:
- Check spelling
- Insert and delete text in slides
- Find and replace text in slides
- Cut, copy, and paste text in slides
- Rearrange text in the Slides/Outline pane
- Size and rearrange placeholders
- Insert, delete, move, and copy slides
- Copy slides between presentations
- Duplicate slides
- Reuse slides
- Use the Help feature

When preparing a presentation, you may need to modify a presentation by inserting and deleting text in slides or finding and replacing specific text. Improve the quality of your presentation by completing a spelling check to ensure that the words in your presentation are spelled correctly. Additional modifications you may need to make to a presentation include sizing and rearranging placeholders and rearranging, inserting, deleting, or copying slides. In this chapter, you will learn how to make these modifications to a presentation as well as how to preview a presentation and use the Help feature. Model answers for this chapter's projects appear on the following pages.

Note: Before beginning the projects, copy to your storage medium the PowerPoint2010C2 subfolder from the PowerPoint2010 folder on the CD that accompanies this textbook and then make PowerPoint2010C2 the active folder.

Model Answers

Project 1 Check Spelling and Manage Text in a Design Presentation P-C2-P1-ElectronicDesign.pptx

Project 2 Cut, Copy, paste, Rearrange, and Manage Slides in a Network Presentation P-C2-P2-NetworkSystem.pptx

Project 3 Insert and Manage Slides in an Adventure Tours Presentation P-C2-P3-AdvTours.pptx

Project 4 Use PowerPoint Help Feature and Create a Presentation P-C2-P4-Shortcuts.pptx

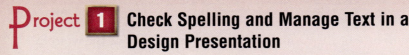

Project 1 **Check Spelling and Manage Text in a Design Presentation** 3 Parts

You will open a presentation on steps for planning a design publication, complete a spelling check on the text in the presentation, and find and replace specific text in slides.

Checking Spelling

When preparing a presentation, perform a spelling check on text in slides using PowerPoint's spelling feature. The spelling feature compares words in slides in a presentation with words in its dictionary. If a match is found, the word is passed over. If a match is not found, the spelling checker selects the word and offers replacement suggestions. To perform a spelling check on a PowerPoint presentation, click the Review tab and then click the Spelling button in the Proofing group. You can also start the spelling checker by pressing the F7 function key on the keyboard.

When you begin spell checking text in a presentation in Project 1a, the spelling checker will stop at the misspelled word *Layuot* and display the Spelling dialog box as shown in Figure 2.1. The options available in the Spelling dialog box are described in Table 2.1.

▼ **Quick Steps**

Complete a Spelling Check
1. Click Review tab.
2. Click Spelling button.
3. Change or ignore errors.
4. Click OK.

Spelling

Chapter 2 ■ Modifying a Presentation and Using Help

Figure 2.1 Spelling Dialog Box

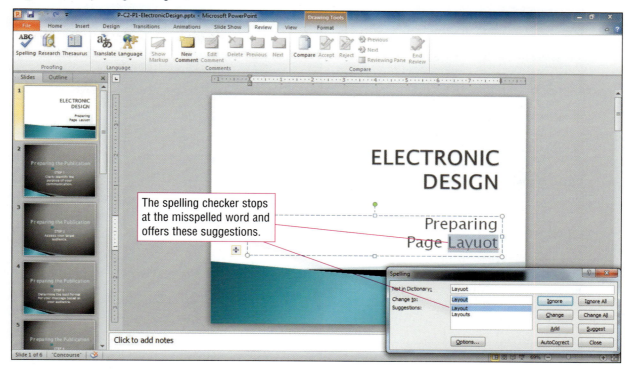

Table 2.1 Spelling Dialog Box Options

Button	Function
Ignore	Skips that occurrence of the word.
Ignore All	Skips that occurrence of the word and all other occurrences of the word in slides.
Change	Replaces selected word in slide with selected word in *Suggestions* list box.
Change All	Replaces selected word in slide with selected word in *Suggestions* list box and all other occurrences of the word.
Add	Adds selected word to the main spelling check dictionary.
Suggest	Makes active the first suggestion in the *Suggestions* list box.
AutoCorrect	Inserts selected word and correct spelling of word in AutoCorrect dialog box.
Close	Closes the Spelling dialog box.
Options	Displays PowerPoint Options dialog box with *Proofing* selected that contains options for customizing a spelling check.

Project 1a — Checking the Spelling in a Presentation — Part 1 of 3

1. Open **ElectronicDesign.pptx** and then save the presentation with Save As and name it **P-C2-P1-ElectronicDesign**.
2. With the presentation in Normal view, complete a spelling check by completing the following steps:
   a. Click the Review tab.
   b. Click the Spelling button in the Proofing group.
   c. When the spelling checker selects the misspelled word *Layuot* and displays the correct spelling (*Layout*) in the *Change to* text box, click the Change button (or Change All button).
   d. When the spelling checker selects the misspelled word *Clerly* and displays the correct spelling (*Clearly*) in the *Change to* text box, click the Change button (or Change All button).

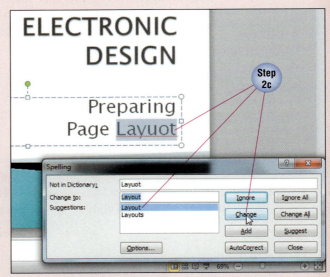

   e. When the spelling checker selects the misspelled word *massege*, click *message* in the *Suggestions* list box and then click the Change button (or Change All button).

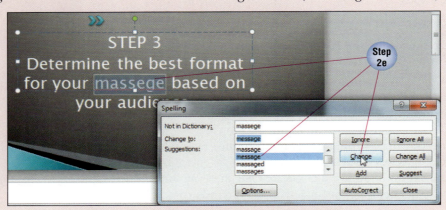

   f. When the spelling checker selects the misspelled word *fo* and displays the correct spelling (*of*) in the *Change to* text box, click the Change button.
   g. At the message telling you that the spelling check is complete, click the OK button.
3. Save **P-C2-P1-ElectronicDesign.pptx**.

Managing Text in Slides

As you enter text in slides or as you manage existing slides, you may need to edit, move, copy, or delete text from slides. You may also want to find specific text in slides and replace it with other text. Text is generally inserted in a slide placeholder and this placeholder can be moved, sized, and/or deleted.

Inserting and Deleting Text in Slides

To insert or delete text in an individual slide, open the presentation, edit the text as needed, and then save the presentation again. If you want to delete more than an individual character, consider selecting the text first. Several methods can be used for selecting text as shown in Table 2.2.

Text in a slide is positioned inside of a placeholder. Slide layouts provide placeholders for text and generally display with a message suggesting the type of text to be entered in the slide. For example, the Title and Content slide layout contains a placeholder with the text *Click to add title* and another with the text *Click to add text*. Click placeholder text and the insertion point is positioned inside the placeholder, the default text is removed, and the placeholder is selected.

Table 2.2 Selecting Text

To do this	Perform this action
Select text mouse pointer passes through	Click and drag mouse
Select entire word	Double-click word
Select entire paragraph	Triple-click anywhere in paragraph
Select entire sentence	Ctrl + click anywhere in sentence
Select all text in selected placeholder	Click Select, Select All or press Ctrl + A

Project 1b Inserting and Deleting Text in Slides   Part 2 of 3

1. With **P-C2-P1-ElectronicDesign.pptx** open and the presentation in Normal view, click the Previous Slide button (or Next Slide button) located at the bottom of the vertical scroll bar until Slide 5 displays.
2. Edit Slide 5 by completing the following steps:
    a. Position the I-beam pointer on the sentence below *STEP 4* and then click the left mouse button. (This selects the placeholder.)
    b. Edit the sentence so it reads *Decide what steps you want readers to take after reading the message.* (Use deleting and inserting commands to edit this sentence.)

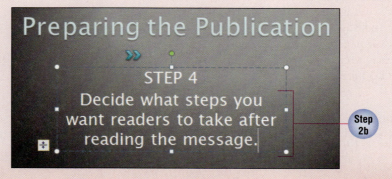

3. Click the Next Slide button to display Slide 6 and then edit Slide 6 in the Slides/Outline pane by completing the following steps:
   a. Click the Outline tab in the Slides/Outline pane.
   b. Click in the sentence below *STEP 5* and then edit the sentence so it reads *Collect and assess examples of effective designs*.
   c. Click the Slides tab.
4. Save **P-C2-P1-ElectronicDesign.pptx**.

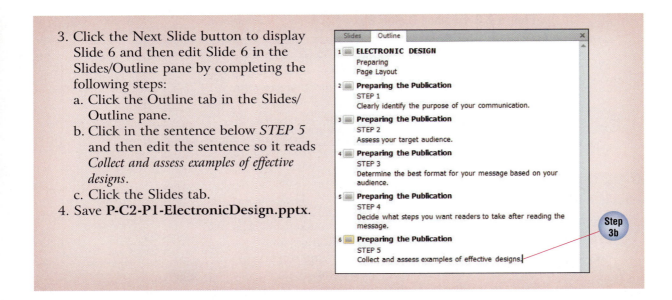

Finding and Replacing Text in Slides

Use the find feature to look for specific text in slides in a presentation and use the find and replace feature to look for specific text in slides in a presentation and replace with other text. Begin a find by clicking the Find button in the Editing group in the Home tab. This displays the Find dialog box shown in Figure 2.2. In the *Find what* text box, type the text you want to find and then click the Find Next button. Continue clicking this button until a message displays telling you that the search is complete. At this message, click OK.

Use options at the Replace dialog box shown in Figure 2.3 to search for text and replace it with other text. Display this dialog box by clicking the Replace button in the Home tab. Type the text you want to find in the *Find what* text box, press the Tab key, and then type the replacement text in the *Replace with* text box. Click the Find Next button to find the next occurrence of the text or click the Replace All button to replace all occurrences in the presentation.

Both the Find and Replace dialog boxes contain two additional options for conducting a find and a find and replace. Insert a check mark in the *Match case* check box to specify that the text should exactly match the case of the text entered in the *Find what* text box. For example, if you search for *Planning*, PowerPoint will stop at *Planning* but not *planning* or *PLANNING*. Insert a check mark in the *Find whole words only* check box to specify that the text is a whole word and not part of a word. For example, if you search for *plan*, and did not check the *Find whole words only* option, PowerPoint would stop at ex*plan*ation, *plan*ned, *plan*et, and so on.

Quick Steps

Find Text
1. Click Find button.
2. Type text for which you are searching.
3. Click Find Next button.

Replace Text
1. Click Replace button.
2. Type text for which you are searching.
3. Press Tab key.
4. Type replacement text.
5. Click Replace All button.

Find

Replace

Figure 2.2 Find Dialog Box

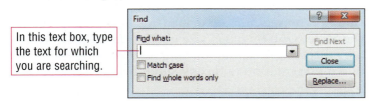

Figure 2.3 Replace Dialog Box

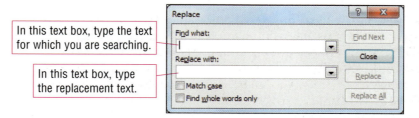

In this text box, type the text for which you are searching.

In this text box, type the replacement text.

Project 1c Finding and Replacing Text Part 3 of 3

1. With **P-C2-P1-ElectronicDesign.pptx** open, make Slide 1 active.
2. Find all occurrences of *Preparing* in the presentation and replace with *Planning* by completing the following steps:
   a. With Slide 1 active, click the Replace button in the Editing group in the Home tab.
   b. At the Replace dialog box, type **Preparing** in the *Find what* text box.
   c. Press the Tab key.
   d. Type **Planning** in the *Replace with* text box.
   e. Click the Replace All button.
   f. At the message telling you that 6 replacements were made, click OK.
   g. Click the Close button to close the Replace dialog box.
3. Find all occurrences of *Publication* and replace with *Newsletter* by completing steps similar to those in Step 2.
4. Save the presentation.
5. Apply a transition and sound of your choosing to all slides in the presentation.
6. Run the presentation.
7. Print Slide 1 by completing the following steps:
   a. Click the File tab and then click the Print tab.
   b. At the Print tab Backstage view, click in the *Slides* text box in the Settings category and then type **1**.
   c. Click the Print button.
8. Print the presentation as a handout with 6 slides horizontally per page. (Change the second gallery in the Settings category to *6 Slides Horizontal* and delete the *1* in the *Slides* text box.)
9. Save and then close **P-C2-P1-ElectronicDesign.pptx**.

Project 2 Cut, Copy, Paste, Rearrange, and Manage Slides in a Network Presentation 5 Parts

You will open a network evaluation presentation and then cut, copy, and paste text in slides; rearrange text in the Slides/Outline pane; size and rearrange placeholders in slides; and manage slides by inserting, deleting, moving, and copying slides. You will also create sections within a presentation and copy slides between presentations.

Cutting, Copying, and Pasting Text in Slides

With buttons in the Clipboard group in the Home tab and also with shortcut menu options, you can cut, copy, and/or paste text in slides. For example, to move text in a slide, click once in the placeholder containing the text to be moved, select the text, and then click the Cut button in the Clipboard group. Position the insertion point where you want the text inserted and then click the Paste button in the Clipboard group. To cut and paste with the shortcut menu, select the text you want to move, right-click the text, and then click *Cut* at the shortcut menu. Position the insertion point where you want the text inserted, right-click the location, and then click *Paste* at the shortcut menu. Complete similar steps to copy and paste text except click the Copy button instead of the Cut button or click the *Copy* option at the shortcut menu instead of the *Cut* option.

Ctrl + X is the keyboard shortcut to cut selected text, Ctrl + C is the keyboard shortcut to copy selected text, and Ctrl + V is the keyboard shortcut to paste cut or copied text.

 Cut

 Copy

 Paste

Project 2a — Cutting, Copying, and Pasting Text in Slides — Part 1 of 5

1. Open **NetworkSystem.pptx** located in the PowerPoint2010C2 folder on your storage medium and then save the presentation with Save As and name it **P-C2-P2-NetworkSystem**.
2. Insert a new slide by completing the following steps:
   a. Make Slide 4 active.
   b. Click the New Slide button in the Slides group in the Home tab.
   c. Click in the *Click to add title* placeholder and then type **TIME**.
3. Cut text from Slide 3 and paste it into Slide 5 by completing the following steps:
   a. Make Slide 3 active.
   b. Click on any character in the bulleted text (in the Slide pane).
   c. Using the mouse, select the text following the bottom three bullets. (The bullets will not be selected.)
   d. With the text selected, click the Cut button in the Clipboard group in the Home tab.

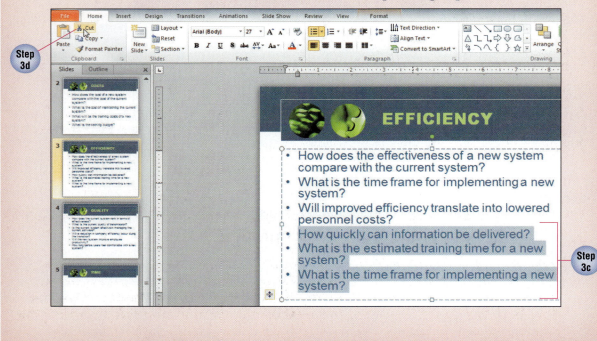

Chapter 2 ■ Modifying a Presentation and Using Help   49

e. Make Slide 5 the active slide (contains the title *TIME*).
f. Click in the *Click to add text* placeholder.
g. Click the Paste button in the Clipboard group.
h. If the insertion point is positioned below the third bulleted item following a bullet, press the Backspace key twice. (This removes the bullet and deletes the blank line below the bullet.)

4. Insert a new slide by completing the following steps:
   a. With Slide 5 the active slide, click the New Slide button in the Slides group in the Home tab.
   b. Click in the *Click to add title* placeholder and then type **EASE OF USE**.

5. Cut text from Slide 4 and paste it into Slide 6 by completing the following steps:
   a. Make Slide 4 active.
   b. Click on any character in the bulleted text.
   c. Select the text following the bottom three bullets.
   d. Click the Cut button in the Clipboard group in the Home tab.
   e. Make Slide 6 active (contains the title *EASE OF USE*).
   f. Click in the *Click to add text* placeholder.
   g. Click the Paste button in the Clipboard group.
   h. If the insertion point is positioned below the third bulleted item following a bullet, press the Backspace key twice.

6. Copy text from Slide 3 to Slide 5 by completing the following steps:
   a. Make Slide 3 active.
   b. Click on any character in the bulleted text.
   c. Position the mouse pointer on the last bullet until the pointer turns into a four-headed arrow and then click the left mouse button. (This selects the text following the bullet.)

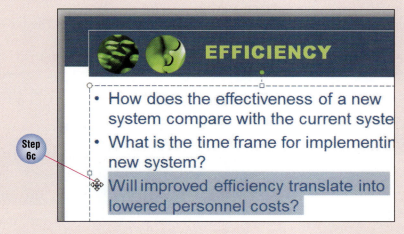

   d. Click the Copy button in the Clipboard group.
   e. Make Slide 5 active.
   f. Click in the bulleted text and then move the insertion point so it is positioned immediately right of the question mark in the second bulleted item.

g. Press the Enter key. (This moves the insertion point down to the next line and inserts another bullet.)
h. Click the Paste button in the Clipboard group.

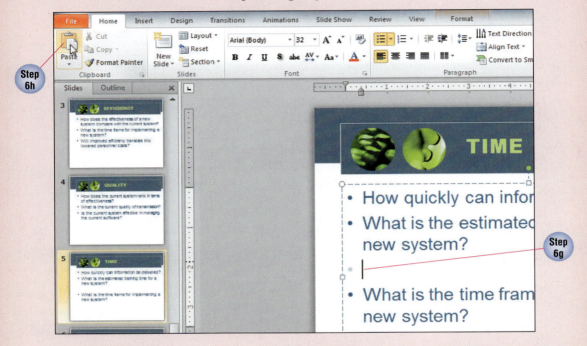

i. If a blank line is inserted between the third and fourth bullets, press the Backspace key twice.
7. Save **P-C2-P2-NetworkSystem.pptx**.

Rearranging Text in the Slides/Outline Pane

You can use the mouse to move text in the Slides/Outline pane with the Outline tab selected. To do this, position the mouse pointer on the slide icon or bullet at the left side of the text until the arrow pointer turns into a four-headed arrow. Hold down the left mouse button, drag the arrow pointer (a thin horizontal line displays) to the desired location, and then release the mouse button.

If you position the arrow pointer on the slide icon and then hold down the left mouse button, all of the text in the slide is selected. If you position the arrow pointer on the bullet and then hold down the left mouse button, all text following that bullet is selected.

Dragging selected text with the mouse moves the selected text to a new location in the presentation. You can also copy selected text. To do this, click the slide icon or click the bullet to select the desired text. Position the arrow pointer in the selected text, hold down the Ctrl key, and then the left mouse button. Drag the arrow pointer (displays with a light gray box and a plus sign attached) to the desired location, release the mouse button, and then release the Ctrl key.

Press Ctrl + Shift + Tab to switch between the Slides and Outline tabs in the Slides/Outline pane.

Project 2b — Rearranging Text in the Slides/Outline Pane — Part 2 of 5

1. With **P-C2-P2-NetworkSystem.pptx** open, make Slide 1 active.
2. Click the Outline tab in the Slides/Outline pane.
3. Move the first bulleted item in Slide 4 to the end of the list by completing the following steps:
   a. Position the mouse pointer on the first bullet below *QUALITY* until it turns into a four-headed arrow.
   b. Hold down the left mouse button, drag the arrow pointer down until a thin horizontal line displays below the last bulleted item, and then release the mouse button.
4. Copy and paste text by completing the following steps:
   a. In the Slides/Outline pane, move the insertion point to the end of the text in Slide 6 and then press the Enter key. (This inserts a new bullet in the slide.)
   b. Scroll up the Slides/Outline pane until the last bulleted item in Slide 2 is visible in the Slides/Outline pane as well as the last bullet in Slide 6.
   c. Position the mouse pointer on the fourth bullet below *COSTS* until it turns into a four-headed arrow and then click the left mouse button. (This selects the text.)
   d. Position the mouse pointer in the selected text, hold down the left mouse button, hold down the Ctrl key, and then drag down until the arrow pointer and light blue vertical line display on the blank line below the text in Slide 6.
   e. Release the mouse button and then release the Ctrl key.
5. Click the Slides tab in the Slides/Outline pane.
6. Save **P-C2-P2-NetworkSystem.pptx**.

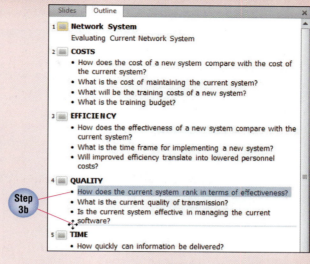

Step 3b

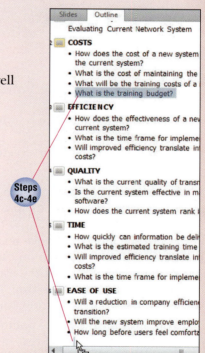

Steps 4c-4e

Sizing and Rearranging Placeholders in a Slide

Click inside a placeholder to select it and white sizing handles and a green rotation handle display around the placeholder border. With the sizing handles, you can increase or decrease the size of the placeholder. You can also move a placeholder by dragging it with the mouse. Increase or decrease the size of a placeholder by positioning the arrow pointer on a sizing handle until the pointer

turns into a double-headed arrow and then dragging the placeholder border to the desired size. To move a placeholder, position the arrow pointer on the placeholder border until the arrow pointer displays with a four-headed arrow attached. Hold down the left mouse button, drag the outline of the placeholder to the desired position, and then release the mouse button.

Dragging a selected placeholder with the mouse moves the placeholder. If you want to copy a placeholder, hold down the Ctrl key while dragging the placeholder. When the outline of the placeholder is in the desired position, release the mouse button, and then release the Ctrl key. If you make a change to the size and/or location of a placeholder, click the Reset button in the Slides group in the Home tab to return the formatting of the placeholder back to the default.

 **Sizing and Rearranging Placeholders**   **Part 3 of 5**

1. With **P-C2-P2-NetworkSystem.pptx** open, make Slide 1 active.
2. Size and move a placeholder by completing the following steps:
    a. Click on any character in the subtitle *Evaluating Current Network System*.
    b. Position the arrow pointer on the sizing handle that displays in the middle of the right border until the pointer turns into a left- and right-pointing arrow.
    c. Hold down the left mouse button, drag to the left until the right border displays just to the right of the text in the placeholder, and then release the mouse button (see image at the top right).
    d. Position the arrow pointer on the border of the placeholder until the pointer turns into a four-headed arrow.
    e. Hold down the left mouse button, drag the placeholder to the right so the placeholder is positioned as shown at the right, and then release the mouse button.
3. Make Slide 4 active.
4. Size and move a placeholder by completing the following steps:
    a. Click on any character in the bulleted text.
    b. Position the arrow pointer on the sizing handle that displays in the middle of the right border until the pointer turns into a left- and right-pointing arrow.
    c. Hold down the left mouse button and then drag to the left until the right border displays just to the right of the word *in* in the third bulleted text (see image above).

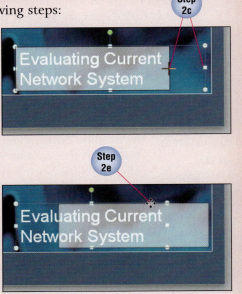

d. Drag the middle sizing handle on the bottom border up until the bottom border of the placeholder displays just below the last bulleted text.
e. Position the arrow pointer on the border of the placeholder until the pointer turns into a four-headed arrow.
f. Hold down the left mouse button and then drag the placeholder to the right so the placeholder is positioned approximately in the middle of the white portion of the slide.

5. Save **P-C2-P2-NetworkSystem.pptx**.

Step 4f

Managing Slides

As you edit a presentation, you may need to reorganize slides and insert a new slide or delete an existing slide. You can manage slides in the Slides/Outline pane or in Slide Sorter view. Switch to Slide Sorter view by clicking the Slide Sorter button in the view area on the Status bar or by clicking the View tab and then clicking Slide Sorter in the Presentation Views group.

Inserting and Deleting Slides

As you learned in Chapter 1, click the New Slide button in the Slides group in the Home tab to insert a new slide in the presentation immediately following the currently active slide. You can also insert a new slide in Slide Sorter view. To do this, click the slide that will immediately precede the new slide and then click the New Slide button in the Slides group. Delete a slide in Normal view by clicking the slide miniature in the Slides/Outline pane and then pressing the Delete key. You can also delete a slide by switching to Slide Sorter view, clicking the slide miniature, and then pressing the Delete key.

Moving Slides

Move slides in a presentation in Normal view or Slide Sorter view. In Normal view, click the desired slide in the Slides/Outline pane (with the Slides tab selected) and then position the mouse pointer on the selected slide. Hold down the left mouse button, drag up or down until a thin horizontal line displays in the desired location, and then release the mouse button. In Slide Sorter view, click the desired slide and then position the mouse pointer on the selected slide. Hold down the left mouse button, drag with the mouse until a thin vertical line displays in the desired location, and then release the mouse button.

▼ **Quick Steps**

Insert Slide
Click New Slide button.
OR
1. Click Slide Sorter button in view area of Status bar.
2. Click slide that will immediately precede new slide.
3. Click New Slide button.

Delete Slide
1. Click slide miniature in Slides/Outline pane.
2. Press Delete key.
OR
1. Click Slide Sorter button in view area of Status bar.
2. Click desired slide.
3. Press Delete key.

Press Ctrl + M to insert a new slide.

Copying a Slide

Slides in some presentations may contain similar text, objects, and formatting. Rather than create a new slide, consider copying a slide. To do this, display the presentation in either Slide Sorter view or in Normal view with the Slides tab selected in the Slides/Outline pane. Position the arrow pointer in the slide, hold down the Ctrl key and then the left mouse button. Drag to the location where you want the slide copied, then release the mouse button and then the Ctrl key.

Press Ctrl + X to cut the selected slide and then press Ctrl + V to insert the cut slide.

Press Ctrl + C to copy the selected slide and then press Ctrl + V to insert the copied slide.

Project 2d Moving and Copying Slides   Part 4 of 5

1. With **P-C2-P2-NetworkSystem.pptx** open in Normal view, move slides by completing the following steps:
   a. Make sure the Slides tab is selected in the Slides/Outline pane.
   b. Click Slide 3 (*EFFICIENCY*) in the Slides/Outline pane.
   c. Position the mouse pointer on Slide 3, hold down the left mouse button, drag up until a thin horizontal line displays between Slides 1 and 2, and then release the mouse button.
   d. Click Slide 4 (*QUALITY*) in the Slides/Outline pane.
   e. Position the mouse pointer on Slide 4, hold down the left mouse button, drag down until a thin horizontal line displays below Slide 6, and then release the mouse button.
2. Move and copy slides in Slide Sorter view by completing the following steps:
   a. Click the Slide Sorter button in the view area on the Status bar.
   b. Click Slide 4 to make it the active slide. (The slide displays with an orange border.)
   c. Position the mouse pointer on Slide 4, hold down the left mouse button, drag to the left until the thin vertical line displays between Slides 1 and 2, and then release the mouse button.

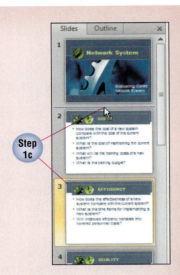

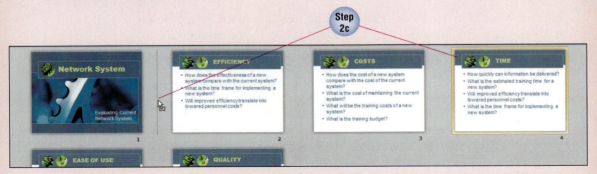

   d. Click Slide 1 to make it the active slide.

Chapter 2 ■ Modifying a Presentation and Using Help

e. Position the mouse pointer on Slide 1, hold down the left mouse button, and then hold down the Ctrl key.
f. Drag down and to the right until the thin vertical line displays immediately right of Slide 6.
g. Release the mouse button and then the Ctrl key.
3. Click the Normal button in the view area on the Status bar.
4. Save **P-C2-P2-NetworkSystem.pptx**.

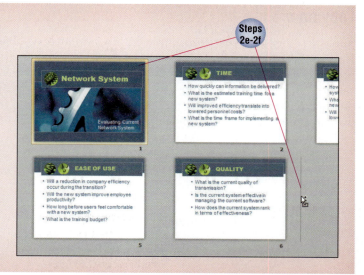

Copying a Slide between Presentations

You can copy slides within a presentation as well as between presentations. To copy a slide, click the slide you want to copy (either in Slide Sorter view or in Normal view with the Slides tab selected in the Slides/Outline pane) and then click the Copy button in the Clipboard group in the Home tab. Open the presentation into which the slide is to be copied (in either Slide Sorter view or Normal view with the Slides tab selected in the Slides/Outline pane). Click in the location where you want the slide positioned and then click the Paste button. The copied slide will take on the design theme of the presentation into which it is copied.

Project 2e Copying Slides between Presentations   Part 5 of 5

1. With **P-C2-P2-NetworkSystem.pptx** open, open the presentation named **EvalNetwork.pptx** located in the PowerPoint2010C2 folder on your storage medium.
2. Copy Slide 2 to the **P-C2-P2-NetworkSystem.pptx** presentation by completing the following steps:
   a. Click Slide 2 in the Slides/Outline pane to make it the active slide.
   b. Click the Copy button in the Clipboard group in the Home tab.
   c. Click the PowerPoint button on the Taskbar and then click the **P-C2-P2-NetworkSystem.pptx** presentation thumbnail.
   d. Click Slide 4 (*COSTS*) in the Slides/Outline pane.
   e. Click the Paste button in the Clipboard group.
   f. Click the PowerPoint button on the Taskbar and then click the **EvalNetwork.pptx** presentation thumbnail.
3. Copy Slide 3 to the **P-C2-P2-NetworkSystem.pptx** by completing the following steps:
   a. Click Slide 3 in the Slides/Outline pane.
   b. Position the mouse pointer on Slide 3 and then click the right mouse button. (This displays a shortcut menu.)

c. Click *Copy* at the shortcut menu.
   d. Click the PowerPoint button on the Taskbar and then click the **P-C2-P2-NetworkSystem.pptx** thumbnail.
   e. Right-click Slide 3 in the Slides/Outline pane.
   f. Click the Use Destination Theme button that displays in the *Paste Options* section.

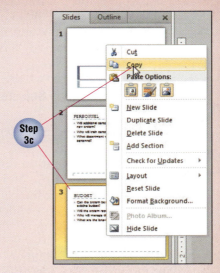

4. Click the PowerPoint button on the Taskbar and then click the **EvalNetwork.pptx** thumbnail.
5. Close the presentation.
6. With **P-C2-P2-NetworkSystem.pptx** open, delete Slide 9 by completing the following steps:
   a. If necessary, scroll down the Slides/Outline pane until Slide 9 is visible.
   b. Click Slide 9 to select it.
   c. Press the Delete key.
7. Save the presentation.
8. Print the presentation as a handout with nine slides horizontally per page.
9. Close **P-C2-P2-NetworkSystem.pptx**.

 **Insert and Manage Slides in an Adventure Tours Presentation**   **3 Parts**

You will open a presentation on Adventure Tours and then insert additional slides in the presentation by duplicating existing slides in the presentation and reusing slides from another presentation. You will also divide the presentation into sections and print a section.

Duplicating Slides

In Project 2, you used the Copy and Paste buttons in the Clipboard group and also options from a shortcut menu to copy slides in a presentation. You can also copy slides in a presentation using the *Duplicate Selected Slides* option from the New Slide button drop-down list or by clicking the Copy button arrow and then clicking *Duplicate* at the drop-down list. In addition to duplicating slides, you can use the *Duplicate* option from the Copy button drop-down list to duplicate a selected object such as a placeholder in a slide.

▼ **Quick Steps**
Duplicate Slides
1. Select desired slides in Slides/Outline pane.
2. Click New Slide button arrow.
3. Click *Duplicate Selected Slides* at drop-down list.

Chapter 2 ■ Modifying a Presentation and Using Help   57

You can duplicate a single slide or selected slides. To select adjacent (sequential) slides, click the first slide in the Slides/Outline pane, hold down the Shift key, and then click the last in the sequence. To select nonadjacent (nonsequential) slides, hold down the Ctrl key while clicking each desired slide.

Project 3a — Duplicating Selected Slides — Part 1 of 3

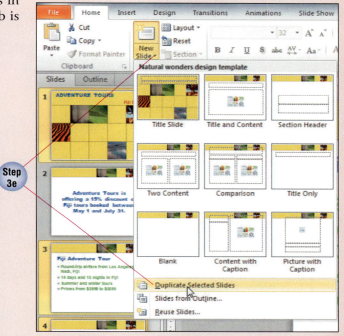

1. Open **AdvTours.pptx** and then save the presentation with Save As and name it **P-C2-P3-AdvTours**.
2. Make sure the presentation displays in Normal view and that the Slides tab is active in the Slides/Outline pane.
3. Select and then duplicate slides by completing the following steps:
   a. Click Slide 1 in the Slides/Outline pane.
   b. Hold down the Ctrl key.
   c. Click Slide 3, Slide 4, and Slide 5.
   d. Release the Ctrl key.
   e. Click the New Slide button arrow in the Slides group in the Home tab and then click *Duplicate Selected Slides* at the drop-down list.
4. With Slide 6 active in the Slide pane, change *Fiji Tour* to *Costa Rica Tour*.
5. Make Slide 7 active, select *Fiji* and then type **Costa Rica**. Select and delete the bulleted text, and then type the following bulleted text:
   - **Round-trip airfare from Los Angeles to San Jose, Costa Rica**
   - **8 days and 7 nights in Costa Rica**
   - **Monthly tours**
   - **Prices from $1099 to $1599**
6. Make Slide 8 active, select and delete the bulleted text, and then type the following bulleted text:
   - **San Jose, Emerald Suites**
   - **Tortuguero, Plantation Spa and Resort**
   - **Fortuna, Pacific Resort**
   - **Jaco, Monteverde Cabanas**
7. Make Slide 9 active, select and delete the bulleted text, and then type the following bulleted text:
   - **San Jose city tour**
   - **Rainforest tram**
   - **Canal cruise**
   - **Forest hike**
8. Save **P-C2-P3-AdvTours.pptx**.

Reusing Slides

PowerPoint provides another method for copying slides from one presentation to another. Click the New Slide button arrow and then click the *Reuse Slides* option at the drop-down list and the Reuse Slides task pane displays at the right side of the screen as shown in Figure 2.4. At this task pane, click the Browse button, click *Browse File* at the drop-down list, and the Browse dialog box displays. At this dialog box, navigate to the desired folder and then double-click the desired presentation. This inserts the presentation slides in the Reuse Slides task pane. Click a slide in the Reuse Slides task pane to insert it in the currently open presentation.

By default, the slides you insert from the Reuse Slides task pane into the currently open presentation take on the formatting of the current presentation. If you want the slides to retain their original formatting when inserted in the presentation, insert a check mark in the *Keep source formatting* check box located toward the bottom of the Reuse Slides task pane.

▼ **Quick Steps**

Reuse Slides
1. Click New Slide button arrow.
2. Click *Reuse Slides*.
3. Click Browse button, *Browse File*.
4. Navigate to desired folder.
5. Double-click desired presentation.
6. Click desired slide in Reuse Slides task pane.

Figure 2.4 Reuse Slides Task Pane

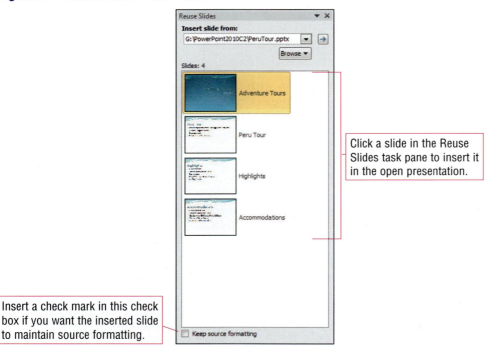

Click a slide in the Reuse Slides task pane to insert it in the open presentation.

Insert a check mark in this check box if you want the inserted slide to maintain source formatting.

Project 3b Reusing Slides   Part 2 of 3

1. With **P-C2-P3-AdvTours.pptx** open, click the New Slide button arrow in the Slides group in the Home tab and then click *Reuse Slides* at the drop-down list. (This displays the Reuse Slides task pane at the right side of the screen.)
2. Click the Browse button in the Reuse Slides task pane and then click *Browse File* at the drop-down list.

3. At the Browse dialog box, navigate to the PowerPoint2010C2 folder on your storage medium and then double-click *PeruTour.pptx*.
4. In the Slides/Outline pane, scroll down the slide thumbnails until Slide 9 displays and then click below Slide 9. (This inserts a thin, horizontal line below the Slide 9 thumbnail in the Slides/Outline pane.)
5. Click the first slide thumbnail (*Adventure Tours*) in the Reuse Slides task pane. (This inserts the slide in the open presentation immediately below Slide 9.)
6. Click the second slide thumbnail (*Peru Tour*) in the Reuse Slides task pane.
7. Click the fourth slide thumbnail (*Accommodations*) in the Reuse Slides task pane.
8. Click the third slide thumbnail (*Highlights*) in the Reuse Slides task pane.
9. Close the Reuse Slides task pane by clicking the Close button (contains an X) located in the upper right corner of the task pane.
10. Save **P-C2-P3-AdvTours.pptx**.

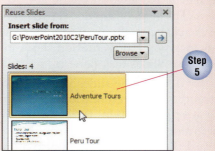

Creating Sections within a Presentation

▼ **Quick Steps**

Create Section
1. Select slides.
2. Click Section button.
3. Click *Add Section*.

Section

If you are working on a presentation with others in a group, or you are working in a presentation containing numerous slides, consider dividing related slides in the presentation into sections. Dividing a presentation into sections allows you to easily navigate and edit slides within a presentation. Create a section by selecting the first slide in the desired section in the Slides/Outline pane, clicking the Section button in the Slides group in the Home tab, and then clicking *Add Section* at the drop-down list. A section title bar displays in the Slides/Outline pane with the Slides tab selected. By default, the section title name is *Untitled Section*. Rename a section by clicking the Section button in the Slides group in the Home tab and then clicking *Rename Section* at the drop-down list. You can also rename a section by right-clicking the section title bar in the Slides/Outline pane and then clicking *Rename Section* at the shortcut menu. You can remove, move, collapse, and expand sections with options in the Section button drop-down list or by right-clicking the section title bar and then clicking the desired option.

When you create sections within a presentation, you can print only desired sections within the presentation. To print a section in a presentation, click the File tab, click the Print tab, click the first gallery in the Settings category, click the desired section in the drop-down list, and then click the Print button.

Project 3c   Creating and Printing Sections   Part 3 of 3

1. With **P-C2-P3-AdvTours.pptx** open, create a section for slides about Fiji by completing the following steps:
   a. Click Slide 1 in the Slides/Outline pane.
   b. Click the Section button in the Slides group in the Home tab and then click *Add Section* at the drop-down list.

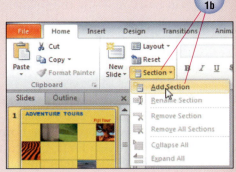
Step 1b

2. Rename the new section by completing the following steps:
   a. Click the Section button and then click *Rename Section* at the drop-down list.
   b. At the Rename Section dialog box, type **Fiji Tour** and then click the Rename button.

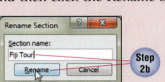
Step 2b

3. Create a section for slides about Costa Rica by completing the following steps:
   a. Click Slide 6 in the Slides/Outline pane.
   b. Click the Section button in the Slides group and then click *Add Section* at the drop-down list.
   c. Right-click on the section title bar (contains the text *Untitled Section*) and then click *Rename Section* at the shortcut menu.
   d. At the Rename Section dialog box, type **Costa Rica Tour** and then press Enter.

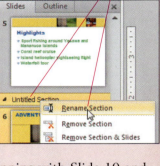
Step 3c

4. Complete steps similar to those in Step 3 to create a section beginning with Slide 10 and then rename the section *Peru Tour*.
5. Display only slides in the Costa Rica Tour section by completing the following steps:
   a. Click the Section button in the Slides group and then click *Collapse All* at the drop-down list.

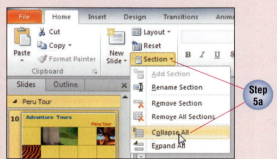
Step 5a

   b. Double-click the *Costa Rica Tour* section bar in the Slides/Outline pane. (Notice that only Slides 6 through 9 display in the Slides/Outline pane and the slides in the Fiji Tour and Peru Tour sections are hidden.)
6. Redisplay the Fiji Tour section slides by double-clicking the *Fiji Tour* section bar in the Slides/Outline pane.
7. Display all sections by clicking the Section button in the Slides group and then clicking *Expand All* at the drop-down list.

Chapter 2 ■ Modifying a Presentation and Using Help

8. Print only the Costa Rica Tour section by completing the following steps:
   a. Click the File tab and then click the Print tab.
   b. At the Print tab Backstage view, click the first gallery in the Settings category and then click *Costa Rica Tour* in the *Sections* section (located toward the bottom of the drop-down list).
   c. Click the *Full Page Slides* option in the Settings category and then click *4 Slides Horizontal* in the *Handouts* section.
   d. Click the Print button.
9. Complete steps similar to those in Step 8 to print only the Peru Tour section.
10. Save and then close **P-C2-P3-AdvTours.pptx**.

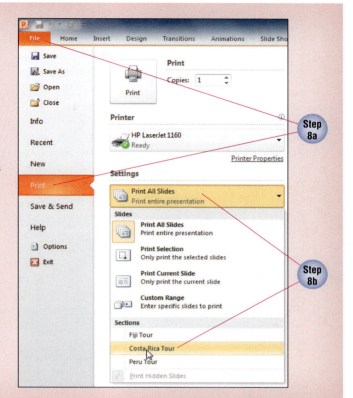

Project 4 Use PowerPoint Help Feature and Create a Presentation 2 Parts

You will use the Help feature to learn more about PowerPoint features. You will also use the Help feature to find information on keyboard shortcuts and then use the information to create a presentation.

Using Help

Help

Microsoft PowerPoint includes a Help feature that contains information about PowerPoint features and commands. This on-screen reference manual is similar to Windows Help and the Help features in Word, Excel, and Access. Click the Microsoft PowerPoint Help button (the circle with the question mark) located in the upper right corner of the screen or press the keyboard shortcut F1 to display the PowerPoint Help window. In this window, type a topic, feature, or question in the Search text box and then press the Enter key. Topics related to the search text display in the PowerPoint Help window. Click a topic that interests you. If the topic window contains a Show All hyperlink in the upper right corner, click this hyperlink and the topic options expand to show additional help information related to the topic. When you click the Show All hyperlink, it becomes the Hide All hyperlink.

Getting Help at the Help Tab Backstage View

The Help tab Backstage view, shown in Figure 2.5, contains an option for displaying the PowerPoint Help window as well as other options. Display this view by clicking the File tab and then clicking the Help tab. Click the Microsoft Office Help button in the Support category to display the PowerPoint Help window and click the Getting Started button to access the Microsoft website that displays information about getting started with PowerPoint 2010. Click the Contact Us button in the Support category and the Microsoft Support website displays. Click the Options button in the Tools for Working With Office category and the PowerPoint Options dialog box displays with options for customizing PowerPoint. Click the Check for Updates button and the Microsoft Update website displays with information on available updates. The right side of the Help tab Backstage view displays information about Office and PowerPoint.

▼ **Quick Steps**

Use the Help Feature
1. Click Microsoft PowerPoint Help button.
2. Type topic or feature.
3. Press Enter.
4. Click desired topic.

Display Help Tab Backstage View
1. Click File tab.
2. Click Help tab.

Getting Help on a Button

When you position the mouse pointer on a button, a ScreenTip displays with information about the button. Some button ScreenTips display with the message "Press F1 for more help." that is preceded by an image of the Help button. With the ScreenTip visible, press the F1 function key on your keyboard and the PowerPoint Help window opens and displays information about the specific button.

Figure 2.5 Help Tab Backstage View

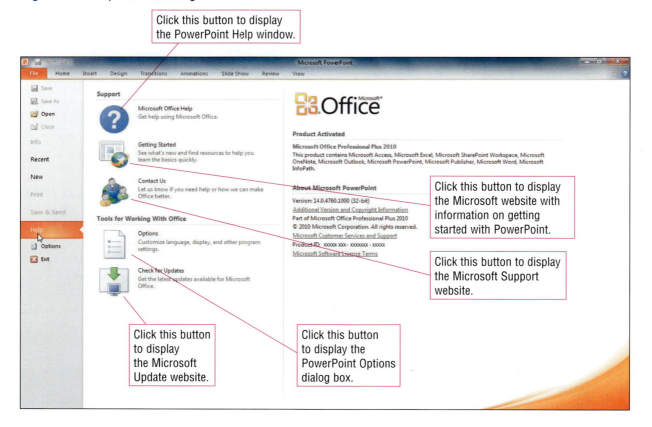

Chapter 2 ■ Modifying a Presentation and Using Help

Project 4a Using the Help Feature Part 1 of 2

1. At the blank screen, press Ctrl + N to display a blank presentation. (Ctrl + N is the keyboard shortcut to open a blank presentation.)
2. Click the Microsoft PowerPoint Help button located in the upper right corner of the screen.
3. At the PowerPoint Help window, type **create a presentation** in the Search text box and then press the Enter key.
4. When the list of topics displays, click the Create a basic PowerPoint presentation hyperlink. (If your PowerPoint Help window does not display the online options, check the lower right corner of the window. If the word *Offline* displays, click *Offline* and then click the *Show content from Office.com* option at the drop-down list.)
5. Scroll down the PowerPoint Help window and then click a hyperlink to an article that interests you.
6. Read the information in the article. (If you want a printing of the information, you can click the Print button located toward the top of the PowerPoint Help window and then click the Print button at the Print dialog box.)
7. Close the PowerPoint Help window by clicking the Close button located in the upper right corner of the window.
8. Click the File tab and then click the Help tab.
9. At the Help tab Backstage view, click the Getting Started button in the Support category. (You must be connected to the Internet to display the web page.)
10. Look at the information that displays at the website and then click the Close button located in the upper right corner of the web page.
11. Click the File tab and then click the Help tab.
12. Click the Contact Us button, look at the information that displays at the website, and then close the web page.
13. At the blank presentation, click the text *Click to add title* and then type **PowerPoint Help**.
14. Click the text *Click to add subtitle* and then type **Keyboard Shortcuts**.
15. Hover the mouse pointer over the Font Color button in the Font group in the Home tab until the ScreenTip displays and then press F1.
16. At the PowerPoint Help window, read the information that displays and then close the window.

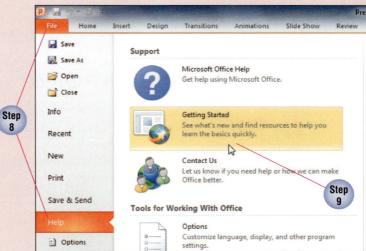

Getting Help in a Dialog Box or Backstage View

Some dialog boxes, as well as the Backstage view, contain a Help button you can click to display a help window with specific information about the dialog box or Backstage view. After reading and/or printing the information, close a dialog box by clicking the Close button located in the upper right corner of the dialog box or close the Backstage view by clicking the File tab or clicking any other tab in the ribbon.

Project 4b — Getting Help in a Dialog Box and Backstage View and Creating a Presentation

Part 2 of 2

1. At the presentation, click the File tab and then click the Save As button.
2. At the Save As dialog box, click the Help button located near the upper right corner of the dialog box.
3. Read the information about saving files that displays in the Windows Help and Support window.
4. Close the window by clicking the Close button located in the upper right corner of the window.
5. At the Save As dialog box, select the text that displays in the *File name* text box, type **P-C2-P4-Shortcuts**, and then press Enter.
6. Click the File tab.
7. At the Backstage view, click the Help button located in the upper right corner of the window.
8. At the PowerPoint Help window, click a hyperlink that interests you.
9. Read the information and then close the PowerPoint Help window by clicking the Close button located in the upper right corner of the window.
10. Click the File tab to return to the presentation.
11. Click the PowerPoint Help button.
12. At the Help window, type **keyboard shortcuts** in the Search text box and then press the Enter key.
13. When the list of topics displays, scroll down the list and then click the Keyboard shortcuts for use while creating a presentation in PowerPoint 2010. (Not all of the hyperlink text will be visible.)
14. Scroll down the list of topics, display the *Common tasks in Microsoft Office PowerPoint* section, and then click the Delete and copy text and objects hyperlink. (This displays a list of keyboard shortcuts.)
15. Select the list of keyboard shortcuts by positioning the mouse pointer at the left side of the heading *TO DO THIS*, hold down the left mouse button, drag down to the lower right corner of the list of keyboard shortcuts, and then release the mouse button. (See image above.)

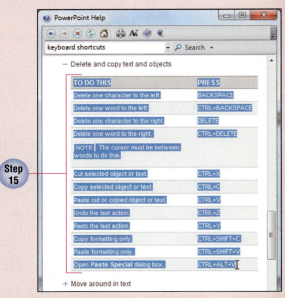

Chapter 2 ■ Modifying a Presentation and Using Help   65

16. With the information selected, click the Print button that displays on the PowerPoint Help window toolbar.
17. At the Print dialog box, click the *Selection* option in the *Page Range* section and then click the Print button.
18. Close the PowerPoint Help window.
19. Using the information you printed, create slides with the following information:
    - Slide 2: Insert the text **Delete Text** as the title and then insert the four delete keyboard shortcuts as bulleted text. (For each keyboard shortcut, type the description followed by a colon and then the keyboard shortcut. For example, type **Delete one character to the left: Backspace** as the first bulleted item in the slide.)
    - Slide 3: Insert the text **Cut, Copy, Paste Text** as the title and then insert the three cut, copy, and paste keyboard shortcuts as bulleted text.
    - Slide 4: Insert the text **Undo and Redo** as the title and then insert the two undo and redo keyboard shortcuts as bulleted text.
    - Slide 5: Insert the text **Copy and Paste Formatting** as the title and then insert the three copy and paste formatting keyboard shortcuts as bulleted text.
20. Apply the Newsprint design theme to the presentation.
21. Apply a transition and sound of your choosing to all slides in the presentation.
22. Print the presentation as a handout with six slides printed horizontally per page.
23. Save and then close **P-C2-P4-Shortcuts.pptx**.

Chapter Summary

- Use the spelling feature to check spelling of slides in a presentation. Begin the spelling checker by clicking the Review tab and then clicking the Spelling button in the Proofing group.
- Click in a placeholder to select the placeholder and position the insertion point inside.
- Display the Find dialog box by clicking the Find button in the Editing group in the Home tab.
- Display the Replace dialog box by clicking the Replace button in the Editing group in the Home tab.
- With buttons in the Clipboard group or with options from a shortcut menu, you can cut and paste or copy and paste text in slides.
- You can use the mouse to move text in the Slides/Outline pane. You can select and then drag it to a new location or hold down the Ctrl key while dragging to copy text to a new location.
- Use the sizing handles that display around a selected placeholder to increase or decrease the size of the placeholder. You can use the mouse to drag a selected placeholder to a new location in the slide.
- Use the New Slide button in the Home tab to insert a slide in a presentation.
- Delete a selected slide by pressing the Delete key.
- You can move or delete a selected slide in Normal view in the Slides/Outline pane or in Slide Sorter view.

- Copy a selected slide by holding down the Ctrl key while dragging the slide to the desired location.
- Use the Copy and Paste buttons in the Clipboard group in the Home tab to copy a slide between presentations.
- Select adjacent slides in the Slides/Outline pane or in Slide Sorter view by clicking the first slide, holding down the Shift key, and then clicking the last slide. Select nonadjacent slides by holding down the Ctrl key while clicking each desired slide.
- Duplicate slides in a presentation by selecting the desired slides in the Slides/Outline pane, clicking the New Slide button arrow, and then clicking the *Duplicate Selected Slides* option or clicking the Copy button arrow and then clicking *Duplicate* at the drop-down list.
- Divide a presentation into sections to easily navigate and edit slides in a presentation.
- You can copy slides from a presentation into the open presentation with options at the Reuse Slides task pane. Display this task pane by clicking the New Slide button arrow and then clicking *Reuse Slides* at the drop-down list.
- Click the Microsoft PowerPoint Help button or press F1 to display the PowerPoint Help window.
- Click the File tab and then the Help tab to display the Help tab Backstage view.
- Some dialog boxes, as well as the Backstage view, contain a Help button you can click to display information specific to the dialog box or Backstage view.

Commands Review

FEATURE	RIBBON TAB, GROUP	BUTTON, OPTION	KEYBOARD SHORTCUT
Spelling check	Review, Proofing		F7
Find dialog box	Home, Editing		Ctrl + F
Replace dialog box	Home, Editing		Ctrl + H
Cut text or slide	Home, Clipboard		Ctrl + X
Copy text or slide	Home, Clipboard		Ctrl + C
Paste text or slide	Home, Clipboard		Ctrl + V
Duplicate slide	Home, Slides	, Duplicate Selected Slides	
Section	Home, Slides	Section ▼	
Reuse Slides task pane	Home, Slides	, Reuse Slides	
PowerPoint Help window			F1

Concepts Check — Test Your Knowledge

Completion: In the space provided at the right, indicate the correct term, symbol, or command.

1. The Spelling button is located in the Proofing group in this tab. _____

2. This is the keyboard shortcut to select all text in a placeholder. _____

3. The Find button is located in this group in the Home tab. _____

4. To copy text to a new location in the Slides/Outline pane with the Outline tab selected, hold down this key while dragging text. _____

5. The border of a selected placeholder displays these handles as well as a green rotation handle. _____

6. You can reorganize slides in a presentation in the Slides/Outline pane or in this view. _____

7. You can copy selected slides in a presentation using this option from the New Slide button drop-down list. _____

8. To select adjacent slides, click the first slide, hold down this key, and then click the last slide. _____

9. Click the New Slide button arrow and then click the *Reuse Slides* option at the drop-down list and this displays. _____

10. Divide a presentation into these to easily navigate and edit slides in a presentation. _____

11. This is the keyboard shortcut to display the PowerPoint Help window. _____

Skills Check Assess Your Performance

Assessment

1 CREATE AN ELECTRONIC DESIGN PRESENTATION

1. Create the presentation shown in Figure 2.6 using a design theme of your choosing. (When typing bulleted text, press the Tab key to move the insertion point to the desired tab level.)
2. After creating the slides, complete a spelling check on the text in the slides.
3. Save the presentation into the PowerPoint2010C2 folder on your storage medium and name the presentation **P-C2-A1-ElecDesign**.
4. Run the presentation.
5. Print the presentation as a handout with four slides horizontally per page.
6. Make the following changes to the presentation:
    a. Change to Slide Sorter view and then move Slide 3 between Slides 1 and 2.
    b. Move Slide 4 between Slides 2 and 3.
    c. Change to Normal view.
    d. Search for the word *document* and replace it with the word *brochure*. (After the replacements, make Slide 1 active and, if necessary, capitalize the "b" in "brochure.")
    e. Add a transition and sound of your choosing to each slide.
7. Save the presentation.
8. Display the Reuse Slides task pane, browse to the PowerPoint2010C2 folder on your storage medium, and then double-click **LayoutTips.pptx**.
9. Insert the *Layout Punctuation Tips* slide below Slide 4.
10. Insert the *Layout Tips* slide below Slide 5.
11. Close the Reuse Slides task pane.
12. Find all occurrences of *Layout* and replace with *Design*. (Insert a check mark in the *Match case* check box.)
13. Move Slide 5 between Slides 1 and 2.
14. Move Slide 6 between Slides 2 and 3.
15. Change to Normal view and then save the presentation.
16. Print the presentation as a handout with six slides horizontally per page.
17. Beginning with Slide 2, create a section named *Design Tips*.
18. Beginning with Slide 4, create a section named *Design Features*.
19. Print only the Design Features section as a handout with four slides horizontally per page.
20. Save and then close **P-C2-A1-ElecDesign.pptx**.

Figure 2.6 Assessment 1

Slide 1	Title	=	Electronic Design and Production
	Subtitle	=	Designing a Document
Slide 2	Title	=	Creating Balance
	Bullets	=	• Symmetrical balance: Balancing similar elements equally on a page (centered alignment) of the document
			• Asymmetrical balance: Balancing contrasting elements on a page of the document
Slide 3	Title	=	Creating Focus
	Bullets	=	• Creating focus with titles, headings, and subheads in a document
			• Creating focus with graphic elements in a document
			o Clip art
			o Watermarks
			o Illustrations
			o Photographs
			o Charts
			o Graphs
Slide 4	Title	=	Providing Proportion
	Bullets	=	• Evaluating proportions in a document
			• Sizing graphic elements in a document
			• Using white space in a document

Assessment 2 CREATE A NETIQUETTE PRESENTATION

1. Create a presentation with the text shown in Figure 2.7. You determine the slide layout. Apply the Pushpin design theme.
2. If necessary, size and move placeholders so the text is positioned attractively on the slide.
3. Select Slides 4 through 6 and then duplicate the slides.
4. Type the following text in place of the existing text in the identified slides:
   a. Slide 7: Select the placeholder netiquette rule text and then type **Do not plagiarize.**
   b. Slide 8: Select the netiquette rule text in the placeholder and then type **Respect and accept people's differences.**
   c. Slide 9: Select the netiquette rule text in the placeholder and then type **Respect others' time.**
5. Complete a spelling check on text in the presentation.
6. Save the presentation and name it **P-C2-A2-InternetApps**.
7. Print the presentation as a handout with nine slides horizontally per page.

8. Make the following edits to the presentation:
   a. Display the presentation in Slide Sorter view.
   b. Move Slide 3 between Slide 5 and Slide 6.
   c. Move Slide 7 between Slide 3 and Slide 4.
9. Add a transition and sound of your choosing to all slides in the presentation.
10. Save the presentation.
11. Run the presentation.
12. Print the presentation as a handout with nine slides horizontally per page.
13. Close **P-C2-A2-InternetApps.pptx**.

Figure 2.7 Assessment 2

Slide	Element		Content
Slide 1	Title	=	INTERNET APPLICATIONS
	Subtitle	=	Internet Community
Slide 2	Title	=	Community Issues
	Bullets	=	• Flaming • Email • Moderated environments • Netiquette
Slide 3	Title	=	Netiquette Rule
	Subtitle	=	Remember you are dealing with people.
Slide 4	Title	=	Netiquette Rule
	Subtitle	=	Adhere to the same standards of behavior online that you follow in real life.
Slide 5	Title	=	Netiquette Rule
	Subtitle	=	Respect the privacy of others.
Slide 6	Title	=	Netiquette Rule
	Subtitle	=	Share expert knowledge.

Assessment 3

DOWNLOAD A DESIGN THEME

1. If your computer is connected to the Internet, Office.com provides a number of design themes you can download to your computer. Display the New tab Backstage view, click in the search text box located to the right of the *Office.com Templates* heading, type **computer**, and then press Enter.
2. In the Office.com Templates section, click the *Computer monitor design template* option and then click the Download button that displays at the right.
3. When the design theme is downloaded and a presentation is opened with the design theme applied, open **P-C2-A2-InternetApps.pptx**.
4. Select the nine slides in the **P-C2-A2-InternetApps.pptx** presentation and then click the Copy button.

5. Click the PowerPoint button on the Taskbar and then click the thumbnail representing the presentation with the downloaded design theme applied.
6. Click the Paste button to paste the nine slides in the current presentation.
7. Delete Slide 1.
8. Scroll through and look at each slide and make any changes required so the text is positioned attractively on each slide.
9. Save the presentation and name it **P-C2-A3-InternetApps**.
10. Run the presentation.
11. Print the presentation as a handout with nine slides horizontally per page.
12. Close **P-C2-A3-InternetApps.pptx** and then close **P-C2-A2-InternetApps.pptx**.

Visual Benchmark Demonstrate Your Proficiency

FORMATTING A PRESENTATION ON ONLINE LEARNING

1. Open **OnlineLearning.pptx** in the PowerPoint2010C2 folder and then save the presentation with Save As and name it **P-C2-VB-OnlineLearning**.
2. Format the presentation so it appears as shown in Figure 2.8 with the following specifications:
   a. Apply the Newsprint design theme.
   b. Use the *Reuse Slides* option from the New Slide button drop-down list to insert the last two additional slides from the **Learning.pptx** presentation.
   c. Arrange the slides to match what you see in Figure 2.8. (Read the slides from left to right.)
   d. Size and/or move placeholders so text displays in each slide as shown in Figure 2.8.
3. Add a transition and sound of your choosing to each slide.
4. Run the presentation.
5. Print the presentation as a handout with six slides horizontally per page.
6. Save and then close **P-C2-VB-OnlineLearning.pptx**.

Figure 2.8 Visual Benchmark

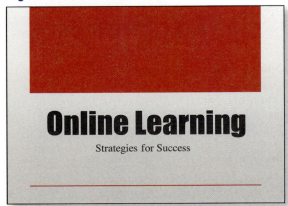

Case Study Apply Your Skills

Part 1

You are the office manager at the Company Connections agency. One of your responsibilities is to conduct workshops for preparing individuals for the job search process. A coworker has given you a presentation for the workshop but the presentation needs some editing and modifying. Open **JobAnalysis.pptx** and then save the presentation with Save As and name it **P-C2-CS-JobAnalysis**. Check each slide in the presentation and then make modifications to maintain consistency in the size and location of placeholders (consider using the Reset button to reset the formatting and size of the placeholders), maintain consistency in heading text, move text from an overcrowded slide to a new slide, complete a spelling check, apply a design theme, and make any other modifications to improve the presentation. Save **P-C2-CS-JobAnalysis.pptx**.

Part 2

After reviewing the presentation, you realize that you need to include slides on resumes. Open the **ResumePres.pptx** presentation and then copy Slides 2 and 3 into the **P-C2-CS-JobAnalysis.pptx** presentation (at the end of the presentation). You want to add additional information on resume writing tips and decide to use the Internet to find information. Locate information on the Internet with tips on writing a resume and then create a slide (or two) with the information you find. Add a transition and sound to all slides in the presentation. Save the **P-C2-CS-JobAnalysis.pptx** presentation.

Part 3

You know that Microsoft Word offers a number of resume templates you can download from the Office.com website. You decide to include information in the presentation on how to find and download resumes. Open Microsoft Word, click the File tab, and then click the New tab. At the New tab Backstage view, click in the search box that displays to the right of the *Office.com Templates* heading, type **resume**, and then press Enter. Scroll through the list of resume templates that displays and then experiment with downloading a template. With the **P-C2-CS-JobAnalysis.pptx** presentation open, add an additional slide to the end of the presentation that provides steps on how to download a resume in Microsoft Word. Print the presentation as a handout with nine slides horizontally per page. Save, run, and then close the presentation.

PowerPoint

Formatting Slides

CHAPTER 3

PERFORMANCE OBJECTIVES

Upon successful completion of Chapter 3, you will be able to:
- Apply font and paragraph formatting to text in slides
- Apply formatting with the Mini toolbar and Format Painter
- Customize bullets and numbers
- Modify theme colors and fonts
- Change slide background
- Change page setup
- Create custom themes including custom theme colors and theme fonts
- Delete custom themes

The Font and Paragraph groups in the Home tab contain a number of buttons and options you can use to format text in slides. PowerPoint also provides a Mini toolbar and the Format Painter feature to help you format text. You can modify the design theme colors and fonts provided by PowerPoint and you can create your own custom themes. You will learn to use these features in this chapter along with how to change page setup options. Model answers for this chapter's projects appear on the following pages.

Note: Before beginning the projects, copy to your storage medium the PowerPoint2010C3 subfolder from the PowerPoint2010 folder on the CD that accompanies this textbook and then make PowerPoint2010C3 the active folder.

75

Model Answers

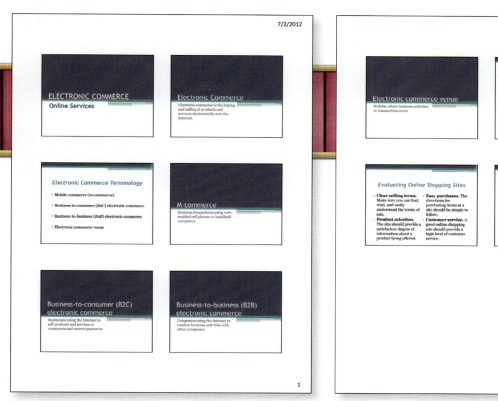

Project 1 Format an E-Commerce Presentation

P-C3-P1-E-Commerce.pptx

Project 2 Customize Bullets and Numbers in a Network Presentation

P-C3-P2-ColorPres.pptx

Project 3 Modify the Theme and Slide Background of a Job Search Presentation

P-C3-P3-JobSearch.pptx

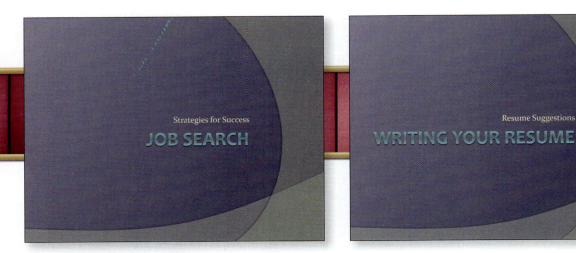

Project 4 Create and Apply Custom Themes to Presentations
P-C3-P4-JobSearch.pptx   P-C3-P4-ResumePres.pptx

Project 1   **Format an E-Commerce Presentation**   **5 Parts**

You will open an e-commerce presentation, apply font and paragraph formatting, apply formatting with Format Painter, apply column formatting to text in placeholders, and rotate and vertically align text in placeholders.

Formatting a Presentation

PowerPoint provides a variety of design themes you can apply to a presentation. These themes contain formatting such as font, color, and graphics. In some situations, the formatting provided by the theme is appropriate; in other situations, you may want to change or enhance the formatting of a slide.

Applying Font Formatting

The Font group in the Home tab contains a number of buttons for applying font formatting to text in a slide such as changing the font, font size, color, and applying font effects. Table 3.1 describes the buttons in the Font group along with any keyboard shortcuts to apply font formatting.

Changing Fonts

Design themes apply a font to text in slides. You may want to change this default to some other font for such reasons as changing the mood of a presentation, enhancing the visual appeal of slides, and increasing the readability of the text in slides. Change the font with the Font and Font Size buttons in the Font group in the Home tab.

When you select text and then click the Font button arrow, a drop-down gallery displays with font options. Hover your mouse pointer over a font option and the selected text in the slide displays with the font applied. You can continue hovering your mouse pointer over different font options to see how the selected text displays in the specified font. The Font button drop-down gallery

HINT Consider using a sans serif typeface for titles and headings and a serif typeface for body text.

HINT Use options at the Font dialog box with the Character Spacing tab selected to increase or decrease spacing between characters and to apply kerning to text.

is an example of the *live preview* feature, which allows you to see how the font formatting affects your text without having to return to the presentation. The live preview feature is also available when you click the Font Size button arrow.

Fonts may be decorative or plain and generally fall into one of two categories: **serif fonts** or **sans serif fonts**. A serif is a small line at the end of a character stroke. A serif font is easier to read and is generally used for large amounts of text. A sans serif font does not have serifs (*sans* is French for *without*) and is generally used for titles and headings.

In addition to buttons in the Font group in the Home tab, you can use options at the Font dialog box shown in Figure 3.1 to apply character formatting to text. Display the Font dialog box by clicking the Font group dialog box launcher or with the keyboard shortcut Ctrl + Shift + F. (The dialog box launcher is the small button containing a diagonal arrow that displays in the lower right corner of the group.) Use options at the Font dialog box to choose a font, font style, font size, and to apply special effects to text in slides such as superscript, subscript, and double strikethrough.

Table 3.1 PowerPoint Home Tab Font Group Buttons

Button	Name	Function	Keyboard Shortcut
Calibri	Font	Changes selected text to a different font.	
32	Font Size	Changes selected text to a different font size.	
A˄	Increase Font Size	Increases font size of selected text to next available larger size.	Ctrl + Shift + >
A˅	Decrease Font Size	Decreases font size of selected text to next available smaller size.	Ctrl + Shift + <
	Clear All Formatting	Clears all character formatting from selected text.	Ctrl + Spacebar
B	Bold	Adds or removes bold formatting to or from selected text.	Ctrl + B
I	Italic	Adds or removes italic formatting to or from selected text.	Ctrl + I
U	Underline	Adds or removes underline formatting to or from selected text.	Ctrl + U
S	Text Shadow	Adds or removes shadow formatting to or from selected text.	
abc	Strikethrough	Inserts or removes a line through the middle of selected text.	
AV	Character Spacing	Adjusts spacing between characters.	
Aa	Change Case	Changes the case of selected text.	Shift + F3
A	Font Color	Changes the font color for selected text.	

Figure 3.1 Font Dialog Box

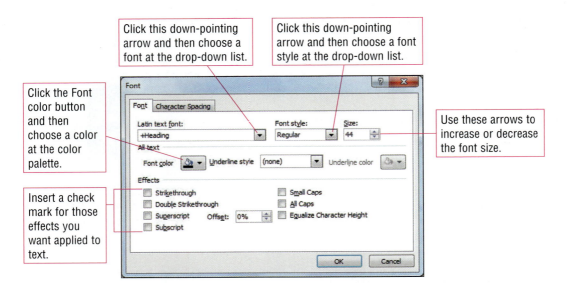

Formatting with the Mini Toolbar

When you select text, the Mini toolbar displays in a dimmed fashion above the selected text. Hover the mouse pointer over the Mini toolbar and it becomes active. Click a button on the Mini toolbar to apply formatting to selected text. If you do not want the Mini toolbar to display when you select text, you can turn it off. To do this, click the File tab and then click the Options button that displays below the Help tab. At the PowerPoint Options dialog box with the *General* option selected in the left panel, click the *Show Mini Toolbar on selection* check box to remove the check mark.

Project 1a   Applying Font Formatting to Text   Part 1 of 5

1. Open **E-Commerce.pptx** and then save the presentation with Save As and name it **P-C3-P1-E-Commerce**.
2. Apply the Urban design theme to the presentation by completing the following steps:
   a. Click the Design tab.
   b. Click the More button located to the right of the theme thumbnails.
   c. Scroll down the drop-down gallery of design themes (the list is alphabetized) and then click the *Urban* theme.
3. Change the font formatting of the Slide 1 subtitle by completing the following steps:
   a. With Slide 1 active, click any character in the subtitle *Online Services*.
   b. Select *Online Services*.
   c. Click the Home tab.
   d. Click the Font button arrow, scroll down the drop-down gallery, and then click *Trebuchet MS*.

Chapter 3 ■ Formatting Slides   79

e. Click the Font Size button arrow and then click *40* at the drop-down gallery.
f. Click the Bold button in the Font Group.
g. Click the Text Shadow button.
h. Click the Font Color button arrow and then click the *Blue-Gray, Accent 6, Darker 25%* option as shown below.

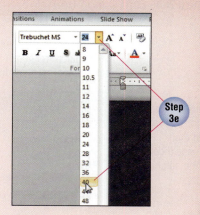

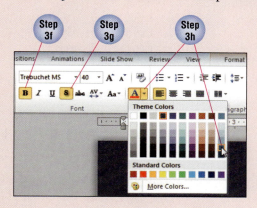

4. Change the size of the title text by completing the following steps:
   a. Click any character in the title *ELECTRONIC COMMERCE* and then select the title.
   b. Click the Increase Font Size button in the Font group.
5. Change the case of text by completing the following steps:
   a. Make Slide 2 active.
   b. Click in the title *ELECTRONIC COMMERCE* and then select the title.
   c. Click the Change Case button in the Font group and then click *Capitalize Each Word* at the drop-down list.

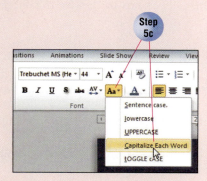

6. Apply and clear formatting to text by completing the following steps:
   a. Make Slide 3 active.
   b. Click in the bulleted text placeholder.
   c. Select *m-commerce* located in the parentheses.
   d. Click the Underline button in the Font group in the Home tab.
   e. Click the Bold button in the Font group.
   f. After looking at the text set with underlining and bold formatting, you decide to remove the formatting by clicking the Clear All Formatting button in the Font group.
   g. With the text still selected, click the Italic button in the Font group in the Home tab.

7. Apply italic formatting with the Mini toolbar by completing the following steps:
   a. Select *B2C*, hover the mouse pointer over the Mini toolbar to make it active, and then click the Italic button.
   b. Select *B2B*, hover the mouse pointer over the Mini toolbar to make it active, and then click the Italic button.
8. Save **P-C3-P1-E-Commerce.pptx**.

Formatting with Format Painter

If you apply character and/or paragraph formatting to text in a slide and want to apply the same formatting to text in the slide or other slides, use the Format Painter. With Format Painter, you can apply the same formatting in more than one location in a slide or slides. To use the Format Painter, apply the desired formatting to text, position the insertion point anywhere in the formatted text, and then double-click the Format Painter button in the Clipboard group in the Home tab. Using the mouse, select the additional text to which you want the formatting applied. After applying the formatting in the desired locations, click the Format Painter button to deactivate it. If you need to apply formatting in only one other location, click the Format Painter button once. The first time you select text, the formatting is applied and the Format Painter is deactivated.

▼ **Quick Steps**

Format with Format Painter
1. Click text containing desired formatting.
2. Double-click Format Painter button.
3. Select or click on text.
4. Click Format Painter button.

HINT
You can also turn off Format Painter by pressing the Esc key.

Format Painter

Project 1b Applying Formatting with Format Painter   Part 2 of 5

1. With **P-C3-P1-E-Commerce.pptx** open, make sure Slide 3 is active.
2. Apply formatting to the title by completing the following steps:
   a. Click in the title text and then select the title *Electronic Commerce Terminology*.
   b. Click the Font group dialog box launcher.

Chapter 3 ■ Formatting Slides

c. At the Font dialog box, click the down-pointing arrow at the right side of the *Font style* option box and then click *Bold Italic* at the drop-down list.
d. Select the current number in the *Size* text box and then type 36.
e. Click the Font color button and then click the *Blue-Gray, Accent 6, Darker 25%* option.

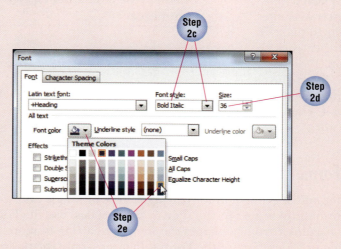

f. Click OK to close the dialog box.
3. Click on any character in the title.
4. Double-click the Format Painter button in the Clipboard group.

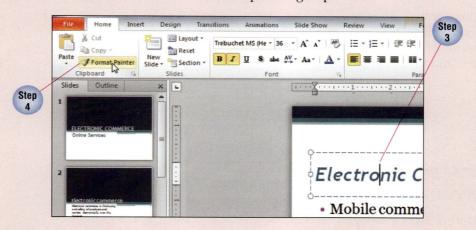

5. Make Slide 8 active.
6. Using the mouse, select the title *Advantages of Online Shopping*. (The mouse pointer displays as an I-beam with a paintbrush attached. You can also click each word in the title to apply the formatting.)
7. Make Slide 9 active and then select the title (or click each word in the title).
8. Make Slide 10 active and then select the title (or click each word in the title).
9. Click the Format Painter button to deactivate it.
10. If necessary, deselect the text.
11. Save **P-C3-P1-E-Commerce.pptx**.

Formatting Paragraphs

The Paragraph group in the Home tab contains a number of buttons for applying paragraph formatting to text in a slide such as applying bullets and numbers, increasing and decreasing list levels, changing the horizontal and vertical alignment of text, changing line spacing, and rotating text in a placeholder. Table 3.2 describes the buttons in the Paragraph group along with any keyboard shortcuts.

Table 3.2 PowerPoint Home Tab Paragraph Group Buttons

Button	Name	Function	Keyboard Shortcut
	Bullets	Adds or removes bullets to or from selected text.	
	Numbering	Adds or removes numbers to or from selected text.	
	Decrease List Level	Moves text to the previous tab stop (level).	Shift + Tab
	Increase List Level	Moves text to the next tab stop (level).	Tab
	Line Spacing	Increases or reduces spacing between lines of text.	
	Align Text Left	Left-aligns text.	Ctrl + L
	Center	Center-aligns text.	Ctrl + E
	Align Text Right	Right-aligns text.	Ctrl + R
	Justify	Justifies text.	
	Columns	Splits text into two or more columns.	
	Text Direction	Rotates or stacks text.	
	Align Text	Changes the alignment of text within a text box.	
	Convert to SmartArt Graphic	Converts selected text to a SmartArt graphic.	

Project 1c — Applying Paragraph Formatting to Text — Part 3 of 5

1. With **P-C3-P1-E-Commerce.pptx** open, change bullets by completing the following steps:
   a. Make Slide 3 active.
   b. Click on any character in the bulleted text.
   c. Select the bulleted text.
   d. Click the Bullets button arrow in the Paragraph group in the Home tab and then click the *Filled Square Bullets* option at the drop-down gallery.

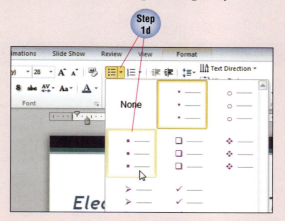

2. Change bullets to numbers by completing the following steps:
   a. Make Slide 8 active.
   b. Click on any character in the bulleted text.
   c. Select the bulleted text.
   d. Click the Numbering button arrow in the Paragraph group in the Home tab and then click the *A. B. C.* option at the drop-down gallery.

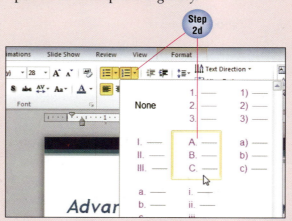

   e. After looking at the numbering, you decide to change to numbers by clicking the Numbering button arrow and then clicking the *1. 2. 3.* option at the drop-down gallery.
3. Decrease and increase list levels by completing the following steps:
   a. With Slide 8 active and the numbered text selected, click the Increase List Level button in the Paragraph group in the Home tab.
   b. With the text still selected, click the Font Color button arrow in the Font group in the Home tab and then click the Dark Blue color (second color from the right in the bottom row).

   c. Make Slide 10 active.
   d. Click on any character in the bulleted text.
   e. Move the insertion point so it is positioned immediately left of the *J.* in *J.C. Penney*.
   f. Click the Decrease List Level button in the Paragraph group in the Home tab.
   g. Move the insertion point so it is positioned immediately left of the *M* in *Macy's*.
   h. Press Shift + Tab.
   i. Move the insertion point so it is positioned immediately left of the first *L.* in *L.L. Bean*.
   j. Click the Increase List Level button in the Paragraph group.
   k. Move the insertion point so it is positioned immediately left of the *T* in *The Gap*.
   l. Press the Tab key.
   m. Complete similar steps to those in 3j or 3l to indent the following text to the next level: *Bloomingdale's*, *Expedia*, *Travelocity*, and *Orbitz*.

4. Change text line spacing by completing the following steps:
   a. Make Slide 3 active.
   b. Click in the bulleted text and then select the bulleted text.
   c. Click the Line Spacing button in the Paragraph group in the Home tab and then click *1.5* at the drop-down list.
   d. Make Slide 8 active.
   e. Click in the numbered text and then select the numbered text.
   f. Click the Line Spacing button and then click *2.0* at the drop-down list.

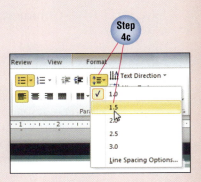

5. Change paragraph alignment by completing the following steps:
   a. Make Slide 3 active, click on any character in the title, and then click the Center button in the Paragraph group.

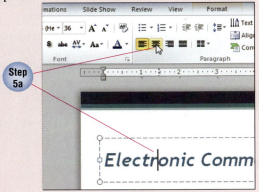

   b. Make Slide 8 active, click on any character in the title, and then click the Center button.
   c. Make Slide 9 active, click on any character in the title, and then click the Center button.
   d. Make Slide 10 active, click on any character in the title, and then click the Center button.

6. Split text into two columns by completing the following steps:
   a. Make Slide 9 active.
   b. Click in the bulleted text and then select the bulleted text.
   c. Click the Columns button in the Paragraph group and then click *Two Columns* at the drop-down list.

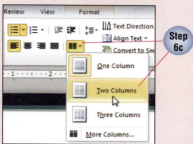

   d. Select the first sentence in the first bulleted paragraph (the sentence *Clear selling terms.*) and then click the Bold button.
   e. Select and then bold the first sentence in the remaining bulleted paragraphs of text in Slide 9.
7. Save **P-C3-P1-E-Commerce.pptx**.

Customizing Paragraphs

Line Spacing

If you want more control over paragraph alignment, indenting, and spacing, click the Paragraph group dialog box launcher. This displays the Paragraph dialog box as shown in Figure 3.2. You can also display this dialog box by clicking the Line Spacing button in the Paragraph group and then clicking *Line Spacing Options* at the drop-down list. Use options at this dialog box to specify text alignment, paragraph indentation, spacing before and after paragraphs, and line spacing.

Figure 3.2 Paragraph Dialog Box

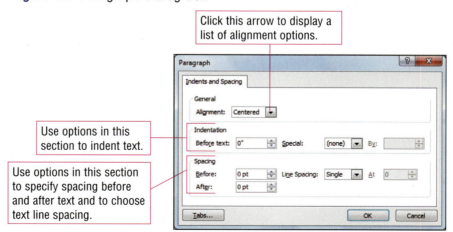

Customizing Columns

Click the Columns button in the Paragraph group and you can choose one, two, or three columns. If you want to choose a number for columns other than the three choices or if you want to control spacing between columns, click the *More Columns* option at the drop-down list. This displays the Columns dialog box shown in Figure 3.3. With options in this dialog box, you can specify the number of columns and the spacing measurement between columns.

Format text into columns to make the text attractive and easy to read.

Columns

Figure 3.3 Columns Dialog Box

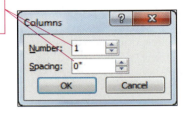

Specify the number of columns and spacing between columns in this dialog box.

Project 1d Customizing Paragraph and Column Formatting — Part 4 of 5

1. With **P-C3-P1-E-Commerce.pptx** open, change line and paragraph spacing by completing the following steps:
   a. Make Slide 3 active.
   b. Click in the bulleted text and then select the bulleted text.
   c. Click the Paragraph group dialog box launcher.
   d. At the Paragraph dialog box, click twice on the up-pointing arrow at the right side of the *Before text* measurement box. (This inserts *0.6"* in the measurement box.)
   e. Click twice on the up-pointing arrow at the right side of the *After* measurement box in the *Spacing* section. (This inserts *12 pt* in the box.)
   f. Click the down-pointing arrow at the right side of the *Line Spacing* option box and then click *Multiple* at the drop-down list.
   g. Select the current measurement in the *At* text box and then type *1.8*.
   h. Click OK.

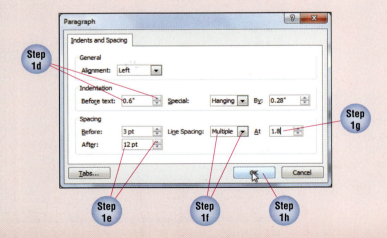

Chapter 3 ■ Formatting Slides

2. Format text in columns by completing the following steps:
   a. Make Slide 10 active.
   b. Click in the bulleted text and then select the text.
   c. Click the Columns button in the Paragraph group and then click *More Columns*.
   d. At the Columns dialog box, click once on the up-pointing arrow at the right side of the *Number* option. (This inserts a *2* in the text box.)
   e. Click the up-pointing arrow at the right side of the *Spacing* measurement box until *0.5"* displays in the box.
   f. Click OK.
   g. With the text still selected, click the Paragraph group dialog box launcher.
   h. At the Paragraph dialog box, click once on the up-pointing arrow at the right side of the *After* measurement box in the *Spacing* section. (This inserts *6 pt* in the box.)
   i. Click OK.
3. Save **P-C3-P1-E-Commerce.pptx**.

Rotating and Vertically Aligning Text

Text Direction

Align Text

If you click the Text Direction button in the Paragraph group, a drop-down list displays with options for rotating and stacking text. Click *More Options* at the drop-down list and the Format Text Effects dialog box with *Text Box* selected in the left panel displays as shown in Figure 3.4. Use options in this dialog box to specify vertical alignment and text direction, autofit contents, and change internal margins. Click the Align Text button in the Paragraph group and a drop-down list displays with options for changing the alignment to top, middle, or bottom of the placeholder.

Figure 3.4 Format Text Effects Dialog Box with *Text Box* Selected

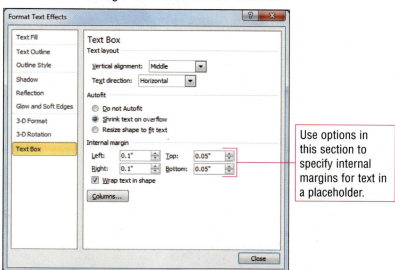

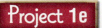 **Rotating and Vertically Aligning Text** Part 5 of 5

1. With **P-C3-P1-E-Commerce.pptx** open, change vertical alignment by completing the following steps:
   a. Make Slide 9 active.
   b. Click on any character in the bulleted text.
   c. Click the Align Text button in the Paragraph group in the Home tab and then click *Middle* at the drop-down list.

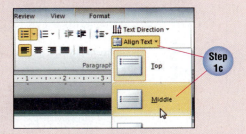

2. Make Slide 8 active and then modify the slide so it displays as shown in Figure 3.5 by completing the following steps:
   a. Click in the numbered text and then select the numbered text.
   b. Click the Bullets button arrow and then click the *Filled Square Bullets* option.
   c. Decrease the size of the bulleted text placeholder so the placeholder borders display just outside the text.
   d. Drag the placeholder so the bulleted text is positioned as shown in Figure 3.5.
   e. Click on any character in the title *Advantages of Online Shopping*.
   f. Delete *of Online Shopping*.
   g. Select *Advantages* and then change the font size to 60.
   h. Drag in the right border of the placeholder to the left so it is positioned just outside the text.
   i. Click the Text Direction button in the Paragraph group and then click *Rotate all text 270°*.

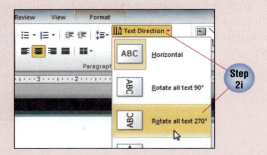

   j. Using the sizing handles that display around the title placeholder, increase the height and decrease the width of the placeholder and then drag the placeholder so the title displays as shown in Figure 3.5.
3. Apply a transition and sound to all slides in the presentation.
4. Print the presentation as a handout with six slides horizontally per page.
5. Save and then close **P-C3-P1-E-Commerce.pptx**.

Figure 3.5 Project 1e, Slide 8

Project 2 — Customize Bullets and Numbers in a Network Presentation — 3 Parts

You will open a presentation on using colors in publications and then create and apply custom bullets and numbering.

Customizing Bullets

▼ Quick Steps

Customize Bullets
1. Click in bulleted text.
2. Click Bullets button arrow.
3. Click *Bullets and Numbering* at drop-down gallery.
4. Make desired changes.
5. Click OK.

Each design theme contains a Title and Content slide layout containing bullets. The appearance and formatting of the bullets varies with each design theme. You can choose to use the bullet provided by the design theme or create custom bullets. Customize bullets with options at the Bullets and Numbering dialog box with the Bulleted tab selected as shown in Figure 3.6. Display this dialog box by clicking in a bulleted list placeholder, clicking the Bullets button arrow, and then clicking *Bullets and Numbering* at the drop-down gallery.

Figure 3.6 Bullets and Numbering Dialog Box with Bulleted Tab Selected

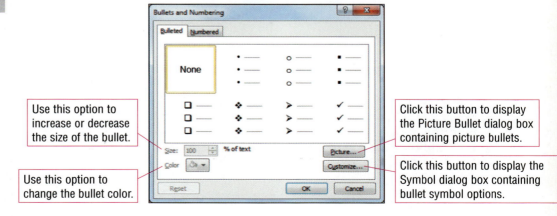

At the Bullets and Numbering dialog box, choose one of the predesigned bullets from the list box, change the size of the bullets by percentage in relation to the text size, change the bullet color, and display bullet pictures and characters. Click the Picture button located toward the bottom of the dialog box and the Picture Bullet dialog box displays. Click the desired bullet in the list box and then click OK. Click the Customize button located toward the bottom of the Bullets and Numbering dialog box and the Symbol dialog box displays. Choose a symbol bullet option at the Symbol dialog box and then click OK. Picture or symbol bullets are particularly effective in adding visual interest.

Choose a custom bullet that matches the theme or mood of the presentation.

Picture

If you want to move the insertion point down to the next line without inserting a bullet, press Shift + Enter. This inserts a line break without inserting a bullet. If you press the Enter key, bulleting is turned back on.

Project 2a Customizing Bullets and Numbers   Part 1 of 3

1. Open **ColorPres.pptx** and then save the presentation with Save As and name it **P-C3-P2-ColorPres**.
2. Increase list level and create custom bullets by completing the following steps:
   a. Make Slide 2 active.
   b. Select the second, third, and fourth bulleted paragraphs.
   c. Click the Increase List Level button in the Paragraph group in the Home tab.
   d. With the three bulleted paragraphs still selected, click the Bullets button arrow and then click *Bullets and Numbering* at the drop-down list.
   e. At the Bullets and Numbering dialog box with the Bulleted tab selected, click the up-pointing arrow at the right side of the *Size* option until *75* displays in the text box.
   f. Click the Picture button located toward the bottom right corner of the dialog box.
   g. At the Picture Bullet dialog box, click a yellow square bullet option like the one shown below.
   h. Click OK to close the Picture Bullet dialog box and the Bullets and Numbering dialog box.

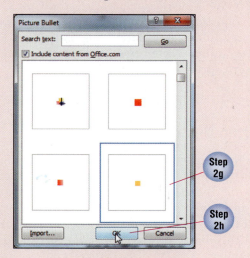

3. Insert symbol bullets by completing the following steps:
   a. Make Slide 3 active.
   b. Select all of the bulleted text.
   c. Click the Bullets button arrow and then click *Bullets and Numbering* at the drop-down list.
   d. At the Bullets and Numbering dialog box with the Bulleted tab selected, click the up-pointing arrow at the right side of the *Size* option until *80* displays in the text box.

e. Click the Customize button located toward the bottom right corner of the dialog box.
f. At the Symbol dialog box, click the down-pointing arrow at the right side of the *Font* option box, scroll down the drop-down list, and then click *Wingdings*. (This option is located toward the bottom of the list.)
g. Scroll to the bottom of the Symbol dialog box list box until the last row of symbols displays and then click the second symbol from the right in the bottom row (check mark inside of a square).
h. Click OK.

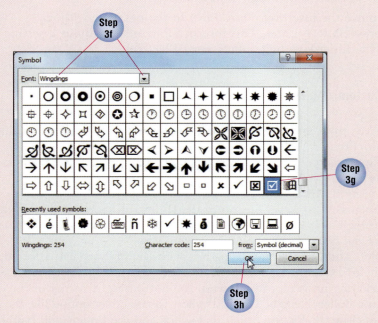

i. At the Bullets and Numbering dialog box, click the Font Color button and then click the Red color (second color from the left in the *Standard Colors* section).
j. Click OK to close the Bullets and Numbering dialog box. (This applies the red check mark symbol bullets to the selected text.)
4. Save **P-C3-P2-ColorPres.pptx**.

Customizing Numbering

▼ **Quick Steps**

Customize Numbering
1. Click in numbered text.
2. Click Numbering button arrow.
3. Click *Bullets and Numbering* at drop-down gallery.
4. Make desired changes.
5. Click OK.

Click the Numbering button arrow in the Paragraph group and several numbering options display in a drop-down gallery. You can customize numbering with options at the Bullets and Numbering dialog box with the Numbered tab selected as shown in Figure 3.7. Display this dialog box by clicking the Numbering button arrow and then clicking *Bullets and Numbering* at the drop-down gallery. Use options at this dialog box to change the size and color of numbers as well as the starting number.

If you want to move the insertion point down to the next line without inserting a number, press Shift + Enter. If you press Enter, numbering is turned back on.

Numbering

Figure 3.7 Bullets and Numbering Dialog Box with Numbered Tab Selected

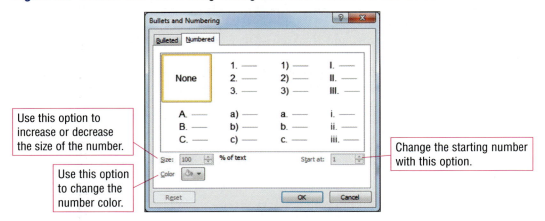

Project 2b Customizing Numbers   Part 2 of 3

1. With **P-C3-P2-ColorPres.pptx** open, make sure the presentation displays in Normal view.
2. Customize and insert numbers by completing the following steps:
   a. Make Slide 4 active.
   b. Select the bulleted text in the slide.
   c. Click the Numbering button arrow in the Paragraph group in the Home tab and then click the *Bullets and Numbering* option at the drop-down list.
   d. At the Bullets and Numbering dialog box with the Numbered tab selected, click the *1. 2. 3.* option (second option from the left in the top row).
   e. Click the up-pointing arrow at the right side of the *Size* option until *80* displays in the text box.
   f. Click the Font Color button and then the Dark Red color (first color option from the left in the *Standard Colors* row).
   g. Click OK.

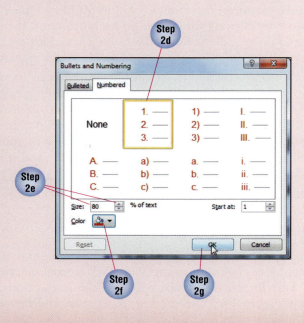

Chapter 3 ■ Formatting Slides   93

h. Make Slide 5 active.
i. Select the bulleted text in the slide.
j. Click the Numbering button arrow and then click the *Bullets and Numbering* option at the drop-down list.
k. At the Bullets and Numbering dialog box with the Numbered tab selected, click the *1. 2. 3.* option (second option from the left in the top row).
l. Click the up-pointing arrow at the right side of the *Size* option until *80* displays in the text box.
m. Click the Font Color button and then click the Dark Red color (first color option from the left in the *Standard Colors* row).
n. Click the up-pointing arrow at the right of the *Start at* option until *6* displays in the text box.
o. Click OK.
3. Add a transition and sound of your choosing to all slides in the presentation.
4. Run the presentation.
5. Save **P-C3-P2-ColorPres.pptx**.

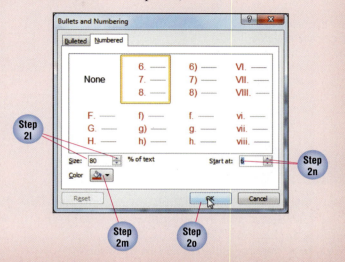

Customizing Placeholders

You can customize a placeholder in a slide with buttons in the Drawing group in the Home tab. For example, you can apply a fill color, an outline, and an effect to a placeholder. You can also customize a placeholder by applying a **Quick Style**. To customize a placeholder, click in the placeholder to select it and then click the desired button in the Drawing group. Apply a Quick Style to the selected placeholder by clicking the Quick Styles button and then clicking the desired style at the drop-down gallery. Click the *Other Theme Fills* option that displays at the bottom of the drop-down gallery and a side menu displays with additional fills.

In addition to the Quick Styles button, you can use the Shape Fill, Shape Outline, and Shape Effects buttons in the Drawing group in the Home tab to customize a placeholder. Click the Shape Fill button arrow and a drop-down gallery displays with options for applying a color, picture, gradient, or texture to the placeholder. Use the Shape Outline button to apply an outline to a placeholder and specify the outline color, weight, and style. With the Shape Effects button, you can choose from a variety of effects such as shadow, reflection, glow, and soft edges.

HINT You can also use options in the Drawing Tools Format tab to customize a placeholder.

Quick Styles

Shape Fill

Shape Outline

Shape Effects

Changing Internal Margins

When you apply formatting to a placeholder, you may need to move text within the placeholder. You can do this with the internal margins measurements in the Format Text Effects dialog box with the *Text Box* option selected in the left panel (shown in Figure 3.4). Use the *Left*, *Right*, *Top*, and *Bottom* measurements boxes to specify internal margins for text inside the placeholder.

Project 2c Customizing Placeholders   Part 3 of 3

1. With **P-C3-P2-ColorPres.pptx** open, customize the title placeholder in Slide 1 by completing the following steps:
   a. If necessary, make Slide 1 active.
   b. Click in the title to select the placeholder.
   c. If necessary, click the Home tab.
   d. Click the Quick Styles button in the Drawing group.
   e. Click the *Moderate Effect - Green, Accent 1* option at the drop-down gallery (second option from the left in the fifth row).
   f. Click the Shape Outline button arrow in the Drawing group and then click *Blue* in the *Standard Colors* section.
   g. Click the Shape Outline button arrow, point to *Weight*, and then click *3 pt* at the side menu.
   h. Click the Shape Effects button, point to *Bevel*, and then click *Cool Slant* at the side menu (last option in the top row in the *Bevel* section).

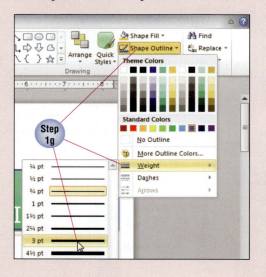

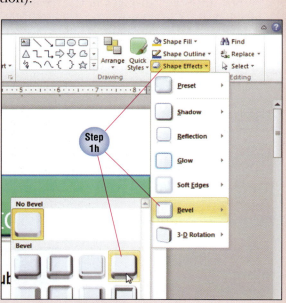

   i. After looking at the fill color, you decide to change it by clicking the Quick Styles button in the Drawing group, pointing to *Other Theme Fills* that displays at the bottom of the drop-down gallery, and then clicking *Style 11* at the side menu (third option from the left in the bottom row).

2. Change the internal margins for the text in the title placeholder by completing the following steps:
    a. With the title placeholder selected, click the Text Direction button in the Paragraph group in the Home tab and then click *More Options* at the drop-down list.
    b. At the Format Text Effects dialog box with *Text Box* selected in the left panel, click the up-pointing arrow at the right side of the *Left* measurement box until *0.6"* displays in the measurement box.

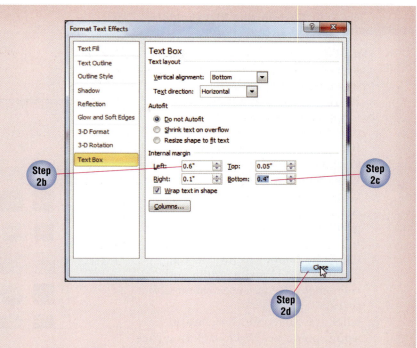

    c. Click the up-pointing arrow at the right side of the *Bottom* measurement box until *0.4"* displays in the measurement box.
    d. Click the Close button to close the dialog box.
3. Customize the subtitle placeholder by completing the following steps:
    a. Click in the subtitle text to select the placeholder.
    b. Click the Shape Fill button arrow in the Drawing group, point to *Texture*, and then click *Water droplets* at the drop-down gallery (first option from the left in the second row).

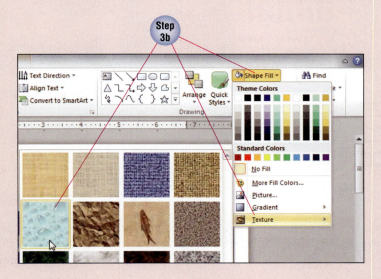

    c. Click the Shape Effects button, point to *Bevel*, and then click *Cool Slant* at the side menu (last option in the top row in the *Bevel* section).

4. Change the internal margins for the text in the subtitle placeholder by completing the following steps:
   a. With the subtitle placeholder selected, click the Text Direction button in the Paragraph group in the Home tab and then click *More Options* at the drop-down list.
   b. At the Format Text Effects dialog box with *Text Box* selected in the left panel, click the up-pointing arrow at the right side of the *Left* measurement box until *0.3"* displays in the measurement box.
   c. Click the up-pointing arrow at the right side of the *Top* measurement box until *0.6"* displays in the measurement box.
   d. Click the Close button to close the dialog box.
5. Make Slide 3 active and then change the spacing after paragraphs by completing the following steps:
   a. Select the bulleted text.
   b. Click the Paragraph group dialog box launcher.
   c. At the Paragraph dialog box, click the up-pointing arrow at the right side of the *After* option in the *Spacing* section to display *6 pt* in the option box.
   d. Click OK to close the dialog box.
6. Customize the placeholder by completing the following steps:

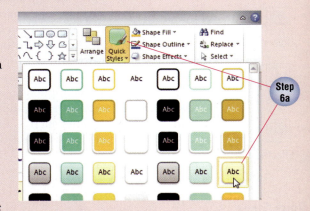

   a. With the bulleted text placeholder selected, click the Quick Styles button in the Drawing group and then click *Subtle Effect - Gold, Accent 6* at the drop-down gallery (last option in the fourth row).
   b. Click the Shape Effects button in the Drawing group, point to *Soft Edges*, and then click *2.5 Point* at the side menu.
   c. Click the Text Direction button in the Paragraph group and then click *More Options* at the drop-down list.
   d. At the Format Text Effects dialog box, change the left, right, top, and bottom measurements to *0.4"*.
   e. Click the Close button to close the dialog box.
   f. Move the placeholder so it is positioned attractively in the slide.
7. Run the presentation.
8. You decide that you do not like the appearance of the formatting of the subtitle placeholder in Slide 1 so you decide to remove the formatting by completing the following steps:
   a. Make Slide 1 active.
   b. Click on any character in the subtitle placeholder text.
   c. Make sure the Home tab is selected.
   d. Click the Quick Styles button in the Drawing group and then click the *Colored Outline - White, Accent 3* option (fourth option from the left in the top row).
9. Print the presentation as a handout with six slides horizontally per page.
10. Save and then close **P-C3-P2-ColorPres.pptx**.

> **Project 3** **Modify the Theme and Slide Background of a Job Search Presentation** **2 Parts**
>
> You will open a job search presentation, apply a design theme, and then change the theme colors and fonts. You will also apply and customize a background style.

Modifying Theme Colors and Fonts

HINT Themes are shared across Office programs such as PowerPoint, Word, and Excel.

A design theme is a set of formatting choices that includes a color theme (a set of colors), a font theme (heading and text fonts), and an effects theme (a set of lines and fill effects). Use buttons at the right side of the Themes group in the Design tab to change design theme colors, fonts, and effects.

A theme contains specific color formatting, which you can change with options from the Colors button in the Themes group. Click this button and a drop-down gallery displays with named color schemes. The names of the color schemes correspond to the names of the themes. Each theme applies specific fonts, which you can change with options from the Fonts button in the Themes group. Click this button and a drop-down gallery displays with font choices. Each font group in the drop-down gallery contains two choices. The first choice in the group is the font that is applied to slide titles and the second choice is the font that is applied to slide subtitles and text. If you are formatting a presentation that contains graphic elements such as illustrations, pictures, clip art, or text boxes, you can specify theme effects with options at the Effects drop-down gallery.

Colors

Fonts

Effects

Changing Slide Background

▼ Quick Steps
Change Slide Background
1. Click Design tab.
2. Click Background Styles button.
3. Click desired style at drop-down gallery.

Background Styles

The Background group in the Design tab contains a button and an option for customizing the background of slides in a presentation. Click the Background Styles button and a drop-down gallery of background styles displays. Click the desired style at this drop-down gallery or click the *Format Background* option to display the Format Background dialog box shown in Figure 3.8. You can also display the dialog box by clicking the Background group dialog box launcher. Use options in this dialog box to customize background fill, gradient, direction, and color. If you make changes to the slide background, you can reset the background to the default by clicking the Reset Background button in the Format Background dialog box. You can also reset the background to the default by clicking the Background Styles button and then clicking *Reset Slide Background* at the drop-down gallery.

Some of the design themes provided by PowerPoint contain a background graphic. You can remove this graphic from a slide by clicking the *Hide Background Graphics* check box in the Background group. This removes the background from the currently active slide. If you want to remove the background from more than one slide, select the slides. You can also remove background graphics from all slides by inserting a check mark in the *Hide background graphics* check box in the Format Background dialog box and then clicking the Apply to All button.

Figure 3.8 Format Background Dialog Box

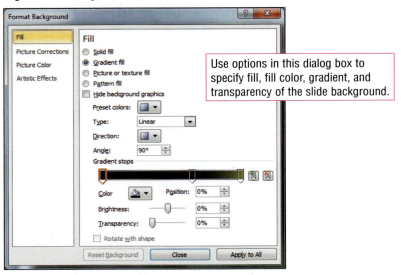

Use options in this dialog box to specify fill, fill color, gradient, and transparency of the slide background.

Project 3a   Customizing Theme Colors and Fonts   Part 1 of 2

1. Open **JobSearch.pptx** and then save the presentation with Save As and name it **P-C3-P3-JobSearch**.
2. Apply a design theme by completing the following steps:
   a. Click the Design tab.
   b. Click the More button at the right side of the design theme thumbnails and then click *Metro* at the drop-down gallery.
3. Change the theme colors by clicking the Colors button in the Themes group, scrolling down the drop-down gallery, and then clicking *Paper*.
4. Change the theme fonts by clicking the Fonts button in the Themes group, scrolling down the drop-down gallery, and then clicking *Solstice*.

5. Change the background style by clicking the Background Styles button in the Background group and then clicking *Style 10* at the drop-down gallery.

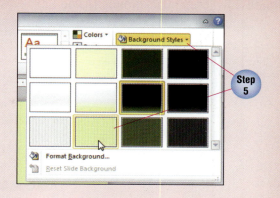

6. With Slide 1 active, run the presentation and notice the formatting applied by the theme, theme colors, theme fonts, and background style.
7. With the presentation in Normal view, change the background style by clicking the Background Styles button in the Background group in the Design tab and then clicking *Style 7* at the drop-down gallery.
8. Apply and customize a background style by completing the following steps:
    a. Click the Background group dialog box launcher.
    b. At the Format Background dialog box, click the *Hide background graphics* check box to insert a check mark.
    c. Click the down-pointing arrow to the right of the *Type* option box and then click *Path* at the drop-down list.
    d. Drag the first button on the *Gradient stops* slider bar until *80%* displays in the Position text box.

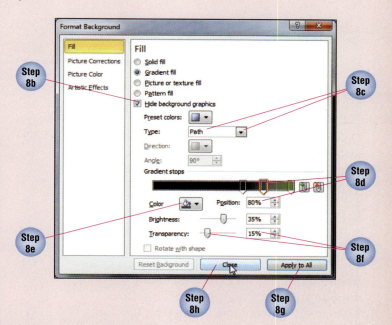

   e. Click the Color button and then click the *Black, Background 1, Lighter 35%* color (located in the first column).
   f. Drag the button on the *Transparency* slider bar until *15%* displays in the percentage box at the right. (You can also click the up-pointing arrow at the right side of the percentage box until *15%* displays.)
   g. Click the Apply to All button.
   h. Click the Close button.
9. Run the presentation and notice the background formatting.
10. Save **P-C3-P3-JobSearch.pptx**.

Changing Page Setup

You can control page setup and the orientation of slides with buttons in the Page Setup group in the Design tab. The default slide orientation is *Landscape*. You can change this to *Portrait* with the Slide Orientation button. Click the Page Setup button and the Page Setup dialog box displays as shown in Figure 3.9. With options at this dialog box, you can specify how you want the slides sized. By default, slides are sized for an on-screen show with a 4:3 ratio. Click the down-pointing arrow at the right side of the *Slides sized for* option and a drop-down list displays with options for changing the slide size ratio and choosing other paper sizes. With other options in the dialog box, you can specify slide width and height and change the starting slide number. You can also change the orientation of slides and the orientation of notes, handouts, and outline pages.

Slide Orientation

Page Setup

Figure 3.9 Page Setup Dialog Box

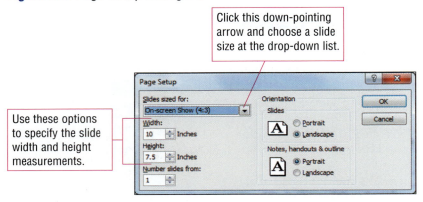

Project 3b   Changing Orientation and Page Setup   Part 2 of 2

1. With **P-C3-P3-JobSearch.pptx** open, change slide orientation by clicking the Design tab, clicking the Slide Orientation button in the Page Setup group, and then clicking *Portrait* at the drop-down list.

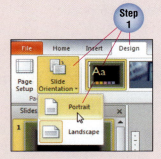

2. Run the presentation and notice how the slides appear in portrait orientation.
3. After running the presentation, click the Slide Orientation button and then click *Landscape* at the drop-down list.

4. Suppose you are going to run the presentation on a wide screen monitor. To do this, you decide to change the slide size ratio by completing the following steps:
   a. Click the Page Setup button in the Page Setup group in the Design tab.
   b. At the Page Setup dialog box, click the down-pointing arrow at the right side of the *Slides sized for* option and then click *On-screen Show (16:10)*. (Notice that the slide height changed from *7.5* to *6.25*.)
   c. Click OK.

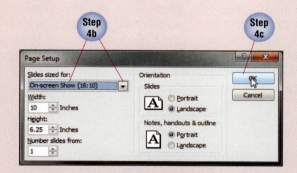

5. Run the presentation.
6. Specify slide width and height by completing the following steps:
   a. Click the Page Setup button in the Page Setup group in the Design tab.
   b. At the Page Setup dialog box, click the down-pointing arrow at the right side of the *Width* measurement box until *9* displays in the box.
   c. Click the down-pointing arrow at the right side of the *Height* measurement box until *6* displays in the box.
   d. Click OK.
7. Run the presentation.
8. Return the slide size to the default by completing the following steps:
   a. Click the Page Setup button in the Page Setup group in the Design tab.
   b. At the Page Setup dialog box, click the down-pointing arrow at the right side of the *Slides sized for* option and then click *On-screen Show (4:3)*.
   c. Click OK.
9. Print the presentation as a handout with nine slides horizontally per page.
10. Save and then close **P-C3-P3-JobSearch.pptx**.

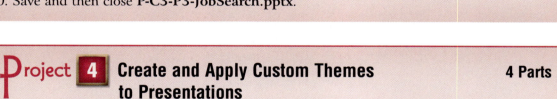

Project 4   **Create and Apply Custom Themes to Presentations**   4 Parts

You will create custom theme colors and custom theme fonts and then save the changes as a custom theme. You will then apply the custom theme to a job search presentation and a resume writing presentation.

Creating Custom Themes

If the default themes, theme colors, and theme fonts do not provide the formatting you desire for your presentation, you can create your own custom theme colors, custom theme fonts, and a custom theme. A theme you create will display in the Themes drop-down gallery under the *Custom* section. To create a custom theme, change the theme colors, theme fonts, and/or theme effects.

The buttons at the right side of the Themes group in the Design tab display a visual representation of the current theme. If you change the theme colors, the colors are reflected in the small color squares on the Colors button. If you change the theme fonts, the *A* on the Fonts button reflects the change.

Creating Custom Theme Colors

To create custom theme colors, click the Design tab, click the Colors button in the Themes group, and then click *Create New Theme Colors* at the drop-down gallery. This displays the Create New Theme Colors dialog box similar to the one shown in Figure 3.10. Theme colors contain four text and background colors, six accent colors, and two hyperlink colors as shown in the *Themes color* section of the dialog box. Change a color in the list box by clicking the color button at the right side of the color option and then clicking the desired color at the color palette.

After you have made all desired changes to colors, click in the *Name* text box, type a name for the custom theme colors, and then click the Save button. This saves the custom theme colors and applies the color changes to the currently open presentation. Display the custom theme colors by clicking the Colors button in the Themes group in the Design tab. Your custom theme colors will display toward the top of the drop-down gallery in the *Custom* section. If you make changes to colors at the Create New Theme Colors dialog box and then decide you do not like the color changes, click the Reset button located in the lower left corner of the dialog box.

▼ **Quick Steps**

Create Custom Theme Colors
1. Click Design tab.
2. Click Colors button in Themes group.
3. Click *Create New Theme Colors*.
4. Change to desired background, accent, and hyperlink colors.
5. Type name for custom theme colors.
6. Click Save button.

Figure 3.10 Create New Theme Colors Dialog Box

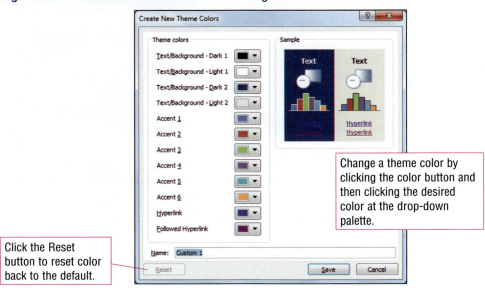

Click the Reset button to reset color back to the default.

Change a theme color by clicking the color button and then clicking the desired color at the drop-down palette.

Chapter 3 ■ Formatting Slides

When you create custom theme colors, you can apply the theme to a presentation by clicking the Colors button in the Themes group in the Design tab and then clicking the custom theme colors that display toward the top of the drop-down gallery in the *Custom* section.

Project 4a   Creating Custom Theme Colors   Part 1 of 4

Note: If you are running PowerPoint 2010 on a computer connected to a network in a public environment such as a school, you may need to complete all four parts of Project 4 during the same session. Network system software may delete your custom themes when you exit PowerPoint. Check with your instructor.

1. At a blank presentation, click the Design tab, click the More button at the right side of the theme thumbnails in the Themes group, and then click *Technic* at the drop-down gallery.
2. Create custom theme colors by completing the following steps:
   a. Click the Colors button in the Themes group and then click the *Create New Theme Colors* option at the drop-down gallery.
   b. At the Create New Theme Colors dialog box, click the color button that displays at the right side of the *Text/Background - Dark 1* option and then click the *Olive Green, Accent 4, Lighter 60%* option.

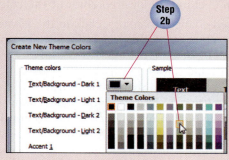

   c. Click the color button that displays at the right side of the *Text/Background - Light 1* option and then click the *Gold, Accent 2, Lighter 80%* option.
   d. Click the color button that displays at the right side of the *Text/Background - Dark 2* option and then click the *Lavender, Accent 3, Darker 25%* option.

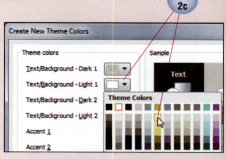

3. Save the custom colors by completing the following steps:
   a. Select the current text in the *Name* text box.
   b. Type your first and last names.
   c. Click the Save button.

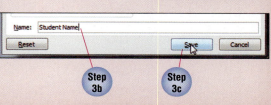

4. Save the presentation and name it **P-C3-P4-CustomTheme**.

Creating Custom Theme Fonts

To create custom theme fonts, click the Design tab, click the Fonts button, and then click *Create New Theme Fonts* at the drop-down gallery. This displays the Create New Theme Fonts dialog box similar to the one shown in Figure 3.11. At this dialog box, choose a heading font and a font for body text. Type a name for the custom theme fonts in the *Name* box and then click the Save button.

Quick Steps

Create Custom Fonts
1. Click Design tab.
2. Click Theme Fonts button.
3. Click *Create New Theme Fonts*.
4. Choose desired fonts.
5. Type name for custom theme fonts.
6. Click Save button.

Figure 3.11 Create New Theme Fonts Dialog Box

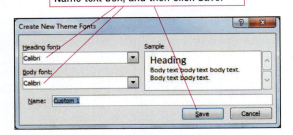

Choose a heading font and body font, type a new name for the theme in the Name text box, and then click Save.

Project 4b Creating Custom Theme Fonts   Part 2 of 4

1. With **P-C3-P4-CustomTheme.pptx** open, create custom theme fonts by completing the following steps:
   a. If necessary, click the Design tab.
   b. Click the Fonts button in the Themes group and then click the *Create New Theme Fonts* option at the drop-down gallery.
   c. At the Create New Theme Fonts dialog box, click the down-pointing arrow at the right side of the *Heading font* option box, scroll up the drop-down list, and then click *Candara*.
   d. Click the down-pointing arrow at the right side of the *Body font* option box, scroll down the drop-down list, and then click *Constantia*.
2. Save the custom theme fonts by completing the following steps:
   a. Select the current text in the *Name* text box.
   b. Type your first and last names.
   c. Click the Save button.
3. Save **P-C3-P4-CustomTheme.pptx**.

▼ **Quick Steps**

Save a Custom Theme
1. Click Design tab.
2. Click More button in Themes group.
3. Click *Save Current Theme*.
4. Type name for custom theme.
5. Click Save button.

Saving a Custom Theme

When you have customized theme colors and fonts, you can save these as a custom theme. To do this, click the More button at the right side of the Themes group in the Design tab and then click *Save Current Theme*. This displays the Save Current Theme dialog box with many of the same options as the Save As dialog box. Type a name for your custom theme in the *File name* text box and then click the Save button. To apply a custom theme, click the More button and then click the desired theme in the *Custom* section of the drop-down gallery.

Project 4c   Saving and Applying a Custom Theme   Part 3 of 4

1. With **P-C3-P4-CustomTheme.pptx** open, save the custom theme colors and fonts as a custom theme by completing the following steps:
   a. If necessary, click the Design tab.
   b. Click the More button at the right side of the theme thumbnails in the Themes group.
   c. Click the *Save Current Theme* option that displays at the bottom of the drop-down gallery.
   d. At the Save Current Theme dialog box, type **C3** and then type your last name in the *File name* text box.
   e. Click the Save button.

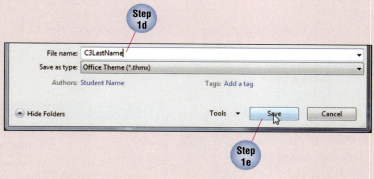

2. Close **P-C3-P4-CustomTheme.pptx**.
3. Open **JobSearch.pptx** and then save the presentation with Save as and name it **P-C3-P4-JobSearch**.
4. Apply your custom theme by completing the following steps:
   a. Click the Design tab.
   b. Click the More button that displays at the right side of the theme thumbnails.
   c. Click the custom theme that begins with *C3* followed by your last name. (The theme will display in the *Custom* section of the drop-down gallery.)
5. Run the presentation and notice how the slides display with the custom theme applied.
6. Print Slide 1 of the presentation.

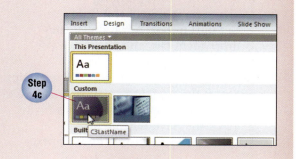

7. Save and then close **P-C3-P4-JobSearch.pptx**.
8. Open **ResumePres.pptx** and then save the presentation with Save As and name it **P-C3-P4-ResumePres**.
9. Apply your custom theme (the theme that displays beginning with *C3* followed by your last name).
10. Make Slide 2 active and then adjust the placeholder containing the bulleted text so it is positioned attractively on the slide.
11. Make Slide 1 active and then run the presentation.
12. Print Slide 1 of the presentation.
13. Save and then close **P-C3-P4-ResumePres.pptx**.

Editing Custom Themes

You can edit the custom theme colors and custom theme fonts. To edit the custom theme colors, click the Colors button in the Themes group in the Design tab. At the drop-down gallery of custom and built-in themes, right-click your custom theme and then click *Edit* at the shortcut menu. This displays the Edit Theme Colors dialog box that contains the same options as the Create New Theme Colors dialog box shown in Figure 3.10 on page 103. Make the desired changes to theme colors and then click the Save button.

To edit custom theme fonts, click the Fonts button in the Themes group in the Design tab, right-click your custom theme fonts, and then click *Edit* at the shortcut menu. This displays the Edit Theme Fonts dialog box that contains the same options as the Create New Theme Fonts dialog box shown in Figure 3.11 on page 105. Make the desired changes and then click the Save button.

Deleting Custom Themes

You can delete custom theme colors from the Colors button drop-down gallery, delete custom theme fonts from the Fonts drop-down gallery, and delete custom themes from the Save Current Theme dialog box. To delete custom theme colors, click the Colors button, right-click the theme you want to delete, and then click *Delete* at the shortcut menu. At the message asking if you want to delete the theme colors, click Yes. Complete similar steps to delete custom theme fonts.

Delete a custom theme at the Save Current Theme dialog box. To display this dialog box, click the More button at the right side of the Themes group in the Design tab and then click *Save Current Theme* at the drop-down gallery. At the dialog box, click the custom theme file name, click the Organize button on the toolbar, and then click *Delete* at the drop-down list. At the message asking if you are sure you want to send the theme to the Recycle Bin, click Yes.

▼ Quick Steps

Edit Custom Theme Colors
1. Click Design tab.
2. Click Colors button in Themes group.
3. Right-click desired custom theme.
4. Click *Edit*.
5. Make desired changes.
6. Click Save button.

Edit Custom Theme Fonts
1. Click Design tab.
2. Click Fonts button in Themes group.
3. Right-click desired custom theme.
4. Click *Edit*.
5. Make desired changes.
6. Click Save button.

Delete Custom Theme Colors
1. Click Design tab.
2. Click Colors button in Themes group.
3. Right-click desired custom theme.
4. Click *Delete*.
5. Click Yes.

Delete Custom Theme Fonts
1. Click Design tab.
2. Click Fonts button in Themes group.
3. Right-click desired custom theme.
4. Click *Delete*.
5. Click Yes.

Delete Custom Theme
1. Click Design tab.
2. Click More button in Themes group.
3. Click *Save Current Theme*.
4. Click custom theme.
5. Click Organize button, *Delete*.
6. Click Yes.

Project 4d Deleting Custom Themes   Part 4 of 4

1. At a blank presentation, delete the custom theme colors by completing the following steps:
   a. Click the Design tab.
   b. Click the Colors button in the Themes group.
   c. Right-click the custom theme colors named with your first and last names.
   d. Click *Delete* at the shortcut menu.

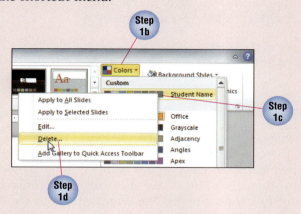

   e. At the message asking if you want to delete the theme colors, click Yes.
2. Complete steps similar to those in Step 1 to delete the custom theme fonts you created named with your first and last names.
3. Delete the custom theme by completing the following steps:
   a. Click the More button that displays at the right side of the theme thumbnails.
   b. Click *Save Current Theme* located toward the bottom of the drop-down gallery.
   c. At the Save Current Theme dialog box, click the custom theme that begins with *C3* followed by your last name.
   d. Click the Organize button on the toolbar and then click *Delete* at the drop-down list.
   e. At the message asking if you are sure you want to send the theme to the Recycle Bin, click Yes.
   f. Click the Cancel button to close the dialog box.
4. Close the presentation without saving it.

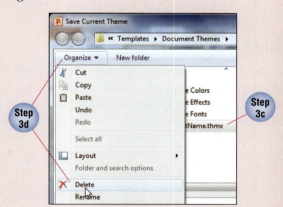

Chapter Summary

- The Font group in the Home tab contains buttons for applying character formatting to text in slides.
- Design themes apply a font to text in slides. You can change this default font with the Font and Font Size buttons in the Font group.
- Some buttons, such as the Font and Font Size buttons, contain the live preview feature, which allows you to see how the formatting affects your text without having to return to the presentation.
- You can also apply character formatting with options at the Font dialog box. Display this dialog box by clicking the Font group dialog box launcher.
- Select text in a slide and the Mini toolbar displays above the selected text in dimmed fashion. Move the mouse pointer to the toolbar and it becomes active.
- Use the Format Painter feature to apply formatting to more than one location in a slide or slides.
- The Paragraph group in the Home tab contains a number of buttons for applying paragraph formatting to text in slides.
- Customize paragraph formatting with options at the Paragraph dialog box with the Indents and Spacing tab selected. Display this dialog box by clicking the Paragraph group dialog box launcher or by clicking the Line Spacing button in the Paragraph group and then clicking *Line Spacing Options* at the drop-down list.
- Use the Columns button in the Paragraph group or options at the Columns dialog box to format selected text into columns. Display the Columns dialog box by clicking the Columns button and then clicking *More Columns* at the drop-down list.
- Use the Text Direction button or options at the Format Text Effects dialog box to rotate or stack text in a slide. Display the Format Text Effects dialog box by clicking the Text Direction button and then clicking *More Options* at the drop-down list.
- Use the Align Text button or options at the Format Text Effects dialog box to vertically align text in a slide.
- Customize bullets with options at the Bullets and Numbering dialog box with the Bulleted tab selected. Display this dialog box by clicking the Bullets button arrow and then clicking *Bullets and Numbering* at the drop-down list.
- Customize numbering with options at the Bullets and Numbering dialog box with the Numbered tab selected. Display this dialog box by clicking the Numbering button arrow and then clicking *Bullets and Numbering* at the drop-down list.
- Click the Quick Styles button in the Drawing group in the Home tab to apply formatting to a placeholder. The Drawing group also contains the Shape Fill, Shape Outline, and Shape Effects buttons you can use to customize a placeholder.
- Use the Colors button in the Themes group in the Design tab to change the theme colors and use the Fonts button to change the theme fonts.

- Use the Background Styles button in the Background group in the Design tab to customize the background of slides and insert a check mark in the *Hide Background Graphics* check box to remove the slide background graphic.
- Click the Page Setup button in the Design tab and the Page Setup dialog box displays containing options for changing the slide size and ratio, starting slide number, and the orientation of slides and notes, handouts, and outline pages.
- Create custom theme colors with options at the Create New Theme Colors dialog box. Display this dialog box by clicking the Colors button in the Themes group in the Design tab and then clicking *Create New Theme Colors* at the drop-down gallery.
- Create custom theme fonts with options at the Create New Theme Fonts dialog box. Display this dialog box by clicking the Fonts button in the Themes group in the Design tab and then clicking *Create New Theme Fonts* at the drop-down gallery.
- Save a custom theme at the Save Current Theme dialog box. Display this dialog box by clicking the Themes button in the Themes group in the Design tab and then clicking *Save Current Theme* at the drop-down gallery.
- Edit custom theme colors with options at the Edit Theme Colors dialog box and edit custom theme fonts with options at the Edit Theme Fonts dialog box.
- Delete custom theme colors by clicking the Theme Colors button, right-clicking the custom theme, and then clicking the *Delete* option.
- Delete custom theme fonts by clicking the Theme Fonts button, right-clicking the custom theme, and then clicking the *Delete* option.
- Delete a custom theme at the Save Current Theme dialog box. Display this dialog box by clicking the Themes button and then clicking *Save Current Theme* at the drop-down gallery.

Commands Review

FEATURE	RIBBON TAB, GROUP	BUTTON, OPTION	KEYBOARD SHORTCUT
Font dialog box	Home, Font		Ctrl + Shift + F
Format Painter	Home, Clipboard		
Paragraph dialog box	Home, Paragraph		
Columns dialog box	Home, Paragraph	, More Columns	
Format Text Effects dialog box	Home, Paragraph	, More Options	
Bullets and Numbering dialog box with Bulleted tab selected	Home, Paragraph	, Bullets and Numbering	
Bullets and Numbering dialog box with Numbered tab selected	Home, Paragraph	, Bullets and Numbering	
Format Background dialog box	Design, Background		
Page Setup dialog box	Design, Page Setup		
Create New Theme Colors dialog box	Design, Themes	, Create New Theme Colors	
Create New Theme Fonts dialog box	Design, Themes	, Create New Theme Fonts	
Save Current Theme dialog box	Design, Themes	, Save Current Theme	

Concepts Check Test Your Knowledge

Completion: In the space provided at the right, indicate the correct term, symbol, or command.

1. The Font button drop-down gallery is an example of this feature, which allows you to see how the font formatting affects your text without having to return to the presentation. _____

2. Click this button to clear character formatting from selected text. _____

3. Click this to display the Font dialog box. _____

4. Select text in a slide and this displays in a dimmed fashion above the selected text. _____

5. The Format Painter button is located in this group in the Home tab. _____

6. Press this key to move text to the next tab stop (level). _____

7. Use options at this dialog box to change text alignment, indentation, and spacing. _____

8. Click this button in the Paragraph group and a drop-down list displays with options for rotating and stacking text. _____

9. Use the Align Text button or options at this dialog box to vertically align text in a slide. _____

10. Customize numbering with options at the Bullets and Numbering dialog box with this tab selected. _____

11. The Quick Styles button is located in this group in the Home tab. _____

12. Click this button to apply fill to a placeholder. _____

13. Create custom theme colors with options at this dialog box. _____

14. Save a custom theme at this dialog box. _____

Skills Check Assess Your Performance

Assessment

1 CREATE, FORMAT, AND MODIFY A BENEFITS PRESENTATION

1. At a blank presentation, create the slides shown in Figure 3.12.
2. Apply the Oriel design theme.
3. Make Slide 1 active and then make the following changes:
   a. Select the title *BENEFITS PROGRAM*, change the font to Candara, the font size to 48, the font color to Ice Blue, Accent 5, Darker 50%, and apply italic formatting.
   b. Select the subtitle *Changes to Plans*, change the font to Candara, the font size to 32, the font color to Orange, Accent 1, Darker 50%, and apply shadow formatting.
   c. Click the title placeholder and then drag the placeholder up until the title is vertically centered on the slide.
   d. Click the subtitle placeholder and then drag the placeholder up so the subtitle is positioned just below the title.
4. Make Slide 2 active and then make the following changes:
   a. Select the title *INTRODUCTION*, change the font to Candara, the font size to 48 points, and apply shadow formatting.
   b. Using Format Painter, apply the title formatting to the titles in the remaining slides.
5. Center-align the titles in Slides 2 through 5.
6. Make Slide 2 active, select the bulleted text, and then change the line spacing to *2.0*.
7. Make Slide 3 active, select the bulleted text, and then change the line spacing to *2.0*.
8. Make Slide 4 active, select the bulleted text, and then change the line spacing to *1.5*.
9. Make Slide 5 active, select the bulleted text, and then change the spacing after paragraphs to *18 pt*. **Hint: Do this at the Paragraph dialog box.**
10. Make Slide 2 active and then select the bulleted text. Display the Bullets and Numbering dialog box with the Numbered tab selected, choose the *1. 2. 3.* option, change the size to *85%*, and then close the dialog box.
11. Make Slide 3 active and then select the bulleted text. Display the Bullets and Numbering dialog box with the Numbered tab selected, choose the *1. 2. 3.* option, change the size to *85%*, change the starting number to *5*, and then close the dialog box.
12. Make Slide 4 active, select the bulleted text, and then change the bullets to *Hollow Square Bullets*.
13. Make Slide 5 active, select the bulleted text, and then change the bullets to *Hollow Square Bullets*.
14. Apply the *Style 5* background style to slides.
15. Save the presentation and name it **P-C3-A1-Benefits**.
16. Print the presentation as a handout with six slides horizontally per page.
17. Change the theme colors to *Solstice*.
18. Apply the *Style 2* background style to slides.
19. Apply a transition and sound of your choosing to each slide.

20. Run the presentation.
21. Print the presentation as a handout with six slides horizontally per page.
22. Save and then close **P-C3-A1-Benefits.pptx**.

Figure 3.12 Assessment 1

Slide 1	Title	=	BENEFITS PROGRAM
	Subtitle	=	Changes to Plans
Slide 2	Title	=	INTRODUCTION
	Subtitle	=	• Changes made for 2013 • Description of eligibility • Instructions for enrolling new members • Overview of medical and dental coverage
Slide 3	Title	=	INTRODUCTION
	Subtitle	=	• Expanded enrollment forms • Glossary defining terms • Telephone directory • Pamphlet with commonly asked questions
Slide 4	Title	=	WHAT'S NEW

	Subtitle	=	• New medical plans
			   ○ Plan 2013
			   ○ Premier Plan
			• Changes in monthly contributions
			• Paying with pretax dollars
			• Contributions toward spouse's coverage

Slide 5	Title	=	COST SHARING
	Subtitle	=	• Increased deductible • New coinsurance amount • Higher coinsurance amount for retail prescription drugs • Co-payment for mail-order medicines • New stop loss limit

Assessment 2 — FORMAT AND MODIFY A PERENNIALS PRESENTATION

1. Open **PerennialsPres.pptx** and then save the presentation with Save As and name it **P-C3-A2-PerennialsPres**.
2. Change the theme fonts to *Opulent*. (Make sure you change the theme fonts and **not** the theme.)
3. Make Slide 3 active, select the bulleted text, and then create and apply a custom bullet using a flower symbol in a complementary color. (You can find a flower symbol in the *Wingdings* font in the Symbol dialog box.)
4. With Slide 3 active, format the bulleted text into two columns and change the line spacing to *2*. Make sure each column contains four bulleted items. If not, make any spacing or other corrections to make the columns even.

5. Make Slide 4 active and then arrange the bulleted text more attractively on the slide. (You determine the formatting and position.)
6. Make Slide 5 active and then format the bulleted text into two columns with three bulleted items in each column. Make any spacing or formatting changes to improve the visual appeal of the slide.
7. Make Slide 6 active and then format the bulleted text into two columns with three bulleted items in each column. Make any spacing or formatting change to improve the visual appeal of the slide.
8. Make any other changes to slides to improve the visual appeal of each slide.
9. Print the presentation with four slides horizontally per page.
10. Add a transition and sound of your choosing to all slides in the presentation.
11. Run the presentation.
12. Save and then close **P-C3-A2-PerennialsPres.pptx**.

Assessment

3 CREATE AND APPLY A CUSTOM THEME TO A TRAVEL PRESENTATION

1. At a blank presentation, apply the *Opulent* design theme.
2. Create custom theme colors named with your first and last names that changes the following colors:
   a. At the Create New Theme Colors dialog box, change the *Text/Background - Light 1* option to *Gold, Accent 4, Lighter 80%*.
   b. Change the *Text/Background - Dark 2* option to *Green* (sixth color from the left in the *Standard Colors* row).
3. Create custom theme fonts named with your first and last names that applies the following fonts:
   a. At the Create New Theme Fonts dialog box, change the *Heading font* to *Copperplate Gothic Bold*.
   b. Change the *Body font* to *Rockwell*.
4. Save the current theme as a custom theme named with your first and last names. **Hint: Do this at the Save Current Theme dialog box.**
5. Close the presentation without saving it.
6. Open **TravelEngland.pptx** and then save the presentation with Save As and name it **P-C3-A3-TravelEngland**.
7. Apply the custom theme named with your first and last names.
8. Improve the visual display of the bulleted text in Slides 2 and 3 by increasing the spacing between items and positioning the bulleted item placeholders attractively in the slides.
9. Make Slide 4 active, increase the spacing between bulleted items and then format the text into two columns. Make sure that each column contains three bulleted items. Consider decreasing the size of the placeholder.
10. Format the bulleted text in Slides 5 and 6 into two columns with four bulleted items in each column. Consider decreasing the size of the placeholder as a handout with six slides horizontally per page.
11. Print the presentation as a handout with six slides horizontally per page.
12. Add a transition and sound of your choosing to all slides in the presentation.
13. Run the presentation.
14. Save and then close **P-C3-A3-TravelEngland.pptx**.
15. Display a blank presentation and then delete the custom theme colors, custom theme fonts, and custom theme you created for this assessment.
16. Close the presentation without saving it.

Assessment

4 PREPARE A PRESENTATION ON ONLINE SHOPPING

1. Open Microsoft Word and then open the document **OnlineShopping.docx** that is located in the PowerPoint2010C3 folder on your storage medium.
2. Print the document by clicking the File tab, clicking the Print tab, and then clicking the Print button at the Print tab Backstage view.
3. Close **OnlineShopping.docx** and then exit Word.
4. At a blank PowerPoint presentation, use the information you printed to create a presentation on online shopping with the following specifications:
    a. Create a slide with the title of your presentation. Type your name as the subtitle.
    b. Create slides (you determine the number of slides) that summarize the information you printed. (Make sure the slides are not crowded with too much information.)
    c. Apply a design theme of your choosing.
    d. Change the design theme colors.
    e. Change the design theme fonts.
    f. Apply a transition and sound of your choosing to all slides.
5. Save the presentation and name it **P-C3-A4-OnlineShopping**.
6. Run the presentation.
7. Print the presentation as a handout with six slides horizontally per page.
8. Close **P-C3-A4-OnlineShopping.pptx**.

Visual Benchmark Demonstrate Your Proficiency

FORMAT A PRESENTATION ON HOME SAFETY

1. Open **HomeSafety.pptx** and then save the presentation with Save As and name it **P-C3-VB-HomeSafety**.
2. Format the presentation so the slides appear as shown in Figure 3.13 with the following specifications.
    a. Apply the *Civic* theme, the *Origin* theme colors, and the *Module* theme fonts.
    b. Apply the *Style 1* background style.
    c. Change the font size of the title in Slide 1 to *48* and apply bold formatting.
    d. Change the font size of the subtitle in Slide 1 to *24* and apply italics.
    e. Change the font of the titles in Slides 2 through 6 to 44-point bold in *Blue-Gray, Accent 1* color.
    f. Change the line spacing, apply column formatting, and then apply other formatting so your slides display similarly to the slides shown in Figure 3.13.
3. Print the presentation as a handout with six slides horizontally per page.
4. Save and then close the presentation.

Figure 3.13 Visual Benchmark

Home Safety
CHILDREN AND BABIES

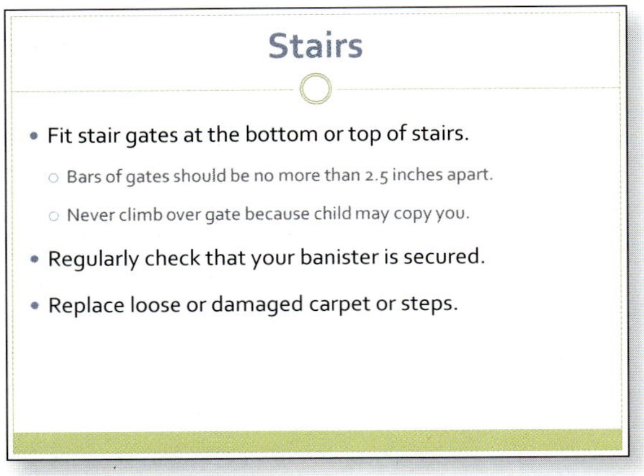

Stairs
- Fit stair gates at the bottom or top of stairs.
  - Bars of gates should be no more than 2.5 inches apart.
  - Never climb over gate because child may copy you.
- Regularly check that your banister is secured.
- Replace loose or damaged carpet or steps.

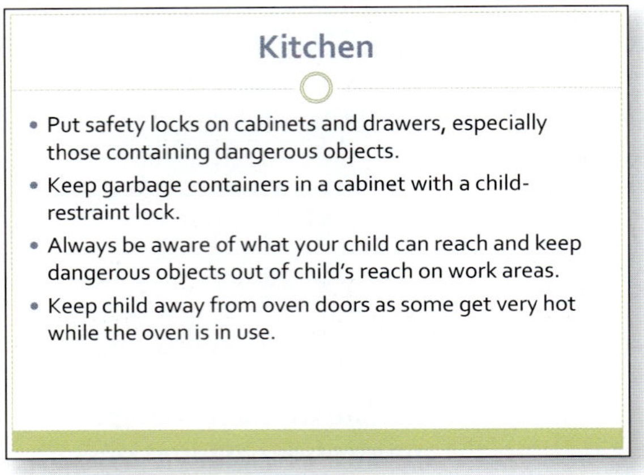

Kitchen
- Put safety locks on cabinets and drawers, especially those containing dangerous objects.
- Keep garbage containers in a cabinet with a child-restraint lock.
- Always be aware of what your child can reach and keep dangerous objects out of child's reach on work areas.
- Keep child away from oven doors as some get very hot while the oven is in use.

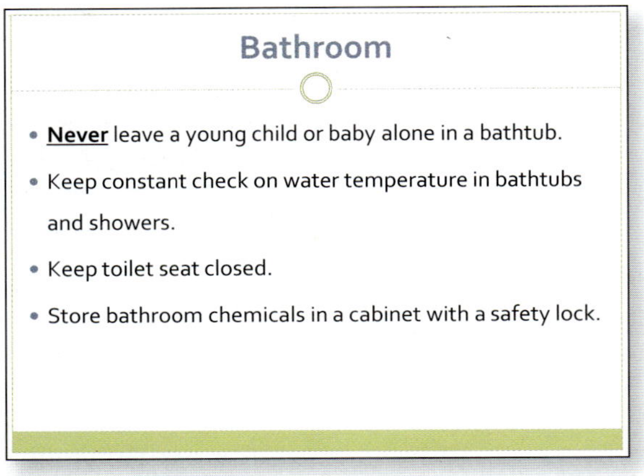

Bathroom
- **Never** leave a young child or baby alone in a bathtub.
- Keep constant check on water temperature in bathtubs and showers.
- Keep toilet seat closed.
- Store bathroom chemicals in a cabinet with a safety lock.

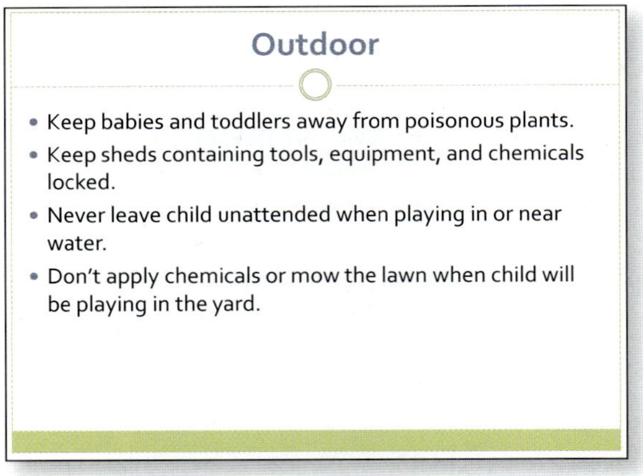

Outdoor
- Keep babies and toddlers away from poisonous plants.
- Keep sheds containing tools, equipment, and chemicals locked.
- Never leave child unattended when playing in or near water.
- Don't apply chemicals or mow the lawn when child will be playing in the yard.

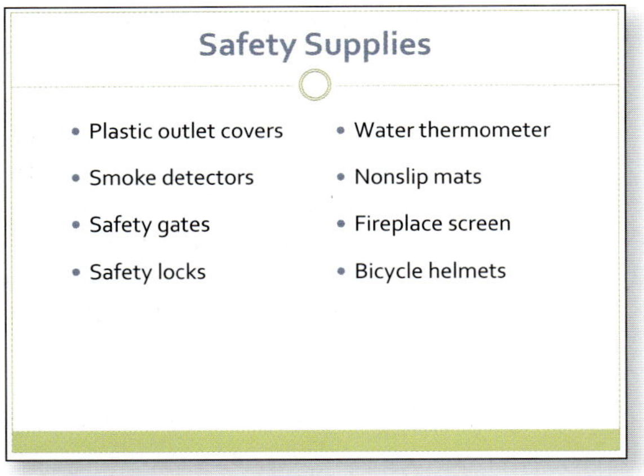

Safety Supplies
- Plastic outlet covers
- Smoke detectors
- Safety gates
- Safety locks
- Water thermometer
- Nonslip mats
- Fireplace screen
- Bicycle helmets

Case Study   Apply Your Skills

Part 1

You are the assistant to Gina Coletti, manager of La Dolce Vita, an Italian restaurant. She has been working on a new lunch menu and wants to present the new menu at the upcoming staff meeting. She has asked you to prepare a presentation she can use at the meeting. Open the Word document named **LunchMenu.docx** and then print the document. Close the document and then exit Word. Using the information you printed, create a presentation and apply the Civic design theme to the presentation. Make any formatting changes to improve the visual appeal of the presentation. Save the presentation and name it **P-C3-CS-LunchMenu**.

Part 2

Ms. Coletti has looked over the presentation and has asked you to apply color and font formatting consistent with other restaurant publications. With **P-C3-CS-LunchMenu.pptx** open, create custom theme colors that change the *Text/Background - Light 2* color to *Dark Yellow, Accent 2, Lighter 80%* and the *Accent 3* color to *Green, Accent 5, Darker 25%*. Create custom theme fonts that apply Monotype Corsiva as the heading font and Garamond as the body font. Save the custom theme and name it *LaDolceVita* followed by your initials. Add a transition and sound to all slides in the presentation. Print the presentation as a handout with six slides horizontally per page. Save and then close **P-C3-CS-LunchMenu.pptx**.

Part 3

Ms. Coletti needs further information for the meeting. She wants you to use the Internet to search for two companies that print restaurant menus, two companies that design restaurant menus, and the names of two restaurant menu design software programs. Prepare a presentation with the information you find on the Internet and then apply your custom theme to the presentation. Make any formatting changes to improve the visual appeal of each slide. Add a transition and sound to each slide in the presentation. Save the presentation and name it **P-C3-CS-RestMenus.pptx**. Print the presentation as a handout with six slides horizontally per page. Close **P-C3-CS-RestMenus.pptx**.

Part 4

When running **P-C3-CS-RestMenus.pptx**, Ms. Coletti would like to link to a couple of the sites you list in the presentation. Use PowerPoint's Help feature to learn how to insert a hyperlink in a slide to a web page or website. Create at least two hyperlinks between sites you list in the presentation and the web page or website. Print the slide(s) containing the hyperlinks. Save and then close **P-C3-CS-RestMenus.pptx**.

Microsoft PowerPoint

Inserting Elements in Slides

CHAPTER 4

PERFORMANCE OBJECTIVES

Upon successful completion of Chapter 4, you will be able to:
- Insert, format, select, and align a text box
- Set tabs in a text box
- Insert, format, and copy shapes
- Display rulers, gridlines, and guides
- Group and ungroup objects
- Insert, crop, size, move, and format a picture
- Insert a picture as a slide background
- Insert, size, scale, rotate, and position a clip art image
- Create and insert a screenshot
- Create and format WordArt text
- Insert objects such as a header, footer, date, slide number, and symbol

A presentation consisting only of text slides may have important information in it that will be overlooked by the audience because a slide contains too much text. Adding visual elements, where appropriate, can help deliver the message to your audience by adding interest and impact to the information. In this chapter, you will learn how to create visual elements on slides such as text boxes, shapes, pictures, clip art images, a screenshot, and WordArt text. These elements will make the delivery of your presentation a dynamic experience for your audience. The model answer for this chapter's project appears on the following page.

Note: Before beginning the project, copy to your storage medium the PowerPoint2010C4 subfolder from the PowerPoint2010 folder on the CD that accompanies this textbook and then make PowerPoint2010C4 the active folder.

119

Project 1 Create a Company Presentation Containing Text Boxes, Shapes, and Images P-C4-P1-AddisonInd.pptx

Project 1 — Create a Company Presentation Containing Text Boxes, Shapes, and Images

14 Parts

You will create a company presentation that includes slides with text boxes, a slide with tabbed text in a text box, slides with shapes and text, slides with pictures, and slides with clip art images. You will also insert elements in slides such as slide numbers, headers, footers, date, and symbols.

▼ Quick Steps
Draw a Text Box
1. Click Insert tab.
2. Click Text Box button.
3. Drag in slide to create box.

OR
1. Click Insert tab.
2. Click Text Box button.
3. Click in slide.

Text Box

Inserting and Formatting Text Boxes

Many of the slide layouts contain placeholders for entering text and other elements in a document. Along with placeholders, you can insert and format a text box. To insert a text box in a slide, click the Insert tab, click the Text Box button in the Text group, and the mouse pointer displays as a thin, down-pointing arrow. Using the mouse, drag in the slide to create the text box. You can also click in the desired location and a small text box is inserted in the slide.

Formatting a Text Box

When you insert a text box in the document, the Home tab displays. Use options in the Drawing group to format the text box by applying a Quick Style or adding a shape fill, outline, or effect. Format a text box in a manner similar to formatting a placeholder. In addition to the options in the Drawing group, you can also apply formatting to a text box with options in the Drawing Tools Format tab. Click this tab and the ribbon displays as shown in Figure 4.1. The Shape Styles group contains the same options as the Drawing group in the Home tab. With other options in the tab, you can apply WordArt formatting to text and arrange and size the text box.

Move a text box in the same manner as you move a placeholder. Click the text box to select it, position the mouse pointer on the text box border until the pointer displays with a four-headed arrow attached, and then drag the text box to the desired position. Change the size of a selected text box using the sizing handles that display around the box. You can also use the *Shape Height* and *Shape Width* measurement boxes in the Size group in the Drawing Tools Format tab to specify the text box height and width.

You can apply the same formatting to text in a text box that you apply to text in a placeholder. For example, you can use the buttons in the Paragraph group in the Home tab to align text horizontally and vertically in a text box, change text direction, set text in columns, and set internal margins for the text in the text box.

HINT Use a text box to place text anywhere in a slide. Text in inserted text boxes does not appear in the Outline view.

▼ Quick Steps
Select All Text Boxes
1. Click Select button.
2. Click *Select All*.
OR
Press Ctrl + A.

Selecting Multiple Objects

You can select multiple text boxes and other objects in a slide and then apply formatting or align and arrange the objects in the slide. To select all objects in a slide, click the Select button in the Editing group in the Home tab and then click *Select All* at the drop-down list. You can also select all objects in a slide with the keyboard shortcut, Ctrl + A. To select specific text boxes or objects in a slide, click the first object, hold down the Shift key, and then click each of the other desired objects.

HINT To select an object that is behind another object, select the top object and then press the Tab key to cycle through and select the other objects.

Select

Aligning Text Boxes

With the Align button in the Arrange group in the Drawing Tools Format tab, you can align the edge of multiple objects in a slide. Click the Align button and a drop-down list of alignment options displays including options for aligning objects vertically and horizontally and distributing objects.

Align

Figure 4.1 Drawing Tools Format Tab

Project 1a — Inserting and Formatting Text Boxes — Part 1 of 14

1. At a blank presentation, apply a design and change colors by completing the following steps:
   a. Click the Design tab.
   b. Click the More button that displays at the right side of the theme thumbnails and then click *Technic* at the drop-down gallery.
   c. Click the Colors button in the Themes group and then click *Trek* at the drop-down gallery.
2. Click in the title placeholder, type **Addison**, press the Enter key, and then type **Industries**.
3. Click in the subtitle placeholder and then type **Annual Report**.
4. Insert a text box in the slide by completing the following steps:
   a. Click the Insert tab.
   b. Click the Text Box button in the Text group.
   c. Click in the lower right corner of the slide. (This inserts a small, selected text box in the slide.)
   d. Type **January 2013**.
   e. Click outside the text box to deselect it.
5. After looking at the slide, you decide to delete the text box by completing the following steps:
   a. Click in the text box to select it.
   b. Position the mouse pointer on the text box border until the mouse pointer displays with a four-headed arrow attached and then click the left mouse button. (This changes the text box border from a dashed border line to a solid border line.)
   c. Press the Delete key.

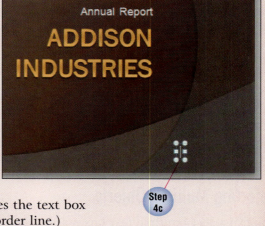

Step 4c

6. Insert a new slide with the *Blank* layout by completing the following steps:
   a. Click the Home tab.
   b. Click the New Slide button arrow.
   c. Click the *Blank* layout at the drop-down list.
7. Insert and format the *Safety* text box shown in Figure 4.2 (on page 124) by completing the following steps:
   a. Click the Insert tab.
   b. Click the Text Box button in the Text group.
   c. Click anywhere in the slide. (This inserts a small, selected text box in the slide.)
   d. Type **Safety**.
   e. Select the text and then change the font to Copperplate Gothic Bold, the font size to 36, and the font color to Orange (third color option from the left in the *Standard Colors* row).
   f. Click the Text Direction button in the Paragraph group in the Home tab and then click *Stacked* at the drop-down list.
   g. Click the Drawing Tools Format tab.
   h. Click the down-pointing arrow at the right side of the *Shape Height* measurement box in the Size group until *4″* displays in the box. (Make sure the measurement in the *Shape Width* box is *0.86″*.)

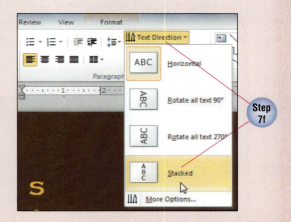

Step 7f

i. Click the More button that displays at the right side of the styles thumbnails in the Shape Styles group and then click the *Moderate Effect - Orange, Accent 6* option (last option in the fifth row).
j. Drag the text box so it is positioned as shown in Figure 4.2.

8. Insert and format the other text box shown in Figure 4.2 by completing the following steps:
   a. Click the Insert tab.
   b. Click the Text Box button in the Text group.
   c. Drag in the slide to create a text box. (Drag to the approximate width of the text box in Figure 4.2.)
   d. Type the text shown in the text box in Figure 4.2 in a single column. Type the text in the first column and then type the text in the second column. (Your text will display as shown at the right in one column, in a smaller font, and in a different line spacing than you see in the figure.)
   e. Select the text and then change the font size to 32.
   f. Click the Line Spacing button in the Paragraph group and then click *2.0* at the drop-down list. (The text may flow off the slide.)
   g. Click the Columns button in the Paragraph group and then click *Two Columns* at the drop-down list.
   h. Click the Drawing Tools Format tab.
   i. Click the down-pointing arrow at the right side of the *Shape Height* measurement box until *4"* displays in the box.
   j. Click the up- or down-pointing arrow at the right side of the *Shape Width* measurement box until *7"* displays in the box.
   k. Click the Shape Fill button arrow in the Shape Styles group and then click *Orange, Accent 6, Lighter 40%* at the drop-down gallery.
   l. Click the Shape Fill button arrow, point to *Gradient*, and then click *Linear Up* in the *Dark Variations* section at the side menu.
   m. Click the Shape Outline button arrow in the Shape Styles group and then click *Dark Red* at the drop-down gallery (first color from the left in the *Standard Colors* row).

Step 7i

Step 8d

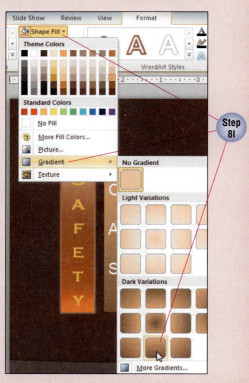

Step 8l

Chapter 4 ■ Inserting Elements in Slides

n. Click the Shape Effects button in the Shape Styles group, point to *Shadow*, and then click *Inside Diagonal Top Right* at the side menu (last option in the top row of the *Inner* section).
o. Change the internal margins by completing the following steps:
   1) Click the Home tab.
   2) Click the Text Direction button and then click *More Options* at the drop-down list.
   3) In the *Internal margin* section of the Format Text Effects dialog box, change the *Left* measurement to *0.6"* and the *Top* and *Bottom* measurements to *0.4"*.
   4) Click the Close button to close the dialog box.
p. With the text box selected, click the Drawing Tools Format tab and then change the shape height measurement to *4"*.
q. Click in the slide outside the text box.

9. Arrange the text boxes by completing the following steps:
   a. Press Ctrl + A to select both text boxes.
   b. Click the Drawing Tools Format tab.
   c. Click the Align button in the Arrange group and then click *Align Bottom* at the drop-down list.
   d. Drag both boxes to the approximate location in the slide as shown in Figure 4.2.
10. Save the presentation and name it **P-C4-P1-AddisonInd**.

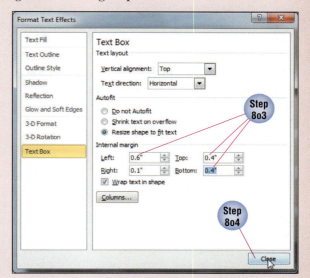
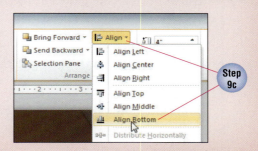

Figure 4.2 Project 1a, Slide 2

Setting Tabs in a Text Box

Inside a text box, you may want to align text in columns using tabs. A text box, by default, contains left alignment tabs that display as light gray marks along the bottom of the horizontal ruler. (If the ruler is not visible, display the horizontal ruler as well as the vertical ruler by clicking the View tab and then clicking the *Ruler* check box in the Show group.) You can change these default left alignment tabs to center, right, or decimal. To change to a different tab alignment, click the Alignment button located at the left side of the horizontal ruler. Display the desired tab alignment symbol and then click at the desired position on the horizontal ruler. When you set a tab on the horizontal ruler, any default tabs to the left of the new tab are deleted. You can move tabs on the horizontal ruler by using the mouse to drag the tab to the desired position. To delete a tab, use the mouse to drag the tab off of the ruler.

You can also set tabs with options at the Tabs dialog box. To display this dialog box, click the Paragraph group dialog box launcher. At the Paragraph dialog box, click the Tabs button that displays in the lower left corner. At the Tabs dialog box, type a tab position in the *Tab stop position* text box, choose a tab alignment with options in the *Alignment* section, and then click the Set button. Clear a specific tab by typing the tab stop position in the *Tab stop position* text box and then clicking the Clear button. Clear all tabs from the horizontal ruler by clicking the Clear All button. When all desired changes are made, click OK to close the Tabs dialog box and then click OK to close the Paragraph dialog box.

HINT Tab stops help you align your text in a slide.

Left Tab

Center Tab

Right Tab

Project 1b — Creating a Text Box and Setting Tabs — Part 2 of 14

1. With **P-C4-P1-AddisonInd.pptx** open, make Slide 1 active and then click the Home tab.
2. Click the New Slide button arrow and then click the *Title Only* layout.
3. Click in the placeholder text *Click to add title* and then type **Executive Officers**.
4. Draw a text box by completing the following steps:
   a. Click the Insert tab.
   b. Click the Text Box button in the Text group.
   c. Draw a text box in the slide that is approximately 8 inches wide and 0.5 inch tall.
5. Change tabs in the text box by completing the following steps:
   a. With the insertion point inside the text box, make sure the horizontal ruler displays. (If not, click the View tab and then click the *Ruler* check box in the Show group.)
   b. Check the alignment button at the left side of the horizontal ruler and make sure the left tab symbol displays.
   c. Position the tip of the mouse pointer on the horizontal ruler below the 0.5-inch mark and then click the left mouse button.

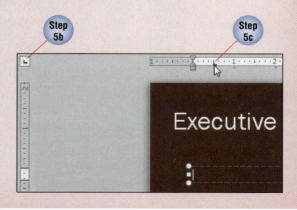

d. Click once on the Alignment button to display the Center alignment symbol.
e. Click on the horizontal ruler immediately below the 4-inch mark on the horizontal ruler.
f. Click once on the Alignment button to display the Right alignment symbol.
g. Click on the horizontal ruler immediately below the 7.5-inch mark. (You may need to expand the size of the text box to set the tab at the 7.5-inch mark.)

6. Type the text in the text box as shown in the slide in Figure 4.3. Make sure you press the Tab key before typing text in the first column. (This moves the insertion point to the first tab, which is a left alignment tab.) Bold the three column headings — *Name*, *Title*, and *Number*.
7. When you are finished typing the text in the text box, press Ctrl + A to select all of the text in the text box and then change the line spacing to 1.5.
8. With the text still selected, drag the left alignment marker on the horizontal ruler from the 0.5-inch mark to the 0.25-inch mark and then drag the right alignment marker on the horizontal ruler from the 7.5-inch mark on the ruler to the 7-inch mark.
9. Position the text box as shown in Figure 4.3.
10. Save **P-C4-P1-AddisonInd.pptx**.

Figure 4.3 Project 1b, Slide 2

Inserting, Formatting, and Copying Shapes

You can draw shapes in a slide using the Shapes button in the Drawing group or with the Shapes button in the Illustrations group in the Insert tab. With the Shapes button drop-down list, you can choose to draw shapes including lines, basic shapes, block arrows, flow chart symbols, callouts, stars, and banners. Click a shape and the mouse pointer displays as crosshairs (plus sign). Click in the slide to insert the shape or position the crosshairs in the slide and then drag to create the shape. Apply formatting to a shape in a manner similar to formatting a text box. Use buttons in the Drawing group in the Home tab and/or buttons in the Drawing Tools Format tab (shown in Figure 4.1) to apply formatting.

If you choose a shape in the *Lines* section of the drop-down list, the shape you draw is considered a ***line drawing***. If you choose an option in the other sections of the drop-down list, the shape you draw is considered an ***enclosed object***. When drawing an enclosed object, you can maintain the proportions of the shape by holding down the Shift key while dragging with the mouse to create the shape.

▼ Quick Steps

Insert a Shape
1. Click Insert tab.
2. Click Shapes button.
3. Click desired shape at drop-down list.
4. Drag in slide to create shape.

HINT
Many shapes have an adjustment handle you can use to change the most prominent feature of the shape.

Shapes

Project 1c — Drawing and Formatting Lines and Shapes — Part 3 of 14

1. With **P-C4-P1-AddisonInd.pptx** open, make Slide 3 active.
2. Click the New Slide button arrow and then click the *Blank* layout at the drop-down list.
3. Insert and format the square shown in the lower left corner of the slide in Figure 4.4 (on page 129) by completing the following steps:
   a. Make sure the Home tab is selected.
   b. Click the More button located to the right of the shape thumbnails in the Drawing group.
   c. Click the *Rectangle* shape in the *Rectangles* section of the drop-down list.
   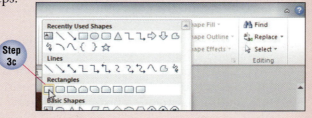
   d. Hold down the Shift key and then draw a square the approximate size of the square shown in Figure 4.4.
   e. With the square selected, click the Quick Styles button in the Drawing group and then click *Moderate Effect - Orange, Accent 1* (second option from the left in the fifth row).

   f. Click the Drawing Tools Format tab.
   g. Change the *Shape Height* and *Shape Width* to 1.6″.
   h. If necessary, drag the square so it is positioned as shown in Figure 4.4.
4. Insert the word *Safety* in the square by completing the following steps:
   a. With the shape selected, type **Safety**.
   b. Select *Safety* and then change the font to Copperplate Gothic Bold, change the font size to 24, and change the font color to Brown, Accent 2, Darker 50%.

5. Draw and format the line shown in Figure 4.4 by completing the following steps:
   a. Click the Insert tab.
   b. Click the Shapes button in the Illustrations group and then click *Arrow* in the *Lines* section.
   c. Position the mouse pointer (cross hairs) in the upper right corner of the square and then drag up to the approximate location shown in Figure 4.4.
   d. With the arrow line selected, click the Drawing Tools Format tab.
   e. Click the Shape Outline button arrow in the Shape Styles group, point to *Weight*, and then click *4½ pt* at the side menu.
   f. Click the Shape Effects button in the Shape Styles group, point to *Bevel*, and then click *Circle* at the side menu (first option from the left in the top row in the *Bevel* section).

6. Draw a text box and type the text shown in the upper left corner of the slide in Figure 4.4 by completing the following steps:
   a. Click the Text Box button in the Insert Shapes group in the Drawing Tools Format tab.
   b. Click in the upper left side of the slide.
   c. With the Home tab active, change the font size to 28 and then click the Bold button in the Font group.
   d. Click the Align Text Right button in the Paragraph group.
   e. Type **2012**, press the Enter key, and then type **Safety Training**.
   f. If necessary, drag the text box so it is positioned as shown in Figure 4.4.

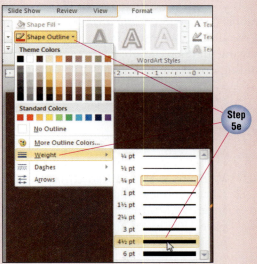

7. Draw and format the text box near the arrow line shown in Figure 4.4 by completing the following steps:
   a. Click the Insert tab.
   b. Click the Text Box button in the Text group.
   c. Click in the slide (you determine the position).
   d. Change the font size to 24, click the Bold button in the Font group in the Home tab, and then change the font color to Orange.
   e. Type **1,000 ASA-trained employees**.
   f. Position the mouse pointer on the green rotation handle, hold down the left mouse button, and then rotate the text box so it is angled as shown in Figure 4.4.
   g. Drag the text box so it is positioned next to the arrow line.
8. Save **P-C4-P1-AddisonInd.pptx**.

Figure 4.4 Project 1c, Slide 4

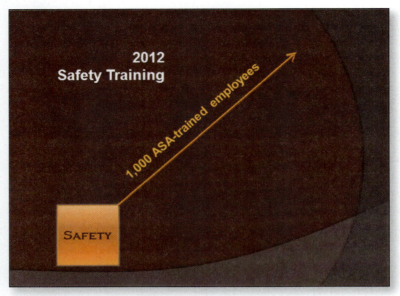

To copy a shape, select the shape and then click the Copy button in the Clipboard group in the Home tab. Position the insertion point at the location where you want the copied image and then click the Paste button. You can also copy a selected shape by holding down the Ctrl key while dragging the shape to the desired location.

Displaying Rulers, Gridlines, and Guides

To help position objects such as placeholders, text boxes, and shapes, consider displaying horizontal and vertical rulers, gridlines, and/or drawing guides as shown in Figure 4.5. You can turn the horizontal and vertical ruler on and off with the *Ruler* check box in the Show group in the View tab. The Show group also contains a *Gridlines* check box. Insert a check mark in this check box and gridlines display in the active slide. Gridlines are intersecting lines that create a grid on the slide and are useful for aligning objects. You can also turn the display of gridlines on and off with the keyboard shortcut, Shift + F9.

Turn on drawing guides to help position objects on a slide. Drawing guides are horizontal and vertical dashed lines that display on the slide in the Slide pane as shown in Figure 4.5. To turn on the drawing guides, display the Grid and Guides dialog box shown in Figure 4.6. Display this dialog box by clicking the Show group dialog box launcher in the View tab. You can also display the Grid and Guides dialog box by selecting an object in the slide, clicking the Drawing Tools Format tab, clicking the Align button in the Arrange group, and then clicking *Grid Settings* at the drop-down list. At the dialog box, insert a check mark in the *Display drawing guides on screen* check box. By default, the horizontal and vertical drawing guides intersect in the middle of the slide. You can move these guides by dragging the guide with the mouse. As you drag the guide, a measurement displays next to the mouse pointer. Drawing guides and gridlines display on the slide but do not print.

▼ **Quick Steps**
Copy a Shape
1. Select desired shape.
2. Click Copy button.
3. Position insertion point at desired location.
4. Click Paste button.
OR
1. Select desired shape.
2. Hold down Ctrl key.
3. Drag shape to desired location.

Figure 4.5 Rulers, Gridlines, and Drawing Guides

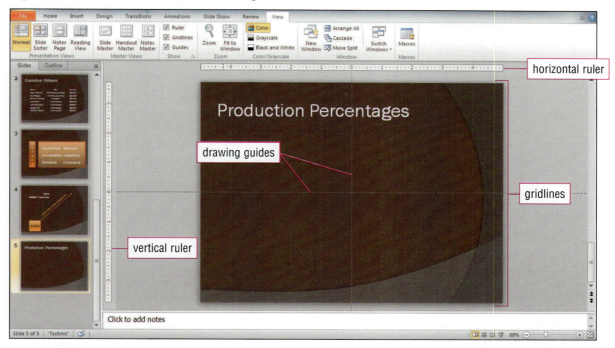

You can turn on gridlines with the *Gridlines* check box in the View tab and you can also turn them on by inserting a check mark in the *Display grid on screen* check box at the Grid and Guides dialog box. The horizontal and vertical spacing between the gridlines is 0.083 inch by default. You can change this measurement with the *Spacing* option at the Grid and Guides dialog box.

As you drag or draw an object on the slide, it is pulled into alignment with the nearest intersection of gridlines. This is because the *Snap objects to grid* option at the Grid and Guides dialog box is active by default. If you want to position an object precisely, you can remove the check mark from the *Snap objects to grid* to turn the feature off or you can hold down the Alt key while dragging an object. If you want an object to be pulled into alignment with another object, insert a check mark in the *Snap objects to other objects* check box.

Figure 4.6 Grid and Guides Dialog Box

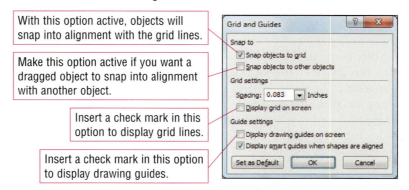

Project 1d Drawing and Formatting Shapes and Text Boxes   Part 4 of 14

1. With **P-C4-P1-AddisonInd.pptx** open, make sure Slide 4 is active and then insert a new slide by clicking the New Slide button arrow in the Slides group in the Home tab and then clicking *Title Only* at the drop-down list.
2. Turn on the display of gridlines by clicking the View tab and then clicking *Gridlines* to insert a check mark in the check box.

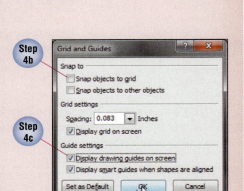

3. Click in the title placeholder and then type **Production Percentages**.
4. Turn on drawing guides and turn off the snap-to-grid feature by completing the following steps:
    a. Make sure the View tab is active and then click the Show group dialog box launcher.
    b. At the Grid and Guides dialog box, click the *Snap objects to grid* check box to remove the check mark.
    c. Click the *Display drawing guides on screen* check box to insert a check mark.
    d. Click OK.
5. Draw the arrow at the left in the slide in Figure 4.7 (on page 133) by completing the following steps:
    a. Click outside the title placeholder to deselect it.
    b. Click the Insert tab.
    c. Click the Shapes button in the Illustrations group and then click the *Up Arrow* shape (third shape from the left in the top row of the *Block Arrows* section).
    d. Position the crosshairs on the intersection of the horizontal drawing guide and the first vertical gridline from the left.
    e. Hold down the left mouse button, drag down and to the right until the crosshairs are positioned on the intersection of the third vertical line from the left and the first horizontal line from the bottom, and then release the mouse button. (Your arrow should be the approximate size shown in Figure 4.7.)

    f. With the arrow selected, click the Drawing Tools Format tab.
    g. Click the Shape Fill button arrow in the Shape Styles group and then click *Light Blue* at the drop-down gallery (seventh color option from the left in the *Standard Colors* section).
    h. Click the Shape Fill button arrow, point to *Gradient*, and then click the *Linear Up* option in the *Dark Variations* section (second option from the left in the bottom row of the *Dark Variations* section).
    i. Click the Shape Effects button, point to *Bevel*, and then click the *Soft round* option (second option from the left in the second row in the *Bevel* section).

6. Insert a text box in the arrow by completing the following steps:
   a. Click the Insert tab.
   b. Click the Text Box button in the Text group.
   c. Drag to create a text box toward the top of the arrow the approximate size shown at the right.
   d. With the Home tab selected, change the font size to 20, turn on Bold, and then change the font color to Dark Blue.
   e. Click the Center button in the Paragraph group.
   f. Type **Plant 3**, press the Enter key, and then type **48%**.
   g. Move and/or size the text box so the text is positioned in the arrow as shown in Figure 4.7.

7. Copy the arrow and text box by completing the following steps:
   a. With the text box selected, hold down the Shift key and then click the arrow. (This selects the arrow and the text box.)
   b. Position the mouse pointer on the border of the selected arrow or text box until the mouse pointer displays with a four-headed arrow attached.
   c. Hold down the Ctrl key and drag the arrow and text box to the right so the tip of the arrow is positioned at the intersection of the horizontal and vertical drawing guides.

8. Move the vertical drawing guide and then copy the arrow and text box by completing the following steps:
   a. Click outside the arrow to deselect the arrow and the text box.
   b. Position the mouse pointer on the vertical drawing guide, hold down the left mouse button, drag right until the mouse pointer displays with *3.00* and a right-pointing arrow in a box, and then release the mouse button.

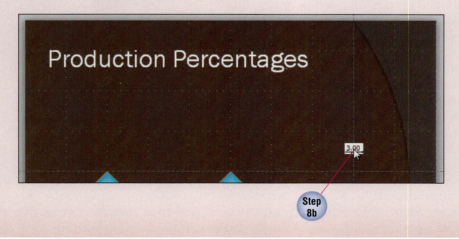

c. Click the arrow at the right, hold down the Shift key, and then click the text box inside the arrow.
   d. Hold down the Ctrl key and drag the arrow and text box to the right so the tip of the arrow is positioned at the intersection of the horizontal and vertical drawing guides.
9. Increase the height of the middle arrow by completing the following steps:
   a. Click the middle arrow to select it.
   b. Using the mouse, drag the top middle sizing handle up to the next horizontal gridline.
   c. Click the text box in the middle arrow and then drag the text box up to the position shown in Figure 4.7.
   d. Complete similar steps to increase the height of the arrow at the right to the second horizontal gridline. Drag the text box to the position shown in Figure 4.7.
   e. Change the text in the text box in the middle arrow to *Plant 1 72%* and change the text in the text box in the arrow at the right to *Plant 2 91%* (see Figure 4.7).
10. Turn off gridlines, drawing guides, and turn on the snap-to-grid feature by completing the following steps:
    a. Click the text in the title placeholder.
    b. Click the Drawing Tools Format tab.
    c. Click the Align button in the Arrange group.
    d. Click the *Grid Settings* option at the drop-down list.
    e. At the Grid and Guides dialog box, click the *Snap objects to grid* check box to insert a check mark.
    f. Click the *Display grid on screen* option to remove the check mark.
    g. Click the *Display drawing guides on screen* check box to remove the check mark.
    h. Click OK.
11. Save **P-C4-P1-AddisonInd.pptx**.

Figure 4.7 Project 1d, Slide 5

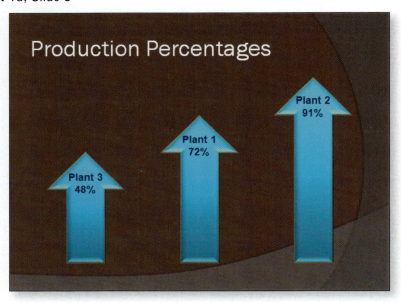

▼ **Quick Steps**

Group Objects
1. Select desired objects.
2. Click Drawing Tools Format tab.
3. Click Group button.
4. Click *Group* at drop-down list.

HINT
Group objects so you can move, size, flip, or rotate objects at one time.

Group

Grouping/Ungrouping Objects

If you want to apply the same formatting or make the same adjustments to the size or rotation of objects, group the objects. If you group objects and then apply a formatting such as a shape fill, effect, or shape style, the formatting is applied to each object within the group. With objects grouped, you can apply formatting more quickly to objects in the slide. To group objects, select the objects you want included in the group. You can do this by clicking each object while holding down the Shift key or you can draw a border around the objects you want included. With the objects selected, click the Drawing Tools Format tab, click the Group button in the Arrange group, and then click *Group* at the drop-down list.

You can format an individual object within a group. To do this, click any object in the group and the group border displays around the objects. Click the individual object and then apply the desired formatting. If you no longer want objects grouped, click the group to select it, click the Drawing Tools Format tab, click the Group button in the Arrange group, and then click *Ungroup* at the drop-down list.

Project 1e Grouping and Formatting Objects   Part 5 of 14

1. With **P-C4-P1-AddisonInd.pptx** open, make Slide 3 active.
2. Group the objects and apply formatting by completing the following steps:
   a. Using the mouse, draw a border around the two text boxes in the slide. (This selects the text boxes.)
   b. Click the Drawing Tools Format tab.
   c. Click the Group button in the Arrange group and then click *Group* at the drop-down list.
   d. Click the More button at the right side of the shape style thumbnails in the Shape Styles group and then click *Moderate Effect - Orange, Accent 6* at the drop-down gallery (last option in the fifth row).
   e. Click the Shape Outline button arrow and then click *Brown, Accent 3, Darker 50%*.
   f. Click the Shape Outline button arrow, point to *Weight*, and then click *4½ pt*.
3. Make Slide 4 active and then group and format objects by completing the following steps:
   a. Using the mouse, draw a border around all objects in the slide.
   b. Click the Drawing Tools Format tab.
   c. Click the Group button in the Arrange group and then click *Group* at the drop-down list.
   d. Click the Home tab.
   e. Click the Font Color button arrow in the Font group and then click the *Orange, Accent 1, Lighter 60%* option.
4. Make Slide 1 active and then run the presentation.
5. After running the presentation you decide that you want to change the color of the square shape and the arrow in Slide 4. Do this by completing the following steps:
   a. Make Slide 4 active.
   b. Click any object in the slide. (This selects the border around all of the objects.)
   c. Click the gold square located in the lower left corner of the slide.
   d. Click the Drawing Tools Format tab.
   e. Click the More button at the right side of the shape style thumbnails in the Shape Styles group and then click *Moderate Effect - Orange, Accent 6* at the drop-down gallery (last option in the fifth row).

6. Ungroup the objects by completing the following steps:
   a. With the group and square selected, click the Group button in the Arrange group and then click *Ungroup* at the drop-down list.
   b. Click outside any object to deselect the objects.
   c. Click the arrow line.
   d. Click the More button at the right side of the shape style thumbnails and then click the *Intense Line - Accent 1* option (second option in the bottom row).

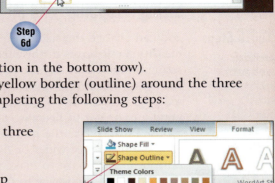

Step 6d

7. You also decide that you do not like the light yellow border (outline) around the three arrows in Slide 5. Remove the outlines by completing the following steps:
   a. Make Slide 5 active.
   b. Using the mouse, draw a border around the three arrows in the slide.
   c. Click the Drawing Tools Format tab.
   d. Click the Group button in the Arrange group and then click *Group* at the drop-down list.
   e. Click the Shape Outline button in the Shape Styles group and then click *No Outline* at the drop-down gallery.
8. Save **P-C4-P1-AddisonInd.pptx**.

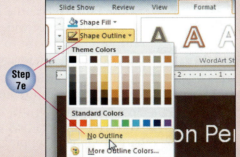

Step 7e

Inserting an Image

You can insert an image such as a picture or clip art in a slide with buttons in the Images group in the Insert tab. Click the Picture button to display the Insert Picture dialog box where you can specify the desired picture file or click the Clip Art button and then choose from a variety of images available at the Clip Art task pane.

Customizing and Formatting an Image

When you insert an image in a slide, the image is selected and the Picture Tools Format tab is active as shown in Figure 4.8. Use buttons in this tab to apply formatting to the image. With options in the Adjust group in the Picture Tools Format tab you can remove unwanted portions of the image, correct the brightness and contrast, change the image color, apply artistic effects, compress the size of the image file, change to a different image, and reset the image back to the original formatting.

Figure 4.8 Picture Tools Format Tab

Use buttons in the Picture Styles group to apply a predesigned style to the image, change the image border, or apply other effects to the image. With options in the Arrange group, you can position the image on the page, specify how text will wrap around it, align the image with other elements in the document, and rotate the image. Use the Crop button in the Size group to remove any unnecessary parts of the image and specify the image size with the *Shape Height* and *Shape Width* measurement boxes.

Sizing, Cropping, and Moving an Image

▼ **Quick Steps**

Insert Picture
1. Click Insert tab.
2. Click Picture button.
3. Navigate to desired folder.
4. Double-click desired picture.

Insert a picture from your camera by downloading the picture to your computer and then copying the picture into PowerPoint.

Crop

You can change the size of an image with the *Shape Height* and *Shape Width* measurement boxes in the Size group in the Picture Tools Format tab or with the sizing handles that display around the selected image. To change size with a sizing handle, position the mouse pointer on a sizing handle until the pointer turns into a double-headed arrow and then hold down the left mouse button. Drag the sizing handle in or out to decrease or increase the size of the image and then release the mouse button. Use the middle sizing handles at the left or right side of the image to make the image wider or thinner. Use the middle sizing handles at the top or bottom of the image to make the image taller or shorter. Use the sizing handles at the corners of the image to change both the width and height at the same time.

The Size group in the Picture Tools Format tab contains a Crop button. Use this button to remove portions of an image. Click the Crop button and the mouse pointer displays with the crop tool attached, which is a black square with overlapping lines, and the image displays with cropping handles around the border. Drag a cropping handle to remove a portion of the image.

Move a selected image by dragging it to the desired location. Move the image by positioning the mouse pointer on the image border until the arrow pointer turns into a four-headed arrow. Hold down the left mouse button, drag the image to the desired position, and then release the mouse button. You can use the arrow keys on the keyboard to move the image in the desired direction. If you want to move the image in small increments (called **nudging**), hold down the Ctrl key while pressing an arrow key.

Use the rotation handle to rotate an image by positioning the mouse pointer on the green, round rotation handle until the pointer displays as a circular arrow. Hold down the left mouse button, drag in the desired direction, and then release the mouse button.

Arranging Objects

Bring Forward

Send Backward

With the Bring Forward and Send Backward buttons in the Arrange group in the Drawing Tools Format tab or the Picture Tools Format tab, you can layer one object on top of another. Click the Bring Forward button and the selected object is moved forward one layer. For example, if you have three objects layered on top of each other, selecting the object at the bottom of the layers and then clicking the Bring Forward button will move the object in front of the second object (but not the first object). If you want to move an object to the top layer, select the object, click the Bring Forward button arrow, and then click the *Bring to Front* option at the drop-down list. To move the selected object back one layer, click the Send Backward button. If you want to move the selected object behind all other objects, click the Send Backward button arrow and then click the *Send to Back* option at the drop-down list.

Inserting a Picture

To insert a picture in a document, click the Insert tab and then click the Picture button in the Images group. At the Insert Picture dialog box, navigate to the folder containing the desired picture and then double-click the picture. Use buttons in the Picture Tools Format tab to format and customize the picture.

Picture

Project 1f — Inserting and Formatting a Picture — Part 6 of 14

1. With **P-C4-P1-AddisonInd.pptx** open, make Slide 5 active and make sure the Home tab is active.
2. Insert a new slide by clicking the New Slide button arrow in the Slides group and then clicking *Blank* at the drop-down list.
3. Insert a text box by completing the following steps:
    a. Click the Insert tab.
    b. Click the Text Box button in the Text group.
    c. Click in the middle of the slide.
    d. Change the font to Arial Black and the font size to 36.
    e. Click the Center button in the Paragraph group.
    f. Type **Alternative**, press the Enter key, and then type **Energy Resources**.
    g. With the text box selected, click the Drawing Tools Format tab.
    h. Click the Align button in the Arrange group and then click *Distribute Horizontally* at the drop-down list.
    i. Click the Align button and then click *Distribute Vertically* at the drop-down list.

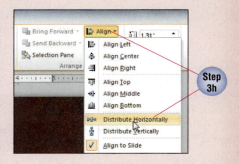
Step 3h

4. Insert a picture by completing the following steps:
    a. Click the Insert tab.
    b. Click the Picture button in the Images group.
    c. At the Insert Picture dialog box, navigate to the PowerPoint2010C4 folder on your storage medium and then double-click **Ocean.jpg**.
5. Crop the picture by completing the following steps:
    a. With the picture selected, click the Crop button in the Size group in the Picture Tools Format tab.
    b. Position the mouse pointer (displays with the crop tool attached) on the cropping handle in the middle of the right side of the picture.
    c. Hold down the left mouse button and then drag to the left approximately 0.25 inch. (Use the guideline that displays on the horizontal ruler to crop the picture 0.25 inch.)
    d. Complete steps similar to those in Steps 5b and 5c to crop approximately 0.25 inch from the top of the picture. (Use the guideline that displays on the vertical ruler to crop the picture 0.25 inch.)
    e. Click the Crop button to turn off cropping.

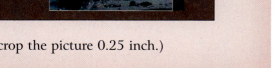
Step 5c

6. Click in the *Shape Height* measurement box in the Size group, type 5, and then press Enter.
7. Click the Send Backward button arrow in the Arrange group and then click the *Send to Back* option at the drop-down list. (This moves the picture behind the text in the text box.)

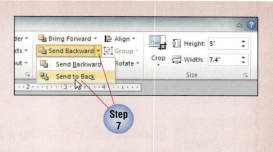

Step 7

8. Align the picture by completing the following steps:
    a. With the picture selected, click the Home tab.
    b. Click the Arrange button in the Drawing group, point to *Align* at the drop-down list, and then click *Distribute Horizontally*.
    c. Click the Arrange button, point to *Align*, and then click *Distribute Vertically*.
9. Format the picture by completing the following steps:
    a. With the picture selected, click the Picture Tools Format tab, click the Color button in the Adjust group, and then click the *Orange, Accent color 6 Dark* option (last option in the second row in the *Recolor* section).

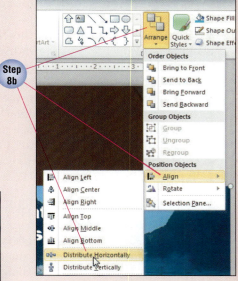

Step 8b

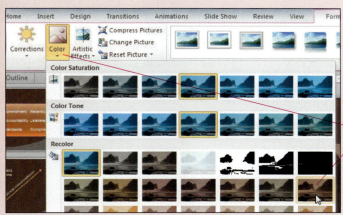

Step 9a

b. Click the Corrections button in the Adjust group and then click *Brightness: +20% Contrast: +20%* (fourth option in the fourth row in the *Brightness and Contrast* section).

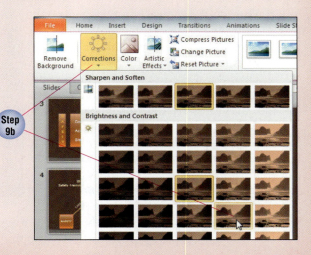

Step 9b

c. Click the Corrections button and then click *Sharpen: 25%* in the *Sharpen and Soften* section.

d. Click the More button that displays at the right side of the picture style thumbnails and then click *Soft Edge Oval* at the drop-down gallery (sixth option from the left in the third row).

e. Click the Compress Pictures button in the Adjust group. At the Compress Pictures dialog box, click OK.

Step 9d

10. With Slide 6 active, insert a new slide by clicking the Home tab, clicking the New Slide button arrow in the Slides group, and then clicking *Title Only* at the drop-down list.
11. Click in the title placeholder and then type **Shipping Contracts**.
12. Insert a picture by completing the following steps:
    a. Click the Insert tab and then click the Picture button.
    b. At the Insert Picture dialog box, make sure the PowerPoint2010C4 folder on your storage medium is active and then double-click **Ship.jpg**.
13. With the ship picture selected, remove some of the background by completing the following steps:
    a. Click the Remove Background button in the Adjust group in the Picture Tools Format tab.
    b. Using the left middle sizing handle, drag the border to the left to include the back of the ship (see image at the right).
    c. Click the Mark Areas to Remove button in the Refine group in the Background Removal tab.
    d. Click anywhere in the water that displays below the ship. (This removes the water from the picture. If all of the water is not removed, you will need to click in the remaining water.)
    e. Using the right middle sizing handle, drag the border to the left so the border is near the front of the ship.
    f. If part of the structure above the front of the ship has been removed, include it in the picture. To begin, click the Mark Areas to Keep button in the Refine group in the Background Removal tab. (The mouse pointer displays as a pencil.)
    g. Using the mouse, position the pencil at the top of the structure (as shown at the right), drag down to the top of the containers on the ship, and then release the mouse button.
    h. Click the Keep Changes button in the Close group in the Background Removal tab.

Step 13b

Step 13g

14. Click the Corrections button in the Adjust group in the Picture Tools Format tab and then click the *Brightness: +40% Contrast: +40%* option at the drop-down gallery (last option in the bottom row in the *Brightness and Contrast* section).
15. Click the Corrections button in the Adjust group and then click the *Sharpen: 50%* option at the drop-down gallery (last option in the *Sharpen and Soften* section).
16. Drag the picture down to the middle of the slide.
17. Click outside the picture to deselect it.
18. Save **P-C4-P1-AddisonInd.pptx**.

Chapter 4 ■ Inserting Elements in Slides   139

▼ **Quick Steps**

Insert Picture as Slide Background
1. Click Design tab.
2. Click Background Styles button, *Format Background*.
3. Click *Picture or texture fill* option.
4. Click File button.
5. Navigate to desired folder.
6. Double-click desired picture.
7. Click Close button.

Inserting a Picture as a Slide Background

You can insert a picture as the background in an entire slide. To do this, click the Design tab, click the Background Styles button in the Background group, and then click *Format Background* at the drop-down list. At the Format Background dialog box, click the *Picture or texture fill* option in the *Fill* section and then click the File button. At the Insert Picture dialog box, navigate to the desired folder, and then double-click the picture. Click the Close button to close the Format Background dialog box. If you want the picture background to display on all slides, click the Apply to All button at the Format Background dialog box.

Project 1g Inserting a Picture as a Slide Background   Part 7 of 14

1. With **P-C4-P1-AddisonInd.pptx** open, make sure Slide 7 is active and the Home tab is active.
2. Click the New Slide button arrow in the Slides group and then click the *Blank* layout at the drop-down list.
3. Insert a picture background on Slide 8 by completing the following steps:
   a. Click the Design tab.
   b. Click the Background Styles button in the Background group and then click *Format Background* at the drop-down gallery.
   c. At the Format Background dialog box, click the *Picture or texture fill* option in the *Fill* section.
   d. Click the File button that displays near the middle of the dialog box.
   e. At the Insert Picture dialog box, navigate to the PowerPoint2010C4 folder on your storage medium and then double-click *EiffelTower.jpg*.
   f. Click the Close button to close the Format Background dialog box.
   g. Remove the background graphic by clicking the *Hide Background Graphics* check box in the Background group in the Design tab to insert a check mark.

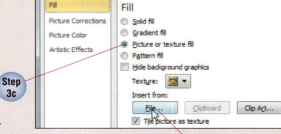

Step 3c

Step 3d

4. Insert a text box by completing the following steps:
   a. Click the Insert tab.
   b. Click the Text Box button in the Text group.
   c. Click in the upper left corner of the slide.
   d. Change the font size to 40.
   e. Type **European** and then press Enter.
   f. Type **Division 2013**.
   g. Drag the text box so it is positioned attractively on the slide in the upper left corner.
5. Change the theme colors by completing the following steps:
   a. Make Slide 3 active.
   b. Click the Design tab.
   c. Click the Colors button in the Themes group and then click *Office* at the drop-down gallery.

6. Change the formatting of slide objects by completing the following steps:

Step 6h

a. Click in the lower right corner of the text box containing the text in columns (this selects the group).
b. Click the Drawing Tools Format tab.
c. Click the More button at the right side of the shape style thumbnails and then click the *Moderate Effect - Blue, Accent 1* option (second option from the left in the fifth row).
d. Make Slide 4 active.
e. Using the mouse, draw a border around all of the objects in the slide, make sure the Home tab is active, and then change the font color to Orange.
f. Make Slide 6 active and then click the picture to select it.
g. Click the Picture Tools Format tab.
h. Click the Color button in the Adjust group and then click the *No Recolor* option in the *Recolor* section.

7. Save **P-C4-P1-AddisonInd.pptx**.

Inserting a Clip Art Image

Microsoft Office includes a gallery of media images you can insert in a slide such as clip art, photographs, and movie images, as well as sound clips. To insert a clip art image in a slide, click the Insert tab and then click the Clip Art button in the Images group. This displays the Clip Art task pane at the right side of the screen as shown in Figure 4.9. You can also choose a slide layout that contains a content placeholder with a Clip Art button.

To view all picture, sound, and motion files, make sure the *Search for* text box in the Clip Art task pane does not contain any text and then click the Go button. When the desired image is visible, click the image to insert it in the document. Use buttons in the Picture Tools Format tab shown in Figure 4.8 to format and customize the clip art image.

If you are searching for specific images, click in the *Search for* text box, type the desired topic, and then click the Go button. For example, if you want to find images related to business, click in the *Search for* text box, type *business*, and then click the Go button. Clip art images related to *business* display in the viewing area of the task pane. If you are connected to the Internet, Word will search for images at the Office.com website matching the topic.

Unless the Clip Art task pane default setting has been customized, the task pane displays all illustrations, photographs, videos, and audio files. The *Results should be* option has a default setting of *All media file types*. Click the down-pointing arrow at the right of this option to display media types. To search for a specific media type, remove the check mark before all options at the drop-down list except for the desired type. For example, if you are searching only for photograph images, remove the check mark before *Illustrations*, *Videos*, and *Audio*.

▼ **Quick Steps**

Insert Clip Art Image
1. Click Insert tab.
2. Click Clip Art button.
3. Type search word or topic.
4. Press Enter.
5. Click desired image.

For additional clip art images, consider buying a commercial package of images.

Preview a clip art image and display properties by positioning the pointer over the image, clicking the arrow that displays, and then clicking *Preview/Properties*.

Clip Art

Chapter 4 ■ Inserting Elements in Slides

Figure 4.9 Clip Art Task Pane

Search for specific images by typing the desired category in this text box and then clicking the Go button.

Project 1h Inserting and Formatting a Clip Art Image   Part 8 of 14

1. With **P-C4-P1-AddisonInd.pptx** open, make Slide 1 active.
2. Insert a clip art image by completing the following steps:
   a. Click the Insert tab.
   b. Click the Clip Art button in the Images group.
   c. At the Clip Art task pane, click the down-pointing arrow at the right side of the *Results should be* option box and then click in the *Photographs*, *Videos*, and *Audio* check boxes to remove the check marks. (The *Illustrations* check box should be the only option with a check mark.)
   d. Select any text that displays in the *Search for* text box, type **industry**, and then press Enter.
   e. Click the clip art image in the list box as shown at the right.
   f. Close the Clip Art task pane by clicking the Close button (contains an X) located in the upper right corner of the task pane.

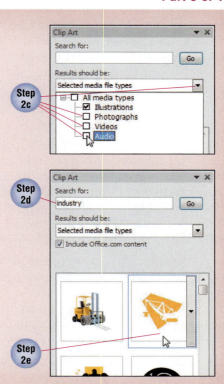

3. Arrange, size, and position the clip art image by completing the following steps:
   a. With the clip art image selected, click the Rotate button in the Arrange group and then click *Flip Horizontal*.
   b. Click in the *Shape Height* measurement box, type 4.5, and then press Enter.
   c. Click the Color button in the Adjust group and then click the *Aqua, Accent color 5 Light* option at the drop-down gallery (second option from the right in the third row).
   d. Click the Corrections button and then click *Brightness: 0% (Normal) Contrast: +20%* at the drop-down gallery (third option from the left in the fourth row).
   e. Click the Send Backward button arrow in the Arrange group and then click *Send to Back* at the drop-down list.
   f. Drag the clip art image so it is positioned as shown in Figure 4.10.
4. Save **P-C4-P1-AddisonInd.pptx**.

Figure 4.10 Project 1h, Slide 1

Sizing, Rotating, and Positioning Objects

As you learned in this chapter, you can use the sizing handles that display around an object to increase and decrease the size, and use the *Shape Height* and *Shape Width* measurement boxes. You also learned to position objects by dragging the object with the mouse. You can also size objects with options at the Format Picture dialog box with *Size* selected in the left panel, as shown in Figure 4.11, and position objects with options at the Format Picture dialog box with *Position* selected in the left panel. Display the Format Picture dialog box with *Size* selected in the left panel by clicking the Size group dialog box launcher. Use options at the dialog box to specify the object size, rotation, and scale. Click *Position* in the left panel of the dialog box and use the options to specify the horizontal and vertical position of the object on the slide.

Shape Height

Shape Width

Chapter 4 ■ Inserting Elements in Slides

Figure 4.11 Size and Position in the Format Picture Dialog Box

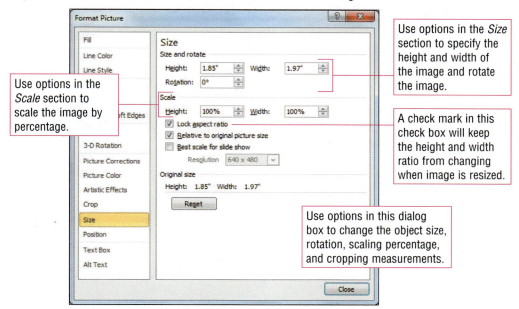

Project 1i — Inserting and Formatting a Clip Art Image

Part 9 of 14

1. With **P-C4-P1-AddisonInd.pptx** open, make Slide 8 active.
2. Click the New Slide button arrow in the Slides group in the Home tab and then click the *Two Content* layout at the drop-down list.
3. Click the placeholder text *Click to add title* and then type **Technology**.
4. Click the placeholder text *Click to add text* located in the right side of the slide.
5. Click the Bullets button in the Paragraph group to turn off bullets.
6. Change the font size to 36, turn on bold, and change the font color to Orange.
7. Press the Enter key.
8. Type **Equipment** and then press the Enter key twice.
9. Type **Software** and then press the Enter key twice.
10. Type **Personnel**.
11. Insert a clip art image by completing the following steps:
    a. Click the Clip Art button that displays in the middle of the placeholder at the left side of the slide.

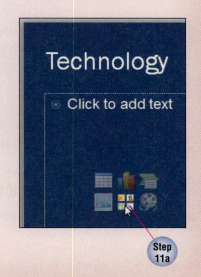

Step 11a

b. At the Clip Art task pane, select any text that displays in the *Search for* text box, type **technology**, and then press Enter.
c. Click the clip art image in the list box as shown at the right.
d. Close the Clip Art task pane by clicking the Close button (contains an X) located in the upper right corner of the task pane.

12. Scale, rotate, and position the clip art image by completing the following steps:
    a. With the clip art image selected, click the Size group dialog box launcher.
    b. Click the down-pointing arrow at the right of the *Rotation* option until *−20°* displays in the option box.
    c. Select the current percentage in the *Height* option box in the *Scale* section and then type **225**.
    d. Click the *Position* option in the left panel.
    e. Click the down-pointing arrow at the right side of the *Horizontal* option until *0.7"* displays in the option box.
    f. Click the down-pointing arrow at the right side of the *Vertical* option until *1.9"* displays in the option box.

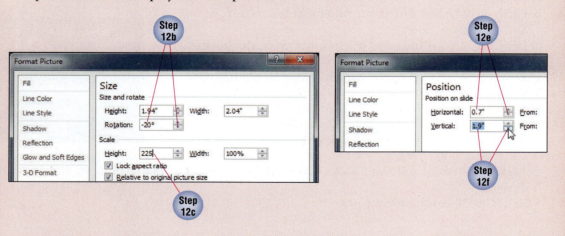

   g. Click the Close button to close the dialog box.
13. Bring the text in front of the clip art image by completing the following steps:
    a. Click in the text to select the text placeholder.
    b. Click the Drawing Tools Format tab.
    c. Click the Bring Forward button in the Arrange group.
14. Save **P-C4-P1-AddisonInd.pptx**.

Copying Objects within and between Presentations

Earlier in this chapter you learned how to copy shapes within a slide. You can also copy shapes as well as other objects to other slides within the same presentation or to slides in another presentation. To copy an object, select the object and then click the Copy button in the Clipboard group in the Home tab. Make the desired

slide active or open another presentation and display the desired slide and then click the Paste button in the Clipboard group. You can also copy an object by right-clicking the object and then clicking *Copy* at the shortcut menu. To paste the object, make the desired slide active, click the right mouse button, and then click *Paste* at the shortcut menu.

Project 1j — Copying an Object within and between Presentations — Part 10 of 14

1. With **P-C4-P1-AddisonInd.pptx** open, make Slide 1 active.
2. Click the clip art image to select it and then press the Delete key.
3. Open **Addison.pptx**.
4. Click the clip art image located in Slide 1 and then click the Copy button in the Clipboard group.
5. Click the PowerPoint button on the Taskbar and then click the thumbnail representing **P-C4-P1-AddisonInd.pptx**.
6. Click the Paste button. (This inserts the clip art image in Slide 1.)
7. Make the **Addison.pptx** presentation active and then close the presentation.
8. With **P-C4-P1-AddisonInd.pptx** open and the clip art image selected, make Slide 2 active and then click the Paste button.
9. Decrease the size and position the clip art by completing the following steps:
   a. Click the Picture Tools Format tab.
   b. Click in the *Shape Height* measurement text box, type **0.8**, and then press Enter.
   c. Drag the clip art image so it is positioned in the upper right corner of the slide.
10. Copy the clip art image to other slides by completing the following steps:
    a. With the clip art image selected in Slide 2, click the Copy button in the Clipboard group in the Home tab.
    b. Make Slide 3 active and then click the Paste button in the Clipboard group.
    c. Make each of the following slides active and then paste the clip art image: Slide 4, 5, 6, 7, and 9.
11. Save **P-C4-P1-AddisonInd.pptx**.

Step 9c

Creating Screenshots

Screenshot

The Images group in the Insert tab contains a Screenshot button you can use to capture the contents of a screen as an image or capture a portion of a screen. This is useful for capturing information from a web page or from a file in another program. If you want to capture the entire screen, display the desired web page or open the desired file from a program, make PowerPoint active, and then open a presentation. Click the Insert tab, click the Screenshot button, and then click the desired screen thumbnail at the drop-down list. The currently active presentation does not display as a thumbnail at the drop-down list, only any other file or program you have open. If you do not have another file or program open, the Windows desktop displays. When you click the desired thumbnail, the screenshot is inserted as an image in the active slide in the open presentation, the image is selected, and the Picture Tools Format tab is active. Use buttons in this tab to customize the screenshot image.

In addition to making a screenshot of an entire screen, you can make a screenshot of a specific portion of the screen by clicking the *Screen Clipping* option at the Screenshot button drop-down list. When you click this option, the open web page, file, or Windows desktop displays in a dimmed manner and the mouse pointer displays as crosshairs. Using the mouse, draw a border around the specific area of the screen you want to capture. The specific area you identify is inserted in the active slide in the presentation as an image, the image is selected, and the Picture Tools Format tab is active.

Quick Steps

Insert Screenshot
1. Open presentation.
2. Open another file.
3. Display desired information.
4. Make presentation active.
5. Click Insert tab.
6. Click Screenshot button.
7. Click desired window at drop-down list.
OR
6. Click Screenshot button, *Screen Clipping*.
7. Drag to specify capture area.

Project 1k Inserting and Formatting a Screenshot   Part 11 of 14

1. With **P-C4-P1-AddisonInd.pptx** open, make sure that no other programs are open.
2. Make Slide 8 active and then insert a new slide by clicking the New Slide button arrow in the Slides group and then clicking the *Title Only* layout.
3. Click in the title placeholder and then type Draft Invitation.
4. Open Word and then open the document named **AddIndInvite.docx** from the PowerPoint2010C4 folder on your storage medium.
5. Click the PowerPoint button on the Taskbar.
6. Insert a screenshot of the draft invitation in the Word document by completing the following steps:
   a. Click the Insert tab.
   b. Click the Screenshot button in the Images group and then click *Screen Clipping* at the drop-down list.

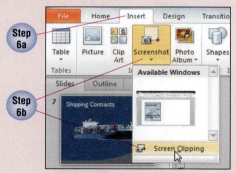
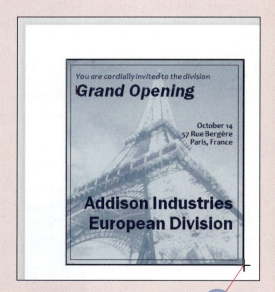

   c. When the **AddIndInvite.docx** document displays in a dimmed manner, position the mouse crosshairs in the upper left corner of the invitation, hold down the left mouse button, drag down to the lower right corner of the invitation, and then release the mouse button. (See image above.)

Chapter 4 ■ Inserting Elements in Slides   147

7. With the screenshot image inserted in the slide in the presentation, make the following changes:
    a. Click in the *Width* measurement box in the Size group in the Picture Tools Format tab, type **4.75**, and then press Enter.
    b. Click the Corrections button in the Adjust group and then click the *Sharpen 25%* option (fourth option from the left in the *Sharpen and Soften* section).
    c. Using the mouse, drag the screenshot image so it is centered on the slide.
8. Click outside the screenshot image to deselect it.
9. Save **P-C4-P1-AddisonInd.pptx**.
10. Click the Word button, close **AddIndInvite.docx**, and then exit Word.

Creating WordArt Text

Quick Steps

Create WordArt Text
1. Click Insert tab.
2. Click WordArt button.
3. Click desired WordArt style.
4. Type WordArt text.

Use WordArt to create interesting text effects in slides.

Edit WordArt by double-clicking the WordArt text.

Use the WordArt feature to insert preformatted, decorative text in a slide. You can also use WordArt to modify text to conform to a variety of shapes. Consider using WordArt to create a company logo, letterhead, flier title, or heading. Insert WordArt in a slide by clicking the Insert tab and then clicking the WordArt button in the Text group. This displays the WordArt drop-down list as shown in Figure 4.12. Click the desired WordArt style at this drop-down list and a text box is inserted in the slide containing the text *Your Text Here*. Type the desired WordArt text and then use the options in the Drawing Tools Format tab to customize the WordArt text.

Formatting WordArt Text

When you insert WordArt text in a document, the Drawing Tools Format tab is active. Use options and buttons in this tab to format the WordArt text. Use the WordArt styles to apply predesigned formatting to the WordArt text. Customize the text with the Text Fill, Text Outline, and Text Effects buttons in the WordArt Styles group. Use the Text Fill button to change the fill color, the Text Outline button to change the text outline color, and use the Text Effects button to apply a variety of text effects and shapes.

Figure 4.12 WordArt Drop-down List

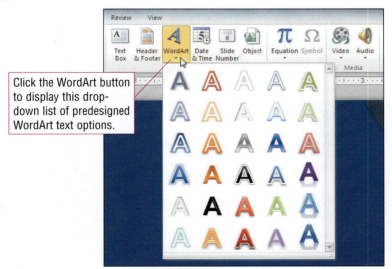

Click the WordArt button to display this drop-down list of predesigned WordArt text options.

Click the Text Effects button and then point to *Transform* and a side menu displays with shaping and warping options as shown in Figure 4.13. Use these options to conform the WordArt text to a specific shape.

WordArt

Text Fill

Text Outline

Text Effects

Figure 4.13 Text Effects Transform Side Menu

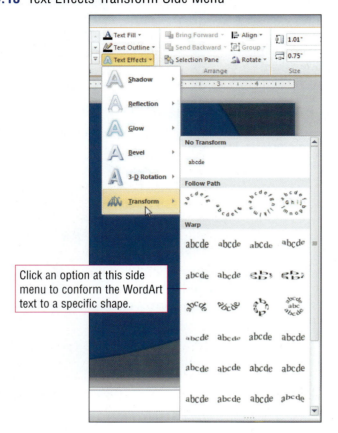

Click an option at this side menu to conform the WordArt text to a specific shape.

Project 1I Inserting and Formatting WordArt Part 12 of 14

1. With **P-C4-P1-AddisonInd.pptx** open, make Slide 10 active and make sure the Home tab is active.
2. Click the New Slide button arrow in the Slides group and then click the *Blank* layout.
3. Click the Insert tab.
4. Click the WordArt button in the Text group and then click the *Gradient Fill - Orange, Accent 6, Inner Shadow* option (second option from the left in the fourth row).
5. Type **Addison Industries**, press the Enter key, and then type **2013**.
6. Click the WordArt text border to change the border from a dashed line to a solid line. (This selects the text box.)

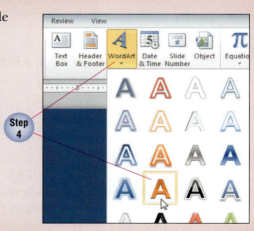

7. Click the Text Outline button arrow in the WordArt Styles group and then click the *Dark Blue* color in the *Standard Colors* section.
8. Click the Text Effects button, point to *Glow*, and then click *Blue, 11 pt glow, Accent color 1* at the side menu (first option from the left in the third row in the *Glow Variations* section).
9. Click the Text Effects button, point to *Transform*, and then click the *Triangle Up* option (third option from the left in the top row of the *Warp* section).
10. Click in the *Shape Height* measurement box, type 3, and then press Enter.
11. Click in the *Shape Width* measurement box, type 8, and then press Enter.
12. Click the Align button in the Arrange group and then click *Distribute Horizontally*.
13. Click the Align button and then click *Distribute Vertically*.
14. Make Slide 6 active.
15. Apply WordArt formatting to the text in the text box by completing the following steps:
    a. Click in the text to select the text box.
    b. Click the text box border to change the border line from a dashed line to a solid line.
    c. Click the Drawing Tools Format tab. Click the More button at the right side of the WordArt style thumbnails, and then click *Fill - Orange, Accent 6, Warm Matte Bevel* option (second option from the left in the bottom row).
16. Save **P-C4-P1-AddisonInd.pptx**.

Inserting Symbols

Symbol

You can insert symbols in a slide in a presentation with options at the Symbol dialog box. Display this dialog box by clicking the Symbol button in the Symbols group in the Insert tab. At the Symbol dialog box, choose a symbol font with the *Font* option in the dialog box, click the desired symbol in the list box, click the Insert button, and then click the Close button. The symbol is inserted in the slide at the location of the insertion point.

Project 1m Inserting Symbols in a Presentation   Part 13 of 14

1. With **P-C4-P1-AddisonInd.pptx** open, insert a symbol by completing the following steps:
   a. Make Slide 2 active.
   b. Click in the text box containing the names, titles, and telephone numbers. (This selects the text box.)
   c. Delete the *n* in *Pena* (the fourth last name).
   d. Click the Insert tab and then click the Symbol button in the Symbols group.
   e. At the Symbol dialog box, click the down-pointing arrow at the right side of the *Font* option box and then click *(normal text)* at the drop-down list (first option in the list).
   f. Scroll down the symbol list box and then click the ñ symbol (located in approximately the eleventh or twelfth row).

g. Click the Insert button and then click the Close button.
2. Insert a text box and a symbol by completing the following steps:
   a. With Slide 2 active, click the Text Box button in the Text group in the Insert tab.
   b. Click in the lower right corner of the slide below the telephone number column.
   c. Change the font size to 24 and the font color to Black.
   d. Click the Insert tab.
   e. Click the Symbol button.
   f. At the Symbol dialog box, click the down-pointing arrow at the right side of the *Font* option, scroll to the end of the list box, and then click *Wingdings*.
   g. Click the telephone symbol (☎) located in the top row.
   h. Click the Insert button and then click the Close button.
   i. If necessary, position the telephone symbol centered below the telephone column.
3. Save **P-C4-P1-AddisonInd.pptx**.

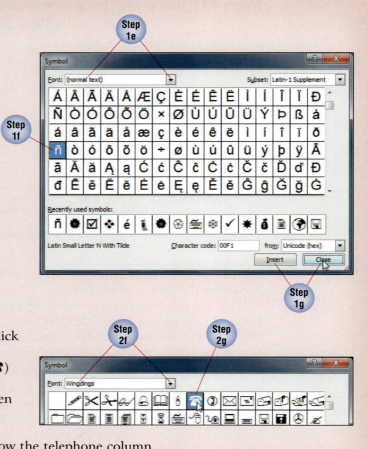

Inserting Headers and Footers

As you learned in Chapter 1, if you print a presentation as a handout or an outline, PowerPoint will automatically print the current date in the upper right corner of the page and the page number in the lower right corner. If you print the presentation as notes pages, PowerPoint will automatically print the page number when you print the individual slides. The date and page numbers are considered header and footer elements. You can modify existing header and footer elements or insert additional elements with options in the Header and Footer dialog box. Display the Header and Footer dialog box shown in Figure 4.14 by clicking the Header & Footer button in the Text group in the Insert tab, clicking the Date & Time button in the Text group, or clicking the Slide Number button in the Text group. You can also display the Header and Footer dialog box by displaying the Print tab Backstage view and then clicking the Edit Header & Footer hyperlink that displays below the galleries in the Settings category.

Header & Footer

Slide Number

   The Header and Footer dialog box has two tabs, the Slide tab and the Notes and Handouts tab, and the options in the dialog box are similar with either tab selected. With options at the dialog box, you can insert the date and time, a header, a footer, and page numbers. If you insert the date and time in a presentation, you

Chapter 4 ■ Inserting Elements in Slides   151

Figure 4.14 Header and Footer Dialog Box with the Notes and Handouts Tab Selected

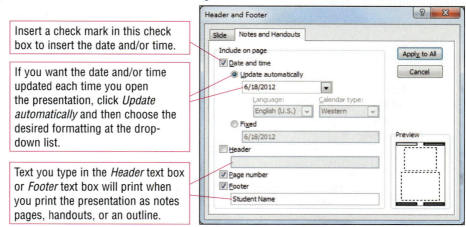

Insert a check mark in this check box to insert the date and/or time.

If you want the date and/or time updated each time you open the presentation, click *Update automatically* and then choose the desired formatting at the drop-down list.

Text you type in the *Header* text box or *Footer* text box will print when you print the presentation as notes pages, handouts, or an outline.

can choose the *Update automatically* option if you want the date and time updated each time the presentation is opened. Choose the date and time formatting by clicking the down-pointing arrow at the right side of the *Update automatically* option box and then choose the desired formatting at the drop-down list. If you choose the *Fixed* option, type the desired date and/or time in the *Fixed* text box. Type header text in the *Header* text box and type footer text in the *Footer* text box.

If you want to print the slide number on slides, insert a check mark in the *Slide number* check box in the Header and Footer dialog box with the Slide tab selected. If you want to include page numbers on handouts, notes pages, or outline pages, insert a check mark in the *Page number* check box in the Header and Footer dialog box with the Notes and Handouts tab selected. If you want all changes you make to the Header and Footer dialog box to apply to all slides or all handouts, notes pages, and outline pages, click the Apply to All button located in the upper right corner of the dialog box.

Project 1n Inserting Headers and Footers   Part 14 of 14

1. With **P-C4-P1-AddisonInd.pptx** open, insert slide numbers on each slide in the presentation by completing the following steps:
   a. Make Slide 1 active.
   b. Click the Insert tab.
   c. Click the Slide Number button in the Text group.
   d. At the Header and Footer dialog box with the Slide tab selected, click the *Slide number* check box to insert a check mark.
   e. Click the Apply to All button.
   f. Scroll through the slides and notice the slide number that displays in the lower right corner of each slide.

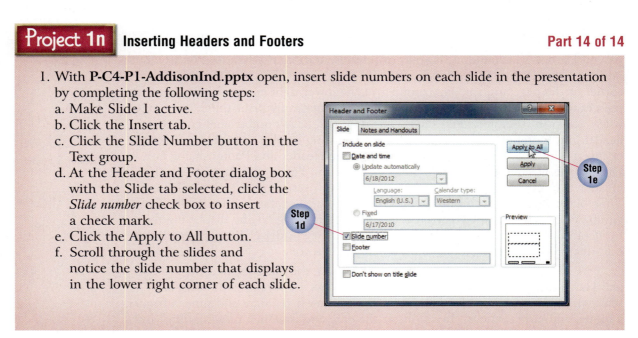

2. Insert your name as a footer that displays on each slide in the presentation by completing the following steps:
   a. Click the Header & Footer button in the Text group.
   b. Click the *Footer* check box to insert a check mark and then type your first and last names.
   c. Click the Apply to All button.
   d. Run the presentation and notice that your name displays at the bottom center of each slide.
3. You decide that you also want your name to print as a footer on handout pages. To do this, complete the following steps:
   a. Click the Header & Footer button in the Text group.
   b. At the Header and Footer dialog box, click the Notes and Handouts tab.
   c. Click the *Footer* check box to insert a check mark and then type your first and last names.
   d. Click the Apply to All button.
4. Insert the current date as a header that prints on handout pages by completing the following steps:
   a. Click the Date & Time button in the Text group.
   b. At the Header and Footer dialog box, click the Notes and Handouts tab.
   c. Click the *Date and time* check box to insert a check mark.
   d. Click the Apply to All button.
5. Insert the presentation name as a header that prints on handout pages by completing the following steps:
   a. Click the File tab and then click the Print tab.
   b. At the Print tab Backstage view, click the <u>Edit Header & Footer</u> hyperlink that displays below the galleries in the Settings category.
   c. At the Header and Footer dialog box, select the Notes and Handouts tab.

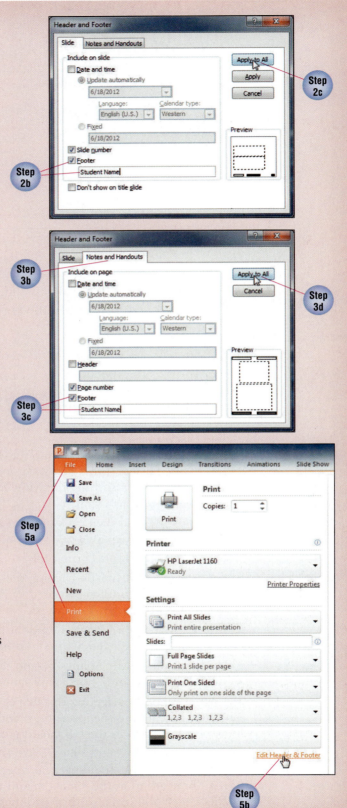

Chapter 4 ■ Inserting Elements in Slides   153

d. Click the *Header* check box to insert a check mark and then type **P-C4-P1-AddisonInd.pptx**.
e. Click the Apply to All button.
f. Click the second gallery in the Settings category and then click *6 Slides Horizontal* at the drop-down list.

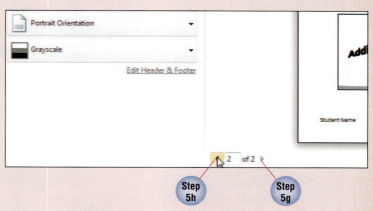

g. Display the next handout page by clicking the Next Page button that displays toward the bottom of the Print tab Backstage view.
h. Click the Previous page button to display the first handout page.
i. Click the Print button to print the presentation as a handout with six slides horizontally per page.
6. Save and then close **P-C4-P1-AddisonInd.pptx**.

Chapter Summary

- Insert a text box in a slide using the Text Box button in the Text group in the Insert tab. Format a text box with options in the Drawing group in the Home tab or with options in the Drawing Tools Format tab.
- Select all objects in a slide by clicking the Select button in the Editing group in the Home tab and then clicking *Select All* or with the keyboard shortcut, Ctrl + A.
- Align selected objects with options from the Align button in the Arrange group in the Drawing Tools Format tab.
- Set tabs in a text box by clicking the Alignment button at the left side of the horizontal ruler until the desired symbol displays and then clicking on a specific location on the ruler. You can set a left, center, right, or decimal tab.
- Insert a shape in a slide with options at the Shapes button in the Drawing group in the Home tab or the Shapes button in the Illustrations group in the Insert tab.
- With options in the Shapes button drop-down list, you can draw a line, basic shapes, block arrows, flow chart symbols, callouts, stars, and banners.
- Copy a shape by selecting the shape, clicking the Copy button in the Clipboard group, positioning the insertion point in the desired position, and then clicking the Paste button in the Clipboard group. You can also copy a shape by holding down the Ctrl key and then dragging the shape to the desired location.
- Turn the horizontal and vertical rulers on and off with the *Ruler* check box in the Show group in the View tab and turn gridlines on and off with the *Gridlines* check box. You can also turn gridlines as well as drawing guides and the snap-to-grid feature on and off with options at the Grid and Guides dialog box.

- You can group objects and then apply the same formatting to objects in the group. To group objects, select the objects, click the Group button in the Arrange group in the Drawing Tools Format tab, and then click *Group* at the drop-down list.
- Size images with the *Shape Height* and *Shape Width* measurement boxes in the Picture Tools Format tab or with the sizing handles that display around a selected image.
- Use the Crop button in the Size group in the Picture Tools Format tab to remove portions of an image.
- Move an image by dragging it to the new location. Move an image in small increments, called nudging, by holding down the Ctrl key while pressing an arrow key.
- Specify how you want to layer objects with the Bring Forward and Send Backward buttons in the Adjust group in the Drawing Tools Format tab or the Picture Tools Format tab.
- Insert a picture in a slide with the Picture button in the Images group in the Insert tab.
- Insert a picture as a slide background with options at the Format Background dialog box. Display this dialog box by clicking the Background Styles button in the Background group in the Design tab and then clicking *Format Background*.
- Insert a clip art image with options in the Clip Art task pane. Display this task pane by clicking the Clip Art button in the Images group in the Insert tab or clicking the Clip Art button in a layout content placeholder.
- You can size objects with options at the Format Picture dialog box with *Size* selected in the left panel. Position an object with options at the Format Picture dialog box with *Position* selected in the left panel.
- Use the Screenshot button in the Images group in the Insert tab to capture the contents of a screen or capture a portion of a screen.
- Use the WordArt feature to distort or modify text to conform to a variety of shapes. Insert WordArt with the WordArt button in the Text group in the Insert tab. Format WordArt with options in the Drawing Tools Format tab.
- Insert symbols in a slide with options at the Symbol dialog box. Display this dialog box by clicking the Symbol button in the Symbols group in the Insert tab.
- Click the Header & Footer button, the Date & Time button, or the Slide Number button to display the Header and Footer dialog box. You can also display the dialog box by clicking the Edit Header & Footer hyperlink at the Print tab Backstage view.

Commands Review

FEATURE	RIBBON TAB, GROUP	BUTTON, OPTION	KEYBOARD SHORTCUT
Text box	Insert, Text		
Shape	Insert, Illustrations OR Home, Drawing		
Gridlines	View, Show	Gridlines	Shift + F9
Rulers	View, Show	Ruler	
Grid and Guides dialog box	View, Show		
Picture	Insert, Images		
Format Background dialog box	Design, Background	, Format Background	
Clip Art task pane	Insert, Images		
Format Picture dialog box	Picture Tools Format, Picture Styles		
Screenshot	Insert, Images		
WordArt	Insert, Text		
Header and Footer	Insert, Text		
Date and Time	Insert, Text		
Slide number	Insert, Text		
Symbol dialog box	Insert, Symbols		

Concepts Check Test Your Knowledge

Completion: In the space provided at the right, indicate the correct term, symbol, or command.

1. The Text Box button is located in the Text group in this tab.

2. Use the sizing handles or these measurement boxes to change the size of a text box.

3. This is the keyboard shortcut to select all objects in a slide.

4. A text box, by default, contains tabs with this alignment. _____

5. The Drawing group in the Home tab and the Illustrations group in this tab each contain a Shapes button. _____

6. When dragging a shape to change the size, hold down this key to maintain the proportions of the shape. _____

7. Copy a shape by holding down this key while dragging the shape to the desired location. _____

8. Turn drawing guides on and off with options in this dialog box. _____

9. The Group button is located in this group in the Drawing Tools Format tab. _____

10. Click the Clip Art button and this displays at the right side of the screen. _____

11. Use this button in the Size group in the Picture Tools Format tab to remove any unnecessary parts of an image. _____

12. With the Bring Forward button and this button in the Arrange group in the Drawing Tools Format tab or the Picture Tools Format tab, you can layer one object on top of another. _____

13. To capture a portion of a screen, click the Screenshot button in the Images group in the Insert tab and then click this option at the drop-down list. _____

14. Use this feature to distort or modify text to conform to a variety of shapes. _____

15. The Symbol button is located in the Symbols group in this tab. _____

16. Click this hyperlink at the Print tab Backstage view to display the Header and Footer dialog box. _____

Skills Check Assess Your Performance

Assessment

1 FORMAT AND ADD ENHANCEMENTS TO A TRAVEL PRESENTATION

1. Open **TravelEngland.pptx** and then save the presentation with Save As and name it **P-C4-A1-TravelEngland**.
2. Apply the Solstice design theme.
3. Insert the slide shown in Figure 4.15 with the following specifications:
   a. Make Slide 6 active and then insert a new slide with the *Title Only* layout.
   b. Type the title *Travel England* as shown in the slide.
   c. Draw a text box in the slide and then type the text shown in Figure 4.15. Select and then change the text font size to 40 and change the font color to *Brown, Accent 5, Darker 50%*.
   d. Apply *Gold, Accent 2, Lighter 80%* shape fill to the text box.
   e. Apply the *Aqua, 18 pt glow, Accent color 1* shape effect (from the *Glow* side menu).
   f. Size and position the text box so it displays as shown in Figure 4.15.
4. Insert the slide shown in Figure 4.16 with the following specifications:
   a. Make Slide 1 active and then insert a new slide with the *Title Only* layout.
   b. Type the title *Upcoming Tours* as shown in the slide.
   c. Draw a text box in the slide and then set a left tab at the 0.5-inch mark on the horizontal ruler, a center tab at the 4-inch mark, and a right tab at the 6.75-inch mark.
   d. Type the text in columns as shown in Figure 4.16. Bold the heading text *Dates*, *Duration*, and *Price*.
   e. After typing the text, select the text, change the font size to 20, the font color to *Brown, Accent 5, Darker 50%*, and change the line spacing to 1.5.
   f. Size and position the text box so it displays as shown in Figure 4.16.
5. Insert a picture in Slide 6 as shown in Figure 4.17 with the following specifications:
   a. Insert the picture named **WhiteHorse.jpg**.
   b. Size and move the picture so it displays as shown in Figure 4.17.
6. Insert a picture in Slide 4 as shown in Figure 4.18 with the following specifications:
   a. Insert the picture named **Stonehenge.jpg**.
   b. Crop the picture so it displays as shown in Figure 4.18.
   c. Send the picture behind the text.
   d. Size and move the picture so it displays as shown in Figure 4.18.
   e. Size and move the bulleted text placeholder so it displays as shown in Figure 4.18.
7. Insert a clip art image in Slide 7 as shown in Figure 4.19 with the following specification:
   a. In the Clip Art task pane, search only for clip art images related to *umbrella*.
   b. At the Clip Art task pane, click the image shown in Figure 4.19. (The original umbrella colors are green and gray. If this image is not available, choose a different umbrella clip art image and then color and size the image as shown in Figure 4.19.)
   c. Flip the umbrella horizontally. **Hint: Do this with the Rotate button in the Arrange group in the Picture Tools Format tab.**

d. Change the color of the umbrella to *Aqua, Accent color 1 Light*.
   e. Size and position the clip art image as shown in Figure 4.19.
8. Insert a picture as background in Slide 1 as shown in Figure 4.20 with the following specifications:
   a. Click the Design tab, click the Background Styles button, and then click *Format Background* at the drop-down list.
   b. At the Format Background dialog box, insert a check mark in the *Hide background graphics*.
   c. Click the File button, navigate to the PowerPoint2010C4 folder on your storage medium, and then double-click **BigBen.jpg**.
   d. At the Format Background dialog box, click the down-pointing arrow at the right side of the *Bottom* option box in the *Stretch Options* section until *-100%* displays in the box.
   e. Close the dialog box.
   f. Size and move the title placeholder so the title displays as shown in Figure 4.20.
   g. Size and move the subtitle placeholder so the subtitle displays as shown in Figure 4.20.
9. Insert the slide shown in Figure 4.21 with the following specifications:
   a. Make Slide 8 active and then insert a new slide with the *Title Only* layout.
   b. Type the title *Travel Discounts!* as shown in Figure 4.21.
   c. Draw the shape shown in the slide in Figure 4.21 using the *Up Ribbon* shape.
   d. Apply the *Subtle Effect - Aqua Accent 1* shape style to the shape.
   e. Apply the *Gold, 8 pt glow, Accent color 2* shape effect (from the *Glow* side menu).
   f. Type the text in the shape as shown in Figure 4.21. Change the font size for the text to 28 and change the font color to *Brown, Accent 5, Darker 50%*.
   g. Size and position the shape so it displays as shown in Figure 4.21.
10. Insert a new slide at the beginning of the presentation with the *Blank* layout. **Hint: Click above the Slide 1 miniature in the Slides/Outline pane and then click the New Slide button arrow.** Insert a logo from another presentation by completing the following steps:
    a. Open **FCTCruise.pptx** and then copy the First Choice Travel logo from Slide 1 to Slide 1 in the **P-C4-A1-TravelEngland.pptx** presentation.
    b. Close **FCTCruise.pptx**.
    c. With Slide 1 of **P-C4-A1-TravelEngland.pptx** active and the logo selected, change the logo (picture) color to *Aqua Accent color 1 Light*.
    d. Position the logo attractively on the slide.
11. Apply a transition and sound of your choosing to each slide.
12. Insert slide numbers on each slide.
13. Insert a footer for notes and handouts pages that prints your first and last names.
14. Run the presentation.
15. Print the presentation as a handout with six slides horizontally per page.
16. Save and then close **P-C4-A1-TravelEngland.pptx**.

Figure 4.15 Assessment 1 Step 3

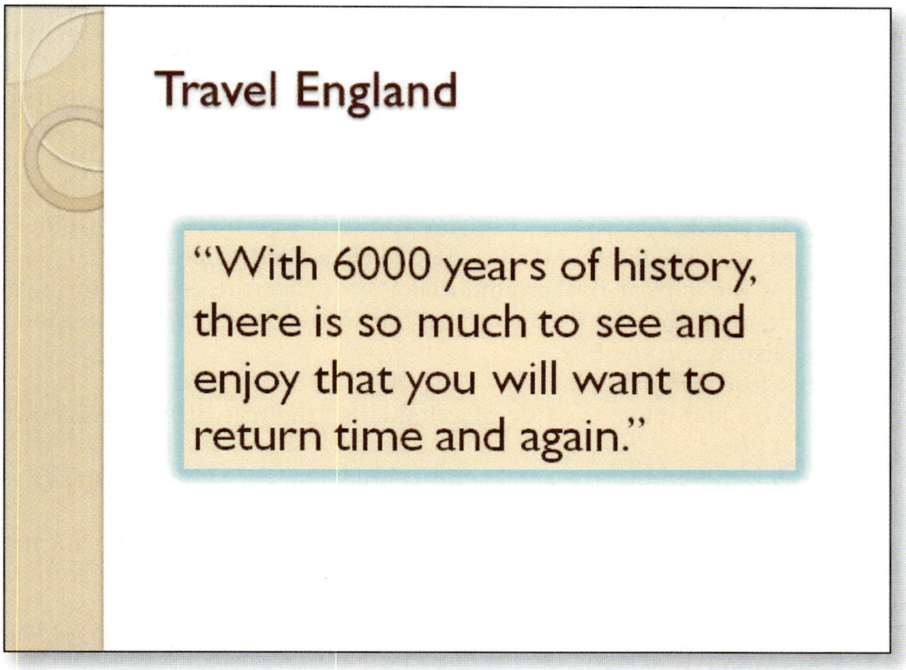

Travel England

"With 6000 years of history, there is so much to see and enjoy that you will want to return time and again."

Figure 4.16 Assessment 1 Step 4

Upcoming Tours

Dates	Duration	Price
April 17 – 24	8 days, 7 nights	$2499
May 15 – 22	8 days, 7 nights	$2499
June 12 – 19	8 days, 7 nights	$2999
July 8 – 18	11 days, 10 nights	$3599
July 24 – 31	8 days, 7 nights	$3099

Figure 4.17 Assessment 1 Step 5

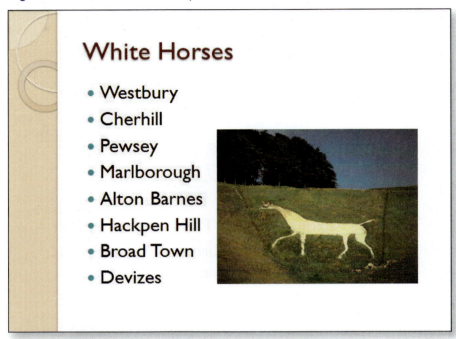

Figure 4.18 Assessment 1 Step 6

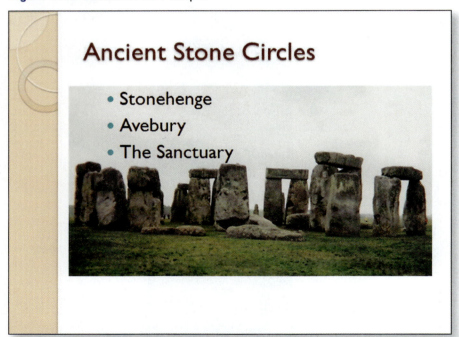

Figure 4.19 Assessment 1 Step 7

Figure 4.20 Assessment 1 Step 8

Figure 4.21 Assessment 1 Step 9

Assessment 2

FORMAT AND ADD ENHANCEMENTS TO A GARDENING PRESENTATION

1. Open **PerennialsPres.pptx** and then save the presentation with Save As and name it **P-C4-A2-PerennialsPres**.
2. Insert the slide shown in Figure 4.22 with the following specifications:
   a. Make Slide 2 active and then insert a new slide with the *Blank* layout.
   b. Hide the background graphics.
   c. Insert the WordArt text using *Gradient Fill - Dark Green, Accent 6, Inner Shadow* (second option from the left in the fourth row).
   d. Change the shape of the WordArt to *Wave 1*. (The *Wave 1* option is the first option in the fifth row in *Warp* section of the Text Effects button Transform side menu.)
   e. Change the height of the WordArt to *3″* and the width to *9″*.
   f. Display the Format Background dialog box (for help, see Assessment 1, Step 8), click the *Gradient fill* option in the *Fill* section, change the *Preset colors* option to *Daybreak*, and then close the dialog box.
   g. Position the WordArt text as shown in Figure 4.22.
3. Insert the slide shown in Figure 4.23 with the following specifications:
   a. Make Slide 8 active and then insert a new slide with the *Title Only* layout.
   b. Insert the title *English/French Translations* as shown in Figure 4.23.
   c. Insert a text box, change the font size to 28, change the font color to *Light Blue, Accent 5, Darker 25%*, set left tabs at the 0.5-inch and the 4-inch marks on the horizontal ruler, and then type the text shown in Figure 4.23 in columns. Bold the headings *English Name* and *French Name* and use the Symbol dialog box to insert the special symbols in the French names.
   d. If necessary, move the text box so it is positioned as shown in Figure 4.23.

4. Make Slide 4 active and then make the following changes:
   a. Select the bulleted text and then change the line spacing to 2.0.
   b. With the bulleted text selected, set the bulleted text in two columns. **Hint: Refer to Project 1c in Chapter 3.**
   c. Make sure four bulleted items display in each column.
5. Make Slide 5 active and then insert a clip art image related to *garden* or *gardening*. Size and position the clip art attractively in the slide.
6. Make Slide 8 active and then insert a clip art image of a flower. Size and position the clip art attractively in the slide.
7. Select and then delete Slide 10.
8. Insert the slide shown in Figure 4.24 with the following specifications:
   a. Make Slide 9 active and then insert a new slide with the *Title Only* layout.
   b. Insert the title *Gardening Magazines*.
   c. Create the top shape using the *Bevel* shape.
   d. Change the font size to 32, turn on bold, turn on italic, change the alignment to Center, and then type the text in the top shape. **Hint: To vertically center the text in the shape, click the Align Text button in the Paragraph group in the Home tab and then click Middle *at the drop-down list.***
   e. Select and then copy the shape two times.
   f. Change the text in the second and third shapes to match what you see in Figure 4.24.
   g. Size and position the shapes and text boxes as shown in Figure 4.24.
9. Make Slide 7 active and then insert a clip art image of your choosing.
10. Make Slide 10 active and then insert a new slide with the *Title Only* layout. Type **Gift Certificates Available!** as the title and then insert a screenshot with the following specifications:
    a. Open Word and then open the document named **GAGiftCert.docx** from the PowerPoint2010C4 folder on your storage medium.
    b. Click the PowerPoint button on the Taskbar and then use the *Screen Clipping* option from the Screenshot button drop-down list to capture only the gift certificate in the Word document.
    c. With the gift certificate screenshot inserted in the slide, size and position the gift certificate attractively on the slide.
    d. Make Word active and then exit Word.
11. Run the presentation.
12. Print the presentation as a handout with six slides horizontally per page.
13. Save **P-C4-A2-PerennialsPres.pptx**.

Figure 4.22 Assessment 2 Step 2

Figure 4.23 Assessment 2 Step 3

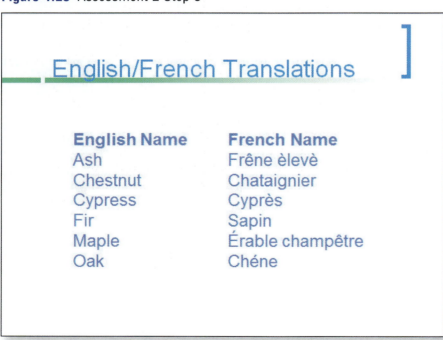

Figure 4.24 Assessment 2 Step 7

Assessment

3 COPY A PICTURE FROM A WEBSITE TO A PRESENTATION

1. With **P-C4-A2-PerennialsPres.pptx** open, make Slide 6 active.
2. Use the Help feature to find information on copying a picture from a web page. (Begin by entering "insert a picture or clip art" in the PowerPoint Help window and then press Enter. Click the Insert a picture or clip art hyperlink and then click the Insert a picture from a Web page hyperlink.)
3. Using the information you learned about inserting a picture from a web page, open your web browser and then use a search engine of your choosing to search for a picture of at least one flower mentioned in the slide.
4. Save the picture to the PowerPoint2010C4 folder on your storage medium and then insert the image in the slide. Size and move the picture so it is positioned attractively in the slide. (Consider inserting at least one more picture of one of the flowers mentioned.)
5. Print only Slide 6.
6. Run the presentation.
7. Save and then close **P-C4-A2-PerennialsPres.pptx**.

Visual Benchmark Demonstrate Your Proficiency

CREATING A STUDY ABROAD PRESENTATION

1. At a blank presentation, create the presentation shown in Figure 4.25 with the following specifications:
    a. Apply the *Slipstream* design theme.
    b. In Slide 1, increase the font size for the subtitle to 32 and then position the subtitle as shown in Figure 4.25.
    c. In Slide 2, insert the WordArt using the *Fill – Turquoise, Accent 2, Matte Bevel* option (located in the *Applies to All Text in the Shape* section) and apply the *Deflate* transform text effect. Size and position the WordArt on the slide as shown in Figure 4.25.
    d. Change the line spacing to *2* for the bulleted text in Slides 3, 4, and 5.
    e. Use the word *apartment* to search for the clip art image in Slide 4. The original color of the clip art image is dark pink. Change the color to *Turquoise, Accent color 2 Light*. (If this clip art image is not available, choose a similar image.)
    f. Insert the picture **Colosseum.jpg** in Slide 5. (This image is located in the PowerPoint2010C4 folder on your storage medium.) Size and position the image as shown in Figure 4.25.
    g. In Slide 6, use the Bevel shape in the *Basic Shapes* section of the Shapes button drop-down list to create the shape and change the fill color to *Turquoise, Accent 2, Darker 50%*.
    h. Make any other changes to placeholders and other objects so your slides display similar to what you see in Figure 4.25.
2. Apply a transition and sound of your choosing to all slides in the presentation.
3. Save the presentation and name it **P-C4-VB-RomeStudy**.
4. Print the presentation as a handout with six slides horizontally per page.
5. Close **P-C4-VB-RomeStudy.pptx**.

Figure 4.25 Visual Benchmark

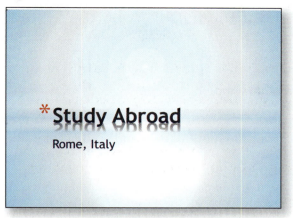
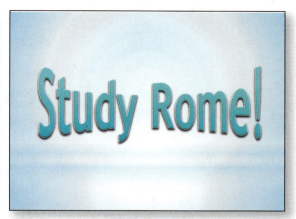
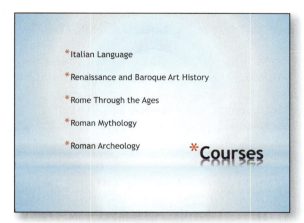

Case Study Apply Your Skills

Part 1

You work for Honoré Financial Services and the Office Manager, Jason Monroe, has asked you to prepare a presentation for a community workshop he will be conducting next week. Open the Word document named **HFS.docx** and then use the information in the document to create a presentation with the following specifications:

- Slide 1: Include the company name Honoré Financial Services (use the Symbol feature to create the é in Honoré) and the subtitle *Managing Your Money*.
- Slide 2: Insert the word *Budgeting* as WordArt.
- Slides 3, 4, and 5: Use the bulleted and numbered information to create these slides.
- Slide 6: Create a text box, set tabs, and then type the information in the *Managing Records* section that is set in columns.
- Slide 7: Create a shape and then insert the following slogan *"Retirement Planning Made Easy"*.
- Include at least one picture and one clip art in the presentation.

Apply a design theme of your choosing and add any additional features to improve the visual appeal of the presentation. Insert a transition and sound to each slide and then run the presentation. Save the presentation and name it **P-C4-CS-HFS.pptx**. Print the presentation as a handout with four slides horizontally per page.

Part 2

Mr. Monroe will be conducting a free workshop titled *Financial Planning for the College Student*. Create a slide in the **P-C4-CS-HFS.pptx** presentation (make it the last slide in the presentation) that includes a shape with text inside that includes information about the workshop. You determine the day, the time, and the location for the workshop. Print the slide.

Part 3

Mr. Monroe would like to post the information about the workshop in various locations in the community and wants to print a number of copies. You decide to copy the shape and then insert it in a blank Word document. In Word, change the orientation of the page to landscape, increase the size of the shape, and then drag the shape to the middle of the page. Save the Word document and name it **P-C4-CS-HFSWorkshop**. Print and then close **P-C4-CS-HFSWorkshop.docx**.

Part 4

Mr. Monroe has asked you to locate online finance and/or budgeting resources such as newsletters and magazines. He would like you to locate resources and then create a slide with hyperlinks to the resources. Locate at least two online resources and then insert this information with the hyperlinks in a new slide at the end of the **P-C4-CS-HFS.pptx** presentation. Print the slide and then save and close the presentation.

UNIT 1

Performance Assessment

Note: Before beginning unit assessments, copy to your storage medium the PowerPoint2010U1 folder from the PowerPoint2010 folder on the CD that accompanies this textbook and then make PowerPoint2010U1 the active folder.

Assessing Proficiency

In this unit, you have learned to create, print, save, close, open, view, run, edit, and format a PowerPoint presentation. You also learned how to add transitions and sound to presentations; rearrange slides; customize presentations by changing the design theme; and add visual appeal to slides by inserting text boxes, shapes, pictures, clip art, screenshots, and symbols.

Assessment 1 Prepare, Format, and Enhance a Conference Presentation

1. Create a presentation with the text shown in Figure U1.1 using the Module design theme. Use the appropriate slide layout for each slide. After creating the slides, complete a spelling check on the text in slides.
2. Add a transition and sound of your choosing to all slides.
3. Save the presentation and name it **P-U1-A1-CSConf**.
4. Run the presentation.
5. Make Slide 1 active and then find all occurrences of *Area* and replace with *Market*.
6. Make the following changes to Slide 2:
   a. Type **Net income per common share** over *Net income*.
   b. Delete *Return on average equity*.
7. Make the following changes to Slide 4:
   a. Delete *Shopping*.
   b. Type **Business finance** between *Personal finance* and *Email*.
8. Rearrange the slides in the presentation so they are in the following order (only the slide titles are shown below):
   - Slide 1 = CORNERSTONE SYSTEMS
   - Slide 2 = Corporate Vision
   - Slide 3 = Future Goals
   - Slide 4 = Industrial Market
   - Slide 5 = Consumer Market
   - Slide 6 = Financial Review
9. Increase spacing to 1.5 for the bulleted text in Slides 2, 3, 5, and 6.
10. Make Slide 4 active, increase the spacing to 2.0 for the bulleted text, and then format the bulleted text into two columns with three entries in each column. (You may need to decrease the size of the placeholder.)

11. Save and then run the presentation.
12. Print the presentation as a handout with six slides horizontally per page.
13. Display the Reuse Slides task pane, browse to the PowerPoint2010U1 folder on your storage medium, and then double-click **CSMktRpt.pptx**.
14. Insert the *Department Reports* slide below Slide 4.
15. Insert the *Services* slide below Slide 2.
16. Close the Reuse Slides task pane.
17. Make Slide 8 active, select the bulleted text, and then create and apply a custom bullet using a dollar sign in a complementary color. (You can find a dollar sign in the normal font in the Symbol dialog box.)
18. With Slide 8 active, insert a clip art image related to *money* or *finances*. Size and position the clip art attractively in the slide.
19. Move Slide 4 (*Future Goals*) to the end of the presentation.
20. Insert a new slide with the *Title and Content* layout at the end of the presentation with the following specifications:
    a. Insert *Future Goals* as the title.
    b. Type **International market** as the first bulleted item and then press Enter.
    c. Copy *Acquisitions*, *Production*, *Technology*, and *Marketing* from Slide 8 and paste them in the content area of the new slide below the first bulleted text. (When copied, the items should be preceded by a bullet. If a bullet displays on a blank line below the last text item, press the Backspace key twice.)
    d. Select the bulleted text and then change the line spacing to 1.5.
21. Make Slide 8 active, select the bulleted items, and then apply numbering.
22. Make Slide 9 active, select the bulleted items, and then apply numbering and change the beginning number to *6*.
23. With Slide 9 active, create a new slide with the *Blank* layout with the following specifications:
    a. Insert the picture named **Nightscape.jpg** as a background picture and hide the background graphics. ***Hint: Do this with the Background Styles button in the Design tab.***
    b. Create a text box toward the top of the slide, change the font color to white, increase the font size to 36, and then change the alignment to center.
    c. Type **National Sales Meeting**, press Enter, type **New York City**, press Enter, and then type **March 6 - 8, 2013**.
    d. Move and/or size the text box so the text is positioned centered above the buildings in the picture.
24. With Slide 10 active, insert a new slide with the *Title Only* layout. Type **Doubletree Guest Suites** as the title and then insert a screenshot with the following specifications:
    a. Open Word and then open the document named **HotelMap.docx** from the PowerPoint2010U1 folder on your storage medium.
    b. Click the PowerPoint button on the Taskbar and then use the *Screen Clipping* option from the Screenshot button drop-down list to capture only the map in the Word document.
    c. With the map screenshot inserted in the slide, apply the *Sharpen: 25%* correction. Size and position the map attractively on the slide.
25. Insert slide numbers on each slide.
26. Insert a footer for notes and handouts pages that prints your first and last names.
27. Save and then run the presentation.
28. Print the presentation as a handout with six slides horizontally per page.
29. Close **P-U1-A1-CSConf.pptx**.

Figure U1.1 Assessment 1

Slide 1	Title	=	CORNERSTONE SYSTEMS
	Subtitle	=	Executive Conference
Slide 2	Title	=	Financial Review
	Bullets	=	• Net revenues
			• Operating income
			• Net income
			• Return on average equity
			• Return on average asset
Slide 3	Title	=	Corporate Vision
	Bullets	=	• Expansion
			• Increased productivity
			• Consumer satisfaction
			• Employee satisfaction
			• Area visibility
Slide 4	Title	=	Consumer Area
	Bullets	=	• Travel
			• Shopping
			• Entertainment
			• Personal finance
			• Email
Slide 5	Title	=	Industrial Area
	Bullets	=	• Finance
			• Education
			• Government
			• Production
			• Manufacturing
			• Utilities
Slide 6	Title	=	Future Goals
	Bullets	=	• Domestic market
			• Acquisitions
			• Production
			• Technology
			• Marketing

Assessment 2 Format and Enhance a Kraft Artworks Presentation

1. Open **KAPres.pptx** and then save the presentation with Save As and name it **P-U1-A2-KAPres**.
2. With Slide 1 active, insert the text *Kraft Artworks* as WordArt and apply at least the following formatting:
   a. Change the shape of the WordArt.
   b. Change the size so the WordArt better fills the slide.
   c. Change the fill to a purple color.
   d. Apply any other formatting to improve the visual appeal of the WordArt.
3. Duplicate Slides 2 and 3.
4. Change the goal number in Slide 4 from *1* to *3* and change the goal text to *Conduct six art workshops at the Community Center*.
5. Change the goal number in Slide 5 from *2* to *4* and change the goal text to *Provide recycled material to public schools for art classes*.
6. With Slide 5 active, insert a new slide with the *Title Only* layout with the following specifications:
   a. Insert the title *Clients* and then format, size, and position the title in the same manner as the title in Slide 5.
   b. Insert a text box, change the font to Comic Sans MS, the font size to 20, the font color to purple, and then type the following text in columns (you determine the tab settings):

School	Contact	Number
Logan Elementary School	Maya Jones	555-0882
Cedar Elementary School	George Ferraro	555-3211
Sunrise Elementary School	Avery Burns	555-3444
Hillside Middle School	Joanna Myers	555-2211
Douglas Middle School	Ray Murphy	555-8100

   c. Select all of the text in the text box and then change the line spacing to 1.5.
7. With Slide 6 active, insert a new slide with the *Blank* layout, hide the background graphic, and then create the slide shown in Figure U1.2 with the following specifications:
   a. Use the *Explosion 1* shape (in the *Stars and Banners* section) to create the first shape.
   b. Change the fill color of the shape to *Gold, Accent 2, Lighter 40%* and apply the *Lavender, 18 pt glow, Accent color 3* glow effect.
   c. With the shape selected, change the font to 40-point Comic Sans MS bold in purple color, change the alignment to center, change the vertical alignment to middle, and then type the text shown in Figure U1.2.
   d. Copy the shape twice and position the shapes as shown in Figure U1.2.
   e. Type the appropriate text in each text box as shown in Figure U1.2.
8. With Slide 7 active, insert a new slide with the *Blank* layout, hide the background graphic, and then create the slide shown in Figure U1.3 with the following specifications:
   a. Set the text in the two text boxes at the left and right sides of the slide in 54-point Comic Sans MS bold and in purple color. Rotate, size, and position the two text boxes as shown in Figure U1.3.
   b. Use the *Explosion 1* shape to create the shape in the middle of the slide.
   c. Change the fill color of the shape to *Gold, Accent 2, Lighter 40%*, apply the *Perspective Diagonal Upper Left* shadow effect, and change the shape outline color to purple and the weight to *2¼ pt*.

    d. Insert the text in the shape and then change the font to 28-point Comic Sans MS bold in purple color, change the alignment to center, and change the vertical alignment to middle.
9. Create a footer that prints your first and last names and the current date on handout pages.
10. Print the presentation as a handout with four slides horizontally per page.
11. Save and then close **P-U1-A2-KAPres.pptx**.

Figure U1.2 Assessment 2, Slide 7

Figure U1.3 Assessment 2, Slide 8

Assessment 3 Create and Apply a Custom Theme to a Job Search Presentation

1. At a blank presentation, apply the *Civic* design theme.
2. Create custom theme colors named with your first and last names that change the following colors:
   a. Change the Text/Background, Dark 1 color, to *Dark Yellow, Followed Hyperlink, Lighter 80%*.
   b. Change the Text/Background, Dark 2 color, to *White, Text 1*.
   c. Change the Text/Background, Light 2 color, to *Turquoise, Hyperlink, Darker 25%*.
   d. Change the Accent 1 color to *Dark Red*.
   e. Change the Accent 2 and the Accent 3 color to *Red, Accent 1, Darker 50%*.
3. Create custom theme fonts named with your first and last names that changes the *Heading font* to Constantia and the *Body font* to Cambria.
4. Save the current theme as a custom theme named with your first and last names. **Hint: Do this at the Save Current Theme dialog box.**
5. Close the presentation without saving it.
6. Open **JobSearch.pptx** and then save the presentation with Save As and name it **P-U1-A3-JobSearch**.
7. Apply the custom theme named with your first and last names.
8. Insert a clip art image in Slide 5 related to *telephone*, *people*, or *Internet*. You determine the size and position of the image.
9. Insert a clip art image in Slide 6 related to *clock* or *time*. You determine the size and position of the image.
10. Improve the visual display of text in Slides 2, 3, 7, 8, and 9 by increasing the spacing between items and positioning the text placeholders attractively in the slides.
11. Insert the current date and slide number on all slides in the presentation. (The slide numbers will appear in the round circle that is part of the design theme.)
12. Create the header *Job Search Seminar*, the footer *Employment Strategies*, and insert the date and page number for notes and handouts.
13. Add the speaker note *Distribute list of Internet employment sites.* to Slide 5.
14. Apply a transition and sound of your choosing to all slides in the presentation.
15. Save and then run the presentation.
16. Print the presentation as a handout with six slides horizontally per page.
17. Print Slide 5 as notes pages.
18. Save and then close **P-U1-A3-JobSearch.pptx**.
19. Display a blank presentation and then delete the custom theme colors, custom theme fonts, and custom theme you created for this assessment.
20. Close the presentation without saving it.

Assessment 4 Format and Enhance a Medical Plans Presentation

1. Open **MedicalPlans.pptx** and then save the presentation with Save As and name it **P-U1-A4-MedicalPlans**.
2. Apply a design theme of your choosing.
3. Create a new slide with a Blank layout between Slides 1 and 2 that contains a shape with the text *Medical Plans 2013 - 2014* inside the shape. You determine the format, position, and size of the shape and the formatting of the text.

4. Change the bullets to custom bullets (you determine the picture or symbol) for the bullets in Slides 3, 4, and 5.
5. Insert a clip art image related to *medicine* in Slide 4. You determine the color, size, and position of the image.
6. Make Slide 5 active, and then apply the following formatting:
   a. Move the insertion point to the beginning of *Eugene* and then press the Enter key.
   b. Select all of the bulleted text and then change the line spacing to 2.0.
   c. With the bulleted text selected, format the text into two columns. (Make sure each column contains four entries.)
   d. Size and/or move the placeholder so the bulleted text displays attractively in the slide.
7. Apply any additional formatting or elements to improve the visual appeal of the slides.
8. Add a transition and sound of your choosing to the presentation.
9. Run the presentation.
10. Print the presentation as a handout with four slides horizontally per page.
11. Save and then close **P-U1-A4-MedicalPlans.pptx**.

Writing Activities

The following activities provide you with the opportunity to practice your writing skills along with demonstrating an understanding of some of the important PowerPoint features you have mastered in this unit. Use correct spelling, grammar, and appropriate word choices.

Activity 1 Prepare and Format a Health Plan Presentation

Open Word and then open, print, and close **KLHPlan.docx**. Looking at the printing of this document, create a presentation in PowerPoint that presents the main points of the plan. (Use bullets in the presentation.) Add a transition and sound to the slides. Apply formatting and/or insert images to enhance the visual appeal of the presentation. Save the presentation and name it **P-U1-Act1-KLHPlan**. Run the presentation. Print the presentation as a handout with six slides horizontally per page. Save and then close **P-U1-Act1-KLHPlan.pptx**.

Activity 2 Prepare and Format a Presentation on Clip Art

At a blank presentation, use the Help feature to find information on inserting a picture or clip art image. *Hint: Display the PowerPoint Help window, type* **insert picture or clip art**, *press Enter, and then click the* **Insert a picture or clip art** *hyperlink that displays in the window.* Print and then read the information and then use the information to create a presentation that includes at least four slides. Format and add visual appeal to the presentation. With the presentation still open, display the Clip Art task pane and then click the Find more at Office.com hyperlink that displays at the bottom of the task pane. (Your computer needs to be connected to the Internet to complete this activity.) At the website, search for information on how to display image categories and then how to specify media types and sizes and how to download images. With the information, create at least three additional slides that contain information about displaying and downloading images from Office.com.

Download and insert at least one image into a slide. Save the completed presentation and name it **P-U1-Act2-ClipArtPres**. Add a transition and sound of your choosing to each slide and then run the presentation. Print the presentation as a handout with four slides horizontally per page. Close **P-U1-Act2-ClipArtPres.pptx**.

Internet Research

Analyze a Magazine Website

Make sure you are connected to the Internet and then explore the *Time*® magazine website at www.time.com. Discover the following information for the site:

- Magazine sections
- The type of information presented in each section
- Information on how to subscribe

Use the information you discovered about the *Time* magazine website and create a PowerPoint presentation that presents the information in a clear, concise, and logical manner. Add formatting and enhancements to the presentation to make it more interesting. When the presentation is completed, save it and name it **P-U1-TimeMag**. Run, print, and then close the presentation.

Microsoft® PowerPoint®

Unit 2 ■ Customizing and Enhancing PowerPoint Presentations

Chapter 5 ■ Creating Tables, Charts, and SmartArt Graphics

Chapter 6 ■ Using Slide Masters and Action Buttons

Chapter 7 ■ Applying Custom Animation and Setting Up Shows

Chapter 8 ■ Integrating, Sharing, and Protecting Presentations

Microsoft® PowerPoint®

Creating Tables, Charts, and SmartArt Graphics

CHAPTER 5

PERFORMANCE OBJECTIVES

Upon successful completion of Chapter 5, you will be able to:
- Create and format a table
- Modify the design and layout of a table
- Insert an image in a table
- Create SmartArt diagrams
- Modify the design and layout of SmartArt
- Create a SmartArt graphic with bulleted text
- Create and format charts
- Modify the design and layout of charts
- Select and format chart elements
- Create, edit, and format a photo album

If you want to present numbers and lists in a slide, consider inserting the information in a table. Use the Tables feature to create data in columns and rows in a manner similar to a spreadsheet. Display data in a slide in a more visual way by creating a SmartArt diagram. The SmartArt feature provides a number of predesigned diagrams and organizational charts. You can create a SmartArt diagram and then modify the design and layout of the diagram.

While a table does an adequate job of representing data, you can create a chart from data to provide a more visual representation of the data. A chart is sometimes referred to as a *graph* and is a picture of numeric data. If you have Microsoft Excel installed on your computer, you can create a chart in a PowerPoint slide. If you do not have Excel installed on your computer, PowerPoint uses the Microsoft Graph feature to create your chart. Projects and assessments in this chapter assume that you have Excel installed on your computer.

You can create a photo album presentation to attractively display personal or business photographs. With the Photo Album feature you can insert pictures and then format the appearance of the pictures in the presentation. Model answers for this chapter's projects appear on the following page.

Note: Before beginning the projects, copy to your storage medium the PowerPoint2010C5 folder from the PowerPoint2010 folder on the CD that accompanies this textbook and then make PowerPoint2010C5 the active folder.

Model Answers

Project 1 Create a Company Sales Conference Presentation
P-C5-P1-Conference.pptx

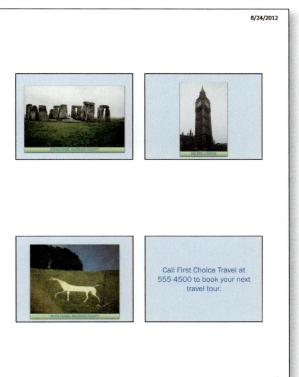

Project 2 Create and Format a Travel Photo Album
P-C5-P2-Album.pptx

> **Project 1 Create a Company Sales Conference Presentation 12 Parts**
>
> You will create a sales conference presentation for Nature's Way that includes a table, a column chart, a pie chart, and four SmartArt graphics.

Creating a Table

Use the Tables feature to create boxes of information called *cells*. A cell is the intersection between a row and a column. A cell can contain text, characters, numbers, data, graphics, or formulas. If you want to arrange the content of a slide in columns and rows, insert a new slide with the slide layout that includes a content placeholder. Click the Insert Table button in the content placeholder and the Insert Table dialog box displays. At the Insert Table dialog box, type the number of columns, press the Tab key, type the number of rows, and then press Enter. You can also insert a table using the Table button in the Tables group in the Insert tab. Click the Table button, drag the mouse down and to the right to select the desired number of columns and rows, and then click the left mouse button.

When you create a table, the insertion point is located in the cell in the upper left corner of the table. Cells in a table contain a cell designation. Columns in a table are lettered from left to right, beginning with *A*. Rows in a table are numbered from top to bottom beginning with *1*. The cell in the upper left corner of the table is cell A1. The cell to the right of A1 is B1, the cell to the right of B1 is C1, and so on.

Entering Text in Cells

With the insertion point positioned in a cell, type or edit text. Move the insertion point to other cells with the mouse by clicking in the desired cell. If you are using the keyboard, press the Tab key to move the insertion point to the next cell or press Shift + Tab to move the insertion point to the previous cell.

If the text you type does not fit on one line, it wraps to the next line within the same cell. Or, if you press Enter within a cell, the insertion point is moved to the next line within the same cell. The cell vertically lengthens to accommodate the text, and all cells in that row also lengthen. Pressing the Tab key in a table causes the insertion point to move to the next cell in the table. If you want to move the insertion point to a tab stop within a cell, press Ctrl + Tab. If the insertion point is located in the last cell of the table and you press the Tab key, PowerPoint adds another row to the table.

Selecting Cells

You can apply formatting to an entire table or to specific cells, rows, or columns in a table. To identify cells for formatting, select the specific cells using the mouse or the keyboard. Press the Tab key to select the next cell or press Shift + Tab to select the previous cell. Refer to Table 5.1 for additional methods for selecting in a table.

▼ **Quick Steps**

Insert a Table
1. Click Insert Table button in content placeholder.
2. Type number of columns.
3. Press Tab.
4. Type number of rows.
5. Click OK.
OR
1. Click Insert tab.
2. Click Table button.
3. Drag in grid to desired number of columns and rows.

Table

Add a row to the bottom of a table by positioning the insertion point in the last cell and then pressing the Tab key.

HINT
You can move text to a different cell by selecting the text and then dragging the selected text to a different cell.

Table 5.1 Selecting in a Table

To select this	Do this
A cell	Position the mouse pointer at left side of cell until pointer turns into a small, black, diagonally pointing arrow and then click the left mouse button.
A row	Position the mouse pointer outside the table at the left edge of the row until the pointer turns into a small, black arrow pointing right and then click the left mouse button. Drag to select multiple rows.
A column	Position the mouse pointer outside the table at the top of the column until the pointer turns into a small, black arrow pointing down and then click the left mouse button. Drag to select multiple columns.
All cells in a table	Drag to select all cells or press Ctrl + A.
Text within a cell	Position the mouse pointer at the beginning of the text and then hold down the left mouse button as you drag the mouse across the text. (When a cell is selected, the cell background color changes to blue. When text within cells is selected, only those lines containing text are selected.)

Project 1a Creating a Table   Part 1 of 12

1. Open **Conference.pptx** and then save the presentation with Save As and name it **P-C5-P1-Conference**.
2. Make Slide 4 active.
3. Insert a table in the slide and enter text into the cells by completing the following steps:
   a. Click the Insert Table button located in the middle of the slide in the content placeholder.
   b. At the Insert Table dialog box, type 2 in the *Number of columns* text box.
   c. Press the Tab key.
   d. Type 5 in the *Number of rows* text box.
   e. Click OK or press Enter.
   f. Type the text as displayed in the table below. Press the Tab key to move the insertion point to the next cell or press Shift + Tab to move the insertion point to the previous cell. Do not press Tab after typing the last cell entry.

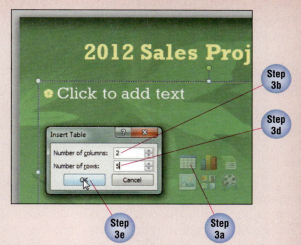

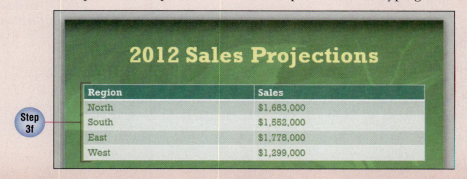

184 PowerPoint ■ Unit 2

4. Apply formatting to text in specific cells by completing the following steps:
   a. With the insertion point positioned in the table, press Ctrl + A to select all of the text in the table.
   b. Click the Home tab and then change the font size to 32.
   c. Looking at the text set in 32 point size, you decide that you want the text below the headings set in a smaller point size. To do this, position the mouse pointer at the left edge of the second row (to the left of the cell containing *North*) until the pointer turns into a small, black, right-pointing arrow. Hold down the left mouse button, drag down so the remaining rows are selected, and then change the font size to 28.
   d. Click outside the table to deselect it.
5. Save **P-C5-P1-Conference.pptx**.

Changing Table Design

When you create a table, the Table Tools Design tab is selected that contains a number of options for enhancing the appearance of the table as shown in Figure 5.1. With options in the Table Styles group, apply a predesigned style that applies color and border lines to a table. Maintain further control over the predesigned style formatting applied to columns and rows with options in the Table Style Options group. For example, if you want your first column to be formatted differently than the other columns in the table, insert a check mark in the *First Column* check box. Apply additional design formatting to cells in a table with the Shading, Borders, and Effects buttons in the Table Styles group. Draw a table or draw additional rows and/or columns in a table by clicking the Draw Table button in the Draw Borders group. Click this button and the mouse pointer turns into a pencil. Drag in the table to create the desired columns and rows. Click the Eraser button and the mouse pointer turns into an eraser. Drag through the column and/or row lines you want to erase in the table.

HINT Draw a freeform table by clicking the Insert tab, clicking the Table button, and then clicking the *Draw Table* option. Drag in the document to create the table.

Figure 5.1 Table Tools Design Tab

Project 1b Modifying the Table Design   Part 2 of 12

1. With **P-C5-P1-Conference.pptx** open, make sure Slide 4 is active, the insertion point is positioned in the table, and then click the Table Tools Design tab.
2. Click the *First Column* check box in the Table Style Options group to insert a check mark. (This applies bold formatting to the text in the first column and applies darker shading to the cell.)

3. Click the More button that displays at the right side of the Table Styles thumbnails and then click the *Themed Style 1 - Accent 6* option (last option in the top row).

4. Select the first row of the table.
5. Click the Quick Styles button in the WordArt Styles group and then click *Fill - Light Green Accent 3, Outline - Text 2* option (last option in the top row).
6. Click the Text Fill button arrow in the WordArt Styles group and then click *Light Yellow, Text 2, Darker 10%*.

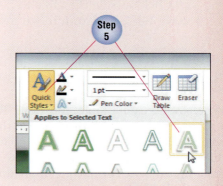

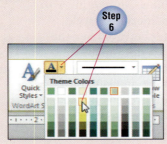

7. Click the Text Outline button arrow in the WordArt Styles group and then click *Green, Accent 6, Lighter 40%*.
8. Click the Pen Weight button arrow in the Draw Borders group and then click *2¼ pt*. (This activates the Draw Table button.)
9. Click the Pen Color button in the Draw Borders group and then click *Green, Accent 6, Darker 25%*.
10. Draw along the border that separates the two columns from the top of the first row to the bottom of the last row.
11. Draw along the border that separates the first row from the second row.
12. Click the Draw Table button to deactivate it.
13. Save **P-C5-P1-Conference.pptx**.

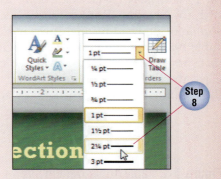

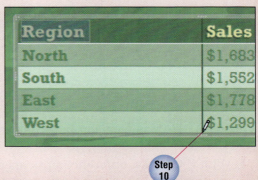

Changing Table Layout

To further customize a table consider changing the table layout by inserting or deleting columns and rows and specifying cell alignments. Change table layout with options at the Table Tools Layout tab shown in Figure 5.2. Use options and buttons in the tab to select specific cells, delete and insert rows and columns, merge and split cells, specify cell and table height and width and text alignment in cells, and arrange elements in a slide.

HINT
If you make a mistake while formatting a table, immediately click the Undo button on the Quick Access toolbar.

Figure 5.2 Table Tools Layout Tab

Project 1c — Modifying Table Layout — Part 3 of 12

1. With **P-C5-P1-Conference.pptx** open, make sure Slide 4 is active.
2. Click in any cell in the table and then click the Table Tools Layout tab.
3. Click in the cell containing the word *East*.
4. Click the Insert Above button in the Rows & Columns group.
5. Type **Central** in the new cell at the left, press the Tab key, and then type **$1,024,000** in the new cell at the right.
6. Click in the cell containing the word *Region*.
7. Click the Insert Left button in the Rows & Columns group.
8. Click the Merge Cells button in the Merge group.
9. Type **Sales Projections** in the new cell.
10. Click the Text Direction button in the Alignment group and then click *Rotate all text 270°* at the drop-down list.
11. Click the Center button in the Alignment group and then click the Center Vertically button in the Alignment group.
12. Click in the Width measurement box in the Cell Size group, type **1.2**, and then press Enter.

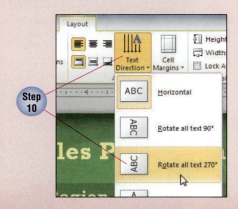

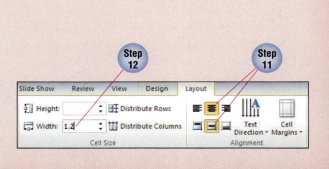

Chapter 5 ■ Creating Tables, Charts, and SmartArt Graphics

13. Click the Table Tools Design tab.
14. Click the Borders button arrow in the Table Styles group (the name of the button changes depending on the last action performed) and then click *Bottom Border* at the drop-down list.
15. Click in the cell containing the text *Sales* and then click the Table Tools Layout tab.
16. Click in the Height measurement box in the Cell Size group and type **0.7**.
17. Click in the Width measurement box in the Cell Size group, type **2.5**, and then press Enter.
18. Click in the cell containing the text *Region*.
19. Click in the Width measurement box in the Cell Size group, type **4**, and then press Enter.
20. Click in the Height measurement box in the Table Size group, type **4.2**, and then press Enter.
21. Click the Select button in the Table group and then click *Select Table* at the drop-down list.
22. Click the Center button and then click the Center Vertically button in the Alignment group.
23. After looking at the text in cells, you decide that you want the text in the second column left-aligned. To do this, complete the following steps:
    a. Click in the cell containing the text *Region*.
    b. Click the Select button in the Table group and then click *Select Column* at the drop-down list.
    c. Click the Align Text Left button in the Alignment group.
    d. Click in any cell in the table.
24. Align the table by completing the following steps:
    a. Click the Home tab.
    b. Click the Arrange button in the Drawing group, point to *Align*, and then click *Distribute Horizontally*.
    c. Click the Arrange button, point to *Align*, and then click *Distribute Vertically*.
    d. Looking at the table, you decide that it should be moved down in the slide. To do this, position the mouse pointer on the table border until the pointer displays with a four-headed arrow attached. Hold down the left mouse button, drag down approximately one-half inch, and then release the mouse button.
25. Insert a clip art image in the table by completing the following steps:
    a. Click the Insert tab.
    b. Click the Clip Art button in the Illustrations group.

Step 13

Step 14

Step 16

Step 17

Step 20

Step 24b

c. Select any text that displays in the *Search for* text box in the Clip Art task pane, type **sales**, and then press Enter.
d. Scroll down the list of clip art images and then click the image shown in Figure 5.3. (If this image is not available, choose a similar clip art image related to sales.)
e. Close the Clip Art task pane.
f. With the image selected, click in the Shape Height measurement box in the Size group in the Picture Tools Format tab, type **2.8**, and then press Enter.
g. Drag the clip art image so it is positioned in the table as shown in Figure 5.3.
h. Click outside the clip art image to deselect it.
26. Save **P-C5-P1-Conference.pptx**.

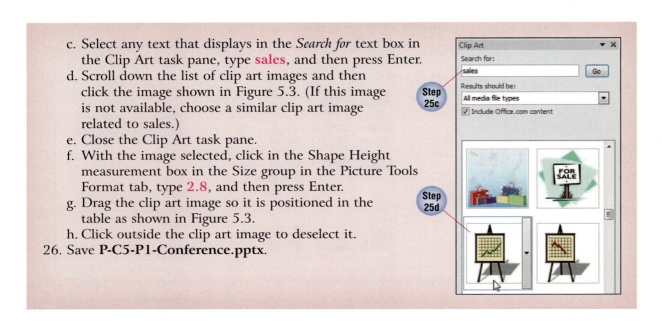

Figure 5.3 Project 1c, Slide 4

Creating SmartArt

With the SmartArt feature you can insert diagrams and organizational charts in a slide. SmartArt offers a variety of predesigned diagrams and organizational charts that are available at the Choose a SmartArt Graphic dialog box shown in Figure 5.4. Display the Choose a SmartArt Graphic dialog box by clicking the Insert SmartArt Graphic button that displays in a content placeholder or by clicking the Insert tab and then clicking the SmartArt button in the Illustrations group. At the dialog box, *All* is selected in the left panel and all available predesigned diagrams display in the middle panel.

▼ Quick Steps

Insert a SmartArt Diagram
1. Click Insert SmartArt Graphic button in content placeholder.
2. Double-click desired diagram.

OR

1. Click Insert tab.
2. Click SmartArt button.
3. Double-click desired diagram.

Chapter 5 ■ Creating Tables, Charts, and SmartArt Graphics   189

Figure 5.4 Choose a SmartArt Graphic Dialog Box

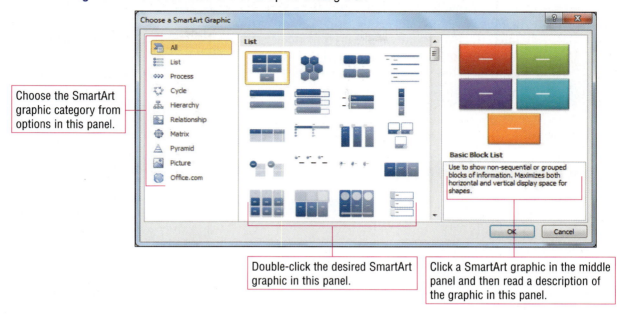

Modifying SmartArt Design

Predesigned diagrams display in the middle panel of the Choose a SmartArt Graphic dialog box. Use the scroll bar at the right side of the middle panel to scroll down the list of diagram choices. Click a diagram in the middle panel and the name of the diagram displays in the right panel along with a description of the diagram type. SmartArt includes diagrams for presenting a list of data; showing data processes, cycles, and relationships; and presenting data in a matrix or pyramid. Double-click a diagram in the middle panel of the dialog box and the diagram is inserted in the slide.

When you double-click a diagram at the dialog box, the diagram is inserted in the slide and a text pane may display at the left side of the diagram. You can type text in the text pane or directly in the diagram. Apply design formatting to a diagram with options at the SmartArt Tools Design tab shown in Figure 5.5. This tab is active when the diagram is inserted in the slide. With options and buttons in this tab you add objects, change the diagram layout, apply a style to the diagram, and reset the diagram back to the original formatting.

SmartArt

Figure 5.5 SmartArt Tools Design Tab

Project 1d Inserting and Modifying a SmartArt Diagram   Part 4 of 12

1. With **P-C5-P1-Conference.pptx** open, make sure Slide 4 is active and then insert a new slide with the *Title and Content* layout.
2. Click in the title placeholder and then type **Division Reorganization**.
3. Click the Insert SmartArt Graphic button located in the middle of the slide in the content placeholder.
4. At the Choose a SmartArt Graphic dialog box, click *Hierarchy* in the left panel of the dialog box.
5. Double-click the *Horizontal Hierarchy* option (last option in the third row).
6. If a *Type your text here* window displays at the left side of the organizational chart, close the pane by clicking the Text Pane button in the Create Graphic group.
7. Delete one of the boxes in the organizational chart by clicking the border of the top box at the right side of the slide (the top box of the three stacked boxes) and then pressing the Delete key. (Make sure that the selection border that surrounds the box is a solid line and not a dashed line. If a dashed line displays, click the box border again. This should change it to a solid line.)
8. Click *[Text]* in the first box at the left, type **Andrew Singh**, press the Enter key, and then type **Director**. Click in each of the remaining boxes and type the text as shown below.

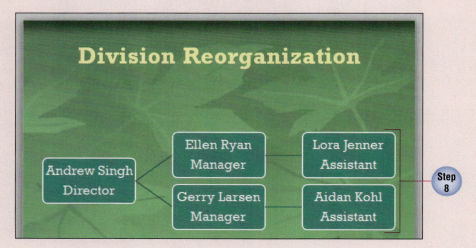

9. Click inside the SmartArt border but outside of any shape.
10. Click the More button located at the right side of the style thumbnails in the SmartArt Styles group and then click the *Polished* style (first option from the left in the top row of the *3-D* section).

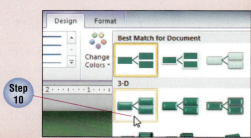

Chapter 5 ■ Creating Tables, Charts, and SmartArt Graphics   191

11. Click the Change Colors button in the SmartArt Styles group and then click *Gradient Range - Accent 2* (third option from the left in the *Accent 2* section).
12. Change the layout of the organizational chart by clicking the More button at the right side of the thumbnails in the Layouts group and then click *Table Hierarchy* at the drop-down list. Your slide should now look like the slide shown in Figure 5.6.

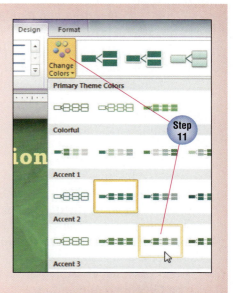

13. Save **P-C5-P1-Conference.pptx**.

Figure 5.6 Project 1d, Slide 5

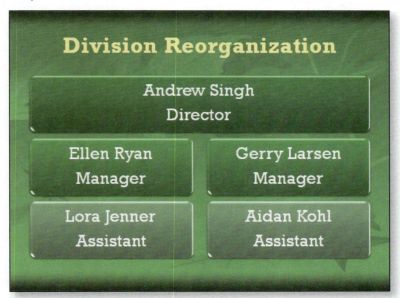

Formatting SmartArt

Nudge selected shape(s) with the up, down, left, or right arrow keys on the keyboard.

Apply formatting to a SmartArt diagram with options at the SmartArt Tools Format tab shown in Figure 5.7. With options and buttons in this tab you can change the size and shape of objects in the diagram; apply shapes styles and WordArt styles; change the shape fill, outline, and effects; and arrange and size the diagram. Move the diagram by positioning the arrow pointer on the diagram border until the pointer turns into a four-headed arrow, holding down the left mouse button, and then dragging the diagram to the desired location.

Figure 5.7 SmartArt Tools Format Tab

Project 1e Inserting and Formatting a Diagram Part 5 of 12

1. With **P-C5-P1-Conference.pptx** open, make Slide 1 active.
2. Click the Insert tab and then click the SmartArt button in the Illustrations group.
3. At the Choose a SmartArt Graphic dialog box, click *Relationship* in the left panel of the dialog box.
4. Double-click the *Basic Venn* option shown at the right.
5. Click in the top shape and type Health.
6. Click in the shape at the left and type Happiness.
7. Click in the shape at the right and type Harmony.
8. Click inside the SmartArt border but outside of any shape.
9. Click the Change Colors button in the SmartArt Styles group and then click *Colored Fill - Accent 2* (second option from the left in the *Accent 2* section).
10. Click the More button at the right side of the thumbnails in the SmartArt Styles group and then click *Polished* at the drop-down gallery (first option from the left in the top row of the *3-D* section).
11. Click the SmartArt Tools Format tab.
12. Click the More button at the right side of the WordArt Styles thumbnails and then click *Fill - Light Green, Accent 3, Powder Bevel* at the drop-down gallery (fourth option from the left in the first row in the *Applies to All Text in the Shape* section).

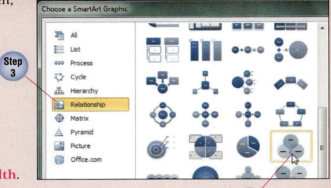

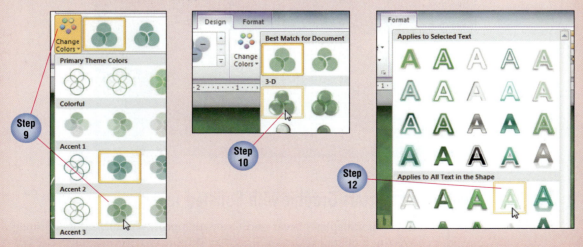

Chapter 5 ■ Creating Tables, Charts, and SmartArt Graphics   193

13. Click the Text Outline button arrow in the WordArt Styles group and then click *Light Yellow, Text 2, Darker 25%*.
14. Click in the Height measurement box in the Size group and then type 3.6.
15. Click in the Width measurement box, type 5.5, and then press Enter.
16. Click the Send Backward button arrow in the Arrange group and then click the *Send to Back* option at the drop-down list.
17. Drag the SmartArt so it is positioned as shown in Figure 5.8.
18. Drag the title and subtitle placeholders so they are positioned as shown in Figure 5.8.
19. You decide to experiment with rotating and changing the orientation of text in a shape. To do this, complete the following steps:
    a. Click the shape containing the word *Happiness*.
    b. Click the Rotate button in the Arrange group in the SmartArt Tools Format tab and then click *Rotate Left 90°* at the drop-down list.
    c. Click the shape containing the word *Harmony*.
    d. Click the Rotate button in the Arrange group and then click *Rotate Left 90°* at the drop-down list.
    e. You decide you do not like the text rotated. Return the text to normal orientation by clicking twice on the Undo button on the Quick Access toolbar.
20. Save **P-C5-P1-Conference.pptx**.

Figure 5.8 Project 1e, Slide 1

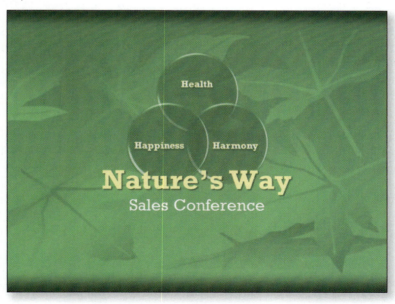

Creating a SmartArt Graphic with Bulleted Text

To improve the visual display of text and to create a professionally designed image, consider converting bulleted text to a SmartArt graphic. To do this, select the placeholder containing the text you want to convert and then click the Convert to

SmartArt Graphic button that displays in the Paragraph group in the Home tab. Click the desired SmartArt graphic at the drop-down gallery or click the *More SmartArt Graphics* option that displays at the bottom of the drop-down gallery. This displays the Choose a SmartArt Graphic dialog box where you can choose a SmartArt graphic.

Project 1f   Creating a SmartArt Graphic with Bulleted Text   Part 6 of 12

1. With **P-C5-P1-Conference.pptx** open, make Slide 6 active.
2. Click on any character in the bulleted text.
3. If necessary, click the Home tab.
4. Click the Convert to SmartArt Graphic button that displays in the Paragraph group.
5. At the drop-down gallery that displays, click the *More SmartArt Graphics* option that displays at the bottom of the gallery.
6. At the Choose a SmartArt Graphic dialog box, click *Cycle* in the left panel, and then double-click *Diverging Radial* in the middle panel.

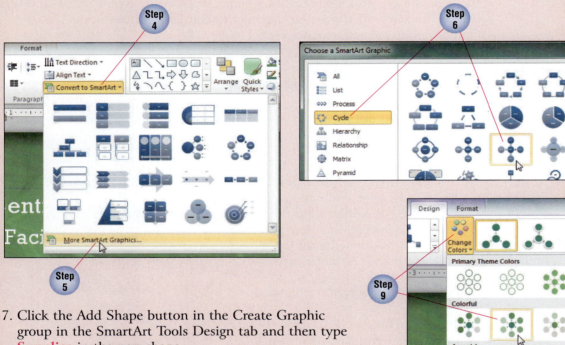

7. Click the Add Shape button in the Create Graphic group in the SmartArt Tools Design tab and then type **Supplies** in the new shape.
8. Change the order of the text in the shapes at the left and right sides of the graphic by clicking the Right to Left button in the Create Graphic group.
9. Click the Change Colors button in the SmartArt Styles group and then click *Colorful Range - Accent Colors 2 to 3* (second option from the left in the *Colorful* section).
10. Click the More button at the right of the SmartArt Styles thumbnails and then click *Inset* (second option from the left in the *3-D* section).
11. Click the SmartArt Tools Format tab.
12. Click the middle circle (contains the text *Central Division*).
13. Click three times on the Larger button in the Shapes group.

Chapter 5 ■ Creating Tables, Charts, and SmartArt Graphics

14. Click inside the SmartArt border but outside of any shape.
15. Click in the Height measurement box in the Size group and then type 6.6.
16. Click in the Width measurement box, type 8.2, and then press Enter.
17. Click the Home tab.
18. With the SmartArt graphic selected, click the Arrange button in the Drawing group, point to *Align*, and then click *Distribute Horizontally*.
19. Click the Arrange button in the Drawing group, point to *Align*, and then click *Distribute Vertically*.
20. Click the Bold button in the Font group.
21. Save **P-C5-P1-Conference.pptx**.

Inserting Text in the Text Pane

You can enter text in a SmartArt shape by clicking in the shape and then typing the text. You can also insert text in a SmartArt shape by typing text in the Text pane. Display the Text pane by clicking the Text Pane button in the Create Graphic group in the SmartArt Tools Design tab.

Project 1g Creating a SmartArt Graphic and Inserting Text in the Text Pane — Part 7 of 12

1. With **P-C5-P1-Conference.pptx** open, make sure Slide 6 is active and then insert a new slide with the *Title and Content* layout.
2. Click the title placeholder and type **Division Planning**.
3. Click the Insert SmartArt Graphic button in the content placeholder.
4. At the Choose a SmartArt Graphic dialog box, click *Process* in the left panel, and then double-click *Alternating Flow* (second option in the second row).
5. If necessary, click the Text Pane button in the Create Graphic group in the SmartArt Tools Design tab to display the *Type your text here* text pane.
6. With the insertion point positioned after the top bullet in the *Type your text here* text pane, type **Facility**.
7. Click *[Text]* that displays below *Facility* and then type **Research market**.
8. Continue clicking occurrences of *[Text]* and typing text so the text pane displays as shown at the right.
9. Close the text pane by clicking the Close button (contains an X) that displays in the upper right corner of the pane. (You can also click the Text Pane button in the Create Graphic group.)
10. Click inside the diagram border but outside any shape. (This deselects any shapes but keeps the diagram selected.)
11. If necessary, click the SmartArt Tools Design tab.

12. Click the Change Colors button in the SmartArt Styles group and then click *Dark 2 Fill*, the last option in the *Primary Theme Colors* section.
13. Click the *Intense Effect* style thumbnail that displays in the SmartArt Styles group. (If this style is not visible, click the More button at the right side of the SmartArt Styles group and then click the last option in the *Best Match for Document* section.)

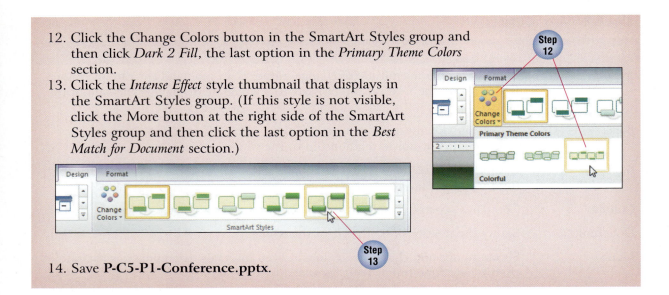

14. Save **P-C5-P1-Conference.pptx**.

Creating a Chart

You can create a variety of charts including bar and column charts, pie charts, area charts, and much more. To create a chart, click the Insert Chart button in a content placeholder or click the Insert tab and then click the Chart button in the Illustrations group. This displays the Insert Chart dialog box shown in Figure 5.9. At this dialog box, choose the desired chart type in the list at the left side, click the chart style, and then click OK. Table 5.2 describes the eleven basic chart types you can create in PowerPoint.

Chart

Figure 5.9 Insert Chart Dialog Box

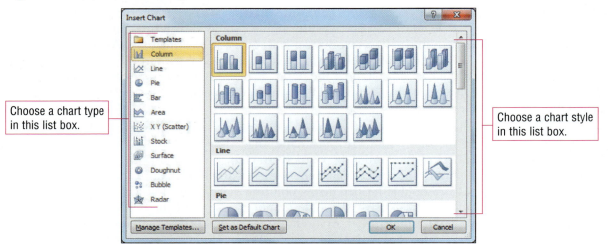

Chapter 5 ■ Creating Tables, Charts, and SmartArt Graphics   197

Table 5.2 Types of Charts

Type	Description
Area	Emphasizes the magnitude of change, rather than time and the rate of change. It also shows the relationship of parts to a whole by displaying the sum of the plotted values.
Bar	Shows individual figures at a specific time, or shows variations between components but not in relationship to the whole.
Bubble	Compares sets of three values in a manner similar to a scatter chart, with the third value displayed as the size of the bubble marker.
Column	Compares separate (noncontinuous) items as they vary over time.
Doughnut	Shows the relationship of parts of the whole.
Line	Shows trends and change over time at even intervals. It emphasizes the rate of change over time rather than the magnitude of change.
Pie	Shows proportions and relationships of parts to the whole.
Radar	Emphasizes differences and amounts of change over time and variations and trends. Each category has its own value axis radiating from the center point. Lines connect all values in the same series.
Stock	Shows four values for a stock — open, high, low, and close.
Surface	Shows trends in values across two dimensions in a continuous curve.
XY (Scatter)	Either shows the relationships among numeric values in several data series or plots the interception points between *x* and *y* values. It shows uneven intervals of data and is commonly used in scientific data.

▼ **Quick Steps**

Insert a Chart
1. Click Insert Chart button in content placeholder.
2. Click desired chart style and type.
3. Enter data in Excel spreadsheet.
4. Close Excel.

OR
1. Click Insert tab.
2. Click Chart button.
3. Click desired chart type and style.
4. Enter data in Excel spreadsheet.
5. Close Excel.

When you click OK at the Insert Chart dialog box, a sample chart is inserted in your slide and Excel opens with sample data as shown in Figure 5.10. Type the desired data in the Excel worksheet cells over the existing data. As you type data, the chart in the slide reflects the typed data. To type data in the Excel worksheet, click in the desired cell, type the data, and then press the Tab key to make the next cell active, press Shift + Tab to make the previous cell active, or press Enter to make the cell below active.

Cells used by Excel to create the chart are surrounded by a blue border and the message "To resize chart data range, drag lower right corner of range." displays below the border. If you need to change the data range, position the mouse pointer on the bottom right corner of the border until the mouse pointer displays as a double-headed arrow pointing diagonally. Hold down the left mouse button and then drag up, down, left, and/or right until the border is in the desired location. You can also click in a cell immediately outside the border and, when you insert data, the border will expand. When all data is entered in the worksheet, click the Close button that displays in the upper right corner of the screen. This closes the Excel window and displays the chart in the slide.

Figure 5.10 Sample Chart

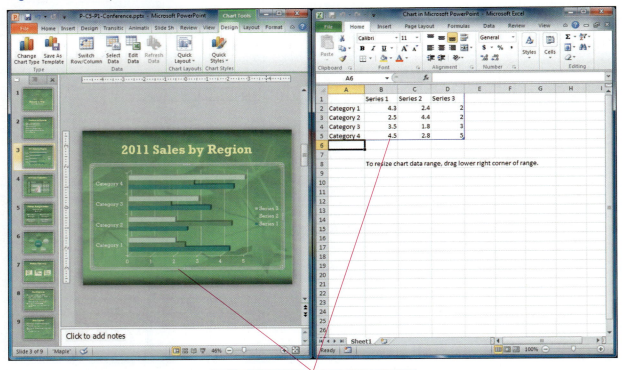

Enter data in cells in the Excel worksheet. The data entered is reflected in the PowerPoint presentation chart.

Project 1h Creating a Chart — Part 8 of 12

1. With **P-C5-P1-Conference.pptx** open, make Slide 3 active.
2. Click the Insert Chart button in the content placeholder.
3. At the Insert Chart dialog box, click *Bar* in the left panel.
4. Click the *Clustered Bar in 3-D* option that displays in the *Bar* section (fourth option from the left) in the middle panel and then click OK.
5. In the Excel worksheet, position the mouse pointer on the bottom right corner of the blue border until the mouse pointer displays as a double-headed arrow pointing diagonally. Hold down the left mouse button, drag to the left until the border displays at the right side of column C, and then release the mouse button.

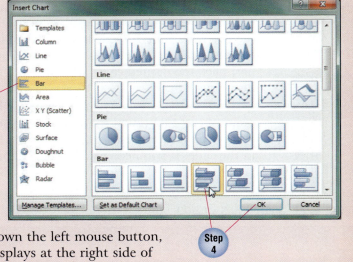

Chapter 5 ■ Creating Tables, Charts, and SmartArt Graphics

6. Position the mouse pointer on the bottom right corner of the blue border until the pointer displays as a double-headed arrow and then drag down until the border displays at the bottom of row 6.
7. Type the text in cells as shown below by completing the following steps:
   a. Click in cell B1 in the Excel worksheet, type **1st Half**, and then press the Tab key.
   b. With cell C1 active, type **2nd Half** and then press the Tab key.
   c. In cell A2, type **North** and then press the Tab key.
   d. Type **$853,000** and then press the Tab key.
   e. Type **$970,000** and then press the Tab key.
   f. Continue typing the remaining data in cells as indicated below.
8. Click the Close button that displays in the upper right corner of the Excel window.

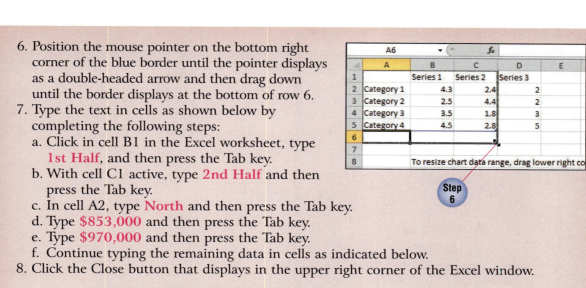

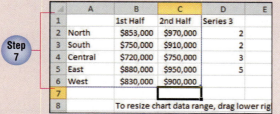

9. Save **P-C5-P1-Conference.pptx**.

Changing Chart Design

▼ **Quick Steps**

Change Chart Type and Style
1. Make the chart active.
2. Click Chart Tools Design tab.
3. Click Change Chart Type button.
4. Click desired chart type.
5. Click desired chart style.
6. Click OK.

When the chart is inserted in the slide, the Chart Tools Design tab is active as shown in Figure 5.11. Use options in this tab to change the chart type, edit chart data, change the chart layout, and apply a chart style.

After you create a chart, you can change the chart type by clicking the Change Chart Type button in the Type group in the Chart Tools Design tab. This displays the Change Chart Type dialog box. This dialog box contains the same options as the Insert Chart dialog box shown in Figure 5.9. At the Change Chart Type dialog box, click the desired chart type in the left panel and click the desired chart style in the right panel.

Use options in the Data group in the Chart Tools Design tab to change the order of the data in the chart, select specific data, edit data, and refresh the data. When you create a chart, the cells in the Excel worksheet are linked to the chart in the slide. If you need to edit data in the chart, click the Edit Data button

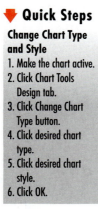

Change Chart Type   Edit Data

Figure 5.11 Chart Tools Design Tab

200   PowerPoint ■ Unit 2

and the Excel worksheet opens. Make the desired changes to cells in the Excel worksheet and then click the Close button.

The chart feature provides a number of predesigned chart layouts and styles you can apply to a chart. Click one of the chart layouts that displays in the Chart Layouts group or click the More button and then click the desired layout at the drop-down list. Apply a chart style to a chart by clicking one of the styles in the Chart Styles group or by clicking the More button and then clicking the desired style at the drop-down list.

HINT Click the Save As Template button in the Chart group in the Chart Tools Design tab to save the current chart as a template.

Project 1i — Changing the Chart Type and Editing Data — Part 9 of 12

1. With **P-C5-P1-Conference.pptx** open, make sure Slide 3 is active.
2. Delete the title placeholder by completing the following steps:
   a. Click on any character in the title *2011 Sales by Region*.
   b. Position the mouse pointer on the placeholder border until the pointer displays with a four-headed arrow attached and then click the left mouse button. (This changes the placeholder border from a dashed line to a solid line.)
   c. Press the Delete key. (This removes the title *2011 Sales by Region* and displays the placeholder text *Click to add title*.)
   d. Position the mouse pointer on the placeholder border until the pointer displays with a four-headed arrow attached and then click the left mouse button. (This changes the placeholder border from a dashed line to a solid line.)
   e. Press the Delete key.
3. Click near the chart (but outside any chart elements) to select the chart. (A light gray border displays around the chart.)
4. Click the Chart Tools Design tab.
5. Looking at the chart, you decide that the bar chart was not the best choice for the data and decide to change to a column chart. To do this, click the Change Chart Type button in the Type group.
6. At the Change Chart Type dialog box, click the *Column* option in the left panel.
7. Click the *3-D Clustered Column* option (fourth option from the left in the top row in the *Column* section of the dialog box).
8. Click OK to close the dialog box.
9. Click the Edit Data button in the Data group.
10. Click in cell B4 (the cell containing the amount $720,000), type **650000** and then press Enter. (When you press Enter, a dollar sign is automatically inserted in front of the number and a thousand separator comma is inserted.)
11. Click in cell B6 (the cell containing the amount $830,000), type **730000**, and then press Enter.
12. Click the Close button that displays in the upper right corner of the Excel window.

13. Click the *Layout 3* thumbnail (third layout from the left) in the Chart Layouts group.
14. Click the More button that displays at the right side of the Chart Styles group and then click the *Style 18* option (second option from the left in the third row).
15. Save **P-C5-P1-Conference.pptx**.

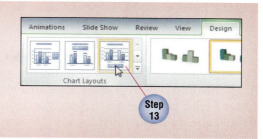

Step 13

Formatting Chart Layout

Quick Steps

Position Labels in Chart
1. Make the chart active.
2. Click Chart Tools Layout tab.
3. Click desired button.
4. Choose desired option at drop-down list.

HINT Right-click text in a chart element to display the Mini toolbar.

Click the Chart Tools Layout tab and options display for changing and customizing chart elements as shown in Figure 5.12. With options in this tab you can specify chart elements, insert objects, add labels to the chart, customize the chart background, and add analysis items to the chart.

To format or modify a specific element in a chart, select the element. Do this by clicking the element or by clicking the Chart Elements button in the Current Selection group in the Chart Tools Layout tab. With the element selected, apply the desired formatting. Click the Format Selection button in the Current Selection group and a dialog box displays with options for formatting the selected element.

Insert objects in a chart with buttons in the Insert group in the Chart Tools Layout tab. Click the Picture button and the Insert Picture dialog box displays. At this dialog box, navigate to the desired folder and then double-click the desired picture. Use the Shapes button to draw a shape in the chart and use the Draw Text Box button to insert a text box in the chart.

Use options in the Labels group in the Chart Tools Layout tab to insert and position labels. For example, click the Chart Title button and a drop-down list displays with options for removing the chart title, centering the title and overlaying on the chart, and displaying the title above the chart. You can also position a label by dragging it. To do this, select the label, position the mouse pointer over the selected label or over the label border until the pointer displays with a four-headed arrow attached, hold down the left mouse button, and then drag the label to the desired location.

With buttons in the Axes, Background, and Analysis groups, you can further customize a chart. Use buttons in the Axes group to specify if you want major and/or minor horizontal and vertical lines in the chart. With buttons in the Background group, you can format the chart wall and floor and rotate the chart. Depending on the type of chart, some of the buttons in the Background group may not be active. Use buttons in the Analysis group to add analysis elements such as trendlines and up and down bars and error bars.

Chart Elements

Format Selection

Picture

Shapes

Text Box

Chart Title

Figure 5.12 Chart Tools Layout Tab

Project 1j Modifying Chart Layout Part 10 of 12

1. With **P-C5-P1-Conference.pptx** open, make sure Slide 3 is active and the chart is selected.
2. Click the Chart Tools Layout tab.
3. Click the Text Box button in the Insert group.
4. Click in the lower left corner of the chart (outside any chart elements).
5. Change the font size to 16, turn on bold, change the font color to Green, Accent 6, Darker 50%, and then type *Nature's Way*.
6. Click the Drawing Tools Format tab.
7. Click in the Shape Height measurement box in the Size group and then type **0.4**.
8. Click in the Shape Width measurement box, type **1.7**, and then press Enter.
9. Drag the text box down to the lower left corner of the chart.

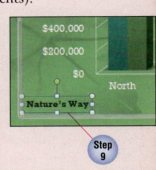
Step 9

10. Click inside the chart border but outside any chart elements and then click the Chart Tools Layout tab.
11. Click the Chart Elements button arrow in the Current Selection group and then click *Chart Title* at the drop-down list.
12. Type **2011 Regional Sales**.
13. Click the Data Table button in the Labels group and then click the *Show Data Table with Legend Keys* option at the drop-down list.
14. After looking at the data table, you decide to remove it by clicking the Data Table button in the Labels group and then clicking *None* at the drop-down list.
15. Click the Gridlines button in the Axes group, point to *Primary Vertical Gridlines*, and then click *Major & Minor Gridlines* at the side menu.

Step 11

Step 15

16. Increase the height of the chart by positioning the mouse pointer on the four dots that display in the middle of the top border until the pointer displays as a two-headed arrow pointing up and down. Hold down the left mouse button, drag up approximately one inch, and then release the mouse button.
17. Click on any character in the chart title *2011 Regional Sales*.
18. Click the Home tab, change the font size to 32, and change the font color to Light Yellow, Text 2, Darker 10%.
19. Save **P-C5-P1-Conference.pptx**.

Changing Chart Formatting

Customize the format of the chart and chart elements with options in the Chart Tools Format tab as shown in Figure 5.13. The tab contains the same Current

Figure 5.13 Chart Tools Format Tab

Chart elements can be repositioned for easier viewing.

Selection group as the Chart Tools Layout tab. With the other options in the tab you can apply a predesigned style to a shape, a predesigned WordArt style to text, and arrange and size the chart.

The Shape Styles group in the Chart Tools Format tab contains predesigned styles you can apply to shapes in the chart. Click the More button at the right side of the style in the group and a drop-down gallery displays of shape styles. Use the buttons that display at the right side of the Shape Styles group to apply fill, an outline, and an effect to a selected shape. The WordArt Styles group contains predesigned styles you can apply to text in a chart. Use the buttons that display at the right side of the WordArt Styles group to apply fill, an outline, or an effect to text in a chart.

Project 1k   Changing Chart Formatting   Part 11 of 12

1. With **P-C5-P1-Conference.pptx** open, make sure Slide 3 is the active slide and the chart is selected.
2. Click the Chart Tools Format tab.
3. Click the Chart Elements button arrow in the Current Selection group and then click *Series "2nd Half"* at the drop-down list. (This selects the green bars in the chart representing second half sales.)
4. Click the More button at the right side of the Shape Styles thumbnails and then click the *Colored Fill - Green, Dark 1* option (first option from the left in the second row).

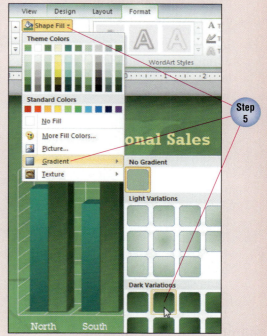

5. With the second half bars still selected, click the Shape Fill button arrow in the Shape Styles group, point to *Gradient*, and then click *Linear Down* in the *Dark Variations* section (second option from the left in the top row).

6. With the second half bars still selected, click the Shape Effects button in the Shape Styles group, point to *Bevel*, and then click the *Circle* option (first option from the left in the *Bevel* section of the side menu).
7. Click one of the teal bars that represent the first half sales amounts. (This selects all teal bars in the chart.)
8. Click the Shape Fill button arrow in the Shape Styles group and then click *Light Yellow, Text 2, Darker 10%*.
9. With the first half bars still selected, click the Shape Effects button in the Shape Styles group, point to *Bevel*, and then click the *Circle* option at the side menu.
10. Save **P-C5-P1-Conference.pptx**.

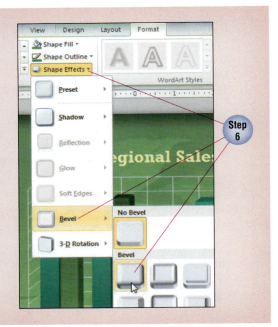

Step 6

Use buttons in the Arrange group to send the chart behind other objects, move it to the front of other objects, specify the alignment, and rotate the chart. You can size a chart by selecting the chart and then dragging a border. You can also size a chart to specific measurements with the Shape Height and Shape Width measurement boxes in the Size group in the Chart Tools Format tab. Change the height or width by clicking the up- or down-pointing arrows that display at the right side of the measurement box or click the current measurement in the measurement box and then type a specific measurement.

▼ **Quick Steps**

Change Chart Height and/or Width
1. Make the chart active.
2. Click Chart Tools Format tab.
3. Insert desired height and/or width in Shape Height and/ or Shape Width measurement boxes.

Shape Height

Shape Width

Project 1l   **Creating and Formatting a Pie Chart**   Part 12 of 12

1. With **P-C5-P1-Conference.pptx** open, make Slide 6 active and then insert a new slide with the *Title and Content* layout.
2. Click the title placeholder text and then type **Division Budget**.
3. Click the Insert tab and then click the Chart button in the Illustrations group.
4. At the Insert Chart dialog box, click *Pie* in the left panel.
5. Click the *Pie in 3-D* option (second option from the left in the *Pie* section) and then click OK.

Chapter 5 ■ Creating Tables, Charts, and SmartArt Graphics   **205**

6. In the Excel worksheet, position the mouse pointer on the bottom right corner of the border until the mouse pointer displays as a double-headed arrow pointing diagonally. Hold down the left mouse button and then drag down until the border displays at the bottom of row 7.
7. Type the text in cells as shown below.
8. When all data is entered, click the Close button that displays in the upper right corner of the Excel window.
9. With the Chart Tools Design tab selected, click the More button at the right side of the Chart Styles group and then click the *Style 26* option (second option from the left in the fourth row).
10. Click the Chart Tools Layout tab.
11. Click the Chart Title button in the Labels group and then click *None* at the drop-down list.
12. Click the Data Labels button in the Labels group and then click *Inside End* at the drop-down list.
13. Click the Chart Tools Format tab.
14. Click the piece of pie containing *10%* and then click it again. (Make sure only the one piece of pie is selected.)
15. Click the Shape Fill button arrow in the Shape Styles group and then click *Light Yellow, Text 2, Darker 75%*.
16. Click the piece of pie containing *9%*. (Make sure only the one piece of pie is selected.)
17. Click the Shape Fill button arrow in the Shape Styles group and then click *Light Green, Accent 5, Darker 50%*.
18. Click the piece of pie containing *12%*. (Make sure only the one piece of pie is selected.)
19. Click the Shape Fill button arrow in the Shape Styles group and then click *Dark Teal, Accent 1, Lighter 40%*.
20. Click the Chart Elements button in the Current Selection group and then click *Chart Area* at the drop-down list.
21. Click in the *Shape Height* measurement box in the Size group, type 6, and then press Enter.
22. Click the Align button in the Arrange group and then click *Distribute Vertically*.
23. Drag the chart down approximately one-half inch.
24. Apply a transition and sound of your choosing to all slides in the presentation.
25. Save **P-C5-P1-Conference.pptx**.
26. Run the presentation.
27. Print the presentation as a handout with six slides horizontally per page and then close **P-C5-P1-Conference.pptx**.

Project 2 Create and Format a Travel Photo Album — 3 Parts

You will use the photo album feature to create a presentation containing travel photographs. You will also apply formatting and insert elements in the presentation.

Creating a Photo Album

With PowerPoint's photo album feature, you can create a presentation containing personal or business pictures. You can customize and format the appearance of pictures by applying interesting layouts, frame shapes, and themes and you can also insert elements such as captions and text boxes. To create a photo album, click the Insert tab, click the Photo Album button arrow, and then click *New Photo Album* at the drop-down list. This displays the Photo Album dialog box as shown in Figure 5.14.

To insert pictures in the photo album, click the File/Disk button and the Insert New Pictures dialog box displays. At this dialog box, navigate to the desired folder and then double-click the picture you want inserted in the album. This inserts the picture name in the *Pictures in album* list box in the dialog box and also previews the picture in the *Preview* section. As you insert pictures in the photo album, the picture names display in the *Pictures in album* list box in the order in which they will appear in the presentation. When you have inserted the desired pictures in the photo album, click the Create button. This creates the photo album as a presentation and displays the first slide. The photo album feature creates the first slide with the title *Photo Album* and inserts the user's name.

▼ **Quick Steps**

Create Photo Album
1. Click Insert tab.
2. Click Photo Album button arrow.
3. Click *New Photo Album*.
4. Click File/Disk button.
5. Double-click desired picture.
6. Repeat steps 4 and 5 for all desired pictures.
7. Make desired changes at Photo Album dialog box.
8. Click Create button.

Photo Album

Figure 5.14 Photo Album Dialog Box

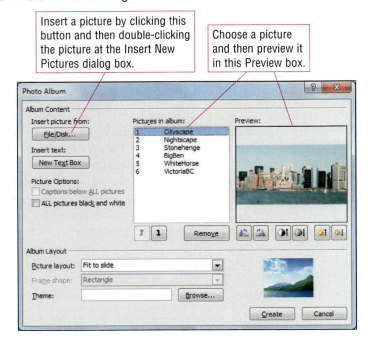

Project 2a — Creating a Travel Photo Album   Part 1 of 3

1. At a blank screen, click the Insert tab, click the Photo Album button arrow, and then click *New Photo Album* at the drop-down list.
2. At the Photo Album dialog box, click the File/Disk button.
3. At the Insert New Pictures dialog box, navigate to the PowerPoint2010C5 folder on your storage medium and then double-click *Cityscape.jpg*.
4. At the Photo Album dialog box, click the File/Disk button, and then double-click *Nightscape.jpg* at the Insert New Pictures dialog box.
5. Insert the following additional pictures: *Stonehenge.jpg*, *BigBen.jpg*, *WhiteHorse.jpg*, and *VictoriaBC.jpg*.
6. Click the Create button. (This opens a presentation with each image in a slide and the first slide containing the default text *Photo Album* followed by your name (or the user name for the computer).
7. Save the presentation and name it **P-C5-P2-Album.pptx**.
8. Run the presentation.

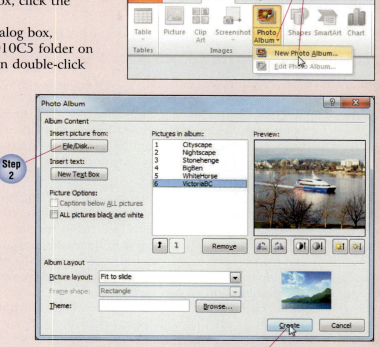

Editing and Formatting a Photo Album

Quick Steps

Edit Photo Album
1. Click Insert tab.
2. Click Photo Album button arrow.
3. Click *Edit Photo Album*.
4. Make desired changes at *Edit Photo Album* dialog box.
5. Click Update button.

If you want to make changes to a photo album presentation, open the presentation, click the Insert tab, click the Photo Album button arrow, and then click *Edit Photo Album* at the drop-down list. This displays the Edit Photo Album dialog box, which contains the same options as the Photo Album dialog box.

Rearrange the order of slides in the photo album presentation by clicking the desired slide in the *Pictures in album* list box and then clicking the button containing the up-pointing arrow to move the slide up in the order or clicking the button containing the down-pointing arrow to move the slide down in the order. Remove a slide by clicking the desired slide in the list box and then clicking the Remove button. With the buttons below the *Preview* box in the Edit Photo Album dialog box, you can rotate the picture in the slide, increase or decrease the contrast, and increase or decrease the brightness of the picture.

The *Picture layout* option in the Album Layout group has a default setting of *Fit to slide*. At this setting the picture in each slide will fill most of the slide. You

can change this setting by clicking the down-pointing arrow at the right side of the option. With options at the drop-down list, you can specify that you want one picture inserted in the slide, two pictures, or four pictures. You can also specify that you want the one, two, or four pictures inserted in slides with titles.

If you change the *Picture layout* option to something other than the default of *Fit to slide*, the *Frame shape* option becomes available. Click the down-pointing arrow at the right side of the option and a drop-down list displays with framing options. You can choose a rounded frame, simple frame, double frame, or a soft or shadow effect frame.

You can apply a theme to the photo album presentation by clicking the Browse button located at the right side of the *Theme* option box and then double-clicking the desired theme in the Choose Theme dialog box. This dialog box contains the predesigned themes provided by PowerPoint.

If you want to include a caption with the pictures, change the *Picture layout* to one, two, or four slides, and then click the *Captions below ALL pictures* check box located in the *Picture Options* section of the dialog box. PowerPoint will insert a caption below each picture that contains the name of the picture. You can edit the caption in the slide in the presentation. If you want to display all of the pictures in your photo album in black and white, click the *ALL pictures black and white* check box in the *Picture Options* section.

Click the New Text Box button in the Edit Photo Album dialog box and a new slide containing a text box is inserted in the presentation. In the presentation, you can edit the information in the text box. When all changes are made to the photo album, click the Update button located toward the bottom right side of the dialog box.

Project 2b Editing and Formatting a Photo Album   Part 2 of 3

1. With **P-C5-P2-Album.pptx** open, click the Insert tab, click the Photo Album button arrow in the Images group, and then click *Edit Photo Album* at the drop-down list.
2. At the Edit Photo Album dialog box, make the following changes:
   a. Click *VictoriaBC* in the *Pictures in album* list box and then click three times on the up-pointing arrow that displays below the list box. (This moves *VictoriaBC* so it is positioned between *Nightscape* and *Stonehenge*).
   b. Click the down-pointing arrow at the right side of the *Picture layout* option and then click *1 picture* at the drop-down list.
   c. Click the down-pointing arrow at the right side of the *Frame shape* option and then click *Center Shadow Rectangle* at the drop-down list.
   d. Click the Browse button located at the right side of the *Theme* option box. At the Choose Theme dialog box, scroll down the list box and then double-click *Trek.thmx*.

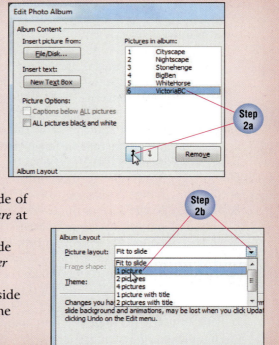

e. Click the *Captions below ALL pictures* check box to insert a check mark.
f. Click *WhiteHorse* in the *Pictures in album* list box and then click the New Text Box button that displays at the left side of the list box. (This inserts a new slide containing a text box at the end of the presentation.)
g. Click the Update button located in the lower right corner of the dialog box.

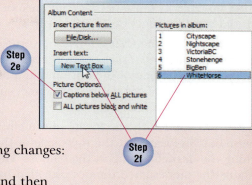

3. At the presentation, make the following formatting changes:
   a. Click the Design tab.
   b. Click the Colors button in the Themes group and then click *Metro* at the drop-down gallery.
   c. Click the Background Styles button in the Background group and then click *Style 2* at the drop-down list.
4. Make Slide 1 active and then make the following changes:
   a. Select the text *PHOTO ALBUM* and then type **travel album**. (The text will display in all caps.)
   b. Select any text that displays after the word *by* and then type your first and last names.
   c. Click the Insert tab and then click the Picture button.
   d. At the Insert Picture dialog box, navigate to the PowerPoint2010C5 folder on your storage medium and then double-click *FCTLogo.jpg*.
   e. Click the Color button in the Adjust group in the Picture Tools Format tab and then click *Set Transparent Color* at the drop-down list.
   f. Move the mouse pointer (pointer displays with a tool attached) to any white portion of the logo and then click the left mouse button. (This changes the white fill to transparent fill and allows the blue background to show through.)
   g. Change the height of the logo to *3.5"* and then position the logo attractively in the slide.

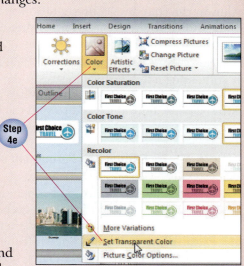

5. Make Slide 2 active and then edit the caption by completing the following steps:
   a. Click on any character in the caption *Cityscape*.
   b. Select *Cityscape* and then type **New York City Skyline**.
6. Complete steps similar to those in Step 5 to change the following captions:
   a. Slide 3: Change *Nightscape* to *New York City at Night*.
   b. Slide 4: Change *VictoriaBC* to *Victoria, British Columbia*.
   c. Slide 5: Change *Stonehenge* to *Stonehenge, Wiltshire County*.
   d. Slide 6: Change *BigBen* to *Big Ben, London*.
   e. Slide 7: Change *WhiteHorse* to *White Horse, Wiltshire County*.
7. Make Slide 8 active and then make the following changes:
   a. Select the text *Text Box* and then type **Call First Choice Travel at 555-4500 to book your next travel tour.**
   b. Select the text, change the font size to 48, change the font color to Blue, and change the alignment to Center.

8. Apply a transition and sound of your choosing to each slide.
9. Run the presentation.
10. Save **P-C5-P2-Album.pptx**.

Formatting Pictures

If you format slides in the presentation instead of the Edit Photo Album dialog box, you may lose some of those changes if you subsequently display the Edit Photo Album dialog box, make changes, and then click the Update button. Consider making your initial editing and formatting changes at the Edit Photo Album dialog box and then make final editing and formatting changes in the presentation.

Since a picture in a slide in a photo album is an object, you can format it with options at the Drawing Tools Format tab and the Picture Tools Format tab. With options at the Drawing Tools Format tab, you can insert shapes, apply a shape style to the picture and caption (if one is displayed), apply a WordArt style to caption text, and arrange and size the picture. Use options in the Picture Tools Format tab to adjust the color of the picture, apply a picture style, and arrange and size the picture.

Project 2c Formatting Pictures in a Presentation   Part 3 of 3

1. With **P-C5-P2-Album.pptx** open, make Slide 2 active.
2. Format the picture in Slide 2 by completing the following steps:
   a. Click the picture to select it.
   b. Click the Drawing Tools Format tab.
   c. Click the More button at the right side of the thumbnails in the Shape Styles group and then click *Subtle Effect - Green, Accent 1* (second option from the left in the fourth row).
3. Apply the same style to the pictures in Slides 3 through 7 by making each slide active, clicking the picture, and then pressing F4. (Pressing F4 repeats the style formatting.)
4. Make Slide 2 active and then apply a WordArt style to the caption text by completing the following steps:
   a. With Slide 2 active, click the picture to select it.
   b. Click the Drawing Tools Format tab.
   c. Click the More button at the right side of the thumbnails in the WordArt Styles group and then click *Gradient Fill - Turquoise, Accent 4, Reflection* (last option in the fourth row).
5. Apply the same WordStyle style to caption text in Slides 3 through 7 by making each slide active, clicking the picture, and then pressing F4.
6. Run the presentation.
7. Print the presentation as a handout with four slides horizontally per page.
8. Save and then close **P-C5-P2-Album.pptx**.

Chapter Summary

- Use the Tables feature to create columns and rows of information.
- Change the table design with options and buttons in the Table Tools Design tab. Change the table layout with options and buttons in the Table Tools Layout tab.
- Use the SmartArt feature to insert predesigned diagrams and organizational charts in a slide.
- Use options and buttons in the SmartArt Tools Design tab to change the diagram layout, apply a style to the diagram, and reset the diagram back to the original formatting.
- Use options and buttons in the SmartArt Tools Format tab to change the size and shapes of objects in the diagram; apply shape styles; change the shape fill, outline, and effects; and arrange and size the diagram.
- You can insert text directly into a SmartArt diagram shape or at the Text pane. Display this pane by clicking the Text Pane button in the Create Graphic group in the SmartArt Tools Design tab.
- A chart is a visual presentation of data and you can create a variety of charts as described in Table 5.2.
- To create a chart, display the Insert Chart dialog box by clicking the Insert Chart button in a content placeholder or clicking the Chart button in the Illustrations group in the Home tab.
- Enter chart data in an Excel worksheet. When entering data, press Tab to make the next cell active, press Shift + Tab to make the previous cell active, and press Enter to make the cell below active.
- Modify a chart design with options and buttons in the Chart Tools Design tab.
- Cells in the Excel worksheet used to create a chart are linked to the chart in the slide. To edit chart data, click the Edit Data button in the Chart Tools Design tab and then make changes to text in the Excel worksheet.
- The Chart Tools Layout tab contains options and buttons for inserting objects in a chart such as a picture, shape, or text box and inserting and removing labels, axes, gridlines, and backgrounds.
- Customize the format of a chart and chart elements with options and buttons in the Chart Tools Format tab. You can select the chart or a specific element, apply a style to a shape, apply a WordArt style to text, and arrange and size the chart.
- Use the Photo Album feature to create a presentation containing pictures and then edit and format the pictures.
- At the Photo Album dialog box (or the Edit Photo Album dialog box), insert pictures and then use options to customize the photo album.
- Use options in the Drawing Tools Format tab and the Picture Tools Format tab to format pictures in a photo album presentation.

Commands Review

FEATURE	RIBBON TAB, GROUP	BUTTON, FILE TAB	PLACEHOLDER BUTTON
Insert Table dialog box	Insert, Tables	, Insert Table	
Choose a SmartArt Graphic dialog box	Insert, Illustrations		
Convert bulleted text to SmartArt	Home, Paragraph		
Text pane	SmartArt Tools Design, Create Graphic		
Insert Chart dialog box	Insert, Illustrations		
Create photo album	Insert, Illustrations	, New Photo Album	
Edit photo album	Insert, Illustrations	, Edit Photo Album	

Concepts Check   Test Your Knowledge

Completion: In the space provided at the right, indicate the correct term, symbol, or command.

1. This term refers to the intersection between a row and a column.

2. Display the Insert Table dialog box by clicking this button in a content placeholder.

3. Use this keyboard shortcut to move the insertion point to the next cell.

4. This is the keyboard shortcut to select all cells in a table.

5. The Table Styles group is located in this tab.

6. Use options and buttons in this tab to delete and insert rows and columns and merge and split cells.

7. Click this button in a content placeholder to display the Choose a SmartArt Graphic dialog box.

8. When you insert a SmartArt diagram in a slide, this tab is active.

9. Create a SmartArt diagram with bulleted text by clicking in the text placeholder, clicking this button, and then clicking the desired SmartArt graphic at the drop-down gallery.

10. Click the Chart button in this group in the Insert tab to display the Insert Chart dialog box.

11. Insert a chart in a slide and this tab is active.

12. To edit data in a chart, click the Edit Data button in this group in the Chart Tools Design tab.

13. This group in the Chart Tools Format tab contains predesigned styles you can apply to shapes in a chart.

14. This group in the Chart Tools Format tab contains predesigned styles you can apply to chart text.

15. To create a photo album, click the Insert tab, click the Photo Album button arrow, and then click this at the drop-down list.

16. Click the down-pointing arrow at the right of this option in the Edit Photo Album dialog box to display a list of framing choices.

17. To insert captions below pictures in a photo album, insert a check mark in this check box in the Edit Photo Album dialog box.

Skills Check Assess Your Performance

Assessment

1 CREATE AND FORMAT TABLES AND SMARTART IN A RESTAURANT PRESENTATION

1. Open **Dockside.pptx** and then save the presentation with Save As and name it **P-C5-A1-Dockside**.
2. Make Slide 6 active and then create the table shown in the slide in Figure 5.15 with the following specifications:
   a. Create a table with three columns and six rows.
   b. Type the text in cells as shown in Figure 5.15.
   c. Apply the *Medium Style 4 - Accent 3* style to the table.
   d. Select all of the text in the table, center the text vertically, change the font size to 20 points, and change the font color to *Turquoise, Accent 2, Darker 50%*.
   e. Change the height of the table to 3.7 inches. (The width should be set at 9 inches.)
   f. Center the text in the first row.
   g. Center the text in the third column.
   h. Make sure the table is positioned as shown in Figure 5.15.

3. Make Slide 4 active and then create the table shown in the slide in Figure 5.16 with the following specifications:
   a. Create a table with four columns and three rows.
   b. Select the entire table, change the vertical alignment to center, and then change the font size to 28.
   c. Merge the cells in the first column, change the text direction to *Rotate all text 270°*, change the alignment to center, change the font size to 40, and then type **Lunch**.
   d. Merge the cells in the third column, change the text direction to *Rotate all text 270°*, change the alignment to center, change the font size to 40, and then type **Dinner**.
   e. Type the remaining text in cells as shown in Figure 5.16.
   f. Change the height of the table to 3 inches.
   g. Change the width of the first and third columns to 1.2 inches.
   h. Change the width of the second and fourth columns to 2.5 inches.
   i. Insert a check mark in the *Banded Columns* check box in the Table Style Options group in the Table Tools Design tab and remove the check marks from the other check boxes in the group.
   j. Apply the *Medium Style 4 - Accent 3* style to the table.
   k. Select all of the text in the table and then change the font color to *Turquoise, Accent 2, Darker 50%*.
   l. Change the height of all of the rows to 1 inch.
   m. Position the table on the slide as shown in Figure 5.16.
4. Make Slide 5 active and then create the SmartArt organizational chart shown in the slide in Figure 5.17 with the following specifications:
   a. Choose the *Half Circle Organization Chart* diagram at the Choose a SmartArt Graphic dialog box.
   b. Delete the second box so your chart appears with the same number of boxes and in the same order as the organizational chart in Figure 5.17.
   c. Type the text in the boxes as shown in Figure 5.17.
   d. Change the color to *Colorful Range - Accent Colors 3 to 4*.
   e. Apply the *Cartoon* SmartArt style.
   f. Apply the *Gradient Fill - Blue, Accent 1* WordArt style to text.
   g. Change the height of the organizational chart to 5 inches and change the width to 8.5 inches.
   h. Position the organizational chart in the slide as shown in Figure 5.17.
5. Make Slide 1 active and then format the title and create the SmartArt diagram shown in the slide in Figure 5.18 with the following specifications:
   a. Select the title *The Dockside Café* and then change the font to Lucida Calligraphy.
   b. Create the SmartArt diagram with the *Linear Venn* option located in the *Relationship* group. Type the text in the shapes as shown in Figure 5.18.
   c. Change the colors to *Colorful - Accent Colors*.
   d. Apply the *Intense Effect* SmartArt style.
   e. Apply the *Fill - White, Drop Shadow* WordArt style to text.
   f. Change the height of the diagram to 4.2 inches and the width to 6.8 inches.
   g. Position the SmartArt diagram on the slide as shown in Figure 5.18.
6. Make Slide 2 active, select the bulleted text placeholder, and then convert the bulleted text to a *Basic Matrix* diagram as shown in the slide in Figure 5.19 with the following specifications:
   a. Change the colors to *Colorful - Accent Colors*.
   b. Apply the *Cartoon* SmartArt style.
   c. Apply the *Fill - White, Drop Shadow* WordArt style to text.
   d. Change the height of the diagram to 4.8 inches and the width to 5.5 inches.
   e. Position the SmartArt diagram on the slide as shown in Figure 5.19.

7. Make Slide 3 active and then insert a clip art image related to "menu." Size and position the image attractively on the slide.
8. Apply a transition and sound of your choosing to all slides in the presentation.
9. Run the presentation.
10. Print the presentation as a handout with six slides horizontally per page.
11. Save and then close **P-C5-A1-Dockside.pptx**.

Figure 5.15 Assessment 1, Slide 6

Figure 5.16 Assessment 1, Slide 4

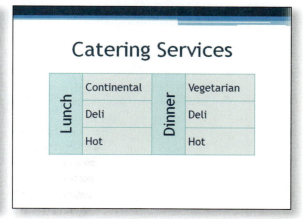

Figure 5.17 Assessment 1, Slide 5

Figure 5.18 Assessment 1, Slide 1

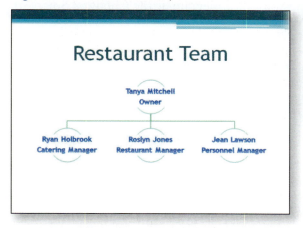
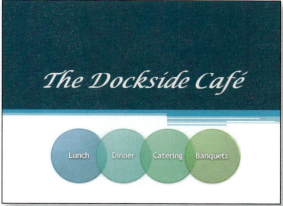

Figure 5.19 Assessment 1, Slide 2

Assessment

2 CREATE AND FORMAT CHARTS IN A MARKETING PRESENTATION

1. Open **MarketingPres.pptx** and save the presentation with Save As and name it **P-C5-A2-MarketingPres**.
2. Make Slide 2 active, insert a new slide with the *Title and Content* layout, and then create the chart shown in the slide in Figure 5.20 with the following specifications:
   a. Type the slide title as shown in Figure 5.20.
   b. Use the pie chart option *Pie in 3-D* to create the chart.
   c. Type the following information in the Excel worksheet:

	Amount
Salaries	47%
Equipment	18%
Supplies	4%
Production	21%
Distribution	10%

   d. Change the chart layout to *Layout 3*.
   e. Insert data labels on the outside end.
   f. Change the shape fill of the piece of pie containing *10%* to *White, Accent 3, Darker 35%*.
3. Print Slide 3.
4. After looking at the slide, you realize that two of the percentages are incorrect. Edit the Excel data and change *47%* to *42%* and change *10%* to *15%*.
5. With Slide 3 active, insert a new slide with the *Title and Content* layout and then create the chart shown in the slide in Figure 5.21 with the following specifications:
   a. Type the slide title as shown in Figure 5.21.
   b. Use the line chart option *Line with Markers* to create the chart.
   c. Type the following information in the Excel worksheet:

	Revenues	Expenses
1st Qtr	$789,560	$670,500
2nd Qtr	$990,450	$765,000
3rd Qtr	$750,340	$780,000
4th Qtr	$980,400	$875,200

   d. Apply the *Style 42* chart style.

Figure 5.20 Assessment 2, Slide 3

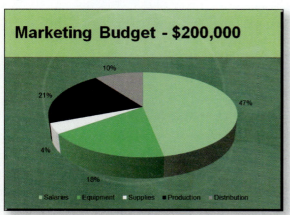

Figure 5.21 Assessment 2, Slide 4

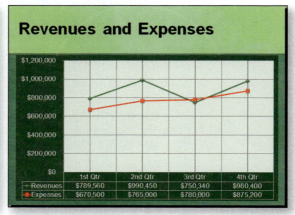

Chapter 5 ■ Creating Tables, Charts, and SmartArt Graphics

e. Click the Data Table button in the Chart Tools Layout tab and then click the *Show Data Table with Legend Keys* option.
  f. Click the Legend button and then click *None* at the drop-down list.
  g. Insert major and minor vertical gridlines.
  h. Select the plot area and then change the shape fill color to *Light Green, Accent 1, Lighter 80%*. (The Shape Fill button is located in the Chart Tools Format tab.)
  i. Select the chart area and then change the shape fill color to *Green, Accent 2, Darker 50%*.
  j. Select the expenses line (*Series "Expenses"*) and then change the shape fill to Red and the shape outline to Red.
  k. Select the revenues line (*Series "Revenues"*) and then change the shape fill and the shape outline to *Light Green, Accent 1, Darker 50%*.
6. Apply a transition and sound of your choosing to each slide in the presentation.
7. Run the presentation.
8. Print the presentation as a handout with three slides per page.
9. Save and then close **P-C5-A2-MarketingPres.pptx**.

Assessment

3 CREATE A SCENERY PHOTO ALBUM

1. At a blank screen, create a new photo album.
2. At the Photo Album dialog box, insert the following images:
   AlderSprings.jpg
   CrookedRiver.jpg
   Mountain.jpg
   Ocean.jpg
   Olympics.jpg
   River.jpg
3. Change the *Picture layout* option to *1 picture with title*.
4. Change the *Frame shape* option to *Simple Frame, White*.
5. Apply the *Paper* theme.
6. Click the Create button.
7. At the presentation, change the theme colors to *Solstice* and the background style to *Style 8*. **Hint: Do this with buttons in the Design tab.**
8. Insert the following titles in the specified slides:
   Slide 2 = Alder Springs, Oregon
   Slide 3 = Crooked River, Oregon
   Slide 4 = Mt. Rainier, Washington
   Slide 5 = Pacific Ocean, Washington
   Slide 6 = Olympic Mountains, Washington
   Slide 7 = Salmon River, Idaho
9. Make Slide 1 active, select any name that follows *by*, and then type your first and last names.
10. Save the presentation and name it **P-C5-A3-PhotoAlbum**.
11. Print the presentation as a handout with four slides horizontally per page.
12. Close **P-C5-A3-PhotoAlbum.pptx**.

Assessment

4 CREATE A SALES AREA CHART

1. Open **P-C5-A2-MarketingPres.pptx** and then save the presentation with Save As and name it **P-C5-A4-MarketingPres**.
2. Make Slide 4 active and then insert a new slide with the *Title and Content* layout.
3. Use Excel's Help feature to learn more about chart types and then create an area chart (use the *Area* chart type) with the data shown below. Apply design, layout, and/or formatting to improve the visual appeal of the chart. Type **Sales by Region** as the slide title.

	Region 1	Region 2	Region 3
Sales 2009	$650,300	$478,100	$225,500
Sales 2010	$623,100	$533,600	$210,000
Sales 2011	$725,600	$478,400	$296,500

4. Print Slide 5.
5. Save and then close **P-C5-A4-MarketingPres.pptx**.

Visual Benchmark Demonstrate Your Proficiency

CREATE AND FORMAT A MEDICAL CENTER PRESENTATION

1. Open **RMCPres.pptx** and then save the presentation with Save As and name it **P-C5-VB-RMCPres**.
2. Create the presentation shown in Figure 5.22 with the following specifications:
   a. Apply the *Aspect* design theme and change the theme colors to *Hardcover*.
   b. In Slide 2, create the SmartArt with the *Hierarchy* relationship diagram and apply the *Colorful Range - Accent Colors 2 to 3* colors to the diagram.
   c. In Slide 3, create the SmartArt with the *Basic Venn* relationship diagram and apply the *Colorful Range - Accent Colors 2 to 3* colors to the diagram.
   d. Use the Bevel shape to create the shape in Slide 4.
   e. Insert the table as shown in Slide 5.
   f. Use the information shown in the legend and the data information shown above the bars to create a 3-D bar chart as shown in Slide 6.
   g. Use the information shown in the legend and the data information at the outside end of each pie to create a 3-D pie chart as shown in Slide 7.
3. Apply a transition and sound of your choosing to all slides in the presentation.
4. Print the presentation as a handout with four slides horizontally per page.
5. Save and then close **P-C5-VB-RMCPres.pptx**.

Figure 5.22 Visual Benchmark

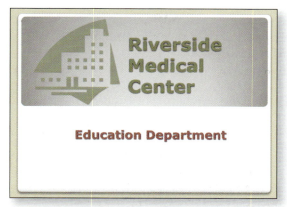

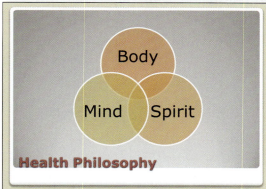
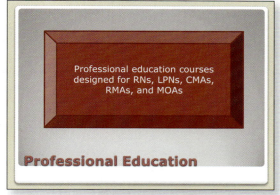
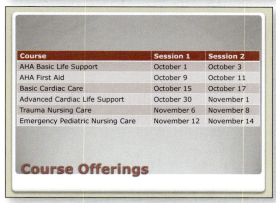

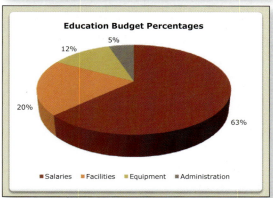

Case Study — Apply Your Skills

Part 1

You are an administrator for Terra Energy Corporation and you are responsible for preparing a presentation for a quarterly meeting. Open the Word document named **TerraEnergy.docx** and then use the information to prepare a presentation with the following specifications:

- Create the first slide with the company name and the subtitle of *Quarterly Meeting*.
- Create a slide that presents the Executive Team information in a table.
- Create a slide that presents the phases information in a table (the three columns of text in the *Research and Development* section). Insert a column at the left side of the table that includes the text *New Product* rotated.
- Create a slide that presents the development team information in a SmartArt organizational chart.
- Create a slide that presents the revenues information in a chart (you determine the type of chart).
- Create a slide that presents the United States sales information in a chart (you determine the type of chart).

Apply a design theme of your choosing and add any additional features to improve the visual appeal of the presentation. Insert a transition and sound to each slide and then run the presentation. Save the presentation and name it **P-C5-CS-TECPres.pptx**. Print the presentation as a handout with four slides horizontally per page.

Part 2

Last year, a production project was completed and you want to display a graphic that illustrates the primary focus of the project. Create a new slide in the **P-C5-CS-TECPres.pptx** presentation and insert a *Funnel* SmartArt graphic (in the *Relationship* group) with the following information in the shapes inside the funnel (turn on the Text pane to type the information in the shapes):

Updated Systems
Safety Programs
Market Expansion

Insert the information *Higher Profits* below the funnel. Apply formatting to the SmartArt graphic to improve the visual appeal. Print the slide and then save **P-C5-CS-TECPres.pptx**.

Part 3

The **P-C5-CS-TECPres.pptx** presentation should include information on the corporation's stock. Use the Help feature to learn about stock charts and then insert a new slide in the presentation and create a high-low-close stock chart in the slide with the following information:

Date	High	Low	Close
01/01/2012	23	20.25	21.875
02/01/2012	28.625	25.25	26.375
03/01/2012	32.375	28	30.125
04/01/2012	27.125	24.5	26.375
05/01/2012	25.125	22.875	24.25

Apply formatting to the chart to improve the readability and appeal of the chart. Print the slide and then save **P-C5-CS-TECPres.pptx**.

Part 4

You have created an Excel chart containing information on department costs. You decide to improve the visual appeal of the chart and then create a link from the presentation to the chart. Open Excel and then open **DepartmentCosts.xlsx**. Apply additional formatting to the pie chart to make it easy to read and understand the data. Save and then close the workbook and exit Excel. Create a new slide in the **P-C5-CS-TECPres.pptx** presentation that includes a hyperlink to the **DepartmentCosts.xlsx** workbook. Run the presentation and when the slide displays containing the hyperlinked text, click the hyperlink, view the chart in Excel, and then exit Excel. Print the presentation as a handout with four slides horizontally per page. Save and then close **P-C5-CS-TECPres.pptx**.

Microsoft PowerPoint

Using Slide Masters and Action Buttons

CHAPTER 6

PERFORMANCE OBJECTIVES

Upon successful completion of Chapter 6, you will be able to:
- Format slides in Slide Master view
- Apply themes and backgrounds in Slide Master view
- Delete placeholders and slide master layouts
- Insert elements in Slide Master view
- Create and rename a custom slide layout
- Insert a new slide master
- Save a presentation as a template
- Customize a handout in Handout Master view
- Customize notes pages in Notes Master view
- Insert action buttons
- Create hyperlinks

If you make design or formatting changes and you want the changes to affect all slides in the presentation, consider making the changes in a slide master in the Slide Master view. Along with the Slide Master view, you can make changes to all pages in a handout with options in the Handout Master view and all notes pages in the Notes Master view. You can insert action buttons in a presentation to connect to slides within the same presentation, connect to another presentation, connect to a website, or connect to another program. You can also connect to a website by inserting a hyperlink to the site. Model answers for this chapter's projects appear on the following pages.

Note: Before beginning the projects, copy to your storage medium the PowerPoint2010C6 folder from the PowerPoint2010 folder on the CD that accompanies this textbook and then make PowerPoint2010C6 the active folder.

Model Answers

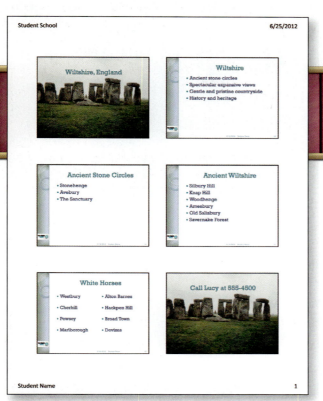

Project 1 Create a Travel Presentation and Apply Formatting in Slide Master View   P-C6-P1-England.pptx

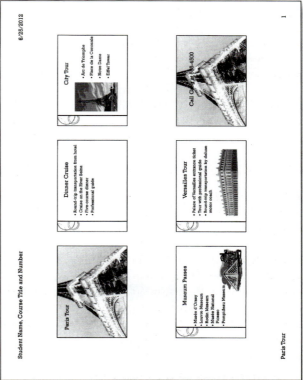

Project 2 Save a Template and Create a Travel Presentation with the Template   P-C6-P2-ParisTour.pptx

Project 3 Insert Action Buttons and Hyperlinks in a Job Search Presentation

P-C6-P3-JobSearch.pptx

Project 1 — Create a Travel Presentation and Apply Formatting in Slide Master View   6 Parts

You will apply formatting to a blank presentation in Slide Master view, insert slides in the presentation, insert elements in Slide Master view, insert a custom slide layout, and insert a new slide master.

Customizing Slide Masters

When creating a presentation, you can apply a design theme to the presentation to provide colors and formatting. If you make changes to a slide and want the changes to affect all slides in the presentation, make the change in a slide master. You can customize a slide master by changing the theme, theme colors, and/or theme fonts; changing the location of and inserting placeholders; applying a background style; and changing the page setup and slide orientation. If you know you want to customize slides, consider making the changes in Slide Master view before you create each slide. If you apply a slide master to an existing presentation, some items on slides may not conform to the new formatting.

To display the Slide Master view, click the View tab and then click the Slide Master button in the Master Views group. This displays the Slide Master tab, a blank slide master in the Slide pane, and inserts slide master thumbnails in the slide thumbnail pane. The largest thumbnail in the pane is the slide master and the other thumbnails represent associated layouts. Position the mouse pointer on a

▼ Quick Steps
Display Slide Master View
1. Click View tab.
2. Click Slide Master button.

HINT
Create a consistent look to your slides by customizing slides in Slide Master view.

Slide Master

Chapter 6 ■ Using Slide Masters and Action Buttons

Figure 6.1 Slide Master View

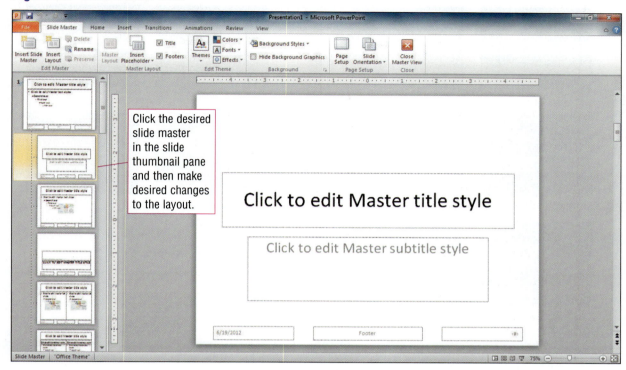

Close Master View

slide thumbnail and the name of the thumbnail displays in a box by the thumbnail. Figure 6.1 displays a blank presentation in Slide Master view. To specify the slide master or layout you want to customize, click the desired thumbnail in the slide thumbnail pane. With the slide master layout displayed in the Slide pane, make the desired changes and then click the Close Master View button.

Applying Themes to Slide Masters

Themes

You can apply themes, theme colors, theme fonts, and theme effects with buttons in the Edit Theme group in the Slide Master tab. Click the Themes button and a drop-down gallery displays with available predesigned themes and also any custom themes you have created. Click the desired theme and the theme formatting is applied to the slide master. Complete similar steps to apply theme colors, theme fonts, and theme effects.

Project 1a   **Formatting a Slide Master**   Part 1 of 6

1. Display a blank presentation.
2. Click the View tab and then click the Slide Master button in the Master Views group.

226   PowerPoint ■ Unit 2

3. Click the top (and largest) slide master thumbnail in the slide thumbnail pane (*Office Theme Slide Master*). (This displays the slide master layout in the Slide pane.)
4. Click the Themes button in the Edit Theme group in the Slide Master tab.
5. Click *Solstice* at the drop-down gallery.
6. Click the Colors button in the Edit Theme group and then click *Metro* at the drop-down gallery.
7. Click the Fonts button in the Edit Theme group and then click the *Foundry* option at the drop-down gallery.
8. Change the font color and alignment for the title style by completing the following steps:
   a. Select the text *Click to edit Master title style* that displays in the slide master in the Slide pane.
   b. Click the Home tab.
   c. Click the Font Color button arrow in the Font group and then click the *Turquoise, Accent 4, Darker 25%* option.
   d. Click the Center button in the Paragraph group.

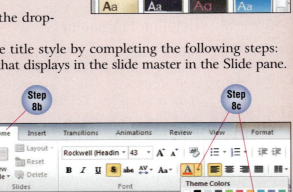

9. Change the font color of the bulleted text in the slide master by completing the following steps:
   a. Select all of the bulleted text in the slide master.
   b. Make sure the Home tab is selected.
   c. Click the Font Color button arrow in the Font group and then click the *Periwinkle, Accent 5, Darker 50%* option.
10. Change the color of the first bullet by completing the following steps:
    a. Select the text following the first bullet.
    b. Click the Bullets button arrow in the Paragraph group in the Home tab and then click *Bullets and Numbering* at the drop-down gallery.
    c. At the Bullets and Numbering dialog box with the Bulleted tab selected, click the Color button and then click the *Turquoise, Accent 4, Darker 25%* color option.
    d. Click OK to close the dialog box.
11. Select the text following the second bullet and then complete steps 10b through 10d to change the bullet color to *Turquoise, Accent 4, Darker 25%*.
12. Click the Slide Master tab.
13. Click the Close Master View button.
14. Save the presentation and name it **P-C6-P1-TravelMaster.pptx**.

Chapter 6 ■ Using Slide Masters and Action Buttons   227

 **Applying and Formatting Backgrounds**

Background styles are derived from the theme colors and background intensities in the theme. If you change the theme, background styles are updated.

Like the Background group in the Design tab, the Background group in the Slide Master tab contains the Background Styles button and the *Hide Background Graphics* check box. If you want to change the background graphic for all slides, make the change at the slide master. To do this, display the presentation in Slide Master view and then click the desired slide master layout in the slide thumbnail pane. Click the Background Styles button and then click a background at the drop-down gallery. Or, click the *Format Background* option and choose the desired options at the Format Background dialog box. If you want to remove the background graphic for slides, click the *Hide Background Graphics* check box to insert a check mark.

▼ **Quick Steps**

Delete Slide Master Layouts
1. Display presentation in Slide Master view.
2. Click desired slide layout thumbnail.
3. Click Delete button.

Deleting Placeholders

If you want to remove a placeholder for all slides in a presentation, consider deleting the placeholder in the Slide Master view. To do this, display the presentation in Slide Master view, click the desired slide master layout in the slide thumbnail pane, click the placeholder border (make sure the border displays as a solid line), and then press the Delete key. You can also remove a title placeholder from a slide master by clicking the *Title* check box in the Master Layout group to remove the check mark. Remove footer placeholders by clicking the *Footer* check box to remove the check mark.

 You can also delete a slide layout by right-clicking the layout in the slide thumbnail pane and then clicking *Delete Layout* at the shortcut menu.

Deleting Slide Master Layouts

In Slide Master view, a slide master displays for each available layout. If you know that you will not be using a particular layout in the presentation, you can delete the layout slide master. To do this, display the presentation in Slide Master view, click the desired slide layout thumbnail in the slide thumbnail pane, and then click the Delete button in the Edit Master group.

Delete

Project 1b — Applying and Formatting Background Graphics — Part 2 of 6

1. With **P-C6-P1-TravelMaster.pptx** open, click the View tab and then click the Slide Master button in the Master Views group.
2. Click the top slide layout thumbnail (*Solstice Slide Master*) in the slide thumbnail pane.
3. Format the background by completing the following steps:
   a. Click the Background Styles button in the Background group in the Slide Master tab and then click *Format Background* at the drop-down gallery.
   b. At the Format Background dialog box, click the *Gradient fill* option.
   c. Click the Preset colors button and then click the *Fog* option at the drop-down list (last option in the second row).

d. Click the down-pointing arrow at the right side of the *Type* option and then click *Path* at the drop-down list.
   e. Click the Close button.
4. Apply a picture to the background of the title slide layout (the picture will appear only on this layout) by completing the following steps:
   a. Click the second slide layout thumbnail (*Title Slide Layout*) in the slide thumbnail pane.
   b. Click the *Hide Background Graphics* check box in the Background group in the Slide Master tab to insert a check mark.
   c. Click the Background Styles button in the Background group and then click *Format Background* at the drop-down list.
   d. At the Format Background dialog box, click the *Picture or texture fill* option.
   e. Click the File button (located in the Insert from group).
   f. At the Insert Picture dialog box, navigate to the PowerPoint2010C6 folder on your storage medium and then double-click **Stonehenge.jpg**.
   g. Click the Close button to close the Format Background dialog box.
   h. Remove the two small green circles that appear in the slide master in the Slide pane by clicking each circle and then pressing the Delete key.
   i. Click on any character in the text *Click to edit Master title style* and then press Ctrl + E. (This is the keyboard shortcut for centering.)
   j. Drag the placeholder so it is positioned above the stones and centered horizontally. (Make sure the bottom border of the placeholder is positioned above the stones.)
   k. Delete the Master subtitle style placeholder by clicking the placeholder border (make sure the border displays as a solid line) and then pressing the Delete key.
   l. Remove the footer placeholders from the layout by clicking the *Footers* check box in the Master Layout group to remove the check mark.
5. Delete slide layouts that you will not be using in the presentation by completing the following steps:
   a. Click the fourth slide layout thumbnail (*Section Header Layout*) in the slide thumbnail pane.
   b. Scroll down the pane until the last slide layout thumbnail is visible.
   c. Hold down the Shift key and then click the last slide layout thumbnail.
   d. Click the Delete button in the Edit Master group. (The slide thumbnail pane should contain the slide master and two associated layouts.)
6. Click the Close Master View button.
7. Delete the slide that currently displays in the Slide pane. (This displays a gray background with the text *Click to add first slide*. The presentation does not contain any slides, just formatting.)
8. Save **P-C6-P1-TravelMaster.pptx**.

Inserting Slides in a Customized Presentation

If you customize slides in a presentation in Slide Master view, you can use the presentation formatting in other presentations. You can save the formatted presentation as a template or you can save the presentation in the normal manner and then open the presentation, save it with a new name, and then type text in slides. You can also insert slides into the current presentation using the Reuse

Slides task pane. (You learned about this task pane in Chapter 2.) To use this task pane, click the Home tab, click the New Slide button arrow, and then click *Reuse Slides* at the drop-down list. This displays the Reuse Slides task pane at the right side of the screen. Click the Browse button and then click the *Browse File* option at the drop-down list. At the Browse dialog box, navigate to the desired folder and then double-click the desired presentation. Insert slides into the current presentation by clicking the desired slide in the task pane.

Project 1c Inserting Slides in a Presentation   Part 3 of 6

1. With **P-C6-P1-TravelMaster.pptx** open, save the presentation with Save As and name it **P-C6-P1-England**.
2. Make sure the Home tab is active, click the New Slide button arrow, and then click *Title Slide* at the drop-down list.

3. Click the *Click to add title* text in the current slide and then type **Wiltshire, England**.
4. Insert slides into the current presentation from an existing presentation by completing the following steps:
   a. Click the New Slide button arrow and then click *Reuse Slides* at the drop-down list.
   b. Click the Browse button in the Reuse Slides task pane and then click *Browse File* at the drop-down list.
   c. At the Browse dialog box, navigate to the PowerPoint2010C6 folder on your storage medium and then double-click *TravelEngland.pptx*.

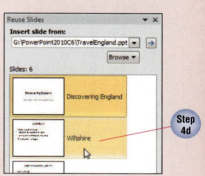

   d. Click the *Wiltshire* slide in the Reuse Slides task pane. (This inserts the slide in the presentation and applies the custom formatting to the slide.)
   e. Click the *Ancient Stone Circles* slide in the Reuse Slides task pane.
   f. Click the *Ancient Wiltshire* slide in the Reuse Slides task pane.
   g. Click the *White Horses* slide in the Reuse Slides task pane.
   h. Click the Close button located in the upper right corner of the Reuse Slides task pane to close the task pane.
5. With Slide 5 active, format the bulleted text into two columns by completing the following steps:
   a. Click in any character in the bulleted text.
   b. Move the insertion point so it is positioned immediately following *Marlborough*.
   c. Press the Enter key (to insert a blank line) and then click the Bullets button in the Paragraph group in the Home tab to remove the bullet.
   d. Press Ctrl + A to select all of the bulleted text.
   e. Click the Line Spacing button in the Paragraph group and then click *2.0* at the drop-down list.
   f. Click the Columns button in the Paragraph group and then click *Two Columns* at the drop-down list.
6. With Slide 5 active, insert a new slide by completing the following steps:
   a. Click the New Slide button arrow and then click the *Title Slide* layout at the drop-down list.
   b. Click in the text *Click to add title* and then type **Call Lucy at 555-4500**.
7. Save **P-C6-P1-England.pptx**.

Inserting Elements in a Slide Master

As you learned in Chapter 4, you can insert a header, footer, or the date and time that print on every slide in the presentation. You can also insert these elements in a slide master. For example, to insert a header or footer in slides, display the presentation in Slide Master view, click the Insert tab, and then click the Header & Footer button in the Text group. At the Header and Footer dialog box with the Slide tab selected, make the desired changes, click the Notes and Handouts tab, make the desired changes, and then click the Apply to All button. You can also insert additional elements in the Slide Master view such as a picture, clip art image, shape, SmartArt graphic, or chart. Insert any of these elements in the normal manner in a slide in Slide Master view.

Project 1d Inserting Elements in Slide Master View   Part 4 of 6

1. With **P-C6-P1-England.pptx** open, insert a header, a footer, and the date and time by completing the following steps:
   a. Click the View tab.
   b. Click the Slide Master button in the Master Views group.
   c. Click the slide master thumbnail (the top slide thumbnail in the slide thumbnail pane).
   d. Click the Insert tab.
   e. Click the Header & Footer button in the Text group.
   f. At the Header and Footer dialog box with the Slide tab selected, click the *Date and time* check box to insert a check mark.
   g. Make sure the *Update automatically* option is selected. (With this option selected, the date and/or time will automatically update each time you open the presentation.)
   h. Click the *Slide number* check box to insert a check mark.
   i. Click the *Footer* check box to insert a check mark and then type your first and last names in the *Footer* text box.
   j. Click the Notes and Handouts tab.
   k. Click the *Date and time* check box to insert a check mark.
   l. Make sure the *Update automatically* option is selected.
   m. Click the *Header* check box and then type the name of your school in the *Header* text box.
   n. Click the *Footer* check box and then type your first and last names in the *Footer* text box.
   o. Click the Apply to All button.

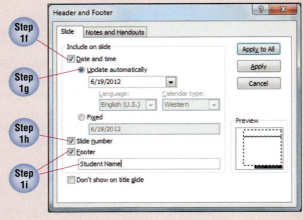

Chapter 6 ■ Using Slide Masters and Action Buttons

2. Insert the First Choice Travel logo in the lower left corner of the slide master by completing the following steps:
    a. Click the Picture button in the Images group.
    b. At the Insert Picture dialog box, navigate to the PowerPoint2010C6 folder on your storage medium and then double-click *FCTLogo.jpg*.
    c. Click in the *Shape Height* measurement box in the Size group in the Picture Tools Format tab, type **0.55**, and then press Enter.
    d. Drag the logo so it is positioned in the lower left corner of the slide as shown at the right.
    e. Click the Send Backward button in the Arrange group.
    f. Click outside the logo to deselect it.
3. With the Slide Master tab selected, click the Close Master View button.
4. Run the presentation and notice the logo and other elements in the slides.
5. Save **P-C6-P1-England.pptx**.

Creating and Renaming a Custom Slide Layout

Insert Layout

Rename

You can create your own custom slide layout in Slide Master view and then customize the layout by inserting or deleting elements and applying formatting to placeholders and text. To create a new slide layout, click the Insert Layout button in the Edit Master group in the Slide Master tab. This inserts in the Slide pane a new slide containing a Master title style placeholder and footer placeholders. Customize the layout by inserting or deleting placeholders and applying formatting to placeholders.

PowerPoint will automatically assign the name *Custom Layout* to a slide layout you create. If you create another slide layout, PowerPoint will name it *1_Custom Layout*, and so on. Consider renaming your custom layout to a name that describes the layout. To rename a layout, make sure the desired slide layout is active, and then click the Rename button in the Edit Master group. At the Rename Layout dialog box, type the desired name, and then click the Rename button.

Inserting Placeholders

Insert Placeholder

Master Layout

You can insert placeholders in a predesigned slide layout or you can insert a custom slide layout and then insert placeholders. Insert a placeholder by clicking the Insert Placeholder button arrow in the Master Layout group and then clicking the desired placeholder option at the drop-down list. If you click the slide master, the Insert Placeholder button is dimmed. If you delete a placeholder from the slide master, you can reinsert the placeholder with options at the Master Layout dialog box. Display this dialog box by clicking the Master Layout button and any placeholder that has been removed from the slide master displays in the dialog box as an active option with an empty check box. Reinsert the placeholder by inserting a check mark in the desired placeholder check box and then clicking OK to close the dialog box.

Creating Custom Prompts

Some placeholders in a custom layout may contain generic text such as *Click to add Master title style* or *Click to edit Master text styles*. In Slide Master view, you can select this generic text and replace it with custom text. You might want to insert text that describes what you want entered into the placeholder.

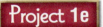 **Inserting a Layout and Placeholder** Part 5 of 6

1. With **P-C6-P1-England.pptx** open, click the View tab and then click the Slide Master button in the Master Views group.
2. Click the bottom slide layout thumbnail in the slide thumbnail pane.
3. Click the Insert Layout button in the Edit Master group. (This inserts in the Slide pane a new slide with a Master title style placeholder, the logo, and the footer information.)
4. Format and move the placeholder by completing the following steps:
   a. Select the text *Click to edit Master title style*.
   b. Click the Home tab, click the Text Shadow button (to turn off shadowing), turn on bold, change the font to Tahoma, change the font size to 28 points, and change the font color to Light Blue.
   c. Move the placeholder so it is positioned along the bottom of the slide just above the footer placeholder.

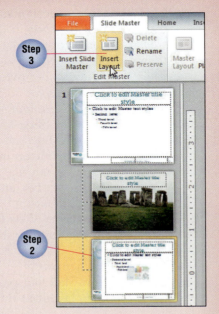

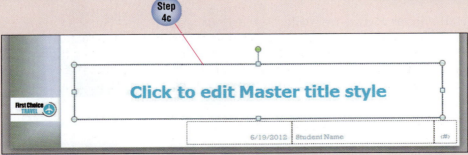

5. Click the Slide Master tab.
6. Insert a Picture placeholder by completing the following steps:
   a. Click the Insert Placeholder button arrow.
   b. Click *Picture* at the drop-down list.
   c. Drag in the slide in the Slide pane to create a placeholder that is approximately 7.5 inches wide and 3.5 inches high.
   d. Click the Drawing Tools Format tab.

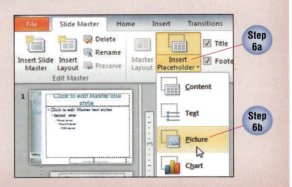

Chapter 6 ■ Using Slide Masters and Action Buttons   **233**

e. Click in the *Shape Height* measurement box and then type **3.5**.
f. Click in the *Shape Width* measurement box, type **7.5**, and then press Enter.
g. Drag the placeholder so it is balanced in the slide.
h. Click anywhere in the word *Picture* in the placeholder. (This removes the word *Picture* and inserts the insertion point in the placeholder.)
i. Type **Insert company logo**.

7. Remove the footer and slide number placeholders by completing the following steps:
   a. Click the footer placeholder. (The placeholder contains your name and is located along the bottom of the slide in the Slide pane.)
   b. Click the border of the placeholder to select it (the border turns into a solid line) and then press the Delete key.
   c. Click the slide number placeholder, click the placeholder border, and then press the Delete key.
   d. Drag the date placeholder so it is positioned at the right side of the slide.
8. If necessary, click the Slide Master tab.
9. Rename the custom slide layout by completing the following steps:
   a. Click the Rename button in the Edit Master group.
   b. At the Rename Layout dialog box, select the text that displays in the *Layout name* text box and then type **Logo**.
   c. Click the Rename button.
10. Click the Close Master View button.
11. Insert a slide using the new slide layout by completing the following steps:
    a. Make Slide 6 active.
    b. Click the New Slide button arrow.
    c. Click the Logo layout at the drop-down list.
    d. Click the Insert Picture from File button in the slide.
    e. At the Insert Picture dialog box, navigate to the PowerPoint2010C6 folder on your storage medium and then double-click *FCTLogo.jpg*.
    f. Click in the text *Click to add title* and then type **Monthly special – 20% discount on Wiltshire tour**.
12. Save **P-C6-P1-England.pptx**.

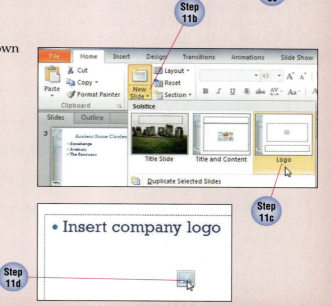

Inserting a New Slide Master

Insert Slide Master

A PowerPoint presentation can contain more than one slide master (and associated layouts). To insert a new slide master, display the presentation in Slide Master view and then click the Insert Slide Master button in the Edit Master group. This

inserts the slide master and all associated layouts below the existing slide master and layouts in the slide thumbnail pane. You can also insert a slide master and all associated layouts with a design theme applied. To do this, click below the existing slide master and associated layouts, click the Themes button in the Edit Theme group, and then click the desired theme at the drop-down gallery. A slide master containing the chosen design theme is inserted below the existing thumbnails.

Preserving Slide Masters

If you delete all slide layouts that follow a slide master, PowerPoint will automatically delete the slide master. You can protect a slide master from being deleted by "preserving" the master. To do this, click the desired slide master thumbnail and then click the Preserve button in the Edit Master group. If you insert a slide master using the Insert Slide Master button, the Preserve button is automatically active. When a slide master is preserved, a preservation icon displays below the slide number in the slide thumbnail pane.

Changing Page Setup

The Page Setup group in the Slide Master tab contains two buttons. By default, slides display in the landscape orientation (wider than tall). You can change this to portrait orientation (taller than wide) by clicking the Slide Orientation button in the Page Setup group and then clicking *Portrait* at the drop-down list. Click the Page Setup button and the Page Setup dialog box displays with options for changing slide width and height; slide numbering; and applying slide orientation to slides or notes, handouts, and outline pages.

▼ **Quick Steps**

Preserve Slide Master
1. Display presentation in Slide Master view.
2. Click desired slide master thumbnail.
3. Click Preserve button.

Preserve

Slide Orientation

Page Setup

Project 1f Applying a Second Slide Master and Changing Slide Numbering   Part 6 of 6

1. With **P-C6-P1-England.pptx** open, insert a second slide master by completing the following steps:
   a. Click the View tab and then click the Slide Master button in the Master Views group.
   b. Click below the bottom slide layout in the slide thumbnail pane. (You want the slide master and associated layouts to display below the original slide master and not take the place of the original.)
   c. Click the Themes button in the Edit Theme group and then click *Flow* at the drop-down gallery. (Notice the slide master and associated layouts that display in the slide thumbnail pane below the original slide master and associated layouts and notice the preservation icon that displays below the slide master number 2.)
   d. Click the new slide master (Flow Slide Master) in the slide thumbnail pane.
   e. Click the Colors button in the Edit Theme group and then click *Apex* at the drop-down gallery.
   f. Click the Fonts button and then click *Foundry* at the drop-down gallery.

Step 1b

2. Insert a footer, the date and time, and slide numbers in the slide master by completing the following steps:
   a. Click the Insert tab.
   b. Click the Header & Footer button in the Text group.
   c. At the Header and Footer dialog box with the Slide tab selected, click the *Date and time* check box to insert a check mark.
   d. Make sure the *Update automatically* option is selected. (With this option selected, the date and/or time will automatically update each time you open the presentation.)
   e. Click the *Slide number* check box to insert a check mark.
   f. Click the *Footer* check box to insert a check mark and then type your first and last names in the *Footer* text box.
   g. Click the Apply to All button.
3. Click the Slide Master tab.
4. Click the third layout below the new slide master (*Section Header Layout*), scroll down to the bottom of the slide thumbnail pane, hold down the Shift key, click the bottom thumbnail, and then click the Delete button in the Edit Master group. (This deletes all but two of the associated layouts with the new slide master.)
5. Format the slide layout below the new slide master by completing the following steps:
   a. Click the first layout (*Title Slide Layout*) below the new slide master.
   b. Click the Background Styles button in the Background group and then click *Format Background*.
   c. At the Format Background dialog box, click the *Picture or texture fill* option.
   d. Click the File button (located in the Insert from group).
   e. At the Insert Picture dialog box, navigate to the PowerPoint2010C6 folder on your storage medium and then double-click **Nightscape.jpg**.
   f. Click the *Hide background graphics* check box to insert a check mark.
   g. Click the Close button.
   h. Click in the text *Click to edit Master title style* and then press Ctrl + E. (This centers the text.)
   i. Drag the placeholder up so the text displays above the buildings.
   j. Select and then delete the subtitle placeholder.
   k. Click the *Footers* check box in the Master Layout group to remove footer placeholders.
6. Click the Close Master View button.
7. Insert a new slide by completing the following steps:
   a. Make Slide 7 active.
   b. Click the New Slide button arrow and then click the Flow Title Slide (the slide with the image of the New York City night skyline).
   c. Click in the text *Click to add title* and then type **New York City Tour**.
8. Insert a new slide by completing the following steps:
   a. With Slide 8 active, click the New Slide button. (This inserts the Flow Title and Content layout.)
   b. Click the text *Click to add title* and then type **Manhattan Tour**.

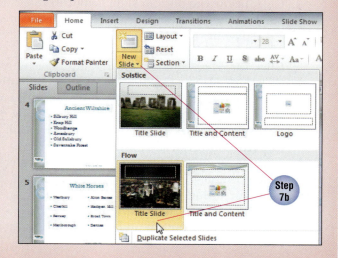

    c. Click the text *Click to add text* and then type the following bulleted text:
- Times Square
- Madison Square Garden
- Greenwich Village
- Soho
- Little Italy
- Battery Park

9. Insert the following text in slides using the Flow Title and Content layout:

    Slide 10   **Dinner Cruise**
- Three-hour cruise
- Manhattan skyline
- Five-course gourmet dinner
- Entertainment
- Dancing

    Slide 11   **City Pass**
- Empire State Building
- Statue of Liberty
- Ellis Island
- Rockefeller Center
- United Nations Building
- Bronx Zoo

    Slide 12   **Museum Passes**
- Museum of Modern Art
- Guggenheim Museum
- American Museum of Natural History
- Metropolitan Museum of Art
- Ellis Island Museum
- Brooklyn Museum of Art

10. Insert a new slide by completing the following steps:
    a. With Slide 12 active, click the New Slide button arrow and then click the Flow Title Slide (the slide with the image of the New York City night skyline).
    b. Click in the text *Click to add text* and then type **Call Beth at 555-4500**.

11. Insert a new slide with the logo layout by completing the following steps:
    a. With Slide 13 active, click the New Slide button arrow and then click the Solstice Logo Layout.
    b. Click the Insert Picture from File button in the slide.
    c. At the Insert Picture dialog box, navigate to the PowerPoint2010C6 folder on your storage medium and then double-click *FCTLogo.jpg*.
    d. Click in the text *Click to add title* and then type **Complimentary airport shuttle when you book your New York tour**.

12. Assume that the presentation is going to be inserted into a larger presentation and that the starting slide number will be 12 (instead of 1). Change the beginning slide number by completing the following steps:
    a. Click the View tab and then click the Slide Master button.
    b. Click the top slide master in the slide thumbnail pane.
    c. Click the Page Setup button in the Page Setup group.

d. At the Page Setup dialog box, select the current number in the *Number slides from* text box and then type 12.
e. Click OK to close the dialog box.
f. Click the Close Master View button.

13. Make Slide 12 active and then run the presentation.
14. Print the presentation as a handout with six slides horizontally per page.
15. Save and then close **P-C6-P1-England.pptx**.

Step 12d
Step 12e

Project 2 Save a Template and Create a Travel Presentation with the Template

4 Parts

You will save a travel presentation as a template and then use the template to create and format a travel presentation. You will insert elements in the presentation in Handout Master view and Notes Master view, change the presentation zoom, and view the presentation in grayscale and black and white.

Saving a Presentation as a Template

▼ Quick Steps

Save Presentation as a Template
1. Click File tab, Save As button.
2. Click *Save as type* option.
3. Click *PowerPoint Template (*.potx)*.
4. Type presentation name.
5. Click Save button.

If you create custom formatting that you will use for future presentations, consider saving the presentation as a template. The advantage to saving your presentation as a template is that you cannot accidentally overwrite the presentation. When you open a template and then click the Save button on the Quick Access toolbar, the Save As dialog box automatically displays.

To save a presentation as a template, click the File tab and then click Save As. At the Save As dialog box, click the *Save as type* option button and then click *PowerPoint Template (*.potx)* at the drop-down list. Type a name for the template in the *File name* text box and then click the Save button. The template is automatically saved in a Templates folder on the hard drive. If you want to save the template to another location, navigate to the desired folder in the Save As dialog box and then save the template.

To create a presentation based on a template, click the File tab and then click the New tab. At the New tab Backstage view, click the *My templates* option in the Available Templates and Themes category. At the New Presentation dialog box, double-click the desired theme in the list box.

If you saved a template in a location other than the default, open a presentation based on the template by displaying the New tab Backstage view and then clicking the *New from existing* option in the Available Templates and Themes category. At the New from Existing Presentation dialog box, navigate to the desired folder and then double-click the desired template.

After opening a presentation template, insert the desired slides and make any other formatting or design changes and then click the Save button on the Quick Access toolbar. At the Save As dialog box, type a name for the presentation and then click the Save button.

If you no longer need a template, delete the template at the New Presentation dialog box. To do this, display the New tab Backstage view and then click the *My templates* option in the Available Templates and Themes category. At the New Presentation dialog box, right-click the template you want to delete and then click *Delete* at the shortcut menu. At the message asking if you want to delete the template, click the Yes button. If you saved a template to a location other than the default, delete the template in the same manner as you delete a presentation. To do this, display the Open dialog box, navigate to the desired folder, click the template you want to delete, click the Organize button, click *Delete* at the drop-down list, and then click Yes at the message that displays.

Project 2a — Saving a Presentation as a Template — Part 1 of 4

1. Open **P-C6-P1-TravelMaster.pptx**.
2. Click the File tab and then click the Save As button.
3. At the Save As dialog box, click the *Save as type* option button and then click *PowerPoint Template (*.potx)* at the drop-down list.

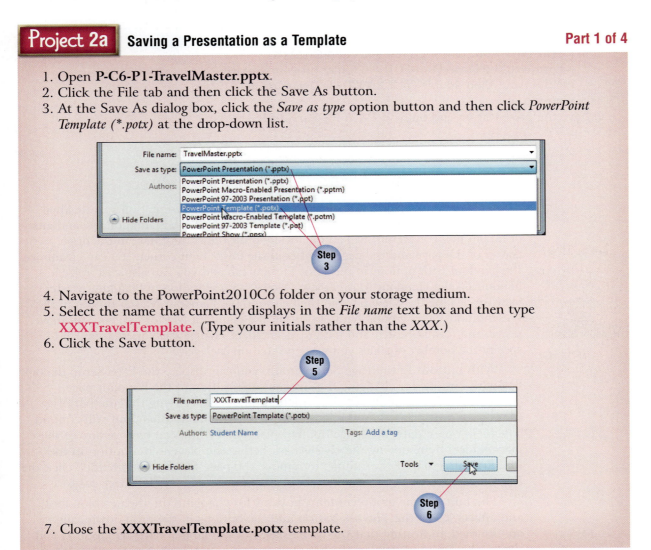

4. Navigate to the PowerPoint2010C6 folder on your storage medium.
5. Select the name that currently displays in the *File name* text box and then type **XXXTravelTemplate**. (Type your initials rather than the *XXX*.)
6. Click the Save button.

7. Close the **XXXTravelTemplate.potx** template.

8. Open the template and save it as a presentation by completing the following steps:
   a. Click the File tab and then click the New tab.
   b. At the New tab Backstage view, click the *New from existing* option in the Available Templates and Themes category.

   c. At the New from Existing Presentation dialog box, navigate to the PowerPoint2010C6 folder on your storage medium and then double-click **XXXTravelTemplate.potx** (where the *XXX* represents your initials).
9. Save the presentation and name it **P-C6-P2-ParisTour**.

Customizing the Handout Master

Handout Master

As you learned in Chapter 1, you can choose to print a presentation as individual slides, handouts, notes pages, or an outline. If you print a presentation as handouts or an outline, PowerPoint will automatically print the current date in the upper right corner of the page and the page number in the lower right corner. You can customize the handout with options in the Print Preview tab and you can also customize a handout in the Handout Master view. Display a presentation in Handout Master view by clicking the View tab and then clicking the Handout Master button in the Presentation Views group. With options in the Handout Master tab, you can move, resize, and format header and footer placeholders, change page orientation, and specify the number of slides you want printed on each page.

With buttons in the Page Setup group, you can display the Page Setup dialog box with options for changing the size and orientation of the handout page, changing the handout and/or slide orientation, and specifying the number of slides you want printed on the handout page. By default, a handout will contain a header, footer, date, and page number placeholder. You can remove any of these placeholders by removing the check mark before the placeholder option in the Placeholders group. For example, to remove the page number placeholder, click the *Page Number* check box in the Placeholders group to remove the check mark.

The Edit Theme group contains buttons for changing the theme color, font, and effects. Click the Themes button and the options in the drop-down gallery are dimmed, indicating that the themes are not available for the handout. If you apply a background style to the handout master, you can change theme colors by clicking the Colors button and then clicking the desired color theme at the drop-down gallery. Apply theme fonts by clicking the Fonts button and then clicking the desired fonts theme at the drop-down gallery.

Apply a background style to the handout page by clicking the Background Styles button in the Background group and then clicking one of the predesigned styles. You can also click the *Format Background* option and then make changes at the Format Background dialog box. Remove any background graphics by clicking the *Hide background graphics* check box to insert a check mark.

Background Styles

Project 2b — Customizing the Handout Master — Part 2 of 4

1. With **P-C6-P2-ParisTour.pptx** open, click the New Slide button arrow and then click *Reuse Slides* at the drop-down list.
2. In the Reuse Slides task pane, click the Browse button, and then click the *Browse File* option at the drop-down list.
3. Navigate to the PowerPoint2010C6 folder on your storage medium and then double-click **ParisTour.pptx**.
4. Insert the second, third, fourth, and fifth slides from the Reuse Slides task pane into the current presentation.
5. Close the Reuse Slides task pane.
6. Edit the Title Slide Layout in Slide Master view by completing the following steps:
   a. Click the View tab and then click the Slide Master button.
   b. Click the second thumbnail in the slide thumbnail pane (*Title Slide Layout*).
   c. Click the Background Styles button in the Background group and then click *Format Background* at the drop-down list.
   d. At the Format Background dialog box, click the File button (displays in the *Insert from* section).
   e. At the Insert Picture dialog box, navigate to the PowerPoint2010C6 folder on your storage medium and then double-click **EiffelTower.jpg**.
   f. Click the Close button to close the Format Background dialog box.
   g. Select the text *Click to edit Master title style*, click the Home tab, click the Font Color button arrow, and then click *Turquoise, Accent 4, Lighter 60%* at the drop-down gallery.
   h. Click the Slide Master tab.
   i. Click the Close Master View button.
7. Make Slide 1 active, click in the text *Click to add title*, and then type **Paris Tour**.
8. Size and move the text placeholder so *Paris Tour* displays in a blue area on the slide (not over the tower).
9. Display each slide and then make adjustments to the position of clip art images and/or placeholders.
10. Make Slide 5 active and then create a new slide with the *Title Slide* layout. Type **Call Greg at 555-4500**.
11. Save **P-C6-P2-ParisTour.pptx**.
12. Click the View tab and then click the Handout Master button in the Master Views group.
13. Click the Handout Orientation button in the Page Setup group and then click *Landscape* at the drop-down list.

Step 12

14. Click in the Header placeholder on the page and then type your first and last names.
15. Click in the Footer placeholder and then type **Paris Tour**.
16. Click the Background Styles button and then click *Style 10* at the drop-down list (second option from the left in the third row).
17. Click the Colors button in the Edit Theme group and then click *Metro* at the drop-down list.
18. Click the Fonts button in the Edit Theme group and then click *Foundry* at the drop-down list.
19. Edit the header text by completing the following steps:
    a. Click in the header placeholder and then click on any character in your name.
    b. Move the insertion point so it is positioned immediately right of the last character in your last name.
    c. Type a comma, press the spacebar, and then type your course number and title.
    d. Click in the handout page outside of any placeholder.
20. Click the Close Master View button.
21. Save **P-C6-P2-ParisTour.pptx**

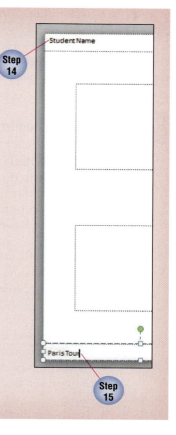

Customizing the Notes Master

Notes Master

You can insert notes in a presentation and then print the presentation as notes pages and the notes will print below the slide. If you want to insert or format text or other elements as notes on all slides in a presentation, consider making the changes in the Notes Master view. Display this view by clicking the View tab and then clicking the Notes Master button in the Master Views group. This displays a notes page along with the Notes Master tab. Many of the buttons and options in this tab are the same as the ones in the Handout Master tab.

Project 2c Customizing the Notes Master Part 3 of 4

1. With **P-C6-P2-ParisTour.pptx** open, click the View tab and then click the Notes Master button in the Master Views group.
2. Click the *Body* check box in the Placeholders group to remove the check mark.
3. Click the Fonts button in the Edit Theme group and then click *Foundry* at the drop-down list.
4. Click the Insert tab.
5. Click the Text Box button in the Text group.
6. Click in the notes page below the slide.
7. Type **Visit www.first-choice.emcp.net for a listing of all upcoming tours.**

8. Size and position the text box below the slide as shown.

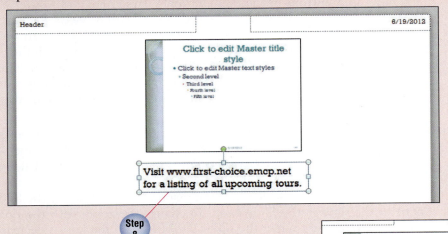

Step 8

9. Click the Insert tab and then click the Picture button in the Images group.
10. At the Insert Picture dialog box, navigate to the PowerPoint2010C6 folder on your storage medium and then double-click *FCTLogo.jpg*.
11. Change the height of the logo to *0.5"*. (This changes the width to *1"*.)
12. Drag the logo so it is positioned below the text.
13. Click the Notes Master tab and then click the Close Master View button.
14. Print Slides 2 and 4 as notes pages by completing the following steps:
    a. Display the Print tab Backstage view.
    b. Click the second gallery in the Settings category and then click *Notes Pages* in the *Print Layout* section.
    c. Click in the *Slides* text box located below the first gallery in the Settings category and then type *2,4*.
    d. Click the Print button.
15. Save **P-C6-P2-ParisTour.pptx**.

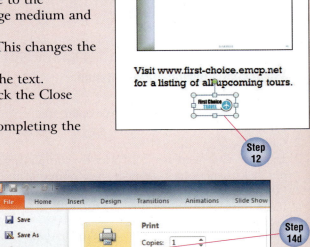

Step 12

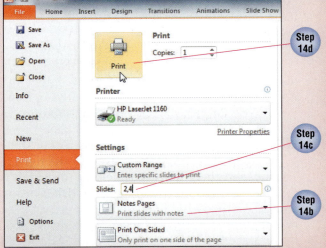

Step 14d

Step 14c

Step 14b

Chapter 6 ■ Using Slide Masters and Action Buttons   243

Using View Tab Options

You have used buttons in the Presentation Views group and Master Views group in the View tab to display your presentation in various views such as Normal, Slide Sorter, Slide Master, Handout Master, and Notes Master. In addition to viewing buttons, the View tab includes options for showing or hiding the ruler and gridlines; zooming in or out in the slide; viewing the slide in color, grayscale, or black and white; and working with windows including opening a new window containing the current presentation and arranging, splitting, and switching windows.

Zoom

You can change the display size of the slide in the Slide pane or slides in the Slides/Outline pane with the Zoom button in the View tab and also with the Zoom slider bar located at the right side of the Status bar. Click the Zoom button in the View tab and the Zoom dialog box displays. Use options in this dialog box to increase or decrease the display size of slides in the Slides/Outline pane or the slide in the Slide pane. To change the zoom with the Zoom slider bar, use the mouse to drag the slider bar button to the left to decrease the display size or to the right to increase the display size. Click the button with the minus symbol that displays at the left side of the Zoom slider bar to decrease the display percentage or click the button with the plus symbol that displays at the right side of the Zoom slider bar to increase the display percentage. Click the percentage number that displays at the left side of the slider bar and the Zoom dialog box displays.

Project 2d — Viewing a Presentation — Part 4 of 4

1. With **P-C6-P2-ParisTour.pptx** open, make Slide 1 active and then click the slide in the Slide pane.
2. Click the View tab.
3. Increase and decrease the zoom by completing the following steps:
   a. Click the Zoom button in the Zoom group. (This displays the Zoom dialog box.)
   b. At the Zoom dialog box, click the *33%* option and then click OK.
   c. Click the Zoom button, click the *100%* option in the Zoom dialog box, and then click OK.
   d. Click the Slide 2 thumbnail in the Slides/Outline pane.
   e. Click the Zoom button, click the *66%* option in the Zoom dialog box, and then click OK. (Because the slide in the Slides/Outline pane was active, the percentage display changed for the thumbnails in the pane.)
   f. Position the mouse pointer on the Zoom slider bar button (located at the right side of the Status bar), drag the button to the right to increase the size of the slide in the Slide pane, and then drag the slider bar to the left to decrease the size of the slide.
   g. Click the percentage number that displays at the left side of the Zoom slider bar (this displays the Zoom dialog box).
   h. Click the *66%* option in the Zoom dialog box and then click OK.
   i. Click the Slide 3 thumbnail in the Slides/Outline pane.
   j. Click the Zoom button in the View tab.
   k. Type **45** in the *Percentage* text box and then click OK. (This changes the zoom display for the slides in the Slides/Outline pane.)

Step 3b

4. View the slides in grayscale by completing the following steps:
    a. Click the slide in the Slides pane to make it active and then click the Grayscale button in the Color/Grayscale group in the View tab.
    b. Click some of the buttons in the Grayscale tab to display the slides in varying grayscale options.
    c. Click the Back To Color View button.

Step 4a

5. View the slides in black and white by completing the following steps:
    a. Click the View tab and then click the Black and White button in the Color/Grayscale group in the View tab.
    b. Click some of the buttons in the Black And White tab to display the slides in varying black and white options.
    c. Click the Back To Color View button.
6. Open a new window and arrange the windows by completing the following steps:
    a. Click the View tab and then click the New Window button in the Window group. (This opens the same presentation in another window. Notice that the name on the title bar displays followed by a colon and the number 2.)

Step 6a

    b. Click the View tab and then click the Arrange All button to arrange the two presentation windows. (This arranges the presentations as tiles with the title bar of each presentation visible as well as a portion of each presentation.)
    c. Click the Window button in either window and then click the Cascade button at the drop-down list. (This arranges the two presentations with the presentations overlapping with the title bar for each presentation visible as well as a portion of the top presentation.)

Step 6c

    d. Click the Switch Windows button and then click the *P-C6-P2-ParisTour.pptx:1* option at the drop-down list. (Notice the presentation name in the title bar now displays followed by a colon and the number 1.)
    e. Click the Close button that displays in the upper right corner of the currently active presentation. (The Close button contains an X.)
    f. Click the Maximize button that displays in the upper right corner of the presentation window. (The Maximize button displays immediately left of the Close button.)

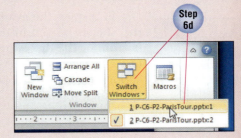

Step 6d

7. With the View tab active, click the Grayscale button in the Color/Grayscale group and then click the Inverse Grayscale button in the Change Selected Object group.
8. Print the presentation by completing the following steps:
    a. Display the Print tab Backstage view.
    b. If any text displays in the *Slides* text box, select and then delete the text.
    c. If you are using a color printer, click the Color gallery that displays at the bottom of the Settings category and then click *Grayscale*. (Skip this step if you are using a black and white printer.)

Chapter 6 ■ Using Slide Masters and Action Buttons

d. Click the second gallery in the Settings category and then click *6 Slides Horizontal* in the Handout section.
e. Click the Print button.
9. Click the Back To Color View button in the Grayscale tab.
10. Make Slide 1 active and then run the presentation.
11. Save and then close **P-C6-P2-ParisTour.pptx**.

Project 3 — Insert Action Buttons and Hyperlinks in a Job Search Presentation — 5 Parts

You will open a job search presentation and then insert action buttons that display the next slide, the first slide, and another presentation. You will also create a hyperlink from text in a slide to a site on the Internet.

▼ Quick Steps
Create Action Button
1. Make desired slide active.
2. Click Insert tab.
3. Click Shapes button.
4. Click desired action button.
5. Drag in slide to create button.
6. Make desired changes at Action Settings dialog box.
7. Click OK.

Apply formatting to an action button with options in the Drawing Tools Format tab.

Inserting Action Buttons

Action buttons are drawn objects on a slide that have a routine attached to them which is activated when the viewer or the speaker clicks the button. For example, you could include an action button that displays the next slide in the presentation, a file in another program, or a specific web page. Creating an action button is a two-step process. You draw the button using an Action Button shape in the Shapes button drop-down list and then you define the action that will take place with options in the Action Settings dialog box. You can customize an action button in the same manner as customizing a drawn object. When the viewer or speaker moves the mouse over an action button during a presentation, the pointer changes to a hand with a finger pointing upward to indicate clicking will result in an action.

To display the available action buttons, click the Insert tab and then click the Shapes button in the Illustrations group. Action buttons display at the bottom of the drop-down list. Hover the mouse pointer over a button and the name as well as the action it performs displays in a box above the button. The action attached to an action button occurs when you run the presentation and then click the button.

Project 3a — Inserting Action Buttons — Part 1 of 5

1. Open **JobSearch.pptx** and then save the presentation with the name **P-C6-P3-JobSearch**.
2. Make the following changes to the presentation:
   a. Change the design theme to *Verve*.
   b. Change the theme colors to *Metro*.
   c. Change the theme fonts to *Concourse*.
   d. Click the Insert tab and then click the Header & Footer button in the Text group.
   e. At the Header and Footer dialog box with the Slide tab selected, click the *Date and time* check box and make sure *Update automatically* is selected.

f. Click the *Slide number* check box to insert a check mark.
　　g. Click the Notes and Handouts tab.
　　h. Click the *Date and time* check box and make sure *Update automatically* is selected.
　　i. Click the *Header* check box and then type the name of your school.
　　j. Click the *Footer* check box and then type your first and last names.
　　k. Click the Apply to All button.
3. Insert an action button in Slide 1 that will display the next slide by completing the following steps:
　　a. Make Slide 1 active.
　　b. Click the Insert tab and then click the Shapes button.
　　c. At the drop-down list, click *Action Button: Forward or Next* (second option from the left in the Action Buttons group) that displays at the bottom of the drop-down list.
　　d. Move the crosshair pointer to the lower right corner of the slide and then drag to create a button as shown below.

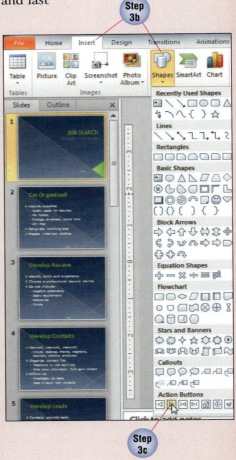

　　e. At the Action Settings dialog box, click OK. (The default setting is *Hyperlink to Next Slide*.)
4. Insert an action button in Slide Master view that will display the next slide by completing the following steps:
　　a. Display the presentation in Slide Master view.
　　b. Click the top slide master thumbnail.
　　c. Click the Insert tab and then click the Shapes button.
　　d. At the drop-down list, click *Action Button: Forward or Next* (second option from the left in the Action Buttons group).
　　e. Move the crosshair pointer to the lower right corner of the slide master and then drag to create a button as shown at the right.
　　f. At the Action Settings dialog box, click OK. (The default setting is *Hyperlink to Next Slide*.)
　　g. Click the Slide Master tab and then click the Close Master View button.

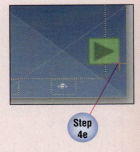

5. Make Slide 1 active and then run the presentation, clicking the action button to advance slides. When you click the action button on the last slide (Slide 9) nothing happens because it is the last slide. Press the Esc key to end the presentation.

Chapter 6 ■ Using Slide Masters and Action Buttons

6. Change the action button on Slide 9 by completing the following steps:
   a. Make Slide 9 active.
   b. Click the Insert tab and then click the Shapes button.
   c. At the drop-down list, click *Action Button: Home* (fifth button from the left in the Action Buttons group).
   d. Drag to create a button on top of the previous action button. (Make sure it completely covers the previous action button.)
   e. At the Action Settings dialog box with the *Hyperlink to: First Slide* option selected, click OK.
   f. Deselect the button.
7. Display Slide 1 in the Slide pane and then run the presentation. Navigate through the slide show by clicking the action button. When you click the action button on the last slide, the first slide displays. End the slide show by pressing the Esc key.
8. Save **P-C6-P3-JobSearch.pptx**.

Step 6c

Applying an Action to an Object

Action

The Links group in the Insert tab contains an Action button you can use to specify an action to a selected object. To use this button, select the desired object in the slide, click the Insert tab, and then click the Action button. This displays the Action Settings dialog box, which is the same dialog box that displays when you draw an action button in a slide.

You can specify that an action button or a selected object link to another PowerPoint presentation or other file as well as a website. To link to another PowerPoint presentation, click the *Hyperlink to* option at the Action Settings dialog box, click the down-pointing arrow at the right side of the *Hyperlink to* option box, and then click *Other PowerPoint Presentation* at the drop-down list. At the Hyperlink to Other PowerPoint Presentation dialog box, navigate to the desired folder, and then double-click the PowerPoint presentation. To link to a website, click the *Hyperlink to* option at the Action Settings dialog box, click the down-pointing arrow at the right side of the *Hyperlink to* option box, and then click *URL* at the drop-down list. At the Hyperlink To URL dialog box, type the web address in the URL text box, and then click OK. Click OK to close the Action Settings dialog box. Other actions you can link to using the *Hyperlink to* drop-down list include: Next Slide, Previous Slide, First Slide, Last Slide, Last Slide Viewed, End Show, Custom Show, Slide, and Other File.

Project 3b Linking to Another Presentation and a Website   Part 2 of 5

1. With **P-C6-P3-JobSearch.pptx** open, add an action button that will link to another presentation by completing the following steps:
   a. Make Slide 4 active.
   b. Click the Insert tab and then click the Shapes button in the Illustrations group.
   c. At the drop-down list, click *Action Button: Help* (second button from the right in the Action Buttons group).

d. Draw the action button to the left of the existing button located in the lower right corner of the slide.
e. At the Action Settings dialog box, click the *Hyperlink to* option.
f. Click the down-pointing arrow at the right side of the *Hyperlink to* option box and then click *Other PowerPoint Presentation* at the drop-down list. (You will need to scroll down the list to display this option.)
g. At the Hyperlink to Other PowerPoint Presentation dialog box, navigate to the PowerPoint2010C6 folder on your storage medium and then double-click **Contacts.pptx**.
h. At the Hyperlink to Slide dialog box, click OK.
i. Click OK to close the Action Settings dialog box.

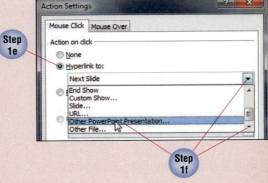

2. Apply an action to the clip art image in Slide 5 that links to a website by completing the following steps:
a. Make Slide 5 active and then click the clip art image to select it.
b. Click the Insert tab and then click the Action button in the Links group.
c. At the Action Settings dialog box, click the *Hyperlink to* option.
d. Click the down-pointing arrow at the right of the *Hyperlink to* option box, and then click *URL* at the drop-down list.
e. At the Hyperlink To URL dialog box, type www.usajobs.gov and then click OK.
f. Click OK to close the Action Settings dialog box.
g. Click outside the clip art image to deselect it.

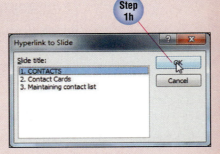

3. Run the presentation by completing the following steps:
a. Make sure you are connected to the Internet.
b. Make Slide 1 active.
c. Click the Slide Show button in the view area on the Status bar.
d. Navigate through the slide show to Slide 4.
e. Click the action button in Slide 4 containing the question mark. (This displays Slide 1 of **Contacts.pptx**.)
f. Navigate through the three slides in **Contacts.pptx**. Continue clicking the mouse button until you return to Slide 4 of **P-C6-P3-JobSearch.pptx**.
g. Display Slide 5 and then click the clip art image. (If you are connected to the Internet, the job site of the United States Federal Government displays.)
h. Click a few links at the website.
i. When you are finished viewing the website, close your web browser.
j. Continue viewing the remainder of the presentation by clicking the action button in the lower right corner of each slide.
k. When Slide 1 displays, press the Esc key to end the presentation.

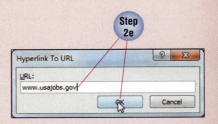

4. Save **P-C6-P3-JobSearch.pptx**.

Inserting Hyperlinks

Quick Steps

Insert Hyperlink
1. Click Insert tab.
2. Click Hyperlink button.
3. Make desired changes at Insert Hyperlink dialog box.
4. Click OK.

In Project 3b, you created hyperlinks with options at the Action Settings dialog box. You can also create hyperlinks with options at the Insert Hyperlink dialog box shown in Figure 6.2. To display this dialog box, select a key word, phrase, or object in a slide, click the Insert tab, and then click the Hyperlink button in the Links group. You can also display the Insert Hyperlink dialog box with the keyboard shortcut Ctrl + K. You can link to a website, another presentation, a place in the current presentation, a new presentation, or to an email address. To insert a hyperlink to a website or an existing presentation, click the Existing File or Web Page button in the *Link to* group at the Insert Hyperlink dialog box.

Figure 6.2 Insert Hyperlink Dialog Box

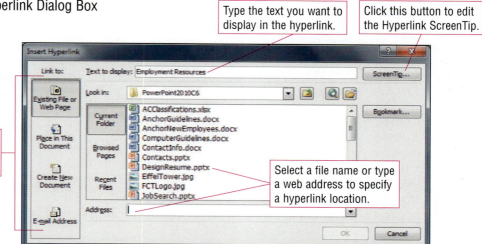

Project 3c   Inserting Hyperlinks to a Website   Part 3 of 5

1. With **P-C6-P3-JobSearch.pptx** open, insert a new slide by completing the following steps:
   a. Make Slide 5 active.
   b. Click the Home tab.
   c. Click the New Slide button arrow and then click the *Title Slide* layout.
   d. Click the text *Click to add title* and then type Internet Job Resources.
   e. Click the text *Click to add subtitle* and then type Employment Resources, press Enter, and then type America's Job Bank.
2. Add a hyperlink to the Employment Resources site by completing the following steps:
   a. Select *Employment Resources* in Slide 6.
   b. Click the Insert tab and then click the Hyperlink button in the Links group.
   c. At the Insert Hyperlink dialog box, type www.employment-resources.com in the *Address* text box. (PowerPoint automatically inserts *http://* at the beginning of the address.)
   d. Click OK to close the Insert Hyperlink dialog box.

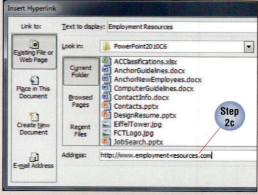

3. Add a hyperlink to the America's Job Bank website by completing the following steps:
   a. Select *America's Job Bank* in Slide 6.
   b. Click the Hyperlink button in the Links group.
   c. At the Insert Hyperlink dialog box, type www.ajb.dni.us in the *Address* text box.
   d. Click OK to close the Insert Hyperlink dialog box.
4. Copy the action button in Slide 1 to Slide 6 by completing the following steps:
   a. Make Slide 1 active.
   b. Click the action button to select it.
   c. Press Ctrl + C to copy the button.
   d. Make Slide 6 active.
   e. Press Ctrl + V to paste the button.
5. Save **P-C6-P3-JobSearch.pptx**.

In addition to linking to a website, you can create a hyperlink to another location in the presentation with the Place in This Document button in the *Link to* group in the Insert Hyperlink dialog box. Click the slide you want to link to in the *Select a place in this document* list box. With the Create New Document button in the Insert Hyperlink dialog box, you can create a hyperlink to a new presentation. When you click this button, you will be prompted to type a name for the new presentation and specify if you want to edit the new presentation now or later.

HINT
Hyperlinks are active when running the presentation, not when creating it.

You can use a graphic such as a clip art image, picture, or text box, to hyperlink to a file or website. To hyperlink with a graphic, select the graphic, click the Insert tab, and then click the Hyperlink button. You can also right-click the graphic and then click *Hyperlink* at the shortcut menu. At the Insert Hyperlink dialog box, specify what you want to link to and the text you want to display in the hyperlink.

You can insert a hyperlink to an email address at the Insert Hyperlink dialog box. To do this, click the E-Mail Address button in the *Link to* group, type the desired address in the *E-mail address* text box, and type a subject for the email in the *Subject* text box. Click in the *Text to display* text box and then type the text you want to display in the document. To use this feature, the email address you use must be set up in Outlook 2010.

Navigate to a hyperlink by clicking the hyperlink in the slide. Hover the mouse over the hyperlink and a ScreenTip displays with the hyperlink. If you want specific information to display in the ScreenTip, click the ScreenTip button in the Insert Hyperlink dialog box, type the desired text in the Set Hyperlink ScreenTip dialog box, and then click OK.

Project 3d Inserting Hyperlinks to Another Presentation and to a Word Document   Part 4 of 5

1. With **P-C6-P3-JobSearch.pptx** open, make Slide 3 active.
2. Create a link to another presentation by completing the following steps:
   a. Move the insertion point immediately right of the word *Picture*, press the Enter key, press Shift + Tab, and then type *Resume design*.
   b. Select *Resume design*.
   c. Make sure the Insert tab is active and then click the Hyperlink button in the Links group.

d. At the Insert Hyperlink dialog box, make sure the Existing File or Web Page button is selected.
   e. Click the down-pointing arrow at the right side of the *Look in* option and then navigate to the PowerPoint2010C6 folder on your storage medium.
   f. Double-click *DesignResume.pptx*.

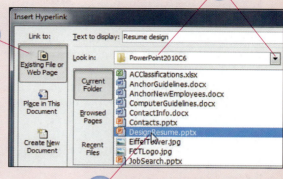

3. Create a hyperlink from a graphic to a Word document by completing the following steps:
   a. Make Slide 4 active.
   b. Right-click the small clip art image that displays in the upper right corner of the slide and then click *Hyperlink* at the shortcut menu.
   c. At the Insert Hyperlink dialog box, make sure the Existing File or Web Page button is selected.
   d. Click the down-pointing arrow at the right side of the *Look in* option and then navigate to the PowerPoint2010C6 folder on your storage medium.
   e. Double-click *ContactInfo.docx*.

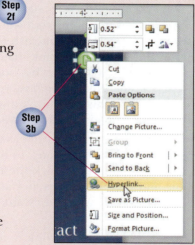

4. Run the presentation by completing the following steps:
   a. Make sure you are connected to the Internet.
   b. Make Slide 1 active.
   c. Click the Slide Show button in the view area on the Status bar.
   d. Navigate through the slides to Slide 3 and then click the Resume design hyperlink in the slide.
   e. Run the **DesignResume.pptx** presentation that displays and then press the Esc key when the presentation has ended.
   f. Click the mouse button to display Slide 4.
   g. Display the Word document by clicking the small clip art image in the upper right corner of the slide.

   h. Look at the information that displays in the Word document and then click the Close button located in the upper right corner of the Word window.
   i. Continue running the presentation to Slide 6.
   j. At Slide 6, click the Employment Resources hyperlink.
   k. Scroll through the employment site and then close the web browser.
   l. Click the America's Job Bank hyperlink.
   m. Scroll through the America's Job Bank site and then close the web browser.
   n. Continue viewing the remainder of the presentation. (When Slide 1 displays, press the Esc key to end the presentation.)
5. Save **P-C6-P3-JobSearch.pptx**.

You can modify or change hyperlink text or the hyperlink destination. To do this, right-click the hyperlink and then click *Edit Hyperlink* at the shortcut menu. At the Edit Hyperlink dialog box, make any desired changes and then close the dialog box. The Edit Hyperlink dialog box contains the same options as the Insert Hyperlink dialog box.

In addition to modifying the hyperlink, you can edit hyperlink text by making the desired editing changes. For example, you can apply a different font or font size, change the text color, and apply a text effect. Remove a hyperlink from a slide by right-clicking on the hyperlinked text and then clicking *Remove Hyperlink* at the shortcut menu.

Project 3e — Modifying, Editing, and Removing a Hyperlink — Part 5 of 5

1. With **P-C6-P3-JobSearch.pptx** open, make Slide 4 active and then modify the hyperlink in the clip art image by completing the following steps:
    a. Position the mouse pointer on the small clip art image in the upper right corner of the slide, click the right mouse button, and then click *Edit Hyperlink* at the shortcut menu.
    b. At the Edit Hyperlink dialog box, click the ScreenTip button located in the upper right corner of the dialog box.
    c. At the Set Hyperlink ScreenTip dialog box, type **Click this image to display information on typing contact information.**
    d. Click OK to close the Set Hyperlink ScreenTip dialog box.
    e. Click OK to close the Edit Hyperlink dialog box.

2. Make Slide 3 active and then remove the Resume design hyperlink by right-clicking the hyperlinked text (the text is dimmed and barely visible) and then clicking *Remove Hyperlink* at the shortcut menu.
3. Run the presentation and click the hyperlinks as they appear in slides.
4. Print the presentation as a handout with six slides horizontally per page.
5. Save and then close **P-C6-P3-JobSearch.pptx**.

Chapter Summary

- Display a presentation in Slide Master view by clicking the View tab and then clicking the Slide Master button in the Master Views group. In Slide Master view, slide master thumbnails display in the slide thumbnail pane.
- Use buttons in the Edit Theme group in the Slide Master tab to apply a design theme, theme colors, and theme fonts.
- Use buttons in the Background group in the Slide Master tab to apply a predesigned background style, display the Format Background dialog box with options for applying background styles, and hide background graphics.

- Delete a placeholder by clicking in the placeholder, clicking the placeholder border, and then pressing the Delete key.
- Delete a slide master in Slide Master view by clicking the desired slide master thumbnail in the slide thumbnail pane and then clicking the Delete button in the Edit Master group.
- In Slide Master view, you can display the Header and Footer dialog box with the Slide tab selected and then insert the date and time, slide number, and/or a footer. At the Header and Footer dialog box with the Notes and Handouts tab selected, you can insert the date and time, a header, page numbers, and/or a footer.
- Create a custom slide layout by clicking the Insert Layout button in the Edit Master group in the Slide Master tab. Rename the custom slide layout with the Rename button in the Edit Master group.
- Insert placeholders in a slide layout or custom slide layout by clicking the Insert Placeholder button arrow in the Master Layout group and then clicking the desired placeholder at the drop-down list.
- In Slide Master view, create custom prompts by selecting generic text in a placeholder and then typing the desired text.
- Click the Insert Slide Master button in Slide Master view to insert a new slide master and associated slide layouts. You can also insert a new slide master by applying a design theme in Slide Master view.
- Save a presentation as a template by changing the *Save as type* option at the Save As dialog box to *PowerPoint Template (*.potx)*.
- Open a presentation based on a template by clicking the My templates button or the New from existing button at the New tab Backstage view.
- You can customize a handout with options in the Handout Master view and customize notes pages with options in the Notes Master view.
- In addition to changing the view, you can use buttons in the View tab to show/hide the ruler and/or gridlines; change the zoom display; view slides in color, grayscale, or black and white; and arrange, split, and switch windows.
- Action buttons are drawn objects in a slide that have a routine attached, such as displaying the next slide, the first slide, a website, or another PowerPoint presentation.
- Create an action button by clicking the Insert tab, clicking the Shapes button, clicking the desired button at the drop-down list, and then dragging in the slide to create the button.
- Apply an action to text or an object in a slide by selecting the text or object, clicking the Insert tab, and then clicking the Action button.
- With options at the Insert Hyperlink dialog box, you can create a hyperlink to a web page, another presentation, a location within a presentation, a new presentation, or to an email. You can also create a hyperlink using a graphic.
- You can modify, edit, and remove hyperlinks.

Commands Review

FEATURE	RIBBON TAB, GROUP	BUTTON, FILE TAB	KEYBOARD SHORTCUT
Slide Master view	View, Master Views		
New tab Backstage view	File	New	
Handout Master view	View, Master Views		
Notes Master view	View, Master Views		
Action buttons	Insert, Illustrations		
Insert Hyperlink dialog box	Insert, Links		Ctrl + K
Action Settings dialog box	Insert, Links		

Concepts Check Test Your Knowledge

Completion: In the space provided at the right, indicate the correct term, symbol, or command.

1. To display a presentation in Slide Master view, click this tab and then click the Slide Master button.

2. Click this button to close Slide Master view.

3. This group in the Slide Master tab contains buttons for applying a theme, theme colors, and theme fonts.

4. This dialog box with the Slide tab selected contains options for inserting the date and time, a slide number, and a footer.

5. To create a new slide layout in Slide Master view, click this button in the Edit Master group.

6. To save a presentation as a template, choose this option at the *Save as type* option drop-down list at the Save As dialog box.

7. Change to this view to customize handouts.

8. Change to this view to customize notes pages.

9. The Zoom slider bar is located at the right side of this bar.

Chapter 6 ■ Using Slide Masters and Action Buttons

10. Click this button to display a drop-down list that includes action buttons. _____

11. Insert this action button in a slide to display the next slide in the presentation. _____

12. Insert this action button in a slide to display the first slide in the presentation. _____

13. This is the keyboard shortcut to display the Insert Hyperlink dialog box. _____

Skills Check Assess Your Performance

Assessment

1 FORMAT A PRESENTATION IN SLIDE MASTER VIEW AND THEN SAVE THE PRESENTATION AS A TEMPLATE

1. Display a blank presentation, click the View tab, and then click the Slide Master button.
2. Click the top slide master thumbnail in the slide thumbnail pane.
3. Apply the *Urban* theme, change the theme colors to *Paper*, and change the theme fonts to *Flow*.
4. Apply the *Style 2* background style.
5. Select the text *Click to edit Master title style*, click the Home tab, change the font color to *Olive Green, Accent 1, Darker 50%*, and then turn on bold.
6. Select the text *Second level* in the slide master and then change the font color to *Orange, Accent 2, Darker 50%*.
7. Insert the **WELogo.jpg** image in the master slide and then change the background of the logo to transparent by clicking the Color button in the Picture Tools Format tab, clicking the *Set Transparent Color* option, and then clicking on a white portion of the logo. This removes the white background so the yellow slide background displays. Change the height of the logo to 0.5 inch and drag the logo to the lower left corner of the slide master.
8. Select the date placeholder and then move the placeholder to the lower right corner of the slide.
9. Select the footer placeholder and then drag it down to the lower right corner of the slide immediately left of the date placeholder.
10. Click the Slide Master tab.
11. Click the first slide layout below the slide master.
12. Click the *Footers* check box in the Master Layout group to remove the footer and date placeholders.
13. Select and then delete the slide layouts from the third layout below the slide master (the *Section Header Layout*) to the last layout.
14. Preserve the slide masters by clicking the top slide master in the slide thumbnail pane, clicking the Slide Master tab, and then clicking the Preserve button in the Edit Master group.

15. Click the Close Master View button.
16. Save the presentation as a template to the PowerPoint2010C6 folder on your storage medium and name the template **XXXPublicationTemplate** (use your initials in place of the *XXX*).
17. Close **XXXPublicationTemplate.potx**.

Assessment

2 USE A TEMPLATE TO CREATE A PUBLICATIONS PRESENTATION

1. Open **XXXPublicationTemplate.potx** (where the *XXX* represents your initials). (To do this, display the New tab Backstage view and then click the New from existing button. At the New from Existing Presentation dialog box, navigate to the PowerPoint2010C6 folder on your storage medium, and then double-click *XXXPublicationTemplate.potx*.)
2. Save the presentation and name it **P-C6-A2-WEnterprises**.
3. Click the *Click to add title* text in the current slide and then type **Worldwide Enterprises**.
4. Click the *Click to add subtitle* text and then type **Company Publications**.
5. Display the Reuse Slides task pane, browse to PowerPoint2010C6 folder on your storage medium, and then double-click **Publications.pptx**.
6. Insert the second, third, fourth, and fifth slides from the Reuse Slides task pane into the current presentation and then close the task pane.
7. Insert a second slide master with the following specifications:
    a. Display the presentation in Slide Master view.
    b. Click in the slide thumbnail pane below the bottom slide layout.
    c. Change the theme to *Foundry*.
    d. Click the Foundry Slide Master thumbnail in the slide thumbnail pane and then change the colors to *Paper* and the fonts to *Flow*.
    e. Apply the *Style 2* background style.
    f. Select the *Click to edit Master title style* text, click the Home tab, turn off text shadow, turn on bold, and change to left alignment.
    g. Select the text *Second level* and then change the font color to *Orange, Accent 2, Darker 50%*.
    h. Click the Slide Master tab.
8. Select and then delete slide layouts from the third layout (*Section Header Layout*) below the new slide master to the last layout.
9. Insert headers, footers, slide numbers, and dates with the following specifications:
    a. Click the Insert tab, display the Header and Footer dialog box with the Slide tab selected, insert the date to update automatically, and insert slide numbers.
    b. Click the Notes and Handouts tab, insert the date to update automatically, insert a header that prints your first and last names, insert a footer that prints *Worldwide Enterprises*, and then click the Apply to All button.
10. Close Slide Master view.
11. Make Slide 5 active and then insert a new slide using the new Foundry Title Slide layout and then type *Worldwide Enterprises* as the title and *Preparing the Company Newsletter* as the subtitle.

12. Insert the following text in slides using the Foundry Title and Content layout:
    Slide 7   Preparing the Newsletter
    - Maintain consistent elements from issue to issue
    - Consider the following when designing the newsletter
        - Focus
        - Balance
        - White space
        - Directional flow
    Slide 8   Preparing the Newsletter
    - Choose paper size and weight
    - Determine margins
    - Specify column layout
    - Choose nameplate layout and format
    - Specify heading format
    - Determine newsletter colors
13. Select the bulleted text in Slide 8 and then change the line spacing to *1.5*.
14. Make Slide 7 active and then insert a clip art image related to newsletters.
15. Insert a transition and sound of your choosing to the presentation.
16. Run the presentation.
17. Print the presentation as a handout with four slides horizontally per page.
18. Save and then close **P-C6-A2-WEnterprises.pptx**.

Assessment

3 INSERT ACTION BUTTONS IN A GARDENING PRESENTATION

1. Open **PerennialsPres.pptx** and then save the presentation with the name **P-C6-A3-PerennialsPres**.
2. Make Slide 1 active and then insert an action button in the lower right corner of the slide that displays the next slide.
3. Display the presentation in Slide Master view, click the top slide master in the slide thumbnail pane, create an action button in the lower right corner of the slide that displays the next slide, and then close Slide Master view.
4. Make Slide 8 active and then create an action button that displays the first slide in the presentation.
5. Make Slide 2 active, click the flowers clip art image, and then create a link to the presentation **MaintenancePres.pptx** (located in the PowerPoint2010C6 folder on your storage medium). *Hint: Use the Action button in the Links group in the Insert tab.*
6. Display Slide 8 and then make the following changes:
    a. Delete text *Better Homes and Gardens®* and then type Organic Gardening®.
    b. Select *Organic Gardening®* and then create a hyperlink with the text to the website www.organicgardening.com.
7. Make sure you are connected to the Internet and then run the presentation beginning with Slide 1. Navigate through the slide show by clicking the next action button and display the connected presentation by clicking the clip art image in Slide 2. At Slide 8, click the Organic Gardening® hyperlink (if you are connected to the Internet). Scroll through the site and click a couple different hyperlinks that interest you. After viewing a few web pages in the magazine, close your web browser. When you click the action button on the last slide, the first slide displays. End the slide show by pressing the Esc key.
8. Print the presentation as a handout with four slides horizontally per page.
9. Save and then close **P-C6-A3-PerennialsPres.pptx**.

Assessment

4 CREATE AN ACTION BUTTONS PRESENTATION

1. In this chapter, you learned to insert a number of action buttons in a slide. Experiment with the other action buttons (click the Insert tab, click the Shapes button, and then point to Action Buttons) and then prepare a PowerPoint presentation with the following specifications:
   a. The first slide should contain the title of your presentation.
   b. Include one slide for each of the action buttons that includes the specific name as well as an explanation of the button.
   c. Apply a design theme of your choosing to the presentation.
2. Save the presentation and name it **P-C6-A4-ActionButtons**.
3. Print the presentation as a handout with six slides horizontally per page.
4. Close **P-C6-A4-ActionButtons.pptx**.

Visual Benchmark Demonstrate Your Proficiency

CREATE AND FORMAT A COMPANY BRANCH OFFICE PRESENTATION

1. Create the presentation shown in Figure 6.3 with the following specifications:
   a. Apply the *Concourse* design theme, the *Module* theme colors, and the *Aspect* theme fonts.
   b. Insert **WELogo.jpg** in Slide 1 and then size and position the logo as shown in the figure. Insert the Forward or Next action button in the lower right corner of the slide as shown in the figure.
   c. Display the presentation in Slide Master view and then click the top slide master thumbnail. Insert **WELogo.jpg**, change the height of the logo to 0.5 inch, and then position the logo in the lower left corner of the side as shown in Figure 6.3. Click the *Click to edit Master Title style* text, click the Home tab, remove the text shadow effect, and then change the font color to *Gold, Accent 1, Darker 25%*. Insert the Forward or Next action button in the lower right corner of the slide master as shown in the figure and then close the Slide Master view.
   d. In Slide 4, create the clustered column chart with the *Style 26* chart style applied using the following numbers:

	>$25,000	>$50,000	>$100,000
Under 25	184	167	0
25 to 44	1,228	524	660
45 to 64	519	1,689	1,402
Over 64	818	831	476

   e. In Slide 5, insert the Information action button that links to the website www.clearwater-fl.com/gov and size and position the action button as shown in the figure.
   f. In Slide 6, insert the clip art image of the hospital (the original clip art image is black and light purple), change the clip art color to *Gold, Accent color 1 Dark*, and then size and position the clip art as shown in the figure. Insert a Home action button over the Forward or Next action button.
   g. Change the line spacing in slides so your slides display similar to the slides in Figure 6.3.

2. Apply a transition and sound of your choosing to all slides in the presentation.
3. Save the presentation and name it **P-C6-VB-WEClearwater**.
4. Run the presentation.
5. Print the presentation as a handout with six slides horizontally per page.
6. Close **P-C6-VB-WEClearwater.pptx**.

Figure 6.3 Visual Benchmark

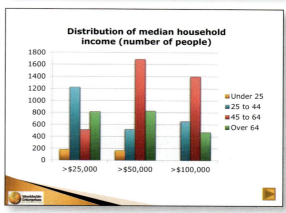

Case Study — Apply Your Skills

Part 1

You are the training manager for Anchor Corporation and one of your job responsibilities is conducting new employee orientations. You decide that a PowerPoint presentation will help you deliver information to new employees during the orientation. You know that you will be creating other PowerPoint presentations so you decide to create a template. Create a presentation template with attractive formatting that includes a design theme, theme colors, theme fonts, and include an anchor clip art image in the lower left corner of most of the slides. Apply any other formatting or design elements to increase the appeal of the presentation. Save the presentation as a template on your storage medium with the name **AnchorTemplate** and make sure it contains the file extension *.potx*. Close the template.

Part 2

You have a document with notes about information on types of employment appointments, employee performance, and compensation. Open the Word document named **AnchorNewEmployees.docx** and then use the information to prepare a presentation using the **AnchorTemplate.potx** template. Save the completed presentation with the name **P-C6-CS-AnchorEmp** and make sure it has the file extension *.pptx*. Apply a transition and sound to each slide in the presentation, print the presentation as a handout, and then close the presentation.

Part 3

Open the Word document named **AnchorGuidelines.docx** and then use the information in the document to prepare a presentation using the **AnchorTemplate.potx** template. Save the completed presentation with the name **P-C6-CS-AnchorGuidelines** and make sure it contains the file extension *.pptx*. Apply a transition and sound to each slide in the presentation, print the presentation as a handout, and then close the presentation.

Part 4

During the new employee presentation you want to refer to a chart of employee classifications, so you decide to create a link to an Excel spreadsheet. Open the **P-C6-CS-AnchorEmp.pptx** presentation and then create a new slide that contains a hyperlink to the Excel workbook named **ACClassifications.xlsx**. Run the presentation, link to the Excel chart, and then continue running the remaining slides in the presentation. Print only the new slide and then save and close **P-C6-CS-AnchorEmp.pptx**.

Part 5

The information you used to create the **P-C6-CS-AnchorGuidelines.pptx** presentation was taken from a document that is part of a new employee handbook. You decide that you want to create a link in your presentation to the Word document to show employees the additional information in the document. Create a new slide in the **P-C6-CS-AnchorGuidelines.pptx** presentation that includes an action button that links to the Word document named **ComputerGuidelines.docx**. Include other action buttons for navigating in the presentation. Run the presentation, link to the Word document, and then continue running the remaining slides in the presentation. Print only the new slide and then save and close **P-C6-CS-AnchorGuidelines.pptx**.

Microsoft PowerPoint
Applying Custom Animation and Setting Up Shows

CHAPTER 7

PERFORMANCE OBJECTIVES

Upon successful completion of Chapter 7, you will be able to:
- Apply animations
- Modify and remove animations
- Apply a build
- Animate shapes, images, SmartArt, and chart elements
- Draw motion paths
- Set up a slide show
- Set rehearse timings for slides
- Hide slides
- Create, run, edit, and print a custom show
- Insert and customize audio and video files

Animation or movement will add visual appeal and interest to your presentation when used appropriately. PowerPoint provides a number of animation effects you can apply to elements in a slide. In this chapter, you will learn how to apply animation effects as well as how to insert audio and video files to create dynamic presentations.

In some situations, you may want to prepare a self-running presentation where the presentation runs on a continuous loop. You can customize a presentation to run continuously and also rehearse the time you want each slide to remain on the screen. You can also create a custom slide show to present only specific slides in a presentation. In this chapter, you will learn how to prepare self-running presentations and how to create and edit custom slide shows. Model answers for this chapter's projects appear on the following pages.

Note: Before beginning the projects, copy to your storage medium the PowerPoint2010C7 folder from the PowerPoint2010 folder on the CD that accompanies this textbook and then make PowerPoint2010C7 the active folder.

Project 1 Apply Animation Effects to Elements in a Marketing Presentation

P-C7-P1-MarketingPres.pptx

The main title appears with Grow and Turn entrance that begins automatically when slides are displayed.

CORNERSTONE SYSTEMS
Marketing Report

The subtitle appears with Grow and Turn entrance on a click.

Department Reports
- Sales
- Public Relations
- Human Resources

Main headings have Spiral animation that begins automatically.

Each bullet is animated with Zoom entrance on a click.

Current Projects
- Corporate Publications
- Marketing Design
- Product Specifications
- Community Outreach

Clip art is animated with Pulse emphasis and appears automatically.

Services
- Project Management
- Research and Development
- Inventory Management
- Quality Control

Project 2 Apply Custom Animation Effects to Elements in Slides in an Online Learning Presentation

P-C7-P2-OLLearning.pptx

ONLINE LEARNING
A Growing Trend in Education

Clip art is animated with a motion path that begins on a click.

Instructional Delivery Methods
- **Traditional:** Classroom environment only
- **Hybrid:** Classroom and online course site
- **Internet:** Online course site only

Each bullet is animated with Split entrance on a click; a pie chart displays when its bullet is clicked.

Student Enrollment

Parts of the bar charts are animated with Dissolve entrance on a click.

Reasons for Growth

Convenient
- Accessible 24 hours a day
- No travel hassles
- No child care expenses

Addresses Multiple Learning Styles
- Audio/video clips
- Hands-on activities
- Student-controlled pace

The SmartArt shapes are animated with either Float In (Up) or Grow and Turn entrance on a click.

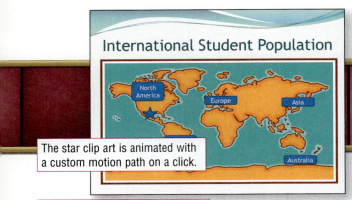

The star clip art is animated with a custom motion path on a click.

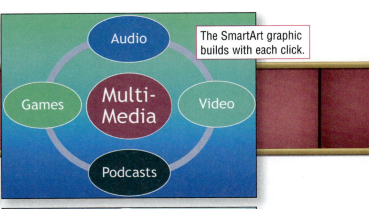

The SmartArt graphic builds with each click.

Each bullet is animated with Fly In entrance on a click and then dims.

The first object (question) spirals out after a click. Then three objects (possible answers) appear with Spinner entrance, each on a click. With a final click one of the objects grows (the correct answer).

Objects are animated with Grow and Turn entrance, two spins, and Swivel entrance—each on a click.

Project 3 Prepare a Self-Running Adventure Presentation and Create Custom Shows

P-C7-P3-AdvTours-Custom.pptx

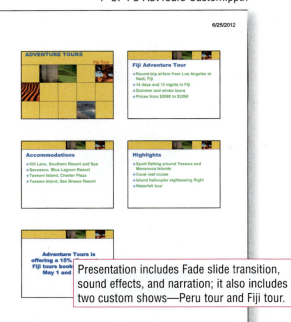

Presentation includes Fade slide transition, sound effects, and narration; it also includes two custom shows—Peru tour and Fiji tour.

Project 4 Insert Audio and Video Files in a Presentation   P-C7-P4-EcoTours.pptx

Video file inserted in slide that plays automatically. Video file deleted and then audio file inserted that plays throughout all slides as each slide advances automatically after five seconds.

Project 1 Apply Animation Effects to Elements in a Marketing Presentation

6 Parts

You will open a marketing presentation and then apply animation effects to the title slide and apply animation effects in Slide Master view to the remaining slides. You will remove some of the animation effects and then apply custom animation effects to elements in slides such as entrance and emphasis effects.

▼ Quick Steps

Apply Animation
1. Click desired item.
2. Click Animations tab.
3. Click More button in Animation group.
4. Click desired animation at drop-down gallery.

You can animate text, objects, graphics, SmartArt diagrams, charts, hyperlinks, and sound.

When you apply an animation effect to an object in a slide, an animation icon displays below the slide number in the Slides/Outline pane.

Effects Options

Preview

Applying and Removing Animation Effects

You can animate items such as text or objects in a slide to add visual interest to your presentation. Displaying items one at a time helps your audience focus on a single topic or point as you present it. PowerPoint includes a number of animations you can apply to items in a slide. These animations can be modified to fit your specific needs. You may want items to appear one right after the other or in groups. You can control the direction that the item comes from and the rate of speed. Try not to overwhelm your audience with too much animation. In general, you want them to remember the content of your presentation and not the visual effects.

To animate an item, click the desired item, click the Animations tab, click the More button at the right side of the animations in the Animation group, and then click the desired animation at the drop-down gallery. Once you have applied an animation, you can specify the animation effects with options in the Effect Options button drop-down gallery. Some of the animation effect options may include the direction from which you want the item to appear, and if you want the items such as bulleted text or SmartArt to appear as one object, all at once, or by paragraph. To apply effects to an animation, apply an animation to an item, click the Effect Options button located in the Animation group, and then click the desired effect at the drop-down gallery. (The appearance of this button changes depending on the selected effect.) Use options in the Timing group of the Animations tab to determine when the animation needs to start on a slide, the duration of the animation, the delay between animations, and the order in which animations should appear on the slide.

If you want to see the animation effects in your slide without running the presentation, click the Preview button in the Animations tab. Click this button and the animation effect you applied to the active slide displays on the slide in the Slide pane. When you apply animation effects to items in a slide, an animation icon displays below the slide number in the Slides/Outline pane.

If you add or change an animation, PowerPoint will automatically preview the animation in the slide. If you want to turn off this feature, click the Preview button arrow and then click *AutoPreview* at the drop-down list to remove the check mark.

Project 1a Applying Animations

Part 1 of 6

1. Open **MarketingPres.pptx** and save the presentation with the name **P-C7-P1-MarketingPres**.
2. Make sure Slide 1 is active and then apply animations to the title and subtitle by completing the following steps:
   a. Click anywhere in the title *CORNERSTONE SYSTEMS*.

b. Click the Animations tab.
c. Click the *Fade* animation in the Animation group. (If you hover the mouse pointer over the animation option, the slide in the Slide pane will preview the animation.)

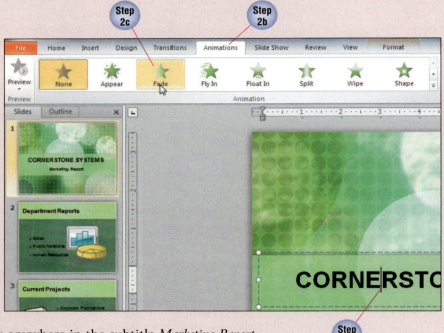

d. Click anywhere in the subtitle *Marketing Report*.
e. Click the *Fade* animation that displays in the Animation group.
f. Click the Effect Options button in the Animation group and then click *All at Once* at the drop-down gallery.
g. Click the Preview button in the Animations tab to see the animation effect in the slide in the Slide pane.

3. Apply animations to Slides 2 through 4 in Slide Master view by completing the following steps:
   a. Click the View tab and then click the Slide Master button in the Master Views group.
   b. Click the third slide master layout in the slide thumbnail pane (*Title and Content Layout*).
   c. Click the text *Click to edit Master title style*.
   d. Click the Animations tab and then click the *Fly In* animation that displays in the Animation group.
   e. Click twice on the up-pointing arrow at the right of the *Duration* option box in the Timing group. (This displays *01.00* in the option box.)

Chapter 7 ■ Applying Custom Animation and Setting Up Shows   267

f. Click the bulleted text *Click to edit Master text styles*.
g. Click the *Fly In* animation that displays in the Animation group.
h. Click twice on the up-pointing arrow at the right of the *Duration* option box in the Timing group. (This displays *01.00* in the option box.)
i. Click the Slide Master tab and then click the Close Master View button.
4. Make Slide 1 active and then run the presentation. Click the mouse button to advance items in slides and advance slides. Notice how the bulleted text in Slides 2 through 4 displays one bulleted item at a time.
5. Save **P-C7-P1-MarketingPres.pptx**.

▼ Quick Steps

Remove Animation
1. Click desired item.
2. Click Animations tab.
3. Click *None* option.

If you want to remove an animation effect from an item, click the item in the slide in the Slides pane, click the Animations tab, and then click the *None* option in the Animation group. You can also remove an animation effect from an item by clicking the item in the Slides pane, clicking the assigned animation button, and then pressing the Delete key. You will need to remove an assigned animation first if you want to apply a different animation. If you do not delete the first animation, both animations will be assigned to the item.

Project 1b Removing Animations   Part 2 of 6

1. With **P-C7-P1-MarketingPres.pptx** open, make Slide 1 active and then remove the animation from the title and subtitle by completing the following steps:
    a. Click the title *CORNERSTONE SYSTEMS*.
    b. Click the Animations tab.
    c. Click the *None* option in the Animation group.
    d. Click the subtitle *Marketing Report*.
    e. Click the *None* option in the Animation group.
2. Remove the animation effects for Slides 2 through 4 by completing the following steps:
    a. Click the View tab and then click the Slide Master button in the Master Views group.
    b. Click the third slide master layout in the slide thumbnail pane (*Title and Content Layout*).
    c. Click in the text *Click to edit Master title style*.
    d. Click the Animations tab and then click the *None* option in the Animation group.
    e. Click in the text *Click to edit Master text styles*.
    f. Click the *None* option in the Animation group.
    g. Click the Slide Master tab and then click the Close Master View button.
3. Make Slide 1 active and then run the presentation.
4. Save **P-C7-P1-MarketingPres.pptx**.

Applying Animation Effects

The Add Animation button in the Advanced Animation group in the Animations tab provides four types of animation effects you can apply to an item. You can apply an effect as an item enters the slide and also as an item exits the slide. You can apply emphasis to an item and you can apply a motion path to an item that will cause it to move in a specific pattern or even off the slide.

To apply an entrance effect to an item, click the Add Animation button in the Advanced Animation group and then click the desired animation effect in the *Entrance* section of the drop-down gallery. Customize the entrance effect by clicking the Effect Options button in the Animation group and then clicking the desired entrance effect. Additional entrance effects are available at the Add Entrance Effect dialog box. Display this dialog box by clicking the Add Animation button and then clicking *More Entrance Effects* at the drop-down gallery. Complete similar steps to apply an emphasis effect and an exit effect. Display additional emphasis effects by clicking the Add Animation button and then clicking *More Emphasis Effects* and display additional exit effects by clicking the Add Animation button and then clicking *More Exit Effects*.

Applying Animations with Animation Painter

If you apply an animation or animations to items in a slide and want to apply the same animation in more than one location in a slide or slides, use the Animation Painter. To use the Animation Painter, apply the desired animation to an item, position the insertion point anywhere in the animated item, and then double-click the Animation Painter button in the Advanced Animation group in the Animations tab. Using the mouse, select or click on additional items to which you want the animation applied. After applying the animation in the desired locations, click the Animation Painter button to deactivate it. If you need to apply animation in only one other location, click the Animation Painter button once. The first time you click an item, the animation is applied and the Animation Painter is deactivated.

Quick Steps

Apply Animation Effect
1. Click desired item.
2. Click Animations tab.
3. Click Add Animation button.
4. Click desired animation effect at drop-down gallery.

Apply Effects with Animation Painter
1. Click item, then apply desired animation effect.
2. Click item with animation effect.
3. Double-click Animation Painter button.
4. Click each item to which you want animation effect applied.
5. Click Animation Painter button to deactivate it.

Add Animation

Animation Painter

Project 1c **Applying Animation Effects**   Part 3 of 6

1. With **P-C7-P1-MarktingPres.pptx** open, apply an animation effect to the title and subtitle in Slide 1 by completing the following steps:
   a. Make Slide 1 active.
   b. Click the title CORNERSTONE SYSTEMS.
   c. Click the Animations tab.
   d. Click the Add Animation button in the Advanced Animation group and then click the *Wipe* animation in the *Entrance* section of the drop-down gallery.

    e. Click the Effect Options button in the Animation group and then click *From Top* at the drop-down gallery.
    f. Click the subtitle *Marketing Report*.
    g. Click the Add Animation button and then click the *Zoom* animation in the *Entrance* section.
2. Apply an animation effect to the title in Slides 2 through 4 by completing the following steps:
    a. Click the View tab and then click the Slide Master button in the Master Views group.
    b. Click the third slide master layout in the slide thumbnail pane (*Title and Content Layout*).
    c. Click in the text *Click to edit Master title style*.
    d. Click the Animations tab, click the Add Animation button in the Advanced Animation group, and then click the *Spin* animation in the *Emphasis* section.
    e. Click the Slide Master tab and then click the Close Master View button.
3. Apply an animation effect to the bulleted text in Slides 2 through 4 using the Animation Painter by completing the following steps:
    a. Make Slide 2 active.
    b. Click anywhere in the bulleted text to make the placeholder active.
    c. Click the Animations tab, click the Add Animation button, and then click the *Split* animation in the *Entrance* section.
    d. Click anywhere in the bulleted text.
    e. Double-click the Animation Painter button in the Advanced Animation group.
    f. Click the Next Slide button to display Slide 3.
    g. Click anywhere in the bulleted text. (The mouse pointer displays as an arrow with a paintbrush attached. The animations are applied to all four bulleted items.)
    h. Make Slide 4 active and then click anywhere in the bulleted text.
    i. Click the Animation Painter button to deactivate it.
4. Click the Preview button to view the animation effects.
5. Make Slide 1 active and then run the presentation by clicking the Slide Show button located toward the bottom of the task pane. Click the mouse button to begin animation effects and to advance slides.
6. Save **P-C7-P1-MarketingPres.pptx**.

Modifying Animation Effects

Start

When you apply an animation effect to an item, you can use options in the Timing group to modify the animation effect. Use the *Start* option drop-down list to specify when you want the item inserted in the slide. Generally, items display in a slide when you click the mouse button. Click the *Start* option down-pointing arrow and then click *With Previous* or *With Next* at the drop-down list to make the item appear on the slide with the previous item or the next item.

Use the *Duration* option to specify the length of an animation. For example, click the up-pointing arrow to the right of the *Duration* option box to increase the length of time the animation takes to display on the slide and click the down-pointing arrow to decrease the length of time the animation takes to display. You can also select the current time in the *Duration* option box and then type the desired time.

Duration

Delay

The *Delay* option allows you to specify when to play an animation after a certain number of seconds. Click the up-pointing arrow to increase the amount of time between when an animation displays and the item that displays before it and click the down-pointing arrow to decrease the amount of time between when an animation displays after the previous animation. You can also select the current time in the *Delay* option box and then type the desired time.

Move Earlier

Move Later

Reordering Items

When you apply an animation effect to an item, the item displays with an assigned animation number in the Slides pane. This number indicates the order in which items will appear in the slide. When more than one item displays in the slide, you can change the order with options in the *Reorder Animation* section of the Timing group in the Animations tab. Click the Move Earlier button to move an item before other items or click the Move Later button to move an item after other items.

▼ **Quick Steps**
Reorder Animation Item
1. Click item in slide.
2. Click Move Earlier or Move Later button.

 **Removing, Modifying, and Reordering Animation Effects**   Part 4 of 6

1. With **P-C7-P1-MarketingPres.pptx** open, make Slide 1 active.
2. Modify the start setting for the slide title animation effect by completing the following steps:
   a. Click anywhere in the title to activate the placeholder.
   b. Click the down-pointing arrow at the right of the *Start* option in the Timing group.
   c. Click *With Previous* at the drop-down list. (At this setting, the title animation effect will begin as soon as the slide displays without you having to click the mouse button. Notice that the number 1 located to the left of the item changed to a zero.)
3. Change the animation effect applied to the subtitle and modify the animation effect by completing the following steps:
   a. Click anywhere in the subtitle *Marketing Report* in the slide.
   b. Click the More button located to the right of the thumbnails in the Animation group and then click the *None* option in the drop-down gallery.
   c. Click the Add Animation button in the Advanced Animation group and then click the *Grow/Shrink* animation in the *Emphasis* section.
   d. Click the down-pointing arrow at the right side of the *Start* option and then click *With Previous* at the drop-down list.
   e. Click four times on the down-pointing arrow at the right side of the *Duration* option. (This displays *01.00* in the option box.)

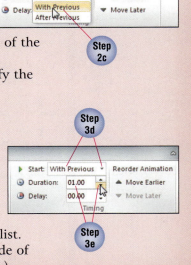

Chapter 7 ■ Applying Custom Animation and Setting Up Shows   271

4. Remove animations from slide titles in Slide Master view by completing the following steps:
   a. Click the View tab and then click the Slide Master button in the Master Views group.
   b. Click the third slide master layout in the slide thumbnail pane (*Title and Content Layout*).
   c. Click in the text *Click to edit Master title style*.
   d. Click the Animations tab.
   e. Click the More button located to the right of the thumbnails in the Animation group and then click the *None* option in the Animation group.
   f. Click the Slide Master tab and then click the Close Master View button.
5. Remove animations from bulleted text in Slides 2 through 4 by completing the following steps:
   a. Make Slide 2 active.
   b. Click in the bulleted text.
   c. Click the *None* option in the Animation group in the Animations tab.
   d. Make Slide 3 active, click in the bulleted text, and then click the *None* option in the Animation group.
   e. Make Slide 4 active, click in the bulleted text, and then click the *None* option in the Animation group.
6. Make Slide 2 active and then apply and customize animation effects by completing the following steps:
   a. Click the title *Department Reports*.
   b. Click the Add Animation button in the Advanced Animation group and then click the *More Entrance Effects* option at the drop-down gallery.
   c. At the Add Entrance Effect dialog box, scroll down the list box and then click *Spiral In* in the *Exciting* section.
   d. Click OK to close the dialog box.

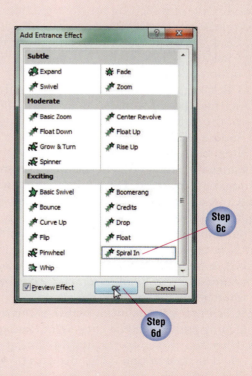

e. Click the bulleted text.
   f. Click the Add Animation button and then click the *Zoom* animation in the *Entrance* section.
   g. Click the clip art image.
   h. Click the Add Animation button and then click the *Zoom* animation in the *Entrance* section.
7. Click the Preview button located at the left side of the Animations tab to view the animation effects.
8. After viewing the animation effects, you decide that you want the clip art to animate before the bulleted text and you want the animation effects to begin with the previous animation (instead of with a mouse click). With Slide 2 active, complete the following steps:
   a. Click the clip art image. (The number 5 will display in the assigned animation button located to the left of the clip art placeholder because the clip art is the fifth item to enter the slide.)
   b. Click the Move Earlier button located in the *Reorder Animation* section of the Timing group. (This displays the number 2 in the assigned animation button because you moved the clip art animation before the three bulleted items.)
   c. Click the down-pointing arrow at the right side of the *Start* option in the Timing group and then click *With Previous* at the drop-down list.
   d. Click the title *Department Reports*.
   e. Click the down-pointing arrow at the right side of the *Start* option in the Timing group and then click *With Previous* at the drop-down list.
9. Make Slide 3 active and then apply the same animation effects you applied in Slide 2. (Do this by completing steps similar to those in Steps 6a through 6h and Steps 8a through 8e.)
10. Make Slide 4 active and then apply the same animation effects you applied to Slide 2. (Do this by completing steps similar to those in Steps 6a through 6e and Steps 8d through 8e.)
11. Make Slide 1 active and then run the presentation. After running the presentation, make any changes or modifications to animation effects.
12. Save **P-C7-P1-MarketingPres.pptx**.

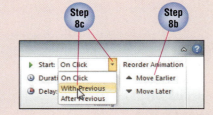

Customizing Animation Effects at the Animation Pane

You can use the Animation Pane to customize and modify animation effects in a presentation. Display the Animation Pane, shown in Figure 7.1, by clicking the Animation Pane button in the Advanced Animation group in the Animations tab. When you apply an animation to an item, the item name or description displays in the *Animation Pane* list box. Hover the mouse pointer over an item and a description of the animation effect applied to the item displays in a box below the item. If you click the down-pointing arrow at the right side of an item in the list box, a drop-down list displays with options for modifying or customizing the animation effect. For example, you can use options at the drop-down list to specify when you want the item inserted in the slide, the delay and duration of the animation, and specify that you want the animation effect removed.

When you apply an effect to an item, the item name and/or description displays in the *Animation Pane* list box preceded by a number. This number indicates the order in which items will appear in the slide. When more than one item displays in the list box, you can change the order of an item by clicking the item in the list box and then clicking the Up Re-Order button or the Down Re-Order button located toward the bottom of the Animation Pane.

Animation Pane

Up Re-Order

Down Re-Order

Figure 7.1 Animation Pane

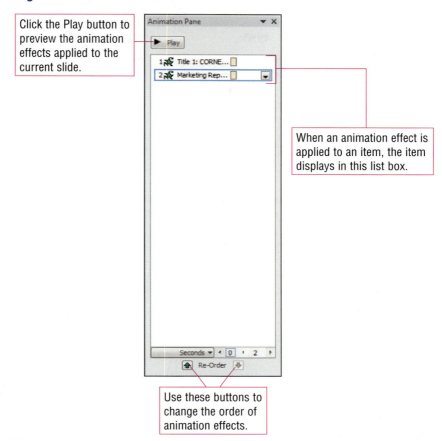

Click the Play button to preview the animation effects applied to the current slide.

When an animation effect is applied to an item, the item displays in this list box.

Use these buttons to change the order of animation effects.

▼ **Quick Steps**

Reorder Animation Items
1. Click item in *Animation Pane* list box.
2. Click Up Re-Order button or Down Re-Order button.

Remove Animation Effect
1. Click item in *Animation Pane* list box.
2. Click down-pointing arrow.
3. Click *Remove*.

When you apply an animation effect or effects to a slide, you can play the animations in the Animation Pane by clicking the Play button at the top of the pane. The animation effects display in the slide in the Slide pane and a time indicator displays along the bottom of the Animation Pane with a vertical line indicating the progression of time (in seconds).

Project 1e Removing, Modifying, and Reordering Animation Effects in the Animation Pane

Part 5 of 6

1. With **P-C7-P1-MarketingPres.pptx** open, make Slide 1 active.
2. Click in the title *CORNERSTONE SYSTEMS*, click the Animations tab, and then click the *None* option in the Animation group.
3. With the title placeholder selected, click the Add Animation button in the Advanced Animation group and then click the *Grow & Turn* animation in the *Entrance* section.
4. Click twice on the down-pointing arrow at the right side of the *Duration* option. (This displays *00.50* in the option box.)
5. Click in the subtitle *Marketing Report*, click the More button located to the right of the animation thumbnails in the Animation group, and then click the *None* option.

6. With the subtitle placeholder selected, click the Add Animation button in the Advanced Animation group and then click the *Grow & Turn* animation in the *Entrance* section.
7. Click twice on the down-pointing arrow at the right side of the *Duration* option. (This displays *00.50* in the option box.)
8. Modify the start setting for the slide title animation effect in the Animation Pane by completing the following steps:

    a. Click the Animation Pane button located in the Advanced Animation group in the Animations tab. (This displays the Animation Pane at the right side of the screen.)

    b. Click the Title 1 item that displays in the Animation Pane list box.

    c. Click the down-pointing arrow at the right side of the item and then click *Start With Previous* at the drop-down list.

    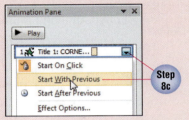

9. Remove animations from slides using the *Animation Pane* by completing the following steps:

    a. Make Slide 2 active.

    b. Click the Picture 3 item in the *Animation Pane* list box.

    c. Click the down-pointing arrow at the right side of the item and then click *Remove* at the drop-down list.

    d. Click the clip art image in the Slides pane, click the Add Animation button in the Advanced Animation group, and then click the *Pulse* animation in the *Emphasis* section.

    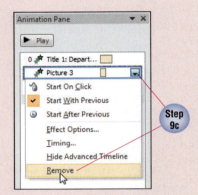

10. Make Slide 3 active and then complete steps similar to those in Steps 9b through 9d to remove the animation effect from the clip art image and add the *Pulse* emphasis effect.
11. Click the Play button located toward the top of the Animation Pane to view the animation effects.

    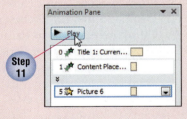

12. After viewing the animation effects, you decide that you want the clip art image to animate before the title and bulleted text and you want the animation effect to begin with the previous animation. With Slide 3 active, complete the following steps:

    a. Click the Picture 6 item in the *Animation Pane* list box.

    b. Click twice on the Up Re-Order button located at the bottom of the task pane. (This moves the Picture 6 item above the Title 1 and the content placeholder items.)

    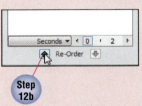

    c. Click the down-pointing arrow at the right side of the Picture 3 item and then click *Start With Previous* at the drop-down list.

13. Reorder animation effects in Slide 2 to match the changes made to Slide 3.
14. Make Slide 1 active and then run the presentation. After running the presentation, make any changes or modifications to animation effects.
15. Close the Animation Pane.
16. Save **P-C7-P1-MarketingPres.pptx**.

Applying a Build

You can group text (in a bulleted text placeholder) at the Effect Options dialog box by first, second, third, fourth, or fifth levels.

In Project 1a, you applied a build to bulleted text in a slide. A ***build*** displays important points on a slide one point at a time, keeping the audience's attention focused on the current point. You can further customize a build by causing a previous point to dim when the next point displays. To customize a build, click the Animation Pane button to display the Animation Pane, click the desired bulleted item in the Animation Pane list box, click the down-pointing arrow at the right side of the item, and then click *Effect Options* at the drop-down list. At the Effect Options dialog box with the Effect tab selected, choose a color option with the *After animation* option.

Project 1f Applying a Build Animation   Part 6 of 6

1. With **P-C7-P1-MarketingPres.pptx** open, make Slide 2 active and then apply a build to the bulleted text by completing the following steps:
   a. Click in the bulleted text.
   b. Open the Animation Pane by clicking the Animation Pane button in the Advanced Animation group in the Animations tab.
   c. Click the down-pointing arrow at the right side of the Content Placeholder item in the Animation Pane list box and then click *Effect Options* at the drop-down list.
   d. At the Zoom dialog box, make sure the Effect tab is selected, click the down-pointing arrow at the right side of the *After animation* option, and then click the light green color (fifth color from the left).
   e. Click OK to close the dialog box.
2. Click in the bulleted text in the slide.
3. Double-click the Animation Painter button.
4. Display Slide 3 and click anywhere in the bulleted text.
5. Display Slide 4 and click anywhere in the bulleted text.
6. Click the Animation Painter button to deactivate it.
7. Close the Animation Pane.
8. Make Slide 1 active and then run the presentation. After running the presentation, make any necessary changes or modifications to animation effects.
9. Save and then close **P-C7-P1-MarketingPres.pptx**.

Project 2 Apply Custom Animation Effects to Elements in Slides in an Online Learning Presentation   6 Parts

You will open an online learning presentation and then apply animation effects to shapes, a clip art image, elements in SmartArt graphics, and elements in a chart. You will also draw a motion path in a slide.

Animating Shapes and Images

You can animate individual shapes or images such as clip art images in a slide in the same manner as animating a title or text content placeholder. You can select more than one shape and then apply the same animation effect to the shapes. To select more than one shape, click the first shape, hold down the Shift key, and then click any additional shapes.

Project 2a Animating Shapes and a Clip Art Image   Part 1 of 6

1. Open **OLLearning.pptx** and then save the presentation with Save As and name it **P-C7-P2-OLLearning**.
2. Make Slide 8 active (this slide contains one large object with three smaller objects hidden behind it) and then animate objects and apply exit effects by completing the following steps:
   a. Click the Animations tab and then click the Animation Pane button in the Advanced Animation group. (This displays the Animation Pane at the right side of the screen.)
   b. Click the large object in the slide.
   c. Click the Add Animation button in the Advanced Animation group.
   d. Click the *More Exit Effects* option at the drop-down gallery.
   e. At the Add Exit Effect dialog box, click the *Spiral Out* option in the *Exciting* section. (You will need to scroll down the list to display this option.) Watch the animation effect in the slide and then click OK.

   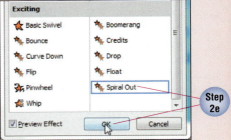
   Step 2e

   f. Click the large object to select it and then drag it down the slide to display a portion of the three objects behind.
   g. Click the small object at the left, click the Add Animation button, and then click the *More Entrance Effects* option at the drop-down gallery.
   h. At the Add Entrance Effect dialog box, click *Spinner* in the *Moderate* section, and then click OK.
   i. Select the middle object, hold down the Shift key, and then click the object at the right. (This selects both objects.)

   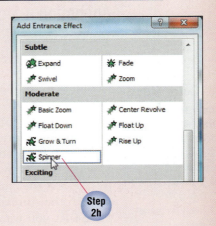
   Step 2h

   j. Click the Add Animation button and then click the *More Entrance Effects* option at the drop-down gallery.
   k. At the Add Entrance Effect dialog box, click *Spinner* in the *Moderate* section and then click OK. (Notice that the two objects are numbered *3* in the Animation Pane list box and are set to enter the slide at the same time. You will change this in the next step.)
   l. Click the small object at the right, click the down-pointing arrow at the right of the *Start* option in the Timing group, and then click *On Click* at the drop-down list.
   m. Apply emphasis to the middle object by clicking the middle object, clicking the Add Animation button, and then clicking the *Grow/Shrink* option in the *Emphasis* section of the drop-down gallery.
   n. Click the large object to select it and then reposition it over the three smaller objects.
   o. Click the Preview button to play the animation effects in the slide.

3. Make Slide 9 active and apply and modify animation effects and change animation order by completing the following steps:
   a. Click in the text *Online learning continues to evolve!* (this selects the text box), click the Add Animation button, and then click *Grow & Turn* in the *Entrance* section.
   b. Click in the text *Stay tuned!* (this selects the text box), click the Add Animation button, and then click the *Swivel* option in the *Entrance* section.
   c. Click the clip art image to select it.
   d. Click the Add Animation button and then click the *Spin* animation in the *Emphasis* section.
   e. Click the Effect Options button in the Animation group and then click *Two Spins* at the drop-down gallery.
   f. Click the down-pointing arrow at the right side of the *Duration* option until *01.00* displays.
   g. Click once on the Up Re-Order button (located toward the bottom of the Animation Pane). This moves the clip art image item in the list box above the *Stay tuned!* text box item.
   h. Click the Preview button to play the animation effects in the slide.
4. Save **P-C7-P2-OLLearning.pptx**.

Animating a SmartArt Graphic

You can apply animation effects to a SmartArt graphic and specify if you want the entire SmartArt graphic to display at once or if you want the individual elements in the SmartArt graphic to display one at a time. Specify a sequence for displaying elements in a SmartArt graphic with the Effect Options button in the Animation group.

When you apply an animation effect to a SmartArt graphic, you can apply animations to individual elements in the graphic. To do this, click the Effect Options button and then click the *One by One* option at the drop-down list. Display the Animation Pane and then expand the list of SmartArt graphic objects by clicking the small double arrows that display in a gray shaded box below the item in the Animation Pane list box. Click the individual item in the Animation Pane that you want to apply a different animation effect to and then click the desired animation in the Animation group.

▼ **Quick Steps**

Animate SmartArt Graphic
1. Click SmartArt graphic.
2. Apply animation effect.
3. Click Effect Options button.
4. Specify the desired sequence.

Project 2b Animating SmartArt   Part 2 of 6

1. With **P-C7-P2-OLLearning.pptx** open, make Slide 4 active and then animate objects in the SmartArt graphic by completing the following steps:
   a. Click the shape in the SmartArt graphic containing the word *Convenient*. (Make sure white sizing handles display only around the shape.)
   b. Make sure the Animations tab is selected and then click the *Float In* animation in the Animation group.

c. Click the Effect Options button in the Animation group and then click *One by One* at the drop-down gallery. (This will allow you to apply different effects to the objects in the SmartArt graphic.)
   d. Make sure the Animation Pane displays.
   e. Expand the list of SmartArt graphic objects in the Animation Pane list box by clicking the small double arrows that display in a gray shaded box below the content placeholder item. (This expands the list to display four items.)
   f. Click the second item in the Animation Pane list box (the item that begins with the number *2*).
   g. Click the More button at the right side of the animations in the Animation group and then click the *Grow & Turn* animation in the *Entrance* section.
   h. Click the fourth item in the Animation Pane list box (the item that begins with the number *4*).
   i. Click the More button at the right side of the animations in the Animation group and then click the *Grow & Turn* animation in the *Entrance* section.
2. Click the Play button located toward the top of the Animation Pane to view the animation effects applied to the SmartArt graphic objects.
3. Make Slide 6 active and then apply animation effects by completing the following steps:
   a. Click the shape in the SmartArt graphic containing the text *Multi-Media*. (Make sure white sizing handles display only around the shape.)
   b. Click the Add Animation button and then click the *More Entrance Effects* option.
   c. At the Add Entrance Effect dialog box, click the *Circle* option in the *Basic* section.
   d. Click OK to close the dialog box.
   e. Click the Effect Options button and then click *Out* in the *Direction* section of the drop-down list.
   f. Click the Effect Options button and then click *One by One* in the *Sequence* section of the drop-down list.
   g. Click the down-pointing arrow at the right of the *Duration* option until *00.50* displays.
4. Click the Play button located toward the top of the Animation Pane to view the animation effects applied to the SmartArt graphic objects.
5. Save **P-C7-P2-OLLearning.pptx**.

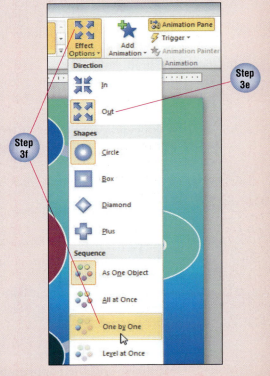

Animating a Chart

Like a SmartArt graphic, you can animate a chart or elements in a chart. Displaying data in a chart may have a more dramatic effect if the chart is animated. Bringing in one element at a time also allows you to discuss each piece of the data as it displays. Specify how you want the chart animated in the slide

and how you want chart elements grouped. For example, you can group chart elements on one object or by series or category. Apply animation to elements in a chart in a manner similar to animating elements in a SmartArt graphic.

Project 2c Animating Elements in a Chart Part 3 of 6

1. With **P-C7-P2-OLLearning.pptx** open, make Slide 3 active and then animate chart elements by completing the following steps:
   a. Click in the chart placeholder to select the chart. (Make sure you do not have a chart element selected.)
   b. Click the Add Animation button and then click the *More Entrance Effects* option.
   c. At the Add Entrance Effect dialog box, click the *Dissolve In* option in the *Basic* section.
   d. Click OK to close the dialog box.
   e. Make sure the Animation Pane displays and then click the down-pointing arrow at the right side of the Content Placeholder item in the list box.
   f. At the drop-down list that displays, click *Effect Options*.
   g. At the Dissolve In dialog box, click the down-pointing arrow at the right side of the *Sound* option, scroll down the drop-down list, and then click the *Click* option.
   h. Click the Timing tab.
   i. Click the down-pointing arrow at the right side of the *Duration* option and then click *1 seconds (Fast)* at the drop-down list.
   j. Click the Chart Animation tab.
   k. Click the down-pointing arrow at the right side of the *Group chart* option and then click *By Category* at the drop-down list.

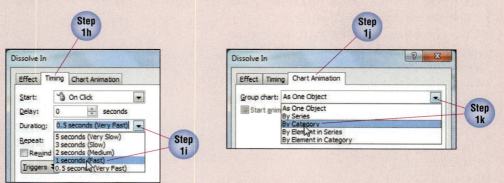

   l. Click OK to close the dialog box.
2. Make Slide 7 active and then apply a build animation effect to the bulleted text by completing the following steps:
   a. Click in the bulleted text.
   b. Click the *Fly In* animation in the Animation group in the Animations tab.
   c. Click the Effect Options button and then click *From Right* at the drop-down gallery.
   d. Make sure the Animation Pane displays, click the down-pointing arrow at the right side of the Content Placeholder item in the list box, and then click *Effect Options* at the drop-down list.

e. At the Fly In dialog box, make sure the Effect tab is selected, click the down-pointing arrow at the right side of the *After animation* option, and then click the yellow color (second from the right).

f. Click OK to close the dialog box.

3. Save **P-C7-P2-OLLearning.pptx**.

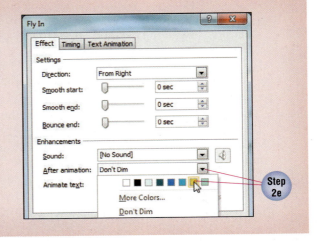

Creating a Motion Path

With options in the *Motion Paths* section of the Add Animation button drop-down gallery, you can specify a motion path. A **motion path** is a path you create for an object that specifies the movements of the object when you run the presentation. Click the Add Animation button in the Advanced Animation group, and a gallery of options for drawing a motion path in a specific direction can be found in the *Motion Paths* section. For example, if you want an item to move left in a line when running the presentation, click the Add Animation button in the Advanced Animation group and then click the *Lines* option in the *Motion Paths* section of the drop-down gallery. Click the Effect Options button in the Animation group and then click *Left* at the drop-down gallery. You can also apply a motion path by clicking the Add Animation button, clicking *More Motion Paths* at the drop-down gallery, and then clicking the desired motion path at the Add Motion Path dialog box.

To draw your own motion path, select the object in the slide you want to move in the slide, click the Add Animation button, and then click the *Custom Path* option in the *Motion Paths* section of the drop-down gallery. Using the mouse, drag in the slide to create the path. When the path is completed, double-click the mouse button.

▼ Quick Steps

Insert Motion Path
1. Click desired item in slide.
2. Click Animations tab.
3. Click Add Animation button.
4. Click desired path in *Motion Path* section.

Draw Motion Path
1. Click desired item in slide.
2. Click Animations tab.
3. Click Add Animation button.
4. Click *Custom Path* in *Motion Path* section.
5. Drag in slide to create path.
6. Double-click mouse button.

Project 2d Drawing a Motion Path   Part 4 of 6

1. With **P-C7-P2-OLLearning.pptx** open, make Slide 1 active and then apply a motion path to the clip art image by completing the following steps:
   a. Click the clip art image.
   b. Click the Add Animation button and then click the *More Motion Paths* option at the drop-down gallery.

Chapter 7 ■ Applying Custom Animation and Setting Up Shows   281

c. At the Add Motion Path dialog box, scroll down the list box and then click the *Spiral Right* option in the *Lines & Curves* section.
d. Click OK to close the dialog box.
e. Notice that a spiral line object displays in the slide and the object is selected. Using the mouse, drag the spiral line object so it is positioned in the middle of the clip art image.
2. Make Slide 5 active and then animate the star on the map by completing the following steps:
   a. Click the star object in the slide (located below the heading *North America*).

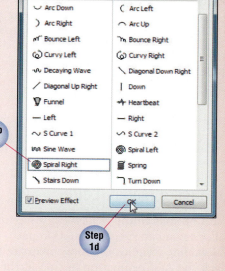

   b. Click the Add Animation button, scroll down the drop-down gallery, and then click the *Custom Path* option in the *Motion Paths* section.
   c. Position the mouse pointer (displays as crosshairs) on the star, hold down the left mouse button, drag a path through each of the five locations on the map ending back in the original location, and then double-click the left mouse button.
3. Run the presentation and click the mouse to advance slides and elements on slides as needed.
4. Save **P-C7-P2-OLLearning.pptx**.

Applying a Trigger

▼ **Quick Steps**

Apply a Trigger
1. Click desired object in slide.
2. Click Animations tab.
3. Click Trigger button, point to *On Click of,* and then click trigger object.

Trigger

With the Trigger button in the Advanced Animation group, you can make an animation effect occur during a slide show by clicking an item on the slide. For example, you can apply a trigger to a specific bulleted item in a presentation. A *trigger* creates a link between two items and triggers another item such as a picture or chart that provides additional information about the bulleted item. When running the presentation, you hover the mouse over the item containing the trigger until the mouse pointer displays as a hand and then you click the mouse button. This displays the trigger item.

The advantage to applying a trigger to an item is that you control whether or not the item displays when running the presentation. For example, suppose you created a presentation with product sales information and you wanted to provide additional specific sales data to one group you will be presenting to but not another group. When presenting to the group that you want to share the additional

sales data, click the item to trigger the display of the data. When presenting to the other group, you would not click the item and the sales data would remain hidden.

To insert a trigger, apply an animation effect to both items, display the Animation Pane, and then click in the list box the item to which you want to apply the trigger. Click the Trigger button in the Advanced Animation group, point to *On Click of*, and then click the item you want triggered at the side menu.

Project 2e Inserting Triggers   Part 5 of 6

1. With **P-C7-P2-OLLearning.pptx** open, make Slide 2 active.
2. Apply animation effects to the text and charts by completing the following steps:
   a. Click anywhere in the bulleted text.
   b. Click the Animations tab.
   c. Click the *Split* animation in the Animation group.
   d. Select the pie chart at the left. (To do this, click outside the chart at the left side. Make sure the chart is selected and not an individual chart element.)
   e. Click the *Split* animation in the Animation group.
   f. Select the middle pie chart and then click the *Split* animation. (Make sure you select the chart and not a chart element.)
   g. Select the pie chart at the right and then click the *Split* animation. (Make sure you select the chart and not a chart element.)
3. Make sure the Animation Pane displays.
4. Apply a trigger to the first bulleted item that, when clicked, will display the chart at the left by completing the following steps:
   a. Click the *Chart 3* item in the list box in the Animation Pane.
   b. Click the Trigger button in the Advanced Animation group, point to *On Click of*, and then click *Content Placeholder 2* at the side menu.
   c. Click the *Chart 4* item in the list box in the Animation Pane, click the Trigger button, point to *On Click of*, and then click *Content Placeholder 2* at the side menu.
   d. Click the *Chart 5* item in the list box in the Animation Pane, click the Trigger button, point to *On Click of*, and then click *Content Placeholder 2* at the side menu.
5. Close the Animation Pane.
6. Run the presentation by completing the following steps:
   a. Run the presentation from the beginning and when you get to Slide 2, click the mouse button until the first bulleted item displays (the item that begins with *Traditional*).
   b. Hover your mouse over the bulleted text until the pointer turns into a hand and then click the left mouse button. (This displays the first chart.)

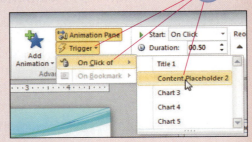

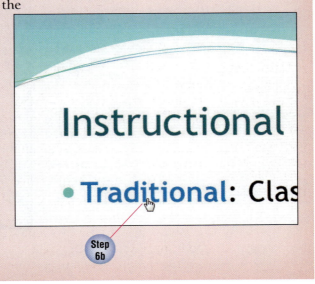

Chapter 7 ■ Applying Custom Animation and Setting Up Shows

c. Position the mouse pointer anywhere in the white background of the slide and then click the left mouse button to display the second bulleted item (the item that begins with *Hybrid*).
d. Hover your mouse over the text in the second bulleted item until the pointer turns into a hand and then click the left mouse button. (This displays the middle chart.)
e. Position the mouse pointer anywhere in the white background of the slide and then click the left mouse button to display the third bulleted item (the item that begins with *Internet*).
f. Hover your mouse over the text in the third bulleted item until the pointer turns into a hand and then click the left mouse button. (This displays the third chart.)
g. Continue running the remaining slides in the presentation.
7. Save **P-C7-P2-OLLearning.pptx**.
8. Print the presentation as a handout with all nine slides printed horizontally on the page.

Setting Up a Slide Show

Set Up Slide Show

You can control how the presentation displays with options at the Set Up Show dialog box shown in Figure 7.2. With options at this dialog box, you can set slide presentation options, specify how you want slides to advance, and set screen resolution. Display the Set Up Show dialog box by clicking the Slide Show tab and then clicking the Set Up Slide Show button in the Set Up group.

▼ **Quick Steps**

Run Presentation without Animation
1. Click Slide Show tab.
2. Click Set Up Slide Show button.
3. Click *Show without animation*.
4. Click OK.

Running a Presentation without Animation

If a presentation contains numerous animation effects, you can choose to run the presentation without the animations. To do this, display the Set Up Show dialog box, click the *Show without animation* check box to insert a check mark, and then click OK. Changes you make to the Set Up Show dialog box are saved with the presentation.

Figure 7.2 Set Up Show Dialog Box

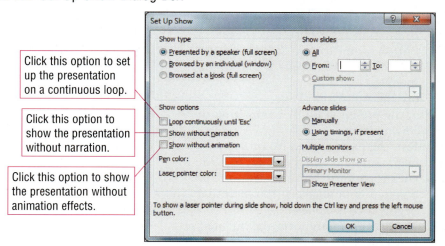

Project 2f Running a Presentation without Animation   Part 6 of 6

1. With **P-C7-P2-OLLearning.pptx** open, specify that you want to run the presentation without animation by completing the following steps:
   a. Click the Slide Show tab.
   b. Click the Set Up Slide Show button in the Set Up group.
   c. At the Set Up Show dialog box, click the *Show without animation* check box to insert a check mark.
   d. Click OK to close the dialog box.
2. Run the presentation and notice that the animation effects do not play.
3. Specify that you want the presentation to run with animations by completing the following steps:
   a. Click the Set Up Slide Show button in the Slide Show tab.
   b. At the Set Up Show dialog box, click the *Show without animation* check box to remove the check mark and then click OK.
4. Save and then close **P-C7-P2-OLLearning.pptx**.

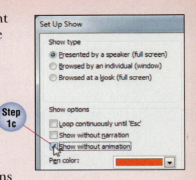
Step 1c

Project 3 Prepare a Self-Running Adventure Presentation and Create Custom Shows   5 Parts

You will open a travel tour presentation and then customize it to be a self-running presentation set on a continuous loop. You will also hide slides and create and edit custom shows.

Setting Up a Presentation to Loop Continuously

In Chapter 1, you learned how to set automatic times for advancing slides. To advance a slide automatically, insert a check mark in the *After* check box in the Advance Slide section of the Timing group in the Transitions tab and then insert the desired number of seconds in the time box. If you want to have the ability to advance a slide more quickly than the time applied, leave the check mark in the *On Mouse Click* option. With this option active, you can let the slide advance the specified number of seconds or you can click the left mouse button to advance the slide sooner. Remove the check mark from the *On Mouse Click* button if you do not want to advance slides with the mouse.

In some situations, such as at a trade show or convention, you may want to prepare a self-running presentation. A self-running presentation is set up on a continuous loop and does not require someone to run the presentation. To design a self-running presentation, display the Set Up Show dialog box and then insert a check mark in the *Loop continuously until 'Esc'* option. With this option active, the presentation will continue running until you press the Esc key.

▼ **Quick Steps**

Loop Presentation Continuously
1. Click Slide Show tab.
2. Click Set Up Slide Show button.
3. Click *Loop continuously until 'Esc'*.
4. Click OK.

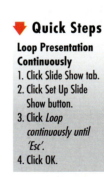

Use a self-running presentation to communicate information without a presenter.

Project 3a — Preparing a Self-Running Presentation — Part 1 of 5

1. Open **AdvTours.pptx** and then save the presentation with the name **P-C7-P3-AdvTours**.
2. Insert slides by completing the following steps:
   a. Click below the last slide thumbnail in the Slides/Outline pane.
   b. Make sure the Home tab is selected, click the New Slide button arrow, and then click *Reuse Slides* at the drop-down list.
   c. At the Reuse Slides task pane, click the Browse button and then click *Browse File*.
   d. At the Browse dialog box, navigate to the PowerPoint2010C7 folder on your storage medium and then double-click **PeruTour.pptx**.
   e. Click each slide in the Reuse Slides task pane in the order in which they display beginning with the top slide.
   f. Close the Reuse Slides task pane.
3. Add transition and sound effects and specify a time for automatically advancing slides by completing the following steps:
   a. Click the Transitions tab.
   b. Click in the *After* check box in the Timing group to insert a check mark.
   c. Click the up-pointing arrow at the right side of the *after* box until *00:05.00* displays.
   d. Click the *On Mouse Click* check box to remove the check mark.
   e. Click the *Fade* slide transition in the Transition to This Slide group.
   f. Click the down-pointing arrow at the right side of the *Sound* option in the Timing group and then click *Breeze* at the drop-down list.
   g. Click the Apply To All button.

4. Set up the presentation to run continuously by completing the following steps:
   a. Click the Slide Show tab.
   b. Click the Set Up Slide Show button in the Set Up group.
   c. At the Set Up Show dialog box, click in the *Loop continuously until 'Esc'* check box to insert a check mark. (Make sure *All* is selected in the *Show slides* section and *Using timings, if present* is selected in the *Advance slides* section.)
   d. Click OK to close the dialog box.
5. Click Slide 1 to select it and then run the presentation. (The slides will advance automatically after five seconds.)
6. After viewing the presentation, press the Esc key on the keyboard.
7. Save **P-C7-P3-AdvTours.pptx**.

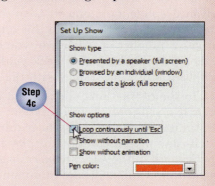

Setting Automatic Times for Slides

Applying the same time to all slides is not very practical unless the same amount of text occurs on every slide. In most cases, some slides should be left on the screen longer than others. Apply specific times to a slide with buttons on the Recording toolbar. Display this toolbar by clicking the Slide Show tab and then clicking the Rehearse Timings button in the Set Up group. This displays the first slide in the presentation in Slide Show view with the Recording toolbar located in the upper left corner of the slide. The buttons on the Recording toolbar are identified in Figure 7.3.

When the slide displays on the screen, the timer on the Recording toolbar begins. Click the Next button on the Recording toolbar when the slide has displayed for the appropriate amount of time. If you want to stop the timer, click the Pause button. Click the Resume Recording button to resume the timer. Use the Repeat button on the Recording toolbar if you get off track and want to reset the time for the current slide. Continue through the presentation until the slide show is complete. After the last slide, a message displays showing the total time for the presentation and asks if you want to record the new slide timings. At this message, click Yes to set the times for each slide recorded during the rehearsal. If you do not want to use the rehearsed timings when running a presentation, click the Slide Show tab and then click in the Use Timings check box to remove the check mark.

The time you apply to each slide will display below slides in the Slide Sorter view. The time that displays below the slide will generally be one second more than the time you applied to the slide. So, if you applied 5 seconds to Slide 1, *00:06* will display below the slide in Slide Sorter view.

▼ **Quick Steps**

Set Automatic Times for Slides
1. Click Slide Show tab.
2. Click Rehearse Timings button.
3. Using Recording toolbar, specify time for each slide.
4. Click Yes.

You can enter a specific recording time by selecting the time in the Slide Time text box, typing the desired time, and then pressing Enter.

Rehearse Timings

Figure 7.3 Recording Toolbar

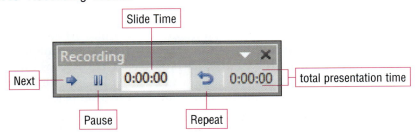

| Project 3b | **Setting Rehearse Timings for Slides** | Part 2 of 5 |

1. With **P-C7-P3-AdvTours.pptx** open, remove the automatic times for slides by completing the following steps:
   a. Click the Slide Show tab.
   b. Click the Set Up Slide Show button.
   c. At the Set Up Show dialog box, click the *Loop continuously until 'Esc'* check box to remove the check mark.
   d. Click OK to close the dialog box.
2. Set times for the slides to display during a slide show by completing the following steps:
   a. Make Slide 1 active.
   b. With the Slide Show tab active, click the Rehearse Timings button in the Set Up group.

c. The first slide displays in Slide Show view and the Recording toolbar displays. Wait until the time displayed for the current slide reaches four seconds and then click Next. (If you miss the time, click the Repeat button to reset the clock back to zero for the current slide.)

d. Set the times for remaining slides as follows:
   Slide 2 = 5 seconds
   Slide 3 = 6 seconds
   Slide 4 = 5 seconds
   Slide 5 = 6 seconds
   Slide 6 = 3 seconds
   Slide 7 = 6 seconds
   Slide 8 = 7 seconds
   Slide 9 = 7 seconds

e. After the last slide displays, click Yes at the message asking if you want to record the new slide timings. (The slide times may display each with one additional second.)

f. Click the Normal button in the view area on the Status bar.

3. Click the Set Up Slide Show button to display the Set Up Show dialog box, click the *Loop continuously until 'Esc'* check box to insert a check mark, and then click OK to close the dialog box.

4. Run the presentation. (The slide show will start and run continuously.) Watch the presentation until it has started for the second time and then end the show by pressing the Esc key.

5. Save **P-C7-P3-AdvTours.pptx**.

Recording Narration

You can record narration with your presentation that will play when the presentation is running. To record narration you must have a microphone connected to your computer. To begin the narration, click the Record Slide Show button in the Set Up group in the Slide Show tab. At the Record Slide Show dialog box, click the Start Recording button. Your presentation begins and the first slide fills the screen. Begin your narration, clicking the mouse to advance each slide. When you have narrated all of the slides in the presentation, your presentation displays in Slide Sorter view.

If you click the Record Slide Show button arrow, a drop-down list displays with three options. Click the *Start Recording from Beginning* option to begin recording your narration with the first slide in the presentation or click the *Start Recording from Current Slide* if you want to begin recording your narration with the currently active slide. Position your mouse on the third option, *Clear*, and a side menu displays with options for clearing the timing on the current slide or all slides and clearing the narration from the current slide or all slides.

When you click the Record Slide Show button in the Slide Show tab, the Record Slide Show dialog box displays. This dialog box contains two options: *Slide and animation timings* and *Narrations and laser pointer*. You can choose to record just the slide timings, just the narration, or both at the same time. With the *Slide and animation timings* option active (contains a check mark), PowerPoint will keep track of the timing for each slide. When you run the presentation, the slides will

remain on the screen the number of seconds recorded. If you want to narrate a presentation but do not want slides timed, remove the check mark from the *Slide and animation timings* check box. With the *Narrations and laser pointer* option active (contains a check mark), you can record your narration and record laser pointer gestures you can make with the mouse. To make laser pointer gestures, hold down the Ctrl key, hold down the left mouse button, and then drag in the slide.

The narration in a presentation plays by default when you run the presentation. You can run the presentation without the narration by displaying the Set Up Show dialog box and then inserting a check mark in the *Show without narration* check box in the *Show options* section.

▼ **Quick Steps**

Record Narration
1. Click Slide Show tab.
2. Click Record Slide Show button.
3. Click Start Recording button.
4. Narrate slides.

Project 3c Recording Narration Part 3 of 5

This is an optional project. Before beginning the project, check with your instructor to determine if you have a microphone available for recording.

1. With **P-C7-P3-AdvTours.pptx** open, save the presentation and name it **P-C7-P3-AdvTours-Narration**.
2. Remove the timings and the continuous loop option by completing the following steps:
   a. Click the Slide Show tab.
   b. Click the Record Slide Show button arrow, point to *Clear* at the drop-down list, and then click *Clear Timings on All Slides* at the side menu.
   c. Click the Set Up Slide Show button.
   d. At the Set Up Show dialog box, click the *Loop continuously until 'Esc'* check box to remove the check mark.
   e. Click OK to close the dialog box.

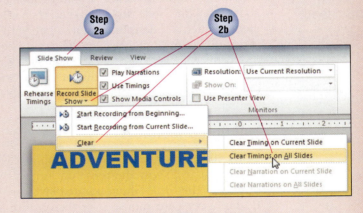

3. Make Slide 1 active and then record narration by completing the following steps:
   a. Click the Record Slide Show button in the Set Up group in the Slide Show tab.
   b. At the Record Slide Show dialog box, make sure both options contain a check mark and then click the Start Recording button.
   c. When the first slide displays, either read the information or provide your own narrative of the slide and then click the left mouse button. (You can also click the Next button on the Recording toolbar that displays in the upper left corner of the slide.)
   d. Continue narrating each slide (either using some of the information in the slides or creating your own narration). Try recording laser pointer gestures by holding down the Ctrl key, holding down the left mouse button, and then dragging in the slide.
   e. After narrating the last slide (the slide about accommodations for the Peru tour), the presentation will display in Slide Sorter view.
4. Make Slide 1 active and then run the presentation. If your computer has speakers, you will hear your narration as the presentation runs.

5. Run the presentation without narration by completing the following steps:
   a. Click the Set Up Slide Show button in the Set Up group in the Slide Show tab.
   b. At the Set Up Show dialog box, click in the *Show without narration* check box to insert a check mark.
   c. Click OK.
   d. Run the presentation beginning with Slide 1. (The presentation will run automatically with the timing established when you were recording your narration but without the narration.)
6. Save and then close **P-C7-P3-AdvTours-Narration.pptx**.

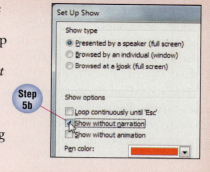

Step 5b

Hiding Slides

Quick Steps

Hide Slide
1. Make slide active.
2. Click Slide Show tab.
3. Click Hide Slide button.

Hide Slide

A presentation you create may be presented to a number of different groups or departments. In some situations, you may want to hide specific slides in a presentation depending on the audience. To hide a slide in a presentation, make the desired slide active, click the Slide Show tab, and then click the Hide Slide button in the Set Up group. When a slide is hidden, a square with a slash through it displays behind the slide number in the Slides/Outline pane. The slide is visible in the Slides/Outline pane in Normal view and also in the Slide Sorter view. To remove the hidden icon and redisplay the slide when running a presentation, click the slide miniature in the Slides/Outline pane, click the Slide Show tab, and then click the Hide Slide button.

Setting Up Monitors

With options in the Monitors group in the Slide Show tab, you can specify screen resolution and show the presentation on two different monitors. The Resolution option in the Slide Show tab displays the default setting of *Use Current Resolution*. If you hover your mouse over the option, an expanded ScreenTip displays with information telling you that you can choose a screen resolution and that a smaller resolution generally displays faster while a larger resolution generally displays the presentation slower but with more visual detail.

If you have two monitors connected to your computer or are running PowerPoint on a laptop with dual-display capabilities, you can choose the *Use Presenter View* option in the Monitors group. With this option active, you display your presentation in full-screen view on one monitor and display your presentation in a special speaker view on the other.

Project 3d Changing Monitor Resolution   Part 4 of 5

Check with your instructor before completing this project to determine if you can change monitor resolution.
1. Open **P-C7-P3-AdvTours.pptx**.
2. Remove the continuous loop option and remove timings by completing the following:
   a. Click the Slide Show tab.

b. Click the Set Up Slide Show button.
c. At the Set Up Show dialog box, click the *Loop continuously until 'Esc'* check box to remove the check mark.
d. Click OK to close the dialog box.
e. Click the Transitions tab.
f. Click the down-pointing arrow at the right side of the *After* option box until *00:00* displays.
g. Click the *After* check box to remove the check mark.
h. Click the *On Mouse Click* option to insert a check mark.
i. Click the Apply To All button.
3. Hide Slide 2 by completing the following steps:
   a. Click the Slide 2 thumbnail in the Slides/Outline pane.
   b. Click the Slide Show tab and then click the Hide Slide button in the Set Up group.

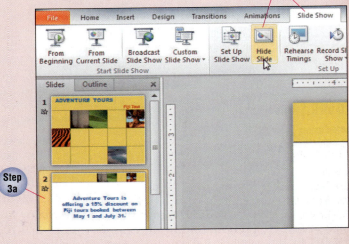

4. Change the monitor resolution by clicking the down-pointing arrow at the right side of the *Resolution* option in the Monitors group and then clicking *800×600* at the drop-down list.
5. Run the presentation and notice the resolution and that Slide 2 does not display (since it is hidden).
6. Unhide Slide 2 by clicking the Slide 2 thumbnail in the Slides/Outline pane and then clicking the Hide Slide button in the Set Up group in the Slide Show tab.
7. Return the monitor resolution to the original setting by clicking the down-pointing arrow at the right side of the *Resolution* option in the Monitors group in the Slide Show tab and then clicking *Use Current Resolution* at the drop-down list.
8. Save **P-C7-P3-AdvTours.pptx**.

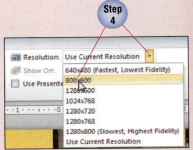

Creating a Custom Show

You can create a ***custom slide show***, which is a presentation within a presentation. This might be useful in situations where you want to show only a select number of slides to a particular audience. To create a custom show, click the Slide Show tab, click the Custom Slide Show button in the Start Slide Show group, and then click *Custom Shows* at the drop-down list. At the Custom Shows dialog box, click the New button and the Define Custom Show dialog box displays similar to what you see in Figure 7.4.

Create custom shows to customize a presentation for a variety of audiences.

Custom Slide Show

Figure 7.4 Define Custom Show Dialog Box

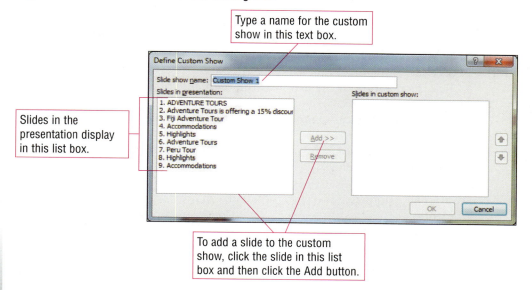

Quick Steps

Create Custom Show
1. Click Slide Show tab.
2. Click Custom Slide Show button.
3. Click *Custom Shows*.
4. Click New button.
5. Make desired changes at Define Custom Show dialog box.
6. Click OK.

Run Custom Show
1. Click Slide Show tab.
2. Click Custom Slide Show button.
3. Click desired custom show.

Edit Custom Show
1. Click Slide Show tab.
2. Click Custom Slide Show button.
3. Click *Custom Shows*.
4. Click desired custom show.
5. Click Edit button.
6. Make desired changes at Define Custom Show dialog box.
7. Click OK.

Print Custom Show
1. Display Print tab Backstage view.
2. Click first gallery in Settings category.
3. Click desired custom show at drop-down list.
4. Click Print button.

At the Define Custom Show dialog box, type a name for the custom presentation in the *Slide show name* text box. To insert a slide in the custom show, click the slide in the *Slides in presentation* list box and then click the Add button. This inserts the slide in the *Slides in custom show* list box. Continue in this manner until all desired slides are added to the custom show. If you want to change the order of the slides in the *Slides in custom show* list box, click one of the arrow keys to move the selected slide up or down in the list box. When the desired slides are inserted in the *Slides in custom show* list box and in the desired order, click OK. You can create more than one custom show in a presentation.

Running a Custom Show

To run a custom show within a presentation, click the Custom Slide Show button in the Slide Show tab and then click the desired custom show at the drop-down list. You can also choose a custom show by displaying the Set Up Show dialog box and then clicking the *Custom show* option. If the presentation contains more than one custom show, click the down-pointing arrow at the right of the *Custom show* option and then click the show name at the drop-down list.

Editing a Custom Show

A custom show is saved with the presentation and can be edited. To edit a custom show, open the presentation, click the Custom Slide Show button in the Slide Show tab, and then click *Custom Shows* at the drop-down list. At the Custom Shows dialog box, click the custom show name you want to edit and then click the Edit button. At the Define Custom Show dialog box, make the desired changes to the custom show such as adding or removing slides or changing the order of slides. When all changes have been made, click the OK button.

Printing a Custom Show

You can print a custom show with options in the Settings category of the Print tab Backstage view. To do this, click the File tab and then click the Print tab to display the Print tab Backstage view. Click the first gallery in the Settings category and then click the desired custom show in the *Custom Shows* section.

Project 3e — Creating, Editing, and Running Custom Shows — Part 5 of 5

1. With **P-C7-P3-AdvTours.pptx** open, save the presentation and name it **P-C7-P3-AdvTours-Custom**.
2. Create two custom shows by completing the following steps:
   a. Click the Slide Show tab, click the Custom Slide Show button, and then click *Custom Shows* at the drop-down list.
   b. At the Custom Shows dialog box, click the New button.
   c. At the Define Custom Show dialog box, type **PeruTourCustom** in the *Slide show name* text box.
   d. Click Slide 6 in the *Slides in presentation* list box and then click the Add button. (This adds the slide to the *Slides in custom show* list box.)
   e. Click each of the following slides in the list box (Slides 7, 8, and 9) and click the Add button.
   f. Click OK to close the Define Custom Show dialog box.
   g. At the Custom Shows dialog box, click the New button.
   h. At the Define Custom Show dialog box, type **FijiTourCustom** in the *Slide show name* text box.
   i. Add Slides 1 through 5 to the *Slides in custom show* list box.
   j. Click OK to close the dialog box.
   k. Click the Close button to close the Custom Shows dialog box.
3. Run the *PeruTourCustom* custom show by completing the following steps:
   a. Click the Custom Slide Show button in the Slide Show tab and then click *PeruTourCustom* at the drop-down list.
   b. Click the left mouse button to advance slides.
   c. Click the Custom Slide Show button, click *FijiTourCustom* at the drop-down list, and then view the presentation. (Click the left mouse button to advance slides.)
4. Edit the FijiTourCustom custom slide show by completing the following steps:
   a. Click the Custom Slide Show button in the Slide Show tab and then click *Custom Shows* at the drop-down list.
   b. At the Custom Shows dialog box, click *FijiTourCustom* in the *Custom shows* list box and then click the Edit button.

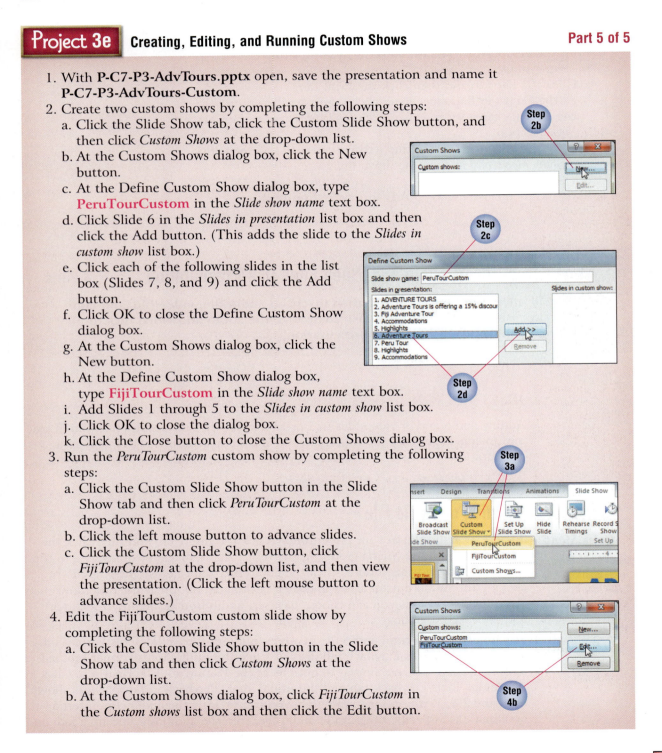

Chapter 7 ■ Applying Custom Animation and Setting Up Shows

c. At the Define Custom Show dialog box, click Slide 2 in the *Slides in custom show* list box and then click three times on the down-pointing arrow at the right side of the list box. (This moves the slide to the bottom of the list.)
d. Click OK to close the dialog box.
e. Click the Close button to close the Custom Shows dialog box.
5. Run the FijiTourCustom custom show.
6. Print the FijiTourCustom custom show by completing the following steps:
a. Click the File tab and then click the Print tab.
b. At the Print tab Backstage view, click the first gallery in the Settings category and then click *FijiTourCustom* in the *Custom Shows* section.
c. Click the second gallery in the Settings category and then click *6 Slides Horizontal* at the drop-down list.
d. Click the Print button.
7. Save and then close **P-C7-P3-AdvTours-Custom.pptx**.

Step 4c

Project 4 Insert Audio and Video Files in a Presentation   4 Parts

You will open a presentation and then insert an audio file, video file, and clip art image with motion. You will also customize the audio and video files to play automatically when running the presentation.

Inserting Audio and Video Files

Adding audio and/or video files to a presentation will turn a slide show into a true multimedia experience for your audience. Including a variety of elements in a presentation will stimulate interest in your presentation and keep the audience motivated.

Inserting an Audio File

Quick Steps
Insert Audio File
1. Click Insert tab.
2. Click Audio button.
3. Double-click desired audio file.

Audio

To add an audio file to your presentation, click the Insert tab and then click the Audio button in the Media group. At the Insert Audio dialog box, navigate to the desired folder and then double-click the audio file. You can also insert audio by clicking the Audio button arrow and then clicking an option at the drop-down list. With the list options you can choose to insert audio from a file, insert a clip art audio, or record audio.

When you insert an audio file in a presentation, the Audio Tools Format tab and the Audio Tools Playback tab display. Click the Audio Tools Format tab and options display that are similar to options in the Picture Tools Format tab. Click the Audio Tools Playback tab and the Audio Tools Playback tab displays as shown in Figure 7.5. With options in the tab, you can preview the audio clip, insert a bookmark at a specific time in the audio file, trim the audio file, specify a fade in and fade out time, and specify how you want the audio file to play.

Figure 7.5 Audio Tools Playback Tab

Project 4a Inserting an Audio File   Part 1 of 4

1. Open **EcoTours.pptx** and then save the presentation with Save As and name it **P-C7-P4-EcoTours**.
2. Insert an audio file that plays music at the end of the presentation by completing the following steps:
   a. Make Slide 8 active.
   b. Click the Insert tab and then click the Audio button in the Media group.
   c. At the Insert Audio dialog box, navigate to the PowerPoint2010C7 folder on your storage medium and then double-click **AudioFile-01.mid**.
   d. Click the Audio Tools Playback tab.
   e. Click the down-pointing arrow at the right side of the *Start* option in the Audio Options group and then click *Automatically* at the drop-down list.
   f. Click the *Hide During Show* check box in the Audio Options group to insert a check mark.
   g. Click the *Loop until Stopped* check box to insert a check mark.
3. Make Slide 1 active and then run the presentation. When the last slide displays, listen to the audio clip and then press the Esc key to return to the Normal view.
4. Save **P-C7-P4-EcoTours.pptx**.

Inserting a Video File

Inserting a video file in a presentation is a similar process to inserting an audio file. Click the Video button in the Media group in the Insert tab to display the Insert Video dialog box. At this dialog box, navigate to the folder containing the video file and then double-click the file. You can also click the Video button arrow and then click *Video from File* to display the Insert Video dialog box.

You can insert a link in a slide to a video file at a website. To do this, click the Video button arrow in the Media group in the Insert tab and then click *Video from Web Site* at the drop-down list. This displays the Insert Video From Web Site dialog box. Information in this dialog box tells you that you can insert a link to a video file you have uploaded to a website by copying the embedded code from the website and pasting it into the dialog box text box. Click the *Clip Art Video* option at the Media button drop-down list and the Clip Art task pane displays with clip art images containing animation effects.

When you insert a video file in a presentation, the Video Tools Format tab and the Video Tools Playback tab display. Click the Video Tools Format tab and

▼ **Quick Steps**

Insert Video File
1. Click Insert tab.
2. Click Video button.
3. Double-click desired video file.

Video

Chapter 7 ■ Applying Custom Animation and Setting Up Shows   **295**

options display for adjusting the video file color and frame, applying video styles, and arranging and sizing the video file. Click the Video Tools Playback tab and options display that are similar to the options in the Audio Tools Playback tab shown in Figure 7.5.

Project 4b Inserting a Video File in a Presentation Part 2 of 4

1. With **P-C7-P4-EcoTours.pptx** open, make Slide 8 active.
2. You will insert a video file in the slide that contains audio so delete the audio file you inserted in Project 4a by clicking the audio file icon that displays in the middle of Slide 8 and then pressing the Delete key.
3. Insert a video file by completing the following steps:
   a. Click the Insert tab and then click the Video button in the Media group.
   b. At the Insert Video dialog box, navigate to the PowerPoint2010C7 folder on your storage medium and then double-click the file named *EcoTours.wmv*. (The **EcoTours.wmv** file is a low-resolution video. If you have access to sample videos in Windows 7, use the **Wildlife.wmv** video located in the Videos folder in the Libraries section of the hard drive. Double-click the Sample Videos folder and then double-click *Wildlife.wmv*. This video is high resolution.)
   c. Click the Play button in the Preview group (left side of the Video Tools Format tab) to preview the video clip. (The video plays for approximately 37 seconds.)
   d. After viewing the video, click the Video Tools Playback tab.
   e. Click the up-pointing arrow at the right side of the *Fade In* text box until *01.00* displays and then click the up-pointing arrow at the right side of the *Fade Out* text box until *01.00* displays.
   f. Click the Volume button in the Video Options group and then click *Low* at the drop-down list.
   g. Click the *Loop until Stopped* check box in the Video Options group to insert a check mark.

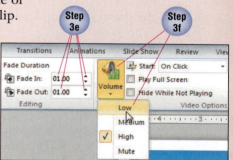

4. Make Slide 1 active and then run the presentation. When the slide containing the video clip displays, move the mouse over the video clip window and then click the Play button located at the bottom left side of the window.
5. After viewing the video a couple of times, press the Esc key twice.
6. Specify that you want the video window to fill the slide, the video to automatically start when the slide displays, and the video to play only once by completing the following steps:
   a. Make sure Slide 8 is active, click the video clip window, and then click the Video Tools Playback tab.
   b. Click the *Play Full Screen* check box in the Video Options group to insert a check mark and click the *Loop until Stopped* check box to remove the check mark.
   c. Click the down-pointing arrow at the right side of the *Start* option in the Video Options group and then click *Automatically* at the drop-down list.
7. Make Slide 1 active and then run the presentation. When the slide displays containing the video, the video will automatically begin. When the video is finished playing, press the Esc key to return to Normal view.
8. Print Slide 8.
9. Save **P-C7-P4-EcoTours.pptx**.

Trimming a Video File

With the Trim Video button in the Video Tools Playback tab, you can trim the beginning and end of your video. This might be helpful in a situation where you want to remove a portion of the video that is not pertinent to the message in your presentation. You are limited in trimming the video to trimming a portion of the beginning of the video or the end.

To trim a video, insert the video file in the slide, click the Video Tools Playback tab, and then click the Trim Video button in the Editing group. At the Trim Video dialog box, specify the time you want the video to start and/or the time you want the video to end. To trim the start of the video, you can insert a specific time in the *Start Time* text box or drag the green start point marker that displays on the slider bar below the video. You can zero in on a very specific starting point by clicking the Next Frame button or the Previous Frame button to move the display of the video a frame at a time. Complete similar steps to trim the ending of the video except use the red end point marker on the slider bar or insert the specific ending time in the *End Time* text box.

Quick Steps
Trim Video
1. Insert video file.
2. Click Video Tools Playback tab.
3. Click Trim Video button.
4. Specify start time and/or end time.
5. Click OK.

Trim Video

Project 4c   Trimming a Video   Part 3 of 4

1. With **P-C7-P4-EcoTour.pptx** open, make Slide 8 active.
2. Trim out the first part of the video that shows the wolf howling by completing the following steps:
   a. Click the video to select it.
   b. Click the Video Tools Playback tab.
   c. Click the Trim Video button in the Editing group.
   d. At the Trim Video dialog box, position the mouse pointer on the green start point marker on the slider bar until the pointer displays as a double-headed arrow pointing left and right. Hold down the left mouse button, drag the start point marker to approximately the *00:04.5* time and then release the mouse button. (If you inserted the high-resolution **Wildlife.wmv** file from Windows 7, trim the horses running from the first part of the video by dragging the start point marker to approximately the *00:04.0* time.)
   e. Click the Next Frame button until the first image of the sunset displays. (Depending on where you dragged the start point marker, you may need to click the Previous Frame button. If you inserted the **Wildlife.wmv** video file, click the Next Frame button until the first image of the birds displays.)
   f. Click the OK button.
3. Run the presentation.
4. Save **P-C7-P4-EcoTours.pptx**.

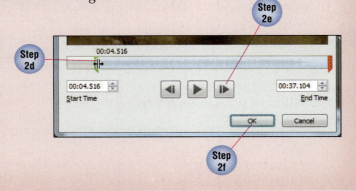

Playing an Audio File throughout a Presentation

In Project 4a, you inserted an audio file that played when a specific slide displayed. You can also insert an audio file in a presentation and have the audio

play continually through all slides in the presentation. Generally you would add an audio file for the entire presentation when setting up a self-running presentation. To specify that you want the audio file to play throughout the presentation, click the down-pointing arrow at the right side of the *Start* option in the Audio Options group in the Audio Tools Playback tab and then click *Play across slides* at the drop-down list. To make the presentation self-running, display the Set Up Show dialog box and then insert a check mark in the *Loop continuously until 'Esc'* check box.

Project 4d Playing an Audio File throughout a Presentation   Part 4 of 4

1. With **P-C7-P4-EcoTours.pptx** open, make Slide 8 active and then make the following changes:
   a. Select and then delete the video file.
   b. Select and then delete the bulleted text placeholder.
   c. Select the title placeholder and then drag the title down to the middle of the slide.
2. Make Slide 1 active and then insert an audio file that plays throughout all files by completing the following steps:
   a. Click the Insert tab and then click the Audio button in the Media group.
   b. At the Insert Audio dialog box, navigate to the PowerPoint2010C7 folder on your storage medium and then double-click **AudioFile-02.mid**.
   c. Click the Audio Tools Playback tab.
   d. Click the down-pointing arrow at the right side of the *Start* option in the Audio Options group and then click *Play across slides* at the drop-down list.
   e. Click the *Hide During Show* check box in the Audio Options group to insert a check mark.
   f. Click the *Loop until Stopped* check box to insert a check mark.
   g. Click the Volume button in the Audio Options group and then click *Medium* at the drop-down list.
3. Specify that you want slides to automatically advance after five seconds by completing the following steps:
   a. Click the Transitions tab.
   b. Click the up-pointing arrow at the right side of the *After* option in the Timing group until *00:05.00* displays.
   c. Click in the *On Mouse Click* check box to remove the check mark.
   d. Click the Apply To All button.

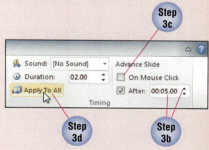

4. Set up the presentation to run continuously by completing the following steps:
   a. Click the Slide Show tab.
   b. Click the Set Up Slide Show button.
   c. At the Set Up Show dialog box, click in the *Loop continuously until 'Esc'* check box to insert a check mark.
   d. Click OK to close the dialog box.
5. Make Slide 1 active and then run the presentation. When the presentation begins for the second time, press the Esc key to return to Normal view.
6. Save and then close **P-C7-P4-EcoTours.pptx**.

Chapter Summary

- Apply animation to an item in a slide with options in the Animation group in the Animations tab. Specify animation effects with options from the Effect Options button drop-down gallery.
- Click the Preview button in the Animations tab to view the animation effects without running the presentation.
- Remove an animation effect from an item in a slide by clicking the *None* option in the Animation group in the Animations tab.
- The Add Animation button in the Advanced Animation group in the Animations tab provides four types of animation effects—entrance, exit, emphasis, and motion paths.
- Use the Animation Painter, located in the Advanced Animation group in the Animations tab, to apply the same animation to items in more than one location in a slide or slides.
- Use options in the Timing group in the Animations tab to determine when an animation starts on a slide, the duration of the animation, the delay between animations, and the order in which animations appear on the slide.
- Use the Animation Pane to customize and modify animation effects. Display the pane by clicking the Animation Pane button in the Advanced Animation group in the Animations tab.
- A build displays important points on a slide one point at a time. You can apply a build that dims the previous bulleted point with the *After animation* option at the effect options dialog box with the Effect tab selected.
- Specify a path you want an item to follow when it displays on the slide with options in the *Motion Paths* section of the Add Animation button drop-down gallery. To draw a motion path, choose the *Custom path* option at the drop-down gallery.
- Use the Trigger button in the Advanced Animation group to specify that you want to make an animation effect occur during a slide show by clicking an item on the slide.
- Customize a slide show with options in the Set Up Show dialog box.
- To prepare a self-running presentation, insert a check mark in the *Loop continuously until 'Esc'* check box at the Set Up Show dialog box.
- To apply specific times to slides, click the Rehearse Timings button in the Set Up group in the Slide Show tab. Use buttons on the Recording toolbar to set, pause, or repeat times.
- To record a narration for a presentation, click the Record Slide Show button in the Set Up group in the Slide Show tab and then click the Start Recording button at the Record Slide Show dialog box.
- Hide or unhide a slide in a presentation by clicking the Hide Slide button in the Set Up group in the Slide Show tab.
- Specify screen resolutions with the *Resolution* option in the Monitors group in the Slide Show tab.

- Create a custom slide show, which is a presentation within a presentation, with options in the Define Custom Show dialog box.
- To run a custom slide show, click the Custom Slide Show button in the Start Slide Show group in the Slide Show tab and then click the desired custom show at the drop-down list.
- Print a custom show at the Print tab Backstage view by clicking the first gallery in the Settings category and then clicking the desired custom show in the *Custom Shows* section.
- Insert an audio file in a slide with the Audio button in the Media group in the Insert tab. Use options in the Audio Tools Format tab and the Audio Tools Playback tab to format and customize the audio file.
- Insert a video file in a slide with the Video button in the Media group in the Insert tab. Use options in the Video Tools Format tab and the Video Tools Playback tab to format and customize the video file.
- With the Trim Video button in the Video Tools Playback tab, you can trim the beginning and end of your video.

Commands Review

FEATURE	RIBBON TAB, GROUP	BUTTON, OPTION
Animations	Animations, Animation	
Add Animations	Animations, Advanced Animation	
Animation Painter	Animations, Advanced Animation	
Animation Pane	Animations, Advanced Animation	
Set Up Show dialog box	Slide Show, Set Up	
Recording toolbar	Slide Show, Set Up	
Hide/unhide slide	Slide Show, Set Up	
Define Custom Show dialog box	Slide Show, Set Up	, Custom Shows, New
Insert audio file	Insert, Media	
Insert video file	Insert, Media	
Trim Video dialog box	Video Tools Playback, Editing	

Concepts Check Test Your Knowledge

Completion: In the space provided at the right, indicate the correct term, symbol, or command.

1. Once you have applied an animation, specify the animation effects with options in this button drop-down gallery. _____

2. Remove an animation effect from an item in a slide by clicking this option in the Animation group in the Animations tab. _____

3. The Add Animation button in the Advanced Animation group in the Animations tab provides four types of animation effects you can apply to an item—entrance, exit, motion paths, and this. _____

4. Use this feature if you apply an animation or animations to items in a slide and want to apply the same animation in more than one location in a slide or slides. _____

5. The *Duration* option is located in this group in the Animations tab. _____

6. Display the Animation Pane by clicking the Animation Pane button in this group in the Animations tab. _____

7. This term refers to displaying important points one at a time in a slide when running a presentation. _____

8. To draw your own motion path in a slide, click the Add Animation button in the Animations tab and then click this option in the *Motion Paths* section of the drop-down gallery. _____

9. The Hide Slide button is located in this tab. _____

10. Specify the slides you want included in a custom show with options at this dialog box. _____

11. The Audio and Video buttons are located in this group in the Insert tab. _____

12. The Volume button for an audio file is located in the Audio Options group in this tab. _____

13. The Trim Video button is located in this tab. _____

Skills Check Assess Your Performance

Assessment 1
APPLY ANIMATION EFFECTS TO A TRAVEL PRESENTATION

1. Open **FCTCruise.pptx** and then save the presentation with Save As and name it **P-C7-A1-FCTCruise**.
2. With Slide 1 active, click the company logo and then apply the *Fade* animation. *Hint: Click the Animations tab*.
3. Click the subtitle *Vacation Cruise* and then apply the *Fly In* animation.
4. Display the presentation in Slide Master view, click the top slide master layout (Japanese Waves Slide Master) in the slide thumbnail pane, apply the *Fade* animation to the title style, and then close the Slide Master view.
5. Make Slide 2 active and then complete the following steps:
    a. Click in the bulleted text.
    b. Apply the *Wipe* animation.
    c. Click in the bulleted text.
    d. Double-click the Animation Painter button.
    e. Make Slide 3 active and then click in the bulleted text.
    f. Make Slide 4 active and then click in the bulleted text.
    g. Make Slide 5 active and then click in the bulleted text.
    h. Click the Animation Painter button to deactivate it.
6. Make Slide 3 active and then insert a trigger by completing the following steps:
    a. Click the banner that displays toward the bottom of the slide and then apply the *Wipe* animation and change the direction to *From Left*. *Hint: Change the direction with the Effect Options button*.
    b. Display the Animation Pane.
    c. Click the *Horizontal Scroll* item in the list box.
    d. Click the Trigger button, point to *On Click of*, and then click *Content Placeholder 2* at the side menu.
    e. Close the Animation Pane.
7. Run the presentation and, when the third bulleted item displays in Slide 3, click the bulleted item to trigger the display of the banner.
8. Save and then close **P-C7-A1-FCTCruise.pptx**.

Assessment 2
APPLY ANIMATION EFFECTS TO AN EMPLOYEE ORIENTATION PRESENTATION

1. Open **GEOrientation.pptx** and then save the presentation with Save As and name it **P-C7-A2-GEOrientation**.
2. Make Slide 2 active and then apply the following animations to the SmartArt graphic:
    a. Apply the *Blinds* entrance animation effect. *Hint: You will need to click the More button at the right of the animations in the Animation group and then click* **More Entrance Effects**.
    b. Change the SmartArt animation so the sequence is *One by One* and change the direction to *Vertical*. *Hint: Do this with the Effect Options button*.

3. Make Slide 3 active and then apply the following animations to the organizational chart.
   a. Apply the *Blinds* entrance animation effect.
   b. Change the SmartArt animation so the sequence is *Level at Once*.
4. Make Slide 4 active and then apply the following animations to the bulleted text (click on any character in the bulleted text):
   a. Apply the *Zoom* entrance animation effect.
   b. Display the Animation Pane and then set the text to dim after animation to a light blue color. ***Hint: Click the down-pointing arrow at the right side of the content placeholder in the Animation Pane list box and then click* Effect Options.**
5. Apply the following animations to the clip art image in Slide 4:
   a. Apply the *Spin* emphasis animation effect.
   b. Set the amount of spin for the clip art image to *Two Spins* and change the duration to *01.00*.
   c. Change the *Start* option to *With Previous*.
   d. Reorder the items in the Animation Pane list box so the clip art displays first when running the presentation.
6. Make Slide 5 active, select the SmartArt graphic, and then apply an animation effect so the elements in the SmartArt graphic fade in one by one.
7. Make Slide 6 active and then apply the following animation effects to the images with the following specifications:
   a. Apply the *Fly Out* exit animation effect to the *Free Education* gift package, change the direction to *To Right*, and change the duration to *00.25*.
   b. Apply the *Shape* entrance animation effect to the diploma/books clip art image and change the duration to *01.00*.
   c. Move the *Free Education* gift package so the bulleted text underneath displays, apply the *Grow & Turn* entrance animation effect to the bulleted text, and then move the gift package back to the original location.
   d. Apply the *Fly Out* exit animation effect to the *Free Toys and Fitness* gift package, change the direction to *To Left*, and change the duration to *00.25*.
   e. Apply the *Shape* entrance animation effect to the notebook computer clip art image and change the duration to *01.00*.
   f. Move the *Free Toys and Fitness* gift package so the bulleted text underneath displays, apply the *Grow & Turn* entrance animation effect to the bulleted text, and then move the gift package back to the original location.
8. Make Slide 1 active and then run the presentation.
9. Save **P-C7-A2-GEOrientation.pptx**.
10. Display the presentation in Slide Master view, click the top slide master layout in the slide thumbnail pane, apply an entrance animation effect of your choosing to the title, and then close Slide Master view.
11. Make Slide 1 active and then apply the following animation effects:
    a. Click the globe clip art image and then draw a motion path (using the *Custom Path* option) so the image will circle around the slide and return back to the original location.
    b. Apply the *Spiral In* entrance animation effect to the *New Employee Orientation* placeholder.
12. Run the presentation.
13. Print the presentation as a handout with nine slides horizontally per page.
14. Save and then close **P-C7-A2-GEOrientation.pptx**.

Assessment

3 APPLY ANIMATION EFFECTS, VIDEO, AND AUDIO TO A JOB SEARCH PRESENTATION

1. Open **JobSearch.pptx** and then save the presentation with Save As and name it **P-C7-A3-JobSearch**.
2. Apply the *Clarity* design theme to the presentation.
3. Add appropriate clip art images to at least two slides.
4. Make Slide 10 active and then insert the video file named **Flight.wmv** from the PowerPoint2010C7 folder on your storage medium. Make the following changes to the video:
   a. Click the Video Tools Format tab and then change the height to 5.3 inches.
   b. Click the Video Tools Playback tab and then specify that you want the video to play automatically (do this with the *Start* option), that you want the video to play full screen, and that you want the video to hide when not playing.
   c. Click the Trim Video button and then trim approximately the first nine seconds from the start of the video. Click OK to close the dialog box.
5. With Slide 10 active, insert the **AudioFile-03.mid** audio file in the slide (located in the PowerPoint2010C7 folder on your storage medium) so it plays automatically, loops until stopped, and is hidden when running the presentation.
6. Run the presentation. After listening to the music for a period of time, end the presentation.
7. Print only Slide 10.
8. Create a custom show named *Interview* that contains Slides 1, 3, 6, 7, and 9.
9. Run the Interview custom show.
10. Print the Interview custom show as a handout with all slides printed horizontally on one page.
11. Edit the Interview custom show by removing Slide 2.
12. Print the Interview custom show again as a handout with all slides printed horizontally on one page.
13. Save and then close **P-C7-A3-JobSearch.pptx**.

Assessment

4 INSERT AN AUDIO CLIP FROM THE CLIP ART TASK PANE

1. Open **JamaicaTour.pptx** and then save the presentation with Save As and name it **P-C7-A4-JamaicaTour**.
2. Click the Insert tab, click the Audio button arrow, and then click *Clip Art Audio*. (This displays the Clip Art task pane with audio files.)
3. Scroll down the list of audio files and then click *Jamaica Bounce (1 or 2)*. (If this audio file is not available, choose another audio file such as *Rainforest music*, *African song*, or a different audio file of your choosing.)
4. Set the audio file to play across all slides and hide when running the presentation.
5. Display the Transitions tab and specify that each slide should advance automatically after five seconds.
6. Set up the presentation to run on an endless loop. (Do this at the Set Up Show dialog box.)
7. Run the presentation.
8. Print the presentation as a handout with six slides horizontally per page.
9. Save and then close **P-C7-A4-JamaicaTour.pptx**.

Visual Benchmark — Demonstrate Your Proficiency

CREATE AND FORMAT A MEDICAL CENTER PRESENTATION

1. Open **RMCPres.pptx** and then save the presentation with Save As and name it **P-C7-VB-RMCPres**.
2. Create the presentation shown in Figure 7.6 with the following specifications:
    a. Apply the *Aspect* design theme and change the theme colors to *Hardcover*.
    b. Find the clip art image for Slide 2 by using the search word *medicine*. Change the color of the clip art to *Gold, Accent color 3 Light*.
    c. Create the SmartArt in Slide 3 using the *Staggered Process* diagram (located in the *Process* section) and apply the *Colorful - Accent Colors* option to the diagram.
    d. Use the information shown in the legend and the data information shown above the bars to create a *3-D Clustered Column* chart as shown in Slide 4.
    e. Use the *Heart* shape (located in the *Basic Shapes* section) to create the hearts in Slide 5.
    f. Use the *Frame* shape (located in the *Basic Shapes* section) to create the shape in Slide 6.
3. Apply the following animation effects to items in slides:
    a. Display the presentation in Slide Master view, click the top slide master layout in the slide thumbnail pane (Aspect Slide Master), apply the *Float In* animation to the title style, and then close the Slide Master view.
    b. Make Slide 1 active and then apply an animation effect of your choosing to the subtitle.
    c. Make Slide 2 active and then apply an animation effect of your choosing to the clip art image and then apply an animation effect to the bulleted text.
    d. Make Slide 3 active and then apply an animation effect of your choosing to the SmartArt and specify a sequence of *One by One*.
    e. Make Slide 4 active and then apply an animation effect of your choosing to the chart and specify a sequence of *By Category*.
    f. Make Slide 5 active and then apply the *Shape* entrance animation effect to the heart at the left side of the slide. Using the Add Animation button, apply the *Pulse* emphasis animation effect. Click the same heart and then use the Animation Painter button to apply the entrance and emphasis animation effect to the middle heart and the heart at the right side of the slide.
    g. Make Slide 6 active and then insert the **AudioFile-04.mid** audio file to play automatically, loop until stopped, and be hidden when running the presentation.
4. Run the presentation.
5. Print the presentation as a handout with six slides horizontally per page.
6. Save and then close **P-C7-VB-RMCPres.pptx**.

Figure 7.6 Visual Benchmark

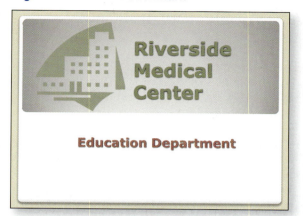

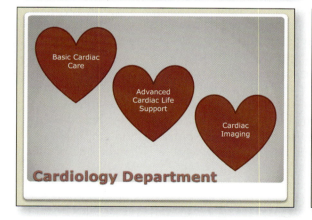

Case Study   Apply Your Skills

Part 1

You are a trainer in the Training Department at Riverside Services. You are responsible for coordinating and conducting software training in the company. Your company hires contract employees and some of those employees work at home and need to have a computer available. You will be conducting a short training for contract employees on how to purchase a personal computer. Open the Word document named **PCBuyGuide.docx** and then use the information in the document to prepare your presentation. Make sure you keep the slides uncluttered and easy to read. Consider inserting clip art or other images in some of the slides. Insert custom animation effects to each slide in the presentation. Run the presentation and then make any necessary changes to the animation effects. Save the presentation and name it **P-C7-CS-PCBuyGuide**. Print the presentation as a handout.

Part 2

Some training sessions on purchasing a personal computer are only scheduled for 20 minutes. For these training sessions, you want to cover only the information about selecting computer hardware components. With the **P-C7-CS-PCBuyGuide.pptx** presentation open, create a custom show (you determine the name) that contains only the slides pertaining to selecting hardware components. Run the custom show and then print the custom show. Save **P-C7-CS-PCBuyGuide.pptx**.

Part 3

You would like to insert an audio file that plays at the end of the presentation and decide to find free audio files on the Internet. Log on to the Internet and then use a search engine to search for "free audio files" or "free audio clips." When you find a site, make sure that you can download and use the audio file without violating copyright laws. Download an audio file and then insert it in the last slide in your presentation. Set up the audio file to play after all of the elements display on the slide. Save and then close **P-C7-CS-PCBuyGuide.pptx**.

Microsoft PowerPoint
Integrating, Sharing, and Protecting Presentations

CHAPTER 8

PERFORMANCE OBJECTIVES

Upon successful completion of Chapter 8, you will be able to:
- Import a Word outline into a presentation
- Send a presentation as an email attachment, broadcast a slide show, and publish slides
- Save a presentation in different file formats
- Export a presentation to Word
- Copy and paste data using the Clipboard
- Link and embed objects
- Download designs
- Insert, edit, and delete comments
- Manage presentation properties
- Protect a presentation
- Add a digital signature
- Inspect and check the accessibility and compatibility of a presentation
- Manage versions of presentations

Share data between programs in the Microsoft Office suite by importing and exporting data, copying and pasting data, copying and embedding data, or copying and linking data. The method you choose depends on how you use the data and whether the data is static or dynamic. Use options in the Save & Send tab Backstage view to send a presentation as an email attachment, save a presentation to a website or SharePoint, broadcast a presentation, and publish slides in a presentation. If you use PowerPoint in a collaborative environment, you may want to insert comments in a presentation and then share the presentation with others. Use options in the Info tab Backstage view to manage presentation properties, password-protect a presentation, insert a digital signature, inspect a presentation, and manage presentation versions. In this chapter, you will learn how to complete these tasks as well as how to download design templates from Office.com. Model answers for this chapter's projects appear on the following pages.

Note: Before beginning the projects, copy to your storage medium the PowerPoint2010C8 subfolder from the PowerPoint2010 folder on the CD that accompanies this textbook and then make PowerPoint2010C8 the active folder.

Model Answers

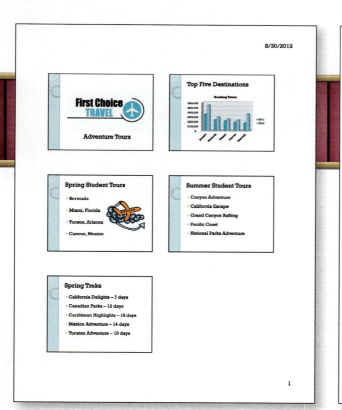
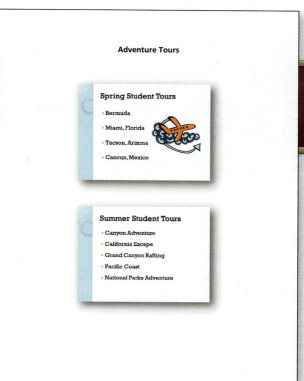

Project 1 Import a Word Outline, Save the Presentation in Different File Formats, and Copy and Paste Objects Between Programs

P-C8-P1-ATTopFive.pptx

P-C8-P1-ATTours.docx

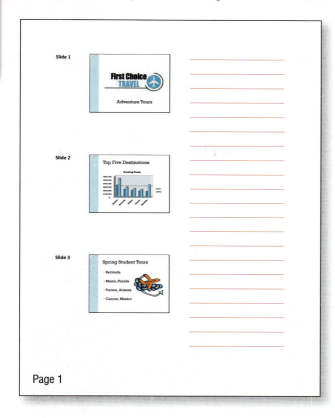
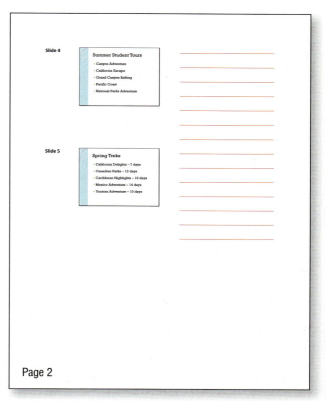

Page 1

Page 2

P-C8-P1-ATTopTours.docx

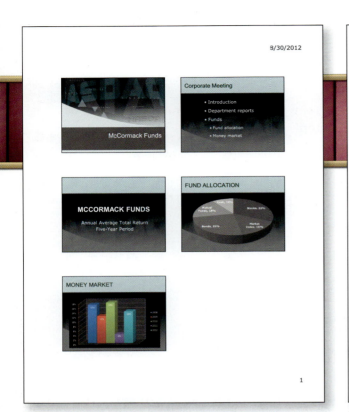

Project 2 Embed and Link Excel Charts to a Presentation
P-C8-P2-FundsPres.pptx

Project 3 Download and Apply a Design Template to a Presentation and Prepare a Presentation for Sharing
P-C8-P3-ISPres.pptx

Project  Import a Word Outline, Save the Presentation in Different File Formats, and Copy and Paste Objects Between Programs — 8 Parts

You will create a PowerPoint presentation using a Word document, save the presentation in different file formats, and then copy and paste an Excel chart and a Word table into slides in the presentation.

Importing a Word Outline

You can import a Word document containing text formatted with heading styles into a PowerPoint presentation. Text formatted with a Heading 1 style becomes the title of a new slide. Text formatted with a Heading 2 style becomes first level text, paragraphs formatted with a Heading 3 style become second level text, and so on. To import a Word outline, open a blank presentation, click the New Slide button arrow in the Slides group in the Home tab, and then click *Slides from Outline* at the drop-down list. At the Insert Outline dialog box, navigate to the folder containing the Word document and then double-click the document. If text in the Word document does not have heading styles applied, PowerPoint creates an outline based on each paragraph of text in the document.

▼ Quick Steps
Import a Word Outline
1. Open blank presentation.
2. Click New Slide button arrow.
3. Click *Slides from Outline*.
4. Double-click desired document.

Chapter 8 ■ Integrating, Sharing, and Protecting Presentations

Project 1a Importing a Word Outline   Part 1 of 8

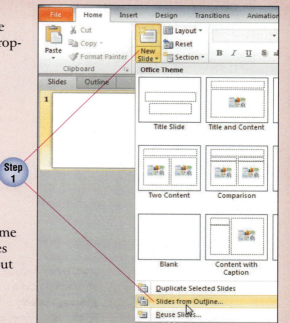

1. At a blank presentation, click the New Slide button arrow in the Slides group in the Home tab and then click *Slides from Outline* at the drop-down list.
2. At the Insert Outline dialog box, navigate to the PowerPoint2010C8 folder on your storage medium and then double-click **ATTopFive.docx**.
3. Apply the *Solstice* design theme, apply the *Metro* theme colors, and apply the *Foundry* theme fonts.
4. Delete Slide 1.
5. Format the current Slide 1 by completing the following steps:
   a. Change the slide layout by clicking the Home tab, clicking the Layout button in the Slides group, and then clicking the *Title Only* layout at the drop-down list.
   b. Click the text *Adventure Tours* to select the placeholder and then drag the placeholder down toward the bottom of the slide and center the text horizontally. (Click the Center button in the Paragraph group in the Home tab.)
   c. Insert the **FCTLogo.jpg** (do this with the Picture button in the Insert tab) and then increase the size of the logo so it fills a good portion of the upper part of the slide.
   d. Set the color to transparent for the background of the logo by clicking the Picture Tools Format tab, clicking the Color button, clicking *Set Transparent Color* at the drop-down list, and then clicking just below the line below *First Choice Travel*.
6. Make Slide 2 active and then change the layout to *Title Only*.
7. Make Slide 3 active, change the line spacing to 2.0 for the bulleted text, and then insert a clip art image of your choosing related to *travel* or *sunshine*.
8. Make Slide 4 active and then change the line spacing to 1.5 for the bulleted text.
9. Save the presentation and name it **P-C8-P1-ATTopFive**.

Copying and Pasting Data

Use the Copy and Paste buttons in the Clipboard group in the Home tab to copy data such as text or an object from one program and then paste it into another program. For example, in Project 1b, you will copy an Excel chart and then paste it into a PowerPoint slide. You can move and size a copied object, such as a chart, like any other object.

Project 1b Copying an Excel Chart to a Slide   Part 2 of 8

1. With **P-C8-P1-ATTopFive.pptx** open, make Slide 2 active.
2. Open Excel and then open the workbook named **Top5Tours.xlsx** located in the PowerPoint2010C8 folder on your storage medium.

3. Click the chart to select it. (Make sure you select the chart and not an element in the chart.)
4. Click the Copy button in the Clipboard group in the Home tab.
5. Close the **Top5Tours.xlsx** workbook and exit Excel.
6. In PowerPoint, with Slide 2 active, click the Paste button in the Clipboard group in the Home tab.
7. Resize and move the chart so it fills a good portion of the slide below the title and to the right of the slide design background.
8. Modify the chart by completing the following steps:
   a. Make sure the chart is selected and then click the Chart Tools Design tab.
   b. Click the More button at the right side of the chart styles thumbnails and then click *Style 38* at the drop-down gallery (sixth option from the left in the fifth row).
   c. Click the Chart Tools Format tab.
   d. Click the Shape Outline button arrow in the Shape Styles group and then click *No Outline* at the drop-down gallery.
9. Display Slide 1 in the Slide pane and then run the presentation.
10. Print only Slide 2.
11. Save **P-C8-P1-ATTopFive.pptx**.

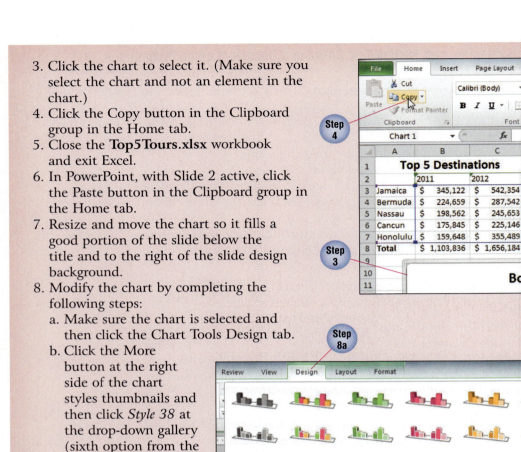

Use the Clipboard task pane to collect and paste multiple items. You can collect up to 24 different items and then paste them in various locations. Turn on the display of the Clipboard task pane by clicking the Clipboard group dialog box launcher. The Clipboard task pane displays at the left side of the screen. Select data or an object you want to copy and then click the Copy button in the Clipboard group.

Continue selecting text or items and clicking the Copy button. To insert an item, position the insertion point in the desired location and then click the button in the Clipboard task pane representing the item. If the copied item is text, the first 50 characters display. When all desired items are inserted, click the Clear All button to remove any remaining items from the Clipboard task pane. If you want to paste all items from the Clipboard task pane at once, click the Paste All button.

HINT Click the Options button at the bottom of the Clipboard task pane to customize the display of the task pane.

Project 1c **Collecting and Pasting Text Between a Document and a Presentation** **Part 3 of 8**

1. With **P-C8-P1-ATTopFive.pptx** open, make Slide 4 active and then insert a new slide with the *Title and Content* layout.
2. Click the text *Click to add title* and then type Spring Treks. Select *Spring Treks* and then change the font color to black.
3. Copy text from Word by completing the following steps:
    a. Open Word and then open **AdvTreks.docx**.
    b. Click the Clipboard group dialog box launcher to display the Clipboard task pane.
    c. If any data displays in the Clipboard task pane, click the Clear All button located toward the top of the task pane.
    d. Select the text *Yucatan Adventure – 10 days* (including the paragraph mark following the text—consider turning on the display of nonprinting characters) and then click the Copy button in the Clipboard group.
    e. Select the text *Mexico Adventure – 14 days* and then click the Copy button.
    f. Select the text *Caribbean Highlights – 16 days* and then click the Copy button.
    g. Select the text *California Delights – 7 days* and then click the Copy button.
    h. Select the text *Canyon Adventure – 10 days* and then click the Copy button.
    i. Select the text *Canadian Parks – 12 days* and then click the Copy button.
    j. Select the text *Royal Canadian Adventure – 14 days* and then click the Copy button.
4. Click the PowerPoint button on the Taskbar and then paste items from the Clipboard task pane by completing the following steps:
    a. With Slide 5 active, click the text *Click to add text*.
    b. Click the Clipboard group dialog box launcher to display the Clipboard task pane.
    c. Click the *California Delights* item in the Clipboard task pane.

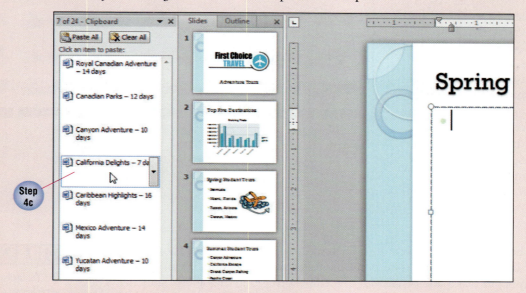

   d. Click the *Canadian Parks* item in the Clipboard task pane.
   e. Click the *Caribbean Highlights* item in the Clipboard task pane.
   f. Click the *Mexico Adventure* item in the Clipboard task pane
   g. Click the *Yucatan Adventure* item in the Clipboard task pane. (Press the Backspace key twice to remove the bullet below *Yucatan Adventure* and the blank line.)

5. Select the bulleted text and then change the line spacing to 1.5.
6. Clear the Clipboard task pane by clicking the Clear All button located in the upper right corner of the task pane.
7. Close the Clipboard task pane by clicking the Close button (contains an *X*) located in the upper right corner of the task pane.
8. Make Slide 1 the active slide and then run the presentation.
9. Print the presentation as a handout with all slides printed horizontally on one page. (Make sure the first gallery in the Settings category displays as *Print All Slides*.)
10. Save **P-C8-P1-ATTopFive.pptx**.
11. Make Word the active program, close the Clipboard task pane, close **AdvTreks.docx**, and then exit Word.

Sharing Presentations

PowerPoint provides a number of options for sharing presentations between programs, sites on the Internet, other computers, and as attachments. Options for sending and sharing presentations are available at the Save & Send tab Backstage view shown in Figure 8.1. Display this view by clicking the File tab and then clicking the Save & Send tab.

Figure 8.1 Save & Send Tab Backstage View

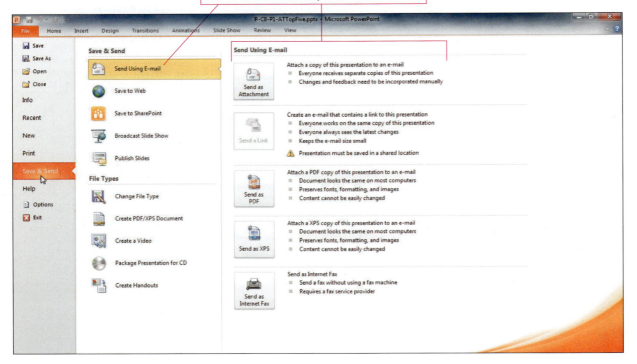

Saving and Sending a Presentation

The Save & Send tab Backstage view contains the Save & Send section with options for sending a presentation as attachment to an email, saving a presentation to the Web or SharePoint, and broadcasting a presentation and publishing slides in a presentation.

With the *Send Using E-mail* option selected, options for sending a presentation display such as sending a copy of the presentation as an attachment to an email, creating an email that contains a link to the presentation, attaching a PDF or XPS copy of the open presentation to an email, and sending an email as an Internet fax. To send the presentation as an attachment, you need to set up an Outlook email account. If you want to create an email that contains a link to the presentation, you need to save the presentation to a web server. Use the last option, *Send as Internet Fax*, to fax the current presentation without using a fax machine. To use this button, you must be signed up with a fax service provider. If you have not previously signed up for a service, you will be prompted to do so.

With the remaining two options in the Send Using E-mail category of the Save & Send tab Backstage view, you can send the presentation in PDF or XPS format. The letters PDF stand for *portable document format*, which is a file format developed by Adobe Systems® that captures all of the elements of a presentation as an electronic image. The XPS format is a Microsoft file format for publishing content in an easily viewable format. The letters XPS stand for *XML paper specification*, and the letters XML stand for *extensible markup language*, which is a set of rules for encoding presentations electronically. The options listed below *Attach a PDF copy of this presentation to an e-mail* and *Attach a XPS copy of this presentation to an e-mail* describe the format and the advantages of saving in the PDF or XPS format.

If you want to share presentations with others, consider saving presentations to Windows Live SkyDrive, which is a file storage and sharing service that allows you to upload files that can be accessed from a web browser. To save a presentation to SkyDrive, you need a Windows Live ID account. If you have a Hotmail, Messenger, or Xbox LIVE account, you have a Windows Live ID account.

Microsoft SharePoint is a collection of products and software that includes a number of components. If your company or organization uses SharePoint, you can save a presentation in a library on your organization's SharePoint site so you and your colleagues have a central location for accessing presentations. To save a presentation to a SharePoint library, open the presentation, click the File tab, click the Save & Send tab, and then click the Save to SharePoint button.

You can save a presentation as a blog post with the Publish as Blog Post button in the Save & Send tab Backstage view. To save a blog post, you must have a blog site established. Click the Publish as Blog Post button and information about supported blog sites displays at the right side of the Save & Send tab Backstage view.

Project 1d Sending a Presentation as an Email Attachment   Part 4 of 8

Note: Before completing this optional exercise, check with your instructor to determine if you have Outlook set up as your email provider.

1. With **P-C8-P1-ATTopFive.pptx** open, click the File tab and then click the Save & Send tab.
2. At the Save & Send tab Backstage view, click the Send as Attachment button in the *Send Using E-mail* category.
3. At the Outlook window, type your instructor's email address in the *To* text box.
4. Click the Send button.

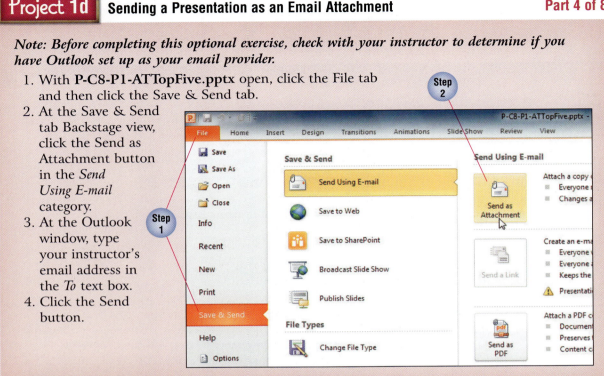

Saving a Presentation in a Different Format

When you save a presentation, it is automatically saved as a PowerPoint presentation. If you need to share a presentation with someone who is using a different presentation program or a different version of PowerPoint, you may want to save the presentation in another format. At the Save & Send tab Backstage view, click the *Change File Type* option in the File Types category and the view displays as shown in Figure 8.2.

With options in the *Presentation File Types* section, you can choose to save a PowerPoint presentation with the default file format, save the presentation in a previous version of PowerPoint, in OpenDocument Presentation format, as a PowerPoint show, or as a PowerPoint picture presentation. You can also save a presentation as an image with the PNG or JPG file extensions. A brief description follows each option.

▼ **Quick Steps**

Save Presentation in Different Format
1. Click File tab.
2. Click Save & Send tab.
3. Click *Change File Type* option in File Types category.
4. Click desired format in Change File Type category.
5. Click Save As button.

Figure 8.2 Save & Send Tab Backstage View with Change File Type Option Selected

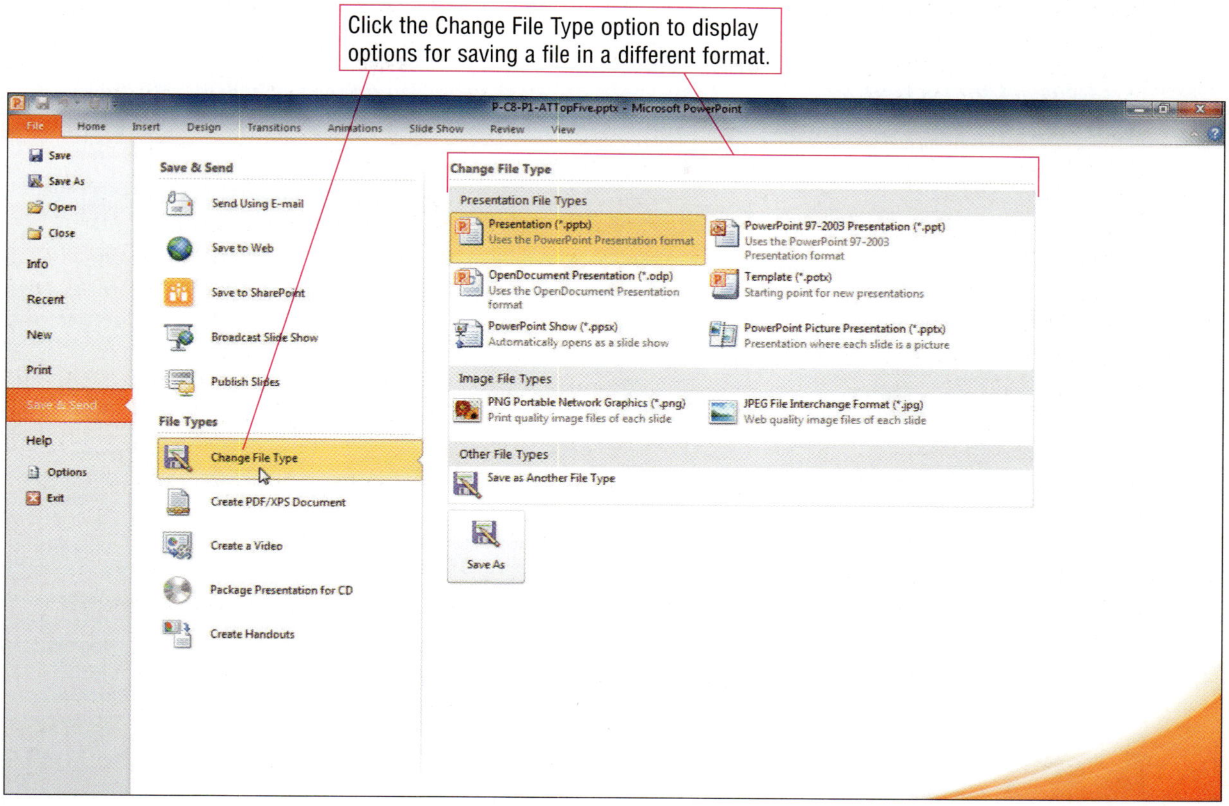
Click the Change File Type option to display options for saving a file in a different format.
P-C8-P1-ATTopFive.pptx - Microsoft PowerPoint
File
Home
Insert
Design
Transitions
Animations
Slide Show
Review
View
Save
Save As
Open
Close
Info
Recent
New
Print
Save & Send
Help
Options
Exit
Save & Send
Send Using E-mail
Save to Web
Save to SharePoint
Broadcast Slide Show
Publish Slides
File Types
Change File Type
Create PDF/XPS Document
Create a Video
Package Presentation for CD
Create Handouts
Change File Type
Presentation File Types
Presentation (*.pptx)
Uses the PowerPoint Presentation format
PowerPoint 97-2003 Presentation (*.ppt)
Uses the PowerPoint 97-2003 Presentation format
OpenDocument Presentation (*.odp)
Uses the OpenDocument Presentation format
Template (*.potx)
Starting point for new presentations
PowerPoint Show (*.ppsx)
Automatically opens as a slide show
PowerPoint Picture Presentation (*.pptx)
Presentation where each slide is a picture
Image File Types
PNG Portable Network Graphics (*.png)
Print quality image files of each slide
JPEG File Interchange Format (*.jpg)
Web quality image files of each slide
Other File Types
Save as Another File Type
Save As

Project 1e Saving a Presentation as a PowerPoint Show and in a Previous Version Part 5 of 8

1. Make sure that **P-C8-P1-ATTopFive.pptx** is open.
2. Save the presentation as a PowerPoint Show by completing the following steps:
   a. Click the File tab and then click the Save & Send tab.
   b. At the Save & Send tab Backstage view, click the *Change File Type* option in the File Types category.
   c. Click the *PowerPoint Show (*.ppsx)* option in the *Presentation File Types* section and then click the Save As button.

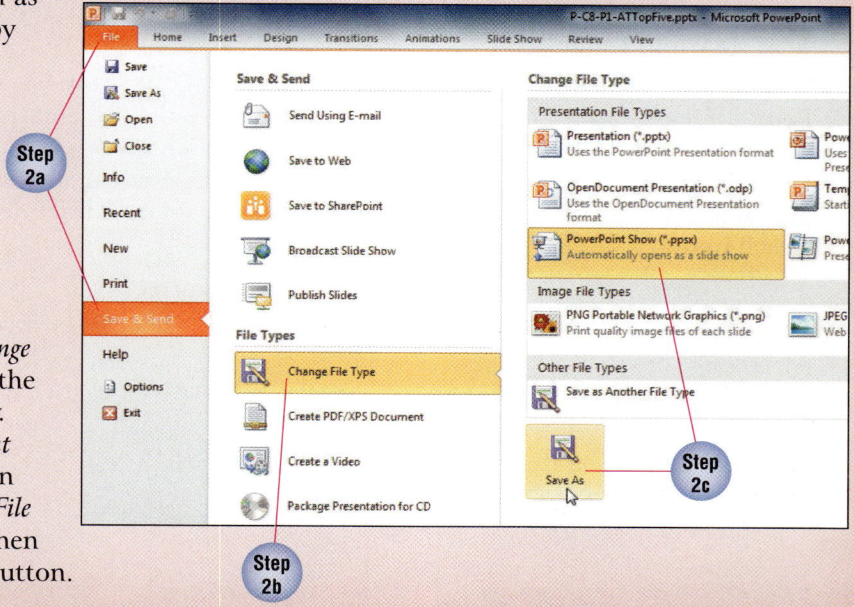
Step 2a
Step 2b
Step 2c
P-C8-P1-ATTopFive.pptx - Microsoft PowerPoint
File
Home
Insert
Design
Transitions
Animations
Slide Show
Review
View
Save
Save As
Open
Close
Info
Recent
New
Print
Save & Send
Help
Options
Exit
Save & Send
Send Using E-mail
Save to Web
Save to SharePoint
Broadcast Slide Show
Publish Slides
File Types
Change File Type
Create PDF/XPS Document
Create a Video
Package Presentation for CD
Change File Type
Presentation File Types
Presentation (*.pptx)
Uses the PowerPoint Presentation format
OpenDocument Presentation (*.odp)
Uses the OpenDocument Presentation format
PowerPoint Show (*.ppsx)
Automatically opens as a slide show
Image File Types
PNG Portable Network Graphics (*.png)
Print quality image files of each slide
Other File Types
Save as Another File Type
Save As

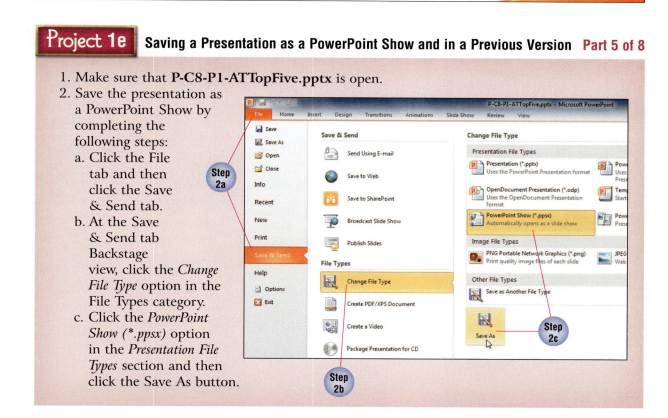

d. At the Save As dialog box, click the Save button. (This saves the presentation with the file extension *.ppsx*.)
3. Close **P-C8-P1-ATTopFive.ppsx**.
4. Open the **P-C8-P1-ATTopFive.ppsx** file in Windows Explorer by completing the following steps:
   a. Click the Windows Explorer button (button containing yellow file folders) on the Taskbar.
   b. In Windows Explorer, double-click the drive representing your storage medium.
   c. Navigate to the PowerPoint2010C8 folder on your storage medium and then double-click ***P-C8-P1-ATTopFive.ppsx***. (This starts the presentation in Slide Show view.)
   d. Run the presentation.
   e. When the presentation has ended, press the Esc key.
   f. Close Windows Explorer by clicking the Windows Explorer button on the Taskbar and then clicking the Close button located in the upper right corner of the window.
5. Open **P-C8-P1-ATTopFive.pptx** (make sure you open the file with the *.pptx* file extension) and then save the presentation in a previous version of PowerPoint by completing the following steps:
   a. Click the File tab and then click the Save & Send tab.
   b. Click the *Change File Type* option in the File Types category.
   c. Click *PowerPoint 97-2003 Presentation (*.ppt)* in the *Presentation File Types* section and then click the Save As button.

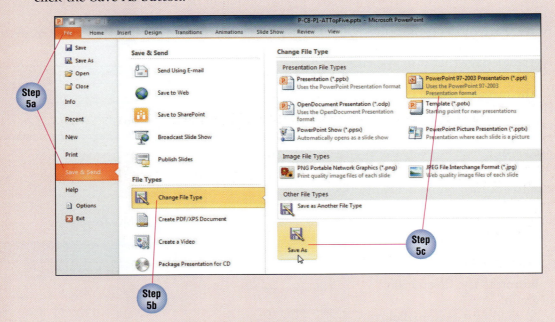

   d. At the Save As dialog box, type **P-C8-P1-ATTopFive-2003format** in the *File name* text box and then click the Save button.
   e. At the Microsoft PowerPoint Compatibility Checker dialog box, click the Continue button.
   f. At the presentation, notice that the file name at the top of the screen displays followed by the words [*Compatibility Mode*].
6. Close **P-C8-P1-ATTopFive-2003format.ppt**.

With options in the *Image File Types* section, you can save slides in a presentation as graphic images as PNG or JPEG files. Save slides as PNG images if you want print quality and save slides as JPEG images if you are going to post the slide images to the Internet. To save a slide or all slides as graphic images, click either the *PNG Portable Network Graphics (*.png)* option or the *JPEG File Interchange Format (*.jpg)* option in the *Image File Types* section and then click the Save As button. At the Save As dialog box, type a name for the slide or presentation and then click the Save button. At the message that displays, click the Every Slide button if you want every slide in the presentation saved as a graphic image or click the Current Slide Only button if you want only the current slide saved as a graphic image. If you click the Every Slide button, a message displays telling you that all slides in the presentation were saved as separate files in a folder. The name of the folder is the name that you type in the *File name* text box in the Save As dialog box.

Project 1f   Saving Slides as Graphic Images   Part 6 of 8

1. Open **P-C8-P1-ATTopFive.pptx**.
2. Click the File tab and then click the Save & Send tab.
3. At the Save & Send tab Backstage view, click the *Change File Type* option in the File Types category.
4. Click the *PNG Portable Network Graphics (*.png)* option in the *Image File Types* section and then click the Save As button.
5. At the Save As dialog box, make sure **P-C8-P1-ATTopFive.png** displays in the *File name* text box and then click the Save button.
6. At the message that displays, click the Every Slide button.
7. At the message telling you that each slide has been saved as a separate file in the P-C8-P1-ATTopFive.png folder, click OK.
8. Open Word.
9. At a blank document, change the font size to 18, turn on bold, change the alignment to center, and then type **Adventure Tours**.
10. Press the Enter key twice and then insert one of the slides saved in PNG format by completing the following steps:
    a. Click the Insert tab and then click the Picture button in the Illustrations group.
    b. At the Insert Picture dialog box, navigate to the P-C8-P1-ATTopFive folder in the PowerPoint2010C8 folder on your storage medium and then double-click *Slide3.PNG*.

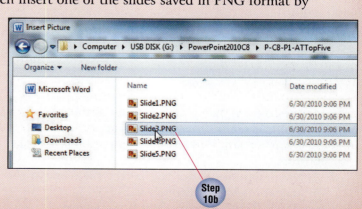

11. Format the image in the document by completing the following steps:
    a. Click in the *Shape Height* measurement box in the Size group in the Picture Tools Format tab, type 2.8, and then press Enter.
    b. Click the *Drop Shadow Rectangle* option in the Picture Styles group.
12. Press Ctrl + End to move the insertion point to the end of the document, press the Enter key, and then complete steps similar to those in Steps 10 and 11 to insert and format the image *Slide4.PNG* in the document.
13. Save the document and name it **P-C8-P1-ATTours**.
14. Print and then close **P-C8-P1-ATTours.docx**.
15. Exit Word.

As you learned earlier, the portable document format (PDF) captures all of the elements of a presentation as an electronic image, and the XPS format is used for publishing content in an easily viewable format. To save a presentation in PDF or XPS format, click the File tab, click the Save & Send tab, click the *Create PDF/XPS Document* option in the File Types category, and then click the Create PDF/XPS button in the Create a PDF/XPS Document category. This displays the Publish as PDF or XPS dialog box with the *PDF (*.pdf)* option selected in the *Save as type* option button. If you want to save the presentation in XPS format, click the *Save as type* option button and then click *XPS Document (*.xps)* at the drop-down list. At the Save As dialog box, type a name in the *File name* text box and then click the Publish button.

If you save the presentation in PDF format, the presentation opens in Adobe Reader and if you save the presentation in XPS format, the presentation opens the XPS Viewer window. You can open a PDF file in Adobe Reader or in your web browser, and you can open an XPS file in your web browser.

With the *Create a Video* option in the File Types category, you can create a video from the presentation that incorporates all of the recorded timings and narrations and preserves animations and transitions. The information at the right side of the Save & Send tab Backstage view describes creating a video and provides a hyperlink to get help on burning a slide show video to a DVD or uploading it to the Web. Click the <u>Get help burning your slide show video to DVD or uploading it to the Web</u> hyperlink and information displays on burning your slide show video to disc, publishing your slide show video to YouTube, and turning your presentation into a video.

Use the *Package Presentation for CD* option to copy a presentation including all of the linked files, embedded items, and fonts. This option will also save the PowerPoint Viewer program in case the destination computer does not have PowerPoint installed. Click the *Package Presentation for CD* option in the File Types category and then click the Package for CD button and the Package for CD dialog box displays. At this dialog box, type a name for the CD and specify the files you want copied. You can copy the presentation to a CD or to a specific folder.

▼ **Quick Steps**

Save Presentation in PDF/XPS Format
1. Open presentation.
2. Click File tab.
3. Click Save & Send tab.
4. Click *Create PDF/XPS Document* option.
5. Click Create PDF/XPS button.
6. At Publish as PDF or XPS dialog box, specify if you want to save in PDF or XPS format.
7. Click Publish button.

Save Presentation as Video
1. Open presentation.
2. Click File tab, Save & Send tab.
3. Click *Create a Video* option.
4. Click Create Video button.

Package Presentation for CD
1. Open presentation.
2. Click File tab, Save & Send tab.
3. Click *Package Presentation for CD* option.
4. Click Package for CD button.
5. Click Copy to CD button or Copy to Folder button.

Project 1g Saving a Presentation in PDF Format, as a Video, and Packaged for CD   Part 7 of 8

1. With **P-C8-P1-ATTopFive.pptx** open, save the presentation in PDF format by completing the following steps:
   a. Click the File tab and then click the Save & Send tab.
   b. Click the *Create PDF/XPS Document* option in the File Types category.
   c. Click the Create PDF/XPS button.
   d. At the Publish as PDF or XPS dialog box, insert a check mark in the *Open file after publishing* check box and then click the Publish button. (In a few moments the presentation displays in PDF format in Adobe Reader.)

   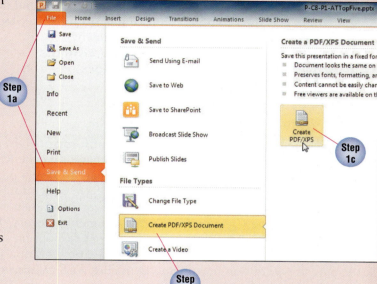

   e. Scroll through the presentation in Adobe Reader.
   f. Click the Close button located in the upper right corner of the window to close Adobe Reader.

2. Save **P-C8-P1-ATTopFive.pptx** as a video by completing the following steps:
   a. Click the File tab and then click the Save & Send tab.
   b. Click the *Create a Video* option in the File Types category.
   c. Click the Create Video button in the *Create a Video* section.
   d. At the Save As dialog box, click the Save button. (Saving to video takes a minute or so. The Status bar displays the saving progress.)

   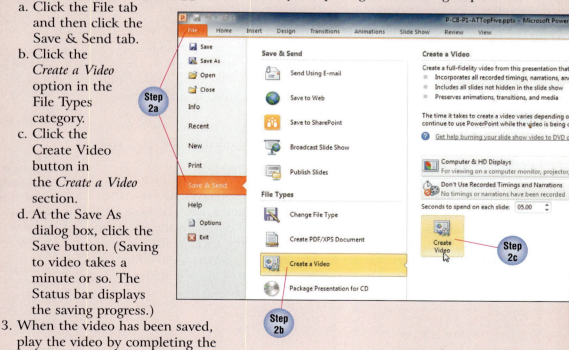

3. When the video has been saved, play the video by completing the following steps:
   a. Click the Windows Explorer button on the Taskbar.

b. Navigate to the PowerPoint2010C8 folder on your storage medium and then double-click *P-C8-P1-ATTopFive.wmv*. (This opens the presentation video in a viewing window.)
c. Watch the presentation video and, when it is finished, close the viewing window.
d. Close Windows Explorer.
4. With **P-C8-P1-ATTopFive.pptx** open, package the presentation by completing the following steps:
   a. Click the File tab and then click the Save & Send tab.
   b. Click the *Package Presentation for CD* option in the File Types category.
   c. Click the Package for CD button.
   d. At the Package for CD dialog box, type **ATTopFiveforCD** in the *Name the CD* text box.
   e. Click the Copy to Folder button.
   f. At the Copy to Folder dialog box, click the Browse button.
   g. Navigate to your storage medium.
   h. Click the Select button.
   i. At the Copy to Folder dialog box, click OK.
   j. At the message asking if you want to include linked files in the presentation, click the Yes button.
   k. When a window displays with the folder name and files, close the window by clicking the Close button in the upper right corner of the window.
   l. Close the Package for CD dialog box by clicking the Close button.

With the *Create Handouts* option in the File Types category at the Save & Send tab Backstage view, you can export a PowerPoint presentation to a Word document. You can print slides as handouts in PowerPoint; however, you may prefer to export the presentation to Word to have greater control over the formatting of the handouts. To export a presentation, open the presentation, click the File tab, click the Save & Send tab, and then click the *Create Handouts* option in the File Types category. This displays the Send To Microsoft Word dialog box shown in Figure 8.3. At this dialog box, select the page layout you want to use in Word and then click OK.

HINT Export a presentation to Word to allow more control in formatting handouts.

Figure 8.3 Send To Microsoft Word Dialog Box

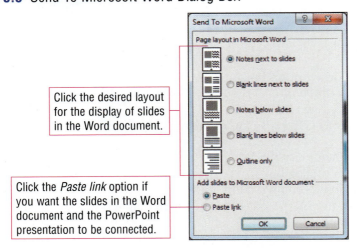

Click the desired layout for the display of slides in the Word document.

Click the *Paste link* option if you want the slides in the Word document and the PowerPoint presentation to be connected.

The first four page layout options will export slides as they appear in PowerPoint with lines to the right or below the slides. The last option will export the text only as an outline. If you select the *Paste link* option, the Word document will be automatically updated whenever changes are made to the PowerPoint presentation.

Project 1h Exporting a Presentation to Word   Part 8 of 8

1. Make sure **P-C8-P1-ATTopFive.pptx** is open, click the File tab, and then click the Save & Send tab.
2. At the Save & Send tab Backstage view, click the *Create Handouts* option in the File Types category.
3. Click the Create Handouts button.
4. At the Send To Microsoft Word dialog box, click the *Blank lines next to slides* option and then click OK.
5. Click the Word button on the Taskbar.
6. In Word, select the first column (the column that contains *Slide 1*, *Slide 2*, and so on) and then turn on bold. (The presentation was inserted in a table in Word.)
7. Select the third column (contains the lines) and then change the font color to red.
8. Save the document and name it **P-C8-P1-ATTopTours**.
9. Print and then close **P-C8-P1-ATTopTours.docx**.
10. Exit Word.
11. In PowerPoint, save and then close **P-C8-P1-ATTopFive.pptx**.
12. Capture an image of the Open dialog box and insert the image in a PowerPoint slide by completing the following steps:
    a. Press Ctrl + N to display a new blank presentation.
    b. Click the Layout button in the Slides group in the Home tab and then click the *Blank* layout at the drop-down list.
    c. Click the File tab and then click the Open button.
    d. At the Open dialog box, click the option button that displays to the right of the *File name* text box (option button that contains the text *All PowerPoint Presentations*) and then click *All Files (*.*)* at the drop-down list.
    e. Make sure that all of your project files display. You may need to scroll down the list box to display the files.
    f. Hold down the Alt key and then press the Print Screen button on your keyboard. (This captures an image of the Open dialog box.)
    g. Click the Cancel button to close the Open dialog box.
    h. Click the Paste button. (This inserts the image of the Open dialog box into the slide.)
13. Print the slide as a full page slide.
14. Close the presentation without saving it.

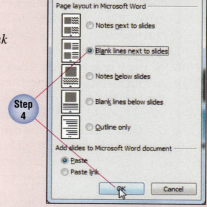

Step 4

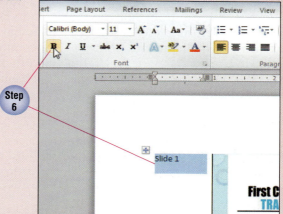

Step 6

Project 2 — Embed and Link Excel Charts to a Presentation — 3 Parts

You will open a company funds presentation and then copy an Excel pie chart and embed it in a PowerPoint slide. You will also copy and link an Excel column chart to a slide and then update the chart in Excel.

Embedding and Linking Objects

One of the reasons the Microsoft Office suite is used extensively in business is because it allows data from an individual program to be seamlessly integrated into another program. For example, a chart depicting sales projections created in Excel can easily be added to a slide in a presentation to the company board of directors on the new budget forecast.

Integration is the process of completing a file by adding parts to it from other sources. Duplicating data that already exist in another program should be a rare instance. Copy and paste objects from one application to another when the content is not likely to change. If the content is dynamic, the copy and paste method becomes problematic and prone to error. To illustrate this point, assume one of the outcomes from the presentation to the board of directors is a revision to the sales projections. The chart that was originally created in Excel has to be updated to reflect the new projections. The existing chart in PowerPoint needs to be deleted and then the revised chart in Excel copied and pasted to the slide. Both Excel and PowerPoint need to be opened and edited to reflect this change in projection. In this case, copying and pasting the chart was not efficient.

To eliminate the inefficiency of the copy and paste method, you can integrate data between programs. An object can be text in a presentation, data in a table, a chart, a picture, a slide, or any combination of data that you would like to share between programs. The program that was used to create the object is called the *source* and the program the object is linked or embedded to is called the *destination*.

Embedding and linking are two methods you can use to integrate data in addition to the copy and paste method. When an object is embedded, the content in the object is stored in both the source and the destination programs. When you edit an embedded object in the destination program, the source program in which the program was created opens. If the content in the object is changed in the source program, the change is not reflected in the destination program and vice versa.

Linking inserts a code into the destination file connecting the destination to the name and location of the source object. The object itself is not stored within the destination file. When linking, if a change is made to the content in the source program, the destination program reflects the change automatically. Your decision to integrate data by embedding or linking will depend on whether the data is dynamic or static. If the data is dynamic, then linking the object is the most efficient method of integration.

Embedding Objects

An object that is embedded will be stored in both the source *and* the destination programs. The content of the object can be edited in *either* the source or the destination; however, a change made in one will not be reflected in the other. The difference between copying and pasting and embedding is that embedded objects can be edited with the source program's editing tabs and options.

HINT Static data remains the same while dynamic data changes periodically or continually.

▼ Quick Steps

Embed an Object
1. Open source program.
2. Select desired object.
3. Click Copy button.
4. Open destination program.
5. Click Paste button arrow.
6. Click *Paste Special*.
7. Click source of object.
8. Click OK.

Since embedded objects are edited within the source program, the source program must reside on the computer when the presentation is opened for editing. If you are preparing a presentation that will be edited on another computer, you may want to check before embedding any objects to verify that the other computer has the same programs.

To embed an object, open both programs and both files. In the source program, click the desired object and then click the Copy button in the Clipboard group in the Home tab. Click the button on the Taskbar representing the destination program file and then position the insertion point at the location where you want the object embedded. Click the Paste button arrow in the Clipboard group and then click *Paste Special* at the drop-down list. At the Paste Special dialog box, click the source of the object in the *As* list box and then click OK.

You can edit an embedded object by double-clicking the object. This displays the object with the source program tabs and options. Make any desired changes and then click outside the object to exit the source program tabs and options. You can apply animation effects to an embedded object with the same techniques you learned in Chapter 7.

Project 2a Embedding an Excel Chart in a Presentation   Part 1 of 3

1. Open **FundsPres.pptx** and then save the presentation with Save As and name it **P-C8-P2-FundsPres**.
2. Open Excel and then open the workbook named **Funds01.xlsx** located in the PowerPoint2010C8 folder on your storage medium.
3. Click the chart to select it. (Make sure the chart is selected and not an element in the chart.)
4. Click the Copy button in the Clipboard group in the Home tab.
5. Click the PowerPoint button on the Taskbar.
6. Make Slide 4 active.
7. Click the Paste button arrow and then click *Paste Special* at the drop-down list.
8. At the Paste Special dialog box, make sure *Microsoft Office Graphic Object* is selected in the *As* list box and then click OK.

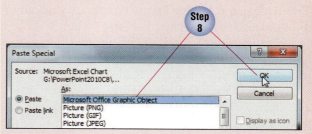

9. With the chart selected, click the Chart Tools Design tab.
10. Click the More button at the right side of the Chart Styles thumbnails and then click *Style 4* (fourth option from the left in the top row).
11. Click the Chart Tools Format tab.
12. Click in the *Shape Height* measurement box and then type 6.
13. Click in the *Shape Width* measurement box, type 9.5, and then press Enter.
14. Press Ctrl + B to bold the text in the pie.
15. Center the pie chart in the slide below the title.
16. Save **P-C8-P2-FundsPres.pptx**.
17. Click the Excel button on the Taskbar, close the workbook, and then exit Excel.

Linking Objects

If the content of the object that you will integrate between programs is likely to change, then link the object from the source program to the destination program. Linking the object establishes a direct connection between the source and destination programs. The object is stored in the source program only. The destination program will have a code inserted into it that indicates the name and location of the source of the object. Whenever the presentation containing the link is opened, a message displays saying that the presentation contains links and the user is prompted to update the links.

To link an object, open both programs and open both program files. In the source program file, click the desired object and then click the Copy button in the Clipboard group in the Home tab. Click the button on the Taskbar representing the destination program file and then position the insertion point in the desired location. Click the Paste button arrow in the Clipboard group in the Home tab and then click *Paste Special* at the drop-down list. At the Paste Special dialog box, click the source program for the object in the *As* list box, click the *Paste link* option located at the left side of the *As* list box, and then click OK.

▼ Quick Steps
Link an Object
1. Open source program.
2. Select desired object.
3. Click Copy button.
4. Open destination program.
5. Click Paste button arrow.
6. Click *Paste Special*.
7. Click *Paste link* option.
8. Click OK.

HINT
Since linking does not increase the size of the file in the destination program, consider linking objects if file size is a consideration.

Project 2b   Linking an Excel Chart to a Presentation   Part 2 of 3

1. With **P-C8-P2-FundsPres.pptx** open, open Excel and then open **Funds02.xlsx** located in the PowerPoint2010C8 folder on your storage medium.
2. Save the workbook with Save As and name it **P-C8-P2-MMFunds**.
3. Copy and link the chart to a slide in the presentation by completing the following steps:
   a. Click the chart to select it.
   b. Click the Copy button in the Clipboard group in the Home tab.
   c. Click the PowerPoint button on the Taskbar.
   d. Make Slide 5 active.
   e. Click the Paste button arrow and then click *Paste Special* at the drop-down list.
   f. At the Paste Special dialog box, click the *Paste Link* option.
   g. Make sure *Microsoft Excel Chart Object* is selected in the *As* list box and then click OK.

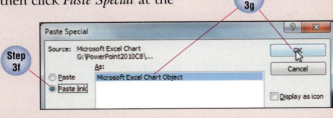

   h. Increase the size of the chart in the slide so it fills a good portion of the slide below the title. Move the chart so it appears balanced below the title.
4. Click the Excel button on the Taskbar, close **P-C8-P2-MMFunds.xlsx**, and then exit Excel.
5. Make Slide 1 active and then run the presentation.
6. Save and then close **P-C8-P2-FundsPres.pptx**.

Editing Linked Objects

Edit linked objects in the source program in which they were created. Open the document, workbook, or presentation containing the object, make the changes as required, and then save and close the file. If both the source and destination programs are open at the same time, the changed content is reflected immediately in both programs.

Project 2c **Editing Linked Data** Part 3 of 3

1. Open Excel and then open **P-C8-P2-MMFunds.xlsx**.
2. Make the following changes to data in the following cells:
   a. Change B2 from *13%* to *17%*.
   b. Change B3 from *9%* to *12%*.
   c. Change B6 from *10%* to *14%*.
3. Click the Save button on the Quick Access toolbar to save the edited workbook.
4. Close **P-C8-P2-MMFunds.xlsx** and then exit Excel.
5. In PowerPoint, open **P-C8-P2-FundsPres.pptx**.
6. At the message telling you that the presentation contains links, click the Update Links button.
7. Make Slide 5 active and then notice the changes in the chart data.
8. Print the presentation as a handout with six slides horizontally per page.
9. Save and then close **P-C8-P2-FundsPres.pptx**.

Project 3 **Download and Apply a Design Template to a Presentation and Prepare a Presentation for Sharing** 9 Parts

You will download a design template from Office.com and apply the template to a company presentation. You will insert, edit, and delete comments in the presentation; modify the presentation properties; inspect the presentation; and encrypt the presentation with a password.

Downloading Designs

Quick Steps

Download a Design
1. Click File tab, New tab.
2. Click *Design slides* option.
3. Click desired category.
4. Click desired design.
5. Click Download button.

PowerPoint 2010 provides a number of design templates you can apply to a presentation. The Office.com website contains additional design templates you can download and apply to a presentation. To view the available design templates for downloading, click the File tab and then click the New tab. At the New tab Backstage view, click the *Design slides* option in the *Office.com Templates* section. This displays categories of design templates. Click a category and design templates in the category display in the *Office.com Templates* section and information about the design displays at the right side of the Backstage view.

Some design options in the middle panel may contain a small logo of shoulders and a head. This indicates that the design template was created by a member of the Microsoft Office Online Community and Microsoft cannot guarantee that the design will work or that the design template is free from viruses or defects.

To download a design template, click the desired template in the *Office.com Templates* section and then click the Download button located at the right side of the Backstage view. A message may display telling you that the templates are only available to customers running genuine Microsoft Office. If this message displays, click the Continue button. When the download is complete, the design template is applied to the open presentation and is also available in the Themes group in the Design tab.

Microsoft checks the validity of your Microsoft Office software when you download a template.

Project 3a — Downloading and Applying a Design Theme — Part 1 of 9

Note: Check with your instructor before downloading a design template. To download a template you must have access to the Internet and access to the hard drive. If the Target the market design template is already downloaded, skip Steps 1 through 8 below. If you do not have access to the design template or cannot download it, open ISPres.pptx, save it with the name P-C8-P3-ISPres, apply a design theme of your choosing, and then continue with Step 10.

1. At a blank presentation, click the File tab and then click the New tab.
2. At the New tab Backstage view, click the *Design slides* option in the *Office.com Templates* section.

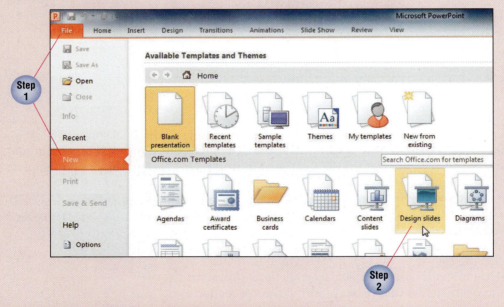

3. Click the *Business* folder in the *Office.com Templates* section.

Chapter 8 ■ Integrating, Sharing, and Protecting Presentations

4. Scroll down the list of design templates and then click the *Target the market design template* (shown below).

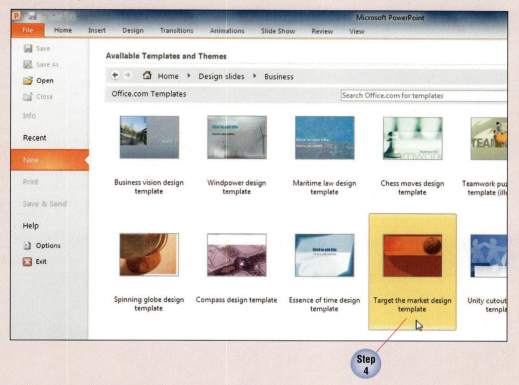

Step 4

5. Click the Download button that displays at the right side of the Backstage view. (If a message displays telling you that the templates are only available to customers running genuine Microsoft Office, click the Continue button.) This applies the design template to the current blank presentation.
6. Close the presentation without saving it.
7. Open **ISPres.pptx** and then save the presentation with the name **P-C8-P3-ISPres**.
8. Apply the new design template by clicking the Design tab, clicking the More button at the right side of the theme thumbnails, and then clicking the *Target the market design template* theme that displays in the *Custom* section of the drop-down gallery.
9. Click the Colors button in the Themes group and then click *Office Theme 5* at the drop-down gallery.
10. Make each slide active and then make any formatting changes to elements so they appear attractively in the slide.
11. Save **P-C8-P3-ISPres.pptx**.

Step 8

Using Comments

If you are sending out a presentation for review and want to ask reviewers specific questions or provide information about slides in a presentation, insert a comment. To insert a comment, display the desired slide and then position the insertion

point where you want the comment to appear. Click the Review tab and then click the New Comment button in the Comments group. At the comment box that displays, type the desired comment. After typing the desired comment, click outside the comment box and a small yellow box displays with the user's initials and a comment number. Comments by individual users are numbered sequentially beginning with 1.

To print comments, display the Print tab Backstage view and then click the second gallery in the Settings category (this is the gallery containing the text *Full Page Slides*). At the drop-down list that displays, make sure the *Print Comments and Ink Markup* check box contains a check mark. Comments print on a separate page after the presentation is printed.

By default, the Show Markup button is active (displays with an orange background) in the Comments group in the Review tab. With this button active, comment boxes display in slides. If you want to hide comment boxes, click the Show Markup button to deactivate it. Use the Next button in the Comments group to display the next comment in a presentation and use the Previous button to display the previous comment. If you turn off the display of comment boxes, you can use the Next and Previous buttons to display comments.

Quick Steps

Insert a Comment
1. Click Review tab.
2. Click New Comment button.
3. Type comment text.

HINT
Move a comment by selecting the comment box and then dragging it to the desired location.

New Comment   Next

Show Markup   Previous

Project 3b Inserting Comments   Part 2 of 9

1. With **P-C8-P3-ISPres.pptx** open, make Slide 2 active and then insert a comment by completing the following steps:
   a. Position the insertion point immediately right of the word *Australia*.
   b. Click the Review tab.
   c. Click the New Comment button in the Comments group.
   d. Type the following in the comment box: **Include information on New Zealand branch.**

Chapter 8 ■ Integrating, Sharing, and Protecting Presentations

2. Make Slide 3 active and then insert a comment by completing the following steps:
   a. Click in the chart to select it. (Make sure you select the chart and not a chart element.)
   b. Click the New Comment button in the Comments group.
   c. Type the following in the comment box: **Include a chart showing profit amounts.**
3. Make Slide 5 active, position the insertion point immediately right of the word *line* at the end of the third bulleted item, and then insert the comment **Provide detailed information on how this goal will be accomplished.**
4. Make Slide 8 active, position the insertion point immediately right of the word *Singapore* in the second bulleted item, and then insert the comment **Who will be managing the Singapore office?**
5. Click the Previous button in the Comments group to display the comment box in Slide 5.
6. Click the Previous button to display the comment box in Slide 3.
7. Click the Show Markup button in the Comments group in the Review tab to turn off the display of comment boxes.
8. Click Slide 5 and notice that the comment box is not visible.
9. Click the Next button to display the comment box in Slide 2.
10. Click the Show Markup button to turn on the display of comment boxes.
11. Print the presentation and the comments by completing the following steps:
    a. Click the File tab and then click the Print tab.
    b. At the Print tab Backstage view, click the second gallery in the Settings category, make sure the *Print Comments and Ink Markup* option contains a check mark, and then click the *9 Slides Horizontal* option.
    c. Click the Print button.
12. Make Slide 1 active and then run the presentation beginning with Slide 1.
13. Save **P-C8-P3-ISPres.pptx**.

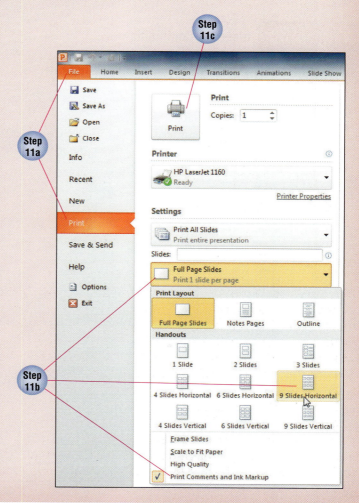

To edit text in a comment box, click the comment box you want to edit and then click the Edit Comment button in the Comments group in the Review tab. This expands the comment box and positions the insertion point inside the box. To delete a comment from a slide, click the small box containing the user's initials and comment number and then click the Delete button in the Comments group in the Review tab. You can also right-click the box containing the initials and then click *Delete* at the shortcut menu.

Edit Comment

Delete

Project 3c Editing and Deleting Comments   Part 3 of 9

1. With **P-C8-P3-ISPres.pptx** open, make Slide 8 active and then edit the comment by completing the following steps:
    a. Click the comment box containing the user's initials and comment number.
    b. Make sure the Review tab is active and then click the Edit Comment button in the Comments group.
    c. Select and delete the text in the comment box and then type **Check with Sandy Cates to determine who will be appointed branch manager.**
2. Delete the comment in Slide 3 by completing the following steps:
    a. Click twice on the Previous button in the Comments group in the Review tab to display Slide 3 and the comment in the slide.
    b. Click the Delete button in the Comments group in the Review tab.
3. Print the presentation as a handout with nine slides horizontally per page and make sure the comments print.
4. Save **P-C8-P3-ISPres.pptx**.

Managing Presentation Information

If you plan to distribute or share a presentation, you should check the presentation information and decide if you want to insert presentation properties in the presentation file, protect the presentation with a password, check the compatibility of the presentation, and access versions of the presentation. You can complete these tasks along with other tasks at the Info tab Backstage view shown in Figure 8.4. Display this view by clicking the File tab and then clicking the Info tab.

Managing Presentation Properties

Each presentation you create has properties associated with it such as the type and location of the presentation and when the presentation was created, modified, and accessed. You can view and modify presentation properties at the Info tab Backstage view and at the document panel.

Property information about a presentation displays at the right side of the Info tab Backstage view. You can add or update a presentation property

Figure 8.4 Info Tab Backstage View

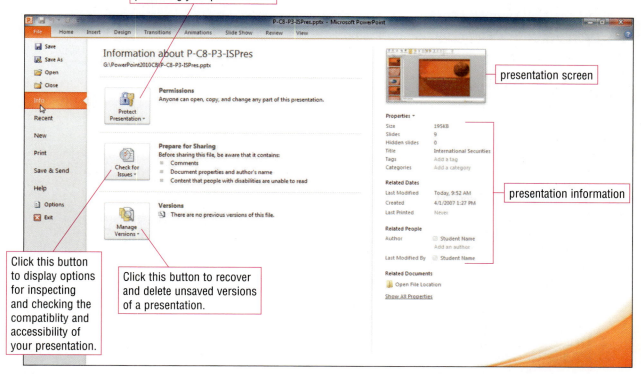

by hovering your mouse over the information that displays at the right of the property (a rectangular box with a light yellow border displays) and then typing the desired information. In the *Related Dates* section, dates display for when the presentation was created and when it was last modified and printed. The *Related People* section displays the name of the author of the presentation and also contains options for adding additional author names. Click the folder below the *Related Documents* section to display the folder contents where the current presentation is located.

You can display additional presentation properties by clicking the Show All Properties hyperlink. You can also manage presentation properties at the document panel shown in Figure 8.5. Display this panel by clicking the Properties button that displays below the thumbnail at the right side of the Info tab Backstage view and then clicking *Show Document Panel* at the drop-down list. Inserting text in some of the text boxes can help you organize and identify your presentations.

Figure 8.5 Document Panel

Project 3d Inserting Presentation Properties   Part 4 of 9

1. With **P-C8-P3-ISPres.pptx** open, click the File tab. (This displays the Info tab Backstage view.)
2. At the Info tab Backstage view, hover your mouse over the text *International Securities* that displays at the right of the *Title* property, click the left mouse button (this selects the text), and then type **IS Sales Meeting**.
3. Display the document panel by clicking the Properties button that displays below the presentation thumbnail and then click *Show Document Panel* at the drop-down list.
4. At the document panel, press the Tab key twice (this makes the *Subject* text box active) and then type **IS Corporate Sales Meeting**.
5. Press the Tab key and then type the following words in the *Keywords* text box: **International Securities, sales, divisions**.
6. Press the Tab key and then type **sales meeting** in the *Category* text box.
7. Press the Tab key twice and then type the following in the *Comments* text box: **This is a presentation prepared for the corporate sales meeting.**
8. Close the document panel by clicking the Close button located in the upper right corner of the panel.

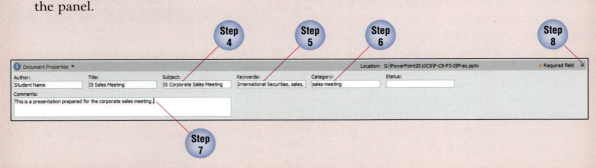

9. Save **P-C8-P3-ISPres.pptx**.

Protecting a Presentation

▼ **Quick Steps**

Mark a Presentation as Final
1. Click File tab.
2. Click Protect Presentation button.
3. Click *Mark as Final*.

Protect Presentation

Click the Protect Presentation button in the middle panel at the Info tab Backstage view and a drop-down list displays with the following options: *Mark as Final*, *Encrypt with Password*, and *Add a Digital Signature*. Click the *Mark as Final* option to save the presentation as a read-only presentation. When you click this option, a message displays telling you that the presentation will be marked and then saved. At this message, click OK. This displays another message telling you that the presentation has been marked as final to indicate that editing is complete and that it is the final version of the presentation. The message further indicates that when a presentation is marked as final, the status property is set to "Final"; typing, editing commands, and proofing marks are turned off; and that the presentation can be identified by the Mark As Final icon, which displays toward the left side of the Status bar. At this message, click OK. After a presentation is marked as final, the message "This presentation has been marked as final to discourage editing." displays to the right of the Protect Presentation button in the Info tab Backstage view.

▼ **Quick Steps**

Encrypt Presentation
1. Click File tab.
2. Click Protect Presentation button.
3. Click *Encrypt with Password*.
4. Type password, press Enter.
5. Type password again, press Enter.

Encrypting a Presentation

You can protect a presentation with a password by clicking the Protect Presentation button at the Info tab Backstage view and then clicking the *Encrypt with Password* option at the drop-down list. At the Encrypt Document dialog box that displays, type your password in the text box (the text will display as round bullets) and then press the Enter key (or click OK). At the Confirm Password dialog box, type your password again (the text will display as round bullets) and then press the Enter key (or click OK). When you apply a password, the message *A password is required to open this document displays* to the right of the Protect Presentation button.

Project 3e Marking a Presentation as Final   Part 5 of 9

1. With **P-C8-P3-ISPres.pptx** open, click the File tab.
2. At the Info tab Backstage view, click the Protect Presentation button and then click *Mark as Final* at the drop-down list.
3. At the message telling you the presentation will be marked as final and saved, click OK.
4. At the next message that displays, click OK. (Notice the message that displays to the right of the Protect Presentation button.)
5. Click the File tab to return to the presentation.
6. At the presentation, notice the message bar that displays above the Ruler.
7. Close the presentation.

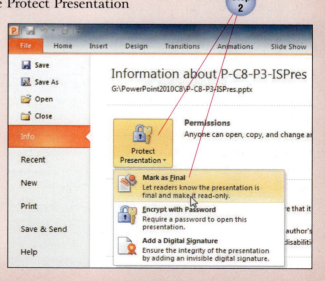

8. Open **P-C8-P3-ISPres.pptx**, click the Edit Anyway button on the yellow message bar, and then save the presentation.
9. Encrypt the presentation with a password by completing the following steps:
    a. Click the File tab, click the Protect Presentation button at the Info tab Backstage view, and then click *Encrypt with Password* at the drop-down list.
    b. At the Encrypt Document dialog box, type your initials in uppercase letters. (Your text will display as round bullets.)
    c. Press the Enter key.
    d. At the Confirm Password dialog box, type your initials again in uppercase letters (your text will display as bullets) and then press the Enter key.

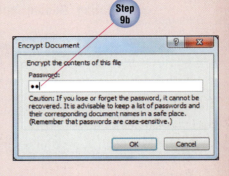

10. Click the File tab to return to the presentation.
11. Save and then close **P-C8-P3-ISPres.pptx**.
12. Open **P-C8-P3-ISPres.pptx**. At the Password dialog box, type your initials in uppercase letters and then press the Enter key.
13. Remove the password protection by completing the following steps:
    a. Click the File tab.
    b. At the Info tab Backstage view, click the Protect Presentation button and then click *Encrypt with Password* at the drop-down list.
    c. At the Encrypt Document dialog box, delete the round bullets in the *Password* text box and then press the Enter key.
    d. Click the File tab to return to the presentation.
14. Save **P-C8-P3-ISPres.pptx**.

Adding a Digital Signature

You can add a ***digital signature***, which is an electronic stamp that vouches for a presentation's authenticity, to a presentation to authenticate it and indicate that you agree with its contents. When you add a digital signature, the presentation is locked so that it cannot be edited or changed unless you remove the digital signature. Before adding a digital signature, you must obtain one. You can obtain a digital signature from a commercial certification authority, or you can create your own digital signature. When you create a digital signature, it is saved on the hard drive or the network. Depending on how your system is set up, you might be prevented from using a digital signature. To add a digital signature, click the Protect Presentation button and then click the *Add a Digital Signature* option at the drop-down list. At the Microsoft PowerPoint digital signature information message, click OK. At the Get a Digital ID dialog box, click the *Create your own digital ID* option and then click OK. At the Create a Digital ID dialog box, insert information and then click Create.

You can remove a digital signature and the presentation is no longer authenticated. Remove the digital signature at the Signatures task pane. Display

▼ Quick Steps

Create a Digital Signature
1. Click File tab.
2. Click Protect Presentation button.
3. Click *Add a Digital Signature*.
4. Click OK.
5. Click *Create your own digital ID*.
6. Click OK.
7. Type information.
8. Click Create button.
9. Type purpose at Sign dialog box.
10. Click Sign button.
11. Click OK.

View Signatures

the Signatures task pane by clicking the Signatures button that displays toward the left side of the Status bar. This button indicates that a digital signature has been applied to the presentation. You can also display the Signatures task pane by clicking the File tab and then clicking the View Signatures button at the Info tab Backstage view. Remove the signature by hovering the mouse pointer over the name in the Signatures task pane, clicking the down-pointing arrow at the right of the name, and then clicking *Remove Signature* at the drop-down list. At the message asking if you want to permanently remove the signature, click Yes and then click OK at the message telling you that the signature has been removed.

Project 3f Creating, Adding, and Removing a Digital Signature   Part 6 of 9

Note: Depending on your system setup, you may not be able to complete this project, or you may need to skip some steps in the project. Please check with your instructor before beginning this project.

1. With **P-C8-P3-ISPres.pptx** open, click the File tab.
2. At the Info tab Backstage view, click the Protect Presentation button and then click *Add a Digital Signature* at the drop-down list.
3. At the Microsoft PowerPoint digital signature information message, click OK.
4. At the Get a Digital ID dialog box, click the *Create your own digital ID* option and then click OK.
5. At the Create a Digital ID dialog box, insert the following information:
   a. Type your name in the *Name* text box.
   b. Type your actual email address or a fictitious email address in the *E-mail address* text box.
   c. Type your school's name in the *Organization* text box.
   d. Type the city in which your school is located in the *Location* text box.
   e. Click the Create button.
6. At the Sign dialog box, type **Agreeing to the contents of the presentation.** in the *Purpose for signing this document* text box.
7. Click the Sign button.
8. At the message saying your signature has been successfully saved, click OK.
9. Click the File tab to return to the presentation and then click each of the ribbon tabs and notice the commands and buttons that are inactive or dimmed.
10. Display the Signatures task pane by clicking the File tab and then clicking the View Signatures button at the Info tab Backstage view.

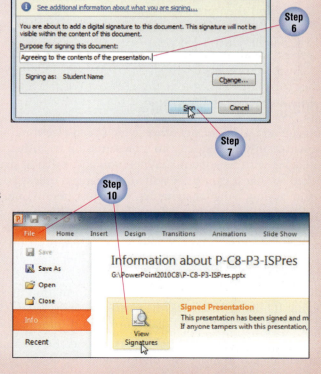

11. View the invisible digital signature details by hovering the mouse pointer over your name in the Signatures task pane, clicking the down-pointing arrow that displays to the right of your name, and then clicking *Signature Details* at the drop-down list.

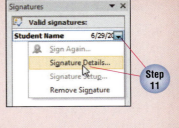

Step 11

12. Notice the signature details, including the information on the inserted digital signature and the purpose of the signature.
13. Click the Close button to close the Signature Details dialog box.
14. Remove the digital signature by completing the following steps:
    a. Hover the mouse pointer over your name in the Signatures task pane, click the down-pointing arrow to the right of your name, and then click *Remove Signature* at the drop-down list.
    b. At the message asking if you want to permanently remove the signature, click Yes.
    c. At the message telling you the signature has been removed and the presentation has been saved, click OK.
15. Close the Signatures task pane.
16. Save **P-C8-P3-ISPres.pptx**.

Inspecting a Presentation

Use options from the Check for Issues button drop-down list at the Info tab Backstage view to inspect a presentation for personal and hidden data and to check a presentation for compatibility and accessibility issues. When you click the Check for Issues button, a drop-down list displays with the options *Inspect Document*, *Check Accessibility*, and *Check Compatibility*.

PowerPoint includes a document inspector feature you can use to inspect your presentation for personal data, hidden data, and metadata. Metadata is data that describes other data, such as presentation properties. You may want to remove some personal or hidden data before you share a presentation with other people. To check your presentation for personal or hidden data, click the File tab, click the Check for Issues button at the Info tab Backstage view, and then click the *Inspect Document* option at the drop-down list. This displays the Document Inspector dialog box.

By default, the document inspector checks all of the items listed in the dialog box. If you do not want the inspector to check a specific item in your presentation, remove the check mark preceding the item. For example, if you know your presentation contains comments and/or annotations, click the *Comments and Annotations* check box to remove the check mark. Click the Inspect button located toward the bottom of the dialog box, and the document inspector scans the presentation to identify information.

When the inspection is complete, the results display in the dialog box. A check mark before an option indicates that the inspector did not find the specific items. If an exclamation point is inserted before an option, the inspector found items and displays a list of the items. If you want to remove the found items, click the Remove All button that displays at the right of the desired option. Click the Reinspect button to ensure that the specific items were removed and then click the Close button.

▼ **Quick Steps**

Inspect a Presentation
1. Click File tab.
2. Click Check for Issues button.
3. Click *Inspect Document*.
4. Remove check mark from items you do not want to inspect.
5. Click Inspect button.
6. Click Close button.

Check for Issues

Project 3g — Inspecting a Presentation — Part 7 of 9

1. With **P-C8-P3-ISPres.pptx** open, click the File tab.
2. At the Info tab Backstage view, click the Check for Issues button and then click *Inspect Document* at the drop-down list.
3. At the Document Inspector dialog box, you decide that you do not want to check the presentation for XML data, so click the *Custom XML Data* check box to remove the check mark.

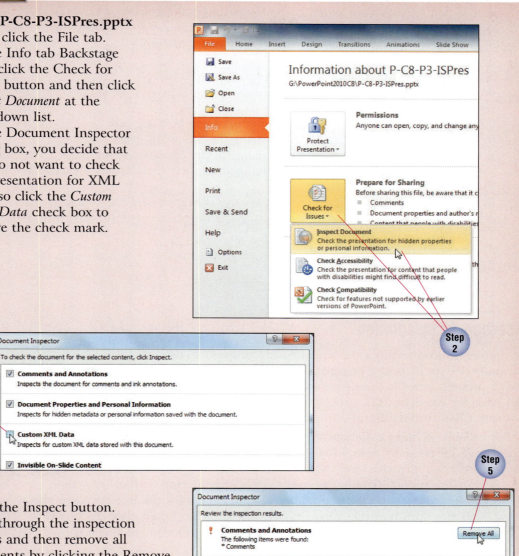

4. Click the Inspect button.
5. Read through the inspection results and then remove all comments by clicking the Remove All button that displays at the right side of the *Comments and Annotations* section.
6. Click the Close button to close the Document Inspector dialog box.
7. Click the File tab to return to the presentation.
8. Save **P-C8-P3-ISPres.pptx**.

Checking the Accessibility of a Presentation

PowerPoint 2010 includes the accessibility checker feature, which checks a presentation for content that a person with disabilities, such as a visual impairment, might find difficult to read. Check the accessibility of a presentation by clicking the Check for Issues button at the Info tab Backstage view and then clicking *Check Accessibility*. The accessibility checker examines the presentation for the most

common accessibility problems in PowerPoint presentations and groups them into three categories: errors—content that is unreadable to a person who is blind; warnings—content that is difficult to read; and tips—content that may or may not be difficult to read. The accessibility checker examines the presentation, closes the Info tab Backstage view, and displays the Accessibility Checker task pane.

At the Accessibility Checker task pane, unreadable errors are grouped in the *Errors* section, content that is difficult to read is grouped in the *Warnings* section, and content that may or may not be difficult to read is grouped in the *Tips* section. Select an issue in one of the sections, and an explanation of how to fix the issue and why displays at the bottom of the task pane.

▼ **Quick Steps**

Check Accessibility
1. Click File tab.
2. Click Check for Issues button.
3. Click *Check Accessibility*.

Project 3h Completing an Accessibility Check   Part 8 of 9

1. With **P-C8-P3-ISPres.pptx** open, click the File tab.
2. At the Info tab Backstage view, click the Check for Issues button and then click *Check Accessibility* at the drop-down list.
3. Notice the Accessibility Checker task pane that displays at the right side of the screen. The task pane displays an *Errors* section. Click *Content Placeholder 3 (Slide 3)* in the *Errors* section and then read the information that displays toward the bottom of the task pane describing why you should fix the error and how to fix it.
4. Add alternative text (which is a text-based representation of the chart) to the chart by completing the following steps:
   a. With Slide 3 active, right-click immediately above the legend in the chart and then click *Format Chart Area* at the shortcut menu.
   b. At the Format Chart Area dialog box, click the *Alt Text* option located at the bottom of the left panel.
   c. Click in the *Title* text box and then type **Division Profit Chart**.
   d. Select and then delete any text that displays in the *Description* text box and then type **Profits: North America, 35%; Europe, 22%; Asia, 17%; Australia, 14%; and Africa, 12%**.
   e. Click the Close button.

> 5. Click the remaining item in the Accessibility Checker task pane and then read the information that displays toward the bottom of the task pane.
> 6. Close the Accessibility Checker task pane by clicking the Close button located in the upper right corner of the task pane.
> 7. Save **P-C8-P3-ISPres.pptx**.

Checking the Compatibility of a Presentation

▼ **Quick Steps**

Check Compatibility
1. Click File tab.
2. Click Check for Issues button.
3. Click *Check Compatibility*.
4. Click OK.

Use one of the Check for Issues button drop-down options, *Check Compatibility*, to check your presentation and identify elements that are either not supported or will act differently in previous versions of PowerPoint from PowerPoint 97 through PowerPoint 2007. To run the compatibility checker, open the desired presentation, click the Check for Issues button at the Info tab Backstage view, and then click *Check Compatibility* at the drop-down list. This displays the Microsoft PowerPoint Compatibility Checker dialog box that displays a summary of the elements in the presentation that are not compatible with previous versions of PowerPoint and indicates what will happen when the presentation is saved and then opened in a previous version.

Managing Versions

▼ **Quick Steps**

Open Autosave Backup Presentation
1. Click File tab.
2. Click presentation name at right of Manage Versions button.

Manage Versions

As you are working in a presentation, PowerPoint is automatically saving your presentation every 10 minutes. This automatic backup feature can be very helpful if you accidentally close your presentation without saving it, or if the power to your computer is disrupted. As PowerPoint is automatically saving a backup of your currently open presentation, the saved presentations are listed to the right of the Manage Versions button in the Info tab Backstage view. Each autosave presentation displays with *Today*, followed by the time and *(autosave)*. When you save and then close your presentation, the autosave backup presentations are deleted.

To open an autosave backup presentation, click the File tab to display the Info tab Backstage view and then click the backup presentation you want to open that displays to the right of the Manage Versions button. The presentation opens as a read-only presentation, and a yellow message bar displays with a Compare button and a Restore button. Click the Compare button and the autosave presentation is compared to the original presentation. You can then decide which changes you want to accept or reject. Click the Restore button and a message displays indicating that you are about to overwrite the last saved version with the selected version. At this message, click OK.

When you save a presentation, the autosave backup presentations are deleted. However, if you are working in a presentation that you close without saving (after 10 minutes) or the power is disrupted, PowerPoint keeps the backup file in the *UnsavedFiles* folder on the hard drive. You can access this folder by clicking the Manage Versions button in the Info tab Backstage view and then clicking *Recover Unsaved Presentations*. At the Open dialog box that displays, double-click the desired backup file you want to open. You can also display the *UnsavedFiles* folder by clicking the File tab, clicking the Recent tab, and then clicking the Recover Unsaved Presentations button that displays toward the bottom of the screen below the *Recent Places* list box.

Project 3i — Checking the Compatibility of Elements in a Presentation and Managing Versions

1. With **P-C8-P3-ISPres.pptx** open, click the File tab.
2. Click the Check for Issues button and then click *Check Compatibility* at the drop-down list.
3. At the Microsoft PowerPoint Compatibility Checker dialog box, read the information that displays in the *Summary* list box.
4. Click OK to close the dialog box.
5. Click the File tab and then check to see if any versions of your presentation display to the right of the Manage Versions button. If so, click the version (or the first version, if more than one displays). This opens the autosave presentation as read-only.
6. Close the read-only presentation.
7. Click the File tab, click the Manage Versions button, and then click *Recover Unsaved Presentations* at the drop-down list.
8. At the Open dialog box, check to see if recovered presentation file names display along with the date and time and then click the Cancel button to close the Open dialog box.
9. Save the presentation, print nine slides horizontally per page, and then close the presentation.

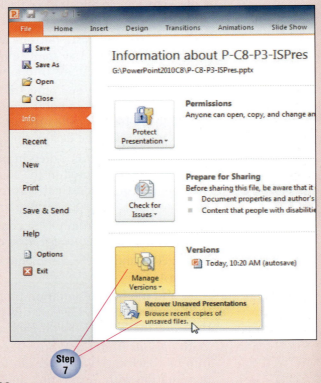

Step 7

Chapter Summary

- Create a PowerPoint presentation by importing a Word document containing text with heading styles applied using the *Slides from Outline* option at the New Slides drop-down list.
- With options at the Save & Send tab Backstage view, you can send a presentation as an email attachment or fax, save your presentation to the Web, SharePoint, or in a different file format, and post your presentation to a special location such as a blog.
- With options in the Send Using E-mail category at the Save & Send tab Backstage view, you can send a presentation in PDF or XPS format.

- Click the *Change File Type* option in the File Types category at the Save & Send tab Backstage view, and options display for saving a presentation in a different file format such as a previous version of PowerPoint, a PowerPoint show, an OpenDocument presentation, and as graphic images.
- At the Save & Send tab Backstage view, you can create a PDF or XPS file with a presentation, create a video, package the presentation in a folder or on a CD, and create handouts.
- Use the Copy and Paste buttons in the Clipboard group to copy data from one program to another. Use the Clipboard task pane to collect and paste up to 24 items and paste the items into a presentation or other program files.
- An object created in one program in the Microsoft Office suite can be copied, linked, or embedded to another program in the suite. The program containing the original object is called the source program and the program the object is pasted to is called the destination program.
- An embedded object is stored in both the source and the destination programs. A linked object is stored in the source program only. Link an object if you want the contents in the destination program to reflect any changes made to the object stored in the source program.
- Download designs from Office.com by displaying the New tab Backstage view and then clicking the *Design slides* option in the *Office.com Templates* section.
- Insert, edit, and delete comments with buttons in the Comments group in the Review tab.
- View and modify presentation properties at the Info tab Backstage view and at the document panel. Display this panel by clicking the Properties button and then clicking *Show Document Panel* at the drop-down list.
- With options from the Protect Presentation button drop-down list at the Info tab Backstage view, you can mark a presentation as final, encrypt the presentation with a password, and add a digital signature.
- With options from the Check for Issues button drop-down list at the Info tab Backstage view, you can inspect a document for personal and hidden data, check a presentation for content that a person with disabilities, such as a visual impairment, might find difficult to read, and check the compatibility of the presentation with previous versions of PowerPoint.
- PowerPoint automatically saves a presentation every 10 minutes. When you save a presentation, the autosave backup presentation(s) are deleted. Use the Manage Versions button at the Info tab Backstage view to open an autosave backup presentation.

Commands Review

FEATURE	RIBBON TAB, GROUP	BUTTON, OPTION
Insert Outline dialog box	Home, Slides	, Slides from Outline
Clipboard task pane	Home, Clipboard	

FEATURE	RIBBON TAB, GROUP	BUTTON, OPTION
Save & Send tab Backstage view	File, Save & Send	
Publish as PDF or XPS dialog box	File, Save & Send	
Package for CD dialog box	File, Save & Send	
Send To Microsoft Word dialog box	File, Save & Send	
Paste Special dialog box	Home, Clipboard	, Paste Special
Encrypt Document dialog box	File, Info	, Encrypt with Password
Document Inspector dialog box	File, Info	, Inspect Document
Accessibility Checker task pane	File, Info	, Check Accessibility
Microsoft PowerPoint Compatibility Checker dialog box	File, Info	, Check Compatibility

Concepts Check Test Your Knowledge

Completion: In the space provided at the right, indicate the correct term, symbol, or command.

1. Display the Insert Outline dialog box by clicking the New Slide button arrow and then clicking this option. _____

2. Click this option at the Save & Send tab Backstage view to display options for sending a copy of a presentation as an attachment to an email. _____

3. Use this task pane to collect and paste multiple items. _____

4. A presentation you save as a PowerPoint show will display with this file extension. _____

5. With options in the *Image File Types* section of the Save & Send tab Backstage view in the Change File Type category, you can save slides in a presentation as graphic images as JPEG files or this type of file. _____

6. If you save the presentation in PDF format, the presentation opens in this. _____

7. With this option in the File Types category at the Save & Send tab Backstage view, you can export a PowerPoint presentation to a Word document. _____

Chapter 8 ■ Integrating, Sharing, and Protecting Presentations

8. Do this to an object if you want the contents in the destination program to reflect any changes made to the object stored in the source program.

9. Download a design template with options at this Backstage view.

10. The New Comment button is located in the Comments group in this tab.

11. Display additional presentation properties at the Info tab Backstage view by clicking this hyperlink.

12. Display the Encrypt Document dialog box by clicking the File tab, clicking the Protect Presentation button at the Info tab Backstage view, and then clicking this option at the drop-down list.

13. Apply this to a presentation to vouch for the authenticity of the presentation.

14. Use this feature to inspect your presentation for personal data, hidden data, and metadata.

15. Use this feature to check a presentation for content that a person with a visual impairment might find difficult to read.

Skills Check Assess Your Performance

Assessment

1 COPY WORD AND EXCEL DATA INTO A SALES CONFERENCE PRESENTATION

1. Open **NWPres.pptx** and then save the presentation with Save As and name it **P-C8-A1-NWPres**.
2. Make Slide 2 active and then complete the following steps:
   a. Open Excel and then open the workbook named **SalesProj.xlsx** (located in the PowerPoint2010C8 folder on your storage medium).
   b. Copy the chart and paste it into Slide 2.
   c. Resize the chart so it fills most of the slide below the title.
   d. Close the workbook and exit Excel.
3. Make Slide 4 active and then complete the following steps:
   a. Draw a text box in the slide.
   b. Open Word and then open the document named **HerbRemedies.docx**.
   c. Copy the first three terms and the paragraph below each term in the document to the text box in Slide 4.
   d. Select the text in the placeholder, change the font to Rockwell, and then change the font size to 24.
   e. Move and/or resize the placeholder so it fills most of the slide below the title.

4. Make Slide 5 active and then complete the following steps:
   a. Draw a text box in the slide.
   b. Make active the **HerbRemedies.docx** Word document.
   c. Copy the last two terms and the paragraph below each term in the document and paste them into Slide 5 in the text box.
   d. Select the text in the text box, change the font to Rockwell, and then change the font size to 24.
   e. Move and/or size the text box so it fills most of the slide below the title.
5. Make Word active, close **HerbRemedies.docx**, and then exit Word.
6. With PowerPoint active, apply animation effects to each item on each slide.
7. Run the presentation.
8. Save **P-C8-A1-NWPres.pptx**.
9. Print the presentation as a handout with six slides horizontally per page.
10. Export the presentation to a Word document that prints blank lines next to slides.
11. Save the Word document and name it **P-C8-A1-NWPresHandout**.
12. Print and then close **P-C8-A1-NWPresHandout.docx** and then exit Word.
13. In PowerPoint, close **P-C8-A1-NWPres.pptx**.

Assessment 2 COPY AND LINK WORD AND EXCEL DATA INTO A COMMUNICATIONS PRESENTATION

1. Open **CommPres.pptx** and then save the presentation with Save As and name it **P-C8-A2-CommPres**.
2. Open Word and then open the document named **VerbalSkills.docx** (located in the PowerPoint2010C8 folder on your storage medium).
3. Copy the table and embed it (use the Paste Special dialog box and click Microsoft Word Document Object in the *As* list box) into Slide 5.
4. Resize the table so it better fills the slide.
5. Make Word active, close the **VerbalSkills.docx** document, and then exit Word.
6. Open Excel and then open the workbook named **NVCues.xlsx** (located in the PowerPoint2010C8 folder on your storage medium).
7. Copy the chart and link it to Slide 6. Resize the chart so it fills a majority of the slide below the title.
8. Save and then close **P-C8-A2-CommPres.pptx**.
9. Make the following changes to the chart in **NVCues.xlsx**:
   a. Select the chart and then apply the *Style 18* chart style. **Hint: Do this in the Chart Tools Design tab**.
   b. Apply the *Gradient Fill – Purple, Accent 4, Reflection* WordArt style. **Hint: Do this in the Chart Tools Format tab**.
   c. Change the shape outline to *No Outline*.
   d. Change the amount in B2 from *35%* to *38%*.
   e. Change the amount in B3 from *25%* to *22%*.
10. Save and then close **NVCues.xlsx** and then exit Excel.
11. In PowerPoint, open **P-C8-A2-CommPress.pptx**. (At the message that displays when you open the presentation, click the Update Links button.)
12. Make Slide 2 active and then insert the following comment after the second bulleted item: Ask Lauren to provide a specific communication example.
13. Make Slide 4 active and then insert the following comment after the third bulleted item: Insert a link here to the writing presentation prepared by Sylvia.

14. Make Slide 8 active and then insert the following comment after the third bulleted item: **Distribute evaluation forms to audience.**
15. Run the presentation.
16. Save the presentation and then print the presentation as a handout with four slides horizontally per page and make sure the comments print.
17. Run the Document Inspector and remove comments.
18. Run the accessibility checker and then create the following alt text (right-click chart, click *Format Object*, click *Alt Text* option) for the chart in Slide 6 with the title *Top Five Nonverbal Cues* and the description *Eye contact, 35%; Smiling, 25%; Posture, 15%; Position, 15%; Gestures, 10%.*
19. Close the Accessibility Checker task pane.
20. Save and then close **P-C8-A2-CommPres.pptx**.

Assessment

3 SAVE A SALES CONFERENCE PRESENTATION IN VARIOUS FORMATS

1. Open **P-C8-A1-NWPres.pptx** and then save the presentation in the PowerPoint 97-2003 Presentation (*.ppt) file format and name the presentation **P-C8-A3-NWPres-2003format**. (At the compatibility checker dialog box, click Continue.)
2. Close **P-C8-A3-NWPres-2003format.ppt**.
3. Open **P-C8-A1-NWPres.pptx** and then save each slide in the presentation as a JPEG image file.
4. Close **P-C8-A1-NWPres.pptx** without saving the changes.
5. Open Word and at a blank document, complete the following steps:
    a. Change the font to Rockwell, change the font size to 24 points, change the alignment to center, and then type **Nature's Way**.
    b. Press the Enter key and then insert the **Slide4.JPG** slide. (Use the Picture button to insert this slide. The slide is located in the **P-C8-A1-NWPres** folder in the PowerPoint2010C8 folder on your storage medium.)
    c. Change the height of the slide to 2.8 inches.
    d. Press Ctrl + End, press the Enter key, and then insert the **Slide5.JPG** slide.
    e. Change the height of the slide to 2.8 inches.
    f. Save the word document and name it **P-C8-A3-Herbs**.
    g. Print and then close **P-C8-A3-Herbs.docx** and then exit Word.
6. Open **P-C8-A1-NWPres.pptx** and then save the presentation in PDF file format. When the presentation displays in Adobe Reader, scroll through the presentation and then close Adobe Reader.
7. In PowerPoint, close **P-C8-A1-NWPres.pptx**.
8. Capture an image of the Open dialog box and insert the image in a PowerPoint slide by completing the following steps:
    a. Press Ctrl + N to display a new blank presentation.
    b. Click the Layout button in the Slides group in the Home tab and then click the *Blank* layout at the drop-down list.
    c. Click the File tab and then click the Open button.
    d. At the Open dialog box, click the option button that displays to the right of the *File name* text box (option button that contains the text *All PowerPoint Presentations*) and then click *All Files (*.*)* at the drop-down list.
    e. Make sure that all of your project and assessment files display. You may need to resize the dialog box to display the files.
    f. Hold down the Alt key and then press the Print Screen button on your keyboard. (This captures an image of the Open dialog box.)

g. Click the Cancel button to close the Open dialog box.
h. Click the Paste button. (This inserts the image of the Open dialog box into the slide.)
9. Print the slide as a full page slide.
10. Close the presentation without saving it.

Assessment

4 DOWNLOAD AND FILL IN A COURSE COMPLETION CERTIFICATE

1. Create the certificate shown in Figure 8.6 with the following specifications:
   a. In PowerPoint, display the New tab Backstage view, click the *Award certificates* option, click the Business folder, and then search for and download the *Excellence award (with eagle)* template.
   b. Type the company name as shown in Figure 8.6, type your name in place of *Student Name*, (the certificate will automatically insert the current date below your name), and type the name and title of the president/CEO as shown in the figure.
2. Save the certificate and name it **P-C8-A4-Certificate**.
3. Print and then close **P-C8-A4-Certificate.pptx**.

Figure 8.6 Assessment 4

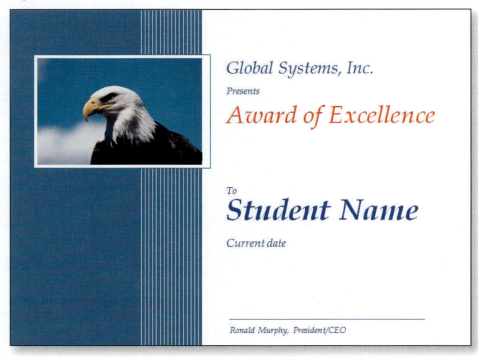

Visual Benchmark Demonstrate Your Proficiency

1 CREATE JPEG IMAGE FILES AND CREATE A WORD DOCUMENT

1. Open **FCTTours.pptx**, save all of the slides in the presentation in the JPEG graphic format, and then close **FCTTours.pptx** without saving the changes.
2. Open Word and, at a blank document, create the document shown in Figure 8.7 with the following specifications:
   a. Set the two lines of text in 24-point Calibri bold.
   b. Insert each slide and change the height of each slide to 2.5 inches, change the text wrapping to *Tight*, and size and position the slides as shown in Figure 8.7.
3. Save the completed Word document and name it **P-C8-VB1-FCTCovers**.
4. Print and then close **P-C8-VB1-FCTCovers.docx** and then exit Word.

2 CREATE A TRAVEL COMPANY PRESENTATION

1. Create the presentation shown in Figure 8.8 with the following specifications:
   a. In PowerPoint, download the design template named *Photo journal design template*. (Find this design template by clicking the *Design slides* option at the New tab Backstage view and then clicking the Travel folder.)
   b. Close the presentation.
   c. At a blank presentation, use the **FCTQtrlyMtg.docx** Word outline document to create the presentation. *Hint: Use the* **Slides from Outline** *option at the New Slide button drop-down list.*
   d. Apply to the presentation the Photo journal design template you downloaded.
   e. Change the layout of Slide 1 to *Blank* and then insert the **FCTLogo.jpg** image. Make the white background of the logo transparent. (Do this with the *Set Transparent Color* option from the Color button drop-down gallery at the Picture Tools Format tab.) Size and position the logo as shown in Figure 8.8.
   f. Make Slide 5 active, change the layout to *Title Only* and then copy and link the Excel chart in **Bookings.xlsx** to the slide. Size and position the chart as shown in Figure 8.8. (Close Excel after inserting the chart.)
   g. Insert the clip art in Slide 2 (use the search word *travel* at the Clip Art task pane) and then make any other formatting changes so your slides appear similar to the slides in Figure 8.8.
2. Save the presentation and name it **P-C8-VB2-FCTQtrlyMtgPres**.
3. Print the presentation as a handout with six slides horizontally per page.
4. Close **P-C8-VB2-FCTQtrlyMtgPres.pptx**.
5. Open Excel, open **Bookings.xlsx**, and then make the following changes to the data in the specified cells:
   C2: Change *45* to *52*
   C3: Change *36* to *41*
   C4: Change *24* to *33*
   C5: Change *19* to *25*
6. After making the changes, save and then close **Bookings.xlsx** and then exit Excel.
7. Open **P-C8-VB2-FCTQtrlyMtgPres.pptx** and update the links.
8. Print the presentation as a handout with six slides horizontally per page.
9. Save and then close **P-C8-VB2-FCTQtrlyMtgPres.pptx**.

Figure 8.7 Visual Benchmark 1

First Choice Travel

Proposed Tour Package Covers

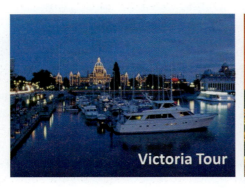

Figure 8.8 Visual Benchmark 2

Case Study — Apply Your Skills

Part 1

You work for Rocky Mountain Family Medicine and are responsible for preparing education and training materials and publications for the center. You want to be able to insert the center logo in publications so you decide to save the logo as a graphic image. To do this, open the presentation (one slide) named **RMFMLogo.pptx** and then save the slide as a JPEG graphic image.

Part 2

You are responsible for presenting information on childhood diseases at an education class at a local community center. Open the Word document named **ChildDiseases.docx** and then use the information to create a presentation with the following specifications:

- Apply the *Flow* design theme.
- Change the layout for the first slide to *Title Only*, type an appropriate title for the presentation, and then move the title to the bottom of the slide. Insert the **RMFMLogo.jpg** graphic image in the first slide and then size and position the logo attractively on the slide. (Consider setting transparent color to the background of the logo graphic image. Do this with the *Set Transparent Color* option in the Color button drop-down list in the Picture Tools Format tab.)
- Create additional slides with the information in the **ChildDiseases.docx** Word document.
- Apply any additional enhancements to improve the presentation.

Run the presentation and then save the presentation with the name **P-C8-CS-RMFMDiseases**. Print the presentation as a handout with six slides horizontally per page and then close the presentation.

Part 3

You need to prepare a presentation for an upcoming education and training meeting. Import the Word outline document named **RMFMOutline.docx** into a PowerPoint presentation and then make the following changes:

- Apply the *Flow* design theme.
- Create the first slide with the *Title Only* layout, insert the **RMFMLogo.jpg** graphic image, and then size and position the logo in the same manner as the first slide in **P-C8-CS-RMFMDiseases.pptx**. Insert the title *Education and Training* in the title placeholder.
- Change the layout to *Title Only* for the Community Contacts slide and then copy the table from the Word document **RMFMContacts.docx** and paste it into the Community Contacts slide. Increase the size of the table so it better fills the slide.
- Change the layout to *Title Only* for the Current Enrollment slide and then copy the chart from the Excel workbook **RMFMEnroll.xlsx** and link it to the Current Enrollment slide.
- Apply any additional enhancements to improve the presentation.

Run the presentation and then save the presentation with the name **P-C8-CS-RMFMClasses**. Print the presentation as a handout with six slides horizontally per page and then close the presentation. You check the enrollments for classes and realize that more people have enrolled so you need to update the numbers in the Excel workbook. Open the **RMFMEnroll.xlsx** Excel workbook and then change *46* to *52*, *38* to *40*, and *24* to *27*. Save and then close the workbook. Open the **P-C8-CS-RMFMClasses.pptx** presentation and then update the links. Print only the Current Enrollment slide and then close the presentation.

Part 4

You decide that you want to include information in the **P-C8-CS-RMFMClasses.pptx** presentation on measles. Using the Internet, search for information on measles such as symptoms, complications, transmission, and prevention. Include this information in new slides in the **P-C8-CS-RMFMClasses.pptx** presentation. Run the presentation and then print only the new slides. Save and then close the presentation.

 Performance Assessment

UNIT 2

 Note: Before beginning unit assessments, copy to your storage medium the PowerPoint2010U2 folder from the PowerPoint2010 folder on the CD that accompanies this textbook and then make PowerPoint2010U2 the active folder.

Assessing Proficiency

In this unit, you have learned to add visual elements to presentations such as tables, charts, and SmartArt graphics; create a photo album; apply formatting in Slide Master view; insert action buttons; apply custom animation effects; and set up slide shows. You also learned how to copy, embed, and link data between programs; how to insert comments; and how to protect and prepare a presentation.

Assessment 1 Save a Slide in JPEG Format and Copy and Link Objects in a Presentation

1. Open **GreenSpaceLogo.pptx**, save the only slide in the presentation as a JPEG graphic image, and then close **GreenSpaceLogo.pptx**.
2. Open **GreenSpacePres.pptx** and then save the presentation with the name **P-U2-A1-GreenSpacePres**.
3. Display the presentation in Slide Master view and then make the following changes:
    a. Click the top slide master thumbnail.
    b. Select the text CLICK TO EDIT MASTER TITLE STYLE and then change the font color to *Green*.
    c. Select the text *Click to edit Master text styles*, change the font color to *Gold, Accent 3, Darker 50%*, and then change the bullet color to *Green*.
    d. Close Slide Master view.
4. Make Slide 1 active and then make the following changes:
    a. Insert the **GreenSpaceLogo.jpg** graphic image.
    b. Set transparent color for the logo background (the white background). (Do this with the *Set Transparent Color* option at the Color button drop-down gallery in the Picture Tools Format tab.)
    c. Size and position the logo so it is positioned attractively on the slide. (Consider offsetting the image slightly to the right to balance it with the slide title.)
5. Make Slide 6 active and then insert the following data in a table. You determine the formatting of the table and the formatting of the data in the table:

Project	Contact	Completion Date
Moyer-Sylvan Complex	Barry MacDonald	07/31/2013
Waterfront Headquarters	Jasmine Jefferson	02/15/2014
Linden Square	Marion Van Horn	09/30/2014
Village Green	Parker Alderton	12/31/2014
Cedar Place Market	Gerry Halderman	03/31/2015

6. Make Slide 7 active and then insert the following data in a SmartArt organizational chart. You determine the organization and formatting of the chart:

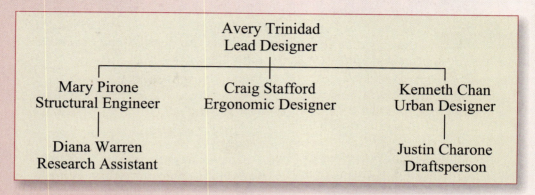

7. Make Slide 5 active and then create a column chart with the following data. Delete the chart title and chart legend. You determine the formatting and layout of the chart.

	Revenues
1st Qtr.	$25,250,000
2nd Qtr.	$34,000,000
3rd Qtr.	$22,750,000
4th Qtr.	$20,500,000

8. Make Slide 8 active and then insert a SmartArt diagram with the *Repeating Bending Process* diagram (found in the *Process* group) with the following information (insert the information in the slides from left to right). You determine the design and formatting of the SmartArt diagram.

   Mission Analysis
   Requirements Analysis
   Function Allocation
   Design
   Verification

9. Check each slide and make any changes that improve the visual appeal of the slide.
10. Make Slide 1 active and then run the presentation.
11. Make Slide 3 active, click immediately right of the slide title, and then insert the comment **Check with Marilyn about adding River View Mall to this list.**
12. Make Slide 4 active, click immediately right of the word *Australia* in the bulleted text, and then insert the comment **What happened to the plans to open an office in Sydney?**
13. Print the presentation as a handout with four slides horizontally per page and make sure the comments print.
14. Save and then close **P-U2-A1-GreenSpacePres.pptx**.

Assessment 2 **Copy and Paste Data between Programs and Insert Action Buttons in a Telecommunications Presentation**

1. Open **TelecomPres.pptx** and then save the presentation with the name **P-U2-A2-TelecomPres**.
2. Make Slide 6 active and then create a new Slide 7 (with the Title and Content layout) with the following specifications:
   a. Insert the title *APPLICATION* in the slide.
   b. Open Word and then open **WordConcepts.docx**.
   c. Display the Clipboard task pane. (Make sure the task pane is empty. If not, click the Clear All button.)
   d. Select and then copy *RECEIVING* and the paragraph below it.
   e. Select and then copy *STORING* and the paragraph below it.
   f. Select and then copy *TRANSMITTING* and the paragraph below it.
   g. Display the **P-U2-A2-TelecomPres.pptx** presentation.
   h. Click in the bulleted text *Click to add text*.
   i. Turn on the display of the Clipboard task pane.
   j. Paste the *TRANSMITTING* item in the slide.
   k. Paste the *RECEIVING* item in the slide.
   l. Clear and then close the Clipboard.
   m. Select all of the bulleted text and then change the font size to 28. Delete the bullet below the last paragraph.
   n. Make the **WordConcepts.docx** document active, close the Clipboard task pane, close the document, and then exit Word.
3. Make Slide 1 active and then insert an action button with the following specifications:
   a. Use the *Action Button: Forward or Next* option to draw the button.
   b. Draw the button in the lower right corner of the slide and make it approximately one-half inch in size.
   c. Change the shape fill of the button to *Blue, Accent 2, Lighter 40%*.
4. Display the presentation in Slide Master view and then make the following changes:
   a. Click the top slide master thumbnail.
   b. Insert an action button in the lower right corner of the slide with the same specifications as those in Step 3.
   c. Close Slide Master view.
5. Run the presentation. (Use the action buttons to advance slides. At the last slide, press the Esc key.)
6. Create a footer that prints your first and last names at the bottom of each slide, create a footer for handouts that prints the presentation title *Telecommunications Technology*, and insert the date in the upper right corner.
7. Print the presentation as a handout with four slides horizontally per page.
8. Save and then close **P-U2-A2-TelecomPres.pptx**.

Assessment 3 **Save a Template Presentation and Copy, Embed, and Link Objects between Programs**

1. Display a blank presentation, click the View tab, and then click the Slide Master button.
2. Click the top slide master thumbnail in the slides thumbnail pane.
3. Apply the *Technic* theme and change the theme colors to *Median*.
4. Apply the *Style 8* background style.

5. Insert **ISLogo.jpg** in the master slide (use the Picture button in the Insert tab), change the height of the logo to one inch, and drag the logo to the lower right corner of the slide master. Set transparent color for the logo background (the white background). (Do this with the *Set Transparent Color* option at the Color button drop-down list in the Picture Tools Format tab.)
6. Close Slide Master view.
7. Save the presentation as a template to the PowerPoint2010U2 folder on your storage medium and name the template **XXXISTemplate** (use your initials in place of the *XXX*).
8. Close **XXXISTemplate.potx**.
9. Open **XXXISTemplate.potx**. (To do this, display the New tab Backstage view and then click *New from existing*. At the New from Existing Presentation dialog box, navigate to the PowerPoint2010U2 folder on your storage medium and then double-click **XXXISTemplate.potx**.)
10. Save the presentation and name it **P-U2-A3-ISMtg**.
11. Format the first slide with the following specifications:
    a. Change to the *Blank* layout.
    b. Use WordArt to create the text *International Securities*. (You determine the shape and formatting of the WordArt text.)
12. Create the second slide with the following specifications:
    a. Choose the *Title Slide* layout.
    b. Type **European Division** as the subtitle.
    c. Type **2012 SALES MEETING** as the title.
13. Create the third slide with the following specifications:
    a. Choose the *Title Only* layout.
    b. Type **REGIONAL SALES** as the title.
    c. Open Excel and then open **ISWorkbook01.xlsx**.
    d. Save the workbook with Save As and name it **ISSalesWorkbook**.
    e. Select cells A1 through D5 (the cells containing data) and then copy and embed the cells in Slide 3.
    f. Increase the size of the cells so they better fill the slide.
14. Create the fourth slide with the following specifications:
    a. Choose the *Title and Content* layout.
    b. Type **2013 GOALS** as the title.
    c. Type the following as the bulleted items:
       ♦ **Increase product sales by 15 percent**
       ♦ **Open a branch office in Spain**
       ♦ **Hire one manager and two additional account managers**
       ♦ **Decrease production costs by 6 percent**
15. Create the fifth slide with the following specifications:
    a. Choose the *Title and Content* layout.
    b. Type **HIRING TIMELINE** as the title.
    c. Create a table with two columns and five rows and then type the following text in the cells in the table. (You determine the formatting of the cells.)

Task	Date
Advertise positions	03/01/2012 to 04/30/2012
Review resumes	05/15/2012 to 06/01/2012
Conduct interviews	06/15/2012 to 07/15/2012
Hire personnel	08/01/2012

16. Create the sixth slide with the following specifications:
    a. Choose the *Title Only* layout.
    b. Type **PRODUCTION EXPENSES** as the title.
    c. Make Excel the active program and then close **ISSalesWorkbook.xlsx**.
    d. Open **ISWorkbook02.xlsx**.
    e. Save the workbook with Save As and name it **ISExpensesWorkbook**.
    f. Copy and then link the pie chart in **ISExpensesWorkbook.xlsx** to Slide 6.
    g. Increase the size of the pie chart so it better fills the slide.
    h. Make Excel active, close **ISExpensesWorkbook.xlsx**, and then exit Excel.
17. Run the presentation.
18. Create a footer that prints your first and last names at the bottom of each slide, create a footer for handouts that prints the presentation title *2012 Sales Meeting*, and insert the date in the upper right corner.
19. Print the presentation as a handout with six slides horizontally per page.
20. Save and then close **P-U2-A3-ISMtg.pptx**.
21. Open Excel and then open **ISExpensesWorkbook.xlsx**.
22. Make the following changes:
    a. B2: Change *38% to 41%*
    b. B3: Change *35% to 32%*
    c. B4: Change *18% to 21%*
    d. B5: Change *9% to 6%*
23. Save, print, and close **ISExpensesWorkbook.xlsx** and then exit Excel.
24. With PowerPoint the active program, open **P-U2-A3-ISMtg.pptx**. (At the message that displays, click the Update Links button.)
25. Display Slide 3, double-click the cells, and then make the following changes to the data in the embedded cells:
    a. C2: Change *2678450* to *2857300*
    b. C3: Change *1753405* to *1598970*
    c. C4: Change *1452540* to *1635400*
26. Run the presentation.
27. Print the slides as a handout with six slides horizontally per page.
28. Save **P-U2-A3-ISMtg.pptx**.
29. Apply a transition and sound of your choosing to all slides in the presentation.
30. Use the Rehearse Timings feature to set the following times for the slides to display during a slide show (your actual time will display with an extra second for each slide):
    Slide 1 = 3 seconds
    Slide 2 = 3 seconds
    Slide 3 = 6 seconds
    Slide 4 = 5 seconds
    Slide 5 = 6 seconds
    Slide 6 = 5 seconds
31. Set up the slide show to run continuously.
32. Run the presentation beginning with Slide 1. Watch the slide show until the presentation has started for the second time and then end the show.
33. Save and then close the presentation.

Assessment 4 Apply Custom Animation Effects to a Travel Presentation

1. Open **AustraliaTour.pptx** and then save the presentation with the name **P-U2-A4-AustraliaTour**.
2. With Slide 1 active, apply a *Fly In* entrance animation effect to the title *Australia Tour* that has the title fly in from the bottom.
3. Display the presentation in Slide Master view and then make the following changes:
   a. Click the third slide master thumbnail.
   b. Apply a *Fly In* entrance animation effect to the title that has the title fly in from the top.
   c. Apply a *Fly In* entrance animation effect to the bulleted text that has the text fly in from the left and then dims to a color of your choosing when the next bullet displays.
   d. Close Slide Master view.
4. Make Slide 5 active, select the sun shape that displays above *Sydney*, and then draw a freeform motion path from Sydney to Melbourne, Tasmania, Adelaide, Perth, Derby, Darwin, Cairns, and then back to Sydney. Change the duration to *04.00*.
5. Make Slide 6 active and then make the following changes:
   a. Click the bottom shape to select it. (You may want to move the top two shapes out of the way.)
   b. Apply the *Grow & Turn* entrance effect.
   c. Click the Add Animation button and then click the *Shrink & Turn* exit effect.
   d. Click the middle shape to select it and then apply the *Grow & Turn* entrance effect.
   e. Click the Add Animation button and then click the *Shrink & Turn* exit effect.
   f. Click the top shape to select it and then apply the *Grow & Turn* entrance effect.
   g. Position the shapes so they are stacked on top of each other so you do not see a portion of the shapes behind.
6. Save **P-U2-A4-AustraliaTour.pptx**.
7. Make Slide 1 active, run the presentation, and make sure the animation effects play correctly.
8. Print the presentation as a handout with all slides printed horizontally on one page.
9. Close **P-U2-A4-AustraliaTour.pptx**.

Assessment 5 Inspect a Presentation and Save a Presentation in Different Formats

1. Open **P-U2-A1-GreenSpacePres.pptx** and then save the presentation with the name **P-U2-A5-GreenSpacePres**.
2. Inspect the presentation using the Document Inspector dialog box and remove comments from the presentation.
3. Run the compatibility checker. (Click OK at the Microsoft Compatibility Checker dialog box.)
4. Save the presentation in *PowerPoint 97-2003* format and name it **P-U2-A5-GreenSpacePres-2003format**. (Click the Continue button at the compatibility checker message.)
5. Close **P-U2-A5-GreenSpacePres-2003format.ppt**.

6. Open **P-U2-A5-GreenSpacePres.pptx** and then save the presentation as a PDF document.
7. View the presentation in Adobe Reader.
8. After viewing all of the slides, close Adobe Reader.
9. Close **P-U2-A5-GreenSpacePres.pptx** without saving the changes.
10. Capture an image of the Open dialog box and insert the image in a PowerPoint slide by completing the following steps:
    a. Press Ctrl + N to display a new blank presentation.
    b. Click the Layout button in the Slides group in the Home tab and then click the *Blank* layout at the drop-down list.
    c. Click the File tab and then click the Open button.
    d. At the Open dialog box, click the option button that displays to the right of the *File name* text box (option button that contains the text *All PowerPoint Presentations*) and then click *All Files (*.*)* at the drop-down list.
    e. Scroll down the Open dialog box list box to display your assessment files.
    f. Hold down the Alt key and then press the Print Screen button on your keyboard. (This captures an image of your Open dialog box.)
    g. Click the Cancel button to close the Open dialog box.
    h. Click the Paste button. (This inserts the image of your Open dialog box into the slide.)
11. Print the slide as a full page slide.
12. Close the presentation without saving it.

Writing Activities

The following activities give you the opportunity to practice your writing skills along with demonstrating an understanding of some of the important PowerPoint features you have mastered in this unit. Use correct grammar, appropriate word choices, and clear sentence structure.

Activity 1 Prepare and Format a Travel Presentation

You work for First Choice Travel and you are responsible for preparing a presentation on travel vacations. Open the Word document named **TravelVacs.docx** and then print the document. Close the document and then exit Word. Using the information in the document, prepare a PowerPoint presentation with the following specifications:

1. Create a presentation that presents the main points of the document.
2. Rehearse and set times for the slides to display during a slide show. You determine the number of seconds for each slide.
3. Insert a song into the first slide from the Clip Art task pane. At the Clip Art task pane, change the *Results should be* option to only *Audio*.
4. Set up the presentation to run on an endless loop and the audio to play across all slides and continuously as long as the presentation is running.
5. Run the presentation. (The slide show will start and run continuously.) Watch the presentation until it has started for the second time and then end the show by pressing the Esc key.
6. Save the presentation and name it **P-U2-Act1-TravelVacs**.
7. Print the presentation as a handout with six slides horizontally per page.
8. Close **P-U2-Act1-TravelVacs.pptx**.

Activity 2 Prepare and Format a Presentation on Media Files

Using PowerPoint's Help feature, learn more about audio and video file formats compatible with PowerPoint 2010. (Search specifically for *compatible audio and video file formats*.) Using the information you find in the Help files, create a presentation with *at least* the following specifications:

- Slide containing the title of the presentation and your name
- Create at least three slides each containing information on a compatible audio file format including the file format, extension, and a brief description of the format.
- Create at least three slides each containing information on a compatible video file format including the file format, extension, and a brief description of the format.
- Optional: If you are connected to the Internet, search for websites where you can download free audio clips and then include this information in a slide as well as a hyperlink to the site.

Save the completed presentation and name it **P-U2-Act2-AudioVideo**. Run the presentation and then print the presentation as a handout with six slides horizontally per page. Close **P-U2-Act2-AudioVideo.pptx**.

Internet Research

Presenting Office 2010

Make sure you are connected to the Internet and then explore the Microsoft website at www.microsoft.com. Browse the various categories and links on the website to familiarize yourself with how information is organized.

Create a PowerPoint presentation that could be delivered to someone who has just purchased Office 2010 and wants to know how to find more information about the software from the Microsoft website. Include points or tips on where to find product release information and technical support. Include hyperlinks to important pages at the Microsoft website. Add formatting and enhancements to make the presentation as dynamic as possible. Save the presentation and name it **P-U2-Int-Office2010**. Run the presentation and then print the presentation as a handout with six slides per page. Close **P-U2-Int-Office2010.pptx**.

Job Study

Creating a Skills Presentation

You are preparing a presentation that you will use when presenting information on jobs at your local job fair. Open the Word document named **JobDescriptions.docx**, print the document, and then close the document and exit Word. Use the information in the document to prepare slides that describe each job (do not include the starting salary). Using the Internet, locate information on two other jobs that interest you and then create a slide for each job that provides information on job responsibilities. Determine the starting salary for the two jobs and then use that information along with the starting salary information for the jobs in the Word document to create a chart that displays the salary amounts. Locate at least two online job search websites and then include them in your presentation along with hyperlinks to the sites. Insert action buttons to move to the next page for the first slide through the second from the end. On your final slide, create an action button to return to the first slide.

Save the presentation and name it **P-U2-JobStudy**. Run the presentation and then print the presentation as a handout with six slides horizontally per page. Close **P-U2-JobStudy.pptx**.

Index

A

accessibility, checking, of presentation, 340–342
Accessibility Checker task pane, 341
action buttons, inserting, 246
Action Settings dialog box, 248
Album Layout group, Picture layout option in, 208–209
alignment
    of text boxes, 121
    vertical, of text, 88–90
animation, 263
    applying, with Animation Painter, 269–270
    of chart, 279–281
    running presentation without, 284–285
    SmartArt graphic, 278–279
animation effects, 269–284
    applying, with Animation Painter, 269–270
    applying and removing, 266–268
    applying build, 276
    applying trigger, 282–284
    of chart, 279–281
    creating motion path, 281–282
    customizing, at Animation Pane, 273–275
    modifying, 270–271
    reordering items, 271–273
    of shapes and images, 277–278
    of SmartArt graphic, 278–279
Animation Painter, 269–270
Animations tab, 266
area chart, 198
audio file
    inserting, 294–295
    playing, throughout presentation, 297–298
Audio Tools Playback tab, 294, 295, 298
AutoCorrect dialog box, 44
automatic advancement of slides, 32
automatic backup, 342
automatic times, setting, for slides, 287

B

background styles, 228
    applying and formatting, 228, 229
Backstage view, getting help in, 65
bar chart, 198
blank presentation, preparing presentation from, 27
blog post, saving presentations as, 316
Browse dialog box, 230
bubble chart, 198
build animation, applying, 276
bulleted text
    applying trigger to, 282
    creating SmartArt graphic with, 194–196
bullets, customizing, 90–92
Bullets and Numbering dialog box, 90, 92, 93
buttons, getting help on, 63

C

cells, 183
    entering text in, 183
    selecting, in table, 183–184
Change Chart Type dialog box, 200
charts, 181, 197–206
    animating, 279–281
    area, 198
    bar, 198
    bubble, 198
    changing design, 200–202
    changing formatting, 203–205
    column, 198
    doughnut, 198
    formatting layout, 202
    line, 198
    pie, 198
    positioning labels in, 202
    radar, 198
    stock, 198
    surface, 198
    types of, 198
    xy (scatter), 198
Chart Tools Design tab, 200
Chart Tools Format tab, 204
    Shape Styles group in, 204
    WordArt Styles group in, 204
Chart Tools Layout tab, 202, 204
Check for Issues button, 339
Choose a SmartArt Graphic dialog box, 189, 190
clip art image
    formatting, 144–145
    inserting, 141–143, 144–145
Clip Art task pane, 141, 142
Clipboard task pane, 313
colors
    creating custom theme, 103–104
    modifying theme, 98, 99–100
column chart, 198
columns, 183
    customizing, 87–88
    dialog box for, 87
    selecting, in table, 184
comments, 330–333
    deleting, 333
    editing, 333
    inserting, 331–332
compatibility, checking, of presentation, 342, 343
Confirm Password dialog box, 336
copy and paste method, inefficiency of, 325
copying
    objects, within and between presentations, 145–146
    slides between presentations, 56–57
    slides in presentations, 55–56
    text in slides, 49–51
Create a Digital ID dialog box, 337
Create New Theme Colors dialog box, 103
Create New Theme Fonts dialog box, 105
creating, custom theme fonts, 105
cropping of images, 136

customizing
    of animation effects at Animation Pane, 273–275
    bullets, 90–92
    columns, 87–88
    Handout Master, 240–242
    images, 135–136
    Notes Master, 242–246
    numbering, 92–94
    paragraphs, 86
    placeholders, 94, 95–97
custom slide layout, creating and renaming, 232
custom slide show, 291–294
    editing, 292
    printing, 293
    running, 292
custom theme colors
    fonts for, 105
custom themes
    colors of, 103–104
    creating, 103–108
    deleting, 107–108
    editing, 107
    fonts for, 105
    saving, 106–107
cutting text in slides, 49–51

D

data, 312–315
Define Custom Show dialog box, 292
deleting
    comments, 333
    custom themes, 107–108
    placeholders, 228
    PowerPoint presentation, 26
    Slide Master layouts, 228
    slides, 54
    text in slides, 46–47
design templates, 328
design theme
    applying, 25–26
    downloading, 328–330
destination, 325
dialog box
    getting help in, 65
    launcher, 78
digital signature
    adding, 337–339
    creating, 337
    removing, 337–338, 339
doughnut chart, 198

drawing
    lines, 127–128
    shapes, 127–128
    table, 185
Drawing Tools Format tab, 121, 211
duplicating slides, 57–58
Duration option, 30

E

Edit Hyperlink dialog box, 253
editing
    comments, 333
    custom show, 292
    custom themes, 107
    hyperlink, 253
    linked objects, 328
    photo album, 208–211
Edit Photo Album dialog box, 211
Edit Theme Colors dialog box, 107
Edit Theme Fonts dialog box, 107
Effect Options button, 266
Effect Options dialog box, 276
elements, inserting, in Slide Master view, 231–232
email address, inserting hyperlink to, 251
email attachment, sending presentation as, 316, 317
embedding objects, 325–326
enclosed object, 127
Encrypt Document dialog box, 336
encrypting, presentation, 336
Excel chart
    copying, to slide, 312–313
    embedding, in presentation, 326
    linking, to presentation, 327

F

File tab, 6
Find and Replace dialog boxes, 47
finding and replacing text in slides, 47–48
Font dialog box, 78
fonts
    applying formatting, 77–81

    changing, 77–78
    creating custom theme, 105
    modifying theme, 98, 99–100
footers, inserting, 151–154
format, saving presentation in different, 317
Format Painter, formatting with, 81–82
Format Picture dialog box, 143
formatting
    chart, 202, 203–205
    clip art image, 144–145
    fonts, 77–81
    with Format Painter, 81–82
    images, 135–136
    lines and shapes, 127–128
    with Mini toolbar, 79
    paragraphs, 83–86
    photo album, 208–211
    pictures, 211
    presentations, 77–98
    screenshots, 147–148
    Slide Master, 226–227
    SmartArt, 192–194
    text box, 121–124
    WordArt text, 148–150

G

galleries, 16
Get a Digital ID dialog box, 337
graphic images, saving slides as, 320–321
graphs, 181
grayscale, 17
Grid and Guides dialog box, 129, 130
gridlines, 129
    displaying, 129–133
grouping/ungrouping objects, 134–135
guides, displaying, 129–133

H

Handout Master, 223
    customizing, 240–242
Header and Footer dialog box, 152, 231
    Notes and Handouts tab on, 151
    Slide tab on, 151
headers, inserting, 151–154

Help, using, 62–65
Help tab Backstage view, getting help at, 63
hidden data, inspecting presentation for, 339–340
Hide all hyperlink, 62
Hide Background Graphics check box, 98
hiding slides, 290
Home tab Font group button, 78
Home tab Paragraph group buttons, 83
horizontal ruler, 125, 129
hyperlinks
   editing, 253
   inserting, 250–253
   modifying, 253
   removing, 253

I
I-beam pointer, 6
images
   animating, 277–278
   customizing and formatting, 135–136
   sizing, cropping, and moving, 136
Info tab Backstage view, 333–334, 339, 342
Insert Audio dialog box, 294
Insert Chart dialog box, 197
Insert Hyperlink dialog box, 250
inserting
   audio file, 294–295
   clip art images, 141–145
   comments, 331–332
   footers, 151–154
   headers, 151–154
   hyperlinks, 250–253
   picture, 137–141
   screenshots, 147–148
   slides, 54
   symbols, 150–151
   text in slides, 46–47
   video file, 295–296
insertion point, 6
Insert Outline dialog box, 311
Insert Picture dialog box, 137–139
Insert Table dialog box, 183

integration, 325
internal margins, changing, 94
Internet fax, saving and sending presentation as, 316
items, reordering, 271–273

J
JPEG File Interchange Format (*.jpg) option, 320
JPG file extension, 317

K
keyboard, in displaying slides, in presentation, 14

L
labels, positioning, in chart, 202
landscape orientation, 101, 235
layout
   changing table, 187–189
   maintaining consistent, 9
left alignment tabs, 125
line chart, 198
line drawing, 127
lines, drawing and formatting, 127–128
Line Spacing Options, 86
linking objects, 327
live preview feature, 25, 78

M
margins, changing internal, 94
Media Tools Format tab, 295–296
Media Tools Playback tab, 295
metadata, 339
   inspecting presentation for, 339–340
Microsoft, predesigned presentation templates of, 7
Microsoft Graph feature, 181
Microsoft PowerPoint Help button, 62
Microsoft SharePoint, 316
Microsoft Word, exporting presentation to, 324
Mini toolbar, 202
   formatting with, 79
modifying hyperlink, 253

monitors
   changing resolution, 290–291
   setting up, 290
motion path, 281
   drawing, 281–282
movement, 263
moving
   images, 136
   slides, 54, 55–56
multiple objects, selecting, 121

N
narration, recording, 288–290
navigating in PowerPoint presentation, 14–16
New from Existing Presentation dialog box, 238
New Pictures dialog box, 207
New Presentation dialog box, 239
New Slide button in Slides group, 54
New tab Backstage view
   Available Templates and Themes category in, 10
   Blank presentation option in, 27
   choosing theme template at, 10, 25
   Design slides option in, 328
   displaying of installed templates and themes, 7
   My templates option in, 238
   New from existing option in, 22, 238
Next Page button, 17
Next Slide button, 14
normal view, 5, 14, 54
Notes Master, 223
   customizing, 242–246
Notes Page view, 14
Notes pane, 6
nudging, 136, 192
numbering, customizing, 92–94

O
objects
   arranging, 136
   copying, within and between, 145–146
   editing linked, 328

embedding, 325–326
grouping/ungrouping, 134–135
linking, 327
sizing, rotating, and positioning, 143–144
Open button at Backstage view, 7
Open dialog box, 7, 22, 26
Options dialog box, 44
orientation
landscape, 101, 235
portrait, 101, 235
Outlook email account, 316
output, determining, 9, 10

P

Package Presentation for CD option, 321
saving presentation in PDF format as, 322–323
page setup, changing, 101–102, 235
Page Setup dialog box, 101
Paragraph dialog box, 86
paragraphs
customizing, 86
formatting, 83–86
password in encrypting presentation, 336
pasting, text in slides, 49–51
PDF (portable document format), 316
saving presentation in, 321, 322–323
personal data, inspecting presentation for, 339–340
photo album, 207–211
editing and formatting, 208–211
formatting pictures, 211
presentation, 181
Photo Album dialog box, 207
Picture layout option in Album Layout group, 208–209
pictures
formatting, 211
inserting as slide background, 140–141
inserting in document, 137–141

Picture Tools Format tab, 135, 211
pie chart, 198
creating and formatting, 205–206
placeholders
customizing, 94, 95–97
deleting, 228
inserting, 232, 233–234
sizing and rearranging, in slide, 52–54
PNG file extension, 317
PNG Portable Network Graphics (*.png) option, 320
portrait orientation, 101, 235
positioning of objects, 143–144
PowerPoint, 3
Screen Tips for, 5
PowerPoint presentations
accessibility of, 340–342
adding transition and sound effects, 29–31
advancing slides, 32
applying design theme, 25–26
changing views, 14
choosing slide layout, 11
closing, 8
compatibility of, 342, 343
copying objects within and between, 145–146
copying slide between, 56–57
creating, 5–6
creating, from existing presentation, 22–24
creating, using theme templates, 10, 11–13
creating sections within, 60–62
deleting, 26
determining main purpose of, 9
display of, in *Recent Presentations* list, 7
embedding Excel chart in, 326
encrypting, 336
exporting, to Word, 324
formatting, 77–98
formatting pictures in, 211

importing Word outline, 311–312
inserting hyperlinks to another, 251–252
inserting new slide, 11
inserting slides in customized, 229–230
inserting symbols in, 150–151
inserting text in slides, 10
inspecting, 339–340
linking Excel chart to, 327
linking website to another, 248–249
managing information, 333–343
managing versions, 342
marking, as final, 336–337
modifying, 41–66
navigating, 14–16
opening, 7
planning, 9–10
playing audio file throughout, 297–298
preparing, from blank presentation, 27
preparing, in Slides/Outline pane, 27–29
previewing, 16–20
printing, 16–20
protecting, 336
running, without animation, 284–285
running slide show, 20–22
saving, 11
saving, in different format, 317
saving, and sending, 316–317
saving, as template, 238–240
self-running, 285
setting up, to loop continuously, 285–286
sharing, 315–324
starting, 8
viewing, 244–246
PowerPoint window, 5, 6
elements of, 6
presentation properties
inserting, 335
managing, 333–335

Presentation Views group in View tab, 14
previewing PowerPoint presentation, 16–20
Previous Slide button, 14
printing
   custom show, 293
   PowerPoint presentation, 16–20
Print tab Backstage view, 16, 17, 331
prompts, creating custom, 233
Protect Presentation button, 336

Q

Quick Access toolbar, 6, 7
Quick Style, applying, 94
Quick Styles button, 94

R

radar chart, 198
Reading view, 14
recording toolbar, 287
Record Slide Show dialog box, 288
rehearse timings, setting, for slides, 287–288
removing, hyperlink, 253
Replace dialog box, 47
Reuse Slides task pane, 59, 230
reusing slides, 59–60
ribbon, 6
rotating
   objects, 143–144
   text, 88–90
rotation handle in rotating images, 136
rows, 183
   selecting, in table, 184
rulers, displaying, 129–133
running custom show, 292

S

sans serif fonts, 78
Save As dialog box, 11, 26, 238
Save As Template button, 201
Save Current Theme, 106, 107
Save & Send tab Backstage view, 309, 315, 316
saving
   custom theme, 106–107

PowerPoint presentation, 11
screenshots
   creating, 146–148
   formatting, 147–148
   inserting, 147–148
Search for text box, 141
sections, creating, within presentations, 60–62
self-running presentation, 285
   preparing, 286
Send To Microsoft Word dialog box, 323
serif fonts, 78
Set Up Show dialog box, 284
shapes
   animating, 277–278
   drawing and formatting, 127–128
Shapes button drop-down list, 127
Shape Styles group in Chart Tools Format tab, 204
<u>Show All</u> hyperlink, 62
<u>Show All Properties</u> hyperlink, 334–335
Show Markup button, 331
Signatures task pane, 337–338
Size and Position dialog box, 144
sizing
   images, 136
   objects, 143–144
slide
   copying, 55–56
   copying, between presentations, 56–57
   copying Excel chart to, 312–313
   inserting new, 11
   showing one idea per, 9
   sizing and rearranging placeholders in, 52–54
slide background
   changing, 98
   inserting picture as, 140–141
slide layout, choosing, 11
Slide Masters, 223, 225–238
   applying and formatting backgrounds, 228, 229
   applying themes to, 226
   changing page setup, 235

creating and renaming custom slide layout, 232
creating custom prompts, 233
deleting layouts, 228
deleting placeholders, 228
formatting, 226–227
inserting elements in, 231–232
inserting new, 234–235
inserting placeholders, 232, 233–234
inserting slides in customized presentation, 229–230
preserving, 235
slide number, printing, on slides, 152
Slide Orientation button, 235
Slide pane, 6
slides
   advancing automatically, 32
   cutting, copying, and pasting text in, 49–51
   deleting, 54
   deleting text in, 46–47
   duplicating, 57–58
   finding and replacing text in, 47–48
   hiding, 290
   inserting, 54
   inserting, in customized presentation, 229–230
   inserting text in, 10, 46–47
   keeping easy to read and uncluttered, 10
   managing, 54–60
   moving, 54, 55–56
   printing number on, 152
   reusing, 59–60
   saving, as graphic images, 320–321
   setting automatic times for, 287
   setting rehearse timings for, 287–288
Slides group, New Slide button in, 54
slide show
   running, 20–22
   setting up, 284–291
Slide Show button, 8, 20

Slide Show Help window, 21
Slide Show tab, 8
Slide Show toolbar, 20–22
    pen button, 21–22
Slide Show view, 14
Slide Sorter view, 14, 29, 54
Slides/Outline pane, 6
    managing slides in, 54
    preparing presentation in, 27–29
    rearranging text in, 51–52
    visibility of slide in, 290
SmartArt, 189–197
    animating, 278–279
    creating graphic with bulleted text, 194–196
    formatting, 192–194
    inserting text in Text pane, 196–197
    modifying design, 190–192
SmartArt Tools Design tab, 190
SmartArt Tools Format tab, 193
sound effects, adding, to PowerPoint presentation, 29–31
sounds, removing, 30
source, 325
spelling, checking, 43–45
Spelling dialog box, 44
    options in, 44
Start Slide Show group, 8, 20
status bar, 6
stock chart, 198
Suggestions list box, 44
surface chart, 198
symbols, inserting, 150–151

T

table, 183–189
    changing design, 185–186
    changing layout, 187–189
    columns in, 183
    drawing freeform, 185
    entering text in cells, 183
    rows in, 183
    selecting cells, 183–184
    selecting columns, 184
    selecting rows, 184
Table Tools Design tab, 185
Table Tools Layout tab, 187

tabs, 6
    setting, in text box, 125–126
templates
    open an installed, 7
    saving presentation as, 238–240
text
    applying paragraph formatting to, 83–86
    cutting, copying, and pasting, in slides, 49–51
    deleting, in slides, 46–47
    entering, in cells, 183
    finding and replacing, in slides, 47–48
    inserting, in slides, 10, 46–47
    inserting, in Text pane, 196–197
    rearranging, in Slides/Outline pane, 51–52
    rotating and vertically aligning, 88–90
text boxes
    aligning, 121
    formatting, 121–124
    inserting and formatting, 120–126
    setting tabs in, 125–126
Text Effects Transform side menu, 149
Text pane, inserting text in, 196–197
theme colors and fonts, modifying, 98, 99–100
themes, applying, to Slide Masters, 226
theme templates, 10
    creating presentation using, 10, 11–13
Title bar, 6
Title default slide layout, 10
Title Slide layout, 11
transitions
    adding, to PowerPoint presentation, 29–31
    defined, 29
    removing, 30
trigger, applying, for animation, 282–284
trimming, video file, 297
Trim Video button, 297

V

vertical alignment of text, 88–90
vertical ruler, 125, 129
vertical scroll bar, 6, 14
video
    saving presentation as, 321
    saving presentation in PDF format as, 322–323
video file
    inserting, 295–296
    trimming, 297
Video Tools Playback tab, 296
view area, 6
views, changing, 14
View tab, 244–249
    Presentation Views group in, 14
visual aids, 3

W

website
    inserting hyperlinks to, 250–251
    linking, to another presentation, 248–249
Windows Live ID account, 316
Windows Live SkyDrive, 316
WordArt drop-down list, 148
WordArt Styles group in Chart Tools Format tab, 204
WordArt text, formatting, 148–150
Word document
    exporting PowerPoint presentation to, 323
    inserting hyperlinks to, 251–252
Word outline, importing, 311–312

X

XML (extensible markup language), 316
XPS format (XML paper specification), 316
xy (scatter) chart, 198

Z

Zoom dialog box, 244
Zoom slider bar, 17, 244